THE OXFORD

INDIA

THE OXFORD HISTORY OF
INDIA

BY THE LATE VINCENT A. SMITH, C.I.E.

FOURTH EDITION
EDITED BY PERCIVAL SPEAR

PART I

REVISED BY SIR MORTIMER WHEELER
AND A.L. BASHAM

PART II

REVISED BY J.B. HARRISON

PART III

REWRITTEN BY PERCIVAL SPEAR

OXFORD
UNIVERSITY PRESS

OXFORD
UNIVERSITY PRESS

YMCA Library Building, Jai Singh Road, New Delhi 110 001

Oxford University Press is a department of the University of Oxford. It furthers the
University's objective of excellence in research, scholarship, and education
by publishing worldwide in

Oxford   New York

Auckland   Bangkok   Buenos Aires   Cape Town   Chennai
Dar es Salaam   Delhi   Hong Kong   Istanbul   Karachi   Kolkata
Kuala Lumpur   Madrid   Melbourne   Mexico City   Mumbai   Nairobi
São Paolo   Shanghai   Taipei   Tokyo   Toronto

Oxford is a registered trade mark of Oxford University Press
in the UK and in certain other countries

Published in India
By Oxford University Press, New Delhi

© Oxford University Press 1958

First published 1919 by the Clarendon Press Oxford
Twenty-first impression 2004

ISBN 019 561297 3

Printed in India at Anand Sons, Delhi 110 092
Published by Manzar Khan, Oxford University Press
YMCA Library Building, Jai Singh Road, New Delhi 110 001

PREFACE TO THE THIRD EDITION

THE *Oxford History of India* was first published in 1919 carrying the Indian story down to 1911. It was entirely the work of the late Vincent Smith and was at once hailed as a monument of wide learning, of concise statement, and of forthright opinion. It came to be regarded as an invaluable compendium of the subject, and its solid merits have been such that it remains a live work after forty years of rapid change, not only in India itself but in opinion about its history. Smith's history has been disparaged as dull and pilloried as prejudiced, but there are few persistent readers who have not found the dullness allied to a regard for accuracy, and most of the prejudice to be expressions of honest even if sometimes mistaken judgement. Vincent Smith's history has lived because it was basically founded on sound knowledge and shrewd judgement, and because these qualities were compounded with a vivid personality which made the book 'alive' in spite of its matter-of-fact approach. The fact that a work composed at the end of the imperial British age and in the spirit of that age is still read in contemporary independent India is sufficient evidence of its solid worth and enduring quality.

A second edition appeared in 1923. The book was revised by the late S. M. Edwardes who added a section bringing the record to 1921.

Since then an era in Indian history which seemed likely in 1912 to persist indefinitely has come to an end; not only maps but thought and a whole climate of opinion have changed; it is therefore inevitable that there should be considerable changes in any new edition. Nevertheless it has been found practicable to retain much of Smith's work in Parts I and II. In the third edition a new chapter on the Indian prehistory which has come to light since Vincent Smith's death has been written by Sir R. Mortimer Wheeler. The remainder of the Ancient Indian period (Books I–III) has been revised by Professor A. L. Basham of the London School of Oriental and African Studies. The medieval or Muslim period (Books IV–VI) has been similarly revised by Mr. J. B. Harrison of the same School. It is revealing of Smith's outlook and characteristic of his work that the revision of the medieval period should be more extensive than the ancient. For the British period, however, such methods would not suffice. The change in perspective has been too great; repair of the garment would have produced a patchwork, not a renovated piece. The whole part (Books VII–X) has therefore been rewritten by a single hand from what must be plainly stated to be a different point of view. The whole British period has been treated as a completed episode. It has been regarded, not as the story of the rise and decline of British power in India, but as the story of the transformation of Indian under the impact of western power, techniques, and ideas, of which the East India Company was the harbinger and Britain the creative intermediary.

This fresh treatment of the British period has involved some problems of adjustment between Parts II and III. If Part III was to be a history of India in the time of the British rather than a history of the British in India, more attention had clearly to be paid to Indian India at the outset. This meant that either sections of Part II must be omitted or some repetition incurred in Part III. I have thought the integration of the Mughul and British periods, and the weaving together of the British and Indian strands so important as to justify some overlapping in the periods and some repetition of topics. Only thus can a proper historical perspective be achieved. These traits will be noticed in passages dealing with the Marathas, the Afghans in the eighteenth century, the Sikhs, and the closing scenes of the Mughul empire.

The provision of notes on authorities at the end of each chapter has been retained throughout the book. Chronological tables have been similarly retained in Parts I and II, but in Part III synchronistic chronological tables for each of the four Books VII–X have been insterted at the end of the Part. The maps and illustrations have both been completely revised.

The problem of the transliteration of Indian names and words has been a difficult one. A book hoping to be read by a wide public should be as clear as possible in its treatment of names and technical terms, but at the same time there must be some consistency and conformance to scientific usage. A further difficulty is that many Indian words have become naturalized in the English language with spellings which are familiar rather than scientific. Thus we have 'Meerut' for 'Mīrat', 'hookah' for 'hūqa', and 'thug' for 'thag'. The last example illustrates a further complication, that of a word undergoing a change of meaning (ritual strangler to general gangster) as well as a change of spelling. The methods adopted have been as follows. In Parts I and II words have been transliterated on accepted Hunterian principles with the usual diacritical marks. The exceptions are certain well-known names such as Akbar and Bengal. In Part III the problem has been more difficult because of the large number of Indian words naturalized into English. Here it has been felt that some sacrifice in accuracy would be well compensated by gain in intelligibility. The Hunterian system of spelling has been generally followed but diacritical marks have been usually omitted. Familiar spellings such as Cawnpore and Lucknow have been retained, but where a word has changed in meaning as well as spelling in passing into English, as 'thug', the correct transliteration has been given. The *Concise Oxford Dictionary* has been used as a guide to naturalization of Indian words into English.

Book X, Chapters 6–9, are a revised version of chapters contributed to the third edition of P. E. Roberts's *History of British India*.

In preparing Part III I have received much help from many quarters. But chiefly I should like to thank my wife whose encouragement and sensitive judgement have contributed so much to the completion of the work.

June 1957

T. G. P. S.

CONTENTS

PART II

INDIA IN THE MUSLIM PERIOD

BOOK IV. *The Muslim Powers of Northern India*

BOOK V. *The Southern Powers*

BOOK VI. *The Mughul Empire*

CONTENTS

PART III

INDIA IN THE BRITISH PERIOD

BOOK X. *National India, 1905–47*

BOOK XI. *Independent India, 1947–75*

TEXT-FIGURES

PLATES

LIST OF ILLUSTRATIONS

LIST OF ILLUSTRATIONS

ABBREVIATIONS

A.D.	Anno Domini.
A.H.	Anno Hijrae (Hegirae).[1]
Āīn.	*Āīn-i Akbarī,* by Abu-l Fazl, transl. Blochmann and Jarrett.
A.S.	Archaeological Survey.
A.S.B.	Asiatic Society of Bengal.
A.S.W.I.	Archaeological Survey of Western India.
A.V.	*Atharvaveda.*
B.C.	Before Christ.
B.M.	British Museum.
B.S.O.A.S.	*Bulletin of the School of Oriental & African Studies,* London.
C.H.I.	*Cambridge History of India.*
E.H.I.	*The Early History of India,* by Vincent A. Smith, 4th ed. (Oxford, Clarendon Press, 1923).
E.I.Co.	East India Company.
Ep. Ind.	*Epigraphia Indica,* Calcutta, in progress.
Gaz.	*Gazetteer.*
Grundriss.	*Grundriss der Indo-Anschen Philologie und Alterthumskunde,* Strassburg.
H.F.A.	*A History of Fine Art in India and Ceylon,* by Vincent A. Smith (Oxford, Clarendon Press, 1911).
I.G.	*Imperial Gazetteer of India* (Oxford, Clarendon Press, 1907, 1908).
I.H.Q.	*Indian Historical Quarterly,* Calcutta.
Ind. Ant.	*Indian Antiquary,* Bombay, 1872 to date.
J. & Proc. A.S.B.	*Journal and Proceedings of the Asiatic Society of Bengal.* Calcutta.
J.As.	*Journal Asiatique,* Paris.
J.A.S.B.	*Journal of the Asiatic Society of Bengal,* Calcutta.
J.B.O. (or *J.B. & O.*) *Res. Soc.*	*Journal of the Bihar and Orissa Research Society.*
J.I.A.	*Journal of Indian Art and Industry.*
J.P.H.S.	*Journal of the Panjab Historical Society.*
J.R.A.S.	*Journal of the Royal Asiatic Society,* London.
MM.	Mahāmahopādhyāya, a title.
P.H.A.I.	*Political History of Ancient India,* by H. C. Raychaudhuri, 6th ed. (Calcutta, 1954).
Proc. A.S.B.	*Proceedings of the Asiatic Society of Bengal.*
Prog. (*Progr.*) *Rep.*	*Progress Report.*
R.V.	*Rigveda.*
S.B.E.	*Sacred Books of the East.*

NOTE.—An index number following the title of a book indicates the edition; e.g. *Annals of Rural Bengal*[7] means the seventh edition of that work.

[1] The word *hijra* is rendered by 'withdrawal' more precisely than by 'flight', the equivalent usually given.

PART I

ANCIENT AND HINDU INDIA

INTRODUCTION

1. General

The geographical unit. The India of this book is almost exclusively the geographical unit called by that name on the ordinary maps of the days before partition, bounded on the north, north-west, and north-east by mountain ranges, and elsewhere by the sea. The extensive Burmese territories, although for a time governed as part of the Indian empire, cannot be described as being part of India. Burma has a separate history, rarely touching on that of India prior to the nineteenth century. Similarly, Ceylon, although geologically a fragment detached from the peninsula in relatively recent times, always has had a distinct political existence, requiring separate historical treatment, and its affairs will not be discussed in this work, except incidentally.

Vast extent of area. Formal, technical descriptions of the geographical and physical features of India may be found in many easily accessible books, and need not be reproduced here. But certain geographical facts with a direct bearing on the history require brief comment, because, as Richard Hakluyt truly observed long ago, 'geography and chronology are the sun and the moon, the right eye and the left eye of all history'. The large extent of the area of India, which may be correctly designated as a sub-continent, is a material geographical fact. The history of a region so vast, bounded by a coast-line of about 3,400 miles, more or less, and a mountain barrier on the north some 1,600 miles in length, and inhabited by a population numbering nearly 400 millions, necessarily must be long and intricate. The detailed treatment suitable to the story of a small country cannot be applied in a general history of India. The author of such a book must be content to sketch his picture in outlines boldly drawn, and to leave out multitudes of recorded particulars.

Continental and peninsular regions. Another geographical fact, namely that India comprises both a large continental, sub-tropical area, and an approximately equal peninsular, tropical area, has had immense influence upon the history.

Three territorial compartments. Geographical conditions divided Indian history, until the nineteenth century, into three well marked territorial compartments, not to mention minor distinct areas, such as the Konkan, the Himalayan region, and others. The three are: (1) the northern plains forming the basins of the Indus and Ganges; (2) the Deccan plateau lying to the south of the Narbada, and to the north of the Krishna and Tungabhadra rivers; and (3) the far south, beyond those rivers, comprising the group of Tamil states. Ordinarily, each of those three geographical compartments has had a distinct.

highly complex story of its own. The points of contact between the three histories are not very numerous.

Dominance of the north. Usually the northern plains, the Āryā-varta of the Hindu period, and the Hindustan of more recent times, have been the seat of the principal empires and the scene of the events most interesting to the outer world. The wide waterways of the great snow-fed rivers and the fertile level plains are natural advantages which have inevitably attracted a teeming population from time immemorial. The open nature of the country, easily accessible to martial invaders from the north-west, has given frequent occasion for the formation of powerful kingdoms ruled by vigorous foreigners. The peninsular, tropical section of India, isolated from the rest of the world by its position, and in contact with other countries only by sea-borne commerce, has pursued its own course, little noticed by and caring little for foreigners. The historian of India is bound by the nature of things to direct his attention primarily to the north, and is able to give only a secondary place to the story of the Deccan plateau and the far south.

No southern power could ever succeed in mastering the north, but the more ambitious rulers of Āryāvarta or Hindustan often have extended their sway far beyond the dividing-line of the Narbada. When Dupleix in the eighteenth century dreamed of a Franco-Indian empire with its base in the peninsula he was bound to fail. The success of the English was dependent on their acquisition of rich Bengal and their command of the Gangetic waterway. In a later stage of the British advance the conquest of the Panjab was conditioned by the control of the Indus navigation, previously secured by the rather unscrupulous proceedings of Lords Auckland and Ellenborough. The rivers of the peninsula do not offer similar facilities for penetration of the interior.

Changes in rivers. The foregoing general observations indicate broadly the ways in which the geographical position and configuration of India have affected the course of her history. But the subject will bear a little more elaboration and the discussion of certain less conspicuous illustrations of the bearing of geography upon history. Let us consider for a moment the changes in the great rivers of India, which, when seen in full flood, suggest thoughts of the ocean rather than of inland streams. Unless one has battled in an open ferry-boat with one of those mighty masses of surging water in the height of the rains, it is difficult to realize their demoniac power. They cut and carve the soft alluvial plains at their will, recking of nothing. Old beds of the Sutlej can be traced across a space eighty-five miles wide. The Indus, the Ganges, the Kosi, the Brahmaputra, and scores of other rivers behave, each according to its ability, in the same way, despising all barriers, natural or artificial. Who can tell where the Indus flowed in the days of Alexander the Great? Yet books, professedly learned, are not afraid to trace his course minutely through the Panjab and Sind by the help of some modern map, and to offer pretended identifications of sites upon the banks of rivers which certainly were somewhere else twenty-two centuries ago. We know that they must have been somewhere else, but where they were no man can tell. So with the Vedic rivers, several of which bear the ancient names. The rivers of the Rishis were not the rivers of today. The descriptions prove that in the old, old days their character often differed completely from what it now is, and experience teaches that their courses must have been widely divergent. Commentators in their arm-chairs with the latest edition of the Indian *Atlas* opened out before them are not always willing to be bothered with such inconvenient facts. Even since the early Muslim invasions the changes in the rivers have been enormous, and the contemporary histories of the foreign conquerors cannot be understood unless the reality and extent of those changes be borne constantly in mind. One large river-system, based on the extinct Hakra or Wahindah river, which once flowed down from the mountains through Bahawalpur, has wholly disappeared, the final stages having been deferred until the eighteenth century. Scores of mounds, silent witnesses to the existence of numberless forgotten and often nameless towns, bear testimony to the desolation wrought when the waters of life desert their channels. A large and fascinating volume might be devoted to the study and description of the freaks of Indian rivers.

Position of cities. In connexion with that topic another point may be mentioned. The founders of the more important old cities almost invariably built, if possible, on the bank of a river, and not only that, but between two rivers in the triangle above the confluence. Dozens of examples might be cited, but one must suffice. The ancient imperial capital, Pātaliputra, represented by the modern Patna, occupied such a secure position between the guarding waters of the Son and the Ganges. The existing city, twelve miles or so below the confluence, has lost the strategical advantages of its predecessor. Historians who forget the position of Pātaliputra in relation to the rivers go hopelessly wrong in their comments on the texts of the ancient Indian and foreign authors.

Changes of the land. Changes in the coast-line and the level of the land have greatly modified the course of history, and must be remembered by the historian who desires to avoid ludicrous blunders. The story of the voyage of Nearchos, for instance, cannot be properly appreciated by any student who fails to compare the descriptions recorded by the Greeks with the surveys of modern geographers. When the changes in the coast-line are understood, statements of the old authors which looked erroneous at first sight are found to be correct. The utter destruction of the once wealthy commercial cities of Korkai and Kāyal on the Tinnevelly coast, now miles from the sea and buried under sand dunes, ceases to be a mystery when we know, as we do, that the coast level has risen. In other localities, some not very distant from the places named, the converse has happened, and the sea has advanced, or, in other words, the land has sunk. The careful investigator of ancient history needs to be continually on his guard against the insidious deceptions of the modern map. Many learned professors, German and others, have tumbled headlong into the pit. The subject being a hobby of mine I must not ride the steed too far.

The scenes of Indian history. Emphasis has been laid on the fact that most of the notable events of Indian history occurred in one or other of the three great regions separated from each other by natural barriers. Hindustan, the Deccan, and the far south continued to be thus kept apart until the rapid progress of scientific discovery during the nineteenth century overthrew the boundaries set by nature. The mighty Indus and Ganges are now spanned by railway bridges as securely as a petty watercourse is crossed by a 6-foot culvert. The No Man's Land of Gondwana—the wild country along the banks of the Narbada and among the neighbouring hills—no longer hides any secrets. Roads and railways climb the steepest passes of the Western Ghats, which more than once tried the nerves of British soldiers in the old wars. The magnificent natural haven of Bombay always was as good as it is now, but it was of no use to anybody as long as it was cut off from the interior of India by creeks, swamps, and mountains.

Fortresses. The progress of modern science has not only destroyed the political and strategical value of the natural barriers offered by mountains, rivers, and forests. It has also rendered useless the ancient fortresses, which used to be considered impregnable, and were more often won by bribery than by assault. Asirgarh in Khandesh, which in the sixteenth and seventeenth centuries was reckoned to be one of the wonders of the world, so that it was 'impossible to conceive a stronger fortress', defied the arms of Akbar, yielding only to his gold. Now it stands desolate, without a single soldier to guard it. When Lord Dufferin decided to pay Sindia the compliment of restoring Gwalior Fort to his keeping, the transfer could be effected without the slightest danger to the safety of the empire. The numberless strongholds on the tops of the hills of the Deccan before which Aurangzeb wasted so many years are now open to any sightseer. The strategical points which dominated the military action of the Hindu and Muslim sovereigns are for the most part of no account in these days. The sieges of fortresses which occupy so large a space in the earlier history will never occur again. Modern generals think much more of a railway junction than of the most inaccessible castle.

The northern record. One reason why the historian must devote most of his space to the narrative of events occurring in northern India has been mentioned. Another is that the northern record is far less imperfect than that of the peninsula. Very little is known concerning the southern kingdoms before the beginning of the Christian era, whereas the history of Hindustan may be carried back twelve centuries earlier. The extreme deficiency of really ancient records concerning the peninsula leaves an immense gap in the history of India which cannot be filled.

Sea-power. The arrival of Vasco da Gama's three little ships at Calicut in 1498 revolutionized Indian history by opening up the country to bold adventurers coming by sea. The earlier maritime visitors to the coasts had come solely for purposes of commerce without any thought of occupation or conquest. It is needless here to recall how the Portuguese pointed out to their successors, Dutch, French, and English, the path of conquest, and so made possible the British empire of India. The strategical importance of the north-western passes has declined somewhat as that of Bombay and Karachi has risen.

Endless diversity. The endless diversity in the Indian subcontinent is apparent and has been the subject of many trite remarks. From the physical point of view we find every extreme of altitude, temperature, rainfall, and all the elements of climate. The variety of the flora and fauna, largely dependent upon climatic conditions, is equally obvious. From the human point of view India has been often described as an ethnological museum, in which numberless races of mankind may be studied, ranging from savages of low degree to polished philosophers. That variety of races, languages, manners, and customs is largely the cause of the innumerable political subdivisions which characterize Indian history before the unification effected by the British supremacy. Megasthenes in the fourth century B.C. heard of 118 kingdoms, and the actual number may well have been more. In all ages the crowd of principalities and powers has been almost past counting. From time to time a strong paramount power has arisen and succeeded for a few years in introducing a certain amount of political unity, but such occasions were rare. When no such power existed, the states, hundreds in number, might be likened to a swarm of free, mutually repellent molecules in a state of incessant movement, now flying apart, and again coalescing.

Unity in diversity. How then, in the face of such bewildering diversity, can a history of India be written and compressed into a single volume of moderate bulk? The difficulties arising from the manifold diversities summarily indicated above are real, and present serious obstacles both to the writer and to the reader of Indian history. A chronicle of all the kingdoms for thousands of years is manifestly impracticable. The answer to the query is found in the fact that India offers unity in diversity. The underlying unity being less obvious than the superficial diversity, its nature and limitations merit exposition. The mere fact that the name India conveniently designates a subcontinental area does not help to unify history any more than the existence of the name Asia could make a history of that continent feasible. The unity sought must be of a nature more fundamental than that implied in the currency of a geographical term.

Political union. Political union attained by the subjection of all India to one monarch or paramount authority would, of course, be sufficient to make smooth the path of the historian. Such political union never was enjoyed by all India until the full establishment of the British sovereignty, which may be dated in one sense so recently as 1877, when Queen Victoria became Empress of India; in another sense from 1858, when Her Majesty assumed the direct government of British India; and in a third sense from 1818, when the Marquess of Hastings shattered the Maratha power, and openly proclaimed the fact that the East India Company had become the paramount authority throughout the whole country. Very few rulers, Hindu or Muslim, attained sovereignty even as extensive as that claimed by the Marquess of Hastings. The Mauryas, who after the defeat of Seleukos Nikator held the country now called Afghanistan as far as the Hindu Kush, exercised authority more or less direct over all India proper down to the northern parts of Mysore. But even Aśoka did not attempt to bring the Tamil kingdoms under his dominion. The empires of the Kushāns and Guptas were confined to the north. In the fourteenth century Muhammad bin Tughluq for a few years exercised imperfect sovereign powers over very nearly the whole of India. Akbar and his historians never mention the Tamil states, or even the powerful Hindu empire of Vijayanagar, which broke up in 1565. But the Great Mughul cherished a passionate desire to subdue the kingdoms of the Deccan plateau. His success, however, was incomplete, and did not extend beyond Ahmadnagar in the latitude of Bombay. His descendants pursued his policy, and at the close of the eighteenth century Aurangzeb's officers levied tribute two or three times from Tanjore and Trichinopoly. Thus Aurangzeb might be regarded as being in a very loose sense the suzerain of almost all India. The Kabul territory continued to be part of the empire until 1739. The periods of partial political unification thus summarily indicated afford welcome footholds to the historian, and are far easier to deal with than the much longer intervals when no power with any serious claim to paramountcy existed.

The political unity of all India, although never attained perfectly in fact, always was the ideal of the people throughout the centuries. The conception of the universal sovereign as the Chakravartin Raja runs through Sanskrit literature and is emphasized in scores of inscriptions. The story of the gathering of the nations to the battle of Kurukshetra, as told in the *Mahābhārata*, implies the belief that all the Indian peoples, including those of the extreme south, were united by real bonds and concerned in interests common to all. European writers, as a rule, have been more conscious of the diversity than of the unity of India. Joseph Cunningham, an author of unusually independent spirit, is an exception. When describing the Sikh fears of British aggression in 1845, he recorded the acute and true observation that 'Hindostan, moreover, from Caubul to the valley of Assam, and the island of Ceylon, is regarded as one country, and dominion in it is associated in the minds of the people with the predominance of one monarch or one race.'[1] India therefore possesses, and always has possessed for con-

---

[1] *History of the Sikhs*[2] (1853), p. 283.

siderably more than 2,000 years, ideal political unity, in spite of the fact that actual complete union under one sovereign, universally acknowledged by all other princes and potentates, dates only from 1877. The immemorial persistence of that ideal goes a long way to explain both the long acquiescence of India in British rule, and the rapid growth of the All India National Congress, under the leadership of Mahātma Gandhi, from a small party of intellectuals to a mighty mass movement covering the whole sub-continent.

Fundamental unity of Hinduism. The most essentially fundamental Indian unity rests upon the fact that the diverse peoples of India have developed a peculiar type of culture or civilization utterly different from any other type in the world. That civilization may be summed up in the term Hinduism. India primarily is a Hindu country, the land of the Brahmans, who have succeeded by means of peaceful penetration, not by the sword, in carrying their ideas into every corner of India. Caste, the characteristic Brahman institution, utterly unknown in Burma, Tibet, and other borderlands, dominates the whole of Hindu India, and exercises no small influence over the powerful Muslim minority. Nearly all Hindus reverence Brahmans,[1] and all may be said to venerate the cow. Few deny the authority of the Vedas and the other ancient scriptures. Sanskrit everywhere is the sacred language. The great gods, Vishnu and Śiva, are recognized and more or less worshipped in all parts of India. The pious pilgrim, when going the round of the holy places, is equally at home among the snows of Badrinath or on the burning sands of Rāma's Bridge. The seven sacred cities include places in the far south as well as in Hindustan. Similarly, the cult of rivers is common to all Hindus, and all alike share in the affection felt for the tales of the *Mahābhārata* and *Rāmāyana*.

India beyond all doubt possesses a deep underlying fundamental unity, far more profound than that produced either by geographical isolation or by political suzerainty. That unity transcends the innumerable diversities of blood, colour, language, dress, manners, and sect.

Limitations of unity. But the limitations are many. Caste, which, looked at broadly, unites all Hindus by differentiating them from the rest of mankind, disintegrates them by breaking them up into thousands of mutually exclusive and often hostile sections. It has tended to make combined political or social action difficult, and in many cases impossible; while it shuts off all Hindus in large measure from sympathy with the numerous non-Hindu population. The Muslims, by far the largest part of that population, being largely converts from Hinduism, are not entire strangers to Hindu ideas. Yet an Indian Muslim may be, and often is, more in sympathy with an Arab or Persian fellow believer than he is with his Hindu neighbour. The rapid growth of Muslim nationalism in India, and the foundation of Pakistan, are clear evidence of the

---

[1] The Lingāyats of the Kanarese country are the principal exception, but others exist.

very real differences between the two communities. The smaller communities, Christians, Jews, Parsis, and others, are still more distant from the Hindu point of view.

Nevertheless, when all allowances are made for the limitations, the fundamental unity of Hindu culture alone makes a general history of India feasible.

Dravidian culture. The Brahmanical ideas and institutions, although universally diffused in every province, have not been wholly victorious. Prehistoric forms of worship and many quite un-Aryan social practices survive, especially in the peninsula among the peoples speaking Dravidian languages. We see there the strange spectacle of an exaggerated regard for caste coexisting with all sorts of weird notions and customs alien to Brahman tradition. The materials available for the study of early Dravidian institutions are not yet sufficiently explored, and the historian's attention necessarily must be directed chiefly to the Indo-Aryan institutions of the north, which are much more fully recorded than those of the south. An enthusiastic southern scholar has expressed the opinion that 'the scientific historian of India . . . ought to begin his study with the basin of the Krishna, of the Cauvery, of the Vaigai [in Madura and the Pāndya country] rather than with the Gangetic plain, as it has been now long, too long, the fashion'. That advice, however sound it may be in principle, cannot be followed in practice at present; and, so far as I can see, it is not likely that for the present it will be practicable to begin writing Indian history in the manner suggested.

Lack of political evolution. The interest attaching to the gradual evolution of political institutions is lacking in Indian history. The early tribal constitutions of a republican, or at any rate, oligarchical character, which are known to have existed among the Mālavas, Kshudrakas, and other nations in the time of Alexander the Great, as well as among the Lichchhavis and Yaudhēyas at much later dates, all perished without leaving a trace. Autocracy is substantially the only form of government with which the historian of India is concerned. Despotism does not admit of development. Individual monarchs vary infinitely in ability and character, but the nature of a despotic government remains much the same at all times and in all places, whether the ruler be a saint or a tyrant.

Extinction of tribal constitutions. The reason for the extinction of the tribal constitutions appears to be that they were a Mongolian institution, the term Mongolian being used to mean tribes racially allied to the Tibetans, Gurkhas, and other Himalayan nations. The Mongolian element in the population of northern India before and after the Christian era was, I believe, much larger than is usually admitted. When the Mongolian people and ideas were overborne in course of time by the strangers who followed the Indo-Aryan or Brahmanical cult and customs, the tribal constitutions disappeared along with many other non-Aryan institutions. The Brahmanical **people**

always were content with autocracy.[1] I use the term 'autocracy' or the equivalent 'despotism' without qualification intentionally, because I do not believe in the theory advocated by several modern Indian authors that the ancient Indian king was a 'limited' or constitutional monarch. Those authors have been misled by taking too seriously the admonitions of the textbook writers that the ideal king should be endowed with all the virtues and should follow the advice of sage counsellors. In reality every Indian despot who was strong enough did exactly what he pleased. If any limitations on his authority were operative, they took effect only because he was weak. A strong sovereign like Chandragupta Maurya was not to be bound by the cobweb of texts. Long afterwards, Akbar, notwithstanding his taste for sententious moral aphorisms, was equally self-willed.

Village and municipal institutions. Much sentimental rhetoric with little relation to the actual facts has been written about the supposed indestructible constitution of the Indo-Aryan village in the north. The student of highly developed village institutions, involving real local self-government administered on an elaborately organized system, should turn to the south and examine the constitution of the villages in the Chola kingdom as recorded for the period from the tenth to the twelfth centuries of the Christian era, and no doubt of extremely ancient origin.[2] Those institutions, like the tribal constitutions of the north, perished long ago, being killed by rulers who had no respect for the old indigenous modes of administration. The development of municipal institutions, which furnishes material for so many interesting chapters in European history, is almost a blank page in the history of early and medieval India.

History of Indian thought. The limitations in the subject-matter of Indian history pointed out in the foregoing observations undoubtedly tend to make the political history of the country rather dry reading. The more attractive story of the development of Indian thought as expressed in religion and philosophy, literature, art, and science cannot be written intelligibly unless it is built on the solid foundation of dynastic history, which alone can furnish the indispensable chronological basis. Readers who may be disposed to turn away with weariness from the endless procession of kingdoms and despots may console themselves by the reflection that a working acquaintance with the political history of India is absolutely essential as a preliminary for the satisfactory treatment of the story of the development of her ideas.

---

[1] On this obscure subject see the author's papers entitled 'Tibetan Affinities of the Lichchhavis' (*Ind. Ant.*, vol. xxxii (1903), pp. 238 ff.; and 'Tibetan Illustration of the Yaudhēya Tribal Organization' (ibid., vol. xxxv (1906), p. 290); and B. C. Law, *Some Kshatriya Tribes of Ancient India* (Calcutta, 1923), *Some Ancient Mid-Indian Kshatriya Tribes* (Calcutta, 1924). Dr. Smith's views on the Tibetan or Mongoloid origin of these peoples have been much criticized by Dr. Law and other authorities. [Ed.]

[2] *E.H.I.*[4] (1923), pp. 479, 484, with references; K. A. N. Sastri, *The Colas* (2 vols. in 3, Madras, 1935-7), *Studies in Cola History and Administration* (Madras, 1932).

I have tried to give in this work, so far as unavoidable limitations permit, an outline of the evolution of Indian thought in various fields. Students who desire further information must consult special treatises when such exist.

Divisions of the history. The main divisions of a book on Indian history hardly admit of variation. I have drawn the line between the Ancient period and the Hindu period at the beginning of the Maurya dynasty as a matter of convenience. In the Hindu period the death of Harsha in A.D. 647 marks a suitable place for beginning a fresh section. The subdivisions of the Muslim period, occupying Books IV, V, VI, and including the Hindu empire of Vijayanagar, are almost equally self-evident. Four books, VII, VIII, IX, and X, are devoted to the British period. The dividing line between Books VII and VIII should be drawn in my opinion at the year 1818, and not at the close of the administration of the Marquess of Hastings. The significance of the events of 1858, when the series of Viceroys begins, cannot be mistaken.

AUTHORITIES

THE subject-matter of this section has been treated previously by the author in several publications, namely, in *E.H.I.*[4] (1923), Introduction; *Oxford Student's History of India*, latest ed., chap. i; and the *Oxford Survey of the British Empire* (1914), chap. vii. A good formal geographical book is the *Geography of India* by G. PATTERSON (Christian Literature Soc. for India, London, 1909). The first chapter of *C.H.I.*, vol. i, by Sir H. MACKINDER, forms a useful short introduction to the geography of India. Very valuable are the relevant chapters of L. D. STAMP's *Asia, a Regional and Economic Geography* (8th ed., London, 1950). See also *I.G.* (Indian Empire), 1907, vol. i, and the Atlas of the same work (1909). The little book entitled *The Fundamental Unity of India* (Longmans, 1914), by RADHAKUMUD MOOKERJI, is well written, learned, and accurate, notwithstanding its avowed political purpose. The influence of sea-power upon Indian history is expounded by Sir A. LYALL in *The Rise and Expansion of the British Dominion in India* (Murray, 1910). A recent valuable geographical survey is O. K. SPATE's *Geography of India and Pakistan*.

2. Sources

Undated history before 650 B.C. A body of history strictly so-called must be built upon a skeleton of chronology, that is to say, on a series of dates more or less precise. In India, as in Greece, such a series begins about the middle or close of the seventh century before Christ.[1] Nothing approaching exact chronology being attainable for earlier times, the account which the historian can offer of those times necessarily is wanting in definiteness and precision. It is often difficult to determine even the sequence or successive order of events. Nevertheless no historian of India and the Indians can escape from the obligation of offering some sort of picture of the life of undated ancient India,

[1] 'The first exact date we have bearing on the history of Greece' is 6 Apr. 648 B.C., when an eclipse of the sun occurred which was witnessed and noted by the poet Archilochus (Bury, *Hist. of Greece*, ed. 1904, p. 119). But the earliest really historical date known with any approach to accuracy seems to be that of Cylon's conspiracy at Athens, which is placed *about* 632 B.C. The archonship of Solon is put in either 594–593 or 592–591 B.C. (ibid., pp. 178, 182).

in its political, social, religious, literary, and artistic aspects, previous to the dawn of exact history. The early literature, composed chiefly in the Sanskrit, Pali, and Tamil languages, supplies abundant material, much of which is accessible in one or other European tongue. The thorough exploration of the gigantic mass of literature, especially that of the southern books, is a task so vast that it cannot ever be completed. Large fields of study have been hardly investigated at all. But a great deal of good work has been accomplished, and the labours of innumerable scholars, European, American, and Indian have won results sufficiently certain to warrant the drawing of an outline sketch of the beginnings of Indian life and history. Although the lines of the sketch are somewhat wanting in clearness, especially with reference to the Vedic age and the early Dravidian civilization, we moderns can form a tolerably distinct mental picture of several stages of Indian history prior to the earliest date ascertained with even approximate accuracy. Such an outline sketch or picture will be presented in the second chapter of Book I.

Chronological puzzles. Definite chronological history begins about 650 B.C. for northern India. No positive historical statement can be made concerning the peninsula until a date much later. Even in the north all approximate dates before the invasion of Alexander in 326 B.C. are obtained only by reasoning back from the known to the unknown. The earliest absolutely certain precise date is that just named, 326 B.C.

The student may be glad to have in this place a brief exposition of the special difficulties which lie in the way of ascertaining precise dates for the events of early Hindu history. Numerous dates are recorded in one fashion or another, but the various authorities are often contradictory, and usually open to more than one interpretation. Dates expressed only in regnal years, such as 'in the 8th year after the coronation of King A. B.', are not of much use unless we can find out by other means the time when King A. B. lived. Very often the year is given as simply 'the year 215', or the like, without mention of the era used, which to the writer needed no specification. In the same way when modern Europeans speak of the 'year 1914', everybody understands that to mean 'after Christ', A.D. or A.C. In other cases an era may be named, but it is not certain from what date the era is to be reckoned. For example, many dates recorded in the Gupta era were known long before historians could make confident use of them. When Fleet was able to prove that Gupta era, year 1 = A.D. 320-1, the whole Gupta dynasty dropped at once into its proper historical setting. The fixation of that one date brought order into several centuries of early Indian history. Dated inscriptions of the Indo-Scythian or Kushān kings are even more abundant, but up to the present time we do not know to which era a record of theirs dated, say, 'in the year 98' should be referred; and in consequence an important section of Indian history continues to be the sport of conjecture, so that it is impossible to write with assurance a narrative of the events connected with one of the most interesting dynasties. That chronological uncertainty spoils the history of religion, art, and literature, as well as the purely political chronicle, for the first two centuries of the Christian era.

More than thirty different eras have been used in Indian annals from time to time.[1] Difficulties of various kinds, astronomical and other, are involved in the attempt to determine the dates on which the various eras begin. Although those difficulties have been surmounted to a large extent many obscurities remain.

Synchronisms; old and new styles. Several puzzles have been solved by the use of 'synchronisms', that is to say, by the use of stray bits of information showing that King A. of unknown date was contemporary with King B. of known date. The standard example is that of Chandragupta Maurya, the contemporary of Alexander the Great for some years. The approximate date of King Meghavarna of Ceylon in the fourth century A.C. is similarly indicated by the 'synchronism' with the Indian King Samudragupta; many other cases might be cited.

The testimony of foreign authors is specially useful in this connexion, because they often give dates the meaning of which is known with certainty. Indian historians obtain much help in that way from the chronicles of Greece, China, and Ceylon, all of which have well-known systems of chronology. The subject might be further illustrated at great length, but what has been said may suffice to give the student a notion of the difficulties of Hindu chronology, and some of the ways in which many of them have been cleared away.

In the Muslim period chronological puzzles are mostly due to the innumerable contradictions of the authorities, but trouble is often experienced in converting Muslim Hijrī dates exactly into the terms of the Christian era. Akbar's fanciful Ilāhī, or Divine era, and Tipu Sultan's still more whimsical chronology present special conundrums. In the British period nearly all dates are ascertained with ease and certainty, subject to occasional conflict of evidence or confusion between the old and new styles, which differ by ten days in the seventeenth and by eleven days in the eighteenth century.[2]

Six classes of sources of Hindu history. The nature of the sources of or original authorities for Hindu history from 650 B.C. will now be considered briefly. The native or indigenous sources may be classified under five heads, namely: (1) inscriptions, or epigraphic evidence; (2) coins, or numismatic evidence; (3) monuments, buildings,

---

[1] Cunningham's *Book of Indian Eras* (1883) discusses twenty-seven, and many more are mentioned in records.

[2] Pope Gregory XIII undertook to reform the Roman calendar by correcting the error which had gradually grown to inconvenient dimensions in the course of centuries. Accordingly he decreed in 1582 that 5 Oct. by the old calendar of that year should be called 15 Oct. The reform was adopted either immediately or soon by Portugal, France, and several other nations; but in Great Britain and Ireland the change was not effected until 1752, Parliament having passed an Act enacting that 3 Sept. of that year should be deemed to be 14 Sept., new style; eleven days being dropped out of the reckoning. Russia still adhered to the old style until 1917 and was then nearly thirteen days in error.

and works of art, or archaeological evidence; (4) tradition, as recorded in literature; and (5) ancient historical writings, sometimes contemporary with the events narrated. The sixth source, foreign testimony, is mostly supplied either by the works of travellers of various nations, or by regular historians, especially Sinhalese, Greek, and Chinese. The value of each class of evidence will now be explained.

Inscriptions. Inscriptions have been given the first place in the list because they are, on the whole, the most important and trustworthy source of our knowledge. Unfortunately, they do not at present go farther back than the third century B.C. with certainty, although it is not unlikely that records considerably earlier may be discovered, and it is possible that a very few known documents may go back beyond the reign of Aśoka. Indian inscriptions, which usually are incised on either stone or metal, may be either official documents set forth by kings or other authorities, or records made by private persons for various purposes. Most of the inscriptions on stone either commemorate particular events or record the dedication of buildings or images. The commemorative documents range from the simple signature of a pilgrim to long and elaborate Sanskrit poems detailing the achievements of victorious kings. Such poems are called *praśasti*. The inscriptions on metal are for the most part grants of land inscribed on plates of copper. They are sometimes extremely long, especially in the south, and usually include information about the reigning king and his ancestors. Exact knowledge of the dates of events in early Hindu history, so far as it has been attained, rests chiefly on the testimony of inscriptions.

Records of an exceptional kind occur occasionally. The most remarkable of such documents are the edicts of Aśoka, which in the main are sermons on *dharma*, the Law of Piety or Duty. At Ajmer in Rajasthan and at Dhar in central India fragments of plays have been found inscribed on stone tablets. Part of a treatise on architecture is incised on one of the towers at Chitor, and a score of music for the *vīnā*, or Indian lute, has been found in the former Pudukottai State, Madras. A few of the metal inscriptions are dedications, and one very ancient document on copper, the Sohgaura plate from the Gorakhpur District, is concerned with government storehouses.

The inscriptions which have been catalogued and published more or less fully aggregate many thousands. The numbers in the peninsula especially are enormous.

Coins. The legends on coins really are a class of inscriptions on metal, but it is more convenient to treat them separately. The science of numismatics, or the study of ancient coins, requires special expert knowledge. Coins, including those without any legends, can be made to yield much information concerning the condition of the country in the distant past. The dates frequently recorded on them afford invaluable evidence for fixing chronology. Even when the outline of the history is well known from books, as is the case for most of the Muslim period, the numismatic testimony helps greatly in settling doubtful dates, and in illustrating details of many kinds. Our scanty knowledge of the Bactrian, Indo-Greek, and Indo-Parthian dynasties rests chiefly on inferences drawn from the study of coins.

Archaeological evidence. The archaeological evidence, regarded as distinct from that of inscriptions and coins, is obtained by the systematic skilled examination of buildings, monuments, and works of art. For our knowledge of the pre-Aryan Indus civilization we are entirely indebted to the archaeologist. Careful registration of the stratification of the ruins on ancient sites, that is to say, of the exact order in which the remains of one period follow those of another, often gives valuable proof of date. The excavations on the site of Taxila, for instance, have done much to clear up the puzzle of the Kushān or Indo-Scythian chronology already mentioned. The scientific description of buildings erected for religious or civil purposes, such as temples, *stūpas*, palaces, and private houses, throws welcome light on the conditions prevailing in ancient times. The study of works of art, including images, frescoes and other objects, enables us to draw in outline the history of Indian art, and often affords a most illuminating commentary on the statements in books. The history of Indian religions cannot be properly understood by students who confine their attention to literary evidence. The testimony of the monuments and works of art is equally important, and, in fact, those remains tell much which is not to be learned from books. Intelligent appreciation of the material works wrought by the ancients is necessary for the formation of a true mental picture of the past. Such observations apply equally to the Hindu and the Muslim periods.

Tradition almost the sole source of undated history. The knowledge, necessarily extremely imperfect, which we possess concerning ancient India between 650 and 326 B.C. is almost wholly derived from tradition as recorded in literature of various kinds, chiefly composed in the Sanskrit, Pali, and Prakrit languages. Most of the early literature is of a religious kind, and the strictly historical facts have to be collected laboriously, bit by bit, from works which were not intended to serve as histories. Some valuable scraps of historical tradition have been picked out of the writings of grammarians; and several plays, based on historical facts, yield important testimony. Tradition continues to be a rich source of historical information long after 326 B.C.

Absence of Hindu historical literature explained. The trite observation that Indian literature, prior to the Muslim period, does not include formal histories, although true in a sense, does not present the whole truth. Most of the Sanskrit books were composed by Brahmans, who certainly had not a taste for writing histories, their interest being engaged in other pursuits. But the Rajas were eager to preserve annals of their own doings, and took much pain to secure ample and permanent record of their achievements. They are not to blame for the melancholy fact that their efforts have had little success. The records

laboriously prepared and regularly maintained have perished almost
completely in consequence of the climate, including insect pests in that
term, and of the innumerable political revolutions from which India
has suffered. Every court in the old Hindu kingdoms maintained official
bards and chroniclers whose duty it was to record and keep up the
annals of the state. Some portion of such chronicles has been preserved
and published by Colonel Tod, the author of the famous book, *Annals
and Antiquities of Rajasthan*, first published in 1829, but that work
stands almost alone. The great mass of the Rajas' annals has perished
beyond recall. Some fragments of the early chronicles clearly are preserved in the royal genealogies and connected historical observations
recorded in the more ancient Purānas; and numerous extracts from
local records are given in the prefaces to many inscriptions. Thus it
appears that the Hindus were not indifferent to history, although the
Brahmans, the principal literary class, cared little for historical composition as a form of literature, except in the form of *praśastis*, some
of which are poems of considerable literary merit. Such Sanskrit histories as exist usually were produced in the border countries, the best
being the metrical chronicle of Kashmir, called the *Rāja-tarangiṇī*,
composed in the twelfth century. Even that work does not attain
exactly to the European ideal of a formal history. Several Brahman
authors, notably Bāna in the seventh century, wrote interesting works,
half history and half romance, which contain a good deal of authentic
historical matter. Our exceptionally full knowledge of the story of
Harsha-vardhana, King of Thanesar and Kanauj, is derived largely
from the work of Bāna entitled 'The Deeds of Harsha'.

Historical or semi-historical compositions are numerous in the
languages of the south. The Mackenzie collection of manuscripts catalogued by H. H. Wilson contains a large number of texts which may
be regarded as histories in some degree.

Foreign evidence. The indigenous or native sources enumerated
above, which must necessarily be the basis of early Hindu history, are
supplemented to a most important extent by the writings of foreigners.
Hearsay notes recorded by the Greek authors Herodotus and Ktesias
in the fifth century B.C. record some scraps of information, but Europe
was almost ignorant of India until the veil was lifted by the operations
of Alexander (326 to 323 B.C.) and the reports of his officers. Those
reports, lost as a whole, survive in considerable extracts quoted in
the writings of later authors, Greek and Roman. The expedition of
Alexander the Great is not mentioned distinctly by any Hindu author,
and the references to the subject by Muslim authors are of little
value. Megasthenes, the ambassador of Seleukos Nikator to Chandragupta Maurya in the closing years of the fourth century, wrote a highly
valuable account of India, much of which has been preserved in fragments.

Formal Chinese histories from about 120 B.C. have something to tell
us, but by far the most important and interesting of all the foreign

witnesses are the numerous Chinese pilgrims who visited the Holy Land of Buddhism, between A.D. 400 and 700. Fa-hsian, the earliest of them (A.D. 399–414), gives life to the bald chronicle of Chandragupta Vikramāditya, as constructed from inscriptions and coins. The learned Hsüan Tsang, or Yuan Chwang, in the seventh century, does the same for Harsha-vardhana, and also records innumerable matters of interest concerning every part of India. I-tsing and more than sixty other pilgrims have left valuable notes of their travels. A book on the early history of Hindu India would be a very meagre and dry record but for the narratives of the pilgrims, which are full of vivid detail.

Albērūnī. Albērūnī, justly entitled the Master, a profoundly learned mathematician and astronomer, who entered India in the train of Mahmūd of Ghazni early in the eleventh century, applied his powerful intellect to the thorough study of the whole life of the Indians. He mastered the difficult Sanskrit language, and produced a truly scientific treatise, entitled 'An Enquiry into India' (*Tahkīk-i Hind*) which is a marvel of well-digested erudition. More than five centuries later that great book served as a model to Abu-l Fazl, whose 'Institutes of Akbar' (*Āīn-i Akbarī*) plainly betray the unacknowledged debt due to Albērūnī.

Muslim histories. Muslims, unlike the Brahmans, always have shown a liking and aptitude for the writing of professed histories, so that every Muslim dynasty in Asia has found its chronicler. The authors who deal with Indian history wrote, as a rule, in the Persian language. Most of the books are general histories of the Muslim world, in which Indian affairs occupy a comparatively small space, but a few works are confined to Indian subjects. The most celebrated was the conscientious compilation composed by Firishta (Ferishta) in the reigns of Akbar and Jahāngīr, which formed the basis of Elphinstone's *History of India*.

A comprehensive general view of the Indian histories in Persian is to be obtained from the translations and summaries in the eight volumes of *The History of India as told by its own Historians* (London, 1867–77) by Sir Henry Elliot and Professor John Dowson, supplemented by S. H. Hodivala's *Studies in Indo-Muslim History* (Bombay, 1939), a critical commentary on Elliot and Dowson. Sir Edward Bayley's incomplete work entitled the *History of Gujarāt* is a supplement to Elliot and Dowson's collection. The English translations of the *Tabaqāt-i Nāsirī* by Raverty; of the *Āīn-i Akbarī* by Blochmann and Jarrett; of the *Akbarnāma* and the *Memoirs of Jahāngīr* by H. Beveridge; of Badāonī's book by Ranking and Lowe; and Professor Jadunath Sarkar's learned account of Aurangzeb's reign may be specially mentioned. S. R. Sharma, *A Bibliography of Mughul India*, discusses the original authorities, available in India, for the reigns of Babur to Aurangzeb. Many other important books exist. The author of this volume has published a detailed biography of Akbar.

The modern historian of India, therefore, when he comes to the

Muslim period, finds plenty of history books ready made from which he can draw most of his material. He is not reduced to the necessity of piecing together his story by combining fragments of information laboriously collected from inscriptions, coins, traditions, and passing literary references, as he is compelled to do when treating of the Hindu period. His principal difficulties arise from the contradictions of his authorities, the defects of their mode of composition, and endless minor chronological puzzles.

The epigraphic, numismatic, and monumental testimony is needed only for the completion and correction of details.

The histories written in Persian have many faults when judged by modern critical standards, but, whatever may be the opinion held concerning these defects, it is impossible to write the history of Muslim India without using the Persian chronicles as its foundation. The fullest review of the Persian material is given in Storey's *Bio-bibliographical Survey of Persian Literature*, vol. iv.

Foreign evidence for the Muslim period. Foreign testimony is as valuable for the Muslim period as it is for the Hindu. From the ninth century onwards Muslim merchants and other travellers throw light upon the history of medieval India. Some scanty notes recorded by European observers in the fifteenth century have been preserved; and from the sixteenth century numerous works by European travellers present a mass of authentic information supplementary to that recorded by the Muslim historians, who looked at things from a different point of view, and omitted mention of many matters interesting to foreign observers and modern readers. The reports of the Jesuit missionaries for the Mughul period possess special value, having been written by men highly educated, specially trained, and endowed with powers of keen observation. Large use is made in this volume of those reports which have been too often neglected by writers. References to the works of the leading Jesuits and the other foreign travellers will be given in due course.

Authorities for Indo-European history and British period. State papers and private original documents of many kinds dating as far back as 1,000 years ago are fairly abundant in most countries of Europe, and supply a vast quarry of material for the historian. In India they are wholly wanting for both the Hindu and the pre-Mughul Muslim periods, except in so far as their place is supplied by inscriptions on stone and metal. Some documents from the reigns of Akbar and his successors survive, but much of what we know about the Mughuls is derived from the secondary evidence of historians, as supplemented by the testimony of the foreign travellers, inscriptions, and coins. The case changes in the eighteenth century. The Marathas left numerous records which are preserved in the Peshwa's *daftar*. The records of the East India Company go back to the beginning of the seventeenth century, and the Portuguese and Dutch archives contain numerous documents of the sixteenth century.

From the middle of the eighteenth century, the commencement of the British period, the mass of contemporary papers, public and private, is almost infinite. Considerable portions of the records have been either printed at length or catalogued, and much of the printed material has been worked up by writers on special sections of the history, but an enormous quantity remains unused. In the composition of this work I have not attempted to explore manuscript collections, and have necessarily been obliged to content myself with printed matter only so far as I could manage to read and digest it. No person can read it all, or nearly all. The leading authorities consulted will be noted at the end of each chapter.

Present state of Indian historical studies. A brief survey of the present state of Indian historical studies will not be out of place in connexion with the foregoing review of the original authorities.

No general history of the Hindu period was in existence before the publication in 1904 of the first edition of the *Early History of India*. The more condensed treatment of the subject in this volume is largely based on the fourth edition of that work, published in 1923, but much new material has been used; and the subject has been treated from a point of view to some extent changed. Many sections of the story need further elucidation, and it is certain that research will add greatly to our knowledge of the period in the near future.

The Muslim period. The publication in 1841 of Elphinstone's justly famous *History of India* made possible for the first time systematic study of the Indo-Muslim history of Hindustan or northern India down to the battle of Panipat in 1761. Although Elphinstone's book, mainly based on the compilations of Firishta and Khāfī Khān, is of permanent value, it is no disparagement of its high merit to say that in these changed times it is no longer adequate for the needs of either the close student or the general reader. Since Elphinstone wrote many authorities unknown to him have become accessible, archaeological discoveries have been numerous, and corrections of various kinds have become necessary. Moreover, the attitude of readers has been modified. They now ask for something more than is to be found in the austere pages of Elphinstone, who modelled his work on the lines adopted by Muslim chroniclers.

The history of the Sultans of Delhi is in an unsatisfactory state. A foundation of specialized detailed studies is always needed before a concise narrative can be composed with confidence and accuracy, and many years may elapse before a thoroughly sound account of the Sultanate of Delhi can be written. Although considerable advance has been made in the study of the history of the Bāhmanī empire and other Muslim kingdoms which became independent of Delhi in the fourteenth century, there is plenty of room for further investigation. The story of the extensive Hindu empire of Vijayanagar (1336–1565) was originally elucidated by the labours of Robert Sewell, whose excellent work has been continued and in certain matters corrected by several Indian authors. In these days most of the best research in Indian history is done by Indian scholars, a fact which has resulted in a profound change in the presentation of the history of their land. The public addressed by a modern historian differs essentially in composition and character from that addressed by Elphinstone or Mill.

The true history of the Mughul dynasty is beginning to be known. The story of Bābur, Humāyūn, and Akbar has been illuminated by the researches of Mr. and Mrs. Henry Beveridge, and the study of Akbar's life by the author of this volume includes much novel matter. The interesting reign of Jahāngīr, which was badly handled by Elphinstone, has now been fully treated in the *History of Jahangir*, by Beni Prasad. Jahangir's own memoirs are available in an English translation by A. Rogers, and there are numerous European sources, listed in Beni Prasad.

The reign of Shāhjahān, prior to the war of succession, awaits further critical study, based on the original authorities; but my treatment of the material available will be found to present a certain amount of novelty. The long and difficult reign of Aurangzeb has been discussed by Professor Jadunath Sarkar with adequate care and learning. His work is an indispensable authority. The history of the later Mughuls has been considerably elucidated in the works by Irvine, Sarkar, and Dr. Spear.

The British period. James Mill's famous book, the *History of British India*, published in 1817, brought together for the first time, to use the author's words, 'a history of that part of the British transactions which have an immediate relation to India'. Mill's book, continued by H. H. Wilson from 1805 to 1835, notwithstanding its well-known faults, will always be valuable for reference. But it is a hundred and forty years old and can no longer be regarded as more than an introduction to the subject.

The British period can now be regarded as a completed whole, but no fully satisfactory work has yet been written from this point of view. The best expression of the imperialist view is Sir A. Lyall's *British Dominion in India*. A masterpiece of liberal imperial history was lost when Sir W. W. Hunter's *History of British India* was cut short after the issue of the first two volumes. His one-time assistant, the late P. E. Roberts, did something to fill the gap in his scholarly and graceful *History of British India*, now continued from 1932 to 1947 in a third edition. But this work is less satisfactory after the Mutiny than before; the more the implications of liberalism came to be realized, the more nervous Roberts became of them. The two volumes of *The Cambridge History of India* (v and vi) end on the threshold of the Montford era in 1918. Though they contain much excellent work, they are so weighed down on the administrative side as hardly to merit the title of a general history. Vol. v is to be preferred to vol. vi. Edward Thompson and G. T. Garratt in their *Rise and Fulfilment of British Rule in India* (1934) showed an awareness of new trends, of the 'Indianness' of British

Indian history. But its overload of quotations and its incessant opinion-ativeness make it less readable than its authors expected and deprive it of the authority for which they hoped. An impressive modern work is the Chatham House study edited by the late L. S. S. O'Malley, *Modern India and the West* (1941) which is concerned with the interaction of the Western and Indian cultures. Mention may finally be made of Messrs. R. C. Majumdar, H. C. Raychaudhuri, and K. K. Datta's joint work, an *Advanced History of India*, first published in 1946. The third part carries the treatment of the British period farther along the lines of Thompson and Garratt, if with less brilliance, certainly with much more sobriety and balance.

Changed methods. It will be apparent from the foregoing sum-mary review of the present condition of Indian historical studies that the writer of a comparatively short history, while enjoying various advantages denied to his predecessors even a few years ago, is not at present in a position to supply a uniformly authentic and digested narrative in all the sections of his work. In some fields the ground has been thoroughly, or at any rate laboriously, cultivated, whereas in others it has been but lightly scratched by the plough of investigation.

The value and interest of history depend largely on the degree in which the present is illuminated by the past. Our existing conditions differ so radically from those which prevailed in the times of our grand-fathers and great-grandfathers, and our positive knowledge of the facts of the past has increased so enormously that a new book on Indian history—even though avowedly compressed—must be composed in a new spirit, as it is addressed to a new audience. Certain it is that the history of India does not begin with the battle of Plassey, as some people thought it ought to begin, and that a sound, even if not profound, knowledge of the older history will always be a valuable aid in the attempt to solve the numerous problems of modern India. Indian history must be seen as a whole if we are to understand any part of it, and specially its recent period, aright.

AUTHORITIES

THE references here given for pre-Muslim history are supplementary to those in *E.H.I.*[4] (1923).

On systems of chronology and the Hindu calendar see the *Book of Indian Eras* by Sir ALEXANDER CUNNINGHAM (Calcutta, 1883), and *The Indian Calendar* by R. SEWELL and S. B. DIKSHIT (London, 1898). Chronological lists are given in *The Chronology of India from the Earliest Times to the Beginning of the Sixteenth Century* by C. MABEL DUFF (Mrs. W. R. RICKMERS) (Westminster, 1899), a good book, but in many respects out of date; and in *The Chronology of Modern India for Four Hundred Years from the Close of the Fifteenth Century* (A.D. 1494–1894) by J. BURGESS (Edinburgh, 1913); BARNETT's *Antiquities of India*, mentioned below, also contains a detailed chronological table of the Hindu period.

Of histories of ancient and Hindu India in greater detail than the present work, besides the author's *E.H.I.*[4], reference should be made to the *Cambridge History of*

India (vol. i, from the earliest times to the beginning of the Christian era, ed. by E. J. RAPSON, 1922); the invaluable work of H. C. RAYCHAUDHURI, *Political History of Ancient India* (6th ed., Calcutta, 1954); and, in French, the three excellent but rather forbidding volumes of L. DE LA VALLÉE POUSSIN (*Indo-Européens et Indo-Iraniens, l'Inde jusque vers 300 av. J.-C.*, 2nd ed., 1936; *L'Inde aux temps des Mauryas et des Barbares, Grecs, Scythes, Parthes et Yueh-tchi*, 1930; and *Dynasties et histoire de l'Inde depuis Kanishka jusqu'aux invasions musulmanes*, 1935; all published in the Histoire du monde series by Boccard, Paris). Very important is the ten-volume *History and Culture of the Indian People*, published by the Bhāratīya Vidyā Bhavan, Bombay, under the editorship of R. C. MAJUMDAR. Three volumes of this series have already appeared (*The Vedic Age*, 1951, *The Age of Imperial Unity*, 1951, and *The Classical Age*, 1954), bringing the history of India down to the eighth century A.D.; of these the first is open to much criticism for its rather credulous use of Purānic legend, but the other two are excellent. Less detailed are the relevant sections of *The Cambridge Shorter History of India* (ed. by H. H. DODWELL, 1934, the pre-Muslim period by J. ALLAN), and the first volume of K. A. NILAKANTA SASTRI's *History of India* (Madras, 1950).

Inscriptions are published, usually with translation or synopsis of contents, in the volumes of *Corpus Inscriptionum Indicarum, Epigraphia Indica, Epigraphia Carnatica, South Indian Inscriptions*, in publications of the Archaeological Survey of India and of the Indian States and in various learned journals too numerous to mention. A valuable collection of the most important inscriptions down to the end of the Imperial Guptas is D. C. SIRCAR's *Select Inscriptions Bearing on Indian History and Civilization*, vol. i (Calcutta, 1942). This is well annotated, but does not contain English translations.

Numismatics are dealt with in the catalogues of Indian coins in the B.M. and in various Indian museums, and in the *Journal of the Numismatic Society of India*. The most useful general outline is E. J. RAPSON's *Indian Coins* (*Grundriss*, ii. 3, B, Strassburg, 1897).

Archaeological discoveries are reported in the numerous excellent publications of the Archaeological Survey of India.

The more important translations and studies of literary sources are mentioned in the bibliographies to the relevant chapters of this work.

On ancient Indian culture the reader is recommended to L. D. BARNETT's *Antiquities of India* (London, 1913), *Ancient India and Indian Civilization* by P. MASSON-OURSEL and others (tr. by M. R. DOBIE in the History of Civilization series, London, 1934) and A. L. BASHAM's *The Wonder that was India* (London, 1954). *The Legacy of India*, edited by G. T. GARRATT (Oxford, 1937), is an excellent symposium. A detailed and excellent work in French is *L'Inde classique* by L. RENOU and J. FILLIOZAT, with other contributors. Of this two volumes have appeared (Paris, 1949 and 1954), and a further volume is eagerly awaited. Also valuable is RENOU's shorter work, *La Civilisation de l'Inde ancienne* (Paris, 1950). Works on political life and thought in ancient India are mentioned in the bibliography to Book II, Chapter 1, below.

BOOK I

Ancient India

CHAPTER 1[1]

Prehistoric India: Elements of the Population

Antiquity of man. On modern computation, species of men have existed on the earth for something like 500,000 years. For the greater part of that time our knowledge of them is confined to certain of their more durable artifacts or, in comparatively rare instances, to their skeletal remains. The earliest written records—those of Egypt and Mesopotamia—take us back no more than 5,000 years, and the oral traditions of India begin nearly two millennia later. Indeed, the first unquestioned historical records of the sub-continent are not earlier than the end of the sixth century B.C., when north-western India became a province of the Achaemenid empire.

Palaeolithic man. In appreciating the significance of the most ancient vestiges of man, in India as elsewhere, two points may be emphasized at the outset. First, in a sparsely inhabited world devoid of systematic communication, immense periods of time may be represented even by relatively simple technical developments; a quarter of a million years may have gone to a slight improvement in the shaping of a stone. Secondly the evidence, limited as it is to imperishable materials, is not a fair index of cultural range and progress, of cultural pattern, and may tend therefore to exaggerate the appearance of stagnation. To these factors, in India a third may be added. In Europe and North Africa the geological phases contemporary with early man have been systematized and can in some measure be related to one another regionally. But how far they can be equated with the geological phases which have been recognized sporadically in the Indian sub-continent is much less certain. In the absence of such equation, the comparison of artifacts and technical methods in Europe and India remains of uncertain significance, and only provisional deductions can be drawn. Thus 'hand-axes' from Abbeville on the Somme and from the neighbourhood of Madras may be almost

[1] Advances in the study of ancient man in India have made it necessary for the editors to rewrite most of this chapter.

identical in form and workmanship; but whether they represent a proximate moment in time is still matter for much further inquiry.

In central Europe it is now agreed that in the Pleistocene geological period, during which man in various specific forms is known to have existed, there were four major and a number of minor phases of acute cold, marked by advances of the ice-field from the mountain zones on to the adjacent lowlands. These periods of glaciation have left identifiable deposits which serve to punctuate the appearances of human and animal life. In northern India, and more particularly in the Rāwalpindi district of the north-west, in the valley of the river Sohān or Soan, the evidence of four major glaciations has been equated tentatively with the four major glaciations of the European series, with the addition of a fifth advance of the ice in post-Pleistocene times. Much further fieldwork is required to confirm and amplify this equation, but meanwhile it will serve as the basis of a working classification. Less useful is the hypothetical equation of rainy or 'pluvial' periods farther south with the northern glaciations. Particularly in the tropical zone, the interrelationship of the two phenomena is quite uncertain.

To the first glacial period and to the milder interglacial period which followed it, no trace of human occupation is at present attributed. Not, it seems, until the formation of the topmost gravels of the second glacial period (perhaps the *Mindel* of Europe) did man begin to drop crude but recognizable implements of quartzite upon the ground, split pebbles and large flakes chipped mainly on one side, with large 'bulbs of percussion' and small striking-platforms. These rough implements have been named 'Pre-Sohān', to distinguish them from the slightly more sophisticated 'Sohān' industry which began to appear in the succeeding second interglacial phase.

The Sohān industry continued in developing forms until the third (*Riss*?) glaciation and possibly, as the so-called 'Evolved Sohān', until the fourth (*Würm*?). It consists typically of pebble and flake tools amongst which chopper-like implements predominate. Some of the pebble tools are struck from the original pebble surface without the more usual prepared striking-platform. The flake tools on the other hand not infrequently show high-angled platforms reminiscent of the Clactonian industry of England. As time went on, the proportion of pebble implements tended to diminish, and the flakes approximated more nearly to the Levalloisian of the European mid-palaeolithic. In terms of years, an antiquity of 400,000 years has been ascribed to the beginnings of the industry, but necessarily with a wide margin; its duration was immense, probably more than 300,000 years.

Alongside the Sohān industry, both in its earlier and in its later aspects, appeared another of a different kind, based not on flakes but upon shaped cores; in other words, upon implements which have been shaped, in a manner which has been compared to sculpture, by the reduction of a lump of quartzite to the desired form through the removal of surplus material. At first, stone hammers were used for this purpose, but later more sensitive instruments, bars of wood or horn, were partially substituted with the result that shallower flake-scars were produced, resulting in a more shapely tool. The characteristic form was a pear-shaped hand-axe, of a type widely distributed in Europe and Africa and approximating to the 'Acheul' of the classical typology.

Although in north-western India and sometimes elsewhere the flake industries and the core industries overlap, they appear to be basically of diverse origin and to represent, indeed, diverse human types. At Swanscombe in Kent a skull essentially modern in type has been found in gravels containing core-artifacts with which it was contemporary, whilst on the other hand there is a tendency for the earlier flake industries to group with obsolete human species representing decadent collateral branches from the human stem. But whether the mixed Indian industries imply the partial coexistence of widely divergent human types in the sub-continent cannot be guessed in the present complete absence of associated human bones. The recovery of human skeletons of palaeolithic age is one of the major needs of Indian archaeology.

In the south of India the hand-axe is the dominant palaeolithic form, and the term 'Madras industry' has been applied to the complex which it represents. But its dominance in peninsular India must not obscure its wide distribution also in the north, not only in the Sohān valley but also in Gujarat, where, for instance, hand-axes of late Acheulian type from the terraces of the Sabarmatī river have been ascribed to the period of the third glaciation, perhaps 150,000–200,000 years ago. Here again, more work is needed.

On meagre evidence of the kind recounted, little can be said of the way of life of these ancient populations. They were doubtless, in India as elsewhere, hunters and food-gatherers, lacking domesticated animals and ignorant of agriculture, although not perhaps unaware of the nutritive value of wild grasses. Their communities must have been exceedingly small and at least semi-nomadic. They may be imagined as foregathering here and there beside the rivers, living in rock-shelters or under huts roofed with thatch or skins, and supplementing their stone equipment with bone, wood, and fibre. Speech of a primitive character may be supposed to have assisted the occasional interchange of knowledge and experience, but the sparseness and isolation of the family or small tribal groups must largely have nullified the accumulation and transmission of tradition on any effective scale. For millennium after millennium an unenterprising uniformity characterized these incipient societies.

Mesolithic industries. In northern and western Europe, following the long palaeolithic phase of the Pleistocene age, archaeologists have recognized a phase in which men lived by hunting and fishing with the aid of implements of bone and flint, the latter often of minute size for use as fish-throttles or, set in bone, as composite tools. Pottery was added as time went on, and the hunter's equipment was supplemented by the domestic dog. This phase, which began after 10,000 B.C. and was generally superseded by about 2500 B.C., is known as the 'meso-lithic', and the small flint implements specially characteristic of it are called 'microliths'. There ensued a phase in which agriculture, already long familiar in the Near East, penetrated into the western outlands, in association with a craftsmanship soon rich in pottery and in flint or stone implements, of which some were ground and polished. This phase is known as the 'neolithic'. It lasted on the average for something like a millennium, but the date of its ending varied widely in different localities.

Attempts to apply this cultural scheme to India are unlikely to be helpful and may readily be misleading. Microliths occur in abundance, but their context is generally undetermined. Some at least are quite late. At Brahmagiri in Mysore State rough microlithic flakes of jasper, agate, carnelian, and other stones occurred with polished stone axes and a little copper and bronze, together with hand-made pottery, in a context indicating a terminal date about 200 B.C. Other microlithic industries more nearly resembling the Tardenoisian of Europe and including crescents, rhomboids, and burins with good secondary work-ing occur in the Vindhyas, beside the Narbadā river and elsewhere; at Langhnaj in Gujarat microliths have been found both with pottery and saddle-querns and, in more deeply stratified deposits, without pottery but with semi-fossilized human skeletons of modern types. It is presumed that these pre-ceramic industries are earlier, perhaps considerably earlier, than the Mysore series, but their absolute date is unknown. Whilst therefore there is a likelihood of a distinct mesolithic period in India, it is certain that some microliths are of a relatively late period.

Agriculture. How far agriculture was practised by these and other pre-pottery folk is not known. At Langhnāj a considerable variety of animal bones, including sheep or goat, large cattle, deer, pig, horse, and dog, and possibly rhinoceros, indicate both pastoralism and hunt-ing as sources of supply. (The presence of the horse is noteworthy, but details are not forthcoming.) On the other hand, at Kile Gul Muham-mad near Quetta the lowest occupation represented a lithic village culture without pottery though otherwise comparable with its more sophisticated successors. Similar settled communities, seemingly in an early agricultural phase, have recently been identified at Jericho in Jordan and at Jarmo in northern Iraq, whose radiocarbon dating indicates a period about 4700 B.C. and earlier. Without clear evidence, however, a knowledge of agriculture in such instances cannot be as-sumed and generalization would be premature.

Neolithic and chalcolithic phases. The normal characteristics of the neolithic phase are the exclusive use of non-metal implements and a knowledge of agriculture with, as a corollary, the development of village life. In India the phase has been inadequately studied and cannot at present be isolated from the so-called chalcolithic phase in which the use of stone was supplemented by that of copper or its alloy, bronze. In the latter phase village economy continued on the old lines, but out of it grew the great chalcolithic civilization of which more will be said shortly.

In north-western India, now West Pakistan, this transitional village life constituted a reasonably coherent cultural complex in the third millennium B.C. and doubtless earlier. Its primary links are with the Persian plateau, but it extended downwards through the glens of Baluchistan to the great river-plain of the Indus and of the parallel system of the former Ghaggar or Sarasvatī which ran from the Himalayas through Bikaner and Bahāwalpur States and probably reached the Arabian Sea south of the Indus. Since the fifth millennium, if not before, the Persian plateau had been occupied by small hill-divided communities of farmers and stock-keepers, exhibiting a considerable measure of local cultural and doubtless political independence. It is postulated that early in the fourth millennium some of these communities made their way south-westwards towards the lengthening valleys of the Tigris and the Euphrates, and there evolved the Bronze Age riverine civilization of Mesopotamia. Towards the south-east, that is towards the Indian sub-continent, a corresponding valleyward advance may have been slower but was certainly in progress by the beginning of the third millennium if not earlier. The details of this advance are at present unknown, and rough cultural and chronological classifications based mainly on surface potsherds await confirmation with the spade. The process was not a rapid one. The settlements are represented by mounds rarely more than 2 acres in extent but sometimes up to 100 feet in height, formed by the accumulation of successive floors and buildings and associated in some instances with irrigation dams across the adjacent valleys. The implication is that, within the limits imposed by a highland environment or origin, these village communities had evolved a settled economy of considerable duration.

Here and there are traces of chert industries which may have anteceded these developments. Flake industries, for example, at Sukkur and Rohri in Sind may be ancestral to the blade industry of the Indus civilization (below) but are not independently dated, nor is anything at present known about their cultural background.

In southern and eastern India, as far as Assam and Burma, a widespread stone type is the pecked and polished axe with pointed butt and oval section. At Brahmagiri (Mysore State) the type occurred with rough microlithic flakes, hand-made pottery, and occasional scraps of copper and bronze at least as late as c. 200 B.C., and it must provisionally be regarded as a first-millennium form which may have had a long life. The concurrence of relatively primitive stone-using societies alongside others with more advanced equipment was doubtless a phenomenon of ancient as of more modern India.

The Indus civilization. In the Indus and Ghaggar valleys the

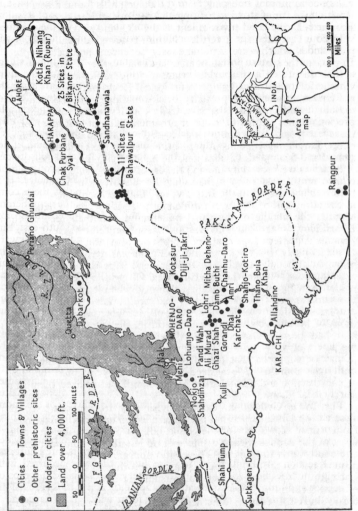

THE INDUS CIVILIZATION

village communities emerging from the Baluch hills found a new challenge which stimulated a surprising and perhaps sudden development. For the self-contained environment of the highland glen was now substituted a vast expanse of fertile alluvium renewed annually by huge river-floods which were simultaneously beneficent and catastrophic. In place of the narrow portals of an upland valley, the villagers now had at their doors a series of arterial streams inviting traffic and interchange, whether of peaceful or less peaceful kinds. Rocks and minerals were no longer immediately present; brick-building took the place of masonry; and only an expensive trade could win the minerals and precious stones required for use or ornament. The urgent moral of all these needs and opportunities was co-ordination and amplification of effort. Larger aggregations of population were at the same time necessitated and facilitated. Civilization, the habit of city life, was born.

So far as we know, city life and the art of writing which was closely related and necessary to it, had alike been evolved in Mesopotamia before they emerged in the Indus valley. Both in Mesopotamia began in the latter half of the fourth millennium, and it seems to have been towards the middle of the third millennium that both reached the Indus. How far the Indus civilization was influenced by that of Mesopotamia is matter of speculation. Egypt may provide a partial analogy. It seems likely that brick-building in Egypt was derived from Mesopotamia, although only in the earliest period are there close formal resemblances between the two countries. Of writing there is no good evidence in Egypt before the First dynasty, when it appears in much the same stage of development as had been attained through some centuries by the Proto-literate writing of Mesopotamia. In both cases, those of building-construction and writing, the inference is that the *idea* had been borrowed from Mesopotamia but had, either immediately or very quickly, been given a local expression. Similarly, it may be supposed that the early citizens of the Indus valley had, under the stimulus of local need and opportunity, adapted the *ideas* of construction and writing from Mesopotamia but utilized them in a purely local idiom.

The Indus civilization, dated provisionally from about 2500 to 1500 B.C. or a little earlier, has been identified on upwards of sixty sites, from Rūpar at the foot of the Simla hills to Sutkagen-dor near the coast of the Arabian Sea, a distance of no less than a thousand miles, and southwards to Gujarat. These sites appear to fall into two main groups, one on the middle Indus system, the other on the lower Indus. Each group is focused on a city of outstanding size, with a periphery of some three miles: Harappā (Panjab) in the former group, Mohenjo-daro (Sind) in the latter. Whether the two cities were complementary capitals of a consolidated empire, or whether they represent two separate régimes, is a matter of guesswork, but of their metropolitan status there can be no doubt.

Of the beginnings of this far-flung civilization, almost nothing is at

PLATE I

b. Mohenjo-daro: Street with drains

a. Mohenjo-daro: 'Low Lane'

PLATE 2

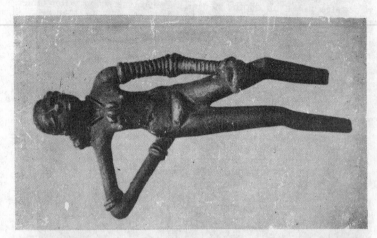

b. Mohenjo-daro: Bronze figure ($\frac{1}{2}$)

a. Mohenjo-daro: Stone head ($\frac{2}{3}$)

present known. Only in a tiny area at Harappā have archaeologists penetrated to its full depth; at Mohenjo-daro the rising water-table makes deep research difficult. But so far as it is known, the civilization presents an astonishing measure of uniformity, exaggerated doubtless by summary methods of research but none the less unmistakable. In its latter stages, indeed, there is evidence at both capitals of a lowering of social standards, of the supercession of major buildings by ill constructed warrens, indicating a swarming population of lower grade. The change, however, was one of degree rather than of kind. For a thousand years the citizens of the Indus valley lived according to their rule, having, as it seems, achieved a balanced pattern at the outset and lacking, therefore, the stimulus for radical change. Their mode of life was rooted in a civic discipline of no uncertain kind; at Mohenjo-daro, and to a less-known extent at Harappā, the urban layout bespeaks authority. At both sites the main body of the city is dominated towards the west by a citadel some 400 × 200 yards in extent and built up to a height of 20–50 feet by piled mud and mud-brick, wholly or partly encompassed by walls and towers of baked and unbaked brick and of formidable size. At Mohenjo-daro, where some of the internal buildings of the citadel have been recovered, these include a sacred bath, a large residence or college (for the priests?), halls of assembly, and a great granary where, it may be supposed, tribute in kind was received and stored. At Harappā equivalent granaries were grouped below the citadel near the (former) river and were associated with serried lines of circular brick platforms for pounding grain, and with barrack-like workmen's quarters. The geometrical planning clearly reflects centralized and effective control of an autocratic or bureaucratic kind.

At Mohenjo-daro, and by inference at Harappā, the lower city was marshalled into blocks or *insulae*, each about the same size superficially as the citadel and bounded by straight unpaved streets some 30 feet wide. The blocks were subdivided by lanes, and both lanes and streets carried brick-lined drains equipped at intervals with manholes to facilitate clearing. The houses were typically of courtyard plan, with brick staircases to upper storeys or flat roofs. Temples have not been definitely recognized, though small stone sculptures of squatting bearded figures probably represent gods, and there is other evidence for a complex religion or religions having affinities with later Hinduism, particularly in the form of a horned Śiva-like figure. The architecture throughout, as preserved, is of the plainest; in a climate evidently moister than today, baked bricks were almost universal, with traces here and there of a rendering of mud-plaster. The rare arches are all corbelled, the voussoir-arch being unknown.

The equipment of the Indus folk included both simple chert blades and implements of copper and bronze—flat axes, knives, saws, spears, and occasionally short swords or dirks. An extensive terracotta industry produced innumerable figurines of animals, particularly bulls, and distinctive female 'dolls' which may sometimes have been votive. The pottery, characteristically red with black patterns of scales, intersecting circles, pipal-leaves, and peacocks, is without close analogy. But amongst small objects the most remarkable are the steatite seal-stones bearing vivid representations of animals and, rarely, of human figures. The animals include cattle of various kinds, tiger, rhinoceros, elephant, and crocodile, in some instances associated with objects which probably

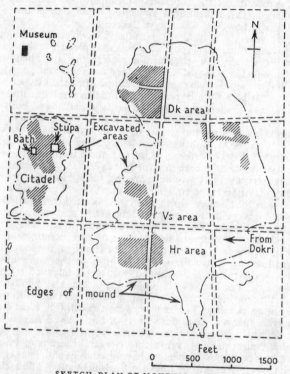

SKETCH-PLAN OF MOHENJO-DARO

indicate animal worship. These seals, or derivatives from them, are occasionally found, with other Indus objects, on Mesopotamian sites, particularly in the Sargonid period about 2350 B.C. The primary utility of these contacts is that they give an approximate date for a flourishing period of the Indus civilization, but there is no evidence that the Western trade which they presumably represent was of any great extent.

Most of the seals bear inscriptions in the pictographic script which

PLAN OF THE CITADEL, HARAPPĀ

still constitutes one of the major mysteries of the Indus civilization. Attempts to interpret it have hitherto failed. The number of signs shows that it cannot be alphabetic; it is probably syllabic, and was read in alternate lines from right to left and from left to right, i.e. boustrophedon. It is unrelated to any known script, although, as already remarked, this fact does not rule out the likelihood that the initial *idea* of writing came from the west. The claim that it was the parent of the Brāhmī script of India awaits confirmation.

A long period of structural decadence at Mohenjo-daro ended in violence which has left dramatic groups of contorted skeletons in the streets and houses of the highest level. The episode has been tentatively interpreted in the light of the hymns of the *Rigveda*, which refer frequently to the storming of the fortified native cities of the Land of the Five (or Seven) Rivers by the Aryan invaders. The date of the Aryan invasions of India has been much disputed, but the trend of opinion is towards the fifteenth century B.C., and the rigid oral tradition perpetuated in the older books of the *Rigveda* is thought to be of almost equal antiquity. The literary evidence and the archaeological evidence as recently reassessed converge sufficiently to render the view likely that the Indus civilization was in fact obliterated a little before 1500 B.C. by an insurgent barbarism, instinct with the heroic qualities which barbarism is likely to assume but not sympathetic to the vestiges of urban discipline. On the other hand, if the relics of the Indus religion are rightly understood, it would appear that some elements of it passed over from the conquered into the religion of the invaders and ultimately into that of modern India. The recurrent figures of the proto-Śiva already noted from the Indus cities, evidences of phallic worship and of reverence paid to animals, particularly the bull, have nothing to do with the Vedic faith of the Aryans but anticipate dominant elements of the historic Brahmanism in spite of its Aryan garb.

The Aryan invaders. For the next thousand years, roughly 1500–500 B.C.—the 'Dark Millennium'—our knowledge of events and cultures in India is dependent mainly upon a dubious literary (or, rather, oral) tradition supplemented by an inadequate but increasing body of material evidence. From the Vedic hymns it has been possible to piece together a reasonably coherent picture of the Aryan invaders on their first impact with the black, noseless (flat-nosed) *dasyus* who comprised their native opponents and subjects. The archetype of the invaders was their war-god, Indra; like him, the Aryan hero was strong, bearded, of mighty appetite, and a great drinker of the divine liquid, *soma*, a drink of unknown composition but equivalent to the nectar of the Greek world. For war or for racing he was mounted in a two-horsed, two-wheeled chariot, armed with a bow or a spear and with a charioteer crouching beside him. The hearth was the centre of domestic life, but we are told little of the dwellings themselves, save that they were of timber, rectangular, and thatched. There were also assembly halls where the men transacted business and gambled. Temples are

PLATE 3

Right Stone 'choppers' and *left* Stone hand-axes from the Sohan Valley, Panjab

PLATE 4

Steatite seals and impressions from Mohenjo-daro

not described, but there were turf altars and animal sacrifices at which the victims were tied to posts. Music and dancing were indulged in, and there were drums, flutes, and seven-stringed harps.

Flocks of sheep and goats were pastured, but the Aryans were first and foremost cattle-breeders and beef-eaters—in the latter respect differing markedly from their medieval and modern successors in India. Grain, possibly barley, was grown and the plough was used; but this stabilizing element does not appreciably modify the general picture of an essentially mobile society of a kind typical of the heroic age in other lands—in Homeric Greece, for example, and in the Celtic West. It is that of a warrior aristocracy, interested in feeding and fighting but little concerned with its humbler foot-slogging peasantry.

After the Indus civilization. The prolonged chaos which must have ensued from the intrusion of these vigorous barbarians into the settled and probably effete populations of north-western India may be supposed to have left widespread traces, both positive and negative, could we but clearly recognize them. Village mounds such as Rānā Ghundāī in the Zhob region of northern Baluchistan or Nāl, farther south, show evidence of conflagrations at an appropriate level; so much so that the Nāl mound is known locally as the Sohr Damb or Red Mound from its fire-reddened soil. At Chanhu-daro, a town of the Indus civilization eighty miles south of Mohenjo-daro, the Indus population deserted their homes and were succeeded by a poorer folk (known to archaeologists as representatives of the 'Jhukar' culture) who re-used some of the derelict houses and supplemented them with rectangular hovels of matting paved with broken brick. The new-comers had circular uninscribed seals or seal-amulets of pottery or faïence bearing a crude decoration lacking all the delicate realism of the Indus series. Similar seals, but of copper, were found at Shahi-tump in southern Baluchistan, in a cemetery perhaps of the second millennium B.C. inserted into a derelict village that had been in contact with the Indus peoples. And at Harappā itself, after the abandonment of the city, a strange folk of unknown origin arrived and built shoddy houses among the ruins. Their burial-rite was at first inhumation, but later the custom was introduced of exposing the dead and subsequently interring selected bones in urns. These 'Cemetery H' people, as they are called, have been tentatively recognized as Aryans, but little is known about them, nor is it easy to guess how long after the departure or subjugation of the Indus people their arrival should be placed.

Certain other groups of 'finds' may be ascribed to the thousand years now in question, though only preliminary information is at present available. The Drishadvatī valley of Bikaner, and Hastināpur on the upper reaches of the Jumna, have produced a crude, ill-fired pottery washed with ochre and known therefore as 'Ochre Ware', which seems to follow the Indus phase at no great interval of time. More certain is it that a fine wheel-turned grey ware, mostly in the form of semicircular bowls and convex-sided dishes with rough linear patterns in brown or black,

was popular during and perhaps before the first half of the last millennium B.C. in the valleys of the Satlej, Sarasvatī, and Drishadvatī, i.e.
the Panjāb-Bikaner area. With it are associated mud houses, agriculture,
and cattle-breeding, and it seems to represent a settled population
with a bronze-age culture (copper or bronze arrow-heads) and an
increasing trend towards something approaching town life. Whether
the Grey Ware culture occurs in the main valley of the Indus is not yet
known; but in the central Ganges valley it appears to represent an
initial phase of jungle-clearing and settlement. It or the Ochre Ware may
there equate with the remarkable hoards of bronze implements which
have been found on some twenty sites from the Ganges–Jumna valleys
as far south as Gungeria in the Deccan. The hoards comprise a distinctive assemblage of flat and shouldered axes, elongated 'bar-celts',
barbed harpoons bearing a superficial resemblance to the bone (or
horn) harpoon-heads of mesolithic Europe, and swords with antenna-
like pommels. Unfortunately their stratigraphical position is unknown,
and their ascription to the period 1500–500 B.C., whilst safe enough, is
too vague for use. Whether they and the Grey Ware, or even the Ochre
Ware, are parallel manifestations of the Aryan invasions of northern
India rests, therefore, in the realm of conjecture.

Alternative or supplementary identifications between material
evidence and the complex episode of the Aryan invasions have been
mooted. Thus certain Iron Age cairn-burials in northern Baluchistan
have been regarded in some vague sense as 'Aryan'. A series at Mughul
Ghundāi produced a distinctive tripod jar, a bracelet, bells, rings, and
arrow-heads, all of bronze, of types characteristic of 'Sialk B' in Persia
and attributable to the period before and after 1000 B.C. The association of these groups with early bearers of the Aryan tongue is without
warrant. If a word of warning be appropriate, it is the desirability of
avoiding an excessively Aryan 'preoccupation' in the present stage of
knowledge. Many of the cultures in the wide period and region in
question may be supposed to have had little to do with Aryan speakers;
if anything, the influence may in any particular instance have operated
in the reverse direction.

In the sixth century B.C., when the dominance of Grey Ware on the
northern plains was dwindling, a new and equally distinctive ceramic
came into use in and beyond the central valley of the Ganges. This
took the form of bowls and dishes with a peculiarly lustrous black or
dark grey surface on a whitish core, and has been christened Northern
Black Polished Ware. It is characteristic of the full development of
urbanization in the neighbourhood of the Ganges and the Jumna, an
event which seems to have begun more than half a millennium after
the decline of city life in the Indus valley farther west. No doubt the
dense and widespread jungles of the Ganges plain had combined with
other factors to delay this development in spite of the relative proximity
of the Indus model. With or shortly after the appearance of the Northern Black Polished Ware, iron came generally into use, in the form of

barbed arrow-heads, chisels, sickles, and other implements; and at the same time the regular use of burnt brick and the construction of impressively large houses once more became normal. Preceding the Black Polished Ware and in part apparently synchronizing with it, another ceramic series appeared on the Mālwā plateau and in central India, in the valleys of the Narbadā and the Chambal; it was marked by simple black patterns on a red or cream slip, and is sometimes associated with one of the long-lived microlithic blade industries, though it is also found with flat copper axes. There is at present no good evidence in India for the use of iron before the sixth century B.C.

South India in the late prehistoric period. North-western India may be said to have entered the historic period, however uncertainly, when it was incorporated in the Achaemenid empire by Darius, the Great King of Persia, shortly before 500 B.C., and in 326 B.C. Alexander the Great brought his own historians into the land (pp. 73 and 84). In the south, even this limited measure of definition is difficult to achieve. The inscriptions of Aśoka carry the admonitions of the royal evangelist as far south as the north of Mysore State about 250 B.C. (pp. 117–23) but scarcely illumine the surrounding darkness. By the first century A.D. trade between the Roman world and the Indian peninsula had introduced the sub-continent to the Western geographers, and there are faint

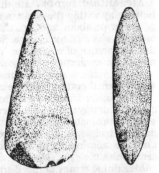

TYPICAL STONE-AXE FROM SOUTHERN INDIA ($\frac{1}{2}$)

reactions in Indian epigraphy and literature. For what such classifications are worth, it may be affirmed that the prehistory of southern India came to an end somewhere between 250 B.C. and A.D. 100, although long after A.D. 100 the methods of prehistoric research must still dominate our inquiry. For greater precision it will be convenient to end the prehistoric period in the south with the organization of Indo-Roman trade in the principate of Augustus, at the beginning of the first century A.D. (p. 160). From that time onwards, impact with the historic West begins to introduce a new element of exactness into the affairs of the peninsula, and the powerful Sātavāhana empire of the Deccan adds a useful quota.

Reference has already been made to the 'stone axe' culture which has been shown by excavation at Brahmagiri in Mysore State and in the neighbouring Bellary District to have been prevalent in the Deccan for some considerable period prior to c. 200 B.C. Between Burma and Cape Comorin, many hundreds of these distinctive polished 'pointed-butt' axes have been found; but the great majority have been surface finds without cultural context, and it must not be assumed that throughout this vast area they represent an identical culture or period. The extent in time and space of the Brahmagiri-Bellary culture can only be proved by further excavation at widely separated points. Meanwhile the evidence indicates that, in the southern area investigated, before and after the middle of the first millennium B.C. the population was housed in wooden huts, and produced hand-made pottery decorated at first with incisions or occasionally with rough geometrical or plant patterns applied in ochre after firing. Rough microlithic flakes and, rarely, an implement of copper or bronze completed the surviving equipment. Burial seems to have been by inhumation, the bodies of children being enclosed in round-bottomed pots.

Megalithic tombs. In the third century B.C. Brahmagiri and Bellary lay within the Mauryan empire (p. 127), but after the death of Aśoka in or about 236 B.C. the empire rapidly melted away and the moment was ripe for change. Whether that was in fact the context for the appearance of a series of 'megalithic' cultures in the peninsula is matter for conjecture; but now if not earlier there appeared upon the southern scene a new folk bringing an elaborate equipment of iron, wheel-turned pottery, and the custom of burying the dead collectively, after exposure and excarnation, in megalithic cists with a round port-hole or doorway in one end. Survivors of the older population continued as a subordinate element, but the megalith-builders were now the dominant class, and, in this region at any rate, remained dominant until the culmination of the Śātavāhana empire in the first and second centuries A.D.

Megalithic tombs of this distinctive type, covered by large capstones and a low circular cairn or barrow and surrounded by stone circles, are very numerous in the peninsula south of Hyderabad (Deccan). They are normally associated with polished red-and-black pottery of a distinctive kind, and with a rich assortment of iron objects including knives, swords, arrowheads, sickles, wedges, chisels, and all-metal spears or lances sometimes over 6 feet in length. Of the origin and growth of this culture we have little knowledge; when it reached Brahmagiri it was obviously in a mature stage, and all that can be predicated about it is that it must have come from the north or north-west. East of India there is no hint of any analogous culture. Far to the north-west, in western Asia, northern Africa, and Europe, are comparable tombs, usually of considerably earlier date. Whether any integral relationship ever existed between the Indian and the Western series, we do not know. In the neighbourhood of Karachi are megalithic cists—not, so far as limited information goes, with the distinctive 'porthole'—which may have constituted a link between the two. But much further investigation over wide areas of Asia and possibly Africa is needed before the south Indian megaliths can be rooted in the West. All that can be said at present is that the associated red-and-black pottery, though absent from the Gangetic plain, occurs in the

Narbadā valley and the Vindhyas at least as early as the Northern Black Polished Ware, and thence extends southwards throughout peninsular India.

Urnfields. To some extent contemporaneous with the cists are the urnfields which are numerous in southern India and may cover 100 acres or more, indicating either large or long-settled populations. One of the best known of these is beside the Tāmraparnī river in the Tinnevelly District, but others are to be found near Madras, near Pondicherry, and in many other localities. The dead are usually buried in large pear-shaped urns associated with smaller urns, but sometimes in the Madras area a terra-cotta sarcophagus on legs is substituted. The latter occurs on occasion within a circle of boulder-like stones or even in a rough cist. The numerous varieties of urn-burial, like those of megalithic burial, await analysis; meanwhile, it must suffice to note the problem. The actual dwelling-places of the urnfield folk have not been identified with certainty, but a very little research should reveal them.

The Greeks and the Śakas. For the north about this time a little more information is available. Small communities of Greek or semi-Greek origin settled in the Panjāb and North-west Frontier consequent on Alexander's invasion in 326 B.C., and the Bactrian kingdom and its offshoots were in some measure the seat of a provincial Hellenism between 246 B.C. and A.D. 50. The next extensive immigration of which any definite knowledge has survived is that of the Śakas, which began in the second or first century B.C. The term Śaka was used by the Indians in a vague way to denote all foreigners from the other side of the passes, without nice distinction of race or tribe. It may have included both squat, narrow-eyed Mongols, and handsome races like the Turks, who resemble the traditional Aryans in physique. The Sakas formed kingdoms in the Panjāb, at Mathurā, and in the Kāthiā-wār peninsula.

The Yueh-chi. In the first century after Christ another nomad tribe from central Asia called the Yueh-chi descended upon the plains of northern India. Their leading clan, the Kushāns, founded a great empire which extended southwards apparently as far as the Narbadā. The Kushāns appear to have been big fair-complexioned men, probably of Turkī race, and possibly akin to the Iranian or Persian Aryans. The Śaka and Yueh-chi conquests must have introduced a large element of foreign blood into the Indian population. Obscure indications exist of Iranian invasions in the third century of the Christian era, but nothing definite has been ascertained about them, if they really occurred.

The Hūnas or Huns. There is no doubt that during the fifth and sixth centuries great multitudes of fierce folk from the central Asian steppes swooped down on both Persia and India. Those invaders are called by the Indians Hūnas, or in English Huns, a term used in a general sense like the earlier term Śakas, to cover a mass of various tribes.[1] Other Huns who invaded Europe are known to have been fierce tribesmen of the Mongolian kind; but the assailants of India are distinguished as Ephthalites or White Huns, a name which may imply that they were fair people like the Turks. Many of the Rājpūt castes or clans, as well as the Jāts, Gūjars, and certain other existing communities, are descended either from the Hūnas or from allied hordes which arrived about the same time. The appearance of the existing castes so descended indicates that their foreign ancestors must have been mostly of the tall, fair, good-looking type. The population of the Panjāb and the United Provinces is free from Mongolian features except in the sub-Himalayan and Himalayan regions.

The Hun irruptions mark a distinct epoch in the history of northern India, the significance of which will be explained later. They are mentioned prominently in this place because they contributed some of the best elements to the population.

Type of Muslim settlers. The last movement which introduced a large new class of recruits to the Indian population was that of the Muslims, beginning with the inroads of the Arabs at the commencement of the eighth century and ending with the establishment of the Mughul dynasty in the sixteenth century. Subsequent Muslim immigration has been on a small scale. The Muslim invaders and settlers, other than the Arab conquerors of Sind, belonged to various Asiatic races, including a certain number of narrow-eyed, yellow-tinted, beardless Mongols. But the majority were collected from nations or tribes of different appearance, and were tall, good-looking, fair-complexioned, bearded men. They comprised Iranian Persians akin to the Indo-Aryans, Turks, Afghans of many varieties, and sundry peoples of mixed descent. The admixture of Mongol blood having been overborne by the other elements has left little trace in the features of modern Indian Muslims. The effect of the immigration on the whole has been to increase materially the proportion of tall, fair-complexioned people in the country. The physical type of the Muslim immigrants was far more like that of the Indo-Aryan Brahmans than it was to the dark 'aboriginal' type indigenous in India.

Rapid spread of Islām. The rapidity of the spread of Islām, the religion of Muhammad, and the dramatic suddenness with which the adherents of his creed rose to a position of dominant sovereignty constitute one of the marvels, or it might be said the miracles of history. No cut-and-dried explanation that can be offered is felt to account adequately for the astounding facts. But history records not a few other unexplained marvels, and we must be content to acknowledge that many things in the past, as in the present, pass man's understanding.

The Prophet Muhammad, a native of Mecca, was more than fifty years of age before he attained any considerable success. He believed

---

[1] A Brahman author, writing about A.D. 1600, applied the term to the Portuguese, and the poet Śrinivāsa, writing in the eighteenth century, referred to the French of Pondicherry as *Prāmśu-Hūnas*.

himself to be the divinely appointed messenger of a revelation destined to supersede the Jewish and Christian religions, as well as the rude paganism of his countrymen. His fellow citizens at Mecca were so hostile that in A.D. 622 he was obliged to quit his birthplace and take refuge at Medina. That event, renowned as the Flight, or Hijra, is the epoch of the Muslim Hijrī era, vulgarly called the Hegira.[1] The remaining ten years of his life sufficed to make him substantially the sovereign of Arabia and the accepted Prophet of the Arabs. Soon after his death in A.D. 632 his successors, the early Khalīfs ('Caliphs'), found themselves in conflict with the mighty Persian and Byzantine empires. Nothing could withstand the furious enthusiasm of the Arabs from the desert, beneath whose attack ancient thrones tottered and fell.

Within the brief space of eighty years from the Prophet's death his Arab followers had become the masters, not only of Arabia, but of Persia, Syria, western Turkistan, Sind, Egypt, and southern Spain. They carried their new religion with them, and either imposed it on their opponents at the point of the sword, or compelled them to ransom their lives by heavy payments.

Islām in the borderlands. The Indian borderlands soon attracted the attention of the Khalīfs. The Arabs reached the coast of Makrān as early as A.D. 643. The conquest of Sind was effected by Muhammad bin Qāsim in A.D. 712, and thenceforward for centuries that country remained under Arab rule. Kābul was subdued or made tributary at a later date. From the beginning of the eighth century many Arabs and Muslims of other nations must have settled in Sind and the neighbouring countries, effecting a marked change in the character of the population. But India proper remained substantially unaffected, although Arab traders occasionally visited the western kingdoms for business purposes and the Arab chiefs of Sind made several raids on Hindu territory. The Indian Rājās rarely troubled themselves about events taking place to the west of the Hakrā river, then the boundary between Sind and Hind.[2]

Islām in India proper. The annexation of the Panjab to the Ghaznī kingdom about A.D. 1020 by Sultan Mahmūd necessarily involved extensive settlement of Muslim strangers in that province, although the rest of India continued to be free from their presence. From the closing years of the twelfth century, when Muhammad of Ghōr began the systematic conquest of the country, a constant stream of Muslim immigrants continued to flow in; and during the period of the growth of the Sultanate of Delhi new-comers arrived without ceasing. During the decline of the Sultanate from 1340 to 1526 the immigration must have diminished, but in the latter year it received a

---

[1] Muslim dates are usually designated as A.H. (*anno hegirae*). For example, A.H. 1335 = A.D. 1916–17, from October to October. The Hijri year is lunar, of about 354 days, and so is 11 days shorter than the solar year.

[2] The Hakrā, which finally dried up in the eighteenth century, used to flow through the Bahāwalpur State and the region which is now the Sind desert.

fresh impetus from the victories of Bābur. During the next two centuries a certain number of Muslims from beyond the border effected a
lodgement, although the total was not very great. The older colonies,
however, multiplied, crowds of converts from Hinduism were made,
and intermarriages between the old and new Muslims took place.
The tendency of the Muslim population is to increase, its fertility
being superior to that of the Hindus. The immigrant Muslims, although
thoroughly naturalized, retain their distinctness and never become
merged in the Hindu majority, as their predecessors the Śakas, Hūnas,
and the rest were absorbed. The reason is to be found in the definite
character of the Muslim creed, resting on scriptures of known date, and
consisting essentially of only two doctrines, the unity of God and the
divine mission of Muhammad. That simple creed inspires intense
devotion and offers unbroken resistance to the seductions of Hinduism,
although Indo-Muslim social practice is affected considerably by its
surroundings. The looser beliefs of the early immigrants from central
Asia were not strong enough to withstand the subtle influence of the
Brahmanical environment. The Shamanism of the nomad invaders,
like the chthonic cults of the Dravidians, yielded before the attractive
force of the Hindu system, so that each successive wave of pre-Muslim
foreigners quickly melted away in the ocean of caste.

Smaller foreign communities. Since the fifteenth century a
considerable population of mixed Indo-European blood, originating
from unions of Portuguese, English, and other Europeans with Indian
women, has grown up, which forms an important element in the
population of the great cities, the Bombay Konkan, and the settlements
on the lower Himalayan ranges.

The Jews, Parsis, Armenians, and certain other small foreign
communities maintain their isolation so strictly that they hardly affect
the racial character of the general population.

Language no proof of race. Sanskrit, with its derivative vernaculars; the old Persian, or Zend language; Greek, Latin, German,
English, and many other European tongues, form a well-defined group
or family of languages which is designated either as Indo-Germanic
or as Aryan. Many authors have shown a tendency to assume that the
various peoples who speak Aryan tongues must be of Aryan race,
connected one with the other more or less closely by ties of blood.
That assumption is wholly unwarranted. Community of language is no
proof of community of blood. The population of India, as we have seen,
comprises extremely various elements, descended from all sorts of
people who formerly spoke all sorts of languages. In the north, for
instance, no trace remains of the central Asian tongues spoken by the
diverse tribes comprised under the terms Śaka, Hūna, or Yueh-chi.
The descendants of those people now speak Hindī and other languages
closely related to Sanskrit. Similar cases may be observed all over the
world. Languages become extinct and are replaced by others spoken
by races whose position gives them an advantage. Thus, in Great

Britain, the Cornish language is absolutely extinct, and the Cornish people, who are of different race from the English, now speak nothing but English.

Aryan ideas and institutions have shown marvellous power and vitality in all parts of India, but the proportion of Aryan blood in the veins of the population, which is small almost everywhere, is non-existent in some provinces.

Languages. The most important family of Indian languages, the Indo-Aryan, comprises all the principal languages of northern and western India, Hindī, Bengālī, Marāthī, Gujarātī, and many others, descended from ancient vernaculars or Prākrits, closely akin both to the Vedic and to the later literary forms of Sanskrit.

The family or group of tongues second in importance is the Dravidian in the peninsula, comprising Tamil, Telugu, Malayālam, Kanarese, and Tulu, besides some minor tongues. Both Tamil and Telugu have rich literatures. The Tamil is the principal and perhaps the oldest language of the group. The grammar and structure of the Dravidian speech differ wholly from the Aryan type. The most ancient Tamil literature, dating from the early centuries of the Christian era, or even earlier, was composed on Dravidian lines and independent of Sanskrit models. The later literature in all the languages has been largely influenced by Brahmanical ideas and diction. The linguistic family is called Dravidian because Dravida was the ancient name of the Tamil country in the far south. In fact, Tamil is really the same word as the adjective Drāvida. Three other families of languages, namely, the Munda, the Mon-Khmēr, and the Tibeto-Chinese, are represented on Indian soil, but as they possess little or no literature, and are mostly spoken by rude, savage, or half-civilized tribes, it is unnecessary to discuss their peculiarities. The speakers of those tongues have had small influence on the course of history.

The Indo-Aryan movement. The Indo-Aryans, after they had entered the Panjab—the 'land of the five rivers', or 'of the seven rivers' according to an ancient reckoning—travelled generally in a south-easterly direction. For reasons unknown they called the south *dakshina*, or 'right-hand', a word familiar in its English corruption as 'the Deccan'. The larger part of the tribes crossed the Panjab and then moved along the courses of the Ganges and Jumna, but some sections at an early period had advanced a considerable distance down the Indus, while others, at a later date, apparently marched eastward along the base of the mountains into Mithilā or Tirhūt. While resident in the Panjab the strangers had not yet become Hindus, but were only Hindus in the making. The distinctive Brahmanical system appears to have been evolved, after the Sutlaj had been passed, in the country to the north of Delhi. The apparently small tract between the rivers Saras-vatī and Drishadvatī, which it is difficult to identify with precision, is specially honoured by Manu as Brahmāvarta, 'the land of the gods'; the less-exalted title of Brahmarshi-deśa, 'the land of divine sages', being given to the larger region comprising Brahmāvarta or Kuruk-shetra, roughly equivalent to the tract about Thānēsar, with the addition of Matsya or eastern Rajasthan, Panchāla, or the Doāb between the Ganges and Jumna, and Surasena, or the Mathura District.[1]

When the legal treatise ascribed to Manu had assumed its present shape, perhaps about A.D. 200 or earlier, the whole space between the Himālaya and the Vindhyas from sea to sea was recognized as Āryā-varta, or 'Aryan territory'. The advance thus indicated evidently was a slow business and occupied a long time. The dark-skinned inhabitants of the country subdued by the invaders were called Dasyus and by other names. They are now represented generally by the lower castes in the plains and by certain tribes in hilly regions.

Aryan penetration of the south. Although there is no reason to believe that any large Indo-Aryan tribal body ever marched into the peninsula, which was well protected by the broad belt of hills and forests marked by the Narbadā river and the Sātpura and Vindhya ranges, the peaceful penetration of the Deccan by Indo-Aryan emissaries began many centuries before the Christian era. Tradition credits the Vedic Rishi Agastya, or a namesake of his, with the introduction of Aryan ideas and institutions into the Dravidian south. Probably the chief line of communication was along the eastern coast, and certainly the propagation of the new ideas was effected by Brahmans. The obscure story of the gradual advance of the caste system and other Indo-aryan institutions in India to the south of the Narbadā has not yet been thoroughly investigated, and it is impossible to discuss the subject in these pages.

Distinct Dravidian civilization. When the Brahmans succeeded in making their way into the kingdoms of the peninsula, including the realms of the Āndhras, Cheras, Cholas, and Pāndyas, they found a civilized society, not merely a collection of rude barbarian tribes. The Dravidian religion and social customs differed widely from those of northern India. Caste was unknown, as it now is in Burma, and the religion was centred on the ecstatic and often orgiastic worship of chthonic deities, the chief of whom was the hill god, Murugan. The original divinities have since been adopted by the Brahmans, given new names, and identified with orthodox Hindu gods and goddesses. The Hindu theory that mankind is divided into four *varnas*, or groups of castes—Brahman, Kshatriya, Vaiśya, and Śūdra—was wholly foreign to the southerners. To this day Kshatriyas and Vaiśyas do not exist

[1] The difficulty in precise identification of the Sarasvatī and Drishadvatī is due to the extensive changes in the course of the rivers of northern India which are known to have occurred. Modern maps are utterly misleading, and it is impossible to construct maps of the ancient river system for any time preceding the Muslim invasions. The following passage may be commended to the attention of careful students: 'It is, however, a reasonable conjecture that within the period of history the Sutlej united with the Saᵃasvatī and Ghaggar to form the great river [sc. Hakrā] which once flowed into the Indus through Bahāwalpur, and that then Brahmāvarta was a Doāb [space between rivers] which might be compared with that of the Ganges and Jumna' (C. Pearson, 'Alexander, Porus, and the Panjab', in *Ind. Ant.*, vol. xxxiv, 1905, p. 254).

among them.[1] The laws of marriage and inheritance also differed completely from those of the Brahmans. Even now, when Hinduism, with its strict caste rules and its recognized system of law, has gained the mastery, the old and quite different Dravidian ideas may be traced in a thousand directions. The ancient Dravidian alphabet called Vatteluttu, of semitic origin, is very different from any of the northern alphabets. Tradition as recorded in the ancient Tamil literature indicates that from very early times wealthy cities existed in the south and that many of the refinements and luxuries of life were in common use. The good fortune of Tamil Land (*Tamilakam*) in possessing such eagerly desired commodities as gold, pearls, conch-shells, pepper, beryls, and choice cotton goods attracted foreign traders from the earliest ages.[2] Commerce supplied the wealth required for life on civilized lines, and the Dravidians were not afraid to cross the seas. Some day, perhaps, the history of Dravidian civilization may be written by a competent scholar skilled in all the lore and languages required for the study of the subject, but at present the literature concerned with it is too fragmentary, defective, and controversial to permit of condensation. Early Indian history, as a whole, cannot be viewed in true perspective until the non-Aryan institutions of the south receive adequate treatment. Hitherto most historians of ancient India have written as if the south did not exist.

AUTHORITIES

Prehistoric India. V. A. SMITH, 'Prehistoric Antiquities', chap. iv, vol. ii, *I.G.*, 1908, with a large number of selected references, was the first general outline of the subject. But all previous general works have been superseded by STUART PIGGOTT, *Prehistoric India down to 1000 B.C.* (London, Pelican Series, 1950). For recent excavations see the periodical *Ancient India* published since 1946 by the Archaeological Department of India, New Delhi. See also MORTIMER WHEELER, *The Indus Civilization* (Cambridge, 1953).

Languages. Sir G. GRIERSON, (1) chap. vii in vol. i, *I.G.*, 1907, with ample list of references; (2) *The Languages of India*, Calcutta, 1903, reprinted from *Census Report, India*, 1901; (3) *Linguistic Survey of India* (Calcutta, 1903–28). The work is on a vast scale, in twenty large quarto volumes.

Dravidian civilization. On early Dravidian culture much has been written but little is scholarly, adequate, or reliable. Perhaps the best works are P. T. S. IVENGAR's *History of the Tamils to A.D. 600* (Madras, 1929), of which the first few chapters are useless, and V. R. RAMACHANDRA DIKSHITAR's *Studies in Tamil Literature and History* (Madras, 1936). For Dravidian religion see WHITEHEAD, *The Village Gods of South India*, Oxford University Press, 1916; ELMORE, *Dravidian Gods in Modern Hinduism*, Hamilton, N.Y., 1915 (reprinted from University Studies of the University of Nebraska, 1915).

[1] The fact is not affected by the efforts of certain castes to obtain recognition as Kshatriyas.

[2] The Tamil Land of early ages was much more extensive than the area in which Tamil is now spoken. It included the Kanarese, Malayālam, and Tulu-speaking countries. Ceylon, too, was in close relations with the Tamil-speaking peoples of the mainland. The jewels and spices of the island may therefore be reckoned among the attractions of Tamil Land. The Telugu-speaking country possessed cotton manufactures and diamond mines.

CHAPTER 2

Literature and civilization of the Vedic and Epic periods; the Purānas; caste

Isolation of the oldest literature. The Vedic Indo-Aryans, whose progress has been sketched in bare outline, are known to us through their literature only, which is all, or almost all, so ancient that it cannot be illustrated either by contemporary books or from monuments. No comparable literature in any Indo-European or Aryan language is nearly as old as the hymns of the *Rigveda*, which 'stands quite by itself, high up on an isolated peak of remote antiquity'; and even if some literary fragments from Egypt or Babylonia in languages of different families be as old, they do not help us to understand the Vedic scriptures. No buildings of the period after the fall of the Indus cities survive in India, nor are there any contemporary material remains, except the copper tools and weapons of the north already mentioned, which may be reasonably assigned to an early stage of the Vedic period. The oldest Indo-Aryan literature, as a rule, must be interpreted by means of itself, and we must be content to learn from it alone what we can discover about the Indo-Aryans whose Rishis composed that literature. External sources of information are almost wholly wanting, but the *Avesta*, the scriptures of the ancient Iranians or Persians, although not so old as the Veda, contributes illustrative matter of value.

The Veda; faith and science. The oldest literature of the Indo-Aryans is known collectively as Veda, which means 'knowledge'—the best of all knowledge in Hindu eyes. It is also designated in the plural as 'the Vedas', 'the three Vedas', or 'the four Vedas'. Most orthodox Hindus accept the whole Veda, forming in itself an enormous literature, as inspired revelation (*śruti*) in opposition to later venerable books classed as traditional learning (*smriti*). But the adherents of the Ārya Samāj, and possibly those of some other sects, allow the rank of revealed matter to the hymns alone, while denying it to the rest of the Veda. The belief that the Vedas were revealed complete as they stand without any process of development seems to be widely held,[1] and means for reconciling such belief with the results of scientific investigation of the documents may not be beyond the powers of human ingenuity. In these pages theories of inspiration will not be further noticed, and the Vedic literature will be treated merely as what it professes to be, the production of individual men and a few women, who composed their

[1] Hopkins (p. 3) quotes the saying:

Na hi chhandānsi kriyante, nityāni chhandānsi;
'Vedic verses are not made, they are eternal.'

works at times widely separated and with varying degrees of literary power.

The Veda, regarded as literature, demands from students of humanity the most respectful attention on account of its remote antiquity, its unique character, and the light which it sheds upon the evolution of mankind, especially in India. The *Rigveda*, as Whitney observes, contains 'the germs of the whole after-development of Indian religion and polity'.

Definition of the Veda. Opinions have varied concerning the definition of the Veda. Kautilya, in the *Arthaśāstra* ascribed to the fourth century B.C., states that 'the three Vedas, Sāma, Rik, and Yajus, constitute the triple Vedas. These together with Atharvaveda and the Itihāsaveda are known as the Vedas. . . . Purāna, Itivritta (history), Ākhyāyika (tales), Udāharana (illustrative stories), Dharmaśāstra, and Arthaśāstra are (known by the name) Itihāsa.'[1]

Kautilya's definition is wider than that ordinarily accepted, which excludes the later, although ancient literature comprised by him under the comprehensive term *Itihāsa*. Common usage recognizes four and only four Vedas, namely (1) the *Rigveda*,[2] (2) the *Sāmaveda*, (3) the *Yajurveda*, and (4) the *Atharvaveda*.

The claim of the last named to be included in the canon has not always been recognized, and not long ago it could be said that 'the most influential Brahmans of southern India still refuse to accept the authority of the fourth Veda, and deny its genuineness'.

But for most people the Vedas are four, and must be described as such.

Contents of the Veda. The essential fundamental part of each of the four Vedas is a *samhitā*, or collection of metrical hymns, prayers, spells, or charms, mixed in some cases with prose passages. But certain supplementary writings are also considered by general consent to be actually part of the Vedas, and are regarded by many Hindus as inspired revelation like the *samhitās*. Those supplements written in prose are the *Brāhmanas* and the *Upanishads*. The *Brāhmanas* are theological and ritual treatises designed as manuals of worship and explanations of the *samhitās*. They are of considerably later date than the verses but still very ancient, and in some cases preserve the written accent, which was disused very early. The *Brāhmanas* include certain mystic treatises called *Āranyakas*, or 'Forest-books', supposed to be 'imparted or studied in the solitude of the forest'. The *Upanishads*,

[1] *Arthaśāstra*, revised translation by R. Shama Sastri (3rd ed., Mysore, 1929), Book I, chaps. 3, 5. Kautilya, it will be observed, places the *Sāmaveda* first.

[2] The name *Rigveda* is a compound of the words *rich* and *veda*, *ch* becoming *g* by the rules of *sandhi*. *Rich* signifies 'any prayer or hymn in which a deity is praised. As these are mostly in verse, the term becomes also applicable to such passages of any *Veda* as are reducible to measure according to the rules of prosody. The first *Veda*, in Vyāsa's compilation, comprehending most of these texts, is called the *Rigveda*; or as expressed in the Commentary on the Index, "because it abounds in such texts (*rich*)" ' (Colebrooke).

exceeding a hundred in number, are philosophical tracts or books, 'which belong to the latest stage of Brāhmana literature'. Certain of the *Upanishads* are the parts of the Veda best known to Hindu readers in modern days, as being the foundation of the later and more systematic Vedānta philosophy.

The Sūtras. The *Sūtras*, 'compendious treatises dealing with Vedic ritual on the one hand, and with customary law on the other', are admitted by all to rank only as traditional learning (*smriti*), but they are usually regarded as included in the Veda. They are written in a laboriously compressed style, sometimes approaching the structure of algebraic formulas, unintelligible without the help of authoritative commentaries. Such exaggerated value used to be attached to mere brevity of expression that a *sūtra* writer was supposed to derive as much pleasure from the saving of a short vowel as from the birth of a son. The *Sūtras* comprise the *Śrauta*, dealing with the ritual of the greater sacrifices; the *Grihya*, explaining the ceremonial of household worship; and *Dharma*, treating of social and legal usage. The third section is that which mainly concerns the historian, being the foundation of the *Dharmaśāstras*, such as the well-known *Laws of Manu*, so called.

Sāma- and Yajurvedas. Having enumerated the principal classses of works usually included in the Veda, we return to the metrical *samhitās* which are the real Veda. Only two need be noticed particularly, because the *Sāma-* and *Yajurvedas* are comparatively unimportant. The former is a hymn-book, 'practically of no independent value, for it consists entirely of stanzas (excepting only 75) taken from the *Rigveda* and arranged solely with reference to their place in the Soma sacrifice'. The *Yajurveda*, which also borrows much matter from the *Rigveda* and exists in several forms, is a book of sacrificial prayers, and includes some prose formulas.

The Rigveda samhitā. The *Rigveda* unquestionably is the oldest part of the literature and the most important of the Vedas from the literary point of view. The *samhitā* contains 1,017 (or by another reckoning 1,028) hymns, arranged in ten books, of which the tenth certainly is the latest. The collection about equals in bulk the *Iliad* and *Odyssey* together. Books II–VII, known as the 'family books', because they are attributed to the members of certain families, form 'the nucleus of the *Rigveda*, to which the remaining books were successively added'.

Difficulties of the Vedic hymns. The Vedic hymns present innumerable difficulties to the student. The language and grammar, which differ widely from those of the 'classical' Sanskrit, require profound expert investigation before the verses can be compelled to yield sense so as to permit the text to be construed. Even when a literal version in more or less grammatical English has been produced, the meaning behind the words often eludes the translator. The ideas of the Rishis are so remote from those of the modern world that the most learned Sanskritist, whether Indian or foreign, may fail to gras them.

Interpretations consequently differ to an enormous extent, and after all possible has been said and done much remains obscure. Subject to such inherent difficulties and to necessary limitations of space, I will try to give the reader some slight notion of the contents of the *Rigveda* and *Atharvaveda* hymnals, to indicate the nature of the poets' religion, and to draw a faint sketch of the social condition of the Indo-Aryans.

The poetry of the Veda. Professor Macdonell observes that 'by far the greater part of the poetry of the *Rigveda* consists of religious lyrics, only the tenth [and latest] book containing some secular poems. . . . The *Rigveda* is not a collection of primitive popular poetry. . . . It is rather a body of skilfully composed hymns produced by a sacerdotal class', for use in a ritual which was not so simple as has been sometimes supposed. The metres and arrangement are the highly artificial work of persons who may be justly called learned, although probably ignorant of the art of writing. The same competent critic holds that, although the poetry is often marred for our taste by obvious blemishes, the diction is generally simple and unaffected, the thought direct, and the imagery frequently beautiful or even noble. The poems naturally vary much in literary merit, having been composed by many diverse authors at different times. The best may be fairly called sublime, while the worst are mechanical and commonplace.

Subject-matter. Most of the hymns are invocations addressed to the gods, conceived as the powers of nature personified. Agni, or Fire, and Indra, primarily the god of thunder, and secondarily the god of battle, are the favourite deities. Indeed the religion may be regarded as being based upon fire-worship. The gods are represented as great and powerful, disposed to do good to their worshippers, and engaged in unceasing conflict with the powers of evil. The poets usually beg for material favours and seek to win the deity's good will by means of prayers and sacrifices. Nothing indicates that images were used as aids to worship. The Heaven or Sky, personified as Varuna, is the subject of striking poems, and the Sun is addressed as Sūrya, or by other names in several compositions of much merit.

Two specimens of *Rigveda* poetry may help readers to form some estimate of the poetic skill of the Rishis and to appreciate their religious aspirations.

Hymn to the Dawn. The first is part of a hymn to the Dawn (*Ushas*), who is styled by Professor Macdonell 'this fairest creation of Vedic poetry'. The rendering is his.

To the Dawn

(*R.V.* i. 113; *Hist. of Sanskrit Liter.* (1900), p. 83)

There Heaven's Daughter has appeared before us
The maiden flushing in her brilliant garments.
Thou sovran lady of all earthly treasure,
Auspicious Dawn, flush here to-day upon us

In the sky's framework she has shone with splendour;
The goddess has cast off the robe of darkness.
Wakening up the world with ruddy horses,
Upon her well-yoked chariot Dawn is coming.

Bringing upon it many bounteous blessings,
Brightly shining, she spreads her brilliant lustre.
Last of the countless morns that have gone by,
First of bright morns to come has Dawn arisen.

Arise! the breath, the life, again has reached us:
Darkness has gone away and light is coming.
She leaves a pathway for the sun to travel:
We have arrived where men prolong existence.

The tenth book. Commentators have different views concerning
the exact meaning of the Rigvedic mythology, some denying that
the gods addressed severally were really regarded as separate beings.
However that may be, the latest book, the tenth, exhibits a somewhat
advanced aspect of religious thought which prepares the way for the
speculations of the Upanishads and the Vedānta. From among the
many versions of the celebrated Creation Hymn, 'the earliest specimen
of Aryan philosophic thought', I choose the metrical rendering by
Max Müller, who wrote it with the aid of a friend.

CREATION HYMN

(*R.V.* x. 129; *Chips from a German Workshop* (1869), vol. i, p. 78)

Nor Aught nor Nought existed; yon bright sky
Was not, nor heaven's broad woof outstretched above.
What covered all? what sheltered? what concealed?
Was it the water's fathomless abyss?
There was not death—yet was there nought immortal,
There was no confine betwixt day and night;
The only One breathed breathless by itself,
Other than It there nothing since has been.
Darkness there was, and all at first was veiled
In gloom profound—an ocean without light—
The germ that still lay covered in the husk
Burst forth, one nature, from the fervent heat.
Then first came love upon it, the new spring
Of mind[1]—yea, poets in their hearts discerned,
Pondering, this bond between created things
And uncreated. Comes this spark from earth
Piercing and all-pervading, or from heaven?
Then seeds were sown, and mighty powers arose—
Nature below, and power and will above—
Who knows the secret? who proclaimed it here,
Whence, whence this manifold creation sprang?

[1] Macdoneil translates better:

Desire then at the first arose within it,
Desire, which was the earliest seed of spirit.

The Gods themselves came later into being—
Who knows from whence this great creation sprang?
He from whom all this great creation came,
Whether his will created or was mute,
The Most High Seer that is in highest heaven,
He knows it—or perchance even He knows not.

The Atharvaveda. The *Atharvaveda* or *Atharvana* is described as being on the whole 'a heterogeneous collection of spells . . . a collection of the most popular spells current among the masses', and consequently breathing the spirit of a prehistoric age. Some of its formulas may go back to the most remote ages prior even to the separation of the Indo-Aryans from the Iranians. The fact that the book preserves so much old-world lore makes it rather more interesting and important for the history of civilization than the *Rigveda* itself. But it is far inferior as literature. The *Atharvaveda* may be read in the literal annotated version by Whitney as revised by Lanman. Although every line has been Englished word for word, much remains unintelligible as it stands in the translation.

A specimen spell. A specimen, selected chiefly because it is short, will illustrate the character of the spells, and the extreme obscurity of the subject-matter.

AGAINST THE POISON OF SNAKES

(*A.V.* vi. 12; Whitney and Lanman, vol. i, p. 289)

1. I have gone about the race of snakes, as the sun about the sky, as night about living creatures other than the swan; thereby do I ward off thy poison.
2. What was known of old by priests, what by seers, what by gods; what is to be, that has a mouth—therewith do I ward off thy poison.
3. With honey I mix the streams; the rugged mountains are honey; honey is the Pārushnī [a river], the Sipālā; weal be to thy mouth, weal to thy heart.

Such sentences read very like nonsense at first sight. They must, of course, have had a definite meaning for the author, which may be discoverable, but it is not easy to make sense of them. The spell quoted is a perfectly fair sample of the collection and the translation.

A notable poem. Fortunately, the *Atharvaveda* includes some compositions of a higher order, although, as Lanman observes, they are 'few indeed'. The best known of such passages, that expressing the omniscience of the heavens personified as Varuna, deserves quotation. The sentiments and diction find many echoes in the Hebrew poetry of the Old Testament.

THE OMNISCIENCE OF VARUNA

(*A.V.* iv. 16. 1–5; after Muir, in Kaegi, p. 65)

As guardian, the Lord of worlds
Sees all things as if near at hand.
In secret what 'tis thought to do
That to the gods is all displayed.

Whoever moves or stands, who glides in secret,
Who seeks a hiding-place, or hastens from it,
What thing two men may plan in secret council,
A third, King Varuna, perceives it also.

And all this earth King Varuna possesses,
His the remotest ends of yon broad heaven;
And both the seas in Varuna lie hidden,[1]
But yet the smallest water-drop contains him

Although I climbed the furthest heaven, fleeing,
I should not there escape the monarch's power;
From heaven his spies descending hasten hither,
With all their thousand eyes the world surveying.

Whate'er exists between the earth and heaven,
Or both beyond, to Varuna lies open.
The winkings of each mortal eye he numbers,
He wields the universe, as dice a player.

The Indo-Aryan tribes. The Indo-Aryan invasion or immigration evidently was a prolonged movement of a considerable number of tribes, five or more, apparently related one to the other, who called themselves collectively Āryas, as the Iranians did.[2] The term *Ārya*, which seems originally to have meant merely 'kinsman', was understood in later times to imply nobility or respectability of birth, as contrasted with *Anārya*, 'ignoble'. The habits of the tribes, while dwelling to the west of the Indus, were those of an agricultural and pastoral people, who reckoned their wealth in terms of cows. The description of the Indo-Aryans by some writers of authority as 'nomads' is opposed to the evidence of the hymns. Many passages of the *Rigveda*, both in the earliest and the latest books, testify to the habitual cultivation of *yava*, which primarily means 'barley', but may include wheat, which is not mentioned separately.[3]

The tribes as they settled down in interior India naturally would have become more agricultural and less pastoral, like the Gūjars and Āhīrs of later ages. Some of the tribal names, as, for example, Pūru and Chedi,[4] survived into the Epic period, while many died out. Each tribe was a group of families, and in each family the father was master. The whole tribe was governed by a Rājā, whose power was checked to

[1] 'Also the two oceans are Varuna's paunches' (Lanman);
'The loins of Varuna are these two oceans' (Macdonell).

[2] Compare the story of the gradual Hellenization of the land of Greece (Bury, chap. i, sec. 4).

[3] e.g. *R.V.* x. 134. 2, 'As men whose fields are full of barley reap the ripe corn removing it in order'; and vii. 67. 10, 'barley cut or gathered up' (Griffith). Barley is grown all over north-western India, in Afghanistan, and in the Himalayan valleys up to a height of 14,000 feet. Rice, unknown to the *Rigveda*, is often mentioned in the *Atharvaveda*, e.g. iv. 34, 35. But the theory that the Indians originally were nomads is supported by Megasthenes, who was told that 'the Indians were in old times nomads like those Scythians who do not plough but wander about in their waggons, &c.' (Arrian, *Indika*, chap. 7).

[4] Pūru seems to be the Pŏros of Greek authors.

an undefined extent by a tribal council. The tribes dwelt in fortified villages, but there were no towns. The details recorded suggest that the life of the people was not unlike that of many tribes of Afghanistan in modern times before the introduction of fire-arms.[1]

Arts of peace and war. The bow and arrow were the principal weapons, but spears and battle-axes were not unknown. Chariots, each carrying a driver and a fighting man, were employed in battle, a fact which implies considerable advance in the mechanical arts. Armour was worn. The Rigvedic Indo-Aryans were also acquainted with the processes of weaving, tanning, and metallurgy, although they had no knowledge of iron. We have seen that the bronze and copper implements of the Gangetic basin may reasonably be referred to Vedic times. Gold was familiar and was made into jewellery. The tribes fought with each other when so disposed, but all united in hostility to the dark-skinned Indians, whom they despised, and whose lands they annexed.

Diet. The Indo-Aryans, while sharing the ancient Iranian veneration for the cow, felt no scruple about sacrificing both bulls and cows at weddings or on other important occasions. The persons who took part in the sacrifice ate the flesh of the victim, whether bull, cow, or horse. But meat was eaten only as an exception. Milk was an important article of food, and was supplemented by cakes of barley or wheat (*yava*), vegetables, and fruit.

Strong drinks. The people freely indulged in two kinds of intoxicating liquor, called *soma* and *surā*. The Parsees of Yezd and Kirmān in Persia, as well as those of the Deccan and Bombay in India, who still occasionally offer *soma* sacrifices, identify the plant with one or other species of *Asclepias* or *Sarcostemma*. The plants of that genus have a milky juice which can be transformed into a rather unpleasant drink. But the real *soma* plant may have been different, and has not yet been clearly identified.[2] *Surā* probably was a kind of beer. *Soma* juice was considered to be particularly acceptable to the gods, and was offered with elaborate ceremonial. The *Sāmaveda* provides the chants appropriate for the ceremonies.

Amusements. Amusements included dancing, music, chariot-racing, and dicing. Gambling with dice is mentioned so frequently in both the *Rigveda* and the later documents that the prevalence of the practice is beyond doubt. One stanza from the well-known 'Gambler's Lament' (*R.V.* x. 34, in Kaegi, p. 84) may be quoted:

> My wife rejects me and her mother hates me;
> The gamester finds no pity for his troubles.
> No better use can I see for a gambler,
> Than for a costly horse worn out and aged.

[1] Discussion concerning the original seat or home of the Aryans is omitted purposely, because no hypothesis on the subject seems to be finally established.

[2] Kautilya prescribes that 'Brāhmans shall be provided with forests for *soma* plantation' (*Arthaśāstra*, Book II, chap. 2). See also *Jātakas*, Nos. 525 and 537.

Dimness of the picture. When all possible care has been bestowed on the drawing of the outline, it must be confessed that the picture of the Indo-Aryans in the Rigvedic period remains indistinct and shadowy. The impossibility of fixing the age of the poems or of the life which they illustrate within limits defined even approximately leaves the Indo-Aryans suspended in the air, so to speak, and unconnected with any ascertained historical realities. The difficulties of the language of the poems, the strange modes of expression, and the remoteness of the ideas hinder a vivid realization of the people by whom and for whom the literature was produced. The matter of the greater part of the *Atharvaveda*, as already observed, produces an impression of prehistoric antiquity even deeper than that produced by the *Rigveda*, although it is certain that the book, as a book, is later in date.

Vedic Aryans and Hinduism. However dim may be the picture of the life of the Vedic Indo-Aryans, it is plain that their religion and habits differed materially from those of Hindus in modern or even in early historical times. The detestation of cow-slaughter and the loathing for beef, which are today the most prominent outward marks of Hinduism, have been so for many centuries, perhaps for something like 2,000 years. The Indo-Aryans had not those marks. It is quite certain that they freely sacrificed bulls and cows and ate both beef and horse flesh on ceremonial occasions. Nevertheless, it is true that the roots of Hinduism go down into the Rigvedic age and even deeper, to the Harappā culture. The pantheon, that is to say, the gods viewed collectively, although widely different from that of Hinduism, contains the germs of many later Hindu developments. Even now the Vedic deities are not wholly without honour, and in southern India the Nambudri Brahmans[1] of Malabar devote their lives to keeping up Vedic ritual as they understand it. The predominance of the Brahman had already begun when the *Rigveda* was composed, and the foundations of the caste system had thus been laid. The *Yajurveda* helps to bridge the gap between the *Rigveda* and Hinduism. It refers to the country between the Sutlaj and the Jumna, not to the Indus basin. The god Śiva is introduced under that name, while Vishnu is more prominent than in the earlier work. The old nature worship has dropped into the background, and a much more mechanical form of religion, depending on elaborate ceremonies and highly skilled priests, is described.

Vedic political history. The hymns of the *Rigveda* contain some material for political history in the shape of names of kings, kingdoms, and tribes. They even describe battles and other incidents. The references occur in a manner so natural and incidental that in all probability they record a genuine tradition and are concerned with real events. But the utter impossibility of determining an even approximate chronology for either the hymns or the events mentioned in them renders the information almost valueless for historical purposes. The

---

[1] The name is also written Nambutiri or Nāmburi.

attempts made to connect the Vedic names with Hindu history by means of the long genealogies preserved in the Purānas and other works have failed to yield tangible results. Bharata, Sudās, Janamejaya, and other kings named in the hymns, although they may be accepted as real persons, cannot be invested with much interest from the historian's point of view.

Historical geography. The study of the geographical data in the hymns is more fruitful, and throws a certain amount of light on the course of the Indo-Aryan migration and the origins of Hinduism. In fact, the accepted belief in the Indo-Aryan immigration from central Asia depends largely on the interpretation of the geographical allusions in the *Rigveda* and *Yajurveda*. Direct testimony to the assumed fact is lacking, and no tradition of an early home beyond the frontier survives in India. The amount of geographical knowledge implied in the literature is considerable. Such knowledge in those ancient days could have been acquired only by actual travelling. The hymn 'In Praise of the Rivers (*Nadī-stuti*)' in the tenth book (x. 75) is specially interesting as a display of geographical information. The author, while devoting his skill chiefly to the praises of the Sindhu or Indus, enumerates at least nineteen rivers, including the Ganges.

The fifth stanza, which gives a list of ten streams, small and great, in order from east to west, is remarkable:

> Attend to this my song of praise, O Gangā,
> Yamunā, Sarasvatī, Śutudrī, Parushnī;
> Together with Asiknī, O Marudvridhā, and with
> Vitastā, O Ārjīkīyā, listen with Sushomā.

The names of the Ganges, Jumna, and Sarasvatī remain unchanged. The Śutudrī is the modern Sutlaj, although its course has been greatly altered. The Parushnī is supposed to be the Rāvī. The Asiknī and Vitastā undoubtedly mean respectively the Akesines or Chināb, and the Vyath or Jhelum. The Marudvridhā is the Maruwārdwan, which flows from north to south through the Maru valley of the Kashmīr-Jammū State, and joins the Chināb on its northern bank at Kashtwār. The Sushomā is the Sohān in the Rāwalpindi District, and the Ārjīkīyā probably is the Kanshi in the same district.

The mention of the Marudvridhā is surprising, and it is difficult to understand how a stream of so little importance, hidden away among high mountains in an almost inaccessible valley, can have come to the knowledge of the author. The list suggests matter for curious speculation.[1]

River changes. It is of much importance, as already observed, that careful students of early Indian history and interpreters of the

---

[1] See Max Müller, *India, What can it Teach us?* (1883), pp. 163–75; Stein in *J.R.A.S.*, 1917, p. 91; and the translations by Griffith and others. I think the Ārjīkīyā must be the Kanshi, and not as Stein suggests.

Vedas or other ancient records should bear in mind the fact that the snow-fed rivers of northern India have undergone immense changes even within historical times. The entire Indus system has been subject to tremendous transformations both in the mountains and in the plains. Earthquakes, elevations, subsidences, and landslips have affected the upper courses of the rivers, while the changes in the soft alluvium of the plains have occurred frequently on a gigantic scale and are still in progress. Some rivers, notably the Hakrā or Wahindah, which once formed the boundary between Sind and Hind, have ceased to exist. Others, like the Kurram in the west and the Sarasvatī in the east, which once were violent and impetuous, have dwindled into feeble, inconsiderable streams. The positions of the confluences in both the Indus and the Gangetic systems have shifted many miles. The existing delta of the Indus has been formed since the time of Alexander the Great. The whole group of rivers connected with or related to the Sutlaj has been completely transformed more than once. The Sutlaj itself has wandered over a bed eighty-five miles in width. Illustrations of the subject might be adduced in endless detail. What has been said may suffice to inspire caution in the interpretation of ancient texts and in attempts to identify places mentioned in those texts.[1]

Vedāngas and Upavedas. Two supplementary sections of the vast Vedic literature which are known as Vedāngas ('members of the Veda') and Upavedas ('subsidiary Vedas') may be briefly mentioned.

The Vedāngas comprise six groups of treatises written in the *sūtra* style on subjects more or less closely connected with ritual or the preservation of the Vedic texts. The subjects are: (1) phonetics or pronunciation (*śikshā*); (2) metre (*chhandas*); (3) grammar (*vyākarana*); (4) etymology (*nirukti* or *nirukta*); (5) religious practice (*kalpa*); and (6) astronomy, or rather astrology (*jyotisha*).

The Upavedas treat of more distinctly secular subjects, namely: (1) medicine (*Āyurveda*); (2) war, or literally 'archery' (*Dhanurveda*); (3) music (*Gandharvaveda*); and (4) architecture and art (*Śilpaśāstra*).[2]

Vedānta. The term Vedānta ('end of the Veda') is now commonly applied to the philosophy taught in most of the Upanishads. So used it is interpreted to mean the 'final goal of the Veda'. In practice many people when speaking of the Vedas mean the Upanishads, and by them

---

[1] Students who desire to appreciate the force of the remarks in the text should read, mark, and digest Raverty's difficult memoir entitled 'The Mihrān of Sind and its Tributaries; a Geographical and Historical Study' in *J.A.S.B.*, vol. lxi, part 1, 1892. Unfortunately the copious matter is ill arranged, so that the treatise is exceptionally hard reading. It deals chiefly with the Indus, pp. 297–317; Hydaspes or Vitastā, pp. 318–36; Chināb, pp. 336–52; Rāvī, pp. 352–71; Biās, pp. 372–90; Sutlaj, pp. 391–418; Hakrā, pp. 418–22 and 454–66. Discussion of results occupies pp. 469–508. I have learned much by repeated reading of the disquisition. For extensive changes in the rivers of the far south see K S. Pillai, *The Tamils Eighteen Hundred Years Ago*, 1904, p. 236.

[2] The fourth Upaveda is also called *Sthapatya-veda*. The term *Arthaśāstra* given by Dr. Smith in earlier editions, on the basis of Weber (*History of Indian Literature*, 1882, pp. 271, 273), is unusual in this context. [Ed.]

the Vedānta is regarded as 'the ultimate bound of knowledge'. In a more literal sense the term means the treatises, namely, the Upanishads, appended to the end of the Brāhmanas. The concise phrase *tat tvam asi*, 'that art thou', is accepted as summing up the ontology of the Vedānta.

The epics. When passing from the Vedic lyrics to the Sanskrit epics we enter a new world. Not only are the grammar, vocabulary, metres, and style different, but the religion has been transformed and social conditions have been profoundly modified. Before those changes can be further considered it is necessary to explain briefly the character of the epics regarded as books.

Two huge poems or masses of verses, the *Rāmāyana* and the *Mahābhārata*, are commonly described as epics.

The Rāmāyana. The *Rāmāyana* deserves the name of epic because it is essentially a single long narrative poem composed by one author named Vālmīki, and is devoted to the celebration of the deeds of the hero Rāma with due regard to the rules of poesy. The work is in fact the first example of the Sanskrit *Kāvya* or artificially designed narrative poem. The simple, easily intelligible style, while free from the ingenuities and verbal gymnastics favoured by later authors, is by no means devoid of ornament. Five out of the seven books seem to constitute the epic as conceived by Vālmīki. Critics regard the first and last books as later additions. Episodes unconnected with the story are few. The grammar and language, which are remote from those of the Veda, closely approximate to those of 'classical' Sanskrit. The poem is known in three different recensions, the variations being due to the liberties taken by professional reciters. It is not possible to determine which form represents the original composed by Vālmīki, but the Bombay recension on the whole seems to preserve the oldest text. The text of narrative poems not being regarded as sacred like that of the Vedas, no obligation to preserve its purity was recognized. The seven books contain about 24,000 *ślokas*, or 48,000 lines.

Theme of the Rāmāyana. The main theme is the story of Prince Rāma, the son of King Daśaratha of Ayodhyā by Queen Kausalyā. The jealousy of Kaikeyī, the second queen, drove Rāma into exile and secured possession of the throne for her son, Bharata. Lakshmana, the third prince, voluntarily shared the exile of Rāma and Sītā his beloved wife. The adventures of the banished prince, the abduction of Sītā by Rāvana, the giant king of Lankā, the aid given to the prince by Hanumān, king of the monkeys, the vindication of Sītā from unjust aspersions on her chastity, and a thousand other incidents are even more familiar to Hindus in every part of India than the Bible stories are to the average European Christian. The story ends happily, and Rāma shares the kingdom with Bharata.

The heroic legend thus indicated has been edited by Brahmans so as to transform the poem into a book of devotion consecrated to the service of God in the form of Vishnu. Rāma, who is pictured as an incarnation of the deity, has thus become the man-god and saviour of mankind in the eyes of millions of devout worshippers, who have his name in the ejaculation, 'Rām, Rām', continually on their lips. He is venerated as the ideal man, while his wife, Sītā, is reverenced as the model of womanhood. Hindus unacquainted with Sanskrit bathe in 'the lake of the deeds of Rām' by the help of vernacular translations or imitations, among which the most celebrated is the noble poem entitled the *Rām-charit-mānas*, composed by Tulsī Dās in the days of Akbar. The moral teaching of the *Rāmāyana* in all its forms tends to edification, and the influence of Tulsī Dās in particular may be truly described as wholly on the side of goodness.

The Mahābhārata. The *Mahābhārata*, as we possess it in two recensions, a northern and a southern, cannot be designated correctly as an epic poem. It is a gigantic mass of compositions by diverse authors of various dates extending over many centuries, arranged in eighteen books or *parvans*, with a supplement called the *Harivamśa*, which may be reckoned as the nineteenth book. The number of *ślokas* exceeds 100,000, and the lines consequently are more than 200,000. The *Harivamśa* contains over 16,000 *ślokas*. The episodes, connected by the slightest possible bonds with the original narrative nucleus, constitute about four-fifths of the whole complex mass, which has the character of an 'encyclopaedia of moral teaching' as conceived by the Brahman mind.

The epic portion. The subject of the truly epic portion of the *Mahābhārata* is the Great War between the Kauravas, the hundred sons of Dhritarāshtra, led by Duryodhana, and the Pāndavas, the five sons of Pāndu, brother of Dhritarāshtra, led by Yudhishthira. The poet relates all the circumstances leading up to the war, and then narrates the tale of the fierce conflict which raged for eighteen days on the plain of Kurukshetra near Thānēsar, to the north of modern Delhi and the ancient Indraprastha. All the nations and tribes of India from the Himālaya to the farthest south are represented as taking part in this combat of giants. The Pāndava host comprised the armies of the states situated in the countries equivalent to the state of Uttar Pradesh, Western Bihār, and Eastern Rājputāna, with contingents from Gujarāt in the west and from the Dravidian kingdoms of the extreme south. The Kaurava cause was upheld by the forces of Eastern Bihār, Bengal, the Himālaya, and the Panjāb. The battles ended in the utter destruction of nearly all the combatants on both sides, excepting Dhritarāshtra and the Pāndavas. But a reconciliation was effected between the few survivors, and Yudhishthira Pāndava was recognized as king of Hastināpura on the Ganges. Ultimately, the five sons of Pāndu, accompanied by Draupadī, the beloved wife of them all, and attended by a faithful dog, quitted their royal state, and journeying to Mount Meru were admitted into Indra's heaven.

The epic narrative, thus inadequately summarized, now occupies about 20,000 *ślokas*, but in its earliest form comprised only 8,800. That fact, which is clearly recorded, proves beyond doubt the unlimited rehandling which the *Mahābhārata* has undergone at the hands of professional reciters, poets of different ages, and Brahman editors. The medieval Hindī epic, the *Chand-Rāisā*, has been subjected to similar treatment and expanded from 5,000 to 125,000 verses. The original form of that poem is said to be still in existence.

The Bhagavad-Gītā, &c. The profound philosophical poem called the *Bhagavad-Gītā*, which may be Englished as 'the Lord's Song', or in Edwin Arnold's phrase as 'the Song Celestial', divided into eighteen chapters or discourses, has been thrust into the sixth book of the *Mahābhārata*.

Other notable episodes, or inserted poems, are the charming tale of Nala and Damayantī, accessible in Milman's elegant English version; the story of Śakuntalā, forming the groundwork of Kālidāsa's play; and the legend of Sāvitrī, the Hindu Alcestis.

Age of the epics. The separate heroic and legendary tales imbedded in both the *Rāmāyana* and the *Mahābhārata* may in some cases go back to the most remote antiquity, but both of the epics in their existing form are far later than any of the Vedic hymns, and probably posterior to all the *Brāhmanas*. The two epics, as Hopkins has proved in detail, are intimately related and include a large number of substantially identical verses. The language of both belongs essentially to the same period in the development of Sanskrit. Probably the greater part of the existing text of the *Mahābhārata* was complete by A.D. 200, but the work as a whole cannot be said to belong to any one era. The original work of Vālmīki, that is to say, Books II–VI of the *Rāmāyana*, is believed by Professor Macdonell to have been completed before the epic kernel of the *Mahābhārata* had assumed definite shape.

The Rāmāyana not historical. Most Hindus regard the epic narratives as statements of absolute historical facts, and would not be disturbed by sceptical criticism more than the ordinary unlearned Christian is by the so-called 'higher criticism' of the Gospels.[1] Scholars naturally look upon the poets' tales in a different light. Professors Jacobi and Macdonell, for instance, regard the *Rāmāyana* as being neither historical nor allegorical, but a poetic creation based on mythology. That interpretation sees in Sītā ('the furrow') an earth-goddess, and in Rāma an equivalent of Indra. Such speculations may or may not be accepted, but I feel fairly certain that the *Rāmāyana* does not hand down much genuine historical tradition of real events, either at Ayodhyā or in the peninsula. The poem seems to me to be essentially a work of imagination, probably founded on vague traditions of the kingdom of Kosala and its capital Ayodhyā. Daśaratha, Rāma, and the rest may or may not be the names of real kings of Kosala, as recorded in the long genealogy of the solar line given in the *Purānas*. But the investigation

[1] 'According to the Hindu notion the stories which are called mythology by Europeans are nothing short of history' (Ketkar, vol. ii, p. 477).

of the genealogies, on which a distinguished scholar has lavished infinite pains, is inconclusive, and the story of the epic is so interwoven with mythological fiction that it is impossible to disentangle the authentic history. The attempts to fix an approximately definite date for the adventures of Rāma rest on a series of guesses and are altogether unconvincing to my mind.

The Great War. The traditional belief that the Great War of the Mahābhārata actually was fought in the year 3102 B.C., the era of Yudhishthira, is strongly held. Although that date will hardly bear criticism, most people seem to be agreed that the poet of the original epic based his tale on the genuine tradition of a real Great War, just as the author of the *Iliad* had his imagination guided by dim recollections of an actual siege of Troy. The story, however, has been so much edited and moralized by different hands at times widely apart that little genuine tradition can be left. Persistent local memory undoubtedly has always recognized the sites of Hastināpura on the Ganges, the original Kaurava capital, and of Indraprastha on the Jumna, the newer town founded by the Pāndavas. Hastināpura is supposed to be marked by a small hamlet of the same name on the high bank of the Ganges in the Meerut District, and recent excavations have revealed there the existence of a city going back to pre-Buddhist times. Every tourist is familiar with the fact that the enclosure of the Purana Qila, situated near the bank of the Jumna between Shāhjahān's Delhi and Humāyūn's tomb, is pointed out as occupying part of the site of Indraprastha. The Nigambōdh Ghāt, or river stairs, and the Nīlīchatrī temple farther north, near Salīmgarh, are believed to have been included in the ancient city, the northern limit of which is supposed to have extended to 'the north-eastern end of the street called Darība—almost in the heart of the modern city'.[1] No ancient remains of any sort have been found to support the identification of the site. The traditions fixing the positions of the two towns, however, may be accepted, and we may believe that a famous local war between the chiefs of Indraprastha and Hastināpura, supported severally by many tribes of northern India, occurred at a very remote date. Beyond that it is difficult to go. The reasons for believing that the Pāndavas were, as Hopkins suggests, 'a new people from without the pale', and for discrediting the alleged relationship between them and the Kauravas, are strong and cut at the root of the whole story. If the Pāndavas were non-Aryan hill-men, which in my judgement is probable, the poets and editors have transformed the story of their doings to such an extent that nothing truly historical is left.

The allegation that the chiefs of all India, including even the Pāndyas from the extreme south of the peninsula, took part in the fray is absolutely incredible.[2] Whether the date of the battle be placed

[1] Carr Stephen, *Archaeology and Monumental Remains of Delhi*, Lūdiāna and Calcutta, 1876, p. 5.
[2] Compare the 'catalogue of ships' interpolated in the *Iliad*. As all Greece desired

about 3000 B.C., as tradition maintains, or 2,000 years later, as seems much more probable, it is impossible that at either period distant powers like the Pāndyas or the King of Assam (Prāgjyotisha) should have been interested in the local quarrels between the Kauravas and Pāndavas, which directly concerned only a small area in the neighbourhood of the city now called Delhi. The entire framework of the story is essentially incredible and unhistorical. It may be that the royal genealogies for ages before and after the Great War, as recorded in the Purānas at length and in the epics less fully, are not wholly fictitious. But even if it be admitted that the lists often give the names in the proper order with approximate correctness, and indicate the existence of certain real relations friendly or hostile between the princes of certain dynasties, we are still a long way from finding intelligible history. The attempt to construct a rationalized narrative out of the materials available rests on a series of assumptions and guesses which can never lead to conclusions of much value. I confess my inability to extract anything deserving the name of political history from the epic tales of either the Rāmāyana or the Mahābhārata.

Social conditions. Both poems describe much the same state of society; but that proposition is subject to the qualification that certain parts of the Mahābhārata retain distinct traces of early practices, such as cow-killing and human sacrifice, which were regarded with horror when the later parts of the work were composed.[1] Other features are clearly non-Aryan, notably the polyandry of the Pāndavas, who all shared the one wife, Draupadī, after the manner of the Tibetans and certain other Himalayan tribes in the present day. The name Pāndava means 'pale-face', and the conjecture seems to be legitimate that the sons of Pāndu may have been the representatives of a yellow-tinted, Himalayan, non-Aryan tribe, which practised polyandry. That hypothesis involves the further inference (which may be supported for other reasons) that the alleged relationship between the Pāndavas and the Kauravas was an invention of the Brahman editors who undertook to moralize the old tales and bring them all into the Aryan fold. The subject is too speculative for further discussion in this place.

When the epics were finally recast in their present shape, be the date A.D. 200 or another, the doctrine of ahimsā, or non-injury to living creatures, had gained the upper hand. It is taught emphatically in many passages, although others, as observed above, retain memories of older practices.

The Vedic nature-worship had been mostly superseded by the cult of Brahmā, Vishnu, and Śiva. New gods and goddesses unknown to the Veda, such as Ganēśa and Pārvati, had arisen; and the Vedic deities had been reduced to a subordinate position, except Indra, who still retained high rank as the king of the heaven which warriors hoped

to be credited with a share in the Trojan war after it had been made famous by Homer, so all India claimed places in the Great War of the Mahābhārata.
[1] For details and references see Vidya, p. 118, and Hopkins, p. 378.

to attain. The doctrine of rebirth, often loosely called transmigration of souls, had become generally accepted, and the belief in the incarnations of Vishnu had been formulated. The *Bhagavad-Gītā*, of which the date is quite uncertain, presents the Supreme Deity incarnate in the guise of the charioteer Krishna, who expounds the religion of duty, subject to the limitations of the four orders or *varnas*, in 'plain but noble language'. The tribal organization of the state is much less prominent than it was in the Vedic period, and territorial kingdoms had arisen. The life of the court of Ayodhyā as depicted in the *Rāmāyana* is much the same as that of any old-fashioned Hindu state in recent times. Caste was already an ancient institution, and it may be said with confidence that the atmosphere of the epic world is that of familiar Hinduism, with certain exceptions indicated above, which occur chiefly in the *Mahābhārata*. The kingdoms mentioned were numerous and comparatively small. No hint seems to be given that a great paramount power existed. But it is not safe to affirm that the political and social conditions depicted in the epics are those of any one definite age. Both works as literary compositions may be roughly placed between 400 B.C. and A.D. 200. The *Rāmāyana* in its original form may have been composed by Vālmīki in the earlier half of the six centuries thus indicated, and it seems probable that the redaction of the *Mahābhārata* to something like its present shape took place in the later half of the same period. But determination of the dates of composition of the poems, if it could be effected, would not throw any light on the historical place of Rāma, Arjuna, and the other epic heroes. They are, I think, the creatures of imagination, guided more or less by dim traditions of half-forgotten stirring events which happened 'once upon a time', but cannot be treated as ascertained facts which came into existence at any particular period. The Indian epic heroes, in short, seem to me to occupy a position like that of the Knights of the Round Table in British legend, and it is as futile to attempt the distillation of matter-of-fact history, whether political or social, from the *Mahābhārata* and *Rāmāyana* as it would be to reconstruct the early history of Britain from the *Morte d'Arthur* or from its modern version, the *Idylls of the King*.

The Purānas. The nature of the works called *Purānas* which have been referred to demands brief explanation. The *Purānas* commonly recognized in the north of India are eighteen in number. Others, about which little is known to European scholars, are used in the south. A *Purāna*, according to the Indian definition, best exemplified by the *Vishnu Purāna*, should treat of five subjects, namely, primary creation, secondary creation, genealogies of gods and patriarchs, reigns of various Manus, and the history of ancient dynasties. The treatises consequently are bulky and crowded with legendary matter of various kinds. They have been well described by Bühler as 'popular sectarian compilations of mythology, philosophy, history, and the sacred law; intended, as they are now used, for the instruction of the unlettered classes, including the upper divisions of the Śūdra *varna*'.[1] Much of the contents comes down from remote antiquity, as the name *Purāna*, meaning 'old', testifies, but the books as they stand are of various dates. The *Vāyu Purāna*, one of the oldest, finally edited perhaps in the fourth century after Christ, is closely connected with the supplement to the *Mahābhārata* entitled the *Harivamśa*, already mentioned. The Puranic genealogies of kings in prehistoric times, as intimated above, seem to be of doubtful value, but those of the historical period or Kali age, from about 600 B.C., are records of high importance and extremely helpful in the laborious task of reconstructing the early political history of India. Each of the *Purānas* is more or less specially consecrated to the service of a particular form of the godhead.

Caste. The existing institution of caste is peculiar to India, and is 'the most vital principle of Hinduism', dominating Indian social life, manners, morals, and thought. It consists essentially in the division of Hindu mankind into about 3,000 hereditary groups, each internally bound together by rules of ceremonial purity, and externally separated by the same rules from all other groups. Those propositions describing the institution of caste as it exists today in general terms are as accurate as any brief abstract description of an institution so complex can be.

Definition of a caste. A caste may be defined as a group of families internally united by peculiar rules for the observance of ceremonial purity, especially in the matters of diet and marriage. The same rules serve to fence it off from all the other groups, each of which has its own set of rules. Admission to an established caste in long settled territory can be obtained nowadays by birth only, and transitions from one caste to another, which used to be feasible in ancient times, are no longer possible, except in frontier regions like Manipur. The families composing a caste may or may not have traditions of descent from a common ancestor, and, as a matter of fact, may or may not belong to one stock. Race, that is to say, descent by blood, has little concern with caste, in northern India, at all events, whatever may be the case in the south. The individual members of a caste may or may not be restricted to any particular occupation or occupations. The members may believe or disbelieve any creed or doctrine, religious or philosophical, without affecting their caste position. That can be forfeited only by breach of the caste regulations concerning the *dharma*, or practical duty of members belonging to the group. Each caste has its own *dharma*, in addition to the common rules of morality as accepted by Hindus generally, and considered to be the *dharma* of mankind. The general Hindu *dharma* exacts among other things reverence to Brahmans, respect for the sanctity of animal life in varying degrees, and especially veneration for horned cattle, pre-eminently the cow. Every caste man is expected to observe accurately the rules of his own group, and to refrain from doing violence to the feelings of other groups concerning

[1] *Laws of Manu, S.B.E.*, vol. xxv, p. xci.

their rules. The essential duty of the member of a caste is to follow the custom of his group, more particularly in relation to diet or marriage.[1] Violation of the rules on those subjects, if detected, usually involves unpleasant and costly social expiation and may result in expulsion from the caste, which means social ruin and grave inconvenience.

The Hindus have not any name for the caste institution, which seems to them part of the order of nature. It is almost impossible for a Hindu to regard himself otherwise than as a member of some particular caste, or species of Hindu mankind. Everybody else who disregards Hindu *dharma* is an 'outer barbarian' (*mlēchchha*) no matter how exalted his worldly rank or how vast his wealth may be. The proper Sanskrit and vernacular term for 'a caste' is *jāti* (*jāt*), 'species', although, as noted above, the members of a *jāti* are not necessarily descended from a common ancestor. Indeed, as a matter of fact, they are rarely, if ever, so descended. Their special caste rules make their community in effect a distinct species, whoever their ancestors may have been.

The fiction of four original castes. The common notion that there were four original castes, Brahman, Kshatriya or Rājanya, Vaiśya, and Śūdra, is false. The ancient Hindu writers classified mankind under four *varnas* or 'orders', with reference to their occupations, namely: (1) the learned, literate, and priestly order, or Brahmans; (2) the fighting and governing classes, who were grouped together as Rājanyas or Kshatriyas, irrespective of race, meaning by that term ancestry; (3) the trading and agricultural people, or Vaiśyas; and (4) common, humble folk, day labourers, and so forth, whose business it was to serve their betters. Every family and caste (*jāti*) observing Hindu *dharma* necessarily fell under one or other of those four heads. Various half-wild tribes, and also communities like sweepers, whose occupations are obviously unclean, were regarded as standing outside the four orders or *varnas*. Such unclean communities have usually imitated the Hindu caste organization and developed an elaborate system of castes of their own, which may be described by the paradoxical term 'out-caste castes'.

Nobody can understand the caste system until he has freed himself from the mistaken notion based on the current interpretation of the so-called *Institutes of Manu*, that there were 'four original castes'. No four original castes ever existed at any time or place, and at the present moment the terms Kshatriya, Vaiśya, and Śūdra have no exact meaning as a classification of existing castes. In northern India the names Vaiśya and Śūdra are not used except in books or disputes about questions of caste precedence. In the south all Hindus who are not Brahmans fall under the denomination of Śūdra, while the designations Kshatriya and Vaiśya are practically unknown.[2]

---

[1] 'Caste means a social exclusiveness with reference to diet and marriage. . . . Birth and rituals are secondary' (Shama Sastri, *The Evolution of Caste*, p. 13).

[2] According to the Census of 1901 for the Madras Presidency the figures are:

The Purusha-sūkta hymn. The famous *Purusha-sūkta* hymn included in the latest book of the *Rigveda* (x. 90), and commonly supposed to be 'the only passage in the Veda which enumerates the four castes', has nothing to do with caste. The hymn has for its subject a cosmogony or theory of creation. The poet tries to picture creation as the result of immolating and cutting up Purusha, that is to say 'embodied spirit, or Man personified and regarded as the soul and original source of the universe, the personal and life-giving principle in all animated beings'. The Vedas, horses, cattle, goats, and sheep, the creatures of the air, and animals both wild and tame are depicted as being products of that 'great general sacrifice'. The poet proceeds next to expound the creation of the human race, and finally, of the sun, moon, and elements. I quote Colebrooke's version because it is free from the effect of the prepossession of other translators, who, under the influence of Manu and his followers, have assumed the reality of a reference to the supposed 'four original castes'.[1]

10. Into how many portions did they divide this being whom they immolated? what did his mouth become? what are his arms, his thighs, and his feet now called?

11. His mouth became a priest [*Brāhmana*]; his arm was made a soldier [*Rājanya*]; his thigh was transformed into a husbandman [*Vaiśya*]; from his feet sprang the servile man [*Śūdra*].

12. The moon was produced from his mind; the sun sprang from his eye; air and breath proceeded from his ear; and fire rose from his mouth.

13. The subtile element was produced from his navel; the sky from his head; the earth from his feet; and space from his ear; thus did he frame worlds....

The general drift of the whole passage is plain enough. The verses give a highly figurative, imaginative theory of creation. Both the Brahman and fire come from Purusha's mouth, just as the servile man or Śūdra and earth both proceed from his feet. No suggestion of the existence of caste groups is made. Mankind is simply and roughly classified under four heads according to occupation, the more honourable professions being naturally assigned the more honourable symbolical origin. It is absurd to treat the symbolical language of the poem as a narrative of supposed facts.

Distinctions between varna and jāti. Most of the misunderstanding on the subject has arisen from the persistent mistranslation of Manu's term *varna* as 'caste', whereas it should be rendered 'class' or 'order', or by some equivalent term.

The compiler of the *Institutes of Manu* was well aware of the distinction between *varna* and *jāti*. While he mentions about fifty different castes, he lays much stress on the fact that there were only four *varnas*.

Brahman, 3·4 per cent.; Śūdra, 94·3 = 97·7 per cent. The small residuum is made up of a few Telingas and Kanarese who called themselves Kshatriyas or Vaiśyas (Richards, *The Dravidian Problem*, p. 31).
[1] Colebrooke, *Miscellaneous Essays*, 1873, vol. i, p. 184.

The two terms are carelessly confused in one passage (x. 31), but in that only. Separate castes existed from an early date. Their relations to one another remain unaffected whether they are grouped theoretically under four occupational headings or not.

Enormous number of existing castes. My statement that 3,000 distinct castes, more or less, exist at the present day is made on the authority of an estimate by Ketkar. Whether the number be taken as 2,000, 3,000, or 4,000 is immaterial, because the figure certainly is of that order. Many reasons, which it would be tedious to specify, forbid the preparation of an exact list of castes. One of those reasons is that new castes have been and still are formed from time to time. But the intricacies of the caste system in its actual working must be studied in the numerous special treatises devoted to the subject, which it is impossible to discuss in this work.

Antiquity of the institution. We know that caste existed before 300 B.C., because the most obvious features of the institution are noticed by the Greek authors of ascertained date; and it is reasonable to believe that castes, separated from one another by rules of ceremonial purity, as they now are, were in existence some centuries earlier. I do not find any indication of the existence of caste in Rigvedic times. But the pre-eminence of the 'Brahman sacrificers', which was well assured even in that remote age, is the foundation of the later caste system. The people of the *Rigveda* had not yet become Hindus.

The learned, priestly, and intellectually superior class of the Indo-Aryans who were called Brahmans gradually framed extremely strict rules to guard their own ceremonial purity against defilement through unholy food or undesirable marriages. The enforcement of such rules on themselves by the most respected members of the Indo-Aryan community naturally attracted the admiration of the more worldly classes of society, who sought to emulate and imitate the virtuous self-restraint of the Brahmans. It being clearly impossible that ordinary soldiers, business men, peasants, and servants could afford to be as scrupulous as saintly, or at least professedly religious Brahmans, a separate standard of *dharma* for each section of society necessarily grew up by degrees. Kings, for instance, might properly and must do things which subjects could not do without sin, and so on. The long-continued conflict with the aboriginal Indians, who held quite different ideals of conduct, made both the Brahmans and their imitators more and more eager to assert their superiority and exclusiveness by ever-increasing scrupulosity concerning both diet and marriage.

The evolution of caste. The geographical isolation of interior India favoured the evolution of a distinct and peculiar social system. A student of the *Rigveda* texts, without knowledge of historical facts, might reasonably presume that the Indus basin where the immigrants first settled would have become the Holy Land of Hinduism. The Rishis never tire of singing the praises of the mighty Indus with its tributary streams. But the strange fact is that the basin of the Indus, and even the Panjab beyo.id the Sutlaj, came to be regarded as impure lands by the Brahmans of interior India at quite an early date.[1] Ortho-dox Hindus are still unwilling to cross the Indus, and the whole Panjab between that river and the Sutlaj is condemned as unholy ground, unfitted for the residence of strict votaries of *dharma*. The reason apparently is that the north-western territories continued to be over-run by successive swarms of foreigners from central Asia, who dis-regarded Brahmans and followed their own customs. The inroads of those foreigners blotted out the memory of the Indo-Aryan immigra-tion from the north-west, which is not traceable either in the popular Puran'c literature or in the oral traditions of the people. To the east of the Sarasvatī and Sutlaj the Indo-Aryans were usually safe from foreign invasion and free to work out their own rule of life undisturbed. They proceeded to do so and thus to create Hinduism with its inseparable institution of caste. Internally the Indian territory was broken up into a multitude of small units, each of which had a tendency towards an exclusive, detached way of living.

Effect of ahimsā on caste. The sentiment in favour of respecting animal life, technically called the *ahimsā* doctrine, had a large share in fixing on the necks of the people burdensome rules of conduct. That sentiment, which is known to have been actively encouraged by Jain and Buddhist teachers from about 500 B.C., probably originated at a much earlier date. The propagation of *ahimsā* necessarily produced a sharp conflict of ideas and principles of conduct between the adherents of the doctrine and the old-fashioned people who clung to bloody sacrifices, cow-killing, and meat eating. Communities which had renounced the old practices and condemned them as revolting impieties naturally separated themselves from their more easy-going and self-indulgent neighbours, and formed castes bound strictly to maintain the novel code of ethics. The *Mahābhārata*, as already noted, contains many inconsistent passages which indicate the transition from the ancient ideas to the new. The same conflict of ideals and practice still goes on, and may be observed in many localities of both southern and northern India. The first Rock Edict of Aśoka, published about 256 B.C., enables us to fix one date in the long story and to mark an early instance of the change of attitude produced by Buddhist teaching.

Formerly, in the kitchen of His Sacred and Gracious Majesty the King each day many [hundred] thousands of living creatures were slaughtered to make curries. But now, when this pious edict is being written, only three living creatures are slaughtered daily for curry, to wit, two peacocks and one antelope—the antelope, however, not invariably. Even those three living creatures henceforth shall not be slaughtered.

Any person acquainted with modern India does not need to be told

---

[1] The combined testimony of the *Jātakas* and the Greek authors proves that in the fourth century B.C. Taxila in the north-western Panjab still was a centre of Vedic learning. The change may have been due to the Indo-Scythian rule in the first two centuries A.C.

how the habit of flesh or fish eating separates certain castes from their vegetarian brethren.

Effect of the Muslim conquest. It is impossible to pursue the subject, which branches off into endless ramifications. One more observation may be recorded to the effect that the process of the Muslim conquest, from the time of Mahmūd of Ghaznī, tended to tighten the bonds of caste. The Hindus, unable on the whole to resist the Muslims in the field, defended themselves passively by the increased rigidity of caste association. The system of close caste brotherhoods undoubtedly protected Hindus and Hinduism during many centuries of Muslim rule. Modern Hinduism is incapable of accepting the old legal fiction that foreign outsiders should be regarded as fallen Kshatriyas. When the compiler of the *Laws of Manu* was writing it seemed quite natural to treat Persians, Dards, and certain other foreign nations as Kshatriyas who had sunk to the condition of Śūdras by reason of their neglect of sacred rites and their failure to consult Brahmans (x. 44). The change in the Hindu attitude towards foreigners seems to be mainly due to the Muslim conquest. We may take it that from the eleventh and twelfth centuries of the Christian era the caste institution has subsisted in substantially its modern form. That proposition is subject to the qualification that minor local and superficial modifications are taking place continually. But the institution as a whole remains unchanged and unshaken.

Demerits of caste.[1] The demerits of the peculiar Hindu institution are obvious. Anybody can perceive that it shuts off Indians from free association with foreigners, thus making it difficult for the Indian to understand the foreigner, and for the stranger to understand the Indian. It is easier for the European to attain full sympathy with the casteless Burman than it is for him to draw aside the veil which hides the inmost thoughts of the Chitpāwan or Nambūdri Brahman. No small part of the mystery which ordinarily confines interest in Indian subjects to a narrow circle of experts is due ultimately to caste. It is not pleasant for an Englishman or Frenchman to know that, however distinguished he may be personally, the touch of his hand is regarded as a pollution by his high-caste acquaintance. Yet that is the disagreeable fact. Within India caste breaks up society into thousands of separate units, frequently hostile one to the other, and always jealous. The institution necessarily tends to hinder active hearty co-operation for any purpose, religious, political, or social. All reformers are conscious of the difficulties thus placed in their path. Each individual finds his personal liberty of action checked in hundreds of ways unknown to the dwellers in other lands. The restrictions of caste rules collide continually with the conditions of modern life, and are the source of endless inconveniences. The institution is a relic of the

---

[1] This section and the next following have been left as Dr. Smith wrote them. Needless to say the past thirty years have seen a great weakening of the more rigid caste prejudices among much of the urban population of India. [Ed.]

ancient past and does not readily adapt itself to the requirements of the twentieth century. Although necessity compels even the strictest Brahmans to make some concessions to practical convenience, as, for instance, in the matters of railway travelling and drinking pipe water, the modifications thus introduced are merely superficial. The innate antique sentiment of caste exclusiveness survives in full strength and is not weakened materially even by considerable laxity of practice. The conflict between caste regulations and modern civilization is incessant, but caste survives. Further, the institution fosters intense class pride fatal to a feeling of brotherhood between man and man. The Malabar Brahman who considers himself defiled if an outcaste stands within twenty paces of him cannot possibly be interested in a creature so despised. The sentiment pervades all classes of Hindu society in varying degrees of intensity. Such objections to the caste institution, with many others which might be advanced, go far to justify, or at any rate explain, the vigorous denunciations of the system found abundantly in Indian literature as well as in the writings of foreigners. Four stanzas by Vemana, the Telugu poet, may serve as a summary of the numerous Indian diatribes on the subject.

CASTE

If we look through all the earth,
Men, we see, have equal birth,
Made in one great brotherhood,
Equal in the sight of God.

Food or caste or place of birth
Cannot alter human worth.
Why let caste be so supreme?
'Tis but folly's passing stream.

Empty is a caste-dispute:
All the castes have but one root.
Who on earth can e'er decide
Whom to praise and whom deride?

Why should we the Pariah scorn,
When his flesh and blood were born
Like to ours? What caste is He
Who doth dwell in all we see?[1]

The dictum of Sir Henry Maine, the eminent jurist, that caste is 'the most disastrous and blighting of human institutions' may suffice as a sample of adverse opinions expressed by European writers.

The merits of caste. The hostile critics have not got hold of the whole truth. Much may be said on the other side, which needs to be presented. An institution which has lasted for thousands of years, and

[1] Gover, *The Folk-songs of Southern India*, London, Trübner, 1872, p. 275; a charming and instructive book.

has forced its passage down through the peninsula all the way to Cape
Comorin in the face of the strongest opposition, must have merits to
justify its existence and universal prevalence within the limits of India.[1]
The most ardent defenders of caste, of course, must admit its unsuit-
ability for other lands. 'Thinking men', as Sir Madhava Row observed,
'must beware lest the vast and elaborate social structure which has
arisen in the course of thousands of years of valuable experience should
be injured or destroyed without anything to substitute, or with a far
worse structure to replace it.' The institution of caste cannot be treated
properly as a thing by itself. It is an integral part of Hinduism, that is
to say, of the Hindu social and economic system. It is, as Ketkar justly
observes, intimately associated with the Hindu philosophical ideas of
karma, rebirth, and the theory of the three *gunas*. But such abstract
ideas cannot be discussed in this place. More writers than one have
observed that the chief attribute of the caste system regarded historically is its stability. The Hindu mind clings to custom, and caste rules
are solidified custom. That stability, although not absolute, has been
the main agent in preserving Hindu ideas of religion, morals, art, and
craftsmanship. The Abbé Dubois was much impressed by the services
which the institution renders to social order. Monier Williams concisely
observes that 'caste has been useful in promoting self-sacrifice, in
securing subordination of the individual to an organized body, in
restraining vice, [and] in preventing pauperism'. Similar quotations
might be largely multiplied.[2]

The **future of caste**. The institutions of *varna* and caste, which
have existed in some form for 3,000 years or more, and are rooted in
the most ancient stratum of India's culture, are now rapidly weakening,
though still a very real element in her civilization. The growth of the
social conscience and the organization of the depressed classes are
already removing the worst aspects of untouchability; but with some
sections of the population, especially in the rural areas, it may well be
that traces of caste prejudice will remain for many generations. The
deep waters of Hinduism are not easily stirred. Ripples on the surface
leave the depths unmoved.

The **'Laws of Manu'**. In connexion with the subject of the evolution of caste, the famous law-book commonly called the 'Laws', or
'Code', or 'Institutes of Manu' (*Mānava-dharmaśāstra* in Sanskrit)
demands notice. The treatise, written in concise Sanskrit verse of the
'epic' type, comprises 2,684 couplets (*śloka*) arranged in twelve chapters; and is the earliest of the metrical law-books. It professes to be

---

[1] 'The hatred which existed between the early Dravidians and the Aryans is best
preserved in the Kuricchans' (a hill tribe in Malabar, corresponding to the Kuravas
of the Tamil country) custom of plastering their huts with cow-dung to remove the
pollution caused by the entrance of a Brahman' (*Tamil Studies*, p. 90). The Kuravas
in Travancore rank very low and bury their dead (*The Travancore State Manual*,
vol. ii, p. 402).
[2] Some of the quotations are taken from Aiya, *The Travancore State Manual*,
1906, vol. ii, pp. 229 ff.

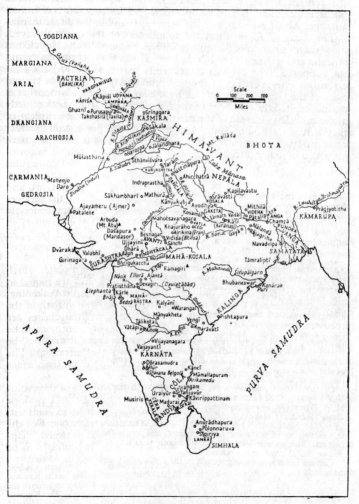

ANCIENT INDIA

the composition of a sage named Bhrigu, who used the works of predecessors. The date of composition may lie between 200 B.C. and A.D. 200. About one-tenth of the verses is found in the *Mahābhārata*.

The *Laws of Manu* form the foundation of the queer medley of inconsistent systems of jurisprudence administered by the High Courts of India under the name of Hindu Law. The prevalent error concerning the supposed 'four original castes' rests partly, as proved above, on erroneous interpretation of the text, and partly on fictitious explanations of the facts of caste offered by the author. The early Sanskritists unduly exalted the authority of the *Laws of Manu*, which they regarded as veritable laws instead of the mere rulings of a textbook writer, which they actually are. The fuller knowledge of the present day sees the book in truer perspective, but the old errors still exert a baneful influence in many directions.

AUTHORITIES

On ancient Indian literature still very valuable is A. A. MACDONELL's *History of Sanskrit Literature* (London, 1900), a masterly summary of an enormous subject. M. WINTERNITZ's *History of Indian Literature* (tr. Mrs. S. KETKAR, Calcutta, 1927) is more detailed. The fine works of Sir A. B. KEITH, *History of Sanskrit Literature* (Oxford, 1928) and *The Sanskrit Drama* (Oxford, 1924), deal only with the literature of the classical period, as does S. N. DAS GUPTA's and S. K. DE's *History of Sanskrit Literature* (vol. i, Calcutta, 1947).

On the Vedic period KEITH's *Religion and Philosophy of the Veda and Upanishads* (Cambridge, Mass., 1925) is of great value, as is MACDONNELL and KEITH's work of reference, the *Vedic Index* (2 vols., London, 1912). The metrical version of the *Hymns of the Rig Veda* by GRIFFITHS (2 vols., 2nd ed., Benares, 1896) is still the only complete translation in English. *The Vedic Age* by a number of Indian scholars (ed. R. C. MAJUMDAR, London 1951; see p. 21) is of varying quality. Still useful as a brief account are chaps. iv and v in *C.H.I.*, vol. i, by KEITH.

For the 'Epic period' HOPKINS's *The Great Epic of India* (New York and London, 1901) is still of value, as are the same author's chapters in *C.H.I.*, vol. i. F. E. PARGITER's efforts at extracting sober history from the Purānic king-lists are contained in *Dynasties of the Kali Age* (Oxford, 1913), and *The Ancient Indian Historical Tradition* (London, 1922). H. C. RAYCHAUDHURI attempts a cautious reconstruction of the political history of the period between the shadowy Mahābhārata War and the time of the Buddha in *P.H.A.I.*, part i.

Of the many works on caste, S. V. KETKAR, *History of Caste in India* (Ithaca, N.Y., 1909); E. SENART, *Caste in India* (tr. Sir E. DENISON ROSS, London, 1930); N. K. DUTT, *Origin and Growth of Caste in India* (Calcutta, 1931); and J. H. HUTTON, *Caste in India* (Cambridge, 1946), are among the best. Professor Hutton's work is an anthropological study of great merit, in which he claims to find caste-like features in the culture of primitive Indian tribes, and traces the institution to pre-Aryan origins. The standard translation of Manu is still that of BÜHLER (*The Laws of Manu*, S.B.E., vol. xxv, Oxford, 1886).

Certain other writers are quoted in the notes and a very long list of books might be given.

CHAPTER 3

*The pre-Maurya states; the rise of Jainism and Buddhism;
the invasion of Alexander the Great; India in the fourth
century B.C.*

Continuity of Indian civilization. China excepted, no region of the world can boast of an ancient civilization so continuous and unbroken as that of India. Civilized life may have begun earlier in Egypt and Babylonia, but in those countries the chain connecting the distant past with the present was rudely snapped long ago. No living memory of the Sumerians and Pharaohs or of their institutions survives. In India the ideas of the Vedic period still are a vital force, and even the ritual of the Rishis is not wholly disused. The lack of ancient records inscribed on imperishable material, such as abound in Egypt and Babylonia, forbids the writing of early Indian history in a manner at all comparable with that feasible in the countries named. The historian of India has nothing but tradition to guide him until quite a late period, and his handling of really ancient times is necessarily devoid of any chronological framework, being vague and sketchy.

Dated history begins in seventh century B.C. No attempt Indian history dated even in the roughest fashion can be made before the seventh century B.C. The first exact date known, as already mentioned, is 326 B.C., the year of Alexander's invasion. By reckoning back from that fixed point, or from certain closely approximate Maurya dates slightly later, and by making use of the historical traditions recorded in literature, a little information can be gleaned concerning a few kingdoms of northern India in the seventh century. No definite affirmation of any kind can be made about specific events in either the peninsula or Bengal before 300 B.C. The scanty record of events in the northern kingdoms has to be mostly picked out of books written primarily to serve religious purposes. Those books, Jain, Buddhist, and Brahmanical, naturally deal chiefly with the countries in which religious movements were most active. The traditionary accounts are deeply tinged by the sectarian prejudices of the writers, and often hopelessly discordant.

India in the seventh century B.C. In the seventh century B.C. we may be assured that although vast territories in most parts of India were still covered by forest, the home of wild beasts and scanty tribes of savage men, extensive civilized settlements of long standing existed in the plains of the Indus and Ganges basins.

Ujjain in Vindhya Pradesh, still a considerable town retaining its ancient name unchanged, ranks as one of the seven sacred cities of

India, and rivals Benares in its claims on Hindu veneration.[1] In the seventh century it was the capital of the kingdom of Avanti, known later as Malwa, which evidently was one of the leading Indian powers for a considerable time until the supremacy passed into the hands of Magadha. Kosala, or Northern Oudh, of which the capital was Śrāvastī on the Rāptī, probably represented by Sahet-Mahet, was another important state which competed with Magadha for the headship of Āryāvarta.

Magadha. Magadha, or South Bihar, the seat of the Magadha tribe, rose to unquestioned pre-eminence in the fourth century B.C., and at a much earlier date had been intimately associated with the development of historical Jainism and Buddhism. The literary traditions of northern India consequently are mostly devoted to the affairs of Magadha, and the history of that state has to do duty as the history of India, because hardly anything is known about the annals of less prominent kingdoms.

King Bimbisāra. The regular story of Magadha begins with the Śaiśunāga dynasty, established before 600 B.C., perhaps in 642 B.C., by a chieftain of Benares named Śiśunāga (or Śiśunāka), who fixed his capital at Girivraja or old Rājagriha, among the hills of the Gaya District.[2]

The first monarch about whom anything substantial has been recorded is the fifth king, Bimbisāra or Śrēnika, who extended his paternal dominions by the conquest of Anga, the modern Bhagalpur and Monghyr Districts. He built the town of New Rājagriha (Rajgir), and may be regarded as the founder of the greatness of Magadha. Both Buddhists and Jains in later days claimed that he was a patron and follower of their respective founders. He reigned, according to the Purānas, for twenty-eight years, or for fifty-two according to the Sinhalese tradition. His death occurred some seven years before that of the Buddha, which, according to the system of chronology employed in this work, took place in 487 B.C. Thus the probable date of Bimbisāra's death was approximately 494 B.C.

Persian occupation of Indus valley. During the period of his rule, at a date subsequent to 516 B.C., Darius, son of Hystaspes, the capable autocrat of Persia (521–485 B.C.), dispatched an expedition commanded by Skylax of Karyanda in Karia with orders to prove the feasibility of a sea passage from the mouths of the Indus to Persia. Skylax equipped a fleet on the upper waters of the Panjab rivers in the

---

[1] The seven sacred cities are Benares (Kāśī), Hardwar (Māyā), Kānchī (Conjeeveram), Ayodhyā (Oudh), Dvāravatī (Dvārikā), Mathura, and Ujjain or Avantikā.

[2] See Jackson, 'Notes on Old Rājagriha', *Ann. Rep. A.S. India*, 1913–14 (1917), pp. 265–71, pl. lxxi.

The chronology adopted by Dr. Smith has been strongly criticized by Professor H. C. Raychaudhuri and others. Raychaudhuri, basing his view on the evidence of the Ceylon chronicle, places Śiśunāga after Bimbisāra, and believes that he was the founder of a new dynasty (*P.H.A.I.*[6], pp. 115 ff.). Some scholars, however, would still support Dr. Smith's chronology. [Ed.]

Gandhāra country, made his way down to the coast, and in the thirteenth month reached the sea. Darius was thus enabled to annex the Indus valley and to send his fleet into the Indian Ocean. The archers from India supplied a contingent to the army of Xerxes, the son of Darius, and shared the defeat of Mardonius at Plataea in Greece in 479 B.C.

The province on the Indus annexed by Darius was formed into the twentieth satrapy, which was considered to be the richest and most populous province of the Persian empire. It paid a tribute of 360 Euboic talents of gold-dust, equivalent to at least a million sterling, and constituting about one-third of the total bullion revenue of the Asiatic provinces. The Indian satrapy, which was distinct from Aria (Herat), Arachosia (Qandahar), and Gandharia (Taxila and the north-western frontier), must have extended from the Salt Range to the sea, and probably included part of the Panjab to the east of the Indus. The courses of the rivers in those days were quite different from what they now are, and there is reason for believing that extensive tracts now desert were then rich and populous. The high tribute paid is thus explained.

No distinct evidence exists to show that there was any communication in the fifth century B.C. between the Persian province on the Indus and the growing kingdom of Magadha. But it would be extremely rash to affirm that no such communication existed. It is not known at what date Persia ceased to exercise effective control over the twentieth satrapy. At the time of Alexander's invasion the Indus was still recognized as the official boundary between the Persian empire and India, but the authorities do not mention the presence of Persian officials along the course of the river, the banks of which were occupied by sundry small states with rulers of their own, and seemingly independent.

The Kharoshthī alphabet, derived from the Aramaic script, and written from right to left, which continued to be used on the north-western frontier until about the fourth century of the Christian era, appears to have been introduced by Persian officials and may be regarded as a memorial of the days when the Indus valley was part of the Achaemenian empire.

King Ajātaśatru. Bimbisāra was succeeded about 494 B.C. by his son Ajātaśatru or Kūnika, whose reign may be taken as having lasted for twenty-seven years. He built the fortress of Pātali on the Son, which afterwards developed into the imperial city of Pātaliputra. His mother was a lady of the famous Lichchhavi tribe, and he was married to a princess of Kosala. He waged successful wars against both the Lichchhavis and his consort's kingdom. Kosala disappears from history as an independent kingdom, and evidently was absorbed by Magadha.

The Lichchhavis. The Lichchhavi nation, tribe, or clan, which played a prominent part in Indian legend and history for more than a thousand years, claims a few words of notice.[1] The Lichchhavis dwelt

---

[1] The spelling of the name varies.

in the land of the Vrijjis, the region now called the Muzaffarpur District of Bihar to the north of the Ganges. Their capital was Vaiśāli, a noble city ten or twelve miles in circuit, represented by the villages and ruins at or near Basārh, twenty miles to the north of Hājīpur, and on the northern side of the river about twenty-seven miles distant in a direct line from Pātaliputra (Patna). The Lichchhavis were governed by an assembly of notables, presided over by an elected chief (nāyaka). Good reason exists for believing that they were hill-men of the Mongolian type akin to the Tibetans. They certainly followed the unpleasant Tibetan custom of exposing the bodies of the dead, which were sometimes hung upon trees, and their judicial procedure in criminal cases was similar to the Tibetan. The first Tibetan king is said to have belonged to the family of Śākya the Lichchhavi, a kinsman of Gautama, the sage of another branch of the Śākyas. The more I consider the evidence of such traditions and the unmistakable testimony of the early sculptures as at Barhut and Sānchī, dating from about 200 B.C., the more I am convinced that the Mongolian or hill-man element formed a large percentage in the population of northern India during the centuries immediately preceding and following the Christian era. I think it highly probable that Gautama Buddha, the sage of the Śākyas, and the founder of historical Buddhism, was a Mongolian by birth, that is to say, a hill-man like a Gūrkha with Mongolian features, and akin to the Tibetans. Similar views were expressed long ago by Beal and Fergusson, who used the terms Scythic or Turanian in the sense in which I use Mongolian.[1]

The Lichchhavis retained an influential position for many centuries. The marriage of Chandragupta I with a Lichchhavi princess at the close of the third century A.C. laid the foundation of the greatness of the Imperial Gupta dynasty, and the tribe supplied a line of rulers in the Nepal valley up to the seventh century.

In early times the Mallas of Pāvā and Kuśinagara, who are often mentioned in Buddhist legends, probably were akin to the Lichchhavis.

Mahāvīra, the founder of historical Jainism, likewise may have been a Mongolian hill-man. The Brahman writers regarded the Lichchhavis as degraded Kshatriyas, a purely fictitious mode of expression.

Kings Darśaka and Udaya. Ajātaśatru was succeeded about 467 B.C. by his son Darśaka, who is mentioned in a play by the early dramatist Bhāsa, which came to light in 1910. He was followed about 443 by his son Udaya, who built the city of Kusumapura on the Ganges, a few miles from Pātaliputra on the Son. The two names are sometimes used as synonyms. The position of the confluence of the Son with the Ganges and the courses of both rivers in the neighbourhood of Pātaliputra have undergone extensive changes since the days of Udaya.

Parricide story. Buddhist tradition from various sources is

[1] This theory has been strongly criticized by several Indian authorities, but in the editor's opinion is still tenable.

unanimous in affirming that Ajātaśatru, weary of awaiting the course of nature, murdered his father, and the crime is said to have been instigated by Devadatta, the heretical cousin of the Buddha. The Jains, though representing Ajātaśatru as a devout follower of their religion who 'ruled the country for eighty years according to the laws of his father', admit that he usurped the throne, but state that Bimbisāra committed suicide in prison. This degree of agreement between independent traditions indicates that there is truth in the story of the usurpation at least, and the respect in which Ajātaśatru was held by the Jains suggests that their account of Bimbisāra's suicide is an effort to conceal the parricide of Ajātaśatru.[1]

Kings and prophets. The main interest of the reigns of Bimbisāra and his son lies in the close association of both kings with the lives of Gautama Buddha and Vardhamāna Mahāvīra Tīrthankara, who are usually described respectively as the founders of Buddhism and Jainism. The traditions concerning the intercourse of the kings with the prophets are discrepant in many particulars which need not be discussed, but it seems to be fairly certain that King Bimbisāra was related to Mahāvīra, and was contemporary for some years with both him and Gautama Buddha.

Credible evidence affirms that Ajātaśatru visited both of those teachers, and that during his reign Gautama Buddha died. According to the modern Sinhalese reckoning the death of the Buddha occurred about 543 B.C., but authorities are almost unanimous in agreeing that the event actually took place some sixty years later. The date 487 B.C. here adopted is approximately indicated by the very old Sinhalese tradition that the death of the Buddha occurred 218 years before the consecration of Asoka, and is confirmed by an independent Chinese Buddhist tradition.

Religion in sixth century B.C. The sixth century B.C. was a time when men's minds in several widely separated parts of the world were deeply stirred by the problems of religion and salvation. The Indian movement was specially active in Magadha and the neighbouring regions where the Hinduizing of the population was incomplete and distinctions of race were clearly marked. Intelligent members of the governing classes, who were regarded as Kshatriyas by the Brahmans from the west, were inclined to consider themselves better men than their spiritual guides, whose arrogant class-pride aroused warm opposition. It seems to me almost certain, as already indicated, that the Śaiśunāgas, Lichchhavis, and several other ruling families or clans in or near Magadha were not Indo-Aryan by blood. They were, I think, hill-men of the Mongolian type, resembling the Tibetans, Gurkhas, Bhūtias, and other Himalayan tribes of the present day. The racial distinction between the Brahmans and their pupils necessarily evoked

[1] The complete rejection of the Buddhist account of the parricide of Ajātaśatru, as in earlier editions of this work, is hardly possible in view of the similar story in the Jaina *Nirayāvalikā Sūtra*, which was evidently not known to Dr. Smith. [Ed.]

and encouraged the growth of independent views on philosophy and religion. The educated men of the upper classes, called Kshatriyas by the Brahmans, rebelled against the claim of the strangers to the exclusive possession of superior knowledge and the key of the door to salvation.

Many sects arose advocating the most diverse opinions concerning the nature of God and the soul, the relation between God and man, and the best way of attaining salvation. Most Indian thinkers contemplate salvation or deliverance (*moksha*) as meaning the release of the soul from all liability to future rebirths. At that time the religion favoured by the Brahmans, as depicted in the treatises called *Brāhmanas*, was of a mechanical, lifeless character, overlaid with cumbrous ceremonial. The formalities of the irksome ritual galled many persons, while the cruelty of the numerous bloody sacrifices was repugnant to others. People sought eagerly for some better path to the goal of salvation desired by all. Some, who hoped to win their object by means of transcendental knowledge, sounded the depths of novel systems of philosophy. Others sought to subdue the body and free the soul by inflicting on themselves the most austere mortifications and cruel self-tortures.

Jainism and Buddhism. All the numerous schools and sects which then sprang up or flourished died out in the course of time save two. The doctrines of the two surviving sects now known as Jainism and Buddhism have brought into existence two powerful churches or religious organizations which still affect profoundly the thoughts of mankind.

Buddhism, although almost extinct in the land of its birth, is at this day one of the greatest spiritual forces in the world, dominating, as it does in various forms, Ceylon, Burma, Siam, Tibet, Mongolia, China, and Japan. Jainism, which never aspired to such wide conquests, now claims but a comparatively small number of adherents, resident chiefly in Rajasthan and western India. The influence of the religion, however, even now is much greater than that indicated by the census returns. In former times it pervaded almost every province of India and enjoyed the patronage of mighty kings.

Both Jainism and Buddhism as historical religions originated in Magadha or the territories adjoining that kingdom in the reigns of Bimbisāra and his son Ajātaśatru. Those two faiths, it need hardly be said, did not come into being independently of previous conditions. The teaching of Mahāvīra the Jain and of Gautama the Buddha was based on the doctrine of earlier prophets. Mahāvīra started his religious life as a reformer of an ancient ascetic order said to have been founded by Pārśvanātha two centuries and a half earlier. Gautama's preaching was related to the cult of the 'former Buddhas', whose prophet was Devadatta, Gautama's cousin. But we need not trouble about the obscure precursors of Jainism and Buddhism, who may be left to the research of antiquarians. The history of India is concerned seriously only with those historical religions as started respectively by Mahāvīra and Gautama. Although the stories of the lives of both prophets are obscured by a veil of legend and mythology, certain facts seem to be established with sufficient certainty. We will take first Jainism, the minor and probably the older religion of the two.

Career of Mahāvīra. Vardhamāna, better known by his title in religion of Mahāvīra, was the son of a Lichchhavi noble of Vaiśāli. He gave up his honourable rank and joined the ascetic order of Pārśvanātha, in which he remained for some years. Becoming dissatisfied with the rules of that order, he started on his own account as a religious leader when about forty years of age. During the remainder of his life, which lasted more than thirty years, he travelled as a preacher through Magadha or South Bihar; Videha, otherwise called Mithilā or Tirhut; and Anga or Bhagalpur. In the course of his ministry he organized a new religious order consisting of professed friars and nuns, lay brethren and lay sisters. When he died at Pāvā in the Patna District his adherents are said to have exceeded 14,000 in number. Being related through his mother to the reigning kings of Videha, Magadha, and Anga, he was in a position to gain official patronage for his teaching, and is recorded to have been in personal touch with both Bimbisāra and Ajātaśatru. The traditional dates for his death vary so much that it is impossible to obtain certainty in the matter. The date most commonly accepted by the Jains, 527 B.C., is difficult to reconcile with the well attested fact of his interview with Ajātaśatru and with the Jain tradition that he was alive at the time of Ajātaśatru's war with the Lichchhavis. Professor Jacobi advocated 467 B.C. as the approximate year of the decease of Mahāvīra.

Career of Buddha. The career of Gautama, the sage of the Śākyas (Śākyamuni), known generally as Buddha or the Buddha, because he claimed to have attained supreme knowledge of things spiritual (*bodhi*), was very similar to that of Mahāvīra. Gautama, like his rival prophet, was the son of a noble Sākya, the Rājā of Kapilavastu in the Nepalese Taraī, a dependency of Kosala, and was classed by the Brahmans as a Kshatriya. The legends relate in endless imaginative detail the story of the young prince's disgust for the luxurious life of a palace, and of his resolve to effect the Great Renunciation. Leaving his home, he went to Gaya and there sought salvation by subjecting his body to the severest penances. But he made the discovery that mere asceticism was futile, and decided to spend the rest of his life in preaching the truth as he saw it. He proceeded to the Deer Park at Sārnāth near Benares, where five disciples joined him. From that small beginning arose the great Buddhist *Sangha* or Order. Gautama continued his preaching for forty-five years and died aged eighty at Kuśinagara, which probably was situated in Nepalese territory at the junction of the Little Rāptī with the Gandak near Bhavēsar Ghat. The well-known remains near Kasiā in the Gorakhpur District appear to be those of the monastic establishment of Vēthadīpa, subordinate to the head monastery at Kuśinagara.

Both were called *Parinirvāna* monasteries as being connected with the death of Buddha.[1] The date of his decease, like that of Mahāvīra's, cannot be determined with accuracy. It appears that both Mahāvīra and Buddha were contemporary with Kings Bimbisāra and Ajātaśatru, both dying in the reign of the latter.

Jainism and Buddhism contrasted. The close parallelism of the careers of the two prophets, combined with certain superficial resemblances between the doctrines of the sects which they founded, induced some of the older scholars to regard Jainism as a sect of Buddhism. That opinion is now recognized to be erroneous. The two systems, whether regarded as philosophies or religions, are essentially different. The word 'sects' as applied above to the Jain and Buddhist churches is correctly used, because both Mahāvīra and Buddha may be justly regarded as having been originally Hindu reformers. Neither prophet endeavoured directly to overthrow the caste framework of Hindu society so far as it had been established in their time, although both rejected the authority of the Vedas and opposed the practice of animal sacrifice. Followers of either Mahāvīra or Gautama were not asked to give up their belief in the Hindu gods, which always have received veneration from both Jains and Buddhists. Indra, Brahmā, and other gods play a prominent part in Buddhist legend and belief. In Ceylon even the great gods Śiva and Vishnu are worshipped as satellites of Buddha. The Jains of the present day continue, as their forefathers always did, to employ Brahmans as their domestic chaplains for the performance of birth or death ceremonies, and even sometimes, it is said, for temple worship. Jainism has never cut itself away from its roots in Hinduism. Many Jains consider themselves to be Hindus, and describe their religion accordingly in census returns. That continuous close connexion between Brahmanical Hinduism and Jainism probably is the principal reason why the latter faith made no conquests outside of India.

Buddhism developed a much more independent existence. Both as a philosophy and a religion it so adapted itself to the needs of foreigners that in the course of time it nearly died out in India while acquiring new life in foreign lands. The Jains give the laity a prominent place, while the Buddhists rely mainly on their organized *Sangha*—the Community or Order of ordained friars. That organized Order has been the main instrument of Buddhist missionary expansion. No avowed Buddhist in any country would dream of describing himself as a Hindu by religion.[2] Readers who desire to understand thoroughly the philosophical, ethical, and theological tenets of Jainism and Buddhism, the

---

[1] See the author's article 'Kuśinagara' in Hastings, *Encycl. of Religion and Ethics.* Kasiā cannot represent Kuśinagara, because that site was and long had been deserted in the time of the Chinese pilgrims, whereas building was continuous at Kasiā all through the Gupta period and afterwards.

[2] For unavowed, veiled, or crypto-Indian Buddhists see Nagendra Nāth Vasu, *The Modern Buddhism and its Followers in Orissa* (Hare Press, Calcutta, 1911), with the extremely learned Introduction by M. M. H. P. Sāstri.

points of agreement or divergence in the two systems, and the church regulations must study some or other of the many excellent books now available. Only a few points can be noted here.

Jain doctrines. Jain teaching lays stress upon the doctrine that man's personality is dual, comprising both material and spiritual natures. It rejects the Vedantist doctrine of the universal soul. Jains believe that not only men and animals, but also plants, minerals capable of growth, air, wind, and fire possess souls (*jīva*) endowed with various degrees of consciousness.[1] They hold that it is possible to inflict pain on a stone, or even on air or water. The belief in a supreme Deity, the creator of the universe, is emphatically denied. God is defined as being 'only the highest, the noblest, and the fullest manifestation of all the powers which lie latent in the soul of man'. From that point of view Jainism may be said to anticipate Comte's 'religion of humanity'.

In ethics or practical morality 'the first principle is *ahimsā*, non-hurting of any kind of life, howsoever low may be the stage of its evolution'. The strange doctrine affirming the existence of *jīvas* in objects commonly called inanimate extends the Jain idea of *ahimsā* far beyond the Brahmanical or Buddhist notions.

The reader of Indian history is sometimes perplexed by the apparent contradiction of principles involved when a king orders the execution of a convict, guilty perhaps only of the killing of an animal. The following authoritative ruling on the subject helps to make intelligible the position taken up by Kumārapāla, King of Gujarat in the twelfth century, who ruthlessly inflicted the capital penalty on all persons who in any way offended against the *ahimsā* doctrine:

A true Jaina will do nothing to hurt the feelings of another person, man woman, or child; nor will he violate the principles of Jainism. Jaina ethics are meant for men of all positions—for kings, warriors, traders, artisans, agriculturists, and indeed for men and women in every walk of life. . . . 'Do your duty. Do it as humanely as you can.' This, in brief, is the primary principle of Jainism. Non-killing cannot interfere with one's duties. The king, or the judge, has to hang a murderer. The murderer's act is the negation of a right of the murdered. The king's, or the judge's, order is the negation of this negation, and is enjoined by Jainism as a duty. Similarly, the soldier's killing on the battle-field.

Jainism is an austere religion, demanding severe self-control in diverse ways, and imposing many inconvenient restraints. The teaching theoretically condemns caste, but in practice 'the modern Jaina is as fast bound as his Hindu brother in the iron fetters of caste'.

[1] Compare Wordsworth, *Prelude* (2nd ed., 1851), Book III, p. 49:

> To every natural form, rock, fruit, or flower,
> Even the loose stones that cover the high-way,
> I gave a moral life: I saw them feel,
> Or linked them to some feeling: the great mass
> Lay bedded in a quickening soul, and all
> That I beheld respired with inward meaning.

The poet felt those sentiments while he was an undergraduate at Cambridge.

The Jains are divided into two main sects, the Śvetāmbara, or 'white-robed', and the Digambara, or 'sky-clad', that is to say nude, which separated about the beginning of the second century A.D. Each sect has its own scriptures. A modern offshoot of the Śvetāmbaras, called Sthānakavāsī, rejects the use of idols in worship.

Jains highly approve of suicide by slow starvation. The practice, abhorred by Buddhists, seems to outsiders inconsistent with the *ahimsā* doctrine, but Jain philosophy has an explanation, which will be found expounded in Mrs. Stevenson's book.

The teaching of Buddha. Gautama Buddha, like Mahāvīra and almost all prophets in his country, took over from the common stock of Indian ideas the theories of rebirth and *karma*, accepted generally by Indian thinkers as truths needing no proof. The *karma* doctrine means that the merits and demerits of a being in past existences determine his condition in the present life. Buddha held that to be born is an evil, that the highest good is deliverance from rebirth, that good *karma* will effect such deliverance, and that the acquisition of good *karma* requires a strictly moral life. His disciples were admonished to aim at purity in deed, word, and thought; observing ten vows, namely not to kill or injure living beings, not to steal, to remain celibate, not to lie or slander, to abstain from intoxicants, not to eat after noon, to abstain from dancing and singing and attendance at entertainments, to abstain from the use of garlands, scents, and ornaments, not to sleep on a raised bed, and not to receive money or valuables. Only the first five vows were binding on laymen, for whom the third is modified to allow lawful marriage. Special stress was laid on the virtues of truthfulness, reverence to superiors, and respect for animal life.

He held that men should follow what he called the 'Noble Eightfold Path', practising right belief, right thought, right speech, right action, right means of livelihood, right exertion, right remembrance, and right meditation. That path was also described as the Middle Path, lying midway between sensuality and asceticism. Men and women of the laity could attain much success in travelling the way of holiness, but full satisfaction could be obtained only by joining the *Sangha* or Order of ordained monks, or rather friars. Women were permitted to become nuns, but nuns never occupied an important place in Buddhism. The *Sangha* of monks developed into a highly organized, wealthy, and powerful fraternity, which became the efficient instrument for the wide diffusion of Buddhism in Asia.

Popular Buddhism. Buddha can hardly be said to have intended to found a new religion. He taught an abstruse doctrine of metaphysics, which he used chiefly as the rational basis of his practical moral code. He was unwilling to discuss questions concerning the nature of God or the soul, the infinity of the universe, and so forth, holding that such discussions are unprofitable. Without formally denying the existence of Almighty God, the Creator, he ignored Him. Buddha, although he denied the authority of the Vedas, did not seek to interfere with the current beliefs in the Hindu gods or with familiar superstitions; and, as a matter of fact, popular Buddhism from the very earliest times has always differed much from the austere religion of the books. Modern Burma, where everybody worships the Nats or spirits, while accepting without question the orthodox teaching of the monks, offers the best illustration of the state of things in ancient Buddhist India, as vividly represented in the sculptures. Buddhism in practice was a cheerful religion in India long ago, as it is in Burma now.

Transformation of Buddhism. The person of Buddha inspired in his disciples such ardent affection and devotion that very soon after his death, or perhaps even during his lifetime, he was regarded as being something more than a man. By the beginning of the Christian era, if not earlier, he had become a god to whom prayer might be offered. The primitive Buddhism which ignored the Divine was known in later times as the Hīnayāna, or Lesser Vehicle of salvation, while the modified religion which recognized the value of prayer and acknowledged Buddha as the incarnation of an eternal heavenly Buddha was called the Mahāyāna, or the Greater Vehicle.

While the original official Buddhism was a dry, highly moralized philosophy much resembling in its practical operation the Stoic schools of Greece and Rome, the later emotional Buddhism approached closely to Christian doctrines in substance, although not in name. In another direction it became almost indistinguishable from Hinduism.

No Buddhist period. It must be clearly understood that Brahmanical Hinduism continued to exist and to claim innumerable adherents throughout the ages. It may well be doubted if Buddhism can be correctly described as having been the prevailing religion in India as a whole at any time. The phrase 'Buddhist period', to be found in many books, is false and misleading. Neither a Buddhist nor a Jain period ever existed. From time to time either Buddhism or Jainism obtained exceptional success and an unusually large percentage of adherents in the population of one kingdom or another, but neither heresy ever superseded Brahmanical Hinduism. Mahāvīra, as has been mentioned, had about 14,000 disciples when he died, a mere drop in the ocean of India's millions. Subsequent royal patronage largely extended his following, and at times Jainism became the state religion of certain kingdoms, in the sense that it was adopted and encouraged by certain kings, who carried with them many of their subjects. Instances of kings changing their creed are numerous. Buddhism probably continued to be an obscure local sect, confined to Magadha and the neighbouring regions, until Aśoka gave it his powerful patronage more than two centuries after the death of Buddha. The fortune of Buddhism was made by Aśoka, but even he never attempted to force all his subjects to enter the Buddhist fold. While he insisted on certain rules of conduct concerning diet and other matters being observed by everybody in accordance with the orders of government, he did not interfere with anybody's faith. Akbar pursued the same policy in the sixteenth century. Even in Aśoka's age it is likely that the majority of the people in many, if not in most, provinces followed the guidance of the Brahmans. The relative proportions of orthodox Hindus and Buddhist dissenters varied enormously according to locality. Many details on the subject can be extracted from the narratives of the Chinese pilgrims in the fifth and seventh centuries after Christ, and there can be no doubt that similar relations between the various Indian sects or religions must have existed in earlier times.

The Hinduism of the Brahmans did not remain unchanged. The attacks delivered by Mahāvīra, Buddha, and other less celebrated prophets on the elaborate ritual and bloody sacrifices favoured by the Brahmans of the sixth century B.C. resulted, not only in the development of Jainism and Buddhism as distinct sects or religions, but in profound modification in the ideas of those Hindus who still professed obedience to the Vedas and to Brahman gurus. The *ahimsā* principle of non-injury to animal life gained many adherents, so that the more shocking elements in the old Hindu ritual tended to fall into disrepute. The change of feeling, as already noted, can be traced in many passages of the *Mahābhārata*. Bloody sacrifices still retain the approval of considerable sections of the population, but the general tendency during the last 2,000 years has been to discredit them. The movement of sentiment on the subject continues to this day, and may be observed on a large scale in the peninsula. The slaughter of victims in appalling numbers is still practised in the Telugu country. For instance, at Ellore in the Kistna (Krishnā) District, a thousand victims may be slain on one day at a certain festival, so that the blood flows down from the place of sacrifice 'in a regular flood'. But in the Tamil country 'there is a widespread idea that animal sacrifices are distasteful to good and respectable deities', with the result that such offerings are going out of fashion.[1]

Brahmanical cults. The reaction against the atheistic tendency of both Jainism and Buddhism on the one hand and against the formalism of a religion of ritual on the other resulted in the evolution among Brahmanical Hindus of the religion of *bhakti*, or lively loving faith in a personal, fatherly God. Although it is impossible to fix dates, Bhandarkar has shown that such devotion to the Deity under the name of Vāsudeva may be traced back as far as the time of the great grammarian Pāṇini, whatever that was.[2] Other facts indicate the existence of the worship of Vāsudeva in the two centuries immediately preceding the Christian era. The noble *Bhagavad-Gītā*, the date of which cannot be determined, offers the earliest formal exposition of the *bhakti* doctrine, the Deity being represented under the name and person of Krishna.

---

[1] Whitehead, *The Village Gods of Southern India* (1916), pp. 66, 94. Modern reform movements have probably considerably reduced animal sacrifice since Dr. Smith wrote; but it still takes place. [Ed.]
[2] Most probably the fourth century B.C.

The practice of *bhakti* seems to have arisen in the Brahmarshi region in the neighbourhood of Mathura and Delhi. Vāsudeva and Krishna both became identified with Vishnu, whose cult has a long history. Simultaneously the cults of Śiva and other forms of the Deity were developed, especially in the south. It is impossible to trace the details of religious evolution in a general history, but it is important to remember that much was happening inside the fold of Brahmanical Hinduism while Buddhism and Jainism were being founded and started on their more conspicuous adventures outside.

The 'Nine Nandas'. The dynastic lists of the older Purānas, which are the best authority on the subject, state that the Śaiśunāga dynasty comprised ten kings, of whom the last two were named Nandi-vardhana and Mahānandin. Their reigns are said to have covered eighty-three years. The Ceylon tradition makes no mention of these kings, and the lengths of their reigns are evidently too long; but all sources are agreed on the historicity of their successors, the 'Nine' or 'New' Nandas, namely, King Mahāpadma and his eight sons, whose rule altogether is variously said to have lasted 100, 40, or 22 years.[1] It is clear that the history has been falsified in some way and that the chronology cannot be right. The traditions about the Nandas as recorded in the Purānas, sundry Jain and Buddhist books, the *Mudrā Rākshasa* drama, perhaps composed in the fourth or fifth century A.D., and by the Greek writers, are hopelessly discrepant in many respects, but it is certain that the king deposed and slain by Chandragupta Maurya with the aid of his Brahman minister Chānakya, alias Kautilya or Vishnugupta, was a Nanda, that he was of low caste, that he was a heretic hostile to the Brahmans and Kshatriyas, and that he was a rich, powerful sovereign, believed by the Greeks to control an army of 20,000 horse, 200,000 foot, 2,000 chariots, and 3,000 or 4,000 elephants. The Hāthīgumphā inscription of Khāravela indicates that Orissa was at one time in the possession of the Nandas and there are vague traditions that they exerted some influence in the Deccan, so it would appear that, despite their unpopularity, they successfully extended the power of Magadha. Many unsuccessful attempts have been made to harmonize the conflicting traditions and to evolve a reasonable scheme of chronology. I cannot pretend to solve the puzzle. The Nanda king dethroned by Chandragupta Maurya was certainly a heretic in Hindu eyes, because the concluding verse of Kautilya's *Arthaśāstra* states that 'this *Śāstra* (scripture) has been made by him who from intolerance (of misrule) quickly rescued the scriptures (*śāstram*) and the science of weapons (*śastram*) and the earth which had passed to the Nanda king'.[2] The necessary inference seems to be that the hated Nanda king was either a Jain or a Buddhist, whom orthodox writers did not care to acknowledge as a lawful sovereign. The supposi-

---

[1] For the interpretation of *Navanandāh* as the 'New' or 'Later' Nandas see *J.B.O. Res. Soc.*, vol. iv, pp. 91-95.

[2] The rendering of the *Arthaśāstra* text is that of Shāma Sastri.

tion that the last Nanda was a follower of Mahāvīra is strengthened by the comparatively friendly references to the Nandas in Jain literature. A certain obscure passage in the Jain *Bhagavatī Sūtra* suggests that he may have been a follower of the Ājīvika sect.

Invasion of Alexander the Great. The invasion of India by Alexander the Great of Macedon in 326 B.C., which occurred during the rule of the Nandas in Magadha and is more interesting than any other episode of early Indian history to most European readers, made so little impression on the minds of the inhabitants of the country that no distinct reference to it is to be found in any branch of ancient Indian literature. Our detailed knowledge of his proceedings is derived solely from Greek authors.[1] The name of Sikandar or Alexander is often on the lips of the people in the Panjab, but it is doubtful how far a genuine tradition of the Macedonian invader survives in that country. Spurious traditions are apt to be generated from confused recollections of the investigations and talk of modern archaeologists. There is also reason to believe that the popular memory sometimes confounds Sikandar of Macedon with his namesakes, the Lodī Sultan of Delhi (1489–1517) and the image-breaking Sultan of Kashmir (1394–1420). A genuine tradition of Philip's son has possibly been preserved in the families of no less than eight chieftains in the neighbourhood of the Indus and Oxus, all of whom claim the honour of descent from Alexander. The claims may be well founded to some extent, because the historians record that Kleophis, Queen of the Assakēnoi, was reputed to have borne a son to Alexander.[2] The Tungani soldiers who formed the garrison of Yarkand in 1835 also alleged that Macedonian soldier colonists left behind by the conqueror were their ancestors.

Alexander, after completing the conquest of Bactria to the south of the Oxus, resolved to execute his cherished purpose of surpassing the mythical exploits of Herakles his reputed ancestor, Semiramis the fabled Assyrian queen, Cyrus, King of Persia, and the divine Dionysos, by effecting the subjugation of India. When he undertook the task very little accurate information about the scene of the proposed conquests was at his disposal. The sacred soil of India had never been violated by any earlier European invader, nor had the country been visited by travellers from the west, so far as is known. Wild tales concerning the marvels to be seen beyond the Indus were current, but nothing authentic seems to have been on record, and the bold adventurer was obliged to collect the necessary intelligence as he advanced.

Alexander, however, although adventurous, was not imprudent. He never moved without taking adequate precautions to maintain communication with his distant base in Macedon thousands of miles

[1] Archaeological evidence, chiefly numismatic, corroborates the Greek historians in certain details.

[2] The chieftains referred to are: (1) the former Mirs of Badakhshan, dispossessed about 1822; (2–5) the chiefs of Darwāz, Kulāb, Shighnān, and Wakhan; and (6–8) the chiefs of Chitral, Gilgit, and Iskardo (Burnes, *Travels into Bokhara*, &c., 2nd ed., 1835, vol. iii, pp. 186–90).

away, and to protect his flanks from hostile attack. His intelligence department seems to have provided him with information accurate enough to ensure the success of each operation.

Campaign in the hills. He crossed the Hindu Kush mountains in May 327 B.C., and after garrisoning either Kabul itself or a stronghold in the neighbourhood, spent the remainder of the year in subduing the fierce tribes which then as now inhabited the valleys of Suwāt (Swat) and Bājaur. He gave them a lesson such as they have never received since from Afghans, Mughuls, or English, and penetrated into secluded fastnesses which no European has ever seen again. His ruthless operations effected their purpose so thoroughly that his communications were never harassed by the tribes.

The Indus crossed. In February 326 B.C., at the beginning of spring, he crossed the Indus, then regarded as the frontier of the Persian empire, by a bridge of boats built at Und or Ohind above Attock. Thence he advanced to Takshasilā or Taxila, 'a great and flourishing city', the capital of Āmbhi, ruler of the region between the Indus and the Hydaspes or Jihlam (Jhelum) river. Āmbhi, who was at feud with the chiefs of neighbouring principalities, welcomed the invader and received him hospitably at his capital. The rich presents offered by the Indian king were requited tenfold by his generous and politic guest. It is worthy of note that the supplies tendered by Āmbhi comprised '3,000 oxen fatted for the shambles' besides 10,000 or more sheep. That statement, made incidentally, is good evidence that in 326 B.C. the people of Taxila were still willing to fatten cattle for slaughter and the feeding of honoured guests, in Vedic fashion.

Taxila. The situation of Taxila in a pleasant valley, amply supplied with water, well adapted for defence, and lying on the highroad from central Asia to the interior of India, was admirably suited for the site of a great city. The remains of the ancient capital, or rather series of successive capitals, gradually shifted from south to north, cover a space of at least twelve square miles at Hasan Abdal and several other villages situated about twenty miles to the north-west of Rawalpindi, which is the strategical representative of Taxila. The line of the ancient highway has been followed by the Grand Trunk Road and the North-Western Railway.

In the time of Alexander the Panjab was divided among a large number of small states, Taxila being the capital only of the tract between the Indus and the Hydaspes. Its military importance, therefore, was less than that of its modern representative. The invader having been received by the local king as a friend, no fighting took place in the neighbourhood of Taxila, and no information concerning its defences is recorded. Āmbhi supplied a contingent of 5,000 men to help Alexander.

The testimony of the Buddhist *Jātaka* or Birth stories, which, although undated, may be applied fairly to the age of Alexander, proves by a multitude of incidental allusions that Taxila was then the leading seat of Hindu learning, where crowds of pupils from all quarters were taught the 'three Vedas and the eighteen accomplishments'. It was the fashion to send princes and the sons of well-to-do Brahmans on attaining the age of sixteen to complete their education at Taxila, which may be properly described as a university town. The medical school there enjoyed a special reputation, but all arts and sciences could be studied under the most eminent professors.

Strange Taxilan customs. The willing offering of 3,000 oxen to be converted into beef has been noted as a remarkable feature in the social usage of the Taxilans. They had also several peculiar customs, which struck the Greek observers as 'strange and unusual'. The practices described are so startling that it is well to quote the exact words of Strabo, who copied Aristoboulos, a companion of Alexander, and an author deserving of the fullest credit.

He makes mention of some strange and unusual customs which existed. Those who are unable from poverty to bestow their daughters in marriage expose them for sale in the market-place in the flower of their age, a crowd being assembled by sound of the [conch] shells and drums, which are also used for sounding the war-note. When any person steps forward, first the back of the girl as far as the shoulders is uncovered for his examination and then the parts in front, and if she pleases him and allows herself at the same time to be persuaded, they cohabit on such terms as may be agreed upon. The dead are thrown out to be devoured by vultures. The custom of having many wives prevails here and is common among other races. He says that he had heard from some persons of wives burning themselves along with their deceased husbands and doing so gladly; and that those women who refused to burn themselves were held in disgrace. The same things have been stated by other writers.[1]

The marriage market obviously suggests comparison with the similar institution in the territory of Babylon, fully described with approval by Herodotus (1. 196), who observes that the sales took place once a year in every village. He heard that the Venetians of Illyria had a like custom. The casting out of the dead to be devoured by vultures was a practice of the Zoroastrian Iranians, and also of the Tibetans. The definite proof of the usage of widow-burning or satī at such an early certain date is interesting. Among the Kathaioi of the eastern Panjab also 'the custom prevailed that widows should be burned with their husbands'. The scanty evidence as to Taxilan institutions taken as a whole suggests that the civilization of the people was compounded of various elements, Babylonian, Iranian, Scythian, and Vedic. Satī was probably a Scythian rite introduced from central Asia. There is some indication that it was practised by the Aryans in pre-Vedic times, before their entry into India.

Religion and civilization. When the fact is remembered that in

---

[1] Strabo, Book XV, chap. i, sec. 62; transl. McCrindle in *Ancient India as described in Classical Literature* (Constable, 1901), p. 69. In sec. 28 Strabo observes that Taxila was governed by 'good laws'.

later times the Panjab came to be regarded as an unholy, non-Aryan country, it is worthy of note that the *Jātakas* represent Taxila as the seat of study of the three Vedas and all the other branches of Hindu learning. The population of the Panjab in Alexander's time probably included many divers races. Strabo (Book XV, chap. i, secs. 61, 63–68) gives an interesting account of the Brahman ascetics of Taxila, chiefly derived from the works of Aristoboulos and Onesikritos. It is clear that the Brahmanical religion was firmly established, notwithstanding the survival of strange customs, and in all likelihood the coexistence of Zoroastrian or Magian fire-worship and other foreign cults. It is manifest that a high degree of material civilization had been attained, and that all the arts and crafts incident to the life of a wealthy, cultured city were familiar. The notices recorded by Alexander's officers permit no doubt that in the fourth century B.C. the history of Indian civilization was already a long one. Their statements have a material bearing upon discussions concerning the date of the introduction of writing and the chronology of Vedic literature.

Advance against Pŏros. Alexander, after allowing his army a pleasant rest at hospitable Taxila, advanced eastward, to attack Pŏros, or Pūru, the king of the country between the Hydaspes (Jihlam) and Akesines (Chinab), who felt himself strong enough to defy the invader. The Greeks, who were much impressed by the high stature of the men in the Panjab, acknowledged that 'in the art of war they were far superior to the other nations by which Asia was at that time inhabited'. The resolute opposition of Pŏros consequently was not to be despised. Alexander experienced much difficulty in crossing the Hydaspes river, then, at the end of June or the beginning of July, in full flood and guarded by a superior force. His horses would not face the elephants on the opposite bank. After a delay of several weeks he succeeded in stealing a passage at a sharp bend in the river some sixteen miles above his camp and getting across with the help of a convenient island. The hostile armies met in the Karri plain marked by the villages Sirwāl and Pakral.

Battle of the Hydaspes. The army of Pŏros, consisting of 30,000 infantry, 4,000 cavalry, 300 chariots, and 200 mighty war elephants, was defeated after a hard fight, and annihilated. All the elephants were captured or killed, the chariots were destroyed, 12,000 men were slain, and 9,000 taken prisoners. The total Macedonian casualties did not exceed a thousand. The primary cause of the Greek victory was the consummate leadership of Alexander, the greatest general in the history of the world. Pŏros, a giant 6½ feet in height, fought to the last, and received nine wounds before he was taken prisoner: The victor, who willingly responded to his captive's proud request that he might be treated as a king, secured the alliance of the Indian monarch by prudent generosity.

The elephants on which Pŏros had relied proved unmanageable in the battle and did more harm to their friends than to their foes. The archers in the chariots were not a match for the mounted bowmen of Alexander; and the slippery state of the ground hindered the Indian infantry from making full use of their formidable bows, which they were accustomed to draw after resting one end upon the earth, and pressing it with the left foot. The Indian infantryman also carried a heavy two-handed sword slung from the left shoulder, a buckler of undressed ox-hide, and sometimes javelins in place of a bow.

Advance to the Hyphasis. In due course Alexander advanced eastwards, regardless of the rain, defeated the Glausai or Glaukanikoi, crossed both the Akesines (Chinab) and the Hydraotes or Ravi, stormed Sangala, the stronghold of the Kathaioi, and threatened the Kshudrakas (Oxydrakai), who dwelt on the farther bank of the Ravi. The king then advanced as far as the Hyphasis or Bias, where he was stopped by his soldiers, who refused firmly to plunge farther into unknown lands occupied by formidable kingdoms. The limits of the Greek advance were marked by the erection of twelve altars of cut stone on the northern bank of the Bias, at a point where it flows from east to west between Indaura in the Kangra and Mirthal in the Gurdaspur District, close to the foot of the hills. The cutting back of the northern bank, which has extended for about five miles, has swept away all traces of the massive buildings.[1]

Retreat and river voyage. Alexander, intensely disappointed, was forced to return along the way by which he had come. He appointed Pōros to act as his viceroy over seven nations which shared the territory between the Hyphasis and Hydaspes, while he himself made preparations for executing the astonishingly bold project of taking his army down the course of the Panjab rivers to the sea. A fleet, numbering perhaps 2,000 vessels of all sizes, had been built by his officers on the upper waters of the Hydaspes. When all was ready in October 326 B.C., the voyage began, the ships being escorted by an army of 120,000 men marching along the banks. The extensive changes in the courses of the rivers of the Panjab and Sind, as mentioned more than once, forbid the tracing of Alexander's progress in detail, but he certainly passed through the Śibi country, now in the Jhang District, and then inhabited by rude folk clad in skins and armed with clubs, who submitted and were spared. Seven centuries later, when Śibi had become more civilized, its capital was Śivipura or Shōrkōt.[2] A neighbouring tribe, called Agalassoi by the Greeks, who dared to resist the invader, met with a terrible fate. The inhabitants of one town to the number of 20,000 set fire to their dwellings and cast themselves with their wives and children into the flames—an early and appalling instance of the practice of *jauhar* so often recorded in Muslim times.

The most formidable opposition to the Greek invaders was offered by a confederacy of the Mālavas (Malloi), Kshudrakas (Oxydrakai),

---

[1] *E.H.I.*[4] (1923), p. 76.
[2] The name Śibipura occurs in a Buddhist inscription from Shōrkōt dated 83 [G.E.] = A.D. 402–3 (Vogel in *J.P.H.S.*, vol. i, p. 174).

and other tribes dwelling along the Ravi and Bias. The confederate forces, said to have numbered 80,000 or 90,000 well equipped infantry, 10,000 cavalry, and 700 or 800 chariots, should have sufficed to destroy the Macedonian army, but the superior generalship of Alexander as usual gave him decisive victory. The survivors of the Mālavas submitted. The Kshudrakas, luckily for themselves, had been late for the fighting and so escaped the ruthless slaughter which befell their allies.

Wealth of the Mālavas. The presents offered by the envoys of the Mālavas and their allies indicate the wealth of the community and the advanced state of their material civilization. The gifts comprised 1,030 (or according to another account 500) four-horsed chariots; 1,000 bucklers; a great quantity of cotton cloth; 100 talents of 'white iron', probably meaning steel; the skins of crocodiles ('very large lizards'); a quantity of tortoise shell; and some tame lions and tigers of extraordinary size.

Patala. Several nations in Upper Sind having been subdued, Alexander reached Patala at the apex of the delta as it then existed. The town was not far from Bahmanābād, the ancient city subsequently superseded by Mansūriya. It is impossible to fix localities with accuracy for the reason already stated. Alexander made arrangements for establishing a strong naval station at Patala.

Movements of Alexander and Nearchos. He sent Krateros with elephants and heavy troops into Persia through the Mulla Pass and across Baluchistan, while he himself advanced to the mouths of the Indus, then in a position very different from that which they now occupy. In those days the Rann of Cutch was a gulf of the sea and one arm of the Indus emptied itself into it. Most of the existing delta has been formed since Alexander's time.

Early in October 325 B.C. Alexander, having spent about ten months on the voyage down the rivers, quitted the neighbourhood of the modern Karachi with his remaining troops, crossed the Arabis or Habb river forming the boundary between India and Gedrosia,[1] and started to march for Persia through absolutely unknown country. The troops suffered terribly from heat and thirst, which destroyed multitudes of the camp followers, but in February the remnant of the soldiers emerged in Karmania, having got into touch with the fleet which had started late in October and sailed round the coast under Admiral Nearchos. The story of the adventures of both Alexander and Nearchos is of surpassing interest, but unfortunately far too long for insertion. Its interest depends on the details. In May 324 B.C. Alexander arrived safely at Sūsa in Persia. His Indian expedition had lasted just three years. He died at Babylon, near the modern Baghdad, in June 323 B.C., in the thirty-third year of his age. 'Into thirteen years he had compressed the energies of many lifetimes.'

Disappearance of Greek authority. Alexander undoubtedly had intended to annex permanently the Indian provinces in the basin of

[1] *E.H.I.*[4] (1923), p. 106.

the Indus and to include them in his vast empire extending across Asia into Greece. The arrangements which he made to carry out his intention were suitable and adequate, but his premature death rendered his plans fruitless. When the second partition of the empire was effected at Triparadeisos in 321 B.C., Antipater appointed Pōros and Āmbhi as a matter of form to the charge of the Indus valley and the Panjab. The conditions, however, did not permit them to fulfil their commission, and by 317 at latest all trace of Macedonian authority in India had vanished.

Effect on India of the invasion. Although the direct effects of Alexander's expedition on India appear to have been small, his proceedings had an appreciable influence on the history of the country. They broke down the wall of separation between west and east, and opened up four distinct lines of communication, three by land and one by sea. The land routes which he proved to be practicable were those through Kabul, the Mulla Pass in Baluchistan, and Gedrosia. Nearchos demonstrated that the sea voyage round the coast of Makran offered few difficulties to sailors, once the necessary local information had been gained, which he lacked. The immediate formation of Greek kingdoms in western Asia ensured from the first a certain amount of exchange of ideas between India and Europe. The establishment of the Graeco-Bactrian monarchy in the middle of the third century B.C. brought about the actual subjugation of certain Indian districts by Greek kings. The Hellenistic influence on Indian art, which is most plainly manifested in the Gandhāra sculptures dating from the early centuries of the Christian era, may be traced less conspicuously in other directions. There is good reason to believe that Buddhist teaching was considerably modified by contact with the Greek gods, and that the use of images in particular as an essential element in the Buddhist cult was mainly due to Greek example.[1] In astronomy Hellenic influence is indisputable; many Indian astronomical terms are evidently derived from the Greek. Whatever Hellenistic elements in Indian civilization can be detected were all indirect consequences of Alexander's invasion. The Greek influence never penetrated deeply. Indian polity and the structure of society resting on the caste basis remained substantially unchanged, and even in military science Indians showed no disposition to learn the lessons taught by the sharp sword of Alexander. The kings of India preferred to go on in the old way, trusting to their elephants and chariots, supported by enormous hosts of inferior infantry. They never mastered the shock tactics of Alexander's cavalry, which were repeated by Babur in the sixteenth century with equal success.

Indian influence on Europe. On the other hand, the West learned something from India in consequence of the communications opened up by Alexander's adventure. Our knowledge of the facts is so scanty

---

[1] Hervey (*Some Records of Crime*, vol. i, p. 209) finds a trace of Greek art in the Grecian ram's head on the hilt of weapons in Bikaner. There are Greek survivals also among the Kafirs of the Hindu Kush.

and fragmentary that it is difficult to make any positive assertions with confidence, but it is safe to say that the influence of Buddhist ideas on Christian doctrine may be traced in the Gnostic forms of Christianity, if not elsewhere. The notions of Indian philosophy and religion which filtered into the Roman empire flowed through channels opened by Alexander.

The information about India collected by Alexander's officers under his intelligent direction received no material additions until the closing years of the fifteenth century, when Vasco da Gama finally rent the veil which had so long hidden India from Europe and Europe from India.

India in the fourth century B.C. Although it is impossible to write the history of any Indian state in the fourth century B.C., except that of Magadha to a certain extent, we are not altogether ignorant of the conditions, political, social, economical, and religious which prevailed in that age. It is clear that no paramount imperial power existed. In the Panjab and Sind, the two provinces actually visited by Alexander, the separate states were numerous and independent. The country between the Hydaspes and the Hyphasis alone was occupied by seven distinct nations or tribes. Some of the states, like Taxila and the realm of Pôros, were ruled by Rajas. Others, like the territories of the Mālavas and Kshudrakas (Malloi and Oxydrakai), were governed as republics, apparently by aristocratic oligarchies. The Kshudrakas, who sent 150 of their most eminent men to negotiate terms, pleaded their special attachment to freedom and self-government from the most ancient times. Unfortunately the nature of the government in the numerous republican states of ancient India is imperfectly recorded. The existence of such states is noticed in the *Arthaśāstra* and in the Buddhist and Jain scriptures, and their characteristics are the subject of a special section of the *Mahābhārata*.[1]

The statement made by Megasthenes twenty years or so after Alexander's invasion that 118 distinct nations or tribes were said to exist in the whole of India proves that the large number of distinct governments in the Panjab and Sind was in no way exceptional. Such states were engaged in unceasing wars among themselves, with endless changes of rank and frontiers. Alexander profited by the dissensions of the Panjab Rajas, and the *Arthaśāstra* frankly lays down the principles:

Whoever is superior in power shall wage war. Whoever is rising in power may break the agreement of peace.

The king who is situated anywhere on the circumference of the conqueror's territory is termed the enemy.

Such maxims could not but result in chronic warfare.

---

[1] *Śānti Parva*, p. 107; transcribed and translated by K. P. Jayaswal, 'Republics in the *Mahābhārata*' (*J.B.O. Res. Soc.*, vol. i (1915), p. 173). The subject has been discussed with much learning and at considerable length by R. C. Majumdar in *Corporate Life in Ancient India*, chap. iii, Calcutta, 1918.

Extensive commerce. The numerous details recorded both by the Greeks and by the *Arthaśāstra* prove beyond doubt that the Indians of the fourth century B.C. were advanced in material civilization, that they conducted extensive commerce internal and foreign, and were amply supplied with the luxuries of life. Incidental observations show that the countries of the extreme south were well known in the north, and that active intercourse for business purposes bound together all parts of India. A few details will establish the accuracy of that proposition.

We learn that the best elephants came from the eastern realms; Anga (Bhagalpur and Monghyr), Kalinga (Orissa), and Karūśa (Shāhābād) being specially named. The worst animals came from Saurashtra (Kathiawar) and Panchajana (probably the Pānch Mahāls in Gujarat). Those of medium quality were obtained along the Dasān river of Bundelkhand and farther west.

The *Arthaśāstra* was of opinion that the commerce with the south was of greater importance than that with the north, because the more precious commodities came from the peninsula, while the northern regions supplied only blankets, skins, and horses. Gold, diamonds, pearls, other gems, and conch shells are specified as products of the south. The Tāmraparnī river in Tinnevelly, the Pāndya country of Madura, and Ceylon are named. Commerce by land and sea with foreign countries was regulated by many ordinances, and passports were required by all persons entering or leaving an Indian kingdom.[1] The coinage was of a primitive character. The coins most commonly used were of the kind called 'punchmarked', because their surface is stamped with separate marks made at different times by different punches. Such coins in base silver are found all over India. Specimens in copper occur, but are rare. The greater number are roughly square or oblong bits of metal cut out of a strip. The circular pieces are scarce. Roughly cast coins of early date are common in some localities.

Religion. Certain matters concerning the history of religions have been discussed in connexion with Taxila. A few other miscellaneous observations will not be out of place. The deities specifically mentioned include Zeus Ombrios—the rain-god—which term must be intended to denote Indra; the Indian Herakles worshipped by the Surasenas of Mathura, who may be identified with Krishna's brother Balarāma or with Krishna himself; and the river Ganges.[2] The dated references to the Krishna cult and the veneration of the Ganges are worth noting.

The authority of the Brahmans was secure and fully recognized. They occupied a town in the Mālava territory, which probably was an *agrahāra* or proprietary grant, and everywhere they were the councillors of the Rajas. In Sind they used their influence to induce the local chiefs to resist the invader, and paid with their lives for their advice.[3]

---

[1] *Arthaśāstra*, Book II, chaps. 2, 11, 16, 28, 34; Book VII, chap. 12.
[2] Strabo, Book XV, chap. i, secs. 59, 69; Arrian, *Indikē*, chap. 8.
[3] Arrian, *Anab.*, Book VI, chaps. 7, 17.

Quintus Curtius notes the cult of trees, and asserts that violation of sacred trees was a capital offence. Brahmans are said to have been accustomed to eat flesh, but not that of animals which assist man in his labours. That remark seems to imply the sacredness of horned cattle in the eyes of Brahmans, although other people might still eat beef.

TENTATIVE CHRONOLOGY OF THE ŚAIŚUNĀGA AND NANDA DYNASTIES[1]

Serial No.	King, as in Matsya Purāna	Probable date of accession B.C.	Remarks
	Saisunāgas		
1	Śiśunāga	c. 650	
2	Kākavarna		Originally Raja of Kāśi or Banaras.
3	Kshemadharman		No events recorded.
4	Kshemajit or Kshatraujas		
5	Bimbisāra or Śrenika	522	Built New Rājagriha; conquered Anga; contemporary with Mahāvīra and Buddha; reputed to be a Jain.
6	Ajātaśatru or Kūnika	494	Built fort of Pātaliputra; defeated rulers of Vaiśāli and Kosala; death of Buddha; death of Mahāvīra.
7	Darśaka	467	Mentioned in *Svapna-Vāsavadattā* of Bhāsa.
8	Udāsin or Udaya	443	Built city of Kusumapura on the Ganges near Pātaliputra on the Son.
9	Nandivardhana	410	No events recorded.
10	Mahānandin		
	The Nine Nandas		
11	Mahāpadma and 8 sons, 2 genera-tions	362	Low caste heretics, hostile to Brahmans and Kshatriyas; destroyed by Chandragupta and Kautilya.
12			
	Mauryas		
13	Chandragupta	322	Date approximately correct.

[1] In revising this table I have retained, though with many misgivings, the succession of the *Matsya Purāna* king-list supported by Dr. Smith. Professor H. C. Raychaudhuri (*P.H.A.I.*[6], pp. 115 ff.) and others have given weighty reasons for rejecting the Purānic chronology in favour of that of the *Mahāvamsa*; but Dr. Smith's distrust of the Ceylon tradition was so strong that I feel that even now he would not have accepted it, and the Purānic succession is not definitely disproved. The dates I have amended on the basis of a date of the Buddha's *nirvāna*, which was earlier supported by Dr. Smith (*E.H.I.*[3], p. 48) and still has the backing of some authorities. Despite Dr. Smith's misgivings I have relied on the Ceylon tradition that the *nirvāna* occurred in the eighth year of Ajātaśatru's reign. Even though the list of kings of Magadha given in the chronicles may be unreliable, this synchronism, which fits well with the account of Buddha's life in the Pāli scriptures, seems to me to be probably correct. The dates of accessions are based on the lengths of reigns given in the Purānas. I adopt the *Vāyu Purāna*'s figure of forty years for the reigns of Mahāpadma and his sons. The reigns of Nandivardhana and Mahānandin, totalling according to the Purānas over eighty years, have been much reduced to fit the approximately certain dates of Chandragupta and the *nirvāna*. [Ed.]

CHRONOLOGY

Of Alexander the Great

(Dates accurate)

B.C.

334. A. started on campaign against Persia; battle of the Granīcus (Thargelion).
333. Battle of Issus.
332. Conquest of Egypt.
331. Foundation of Alexandria in Egypt; battle of Gaugamela (Arbela).
330. A. in Persia; death of Darius.
328–7. A. in Bactria.

Indian Expedition (leading dates only)

327. May. Crossing of Hindu Kush range.
327. June to December. Campaign in the hills of Bājaur and Suwāt (Swat).
326. February. Crossing of the Indus.
326. Beginning of July. Battle of Hydaspes.
326. September. Arrival at the Hyphasis; erection of altars; forced return.
326. End of October. Beginning of voyage down the rivers.
325. January. Defeat of the Mālavas (Malloi).
325. October, beginning of. A. started on march through Gedrosia.
325. October, end of. Nearchos started on voyage along the coast to Persian Gulf.
324. February. A. and the remains of his army in Karmania.
324. May. A. at Susa in Persia.
323. June. Death of Alexander at Babylon.

AUTHORITIES

THE references given here are supplementary to those in *E.H.I.*[4] (1923), and in the footnotes to this chapter.

On Taxila Sir J. MARSHALL's monumental *Taxila* (3 vols., Cambridge, 1951).

On the Buddhist period T. W. RHYS DAVIDS's *Buddhist India* (London, 1903) is still valuable, as are chaps. vii and viii of *C.H.I.*, vol. i. On Hīnayāna Buddhism the works of Professor Rhys Davids are still among the most important, as are those of his wife, Mrs. C. A. RHYS DAVIDS, who believed that the original teaching of the Buddha was closer to that of the Upanishads than hitherto thought. See also bibliography to Book II, chap. 3.

On Jainism the most useful work in English is probably Mrs. SINCLAIR STEVENSON's *The Heart of Jainism* (Oxford, 1915). The important works of SCHUBRING (*Die Lehre der Jainas, Grundriss*, iii. 7, Berlin, 1935), GLASENAPP (*Der Jainismus*, Berlin, 1925), and GUÉRINOT (*La Religion Djaïna*, Paris, 1926) have unfortunately not been translated.

Sir R. G. BHANDARKAR's treatise on Vaishnavism, &c., in the *Grundriss* (Strassburg, 1913) is important, as is H. C. RAYCHAUDHURI's *Materials for the Study of the Early History of the Vaishnava Sect* (Calcutta, 1920).

For the *Arthaśāstra* see bibliography to the following chapter.

A detailed study of Alexander's campaign in Asia is that of W. W. TARN, *Alexander the Great* (2 vols., Cambridge, 1948). A very full account of the Indian campaign will be found in *E.H.I.*[4] The classical sources are translated by J. W. M'CRINDLE in *The Invasion of India by Alexander the Great* (2nd ed., Westminster, 1896).

The second volume of the *History and Culture of the Indian People*, entitled *The Age of Imperial Unity* (ed. R. C. MAJUMDAR, Bombay, 1951) provides an up-to-date survey of the history of the period covered in this and the three following chapters.

BOOK II

Hindu India from the Beginning of the Maurya Dynasty in 322 B.C. to the Seventh Century A.D.

CHAPTER 1

Chandragupta Maurya, the first historical Emperor of India, and his institutions; Bindusāra

From darkness to light. The advent of the Maurya dynasty marks the passage from darkness to light for the historian. Chronology suddenly becomes definite, almost precise; a huge empire springs into existence, unifying the innumerable fragments of distracted India; the kings, who may be described with justice as emperors, are men of renown, outstanding personalities whose qualities can be discerned, albeit dimly, through the mists of time; gigantic world-wide religious movements are initiated, of which the effects are still felt; and the affairs of secluded India are brought into close touch with those of the outer world.

Authorities for the Maurya age. Our much clearer knowledge of this period mainly depends on three sources; the accounts of the Greeks who visited India either with Alexander or a generation later, which are recorded by a number of classical authors; the wonderful inscriptions of Aśoka, inscribed on rocks and pillars; and a treatise on statecraft, the *Arthaśāstra*, attributed to Chandragupta Maurya's able minister, the Brahman variously known as Vishnugupta, Kautilya (Kautalya), or Chānakya. The latter source, though of great value, is often of dubious reliability as far as the Mauryan period is concerned. In its existing form it is certainly several centuries later than Chandragupta. This is shown by numerous indications. For instance, it mentions peoples who cannot well have been known to the Indians at this time,[1] and though it recognizes the possibility of a large empire it

---

[1] This is certain in the case of the Chinese, who cannot have been known by this name until the Ch'in dynasty, which arose in the mid-third century B.C. It has been suggested that *Cina* in the *Arthaśāstra* refers to the small state of Ch'in which later gave its name to the whole of China, but this is very unlikely. Efforts of some scholars to explain away the *Cīnas* of the *Arthaśāstra* as early representatives of modern hill tribes (Shinas of the Himalaya or Chins of Burma) are equally unconvincing.

accepts as the unit of government a comparatively small kingdom.[1] Thus it is not, as some earlier authorities believed, an official manual of instruction for the Mauryan emperor and his court. It must also be remembered that the work, like the relevant portions of the Dharma-śāstras, outlines the views of the author on the best means of governing the state rather than the actual system of government at the time. But with these serious reservations the *Arthaśāstra* of Kautilya may still be used as a general guide to Mauryan polity. Though the work is almost certainly post-Mauryan, it is equally certain that it is pre-Guptan, and the system of government envisaged in the text corresponds more closely to what we know of that of the Mauryas than to that of later times. The detailed instructions for the organization of the depart-ments of state strongly suggest that the author, though he himself may have been a theorist, had at his disposal the work of a practical politician, whether the great minister of Chandragupta or another, who probably lived in Mauryan times.

Besides these three sources Indian *tradition recorded in various forms, combined with critical study of the monuments which have defied the ravenous tooth of time, enables the historian to fill in the outline of his picture with certain additional details. The external political facts, although on record to a considerable extent, are known far less perfectly than the particulars of the internal government and administration.

The revolution in Magadha. The exact course of the events which led to the overthrow of the Nandas and the establishment of the Mauryas in their royal seat is not fully ascertained. Many alleged incidents of the revolution in Magadha are depicted vividly in the ancient political drama entitled the 'Signet of Rākshasa' (*Mudrā-Rākshasa*), written at the earliest in the fifth century after Christ. But it would be obviously unsafe to rely for a matter-of-fact historical narrative on a work of imagination composed some seven centuries after the events dramatized. The information gleaned from other authorities is scanty, and in some respects discrepant. Chandragupta, who when quite young had met Alexander in 326 or 325 B.C., may have been a scion of the Nanda stock. According to some accounts he was a son of the last Nanda king by a low-born woman. Buddhist tradition, on the other hand, states that he was a member of the clan of the Moriyas (the Pāli form of Maurya) of Pipphalivana, who are first met as recipients of a share of the Buddha's ashes. Acting under the guidance of his astute Brahman preceptor, Vishnugupta, better known by his patronymic Chanakya, or his surname Kautilya or Kautalya, Chandra-gupta, who had been exiled from Magadha, attacked the Macedonian officers in command of the garrisons in the Indus basin after Alexander's

---

[1] The view that Kautilya composed the *Arthaśāstra* before the setting up of the Mauryan empire, and therefore looked on the small state as the unit, is not feasible. The Nandas, at whose court Kautilya is said to have served, were themselves lords of a great empire, covering most of northern India with the exception of the Panjab.

death, and destroyed them, with the aid of the northern nations. About the same time the youthful adventurer and his wily counsellor effected a revolution at Pātaliputra (Patna), the capital of the Magadhan monarchy, and exterminated the Nanda family. It is not clear whether the Magadhan revolution preceded or followed the attack on the Macedonian garrisons. However that may have been, Chandragupta undoubtedly succeeded to the throne of Pātaliputra, secured his position against all enemies, and established a gigantic empire. He is the first strictly historical person who can be properly described as Emperor of India.

Chronology. Alexander having died at Babylon in June 323 B.C., the news of his passing must have reached the Panjab a month or two later. It may be assumed with safety that the campaign against the foreign garrisons began in the following cold season of 323 to 322, and we cannot be far wrong if we date Chandragupta's accession in 322 B.C. The Magadhan revolution seems to have occupied at least a year from beginning to end.[1] If it had been completed before Alexander's death, which is possible, the change of dynasty might be antedated to 325 B.C. The true date probably lies between 325 and 320 inclusive, which is sufficiently precise for most purposes.[2]

War and peace with Seleukos. Alexander not having left an heir capable of wielding his sceptre, his dominions were divided among his generals. The supreme power in Asia was disputed by Antigonos and Seleukos. After a long struggle the latter recovered Babylon in 312, and assumed the style of king six years later. He is known in history as Seleukos Nikator, the Conqueror, and is called King of Syria, but would be more accurately described as the King of Western Asia. Hoping to recover Alexander's Indian provinces, he crossed the Indus to attack the reigning Indian sovereign, Chandragupta Maurya. The invader was defeated, probably somewhere in the Panjab, and compelled to retire beyond the frontier. The terms of peace involved the cession by Seleukos to Chandragupta of the provinces of the Paropanisadai, Aria, and Arachosia, the capitals of which were respectively Kabul, Herat, and Qandahar, and also Gedrosia, the modern Baluchistan. The Indian king gave in exchange a comparatively small equivalent in the shape of 500 elephants, which Seleukos needed for the wars with his western enemies. A matrimonial alliance also was arranged, which may be interpreted as meaning that a daughter of Seleukos was married to Chandragupta, but may also imply the recognition of the right of connubium between the subjects of the two monarchs.

Megasthenes. The peace so concluded between Syria and India remained inviolate, and Seleukos, in or about the year 302 B.C., sent as

---

[1] Malayaketu, son of the king of the mountains, says:

> Nine months have o'er us passed since that sad day
> My father perished.   (*Mudrā-Rākshasa*, Act IV.)

[2] In recent years efforts have been made in India and France to establish a Jain tradition that Chandragupta came to the throne in 313 B.C.

his envoy to the court of Pātaliputra an officer named Megasthenes, who had served in Arachosia (Qandahar). The ambassador employed his leisure in compiling an excellent account of the geography, products, and institutions of India, which continued to be the principal authority on ancient India until the nineteenth century. Unfortunately his book is no longer extant as a whole, but a great part of it has been preserved in the form of extracts made by other authors. Megasthenes is a thoroughly trustworthy witness concerning matters which came under his own observation. His work has been sometimes discredited unfairly because he permitted himself to embellish his text by the insertion of certain incredible marvels on hearsay testimony.

Chandragupta's empire. Little more than what has been stated is known concerning the political events of Chandragupta's reign, which lasted for twenty-four years. His dominions certainly included the country now called Afghanistan, the ancient Ariana, as far as the Hindu Kush range; the Panjab; the territories now known as Uttar Pradesh (formerly United Provinces), Bihar, and the peninsula of Kathiawar in the far west. Probably they also comprised Bengal. It is safe to affirm that Chandragupta, when his reign terminated about 298 B.C., was master of all India north of the Narbada, as well as of Afghanistan. At present there is no good evidence that his conquests extended into the Deccan, but it is possible that he may have carried his victorious arms across the Narbada. Late traditions in Mysore go so far as to assert the extension of the Nanda dominion to that country.

Chandragupta's severity. The Roman historian Justin, who affirms that Chandragupta was the author of India's liberty after Alexander's death, adds the comment that 'when he had gained the victory and ascended the throne, he transformed nominal liberty into slavery, inasmuch as he oppressed with servitude the people whom he had rescued from foreign rule'.

The known facts concerning his administration prove that he was a stern despot, who lived in daily fear of his life, and enforced strict order by a highly organized autocracy supported by punishments of ruthless severity. All tradition agrees that the ship of state was steered with exceptional ability by his Brahman minister, and that his statecraft was not hampered by any moral scruples. The date or manner of the minister's disappearance from the scene is not recorded. According to the confused traditions collected in the seventeenth century by the Tibetan author Tāranātha, Chānakya continued to guide the counsels of Chandragupta's successor, Bindusāra. The statement may be well founded.[1]

The fate of Chandragupta. The only direct evidence throwing

---

[1] Wilford printed a story that the wicked minister repented and retired to 'Shookul Teerth, near Broach, on the banks of the Nerbudda', where he died. Chandragupta is said to have accompanied Chānakya (*As. Res.*, vol. ix, p. 96). One version of the story is said to be based on the *Agni Purāna*, and another on alleged traditions related by Wilford's Pandit. See *Rāsmālā*, vol. i, p. 69 n.

light on the manner in which the eventful reign of Chandragupta Maurya came to an end is that of Jain tradition. The Jains always treat the great emperor as having been a Jain like Bimbisāra, and it may be that he embraced Jainism towards the end of his reign. The Jain religion undoubtedly was extremely influential in Magadha during the time of the later Śaiśunāgas, the Nandas, and the Mauryas. The fact that Chandragupta won the throne by the contrivance of a learned Brahman is not inconsistent with the supposition that Jainism was the royal faith. Jains habitually employ Brahmans for their domestic ceremonies, and in the drama cited above a Jain ascetic is mentioned as being a special friend of the minister Rākshasa, who served first the Nanda and then the new sovereign.

Once the fact that Chandragupta was or became a Jain is admitted, the tradition that he abdicated and committed suicide by slow starvation in the approved Jain manner becomes readily credible. The story is to the effect that when the Jain saint Bhadrabāhu predicted a famine in northern India which would last for twelve years, and the prophecy began to be fulfilled, the saint led 12,000 Jains to the south in search of more favoured lands. King Chandragupta abdicated and accompanied the emigrants, who made their way to Śravana Belgola ('the white Jain tank') in Mysore, where Bhadrabāhu soon died. The ex-Emperor Chandragupta, having survived him for twelve years, starved himself to death. The tradition is supported by the names of the buildings at Śravana Belgola, inscriptions from the seventh century after Christ, and a literary work of the tenth century. The evidence cannot be described as conclusive, but after much consideration I am disposed to accept the main facts as affirmed by tradition. It being certain that Chandragupta was quite young and inexperienced when he ascended the throne in or about 322 B.C., he must have been under fifty when his reign terminated twenty-four years later. His abdication is an adequate explanation of his disappearance at such an early age. Similar renunciations of royal dignity are on record, and the twelve years' famine is not incredible. In short, the Jain tradition holds the field, and no alternative account exists.

King Bindusāra. Chandragupta was succeeded by his son Bindusāra, whose title Amitraghāta, 'slayer of enemies', suggests a martial career. Unfortunately nothing definite is recorded concerning him except a trivial anecdote showing that he maintained friendly correspondence with Antiochos Soter, whose ambassador, Deïmachos, replaced Megasthenes. An envoy named Dionysios sent by Ptolemy Philadelphos of Egypt (285–247 B.C.) to the court of Pātaliputra must have presented his credentials to either Bindusāra or his son Aśoka. A tradition recorded by Tāranātha represents Bindusāra as having conquered the country between the eastern and the western seas. The tradition is probably founded on fact, because the immense extent of Aśoka's empire is known, and he himself made no known conquests except that of Kalinga. Aśoka's dominion in the peninsula extended over the northern districts of Mysore, and it seems likely that the conquest of the Deccan was effected by Bindusāra.

Maurya organization. The narrative of political events will now be interrupted to permit of a survey of the institutions of the Maurya empire according to the authorities above mentioned. Most of the arrangements adopted by Chandragupta remained in force during the reigns of his son and grandson. The modifications introduced by Aśoka will be noticed in due course. The reader should understand that the Nanda kingdom of Magadha was strong, rich, extensive, protected by a numerous army, and no doubt administered on the system described in the *Arthaśāstra*. The enlargement of the kingdom into an empire did not necessarily involve radical changes in the administrative machinery, although it is reasonable to credit Chandragupta and his prime minister with effecting improvements and increasing the efficiency of the mechanism of government. The Maurya State was organized elaborately with a full supply of departments and carefully graded officials with well defined duties. The accounts leave on my mind the impression that it was much better organized than was the Mughul empire under Akbar, as described in Abu-l Fazl's survey. Akbar's officials, except certain judicial functionaries, all ranked as military officers. Even the underlings in the imperial kitchen were rated and paid as foot soldiers. The bulk of the army was composed of irregular contingents supplied either by subordinate ruling chiefs or by high officials with territorial jurisdiction, and the standing army was quite small. The Mauryas, on the contrary, had a regular civil administration and maintained a huge standing army paid directly by the Crown—an instrument of power infinitely more efficient than Akbar's militia, which failed miserably when confronted with small Portuguese forces, whereas the Maurya was more than a match for Seleukos. The control of the Maurya central government over distant provinces and subordinate officials appears to have been far more stringent than that exercised by Akbar, who did not possess the terrible secret service of his early predecessor. The Maurya government, in short, was a highly organized and thoroughly efficient autocracy, capable of controlling an empire more extensive than that of Akbar as long as the sovereigns possessed the necessary personal ability. They were equal to the task for three generations. Although the figure of Bindusāra is shadowy, and absolutely nothing definite is known about his acts, he must have been a competent ruler. Otherwise he could not have reigned for a quarter of a century and transmitted to his son Aśoka the gigantic empire created by and inherited from his father Chandragupta, probably enlarged by additions in the south.

Pātaliputra, the capital. Pātaliputra, Chandragupta's capital, was a great and noble city extending along the northern bank of the Son for about nine miles, with a depth of less than two miles. Much of the area is now covered by Patna, Bankipore, and sundry neighbouring villages. Kusumapura, the more ancient site, stood on the Ganges, and evidently became merged in Pātaliputra, for the two names are often used as synonyms. The Maurya city was built in the tongue of land formed by the junction of the Son with the Ganges, a defensible position recommended by the writers of textbooks and frequently adopted by the ancient Indians in actual practice. Modern Patna no longer enjoys the strategical security of its predecessor, the confluence being now at the cantonment of Dinapore, about twelve miles above Patna. The old river beds and even the ancient embankments or quays may still be traced. The city was defended by a massive timber palisade, of which the remains have been found at several places. The gates were 64, and the towers 570 in number. The palisade was protected by a deep moat filled with water from the Son.

The palace. The imperial palace, which probably stood close to the modern village of Kumrahār, was chiefly constructed of timber, like the splendid regal edifices of Mandalay in Burma. Its gilded pillars were adorned with golden vines and silver birds, and a fine ornamental park studded with fish-ponds and well furnished with trees and shrubs served as setting for the edifices. Excavations at the site support the belief that the buildings were designed in imitation of the Persian palace at Persepolis.[1]

According to a Greek author the abode of Chandragupta excelled the palaces of Susa and Ekbatana in splendour, and there is no reason to doubt the truth of the statement. The court was maintained and served with luxurious ostentation. Gold vessels measuring 6 feet across are said to have been used. The king, when he appeared in public, was either carried in a golden palanquin or mounted on an elephant with gorgeous trappings. He was clothed in fine muslin embroidered with purple and gold. The luxuries of much of Asia were at his disposal. Within the spacious precincts of the palace the sovereign relied for protection chiefly on his Amazonian bodyguard of armed women. It was considered lucky that when he got up in the morning he should be received by his female archers. The harem or women's quarters were on an extensive scale and carefully guarded. No commodities were allowed to pass in or out except under seal.

Royal amusements. Although the early Brahman writers repeatedly condemned hunting as a grave form of vice, and solemnly debated whether it or gambling should be considered the worse, the ancient kings indulged freely in the pleasures of the chase. Large game preserves were enclosed for the exclusive royal use, and the slightest interference with the sport of kings entailed instant capital punishment. The tradition of the sanctity of the imperial hunting-ground long survived. Jahangir in the seventeenth century did not hesitate to kill or mutilate some unlucky men who had accidentally spoiled his shot at a blue bull. In England the Norman kings were equally tenacious of their sporting privileges. Aśoka kept up the practice of hunting for many years, but abandoned it, as will be narrated presently, when he adopted

[1] *Ann. Rep. A.S.I. East Circle,* 1912–13, 1913–14, 1914–15.

Buddhist ideas. Chandragupta, who still followed the chase when Megasthenes was at his court late in his reign, is alleged to have been a Jain. As we shall see in the case of Khāravela (pp. 140–1), Jainism did not necessarily involve the renunciation of all bloodshed for a ruling monarch; but it may be that Chandragupta was a Brahmanical worshipper of Śiva for the greater part of his reign, and that he was not converted to Jainism by Bhadrabāhu until almost the end.[1] Gladiatorial combats, such as even Akbar enjoyed watching, and the fights between animals, such as were to be witnessed until quite recently in the native states, were included in the list of royal amusements. The races run with chariots, to each of which a mixed team of horses and oxen was harnessed, with horses in the centre and an ox at each side, were a curious kind of diversion. Such races are not to be seen nowadays in India, so far as I know, although good trotting oxen are still to be found. The course measured about 6,000 yards and the races were made the subject of keen betting.[2]

Courtesan attendants. Accomplished courtesans of the dancing-girl class enjoyed a privileged position at court, an evil practice continued by most Indian princes up to recent times, and perhaps, in some cases, to the present day. Such women were employed as housemaids, shampooers, and garland makers. They were entitled to present the king with water, perfumes, dress, and garlands. They held the royal umbrella, fan, and golden pitcher, and attended the sovereign when he was seated on his throne, or riding in a litter or chariot. They were subject to strict official control, and those who practised their profession paid licence fees to the treasury. Similar customs at Vijayanagar in the south are recorded in the sixteenth century. The secret service of the Maurya government did not disdain to make use of intelligence collected by the public women.

Iranian influence. Up to the time of Alexander's invasion the Indus was regarded as the traditional frontier of the Persian empire,

---

[1] *Arthaśāstra* (Book II, chap. 4) prescribes that in the centre of the capital city shrines should be provided for Aparājita, Apratihata, Jayanta, Vaijayanta, Śiva, Vaiśravana (i.e. Kuvera), and the Aśvins. The first four are Jain deities.

[2] Dr. Coomaraswamy informs me that 'bull-racing' is a 'very common pastime in Ceylon, and creates immense excitement. The bulls are harnessed to the light cars called "hackeries".' In 1679, when Dr. Fryer was at Surat, ox-races were still in favour. He describes them in his customary quaint fashion: 'The Coaches . . . Those for Journeying are something stronger than those for the Merchants to ride about the City or to take the Air on: which with their nimble Oxen they will, when they meet in the fields, run races on, and contend for the Garland as much as for an Olympiak Prize: which is a Diversion *To see a Cow gallop*, as we say in scorn; but these not only pluck up their Heels apace, but are taught to amble, they often riding on them' (Fryer, *A New Account*, &c., ed. Crooke, Hakluyt Soc., 1915, vol. iii, pp. 157, 158). I have not found anywhere a notice of mixed teams of horses and oxen. The *Arthaśāstra* (Book IV, chap. 20) provides official rules for gambling. Superintendents of gambling and betting collected the licence fee, and 5 per cent. of the winnings, as well as the charges for hire of the accessories and for water-supply and accommodation in gaming houses. On bull-races in India see W. Crooke's article in *Folk-Lore*, vol. xxviii, pp. 141 ff.

although at that date the Great King does not seem to have actually asserted his authority over the Indian satrapy conquered in the time of Darius the son of Hystaspes. The proximity of the Panjab to territory which was a Persian province for a century or more, and the constant although unrecorded intercourse which must have existed between the Achaemenian monarchy and the Indian kingdoms, cannot have failed to make Persian institutions familiar to the people of India. At a somewhat later date the continuance of strong Persian influence upon India is indicated by the prevalence of the Kharoshthī script, a variety of Aramaic, in the provinces near the frontier; by the long continued use of the Persian title of Satrap; by the form of the Aśoka inscriptions; and by the architecture. Some small particulars which happen to be recorded are sufficient to show that in the time of the first Maurya emperor the court was affected by Iranian practices. The *Arthaśāstra* rule that the king, when consulting physicians and ascetics, should be seated 'in the room where the sacred fire has been kept' seems to be an indication that Magian ritual was honoured at the Maurya court. We are told also that the ceremonial washing of the king's hair was made the occasion of a splendid festival when the courtiers offered rich presents to the king. That observance recalls the Persian hair-washing ceremony on the sovereign's birthday, as described by Herodotus, and is based upon a widespread primitive rule or taboo.[1] The undoubted close relationship between Vedic religion and that of Iran must be borne in mind. Legendary accounts of the early connexion of Persia with India may be read in Firishta and other authors. Whatever may be the fate of the various hypotheses debated by scholars, there can be no doubt that ancient India was to some extent indebted to Iranian ideas and practices.[2]

Autocracy. The normal government of an Indian kingdom appears to have been always autocracy or despotism.[3] The royal will was not controlled by any law, and the customary respect shown to Brahmans was often an ineffective check upon a sovereign resolved to have his own way. According to the *Arthaśāstra* a Brahman convicted of ordinary heinous crime, murder included, was exempt from torture, and should be either banished or sentenced to the mines for life. But the author expressly authorizes the execution by drowning of a Brahman guilty of high treason, whereas other traitors were to be burnt alive. A strong, tyrannous man like Chandragupta would not have allowed himself to be hampered by nice regard for Brahman privileges. The sovereign was not bound to consult anybody, but in practice the most selfwilled despot is obliged to depend largely upon his ministers. 'Sovereignty is possible only with assistance. A single wheel can never

---

[1] Frazer, *The Golden Bough*[3], vol. ii, pp. 253 ff.

[2] The Ionic Jandiāla temple in the Sirkap section of Taxila appears to have been a fire-temple (*J.P.H.S.*, vol. iii, p. 77; *Ann. Rep. A.S. India*, 1912–13, p. 35, pl. xxxiv, *b*). It dates from about the beginning of the Christian era.

[3] The text refers only to monarchical governments; and not to the tribal republics or oligarchies, such as those of the Mālavas, Kshudrakas, Lichchhavis, and Yaudheyas

move. Hence he [the king] shall employ ministers and hear their opinion.'[1] The Maurya monarch, according to the ruling of the *Arthaśāstra*, was not constrained to limit his privy council to any particular number of ministers. The council should 'consist of as many members as the needs of his dominion require'. The sovereign was recommended to be content with the advice of not more than four ministers on any given matter. In any case the decision rested with him alone. Akbar in the sixteenth century, although it is unlikely that he had ever heard of Chānakya or his treatise, acted on the principles laid down in that work so far as his relations with his ministers were concerned.

The only real check. The only real check upon the arbitrary royal authority was the ever-present fear of revolution and assassination. A king who trampled on custom and overstrained his power was apt to come to an untimely end. Chandragupta, who had won the throne by rebellion and the extermination of his predecessor's family, naturally led an uneasy life, and was obliged to take unceasing precautions against conspiracies. According to Megasthenes he dared not incur the risk either of sleeping in the day-time or occupying the same bedroom two nights in succession. A king of Burma at the beginning of the nineteenth century is recorded to have taken similar precautions. The dramatist already cited, who tells the traditional story of the revolution which overthrew the Nandas, gives a vivid account of the varied expedients by which the adherents of the old dynasty sought to destroy the young usurper, and how all failed, so that the disappointed ex-minister exclaims:

> 'Tis ever thus.—Fortune in all befriends
> The cruel Chandragupta. When I send
> A messenger of certain death to slay him,
> She wields the instrument against his rival,
> Who should have spoiled him of one-half his kingdom;
> And arms, and drugs, and stratagems are turned
> In his behalf against my friends and servants;
> So that whate'er I plot against his power
> Serves but to yield him unexpected profit.

The usurper's powerful military force, which will be now described, secured him in possession of his dangerous throne.

The normal Indian army. An Indian army, in accordance with immemorial tradition, comprised four 'arms'—namely elephants, chariots, cavalry, and infantry. The war-elephants were regarded as the most important because 'the victory of Kings depends mainly upon elephants; for elephants, being of large bodily frame, are able not only to destroy the arrayed army of an enemy, his fortifications, and en- campments, but also to undertake works that are dangerous to life'. The high value thus set upon elephants, justified by the conditions and

[1] *Arthaśāstra*, Book I, chap. 7.

experience of purely Indian warfare, was discredited when a bold
general like Alexander confounded the traditional Indian tactics by
novel methods of attack.

Chariots, which had been in use in Rigvedic times, played an important part in ancient Indian warfare for many centuries. It is not known
with certainty when or why they went out of fashion. The Chinese
pilgrim Hiuen Tsang, writing in the middle of the seventh century,
when giving a general description of India, states that the army was
composed of the four divisions or 'arms' above mentioned, and remarks
that officers used to ride in chariots.

The army is composed of Foot, Horse, Chariot, and Elephant soldiers.
The war-elephant is covered with coat-of-mail, and his tusks are provided
with sharp barbs. On him rides the Commander-in-Chief, who has a soldier
on each side to manage the elephant. The chariot in which an officer sits is
drawn by four horses, whilst infantry guard it on both sides.[1]

Apparently at that time chariots were used by officers only.

The same author, when describing the army organized by his contemporary, Harsha of Kanauj, credits that powerful king with possessing originally 5,000 elephants, 20,000 cavalry, and 50,000 foot. After
some years he is said to have increased his war elephants to 60,000,
and his cavalry to 100,000.[2] No mention of chariots is made. It is
legitimate to infer that the use of chariots was obsolescent in the
pilgrim's time, and did not survive the seventh century. I do not know
of any subsequent mention of their employment in warfare.

The Rajput horsemen in later ages were renowned for their courage
and the undisciplined fury of their charges. The only authentic record
we possess of action by cavalry in ancient times is in the Greek narratives of the battle of the Hydaspes. The mounted troops of Pōros on
that occasion did their best, but could not resist effectively the Macedonian cavalry. The Indians were almost all destroyed. It was customary in India to employ enormous hosts of foot soldiers, but the line
between soldiers and followers not being strictly drawn, the military
value of the infantry often was very small.

The Maurya army. Chandragupta maintained the traditional
'fourfold' army. His military organization does not betray any trace of
Greek ideas. The force at the command of the last Nanda was formidable, being estimated at 80,000 horse, 200,000 foot, 8,000 chariots, and
6,000 fighting elephants. The Maurya raised the numbers of the
infantry to 600,000, and of the elephants to 9,000. But his cavalry is
said to have mustered only 30,000. The number of his chariots is not

[1] Watters, *On Yuan Chwang*, vol. i, p. 171. The translation by Beal (*Records*,
vol. i, p. 83) differs materially and appears to be erroneous.
[2] Watters summarizes the passage, omitting details. Beal (vol. i, p. 213) accidentally
gives 2,000 as being Harsha's original cavalry force. Julien clearly is right in stating
20,000 as the number. The figures of elephants and cavalry seem grossly exaggerated,
as may be inferred from the more modest figures given in other sources for the size
of these elements of the armies of ancient Indian kings.

recorded. Assuming that he maintained them as in the time of his predecessor, that each chariot required at least three, and that each elephant carried at least four men, his total force must have amounted to not less than 690,000, or in round numbers 700,000 men. Megasthenes expressly states that the soldiers were paid and equipped by the state. They were not a mere militia of contingents. It is not surprising that an army so strong was able both to 'overrun and subdue all India', as Plutarch asserts, and also to defeat the invasion of Seleukos, whose force must have been far inferior in numbers. According to the *Arthaśāstra* an Indian army was organized in squads of ten men, companies of a hundred, and battalions of a thousand each. Chandragupta probably followed the same practice. The author of the treatise contemplated India as being divided in the normal manner into a multitude of small states, and does not describe the constitution of an empire. He therefore treats the Raja as the commander-in-chief of the army, and betrays no knowledge of any professional headquarters organization. But Megasthenes informs us that Chandragupta's host was controlled and administered under the direction of a War Office elaborately constituted. A commission of thirty members was divided into six boards (*panchāyats*), each with five members, and severally charged with the administration of the following departments, namely: Board No. I (in conjunction with the admiral), Admiralty; Board No. II, Transport, Commissariat, and Army Service; Board No. III, Infantry; Board No. IV, Cavalry; Board No. V, War-chariots; and Board No. VI, Elephants.

No similar organization is recorded elsewhere, and the credit of devising such efficient machinery must be divided between Chandragupta and his exceptionally able minister.

Equipment. The equipment of the army was effective and adequate. A fighting elephant carried at least three archers besides the driver. The chariots usually were four-horsed, but two-horsed cars also were in use. Each chariot had at least two fighting men in addition to the driver. Six men formed the complement of each of the four-horsed chariots employed by Pŏros at the battle of the Hydaspes. Each horseman was armed with two lances resembling the Greek *saunia*, and was protected by a buckler. The principal weapon of the infantry was a straight broadsword suspended by a belt from the shoulder.[1] Javelins and bows and arrows were additional arms. The arrow was discharged with the aid of pressure from the left foot on the extremity of the bow resting on the ground, and with such force that neither shield nor breastplate could withstand it. At the Hydaspes the Indian archers were rendered ineffective by the greasy condition of the ground which prevented the soldier from securing a firm rest for the end of his bow.

Defensive armour was supplied to men, elephants, and horses.

The transport animals included horses, mules, and oxen.

[1] Col. Hendley noted that many Rajputs in recent times carried the sword in the same way (*J.I.A.*, No. 130, 1915, p. 8).

According to the *Arthaśāstra*, an ambulance service was provided in the rear during an action, consisting of surgeons supplied with instruments, medicines, and dressings, and of women with prepared food and beverages (Book X, chap. 3).

It is clear, therefore, that the army, as improved by Chandragupta, was extremely formidable.

Diplomacy and force. But the Maurya did not rely solely on his armed strength. Indian statesmen have always shown a leaning towards the employment of diplomacy in preference to force. The dictum of the *Arthaśāstra* that 'intrigue, spies, winning over the enemy's people, siege, and assault are the five means to capture a fort' is characteristic, and indicates the nature of the subsidiary means employed to create the Maurya empire. Long afterwards, Akbar was content to secure by bribery the fortress of Asirgarh, which his arms were unable to reduce, and Aurangzeb gained possession of Maratha forts usually by the same ignoble means. The writers of textbooks debated the relative value of force and diplomacy. The author of the *Arthaśāstra* had no hesitation in deciding that 'skill in intrigue (or "diplomacy") is better', because the crafty intriguer can always overthrow kings who are superior in warlike spirit and power (Book IX, chap. 1).

Similarly, Machiavelli was prepared to prove by many examples that the prince who 'best personated the fox had the better success'.[1] The theory of politics expounded in the *Arthaśāstra* is substantially identical with that of *The Prince*.

Bāna's criticism of Kautilya or Chānakya. It is right to add that the cynical principles of the *Arthaśāstra*, worked out 'on ground cleared of the hindrances of private justice', did not meet with universal acceptance. King Harsha's friend Bāna in the seventh century regarded them with horror:

Is there anything [he exclaims], that is righteous for those for whom the science of Kautilya, merciless in its precepts, rich in cruelty, is an authority; whose teachers are priests habitually hard-hearted with practice of witchcraft; to whom ministers, always inclined to deceive others, are councillors; whose desire is always for the goddess of wealth that has been cast away by thousands of kings; who are devoted to the application of destructive sciences; and to whom brothers, affectionate with natural cordial love, are fit victims to be murdered?

The treatise criticized having been written avowedly 'for the benefit of the Maurya', we may feel assured that Bāna's scruples were not shared by Chandragupta, who evidently acted, as Justin indicates, in accordance with the principles of his preceptor. The late conversion of the first Maurya emperor to the merciful creed of Jainism, if it be a fact, as I think it was, may be ascribed to a revulsion of conscience from the hateful teaching of the Atharvan Brahman.[2]

[1] *The Prince*, transl. in Universal Library ed., Routledge, 1893, p. 110.

[2] Many passages in the *Arthaśāstra* prove that the author was an admirer of the *Atharva*, the Veda of magic and spells. Book XIV, entitled 'Secret Means', treats of weird sorceries supposed to compass the destruction of an enemy.

Severity of the government. Whatever we may think about the principles of Chandragupta, his masterful government was effective. The textbooks define the art of governing as *dandanīti*, 'the science of punishment'. The details preserved show clearly that that definition was accepted heartily by Chandragupta, who acted on it without hesitation. Whether we consult the *Arthaśāstra* or the Greek authorities we receive the same impression of ruthless severity in the enforcement of fiscal regulations for the benefit of the treasury, and of stern repression of crime. Megasthenes noted that while he resided in the imperial camp with a population of 400,000 people the daily thefts reported did not exceed 200 drachmae in value, equivalent to about £8 sterling. Such security of property was attained by the application of a terribly severe code, based, as Chānakya observes, on the precepts laid down 'in the scriptures of great sages'. When we come to the history of the purely Hindu empire of Vijayanagar in the sixteenth century we shall find that property in that realm was protected by the most appalling penalties for even petty thefts.

Torture. A person in the Maurya dominion accused of theft and arrested within three days after the commission of the crime was ordinarily (with certain exceptions) subjected to torture in order to elicit a confession, unless he could prove either an alibi or enmity on the part of the complainant. Although the author of the *Arthaśāstra* was fully aware of the danger of eliciting false confessions by torture and insists on the necessity for the production of conclusive evidence, it seems clear that the police must have relied chiefly on the use of torture. The general principle is laid down that 'those whose guilt is believed to be true shall be subjected to torture'. In the face of such a comprehensive rule exceptions would have had little practical effect. All experienced magistrates, among whom the author of this book may be included, know how deeply the tradition of torturing a prisoner in order to extort a confession, true or false, is engrained in the mind of every Indian policeman and how difficult it is to check the practice even under modern conditions. The author of the *Arthaśāstra* gives a horrible list of eighteen kinds of torture, remarking calmly that 'each day a fresh kind of the torture may be employed', and that in certain aggravated cases, by special order, the prisoner might be 'subjected once or many times to one or all of the above kinds of torture'.

When the prisoner had been convicted, the modes of punishment were many, including fines, mutilation, and death in various forms, with or without torment.

Mutilation could sometimes be compounded for by a fine. The caste and rank of the offender were taken into consideration. A Brahman could not be tortured, but might be branded, exiled, or sent to the mines for life. The authorities were instructed to take notice of 'equitable distinctions among offenders, whether belonging to the royal family or to the common people'.

Theft to the value of 40 or 50 silver *panas* was punishable with death.

Among other capital offences were homicide, housebreaking, breaching the dam of a tank, and damage to royal property, with many more. Megasthenes notes that death was the penalty for injury to an artisan in the royal employment, and that even evasion of the municipal tithe on goods sold was punished in the same drastic fashion.

There is no reason to suppose that the severity of the criminal code was seriously modified under the Buddhist government of Aśoka. His censors were specially charged to deal with cases of unjust imprisonment or corporal punishment, and prisoners lying under sentence of death are mentioned.

The *Arthaśāstra* prescribes the modest fine of only 48 *panas* on the superintendent of a jail for inflicting unjust torture; and even if he beat a prisoner to death he was merely to be fined 1,000 *panas*. Aśoka's institution of censors may, perhaps, have rendered the redress of such wrongs somewhat easier than it can have been in the time of his grandfather; but it is always difficult to detect or punish the misdoings of officials.

Town prefect and census. The author of the *Arthaśāstra* contemplated the division of a normal small kingdom into four provinces, each administered by a governor. He applied the same principle to the administration of the capital city, and presumably to that of other large towns. The capital was divided into four quarters or wards, each in charge of a sub-prefect (*sthānika*), who was assisted by subordinates (*gopa*), each responsible for from ten to forty households. The whole city was administered by a prefect (*nāgaraka*), whose duties resembled those of the *kotwāl* in later times.

The town authorities were expected to know everything about everybody within their jurisdiction, and to keep a sharp watch upon all comings and goings. The official activities included the maintenance of a permanent census, the *gopa* being required to 'know not only the caste, *gotra* [caste subdivision], the name, and occupation of both men and women in the households of his block, but also to ascertain their income and expenditure'. Such inquisitorial registration enormously enhanced the power of the central government for taxation and all purposes.

Precautions against fire and simple sanitary regulations were enforced. A person who intentionally set fire to a house was to be thrown into the same fire. Fines were imposed for depositing refuse on the streets. A strict curfew was imposed, under penalty of a fine, mainly with the purpose of repressing crime.

Maurya municipal commission. Chandragupta's municipal organization for his huge imperial capital was more complex. According to Megasthenes he provided a commission of thirty members, divided like that for the War Office, into six boards or committees. The commissioners in their collective capacity had charge, in addition to their special departments, of all matters concerning the public welfare, including the repairs of public works, the maintenance of markets, harbours, and temples, and the regulation of prices. The departmental functions of the six boards or committees were as follows: (1) industrial arts; (2) care of foreigners; (3) registration of births and deaths; (4) retail trade and barter, with supervision of weights and measures, and the due stamping of produce sold; (5) supervision of manufactures and sale of the same duly stamped; and (6) collection of the tithe on the price of goods sold.

The perfection of the arrangements thus indicated is astonishing, even when exhibited in outline. Examination of the departmental details increases our wonder that such an organization could have been planned and efficiently operated in India in 300 B.C. Akbar had nothing like it, and it may be doubted if any of the ancient Greek cities were better organized.

Board No. 1 ; arts. Artisans were regarded as being devoted in a special manner to the royal service, and capital punishment was inflicted on any person who impaired the efficiency of a craftsman by causing the loss of a hand or eye. Board No. 1 no doubt regulated wages, enforced the use of pure and sound materials, and exacted a full tale of work in exchange for the proper wage. The subject might be illustrated at length from the rules of the *Arthaśāstra* concerning the duties of departmental officers as described in that work, and from the practice of later ages, but it is impossible here to follow out the details.

Board No. 2 ; foreigners. Board No. 2 performed duties which in modern times are entrusted to consuls and in ancient Greece were carried out by the officers called *proxenoi*. The members of the board were required to find lodgings for foreigners, to keep them under observation, to escort them out of the country; and in case of sickness or death to provide for the treatment or burial of the stranger, whose property they were obliged to protect and account for. The existence of such officials and regulations affords conclusive proof that the Maurya empire was in constant intercourse with foreign states and that many strangers visited the capital on business.

Board No. 3 ; births and deaths. The registration of births and deaths was expressly designed both to facilitate taxation, probably a poll-tax of so much per head, and for the information of the government. It was a development and necessary consequence of the register or permanent census described in the *Arthaśāstra*. It may be assumed that the exceptionally efficient government of Chandragupta introduced improvements on the arrangements of his predecessors.

Boards 4–6 ; trade and tolls. It has always been the practice of Indian rulers to exercise strict supervision over private trade and to levy duties on sales, the goods being stamped officially to guarantee payment. Manufactures were treated on the same principles. Procedure in such matters varied so little in India from age to age that the best comment on the statement of Megasthenes is afforded by an extract from the travels of Tavernier, the French jeweller who journeyed through India on business in the seventeenth century. He states that at Benares there were

two galleries where they sell cottons, silken stuffs, and other kinds of mer-chandise. The majority of those who vend the goods are the workers who have made the pieces, and in this manner foreigners obtain them at first hand. These workers, before exposing anything for sale, have to go to him who holds the contract [sc. for collecting the tax on sales], in order to get the king's stamp impressed on the pieces of calico or silk, otherwise they are fined and flogged.

The stamp usually was impressed in vermilion. It is called 'identity-stamp' (*abhijnāna-mudrā*) in the *Arthaśāstra*, and is the *sussēmon* of the Greek accounts.[1] False statements made by importers or vendors were punishable as theft, that is to say, by fine, mutilation, or even death. Evasion of the municipal tithe collected by the sixth board was specially made a capital offence, as already noted.

Full particulars of the methods of collection of duties on sales and manufactures will be found in the *Arthaśāstra*, and some indication of the nature of Indian trade in the fourth century B.C. has been given in the account of the Nanda dynasty.

Viceroys. We have seen that according to the *Arthaśāstra* the normal small kingdom described in that book should be divided into four provinces, each under a governor (*sthānika*). We do not know positively how many Viceroys were required for Chandragupta's immense empire extending from the Hindu Kush to at least as far as the Narbada, but it is noticeable that four Viceroys seem to have sufficed for the still larger empire of Aśoka. They will be mentioned more particularly in the history of his reign.

Departments. The *Arthaśāstra* describes in much detail the duties of the heads of the numerous departments in the administration of a properly regulated Hindu state. The book refers to about thirty such departments. The Greek accounts prove that the departmental organiza-tion was maintained by Chandragupta. We hear specifically of officers in charge of markets, rivers, canal irrigation, public works, and sundry branches of fiscal business, besides the superintendents of hunters, wood-cutters, blacksmiths, carpenters, and miners. Innumerable details might be filled in from the *Arthaśāstra*, but limitations of space permit notice of only a few selected topics.

Official corruption. In spite of the drastic penal code and the enhanced severities visited upon offending officials the public service suffered from corruption. The author of the *Arthaśāstra* records his opinion that

just as it is impossible not to taste the honey or the poison that finds itself at the tip of the tongue, so it is impossible for a government servant not to eat up, at least, a bit of the King's revenue. Just as with fish moving under water it cannot possibly be discerned whether they are drinking water or not, so it

---

[1] McCrindle repeatedly mistranslated the words ἀπὸ συσσήμου as meaning 'by public notice'.

is impossible to detect government servants employed on official duties when helping themselves to money. It is possible to mark the movements of birds flying high up in the sky; but it is not possible to ascertain the secret movements of government servants.

'There are', the same authority observes, 'about forty ways of embezzlement; what is realized earlier is entered later on; what is realized later is entered earlier; what ought to be realized is not realized'; and so on through the whole list.

Rewards were promised to informers who disclosed cases of defalcation; but, on the other hand, the informer who failed to prove his charges was liable to severe punishment, which might be capital.

Secret service. The secret service to which reference has been made may be described as the mainstay of the government, next to the army. The king employed hosts of spies or detectives, masquerading in disguises of all kinds, who were controlled by an espionage bureau. Cipher writing was used and the services of carrier pigeons were enlisted. The doctrine of the necessity for constant espionage in every branch of the administration pervades the whole of the *Arthaśāstra*, which treats every form of villainy as legitimate when employed in the business of the state. The evidence of Chānakya's treatise is corroborated by the Greek testimony. News writers at the headquarters of provincial administrations supplied secret reports to the government, and the information obtained from courtesans was not despised. We are told that the king, having set up spies over his ministers, 'shall proceed to espy both citizens and country people'. The drama already cited more than once exhibits the system at work. The secret service was not, however, a mere political police; it also had the task of criminal investigation and the positive function of encouraging loyalty to the king and spreading tales calculated to enhance his prestige and reputation.

Property in land. The question whether or not private property in land existed in ancient India has been often debated, but without any satisfactory result, by reason of the ambiguity lurking in the term property. The disputants who affirm the existence of private property in land use the term in one sense and their opponents in another. The clearest example of absolute private property in land, apparently closely resembling the English freehold, is to be found in Malabar, the home of the Nāyars (Nairs), Coorgs, and Tulus, whom Dubois regarded as the three aboriginal tribes of the western coast. He expressed the opinion that Malabar 'is the only province in India where proprietary right has been preserved intact until the present day. Everywhere else the soil belongs to the ruler, and the cultivator is merely his tenant.'

The abbé then proceeds to explain at considerable length exactly what he means.[1]

---

[1] *Hindu Manners*, &c., ed. Beauchamp, 3rd ed. (1906), p.56. See *The Travancore State Manual*, Trivandrum, 1906, for the theory and details of the Malabar 'birthright' tenure.

The proposition enunciated by Dubois that 'everywhere else the soil belongs to the ruler' has been generally accepted in northern and western India, and was until recently, as Baden-Powell testifies, the doctrine current in the native states.

The commentator on the *Arthaśāstra* (Book II, chap. 24) had no doubt on the subject. He declares that 'those who are well versed in the scriptures admit that the King is the owner of both land and water, and that the people can exercise their right of ownership over all other things excepting these two'. The author of the treatise, as a whole, seems to accept that view. The rules in chapter 1 of Book II, for instance, instruct the king that 'lands prepared for cultivation shall be given to tax-payers (*karada*) only for life (*ekapurushikāni*)'; and that 'lands may be confiscated from those who do not cultivate them, and given to others'. The author evidently held that land of all kinds was at the disposal of the government. Most native Indian governments, including those of the Muslim dynasties, have taken in the shape of land revenue and cesses so large a proportion of the produce that the actual cultivator was left at most a bare subsistence. The government share, it is true, was always limited theoretically, but in practice the state usually took all it could extort. In those circumstances no room was left for economic rent, or for a landlord class receiving rent. Nothing intervened between the poverty-stricken peasant and the state. Ordinarily the peasant's customary right to retain his land as long as he paid all official demands was respected, but his ill-defined right of occupancy, which was not protected by positive law, differed widely from ownership. In Bombay, where the state still deals directly with the cultivating peasant or 'ryot', the ownership of the government is expressly recognized by law.

In Bengal and Uttar Pradesh the British authorities went out of their way to develop, or even to create a class of rent-receiving land-lords, whose rights are often described as amounting to full ownership. But in the background there is always the lien of the state on the soil to enforce the punctual payment of the land revenue, that is to say, the cash commutation for the share of the produce to which every Indian government is entitled by immemorial tradition. The so-called 'ownership' was in former times and still is also subject to the customary rights of subordinate tenure-holders and of the cultivating peasants; those rights being substantial, although undefined by law and inadequately secured before the middle of the nineteenth century.

Land revenue. The land revenue, or state share of the produce, which always has been the mainstay of Indian finance, may be regarded as rent rather than as taxation on the assumption that the ultimate property in land is vested in the state. The normal share of the produce admitted in the *Arthaśāstra* to be claimable by the government was one-fourth. The religious law-books give the standard rate as one-sixth, and this might be reduced for poor land. But Akbar took one-third, and the Sultans of Kashmir claimed one-half. The nominal percentage of land revenue to the produce did not much matter, because the government usually made up for any deficiency by exacting a multitude of extra periodical cesses, not to speak of occasional forced contributions. The ordinary result was that the peasant might consider himself lucky if he was left enough to fill tolerably the stomachs of himself and family and to provide seed. Nothing was available for the payment of rent to a private landlord.

In Anglo-Indian official phraseology the term 'settlement', a translation of the Persian word *bandobast*, is applied to the whole process by which the amount of the land revenue or crown-rent is assessed, and the officer who carries out the operations is called a 'settlement officer'. The authorities do not explain the nature of the 'settlements' made in Maurya times, and we do not know whether the assessment was varied yearly or fixed for longer periods.

Irrigation. Irrigation, which is essential in most parts of India for the security of the crops and consequently of the revenue, received close attention, and was under the supervision of departmental officers. A system of canals with sluices was maintained, and water-rates of varying amounts were levied as they are now.

Roads. The main roads were kept in order by the proper department, and pillars marking the distances, equivalent to our milestones and the Mughul *kōs mīnārs*, were set up at intervals of ten *stadia*, or about 2,022½ English yards, half a *kōs* by Indian reckoning. The Mughul emperors were content with a pillar for each *kōs*. A great highway, now represented by Lord Dalhousie's Grand Trunk Road, connected Taxila and the north-western frontier with Pātaliputra, the capital. The *Arthaśāstra* mentions the construction of roads as one of the duties of a king. Rules were laid down concerning the correct width of each class of road.

Liquor. The drinking of and traffic in liquor were recognized officially and encouraged as a source of revenue. The whole business was under the control of a superintendent, who was responsible for the necessary police and licensing arrangements, as well as for the collection of the government dues. Public-houses or drinking-shops were not to be close together, and the consumption, whether on or off the premises, was duly regulated. The shops were to be made attractive by the provision of seats, couches, scents, garlands, water, and other comforts suitable to the varying seasons. The *Arthaśāstra* mentions six principal kinds of liquor. Special licences for manufacture were granted for a term of four days on the occasions of festivals, fairs, and pilgrimages.

General observations. It is impossible to reproduce in a reasonable space nearly all the information on record concerning the institutions of Chandragupta Maurya and his immediate predecessors. The particulars recounted in the foregoing pages may suffice to give the modern student a fairly accurate and vivid notion of the nature of the civilization of northern India at the close of the fourth century B.C.

Many readers probably will be surprised to learn of the existence at such an early date of a government so thoroughly organized, which anticipated in many respects the institutions of modern times. The dark spots on the picture are the appalling wickedness of the statecraft taught in the *Arthaśāstra* and the hateful espionage which tainted the whole administration and was inspired by the cynical statecraft of the books. The policy of Kautilya or Chānakya was not the invention of that unscrupulous minister. The book attributed to him is avowedly founded upon many earlier treatises no longer extant, all of which seem to have advocated the same principles. The author of the *Arthaśāstra*, while frequently disagreeing with his predecessors concerning details, clearly was in general agreement with them concerning the policy to be pursued. Attention has been drawn to the emphatic repudiation of the *Arthaśāstra* doctrines by Bāna in the seventh century after Christ. He does not stand quite alone, although it might be difficult to cite any passage exactly similar from other authors. The spirit of the *Dharma-śāstra* is in some respects far more humane than that of Chānakya's ruthless treatise, and the story of Rāma, whether told in Sanskrit or Hindī, is that of a noble prince. Kāmandaka, on the other hand, describes the author of the *Arthaśāstra* as 'wise and Brahma (god)-like'; and Dandin calls him 'a revered teacher'.

How did the cynical policy taught in the books of the *Arthaśāstra* class originate and gain wide acceptance? The minister professes to write in accordance with the 'customs of the Āryas', and to revere the 'triple Veda', but his practical advice, so far as it has a Vedic foundation, is based on the fourth Veda, the *Atharva*, a storehouse of sorcery and spells. The question which I have asked suggests curious speculations.[1]

AUTHORITIES

THE only English translation of the *Arthaśāstra* is that of R. SHAMASASTRY (3rd ed., Mysore, 1929). An excellent and fully annotated translation in German is that of J. J. MEYER (Hanover, 1926). Valuable studies by O. STEIN (*Megasthenes und Kautilya*, Vienna, 1922) and B. BRELOER (*Kautalīya Studien*, 3 vols., Bonn, 1927–34) are unfortunately not available in English translation. Since its publication certain Indian scholars have been waging a losing battle in favour of its authenticity as a production of Kautilya. In Europe this view is now almost universally abandoned. On this thorny question see the bibliography in BENI PRASAD's *The State in Ancient India* (Allahābād, 1928), p. 251, n. 1, to which must be added KEITH in *Asutosh Mookerjee Commemoration Volume* (pt. 1, Patna, 1926), pp. 8–22.

[1] The 'triple Veda' (*trayī*) is defined as comprising the '*Sāma, Rik,* and *Yajus*'. The order of enumeration is noteworthy. The author, when specifying the 'four sciences', places first *Anvikshakī* or philosophy (comprising *Sānkhya, Yoga,* and *Lokāyata*); and assigns the 'triple Veda' to the second place. The third science called *Vārta* deals with the practical affairs of common life, namely, agriculture, cattle-breeding, and trade; the fourth, styled alternatively *Arthaśāstra* or *Dandanīti*, is the subject of his treatise. 'This *Arthaśāstra*', he says in his opening sentence, 'is made as a compendium of almost all the *Arthaśāstras*, which, in view of acquisition and maintenance of the earth, have been composed by ancient teachers.' See Book I, chaps. 1–4, and the concluding chapter of the work.

The fragments of Megasthenes have been collated and translated by J. W. M'CRINDLE in *Ancient India as described by Megasthenes and Arrian* (London, 1877).

Among studies of the reign of Chandragupta and of the Mauryas are R. K. MOOKERJI, *Chandragupta Maurya and his Times* (Madras, 1943), and V. R. R. DIKSHITAR, *The Mauryan Polity* (Madras, 1932). These works should be read with some caution, bearing in mind our reservations on the reliability of the *Arthaśāstra*.

Of the numerous works on ancient Indian political life and thought among the best are that of BENI PRASAD above mentioned, and his *Theory of Government in Ancient India* (Allahābād, 1927). The works of U. N. GHOSHAL (*History of Hindu Political Theories*, London, 1923; *The Hindu Revenue System*, Calcutta, 1929; *The Agrarian System in Ancient India*, Calcutta, 1930; *History of Hindu Public Life*, vol. i, Calcutta, 1945; &c.) are solid and thorough. On economic conditions ATINDRANATH BOSE's *Social and Rural Economy of Northern India*, c. 600 B.C.–200 A.D. (2 vols., Calcutta, 1942–5) is the most detailed work so far produced.

Many of the works referred to in *E.H.I.*[4] (1923) are still of value.

CHAPTER 2

Aśoka Maurya and his institutions; diffusion of Buddhism; end of the Maurya dynasty; the successors of the Mauryas

Accession of Aśoka. When the reign of Bindusāra terminated in 273 B.C. he was succeeded by one of his sons named Aśokavardhana, commonly called Aśoka, who seems to have been selected by his father as heir apparent, and possibly may have enjoyed for some time the rank of sub-king or *uparājā*. According to tradition he had served as Viceroy, first at Taxila in the north-west, and subsequently at Ujjain in Malwa. The fact that his formal consecration or coronation (*abhisheka*) was delayed for some four years until 269 B.C. confirms the tradition that his succession was contested, and it may be true that his rival was an elder brother named Susīma, as affirmed by one of the many wild legends which have gathered round Aśoka's name. The story told by the monks of Ceylon that he slaughtered ninety-eight or ninety-nine brothers in order to clear his way to the throne is absurd and false; the fact being, as the inscriptions prove, that Aśoka took good care of his brothers and sisters long after his succession. The grotesque tales about Aśoka's alleged abnormal wickedness prior to his conversion to Buddhism, which were current in the north as well as the south, are equally baseless and obviously concocted for purposes of edification.

Authorities. The monkish legends, whether of Ceylon or other countries, do not afford a safe basis for a matter-of-fact history of the great Buddhist emperor, although some of the Ceylon dates seem to be correct, while others are erroneous. The only sound foundation for his history is to be found in his numerous and wonderful inscriptions, which may be fairly considered the most remarkable set of inscriptions in the world. Their testimony is supplemented by that of a few other epigraphs, by literary tradition in many forms and languages, and by inferences deduced from study of the extant monuments and their distribution. The coins of Aśoka's age, which do not bear his name or titles, are of little use to the historian. The *Arthaśāstra* and certain other books in various languages provide materials for illustrative comment on the narrative.

Little political activity. Aśoka having been a man of peace for the greater part of his long reign, the recorded political events during it are few, and nothing is known about his military force. The interest of the story is centred on the movement initiated by him which transformed Buddhism from a local sect into one of the world-religions and on the gradual development of the emperor's personal character and policy. His imperishable records constitute in large measure his auto-biography written in terms manifestly dictated by himself.

As far as is known Aśoka waged only one war of aggression, that directed to the acquisition of Kalinga on the coast of the Bay of Bengal. His gigantic empire, which extended from the Hindu Kush to the northern districts of Mysore, consequently seems to have been in-herited, with the exception of Kalinga, from. his father, and was probably acquired either by Bindusāra or by Chandragupta, or by both.

Chronology. His inscriptions date the events of the reign by regnal years reckoned from the time of his consecration or coronation in 269 B.C. The month in which that ceremony took place not being known, it is impossible to equate accurately the regnal with the calendar years. Nor is it practicable to define the dates B.C. with absolute pre-cision for various reasons. Two of the chief of those reasons are that the exact year of Chandragupta's accession is not ascertainable, and that the length of Bindusāra's reign is variously stated as either twenty-five or twenty-eight years. For convenience dates will be given in this chapter as if they were precise, but the reader is invited to bear in mind that they are subject to slight correction for possible error, probably not exceeding two years. Aśoka's reign, as counted from his father's death, extended to forty or forty-one years; or, as counted from his consecration, to thirty-six or thirty-seven years. The dated inscriptions begin in the ninth and come down to the twenty-eighth regnal year, equivalent approximately to the period including 261 and 242 B.C. The reign is taken as extending from 273 to 232 B.C.

Aśoka's early years. No definite political event can be assigned to the early years of Aśoka's government. His personal reminiscences prove that he then lived the life of his predecessors, consuming flesh food freely, enjoying the pleasures of the chase, and encouraging festive assemblies accompanied by dancing and drinking. No sound reason exists for believing that his conduct was particularly sinful or vicious. The nature of his diet and amusements in those days affords conclusive evidence that he cannot have been an earnest follower of the Jain religion. It may be presumed that he was a Brahmanical Hindu, and most likely a worshipper of Śiva. The sudden change in his beliefs and habits was produced by the remorse which he felt for the unmerited sorrows inflicted upon the people of the kingdom of Kalinga in the east by his attack on and annexation of that country in 261 B.C.

The Kalinga war. The Kalinga war, which was the turning-point in Aśoka's career, thus became one of the decisive events in the history of the world. The miseries of the campaign, the sufferings of the prisoners, and the wailings for the dead were soon forgotten by the vanquished, as they have been forgotten by other conquered nations after thousands of wars; but the effect which they produced upon the conscience of the victor is still traceable in the world of the twentieth century.

Aśoka himself tells us in the striking language of his longest Rock Edict (No. XIII) how he was haunted by remorse for the calamities caused by his ambition, and was driven to take refuge in the Law of Piety or Duty, which he identifies elsewhere with the doctrine of the Buddha.

Kalinga was conquered by His Sacred and Gracious Majesty when he had been consecrated eight years [261 B.C.]. 150,000 persons were thence carried away captive, 100,000 were there slain, and many times that number died.

Directly after the annexation of the Kalingas began His Sacred Majesty's zealous protection of the Law of Piety, his love of that Law, and his inculcation of that Law (*dharma*). Thus arose His Sacred Majesty's remorse for having conquered the Kalingas, because the conquest of a country previously unconquered involves the slaughter, death, and carrying away captive of the people. That is a matter of profound sorrow and regret to His Sacred Majesty.

The royal author proceeds to develop in detail the sentiment above expressed in general terms, and continues:

So that, of all the people who were then slain, done to death, or carried away captive in Kalinga, if the hundredth or the thousandth part were now to suffer the same fate, it would be matter of regret to His Sacred Majesty. Moreover, should any one do him wrong, that too must be borne with by His Sacred Majesty, so far as it can possibly be borne with. Even upon the forest folk in his dominions His Sacred Majesty looks kindly and he seeks to make them think aright, for, if he did not, repentance would come upon His Sacred Majesty. They are bidden to turn from evil ways that they be not chastised. For His Sacred Majesty desires that all animate beings should have security, self-control, peace of mind, and joyousness.

True conquest. Aśoka goes on to explain that true conquest consists in the conquest of men's hearts by the Law of Duty or Piety,[1] and to relate that he had already won such real victories, not only in his own dominions, but in kingdoms 600 leagues away, including the realm of the Greek king Antiochos, and the dominions of the four kings severally named Ptolemy, Antigonos, Magas, and Alexander, who dwell beyond (or 'to the north of') 'that Antiochos'; and likewise to the south, in the kingdoms of the Cholas and the Pāndyas, as far as Tāmraparnī;[2] and also in the king's dominions among the various

---

[1] Milton offers a surprisingly exact parallel passage:

> They err, who count it glorious to subdue
> By conquest far and wide, to overrun
> Large countries, and in fields great battles win,
> Great cities by assault . . .
> But if there be in glory aught of good,
> It may by means far different be attained
> Without ambition, war, or violence;
> By deeds of peace, by wisdom eminent,
> By patience, temperance. . . .   (*Paradise Regained*, iii. 71–92.)

[2] A common ancient name of Ceylon. Here, however, Dr. Smith believed that the word referred to a small river in the extreme south of the peninsula (see below, p. 121, n. 2). In my opinion his arguments are not wholly convincing. [Ed.]

tribes or nations called Yonas, Kāmbojas, Nabhapamtis of Nābhaka, Bhojas, and Pitinikas, as well as among the Āndhras and Pulindas[1]—in fact, 'everywhere', he says, 'men hearing His Sacred Majesty's ordinance based on the Law of Piety and his instruction in that Law, practise and will practise the Law'.

The royal preacher then extols the true conquest wrought by the Law as being full, not only of transitory delight, but of precious fruit which remains sound in the next world. He concludes by exhorting his sons and grandsons to pursue the path of true conquest; and, if perchance they should become involved in a conquest by force of arms (or 'from self-will', as Hultzsch), to take their pleasure in patience and gentleness, so that they may by effort attain that joy of spirit which avails for both this world and the next.

Special Kalinga edicts. The subject is continued in the two special edicts which the victor composed a little later for the benefit of the conquered provinces, one being addressed to the high officers of a town named Samāpā, and the other to those of a second town called Tosali. A postscript enjoins the Viceroys of Taxila and Ujjain, the governments which Aśoka himself had held as prince, to apply the principles enunciated, and to take effectual steps by means of periodical tours and public proclamations on certain holidays to see that the imperial commands were translated into practice.

The emperor starts by affirming that 'all men are my children', echoing a saying attributed to Buddha. He then seeks to win the confidence of the unsubdued border tribes, and announces that specially trained officers will be sent to look after their interests. He laments that some servants of the state, failing to realize his paternal sentiments, had at times gone so far as to inflict unjust imprisonment or torture. He warns his officers that they must beware of yielding to the vices of 'envy, lack of perseverance, harshness, impatience, want of application, laziness, and indolence', threatening them with his displeasure if they should fail in their duty.

Those admirable instructions, which could not be bettered today, show how Aśoka's remorse for the horrors of his one aggressive war bore fruit in the practical administration of his frontier provinces.

Contemporary powers. The references in the edict first quoted to other potentates, nations, and tribes obviously have much historical importance. When duly interpreted they prove that Aśoka was contemporary with Antiochos Theos, grandson of Seleukos Nikator, the foe and afterwards the ally of Aśoka's grandfather; with Ptolemy Philadelphos of Egypt;[2] with Magas, the ruler of Cyrene to the west of Egypt; and with an Alexander, probably King of Epirus. Chronologists

---

[1] Rock Edict V adds the Rāshtrikas of the Marāthā country, and the Gāndhāras of the north-western frontier.

[2] Ptolemy was a king with great power and wealth, and a liberal patron of literature and science. Euclid lived at Alexandria in his time. Ptolemy founded colonies on the Red Sea coast

show that the last year in which those four princes were alive together appears to have been 258 B.C., and that the edict consequently cannot be much later in date. It is actually dated in either the thirteenth or fourteenth regnal year, equivalent to 257 or 256 B.C. The document further proves that the emperor of India enjoyed the privilege of friendly intercourse with the Hellenistic kings named, that he was at liberty to conduct Buddhist propaganda in their dominions, and that he succeeded in gaining attention to his teaching. We also learn that the Tamil kingdoms of the Cholas and Pāndyas were then in existence, the Maurya emissaries penetrating as far as the Tāmraparnī river in Tinne-velly,[1] the seat of the pearl and the conch-shell trade, chiefly conducted at the now vanished port of Korkai. Another edict mentions two more Tamil kingdoms, namely that of Keralaputra, or the Malabar coast, and that of Satiyaputra, probably equivalent to the Satyamangalam province of the later kingdom of Madura. That province skirted the borders of Mysore, Malabar, Coimbatore, and Madura, along the line of the Western Ghats. We thus obtain a welcome glimpse of the history of the Far South at a definite date; the first, and for a long time the only chronological foothold in the story of the Tamil kingdoms.

We are further informed concerning the names of sundry consider-able tribes or nations who were included more or less completely in Aśoka's dominions or had been brought under his influence.

The accuracy of the Greek accounts concerning the relations be-tween Seleukos Nikator and Chandragupta is confirmed by the edicts, which disclose the friendship of the grandson of Seleukos with the grandson of Chandragupta.[2]

Foreign Buddhist missions. The surprising intimation that Buddhist missions were dispatched in the middle of the third century B.C. to distant Hellenistic kingdoms in Asia and Africa, and perhaps in Europe, opens up a wide field for reflection and speculation.

While the primary authority for the history of Aśoka must always be his inscriptions, much valuable supplementary information is ob-tained from other sources. One of those sources is to be found in the chronicles of Ceylon called the *Mahāvamsa* and *Dīpavamsa*. The latter,

---

[1] But see p. 119, n. 2.

[2] The versions of the edicts are extracted from those in *Aśoka*[3], Oxford, 1920. The name of the conquered province is written in the edict both in the singular and the plural. It was sometimes known as the 'Three Kalingas'.

The name Tāmraparnī refers to the river in the Tinnevelly District, as stated in *Aśoka*[3], p. 162. The intercourse of Aśoka with the island did not begin until after the accession of Devānampiya Tissa, several years subsequent to the date in the thirteenth and partly in the fourteenth regnal year, equivalent to about 257 and 256 B.C. Tissa's accession may be dated about 251 B.C. Exact dates in the early his-tory of Ceylon cannot be determined with complete certainty. The Satiyaputra kingdom should be identified as in the text, as in *E.H.I.*[4], Oxford, 1923, pp. 171, 194, 464. See *Ind. Ant.*, vol. xli (1912), p. 231; vol. xlv (1916), p. 200.

For the meaning of *Devānampiya* and *Piyadasi* used as royal titles see *Aśoka*,[3] p. 22. Mr. Yazdani interprets *Piyadasi* as meaning 'the well-wisher (of all)'. However the titles may be analysed etymologically they were used merely as formal royal style or *protocole*, and are best translated by approximate equivalents.

the older of the two, seems to have been composed in the fourth or fifth century A.D. The statements of the edicts concerning the imperial Buddhist propaganda are amplified by the Ceylonese chroniclers, who describe nine distinct missions, which embraced seven Indian countries lying between the Himalayas and Peshawar in the north and a region called Mahishamandala in the south, usually identified with the southern portion of the Mysore State. Two other missions are said to have been dispatched to countries outside India proper, namely, Suvarnabhūmi, or Lower Burma, and Lankā, or Ceylon. The chronicler gives the names of the missionaries employed in each case, and some of those names are also recorded in inscriptions from the Bhīlsā stūpas. The list may be accepted as correct, subject to the remark that the propaganda in Lower Burma seems to have had little effect. The earliest form of Buddhism in that country, so far as definite evidence goes, was of the Mahāyāna kind, different from the Buddhism of Aścka, and apparently imported from northern India.

Mission to Ceylon. The mission to Ceylon was a complete success, although the conversion of the island was not suddenly effected by a series of astounding miracles as related in the monkish stories. It was, no doubt, a gradual, although tolerably rapid process, aided materially by powerful royal encouragement.[1] The mission came in c. 251 or 250 B.C. on the initiative of King Tissa, who ascended the throne about that time, and reigned, like his friend Aśoka, for forty years. During his rule he expended most of his energy in measures for the propagation of the Buddhist religion, and in erecting splendid buildings for its service. The leading missionary was Mahendra or Mahinda, said to have been Aśoka's son or younger brother, who settled down in the island and died there about 204 B.C. His memory is perpetuated by monuments which bear his name. He was aided by his sister, who is remembered by her title Sanghamitrā, 'Friend of the Church', or 'Order', and was as successful among the women as Mahendra was among the men. The Indian tradition which represents Mahendra as the younger brother of Aśoka is of greater authority than the island legends which describe him as a son of the emperor.

Buddhism won a decisive victory in Ceylon during the long reign of Tissa, and has never lost its hold on the island, where its influence, on the whole, has been for good. A well informed and sympathetic writer observes that:

The missions of King Aśoka are amongst the greatest civilizing influences in the world's history; for they entered countries for the most part barbarous and full of superstition, and amongst these animistic peoples Buddhism spread as a wholesome leaven.

The history of Ceylon and Burma, as of Siam, Japan, and Tibet, may be said to begin with the entrance into them of Buddhism; and in these lands

---

[1] I believe that the missionaries came from Mahendra's monastery at Madura in Pāndya territory.

it spread far more rapidly and made a far deeper impression than in China with its already ancient civilization.

As to-day Christianity spreads very rapidly amongst the animistic peoples of Africa, India, and the South Sea islands, exerting a strong influence and replacing superstition and chaos by a reasonable belief in One God and an orderly universe, so Buddhism in these eastern lands has exerted a beneficent influence by putting Karma, the law of cause and effect, in the place of the caprice of demons and tribal gods, and a lofty system of morals in the place of tribal custom and *taboo*.

The Buddhist missionaries, moreover, brought with them much of the culture of their own land. It seems clear, for instance, that it was Mahinda who brought into Ceylon the arts of stone carving and of irrigation which his father had so successfully practised in India; and the Ceylon Buddhist of today thinks of his religion as the force to which his country owes the greatness of her past history. . . . Not far from the ruined city of Anurādhapura a lovely rocky hill rises out of a dense sea of jungle, and here is the rock-hewn 'study' and the tomb of the great and gentle prince Mahinda, who about 250 B.C. brought Buddhism to Ceylon.

From that day to this Buddhism has been the dominant religion of the island. Its king, Tissa, entered into alliance with Aśoka, and did all he could to foster the religion of Gautama; and he and all his successors built the great Sacred City of Anurādhapura, in which vast hill-like dāgobas, higher than St. Paul's Cathedral and covering many acres of ground, rear their mighty domes above the trees of a royal park and royal baths and palaces given to the Sangha. . . . The 7,774 Bhikkhus [monks or friars] who to-day keep alive the religion are thus descendants in an unbroken succession of the great Mahinda himself, and in Ceylon monasticism has had a unique chance of proving its worth.[1]

Anurādhapura, the Buddhist Rome, may serve as the measure and symbol of Aśoka's influence on the world.

Council of Pātaliputra. But the monkish authors of Ceylon, whom many European writers on Buddhism have been too ready to accept as primary authorities, give little of the credit to the emperor. According to them, the conversion of the island and other lands was the work of the saint or *thera* named Tissa, who convoked a church council at Pātaliputra and then sent out his emissaries. The Ceylonese stories, written many centuries after the events described, have no just claim to be regarded as authorities superior to the words of Aśoka, who never mentions either the saint or the council, while emphatically presenting all the measures taken for the furtherance of religion as having been initiated by himself. I believe Aśoka's word. The Council of Pātaliputra may be accepted as a fact, because it is vouched for by Indian as well as Ceylonese tradition. But, in my opinion, the monks have dated it wrongly. The probability is that it was convoked towards the close of the reign of Aśoka, after the publication of his principal sets of inscriptions, the Fourteen Rock Edicts, and the Seven Pillar Edicts.

[1] K. J. Saunders, *The Story of Buddhism*, Oxford University Press, 1916, pp. 76–79. 'Rome of to-day is a mean thing, the Forum a mean jostle of littleness, compared with the extended enormous ruin of the Sacred City—vast, resigned, silent, leisurely, with full consciousness of an eternity of desolation to face' (Farrer, *In Old Ceylon*, 1908, p. 346).

It may have been the occasion for the promulgation of his latest known records, the Minor Pillar Edicts, which deal specially with the deadly sin of schism, although those documents do not refer expressly to the council.

Upagupta and Thera Tissa. Northern tradition, which was much more likely to be well founded than the tales composed by the Ceylon monks and distorted by theological bias, testifies that the instructor of Aśoka in Buddhism was Upagupta of Mathura, son of Gupta the perfumer of Benares. A monastery bearing his name still existed in the seventh century A.D. at Mathura. No doubt is possible that Upagupta was a real historical person, the fourth patriarch of the Buddhist church. The incidents of his story have been transferred by the Ceylon chroniclers to the Thera Tissa, the son of Moggali. The proof that the two names refer to the same person is absolutely conclusive.

Aśoka a monk. The admonitions of Upagupta produced many effects besides the dispatch of missionaries. He took his imperial pupil in 249 B.C. on a tour round the principal holy places of the faith,[1] beginning with the Lumbini Garden, the modern Rummindēī in the Nepalese Tarai, where the perfect inscription on a pillar still standing commemorates the emperor's visit. Aśoka also gave up hunting and the practice of eating meat, in which he had previously indulged. All slaughter of animals for the royal kitchen was prohibited. Aśoka at least once temporarily assumed the garb of a monk. Long afterwards the Chinese pilgrim I-tsing saw a statue representing him as so robed. Buddhist 'orders' not being irrevocable, it is open to any layman to become a monk for a short time and then to return to the world. In fact, every male Burmese at the present day is expected to make a stay, long or short, in a monastery.

Imperial review of policy. In 242 B.C. Aśoka, who was then growing old, and had been on the throne for over thirty years, undertook to review the measures taken during his reign for the promotion of religion, the teaching of moral duty, and the welfare of his subjects. That review was embodied in a series of edicts inscribed on pillars, and hence called the Seven Pillar Edicts, which must be read as an appendix or supplement to the earlier proclamations engraved on rocks. The foreign missions are not mentioned; I do not know why.

Ahimsā. The fifth Pillar Edict expresses the emperor's matured views on the subject of *ahimsā*, or abstention from injury to or slaughter of animals. He indicates his disapproval of the practice of castration or caponing, and publishes many rules for the protection of living creatures. It is a surprising fact that horned cattle are not included in the list of animals the slaughter of which was forbidden; whereas the *Arthaśāstra* (Book II, chap. 26) contains the clause: 'Cattle such as a calf, a bull, or a milch cow shall not be slaughtered.'[2]

---

[1] M. Foucher has proved that a sculpture on the eastern gate at Sānchī must represent the solemn visit of Aśoka to the sacred tree at Bodh Gayā (*La Porte orientale du Stūpa de Sānchī*, Paris, 1910, pp. 30, 75).

[2] Further evidence that the *Arthaśāstra* is post-Mauryan in its present form. [Ed.]

PLATE 5

a. Brāhmī Script

b. A Copper-plate Grant

PLATE 6

a. Remains of Fortifications, Pātaliputra

b. Capital of an Aśokan Column
Sārnāth

c. Aśokan Column, Lauriyā-
Nandangarh

We have seen that the government of Taxila had felt no scruple in presenting Alexander with thousands of cattle fatted for slaughter. That Taxilan sentiment probably explains Aśoka's abstention from forbidding a practice which his old subjects in the north-west would not readily abandon. It is unlikely that the feelings of the public of Taxila had changed materially during the seventy-four years which had elapsed since the Macedonian visit to their city. The facts thus noted throw light on the obscure problem of the development of the passionate feeling in favour of the sanctity of the cow, which is now one of the most conspicuous outward marks of Hinduism. It is clear that the feeling in anything like its present vehemence was not fully developed in the days of either Alexander or Aśoka.

The prohibitions against animal slaughter in Pillar Edict V coincide to a considerable extent with those recorded in the *Arthaśāstra*. Both documents, for instance, forbid the killing of parrots, starlings, and 'Brahminy' ducks.

Aśoka's last years. The publication of the Seven Pillar Edicts in 242 B.C. is the last event in Aśoka's reign which can be precisely dated. The Council of Pāṭaliputra may be placed, as already observed, a little later, somewhere about 240 B.C., and I would assign the same date approximately to the Minor Pillar Edicts which denounce the sin of schism. The council is said to have been convoked in order to repress heresy, and the publication of the special edicts directed against divisions in the church may be reasonably regarded as a result of the deliberations of the council. Some traditions represent Aśoka as having become in his old age a doting devotee, who wasted the resources of the empire in indiscriminate charity to monks and monasteries. It has also been asserted that he abdicated. His authentic records give no support to such legends or notions. They exhibit him to the last as a masterful autocrat ruling church and state alike with a strong hand, as Charlemagne did in Europe more than a thousand years later. It is possible, of course, that Aśoka may have descended from the throne towards the close of his life and devoted the short remainder of his days to religious exercises, but there is no good evidence that he actually did so.

Classes of inscriptions. It will be convenient at this point to explain briefly the nature and distribution of the remarkable inscriptions so often cited. They fall naturally into two main classes, those inscribed on rocks *in situ* or on detached boulders, and those inscribed on highly finished monolithic columns or pillars. The rock edicts, which are the earlier in date, occur mostly in the more distant and out-of-the-way localities. The columns or pillars are found in the home provinces, where the fine sandstone needed for their construction was procurable.

The records, of which many are substantially and some absolutely perfect, may be arranged in eight groups in chronological order as follows:

(i) The Minor Rock Edicts; two documents dating from about 258 or 257 B.C. No. 1 is found in variant recensions at eight localities; but No. 2 is known at two only.

(ii) The Bhābrū Edict, on a detached boulder, now in Calcutta. The purport of the record is unique. The date probably is the same as that of the Minor Rock Edicts.

(iii) The Fourteen Rock Edicts, in eight more or less complete recensions, varying considerably, and dating after 257 and 256 B.C.

(iv) The Kalinga Edicts, in two recensions, referring only to the conquered province, and substituted for certain of the Fourteen Rock Edicts; they may be dated in 256 B.C.

(v) The Cave Inscriptions, being records of dedications inscribed on the walls of three caves hewn in the rock of the Barābar hills near Gayā, in 257 and 250 B.C.

(vi) The Tarai Pillar Inscriptions, being two commemorative records on columns in the Nepalese Tarai, erected in 249 B.C.

(vii) The Seven Pillar Edicts in six recensions (excepting Edict 7, which is found at one place only), dating from 243 and 242 B.C.

(viii) The Minor Pillar Edicts, four in number, dating between 242 and 232 B.C. Two documents, one at Sarnath, and the other at Sanchi, are inscribed on separate columns; the others are postscripts to the Pillar Edicts at Allahabad.

Distribution of inscriptions. The distribution of the inscriptions is indicated on the map of Aśoka's empire. The Rock Edicts, including the Minor Rock Edicts, the Bhābrū Edict, and the Cave Inscriptions, are widely distributed from the extreme north-western corner of the Panjab to the northern districts of Mysore. They are found on the coasts of both the Bay of Bengal and the Arabian Sea, so that they may be said to cover an area extending from 34° 20′ to 14° 49′ N. lat., and from about 72° 15′ to 85° 50′ E. long., that is to say, twenty degrees of latitude and thirteen degrees of longitude. Additions to the list are still being discovered. The Maski inscription in the Nizam's dominions was not noticed until 1915. It is particularly precious because it is the only record which specifies the emperor's personal name Aśoka.[1] All the other documents describe him by his titles only. In recent years a further series of edicts has been discovered at Erragudi, in the Karnal District of Madras, and is not yet fully published. Two fragmentary Aramaic inscriptions, apparently edicts of Aśoka, have been found at Laghmān (near Jalalabad, Afghanistan) and Taxila respectively. Although some of the sites of the Rock Edicts are now in the wilderness, every one of the localities in Aśoka's time was frequented either as a place of pilgrimage or for other good reason.

The positions of more than thirty monolithic columns or pillars of Aśoka are recorded. Ten of those now visible are inscribed. The area of their distribution is not so large as that of the rock inscriptions, probably owing to the difficulty of obtaining suitable blocks of stone. The pillar formerly at Topra, a village in the Ambāla District, Panjab,

[1] It begins with the words *Devānampiyasa Asokasa*.

and that from Mīrathare is now at Delhi. Others still exist at Sanchi in the former Bhopal State, central India. Those two localities are the most remote from Pātaliputra the capital.

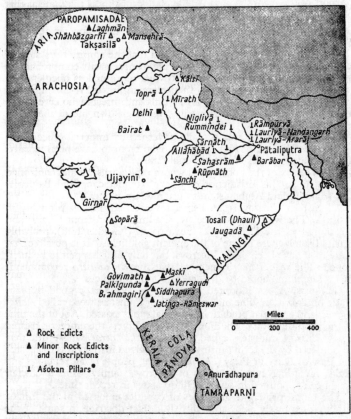

INDIA IN THE REIGN OF AŚOKA

Extent of the empire. The extent of Aśoka's empire is known with sufficient precision from the details of the distribution of his monuments, from the internal testimony of his inscriptions, and from various forms of literary historical tradition.

The empire comprised the countries now known as Afghanistan, as far as the Hindu Kush; Baluchistan and Makran, Sind, Cutch (Kachchh); the Swat (Suwāt) valley, with adjoining tribal territories,

Kashmir, Nepal, and the whole of India proper, excepting Assam, as far south as the northern districts of Mysore and part of north-west Madras. The Tamil states of the extreme south were independent. It is possible, but not clearly proved, or perhaps probable, that the emperor also exercised jurisdiction in Khotan, now in Chinese Turkistan.

The reader, of course, will understand that the empire thus defined was not all under the direct imperial rule. It necessarily comprehended numerous small autonomous states, owing more or less obedience or paying some sort of homage to the sovereign power. It also included many wild or half-wild tribes in the hills and forests who cared little for any government, and ordinarily lived their own life in their own way.

Viceroys. But the area actually governed by imperial officers was enormous. We hear of four Viceroys, who seem to have been usually, if not always, princes of the imperial family.

The Viceroy of the north-west, whose capital was Taxila, controlled the Panjab, and his jurisdiction may have extended over Sind, Baluchistan, Makran, and Afghanistan, to use modern names.

An eastern Viceroy resided at a town called Tosali, probably in Kalinga. The western provinces were administered from Ujjain; and the capital of the Deccan was Suvarnagiri ('Golden hill'), probably situated somewhere in one of the ancient goldfields.[1] It is possible that there may have been other Viceroys, but only four happen to be mentioned. The reader may remember that the *Arthaśāstra* recommends that a kingdom should be divided into four provinces.

Censors. Aśoka inherited from his predecessors a good bureaucratic organization. The higher officials or ministers were called *mahāmātras*, and a regular gradation of official ranks existed. About the time of the promulgation of the Fourteen Rock Edicts the emperor created a new class of ministers called *Dharma-mahāmātras*, whose title may be rendered by the term censors. They received instructions to enforce the Law of Duty or Piety (*dharma*) among people of all religions and ranks, including even members of the royal family. Similar officials have been appointed in several Hindu states in recent times.[2]

The moral principles and rules of conduct enjoined in the Edicts, although expressly associated with Buddhist doctrine in some of the documents, were suitable to a large extent for the adherents of any denomination The stringency of the regulations prohibiting the slaughter or mutilation of animals, increasing with Aśoka's years, no doubt pressed hardly on many classes. The imperial legislation, which directly affected the Brahmanical custom of bloody sacrifices, hampered

---

[1] Maski, where the Aśoka inscription was discovered in 1915, is situated in country which 'abounds in numerous ancient gold workings'. The shaft at Hutti is 'the deepest in the world' (Hyderabad Archaeol. Series, No. 1, 1915). Maski was an important settlement even in the late neolithic period (*Foote Coll. Indian Prehistoric*, vol. of notes, pp. 31, 125, 126).

[2] The *muhtasibs* appointed by Aurangzeb to enforce Islamic law had similar duties.

the activities of hunters, fishermen, and many other poor people. It is likely that the discontent which must have been caused by the strict enforcement may have had much to do with the break-up of the empire which ensued on Aśoka's decease. It was the business of the censors to see that the imperial commands were obeyed. It is easy to imagine the many openings which were offered for vexatious interference with private life, for malicious accusations, and for bribery to secure immunity from penalties. If we may judge from the history of later Hindu and Jain kings who pursued the same ideals and issued similar regulations, it may be assumed that offenders were liable even to capital punishment.

Summary of moral code. Aśoka's moral code is most concisely formulated in the second Minor Rock Edict.

> Thus saith His Majesty:
> 'Father and mother must be obeyed; similarly respect for living creatures must be enforced; truth must be spoken. These are the virtues of the Law of Duty (or "Piety", *dharma*) which must be practised. Similarly, the teacher must be reverenced by the pupil, and proper courtesy must be shown to relations.
> This is the ancient standard of duty (or "piety")—leads to length of days, and according to this men must act.'[1]

The three obligations—of showing reverence, respecting animal life, and telling the truth—are inculcated over and over again in the edicts. In the summary quoted above reverence is placed first, but the general tenor of the teaching is to lay stress primarily on the respect for life, both human and animal.

Sundry virtues taught. The imperial moralist did not limit his catalogue of indispensable virtues to the three named in the summary. He took much pains to inculcate the duties of compassion to all, kind treatment of slaves and hired servants, almsgiving, and toleration for the creeds of other people. Moreover, he displayed anxious solicitude for the bodily well-being of his subjects. Special attention was paid to the comfort of travellers by the provision of wells, rest-houses, and trees planted along the roads to supply both shade and fruit. Arrangements for the healing of man and beast alike were made, not only within the limits of the empire, but also in the territories of friendly independent kingdoms.

Extracts from the edicts. A few brief extracts from the edicts serve better than any paraphrase to enable the student to appreciate their spirit.

> Everywhere in my dominions the subordinate officials, and the Commissioner and the District Officers every five years must proceed on circuit, as well for their other business as for this special purpose, namely, to give

---

[1] Mr. Yazdani compares the style of this document with that of the *Śikshāvalli* section of the *Taittirīya Upanishad*, transl. in *S.B.E.*, vol. xv, part ii. There is some resemblance.

instruction in the Law of Duty (or 'Piety') to wit—'A meritorious ("excellent") thing is the hearkening to father and mother; a meritorious thing is liberality to friends, acquaintances, relations, Brahmans, and ascetics; a mertorious thing is abstention from the slaughter of living creatures; a meritorious thing is small expense and small accumulation' (*Rock Edict III*).

There is no such almsgiving as the almsgiving of the Law of Duty (or 'Piety')—friendship in duty, liberality in duty, association in duty.

Herein does it consist—in proper treatment of slaves and servants, hearkening to father and mother, &c. (*Rock Edict XI*).

A man must not do reverence to his own sect or disparage that of another man without reason. Depreciation should be for specific reasons only, because the sects of other people all deserve reverence for one reason or another.

By thus acting, a man exalts his own sect, and at the same time does service to the sects of other people. By acting contrariwise, a man hurts his own sect, and does disservice to the sects of other people (*Rock Edict XII*).[1]

Both this world and the next are difficult to secure save by intense love of the Law of Duty (or 'Piety'), intense self-examination, intense obedience, intense dread, intense effort (*Pillar Edict I*).

'The Law of Duty is excellent.'

But wherein consists the Law of Duty? In these things, to wit—little impiety, many good deeds, compassion, liberality, truthfulness, and purity (*Pillar Edict II*).

With various blessings has mankind been blessed by former kings, as by me also; by me, however, with the intent that men may conform to the Law of Duty (or 'Piety'), has it been done even as I thought (*Pillar Edict VII*).

It would be easy to illustrate in detail every one of Aśoka's precepts from Buddhist books, as well as from the existing practice in countries where Buddhism now prevails. Jain and Brahmanical writings also might be quoted to show that the morality inculcated was, on the whole, common to all the Indian religions. The Jains, however, go even farther than the Buddhists in applying the principle of *ahimsā*, or non-injury to living creatures, while those Brahmanical Hindus who considered bloody sacrifices indispensable necessarily were unable to give complete assent to the imperial doctrine. The gradual growth of a feeling of distaste for animal sacrifices discussed in an earlier chapter of this work undoubtedly was stimulated by the action of Aśoka continued for many years and supported by all the power of an efficient imperial organization. The Buddhist teaching was superior to that of the rival religions in the prominence it gave to the 'happiness of all creatures' as the main object of morality. Buddhism, in spite of its agnostic, pessimistic philosophy, is in practice a creed which tends to cheerfulness; a fact apparent to all observers in Burma.

Aśoka an ardent Buddhist. Aśoka, although tolerant of competing creeds, and even willing to pursue the policy of concurrent endowment, as proved by his costly gifts to the Ājīvika ascetics, an independent order similar to the Digambara or nude Jains, was personally an ardent Buddhist. His zeal for the teaching of Gautama

---

[1] 'Every sect favourably regards him who is faithful to its precepts, and in truth he is to be commended' (Akbar's 'Happy Sayings', *Āīn*, vol. iii, tr. Jarrett, p. 391).

Buddha is expressed emphatically in the unique Bhābrū Edict of early date, inscribed on a boulder in Eastern Rajasthan and addressed to the Church.

You know, Reverend Sirs, how far extend my respect for and faith in the Buddha, the Sacred Law, and the Church.

Whatsoever, Reverend Sirs, has been said by the Venerable Buddha, all that has been well said.

He then proceeds to enumerate seven passages or texts from the Sacred Law, which he commends to the study of monks and nuns, as well as of the laity, male and female. All of those passages have been at least tentatively identified in the Canon. They begin with the well-known First Sermon, and end with the remarkable admonition by Buddha to his son Rahula on the necessity of speaking the exact truth.[1]

Three of the Minor Pillar Edicts (Sārnāth, Sanchi, and Kausāmbī), which prescribe the penalty of excommunication for schism, and the two Tarai Pillar Edicts are equally Buddhist.

Aśoka's hard work. Aśoka worked hard, very hard.

If a king is energetic [says the author of the *Arthaśāstra*], his subjects will be equally energetic . . . when in court, he shall never cause his petitioners to wait at the door. . . . He shall, therefore, personally attend to the business of gods, of heretics, of Brahmans learned in the Vedas, of earth, of sacred places, of minors, the aged, the afflicted, and the helpless, and of women; all this in order, or according to the urgency or pressure of such kinds of business.

All urgent calls he shall hear at once, and never put off; for when postponed they will prove too hard or even impossible to accomplish. . . . Of a king the religious vow is his readiness for action; satisfactory discharge of duties in his performance of sacrifice; equal attention to all is as the offer of fees and ablution towards consecration.

In the happiness of his subjects lies his happiness; in their welfare his welfare; whatever pleases himself he shall not consider as good, but whatever pleases his subjects he shall consider as good.

Hence the king shall ever be active and discharge his duties; the root of wealth is activity, and of evil its reverse.

Asian idea of kingship. The Asian idea of kingship has ordinarily required that the monarch should hear personally as many causes and complaints as possible, should dispose of them on the spot by final orders untrammelled by legal formalities, and that he should be easily accessible to the meanest of his subjects, even at the cost of much personal inconvenience. Long after Aśoka's time the Timūrid emperors of India acted on those principles, and made the daily public audiences an essential feature of their policy. Even Jahangir, who sometimes failed in the higher duties of his station, was extremely particular

---

[1] The identification of the *Vinaya-samukase* of the Bairāt edict with the sermon preached by Buddha in the Deer Park at Sārnāth to his first five disciples is very doubtful, and alternatives have been suggested. Two admonitions to Rahula are translated by Lord Chalmers in *Further Dialogues of the Buddha* (London, 1926–7) vol. i, p. 300, and vol. ii, p. 313.

to do justice as he conceived it in person, and to appear in public three times a day.

A saying of Akbar that 'divine worship in monarchs consists in their justice and good administration' reproduces one of the sentiments quoted above from the *Arthaśāstra*.

Aśoka on himself. Aśoka expressed similar ideas with all possible emphasis:

For a long time past it has not happened that business has been dispatched and that reports have been received at all hours.

Now by me this arrangement has been made that at all hours and in all places—whether I am dining, or in the ladies' apartments, or in my private room, or in the mews, or in my (?) conveyance, or in the palace gardens—the official Reporters should report to me on the people's business; and I am ready to do the people's business in all places. . . . I have commanded that immediate report must be made to me at any hour and in any place, because I never feel full satisfaction in my efforts and dispatch of business. For the welfare of all folk is what I must work for—and the root of that, again, is in effort and the dispatch of business. And whatsoever exertions I make are for the end that I may discharge my debt to animate beings, and that while I make some happy here, they may in the next world gain heaven (*Rock Edict VI*, amended version).

It is easy to criticize such regulations from the point of view of an official in Europe and to prove that the orderly dispatch of business would be hindered and obstructed by constant interruptions. The criticism would be sound whether in Europe or Asia, but the extreme importance attached by the Eastern nations to the personal intervention and the accessibility of their rulers wins so much popularity for a sovereign who satisfies the sentiment of his people that a king may find it worth his while to submit to the inconveniences which necessarily result from regulations such as those laid down by Aśoka.

Maurya art. When writing on another occasion about the art of the Gupta period, I recorded an observation which is equally applicable to the Maurya age, especially to the reign of Aśoka, and may be repeated here, as I cannot express my meaning better.

In India the establishment of a vigorous dynasty ruling over wide dominions has invariably resulted in the application of a strong stimulus to the development of man's intellectual and artistic powers. Such a dynasty, exercising its administrative duties effectively, fostering commerce, maintaining active intercourse, commercial and diplomatic, with foreign states, and displaying the pomp of a magnificent court, both encourages the desire to do great things, and provides the material patronage without which authors and artists cannot live.[1]

The reign of Aśoka presents in perfection all the conditions enumerated in that extract as being favourable to the development of notable schools of art and literature. It may be that art had flourished

[1] *Ostasiatische Zeitschrift*, April–June, 1914, p. 1.

almost in equal measure under the rule of his father Bindusāra and his grandfather Chandragupta. In fact, there are substantial grounds for believing that buildings of exceptional magnificence were erected in the time of the first Maurya emperor. Splendid architecture necessarily involves the successful cultivation of sculpture, painting, and all the decorative arts. Greek testimony, as already mentioned, declares that the palace of Chandragupta surpassed the royal abodes of Persia, and records some details of the rich ornament of the building. But the whole has vanished, and the excavations at Taxila and Pātaliputra have not revealed much work of the time of the early Maurya kings preserved well enough to furnish material for satisfactory aesthetic criticism. The principal reason is that, so far as our present knowledge extends, the great edifices built by Asoka's predecessors were constructed mainly of perishable wood, just as the magnificent structures at Mandalay were constructed by the latest Burman sovereigns. In the time of Chandragupta Maurya and his son brick and stone seem to have been used chiefly for the foundations and plinths of timber superstructures. Wooden architecture implies the execution of most of the decorative features in material equally perishable. Unless the progress of exploration should disclose an unexpected treasure of early Maurya sculpture in stone or terra-cotta, materials for the history of art during the reigns of Chandragupta and Bindusāra must continue to be scanty. The general use of stone in northern India for building, sculpture, and decoration certainly dates from the reign of Asoka, who was influenced by Persian and Greek example. I do not either assert or believe that prior to the days of Asoka the art of building in stone was absolutely unknown in India, or that all artistic work was executed in perishable material; but the ascertained facts indicate that previous to his reign permanent materials were used rarely and sparingly either for architecture or for ornament. When Megasthenes was at Pātaliputra the city was defended by a wooden palisade. The walls, the stone palace within the city, and many sacred edifices are ascribed to Asoka.[1]

The definite history of Indian art, therefore, still begins with Asoka. At present it is impossible to write any earlier chapter.

Asokan sculpture. No building of Asoka's age is standing, unless some of the *stūpas* near Bhilsa may have been built by him. An early *stūpa*, being merely a domical mound of masonry, does not offer much scope for architectural design. We can judge of Asokan art better from sculpture than from architecture. The noble sculpture of Asoka's age exhibits a mature form of art, the evolution of which through earlier attempts is hidden from our eyes for the reasons explained above. Many details indicate that the artist in stone closely

---

[1] The text refers only to Asoka's empire, and more especially to northern India. In the Tamil countries, during the early centuries of the Christian era, Hindu temples were built of wood or brick. Stone structures did not come into fashion until late in the sixth century, in the Pallava kingdom (Jouveau-Dubreuil, *Pallava Antiquities*. Probsthain, London, 1916, p. 74).

followed the example set by his fellow craftsmen in wood and ivory. Indeed, ordinary Indian usage seems to have favoured the exercise of his skill by a carver in any material that came to his hand. If Aśoka insisted, as he did, on his statuary and reliefs being executed in enduring stone, he was able to utilize the services of skilled Indian workmen accustomed to work in more perishable materials, who were clever enough to adapt their technique to the permanent medium. The art of his time, although obviously affected by Persian and Hellenistic influences, is mainly Indian in both spirit and execution. Take, for instance, the celebrated Sārnāth capital, which has been adopted by the Indian Republic as the device of its national seal. Much of the design was suggested by Persia. But even the lions in the round are wholly different from and far superior to their Persian prototypes in pose and style, while the bas-reliefs of the guardian animals of the four quarters on the sides of the abacus are purely Indian. It is improbable that they could have been executed by any sculptor who had not been soaked in ancient Indian tradition, although his previous practical experience might have been gained by working in wood or ivory.

Perfect execution. The perfection of the execution of the best examples of Aśokan sculpture is astonishing. Sir John Marshall, who has had wide experience of Greek art, praises the Sārnāth capital in the following terms:

Lying near the column were the broken portions of the upper part of the shaft and a magnificent capital of the well-known Persepolitan bell-shaped type with four lions above, supporting in their midst a stone wheel or *dharmachakra*, the symbol of the law first promulgated at Sārnāth. Both bell and lions are in an excellent state of preservation and masterpieces in point of both style and technique—the finest carvings, indeed, that India has yet produced, and unsurpassed, I venture to think, by anything of their kind in the ancient world.

The same expert critic elsewhere comments on 'the extraordinary precision and accuracy which characterizes all Maurya work, and which has never, we venture to say, been surpassed even by the finest workmanship on Athenian buildings'.

The skill of the stone-cutters of the age could not be surpassed. The monolithic columns of fine-grained sandstone, some of which exceed forty feet in height, exclusive of the separate capital, are marvels of technical execution. The art of polishing hard stone was carried to such perfection that it is said to have become a lost art beyond modern powers. The sides of the Barābar caves excavated in most refractory gneiss rock are polished like glass mirrors. The burnishing of Fīrōz Shāh's *Lāt*, the column from Topra, now at Delhi, is so exquisite that several observers have believed the column to be metallic. Quaint Tom Coryat in the seventeenth century described the monument as 'a brazen pillar'; and even Bishop Heber, early in the nineteenth century, received the impression that it was 'a high black pillar of cast metal'. The stonework of Aśoka's time is equally well finished in all other respects. Most of the inscriptions are incised with extreme accuracy in beautifully cut letters. Dr. Spooner notes similar 'absolute perfection' in the carpentry of the mysterious wooden platforms at Kumrahār, probably dating from the reign of Chandragupta.

Skill in all arts. The engineering ability displayed in the handling and transport of huge monolithic columns conveyed over immense distances is remarkable. The combined testimony of books, material remains, and pictorial relief sculpture proves that in the fourth and third centuries B.C. the command of the Maurya monarchs over luxuries of all kinds and skilled craftsmanship in all the manual arts was not inferior to that enjoyed by the Mughal emperors eighteen centuries later. Some fine jewellery, dating from 250 B.C. and associated with a gold coin of Diodotos and debased silver punch-marked coins, has been found in the Bhir mound, the oldest part of the Taxila site.[1] The relief sculptures at Bharhut (Barhut) and Sanchi, some of which are little later than the time of Aśoka, and may be regarded as pictures executed in stone, exhibit most vividly all the details of the life of the age. It was a bustling, cheerful life, full of wholesome activity and movement. The artists delighted in representing it with frank realism, and in decorating their panels with ornaments of charming design treated with good taste.

Education. Aśoka's decision to publish his views on Buddhist doctrine and the moral code deemed suitable for 'all sorts and conditions of men' in documents composed in vernacular dialects and inscribed in two distinct scripts implies a comparatively wide diffusion of education in his empire. The sites of all the inscriptions were carefully chosen at places where crowds of people either passed or congregated for one reason or another. The heavy cost of publication in such an enduring form would have been wasted if people could not read the edicts. Probably the numerous Buddhist monasteries served the purpose of schools, as they still do to some extent in Burma, and so produced a higher general percentage of literacy among the population than that existing at present. Most of the records are incised in the Brāhmī script, the ancient form of the modern characters used in writing Sanskrit and the allied languages of northern and western India; but two sets of the Fourteen Rock Edicts placed near the north-western frontier were engraved in the Kharoshthī script, a form of Aramaic writing used in that region. The language of the records exhibits several dialectic varieties, suitable for the different provinces.

Literature. The style of the Aśoka inscriptions is not wanting in force and dignity. It recalls in some cases that of certain Upanishads. The most interesting of the documents present unmistakable internal evidence of being essentially the composition of the emperor himself. The chronology of ancient Indian literature is so ill defined that it would be difficult to name any other literary works as dating from the

[1] *J.P.H.S.*, vol. iii, p. 9; *Ann. Rep. A.S. India*, 1912–13, p. 41, pl. xxxix.

Maurya age. Professor Rhys Davids's belief that the *Kathāvatthu*, an important Buddhist treatise in Pāli, was actually composed in the time of Aśoka is not shared by all scholars. But it is certain that the reigns of three emperors covering ninety years, during which magnificent courts were maintained and every form of art and luxury was cultivated with success, cannot have been unadorned by the works of eminent authors. It is clear that in the fourth century B.C. Indian literature could look back on a long past extending over many generations. Its history cannot have been interrupted in the third century at a time when the Indian empire had attained its widest extent and was in close touch with the civilizations of western Asia and northern Africa.

Aśoka and Akbar. Few if any students of Indian history will be disposed to dispute the proposition that the most conspicuous and interesting names in the long roll of Indian monarchs are those of Aśoka and Akbar. It so happens, as already observed, that both are better known to us than any others. Although it is impossible to draw a portrait of Aśoka, he has disclosed so much of his character in his edicts that he seems to me at all events, after many years of special study, a very real and familiar figure. His remorse for the sufferings caused by the Kalinga war would have amused Akbar, who was one of the most ambitious of men and eager for the fame of a successful warrior, *gloriae percupidus*, as the Jesuit says. Akbar never was disturbed because his numerous aggressive wars caused infinite suffering. In that respect he resembled most ambitious kings. The attitude of Aśoka was peculiar and obviously sincere. He has his reward in the vast diffusion of Buddhism, which constitutes his special work in the world, and may be counted to his credit as that 'true conquest' which was his ideal.

Aśoka, although devout and zealous in the cause of his religion, was equally energetic in performing his kingly duties. There is no occasion for doubting that he did his best to live up to the admirable principles which he took so much pains to inculcate. Nothing could be better than the instructions addressed to his officers in the newly conquered province of Kalinga, which have been quoted.

A proclamation issued by Mr. Robert Cust to the Sikhs in the year 1848, between the first and the second Sikh wars, under instructions from John Lawrence, is strangely similar in both sentiment and expression:

> If any of your relations have joined the rebels, write to them to come back before blood is shed; if they do so, their fault will be forgiven . . . what is your injury I consider mine: what is gain to you I consider my gain. . . . Consider what I have said and talk it over with your relations . . . and tell those who have joined in the rebellion to return to me, as children who have committed a fault return to their fathers, and their faults will be forgiven them. . . . In two days I shall be in the midst of you with a force which you will be unable to resist.[1]

[1] Issued under direction of John Lawrence to the headmen of the Hoshiarpur District (Aitchison, *Lord Lawrence* (Rulers of India), 1905, p. 45 n.).

I think that Aśoka, who was a capable man of affairs, as well as a pious devotee, always kept an iron hand within the velvet glove, like John Lawrence, who was equally pious and equally practical.

The excellence of the art of Aśoka's reign indicates that the Maurya emperor resembled Akbar in being a man of good taste. He spared no cost or pains, and knew how to employ people who used sound materials and did honest work. The administration of the Mauryas strikes me as having been singularly efficient all round in peace and war. The 'extraordinary precision and accuracy' noted by Sir John Marshall as characteristic of Maurya work in stone are the outward expression of similar accuracy and precision in the working of the government machine. Living under the eyes of the innumerable spies employed by the Maurya kings must have been dangerous and unpleasant for individuals at times; but the espionage system, worked as the *Arthaśāstra* describes it, was an instrument of extraordinary power in the hands of a strong, capable sovereign. If Aśoka had not been capable he could not have ruled his huge empire with success for forty years, and left behind a name which is still fresh in the memory of men after the lapse of more than two millenniums.

Aśoka's sons. We do not know how or where Aśoka passed away from the scene of his strenuous labours. A Tibetan tradition is said to affirm that he died at Taxila. The names of several of his sons are on record. One, named Tīvara, is mentioned in an inscription. Another, called Kunāla and by other names, is the centre of a cycle of wild legends of the folklore type. A third, named Jalauka, the subject of a long passage in the Kashmir chronicle, clearly was a real personage, although certain fabulous stories are attached to his name. Several localities still identifiable are associated with his memory. He did not share his father's devotion to Buddhism, but on the contrary was an ardent worshipper of Śiva, as was his consort Īśānadēvī. He is also credited with the expulsion from the valley of certain unnamed non-Hindu foreigners (*mlēchchhas*). He may have been the Viceroy of his father and become independent after the death of Aśoka. The chronicler includes both Aśoka and Jalauka in the list of the kings of Kashmir.

Aśoka's grandsons. Aśoka seems to have been succeeded directly by two grandsons, Daśaratha in the eastern, and Samprati, son of Kunāla, in the western provinces. The real existence of the former is vouched for by brief dedicatory inscriptions in caves granted to the Ājīvika ascetics, and not far from the similar caves bestowed on the same order by Aśoka. The inscriptions, which were recorded immediately after the accession of Daśaratha, are conclusive evidence of that prince's rule in Magadha.

The existence of the other grandson named Samprati has not yet been verified by any early inscription. But there is no reason to doubt that he actually ruled the western provinces after his grandfather's death. According to Jain authorities Ujjain was his capital. His name has been handed down by numerous local traditions extending from

Ajmer in Rajasthan to Śatrunjaya in Saurashtra, where the most ancient of the crowd of Jain temples is said to have been founded by him. He is also credited with the erection of a temple at Nādlai in Jodhpur, now represented by a more modern building on the site; and with the foundation of the fortress of Jahāzpur, which guarded the pass leading from Mewar to Bundi. He is reputed to have been as zealous in promoting the cause of Jainism as Aśoka had been in propagating the religion of Gautama.[1]

It thus seems reasonable to assume that Asoka's empire was divided in the first instance between his two grandsons; but no decisive proof of the supposed fact has been discovered, and nothing is known about the further history of either Daśaratha or Samprati.

The last Maurya. The Purānas record the names of several other successors of Aśoka, with various readings, which need not be recited, as nothing material is known about the princes named. It is impossible to determine the extent of the dominions ruled by those later Mauryas. Brihadratha, the last prince of the dynasty, was slain about 185 B.C. by his commander-in-chief, Pushyamitra (or Pushpamitra) Sunga.

The Śunga dynasty. The usurper established a new dynasty known as that of the Śungas, which is said to have lasted for 112 years until 73 B.C. Their dominions apparently included Magadha and certain neighbouring provinces, extending southwards as far as the Narbada. The names of the founder of the dynasty and some of his descendants ending in *mitra* have suggested the hypothesis that Pushyamitra may have been an Iranian, a worshipper of the sun (Mithra), but he twice celebrated the *aśvamedha* or horse sacrifice, a rite certainly associated with Brahmanic orthodoxy. It marked the successful assertion by the prince performing it of a claim to have vanquished all his neighbours.

Graeco-Bactrian invasion. Pushyamitra repelled the invasion of a Greek king, either Demetrios son of Euthydemos, or perhaps Menander, the Milinda of Buddhist tradition, King of the Panjab. He advanced (about 175 B.C.) with a strong force into the interior of India; annexed the Indus delta, with the peninsula of Saurashtra (Kathiawar), and some other territories on the western coast; occupied Mathura on the Jumna; besieged Madhyamikā, now Nagari near Chitor in Rajasthan; invested Sākēta in southern Oudh; and threatened, or perhaps took Pātaliputra, the Śunga capital.

Madhyamikā, then the chief town of a branch of the Śibi people, who seem to have emigrated from the Panjab, was in those days a place of much importance, which an invader could not safely pass by. Although the ruins have supplied much material for the building of Chitor, traces of a Maurya edifice can still be discerned, and two inscriptions of the Śunga period have been found, which record the performance of *aśvamedha* and *vājapeya* sacrifices.

---

[1] Tod, *Annals of Mewār*, chap. iv (pop. ed., vol. i, p. 201 n.); Forbes, *Rāsmālā* (1856), vol. i, p. 7; *Rājputāna Gaz.* (Simla, 1880), vol. iii, p. 52; *Bombay Gaz.* (1896), vol. i, part 1, p. 15.

Brahmanical reaction. Pushyamitra, whatever his origin may have been, was reckoned to be a Hindu. Sun-worship is consistent with Hinduism, and even at this day sects of Sauras or sun-worshippers exist. Good reasons warrant the belief that in ancient times the cult of the sun in north-western India, Saurashtra, and Rajasthan was much more prominent than it is now. Tradition represents the first Śunga king as a fierce enemy of Buddhism and relates that he burnt a multitude of monasteries, carrying his ravages as far north as Jālandhar. The reign of Pushyamitra appears to mark a violent Brahmanical reaction against Buddhism, which had enjoyed so much favour in the time of Aśoka, but it is very probable that the Buddhist account of Pushyamitra's persecutions is much exaggerated. It is possible that the Hinduism of the Śungas may have been coloured by Magian practices. They were followers of the sacrificial Sāmaveda.[1]

The celebrated grammarian Patanjali was perhaps a contemporary of Pushyamitra, whose story is partly told in 'Mālavikā and Agnimitra' (*Mālavikāgnimitra*), a play by Kālidāsa, composed probably in the fifth century A.D.

The Kānva dynasty. Devabhūti, or Devabhūmi, the last of the Śungas, a man of licentious habits, lost his life while engaged in a scandalous intrigue. His death was contrived by his Brahman minister, Vasudeva, who seated himself on the vacant throne, and so founded a short-lived dynasty of four kings, whose reigns collectively occupied only forty-five years. The brevity of the rule of each indicates a period of disturbance, and it may be that descendants of the Śungas still ruled in part of their old possessions. Nothing is known about the doings of the Brahman kings, whose dynasty is called Kānva or Kānvāyana. The last of them was killed, about 28 B.C., by an Āndhra king whose identity is doubtful but who may have been Simuka, the first of the line.

The Śātavāhanas or Āndhras. It will be convenient here to give a brief notice of the Śātavāhana dynasty, called in the Purānas the Āndhras. The texts mention the names of thirty kings, whose rule is said to have endured for the exceptionally long period of four centuries and a half in round numbers, though this is probably at least a century too long. Some of the Purānic names are also to be found on inscriptions and coins, but many are not attested epigraphically, and several royal names on coins apparently of this dynasty do not occur in the Purānic lists. The inscriptions and coins do not refer to the kings as Āndhras, and their earliest records are found in the north-western Deccan, where their capital appears to have been Pratishthāna (now Paithan) on the upper Godavari. They do not appear to have exerted much power in the region later called Andhra (the lower Godavari and Krishna) until the second century A.D.

The first king of the line, Simuka, probably ruled in the first century B.C., since he is said by the Purānas to have destroyed the Kānvas. His successors, Krishna and Śātakarnī, are mentioned in contemporary

[1] M. M. Haraprashād Sāstri, in *J. & Proc. A.S.B.*, 1912, p. 287.

inscriptions found near the upper Godavari. Towards the end of the following century the western Deccan was occupied by Śakas of the line of the Kshaharātas, whose Satrap Nahapāna succeeded in temporarily expelling the Śātavāhanas from their ancestral domains. But by about A.D. 126 the Śātavāhana Gautamīputra Śātakarni again controlled the western Deccan, restriking Nahapāna's coins. He was succeeded, probably soon after A.D. 130, by Vāsishthīputra Pulumāyi, from whose reign there is clear evidence of Śātavāhana power in the modern Andhra country. The most powerful of the later Āndhras was Gautamīputra Yajna Śrī, who reigned for about thirty years in the latter half of the second century. The story of the decline and fall of the dynasty has not been fully recovered. The end of it may be placed somewhere about A.D. 225, although a branch line, the Chutus, continued to rule around the important city of Vanavāsī (on the upper Tungabhadra in south Bombay) until towards the end of the third century. Although the Śātavāhanas may at some time or other have controlled Magadha and the ancient imperial capital, Pātaliputra, clear evidence that they did so has not yet come to light. On the other hand it seems certain that their influence was often felt north of the Narbada before the rise of the Śaka Satraps of Ujjain in the second century A.D. In general they appear to have been supporters of Brahmanic orthodoxy, although many Buddhist donations were made in their domains.

Khāravela. Another important king of the post-Mauryan period was Khāravela of Kalinga, which included the modern Orissa and part of northern Andhra. Our knowledge of him depends entirely on a single inscription in a Jain cave in the Udayagiri Hills in the district of Puri. The Hāthīgumphā Inscription has suffered very badly at the hands of time, and is in places illegible, while much of it is only partly decipherable. Hence this tantalizing record has been the source of much speculation, and many rash theories have been based on tentative reconstructions of its text or on claims to have recognized letters and words in the vague and eroded lines of its more defective portions.

Khāravela was an earnest Jain, but this did not prevent him from carrying out successful and audacious campaigns over much of India. He appears to have temporarily occupied Magadha, and perhaps attacked even the realm of the Pāndyas in the extreme south. It seems that he also fought with a Yavana[1] King of Mathura, whose name some authorities have claimed to read as Demetrios, and who has been identified with the invader of India at the time of Pushyamitra; the reading is, however, very uncertain, and the identification almost certainly false. The inscription clearly contains a reference to a King Śātakarni, who may have been the first of this name of the Śātavāhana line.

The best view is that Khāravela lived in the latter half of the first

---

[1] The term *Yavana*, strictly an Ionian or Greek, was often very loosely used for any of the inhabitants of the north-west. It is possible that the king defeated by Khāravela was actually a Śaka.

century B.C.; this is indicated both by the epigraphy and by the fact that the inscription mentions a canal dug by a Nanda king 300 years earlier. Even allowing for the exaggerations of the panegyrist Khāravela appears to have been a very powerful king, who found time from his campaigning to devote to works of piety and public utility. His successors were apparently insignificant, and Orissa was never again an important element in the politics of India as a whole.[1]

CHRONOLOGY

(Dates nearly correct, but the Indian ones not guaranteed exact)

Maurya Dynasty

B.C.	*Event.*
326 or 325.	Chandragupta Maurya in his youth met Alexander.
323, June.	Death of Alexander at Babylon.
323–322.	Expulsion of Macedonian garrisons.
322.	Accession of **Chandragupta Maurya**. [Date possibly earlier.]
312.	Seleukos Nikator recovered Babylon and established Seleukidan era.
306.	Seleukos assumed title of king.
305.	Seleukos invaded India unsuccessfully.
302.	Megasthenes sent to Pātaliputra as ambassador.
298.	Accession of **Bindusāra Amitraghāta**.
	Deïmachos succeeded Megasthenes as ambassador.
285.	Ptolemy Philadelphos, King of Egypt, acc.
280.	Seleukos Nikator died; Antiochos Soter acc.
278 or 277.	Antigonos Gonatas, King of Macedonia, acc.
273.	Aśoka[-vardhana] acc.
272.	Alexander, King of Epirus, acc.
269.	Consecration or coronation (*abhisheka*) of Aśoka. [218 A.B. (*anno Buddhae*) in chronology of Ceylon.]
261.	Antiochos Theos, King of Syria, acc.; the Kalinga war.
259.	Aśoka abolished the imperial hunt, and dispatched missionaries.
258.	Magas, King of Cyrene died; ? Alexander, King of Epirus, died.
257, 256.	The Fourteen Rock Edicts, the Kalinga Edicts, and appointment of censors.
254.	Aśoka enlarged for the second time the *stūpa* of Konagamana.
251.	Tissa, King of Ceylon, acc.
251 or 250.	Mission of Mahendra (Mahinda) to Ceylon. [236 A.B.]
249.	Aśoka's pilgrimage to the holy places.
? 248.	Independence of Bactria and Parthia.
247.	Ptolemy Philadelphos, King of Egypt, died.
247 or 246.	Antiochos Theos, King of Syria, died.
246.	She-hwang-ti became ruler of Ch'in in China.

[1] This section has been added to Dr. Smith's original text and that on the Sātavāhanas completely recast. Though a few authorities might still be found to support him in placing Khāravela and the early Sātavāhanas alike over a century earlier, I feel strongly that the numerous arguments against this chronology put forward since his death would have convinced him. The chronology here followed is substantially that of Professor H. C. Raychaudhuri, for which see the relevant chapters of *P.H.A.I.*[6] [Ed.]

B.C.	*Event*
242.	Publication of the Seven Pillar Edicts.
242 or 239.	Antigonos Gonatas, King of Macedonia, died.
240–232.	Council of Pātaliputra; Minor Pillar Edicts condemning schism.
232.	Aśoka died; his grandson **Daśaratha** acc. in eastern provinces; and probably **Samprati**, another grandson, acc. in western provinces.
221.	She-hwang-ti became Emperor of China.
211.	Tissa, King of Ceylon, died; Uttiya acc.
204.	Mahendra (Mahinda) died in Ceylon.
203.	Sanghamitrā, sister of Mahendra, died in Ceylon
185.	**Bridhadratha**, the last Maurya king, killed.

Śunga Dynasty

185.	**Pushyamitra (Pushpamitra)** acc. Brahmanical reaction; Patanjali.
175.	Invasion of Bactrian Greeks.
73.	**Devabhūti (-bhūmi)**, the last Śunga king, killed.

73–28.	*Kānva* or *Kānvāyana Dynasty*.

Śātavāhana Dynasty

c. 50.	Simuka in north-west Deccan.
	Krishna in north-west Deccan.
	Sātakarni in north-west Deccan. Khāravela in Kalinga.

A.D.	
c. 80.	Kshaharāta Śakas occupy west Deccan.
c. 126.	Gautamīputra Sātakarni expels Śakas.
c. 130.	Vāsishthīputra Śātakarni. Evidence of Śātavāhana power in Āndhra country.
c. 170–200.	Yajna Śrī.
c. 225.	End of dynasty. Chutus in Vanavāsi.

AUTHORITIES

HULTZSCH's edition of the Aśokan inscriptions (*Corpus Inscriptionum Indicarum*, vol. i, Oxford, 1925) is still the standard edition and contains a valuable introduction. In smaller compass is the edition of BLOCH with French translation (*Les Inscriptions d'Aśoka*, Paris, 1951).

Of monographs on Aśoka the author's *Aśoka* in the Rulers of India series (3rd ed., Oxford, 1920) is still of value. Also R. K. MOOKERJI's *Aśoka* (London, 1928), D. R. BHANDARKAR's *Aśoka* (Calcutta, 1925), and B. M. BARUA's *Aśoka and his Inscriptions* (Calcutta, 1946). The relevant chapter of *C.H.I.*, vol. i, by F. W. THOMAS, is also still useful as a brief account. E. J. RAPSON's *Ancient India* (Cambridge, 1914) is a good sketch of the period. For the Ājīvikas see A. L. BASHAM's *History and Doctrines of the Ājīvikas* (London, 1951). The second volume of the *History and Culture of the Indian People* (*The Age of Imperial Unity*, Bombay, 1951), ed. R. C. MAJUMDAR, contains useful chapters on the period.

The only one of the Erragudi Inscriptions to have been edited (by B. M. BARUA) will be found in *I.H.Q.*, vol. xiii, pp. 132 ff. The Aramaic inscription of Taxila has been studied by HERZFELD (*Epi. Ind.*, vol. xix, p. 251) and that of Laghmān by W. HENNING (*B.S.O.A.S.*, vol. xiii, p. 80).

The chronology of the Śātavāhanas here adopted has been mainly based on that of H. C. RAYCHAUDHURI (*P.H.A.I.*[6], pp. 403 ff., 483 ff.). For Khāravela see the bibliography in D. C. SIRCAR's *Select Inscriptions* (Calcutta, 1942), p. 206.

Many of the references in the author's *E.H.I.*[4] and *Asoka*[3] are still of importance.

CHAPTER 3

The Indo-Greek and other foreign dynasties of north-western India; the Kushāns or Indo-Scythians; Greek influence; foreign commerce; beginning of Chola history

Revolt of Bactria and Parthia. About the middle of the third century, within a year or two of 250 B.C., while Aśoka was at the height of his power, two important provinces, Bactria and Parthia, broke away from the Seleukidan empire, and set up almost simultaneously as independent kingdoms, with results which subsequently had considerable effect upon India.

Parthia. The movement in Parthia, the territory lying to the south-east of the Caspian Sea and inhabited by hardy horsemen with habits similar to those of the later Turkomans, was of a national character, and seems to have lasted for several years. The independence of the kingdom may be dated approximately in 248 B.C. The chief named Arsakes, who had led his countrymen in their fight for liberty, founded the Arsakidan dynasty of Persia which lasted for nearly five centuries until it was superseded by the Sassanians in A.D. 226. The Parthian power gradually extended eastwards until it comprised most of the dominions once ruled by the Achaemenian dynasty of Persia; but its influence on India did not make itself felt until more than a century after the foundation of the kingdom.

Bactria. The revolution in Bactria, the rich and civilized region between the Hindu Kush and the Oxus, which was reputed to contain a thousand towns and had been regarded as the premier province of the empire in Achaemenian times, was effected in the ordinary Asiatic manner by the rebellion of a governor named Diodotos.

Inasmuch as the newly formed kingdom adjoined Aśoka's Kabul or Paropanisadai province, echoes of the revolution must have been heard at the court of Pātaliputra, although Indian documents are silent on the subject. While Aśoka lived his strong arm and his friendly relations with the Hellenistic princes protected India against the ambition of Alexander's successors. When he had vanished from the scene and his empire had crumbled to pieces, many years did not elapse until the provinces beyond the Indus became the object of Greek aggression.

Syrian raid on Kabul. Euthydemos, the third King of Bactria, had become involved in a quarrel with Antiochos the Great of Syria, which was ended about 208 B.C. by the formal recognition of Bactrian independence. Shortly afterwards Antiochos crossed the Hindu Kush, and attacked an Indian prince named Subhāgasena (Sophagasenas), ruler of the Kabul valley. The invader, having extorted a large cash indemnity and many elephants, went home through Arachosia (Qandahar) and Drangiana. That raid had no permanent effect.

Demetrios, King of the Indians. But Demetrios, the fourth King of Bactria, and son of Euthydemos, became so powerful that he was able to subdue all Ariana or Afghanistan, and even to annex considerable territories in the Panjab and western India.[1] Either he or Menander (or perhaps both) led a great raid into the heart of India, which, as we have seen, was repelled by Pushyamitra Śunga. Hence he was known as 'King of the Indians'. The nearly contemporary square coins of Pantaleon and Agathokles present Indian features derived from the native coinage of Taxila and prove that Greek principalities, connected in some way with the conquests made by Demetrios, were established on the north-western frontier late in the second century B.C. A rival named Eukratides deprived Demetrios of Bactria about 175 B.C. and founded a new line of frontier princes. The names of about forty such rulers are known from coins. It is impossible to ascertain the exact relationship between the princes or to specify their respective territories with precision.

Menander. The most remarkable king was Menander, who reigned in the Panjab from about 160 to 140 B.C. He is remembered in a famous Buddhist text, *The Questions of Milinda*, where he is said to have embraced Buddhism. He acquired a widespread reputation, and it is said that when he died various cities contended for the honour of giving sepulture to his ashes. His fine coinage is abundant in many interesting types. Specimens have been found in India even to the south of the Jumna.

Antialkidas. We obtain an unexpected and startling glimpse of a slightly later king named Antialkidas, who ruled at Taxila, from an inscription at Besnagar near Bhilsa in central India, which was probably erected towards the end of the second century B.C., or at the beginning of the first. The record was incised by direction of Dion's son, Heliodoros of Taxila, who was sent as envoy to the ruler of Besnagar by King Antialkidas. Heliodoros dedicated a monolithic column to the honour of Vāsudeva, a form of Vishnu, whose worshipper he professed himself to be. The document is of value in the history of Indian religions as giving an early date for the *bhakti* cult of Vāsudeva, and as proving that people with Greek names and in the service of Greek kings had become the followers of Hindu gods.

End of Bactrian monarchy. In the interval between 140 and 120 B.C. a swarm of nomad tribes from the interior of Asia, consisting of Śakas and others, attacked both Parthia and Bactria.[2] Two Parthian

---

[1] Many numismatists now believe that there were two kings of the name of Demetrios, and that most of the coins of Indian type hitherto attributed to Demetrios I are in fact those of Demetrios II. There is now considerable doubt as to the extent of Demetrios I's conquests in India, and he may not have penetrated far beyond the Hindu Kush. [Ed.]

[2] Indians used the term Śaka (Saka, Shaka) vaguely to denote foreigners from

kings were killed, and Greek rule in Bactria was extinguished. The last Graeco-Bactrian king was Heliokles, a member of the family of Eukratides.[1] The end of the Bactrian monarchy, which had lasted little more than a century, may be placed somewhere between 140 and 130 B.C. Precise dates are not ascertainable.

Parthia and India. Mithridates I of Parthia (c. 171 to 136 B.C.) had annexed the country between the Indus and the Hydaspes, that is to say, the kingdom of Taxila, towards the close of his reign, about 138 B.C.[2] The kings of Parthia were not able to retain effective control of the territory thus annexed, but the connexion established between the Parthian or Persian kingdom and India was sufficiently close to bring about the adoption of the Persian title of Satrap or Great Satrap by many Indian rulers of foreign origin. The use of that title continued for several hundred years. The last ruler to use it was the Śaka Satrap of Saurashtra who was conquered and dethroned by the Gupta emperor towards the close of the fourth century A.D.

Indo-Greek and Indo-Parthian princes. Although Heliokles, the last Greek King of Bactria, probably had disappeared before 130 B.C., numerous princes with Greek names continued to govern principalities in the Kabul country and along the north-western frontier of India much longer. The last of them was named Hermaios, who ruled in the first century after Christ.

During the interval sundry ruling families of foreigners appear in the frontier provinces, some of the princes having distinctly Parthian names. The details are too obscure and doubtful for discussion in this work.

Gondophernes and St. Thomas. The most interesting personage among those princes is Gondophernes, whose name is clearly Persian or Parthian. His reign may be placed between A.D. 20 and 48. He ruled an extensive realm which included Arachosia or the Qandahar country, Kabul, and the kingdom of Taxila. The name of Gondophernes or Gondophares has become more or less familiar to European readers because early ecclesiastical legends, going back to the third century A.D., affirm that the apostle St. Thomas preached Christianity in his dominions and was there martyred. Another group of traditions alleges that the same apostle was martyred at Mailāpur (Mylapore) near Madras. Both stories obviously cannot be true; even an apostle can die but once. My personal impression, formed after much examination of the evidence, is that the story of the martyrdom in southern India is the better supported of the two versions of the saint's death. But it is by no means certain that St. Thomas was martyred at all. An early writer,

beyond the passes. In later times the name was often applied to Muslims, as in the *Ekalinga Mahātmya.*

[1] The recent discoveries of Attic tetradrachms, purely Greek in style and legend, issued by later kings down to Hermaios, suggest that some parts of Bactria at least remained in Greek hands until the end of the Greek kingdoms. [Ed.]

[2] This statement, based on an ambiguous passage in Orosius, is by no means certain. [Ed.]

Heracleon the Gnostic, asserts that he ended his days in peace. The tale of his visit to the kingdom of Gondophernes may have originated as an explanation of the early presence in that region of 'Christians of St. Thomas', disciples who followed the practices associated with the name of the apostle. Some writers try to reconcile the two stories in some measure by guessing that St. Thomas may have first visited the kingdom of Gondophernes and then gone on to the peninsula. But that guess is no real explanation. The subject has been discussed by many authors from every possible point of view, and immense learning has been invoked in the hope of establishing one or other hypothesis, without reaching any conclusion approaching certainty. There is no reason to expect that additional evidence will be discovered.

The puzzle of Kushān dates. The principal puzzle of Indian history still awaiting solution is that concerning the chronology of the powerful foreign kings of Kabul and north-western India who belonged to the Kushān clan or sept of the Yueh-chi horde of nomads. The most famous of those kings being Kanishka, the problem is often stated as being 'the question of the date of Kanishka'. Until it is solved, the history of northern India for three centuries or so must remain in an unsatisfactory condition. But definite progress towards a conclusive solution of the problem based upon solid facts has been made. It may now be affirmed with confidence that the order of the five leading Kushān kings is finally settled,[1] and that the uncertainty as to the chronology has been reduced to a period of sixty years in round numbers. Or to state it otherwise, the question is, 'Did Kanishka come to the throne in A.D. 78, or about forty or sixty years later?'

When the third edition of the *Early History of India* was published in 1914, my narrative was based upon the working hypothesis that Kanishka's accession took place in A.D. 78; although it was admitted to be possible that the true date might be later. Further consideration of the evidence now available leads me to follow Sir John Marshall and Professor Sten Konow in dating the beginning of Kanishka's reign approximately in A.D. 120, a date which I had advocated many years ago on different grounds. In the following narrative the correctness of that hypothesis will be assumed without any examination of the intricate archaeological evidence, which cannot be presented advantageously in a brief summary.[2]

---

[1] The five referred to are Kadphises I, Kadphises II, Kanishka, Huvishka, and Vāsudeva I. The word Englished as Kushān appears in various forms in diverse scripts and languages. The long vowel in the second syllable is correct. The name of the sept may have been really Kuṣi or Kushi (nom. from stem *Kuṣa*); the word represented by 'Kushān' being a genitive plural. It would, perhaps, be more correct to speak of the Kushi (Kuṣi) sept, but I retain Kushān as being familiar and in accordance with the views of some scholars.

[2] This section is left virtually as Dr. Smith wrote it. The last thirty years have brought us little nearer an agreed date for Kanishka. Of the two most recent students of the problem Dr. Ghirshman advocates A.D. 144, and Mme Lohuizen de Leeuw A.D. 78. The date suggested by Professor Konow, A.D. 128, still has its supporters. Dr. Smith's approximation is substantially in agreement with it. [Ed.]

The Yueh-chi migration. The horde of nomads called the Great Yueh-chi, who were driven out of western China between 174 and 160 B.C., migrated westwards along the road to the north of the Taklamakān (Gobi) desert. In the course of their long wanderings they encountered another nomad nation, the Sakai or Śakas (Se or Sai of the Chinese), who dwelt to the north of the Jaxartes or Syr Darya river. The Sakai, being defeated by the Yueh-chi, were constrained to yield their pasture-grounds to the victors, and themselves to seek new quarters in the borderlands of India.

The victorious Yueh-chi, in their turn, were vanquished by a third horde named Wu-sun and driven from the lands which had been wrested from the Śakas. The Yueh-chi then settled in the valley of the Oxus, with their headquarters to the north of the river, but probably exercising more or less authority over Bactria to the south.

Kadphises I. In the course of time, which cannot be defined precisely, the Great Yueh-chi horde lost their nomad habits and occupied the Bactrian lands, becoming divided into five principalities, at a date which cannot be determined with any approach to exactness. More than a century later, the Kushān section or sept of the Yueh-chi attained a predominant position over the other sections of the horde, under the leadership of a chieftain named Kujula-Kara-Kadphises, who is conveniently designated by modern historians as Kadphises I. He may be regarded as having become King of the Kushāns or Yueh-chi from somewhere about A.D. 40.[1]

Kadphises I was soon impelled to attack the rich territories to the south of the Hindu Kush, presumably finding the limits of Bactria too narrow for the growing population of his dominions.

He enjoyed a long life and prosperous reign, in the course of which he consolidated his strength in Bactria and conquered the Kabul region south of the mountains. He annexed Ki-pin, which may be interpreted with good reason as meaning Gandhāra, including the kingdom of Taxila to the east of the Indus, where he seems to have succeeded Gondophernes in A.D. 48. He also attacked the Parthians.

The operations indicated must have occupied many years, during which the Kushān or Indo-Scythian rule gradually replaced that of the Indo-Greek, Śaka, and Indo-Parthian princes in the Indian borderlands. Kadphises I attained the age of eighty, and may be assumed to have died about A.D. 77 or 78.

Kadphises II. He was succeeded by his son Wima Kadphises, whose personal name is transliterated as Wēmo (Ooēmo) in his Greek coin legends, and is given as Yen-kao-ching by Chinese historians. It is convenient to designate him as Kadphises II. He set himself to accomplish the conquest of northern India, and effected his purpose. It is reasonable to believe, although strict proof is lacking, that the Śaka era of A.D. 78 dates from the beginning of his reign,

[1] Between A.D. 25 and 81, but nearer to the earlier year, according to Franke, pp. 72, 73.

either from his actual accession or from his formal enthronement a little·later. That hypothesis seems now to present less difficulties than any other.[1] The evidence for the extent of the Indian conquests of Kadphises II is meagre and rests largely on the distribution of his extremely numerous coins. The abundance of his coinage certainly implies a long reign. He seems to have secured the supremacy in the Gangetic valley at least as far down as Benares, and also of the Indus basin. It may be that his power extended southwards as far as the Narbada. The Śaka Satraps in Malwa and western India appear to have owned him as their overlord.

Collision with China. The course of his conquests brought him into collision with the Chinese, who had first entered into relations with western Asia in the reign of the Emperor Wu-ti (140 to 86 B.C.), when an embassy under Chang-kien was dispatched from the Middle Kingdom to the powers on the Oxus. Chang-kien returned home about 120 B.C., the exact date being stated variously by different authorities. For some reason or other Chinese intercourse with the western regions ceased in A.D. 8; and when the first Han dynasty came to an end in A.D. 23, Chinese influence in those countries had been reduced to nothing.

Fifty years later Chinese ambition reasserted itself, and General Pan-chao, in the time from A.D. 73 to 102, advanced victoriously through Khotan and the other districts now called Chinese Turkistan and across Persia, until he carried his country's flag right into Parthia and to the shores of the Caspian Sea.

The advance through Khotan opened up the road to the south of the Taklamakān (Gobi) desert. The route to the north of that desert was cleared in A.D. 94 by the reduction of Kucha and Karāshahr.

Chinese victory. The progress of Chinese arms alarmed the Kushān monarch, namely Kadphises II, according to the chronology adopted in this chapter. In A.D. 87 he boldly asserted his equality with the Son of Heaven by demanding in marriage the hand of a Chinese princess. The proposal being resented as an insult, General Pan-chao arrested the Kushān envoy and sent him home. Kadphises II then prepared a formidable force of 70,000 cavalry under the command of his Viceroy Si, which was dispatched across the Tsung-ling range or Tāghdum-bāsh Pamir. The appalling difficulties of the route, involving the crossing of the Tāshkurghān Pass, 14,000 feet high, so shattered the Kushān host that when it emerged in the plain of either Kāshgar or Yarkand it was easily defeated. Kadphises II was compelled to pay tribute to China, and the Chinese annals note that in the reign of the Emperor Ho-ti (A.D. 89–105) the Indians often sent missions to China bearing presents which were regarded as tribute.

Interval between Kadphises II and Kanishka. The extensive issues of coin by Kadphises II prove, as already observed, that he

---

[1] Other authorities believe that this era was founded either by Kanishka, by Kadphises I, or by the Kshaharāta Satrap Nahapāna (above, p. 140). [Ed.]

enjoyed a reign of considerable length. But, inasmuch as his father, according to Chinese authority, had died at the age of eighty, it is unlikely that Kadphises II can have reigned for much more than thirty years. The close of his life and rule may be placed somewhere about A.D. 110. It is recorded that he appointed military governors to rule the Indian provinces, and it is possible that those officers controlled India for some years after his decease. They may have issued the anonymous coins of the so-called Nameless King, who used the title of Sotēr Megas or Great Saviour, and certainly was closely associated with Kadphises II. Kanishka, the next king, was not a son of Kadphises II, and his father's name may have been Vajheshka; and there is some reason for believing that he was a member of the Little Yueh-chi section of the horde, who seem to have settled in the Khotan region, whereas his predecessor was a Great Yueh-chi from Bactria. On the whole, it seems to be probable that an appreciable space of time intervened between the death of Kadphises II, which may be dated in or about A.D. 110, and the accession of Kanishka, which may be assigned to A.D. 120 approximately. Nothing is on record to show how the sceptre was transferred from the hands of Kadphises II to those of Kanishka.

Era of Kanishka. A new era running from the accession of Kanishka, or perhaps from his formal enthronement a little later, came into use in northern India, including Kabul. The regnal reckoning thus started either by Kanishka himself, or by his subjects, continued to be used by people in the reigns of his successors. Private inscriptions certainly so dated extend from the year 3 to the year 99. Consequently, if the date of Kanishka's accession was known, the chronology of the period would exhibit few difficulties.

Kanishka's dominions. Kanishka is described as having been King of Gandhāra. The capital of his Indian dominions, and apparently the seat of his central government, was Purushapura or Peshawar, where he erected remarkable Buddhist buildings. Portions of those edifices have been disclosed by the researches of the Archaeological Department. Kanishka in his earlier years annexed the valley of Kashmir, consolidated his government in the basins of the Indus and Ganges, and warred with the Parthians. At a later date he avenged his predecessor's defeat in Chinese Turkistan. There seems to be no doubt that he succeeded in accomplishing the supremely difficult feat of conveying an effective army across the Pamirs and subduing the chiefs or petty kings in the Khotan, Yarkand, and Kashgar regions who had been tributary to China. He exacted from one of those princes hostages who were assigned residences in the Panjab and the Kabul province. Tradition affirms that Kanishka, who must have been then an old man, was smothered while on his last northern campaign by officers who had grown weary of exile beyond the passes. Kanishka spent most of his life in waging successful wars. While absent on his distant expeditions he left the government of the Indian province in the hands, first of Vāsishka, apparently his elder, and then of Huvishka, apparently his younger son. Those princes, while acting as their father's colleagues, were allowed to assume full regal titles. Vāsishka evidently predeceased Kanishka, but Huvishka lived to ascend the imperial throne, which he occupied for at least twelve, and perhaps for twenty, years. No coins bearing the name of Vāsishka are known. The extensive and varied coinage of Huvishka may have been issued only after Kanishka's death, but it is possible that part of it was minted while Huvishka occupied the position of his father's colleague.[1]

The Chinese admissions that their information concerning the Western countries was interrupted by the death in A.D. 124 of Pan-yang, the historian, who had succeeded his father Pan-chao as Governor of Turkistan, and that Khotan was lost to the empire in A.D. 152 as the result of a local revolution in the course of which Governor Wang-king was killed, are in agreement with the belief that Kanishka established his suzerainty over the chiefs or petty kings of Chinese Turkistan between the years 125 and 160. The silence of Chinese annalists, as distinguished from Buddhist story-tellers, concerning Kanishka is explained by the well-known unwillingness of the historians of the Middle Kingdom to dwell on events discreditable to the imperial court.

Kanishka's religion. Modern research has disclosed the existence of a large number of inscriptions incised in the reigns of Kanishka and his successors, which give some indications of the extent of his dominions and other particulars concerning him. But his fame rests mainly on the fact that in the latter part of his career he became an active and liberal patron of the Buddhist church. Buddhist authors, writing for purposes of edification, consequently treat him as having been a second Aśoka. We do not know what reasons induced Kanishka to show favour to the Buddhist church. The explanations given in the books look like an adaptation of the stories about the conversion of Aśoka. Kanishka, as his coins prove, honoured a curiously mixed assortment of Zoroastrian, Greek, and Mithraic gods, to which Indian deities were added. We find the Sun and Moon with their Greek names, Hēlios and Selēnē (spelt 'Salēnē'), as well as Herakles. The moon again appears as an Iranian deity under the name of Māo. Other strangely named gods, obviously Iranian or Persian, are Athro, or Fire, Miiro, or the Sun, Nāna, Oaninda, Lrooaspo, &c. The Indian

---

[1] The theory stated in the text, first suggested by R. D. Banerji, is the most adequate explanation of the facts. The known dates include:

Kanishka—year 3 (Sārnāth); 18 (Mānikyāla); and 41 (Āra).

Vāsishka—with full titles, year 24 in words and figures (Isāpur, Mathura); year ? 28 (Sanchi, probable); year 29 (Mathura, possible):

Huvishka—year 33 (Mathura); 51 (Wardak, west of Kabul); and 60 (Mathura):

Vāsudeva—74 (Mathura); 80, 83, 87, 98 (same place).

Others have suggested that the Āra Inscription is of a second Kanishka, or merely records a date in the era founded by him.

All the dated inscriptions were recorded by private persons; none are official.

Śiva, who had already appeared in a two-armed form on the coins of the Parthian Gondophernes and the Great Yueh-chi, Kadphises II, is seen on Kanishka's coins in both the two-armed and four-armed forms. Buddha (Boddo) is figured standing and clad in Greek costume; and also seated in the Indian manner. The queer assembly of deities offers an unlimited field for speculation. Perhaps it may be safely said that Kanishka followed the practice of his Parthian predecessors in adopting a loose form of Zoroastrianism which freely admitted the deities of other creeds. We know that Indian monarchs, as, for example, Harsha of Kanauj in the seventh century, often felt themselves at liberty to mix Buddhism with other cults; and it is probable that Kanishka, even after his alleged 'conversion', continued to honour his old gods. His successor, Huvishka, certainly did so. It is obvious that the character of Buddhism in north-western India and the neighbouring countries must have been profoundly modified by the lax practices to which the coinage of Kanishka and Huvishka bears witness.

Kanishka's Council. Kanishka followed the example set by Aśoka in convening a council of theologians to settle disputed questions of Buddhist faith and practice. The decrees of the council took the form of authorized commentaries on the Canon, which were engraved on sheets of copper, enclosed in a stone coffer, and placed for safety in a *stūpa* erected for the purpose at the capital of Kashmir where the council met. It is just possible that the documents may be still in existence and may be disclosed by some lucky excavation. The Buddhist sect which alone sent delegates to Kanishka's Council was formally classed as belonging to the *Hīna-yāna*, or Lesser Vehicle, the more primitive form of Buddhism. But the cult actually practised more extensively in Kanishka's time was that usually associated with the *Mahā-yāna*, or Great Vehicle, as is clearly proved by the numerous sculptures of the age.

Images of Buddha. The early Buddhists, whose doctrines are expressed in the stone pictures of Sanchi and Barhut (Bharhut), did not dare to form an image of their dead teacher. When they wished to indicate his presence in a scene they merely suggested it by a symbol, an empty seat, a pair of footprints, and so forth.

The Buddhists of the Kushān age had no such scruples. They loved to picture Gautama as the Sage of the Śākyas, the Bodhisattva, and the Buddha in every incident of his last life as well as of his previous births. His image in endless forms and replicas became the principal element in Buddhist sculpture. The change obviously was the result of foreign influence, chiefly Greek (or more accurately, Hellenistic), and Persian or Iranian.

Transformation of Buddhism. The transformation of Buddhism which was effected for the most part during the first two or three centuries of the Christian era is an event of such significance in the history of India and of the world that it deserves exposition at some length. The observations following, which were printed many years ago, still express my opinion and are, I think, in accordance with the facts. Although they are rather long, it seems worth while to reprint them without material modification.

Buddhism had been introduced into the countries on the north-western frontier of India as early as the reign of Aśoka in the third century B.C.; and in 2 B.C. an unnamed Yueh-chi chieftain was interested in the religion of Gautama so far as to communicate Buddhist scriptures to a Chinese envoy. Buddhist sculpture of some sort must have been known in those regions for centuries before the time of Kanishka, but it was not the product of an organized school under liberal and powerful royal patronage, so that remains of such early Buddhist art are rare. Probably the ancient works were executed chiefly in wood.

When the great monarch Kanishka actively espoused the cause of Buddhism and essayed to play the part of a second Aśoka, the devotion of the adherents of the favoured creed received an impulse which speedily resulted in the copious production of artistic creations of no small merit.

The religious system which found its best artistic exponents in the sculptors of Kanishka's court must have been of foreign origin to a large extent. Primitive Buddhism, as expounded in the *Dialogues*, so well translated by Professor Rhys Davids, was an Indian product based on the Indian ideas of rebirth, of the survival and transmission of *karma*, or the net result of human action, and of the blessedness of escape from the pains of being.

Primitive Buddhism added to those theories, which were the common possession of nearly all schools of Indian thought, an excellent practical system of ethics inculcating a Stoic devotion to duty for its own sake, combined with a tender regard for the feelings of all living creatures, human or animal; and so brought about a combination of intellect with emotion, deserving the name of a religion, even though it had no god.

But when the conversion of Aśoka made the fortune of Buddhism it sowed at the same time the seeds of decay. The missionaries of the imperial preacher and their successors carried the doctrines of Gautama from the banks of the Ganges to the snows of the Himalaya, the deserts of central Asia, and the bazaars of Alexandria.

The teaching which was exactly attuned to the inmost feelings of a congregation in Benares needed fundamental change before it could move the heart of the sturdy mountaineer, the nomad horseman, or the hellenized Alexandrian. The moment Indian Buddhism began its foreign travels it was bound to change. We can see the transformation which was effected, although most of the steps of the evolution are hidden from us.

Influence of the Roman empire. Undoubtedly one of the principal agencies engaged in effecting the momentous change was the unification of the civilized world, excepting India, Parthia, and China, under the sway of the Caesars.[1] The general peace of the Roman empire was not seriously impaired by frontier wars, palace revolutions, or the freaks of half-mad emperors. During that long-continued peace nascent Christianity met full-grown Buddhism in the academies and markets of Asia and Egypt, while both religions were exposed to the influences of surrounding paganism in many forms and of the countless works of art which gave expression to the ideas of polytheism. The ancient religion of Persia contributed to the ferment of human thought, excited by improved facilities for international communication and by the incessant clash of rival civilizations.

Novel ideals. In such environment Buddhism was transmuted from its old Indian self into a practically new religion. The specially Indian ideas upon which it had been founded sank into comparative obscurity, while novel ideals came to the front. The quietist teacher of an order of begging friars, who had counted as a glorious victory the recognition of the truth, as he deemed it, that 'after this present life there would be no beyond'; and that 'on the dissolution of the body, beyond the end of his life, neither gods nor men shall see him', was gradually replaced by a divinity ever present to the hearts of the faithful, with his ears open to their prayers, and served by a hierarchy of Bodhisattvas and other beings, acting as mediators between him and sinful men.

In a word, the veneration for a dead Teacher passed into the worship of a living Saviour. That, so far as I understand the matter, is the essential difference between the old Indian Buddhism, the so-called Hīnayāna, and the newer Buddhism or Mahāyāna. Although the delegates to Kanishka's Council were classed officially as Hīnayānists, the popular cult of the time unquestionably was the expression of Mahāyānist ideas, which were formulated and propagated by Nāgār-juna, who was to some extent the contemporary of Kanishka.

The age from A.D. 105 to 273, during which Palmyra flourished as the chief emporium for the commerce between East and West, and the Kushān kings ruled in north-western India, may be taken as marking the time when the Mahāyāna system was developed and the art forming its outward expression attained its highest achievement. It is hardly necessary to add that the movements of the human mind never fit themselves into accurately demarcated chronological compartments, and that all evolutions, such as that of the new Buddhism, have had their beginnings long before the process of change becomes clearly visible. The rigorous doctrine of the earliest form of Buddhism was too chilly to retain a hold upon the hearts of men unless when warmed and quickened by human emotion. The Buddhism of the people in every

---

[1] I agree with Lüders that in the Āra inscription Kanishka took the title of 'Caesar' (Kaïsarasa); but, as it is possible to dispute the reading, it is better not to lay stress upon it. Kanishka's accumulated titles imply a claim to the sovereignty of the four quarters of the world (Sitzungsber. d. königl. Preuss. Akad. der Wissenschaften, 1912, p. 829).

country always has been different from that of the Canon, although the authority of the scriptures is nowhere formally disputed. When it is said that the development of the Mahāyāna was mainly the result of foreign influence, I must not be understood as denying that the germs of the transformed religion may have existed in India from a very early stage in the history of the Buddhist church.

Literature and art. In literature the memory of Kanishka is associated with the names of the eminent Buddhist writers Nāgārjuna, Aśvaghosha, and Vasumitra. Aśvaghosha is described as having been a poet, musician, scholar, religious controversialist, and zealous Buddhist monk, orthodox in creed, and a strict observer of discipline. Charaka, the most celebrated of the early Indian authors treating of medical science, is reputed to have been the court physician of Kanishka.

Architecture, with its subsidiary art of sculpture, enjoyed the liberal patronage of Kanishka, who was, like Aśoka, a great builder. The tower at Peshawar, built over the relics of Buddha, and chiefly constructed of timber, stood 400 feet high. The Sir Sukh section of Taxila hides the ruins of the city built by Kanishka. A town in Kashmir, still represented by a village, bore the king's name; and Mathura (Muttra) on the Jumna was adorned by numerous fine buildings and artistic sculptures during the reigns of Kanishka and his successors. A remarkable portrait statue of Kanishka, unluckily lacking the head, has been found near Mathura, with similar statues of other princes of his line. Those works do not betray any marks of Greek influence.

The Gandhāra school. Much of the Buddhist sculpture of the time of Kanishka and his successors is executed in the style of Gandhāra, the province on the frontier which included both Peshawar and Taxila. That style is often and properly called Graeco-Buddhist because the forms of Greek art were applied to Buddhist subjects, with considerable artistic success in many cases. Images of Buddha appear in the likeness of Apollo, the Yaksha Kuvera is posed in the fashion of the Phidian Zeus, and so on. The drapery follows Hellenistic models. The style was transmitted to the Far East through Chinese Turkistan, and the figures of Buddha now made in China and Japan exhibit distinct traces of the Hellenistic modes in vogue at the court of Kanishka. The explorations of Sir M. A. Stein and other archaeologists have proved that the Khotan region in Chinese Turkistan was the meeting place of four civilizations—Greek, Indian, Iranian, and Chinese—during the early centuries of the Christian era, including the reign of Kanishka. The eastward advance of the Roman frontier in the days of Trajan and Hadrian (A.D. 98–138) was favourable to the spread of Hellenistic ideas and artistic forms in India and other Asiatic countries. The Indo-Greek artists found their inspiration in the schools of Alexandria, and of Pergamon, Ephesus, and other places in Asia Minor rather than in the works of the earlier artists of Greece. In other words, the Gandhāra style is Graeco-Roman, based on the cosmopolitan art of Asia Minor

PLATE 7

a. The Great Stupa, Sanchi

b. Bodhisattva,
Gandhāra School

c. Buddha, Sārnāth.
Fifth century

PLATE 8

a. Headless Statue of Kanishka,
Mathurā

b. Medallion, Amarāvatī

c. Indian Ivory
Goddess from
Herculaneum

and the Roman empire as practised in the first three centuries of the Christian era. Much of the best work in that style was executed during the second century A.D. in the reigns of Kanishka and Huvishka.

Other sculpture. Although the Gandhāra school of sculpture was the most prolific, the art of other centres in the age of Kanishka and Huvishka was not negligible in either quantity or quality. Sārnāth near Benares, Mathura on the Jumna, and Amarāvatī on the Krishna (Kistna) river in the Guntur District, Madras, offer many examples of excellent sculpture. Each of the three localities named had a distinctive style. The best known works are the elaborate bas-reliefs from Amarāvatī, more or less familiar to all visitors to the British Museum from the exhibition of a series of specimens in the entrance hall of that institution. Tradition connects the buildings at Amarāvatī with Nāgārjuna. The work there extended over many years, but most of it probably was executed in Huvishka's reign.

Huvishka. Huvishka or Hushka, presumably Kanishka's son, who had governed the Indian provinces for many years on behalf of his father, while he was engaged in distant wars, succeeded to the imperial throne about A.D. 162. Little is known about the events of his reign. His coinage, which exhibits considerable artistic merit, is even more varied than that of Kanishka, and presents recognizable portraits of the king as a burly, middle-aged or elderly man with a large nose. The Yueh-chi princes had no resemblance to the 'narrow-eyed' Mongolians. They were big pink-faced men, built on a large scale, and may possibly have been related to the Turks. They dressed in long-skirted coats, wore soft leather boots, and sat on chairs in European fashion. Their language was an Iranian form of speech; and their religion, as we have seen, was a modified Zoroastrianism. The name of Huvishka was associated with a town in Kashmir and with a Buddhist monastery at Mathura. His coin types exhibit the strange medley of Greek, Indian, and Iranian deities seen on the coinage of Kanishka, but no distinctively Buddhist coins have been found. So far as appears, he retained possession of the extensive territories ruled by Kanishka. His death may be dated somewhere about A.D. 180 or 185. He must have been an old or elderly man, because his inscriptions, which overlap those of his predecessor, range from the year 33 to the year 60 of Kanishka's regnal era.

End of the Kushān empire. Huvishka's successor was Vāsudeva I, in whose time the empire began to break up. The manner in which the Kushān power in India came to an end has not been clearly ascertained, but there is no doubt that Huvishka was the last monarch to maintain an extensive empire until his death. Such indications as exist concerning the decay of the empire are chiefly derived from the study of coins, and the inferences drawn from material so scanty are necessarily dubious. But it is certain that the coinage of the successors of Vāsudeva, some of whom bore the same name, became gradually persianized, and the suggestion seems to be reasonable that the dissolution of the Kushān empire in India was connected in some way with the rise of the Sassanian power in A.D. 226, and the subsequent conquests of Ardashīr Pāpakān, the first Sassanian king, and his successors, which are alleged to have extended to the Indus, but without sufficient evidence. Strong Kushān dynasties continued to exist in Kabul and the neighbouring countries until the Hun invasions of the fifth century; and some principalities survived even until the Arab conquest of Persia in the seventh century.

The name of Vāsudeva proves the rapidity with which the Kushāns had been changed into Hindus. Its form suggests the worship of Vishnu as Vāsudeva, but the coins bear the images of Śiva and his bull, which had already appeared on the coins of Kadphises II. The history of the third century, whether religious or political, is too obscure and uncertain for further discussion in these pages.

Greek influence. The question as to the extent of Greek, or, more accurately, Hellenistic influence upon Indian civilization is of interest, and always has been warmly debated by European scholars, who naturally desire to find links connecting the unfamiliar doings of isolated India with the familiar Greek ideas and institutions to which Europe owes so much. It will be well, therefore, to devote a few pages to the consideration of the facts bearing on the question. The trade relations between the Hellenistic world and India which existed for centuries, and will be noticed presently, are not relevant in this connexion. Such relations had little effect on the ideas or institutions of either India or Europe. The business people, then, as they usually do in all ages, confined themselves to their trade affairs without troubling about anything else. They left no records, and, so far as appears, did not communicate much information to scholarly persons like Pliny and Strabo. If modern Europe had to depend upon Bombay and Calcutta merchants for its knowledge of India it would not know much.

Effects of Alexander's campaign. Alexander's fierce campaign produced no direct effects upon either the ideas or the institutions of India. During his brief stay in the basin of the Indus he was occupied almost solely with fighting. Presumably he was remembered by the ordinary natives of the regions which he harried merely as a demon-like outer barbarian who hanged Brahmans without scruple and won battles by impious methods in defiance of the scriptures. The Indians felt no desire to learn from such a person. They declined to learn from him even the art of war, in which he was a master; preferring to go on in their own traditional way, trusting to a 'fourfold' army and hosts of elephants. When Chandragupta Maurya swept the Macedonian garrisons out of the Panjab, that was the end of Hellenism on Indian soil for the time. The failure of the invasion by Seleukos Nikator a few years later secured India from all further Greek aggression.

Maurya civilization. Then followed seventy or eighty years of peaceful, friendly intercourse between the Maurya court and the

Hellenistic princes of Asia and Africa, to which we are indebted for the valuable account of the Maurya empire compiled by Megasthenes. His book does not indicate any trace of Hellenic influence upon the political or social institutions of India. On the contrary, the close agreement of the testimony recorded by the Greek ambassador with the statements of the Sanskrit books proves clearly that the Maurya government managed its affairs after its own fashion in general accordance with Hindu tradition, borrowing something from Persia but nothing from Greece. Even the Maurya coinage continued to be purely Indian, or at any rate Asiatic, in character. Aśoka did not care to imitate the beautiful Bactrian issues, or to follow Greek example by putting his image and superscription on his coins. He was content to use the primitive punch-marked, cast, or rudely struck coins which had formed the currency of India before his time.

In the domain of the fine arts some indications of the operation of Greek example and good taste may be discerned. The high quality of Maurya sculpture clearly was due to the happy blending of Indian, Iranian, and Hellenic factors.

It is reasonable also to connect Aśoka's preference for the use of stone in building and sculpture with the opportunities which he enjoyed for studying the Hellenistic practice of working in permanent material.

The design of Indian buildings, so far as is known, rarely owed anything to Greek principles, but the excavations at Taxila suggest, or perhaps prove, that in some cases Greek models may have been imitated in that region. Columns of the Ionic order undoubtedly were inserted in Taxilan buildings. Taxila, however, was half-foreign and only half-Indian, so that practices considered legitimate there would not have been approved in the interior provinces.

Demetrios and others. Direct contact between the Hellenistic states and the Panjab was brought about early in the second century B.C., forty or fifty years after Aśoka's death, by the conquests of the Bactrian sovereign Demetrios, 'King of the Indians'. The elephant's head on his coins is a record of his Indian connexions. A little later we find a king with the Greek name of Pantaleon striking coins in the square Indian shape, copied from the indigenous coinage of Taxila. About the same time Agathokles also adopted bilingual legends, first employed by Demetrios, giving his regal style in both Greek and a kind of Prakrit. The Indian tongue is inscribed in Brāhmī, an old form of the script now called Nāgarī or Devanāgarī. Bilingual legends continued to be used by many kings.

Coin types. Antialkidas, the King of Taxila who sent Heliodoros as envoy to the Raja of Besnagar, adopted the Indian standard of weight for his coins. The idea of striking coins with two dies, obverse and reverse, one side bearing the effigy and titles of the king, was foreign to India, and was gradually adopted by Indian princes in imitation of the issues minted by dynasties of foreign origin—Śakas, Parthians,

Yueh-chi, and the rest. Indian artists, who attained brilliant success in other fields, never cared greatly about die-cutting, and consequently never produced a really fine coin. The best Indian coins, being a few gold pieces struck by the Gupta kings before and after A.D. 400 under the influence of Western models, although good, are not first rate, and do not bear comparison with the magnificent dies of the earlier Bactrian kings, not to speak of Syracusan masterpieces.

Indo-Roman gold coinage. The Yueh-chi, Indo Scythian, or Kushān kings of the first and second centuries A.D. evidently maintained active trade communications with the Roman empire, then far extended eastwards. Hence we find an unmistakable copy of the head of either Augustus, Tiberius, or Claudius on certain coins of Kadphises I. Kadphises II carried much farther his imitation of Roman usage by striking an abundant and excellent issue of gold coins agreeing closely with the Caesarian *aurei* in weight and not much inferior in fineness. Imported Roman coins have been often found in the Panjab, Kabul, and neighbouring territories, but the bulk of the considerable inflow into India of Roman gold, as testified to by Pliny in A.D. 77, seems so far as the northern kingdom was concerned, to have been melted down and reissued as orientalized *aurei*, first by Kadphises II, and afterwards by Kanishka, Huvishka, and Vāsudeva. In peninsular India the Roman *aureus* circulated as currency, just as the British sovereign once passed current in many lands. The gold indigenous currency of the south, introduced apparently at a later date, has never had any connexion with European models.

Greek script and gods. Kanishka, Huvishka, and Vāsudeva used for their coin legends their own language, a near relative of the Śaka tongue, but engraved it in a form of Greek characters only. For some reason or other they did not use any Asiatic script. The strange mixture of deities found in the coin types of Kanishka and Huvishka and the peculiarities of the Graeco-Buddhist school of sculpture have been sufficiently discussed above. The presumed influence of Hellenistic polytheism on the development of the later Buddhism has also been examined. The evidence of all kinds shows that, while foreigners like Heliodoros were ready to adopt Indian gods, the Indians were slow to worship Greek deities. The few Greek deities named on the Kanishka and Huvishka coins belonged also to the Persian pantheon and were taken over from the Parthians. The tendency certainly was for Indo-Greek princes and people to become hinduized, rather than for the Indian Rajas and their subjects to become hellenized. The Brahmans were well able to take care of themselves and to keep at arm's length any foreign notions which they did not wish to assimilate.

Scanty traces of Greek rule. The visible traces of the long-continued Greek rule on the north-western frontier of India are surprisingly scanty, if the coin legends be excluded from consideration. No inscription in the Greek language or script has yet been found, and the Greek names occurring in inscriptions are few, perhaps half a dozen. Two records, one of which comes from Taxila, mention the district officer serving under some Indo-Greek king by the designation of 'meridarch', a detail which indicates the use of Greek for official purposes to a certain extent. Greek must have been spoken at the courts of the Indo-Greek kings, but the language does not seem to have spread among any Indian nation. The exclusive use of a Greek script to express the legends on the coins of Kanishka and his successors may be due, as has been suggested, to the language having been first reduced to writing in the Greek character. The Greek lettering on the coins does not imply a popular knowledge of the Greek alphabet. Only a small proportion of the Indian population has ever been able to read coin legends, whatever the language or script might be. The coins of the ruling power for the time being are accepted as currency without the slightest regard to the inscriptions on them.

Summary. To sum up, it may be said that Greek or Hellenistic influence upon India was slight and superficial, much less in amount than I believed it to be when the subject first attracted me. If any considerable modification of the Indian religions was effected by contact with Hellenism, Buddhism alone was concerned, Jainism and Brahmanical Hinduism remaining untouched. The remarkable local school of Graeco-Buddhist sculpture in the Gandhāra frontier province, which was imitated to some extent in the interior, permanently determined the type of Chinese and Japanese Buddhist images. Some details of Hellenistic ornament became widely diffused throughout India. An undefinable but, I think, real element of Greek feeling may be discerned in the excellent sculpture of Aśoka's age. If any buildings on a Greek plan were erected they were apparently confined to Gandhāra. Indian artists never produced fine coin-dies. Any at all good were copied from or suggested by Graeco-Roman models. The Greek language never obtained wide currency in India, but must have been used to some extent at the courts of the border princes with Greek names. Many of those princes must have been of mixed blood. 'The Indo-Bactrian Greeks', it has been said, 'were the Goanese of antiquity.' The early medical knowledge as expounded by Charaka, Kanishka's physician, has been supposed to betray some acquaintance with the works of Hippocrates, but the proof does not seem to be convincing.

Long after the period treated in this chapter, Western influence again made itself felt in Indian art, literature, and science during the rule of the Gupta emperors. That subject will be noticed in due course.

Commerce by land. Some reference has been made to the commerce between India and the Roman empire during the rule of the Kushān kings. The overland commerce of India with western Asia dated from remote times and was conducted by several routes across Persia, Mesopotamia, and Asia Minor. The Chinese silk trade followed the same roads. From time to time these trans-Asian routes were blocked by Parthian rivalry with Rome, and traffic was diverted to the west-coast ports of India, notably Barygaza or Broach, whence it was sea-borne to the Persian Gulf or the Red Sea.

Commerce by sea. The sea-borne trade of the peninsula with Europe through Egypt does not seem to have been considerable before the time of Claudius, when the course of the monsoons is said to have become known to the Roman merchants. But a certain amount of commerce with Egypt must have existed from much earlier days. In 20 B.C. we hear of a mission to Augustus from 'King Pandion', the Pāndya King of Madura in the far south. During the first and second centuries of the Christian era the trade between southern India and the Roman empire was extensive. Merchants could sail from an Arabian port to Muziris or Cranganore on the Malabar coast in forty days during July and August and return in December or January after transacting their business. There is reason to believe that Roman subjects lived at Muziris and other towns. The trade was checked, and perhaps temporarily stopped, by Caracalla's massacre of the people of Alexandria in A.D. 215. Payment for the Indian goods was made in *aurei* and *denarii*, of which large hoards have been found. In recent years many fragments of Roman pottery have been found at the site of a trading station at Arikamedu near Pondicherry, the Podoukē of the classical geographers.

Goods and ports. The goods most sought by the foreign visitors were pearls from the fisheries of the Tāmraparnī river in Tinnevelly; beryls from several mines in Mysore and Coimbatore; corundum from the same region; gems of various kinds from Ceylon; and pepper with other spices from the Malabar coast. The list is not exhaustive. The two principal ports on the Malabar coast were Muziris or Cranganore, and Bakarai or Vaikkarai, the haven of Kottayam, now in the Travancore State. Korkai on the Tāmraparnī river was the principal seat of the pearl trade. Puhār, also called Pukār or Kāviripattinam, then at the mouth of the Kaveri (Cauvery) river, was for some time a rich and prosperous port. It, with the other ancient ports in that region, is now desolate, a gradual elevation of the land having changed the coast-line.

The Tamil states. The Tamil states of the far south became wealthy and prosperous in virtue of their valuable foreign trade, and attained a high degree of material civilization at an early period. Megasthenes heard of the power of the Pāndya kingdom, and the names of the states are mentioned in Aśoka's edicts. Boundaries varied much from age to age, but three principal powers, the Pāndya, Chera or Kerala, and Chola, were always recognized. Aśoka named a fourth minor kingdom, the Satiya-putra, absorbed subsequently in the Pāndya realm, which was reputed the most ancient of the states, and may be described roughly as embracing the Madura and Tinnevelly Districts. The Kerala or Chera kingdom included the Malabar District with the modern Cochin and Travancore States, and sometimes extended eastwards. The Chola kingdom occupied the Coromandel or Madras coast. Cotton cloth formed an important item in the commerce of the Cholas, who maintained an active fleet, which was not afraid to sail as far as the mouths of the Irrawaddy and Ganges, or even to the islands of the Malay Archipelago.

Tamil literature. During the early centuries of the Christian era Tamil was the language of all the kingdoms named, Malayālam not having then come into being. A rich literature grew up, of which the golden age may be assigned to the first three centuries A.D. Madura may be called the literary capital. To this period belong the 'Eight Anthologies', a large collection of mainly secular poems showing little Aryan influence in style, technique, or content. Somewhat later are the *Kural*, the *Epic of the Anklet*, and *Manimēkalai*. Here northern influence is more apparent. The *Kural* is described as being 'the most venerated and popular book south of the Godavari . . . the literary treasure, the poetic mouthpiece, the highest type of verbal and moral excellence among the Tamil people'. The author taught ethical doctrine oı singular purity and beauty, which cannot, so far as I know, be equalled in the Sanskrit literature of the north. A few stanzas from Gover's excellent versions may be quoted:

LOVE

Loveless natures, cold and hard,
  Live for self alone.
Hearts where love abides regard
  Self as scarce their own. . .

Where the body hath a soul,
  Love hath gone before.
Where no love infils the whole,
  Dust it is—no more.

PATIENCE

How good are they who bear with scorn
  And think not to return it?
They're like the earth that giveth corn
  To those who dig and burn it. . . .

Though men should injure you, their pain
  Should lead thee to compassion.
Do nought but good to them again,
  Else look to thy transgression.

Dynastic history. Only a very vague narrative of political events in the Tamil kingdoms can be constructed for the period dealt with in this chapter, or, indeed, until centuries later. But the literature gives a few glimpses of dynastic history. Karikkāl or Karikāla, the earliest known Chola king, whose mean date may be taken as A.D. 100, contemporary with Kadphises II, is credited with the foundation of

Puhār or Pukār, and with the construction of a hundred miles of embankment along the Kaveri river (Cauvery), built by the labour of captives from Ceylon. Almost continual war with the island princes is a leading feature in the story of the Tamil kingdoms for many centuries. It need hardly be added that the kings fought among themselves still more continuously. The first historical Pāndya king was contemporary more or less exactly with Karikāla Chola's grandson, with a certain powerful Chera monarch, and with Gajabāhu, King of Ceylon, who reigned in the last quarter of the second century, and gives the clue to the chronology. After that time no more dynastic history is possible until the Pallavas make their appearance in the fourth century.

SYNCHRONISTIC TABLE OF THE FOREIGN DYNASTIES AND THEIR CONTEMPORARIES

(All Indian dates of events are merely approximate and authorities differ sometimes by as much as sixty years)

B.C.

- c. 250–248. Revolts of Bactria and Parthia.
- c. 232. Death of Aśoka.
- c. 208. Recognition of Bactrian independence.
- c. 200–190. Demetrios, 'King of the Indians'.
- c. 190–180. Pantaleon and Agathokles, kings of Taxila.
- c. 174–160. Western migration of the Great Yueh-chi from China.
- c. 180–160. Menander (Milinda), King of Kabul.
- c. 140–130. Antialkidas, King of Taxila; Heliokles, last Greek King of Bactria; invasions of Śakas; &c.
- c. 138. Temporary conquest of kingdom of Taxila by Mithridates I, King of Parthia (?).
- c. 122–120. Return of Chang-K'ien to China.
- c. 95. Maues, Śaka or Indo-Parthian King of Arachosia and Panjab, acc.
- c. 58. Azes I acc. in same regions; 58–57, epoch of Vikrama era.
- 30. Roman conquest of Egypt.

A.D.

- 14. Augustus Caesar died; Tiberius, Roman emperor, acc.
- c. 20–48. Gondophernes (Gondophares, &c.); King of Taxila, &c.; probably succeeded Azes II.
- 23. End of First Han dynasty of China.
- c. 40. Kadphises I (Kujula Kara Kadphises, &c.), Kushān, became King of all the Great Yueh-chi.
- 41. Claudius, Roman emperor, acc.
- c. 48. Kadphises I succeeded Gondophernes at Taxila.
- c. 77 or 78. Death of Kadphises I.
- 78. ? Kadphises II acc.; epoch of the Śaka era.
- 89–105. Ho-ti, Chinese emperor.
- c. 87. Defeat of Kadphises II by Pan-chao, Chinese general.
- 98. Trajan, Roman emperor, acc.
- 105. Rise of Palmyra to importance.
- c. 110. Death of Kadphises II.

A.D.

c. 110–20. ? The 'Nameless King' in north-west India.
116. Conquest of Mesopotamia by Trajan.
117. Hadrian, Roman emperor, acc.; retrocession of Mesopotamia.
c. 120. Kanishka Kushān acc.; year 1 of his regnal era.
c. 123. Sārnāth inscription of Kanishka (year 3).
c. 138. Mānikyāla inscription of Kanishka (year 18); Antoninus Pius, Roman emperor, acc.
c. 144–50. Vāsishka, (?) son and viceregal colleague of Kanishka in India (year 24 to (?) 30).
c. 150–62. Huvishka, (?) son and viceregal colleague of Kanishka in India (years 30–42).
c. 161. Āra inscription of Kanishka (year 41); Marcus Aurelius, Roman emperor, acc.
c. 162. Huvishka succeeded Kanishka as Kushān emperor.
c. 182. Vāsudeva I acc.
193. Septimius Severus, Roman emperor, acc.
c. 194–218. Inscriptions of Vāsudeva I (years 74–98).
c. 220. Death of Vāsudeva I.
226. Establishment of Sassanian dynasty of Persia by Ardashīr I
240. Shāpur (Sapor) I acc. in Persia.
273. Destruction of Palmyra by Aurelian.

AUTHORITIES

ON the Graeco-Bactrian dynasties the relevant chapters of *C.H.I.*, vol. i, are still important. Sir W. W. TARN, in *The Greeks in Bactria and India* (Cambridge, 2nd ed., 1951) treats of the subject very fully, if rather adventurously. Very recently A. K. NARAIN, in *The Indo-Greeks* (Oxford, 1956), has strongly criticized many of Tarn's conclusions.

On the chronology of the period MARSHALL's latest conclusions are contained in his *Taxila* (3 vols., Cambridge, 1951). KONOW's *Kharoshthī Inscriptions* (*Corpus Inscriptionum Indicarum*, vol. ii, Oxford, 1929) has an important introduction. Among recent works are R. GHIRSHMAN's *Bégram, Recherches archéologiques et historiques sur les Kouchans* (Cairo, 1946) and J. E. VAN LOHUIZEN DE LEEUW's *The 'Scythian' Period* (Leiden, 1949). DE LA VALLÉE POUSSIN's *L'Inde aux temps des Mauryas . . .* (Paris, 1930) gives a very fair review of all the main theories to the date of publication. Important articles in learned journals are too numerous to mention.

On contact with the West see G. N. BANERJEE, *Hellenism in Ancient India* (London 1919), H. G. RAWLINSON, *Intercourse between India and the Western World* (Cambridge, 1916), E. H. WARMINGTON, *Commerce between the Roman Empire and India* (Cambridge, 1928), and R. E. M. WHEELER, 'Roman contact with India', in *Aspects of Archaeology, Essays Presented to O. G. S. Crawford* (London, 1951). FOUCHER's *L'Art gréco-bouddhique du Gandhāra* (Paris, 1905–23), is the standard authority on Gandhāra sculpture.

For works on early Tamil culture see p. 43. The political history of the early Tamils has been brilliantly reconstructed, though from rather dubious sources, by K. N. SIVARAJA PILLAI in *The Chronology of the Early Tamils* (Madras, 1932).

Of the many works on Mahāyāna Buddhism the relevant portions of ELIOT's *Hinduism and Buddhism* (3 vols., London, 1921) are readable and reliable. The most important recent work on the subject is E. CONZE, *Buddhism, its Essence and Development*, 2nd ed., Oxford, 1953. DE LA VALLÉE POUSSIN discourses exhaustively on Bodhisattvas in Hastings's *Encyclopaedia of Religion and Ethics, s.v.*

Many of the references in *E.H.I.*⁴ (1923) are still significant.

CHAPTER 4

The Gupta period; a golden age; literature, art, and science;
Hindu renaissance; the Huns; King Harsha; the Chālukyas;
disorder in northern India

Definite chronology from A.D. 320. The transition from the unsettled and hotly disputed history of the foreign dynasties to the comparatively serene atmosphere of the Gupta period is no less agreeable to the historian than the similar passage from the uncertainties of the Nandas to the ascertained verities of the Mauryas. In both cases the experience is like that of a man in an open boat suddenly gliding from the misery of a choppy sea outside into the calm water of a harbour.

The chronology of the Gupta period, taking that period in a wide sense as extending from A.D. 320, or in round numbers from A.D. 300, to A.D. 647, or the middle of the seventh century, is not only certain in all its main outlines, but also precise in detail to a large extent, except for the latter half of the sixth century.

It is possible, therefore, to construct a continuous narrative of the history of northern and western India for the greater part of three centuries and a half, without the embarrassment which clogs all attempts at narrative when the necessary chronological framework is insecure.

Rise of the Gupta dynasty. The exact course of events which brought about the collapse of the Indo-Scythian or Kushān empire in India at some time in the third century is not known. The disturbed state of the country seems to be the explanation of the lack of contemporary inscriptions or other memorials of the time, and of the hopeless confusion of tradition as recorded in books. Many independent states must have been formed when the control of a paramount authority was withdrawn. The Lichchhavis of Vaiśāli, last heard of in the days of Buddha, now emerge again after 800 years of silence. It would seem that the clan or nation obtained possession of Pātaliputra, the ancient imperial capital, and perhaps ruled there as tributaries or feudatories of the Kushāns, whose headquarters were at Peshawar. Early in the fourth century a Lichchhavi princess gave her hand to a Rājā in Magadha who bore the historic name of Chandragupta. The matrimonial alliance with the Lichchhavis so enhanced his power that he was able to extend his dominion over Oudh as well as Magadha, and along the Ganges as far as Prayāga or Allahabad. Chandragupta recognized his dependence on his wife's people by striking his gold coins in the joint names of himself, his queen (Kumāra Dēvī), and the Lichchhavi

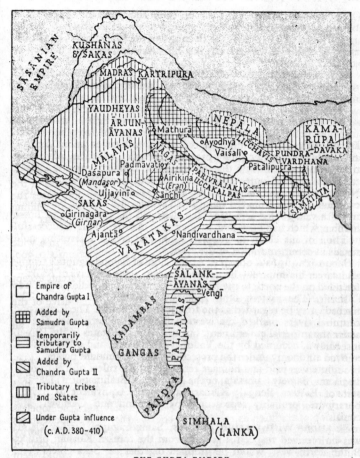

THE GUPTA EMPIRE

Map legend:

- Empire of Chandra Gupta I
- Added by Samudra Gupta
- Temporarily tributary to Samudra Gupta
- Added by Chandra Gupta II
- Tributary tribes and States
- Under Gupta influence (c. A.D. 380–410)

nation.[1] He felt himself sufficiently important to be justified in establishing a new era, the Gupta, of which the year 1 ran from 26 February 320, presumably the date of his enthronement or coronation, to 13 March 321. The era continued in use in parts of India for several centuries.

[1] That seems to me the natural interpretation of the coin legends. Mr. Allan, of the British Museum, regards the coins as having been struck by Samudragupta in honour of his parents, a view which I cannot accept.

The reign of Chandragupta I was probably short, and may have ended about A.D. 330. His son and successor was always careful to describe himself as being 'the son of the daughter of the Lichchhavi', a formula implying the acknowledgement that his royal authority was derived in part from his mother.

Samudragupta. Samudragupta, the second Gupta monarch,[1] who reigned for forty or fifty years, was one of the most remarkable and accomplished kings recorded in Indian history. He undertook and succeeded in accomplishing the formidable task of making himself the paramount power in India. He spent some years first in thoroughly subduing such princes in the Gangetic plain as declined to acknowledge his authority. He then brought the wild forest tribes under control, and finally executed a military progress through the Deccan, advancing so far into the peninsula that he came into conflict with the Pallava ruler of Kanchi (Conjeeveram) near Madras. Samudragupta did not attempt to retain permanently his conquests in the south, being content to receive homage from the vanquished princes and to bring back to his capital a vast golden treasure. He celebrated the *aśvamedha* or horse sacrifice, which had been long in abeyance, in order to mark successful assertion of his claim to imperial rank, and struck interesting gold medals in commemoration of the event.

Samudragupta's empire. At the close of Samudragupta's triumphal career his empire—the greatest in India since the days of Aśoka—extended on the north to the base of the mountains, but did not include Kashmir. The eastern limit probably was the Brahmaputra. The Narbadā may be regarded as the frontier on the south. The Jumna and Chambal rivers marked the western limit of the territories directly under the imperial government, but various tribal states in the Panjab and Malwa, occupied by the Yaudhēyas, Mālavas, and other nations, enjoyed autonomy under the protection of the paramount power.

Tribute was paid and homage rendered by the rulers of five frontier kingdoms, namely Samatata, or the delta of the Brahmaputra; Davāka, perhaps Eastern Bengal; Kāmarūpa, roughly equivalent to Assam; Kartripura, probably represented by Kumaon and Garhwal; and Nepal.

Relations with foreign powers. Samudragupta further claims that he received respectful service from the foreign Kushān princes of the north-west, whom he grouped together as 'Śaka chiefs', and even from the Sinhalese.[2] It is clear, therefore, that his name was

---

[1] Kācha (Kacha), who struck a few gold coins, may have intervened for a few months either before or after Samudragupta, if he was distinct from him; but the general opinion is that they were identical.

[2] The great inscription, which records in line 23 the rendering of 'acts of respectful service' by 'Daivaputra-Shāhi-Shāhānushāhi-Saka-murundas, Sinhalese, and others', must be interpreted in the light of modern research as meaning that the civilities were tendered by Meghavarna, King of Ceylon, and by sundry Kushān princes of the north-west, described collectively as 'Saka-murundas', or 'Saka chiefs', who used the styles of Daivaputra (= Chinese 'Son of Heaven'), Shāhi, or 'king'; and

known and honoured over the whole of India proper. He did not attempt to carry his arms across the Sutlaj or to dispute the authority of the Kushān kings who continued to rule in and beyond the Indus basin. The fact of the existence of friendly relations with Ceylon about A.D. 360 is confirmed by a Chinese historian who relates that King Meghavarna of Ceylon (c. 352–79) sent an embassy with gifts to Samudragupta and obtained his permission to erect a splendid monastery to the north of the holy tree at Bōdh Gayā for the use of pilgrims from the island.

Personal gifts. Samudragupta was a man of exceptional personal capacity and unusually varied gifts. His skill in music and song is commemorated by certain rare gold coins or medals which depict the king seated on a couch playing the Indian lute (vīnā). He was equally proficient in the allied art of poetry, and is said to have composed numerous works worthy of the reputation of a professional author. He took much delight in the society of the learned, whose services he engaged in the defence of the sacred scriptures. He was a Brahmanical Hindu with a special devotion to Vishnu, like the other members of his house.

The exact date of Samudragupta's death is not known; but he certainly lived to an advanced age, and when he passed away had enjoyed a reign of apparently uninterrupted prosperity for nearly half a century.

Chandragupta II. About A.D. 380, or perhaps some five years earlier, he was succeeded by a son specially selected as the most worthy of the crown, who assumed his grandfather's name and is therefore known to history as Chandragupta II. Later in life he took the additional title of Vikramāditya ('Sun of prowess'), which is associated by tradition with the Raja of Ujjain who is believed to have defeated the Śakas and established the Vikrama era in 58–57 B.C. It is possible that such a Raja may really have existed, although the tradition has not yet been verified by the discovery of inscriptions, coins, or monuments. The popular legends concerning 'Raja Bikram' probably have been coloured by indistinct memories of Chandragupta II, whose principal military achievement was the conquest of Malwa, Gujarat, and Saurashtra or Kathiawar, countries which had been ruled for several centuries by Śaka chiefs. Those chiefs, who had been tributary to the Kushāns, called themselves Satraps or Great Satraps. The conquest was effected between the years A.D. 388 and 401. 395 may be taken as the mean date of the operations, which must have lasted for several years. The advance of the imperial arms involved the subjugation of the Mālavas and certain other tribes which had remained outside the frontier of Samudragupta, although enjoying his protection. Rudrasimha, the last of the Satraps, was killed. A

Shāhānushāhi or 'King of Kings'. *Shāhānu* is a genitive plural. The Purānas treat the Murundas as distinct from the Śakas, but originally the word meant simply 'chief = Chinese *wang*. In practice the name Murunda was employed to denote a section of the Śakas.

scandalous tradition, recorded by an author of the seventh century, affirmed that the king of the Śakas, 'while courting another man's wife, was butchered by Chandragupta, concealed in his mistress's dress'. The fragmentary play *Devicandraguptam* treats of this event as occurring during the reign of a weak elder brother of Chandragupta, named Rāmagupta, and adds that Chandragupta killed Rāmagupta and married his queen. The story is disbelieved by most competent authorities, but may contain a germ of truth.

Trade with west; Ujjain. The annexation of the Satraps' territories added provinces of exceptional wealth and fertility to the northern empire, which had become an extremely rich and powerful state at the beginning of the fifth century. The income from the customs duties collected at the numerous ports on the western coast which were now brought under Gupta rule must have been a valuable financial resource. From time immemorial Bharōch (Broach), Sopāra, Cambay, and a multitude of other ports had carried on an active sea-borne trade with the countries of the west. Ujjain appears to have been the inland centre upon which most of the trade routes converged. The city, dating from immemorial antiquity, which still retains its ancient name unchanged and exists as a prosperous town in Madhya Bharat, has been always reckoned as one of the seven sacred Hindu cities, little inferior to Banaras in sanctity. Longitudes were reckoned from its meridian in ancient times. The favourable position of the city for trade evidently was the foundation both of its material prosperity and of the sanctity attaching to a site which enjoyed the favour of successive ruling powers by whom religious establishments of all kinds were founded from time to time.

The Great Satraps of Maharashtra. Two dynasties of Śaka princes, not certainly related, using the style of Great Satrap ruled in western India, and should not be confounded by being lumped together under a single designation as the 'Western Satraps'.

The earlier dynasty ruled in Maharashtra or the region of the Western Ghats, its capital apparently being at or near Nasik. The date of its establishment is not known, and so far the names of only two princes, Bhūmaka and Nahapāna, have been recovered, but others may have existed. These we have met before, in connexion with the line of Sātavāhanas or Āndhras (p. 140, above).

The Great Satraps of Ujjain. At nearly the same time, or probably a few years earlier, a chieftain named Chashtana became Great Satrap of Malwa, with his capital at Ujjain. He may have been a subordinate of Kadphises II. His reign was not long, and his son did not come to the throne. Possibly he was killed in battle, for the times were troubled. Chashtana's grandson, named Rudradāman, who was ruling conjointly with his grandfather in A.D. 130, won afresh for himself the position of Great Satrap, if our chronology is correct, under the suzerainty cf Kanishka, and became the ruler of western India, including the provinces north of the Narbada which the Sātavāhana had wrested from the Satrap of Maharashtra a few years previously. Chashtana's successors must have continued to be tributaries of Huvishka. When the Kushān empire broke up, the rulers of the west, who continued to style themselves Great Satraps, became independent, and preserved their authority until the twenty-first Great Satrap was killed by Chandragupta II at the close of the fourth century, when his country was incorporated in the Gupta empire, as already mentioned. The names and dates of the Great Satraps of Ujjain have been well ascertained, chiefly from coins, but little is known about the details of their history.[1]

Character of Chandragupta II. The principal Gupta kings, except the founder of the dynasty, all enjoyed long reigns, like Akbar and his successors in a later age. Chandragupta Vikramāditya occupied the throne for nearly forty years until at least A.D. 413. The ascertained facts of his career prove that he was a strong and vigorous ruler, well qualified to govern and augment an extensive empire. He loved sounding titles which proclaimed his martial prowess, and was fond of depicting himself on his coins as engaged in the sport of kings, personal combat with a lion. Lions were numerous in the northern parts of the Uttar Pradesh as late as the time of Bishop Heber in 1824, but are now found only in Saurashtra. The last specimen recorded in northern India was killed in the Gwalior State in 1872.

Fa-hien, Chinese pilgrim. The indispensable chronological skeleton of Gupta history constructed from the testimony of numerous dated inscriptions and coins is clothed with flesh chiefly by the help of foreign travellers, the pilgrims from China who crowded into India as the Holy Land of Buddhism from the beginning of the fifth century. Fa-hien or Fa-hsien, the earliest of those pilgrims to have left an account of his journey, was on his travels from A.D. 399 to 414. His laborious journey was undertaken in order to procure authentic texts of the *Vinaya-pitaka*, or Buddhist books on monastic discipline. The daring traveller after leaving western China followed the route to the south of the Taklamakān (Gobi) Desert, through Sha-chow and Lop-nor to Khotan, where the population was wholly Buddhist, and chiefly devoted to the Mahāyāna doctrine.[2] He then crossed the Pamirs with infinite difficulty and made his way into Udyāna or Suwāt (Swat), and so on to Taxila and Purushapura or Peshawar. He spent three years at Pātaliputra and two at Tāmralipti, now represented by Tamluk in the Midnapore District of Bengal. In those days Tāmralipti was an important port. Its modern successor is a small town at least sixty miles distant from the sea. Fa-hien sailed from Tāmralipti on his return journey, going home by sea, and visiting Ceylon and Java on the way.

---

[1] Much difference of opinion has been expressed concerning the date of Nahapāna, and the question has not been settled.

[2] The details of the pilgrim's route from Lop-nor to Khotan have not been worked out properly by any of the translators and are obscure; but he certainly passed Lop-nor.

His stay in India proper, extending from A.D. 401 to 410, thus fell wholly within the limits of the reign of Chandragupta II. About six years were spent in the dominions of that monarch.

The enthusiastic pilgrim was so absorbed in the religious task to which his life was devoted that he never even mentions the name of any reigning sovereign. His references to the facts of ordinary life are made in a casual, accidental fashion, which guarantees the trustworthiness of his observations. Although we moderns should be better pleased if the pious traveller had paid more attention to worldly affairs, we may be thankful for his brief notes, which give a pleasing and fairly vivid picture of the condition of the Gangetic provinces in the reign of Chandragupta II. He calls the Gangetic plain Mid-India or the Middle Kingdom, which may be taken as equivalent roughly to the modern Bihar, Uttar Pradesh, Malwa, and part of Rajasthan. The whole of Mid-India was under the rule of the Gupta emperor.

State of the country. The towns of Magadha or South Bihar were large; the people were rich and prosperous; charitable institutions were numerous; rest-houses for travellers were provided on the highways, and the capital possessed an excellent free hospital endowed by benevolent and educated citizens. Pāṭaliputra was still a flourishing city, specially interesting to Fa-hien because it possessed two monasteries—one of the Little, and one of the Great Vehicle, where 600 or 700 monks resided, who were so famous for their learning that students from all quarters attended their lectures. Fa-hien spent three happy years at the ancient imperial capital in the study of the Sanskrit language and Buddhist scriptures. He was deeply impressed by the palace and halls erected by Aśoka in the middle of the city, and still standing in the time of the pilgrim. The massive stone work, richly adorned with sculpture and decorative carving, seemed to him to be the work of spirits, beyond the capacity of merely human craftsmen. The site of that palace has been identified at Kumrāhār village, to the south of the modern city.

Pāṭaliputra probably continued to be the principal royal residence in the reign of Samudragupta, but there are indications that in the time of his successor Ayodhyā was found to be more convenient as the headquarters of the government.

In the course of a journey of some 500 miles from the Indus to Mathura on the Jumna the traveller passed a succession of Buddhist monasteries tenanted by thousands of men. Mathura alone had twenty such institutions with 3,000 residents. Fa-hien noted that Buddhism was particularly flourishing along the course of the Jumna.

Administration. He liked the climate and was pleased with the mildness of the administration. He notes that people were free to come or go as they thought fit without the necessity of being registered or obtaining passes; that offences were ordinarily punished by fine only; the capital penalty not being inflicted, and mutilation being confined to the case of obstinate rebellion, meaning probably professional brigandage. Persons guilty of that crime were liable to suffer amputation of the right hand. The revenue was derived mainly from the rent of the crown lands, 'land revenue' in modern language. The royal guards and officers were paid regular salaries.

Habits of the people. The Buddhist rule of life was generally observed. 'Throughout the country', we are told, 'no one kills any living thing, or drinks wine, or eats onions or garlic . . . they do not keep pigs or fowls; there are no dealings in cattle, no butchers' shops or distilleries in their market-places.' The Chandālas or outcastes, who did not observe the rules of purity, were obliged to live apart, and were required when entering a town or bazaar to strike a piece of wood as a warning of their approach, in order that other folk might not be polluted by contact with them.

Those observations prove that a great change had occurred in the manners of the people and the attitude of the government since the time of the Mauryas. The people of Taxila had had no scruple in supplying Alexander with herds of fat beasts fit for the butcher; even Aśoka did not definitely forbid the slaughter of kine; while the *Arthaśāstra* not only treated the liquor trade as a legitimate source of revenue, but directed that public-houses should be made attractive to customers. Fa-hien's statements may be, and probably are, expressed in terms too comprehensive, and without the necessary qualifications. Sacrifice, for instance, must have been practised by many Brahmanical Hindus. It is hardly credible that in A.D. 400, 'throughout the whole country', nobody except the lowest outcastes would kill any living thing, drink strong liquor, or eat onions or garlic.[1] But Fa-hien's testimony may be accepted as proving that the *ahimsā* sentiment was extraordinarily strong in 'Mid-India' when he resided there. Evidently it was far more generally accepted than it is at the present day, when Buddhism has been long extinct. The pilgrim's statements, no doubt, apply primarily to the Buddhists. The traveller's account of the precautions enforced on Chandāla outcastes in order to protect caste people from defilement may be illustrated by modern descriptions of the customs prevalent not long ago in the extreme south of the peninsula; and a somewhat similar attitude towards certain classes like the Mahārs, Doms, Chuhras, and Chamārs is still observable in Bombay and northern India, though the impact of Western civilization and modern reform movements have considerably mitigated the extreme rigour of caste rules.[2]

Good government. Fa-hien's incidental observations taken as a whole indicate that the Gupta empire at the beginning of the fifth century was well governed. The government let the people live their

---

[1] The assertion in the same chap. xvi that 'in buying and selling they use cowries' must not be pressed to mean that coins were unknown. Chandragupta II coined freely in gold, and more sparingly in silver and copper.

[2] See article on 'Outcastes' in Hastings, *Encyclopaedia of Religion and Ethics*, vol. ix, pp. 581 ff.

own lives without needless interference; was temperate in the repression of crime, and tolerant in matters of religion. The foreign pilgrim was able to pursue his studies in peace wherever he chose to reside, and could travel all over India without molestation. He makes no mention of any adventures with robbers, and when he ultimately returned home he carried to his native land his collections of manuscripts, images, and paintings. Many other Chinese pilgrims followed his example, the most illustrious being Hiuen Tsang or Yuan Chwang in the seventh century.

Kumāragupta I. In A.D. 415 Chandragupta II was succeeded by a son named Kumāragupta who ruled the empire for about forty years. Details of the events of his reign are not on record, but it is probable that he added to his inherited dominions, because he is known to have celebrated the horse sacrifice, which he would not have ventured to do unless he had gained military successes.

Skandagupta, the last great Gupta. Kumāragupta died in A.D. 455 or a little earlier, when the sceptre passed into the hands of his son Skandagupta. In the latter part of Kumāragupta's reign the empire had been attacked by a tribe or nation called Pushyamitra,[1] perhaps Iranians, who were repulsed. Soon after the accession of Skandagupta a horde of Hūnas, or Huns, fierce nomads from central Asia, made a more formidable inroad, which, too, was successfully repelled. But fresh waves of invaders arrived and shattered the fabric of the Gupta empire. The dynasty was not destroyed. It continued to rule diminished dominions with reduced power for several generations. Skandagupta, however, was the last of the great imperial Guptas, as Aurangzeb Alamgir was the last of the Great Mughuls.

The Gupta golden age. Before we deal more closely with the Hun invasions and their consequences we shall offer a summary review of the golden age of the Guptas, which may be reckoned as extending from A.D. 320 to 480, comprising the reigns of Chandragupta I; Samudragupta; Chandragupta II, Vikramāditya; Kumāragupta I; and Skandagupta, who followed his grandfather's example in taking the title Vikramāditya.

A learned European scholar declares that 'the Gupta period is in the annals of classical India almost what the Periclean age is in the history of Greece'. An Indian author regards the time as that of 'the Hindu Renaissance'. Both phrases are justified. The age of the great Gupta kings presents a more agreeable and satisfactory picture than any other period in the history of Hindu India. Fa-hien's testimony above quoted proves that the government was free from cruelty and was not debased by the system of espionage advocated by Kautilya and actually practised by the Mauryas. Literature, art, and science flourished in a degree beyond the ordinary, and gradual changes in religion were

---

[1] The reading of this word in Skandagupta's Bhitari Inscription is questioned. Some have suggested, for *Pushyamitrān*, *yudhy amitrān* 'his enemies in battle' [Ed.]

effected without persecution. Those propositions will now be developed in some detail.

Hindu renaissance. The energetic and long-continued zeal of Aśoka probably succeeded in making Buddhism the religion of the majority of the people in northern India, during the latter part of his reign. But neither Brahmanical Hinduism nor Jainism ever died out. The relative prevalence of each of the three religions varied immensely from time to time and from province to province. The Buddhist convictions of the Kushān kings, Kanishka and Huvishka, do not seem to have been deep. In fact, the personal faith of those monarchs apparently was a corrupt Zoroastrianism or Magism more than anything else. Their predecessor, Kadphises II, placed the image of Śiva and his bull on his coins, a practice renewed by Huvishka's successor, Vāsudeva I. The Satraps of Ujjain, although tolerant of Buddhism, were themselves Brahmanical Hindus. The Gupta kings, while showing as a family preference for devotion to the Deity under the name of Vishnu or Bhagavat, allowed Buddhists and Jains perfect freedom of worship and full liberty to endow their sacred places. Although we moderns can discern from our distant point of view that the Hindu renaissance or reaction had begun the conquest of Buddhism in the fifth century, or even from an earlier date, Fa-hien was not conscious of the movement. India was simply the Buddhist Holy Land in his eyes, and the country in which the precepts of his religion were observed.

Sanskrit. The growing power of the Brahmans, as compared with the gradually waning influence of the Jain and Buddhist churches, was closely associated with the increased use of Sanskrit, the sacred language of the Brahmans. Aśoka never used Sanskrit officially. All his proclamations were composed and published in easily intelligible varieties of the vernacular tongue, and so were accessible to anybody who knew how to read. The Śātavāhana kings too used Prākrit. The earliest known inscriptions written in grammatical standard Sanskrit date from the time of Kanishka, when we find a short record at Mathura dated in the year 24 of the Kanishka era, and a long literary composition at Girnār in Surashtra, recorded about A.D. 150, which recites the conquests of the Great Satrap Rudradāman.

Literature; Kālidāsa. The increasing use of Sanskrit is further marked by the legends of the Gupta coins, which are in that language, and by the development of Sanskrit literature of the highest quality. Critics are agreed that Kālidāsa surpasses all rivals writing in Sanskrit whether as dramatist or as poet. Something like general assent has been won to the proposition that the literary work of the most renowned of Indian poets was accomplished in the fifth century under the patronage of the Gupta kings. Good reason has been shown for believing that Kālidāsa was a native of Mandasor in Malwa (now in Madhya Bharat), or of some place in the immediate neighbourhood of that once famous town. He was thus brought up in close touch with the court of Ujjain, and the active commercial and intellectual life which centred in that capital of western India. His early descriptive poems, the *Ritusamhāra* and the *Meghadūta*, may be assigned to the reign of Chandragupta II, Vikramāditya, the conqueror of Ujjain, and his dramas to that of Kumāragupta I (A.D. 413–55); but it is probable that his true dates may be slightly later. *Sakuntalā*, the most famous of his plays, secured enthusiastic admiration from European critics the moment it was brought to their notice, and the poet's pre-eminence has never been questioned in either East or West.[1]

Other literature. Good authorities are now disposed to assign the political drama entitled the 'Signet of the Minister' (*Mudrā Rākshasa*) to the Gupta period, probably in its later centuries; and the interesting play called 'The Little Clay Cart' (*Mrichchhakatikā*) may be a little earlier. The *Vāyu Purāna*, one of the most ancient of the existing Purānas, may be assigned to the first half of the fourth century in its present form. All the Purānas contain matter of various ages, some parts being extremely ancient; any date assigned to such a composition refers only to the final literary form of the work.

Science. The sciences of mathematics and astronomy, including astrology, were cultivated with much success during the Gupta period. The most famous writers on those subjects are Āryabhata, born in A.D. 476, who taught the system studied at Pātaliputra, and included Greek elements; Varāhamihira (A.D. 505–87), who was deeply learned in Greek science and used many Greek technical terms; and, at the close of the period, Brahmagupta, who was born in A.D. 598. By this time there is evidence that Indians had devised the decimal system for the notation of numerals, expressing tens, hundreds, &c., by position, and employing a special sign for zero. This system, India's greatest legacy to the world in the sphere of practical knowledge, was not used in inscriptions until about a century after Āryabhata.

Fine arts. The skill of Samudragupta in music has been recorded. We may be assured that the professors of that art, as the recipients of liberal royal patronage, were numerous and prosperous. The three closely allied arts of architecture, sculpture, and painting attained an extraordinarily high point of achievement. The accident that the Gupta empire consisted for the most part of the provinces permanently occupied at an early date by the Muslims, who systematically destroyed Hindu buildings for several centuries, obscures the history of Gupta architecture. No large building of the period has survived, and the smaller edifices which escaped destruction are hidden in remote localities away from the track of the Muslim armies, chiefly in central India and Madhya Pradesh (the former Central Provinces). They closely resemble rock-cut temples.

The most important and interesting extant stone temple of the Gupta age is one of moderate dimensions at Deogarh in the Lalitpur subdivision

[1] For Kālidāsa's birthplace see M. M. Haraprasad Shastri in *J. B. & O. R. Soc.*, vol. i, pp. 197–212. I accept the continuous tradition that the *Ritusamhāra* is an early work of Kālidāsa.

of the Jhansī District, U.P., which may be assigned to the first half
of the sixth, or perhaps to the fifth, century. The panels of the walls
contain some of the finest specimens of Indian sculpture. The larger
brick temple at Bhītargāon in the Cawnpore District, U.P., may be
ascribed to the reign of Chandragupta II. It is remarkable for vigorous
and well-designed sculpture in terra-cotta. Fragments, including some
beautiful sculptures, indicate that magnificent stone temples of Gupta
age stood at Sārnāth near Benares and elsewhere. Sārnāth has proved
to be a treasure-house of Gupta figures and reliefs, among which are
many of high quality dating from the time of Samudragupta and his
successors. The Gupta artists and craftsmen were no less capable in
working metals. The pillar at Delhi, made of wrought iron in the time
of Kumāragupta I, is a marvel of metallurgical skill. The art of casting
copper statues on a large scale by the *cire perdue* process was practised
with conspicuous success. A copper image of Buddha about 80 feet
high is said to have been erected at Nālandā in Bihar at the close of
the sixth century; and the fine Sultānganj Buddha, 7½ feet high, is still
to be seen in the museum at Birmingham. It dates from the reign of
Chandragupta II. The highest development of the arts may be assigned
to the fifth century, the age of Kālidāsa, in the reigns of Chandragupta
II and his son. Two of the finest caves at Ajantā, Nos. XVI and XVII,
were excavated in the same century of brilliant achievement.[1] It is needless to dwell upon the high merits of the paintings in the Ajantā caves,
which are now freely recognized. A Danish artist, who has published a
valuable professional criticism, declares that 'they represent the climax
to which genuine Indian art has attained'; and that 'everything in these
pictures from the composition as a whole to the smallest pearl or flower
testifies to depth of insight coupled with the greatest technical skill'.[2]

The closely related frescoes at Sīgiriya in Ceylon were executed
between A.D. 479 and 497, soon after the close of the reign of Skandagupta.

Hindu art at its best. The facts thus indicated in outline permit no
doubt that the fine arts of music, architecture, sculpture, and painting
attained a high level of excellence during the Gupta period, and more
especially in the fifth century, which in my judgement was the time
when Hindu art was at its best. The Gupta sculpture exhibits pleasing
characteristics which usually enable a student familiar with standard
examples to decide with confidence whether or not a given work is of
Gupta age. The physical beauty of the figures, the gracious dignity of
their attitude, and the refined restraint of the treatment are qualities
not to be found elsewhere in Indian sculpture in the same degree.
Certain more obvious technical marks are equally distinctive. Such
are the plain robes showing the body as if they were transparent, the
elaborate haloes, and the curious wigs. Others might be enumerated.
Many of the sculptures are dated.

[1] *J.R.A.S.*, 1914, p. 335.
[2] *Ann. Rep. Archaeol. Dept. Nizam's Dom.*, for 1914–15, App. H, by Axel Jarl.

Exchange of ideas. The extraordinary intellectual vitality of the Gupta period undoubtedly was largely due to the constant and lively exchange of ideas with foreign lands in both East and West.

The desert sands of central Asia have revealed the existence of kingdoms dating from about the beginning of the Christian era, where elements of Indian culture, introduced through Buddhism, combined with those of Iran and China. The most important of these kingdoms was that of Khotan, the Tarim basin of Chinese Turkistan, which was probably founded in the first century A.D. under the influence of the Kushāns. Its early kings bore Indian names and their state documents were in Prākrit, written in Kharoshthī characters. These were later replaced by a form of Gupta character, from which the modern Tibetan script is derived. Both archaeology and the accounts of Chinese travellers show that these lands had strong Buddhist communities, and contained many monasteries and temples, the remains of which have produced numerous precious manuscripts in Sanskrit and the local vernaculars, and beautiful paintings showing a blending of Indian, Iranian, and Chinese influence. Buddhism survived here until after the coming of Islam, while Tibet has remained a centre of Tantric Buddhism, imported from the medieval Pāla empire of Bihar and Bengal, down to the present day.

It was from central Asia that Buddhism was introduced into China. Though a few Buddhist missionaries may have visited China earlier, the religion first found a foothold there when, in A.D. 65, under the patronage of the Han Emperor Ming-ti, two central Asian monks, Dharmaratna and Kāśyapa Mātanga, established the White Horse monastery at Lo-yang. They were followed by other missionary monks, and soon Buddhism began to make headway, and the scriptures were translated into Chinese. Numerous Chinese Buddhist monks visited India, to do reverence to the sacred spots of the faith, and to improve their knowledge of Sanskrit, and, from Gupta times onwards, many embassies were sent to China from one part of India or another. India has little affected Chinese culture except through Buddhism, but by this means it has exerted a subtle influence which has permeated the whole of Chinese life and thought.

Active communication between the Indian coasts and the islands of the Archipelago was maintained. The Chinese say that the conversion of the Javanese to Buddhism was effected by Gunavarman, Crown Prince of Kashmir, who died at Nanking in China in A.D. 431. From the end of the fourth century onwards numerous inscriptions in south-east Asia and Indonesia show conclusively that the local kings had already adopted Hindu customs; they performed Brahmanical sacrifices, and employed Sanskrit as their official language. This topic is discussed at greater length in an appendix at the end of this chapter. The Ajantā frescoes record intercourse between western India and Persia early in the seventh century. Three missions to Roman emperors in A.D. 336, 361, and 530 are mentioned. The coinage bears unmistak-

a. Monkeys, Ajantā

b. Woman and child, Ajantā

c. Hippogryph, Gupta period

PLATE 10

a. Kandariya Māhadeo Temple, Khajurāho

b. Pāla sculpture

c. Kailāsanātha Temple, Ellora

able testimony to the reality of Roman influence, and the word *dīnāra*, the Latin *denarius*, was commonly used to mean a gold coin.

The conquest of western India by Chandragupta II at the close of the fourth ceutury brought the Gangetic provinces into direct communication with the western ports, and so with Alexandria and Europe. Trade also followed the land routes through Persia. The effect of easy communication with Europe is plainly visible in the astronomy of Āryabhata and Varāhamihira, who must have known Greek. The belief of Windisch that the many striking resemblances in form between the classical Indian dramas and the plays of the school of Menander are not accidental rests on substantial arguments. The influence of Greek taste on the sculpture of the Gupta age, although necessarily less obvious, is not less certain. The works are truly Indian. They are not copies or even imitations of Greek originals, and yet manifest the Greek spirit, forming a charming combination of East and West, such as we see on a vast scale in the inimitable Tāj many centuries later. When the intercourse with Europe died away in the seventh century India developed new schools of sculpture in which no trace of foreign example can be detected. Some expert critics maintain that the works of the eighth century mark the highest achievement of Indian art; but those of the fifth century commend themselves, as already observed, to my taste, and appear to me to be on the whole superior to those of any other age.

The Huns. The meagre annals of the Gupta monarchs subsequent to Skandagupta present little matter of interest, and may be passed by with a mere allusion. But the nature of the foreign inroads which broke down the stately fabric of the Gupta empire demands explanation. The work of destruction was effected by hordes of nomads from central Asia who swarmed across the north-western passes, as the Śakas and Yueh-chi had done in previous ages. The Indians generally spoke of all the later barbarians as Hūnas or Huns, but the Huns proper were accompanied by Gurjaras and other tribes. The section which encamped in the Oxus valley in the fifth century was distinguished as the White Huns or Ephthalites. They gradually occupied both Persia and Kabul, killing the Sassanian King Fīrōz in A.D. 484. Their first attack on the Gupta empire about A.D. 455 was repulsed, but the collapse of Persian resistance opened the flood-gates and allowed irresistible numbers to pour into India. Their leader, Toramāna, who was established in Malwa about A.D. 500, was succeeded soon after by his son Mihiragula ('Sun-flower'), whose Indian capital appears to have been Sākala or Sialkot in the Panjab.

India at that time was only one province of the Hun empire which extended from Persia on the west to Khotan on the east, comprising forty provinces. The headquarters of the horde were at Bamyan near Herat, and the ancient city of Balkh served as a secondary capital. The power of Mihiragula in India was broken about A.D. 528 by Yaśo-dharman, King of Malwa, and by Bālāditya, usually identified with

Narasimha, the Gupta King of Magadha. Mihiragula retired to Kashmir, where he seized the throne, and died. His history is obscured by fanciful legends.

Soon after the middle of the sixth century the Hun kingdom on the Oxus was overthrown by the Turks, who became masters of the greater part of the short-lived Hun empire.

A turning-point in history. The barbarian invasions of the fifth and sixth centuries, although slurred over by the Indian authorities, constitute a turning-point in the history of northern and western India, both political and social. The political system of the Gupta period was completely broken up, and new kingdoms were formed. No authentic family or clan traditions go back beyond the Hun invasions. All genuine tradition of the earlier dynasties has been absolutely lost. The history of the Mauryas, Kushāns, and Guptas, so far as it is known, has been recovered laboriously by the researches of scholars, without material help from living tradition.[1] The process by which the foreigners became hinduized and the Rajput clans were formed will be discussed in the next chapter.

Maukharis and 'Guptas of Magadha'. After the decline of the imperial Guptas another line of kings with names ending in -gupta rose in Magadha. Their genealogies give no clear evidence of relationship to the earlier Gupta line. Simultaneously a line of Maukhari kings grew in importance to the north of the Ganges. Traces of the existence of a martial Maukhari clan are to be found from Maurya times onwards. In the latter half of the fifth century Maukhari chieftains held the Gaya District under Gupta suzerainty. In the sixth century they appear to have established their independence, and to have made Kanauj their capital, the first important house to have ruled from this city, which had been comparatively small and insignificant in earlier centuries. The latter half of the sixth century saw almost continuous warfare between the kings of the two houses which shared the control of much of the Gangetic basin. Towards the end of the century the Maukharis seem to have driven the Guptas from their ancestral domains and to have occupied part or the whole of Magadha. Th Guptas are referred to in Bāna's account of the rise of the Emperor Harsha as kings of Malwa, so it may be assumed that they were forced to take refuge in the eastern part of their possessions, where they came under the influence of Harsha's father, Prabhākara-vardhana of Thanesar. Princes of this line are mentioned both by Bāna and the Chinese traveller Hiuen Tsang as Harsha's vassals.

The Maukhari empire ended very early in the seventh century with the defeat and death of the last of the line, Grahavarman, at the hands of the 'wicked king of Malwa', who appears to be the same as Devagupta, referred to in one of Harsha's inscriptions. On the death of Grahavarman without heirs Kanauj passed to his brother-in-law,

[1] The Jain traditions of Samprati constitute a small exception to the statement in the text.

Harsha, whose reign is discussed below. On the fall of Harsha's empire at his death the Guptas again rose to prominence under Ādityasena (c. 675). They disappeared in the eighth century, perhaps at the hands of Yaśovarman of Kanauj (p. 199, below), who may have been of Maukhari descent.

Valabhī and other kingdoms. When the Gupta power became restricted at the close of the fifth century western India gradually passed under the control of rulers belonging to a foreign tribe called Maitraka, possibly Iranian in origin. The Maitrakas established a dynasty with its capital at Valabhī (Walā, or Vala of *I.G.*, Wullubheepoor of the *Rās Mālā*), in the Saurashtra peninsula, which lasted until about 770, when it seems to have been overthrown by the Arabs. The names and dates of the long line of the kings of Valabhī, who used the Gupta era, are known with sufficient accuracy. The kingdom attained considerable wealth and importance. In the sixth century the capital was the residence of renowned Buddhist teachers, and in the seventh it rivalled Nālandā in Bihar as a centre of Buddhist learning. The modern town is insignificant and shows few signs of its ancient greatness.

After the overthrow of Valabhī its place as the chief city of western India was taken by Anhilwāra (Nahrwālah, &c., or Patan), which in its turn was superseded in the fifteenth century by Ahmadabad.

The Gurjaras, who have been mentioned as associated with the Huns, founded kingdoms at Bharōch (Broach) and at Bhinmāl in southern Rajasthan.

The history of India during the sixth century is exceedingly obscure. The times evidently were much disturbed.

Nothing definite of moment can be stated about the Tamil kingdoms of the Far South during the period dealt with in this chapter.

Ample material for seventh century. The embarrassing lack of material for the history of the latter half of the sixth century is no longer felt when the story of the seventh has to be told. The invaluable description of India recorded by Hiuen Tsang or Yuan Chwang, the eminent Chinese pilgrim; his biography written by his friends; the official Chinese historical works; and an historical romance composed by Bāna, a learned Brahman who enjoyed the friendship of King Harsha, when combined with a considerable amount of information derived from inscriptions, coins, and other sources, supply us with knowledge surpassing in fullness and precision that available for any other period of early Hindu history, except that of the Mauryas. Harsha of Kanauj, the able monarch who reduced anarchy to order in northern India, and reigned for forty-one years; as Aśoka had done, is not merely a name in a genealogy. His personal characteristics and the details of his administration, as recorded by men who knew him intimately, enable us to realize him as a living person who achieved greatness by his capacity and energy.

King Harsha, A.D. 606–47. Harsha, or Harsha-vardhana, was the younger son of Prabhākara-vardhana, Raja of Thanesar, the famous holy town to the north of Delhi, who had won considerable military successes over his neighbours—the Gurjaras, Mālavas, and others, in the latter part of the sixth century. His unexpected death in A.D. 604 was quickly followed by that of his elder son, who was treacherously assassinated by Śaśānka, King of Gauda, or central Bengal. His younger son, Harsha, then only sixteen or seventeen years of age, was constrained by his nobles to accept the vacant throne, and to undertake the difficult task of bringing northern India into subjection and tolerable order. The young sovereign, who reluctantly accepted the trust imposed upon him in October 606, was obliged to spend five years and a half in constant fighting. Soon after his accession he gained control of Kanauj, the kingdom of his brother-in-law Grahavarman Maukhari, who had been killed in battle by the King of Malwa, probably Devagupta, and had apparently left no heirs. According to Hiuen Tsang Harsha was invited to accept the throne of Kanauj by a great meeting of the nobles and dignitaries of the kingdom. His sister Rājyaśrī appears to have played an important part in affairs, no doubt by virtue of her position as widow of the last of the Maukharis. Soon after these events Harsha moved his capital from Thanesar to Kanauj.

The Chinese pilgrim who came to India a few years later tells us that Harsha 'went from east to west subduing all who were not obedient; the elephants were not unharnessed, nor the soldiers unhelmeted'. His conquests were achieved with a force of 5,000 elephants, 20,000 cavalry, and 50,000 infantry. He seems to have discarded chariots. When he had finished his task the cavalry had increased to 100,000, and the elephants are said to have numbered 60,000, a figure hardly credible, and probably erroneous. Harsha's subjugation of upper India, excluding the Panjab, but including Bihar and at least the greater part of Bengal, was completed in 612, when he appears to have been solemnly enthroned. But the new era established by him, which attained wide currency, was reckoned from the beginning of his reign in October 606. His last recorded campaign in 643 was directed against Ganjam on the coast of the Bay of Bengal. A few years earlier he had waged a successful war with Valabhī, which resulted in the recognition of Harsha's suzerainty by the western powers. In the east his name was so feared that even the king of distant Assam was obliged to obey his imperious commands and to attend his court.

War with the Chālukyas. The Chālukya kingdom in the Deccan, founded in the middle of the sixth century, was raised to a paramount position by its king, Pulakeśin II, the contemporary of Harsha. The northern monarch, impatient of a rival, attacked Pulakeśin about A.D. 620, but was defeated, and obliged to accept the Narbada as his southern frontier. So far as is known that defeat was Harsha's only failure. During the greater part of his reign, although his armies may have been given occupation from time to time, he was free to devote his exceptional powers to the work of administration and to consecrate an extraordinarily large share of his time to religious exercises and discussions.

Kanauj the capital. The ancient town of Kanauj (Kanyākubja) on the Ganges, which was selected by Harsha as his capital, was converted into a magnificent, wealthy, and well-fortified city, nearly four miles long and a mile broad, furnished with numerous lofty buildings, and adorned with many tanks and gardens. The Buddhist monasteries, of which only two had existed in the fifth century, numbered more than a hundred in Harsha's time, when Brahmanical temples existed in even larger numbers. The inhabitants were more or less equally divided in their allegiance to Hinduism and Buddhism. The city, after enduring many vicissitudes, was finally destroyed by Sher Shah in the sixteenth century. It is now represented by a petty Muslim country town and miles of shapeless mounds which serve as a quarry for railway ballast. No building erected in Harsha's reign can be identified either at Kanauj or elsewhere

Administration; literature. Harsha, who was only fifty-seven or fifty-eight years of age when he died late in A.D. 646 or early in 647, was in the prime of life throughout most of his long reign. We hear nothing of the elaborate bureaucratic system of the Mauryas, although an organized civil service must have existed. The king seems to have trusted chiefly to incessant personal supervision of his extensive empire, which he effected by constantly moving about, except in the rainy season when the roads were impassable. He marched in state to the music of golden drums, and was accommodated, like the Burmese kings of modern times, in temporary structures built of wood and bamboo, which were burnt on his departure. Many provinces were governed in detail by tributary Rajas. The Chinese pilgrim thought well of the royal administration, although it was less mild than that of the Guptas in the fifth century. The penalty of imprisonment, inflicted after the cruel Tibetan fashion, which left the prisoner to live or die, was freely awarded, and mutilation was often adjudged. The roads, apparently, were not as safe as they had been in the days of Vikramāditya. Official records of all events were kept up in each province by special officers. Education was widely diffused, and the great Buddhist monasteries at Nālandā in Magadha and other places were centres of learning and the arts. The king himself was an accomplished scholar. He is credited with the composition of a grammatical work, sundry poems, and three extant Sanskrit plays, one of which, the *Nāgānanda*, with an edifying Buddhist legend for its subject, is highly esteemed and has been translated into English. A Brahman named Bāna, who was an intimate friend of the king, wrote an account of part of his master's reign in the form of an historical romance, which gives much accurate and valuable information wrapped up in tedious, affected rhetoric, as tiresome as that of Abu-l Fazl in the *Akbarnāma*.

Religion. Harsha, who was extremely devout, assigned many hours of each day to devotional exercises. Primarily a worshipper of Śiva, he permitted himself also to honour the Sun and Buddha. In the latter part of his reign he became more and more Buddhist in sentiment, and apparently set himself the task of emulating Aśoka. He 'sought to plant the tree of religious merit to such an extent that he forgot to sleep or eat'; and is said to have forbidden the slaughter of any living thing or the use of flesh as food throughout the 'Five Indies', under pain of death without hope of pardon.

The details of his proceedings make interesting reading; indeed, the historical material is so abundant that it would be easy to write a large volume devoted solely to his reign. Hiuen Tsang or Yuan Chwang, the most renowned of the Chinese pilgrims, being our leading authority, it is desirable to give a brief account of his memorable career.

Hiuen Tsang or Yuan Chwang. He was the fourth son of a learned Chinese gentleman of honourable lineage, and from childhood was a grave and ardent student of things sacred. When he started on his travels at the age of twenty-nine (A.D. 629) he was already famous as a Buddhist sage. His intense desire to obtain access to the authentic scriptures in the Holy Land of India nerved him to defy the imperial prohibition of travelling westward, and sustained him through all the perils of his dangerous journey, which exceeded 3,000 miles in length, as reckoned from his starting place in western China to Kabul, at the gates of India. The narrative of his adventures, which we possess in detail, is as interesting as a romance. The dauntless pilgrim travelled by the northern route, and after passing Lake Issik Kul, Tashkend, Samarqand, and Qunduz arrived in the kingdom of Gandhāra about the beginning of October 630. Between that date and the close of 643 he visited almost every province in India, recording numberless exact observations on the country, monuments, people, and religion, which entitle him to be called 'the Indian Pausanias'.[1]

He returned by the southern route, crossing the Pamirs, and passing Kashgar, Yarkand, Khotan, and Lop-nor—a truly wonderful journey. Eight years, 635 to 643, had been mostly spent in Harsha's dominions. Early in 645 he reached his native land, bringing with him a large and valuable collection of manuscripts, images, and relics. He occupied the remainder of his life in working up the results of his expedition with the aid of a staff of scholars, and died in 664 at the age of sixty-four or sixty-five. His high character, undaunted courage, and profound learning deservedly won the respect and affection of the Chinese emperor and all his people. The memory of the Master of the Law, the title bestowed upon him by universal consent, is still as fresh in Buddhist lands as it was 1,200 years ago.

[1] See map prepared by the author at the end of vol. ii of Watters, *On Yuan Chwang's Travels in India* (1905). For the benefit of readers unfamiliar with Greek history it may be mentioned that Pausanias travelled through Greece in the second century A.D. and recorded his detailed observations in the form of an *Itinerary* divided into ten books. The Chinese pilgrim's *Travels* or *Records of Western Lands* comprise twelve books (*chuan*); but the last three books, equivalent to chaps. xvi–xviii of Watters, seem to be interpolated and are of inferior authority (Watters, vol. ii, p. 233).

PLATE II

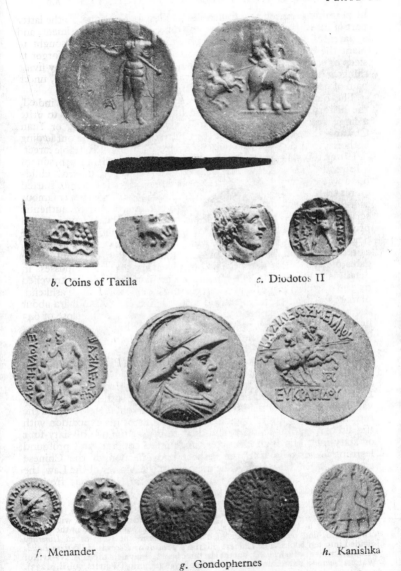

b. Coins of Taxila   *c.* Diodotos II

f. Menander

g. Gondophernes

h. Kanishka

COINS OF ANCIENT INDIA

PLATE 12

a. Candragupta I

b. Samudragupta

c. Candragupta II

d. Toramāṇa

e. Govindacandra Gāhadavāla

f. Pallava

g. Śūdraka

COINS OF ANCIENT INDIA

It is impossible to overestimate the debt which the history of India owes to Hiuen Tsang.

Assemblies at Kanauj and Prayāga. King Harsha, who was in camp in Bengal when he first met the Master, organized in his honour a splendid assembly at Kanauj the capital, which was attended by twenty tributary Rajas, including the King of Assam from the extreme east, and the King of Valabhī from the extreme west. After the close of the proceedings at Kanauj, Harsha carried his honoured guest with him to Prayāga (Allahabad), where another crowded assembly was held, and the royal treasures were distributed to thousands of the holy men of all the Indian religions, Brahmanical, Jain, and Buddhist. On the first day the image of Buddha received honours of the highest class, the effigies of the Sun and Śiva being worshipped respectively on the second and third days with reduced ceremonial. The assembly at Prayāga in 643 was the sixth of its kind, it being Harsha's custom to distribute his accumulated riches at intervals of five years. He did not live to see another celebration. The pilgrim was dismissed with all honour and presented with lavish gifts.

Death of Harsha; results. Either late in 646 or early in 647 the king died, leaving no heir. The withdrawal of his strong arm threw the whole country into disorder, which was aggravated by famine.

Then a strange incident happened. A Chinese envoy named Wang-hiuen-tse was at Harsha's court, attended by an escort of thirty men. A minister who had usurped the vacant throne attacked the envoy, plundered his goods, and killed or captured the men of his escort. Wang-hiuen-tse succeeded in escaping to Nepal, which was then tributary to Tibet. The Tibetan king, the famous Srong-tsan Gampo, who was married to a Chinese princess, assembled a force of Tibetans and Nepalese, who descended into the plains, stormed the chief city of Tirhut, defeated the Indian army with great slaughter, and captured the usurper with his whole family. The captive was sent to China, where he died. Tirhut remained subject to Tibet until A.D. 703.

The death of Harsha having loosened the bonds which had held his empire together, the experiences of the third and sixth centuries were repeated, and a rearrangement of kingdoms was begun, of which the record is obscure. It is impossible to say exactly what happened in most of the provinces for a considerable time after his disappearance from the scene.

His rival, Pulakeśin II, Chālukya, who had successfully defended the Deccan against aggression from the north, had met his fate five years before Harsha's death. He was utterly defeated and presumably killed in 642 by Narasimha-varman, the Pallava King of Kanchi or Conjeeveram in the far south, who thus became the paramount sovereign of the peninsula. The story will be told from the southern point of view in a later chapter.

Unity of history lost. The partial unity of Indian history vanishes with Harsha and is not restored in any considerable measure until the closing years of the twelfth century, when the extensive conquests effected by and for Muhammad of Ghōr brought the most important provinces under the sway of the Sultans of Delhi. The story of Hindu India from the middle of the seventh century until the Muslim conquest, which may be dated approximately in A.D. 1200 for the north and A.D. 1300 for the south, cannot be presented in the form of a single continuous narrative. The subject will be treated in Book III.

CHAPTER 5

Indian Influence in South-east Asia

IT was in the early centuries of the Christian era that the already ancient culture of India began to make a significant impression on the civilizations of south-east Asia. By the end of the Gupta period the whole region had been deeply affected by Indian thought and custom, especially in religion. Thus it is appropriate that we should briefly consider the early kingdoms of south-east Asia here.

Early contacts. There is little doubt that some contact between the islands of Indonesia and India existed before the commencement of the Christian era. The Buddhist *Jātaka* stories, and other sources of the period, frequently mention 'The Land of Gold' and 'The Island of Gold' (*Suvarna-bhūmi* and *Suvarna-dvīpa*), by which terms the lands and islands to the east of India are certainly referred to. Ptolemy's geography, of the second century A.D., proves that by this time there was active commerce between the ports of India and south-east Asia, and several places in the latter region are referred to by Indian names. It is to the intensification of sea-trade, much stimulated by the demands of the Roman empire, that we must chiefly attribute the growth of Indian influence, rather than to any conscious process of colonization. A further factor was Buddhism, which, chiefly in its Mahāyāna form, was carried by courageous monks to the lands beyond the seas, and brought with it many elements of Indian culture. It is significant that the earliest material evidence of Indian contact with south-east Asia takes the form of Buddha images of the school of Amarāvatī, which have been found in Thailand, Cambodia, Annam, Sumatra, Java, and the Celebes. At Oc Eo, in Cambodia, such an image was found in proximity to a gold coin of the Roman emperor Antoninus Pius (A.D. 138–61).

The earliest south-east Asian inscriptions, which are in fairly correct Sanskrit and date from the early fifth century A.D., have been found in Java, Borneo, Malaya, and Cambodia. These show that the region was already ruled by kings with Indian names, many of whom performed Vedic sacrifices. Chinese chronicles tell of the foundation of the kingdom of Fu-nan, the modern Cambodia, in the first century A.D. by a Brahman from India named Kaundinya; we cannot be sure of the accuracy of this account, which is evidently based on a local tradition, since the Chinese source is some centuries later. Late Javanese tradition, however, also tells of the coming of a prince from India, with many followers, to set up the first Javanese kingdom at the end of the first century A.D. The evidence for any such deliberate large-scale settlement is, however, poor, and it is doubtful whether any of the greater south-east Asian kings had more than a little Indian blood in their veins. The traditions of the south-east Asian royal families, connecting them with Indian ancestors, are just such as would be devised by their Brahman advisers to give them prestige and a place in the Hindu order. In the absence of any very clear evidence we may account for the process of Indianization somewhat as follows. By the beginning of the Christian era colonies of Indian merchants had appeared in the busier and more developed coastal settlements of south-east Asia, the inhabitants of which were by no means at the lowest level of barbarism. These colonies increased in numbers and size, and often included Brahmans and Buddhist monks among the settlers. With the growth of Indian settlements, owing to the development of trade in the early Christian centuries, the influence of Indian ideas on the native inhabitants quickly grew, and soon local chiefs became Rajas and Maharajas on the Indian model, performing the royal ceremonies of the Vedas and looking back with pride to usually fictitious Indian ancestors. In many cases intermarriage must have taken place, and here and there an Indian adventurer may have set up a small kingdom. A further probable source of Indian influence was the journeys of south-east Asians themselves to and from India.

Indian influence appears chiefly to have come from the peninsula at this period. The script of the oldest inscriptions resembles that of the early Pallavas, while Amarāvatī provided the earliest Buddha images; but probably every coastal region of India had some cultural influence on south-east Asia, and from the ninth century onwards the religious and cultural influence of the Buddhism of the Pāla kingdom of Bihar and Bengal was very prominent.

In all cases Indian influence in south-east Asia was never sufficient to destroy local customs and religion, and it is evident that the influence was more strongly felt in Indonesia and Malaya than on the mainland; the Buddhism and Hinduism practised in Indonesia had local features distinguishing them from those of India, and the cults of Cambodia and Champā (the southern part of modern Viet-nam) were even more different. A special feature of the state religion of the south-east Asian kingdoms was the deification of the king, who was identified with a god, usually with Śiva, and often worshipped in special temples; in its Śaivite form this worship was directed to the royal *linga*, or phallic emblem, in which the spiritual potency of the divine king was believed to be concentrated. The popular religion was probably little affected by Indian ideas until the coming of Hīnayāna Buddhism from Ceylon, which, in the late Middle Ages, gradually ousted Mahāyāna Buddhism and Hinduism from Burma, Thailand, Cambodia, and Laos. Simultaneously the Indian religions were eclipsed in Indonesia and Malaya by Islam; but a form of Hinduism is practised to this day on the island of Bali, and the Hindu system of the four classes of society is still maintained there.

Malaya and Indonesia. The existence of small Indianized king-

PLATE 13

a. The Stūpa of Barabuḍur, Java

b. The Temple of Angkor Vat, Cambodia

doms in Malaya, Java, and Borneo is attested by inscriptions from the fifth century A.D. onwards. In the late seventh century arose a more important kingdom, that of Śrīvijaya, identified with Palembang in Sumatra, which was conquered in the eighth century by the Śailendra kings of Java, who gained the hegemony of most of Indonesia and Malaya, and for a while of Cambodia. The Śailendra dynasty survived until the eleventh century, but its power was waning, and it received a blow from the invasion of the Cōla emperor Rājendra I from which it never wholly recovered. In the fourteenth century the place of the Śailendras was taken by the kings of Majapahit in Java, which became the centre of a second great island empire, for a while controlling most of Indonesia and Malaya. The empire of Majapahit broke up in the fifteenth century, by which time Islām was making rapid headway in the region, propagated peacefully by merchants from western India. Though Hinduism survived only in Bali, the influence of Hindu India is much in evidence in the culture and language of Indonesia and Malaya even at the present day.

The splendid sculptural and architectural remains of the old kingdoms of Indonesia show the harmonious assimilation of Indian styles and motifs to those native to the region. The most important monument is the famous Barabudūr, the great Buddhist shrine in central Java, erected between about 750 and 850 A.D. Built around a natural hillock, the *stūpa* is surrounded by eleven square concentric terraces, the lowest with a length of 131 yards, all adorned with beautifully sculptured panels, depicting in relief scenes of Buddhist legend.

The mainland of south-east Asia. According to Chinese records an Indianized kingdom existed in the south-eastern part of what is now known as Viet-nam as early as the second century A.D., but inscriptional records of it date from the fifth. This kingdom is generally known as Champā, from the name of its capital city. It survived, suffering much at the hands of Chinese, Annamites, and Khmers (Cambodians), until in the fifteenth century it was conquered by the Annamites.

Farther west a kingdom, known to the Chinese as Fu-nan, is said in Chinese chronicles of the third century A.D. to have had already an existence of two centuries, and to have been founded by an Indian Brahman, Kaundinya, who married a local princess and taught Hindu culture to her subjects. In the seventh century Fu-nan was conquered by one of its vassals, Kambuja (Cambodia), which gave its name to the whole region. For a while, in the eighth century, Kambuja was subject to the Śailendras of Śrīvijaya, but under the great King Jayavarman II (802–50) it regained its independence, and entered on its most prosperous period, which lasted until the end of the twelfth century. During this time Kambuja controlled much of the Indo-Chinese peninsula, including Thailand and Laos. The most impressive monuments of the kingdom of Kambuja are those known today as Angkor Thom and Angkor Vat. The former is a walled city, the capital of Kambuja, as rebuilt by King Jayavarman VII (1181–c. 1218); it is in the form of a perfect square, with walls two miles long on each side, and holds in its centre the fantastic temple known as the Bayon, adorned with relief sculpture of remarkable vigour. The earlier temple of Angkor Vat, to the south of Angkor Thom, is perhaps even more imposing in size and splendour, and is said to be the largest religious building in the world. After the reign of Jayavarman VII the kingdom of Kambuja declined, perhaps exhausted by the immense labour and wealth devoted to the building of the new capital. At the end of the fourteenth century the Annamites, and a new people, the Thais, who had been slowly moving southwards from the Chinese province of Yunnan, divided most of Kambuja between them, though the kingdom has retained its individuality down to the present day. The Thais set up the kingdom of Ayuthia, the ancestor of the present-day Thailand.

Though geographically the closest part of south-east Asia to India, traces of Indian culture in Burma are almost non-existent until the sixth century. In this century there is evidence of the existence of the Buddhist kingdom of Śrīkshetra (modern Prome), which controlled the lower Irrawaddy, and was ruled by a Tibeto-Burman people called Pyu; to the south, in the valley of the Menam in modern Thailand, was another Buddhist kingdom, that of the Mons, called after its capital city Dvāravatī. In the ninth century the Pyus gave way before the kingdom of Pagan, which was ruled by true Burmese, while the centre of the Mon kingdom moved westwards to Pegu. Burma was unified in the eleventh century by Anoratha, King of Pagan (1044–77), whose successors controlled the land until Pagan fell to the Mongols in 1287.

CHRONOLOGY

A.D.

320. Chandragupta I, acc.; epoch of the Gupta era.
c. 330. Samudragupta, acc.
c. 360. Embassy from Meghavarna, King of Ceylon.
c. 380. Chandragupta II, acc.
c. 395. Conquest of western India.
405–11. Travels of Fa-hien in Gupta empire.
415. Kumāragupta I, acc.
455. Skandagupta, acc.; first Hun war.
476. Āryabhata, astronomer, born.
c. 480–90. Partial break-up of Gupta empire.
484. Fīrōz, King of Persia, killed by the Huns.
c. 490–770. Dynasty of Valabhī.
499. Latest date of Budhagupta.
c. 500. Accession of Toramāna in Mālwā.
505. Varāhamihira, astronomer, born.
c. 528. Defeat of Mihiragula the Hun by Indian powers.
c. 540–600. Maukharis and 'Guptas of Magadha' control most of Ganges valley.
578. Brahmagupta, astronomer, born.
c. 605. Defeat and death of Grahavarman, Maukhari King of Kanauj.
606. Harsha-vardhana, acc.; epoch of Harsha era.

A.D.

606–12. Conquest of northern India by Harsha.
  c. 620. Defeat of Harsha by Pulakeśin II, Chālukya.
     622. Flight of Muhammad to Medina; epoch of Hijrī era.
  629–45. Travels of Hiuen Tsang (Yuan Chwang).
     641. Arab conquest of Persia.
     642. Defeat of Pulakeśin II, Chālukya, by the Pallavas.
     643. Harsha's assemblies at Kanauj and Prayāga.
     645. Hiuen Tsang arrived in China.
     647. Death of Harsha; usurpation by minister
     664. Death of Hiuen Tsang.

AUTHORITIES

MANY still important references will be found in *E.H.I.*[4] (1923). A few others are given in notes in the text.

Gupta inscriptions are contained in FLEET's edition (*Corpus Inscriptionum Indicarum*, vol. iii, Calcutta, 1888). Several important inscriptions have come to light since the publication of this volume, and are to be found in various parts of *Epigraphia Indica*. A second edition of the *Corpus*, vol. iii, has been delayed by the death of Professor D. R. Bhandarkar.

On numismatics the B.M. *Catalogue of the Coins of the Gupta Dynasties*, &c., by J. ALLAN (London, 1914) supersedes earlier publications and contains a valuable outline of the history of the period. Later numismatic discoveries are recorded in the *Journal of the Numismatic Society of India* and other learned periodicals.

Among recent monographs on the period the *New History of the Indian People*, vol. vi, edited by R. C. MAJUMDAR and A. S. ALTEKAR (Lahore, 1946), is the most valuable. See also the Bombay *History and Culture of the Indian People* of which the third volume (*The Classical Age*, 1954), also edited by R. C. MAJUMDAR, covers this period. R. K. MOOKERJI's *The Gupta Empire* (Allahabad, 1949) is also a useful work, but inadequately documented.

On the Maukharis see PIRES, *The Maukharis* (Madras, 1934). DE LA VALLÉE POUSSIN's invaluable *Dynasties et Histoire* (Paris, 1935) gives useful chronologies of these and contemporary dynasties, with many references.

On Harsha R. K. MOOKERJI's *Harsha* (Oxford, 1925) is the most recent monograph. R. S. TRIPATHI's *History of Kanauj* (Benares, 1937) devotes much space to Harsha, and is in some respects better than Mookerji's work. The bibliography of translations and studies of Hiuen Tsang will be found in *E.H.I.*[4] To these should be added R. GROUSSET's *In the Footsteps of the Buddha* (tr. M. LEON, London, 1932), a stimulating work on Hiuen Tsang and the Buddhism of the time.

For Gupta art see the author's *Indian Sculpture in the Gupta Period* (*Ostasiatische Zeitung*, April–June 1914), and the relevant chapters of his *History of Fine Art in India* (revised by K. de B. CODRINGTON, Oxford, 1930); also the relevant chapters of P. BROWN's *Indian Architecture, Buddhist and Hindu*, and various reports of the Archaeological Survey. On Ajantā the splendid volumes of the Hyderabad Archaeological Survey by G. YAZDANI (*Ajantā*, London, 1930–3) supersede all earlier works.

Among the many works on the early history of south-east Asia and Indonesia the most valuable single volume is perhaps G. CŒDÈS, *Les États hindouisés d'Indochine et d'Indonésie* (Paris, 1948). In English the best authorities are R. LE MAY, R. C. MAJUMDAR, H. G. QUARITCH WALES, and N. K. SHASTRI, who have produced several important volumes and articles on the subject. D. G. E. HALL's *A History of South-East Asia* (London, 1955) covers the whole period from the earliest times to the present day; its earlier chapters give a very valuable summary of all knowledge to date on the Indianized kingdoms of the region.

BOOK III

The Medieval Hindu Kingdoms from the Death of Harsha in A.D. 647 to the Muslim Conquest

CHAPTER 1

The transitional period; Rajputs; the Himalayan kingdoms and their relations with Tibet and China

A period of transition. The disorder following upon Harsha's death, in which the attack on the Chinese envoy with the consequent subjugation of Tirhut by the Tibetans was an episode, lasted for a considerable number of years concerning which little is known. That time of confusion may be regarded conveniently for purposes of systematic study as forming the transition from Early to Medieval India, during which the hordes of foreign invaders were absorbed into the Hindu body politic and a new grouping of states was gradually evolved. The transitional period was marked by the development of the Rajput clans, never heard of in earlier times, which begin from the eighth century to play a conspicuous part in the history of northern and western India. They become so prominent that the centuries from the death of Harsha to the Muslim conquest of northern India, extending in round numbers from the middle of the seventh to the close of the twelfth century, might be called with propriety the Rajput period. Nearly all the kingdoms were governed by families or clans which for ages past have been called collectively Rajputs. That term, the most generally used, is sometimes replaced by Chhattrī, the vernacular equivalent of the Sanskrit Kshatriya, or by Thakur.

Origin of the Rajputs. The term Rajput, as applied to a social group, has no concern with race, meaning descent or relationship by blood. It merely denotes a tribe, clan, sept, or caste of warlike habits, the members of which claimed aristocratic rank, and were treated by the Brahmans as representing the Kshatriyas of the old books. The huge group of Rajput clan-castes includes people of the most diverse descent. Many of the clans are descended from the foreigners who entered India during the fifth and sixth centuries, while many others are descended from indigenous tribes now represented, so far as the majority of their members is concerned, either by semi-hinduized peoples or by inferior castes.

Probably it would be safe to affirm that all the most distinguished clan-castes of Rajasthan are descended mainly from foreigners, the 'Scythians' of Tod. The upper ranks of the invading hordes of Hūnas, Gurjaras, Maitrakas, and the rest became Rajput clans, while the lower developed into Hindu castes of less honourable social status, such as Gūjars, Āhīrs, Jats, and others.

Such clan-castes of foreign descent are the proud and chivalrous Sīsōdias or Guhilōts of Mewar, the Parihārs (Pratihāras), the Chauhāns (Chāhumānas), the Pawārs (Paramāras), and the 'Solankis, otherwise called Chaulukyas.[1]

The Rāshtrakūtas of the Deccan; the Rathors of Rajasthan, whose name is only a vernacular form of the same designation; the Chandēls and the Bundelas of Bundelkhand, are examples of ennobled indigenous peoples. The Chandēls perhaps originated from among the Gonds, who again were closely associated with the Bhars. It is impossible to pursue farther the subject, which admits of endless illustration.

Brahmans and Kshatriyas. In ancient times the line of demarcation between the Brahmans and the Kshatriyas, that is to say, between the learned and the warrior groups of castes, was not sharply defined. It was often crossed, sometimes by change of occupation, and at other times by intermarriage. Ordinarily, the position of the leading Brahman at court was that of minister, but sometimes the Brahman preferred to rule directly, and himself seized the throne. Thus in early times the Sunga and Kānva royal families were Brahman. Similar cases of Brahman dynasties occur later. In the seventh century Hiuen Tsang noted the existence of several Brahman Rajas, as at Ujjain and in Jijhoti or Bundēlkhand. Usurpations by Brahman ministers also continued to happen. When a Brahman succeeded in founding a dynasty, and so definitely taking up Kshatriya work, his descendants were recognized as Kshatriyas, and allowed to intermarry freely with established Kshatriya families. It must be remembered that the Brahmans themselves are of very diverse origin, and that many of them, as for instance the Nāgar Brahmans, may be descended from the learned or priestly class of the foreign hordes. The Maga Brahmans were probably originally Iranian Magi. During the transitional stage, while a Brahman family was passing into the Kshatriya group of castes, it was often known by the composite designation of Brahma-kshatrī. Several cases of the application of that term to royal families are recorded, the

[1] Pandit Mohanlāl Vishnulāl Pandia admits that Bāpa, the Guhilōt ancestor, was brought up as a concealed or reputed Brahman (*J. & Proc. A. S. B.*, 1912, pp. 62–99); and has not succeeded in refuting the reasoning of D. R. Bhandarkar concerning the origin of the Ranas of Mewar. If the frank statement of facts as revealed by modern research should give offence in any quarter that result is to be regretted. But, as Aśoka observed long ago, 'truth must be spoken'.

most prominent being those of the Sīsōdias of Mewar and the Sēnas of Bengal.

Rajputs not a race. The Rajputs, as already stated, are not to be regarded as a people originally of one race, bound together by ties of blood descent from a common ancestor. Even within the limits of Rajasthan the clans were originally descended from many distinct racial stocks. Such common features as they presented depended on the similarity of their warlike occupations and social habits. Now, of course, the operation of complicated caste rules concerning intermarriage during many centuries has produced an extensive network of blood-relationship between the clans, which have become castes.

These condensed observations may help the student to understand in some measure why the Rajput clans begin to play so prominent a part in Indian history from the eighth century. The Hun invasions and their consequences, as observed in the chapter preceding, broke the chain of historical tradition. Living clan traditions rarely, if ever, go back beyond the eighth century, and few go back as far. The existing clan-castes only began to be formed in the sixth century. The Brahmans found their advantage in treating the new aristocracy, whatever its racial origin, as representing the ancient Kshatriya class of the scriptures, and the novel term Rāja-putra or Rajput, meaning 'king's son', or member of a ruling family or clan, came into use as an equivalent of Kshatriya.

Before entering upon a summary review of outstanding features in the history of the leading Rajput kingdoms of the plains, we must bestow a passing glance on the Himalayan States—Nepal, Kashmir, and Assam—and on their relations with Tibet and China.

China and the Indian border. The short-lived Hun empire was broken up by the Western Turks, who in their turn succumbed to the Chinese. For a few years, from 661 to 665, China enjoyed unparalleled prestige, and the ambassadors in attendance at the imperial court included envoys from the Suwāt valley and from all the countries extending from Persia to Korea. Such glory did not last long. In 670 the Tibetans occupied Kashgaria, and a little later the Turks regained power. In the first half of the eighth century an ambitious emperor, Hiuen-tsung, succeeded in once more establishing Chinese rule over the Western countries. Even kings of Kashmir then received investiture from China. The advance of the Arabs in the middle of the eighth century put an end to Chinese claims to sovereignty over the mountains of Kashmir, and since that time no state of the Indian borderland, except Nepal, has had political relations with China.

Tibet; Srong-tsan Gampo. In the seventh and eighth centuries Tibet was a powerful state, in close touch with India as well as with China. The routes from China through Lhasa and Nepal into India now closed were then open and frequently used by pilgrims and other travellers. Srong-tsan Gampo, the most renowned of Tibetan kings, whose great reign is placed by the best authorities between A.D. 629

and 650, annexed Nepal, defeated the usurper who had dared to occupy the throne vacated by Harsha, occupied Tirhūt, and strengthened his position by marrying a Chinese princess as well as a Nepalese one.[1] Acting under the influence of his Buddhist consorts he introduced their religion into his kingdom, and gave his people the means of acquiring knowledge by importing from India the alphabet now used in Tibet. He founded Lhāsa, for which, according to tradition, he prepared the site by filling up a lake with stones.

In the first half of the eleventh century Atīśa and other eminent monks from the seats of learning in Magadha came to Tibet on the invitation of the reigning king and effected extensive reforms or changes in the Buddhist church, which became the foundation of modern Lamaism.

The object of all these reformations was not, as is often supposed, to go back to the early Buddhism as it was preached by Gautama, but to build up a church which represented the doctrines of the Mahāyāna school of Buddhism in a pure form. The doctrines of Nāgārjuna were propounded by all the great teachers of Tibet. But the Kāla-chakra philosophy with its monotheistic tendencies was also favoured by them.[2]

Nepal. The kingdom of Nepal as at present constituted is an extensive territory lying along the northern frontier of India for about 500 miles, from Kumaon on the west to Sikkim on the east. The Nepal of ancient Indian history means the restricted valley about twenty miles long and fifteen broad, in which the capital, Kāthmandu, and other towns are situated. Some of the adjoining country may have been included at times in the kingdom, but the bulk of the territory now comprised in the Nepal State, whether in the hills or the strip of plain at their base, used to be occupied by independent tribes and principalities.

The valley certainly formed part of Aśoka's empire, but the Kushāns do not seem to have meddled with it. In the fourth century A.D. Nepal acknowledged in some degree the sovereignty of Samudragupta. In the seventh century the influence of Tibet was paramount, and after Harsha's death the country became actually subject to Tibet for half a century.[3] The theory that Harsha conquered Nepal and introduced his era seems to be erroneous. The Gūrkhas who now rule Nepal conquered the country in 1768. From 1815 the foreign policy of the state was controlled by the government of India, though China from time

---

[1] Berthold Laufer (*J.A.O.S.*, vol. 38 (1918), pp. 31–46).

[2] A. H. Francke, *Antiquities of Indian Tibet* (Calcutta, 1914), p. 52. For the Kāla-chakra and other late corrupt forms of Buddhism see the excellent little book by Nagendra Nath Vasu and M. M. H. P. Sastri, entitled *Modern Buddhism and its Followers in Orissa* (Calcutta, 1911).

[3] In A.D. 703 both Nepal and India [*sc.* Tirhūt] threw off the Tibetan sovereignty. The King of Tibet was killed while attempting to reassert his authority (Parker, 'China, Nepaul, &c.', in *J. Manchester Oriental Soc.*, 1911, pp. 129–52). That date, recorded in the histories of the T'ang dynasty, was not known to earlier European writers.

to time has asserted claims to tribute. The long and blood-stained story of the medieval dynasties is not of general interest, and may be left to students specially concerned with the local history.

Modern students of Nepalese affairs have been chiefly interested in the silent conflict of religions which has gone on for centuries and still may be watched in progress. A corrupt form of Buddhism, which allows even the strange institution of married monks, may be seen slowly decaying and yielding to the constant pressure of Brahmanical Hinduism, which is the religion of the government. The Nepalese libraries contain a rich store of Buddhist manuscripts, first made known by the labours of Brian Hodgson between 1820 and 1858, which have supplied much material for the study of the various forms of Buddhist religion and philosophy.

The general current of Indian history has not been affected by the transactions in Nepal, which usually has remained isolated.

Art. The art of Nepal is closely related to that of Tibet. The craftsmen of both countries excel in metal-work, and the Tibetan artists have been eminently successful in producing realistic portrait statuettes of Buddhist saints and similar images of deities belonging to the populous pantheon of later Buddhism. Some of the Tibetan painting has considerable merit. The architecture of Nepal in modern times is usually closer in style to that of China than that of India.

Kashmir. The history of Hindu Kashmir, from the seventh century after Christ, when the trustworthy annals begin, is recorded in ample detail in the metrical chronicle called the *Rājataranginī*, written in the twelfth century by a learned Brahman named Kalhana or Kalyāna, which has been admirably edited and translated by Sir M. A. Stein. The story, although of much interest in itself, has little concern with the general history of India; the reason being that the mountain barriers which enclose the vale of Kashmir have usually sufficed to protect the country against foreign invasion and to preserve its isolated independence. Nevertheless, both the Mauryas and the Kushāns exercised effective authority over the valley. The Guptas did not concern themselves with it, and Harsha, while in a position to bring pressure to bear upon the Raja, did not attempt to annex the country.

The narrative of the doings of the medieval Hindu rulers teems with horrors. Harsha, a half-insane tyrant who reigned in the latter part of the eleventh century, has been justly described as the 'Nero of Kashmir'. Few regions in the world can have had worse luck than Kashmir in the matter of government, a fate due partly to the passive character of the population, which invited oppression. The avowed policy of the Hindu rulers throughout the ages was to fleece the peasantry to the utmost and to leave them at best a bare subsistence. The majority of the people was forced to accept Islām in the fourteenth century, and dynasties of Muslim Sultans ruled until Akbar annexed the kingdom in 1587 with little difficulty. The lot of the common people continued to be hard, whether the government was in the hands of Hindus or

Muslims. In modern times the Kashmīrīs were oppressed successively by the Afghans and the Sikhs, and never enjoyed the advantages of decently good administration until late in the nineteenth century.

But, although Kashmir has ordinarily occupied a position politically isolated from India, the influence of the country on the religion and civilization of its neighbours has been considerable. The valley has been the abode of Sanskrit learning at least from the time of Aśoka, and has played an important part as being the intermediate stage through which Indian civilization and art reached Khotan and the adjoining territories of Chinese Turkistan, and so passed into the Far East. The valley includes many sacred sites both Buddhist and Brahmanical. Jainism does not seem to have entered it. An interesting local style of architecture was developed in the eighth and ninth centuries. The Mārtand temple dedicated to the Sun-god in the reign of Lalitāditya (A.D. 724–60) is the best-known example, but many others exist.

Assam. Assam, roughly equivalent to the ancient Kāmarūpa, resembled Kashmir in being protected by natural fortifications, and was thus enabled, as a rule, to preserve its independence. The country does not seem to have been included in either the Maurya or the Kushān empire, but in the fourth century its ruler, who belonged to an ancient Hindu dynasty, acknowledged in some degree the overlordship of Samudragupta. Buddhism never succeeded in establishing itself. Nevertheless, the ruling king in the seventh century insisted on receiving a visit from Hiuen Tsang, the Chinese Buddhist pilgrim, who was hospitably entertained. The king, although not directly subject to Harsha, was constrained to obey his imperious commands and to attend humbly in his train when summoned. Certain Muslim leaders who invaded the country on several occasions between 1205 and 1662 always met with disaster more or less complete. The Muslim historian who describes the latest venture, that made by Aurangzēb's general Mīr Jumla in the seventeenth century, expresses the horror with which the country and people were regarded by outsiders in striking phrases which deserve quotation.

Assam [he observes] is a wild and dreadful country abounding in danger, ... Its roads are frightful like the path leading to the nook of Death;
Fatal to life is its expanse like the unpeopled city of Destruction. . . .
The air and water of the hills are like the destructive Simoom and deadly poison to natives and strangers alike.
[The inhabitants] resemble men in nothing beyond this, that they walk erect on two feet. [They were reputed to be expert magicians.] In short, every army that entered the limits of this country made its exit from the realm of Life; every caravan that set foot on this land deposited its baggage of residence in the halting-place of Death.[1]

Early in the thirteenth century Assam was invaded by the Āhōms, a Shan tribe from Upper Burma, who gradually acquired the sovereignty

[1] Talish, as transl. by Professor Jadunath Saskar in *J. B. & O. Res. Soc.*, vol. i, pp. 179–95.

of the country, which they retained until it was occupied by the Burmese in 1816 and by the British in 1825. The Āhōms brought with them a tribal religion of their own, which they abandoned in favour of Hinduism about the beginning of the eighteenth century. Their language, too, is almost, if not completely, extinct. The Āhōms have become merged in the Hindu population, and speak Assamese, an Aryan language akin to Sanskrit and Bengālī. When in power they had an efficient, although severe or even cruel, system of administration. They produced a considerable historical literature, and carried the art of carving wood to a high degree of excellence. The Muslim writer quoted expresses unbounded admiration of the decorations of the palace at Garhgāon. No trace of them remains.

Assam is a province of much interest to the student of Indian religion as being the meeting ground of Mongolian and Indian ideas. The contact has resulted in the evolution of a peculiar Tantric form of Hinduism, which offers special honour to female forms of the deity called Śaktis. The temple of Kāmākhyā near Gauhātī is recognized as one of the most important shrines of the cult. All the processes by means of which the members of rude animistic tribes become fanatical Hindus, and strange tribal gods are converted into respectable Brahmanical deities, may be illustrated in Assam.

CHRONOLOGY

A.D.   (MISCELLANEOUS DATES)

629. Srong-tsan Gampo, King of Tibet, acc.
639. Srong-tsan Gampo founded Lhāsa.
641. Srong-tsan Gampo married Chinese and Nepalese princesses.
643. Hiuen Tsang visited Kāmarūpa.
647. Death of Harsha of Kanauj.
670. Tibetans wrested Kashgaria or Chinese Turkistan from China.
703. Nepal and Tirhūt became independent of Tibet.
713. Hiuen-tsung, Chinese emperor, acc.
720, 733. Kings of Kashmir received investiture from China.
751. Chinese defeated by the Arabs.
1038. Mission of Atīśa to Tibet (Waddell, *Lhāsa*³, p. 320).
1089–1111. Harsha, King of Kashmir.
1339. Muslim dynasty established in Kashmir.
1587. Annexation of Kashmir by Akbar.
1768. Gūrkha conquest of Nepal.

AUTHORITIES

THE authorities are indicated sufficiently in the footnotes and in *E.H.I.*⁴ (1923). Since the publication of *E.H.I.*⁴ little new has appeared on Kashmir or Nepal in the pre-Muslim period. On Assam the 2nd ed. of Sir E. GAIT's *History of Assam* (Calcutta, 1925), and K. L. BARUA's *Early History of Kāmarūpa* (Shillong, 1933), should be mentioned. The learned and beautiful book entitled *The Gods of Northern Buddhism*, by ALICE GETTY and J. DENIKER (Clarendon Press, 1914), is a treasury of Tibetan art and mythology. See Laufer, in *J.A.O.S.*, vol. 38 (1918), pp. 31–46.

CHAPTER 2

The northern and western kingdoms of the plains

Countless kingdoms. During the five and a half centuries inter-
vening between the death of Harsha and the Muslim conquest, in which
no permanent foreign occupation was effected, except in the Panjab,
the greater part of India was indifferent to the Muslim power and
knew nothing about it. The numerous Hindu states, which took shape
from time to time, varying continually in number, extent, and in their
relations one with the other, seldom were at peace. It would, however,
be a mistake to suppose that their rulers and people thought of nothing
else than war and rapine. Royal courts of no small magnificence were
maintained, and the arts of peace were cultivated with success. Stately
works of architecture, enriched lavishly with sculptures often of high
merit, were erected in almost every kingdom; and learned men, writing
for the most part in the Sanskrit language, enjoyed liberal and intelligent
patronage from princes who not unfrequently wielded the pen as well
as the sword. Hindī, Bengālī, Gujarātī, and the other languages now
spoken gradually attained the dignity of recognized existence, and the
foundations of vernacular literatures were laid.

In a general history it is impossible to narrate in detail the stories of
the several states, which are recorded in many cases with so much
fullness that they would suffice to fill several volumes each as large as
this work.

The effects of the great foreign invasions in the fifth and sixth
centuries lasted for hundreds of years. The Gurjaras, with their
kinsmen and allies bearing other names, had been converted, as has
been shown, into ruling Rājpūt clans, and had acquired a dominant
position in Rājasthān, which served as the basis of more extended
dominion. In the ninth and tenth centuries the Gurjara-Pratihāras
(Parihārs) became the leading power in north-western India. Bengal
came under the sway of the Pālas, apparently an indigenous dynasty,
for more than four centuries; while Mālwā, Gujarāt, and several other
kingdoms obtained a large share of wealth and power.

The course of history. The history of northern India ordinarily
pursued its own course, regardless of the events happening in the
peninsular kingdoms. But occasionally the rulers of the Deccan made
inroads into the rich plains of Āryāvarta or Hindostan, which resulted
in the temporary extension of their power to the banks of the Ganges.
No northern prince attempted to conquer the Deccan. The Tamil
realms of the Far South formed a world of their own, in comparative
isolation, save for frequent wars with the kings of the Deccan and
Ceylon and for extensive foreign trade.

INDIA c. A.D. 1000
(Kingdoms in brackets became important after this date)

The ancient states of the Pāndyas, Cholas, and Cheras were over-shadowed for a long time, especially in the seventh century, by the Pallava dynasty of uncertain origin, which had its capital at Kānchī (Conjeeveram). In the eleventh century the Chola kingdom became paramount in the south, and probably was the most powerful state in India.

Changes so extensive, disconnected, and incessant as those indicated cannot be described in a single continuous narrative arranged in strict chronological order. The political revolutions were accompanied by silent local modifications in religion, manners, and art equally incapable of comprehensive narration.

The never-ending dynastic wars and revolutions did not bring about any development of political institutions. No republics were formed, no free towns were established. All the states continued to be governed in the old-fashioned way by despotic Rajas, each of whom could do what he pleased, so long as his power lasted, unless he suffered his will to be controlled by Brahman or other religious guides.

It will be convenient to deal in this chapter only with certain outstanding features in the history of some of the more prominent northern and western kingdoms of the plains. The fortune of the peninsular states will similarly form the subject of the chapter following; the few points of contact between the two being duly noted.

Gurjara-Pratihāra kingdom. The Gurjaras, aided by the allied or kindred tribes bearing other names who entered India in the early years of the sixth century, established kingdoms or principalities in various places. The state among those so founded that was most closely associated with the general history of India was the Gurjara kingdom of southern Rājasthān, the capital of which was perhaps Bhinmāl or Bhilmāl to the north-west of Mount Ābū, the site of the fire-pit from which the Parihārs and several other Rājpūt clans originated according to the legend. When Hiuen Tsang visited that Gurjara kingdom in the first half of the seventh century the king, although undoubtedly of foreign descent, was already recognized as a Kshatriya.

About A.D. 725 a new local dynasty was founded by a chief named Nāgabhata, who belonged to the Pratihāra (Parihār) section or sept of the Gurjaras. The dynasty seems to have gained control of Ujjain. Nearly a century later, in or about A.D. 816, his descendant, another Nāgabhata, invaded the Gangetic region, captured Kanauj, deposed the reigning king, and presumably transferred the seat of his own government to the imperial city of Harsha, where his descendants certainly ruled for many generations. The Pratihāras remained in possession for two centuries until 1018–19 when Sultān Mahmūd of Ghaznī occupied Kanauj and forced the Raja to retire to Bārī.

Kanauj. Kanauj must have suffered much during the long-continued troubles which ensued on the decease of Harsha. Nothing definite is known about it until 731 when its king, Yaśovarman by name, sent an embassy to China, probably to invoke the assistance of the emperor against the Raja's powerful enemies. No help came. In or about 740 Yaśovarman was defeated and slain by Lalitāditya, the most renowned of the kings of Kashmir, the builder of the Mārtand temple. Yaśovarman's successor similarly was overthrown by Lalitāditya's son. Again, about 810, Dharmapāla, King of Bengal, deposed the reigning King of Kanauj, replacing him by a nominee of his own. That nominee in his turn was expelled, as related above, by Nāgabhata Pratihāra. Thus, within a space of about seventy-six years (c. A.D. 740–816), four kings

of Kanauj were violently deposed by hostile powers. The fact illustrates
vividly the disturbed condition of northern India in that age.

The Gurjara empire of Bhoja. King Mihira Pratihāra of Kanauj,
commonly known by his cognomen of Bhoja, reigned with great power
and might for half a century (c. A.D. 840–90). His successors being
known to have held both Saurashtra and Oudh, those countries may
be assumed to have formed part of Bhoja's dominions, which were
extensive enough to be described as an empire without exaggeration.
Its limits may be defined as, on the north, the foot of the mountains; on
the north-west, the Sutlaj; on the west, the Hakrā, or 'lost river', forming the boundary of Sind, and then the Mihrān to the Arabian Sea; on
the south, the Jumna, forming the frontier of Jejāka-bhukti; on the
south-west, the lower course of the Narbadā, and on the east, the
frontier of the Pāla kingdom of Magadha. His son, Mahendrapāla
(c. A.D. 890–910), seems to have retained possession of all the dominions
of his father. An inscription of his which mentions the province and
district of Śrāvastī suggests that that famous city was still inhabited in
the tenth century. Magadha or South Bihār seems to have been tributary for a short time.

Hardly anything is known about the internal condition of the
Gurjara or Pratihāra empire of Kanauj. An Arab traveller tells us
that in the middle of the ninth century the king, namely Bhoja, commanded a powerful army, including the best cavalry in India and a
large force of camels. The territories in Rajasthan have always been
famous for their breed of camels, which is still maintained. The extreme
mobility of Bhoja's cavalry and camelry must have given him an immense advantage over the less active armies of the ordinary Hindu
state. The king was extremely rich, and 'no country in India was more
safe from robbers', a brief remark which implies the existence of
efficient internal administration.

Bhoja was a Hindu specially devoted to the worship of Vishnu in
the boar incarnation and of the goddess Bhagavatī or Lakshmī. He
placed on his coins, which are very common, the words *Ādi Varāha*,
meaning 'primeval boar' or Vishnu. The coins, like the other issues
of the White Hun and Gurjara princes, are degenerate imitations of
Sassanian pieces, with reminiscences of the Greek drachma, the name
of which survived in the word *dramma* applied to the Gurjara coins.
The foreign invaders of India in those times never took the trouble to
devise coin types of their own and were content to use barbarous and
degraded derivatives of the Persian coinage.

Mahendrapāla. Mahendrapāla (c. 890–910), the son and successor
of Bhoja, was even more powerful than his father. He drove the Pālas
out of Magadha and left an inscription in western Bengal. He was the
pupil of Rājaśekhara, a poet from the Deccan who attended his court
and was the author of four extant plays. One of those, entitled
Karpūra-manjarī from the name of the heroine, is a curious and interesting work, written wholly in Prākrit. Professor Lanman has published

a clever English translation of it. The dramatist also composed a work on the art of poetry, which has been edited in the Gaikwār's Oriental Series.

Before we proceed to describe the decline and fall of the Gurjara empire and the capture of Kanauj by Sultan Mahmūd of Ghaznī in 1018–19, it will be convenient to give a brief account of the Pāla dynasty of Bengal and the Chandēl rulers of Jijhoti or Bundēlkhand, the two leading kingdoms of northern India which were contemporary with the Gurjara kingdom or empire of Kanauj; adding a slight notice of other states.

Bengal; Ādiśūra. The history of Bengal and Bihār after the decease of Harsha is obscure. For the rest of the century west Bengal was probably controlled by the later Guptas of Magadha. After the victories of Yaśovarman of Kanauj and the sudden disappearance of his empire the fate of Bengal is uncertain.

Bengal tradition has much to say about a king named Ādiśūra, who ruled at Gaur or Lakshmanāvatī, and sought to revive the Brahmanical religion which had suffered from Buddhist predominance. He is believed to have imported five Brahmans from Kanauj, who taught orthodox Hinduism and became the ancestors of the Rādhiya and Vārendra Brahmans. His date may be placed after A.D. 700.

The Pāla dynasty; Dharmapāla. Then Bengal suffered from prolonged anarchy which became so intolerable that the people (c. A.D. 750) elected as their king one Gopāla, of the 'race of the sea', in order to introduce settled government. We do not know the details of the events thus indicated. Gopāla's son, Dharmapāla, who enjoyed an unusually long reign, was the real founder of the greatness of his dynasty, which is conveniently known as that of the 'Pāla Kings' of Bengal, because the names of the sovereigns ended in the word -pāla. Dharmapāla succeeded in carrying his arms far beyond the limits of Bengal and Bihār. He made himself master of most of northern India, and, as already mentioned, was strong enough to depose one Raja of Kanauj and substitute another in his place. He is said to have effected the revolution with the assent of nine northern kings. If this statement of a contemporary inscription is to be believed it indicates that the influence of the Bengal monarch extended even to Gandhāra on the north-western frontier. Those events must have happened about or soon after A.D. 810.

Dharmapāla, like all the members of his house, was a zealous Buddhist. He founded the famous monastery and college of Vikramaśīla, which probably stood at Pattharghāta in the Bhagalpur District. The Buddhism of the Pālas was very different from the religion or philosophy taught by Gautama, and was a corrupt form of Mahāyāna doctrine.

Devapāla. Dharmapāla's son Devapāla, who is reckoned by Bengal tradition to have been the most powerful of the Pālas, also enjoyed a long reign. His rule and that of his father together covered something like 100 years, and may be taken as having extended through almost the whole of the ninth century. Devapāla's general, Lāusena or Lavanasena, is said to have annexed both Assam and Kalinga. At this time the Pālas were in diplomatic contact with the Indonesian kingdom of Śrīvijaya, which controlled much of the archipelago. The King of Śrīvijaya, Bālaputradeva of the Śailendra dynasty, built a monastery at Nālandā. No buildings of Pāla age seem to have survived, but the remembrance of the kings is preserved by many great tanks or artificial lakes excavated under their orders, especially in the Dinājpur District. Sculpture in both stone and metal was practised with remarkable success. The names of two eminent artists, Dhīmān and Bitpālo or Vītapāla, are recorded, and it is possible that some of the numerous extant works may be attributed rightly to them.

Mahīpāla, &c.; the Sēnas. The popular memory has attached itself to Mahīpāla, the ninth king of the dynasty (c. A.D. 978–1030), more than to any other. He reigned for about half a century and underwent the strange experience of being attacked about A.D. 1023 by Rājendra Chola, the Tamil King of the Far South, who prided himself on having advanced as far as the bank of the Ganges. The mission of Atīśa to Tibet, as already mentioned, was dispatched in A.D. 1038, in the reign of Nayapāla, the successor of Mahīpāla.

The dynasty, which underwent various ups and downs of fortune, lasted in Bihār until the Muslim conquest in 1199. Part of Bengal came under the sway of a new dynasty, that of the Senas, early in the eleventh century. Vallāla-sena or Ballāl Sen, who seems to have reigned from about 1158 to 1169, is credited by Bengal tradition with having reorganized the caste system, and introduced the practice of 'Kulīnism' among Brahmans, Baidyas, and Kāyasths.[1] The Senas originally were Brahmans from the Deccan, and their rise seems to have been a result of the Chola invasion in 1023. The details of their chronology and history are obscure.

Chandēl dynasty. The Chandēl dynasty of Jijhoti or Bundēlkhand, although it never attained a position as exalted as that of the greatest Āndhra and Pāla kings, had a still longer history, and played a considerable part on the Indian political stage for about three centuries. The early Chandēl Rajas appear to have been petty Gond chiefs in the territory until recently called the Chhatarpur State in Madhya Pradesh. In the ninth century they overthrew neighbouring Pratihāra (Parihār) chieftains of foreign origin, who must have been connected with the Kanauj dynasty, and advanced their frontier towards the north in the region now called Bundēlkhand, until they approached the Jumna. The principal towns in the kingdom, which was called Jejāka-bhukti or Jijhoti, were Khajurāho in Chhatarpur, Mahoba in the Hamīrpur

---

[1] Under this system the three castes mentioned were divided into sub-castes, among which hypergamy (the marriage of a man of a higher with a woman of a lower sub-caste) was permitted. The practice led to an excess of unmarried girls in the upper (*kulīn*) group, and the marriage of *kulīn* men to a large number of women whom they did not support.

District, and Kâlanjar in the Bāndā District, U.P. The military power of the kingdom depended largely on the possession of the strong fortress of Kālanjar.

The Chandēl Rajas, who probably had been tributary to Bhoja of Kanauj, became fully independent in the tenth century. King Dhanga, whose reign covered the second half of that century, was the most notable prince of his family. He joined the Hindu confederacy formed to resist Amīr Sabuktigīn, the earliest Muslim invader, and shared the disastrous defeat suffered by the allies on the Afghan frontier. Ganda, a later Raja, took part in the opposition to Sultan Mahmūd, which will be noticed presently more particularly. In the second half of the eleventh century Raja Kīrtivarman restored the glories of his house, defeated Karnadeva, the aggressive King of Chedi, the ancient Mahākosala, equivalent in large measure to the modern Madhya Pradesh (formerly Central Provinces), and widely extended the frontiers of his dominions. Kīrtivarman is memorable in literary history as the patron of the curious allegorical play, entitled the *Prabodha-chandrodaya*, or 'Rise of the Moon of Intellect', which was performed at his court about A.D. 1065, and gives in dramatic form a clever exposition of the Vedānta system of philosophy. The Raja's memory is also preserved by the name of the Kīrat Sāgar, a lake situated among the hills near Mahoba.

The last Chandēl Raja to enjoy the position of an independent king of importance was Paramardi or Parmāl, who was defeated by Prithīraj Chauhān in 1182, and by Kutbu-d dīn Ībak in 1203. After that date the Chandēl Rajas sank into obscurity, but long continued to reign as local princes in the jungles of Bundēlkhand. Durgāvatī, the noble Queen of Gondwāna, who so gallantly resisted the unprovoked aggression of Akbar's general, Āsaf Khān, in 1564, was a Chandēl princess. She was married to a Gond Raja, thus renewing the ancient relation between the tribesmen of the forest and their ennobled Rājpūt kinsmen of the plain. The dynasty survived in the line of the Rajas of Gidhaur in the Monghyr (Mungir) District of Bihār, whose ancestor emigrated from Bundēlkhand in the thirteenth century.

Chandēl architecture. One of the beautiful lakes which Chandēl princes formed by damming up valleys among the low forest-clad hills of Bundēlkhand has been mentioned. Many others exist, on the banks of which I often pitched my tents in my youth. The embankments are gigantic structures faced with stone and sometimes crowned by magnificent temples of granite, or rather gneiss. A large group of such temples still standing at Khajurāho is familiar to all students of Indian architecture. Some of the best examples were erected by King Dhanga in the second half of the tenth century. The Jain religion had numerous adherents in the Chandēl dominions during the eleventh and twelfth centuries, although it is now nearly extinct in that region. Ancient Jain temples and dated images may still be seen in many villages. Buddhism had but a slight hold on the country, and Buddhist images, although not unknown, are rare.

Raja Bhoja of Dhār. The Paramāras or Pawārs, one of the clans of foreign origin supposed to have been born from the fire-pit of Mount Ābū, founded a dynasty in Mālwā, which took its share in the wars of the period and attained considerable distinction. The most renowned prince of the dynasty was Raja Bhoja, who reigned for more than forty years, from about 1018 to 1060.[1] He was an accomplished scholar and a liberal patron of Sanskrit learning. His name in consequence has become proverbial as that of the ideal Hindu prince. The defeat of Bhoja in or about 1060 by the allied armies of Gujarāt and Chedi reduced the Raja of Mālwā to a position of little political importance. Dhār or Dhārā, until recently the headquarters of a petty state, was the capital of Bhoja, who adorned the town with handsome edifices, of which some vestiges remain in spite of the long-continued Muslim occupation. The immense Bhojpur lake formed by damming the Betwa river and a smaller stream, and covering an area exceeding 250 square miles, was constructed by Raja Bhoja. Early in the fifteenth century the dam was cut by Hoshang Shāh, Sultan of Mālwā, with the result that a large area of valuable land was reclaimed for cultivation. The railway now traverses the dry bed of the lake.

Saurashtra. A passing reference to the Solanki or Chaulukya dynasty of Saurashtra established by Mūlarāja in the tenth century must suffice, although stories about Mūlarāja occupy a prominent place in the semi-historical legends of the province. If tradition may be believed, Mūlarāja was a son of the King of Kanauj, apparently Mahīpāla, who probably had appointed his son to be Viceroy in the west. Mūlarāja seems to have seized an opportunity to rebel and set up as an independent sovereign. The most important of his successors was Kumārapāla (1143–72), who was a patron of the great Jain doctor Hemacandra, and himself an earnest Jain (see above, p. 79).

We now return to the north and resume the thread of the story of Kanauj with that of other northern kingdoms.

Mahīpāla of Kanauj. The Pratihāra empire began to break up in the reign of Mahīpāla (c. A.D. 910–40), who was a grandson of Bhoja. His power suffered a severe shock in A.D. 916 when Indra III, the Rāshtrakūta King of the Deccan, captured Kanauj. Although the southern monarch did not attempt to secure a permanent dominion on the banks of the Ganges, his successful raid necessarily weakened the authority of Mahīpāla, who could no longer hold the western provinces. The Chandēl king helped Mahīpāla to recover his capital. Some years later Gwālior became independent, but the Kanauj kingdom still continued to be one of the leading states.

Rājā Jaipāl of Bathindah. The rule of the Pratihāras had never extended across the Sutlaj, and the history of the Panjab between the

---

[1] Care should be taken not to confound him with Bhoja or Mihira Pratihāra of Kanauj who reigned from about A.D. 840 to 890, and has been forgotten by Indian tradition. Names like Mahīpāla, Mahendrapāla, and many others occur in distinct dynastic lists, and it is easy to confound the bearers of the names.

seventh and tenth centuries is extremely obscure. At some time not recorded a powerful kingdom had been formed, which extended from the mountains beyond the Indus, eastwards as far as the Hakrā or 'lost river', so that it comprised a large part of the Panjab, as well as probably northern Sind. The capital was Bathindah (Bhatinda), the Tabarhind of Muslim histories, now in the Patiāla State, and for many centuries an important fortress on the military road connecting Mūltān with India proper through Delhi. At that time Delhi, if in existence, was a place of little consideration. In the latter part of the tenth century the Rājā of Bathindah was Jaipāl, probably a Jat or Jāt.

Freedom of the Hindu states. Until almost the end of the tenth century the Indian Rajas were at liberty to do what they pleased, enjoying exemption from foreign invasion and freedom from the control of any paramount authority. Their position was gravely disturbed when an aggressive Muslim power, alien in religion, social customs, ideas, and methods of warfare, appeared on the scene and introduced an absolutely novel element into the interior politics of India, which had not been seriously affected either by the Arab conquest of Sind at the beginning of the eighth century or by the later Muslim occupation of Kābul.

Amīr Sabuktigīn. An ambitious Muslim chief named Sabuktigīn, Amīr of Ghaznī, effected a sudden change. In A.D. 986–7 (A.H. 376) he made his first raid into Indian territory, and came into conflict with Rājā Jaipāl of Bathindah. Two years later the Hindu prince retaliated by an invasion of the Amīr's territory, but being defeated was compelled to sign a treaty binding him to pay a large indemnity and to surrender four forts to the west of the Indus besides many elephants. Jaipāl broke the treaty and was punished for his breach of faith by the devastation of his border-lands and the loss of the Laghmān or Jalālābād District. After a short interval, in or about A.D. 991, Jaipāl made a vigorous effort to ward off the growing Muslim menace by organizing a confederacy of Hindu kings, including among others Rājyapāla, the Pratihāra King of Kanauj, and Dhanga, the ruler of the distant Chandēl kingdom to the south of the Jumna. The allies were defeated disastrously somewhere in or near the Kurram (Kurmah) valley, and Peshāwar passed under Muslim rule.

Sultan Mahmūd. In A.D. 997 the crown of Ghaznī descended after a short interval to Sabuktigīn's son Mahmūd, who assumed the title of Sultan, the royal style preferred by the Muslim kings in India for several centuries. Mahmūd was a zealous Muslim of the ferocious type then prevalent, who felt it to be a duty as well as a pleasure to slay idolaters. He was also greedy of treasure and took good care to derive a handsome profit from his holy wars. Historians are not clear concerning either the exact number or the dates of his raids. The computation of Sir Henry Elliot that Mahmūd made seventeen expeditions may be accepted. Whenever possible he made one each year. Hindu authorities never mention distinctly his proceedings, which are known only from the testimony of Muslim authors, who do not always agree.

It was the custom of the Sultan to quit his capital early in October and utilize the cold weather for his operations. Three months of steady marching brought him into the heart of the rich Gangetic provinces; and by the time he had slain his tens of thousands and collected millions of treasure he was ready at the beginning of the hot season to go home and enjoy himself. He carried off crowds of prisoners as slaves, including no doubt skilled masons and other artisans whom he employed to beautify his capital; as his successors did in later times. It would be tedious to relate in full the story of all his expeditions. Their character will appear sufficiently from a brief notice of the more notable raids.

Early raids. In November 1001, not long after his accession, in the course of his second expedition, he inflicted a severe defeat near Peshāwar on Jaipāl, who was taken prisoner with his family. The captive, who was released on terms after a time, refused to survive his disgrace. He committed suicide by fire and was succeeded by his son Ānandpāl, who continued the struggle with the foreigners, but without success. He followed his father's example and organized a league of Hindu Rajas, including the rulers of Ujjain, Gwālior, Kanauj, Delhi, and Ajmēr, who took the field with a host which was larger than that opposed to Sabuktigīn, and was under the supreme command of Vīsala-deva, the Chauhān Raja of Ajmēr. The hostile forces watched each other on the plain of Peshāwar for forty days, during which the Hindus received reinforcements from the powerful Khokhar tribe of the Panjab, while the Sultan was compelled to form an entrenched camp. The camp was stormed by a rush in force of the new allies, who slew 3,000 or 4,000 Muslims in a few minutes. Victory seemed to be within the grasp of the Hindus when it was snatched from their hands by one of those unlucky accidents which have so often determined the fate of Indian battles. The elephant carrying either Ānandpāl himself or his son Brahmanpāl, for accounts differ as usual, turned and fled. The Indians, on seeing this, broke in disorder. The Muslim cavalry pursued them for two days and nights, killing 8,000 and capturing enormous booty. Loosely organized confederacies of Hindu contingents each under its own independent chief almost always proved incapable of withstanding the attack of fierce foreign cavalry obeying one will.

Kangra. The decisive victory thus gained enabled the Sultan to attack with success the strong fortress of Kangra or Bhīmnagar, with its temple rich in treasure accumulated by the devotion of generations of Hindus (A.D. 1009). Vast quantities of coined money and gold and silver bullion were carried off. The treasure included 'a house of white silver, like to the houses of rich men, the length of which was thirty yards and the breadth fifteen. It could be taken to pieces and put together again. And there was a canopy, made of the fine linen of Rūm, forty yards long and twenty broad, supported on two golden and two silver poles, which had been cast in moulds.' The Sultan returned to Ghaznī with his booty and astonished the ambassadors from foreign powers by the display of 'jewels and unbored pearls and rubies, shining like sparks, or like wine congealed with ice, and emeralds like fresh sprigs of myrtle, and diamonds in size and weight like pomegranates'. The fortress was held by a Muslim garrison for thirty-five years, after which it was recovered by the Hindus. It did not pass finally under Muslim rule until 1620, when it was captured by an officer of Jahāngīr. The buildings were ruined to a great extent by the earthquake of 1905.

Mathurā and Kanauj. The expedition reckoned as the twelfth was directed specially against Kanauj, the imperial city of northern India, then under the rule of Rājyapāla Pratihāra. The Sultan, sweeping away all opposition, crossed the Jumna on 2 December 1018, and was preparing to attack Baran or Bulandshahr when the Raja, by name Haradatta, tendered his submission and with 10,000 of his men accepted the religion of Islām.

Mathurā, the holy city of Krishna, was the next victim. 'In the middle of the city there was a temple larger and finer than the rest, which can neither be described nor painted.' The Sultan was of opinion that 200 years would have been required to build it. The idols included 'five of red gold, each five yards high', with eyes formed of priceless jewels. 'The Sultan gave orders that all the temples should be burnt with naphtha and fire, and levelled with the ground.' Thus perished works of art which must have been among the noblest monuments of ancient India.

Rājyapāla, not daring to attempt the serious defence of his capital, fled across the Ganges. The seven forts which guarded Kanauj were all taken in one day, in January 1019, and the Sultan's troops were let loose to plunder and make captives. It was reported that the city contained nearly 10,000 temples, but it is not said distinctly that they were destroyed. The Sultan, after making an excursion into the Fatehpur District and to the borders of Jijhoti (Bundēlkhand), retired to Ghaznī with his prisoners and plunder.

Collapse of Ganda Chandēl. The cowardly flight of the Kanauj Raja angered his fellow Rajas who, under the command of a Chandēl prince, combined against Rājyapāla, slew him, and replaced him by Trilochanapāla.

Mahmūd, who regarded the slain Raja as his vassal, resolved to punish the chiefs who had dared to defy his might. He marched again in the autumn of A.D. 1019, forced the passage of the Jumna, and entered the territory of Ganda Chandēl, who had assembled a host so vast that the Sultan was frightened. But Ganda, a faint-hearted creature, stole away in the night, and allowed the enemy to carry off to Ghaznī 580 elephants and much other booty. When Mahmūd came back again in 1021-2 Ganda once more refused to fight, and was content to buy off the invader.

Somnāth. The most celebrated and interesting of Mahmūd's expeditions was the sixteenth, undertaken with the object of sacking the temple of Somnāth or Prabhāsa Pattana on the coast of Surāshtra or Kāthiāwar, which was known to be stored with incalculable riches. The authorities differ concerning the chronology of the operations, probably because some of them ignore the fact that Mahmūd spent about a year in Sūrashtra.[1] He seems to have quitted Ghaznī in December, A.D. 1023 (A.H. 414), with a force of 30,000 horsemen besides volunteers. He advanced by Multān and from Ajmēr through the Rajasthan desert to Anhilwāra or Pātan in Saurāshtra. The march through a country lacking in both food and water required extensive commissariat arrangements and a considerable expenditure of time. The Sultan consequently did not appear before Somnāth until the middle of the eleventh month of A.H. 414, or about March, A.D. 1024, or, according to other authorities, 1025. A fiercely contested fight gave the invaders possession of the fortified temple and of an enormous mass of treasure. The number of the slain exceeded 50,000.

The object of worship was a huge stone *lingam* enshrined in the sanctum of a temple constructed mainly of timber. The principal hall had fifty-six columns of wood covered with lead.

The Sultan returned through Sind by a route more westerly than that he had used in coming. His army suffered severely from want of water. He arrived at Ghaznī about April 1026, loaded with plunder.

The Somnāth expedition was the last important military operation of Mahmūd. His final Indian expedition in A.D. 1027 was directed against the Jats in the neighbourhood of Mūltān. The remainder of his life was occupied by domestic troubles, and he died in April, A.D. 1030 (A.H. 421), at the age of sixty-two.

Results of the raids. The Panjab, or a large part of it, was annexed to the Ghaznī Sultanate. That annexation constitutes the sole claim of Mahmūd to be counted as an Indian sovereign. While Muslim historians regard him as one of the glories of Islām, a less partial judgement finds in his proceedings little deserving of admiration. His ruling passion seems to have been avarice. He spent large sums in beautifying his capital and in endowing Muslim institutions in it. Like several Asian conquerors he had a taste for Persian literature, and gained a reputation as a patron of poets and theologians. Firdausī, the author of the immense Persian epic, the *Shāhnāma*, considering himself to have been treated with insufficient generosity, composed a bitter satire upon the Sultan which is extant. Such matters, which occupy a prominent place in the writings of Elphinstone and other authors, really have no relevance to the history of India and need not be noticed further. So far as India was concerned Mahmūd was simply a bandit operating on a large scale, who was too strong for the Hindu Rajas, and was in consequence able to inflict much irreparable damage.

[1] For the year's stay see Forbes, *Rāsmālā*, vol. i, p. 79, and Elphinstone. The *I.G.* (1908), s.v. Somnāth, correctly dates the operations in 1024-6.

a. Dancing śiva, S. India, Cola Period

b. Rājarājeśvara Temple, Tanjore, Cola

c. Temple of Somnāthpur, Mysore, Hoysala

He did not attempt to effect any permanent conquest except in the Panjab, and his raids had no lasting results in the interior beyond the destruction of life, property, and priceless monuments.

Albērūnī. The most distinguished ornament of Sultan Mahmūd's reign was the profound scholar commonly called Albērūnī,[1] who had little reason to feel gratitude to the raiding Sultan, although patronized intelligently by his son Masūd. Albērūnī, who was born in A.D. 973 and died in A.D. 1048, was a native of the Khwārizm or Khiva territory, and was brought to Ghaznī either as a prisoner or as a hostage. When the Sultan succeeded in occupying the Panjab, Albērūnī took up his residence for a time in the newly acquired province, and used the opportunity to make a thorough survey of Hindu philosophy and other branches of Indian science. He mastered the Sanskrit language, and was not too proud to read even the Purānas. He noted carefully and recorded accurately numerous observations on the history, character, manners, and customs of the Hindus, and was thus able to compose the wonderful book conveniently known as 'Albērūnī's India', which is unique in Muslim literature, except in so far as it was imitated without acknowledgement more than five centuries later by Abu-l Fazl in the *Āīn-i Akbarī*. The author, while fully alive to the defects of Hindu literary methods, was fascinated by the Indian philosophy, especially as expounded in the *Bhagavad-Gītā*. He was consumed with a desire to discover truth for its own sake, and laboured conscientiously to that end with a noble disregard of ordinary Muslim prejudices. As his learned translator observes:

His book on India is 'like a magic island of quiet impartial research in the midst of a world of clashing swords, burning towns, and plundered temples'.

His special subjects were 'astronomy, mathematics, chronology, mathematical geography, physics, chemistry, and mineralogy', all treated with such consummate learning that few modern scholars are capable of translating his treatises, and the versions, when accomplished, are often beyond the comprehension of even well-educated readers. Albērūnī undoubtedly was one of the most gifted scientific men known to history. Some of his writings have been lost, and others remain in manuscript. The translation by Sachau of his *Chronology of Ancient Nations*, published in 1879, is a valuable work of reference, but very difficult to understand.

The Gaharwārs of Kanauj. The Pratihāra dynasty of Kanauj came to an end soon after Mahmūd's invasion and was succeeded by Rajas belonging to the Gāhadavāla (Gaharwār) clan, who were connected with the Chandēls and were of indigenous origin. Govindachandra, grandson of the founder of the new dynasty, enjoyed a long reign lasting for more than half a century (c. A.D. 1100 to 1160), and suc-

---

[1] His full designation was Abū-Rīhān (Raīhān) Muhammad, son of Ahmad. He became familiarly known as Bū-Rīhān, Ustād ('Master'), Al-Bērūnī ('the foreigner'). The spellings Al-Bīrūnī and Al-Bērūnī are both legitimate.

ceeded in restoring the glory of the Kanauj kingdom to a considerable extent. Numerous inscriptions of his reign are extant.

Raja Jaichand. His grandson, renowned in popular legend as Raja Jaichand (Jayachchandra), was reputed by the Muslim writers to be the greatest king in India and was known to them as King of Benares, which seems to have been his principal residence. The incident of the abduction of his not unwilling daughter by the gallant Rāi Pithorā or Prithvīrāja Chauhān of Ajmer is a famous theme of bardic lays.

When Jaichand essayed to stem the torrent of Muslim invasion in 1194, Muhammad of Ghōr (Shihābu-d dīn, or Muizzu-d dīn, the son of Sām) defeated the huge Hindu host with immense slaughter at Chandrāwar in the Etawah District near the Jumna. The Raja was among the slain, and his capital, Banaras, was plundered so thoroughly that 1,400 camels were needed to carry away the booty. That battle put an end to the independent kingdom of Kanauj, but local Rajas more or less subordinate to the ruling power of the day long continued to rule in the ancient city. The Gāhadavāla Rajas were succeeded by Chandēls. Innumerable migrations of Rajput clans caused by the early Muslim invasions are recorded in village traditions and rude metrical chronicles kept by court bards.

The Chauhāns ; Prithvīrāja. The Chauhān chiefs of Sāmbhar and Ajmer in Rajasthan fill a large place in Hindu tradition and in the story of the Muslim conquest of northern India. One of them named Vigraharāja (IV) may be mentioned as a noted patron of Sanskrit literature, who was credited with the composition of a drama, fragments of which are preserved on stone tablets at Ajmer. His brother's son was Rāi Pithorā or Prithvīrāja, already mentioned, who carried off Jaichand's daughter about A.D. 1175, and defeated the Chandēls in 1182. He led the resistance to Muhammad of Ghōr ten years later, was defeated at the second battle of Tarāin, captured, and executed. His city of Ajmer was sacked, and the inhabitants were either massacred or enslaved.

He is the most popular hero of northern India to this day, and his exploits are the subject of bards' songs and vernacular epics.

The *Chand Rāisā*. The most celebrated of such epics is the *Chand Rāisā* composed by Prithvīrāja's court poet Chand Bardāi. The poem, written in archaic Hindī, has been constantly enlarged by reciters, as no doubt the Homeric poems were, and is believed to comprise about 125,000 verses. Many other compositions of a similar character are to be found in Rajasthan.

History of Delhi. Delhi, meaning by that term the old town near the Kutb Mīnār, was founded, according to an authority cited by Raverty, in A.D. 993-4.[1] It was held in the eleventh century by Rajas of the Tomara clan, who erected numerous temples, which were

---

[1] But other dates also are recorded.

destroyed by the Muslims, who used the materials for their buildings. In the twelfth century the city was included in the dominions of Prithvīrāja. The wonderful iron pillar, originally erected on the Vishupada Hill, a famous place of pilgrimage not far from Kurukshetra, in the fifth century, seems to have been moved and set up in its present position by the Tomara chief in the middle of the eleventh century. It is a mass of wrought iron nearly 24 feet in length and estimated to weigh more than six tons. The metal is perfectly welded and its manipulation is a triumph of skill in the handling of a refractory material. It is not the only proof that the ancient Indians possessed exceptional mastery over difficult problems of working in iron and other metals.

The current belief that Delhi is a city of immemorial antiquity rests upon the tradition that the existing village of Indarpat marks the site of part of the Indraprastha of the *Mahābhārata* at a very remote age. The tradition may be correct, but there is not a vestige of any prehistoric town now traceable. The first of the many historical cities, known collectively as Delhi, was founded near the close of the tenth century after Christ, and did not attain importance until the time of Ānanga Pāla Tomara in the middle of the eleventh century. Most people probably have a vague impression that Delhi always was the capital of India. If they have, their belief is erroneous. Delhi never figured largely in Hindu history. It was ordinarily the headquarters of the Sultans of Hindostan from 1206 to 1526, but did not become the established Mogul capital until Shāhjahān moved his court from Agra in 1648. It continued to be the usual residence of his successors until 1858 when their dynasty was extinguished. Since 1912 a new Delhi has been declared the official capital of the government of India.

SELECTED DATES

A.D.
- 647. Death of Harsha.
- c. 700. Ādiśūra in Bengal.
- 712. Arab conquest of Sind.
- 731. Embassy to China of Yaśovarman, King of Kanauj.
- c. 740. Yaśovarman defeated by Lalitāditya, King of Kashmīr (A.D. 733–69).
- c. 750. Pāla dynasty of Bengal founded by Gopāla.
- c. 810. Dharmapāla, King of Bengal, deposed a king of Kanauj and appointed another.
- c. 816. Pratihāra capital transferred to Kanauj.
- c. 840–90. Bhoja, or Mihira, the powerful Pratihāra King of Kanauj.
- c. 890–910. Mahendrapāla Pratihāra.
- c. 916. Kanauj captured by Indra III Rāshtrakūta.
- c. 942–97. Mūlarāja, King of Gujarat.
- c. 950–99. Dhanga, the most powerful of the Chandēl kings.
- 973–1048. Albērūnī, scientific author.
- 993–4. Probable date of foundation of Delhi.
- 997. Sultan Mahmūd of Ghaznī, acc.

A.D.
1001. Sultan Mahmūd defeated Jaipāl.
1008–19. The Sultan defeated Ānandpāl and took Kāngrā.
1018–19. The Sultan took Kanauj.
c. 1018–60. Bhoja Paramāra, King of Mālwā.
   c. 1023. Incursion of Rājendra Chola into Bengal.
Dec. 1023–Apr. 1026. Somnāth expedition of Sultan Mahmūd.
   1030. Death of Sultan Mahmūd.
   1038. Atīśa sent on Buddhist mission to Tibet by Nayapāla, King
          of Bengal.
c. 1049–1100. Kīrtivarman, Chandēl king.
c. 1100–60. Govindachandra, Gāhadavāla, King of Kanauj
   1143–72. Kumārapāla, Caulukya, King of Gujarat.
c. 1158–69. Ballāl Sen (Vallāla Sena), King of part of Bengal.
   1182. Parmāl Chandēl defeated by Rājā Prīthvīrāja Chauhān.
   1192. Defeat and death of Prīthvīrāja.

AUTHORITIES

MANY references are given in *E.H.I.*[4] Among more recent works the following should
be noted:

DE LA VALLÉE POUSSIN's *Dynasties et histoire* (see above, p. 189) contains summaries of the history of all the main dynasties, with full references. *C.H.I.*, vol. ii
(in the press), also gives good outline histories. The fourth volume of the *History
and Culture of the Indian People* (*The Age of Imperial Kanauj*), ed. R. C. MAJUMDAR,
Bombay, 1955) is a valuable study of the period, by Indian scholars. R. S. TRIPATHI's
History of Kanauj (Benares, 1937), already mentioned in connexion with the reign
of Harsha, contains the best treatment of the Pratihāras. For the Paramāras see D. C.
GANGULI's *History of the Paramāra Dynasty* (Dacca, 1943). The detailed *History of
Bengal*, of which two volumes have appeared, covers the history of the region down
to the Mughul period. The first volume, edited by R. C. MAJUMDAR, is invaluable
for the Pālas and Senas.

For the advanced study of the later dynasties from the tenth century onward
H. C. RAY's masterly and detailed *Dynastic History of Northern India* (2 vols.,
Calcutta, 1931–6) is essential. For the study of the Ghaznavid sultanate, Mohd.
NAZIM, *Life and Times of Sultan Mahmūd of Ghaznā* (Cambridge, 1931).

closing years of the twelfth century, when the extensive conquests
effected by and for Muhammad of Ghōr brought the most important
provinces under the sway of the Sultans of Delhi. The story of Hindu
India from the middle of the seventh century until the Muslim conquest, which may be dated approximately in A.D. 1200 for the north and
A.D. 1300 for the south, cannot be presented in the form of a single
continuous narrative. The subject will be treated in Book III.

CHAPTER 3

The Kingdoms of the Peninsula

1. The Deccan Proper and Mysore

Groups of states. The medieval history of the peninsula concerns itself chiefly with those of two groups of states, namely, the kingdoms of the Deccan plateau lying between the Narbadā on the north and the Krishna and Tungabhadra on the south, and those beyond those rivers. Mysore, which belongs geographically to the Far South, having been generally more closely connected with the Deccan kingdoms than with the Tamil states, may be treated as an annexe of the Deccan proper. The history of the Tamil group of kingdoms—Pāndya, Chera, Chola, and Pallava—forms a distinct subject. The Deccan proper, Mysore or the Kanarese country, and Tamilakam or Tamil Land were constantly in close touch one with the other, but the points of contact between the peninsular powers and those of northern India were few.

Difficulties of the subject. Although modern research has had much success in piecing together the skeleton of peninsular history, it is not often possible to clothe the dry bones with the flesh of narrative. The greater part of the results of painstaking, praiseworthy, and necessary archaeological study must always remain unattractive to the ordinary reader of history and extremely difficult to remember. The names of the sovereigns and other notables of southern India present peculiar obstacles in the path of the student of history. They are often terribly long, and each king commonly is mentioned by several alternative cumbrous names or titles which are extremely confusing.[1] Names, too, frequently recur in the lists and are liable to be misunderstood. The kingdoms, moreover, were so isolated from the outer world that their history in detail can never possess more than local interest. For those reasons, to which others might be added, the story of the medieval southern kingdoms is even less manageable than that of the northern realms, which is sufficiently perplexing. In this chapter no attempt will be made to narrate consecutively the history of any of the dynasties, the treatment being confined to summary notices of a few leading powers and personages, coupled with observations on the changes which occurred in religion, literature, and art in the course of the centuries. Notwithstanding the political isolation of the south, religious and philosophical movements originated in that region which

---

[1] e.g. an inscription mentions a man called Mēdinī Mīsara Gandakattāri, Trinetra-Sāluva Narasana Nāyaka; and the King Pulakēsin Chalukya I appears also as Satyās-raya, Ranavikrama, and Vallabha. No author who meddles largely with such names can expect to be read.

profoundly affected the thought of the north. The influence exercised by Rāmānuja and other southern sages on the whole country from Cape Comorin to the recesses of the Snowy Mountains is the best evidence of that inner unity of Hindu India which survives the powerful disintegrating forces set in motion by diversity in blood, language, manners, customs, and political allegiance.

Vākātakas. With the disappearance of the Śatavāhanas or Āndhras a number of lesser dynasties arose in central India and the Deccan, of which the most important was that of the Vākātakas. Early in the fourth century Pravarasena I appears to have been a very powerful king, controlling Madhya Pradesh and much of the western Deccan, where he set up a feudatory kingdom at Basīm, in Berar, under his second son Śarvasena. During the reign of the Gupta emperor Chandragupta II the Vākātaka kingdom was much under Gupta influence. Chandragupta's daughter, Prabhāvatī Guptā, the widow of Rudrasena II, governed as regent during the minority of her sons, and issued charters in her own name, giving the Gupta genealogy instead of that of her husband. Her son Pravarasena II came to the throne about A.D. 410 and seems gradually to have thrown off Gupta influence. During the troublous times of the latter half of the fifth century the Vākātakas exerted some temporary power in Malwa. Their last king, Harishena, seems to have been an important monarch, controlling all the central Deccan, but on his death, early in the sixth century, the Vākātaka empire vanished. It was under the Vākātakas that several of the caves of Ajantā were dedicated.

Kadambas. A clan or family called Kadamba enjoyed independent power in the districts now called north and south Kanara and in western Mysore from the third to the sixth century. Their capital Vanavāsī, also known as Jayanti or Vaijayanti, was so ancient that it is mentioned in the Ceylon Buddhist tradition as a city to which Aśoka sent missionaries after the third Buddhist council. The Kadambas resembled several other royal families of distinction in being of Brahman descent, although recognized as Kshatriyas by reason of their occupation as rulers. Their first ruler, Mayūraśarman, is said to have been a Brahman student who revolted against the Pallavas of Kānchī, and raided far and wide in the Deccan. He probably ruled early in the fourth century. Kadamba chiefs in subordinate positions may be traced as late as the beginning of the fourteenth century, and the powerful Rāyas of Vijayanagar, who founded a great kingdom early in that century, are supposed by some authorities to have had Kadamba connexions.

Gangas. An equally distinguished dynasty was that of the Gangas, who ruled over the greater part of Mysore from the second to the eleventh century, and played an important part in the incessant medieval wars. The Gangas of the tenth century were zealous patrons of Jainism, which had a long history in the peninsula from the fourth century B.C. The colossal statue of Gomata, $56\frac{1}{2}$ feet in height, wrought out of a block of gneiss on the top of an eminence at Śravana Belgola, and justly described as being unrivalled in India for daring conception and gigantic dimensions, was executed in about A.D. 983 to the order of Chāmunda Rāya, the minister of a Ganga king.[1]

A branch of the Gangas ruled in Orissa for about a thousand years from the sixth to the sixteenth century.

Early Chālukyas. The most prominent of the early medieval dynasties in the Deccan was that of the Chālukyas, founded in the middle of the sixth century by Pulakeśin I, who established himself as lord of Vātāpi or Bādāmi, now in the Bijāpur District of Bombay.[2] His grandson, Pulakeśin II (608–42), was almost exactly the contemporary of Harsha of Kanauj (606–47), and in the Deccan occupied a paramount position similar to that enjoyed in northern India by his rival. When Harsha, about A.D. 620, sought to bring the Deccan under his dominion, Pulakeśin was too strong for him and repelled his attack, maintaining the Narbada as the frontier between the two empires. The court of the sovereign of the Deccan was visited in A.D. 641 by Hiuen Tsang, the Chinese pilgrim, who was much impressed by the power of Pulakeśin and the loyalty of his warlike vassals. The capital probably was at or near Nāsik, and the traveller experienced much difficulty in penetrating the robber-infested jungles of the Western Ghāts. Even then the country was known as Maharashtra, as it is now. The Buddhist monasteries in the kingdom numbered more than 100 with a population of monks exceeding 5,000. A large proportion of the inhabitants of the realm did not follow the Buddhist religion. Hiuen Tsang gives a brief and indistinct account of the Ajantā caves, which he seems to have visited. Most of the excellent sculptures and paintings in the caves had then been completed.

The fame of Pulakeśin extended even to distant Persia, whose king exchanged embassies with him. The intercourse with Persia is commemorated in the cave frescoes.

The loyal valour of the chieftains of the Deccan did not avail to save their lord from ruin. Only a year after Hiuen Tsang's visit the Chālukya king was utterly defeated and presumably slain by the Pallava King of Kānchī (642), named Narasimhavarman, who thus became the paramount power in the peninsula. The acts of the conqueror will be noticed more particularly as part of the story of the Pallavas.

Thirty-two years later (674) a son of Pulakeśin revenged his father's death and captured Kānchī. The conflict between the Pallavas and the Chālukyas continued for many years, with varying fortune, until the middle of the eighth century (757), when a Rāshtrakūta chieftain, Dantidurga, overthrew the reigning Chālukya. The sovereignty of the Deccan, which had been held by the Chālukyas for some 200 years,

[1] Two similar but smaller colossi of much later date exist at Kārakala or Kārkala and Yenūr in South Kanara. For the former see H.F.A., pl. liii.

[2] The Chālukyas adopted the figure of a boar as their emblem, which was borrowed later by the Rāyas of Vijayanagar and other dynasties.

thus passed to the Rāshtrakūtas, in whose hands it remained for nearly two centuries and a quarter.

Religion. The early Chālukya kings, while tolerant of all religions, like most Indian rulers, were themselves Brahmanical Hindus. In their time Buddhism slowly declined, while the sacrificial form of Hinduism grew in favour, and became the subject of numerous treatises. Handsome temples were erected in many places, and the practice of excavating cave-temples was borrowed by orthodox Hindus from their Jain and Buddhist rivals. The sixth-century Brahmanical caves at Bādāmī contain excellent sculptures in good preservation. The Jain creed had many followers in the southern Marāthā country.

It is needless to detail the wars of the Rāshtrakūtas. The reign of Krishna I (acc. *c.* A.D. 760) is memorable for the rock-cut temple called Kailāsa at Ellora, in the Hyderabad state, which is one of the most marvellous works of human labour. The whole temple, hewn out of the side of a hill and enriched with endless ornament, stands clear as if built in the ordinary way.

Amoghavarsha. King Amoghavarsha (*c.* 815–77) enjoyed one of the longest reigns recorded in history. Sulaimān, the Arab merchant who travelled in western India in the middle of the ninth century, knew the Rāshtrakūta sovereign by his title of Balharā, a corruption of Vallabha Rāi, and states that he was acknowledged not only as the most eminent of the princes of India, but also as the fourth of the great monarchs of the world, the other three being the Khalīfa (Caliph) of Baghdad, the Emperor of China, and the Emperor of Rūm or Constantinople. The Rāshtrakūta kings kept on the best of terms with the Arabs of Sind, and enriched their subjects by encouraging commerce. Amoghavarsha possessed multitudes of horses and elephants, with immense wealth, and maintained a standing army regularly paid. His capital was Mānyakheta, now Mālkhēd in the Hyderabad state. He adopted the Jain religion and showed marked favour to learned Jains of the Digàmbara or nude sect. The rapid progress of Jainism in the Deccan during the ninth and tenth centuries involved a decline in the position of Buddhism.

Chālukyas of Kalyānī. In A.D. 973 the second Chālukya dynasty, with its capital at Kalyānī, was founded by Taila or Tailapa II, who dethroned the last of the Rāshtrakūtas. The kings of the new dynasty fought numerous wars with their neighbours. At the beginning of the eleventh century the Chālukya country was cruelly ravaged by Rājarāja the Great, the Chola king, who threw into it a vast host of hundreds of thousands of merciless soldiers, by whom even Brahmans, women, and children were not spared.

In A.D. 1052 or 1053 Someśvara Chālukya defeated and slew Rājādhirāja, the then reigning Chola king, in a famous battle fought at Koppam on the Krishnā.[1]

---

[1] Fleet (*Ep. Ind.*, vol. xii, p. 298).

Vikramāditya. Vikramāditya or Vikramānka, who reigned from A.D. 1076 to 1126, was the most conspicuous member of his dynasty. He secured his throne by a war with one brother, and later in life had to fight another brother who rebelled. He continued the perennial wars with the southern powers, the Cholas in that age having taken the place of the Pallavas and become the lords of Kānchī, which Vikramānka is said to have occupied more than once. His success in war with his neighbours was so marked that he ventured to found an era bearing his name, which never came into general use. His exploits in war, the chase, and love are recorded at great length in an historical poem composed by Bilhana, his chief pandit, a native of Kashmir. The poem, which recalls Bāna's work on the deeds of Harsha, was discovered by Bühler in a Jain library, and well edited and analysed by him. It is interesting to note that Vikramāditya was chosen by one of his consorts as her husband at a public *svayamvara* in the ancient epic fashion.

The celebrated jurist Vijnāneśvara, author of the *Mitāksharā*, the leading authority on Hindu law outside of Bengal, lived at Kalyānī in the reign of Vikramāditya, whose rule appears to have been prosperous and efficient.

Bijjala Kalachurya During the twelfth century the Chālukya power declined, and after 1190 the Rajas sank into the position of petty chiefs, most of their possessions passing into the hands of new dynasties, the Yādavas of Devagiri and the Hoysalas of Dorasamudra.

A rebel named Bijjala Kalachurya and his sons held the Chālukya throne for some years. Bijjala abdicated in 1167.

The Lingāyat sect. His brief tenure of power was marked by the rise of the Lingāyat or Vīra Śaiva sect, which is still powerful in the Kanarese country, especially among the trading classes. The members of the sect worship Śiva in his phallic (*lingam*) form, reject the authority of the Vedas, disbelieve in the doctrine of rebirth, object to child-marriage, approve of the remarriage of widows, and cherish an intense aversion to Brahmans, notwithstanding that the prophet of their creed was Basava, alleged to have been a Brahman minister of Bijjala, and said by some to have been originally a Jain. The sect when established displayed bitter hostility to Jainism.

Vishnuvardhana Hoysala. The Hoysala or Poysala kings of the Mysore territory were descended from a petty chieftain in the Western Ghāts, and first rose to importance in the time of Bittideva or Bittiga, better known by his later name of Vishnuvardhana, who died in A.D. 1141,[1] after a reign of more than thirty years, more or less in sub-ordination to the Chālukya power. The Hoysalas did not become fully independent until about A.D. 1190. Bittiga engaged in wars of the usual character, which need not be specified, and so extended his dominions; but his substantial claim to remembrance rests on the

---

[1] Lewis Rice in *J.R.A.S.*, 1915, p. 529.

important part played by him in the religious life of the peninsula and on the wonderful development of architecture and sculpture associated with his name and the names of his successors. Bittiga in his early days was a zealous Jain and encouraged his minister Gangarāja to restore the Jain temples which had been destroyed by Chola invaders of the Śaiva persuasion. In those days, although many, perhaps most, Rajas practised the normal Hindu tolerance, political wars were sometimes embittered by sectarian passion, and serious persecution was not unknown. The destruction of Jain temples by the Cholas was an act of fierce intolerance. About the close of the eleventh or the beginning of the twelfth century Bittiga came under the teaching of the famous sage Rāmānuja, who converted him to faith in Vishnu. The king then adopted the name of Vishnuvardhana and devoted himself to the honouring of his new creed by the erection of temples of unsurpassed magnificence. The current Vaishnava story that Vishnuvardhana ground the Jain theologians in oil-mills certainly is not true. The statement seems to be merely a picturesque version of the defeat of the Jain disputants in argument. Good evidence proves that the converted king continued to show toleration for various forms of religion. One of his wives and one of his daughters professed the Jain creed.

Hoysala style of art. The style of the temples built by Vishnuvardhana and his successors in the twelfth and thirteenth centuries, which was used alike by Jains and Brahmanical Hindus, is characterized by a richly carved base or plinth, supporting the temple, which is polygonal, star-shaped in plan, and roofed by a low pyramidal tower, often surmounted by a vase-shaped ornament. In many cases there are several towers, so that the temple may be described as double, triple, or quadruple. The whole of a Hoysala building is generally treated as the background for an extraordinary mass of complicated sculpture, sometimes occurring in great sheets of bas-reliefs, and generally comprising many statues or statuettes, almost or wholly detached. The temple at Halebīd or Dorasamudra is the best known, but many others equally notable exist. Much of the sculpture is of high quality. It was the work of a large school of artists, scores of whom, contrary to the usual Indian practice, have recorded their names on their creations. Artistic skill is not yet dead in Mysore.[1]

Rāmānuja. Rāmānuja, the celebrated Vaishnava philosopher and teacher, who converted the Hoysala king, was educated at Kānchī, and resided at Śrīrangam near Trichinopoly in the reign of Adhirājendra Chola; but owing to the hostility of that king, who professed the Śaiva faith, was obliged to withdraw into Mysore, where he resided until the decease of Adhirājendra freed him from anxiety. He then returned to Śrīrangam, where he remained until his death. The exact chronology of his long life is not easy to determine. His death may be placed about the middle of the twelfth century. His system of metaphysics or

[1] *Ind. Ant.*, 1915, pp. 89 ff.

ontology based on his interpretation of the Upanishads is too abstruse for discussion or analysis in these pages. He is regarded as the leading opponent of the views of Śankarāchārya.[1]

The later Hoysalas. Vīra Ballāla, grandson of Vishnuvardhana, extended the dominions of his house, especially in a northerly direction, where he encountered the Yādavas of Devagiri (A.D. 1191–2). His conquests made the Hoysalas the most powerful dynasty in the Deccan at the close of the twelfth century. Their short-lived dominion was shattered in 1310 by the attack of Malik Kāfūr and Khwāja Hājī, the generals of Alāu-d dīn Khiljī, who ravaged the kingdom and sacked the capital, Dorasamudra or Halebīd, which was finally destroyed by a Muslim force a few years later, in 1326 or 1327. After that date the Hoysalas survived for a while as merely local Rajas.

Yādavas of Devagiri. The Yādavas of Devagiri or Deogir, known in later ages as Aurangābād, were descendants of feudatory nobles of the Chālukya kingdom. In the closing years of the twelfth century, as mentioned above, they were the rivals of the Hoysalas. The most influential member of the dynasty was Singhana early in the thirteenth century, who invaded Gujarāt and other regions, establishing a considerable dominion which lasted only for a few years. In 1294 the reigning Raja was attacked by Alāu-d dīn Khiljī, who carried off an enormous amount of treasure. In 1309 Rāmachandra, the last independent sovereign of the Deccan, submitted to Malik Kāfūr. His son-in-law, Harapāla, having ventured to revolt against the foreigner, paid the penalty by being flayed alive at the order of his barbarous conqueror (1318). That tragedy was the end of the Yādavas.

The story of the Hindu kingdom of Vijayanagar, which was founded about 1336, and developed into an extensive empire to the south of the Krishnā, will be related with considerable detail in a later chapter in connexion with the southern Muslim dynasties.

2. *The Tamil Powers of the Far South*

Origin of the Pallavas. At the close of Chapter 3 of Book II we took a passing glance at the early history of the Tamil kingdoms during the first and second centuries of the Christian era. It is impossible to construct anything like a continuous narrative until a date much later.

After the time of Karikāla Chola and Gajabāhu of Ceylon the power which appears first on the stage of history is that of the Pallavas. In the middle of the fourth century Samudragupta encountered a Pallava king of Kānchī or Conjeeveram, and it is not unlikely that the dynasty may have originated in the third century, after the disappearance of the Sātavāhanas.

[1] For an abstract of the doctrine see *Srī Rāmānujāchārya*, part ii, by T. Rajagopala Chariar, Madras, Natesan & Co., n.d.

The Pallavas constitute one of the mysteries of Indian history. The conjecture that they were Pahlavas, that is to say Parthians or Persians from the north-west, was suggested solely by a superficial verbal similarity and may be summarily dismissed as baseless. Everything known about them indicates that they were a peninsular race, tribe, or clan, probably either identical or closely connected with the Kurumbas, an originally pastoral people, who play a prominent part in early Tamil tradition. The Pallavas are sometimes described as the 'foresters', and seem to have been of the same blood as the Kallars, who were reckoned as belonging to the formidable predatory classes, and were credited up to quite recent times with 'bold, indomitable, and martial habits'. The Raja of Pudukottai, the small state which lay between the Trichinopoly, Tanjore, and Madura Districts, is a Kallar and claims the honour of descent from the Pallava princes.[1]

The history of the Pallavas, although alluded to in some vernacular writings, had been almost wholly forgotten by everybody, and was absolutely unknown to Europeans before 1840, when inscriptions of the dynasty began to come to light. Since that date the patient labours of many investigators have recovered much of the outline of Pallava history and have restored the dynasty to its rightful place in Indian history, a place by no means insignificant.

Limits of the Tamil states. The normal limits of the territories of the three ancient ruling races of the Tamil country were defined by immemorial tradition and well recognized, although the actual frontiers of the kingdoms varied continually and enormously from time to time.

The Pāndya kingdom, as defined by tradition, extended from the Southern Vellāru river (Pudukottai) on the north to Cape Comorin, and from the Coromandel (*Chola-mandala*) coast on the east to the 'great highway', the Achchhankōvil Pass leading into Southern Kērala, or Travancore. It comprised the existing Districts of Madura and Tinnevelly with parts of the Travancore State.

The Chola country, according to the most generally received tradition, extended along the Coromandel coast from Nellore to Pudukottai, where it abutted on the Pāndya territory. On the west it reached the borders of Coorg. The limits thus defined include Madras with several adjoining districts, and a large part of the Mysore State. But the ancient literature does not carry the Tamil Land farther north than

[1] According to Srinivasa Aiyangar, who writes with ample local knowledge, the Pallavas belonged to the ancient Nāga people, who included a primitive Negrito element of Australasian origin and a later mixed race. Their early habitat was the Tondai mandalam, the group of districts round Madras; Tanjore and Trichinopoly being later conquests. The Pallava army was recruited from the martial tribe of Pallis or Kurumbas. The Pallava chiefs were the hereditary enemies of the three Tamil kings, and were regarded as intruders in the southern districts. Hence the term Palava in Tamil has come to mean 'a rogue', while a section of the Pallava subjects who settled in the Chola and Pāndya countries became known as Kallar or 'thieves'. All these people doubtless belonged to the Nāga race. Those statements support the view expressed in the text, as formulated many years ago. See Jouveau-Dubreuil, *The Pallavas*, Pondicherry, 1917.

Pulicat and the Venkata or Tirupathi Hill, about 100 miles to the north-west of Madras. In the middle of the seventh century, when Hiuen Tsang, the Chinese pilgrim, travelled, the Pallavas held most of the Chola traditional territory, and the special Chola principality was restricted to a small and unhealthy area, nearly coincident with the Cuddapah District.

The Chera or Kērala territory consisted in the main of the rugged region of the Western Ghats to the south of the Chandragiri river, which falls into the sea not far from Mangalore, and forms the boundary between the peoples who severally speak Tulu and Malayālam.

No such traditional limits are attributed to the dominions of the Pallavas, although their early habitat, the Tondainādu, comprising the districts near Madras, was well known. They held as much territory as they could grasp, and Kānchī or Conjeeveram, their capital, was in the heart of *Chola-mandalam*. The facts indicate that they overlay the ancient ruling powers, and must have acquired their superior position by means of violence and blackmail, as the Marāthā freebooters did in the eighteenth century.

Outline of Pallava history. For about 200 years from the middle of the sixth to the middle of the eighth century the Pallavas were the dominant power in the Far South. All the princes of the ancient royal families seem to have been more or less subordinate to them in that period. Simhavishnu Pallava, in the last quarter of the sixth century recorded a boast that he had vanquished the Pāndya, Chola, and Chera kings, as well as the ruler of Ceylon.

In the time of their glory the home territories of the Pallavas comprised the modern districts of North Arcot, South Arcot, Chingleput or Madras, Trichinopoly, and Tanjore; while their sovereignty extended from the Orissan frontier on the north to the Ponnaiyār or Southern Pennār river on the south, and from the Bay of Bengal on the east to a line drawn through Salem, Bangalore, and Berar on the west.[1]

Although the Pallavas had to cede the Vengī province between the Krishna and the Godavari to the Chālukyas early in the seventh century, and never recovered it, that century was the time in which they attained their highest point of fame and during which they raised the imperishable monuments which constitute their best claim to remembrance. At the close of the ninth century the sceptre passed definitely from the hands of the Pallavas into those of the Cholas.

Having thus outlined the general course of Pallava history, we proceed to more definite chronicling and to a brief account of Pallava achievements.

Mahendra-varman. Mahendra-varman I (*c*. A.D. 600–25), son and successor of the victorious King Simhavishnu mentioned above, is memorable for his public works, which include rock-cut temples

[1] *I.G.* (1908), s.v. Chingleput District. Trichinopoly and Tanjore were not included in the Tondai nādu.

and caves, the ruined town of Mahendravādi between Arcot and Arconam, and a great reservoir near the same. About A.D. 610 he was defeated by Pulakeśin II Chālukya, who wrested from him the province of Vengī, where a branch Chālukya dynasty was established which endured for centuries.

Narasimha-varman. Mahendra's successor, Narasimha-varman (c. A.D. 625–45), was the most successful and distinguished member of his able dynasty. In A.D. 642 he took Vātāpi (Bādāmi), the Chālukya capital, and presumably killed Pulakeśin II, thus making the Pallavas the dominant power not only in Tamil Land, but also in the Deccan for a short time.

Hiuen Tsang at Kānchī. Two years before that victory Hiuen Tsang, the Chinese pilgrim, had visited Kānchī, which seems to have been the southern terminus of his travels. Civil war in Ceylon prevented him from crossing over to that country. His observations on the island and on the Pāndya territory were based on information collected at Kānchī. The pilgrim does not mention the king's name, nor does he use the term Pallava. To him the kingdom of Kānchī was simply Dravida or the Tamil country. He notes that the soil was fertile and well cultivated, and credits the inhabitants with the virtues of courage, trustworthiness, public spirit, and love of learning. The language, whether spoken or written, differed from that of the north. It was Tamil then as now. The capital of Malakotta, or the Pāndya country, presumably Madura, was a city five or six miles in circumference. A modern observer much admired the plan of Kānchī:

Here [Professor Geddes writes] is not simply a city made monumental by great temples and rich and varied innumerable minor ones; what rejoices me is to find the realization of an exceptionally well-grouped and comprehensive town plan, and this upon a scale of spacious dignity, combined with individual and artistic freedom to which I cannot name any equally surviving parallel whether in India or elsewhere.[1]

That testimony to the good taste of the architect of Pallava times is supported by the excellence of the buildings and sculpture. The kingdom contained more than 100 Buddhist monasteries occupied by over 10,000 monks of the Sthavira school, while non-Buddhist temples, chiefly those of the nude Jain sect, were nearly as numerous. Certain buildings were ascribed to Aśoka. The Buddhist edifices seem to have been taken over and modified or reconstructed by the Hindus, and so have mostly escaped notice.

In 1915 Mr. T. A. Gopinātha Rao, after a few hours' search, discovered five large images of Buddha in Conjeeveram, two being in the Hindu temple of Kāmākshī.[2] Further investigation will assuredly disclose many traces of Buddhism in the Pallava country.

[1] *Town Planning of Ancient Dekhan*, p. 78, by C. P. Venkatarama Aiyar, Madras, 1916.
[2] *Ind. Ant.*, 1915, p. 127.

Pallava art. Narasimha founded the town of Māmallapuram or Mahābalipuram and caused the execution of the wonderful Rathas, or 'Seven Pagodas' at that place, each of which is cut out from a great rock boulder. His artists also wrought the remarkable relief sculptures in the rocks at the same place. The most notable of those works is the celebrated composition which, as commonly stated, depicts the Penance of Arjuna. The alternative explanation, although plausible, seems to be erroneous.[1] The sculptures were continued by Narasimha's successor, but had to be abandoned incomplete about A.D. 670 in consequence of the Chālukya attacks.

The splendid and numerous structural temples at Kānchī and other places are slightly later in date, and were mostly erected in the reign of Rājasimha in the early years of the eighth century.

It thus appears that the history of Indian architecture and sculpture in the south begins at the close of the sixth century under Pallava rule. Earlier works, which were executed in impermanent materials, necessarily have perished. It is impossible here to go further into details, but it may be said that the Pallava school of architecture and sculpture is one of the most important and interesting of the Indian schools. The transition from wood to stone effected for northern India under Aśoka in the third century B.C. was delayed for nearly a thousand years in the Far South. That fact is a good illustration of the immense length of the course of Indian history and of the extreme slowness with which changes have been effected so as ultimately to cover the whole country.

End of the Pallavas. A severe defeat inflicted in A.D. 740 on the reigning Pallava king by the Chālukya may be regarded as the beginning of the end of the Pallava supremacy. The heirs of the Pallavas, however, were not the Chālukyas, who had to make way for the Rāshtrakūtas in A.D. 753, but the Cholas, who, in alliance with the Pāndyas, inflicted a decisive defeat on the Pallavas at the close of the ninth century. Pallava chiefs continued to exist as local rulers down to the thirteenth century, and nobles bearing the name may be traced even later. But after the seventeenth century all trace of the Pallavas as a distinct race or clan disappears, and their blood is now merged in that of the Kallar, Palli, and Vellāla castes.

Religion. The Pallava kings were mostly Brahmanical Hindus, some being specially devoted to the cult of Vishnu, and others to that of Śiva. Mahendra, who originally was a Jain, was converted to the faith of Śiva by a famous Tamil saint, and, with the proverbial zeal of a convert, destroyed the large Jain monastery in South Arcot, which bore the name of Pātaliputtiram, transferred at an early date from the ancient capital of India. The testimony of Hiuen Tsang proves that in the seventh century the nude or Digambara sect of Jains was numerous and influential, and his language implies that the various sects lived

---

[1] *Pallava Antiquities*, vol. i, p. 75. In *H.F.A.* (1911), p. 222, pl. xlvi, I followed the older interpretation, which appears to be correct (*Ind. Ant.*, 1917, pp. 54–57).

together peaceably as a rule, although exceptions may have occurred. The prevailing form of religion throughout the Pallava country in modern times is Śaiva.

Parāntaka I Chola. The Chola chronology is known with accuracy from A.D. 907, the date of the accession of Parāntaka I, son and successor of Āditya, the conqueror of the Pallavas. Parāntaka, who reigned for forty-two years, was an ambitious warrior king, and among other achievements drove the Pāndya king into exile, captured Madura his capital, and invaded Ceylon. Wars between the Tamil sovereigns and the rulers of Ceylon were almost incessant. The events are recorded in a multitude of Indian inscriptions as well as in the chronicles of the island.

Rājarāja the Great. The most prominent of the Chola monarchs were Rājarāja-deva the Great, who came to the throne in A.D. 985, and his son Rājendra Choladeva I, whose reign ended in A.D. 1035. The interval of fifty years covers the period of the most decisive Chola supremacy over the other Tamil powers. The Pāndyas, who never admitted willingly the pretensions of their rivals, which they long resisted, were forced to submit more or less completely to their overlordship.

The exploits of both Rājarāja and his at least equally aggressive son are celebrated in numerous inscriptions beginning from the eighth year of Rājarāja, whose earliest conquest was that of the Chera kingdom.[1]

His conquests on the mainland up to his fourteenth year comprised the Eastern Chālukya kingdom of Vengī, which had been wrested from the Pallavas at the beginning of the seventh century, Coorg, the Pāndya country, and large areas in the table-land of the Deccan. During subsequent years he subdued Quilon or Kollam on the Malabar coast, Kalinga, and Ceylon. About A.D. 1005 he sheathed the sword and spent the rest of his days in peace. During his declining years he associated the crown prince with him in the government, according to the current practice of the southern dynasties.[2] Rājarāja possessed a powerful navy and annexed a large number of islands, probably including the Laccadives and Maldives. When he passed away he left to his son substantially the whole of the modern Madras Presidency, except Madura and Tinnevelly.

Rājendra Choladeva I. Rājendra Choladeva I carried his arms even farther than his father had done. He sent a fleet across the Bay of Bengal, and thus effected the temporary occupation of Pegu, as well as of parts of Sumatra and Malaya and the Andaman and Nicobar islands. He even ventured on an expedition to the north, about A.D. 1023, and defeated Mahīpāla, the Pāla king of Bihar and Bengal. In commemoration of that exploit he assumed the title of Gangaikonda, and built in the Trichinopoly District a new capital city called Gangai-

---

[1] Not of the Chera fleet, as in *E.H.I.*[3], p. 465. The correction is due to T. A. Gopinātha Rao in *Travancore Archaeol. Ser.*, vol. ii, pp. 3–5.
[2] That practice accounts for sundry discrepancies in the accession dates.

konda-Cholapuram, adorned by a magnificent palace, a gigantic temple, and a vast artificial lake. The ruins, which have never been properly described or illustrated, have been much damaged by spoliation for building material.

The later Cholas. The death of Rājendra's son, Rājādhirāja, on the battlefield of Koppam in A.D. 1052 or 1053, when fighting the Chālukya, has been already mentioned. Ten years later the Chālukyas were defeated in their turn in another hard-fought contest.

King Adhirājendra, who was assassinated in A.D. 1074, has been named as having been the enemy of the sage Rāmānuja. Rājendra Kulottunga I, the successor, but not the son of Adhirājendra, was the most conspicuous of the later Cholas, who are known as Chālukya-Cholas, because of their relationship with the Eastern Chālukyas of Vengī. Rājendra, who reigned for forty-nine years, effected extensive conquests, and also directed an elaborate revision of the revenue survey of his dominions in A.D. 1086, the year of the survey for the Anglo-Norman Domesday Book.

During the thirteenth century the Chola power gradually declined, and later in that century the Pāndya kings reasserted themselves and shook off the Chola yoke.

The Muslim inroad in 1310 and the subsequent rise of the Hindu empire of Vijayanagar extinguished the ancient Chola dynasty with its institutions.

Chola administration. The administration of the Chola kingdom was highly systematized and evidently had been organized in very ancient times. Our definite knowledge of the details rests chiefly upon inscriptions dated between A.D. 800 and 1300. Certain records of Parāntaka I supply particularly full information about the actual working of the village assemblies during the first half of the tenth century. The whole fabric of the administration rested upon the basis of the village, or rather of unions of villages. It was usually found more convenient to deal with a group or union of villages (*kūrram*) rather than with a single village as the administrative unit. Each *kūrram* or union (in some parts of the country called *kōttam*) managed its local affairs through the agency of an assembly (*mahāsabhā*), which possessed and exercised extensive powers subject to the control of the royal officers (*adhikārin*). The assembly was elected by an elaborate machinery for casting lots, and the members held office for one year. Each union had its own local treasury, and enjoyed full control over the village lands, being empowered even to sell them in certain contingencies. Committees were appointed to look after tanks, gardens, justice, and other departments.

A certain number of *kūrrams* or unions constituted a district (*nādu*), and a group of districts formed a province(*mandalam*). The kingdom was divided into six provinces. That specially designated as *Cholamandalam* was roughly equivalent to the Tanjore and Trichinopoly Districts.

The theoretical share of the gross produce claimed by the state as land revenue was one-sixth, but petty imposts in great variety were levied. The actual tax levied apparently varied with the nature of the land and, according to Professor N. K. Sastri, might be as much as one-third on very fertile land. Payment could be made either in kind or in gold, but usually the former. The currency unit was the gold *kāsu*, weighing about 28 grains troy. Silver coin was not ordinarily used in the south in ancient times. The lands were regularly surveyed, and a standard measure was recorded.

Details concerning the military organization are lacking. A strong fleet was maintained. Irrigation works were constructed on a vast scale and of good design. The embankment of the artificial lake at Gangai-konda-Cholapuram, for instance, was sixteen miles in length, and the art of throwing great dams or 'anicuts' across the Kāverī (Cauvery) and other large rivers was thoroughly understood. Various public works of imposing dimensions were designed and erected. The single block of stone forming the summit of the steeple of the Tanjore temple is $25\frac{1}{2}$ feet square, and is estimated to weigh 80 tons. According to tradition it was brought into position by being moved up an incline four miles long. It seems that forced labour was employed on such works. The principal roads were carefully maintained. The particulars thus briefly summarized give an impression that the administrative system was well thought out and reasonably efficient. The important place given to the village assemblies assured the central government of considerable popular support, and individuals probably submitted readily to the orders of their fellow villagers who had the force of public opinion behind them. The system appears to have died out along with the Chola dynasty early in the fourteenth century, and ever since that distant time has been quite extinct.

Chola art. The story of south Indian art, meaning by that term architecture and sculpture, because few paintings of significance have survived,[1] is of special interest, inasmuch as the art appears to be wholly of native growth, untouched by foreign influence, and to have moved slowly through a long course of natural evolution. The early works of art, executed in impermanent materials, have perished utterly and cannot be described. But beyond all doubt they existed in large numbers and were the foundation of more enduring works. The artists who designed the Pallava temples and wrought the sculptures on the rocks of Māmallapuram were not novices. They had served their apprenticeship, and when the call came to them to express their ideas in imperishable forms of stone they brought to bear on the new problem the skill acquired by generations of practice. The art of the Chola period is the continuation of that of Pallava times. No violent break separates the two stages. The changes which occurred took place gradually by a process of spontaneous development.

[1] M. Jouveau-Dubreuil has noted some faint traces of Pallava frescoes. A fine series of paintings executed in the fifth century exists at Sigiriya in Ceylon (*H.F.A.*, pls. lviii–lx). Recently some fine Chola murals have been revealed in the Great Temple of Tanjore.

The earliest Chola temple described hitherto is that at Dādāpuram in the South Arcot District dating from the tenth century. The best known examples of Chola architecture, the huge temples of Tanjore and Gangaikonda-Cholapuram, are slightly later in date. Their design pleases the eye because the lofty tower over the shrine dominates the whole composition. In later Chola art the central shrine was reduced to insignificance, while endless labour was lavished on mighty *gopurams* or gateways to the temple enclosure, as at Chidambaram. The result, although imposing, is unsatisfying.

The Hindu temples of Ceylon seem to belong to the school of the earlier Cholas, as exemplified in comparatively small buildings.

The figure sculpture in the panels of the Gangaikonda-Cholapuram temple is of high quality and recalls the best work in Java. Similar sculptures are to be seen elsewhere.

Religion. The Chola kings, apparently without exception, were votaries of the god Śiva, but as a rule were tolerant of the other sects in the normal Indian manner. Sometimes, however, they violated the good custom, as when a Chola army destroyed the Jain temples in the Hoysala country, and a Chola king drove Rāmānuja into exile.

The dynasty is said to have patronized Tamil literature.

The Pāndya kingdom. The remaining Tamil powers—the Pāndya and Chera—require little notice. In the seventh century, Hiuen Tsang, who did not personally visit the Pāndya country, gives no information about the character of the government, nor does he name the capital, which must have been Madura. The Pāndya Rājā at that time presumably was tributary to the Pallavas of Kānchī. Buddhism was almost extinct, the ancient monasteries being mostly in ruins. He was informed that near the east side of the capital the remains of the monastery and *stūpa* built by Aśoka's brother, Mahendra, were still visible.[1] It is to be feared that search for the site is not now likely to be successful. No attempt has been made so far to trace Buddhist monuments in the Pāndya kingdom. Hindu temples were then numerous, and the nude Jain sect had multitudes of adherents.

Persecution of the Jains. Very soon after Hiuen Tsang's stay in the south, the Jains of the Pāndya kingdom suffered a terrible persecution at the hands of the king variously called Kūna, Sundara, or Nedumāran Pāndya, who originally had been a Jain and was converted to faith in Śiva by a Chola queen. He signalized his change of creed by atrocious outrages on the Jains who refused to follow his example. Tradition avers that 8,000 of them were impaled. Memory of the fact has been preserved in various ways, and to this day the Hindus of Madura, where the tragedy took place, celebrate the anniversary of 'the impalement of the Jains' as a festival (*utsava*).[2]

[1] I think it probable that Mahendra undertook the conversion of Ceylon from his base at Madura, and not at all in the manner described in the Buddhist ecclesiastical legends.

[2] T. A. Gopinātha Rao, *Elements of Hindu Iconography*, vol. i, Introd., p. 55; Madras, 1914.

The later Pāndyas. The Pāndya chiefs fought the Pallavas without ceasing, and at the close of the ninth century joined the Cholas in inflicting on their hereditary enemies a decisive defeat. The Pāndyas also engaged frequently in war with Ceylon. In the eleventh and twelfth centuries they were obliged unwillingly to submit to the Chola suzerainty, but in the thirteenth century they regained a better position, and might be considered the leading Tamil power when the Muslim attacks began in 1310. After that time they gradually sank into the position of mere local chiefs.

Marco Polo's visit. A glimpse of the Pāndya kingdom in the days of its revival is obtained from the pages of the Venetian traveller, Marco Polo, who visited Kāyal on the Tāmraparni twice, in 1288 and 1293. That town was then a busy and wealthy port, frequented by crowds of ships from the Arabian coast and China, in one of which the Venetian arrived. He describes Kāyal (Cael)·as 'a great and noble city', where much business was done. The king possessed vast treasures and wore upon his person the most costly jewels. He maintained splendid state, showed favour to merchants and foreigners so that they were glad to visit his city, and administered his realm with equity.

In consequence of the gradual elevation of the land, Old Kāyal is now two or three miles from the sea. Traces of ancient habitations may be discerned for miles, but the site is occupied only by a few miserable fishermen's huts.[1] It would be difficult to find a more striking example of the vicissitudes of fortune. Many ruined buildings must be hidden beneath the sands, but no serious attempt to excavate the locality has been made. Several Jain statues have been noticed both at Kāyal and at the still more ancient neighbouring site of Korkai.

The Chera kingdom. Little is known about the details of the medieval history of the Chera kingdom, which was subject to the more powerful members of the Chola dynasty. The conquest was the first military operation on a large scale undertaken in the reign of Rājarāja Chola, about A.D. 990. The kingdom ordinarily included the greater part of the modern Travancore State. Village assemblies exercised extensive powers, as in the Chola territory. The Kollam or Malabar era of A.D. 824–5, as commonly used in inscriptions, seems to mark the date of the foundation of Kollam or Quilon.

SELECTED DATES

A.D.

c. 600–25. Mahendra-varman Pallava (cave-temples, &c.).
  608–42. Pulakeśin II Chālukya.
  c. 610. Eastern Chālukya dynasty of Vengī founded.
  c. 620. Defeat of Harsha of Kanauj by Pulakeśin.
c. 625–45. Narasimha-varman Pallava (*rathas*, reliefs, &c.).
        Kūna (alias Sundara or Nedumāran) Pāndya, who impaled
        the Jains, was contemporary.

[1] *Ind. Ant.*, vol. vi, pp. 80–83, 215.

A.D.
640. Hiuen Tsang at Kānchī.
641. Hiuen Tsang at the court of Pulakeśin.
642. Defeat and deposition of Pulakeśin by Narasimha-varman Pallava.
740. Defeat of Pallavas by Chālukyas.
757. Overthrow of Early Chālukyas by the Rāshtrakūtas.
c. 760. Krishna I Rāshtrakūta, acc.; Kailāsa temple at Ellora
c. 815–77. Amoghavarsha Rāshtrakūta.
907. Parāntaka I Chola, acc.
973. Taila founded second Chālukya dynasty of Kalyāni.
c. 983. Colossal Jain statue at Śravana Belgola.
985. Rājarāja Chola, acc.
c. 1023. Expedition of Rājendra Choladeva to Bengal.
1052 or 1053. Battle of Koppam; Cholas defeated by Chālukyas.
1076–1126. Vikramānka or Vikramāditya Chālukya.
c. 1110–41. Bittiga or Vishnu-vardhana Hoysala; Rāmānuja.
c. 1160–7. Bijjala usurper; Lingāyat sect founded.
1288, 1293. Marco Polo visited Kāyal.
1310. Invasion by Malik Kāfūr.
1318. Harapāla Yādava flayed alive.
1326–7. Destruction of Dorasamudra and the Hoysala power.
1336. Foundation of Vijayanagar.

AUTHORITIES

MANY still valuable references are contained in *E.H.I.*[4], and others are given in the footnotes. The work of G. JOUVEAU-DUBREUIL deserves prominent notice: *Archéologie du sud de l'Inde* (2 vols., Paris, 1914), *Pallava Antiquities* (vol. i, London, 1916; vol. ii, Pondicherry, 1918), *Dravidian Architecture* (Madras, 1917), *The Pallavas* (Pondicherry, 1917), *Ancient History of the Deccan* (Pondicherry, 1920).

Among more recent works D. C. SIRCAR's *Successors of the Sātavāhanas* (Calcutta, 1939) treats of the early Deccan dynasties ably and in great detail. On the Vākātakas the most recent study is that of A. S. ALTEKAR in *New History of the Indian People* vol. vi (see above, p. 189). A detailed monograph on the Chālukya dynasties is badly needed and is expected shortly from G. C. RAYCHAUDHURI. The Rāshtrakūtas have been ably handled by A. S. ALTEKAR (*Rāshtrakūtas and their Times*, Poona, 1934), whose work gives valuable information on social and economic conditions in the medieval Deccan. On the Pallavas the most important recent works are those of R. GOPALAN (*History of the Pallavas of Kānchī*, Madras, 1928) and C. MINAKSHI (*Administrative and Social Life under the Pallavas*, Madras, 1938). A very detailed monograph on the Kadambas is *The Kadamba Kula* of G. M. MORAES (Bombay, 1931). On the extreme south the works of K. A. NILAKANTA SASTRI deserve special mention as among the most scholarly of those of any Indian historian. His *The Colas* (2nd ed., Madras, 1955), and his *Pāndyan Kingdom* (London, 1929), practically supersede all earlier works on the two dynasties. His *History of South India* has now been published, and the recent *History of India* (vol. i, Madras, 1950) treats of the south Indian dynasties in much greater detail than any work of similar size hitherto published. On the Hoysalas a detailed study by J. D. M. DERRETT will appear shortly. The Eastern or Orissan Gangas together with lesser dynasties of Orissa are thoroughly studied in R. D. BANERJI's *History of Orissa* (2 vols., Calcutta, 1931).

PART II

INDIA IN THE MUSLIM PERIOD

BOOK IV

The Muslim Powers of Northern India

CHAPTER 1

The rise of the Muslim power in India and the sultanate of Delhi
A.D. 1175–1290

Rise and decline of Muslim power. The Muslim conquest of India did not begin until the last quarter of the twelfth century, if the frontier provinces of Kabul, the Panjab, and Sind be excluded from consideration. It may be reckoned to have continued until 1340, when the empire of Sultan Muhammad bin Tughluq attained its maximum extent, comprising twenty-four provinces more or less effectively under the control of the sultan of Delhi.[1] The provinces included a large portion of the Deccan, and even a section of the Malabar or Coromandel coast.

After 1340 the frontiers of the sultanate of Delhi rapidly contracted, many new kingdoms, both Muslim and Hindu, being formed. The quick growth of the Hindu empire of Vijayanagar checked the southern progress of Islam and recovered some territory which had passed under Muslim rule. Elsewhere, too, Hindu chiefs asserted themselves, and it may be affirmed with truth that for more than two centuries, from 1340 to the accession of Akbar in 1556, Islam lost ground on the whole.

Under Akbar and his successors the Muslim frontier was extended from time to time until 1691, when the officers of Aurangzeb were able for a moment to levy tribute from Tanjore and Trichinopoly in the far south. After the date named the Marathas enlarged the borders of Hindu dominion until 1818, when their power was broken and they were forced to acknowledge British supremacy, as based on the conquest of Bengal and Bihar between 1757 and 1765. That, in brief, is the outline of the rise, decline, and fall of Muslim sovereign rule in India. From 1803 to 1858 the empire of Delhi was merely titular.

This chapter and the next will be devoted to a summary account of the progress of the Muslim conquest from A.D. 1175 to 1340. Most of the conquests, after the earliest, were made by or for the sultans of Delhi, whose line began in 1206.

The dynasty of Ghūr (Ghūrī). The first attack was made by a

---

[1] The list is in Thomas, *Chronicles*, p. 203.

chieftain of the obscure principality of Ghūr, hidden away among the mountains of Afghanistan to the south-east of Herat. The fortune of the Ghūr chiefs was made by means of a quarrel with the successors of Sultan Mahmūd of Ghazni, whose power in central Asia had been

NORTH-WEST INDIA AND ADJACENT REGIONS

broken by the growing Seljuk empire. One of those successors named Bāhrām having executed two princes of Ghūr, the blood-feud thus started prompted 'Alā-ud-dīn Husain to take vengeance by sacking Ghazni in A.D. 1151 (= A.H. 544). The unhappy city was given to the flames for seven days and nights, during which 'plunder, devastation, and slaughter were continuous. Every man that was found was slain, and all the women and children were made prisoners. All the palaces and edifices of the Mahmūdi kings which had no equals in the world' were destroyed, save only the tombs of Sultan Mahmūd and two of his relatives. Shortly afterwards Khusrū Shāh, Bāhrām's son, was obliged by an incursion of Ghuzz Turkmāns to leave Ghazni and retire to Lahore (1160). But Ghazni was not incorporated in the dominions of Ghūr until twelve or thirteen years later (1173), when it was wrested from the Turkmāns by Sultan Ghiyās-ud-dīn of Ghūr, who made over the conquered territory with its dependencies, including Kabul, to the government as sultan of his brother Muhammad, the son of Sām, who is also known by his titles of Shihāb-ud-dīn and Muizz-ud-dīn (r-daulat). It is most convenient to designate him as Muhammad Ghūrī, or 'of Ghūr', sultan of Ghazni, and conqueror of Hindustan.

Early operations of Muhammad Ghūrī. He began his Indian operations by a successful attack on Multan (1175–6), which he followed up by the occupation of Uch, obtained through the treachery of a rani. Three years later he moved southwards through the desert and attempted the conquest of rich Gujarat. But Bhīmdev II of Anhilwāra or Patan was too strong for the invader, who was defeated and repulsed with heavy loss (1178). The victory protected Gujarat, as a whole, from any serious Muslim attack for more than a century, although intermediate raids occurred, and Anhilwāra was occupied twenty years later. Such checks to the progress of Islam as Bhīmdev II inflicted were rare.

In 1186 Muhammad Ghūrī deposed Khusrū Malik, the last prince of the line of Sabuktigīn and Mahmūd, and himself occupied the Panjab. Having already secured Sind he was thus in possession of the basin of the Indus, and in a position to make further advances into the fertile plains of India, teeming with tempting riches, and inhabited by idolaters, fit only to be 'sent to hell' according to the simple creed of the invaders.

First battle of Tarāin. The sultan organized a powerful expedition as soon as possible, and in 1191 (A.H. 587) advanced into India. The magnitude of the danger induced the various Hindu kings to lay aside their quarrels for a moment and to form a great confederacy against the invader, as their ancestors had done against Amīr Sabuktigīn and Sultan Mahmūd. All the leading powers of northern India sent contingents, the whole being under the command of Rāi Pithaura or Prithvīrāj, the Chauhān ruler of Ajmer and Delhi. The Hindu host met the army of Islam at Tarāin or Tarāorī, between Karnal and Thānēsar. That region, the modern Karnal District, is marked out by nature as the battlefield in which the invader from the north-west must meet the defenders of Delhi and the basin of the Ganges. The legendary ground of Kurukshetra, where the heroes of the *Mahābhārata* had fought before the dawn of history was not far distant, and Panipat, where three decisive battles were lost and won in later ages, is about thirty miles farther south. The sultan, who met the brother of Prithvīrāj in single combat, was severely wounded, and his army, surrounded and outnumbered, was utterly routed.

Second battle of Tarāin. In the following year the sultan returned, met the Hindu confederates on the same ground, and in his turn defeated them utterly (1192, A.H. 588). Rāi Prithvīrāj, when his cumbrous host had been broken by the onset of 10,000 mounted archers, fled from the field, but was captured and killed. His brother fell in the battle. The victory gave to Muhammad Hansi, Samana, and all northern India to the gates of Delhi. In fact, the second battle of Tarāin in 1192 may be regarded as the decisive contest which ensured the ultimate success of the Muslim attack on Hindustan. No Hindu general in any age was willing to profit by experience and learn the lesson taught by Alexander's operations long ago. Time after time enormous hosts, formed of the contingents supplied by innumerable rajas, and supported by the delusive strength of elephants, were easily routed by quite small bodies of vigorous western soldiers, fighting under one undivided command, and trusting chiefly to well-armed mobile cavalry. Alexander, Muhammad of Ghūr, Babur, Ahmad Shāh Durrānī, and other capable commanders, all used essentially the same tactics by which they secured decisive victories against brave Hindu armies of very large numbers. The Indian caste system was unfavourable to military efficiency as against foreign foes.

Qutb-ud-dīn Aibak. After the victory of Tarāin the sultan returned to Khurasan, leaving the conduct of the Indian campaign in the hands of Qutb-ud-dīn Aibak, a native of Turkistan, who had been bought as a slave, and was still technically in a servile condition while conquering Hindustan. In 1193 (A.H. 589) Qutb-ud-dīn occupied Delhi, and advanced into the Doab. He was there joined by Muhammad Ghūrī in an attack upon Kanauj, whose Rathor ruler, Jai Chand, was defeated and slain. Soon afterward Gwalior fell, and in 1197 Anhilwāra, the capital of Gujarat, was plundered, although the province was not subdued. In the same year Ajmer was occupied and garrisoned.

Conquest of Bihar. The overthrow of the rulers of the eastern kingdoms was effected with astounding facility by Qutb-ud-dīn's general, Muhammad Khiljī, the son of Bakhtyār. The Muslim general, acting independently, after completing several successful plundering expeditions, seized the fort of Bihar in 1193, by an audacious move, and thus mastered the capital of the province of that name. The prevailing religion of Bihar at that time was a corrupt form of Buddhism, which had received liberal patronage from the kings of the Pāla dynasty for more than three centuries. The Muslim historian, indifferent to distinctions among idolaters, states that the majority of the inhabitants were 'shaven-headed Brahmans', who were all put to the sword. He evidently means Buddhist monks, as he was informed that the whole city and fortress were considered to be a college, which the name Bihar signifies. A great library was scattered. The ashes of the Buddhist sanctuaries at Sārnāth near Benares still bear witness to the rage of the image-breakers. Many noble monuments of the ancient civilization of India were irretrievably wrecked in the course of the early Muslim invasions. Those invasions were fatal to the existence of Buddhism as an organized religion in northern India, where its strength resided chiefly in Bihar and certain adjoining territories. The monks who escaped massacre fled, and were scattered over Nepal, Tibet, and the south. After A.D. 1200 the traces of Buddhism in upper India are faint and obscure.

Conquest of Bengal. Bengal, then under the rule of Lakshmana Sēna, an aged and venerated Brahmanical prince, succumbed even more easily a little later, either in 1199 or 1202. Muhammad Khiljī, son of Bakhtyār, riding in advance of the main body of his troops, suddenly appeared before the capital city of Nūdīah (Nuddea) with a party of eighteen troopers, who were supposed by the people to be horse dealers. Thus slenderly escorted he rode up to the raja's palace and boldly attacked the doorkeepers. The raider's audacity succeeded. The raja, who was at his dinner, slipped away by a back door and retired to the neighbourhood of Dacca, where his descendants continued to rule as local chiefs for several generations. The Muslim general destroyed Nūdīah, securing much accumulated treasure, and transferred the seat of government to Lakshmanāvatī or Gaur, an ancient Hindu city. Muhammad secured the approval of his master, Qutb-ud-dīn, by giving him plenty of plunder, and proceeded to organize a Muslim provincial administration, in practical independence. Mosques and other Muslim edifices were erected all over the kingdom. The conquest so easily effected was final. Bengal never escaped from the rule of Muslims for any considerable time until they were superseded in the eighteenth century by the British.

Conquest of Bundelkhand. In 1203 the strong Chandēl fortress of Kalanjar in Bundelkhand was surrendered to Aibak by Aja Deo, the aspiring minister of the late Raja Parmāl.

The gratified historian of the conqueror's exploits states that 'the temples were converted into mosques and abodes of goodness, and the ejaculations of the bead-counters [worshippers using rosaries] and the voices of the summoners to prayer ascended to the highest heaven, and the very name of idolatry was annihilated. . . . Fifty thousand men came under the collar of slavery, and the plain became black as pitch with Hindus.' The victor passed on and occupied Mahoba, the seat of the Chandēl civil government.

Death of Muhammad of Ghūr. In the same year Ghiyās-ud-dīn, the sultan of Ghūr, died and was succeeded by his brother Muhammad, who thus united in his person all the dominions of the family. Muhammad had returned to Ghazni after the capture of Kalanjar. Two years later, in 1205, he was recalled to the Panjab in order to suppress a revolt of the powerful Khokhar tribe. The sultan treated the foe in the drastic manner of the times. But fate overtook him. As he was on the march towards Ghazni in March 1206 (A.H. 602) he was stabbed by an Ismā'īlī fanatic at Dhamiāk, a camping-ground now in the Jhelum District.

The first sultan of Delhi. Qutb-ud-dīn, who had been dignified with the title of sultan by Muhammad Ghūrī's brother's son, Ghiyās-ud-dīn Mahmūd, succeeded Muhammad Ghūrī as sovereign of the new Indian conquests, and from 1206 may be reckoned as the first sultan of Delhi. But his enthronement took place at Lahore. The new sovereign sought to strengthen his position by marriage alliances with influential rival chiefs. He himself married the daughter of Tāj-ud-dīn Yildiz, governor of Kirmān, and he gave his sister to Nāsir-ud-dīn Qabācha, the governor of Sind. Īltutmish (Altamsh), foremost of his slaves, married Qutb-ud-dīn's daughter.

The three persons named, Yildiz, Qabācha, and Īltutmish, had been slaves like Qutb-ud-dīn himself. The dynasty founded by Qutb-ud-dīn and continued by other princes of servile origin is consequently known to history as the Slave dynasty.

Qutb-ud-dīn died in 1210 from the effects of an accident on the polo ground, having ruled as sultan for a little more than four years.

Ferocity of the early invaders. He was a typical specimen of the ferocious central Asian warriors of the time, merciless and fanatical. His valour and profuse liberality to his comrades endeared him to the historian of his age, who praises him as having been a 'beneficent and victorious monarch. . . . His gifts', we are told, 'were bestowed by hundreds of thousands, and his slaughters likewise were by hundreds of thousands.' This attitude of the writer of the *Tabaqāt-i Nāsirī* recurs in many other historians. With its vigorous exaggeration, it doubtless reflects the moral certainty of the Muslim, but also reminds us that the author was writing to flatter a court audience. The invaders' rapid success was largely due to their pitiless 'frightfulness', which made resistance terribly dangerous, and could not always be evaded by humble submission. It was a natural policy for the conquerors, who, few in number, had frequently to deal with revolts among the great mass of Hindus.

But the story of the Muslim conquest as seen from the Hindu point of view was never written, except to some extent in Rajputana. Such narratives as that of Elphinstone, who worked entirely on materials supplied by Muslim authors, too often reflect the prejudices of the historians who wrote in Persian.

Architecture of the early sultans. The prevailing favourable or at least lenient judgement on the merits of the earlier sultans in India is due in no small measure to the admiration deservedly felt for their architectural works. The 'Qutb' group of buildings at Old Delhi, although named after the saint from Ūsh who lies buried there, rather than after the first sultan, undoubtedly is in part the work of Qutb-ud-dīn Aibak, who built the noble screen of arches. The question whether the famous Mīnār was begun by him and completed by Īltutmish, or was wholly built by the later sovereign, has given rise to differences of opinion depending on the interpretation of certain inscriptions.

Indo-Muslim architecture, which derives its peculiar character from the fact that Indian craftsmen necessarily were employed on the edifices of the foreign faith, dates from the short reign of Qutb-ud-dīn Aibak. The masterpieces of the novel form of art cost a heavy price by reason of the destruction of ancient buildings and sculptures in other styles perhaps equally meritorious. The materials of no less than twenty-seven Hindu temples were used in the erection of the 'Qutb' mosque.

The end of Muhammad, son of Bakhtyār. The ludicrous facility with which Bihar and Bengal had been overrun and annexed tempted Muhammad bin Bakhtyār to a more adventurous enterprise. 'The ambition of seizing the country of Turkestan and Tibbat [Tibet] began to torment his brain; and he had an army got ready, and about 10,000 horse were organized.' Unfortunately, the information available is not sufficient to determine exactly either the line of his march or the farthest point of his advance. He seems to have moved through the region now known as the Bogra and Jalpaiguri Districts, and to have crossed a great river supposed to be the Karatoya by a stone bridge of twenty arches, the site of which has not been identified. The rivers have completely changed their courses. The Tista, for instance, now a tributary of the Brahmaputra, formerly joined the Karatoya. He is said to have reached 'the open country of Tibbat', but what that phrase may mean it is not easy to say. Beyond a certain point, perhaps to the north of Darjeeling, he was unable to proceed, and was obliged to retreat. His starving force, finding the bridge broken, attempted to ford the river. All were drowned, except about a hundred including the leader, who struggled across somehow. Muhammad, overcome by shame and remorse, took to his bed and died, or, according to another account, was assassinated by 'Alī Mardān Khaljī. His death occurred in the Hijrī year 602, equivalent to A.D. 1205–6. Early in the reign of Aurangzeb Mīr Jumla invaded Assam and nearly failed as disastrously as his predecessor had done. The mountains to the north of Bengal were never reduced to obedience by any Muslim sovereign.

Sultan Īltutmish. Ārām, the son of Qutb-ud-dīn, who succeeded to the throne, did not inherit his father's abilities, and was quickly displaced (1211) in favour of his sister's husband, Īltutmish, corruptly called Altamsh, who assumed the title of Shams-ud-dīn, 'the sun of religion'. Much of his time was spent in successful fighting with his rival slave chieftains, Yildiz and Qabācha. In 1229 he received a patent of investiture as *Sultān i Āzam* from the reigning khalif of Baghdad. Before he died, in 1236, he had reduced the Khalji Maliks of Bengal to obedience, and had retaken Gwalior, lost at Qutb-ud-dīn's death. He not only brought back under control the territories of his late master, but added to them Malwa and Sind.

The Qutb Mīnār was built, except the basement story, under his direction about A.D. 1232. He made other important additions to the Qutb group of buildings, and is buried there in a beautiful tomb, 'one of the richest examples of Hindu art applied to Muslim purposes that Old Delhi affords'. Īltutmish is also responsible for a magnificent mosque at Ajmer, built like that at Delhi from the materials of Hindu temples.

Chingiz Khān. In his days India narrowly escaped the most terrible of all possible calamities, a visit from Chingiz Khān, the dreaded Great Khān or Khākān of the Mongols.[1] He actually advanced as far as the Indus, in pursuit of Jalāl-ud-dīn Mangbarnī, the fugitive sultan of Khwārizm or Khiva, who sought refuge at the court of Delhi, after surprising adventures. The western Panjab was plundered by the Mongol troopers, but no organized invasion of India took place.

Chingiz Khān was the official title of the Mongol chieftain Temujin or Tamūrchi, born in 1162, who acquired ascendancy early in life over the tribes of Mongolia. About the beginning of the thirteenth century they elected him to be the head of their confederacy and he then adopted the style of Chingiz Khān, probably a corruption of a Chinese title. In the course of a few years he conquered a large portion of China and all the famous kingdoms of central Asia. Balkh, Bokhara, Samarqand, Herat, Ghazni, and many other cities of renown fell under his merciless hand and were reduced to ruins. The vanquished inhabitants, men, women, and children, were slain literally in millions. He carried his victorious hordes far into Russia to the bank of the Dnieper, and when he died in 1227 ruled a gigantic empire extending from the Pacific to the Black Sea.

The author of the *Tabaqāt-i Nāsirī*, who admired a Muslim, but abhorred a heathen slayer of men, has drawn a vivid sketch of the conqueror, which is worth quoting:

Trustworthy persons have related that the Chingiz Khān, at the time when he came into Khurāsān, was sixty-five [lunar] years old, a man of tall stature, of vigorous build, robust in body, the hair on his face scanty and turned white, with cat's eyes, possessed of great energy, discernment, genius, and understanding, awe-striking, a butcher, just, resolute, an overthrower of enemies, intrepid, sanguinary, cruel.

Sultan Raziyyat-ud-dīn. Sultan Īltutmish, knowing the incapacity of his surviving sons, had nominated his daughter Raziyya or Raziyyat-ud-dīn ('accepted by religion') as his successor.[2] But the nobles thought that they knew better and placed on the throne Prince

---

[1] The spelling of the name varies much. Howorth gives Chinghiz as the most correct form. Raverty uses both Chingiz and Chingīz. Chingiz seems to be the simplest and safest spelling. Mongol (Monggol) is the same word as Mughal (Mogul, &c.), but it is convenient to confine the term Mongol to the heathen followers of Chingiz, who were mostly 'narrow-eyed' people, reserving the term Mughul in its various spellings for the more civilized tribes, largely of Turk blood, who became Muslims in the fourteenth century, and from whom sprang the Chagatāi or Jagatāi section of Turks to which Babur and his successors in India belonged. The Turk races ordinarily resemble Europeans in features, and have not the Mongolian 'narrow eyes' strongly marked, but Turks and Mongols intermarried freely, and the Mongol blood often asserted itself. It shows in the portraits of Akbar.

[2] She also bore the title of Jalāl-ud-dīn (Thomas, *Chronicles*, p. 138). Ibn Batūta gives her name simply as Raziyyat—his words are *wa bintari tasmi Raziyyat* (Defrémery, tome iii, p. 166).

Rukn-ud-dīn, a worthless debauchee in 1236. After a scandalous reign of a few months he was put out of the way and replaced by his sister, who assumed the title of sultan and did her best to play the part of a man. She took an active part in the wars with Hindus and rebel Muslim chiefs, riding an elephant in the sight of all men. But her sex was against her. In 1240 the Turkish nobles deposed her. Later that year Altūniya, the governor of Bhatinda and an instrument in her overthrow, finding himself unrewarded, married her and attempted to replace her on the throne. He was defeated, and both she and her husband were killed by certain Hindus. The author of the *Ṭabaqāt-i Nāsirī*, the only contemporary authority for the period, gives Sultan Raziyyat-ud-dīn a high character from his Muslim point of view. She was, he declares,

a great sovereign, and sagacious, just, beneficent, the patron of the learned, a dispenser of justice, the cherisher of her subjects, and of warlike talent, and was endowed with all the admirable attributes and qualifications necessary for kings; but as she did not attain the destiny in her creation of being computed among men, of what advantage were all these excellent qualifications unto her?

Sultan Nāsir-ud-dīn. A son and grandson of Sultan Iltutmish were then successively enthroned. Both proved to be failures and were removed in favour of Nāsir-ud-dīn, a younger son of Iltutmish (1246), who managed to retain his life and office for twenty years. The historian, Minhāj-i Sirāj, who has been quoted more than once, held high office under Nāsir-ud-dīn and called his book by his sovereign's name. His judgement of a liberal patron necessarily is biased, but no other contemporary authority exists, and we must be content with his version of the facts. So far as appears, the sultan lived the life of a fanatical devotee, leaving the conduct of affairs in the hands of Ulugh Khān Balban, his father-in-law and minister.

Mongol raids. The Mongols whom Chingiz Khān had left behind, or who crossed the frontier after his retirement, gave constant trouble during the reign. They had occupied and ruined Lahore in 1241-2 and continued to make many inroads on Sind, including Multan. Nāsir-ud-dīn, who had no family, nominated Ulugh Khān Balban as his successor.[1] He died in 1266.

Suppression of the Meos. In 1258 and 1259 Balban led campaigns against the turbulent Hindus of the Doab, and in 1260 he attacked the Meos south of Delhi. They had infested the approaches to the capital and had ravaged the Bayana District. Now, in a twenty-days' campaign they were slaughtered and pillaged. Two hundred and fifty of their leading men were taken back to Delhi for execution. 'By royal command many of the rebels were cast under the feet of elephants, and the fierce Turks cut the bodies of the Hindus in two. About a hundred met their death at the hands of the flayers, being skinned from

[1] Ibn Batūta alleges that Balban murdered Nāsir-ud-din.

head to foot; their skins were all stuffed with straw, and some of them were hung over every gate of the city. The plain of Hauz-Rānī and the gates of Delhi remembered no punishment like this, nor had one ever heard such a tale of horror.'

Even so a second stroke was needed, in July 1260. 'He fell upon the insurgents unawares, and captured them all, to the number of 12,000—men, women, and children—whom he put to the sword. Thanks be to God for this victory of Islam.'

Sultan Balban. Balban, as Elphinstone observes, 'being already in possession of all the powers of king, found no difficulty in assuming the title'. He had been one of the 'Forty Slaves' attached to Sultan Īltutmish, most of whom attained to high positions. Balban's first care was to execute the survivors of the forty, in order to relieve himself of the dangers of rivalry. He had no regard for human life, and no scruples about shedding blood. He was, indeed, a 'ruthless king'. 'Fear and awe of him took possession of all men's hearts', and he maintained such pomp and dignity at his court that all beholders were impressed with respect for his person. He never laughed. His justice, executed without respect of persons, was stern and bloody. He secured his authority in the provinces by an organized system of espionage, and spies who failed to report incidents of importance were hanged. He refused to employ Hindu officials.

In the early years of his reign, Balban had again to clear the Delhi approaches of Meos, and to hold them down he built a fort and line of police posts. The Doab, which remained rebellious, was distributed in fiefs to nobles who would clear the jungles and root out the Hindu brigands. New forts were built, and Afghan garrisons were settled on the land to guard communications with Bengal.

The threat of the Mongols, now in Ghazni, was checked by the refortification of Lāhore in 1270, and by the prowess of Balban's cousin, Sunqar. With Sunqar's death, by poison, the way for new raids was opened, until Balban appointed his elder son Muhammad to guard the frontier from Multan. The prince utterly routed the invaders in 1279.

The three years from 1279 onwards were spent in suppressing the rebellion in Bengal of a Turki noble named Tughril who had dared to assume royal state. The rebel's family were exterminated. The country-side was terrified at the sight of the rows of gibbets set up in the streets of the provincial capital. The governorship of Bengal continued to be held by members of Balban's family until 1338, when the revolt occurred which resulted in the definite independence of the province. However horrible the cruelty of Balban may appear, it served its purpose and maintained a certain degree of order in rough times. When he died 'all security of life and property was lost, and no one had any confidence in the stability of the kingdom'.

Refugee princes. Balban's magnificent court was honoured by the presence of fifteen kings and princes who had fled to Delhi for refuge from the horrors of the Mongol devastations. Many eminent literary men, the most notable being Amīr Khusrū the poet, were associated with the refugee princes. The sultan's main anxiety was caused by the fear of a Mongol invasion on a large scale, which prevented him from undertaking conquests of new territory. His eldest and best-loved son was killed in a fight with the heathens in March 1285. That sorrow shook the strong constitution of Balban, the 'wary old wolf, who had held possession of Delhi for sixty years'. He died in 1286 at an advanced age.

Sultan Qaiqabad. Balban left no heir fit to succeed him. In those days no definite rule of succession existed and the nobles were accustomed to select whom they pleased by a rough election. Qaiqabad, a grandson of Balban, aged about eighteen years, who was placed on the throne, although his father was living in Bengal, as governor of that province, disgraced himself by scandalous debauchery, and was removed after a short reign.

End of the Slave Kings. Balban's hopes of establishing a dynasty were thus frustrated, and the stormy rule of the Slave Kings came to an end. Their chroniclers present them to us as either fierce fanatics or worthless debauchees. The fanatics possessed the merits of courage and activity in warfare, with a rough sense of justice when dealing with Muslims. Hindu idolaters and Mongol devil-worshippers had no rights in their eyes and deserved no fate better than to be 'sent to hell'. The Muslim historians delight in telling of holy wars and they stress that 'the army is the source and means of government', but it is clear that the sultans were also ready to accept Hindus as vassals, to engage them as officers and troops, and regularly to employ them in the revenue administration. Politically, they acquired a tolerably firm hold on the regions now called the Panjab, Uttar Pradesh, with Bihar, Gwalior, Sind, and some parts of Rajasthan and central India. Bengal was practically independent, although Balban's severities enforced formal submission to the suzerainty of Delhi and the occasional payment of tribute. Yet within this area Hindu Katehr was independent and but rarely invaded, and Hindu chiefs remained in turbulent vigour in the Doab. Malwa, Gujarat, and all the rest of India continued to be governed by numerous Hindu monarchs of widely varying importance to whom the tragedies of the sultanate were matters of indifference. Even their control of the Panjab was disputed by the Mongols, from the time of Chingiz Khān (1221).

CHRONOLOGY

A.D.

Sultan MUHAMMAD OF GHŪR (Ghūri, with titles of Shihāb-ud-din and Muizz-ud-dīn, son of Sām)

	A.D.
Occupied Multan and Uch	1175–6
Defeated by raja of Gujarat	1178
Deposed Khusrū Malik of Lahore . . .	1186
First battle of Tarāin	1191

Sultans of Delhi; the Slave Kings

AUTHORITIES

THE leading contemporary authority, and to a large extent the only one, is the *Tabaqāt-i Nāsirī*, translated in full by RAVERTY (London, 1881), with learned but diffuse annotation. Part of the work is translated in E. & D., vol. ii. Other Persian authorities are given in that volume and vol. iii. FIRISHTA mostly copies from the *Tabaqāt-i Nāsirī* through the *Tabaqāt-i Akbarī*. RAVERTY's *Notes on Afghanistan* (London, 1888), a valuable, though an ill-arranged and bulky book, has been serviceable to me.

Further works include E. THOMAS, *Chronicles of the Pathan Kings of Delhi*, and A. B. M. HABIBULLA, *Foundation of Muslim Rule in India*, Lahore, 1945.

CHAPTER 2

The sultanate of Delhi continued; A.D. 1290 to 1340; the Khiljī and Tughluq dynasties

Sultan Jalāl-ud-dīn Khiljī. Qaiqabad having been brutally killed, a high official named Fīrūz Shāh, of the Khalj or Khiljī tribe, who was placed on the throne by a section of the nobles, assumed the title of Jalāl-ud-dīn. Baranī states that Jalāl-ud-dīn 'came of a race different from the Turks', but in fact the Khiljīs were a Turkish tribe though long settled in the Garmsīr in Afghanistan. Jalāl-ud-dīn was an aged man of about seventy when elected. His election was so unpopular that he did not venture to reside in Delhi, and was obliged to live in Qaiqabad's palace in the village of Kilokhri, a short distance outside, which became known as Naushahr or 'Newtown'. The year after his accession a famine occurred so severe that many Hindus drowned themselves in the Jumna. The administration of the sultan is criticized as having been too lenient, and it seems probable that he was too old for his work. On one occasion he is recorded to have lost his temper and to have cruelly executed an unorthodox holy man named Sīdī Maulā. That irregular execution or murder was believed to have been the cause of the sultan's evil fate. Mongols at least 100,000 strong invaded India in 1292, reached Sunām, but were there defeated by Fīrūz, and agreed to withdraw, unmolested. Many of the Mongols elected to stay in India, becoming nominally Muslims. They were spoken of as New Muslims, and settled down at Kilokhri and other villages near Delhi.

Murder of Jalāl-ud-dīn. In 1294 'Alā-ud-dīn, son of the sultan's brother, and also son-in-law of Jalāl-ud-dīn, obtained permission for an expedition into Malwa. But he went much farther, plunging into the heart of the Deccan, and keeping his movements concealed from the court. He marched through Berar and Khandesh, and having invested his capital compelled Rāmachandra, the Yādava king of Deogiri and the western Deccan, to surrender Ellichpur (Ilichpur). 'Alā-ud-dīn collected treasure to an amount unheard of, and showed no disposition to share it with his sovereign. In fact, his treasonable intentions were patent to everybody except his doting old uncle and father-in-law, who closed his ears against all warnings and behaved like a person infatuated. Ultimately, Jalāl-ud-dīn was persuaded to place himself in his nephew's power at Kara in the Allahabad District. When the sultan grasped the traitor's hand the signal was given. He was thrown down and decapitated. His head was stuck on a spear and carried round the camp. Lavish distribution of gold secured the adhesion of the army to the usurper, and 'Alā-ud-dīn became sultan (July 1296).

Thagi. Jalāl-ud-dīn, although he did not deserve his cruel fate, was wholly unfit to rule. One act of leniency was particularly silly. At some time during his reign about 1,000 *thags* were arrested in Delhi. The sultan would not allow one of them to be executed. He adopted the imbecile plan of putting them into boats and transporting them to Lakhnauti (Gaur), the capital of Bengal. The story, told by Ziā-ud-dīn Baranī, is of special interest as being the earliest known historical notice of *thagi*.

Sultan 'Alā-ud-dīn Khiljī. The African traveller Ibn Batūta in the fourteenth century expressed the opinion that 'Alā-ud-dīn deserved to be considered 'one of the best sultans'.[1] That somewhat surprising verdict is not justified either by the manner in which 'Alā-ud-dīn attained power or by the history of his acts as sultan. Ziā-ud-dīn Baranī, the historian who gives the fullest account of his reign, dwells on his 'crafty cruelty', and on his addiction to disgusting vice. 'He shed more innocent blood than ever Pharaoh was guilty of', and Baranī points the moral, telling us that he 'did not escape retribution for the blood of his patron'. He ruthlessly killed off everybody who could be supposed to endanger his throne, cutting up root and branch all the nobles who had served under his uncle, save three only. Even innocent women and children were not spared, a new horror. 'Up to this time no hand had ever been laid upon wives and children on account of men's misdeeds.' The evil precedent set by 'one of the best sultans' was often followed in later times.

Political events. In 1297 an army was dispatched against Gujarat. The territories of the Baghela Rajput ruler were overrun and annexed, enormous booty was taken from the ports, and Kamalā Devi and Kāfūr, the young eunuch, were secured for 'Alā-ud-dīn.

In 1301 Ranthambhor was captured after a long siege, the Rajput defender Hamīr Deva was taken and killed, while his family committed *jauhar*. To this conquest was added that of Chitor, taken in 1303 and held until 1311. Tod graphically describes the closing scenes of the struggle and the immolation of the Rajput women. The death in battle of the raja of Malwa in 1305 led to the annexation of Ujjain, Mandu, Dhar, and Chanderi.

Expeditions to the south. These successes were followed by a series of most profitable raids into the Deccan, conducted by the sultan's favourite, Kāfūr. He first compelled the submission of Rāmchandradeva, the Yādava ruler of Devagiri who was taken to Delhi, but returned to the Deccan as a tribute-paying vassal. Early in 1310 the Kākatīya ruler of Warangal, Pratāprudradeva I, was besieged in his capital and forced to buy off the raiders. Later in the same year Kāfūr surprised the Hoysala king, Ballāla III, and secured further rich booty on his surrender in February 1311. One further raid into the deep south was then made and the capital of Ma'bar was looted

---

[1] *wa kāna min khaiyār alsalātīn* 'il ut au nombre des meill rs sultans' (Defrémery, tome iii, p. 10)

before Kāfūr was turned back. He arrived at Delhi with an extra-ordinary accumulation of plunder in October 1311. On Rāmchand-radeva's death in 1312, his rebellious son was driven out and Devagiri was annexed.

Mongol raids. Within this period there had been several Mongol incursions into the Panjab. Those of 1296 and 1297 were raids, that of 1299 under Qutlugh Khwāja was planned as a conquest. He was met outside Delhi by the sultan's army, and was there routed. 'Alā-ud-dīn was particularly pleased by this victory, for in achieving it his too brilliant general Zafar Khān lost his life. Later the Mongols were generally held in check by the guardian of the marches, Ghāzī Malik (later Ghiyās-ud-dīn Tughluq). Internal security was achieved by wholesale massacre of the Mongol converts, the New Muslims, who had settled near Delhi.

Administrative measures. These political successes were backed by administrative measures. The conjunction of a Mongol raid to the Jumna, a disaster in Warangal, and a difficult campaign in Rajputana, made an increase in the standing army seem necessary, and a number of rebellions raised the problem of internal security. The standing army at the capital was increased considerably. To provide for it, at a time when prices were inflated, the sultan controlled the price of commodities in the central areas, ordered the payment of the revenue in kind, and stored large quantities of grain. His measures certainly succeeded in preserving an artificial cheapness in the markets of the capital even during years of drought, but at the cost of infinite oppression. Conviviality among the nobles—that cloak for conspiracy—was forbidden. The system of espionage was enlarged and intensified. Above all the means of rebellion were denied to would-be rebels. Baranī says, 'the sultan ordered that wherever there was a village held by proprietary right, in free gift, or as a religious endowment, it should by one stroke of the pen be brought under the exchequer. . . . The people were so absorbed in obtaining the means of livelihood that the very name of rebellion was never mentioned.' Rules were likewise drawn up 'for grinding down the Hindus and for depriving them of that wealth and property which fosters disaffection and rebellion'. The cultivated land was measured and the government took half the gross produce instead of the one-sixth provided by immemorial rule. 'No Hindu could hold up his head, and in their houses no sign of silver or gold . . . or of any superfluity was to be seen.'

Buildings and literature. 'Alā-ud-dīn loved building and exe-cuted many magnificent works. He built a new Delhi called Sīrī on the site now marked by the village of Shāhpur, but his edifices there were pulled down by Sher Shāh and have wholly disappeared. He made extensive additions to the 'Qutb' group of sacred structures, and began a gigantic *mīnār* which was intended to far surpass the noble Qutb Mīnār. The unfinished stump still stands. When building Sīrī he remembered that 'it is a condition that in a new building blood should be sprinkled; he therefore sacrificed some thousands of goat-bearded Mughals for the purpose'.

In early life he was illiterate, but after his accession acquired the art of reading Persian to some extent. In spite of his personal indifference to learning several eminent literary men attended his court, of whom the most famous is Amīr Khusrū, a voluminous and much admired author in both verse and prose.

Death of 'Alā-ud-dīn. The tyrant suffered from many troubles in his latter days, and 'success no longer attended him'. This may perhaps be attributable—as Baranī believed—to his disregard of clerical authority in the pursuit of a purely secular state policy. His naturally violent temper became uncontrollable, and he allowed his guilty infatuation for Malik Kāfūr to influence all his actions. His health failed, dropsy developed, and in January 1316 he died. 'Some say that the infamous Malik Kāfūr helped his disease to a fatal termination.'

Malik Kāfūr placed an infant son of the sultan on the throne, reserving all power to himself. He imprisoned, blinded, or killed most of the other members of the royal family, but his criminal rule lasted only thirty-five days. After the lapse of that time he and his companions were beheaded by their slave guards.

Sultan Qutb-ud-dīn Mubārak. Qutb-ud-dīn or Mubārak Khān, a son of 'Alā-ud-dīn, who had escaped destruction, was taken out of confinement and enthroned. The young sovereign was wholly evil. He was infatuated with a youth named Hasan, originally an outcast *parwārī*, whom he ennobled under the style of Khusrū Khān. 'During his reign of four years and four months, the sultan attended to nothing but drinking, listening to music, debauchery, and pleasure, scattering gifts, and gratifying his lusts.' By good luck the Mongols did not attack. If they had done so no one could have opposed them. Qutb-ud-dīn Mubārak attained two military successes. His officers tightened the hold of his government on Gujarat, and he in person led an army into the Deccan against Deogiri, where the raja, Harpāl Dēo, had revolted. The Hindu prince failed to offer substantial resistance and was barbarously flayed alive (1318). After his triumphant return from the Deccan the sultan became still worse than before.

He gave way to wrath and obscenity, to severity, revenge, and heartlessness. He dipped his hands in innocent blood, and he allowed his tongue to utter disgusting and abusive words to his companions and attendants. . . . He cast aside all regard for decency, and presented himself decked out in the trinkets and apparel of a female before his assembled company;

and did many other evil deeds.

Ultimately the degraded creature was killed by his minion, Khusrū Khān, aided by his outcast brethren, 'and the basis of the dynasty of Alā-ud-dīn was utterly razed'.

The usurper favoured Hindus as against Muslims, and it was said that 'Delhi had once more come under Hindu rule.' The low-born triumph did not last long. After a few months the usurper was defeated and beheaded by Ghāzī Malik, a Qaraunah Turk noble, governor of Debālpur in the Panjab. Everything was in confusion and no male scion of the royal stock had been left in existence.

Ghiyās-ud-dīn Tughluq Shāh. The nobles having thus a free hand, and recognizing the fact that the disordered state required a master, elected Ghāzī Malik to fill the vacant throne. He assumed the style of Ghiyās-ud-dīn Tughluq, and is often called Tughluq Shāh (A.D. 1321). His father, a Turk, had been a slave of Balban; his mother, a Jat woman, was Indian born. His conduct justified the confidence bestowed on him by his colleagues. He restored a reasonable amount of order to the internal administration and took measures to guard against the ever-pressing danger from Mongol inroads.

He sent his son Jūnā Khān into the Deccan, where the countries conquered by ʿAlā-ud-dīn had refused obedience. The prince reached Warangal, now in the eastern part of the Nizam's dominions, and undertook the siege of the fort. The strong walls of mud resisted his efforts, pestilence broke out, his men deserted owing to intrigues among his officers, and he was forced to return to Delhi. But a second expedition was more successful, resulting in the capture of both Bidar and Warangal. At that time Warangal had recovered its independence, and was under the rule of a Hindu raja. The sultan meantime, having been invited to intervene in a disputed succession, had marched across Bengal as far as Sunārgāon near Dacca, and on his way home had annexed Tirhut. He left Bengal practically independent, although he had brought to Delhi as a prisoner one of the claimants to the provincial throne.

Murder of Tughluq Shāh. His son Jūnā, or Muhammad, who had returned from the south, was then in charge of the capital. The sultan desired his son to build for him a temporary reception pavilion or pleasure-house on the bank of the Jumna. Jūnā Khān entrusted the work to Ahmad, afterwards known as Khwāja Jahān, who was head of the public works department and in his confidence. The prince asked and obtained permission to parade the elephants fully accoutred before his father, who took up his station in the new building for afternoon prayers. The confederates arranged that the elephants when passing should collide with the timber structure, which accordingly fell on the sultan and his favourite younger son, Mahmūd, who accompanied him. Jūnā Khān made a pretence of sending for picks and shovels to dig out his father and brother, but purposely hindered action being taken until it was too late. The sultan was found bending over the boy's body, and if he still breathed, as some people assert that he did, he was finished off (A.D. 1325). After nightfall his body was removed and interred in the massive sepulchre which he had prepared for himself in Tughluqābād, the mighty fortress which he had built near Delhi.[1]

---

[1] The facts as recorded by Ibn Batūta (vol. iii, p. 213) are certain, having been related to the traveller by Shaikh Rukn-ud-dīn, the saint, who was present when the carefully arranged 'accident' occurred. No reason whatever exists for giving Jūnā Khān the 'benefit of the doubt'.

Accession of Muhammad bin Tughluq, February 1325. The parricide gathered the fruits of his crime, as ʿAlā-ud-dīn Khiljī had done, and seated himself on the throne without opposition.[1] He occupied it for twenty-six years of tyranny and then died in his bed. Like ʿAlā-ud-dīn he secured favour by lavish largess, scattering without stint the golden treasure stored by his father within the grim walls of Tughluqābād. It was reported that Tughluq Shāh had constructed a reservoir filled with molten gold in a solid mass.

Ibn Batūta; character of the Sultan. Our knowledge of the second sovereign of the Tughluq dynasty, who appears in history as Muhammad bin (son of) Tughluq, is unusually detailed, because, in addition to the narrative of an unusually good Indian historian (Ziā-ud-dīn Baranī), we possess the observations of the African traveller, Ibn Batūta, who spent several years at the court and in the service of the sultan until April 1347, when he succeeded in retiring from his dangerous employment. His account of his Indian experiences, with which alone we are concerned, bears the stamp of truth on every page. Most of his statements concerning Muhammad bin Tughluq are based on direct personal knowledge.[2] Ziā-ud-dīn of Baran (Bulandshahr) also was a contemporary official and wrote in the reign of Muhammad bin Tughluq's cousin and successor, Fīrūz Shāh. Although he naturally does not exhibit the impartial detachment of the foreign observer, his narrative is full of vivid detail.

Notwithstanding that Muhammad bin Tughluq was guilty of acts which the pen shrinks from recording, and that he wrought untold misery in the course of his long reign, he was not wholly evil. He established hospitals and almshouses, and his generosity to learned Muslims was unprecedented. It was even possible to describe him with truth both as 'the humblest of men' and also as an intense egotist. Elphinstone's summary of his enigmatic character deserves quotation:

It is admitted, on all hands, that he was the most eloquent and accomplished prince of his age. His letters, both in Arabic and Persian, were admired for their elegance long after he had ceased to reign. His memory was extraordinary; and, besides a thorough knowledge of logic and the philosophy of the Greeks, he was much attached to mathematics and to physical science; and used himself to attend sick persons for the purpose of watching the symptoms of any extraordinary disease. He was regular in his devotions, abstained from wine, and conformed in his private life to all the moral precepts of his religion. In war he was distinguished for his gallantry and personal activity, so that his contemporaries were justified in esteeming him as one of the wonders of the age.

Yet the whole of these splendid talents and accomplishments were given to him in vain; they were accompanied by a perversion of judgement, which, after every allowance for the intoxication of absolute power, leaves us in doubt whether he was not affected by some degree of insanity.

[1] 'Lorsque le sultan Toghlok fut mort, son fils Mohammed s'empara du royaume, sans rencontrer d'adversaire ni de rebelle.'

[2] 'Quant aux aventures de ce roi-ci, la plupart sont au nombre de ce que j'ai vu durant mon séjour dans ses États' (vol. iii, p. 216).

Moreover, the sultan, like Jahangir afterwards, believed himself to be a just man, and was persuaded that all his atrocities were in accordance with the principles of justice and Muslim law. There is no reason to suppose that his conscience troubled him. On the contrary, he deliberately defended his conduct against criticism and avowed his resolve to continue his course to the end. 'I punish', he said, 'the most trifling act of contumacy with death. This I will do until I die, or until the people act honestly, and give up rebellion and contumacy. . . . I have dispensed great wealth among them, but they have not become friendly and loyal. Thus, he went on, unmoved from his fell purpose, until his inhuman tyranny caused the break-up of the empire of Delhi.

.Premising that the authorities are discrepant concerning the order of events, and that the chronology of the reign is consequently uncertain to some extent, the leading events of the Sultan's rule will now be narrated.

Early rebellions. The first measures of the reign were designed to bring the empire fully under control, and to give order to the administration. By the end of 1328 Muhammad's grip was complete, two rebellions, the one of his cousin Bahā-ud-dīn Garshāsp in the Deccan (1327), the other of Kishlū Khān, the governor of Multan and Sind (1328) having been suppressed by Khwāja Jahān and by the sultan respectively. The defeat of Garshāsp had also involved the destruction of the raja of Kampili, who had given him asylum. The conquest of Warangal, Ma'bar, and Dwarsamudra, and the establishment of Muslim power in Madura in the same period left only the Hoysala power of Ballala III independent in the Deccan.

Administrative measures. Revenue records for all the provinces were ordered to be compiled, and the attempt was made to model all upon the pattern of the central area. With this change went an enhancement of the taxation of the rich but turbulent Doab, a move which echoes that of 'Alā-ud-din Khiljī. Baranī rhetorically states that the demand was increased ten or twentyfold and he gives a harrowing picture of the exactions of officials, the rebellion of the peasants, and the ruthless use of force to suppress them. Baranī perhaps exaggerates through personal interest in this his home country, but that there was distress, added to by local famine, is certain.

Evacuation of Delhi. The movement of the capital from Delhi to Daulatabad in 1327, which involved the court, army, and officials, together with the servants and tradesmen dependent upon them, was another source of discontent and hardship. But suggestions that it was punitive in purpose, a product of Muhammad's petulance, and carried out with ruthless completeness seem rather improbable. Daulatabad was chosen for its position, in an attempt to solve the military and administrative problems of an empire astride the Vindhyas. The need to increase Muslim numbers and influence in the south probably also played a part. Ibn Batūta relates that the very cripples were brutally evicted from Delhi, but the continuance of a mint in

Delhi and of building activity, and the sultan's re-equipment of his
army there only two years later, suggest that the move was for nobles
and officials only.

Forced currency. A more astonishing experiment was the issue,
in 1330, of a token coinage. The motive is not clear, though the
shortage of silver or the needs of the war chest may have been at work.
It does not seem probable that financial stringency was the cause.
For three years the issue of coins of brass or copper, stamped with
legends denoting their value as if the pieces were silver, continued.
But as there was no such close supervision as was exercised over the
paper currency in China, there was widespread fraud.

'The promulgation of this edict turned the house of every Hindu
into a mint, and the Hindus of the various provinces coined millions
and hundreds of thousands of copper coins. With these they paid
their tribute, and with these they purchased horses, arms, and fine
things of all kinds. . . .' Eventually the issue had to be recalled; repay-
ment was made in gold or silver at the face value of the copper coins,
at tremendous cost.

The Mongols. In 1328-9 Tarmāshīrīn, Khān of the Chagatāī
section of the Mongols, crossed into India. He had been heavily defeated in 1326 in his attempt to invade Khurasan, and his rapid move,
almost to Delhi, seems to have been a light raiding venture. The
silence about this raid of Ibn Batūta, who in 1332 met the Khān and
reported a friendship between him and the sultan, rather supports this
view.

Expeditions to the north-west. Muhammad at one point
planned an attack upon Abu Said the profligate Persian ruler, who
suffered a serious revolt by his guardian and a triple change in the
governorship of Khurasan in the years 1329-32. The sultan sought
Egyptian support by the embassy of 1331-2, and was on good terms
with Tarmāshīrīn in Transoxiana. But though a very large army was
assembled and maintained at great cost for a year, the project was
abandoned, possibly owing to the deposition of Tarmāshīrīn.

A second expedition—Ferishta's expedition to China—was directed
against the hill states of the Kumaon region. Though Ibn Batūta says
that this Qarachil expedition did secure the submission of the hill
chiefs, there was a disastrous loss of men among the hills, which made
the venture a costly failure. Nagarkot (Kangra) was, however, taken
in 1337.

But by that date Muhammad's empire, far larger than that under the
rule of any of his Muslim predecessors, was beginning to fall apart.
The early revolts, which were many, had been ruthlessly suppressed.
Later the sultan's tyranny became so intolerable, and the resources
at his command so reduced, that he was unable to resist rebellion or to
prevent the break-up of the empire. The hostility of the native nobility
to the foreign adventurers whom Muhammad favoured, and the
opposition of the Ulama to a ruler who steadily disregarded their

advice and undermined their privileged position hastened the decline.

The turning-point was reached in 1334–5 when Ma'bar, or Coromandal, revolted and escaped from the Delhi tyranny. The decline and fall of the sultanate, which may be dated from that year, will be the subject of the next chapter.

CHAPTER 3

The decline and fall of the sultanate of Delhi, A.D. 1340–1526; the Tughluq dynasty concluded; Timur; the Sayyids; the Lodī dynasty; Islam in Indian life

Rebellion in the south. In 1334 Ahsan Shāh, governor of Ma'bar, rebelled, striking coin in his own name. The sultan marched south from Delhi in 1335 and passed through Bidar to Warangal. There, however, he and most of his army were stricken by pestilence, so that the advance was discontinued. Ma'bar was never recovered.

During the return march Muhammad bin Tughluq was able to view the effects of a disastrous famine in Malwa and around Delhi. A famine relief scheme, with payments for specific agricultural tasks, was introduced, but the people were too exhausted to make use of the money. Later the inhabitants of Delhi were moved to a temporary town in Oudh where adequate supplies were available.

The Warangal disaster, and rumours of the sultan's death, led to a crop of revolts—by the Mongol Hulāgū at Lahore, by Malik Hoshang at Daulatabad, and by the son of Ahsan Shāh at Hansi. These were broken. In Bengal, however, rebellion succeeded.

Revolt of Bengal. Bengal had been ruled since the close of the twelfth century by governors who were expected to recognize the suzerainty of Delhi and to send tribute more or less regularly to court. We have seen how Balban suppressed with merciless ferocity Tughril Khān's attempt to attain formal independence. After the extermination of Tughril Khān and his followers, the governorship was held by Balban's second son, the father of Sultan Qaiqabad, and after him by other members of Balban's family. A contest between two brothers for the viceregal throne resulted, as already mentioned, in the interference of Tughluq Shāh, who marched across Bengal and carried off to Delhi Bahādur Shāh, the claimant whose pretensions had been disallowed. The captive was pardoned and sent back to Bengal by Muhammad bin Tughluq, but rebelled unsuccessfully. He was killed and his stuffed skin was hawked about the empire.

In 1337-8 (A.H. 739) Fakhr-ud-dīn or Fakhra started a rebellion in eastern Bengal, which eventually involved the whole province and brought about its complete separation, under three rulers, from the sultanate of Delhi. Muhammad bin Tugluq was too much occupied elsewhere to be able to assert his sovereignty over Bengal. He let the province go, and it continued to retain its independence until reconquered by Akbar. Occasional ceremonial admissions of the superior rank of the sultan or padshah of Delhi did not impair the substantial independence of the kings of Bengal.

Later revolts. The historians give ample details of the endless revolts which marked the latter years of Muhammad bin Tughluq's disastrous reign, and of his attempts at suppression, in some measure successful. 'The people were never tired of rebelling, nor the king of punishing.' One such was the revolt of Malik Shāhū Lodī in Multan, which ended in the flight of the rebel to Afghanistan. Of this Sir W. Haig says, 'the subsequent rebellions in Gujarat and the Deccan were partly due to the severity of the restrictions placed upon Afghans in India in consequence of Shāhū's revolt'. Another source of trouble lay in the increasing use of the system of farming provinces to the highest bidder, for not merely was the system oppressive to the people, but contractors unable to fulfil their contracts broke into rebellion.

By 1342 order had been restored in the north, but Muhammad felt the need for outside sanction and support. This he sought from the Khalif, living in Egypt, whose envoy, when he arrived with a robe and *farman*, was received with extravagant veneration. Muhammad bin Tughluq professed himself to be merely the vicegerent of the Khalif, removed his own name from the coinage, and replaced it by that of the supreme ruler of Islam. Fīrūz Shāh, the successor of Muhammad, also secured investiture from the Egyptian Khalif, and was as proud of the honour as his cousin had been.

The supersession in 1344-5 of Qutlugh Khān, governor of the Deccan, and the reorganization of the province, with Malwa, into four revenue divisions under new men pledged to increase the revenues caused further unrest. Attacks upon a whole class of officials, the 'centurions', as nuclei of disaffection, only served to spread the disorder to Gujarat.

It is needless to follow the wearisome story through all its horrors. The sultan, after ineffectual efforts to recover the Deccan, where he retained nothing except Daulatabad, moved into Gujarat in order to suppress the disorders of that province, where he spent three rainy seasons. He quitted Gujarat late in 1350 to pursue a rebel, and crossed the Indus into Sind, although his health had failed. While he was still on the bank of the river and a considerable distance from Thatha (Tattah), the capital of Lower Sind, his illness increased and developed into a violent fever which killed him in March 1351. Thus 'the sultan was freed from his people, and the people from their sultan'. It is astonishing that such a monster should have retained power for twenty-six years, and then have died in his bed. The misery caused by his savage misrule is incalculable. Politically, he destroyed the hardly-won supremacy of the Delhi sultanate.

Vijayanagar and Bahmanī kingdoms. A few years earlier the southern expansion of the Muslim power had been checked, and territory had been lost to the Hindus by the rapid rise of the kingdom of the rayas of Vijayanagar to the south of the Krishna. The traditional date for the foundation of the city is 1336. Ten years later the new kingdom had become an important power.

In 1347 the rebellion of Hasan or Zafar Khān, an officer of the sultan, and either an Afghan or a Turk, laid the foundation of the great Bahmanī kingdom, with its capital at Kulbargā or Ahsanābād.

The history of both the Bahmanī and Vijayanagar kingdoms or empires will be narrated with considerable fullness in Book V and need not be pursued farther in this place.

Court of the sultan. The arrangements and ceremonial of the court of Sultan Muhammad bin Tughluq differed widely from those, mainly based upon the Persian model, which were observed by Akbar and his successors, as described in detail by Abu-l Fazl and numerous European travellers. At the sultan's court the proceedings were dominated by the forms of religion, each ceremony being preceded by the ejaculation 'In the name of God', and precedence being given to theologians. The Mughul ceremonial, on the contrary, was purely secular, precedence being given first to members of the royal family and then to officials according to rank.

Executions. The interior of the sultan's palace was approached by three gates in succession. Outside the first gate were platforms on which the executioners sat. The persons condemned were executed outside the gate, where their bodies lay exposed for three days.

Audience-halls. The second gate opened on a spacious audience-hall for the general public.

The 'scribes of the gate' sat at the third portal, which could not be passed without the authorization of the sultan, who gave his formal audiences inside in the 'Hall of a Thousand Columns'. The columns were of varnished wood, and the ceiling was of planks, admirably painted. The formal audience usually was given after prayers in the afternoon, but sometimes at daybreak. Special ceremonial was observed on the occasions of the two great Īd festivals ('Īd-ul fitr and 'Īd-ul kurbān).

Meals in public. The Mughul sovereign always dined alone in the private apartments of the palace. Muhammad bin Tughluq used to dine in the audience-hall and share his meal with about twenty persons of eminence.

He also provided a public banquet twice a day, once before noon and again in the afternoon. The order of precedence was the same as that observed at levées, the judges and theologians being served first. The menu included loaves like cakes; other loaves split and filled with sweet paste; rice, roast meats, fowls, and mince.[1]

Accession of Fīrūz Shāh, 1351. The death of the sultan left his army camped on the bank of the Indus masterless and helpless. The fighting force, as usual in India, was hampered by a crowd of women, children, and camp followers. When it attempted to start on its long

[1] Ibn Batūta, transl. Defrémery and Sanguinetti, tome iii, pp. 217–42. The whole account, which is well worth reading, has not been translated at all in E. & D.; but some details from another and less authoritative author are given in vol iii, pp. 575 ff. For 'Alā-ud-dīn see Ziā-ud-dīn Baranī in E. & D., vol. iii, p. 158.

homeward march it was assailed by Sind rebels and Mongol banditti. Much baggage was lost, and the women and children perished. Fīrūz Shāh, the first cousin of the deceased sovereign and governor of one-fourth of the kingdom, was then in the camp, but was unwilling to assert himself and occupy the seat of his terrible relative. The army endured utter misery for three days by reason of the want of guidance. Then all the chief men, Muslims and Hindus alike, decided that the only person who could deliver the expeditionary force from destruction was Fīrūz Shāh. He was enthroned in the camp on 23 March 1351. The existence of a leader soon effected an improvement, and the new sultan ultimately succeeded in bringing back the survivors of the army to Delhi through Multan and Debalpur.

A pretender. Meanwhile, Khwāja Jahān, the aged governor of Delhi, misled by an untrue report of Fīrūz Shāh's death, had set up as sultan a child, probably, though not certainly, the son of Muhammad bin Tughluq. When Fīrūz Shāh approached the capital, Khwāja Jahān, finding resistance hopeless, surrendered. The sultan spared him, but he was assassinated shortly after.

Personality of Fīrūz. Fīrūz Shāh was scarcely a suitable choice as successor to Muhammad bin Tughluq, for he lacked the generalship necessary for the re-establishment of the authority of Delhi over the lost provinces. In his three main expeditions he showed a vacillating weakness at moments of crisis and despite favourable opportunities he refused even to attempt the subjugation of the Deccan. He led two campaigns against Bengal, in 1353–4 and 1359, and on both occasions after vainly besieging the Bengal ruler in his Brahmaputra stronghold, retreated. The second expedition did, however, include a successful raid on Puri, in Orissa. In 1362 he set out to avenge his sufferings in Sind, assembling some 90,000 cavalry and a supply fleet. The result was disastrous. Thathah was stubbornly defended, supplies failed, and the horses perished of some epidemic disease. Under pressure of dire necessity retreat to Gujarat was ordered. The army, misled, it was alleged, by treacherous guides, suffered unutterable misery in crossing the Rann of Cutch. For six months no news from it reached Delhi, and everybody believed that the sultan had perished. Order was maintained by Khān Jahān, the resourceful minister in charge of the capital, and in due course the sultan with the remnant of his army emerged in Gujarat.

After receiving reinforcements and equipping a fresh force Fīrūz Shāh again advanced into Sind from Gujarat. On this occasion the invaders secured the crops in time, with the result that the people of the country in their turn suffered from famine. When Thathah appeared to be seriously threatened the Jām with another chief surrendered, and accompanied Fīrūz Shāh to Delhi, where they took up their residence, apparently as hostages. A relative of theirs continued to rule at Thathah, so that the government of Delhi failed to secure any substantial benefit from two costly campaigns and a final nominal success.

The only flash of his predecessor's fire was seen in the vengeance, extended over five years, taken upon the raja of Katehr for his assassination of the governor of Budaun: 'in those years not an acre of land was cultivated, no man slept in house, and the death of the three Sayyads was avenged by that of countless thousands of Hindus'.

Personal tastes of Fīrūz Shāh. He was extremely devout, although he allowed himself the kingly privilege of drinking wine, and spent much time in hunting. He was fond of the study of history, and his master-passion was a love for building. He followed the example of his predecessors, by building a new Delhi called Fīrūzābād, which included the site of Indarpat or Indraprastha, famous in epic legend. The two inscribed Aśoka columns now standing near Delhi were brought there by order of Fīrūz Shāh, the one from Toprā in the Ambala District, and the other from Meerut. The contemporary historian Shams-i-Sirāj 'Afīf describes in interesting detail the ingenious devices used to ensure the safe transport and erection of the huge monoliths.

The sultan also founded the cities of Hisār Fīrūza (Hissar, north-west of Delhi), and of Jaunpur (to the north-west of Benares), making use in each case of earlier Hindu towns and buildings. He has left on record under his own hand a list of the principal works executed during his reign of thirty-seven years, comprising towns, forts, mosques, colleges, and many other buildings, besides embankments and canals. The canal constructed to supply Hisār Fīrūza with water was repaired in the reign of Shahjahan and has been utilized in the alignment of the Western Jumna Canal. His chief architect was Malik Ghāzī Shahna whose deputy was Abdul-Hakk, also known as Jāhir Sundhār. Asian kings, as a rule, show no interest in buildings erected by their predecessors, which usually are allowed to decay uncared for. Fīrūz Shāh was peculiar in devoting much attention to the repair and rebuilding of 'the structures of former kings and ancient nobles . . . giving the restoration of those buildings the priority' over his own new constructions.

Internal administration. The internal administration of the country, as distinct from the sultan's personal hobbies, was in the hands of Khān Jahān, the minister, a converted Hindu from Telingana. When he died in 1370–1 (A.H. 772) his place was taken by his son, who assumed the same title of Khān Jahān, and conducted the government to the end of the reign. As Sir W. Haig has it: 'His judgement of character was, indeed, the principal counterpoise to his impatience of the disagreeable details of government. . . .' Sultan 'Alā-ud-dīn, who had been in the habit of paying cash salaries to his officers, had disapproved of the system of payment by *jāgīrs*, or the assignment of revenue, believing that that system tended to produce insubordination and rebellion. But Fīrūz Shāh and his advisers made the grant of *jāgīrs* the rule. Akbar reverted to cash payments from the treasury and direct official administration so far as was practicable.

Alleged prosperity. The statements of Ziā-ud-dīn Baranī in praise of Fīrūz Shāh cannot be accepted without reserve. It is no doubt true that the sultan 'made the laws of the Prophet his guide', and desired to check oppression. But when we are told that

the peasants grew rich and were satisfied. . . . Their houses were replete with grain, property, horses, and furniture; every one had plenty of gold and silver; no woman was without her ornaments, and no house was wanting in excellent beds and couches. Wealth abounded and comforts were general.

the exaggeration of courtly flattery is obvious. The historian states that it had been the practice of previous sultans to leave the peasant only one cow and take away all the rest. The milder rule of Fīrūz Shāh, although it certainly diminished the tyranny practised, cannot have produced a paradise.

Slave-raiding. We are informed by the same author that

the sultan was very diligent in providing slaves, and he carried his care so far as to command his great fief-holders and officers to capture slaves whenever they were at war, and to pick out and send the best for the service of the court. . . . Those chiefs who brought many slaves received the highest favour. . . . About 12,000 slaves became artisans of various kinds. Forty thousand were every day in readiness to attend as guards in the sultan's equipage or at the palace. Altogether, in the city and in the various fiefs, there were 180,000 slaves, for whose maintenance and comfort the sultan took especial care. The institution took root in the very centre of the land, and the sultan looked upon its due regulation as one of his incumbent duties.

Such wholesale slave-raiding clearly must have been the cause of much suffering, even though it be admitted that the slaves after capture were well treated. The slaves, of course, all became Muslims, and the proselytism thus effected probably was the chief reason why the sultan favoured the system.

Abolition of torture. We have the good fortune to possess a tract written by Fīrūz Shāh himself which enumerates his good deeds as he understood them to be. One reform, the abolition of mutilation and torture, deserves unqualified commendation, and the orders must have been acted on to a considerable extent during his lifetime. The enumeration of the 'many varieties of torture' employed under former kings is horrible.

The great and merciful God made me, His servant, hope and seek for His mercy by devoting myself to prevent the unlawful killing of Musalmāns and the infliction of any kind of torture upon them or upon any men.

Intolerance. But Fīrūz Shāh could be fierce when his religious zeal was roused. He records the following facts:

The sect of Shias, also called *Rawāfiz*, had endeavoured to make proselytes. . . I seized them all and I convicted them of their errors and perversions. On the most zealous I inflicted capital punishment (*siyāsat*), and the rest I visited with censure (*tāzīr*), and threats of public punishment. Their books I burnt in public and by the grace of God the influence of this sect was entirely suppressed.

He caused the 'doctors learned in the holy Law' to slay a man who claimed to be the Mahdī, 'and for this good action', he wrote, 'I hope to receive future reward'.

He went in person to a certain village named Malūh, apparently near Delhi, where a religious fair was being held, which was attended even by 'some graceless Musalmāns'.

I ordered that the leaders of these people and the promoters of this abomination should be put to death. I forbade the infliction of any severe punishment on the Hindus in general, but I destroyed their idol temples and instead thereof raised mosques.

The historian witnessed the burning alive of a Brahman who had practised his rites in public.

Those unquestionable facts prove that Fīrūz Shāh carried on the tradition of the early invaders, and believed that he served God by treating as a capital crime the public practice of their religion by the vast majority of his subjects.

Bought conversions. The sultan continues:

I encouraged my infidel subjects to embrace the religion of the prophet, and I proclaimed that every one who repeated the creed and became a Musalmān should be exempt from the *jizya* or poll-tax. Information of this came to the ears of the people at large, and great numbers of Hindus presented themselves, and were admitted to the honour of Islam. Thus they came forward day by day from every quarter, and, adopting the faith, were exonerated from the *jizya*, and were favoured with presents and honours.

Such was the origin of a large part of the existing Muslim population. Several other sovereigns continued the process of conversion by bribery.

The *jizya*. The *jizya* in Delhi was assessed in three grades; namely first class, 40 *tankas*; second class, 20 *tankas*; third class, 10 *tankas*.[1] In former reigns Brahmans had been excused. Fīrūz Shāh, after consultation with his learned lawyers, resolved to include them, and though the Brahmans threatened to fast to death—a decision which Fīrūz applauded—the measure was enforced.

Credit due to the sultan. Fīrūz Shāh, when due allowance is made for his surroundings and education, could not have escaped from the theory and practice of religious intolerance. It was not possible for him in his age to rise, as Akbar did, to the conception that the ruler of Hindustan should cherish all his subjects alike, whether Muslim or Hindu, and allow every man absolute freedom, not only of con-

---

[1] Thomas, *Chronicles*, pp. 218 n., 219 n., 232, 281 n. Sixty-four *jaitals* made one *tanka* in the fourteenth century. A Brahman, consequently, paid about 10 rupees a year. The coin No. 207 of Thomas shows that the word جيتل should be vocalized as *aital*.

science, but of public worship. The Muslims of the fourteenth century were still dominated by the ideas current in the early days of Islam, and were convinced that the tolerance of idolatry was a sin. Fīrūz Shāh, whatever may have been his defects or weaknesses, deserves much credit for having mitigated in some respects the horrible practices of his predecessors, and for having introduced some tincture of humane feeling into the administration. He was naturally a kind if indiscriminately charitable man, and his good deeds included the foundation of a hospital.

Death of Fīrūz Shāh in 1388. Anarchy. Fīrūz Shāh, who had been forty-two years of age when called to the throne, lost capacity for affairs as the infirmities of advancing years increased. Experiments made in the way of associating his sons with himself in the government were not successful, and his minister, the younger Khān Jahān, was tempted to engage in treasonable practices. In September 1388 the old sultan died, aged about eighty-three. The government fell into utter confusion. A series of puppet sultans, all equally wanting in personal merit, pass rapidly across the stage. The kingdom, in fact, ceased to exist, and the governor of every province assumed practical independence. For about three years, from 1394 to 1397, two rival sultans had to find room within the precincts of the Delhi group of cities. Sultan Mahmūd, a boy grandson of Fīrūz Shāh, was recognized as king in Old Delhi, while his relative Nusrat Shāh claimed similar rank in Fīrūzābād a few miles distant. 'Day by day, battles were fought between these two kings, who were like the two kings in the game of chess.' It is not worth while either to remember or record the unmeaning struggles between the many rival claimants to a dishonoured throne.

Mahmūd and his competitor, Nusrat Shāh, were the last of the series of nominal sultans who filled up the interval between the death of Fīrūz Shāh in 1388 and the invasion of Timur ten years later.

Invasion of Timur, 1398. Amīr Tīmūr (Tīmūr-i-lang, the Tamerlane or Tamburlaine of English literature) was a Barlās Turk, whose father was one of the earliest converts to Islam. Born in 1336 Timur attained the throne of Samarqand in 1369, and then entered on a career of distant conquests, rivalling those of Chingiz Khān, whom he equalled in ferocity, although he was a Muslim and equipped with considerable knowledge of Muslim lore. He died in 1405. He needed no formal pretext for his attack on India. The feebleness of the government, the reputed wealth of the country, and the fact that most of the inhabitants were idolaters offered more than sufficient inducement to undertake the conquest.

Late in 1397 his grandson Pīr Muhammad, commanding an advanced guard, laid siege to Uch, and then to Multan, which fell in May 1398. In the autumn Timur himself crossed the Indus, with a large cavalry force, said to number 90,000; sacked Tulamba, to the north-east of Multan, massacring or enslaving the inhabitants. Near Loni, where

Mahmūd Tughlūq essayed to oppose him, the invader won an easy victory.[1] After a second victory near the city Timur occupied Delhi and was proclaimed king. Some resistance by the inhabitants provoked a general massacre. The city was thoroughly plundered for five days, all the accumulated wealth of generations being carried off to Samarqand, along with a multitude of women and other captives. Timur was careful to bring away all the skilled artisans he could find to be employed on the buildings in his capital.

He had no intention of staying in India. He returned through Meerut, storming that city, and slaying everybody. He then visited Hardwar, and marching along the foot of the mountains, where it was easy to cross the rivers, quitted India as he had come by the way of the Panjab, 'leaving anarchy, famine, and pestilence behind him'.

The so-called Sayyids. The appalling atrocities of Timur's raid, which have been barely indicated in the preceding paragraphs, destroyed all semblance of government in Upper India. No regular sultan's government was established at Delhi until fifteen years after Timur's departure. From 1414 to 1450 the affairs of the city and a fluctuating territory adjoining were administered, first by Khizr Khān, who had been governor of the Panjab, and then by three of his successors. They pretended to be Sayyids, and consequently are described in the history textbooks as the Sayyid dynasty. Khizr Khān retained control from the Panjab to the Doab by annual campaigns, which served also to bring in the revenues. But the area in which such operations could be conducted soon dwindled under his successors. The last of the line, named 'Ālam Shāh, was allowed to retire to Budāon, where he lived in peace for many years.

Sultan Buhlūl Lodī. Buhlūl Khān, an Afghan of the Lodī tribe, who had become governor of the Panjab and independent of Delhi, seized the throne in 1451, and was proclaimed sultan. Though many authors erroneously call all the sultans of Delhi from 1206 to 1450 Pathans or Afghans, in reality Buhlūl Lodī was the first Afghan sultan. He engaged in a war with the king of Jaunpur in the east, that kingdom having thrown off its allegiance during the anarchy following on Timur's invasion; and when he died had succeeded in dispossessing Husain Shāh, the king of Jaunpur, and in replacing him by his own son Bārbak Shāh as viceroy. He may be said to have recovered a certain amount of control over territory extending from the foot of the mountains to Benares, and as far south as the borders of Bundelkhand.

Sikandar Lodī. The nobles chose Nizām Khān, a son of Buhlūl, as his father's successor. He assumed the royal style of Sultan Sikandar Ghāzī (1489). The principal political event of his reign was the expulsion of his brother Bārbak Shāh from Jaunpur, and the definite annexation of that kingdom. The sultan also annexed Bihar and levied tribute from Tirhut. The reader must understand that in those day

[1] Mahmūd's opposition led Timur to order the execution of the 100,000 prisoners then in his camp.

'annexation' meant no more than an extremely lax control over the Afghan military chiefs of districts, who were compelled by superior force to yield temporary and imperfect obedience to the sultan of Delhi. Even from the Panjab, the original centre of Lodī power, Sikandar did not venture to exact more than the slightest practical acknowledgement of his supremacy.

Muslim authors speak well of Sultan Sikandar, who was a bigot. He entirely ruined the shrines of Mathura, converting the buildings to Muslim uses, and generally was extremely hostile to Hinduism. Politically he had good cause to be so, for the Hindus of the Doab were always turbulent, and in 1494 a full-scale campaign had to be waged against Hindu rebels in Jaunpur. He strictly followed Quranic law, and was a careful, scrupulous ruler, within the limits of his excessive bigotry. He took a special interest in medical lore. His reign was remarkable for the prevalence of exceptionally low prices for both food and other things, so that 'small means enabled their possessor to live comfortably'.

Agra, which had been ruined by Sultan Mahmūd of Ghazni, and had sunk into insignificance, was improved by Sultan Sikandar, who generally resided there and used it as his base for operations against the powerful raja of Gwalior. Sikandara, where Akbar's tomb stands, is named after the Lodī monarch.

A terrible earthquake, extending to Persia, occurred in 1505, and did much damage in northern India.

Sikandar died a natural death at the close of 1517.

The kingdom of Jaunpur. It will be convenient to notice briefly in this place the history of the short-lived kingdom of Jaunpur, the relations of which with the Lodī sultans supplied the most important political events of their reigns. The foundation of the Muslim city of Jaunpur by Fīrūz Shāh Tughluq has been mentioned. In 1394 Mahmūd Tughluq appointed a powerful eunuch noble entitled Khwāja Jahān to be 'Lord of the East' (*Sultān-ush-Sharq*) with his headquarters at Jaunpur. In those days the control exercised by Delhi was so feeble that every provincial governor was practically independent. After the violence of Timur had shattered the Delhi government in 1398, Khwāja Jahān's adopted son seized the opportunity and set up as an independent king with the style of Mubārak Shāh Sharqī (sc. Eastern), in 1399.

The newly made king was quickly succeeded in 1402 by his younger brother Ibrāhīm, who reigned prosperously for thirty-four years. Like Sikandar Lodī he was 'a steady, if not bloody persecutor'. He won the approval of the historians who shared his religious sentiments, but, as usual, the other side of the case is not on record. Ibrāhīm's son Mahmūd also is spoken of as a successful ruler. Husain Shāh, the last independent king, was overcome by Buhlūl Lodi in or about 1476, and driven to take refuge with his namesake of Bengal.

The expedient attempted at the beginning of Sikandar Lodī's reign of leaving Jaunpur to his elder brother Bārbak Shāh in full sovereignty was a failure, and led to war, in which Delhi was successful.

The experiment, when repeated at the time of Ibrāhīm Lodī's accession, again failed. Jalāl Khān, Ibrāhīm's brother, who had been set up as king of Jaunpur, was defeated and killed. From that time the 'Kingdom of the East' no longer pretended to an independent existence. It may be considered to have come to an end in or about 1476, when Sikandar Lodī expelled his brother Bārbak Shāh.

All the members of the Jaunpur dynasty were patrons of Persian and Arabic literature. Their principal memorial is the group of noble mosques at Jaunpur, designed in a peculiar style, including many Hindu features. The buildings are unusually massive, have no minarets, and are characterized by stately gateways with sloping walls. The mosques date from the reigns of Ibrāhīm, Mahmūd, and Husain Shāh.[1]

Ibrāhīm Lodī. The new Sultan succeeded his father Sikandar after dealing with the attempt of a factious group of nobles to raise a younger brother to an independent throne in Jaunpur. His one great success was the capture of Gwalior, whose stalwart ruler Mān Singh had recently died. But thereafter he could not succeed in keeping on good terms with his Afghan nobles, and his reign was mostly occupied by conflicts with them. When he was victorious he took cruel vengeance. Ultimately the discontent of the Afghan chiefs resulted in an invitation being sent by Daulat Khān Lodī to Babur, the king or padshah of Kabul. Babur, after several indecisive incursions, started on his final invasion in November 1525; and on 21 April 1526 inflicted on Sultan Ibrāhīm a crushing defeat at Panipat, which cost him his throne and life. The battle will be described in connexion with the reign of the victor.

Low prices. The reign of Ibrāhīm was even more remarkable than that of his father for the extreme lowness of prices, due partly to copious rain followed by abundant harvests, and largely to the want of metallic currency. We are told that 'gold and silver were only procurable with the greatest difficulty', and that sellers were ready to offer most extravagant quantities of produce for cash. 'If a traveller wished to proceed from Delhi to Agra, one *bahlōlī* would suffice for the expenses of himself, his horse, and four attendants.'[2]

The coin referred to appears to be the piece weighing about 140 grains, composed of billon or mixed copper and silver in varying proportions, and, by more normal standards, of little intrinsic worth. Timur's invasion, apparently, must have produced tremendous economic effects, which have been very imperfectly recorded. Gold and silver seem to have been still abundant in the time of Fīrūz Shāh Tughluq, before Timur's operations.

The sultanate of Delhi. The annals of the sultanate of Delhi, extending over nearly three centuries and a quarter (1206–1526), are

[1] A. Führer, *The Sharqi Architecture of Jaunpur*, Calcutta, 1889.
[2] Thomas, *Chronicles*, p. 360; E. & D., vol. iv, p. 476.

not pleasant reading. The episodes of Chingiz Khān and Timur are filled with sickening horrors, and the reigns of several sultans offer little but scenes of bloodshed, tyranny, and treachery. All the sultans without exception were convinced Muslims, and acted as such. Even Fīrūz Shāh Tughluq, who exhibited a certain amount of kindly humanity, and felt some desire to do good to his people, was by no means free from the intolerance of his contemporaries. It is to be remembered, however, that the student of the sultanate's history is forced to rely almost entirely upon Muslim authors, and for some periods upon a single witness only. Close examination of the intention of these writers, and steady attention to the exaggeration which a desire to flatter or to denigrate could cause, are at all times required.

Many of the sultans, including the most ferocious, had nice taste in the refinements of Arabic and Persian literature. They liked to be surrounded by men learned in the lore of Islam, and were liberal patrons of the accomplishments which interested them.

They introduced into India several new styles of architecture, based primarily on the model of buildings at Mecca, Damascus, and other cities of the Muslim world, but profoundly modified by Hindu influences. The many Hindu buildings overthrown supplied materials for the new mosques and colleges, for the construction of which the conquerors were compelled to utilize the services of Indian craftsmen. The buildings of the sultanate consequently display characteristics which distinguish them readily from the Muslim edifices in other parts of the world. Numerous authors group all the styles of architecture during the period of the sultanate under the term 'Pathan', a most inappropriate and misleading designation. Several distinct styles current in different localities and at various times during the period of the sultanate may be distinguished, but the subject is too technical for further notice in this place.

Causes of Muslim success. The Muslim invaders undoubtedly were superior to their Hindu opponents in fighting power and so long as they remained uncorrupted by wealth and luxury were practically invincible. The men came from a cool climate in hilly regions, and were for the most part heavier and physically stronger than their opponents. Their flesh diet as compared with the vegetarian habits prevalent in India, combined with their freedom from the restrictions of caste rules concerning food, tended to develop the kind of energy required by an invading force. Their fierce fanaticism, which regarded the destruction of non-Muslims as a service eminently pleasing to God, made them pitiless, and consequently far more terrifying than the ordinary enemies met in India. They were themselves ordinarily saved from fear by their deep conviction that a Ghāzī—a slayer of an infidel—if he should happen to be killed himself, went straight to all the joys of an easily intelligible paradise, winning at the same time undying fame as a martyr. The courage of the invaders was further stimulated by the consciousness that no retreat was open to them. They must either subdue utterly by sheer force the millions confronting their thousands or be completely destroyed. No middle course was available. The enormous wealth in gold, silver, and jewels, not to mention more commonplace valuables, accumulated in the temples, palaces, and towns of India fired their imagination and offered the most splendid conceivable rewards for valour. The Hindu strategy and tactics were old fashioned, based on ancient textbooks, which took no account of foreign methods; and the unity of command on the Indian side was always more or less hampered by tribal, sectarian, and caste divisions. Each horde of the foreigners, on the contrary, obeyed a single leader in the field, and the commanders knew how to make use of shock tactics, that is to say, well-directed cavalry charges, which rarely failed to scatter the Hindu hosts. Elephants, on which Hindu tradition placed excessive reliance, proved to be useless, or worse than useless, when pitted against well-equipped, active cavalry. The Hindu cavalry does not seem to have attained a high standard of efficiency in most parts of the country.

Thus it happened that the Muslims, although insignificant in numbers when compared with the vast Indian population, usually secured easy victories, and were able to keep in subjection for centuries multitudes of Hindus.

Nature of the sultans' government. Bengal, after it had been overrun by a few parties of horsemen at the close of the twelfth century, remained for ages under the heel of foreign chiefs who were sometimes Afghans, and the province never escaped from Muslim rule until it passed under British control. The wars with Bengal of which we read during the period of the sultanate were concerned only with the claim preferred by Delhi to receive homage and tribute from the Muslim rulers of Bengal. Those rulers, in their turn, often seem to have left Hindu rajas undisturbed in their principalities, subject to the payment of tribute with greater or less regularity. Indeed the same practice necessarily prevailed over a large part of the Muslim dominions. Some sort of civil government had to be carried on, and the strangers had not either the numbers or the capacity for civil administration except in a limited area. The sultans left few fruitful ideas or valuable institutions behind them.

The government both at headquarters and in the provinces was an arbitrary despotism, practically unchecked except by rebellion and assassination. A strong autocrat, like 'Alā-ud-dīn, never allowed legal scruples to hamper his will, and Muhammad bin Tughluq, who professed reverence for the sacred law, was the worst tyrant of them all. The succession to the throne usually was effected by means of an irregular election conducted by military chiefs, and the person chosen to be sultan was not necessarily a relative of his predecessor.

Islam in Indian life. The permanent establishment of Muslim governments at Delhi and many other cities, combined with the steady growth of a settled resident Muslim population forming a ruling class in the midst of a vastly more numerous Hindu population, necessar[ily] produced changes in India. The Muslim element increased continually in three ways, namely, by immigration from beyond the north-western frontier, by conversions, whether forcible or purchased, and by birth We do not possess any statistics concerning the growth of the Muslim population in any of the three ways mentioned, but we know that it occurred in all the ways. It was impossible that the presence of a strange element so large should not bring about important modifications of Indian life.

Strength of Muslim religion. The Muslims were not absorbed into the Indian caste system of Hinduism as their foreign predecessors, the Sakas, Huns, and others, had been absorbed in the course of a generation or two. The definiteness of the religion of Islam, founded on a written revelation of known date, preserved its votaries from the fate which befell the adherents of Shamanism and the other vague religions of central Asia. When the Sakas, Huns, and the rest of the early immigrants settled in India and married Hindu women they merged in the Hindu caste system with extraordinary rapidity, chiefly because they possessed no religion sufficiently definite to protect them against the power of the Brahmans. The Muslim with his Quran and his Prophet was in a different position. He believed in his intelligible religion with all his heart, maintained against all comers the noble doctrine of the unity of God, and heartily despised the worshippers of many gods, with their idols and ceremonies. The Muslim settlers consequently regarded themselves, whether rich or poor, as a superior race, and ordinarily kept apart so far as possible from social contact with the idolaters. But, in course of time, the barrier was partially broken down. One cause which promoted a certain degree of intercourse was the necessity of continuing the employment of unconverted Hindus in clerkships and a host of minor official posts which the Muslims could not fill themselves. Another was the large number of conversions effected either by fear of the sword or by purchase. The Hindus thus nominally converted retained most of their old habits and connexions. Even now their descendants are often half Hindu in their mode of life.

Evolution of Urdu. The various necessities which forced the Muslims and Hindus to meet each other involved the evolution of a common language. Some Muslims learned Hindi and even wrote in it, as Malik Muhammad of Jāis did in the time of Humayun. Multitudes of Hindus must have acquired some knowledge of Persian. A convenient compromise between the two languages resulted in the formation of Urdu, the camp language, the name being derived from the Turki word *urdū*, 'camp', the original form of the English word 'horde'. Urdu is a Persianized form of western Hindi, as spoken especially in the neighbourhood of Delhi. Its grammar and structure continue to be Hindi in the main, while the words are largely Persian. The language of Persia after the Muslim conquest became filled with Arabic words, which consequently are numerous in Urdu. No definite date can be assigned to the beginnings of Urdu, which shades off into Hindi by insensible gradations, but it is certain that during the sultanate period the evolution of a language intelligible to both conquerors and the conquered went on unceasingly. Urdu gradually became the vernacular of Indian Muslims and developed a literature. Many Hindi words occur in the writings of Amīr Khusrū, who died in 1325, and is sometimes reckoned as a writer of Urdu.

Modification of Hindu religion. The introduction of the religion of the Prophet as a permanent factor in the life of India could not but modify the notions of Hindu thinkers. Although it is hardly necessary to observe that the idea of the unity of God always has been and still is familiar to even uneducated Hindus, it seems to be true that the prominence given to that doctrine by Muslim teaching encouraged the rise of religious schools which sought for a creed capable of expressing Muslim and Hindu devotion alike.

Rāmānand and Kabīr. The most famous teacher whose doctrine was the basis of such schools was Rāmānand, who lived in the fourteenth century, and came from the south. He preached in Hindi and admitted people of all castes, or of no caste, to his order. He had twelve apostles or chief disciples, who included a Rajput, a currier, a barber, and a Muslim weaver, namely, Kabīr. The verses of Kabīr, which are still familiar in northern India, show clear traces of Muslim influence. He condemned the worship of idols and the institution of caste. Both Muslims and Hindus are included among his followers, who are known as Kabīrpanthīs, or 'travellers on the way of Kabīr', who claimed to be 'at once the child of Allāh and of Rām'.

A few stanzas may be quoted to prove how Hinduism and Islam reacted one upon the other in the days of the Lodī sultans:

I

O Servant, where dost thou seek Me? Lo! I am beside thee.
I am neither in temple nor in mosque; I am neither in Kaaba nor in Kailash:
Neither am I in rites and ceremonies, nor in Yoga and renunciation.
If thou art a true seeker, thou shalt at once see Me: thou shalt meet Me in a
    moment of time.
Kabīr says, 'O Sadhu! God is the breath of all breath.'

II

It is needless to ask of a saint the caste to which he belongs;
For the priest, the warrior, the tradesman, and all the thirty-six castes, alike
    are seeking for God.
It is but folly to ask what the caste of a saint may be;
The barber has sought God, the washer-woman, and the carpenter—
Even Raidas was a seeker after God.
The Rishi Swapacha was a tanner by caste.
Hindus and Muslims alike have achieved that End, where remains no mark
    of distinction.

XLII

There is nothing but water at the holy bathing places; and I know that they are useless, for I have bathed in them.

The images are all lifeless, they cannot speak; I know, for I have cried aloud to them.

The Purana and the Quran are mere words; lifting up the curtain, I have seen.

Kabīr gives utterance to the words of experience; and he knows very well that all other things are untrue.[1]

Such teaching is closely akin to that of the Persian mystics, Jalāl-ud-dīn Rūmī, Hāfiz, and the rest; whose doctrine was embraced in the sixteenth century by Abu-l Fazl and Akbar. Kabīr is the spiritual ancestor of Nānak, the founder of the Sikh sect.

Dr. Farquhar truly observes that

it is a most extraordinary fact that the theology of Kabīr was meant to unite Hindus and Muhammadans in the worship of the one God; yet the most implacable hatred arose between the Sikhs and the Muhammadans; and from that hatred came the Khālsā, the Sikh military order, which created the fiercest enemies the Mughul emperors had. It is also most noteworthy that caste has found its way back into every Hindu sect that has disowned it.[2]

Seclusion of women. Although ancient Indian literature, such as the *Arthaśāstra* of Kautilya, alludes occasionally to the practice of the seclusion of women, many records indicate that the seclusion, even among the wealthy and leisured classes, although practised, was less strict than it is now in most parts of India. The example of the dominant Muslims, combined with the desire of the Hindus to give the female members of their families every possible protection against the foreigners, made the practice of living 'behind the curtain' both more fashionable and more widely prevalent than it used to be in ancient times.

CHRONOLOGY OF THE SULTANATE, 1290–1526
The Khiljī (Khaljī) Dynasty

JALĀL-UD-DĪN (FĪRŪZ SHĀH)	acc. 1290
Famine	1291
Mongol inroad	1292
Annexation of Ellichpur (Ilichpur)	1294
'ALĀ-UD-DĪN, acc.; murder of Jalāl-ud-dīn	1296
Conquest of Gujarat	1297–8
Mongol invasions	1296–1305
Massacre of Mongols at Delhi	? 1298
Southern campaigns of Malik Kāfūr	1302–11
Sack of Chitor	1303

[1] *One Hundred Poems of Kabir*. Translated by Rabindranath Tagore, assisted by Evelyn Underhill. Published by the India Society, London, at the Chiswick Press, 1914. Miss Underhill dates Kabīr from about 1440 to 1518. He used to be placed between 1380 and 1420. A good translation of Kabīr's poems from the Hindi by Mr. Ahmad Shah was published at Hamīrpur, U.P., in 1917.

[2] *Primer of Hinduism*, 2nd ed., Oxford University Press, 1912, p. 138.

AUTHORITIES

THE leading authority for the Khiljī and Tughluq dynasties is the *Tārīkh-i Fīrōz Shāhī* by Ziā-ud-dīn Baranī in E. & D., vol. iii. For the reign of Muhammad bin Tughluq I have made large use of Ibn Batūta's travels, translated into French by DEFRÉMERY and SANGUINETTI (with Arabic text), Paris, 1853–8. Part of that work has been rendered into English in E. & D., vol. iv, App. An abridged version in English has been made by H. A. R. GIBB, London, 1929. Another version of the *Travels* appears in the Hakluyt Society's edition of *Cathay and the Way Thither*, Yule and Cordier, 1916, vol. iv, pp. 1–166, with Introductory Notice, pp. 1–79. The notes are not up to date. Other authors will be found in E. & D., vol. iv; and, of course, FIRISHTA, BADĀONĪ, &c., give abstracts. The history of Timur's invasion, from his own *Memoirs* and other sources, is in E. & D., vol. iv, and the Lodī history in vol. v. I have also found E. THOMAS, *Chronicles of the Pathan Kings of Delhi*, useful. For Kabīr see text ed. by Rev. AHMAD SHAH, Cawnpore, 1911; and excellent transl. by same, Hamīrpur, 1917. More recent works upon personalities and problems include MAHDI HUSAIN, *Rise and Fall of Muhammad bin Tughluq*, Luzac, 1938; ISHWARI PRASAD, *History of the Qaraunah Turks*, Allahabad, 1936; I. H. QURESHI, *Administration of the Sultanate of Delhi*, 2nd ed., Lahore, 1945; W. H. MORELAND, *The Agrarian System of Muslim India*; KUNWAR M. ASHRAF, 'Life and Condition of the people of Hindustan, in *J.A.S.B.*, Letters, 1935; R. S. TRIPATHI, *Some Aspects of Muslim Administration*; TARA CHAND, article in the *Calcutta Review*, 1935, on 'Early Indo-Persian Literature and Amir Khusrav'. On the coinage of the period, H. N. Wright, *The Sultans of Delhi—their Coinage and Metrology*. On the south, R. SEWELL and S. K. AIYANAGAR, *Historical Inscriptions of Southern India*, and S. K. AIYANAGAR, *South India and her Muhammadan Invaders*.

CHAPTER 4

The Muslim kingdoms of Bengal, Malwa, Gujarat, and Kashmir

Scope of this chapter. Although it is impossible in the course of a general survey of Indian history to delineate in detail the story of each outlying kingdom, it is necessary for the completion of the picture to draw a sketch of the prominent events which happened in the more important of such kingdoms. The history of the Muslim Bahmanī kingdom or empire of the Deccan, founded in 1347, which possesses features of special interest; the complicated affairs of the five kingdoms erected on the ruins of the Bahmanī empire; and the history of the Hindu empire of Vijayanagar will be narrated in Book V. The short-lived kingdom of Jaunpur has been already dealt with. This chapter will be devoted to a summary notice of the more interesting passages in the histories of the Muslim kingdoms of Bengal, Malwa, Gujarat, and Kashmir, during the period of the Delhi sultanate. No attempt will be made to write a series of consecutive narratives.

Bengal

The independence of Bengal, that is to say, the definite separation of the Muslim provincial government from the sultanate of Delhi, may be dated from 1338, as the result of Fakhr-ud-dīn's rebellion against the tyranny of Muhammad bin Tughluq. A few years later Fīrūz Shāh Tughluq practically renounced all claim to the suzerainty of Delhi over the revolted province, which continued under a separate government until 1576, when Akbar's generals defeated and killed Dāūd Shāh, the last of the Afghan kings. The vicissitudes of the various dynasties which ruled Bengal between 1340 and 1526, when the sultanate of Delhi came to an end, present few events of intrinsic importance, or such as the memory readily retains. The wars, rebellions, and assassinations which usually fill so large a space in the histories of Muslim dynasties become almost unreadable when the drama is presented on a purely provincial stage isolated from the doings of the larger world. The story of the independent Muslim kings of Bengal seldom offers any points of contact with that world, even within the limits of India. The province ordinarily went its own way, apparently disregarding and disregarded by all other kingdoms, except for certain wars on its frontiers. Very little is known at present concerning the condition of the Hindu population during the period in question, that population being almost wholly ignored by the historians writing in

Persian. Toleration of their religion seems to have been the general rule, though there may have been a wave of conversion in the time of Jalāl-ud-dīn, himself a convert (1414–31).

Husain Shāh. The best and most famous of the Muslim kings of Bengal was Husain Shāh ('Alā-ud-dīn Husain Shāh, A.D. 1493–1519), a Sayyid of Arab descent who had held the office of vizier or prime minister under a tyrant named Shams-ud-dīn Muzaffar Shāh. The tyrant was a negro slave, one of that large body of Abyssinians which had first risen to importance under Rukn-ud-dīn Bārbak (1459–74), and from which three rulers had arisen. When he was deposed and killed the chiefs unanimously elected Husain Shāh to be their sovereign. He justified their choice. His name is still familiar throughout Bengal; and no insurrection or rebellion occurred during his reign, which lasted for twenty-four years. He died at Gaur, having 'enjoyed a peaceable and happy reign, beloved by his subjects, and respected by his neighbours'.

He hospitably received his namesake the fugitive king of Jaunpur.

Nusrat Shāh. Husain Shāh left eighteen sons, the eldest of whom, Nusrat Shāh, was elected by the chiefs as his successor. Nusrat Shāh departed from the usual custom of Asia in regard to his brothers, whom he treated with affection and liberality. He occupied Tirhat, and arranged with Babur honourable terms of peace. He is said to have become a cruel tyrant during his latter years.

Buildings. The mosques of Gaur and the other old cities of Bengal were constructed almost entirely of brick and in a peculiar style. At Gaur the tomb of Husain Shāh and the Lesser Golden Mosque built in his reign, with the Great Golden Mosque and the Kadam Rasūl built by Nusrat Shāh, may be mentioned as being specially noteworthy. The huge Ādīna mosque at Pandua, twenty miles from Gaur, built by Sikandar Shāh in 1368, has about 400 small domes, and is considered to be the most remarkable building in Bengal. The vast ruins of Gaur are estimated to occupy from twenty to thirty square miles.

Hindu literature. The learned historian of Bengali literature states that the most popular book in Bengal is the translation of the Sanskrit *Rāmāyana* made by Krittivāsa, who was born in A.D. 1346. It may be called the Bible of Bengal, where it occupies a position like that held in the upper provinces by the later work of Tulsī Dās. Some of the Muslim kings were not indifferent to the merits of Hindu literature. A Bengali version of the *Mahābhārata* was prepared to the order of Nusrat Shāh, who thus anticipated the similar action of Akbar. An earlier version of the same poem is believed to date from the fourteenth century, and another was composed in the time of Husain Shāh, by command of his general, Parāgal Khān. 'Frequent references are found in old Bengali literature indicating the esteem and trust in which the Emperor Husen Sāhā was held by the Hindus.' In fact, it seems to be true that 'the patronage and favour of the Muslim emperors and chiefs gave the first start towards the recognition of Bengali in the courts of

PLATE 15

a. Babur

b. Humayun

PLATE 16

a. Akbar

b. Jahangir

the Hindu rajas', who, under the guidance of their Brahman te ˑ˕ˑˑ were more inclined to encourage Sanskrit.[1]

Malwa

Malwa (Mālava), the extensive region now included for the most part in Madhya Bharat, and lying between the Narbada on the south, the Chambal on the north, Gujarat on the west, and Bundelkhand on the east, had been the seat of famous kingdoms in the Hindu period. Iltutmish raided the country early in the thirteenth century. In 1310 it was brought more or less into subjection by an officer of ʿAlā-ud-dīn Khiljī and thereafter continued to be ruled by Muslim governors until the break-up of the sultanate of Delhi.

The Ghūrī dynasty. Shortly after Timur's invasion in 1398 the governor, a descendant of the great sultan, Shihāb-ud dīn-Muhammad of Ghūr, set up as king on his own account under the style of Sultan Shihāb-ud-dīn Ghūrī (1401). He had enjoyed his new rank for only four years when he died suddenly, probably having been poisoned by his eldest son. The independent kingdom thus founded lasted for 130 years from 1401 until 1531, when it was annexed by Gujarat. Four years later Humayun brought the country temporarily under the dominion of Delhi, but it did not become finally part of the Mughul empire until the early years of Akbar's reign (1561–4). The political annals of the Muslim kingdom present few features of permanent interest, and the sultans are now remembered chiefly for their magnificent buildings at Mandu.

The first capital of the new kingdom was Dhar, where Raja Bhoja had once reigned, but the second sultan, who assumed the title of Hoshang Shāh, moved his court to Mandu, where he erected many remarkable edifices. He was defeated in a war with Gujarat, and was a prisoner for a year, but was restored to his throne, and retained his ill-gotten power until 1432, when he was succeeded by his son, Sultan Mahmūd, the third and last king of the Ghūrī dynasty, a worthless, drunken creature.

The Khiljī dynasty. Sultan Mahmūd Ghūrī was poisoned in 1436[2] by his minister, Mahmūd Khān, a Khiljī Turk, who seized the throne and founded the Khiljī dynasty, which lasted almost a century. He was by far the most eminent of the sovereigns of Malwa and spent a busy life fighting his neighbours, including the sultan of Gujarat, various rajas of Rajasthān, and Nizām Shāh Bahmanī. Firishta, ignoring the irregularity of the methods by which he won his crown, specially extols his justice and gives him a good general character.

Sultan Mahmūd [we are told] was polite, brave, just, and learned; and during his reign, his subjects, Muslim as well as Hindus, were happy, and

[1] Dinesh Chandra Sen, *History of the Bengali Language and Literature*, Calcutta University, 1911, pp. 12, 14, 170, 184, 201, 203.
[2] A.H. 840—A.D. 16 July 1436–4 July 1437, as proved by coin No. 15 in Wright's *Catalogue*.

maintained a friendly intercourse with each other. Scarcely a year passed that he did not take the field, so that his tent became his home, and his resting-place the field of battle. His leisure hours were devoted to hearing the histories and memoirs of the courts of different kings of the·earth read.

It would be pleasant to be able to believe this eulogy, but Mahmūd's record of temple destruction and enslavement of Hindus makes such belief difficult. The fight with the rana of Chitor apparently must have been indecisive, because the rana commemorated his alleged victory by the erection of a noble Tower of Victory, which still stands at Chitor; while the sultan, making a similar claim for himself, built a remarkable seven-storied tower at Mandu, which unfortunately has collapsed.

Sultan Nāsir-ud-dīn parricide. The next sultan, Ghiyās-ud-dīn (1469–1501), ended a peaceful, if petty-minded reign by handing over power in his own lifetime to his elder son Nāsir-ud-dīn, in 1500. The son, however, faced with widespread rebellions, had his father removed from the scene by poison in 1501. Jahangir, who stayed at Mandu in 1617, and renovated many of the admired buildings, gives a lively, if fanciful, account of these events. He expressed his disgust by destroying Nāsir-ud-dīn's tomb. 'I ordered them to throw his crumbled bones, together with his decayed limbs, into the Narbadda.'[1]

Nāsir-ud-dīn proved to be a cruel brute when in power. He died of fever in 1512, and was succeeded by his son, Mahmūd II, the last king of his race, who was defeated by Bahādur Shāh of Gujarat, and executed. The other male members of the royal family were exterminated, with the exception of one who was at Humayun's court, and the kingdom was annexed to Gujarat (A.H. 937 = A.D. 1531).

Buildings. The fortified city of Mandu, now in ruins, stood on the extensive summit of a commanding hill, protected by walls about twenty-five miles or more in total length. The massive buildings still recognizable are numerous, and of much architectural merit. They include a splendid Jāmi Masjid, or chief mosque, the Hindōlā Mahall, the Jahāz Mahall, the tomb of Hoshang Shāh, and the palaces of Bahādur and Rūpmatī, besides many other remarkable edifices built of sandstone and marble, which have been repaired and conserved to a considerable extent by the officers of the Archaeological department and the authorities of the Dhar state. The hill, which was dangerously infested by tigers and other wild beasts for more than two centuries, can now be visited and explored in the utmost comfort.

Gujarat

The country. The name Gujarat is of wide and indefinite signification. It may be taken in its most extended sense to mean all the terri-

---

[1] *Memoirs of Jahāngīr,* transl. Rogers and Beveridge, R. As. Soc., 1909, vol. i, pp. 365–7. Firishta expresses disbelief in the accusations of parricide preferred against Hoshang Shāh and Nāsir-ud-dīn Shāh, but, so far as I can judge, the charges seem to be true in both cases. As regards the latter, it is highly improbable that both Sher Shāh and Jahangir should have been misinformed.

tory in which the Gujarati language is used, and so to include the peninsula of Cutch (Kachchh), which is not usually reckoned as part of Gujarat.[1] In the ordinary use of the term, Cutch being excluded, Gujarat comprises a considerable region on the mainland and also the peninsula now known as Kathiawar, which used to be called Saurāshtra by the ancient Hindus and Sorath by the Muslims. The definition of the mainland region has varied from time to time. Some people fix the southern boundary at the Narbada, while others extend it to Daman. Certainly, in Muslim times, Surat at the mouth of the Tapti and Daman farther south always were considered as belonging to Gujarat. The Gujarat on the mainland of the Muslim period may be taken as extending north and south from the neighbourhood of Sirohi and Bhinmal in Rajputana to Daman, and east and west from the frontier of Malwa to the sea, and the Rann of Cutch. The region so defined comprises in modern terms six districts of the Bombay state, namely, Ahmadabad, Kaira, Panch Mahals, Broach (Bharōch), Surat, and part of the Thana District, with the late Baroda State or dominions of the Gaikwar, and many smaller states. The peninsula of Kathiawar, which was shared by a great multitude of such states, was in the Muslim period reckoned as part of the Gujarat.

The province, especially the mainland section, enjoys exceptional natural advantages, being fertile, well supplied with manufactures, and possessed of numerous ports where profitable overseas commerce has been practised since the most remote times. A country so desirable necessarily has attracted the attention of all the races which have effected conquests in northern and western India. Sultan Mahmūd of Ghazni's famous raid in A.D. 1024 effected the destruction of the temple at Somnāth and provided his army with much booty, but no attempt at permanent conquest was then made. The Muslim invasions in the latter part of the twelfth century also failed to produce any permanent result, and the country continued to be ruled by Hindu dynasties. In 1297 an officer of ʿAlā-ud-dīn Khiljī annexed it to the sultanate of Delhi. Muslim governors continued to be appointed from the capital after that date as long as the sultanate lasted.

Independence. Zafar Khān, the last governor, who was appointed in 1391, and had been practically independent, formally withdrew his allegiance in 1401.[2] His son, Tātār Khān, in 1403 made his father prisoner and seated himself on the provincial throne as sultan, with the title of Nāsir-ud-dīn Muhammad Shāh. The new sultan seems to have been poisoned by his father in 1404. But in 1407 the old man, who had become Sultan Muzaffar Shāh, was succeeded by his grandson, and heir-designate, who assumed the style of Ahmad Shāh.

Ahmad Shāh. Ahmad Shāh, who reigned for thirty years from 1411

---

[1] Gujarati is the official and literary language of Cutch, but the spoken vernacular is a special dialect of Sindhi.
[2] Wright gives A.H. 806 = A.D. 1403–4; following a paper by G. P. Taylor in *J. Bom. Br. R.A.S.*, for 1902.

to 1441, may be regarded as the real founder of the independent kingdom of Gujarat. His father and grandfather during their few years of power had controlled only a comparatively small territory in the neighbourhood of Ahmadabad, then called Asāwal. Ahmad Shāh devoted his energy and considerable ability to extending his territories, spreading the religion of the Prophet, and improving the administration of his own dominions. Throughout his reign he never suffered a defeat, and his armies invariably prevailed over those of the sultanate of Malwa, the chiefs of Asirgarh, Rajputana, and other neighbouring countries. Sultan Ahmad was a close friend of Sultan Fīrūz Bahmanī, and, like him, was zealous in fighting the infidels and destroying their temples. He built the noble city of Ahmadabad adjoining the old Hindu town of Asāwal. 'Travellers', the local historian avers, 'are agreed that they have found no city in the whole earth so beautiful, charming, and splendid.'

Sultan Mahmūd Bīgarhā. Sultan Mahmūd Begarā or Bīgarhā, a grandson of Ahmad Shāh, ascended the throne at the age of thirteen in (A.H. 863) 1459 and reigned prosperously for fifty-two years until (A.H. 917) 1511. He was by far the most eminent sovereign of his dynasty. Although a mere boy at the time of his accession he seems to have assumed a man's part from the first and to have been able to dispense with a Protector, such as was imposed on Akbar at the same age.

He added glory and lustre to the kingdom of Gujarat, and was the best of all the Gujarat kings, including all who preceded and all who succeeded him; and whether for abounding justice and generosity, for success in religious war, and for the diffusion of the laws of Islam and of Muslims; for soundness of judgement, alike in boyhood, in manhood, and in old age; for power, for valour, and victory—he was a pattern of excellence.

That vigorous eulogy by the leading Muslim historian of his country seems to be justified by the facts as seen from his point of view.

Mahmūd was eminently successful in war. He made himself master of the strong fortresses of Champaner to the north-east of Baroda, and of Junagarh in Kathiawar; overran Cutch and gained victories over the sultan of Ahmadnagar and other potentates.

Towards the end of his reign he came into conflict with the Portuguese and allied himself with the sultan of Egypt and the zamorin of Calicut against them. An Egyptian fleet, built at Suez, commanded by Amīr Husain, reached India in 1507, where it was joined by Indian ships under Malik Ayāz. The combined force surprised a Portuguese squadron at Chaul, defeated it, and killed Dom Lourenço, the viceroy's son, in the battle (January 1508). But in 1509 the Muslim fleet was annihilated in a battle fought off Diu in Kathiawar, then included in the Gujarat kingdom. The foreigners, who finally secured Goa from Bijapur in 1510, were thenceforward always able to maintain their possessions against the Indian powers, but did not obtain a fort at Diu until 1535. Even victorious Akbar was unable to disturb them seriously, although no project was nearer to his heart than the expulsion of the hated intruders from the soil of his richest province.

The personal peculiarities of Mahmūd made a deep impression on his contemporaries, and became known in Europe, as told in fantastic tales chiefly conveyed through the agency of the Italian traveller Ludovico di Varthema. The Sultan's moustaches were so long that he used to tie them over his head and his beard reached to his girdle. His appetite, like that of Akbar's secretary, Abu-l Fazl, was so abnormal that he was credited with eating more than twenty pounds' weight of food daily. He was believed to have been dosed with poison from childhood and thus to have become immune against its effects, while his body was so saturated with venom that if a fly settled on his hand it would drop dead. The legend has found its way into English literature through Samuel Butler's reference to it:

> The Prince of Cambay's daily food
> Is asp, and basilisk, and toad.[1]

Sultan Bahādur Shāh. The latest notable sultan of Gujarat was Mahmūd Bigarhā's grandson, Bahādur Shāh, who reigned from the close of 1526 to February 1537, when his uneasy life was ended by a tragic death at the hands of the Portuguese. He earned a full share of military glory by his defeat of Mahmūd II Khiljī, involving the annexation of Malwa in 1531–2, and by his storm of Chitor in 1534, when the Rajputs made their usual dreadful sacrifice.

In the following year, 1535, Bahādur, through over-confidence in his artillery, was utterly defeated by Humayun Padshah, driven from his kingdom, and forced to take refuge in Malwa. The fortress of Champaner was gallantly taken by Humayun, who was himself among the earliest to escalade the walls. But the Mughul was soon recalled from the scene of his western triumphs by the necessity of meeting his Afghan rival, Sher Khān (Shāh), and Bahādur was then able to return to his kingdom.

Ordinarily the relations between the Portuguese and the government of Gujarat were hostile, but the Mughul pressure forced Bahādur to buy the promise of Portuguese help by the surrender of Bassein, and to conclude a treaty of peace with the proud foreigners. Negotiations on the subject of the port and fortress of Diu, then of much importance as a trading station, induced Bahādur Shāh to visit Nuno da Cunha, the Portuguese governor, and go aboard his ship. No less than eight distinct accounts of what then happened—namely, four Portuguese and four Muslim—are on record, all differing in details. Colonel Watson, who examined them all critically, came to 'the conclusion . . . that on either side the leader hoped by some future treachery to seize the person of the other; and that mutual suspicion turned into a fatal affray a meeting which both parties intended should pass peacefully and lull the other into a false and favourable security'. It is cert

---

[1] *Hudibras*, Part ii, Canto i, published in 1664.

that the sultan of Gujarat, attempting to return, jumped overboard, and while in the water was knocked on the head by a sailor. He was only thirty-one years of age. Manuel de Souza, captain of the port of Diu, also lost his life at the same time.

Bahādur Shāh's intemperance in the use of liquor and drugs clouded his brain and made him prone to acts of ill-considered impulse. He left no son.

Later history. The history of the province from the time of his death in 1537 to its annexation by Akbar after the lightning campaigns of 1572-3 is a record of anarchical confusion, into the details of which it is unnecessary to enter. Disturbances continued to be frequent even after the absorption of the kingdom into the Mughul empire.

Architecture. The exquisite architecture of Gujarat, further beautified by wood-carving of supreme excellence, is the special distinction of the province. The Muslim conquerors adopted with certain modifications the charming designs of the old Hindu and Jain architects, filling Ahmadabad, Cambay, and many other towns with a multitude of buildings singularly pleasing to the eye, and enriched with the most delicate stone lattices and other ornaments. The ancient Hindu monuments of both mainland Gujarat and Kathiawar have been described by Dr. Burgess in two large, finely illustrated quarto volumes of the Archaeological Survey. The same author has described and illustrated with equal copiousness the Muslim architecture on the mainland in three other handsome volumes. The architects of the province still retain much of the skill of their ancestors. Ahmadabad is particularly rich in noble buildings, and during the time of its glory, extending from its foundation to the eighteenth century—a period of about three centuries—undoubtedly was one of the handsomest cities in the world. The population is said to have numbered 900,000, and millionaires were to be found among the merchants. The city is now again wealthy and prosperous, the second largest in the Bombay Presidency, with a population of nearly 800,000 in 1951. According to a local saying the prosperity of Ahmadabad hangs on three threads—silk, gold, and cotton.

Kashmir

The country. In medieval history the name Kashmir refers only to the beautiful valley on the upper course of the Jhelum, which is about eighty-five miles long and from twenty to twenty-five broad. The long the interesting story of the Hindu kingdom of the valley is painful reading on the whole, many of the rajas having been atrocious tyrants.

The first sultan. Early in the fourteenth century a Muslim adventurer from Swat, named Shāh Mīrzā or Mīr, became minister to the Hindu raja of Kashmir. In 1346 he seized the throne, married the late raja's widow, and by his liberal revenue policy secured the position of his dynasty. The third of his sons, who ruled from 135?

1378, further improved the land revenue system, and proved a notable warrior.

Sultan Sikandar. The sixth sultan, Sikandar (1393–1416), who was ruling at the time of Timur's invasion in 1398, managed to avoid meeting that formidable personage, and remained safely protected by his mountain walls. Sikandar, whose generosity attracted the learned from Persia, Arabia, and Mesopotamia, became a gloomy bigot, and his zeal in destroying temples and idols was so intense that he is remembered as the Idol-Breaker. He freely used the sword to propagate Islam and succeeded in forcing the bulk of the population to conform outwardly to the Muslim religion. Most of the Brahmans refused to apostatize, and many of them paid with their lives the penalty for their steadfastness. Many others were exiled, and only a few conformed.

Sultan Zain-ul 'Abidīn. The eighth sultan, Zain-ul 'Abidīn, who had a long and prosperous reign of about half a century from 1420 to 1467, was a man of very different type. He adopted the policy of universal toleration, recalled the exiled Brahmans, repealed the *jizya* or poll-tax on Hindus, and even permitted new temples to be built. He abstained from eating flesh, prohibited the slaughter of kine, and was justly venerated as a saint. He encouraged literature, painting, and music, and caused many translations to be made of works composed in Sanskrit, Arabic, and other languages. His public works included a number of bridges and many irrigation works. In those respects he resembled Akbar, but he differed from that monarch in the continence which enabled him to practise strict fidelity to one wife.

Later history. The reigns of the other sultans are not of sufficient importance or interest to justify the insertion of their annals in this history. For eleven years (1540–51) a relative of Humayun, named Mīrzā Haidar, who had invaded the valley, ruled it, nominally as governor on behalf of Humayun, but in practice as an independent prince. Some years later the Chak dynasty seized the throne.

CHRONOLOGY

(Leading dates only)

Bengal

Independence of Fakhr-ud-dīn	1338
Husain Shāh	1493–1518
Nusrat Shāh	1518–32
Bengal annexed by Akbar	1576

Malwa

Independence of Sultan Shihāb-ud-dīn Ghūrī	1401
Sultan Mahmūd Ghūrī	1432
Sultan Mahmūd Khilji founded Khilji dynasty	1436
Malwa annexed by Bahādur Shāh of Gujarat	1531
Malwa annexed by Akbar	1561–4

AUTHORITIES

FOR my slight notice of the annals of Bengal I have used chiefly FIRISHTA, and STEWART, *History of Bengal*, 1813. See also NALINI K. BHATTASALI, 'Coins and chronology of the Early Independent Sultans of Bengal', and *History of Bengal*, vol. ii, ed. R. D. BANERJEE, Dacca.

FIRISHTA gives the most convenient summary of Malwa history.

The best and most authoritative abstract of Gujarat Muslim history is that by Colonel WATSON in the *Bombay Gazetteer* (1896), vol. i, part i. The same volume contains a good account of Mandu, the capital of Malwa. I have also consulted BAYLEY, *History of Gujarat* (1886); and WHITEWAY, *The Rise of Portuguese Power in India*, 1497–1550 (Constable, 1899).

Various articles in the *I.G.* (1908) are serviceable for all the kingdoms.

The Kashmir history is given by FIRISHTA and ABU-L FAZL (*Āīn*, transl. JARRETT), as well as in the *I.G.*, but many details remain obscure. The story of the sultans was discussed by C. J. RODGERS at considerable length in *J.A.S.B.*, part i, 1885, in a paper on 'The Square Silver Coins of the Sultans of Kashmir'. T. W. HAIG, 'Muhammadan Kings of Kashmir in *J.R.A.S.*, 1918. *Tarikh i Rashidī*, tr. Sir E. DENISON ROSS.

The coins of the various kingdoms are described by H. N. WRIGHT in the *Catalogue of the Coins in the Indian Museum, Calcutta*, vol. ii, Clarendon Press, 1907, with references to other publications.

The works by BURGESS are the leading authority on the art of the province of Gujarat, namely:

1. *Report on the Antiquities of Kāthiāwād and Kachh*, 1876 (A.S.W.I., vol. ii = Imperial Series, vol. ii);
2. *Muhammadan Architecture in Gujarāt*, 1896 (A.S.W.I., vol. vi = Imp. Ser., vol. xxiii);
3. *Muhammadan Architecture of Ahmadābād*, Part I, 1900 (A.S.W.I., vol. vii = Imp. Ser., vol. xxiv);
4. Ibid., Part II, 1905 (A.S.W.I., vol. viii = Imp. Ser., vol. xxxiii);
5. *Architectural Antiquities of Northern Gujarāt*, 1903 (A.S.W.I., vol. ix = Imp. Ser., vol. xxxii).

M. S. Commissariat, *History of Gujarāt*, 1938.

BOOK V

The Southern Powers

CHAPTER 1

The Bahmanī dynasty of the Deccan, 1347–1526

Bahmanī dynasty; Sultan ʿAlā-ud-dīn I. A series of rebellions between the years 1343 and 1351, caused by the tyranny of Muhammad bin Tughluq, left to the sovereign of Delhi only a small portion of the extensive empire which he had controlled for a few years.

Hasan, entitled Zafar Khān, an Afghan or Turki officer of the Delhi sultan, occupied Daulatabad in the Deccan in 1347, and proclaimed his independence before the end of the year. He is known to history as Sultan ʿAlā-ud-dīn I, the founder of the Bahmanī dynasty of the Deccan, which played an important part in India for nearly two centuries, from 1347 to 1526. He assumed the name or title of Bahman, because he claimed descent from the early Persian king so-called, better known as Artaxerxes.

Gulbarga, the capital. The new sultan established his capital at Gulbarga, now in the Nizam's former dominions, to which he gave the Muslim name of Ahsanābād.[1] After the death of Muhammad bin Tughluq in 1351 ʿAlā-ud-dīn undertook the conquest of a large part of the Deccan, and when he passed away in 1358 was master of an extensive dominion, reaching to the sea on the west and including the ports of Goà and Dabhol. The latter place, now a small town in the Ratnagiri District, Bombay, was the principal port of the Konkan from the fourteenth to the sixteenth century. The eastern frontier of the Bahmanī sultanate was marked by Bhōnagir or Bhōngīr (17° 31′ N.; 78° 53′ E.), now a considerable town in the Nizam's former dominions. The Pen Ganga river formed the northern, and the Krishna the southern boundary. For administrative convenience these territories were divided into four provinces or *tarafs*.

---

[1] Ahsanābād, or Hasanābād, with reference to the Sultan's name Hasan (see E. & D., vol. viii, p. 16 n.). The Hyderabad officials use the erroneous form Gulbarga. The name may be correctly written as Kalburgā (कल्बुर्गा), or Kulbargā (कुल्बर्गा), or Kulburgā (कुल्बुर्गा). See King, p. 1 n.

Muhammad Shāh I; wars with Hindus. The reign of the second sultan, Muhammad Shāh I (1358–73), was chiefly occupied by savage wars waged against the Hindu rulers of Vijayanagar and Talingana or Warangal. The ferocious struggle continued until the sultan was reputed to have slain half a million Hindus. At last the butchery was stayed and the parties agreed to spare the lives of prisoners and non-combatants. Muhammad Shāh was as ruthless when dealing with brigandage in his own dominions as he was against his external Hindu foes. Like the Mughul emperors later he sought to suppress robbery by massacres, and in the course of six or seven months sent nearly 8,000 heads of supposed robbers to be piled up near the city gates. He accumulated immense treasures and possessed 3,000 elephants. It was Muhammad Shāh who set the pattern of administration for the Bahmanī kingdom and its successor states. He controlled the provinces by yearly royal tours, reorganized the household guards, and had a group of eight ministers at the centre.

Fīrūz, eighth sultan, 1397–1422. Passing over intermediate revolutions and short reigns, we come to the reign of Fīrūz, the eighth sultan, who was a son of the youngest brother of Muhammad Shāh I.

After a year devoted to the reorganization of the administration— in which increasing numbers of Brahmans were employed—Fīrūz was faced with an invasion by the Vijayanagar ruler Harihara II. The unwieldy Hindu host was surprised during the rains, 1399, Harihara's son was slain, and the army driven in confusion to Vijayanagar. An alliance between Malwa, Gujarat, and Vijayanagar checked the sultan's designs of expansion to the north, but in 1406 he defeated the Hindus, securing a Vijayanagar princess for his harem, and the Tungabhadra for his southern boundary. The Raichur Doab was made a separate province.

He so far violated the principles of his religion as to drink hard and enjoy music. He kept an enormous number of women from many countries, including Europe, and was reputed to be able to talk with each lady in her own tongue. He had facilities for importing European curiosities through Goa and Dabhol. Fīrūz loved building, and constructed a fortified palace at Fīrozābād on the Bhima to the south of the capital. He adorned Gulbarga with many edifices, the most notable being the principal mosque, alleged to have been planned in imitation of the mosque at Cordova in Spain. It is the only large mosque in India which is completely roofed.[1]

Fīrūz went on one expedition too many. About 1420, towards the close of his reign, he suffered a severe defeat at Pāngal, to the r   th of the Krishna, and came home a broken-down old man. He spent the rest of his days in works of piety according to his lights and left affair

---

[1] Gulbarga decayed after the death of Fīrūz, when it ceased to be the capital, and then lay neglected for centuries. It has revived lately, being now a prosperous town of about 30,000 inhabitants with extensive trade. Haig denies that the mosque is copied from that at Cordova (*Historic Landmarks*, p. 94).

of state in the hands of two Turki slaves. Although he gratified his curiosity by reading the Old and New Testament, it is not correct to say, as Meadows Taylor does, that 'in religion he was perfectly tolerant of all sects and creeds'.

Firishta was of opinion that the house of Bahman attained its greatest splendour in the days of Fīrūz.

Ahmad Shāh, 1422–35. The administration of the Turki slaves being displeasing to the sultan's brother Ahmad, that prince, with the aid of a foreign merchant named Khalaf Hasan Basrī, deposed Fīrūz and murdered him with his son. Such tragedies were common in Bahmanī history and do not seem to have offended public opinion. The murderer ascended the throne without opposition, and resumed the war with the Hindus, burning to revenge the losses suffered by the army of Islam in his brother's time. He attacked the Vijayanagar territory, with savagery even greater than that shown by his predecessors.

Ahmad Shāh, without waiting to besiege the Hindu capital, overran the open country; and wherever he went, put to death men, women, and children without mercy, contrary to the compact made by his uncle and predecessor, Muhammad Shāh, and the raya of Vijayanagar. Whenever the number of slain amounted to twenty thousand, he halted three days, and made a festival in celebration of the bloody event. He broke down also the idolatrous temples and destroyed the colleges of the Brahmans.

Ultimately peace was concluded with Vijayanagar. The operation against Warangal in 1424–5 had finally destroyed the independence of that Hindu kingdom, and extended the Bahmanī frontiers to the sea. About the year 1423 the Deccan again suffered from a severe famine.

Ahmad Shāh also engaged in wars with the sultans of Malwa and Gujarat and with the Hindu chiefs of the Konkan. The war with Gujarat was ended by a treaty of alliance offensive and defensive, which subsisted for many years. Nizām Shāh benefited by it in 1462.

Change of capital to Bidar. Ahmad Shāh, who had suffered from illness at Gulbarga, and regarded the place as unlucky, shifted his capital to Bidar (Ahmadabad or Muhammadabad), distant about sixty miles to the north-east. The wisdom of the transfer is fully justified by the description of the new capital recorded by Meadows Taylor:

There is no more healthy or beautiful site for a city in the Deccan than Bidar. The fort had been already erected on the north-east angle of a table-land composed of laterite, at a point where the elevation, which is considerable, or about 2,500 feet above the level of the sea, trends southward and westward, and declines abruptly about 500 feet to the wide plain of the valley of the Manjera, which it overlooks. The fortifications, still perfect, are truly noble; built of blocks of laterite dug out of the ditch, which is very broad. . . . The city adjoined the fort, space being left for an esplanade, and stretched southwards along the crest of the eminence, being regularly laid out with broad streets. There was a plentiful supply of beautiful water, though the wells are deep; and in every respect, whether as regards climate, which is much cooler and healthier than that of Kulbargā, or situation, the new capital was far preferable to the old one. At the present time, though the city has diminished to a provincial town, and the noble monuments of the Bahmani kings have decayed, there is no city of the Deccan which better repays a visit from the traveller than Bīdar.[1]

'Alā-ud-dīn II. Ahmad Shāh was succeeded quietly by his eldest son, 'Alā-ud-dīn II (1435–57). Renewed war with Vijayanagar resulted ultimately in a peace favourable to the sultan. After the termination of the war the sultan neglected his duties and abandoned himself to the fleshly delights of wine and women. The efficiency of the public service was much impaired by the quarrels between two factions—the one comprising the native or Deccani Muslims allied with the Abyssinian (or Habshī) settlers, who were mostly Sunnis; and the other the so-called 'foreigners', that is to say, the Arabs, Turks, Persians, and Mughuls, who usually were Shias. The enmity between the factions led to the commission of a horrid crime by permission of the drunken sultan. When a force under one of his foreign officers had been defeated in the Konkan by the Hindus, the remnant took refuge in a fort named Chākan situated to the north of Poona. The Deccani party, having trumped up false accusations of treasonable intent against the refugees, persuaded the sultan to sanction the extermination of the Sayyids and Mughuls in the fort. The Deccani chiefs secured the confidence of their victims by a show of kindness, and then fell upon them treacherously, slaying every male, including 1,200 Sayyids of pure descent and about 1,000 other foreigners. Khalaf Hasan, the man who had helped Ahmad Shāh to gain the throne, and had subsequently become prime minister, was among the slain. The women were treated 'with all the insult that lust or brutality could invoke'. The sultan, when he found that he had been deceived, punished the authors of the massacre.

Humāyūn. 'Alā-ud-dīn was followed by his eldest son Humāyūn (1457–61), who had already earned a terrible reputation for cruelty. An attempt to displace him in favour of a younger brother was easily defeated, and the new sultan was free to indulge his maniacal passion for the infliction of pain. Men and women, suspected without reason of favouring rebellion, were stabbed with daggers, hewn in pieces with hatchets, or scalded to death by boiling water or hot oil.

The fire of his rage blazed up in such a way that it burned up land and water; and the broker of his violence used to sell the guilty and innocent by one tariff. The nobles and generals when they went to salute the sultan used to bid farewell to their wives and children and make their wills. Most of the nobles, ministers, princes, and heirs to the sovereignty were put to the sword.

Humāyūn is remembered by the epithet Zālim, or the Tyrant. Some authorities suggest that he died a natural death, but the more probable account avers that while intoxicated he was assassinated by his servants. A versifier ingeniously expressed the universal joy at the death of the monster by the chronogram:

> Humāyūn Shāh has passed away from the world.
> God Almighty, what a blessing was the death of Humāyūn!
> On the date of his death the world was full of delight,
> So 'delight of the world' gives the date of his death.[1]

Strange to say the tyrant was served by an excellent minister, Khwāja Mahmūd Gāwān,[2] who apparently was unable to check his master's furious rage. The minister lived long enough to do good service under Humāyūn's successors, and to be murdered for his pains.

Muhammad Shāh III; conquests; famine. The next sultan of importance was Muhammad Shāh III, who reigned for nearly twenty years (1463–82), and enjoyed the services of Khwāja Mahmūd Gāwān, the capable minister who had served Humāyūn, and was equally competent as a general and as a civil administrator. The Khwāja took the strong fortress of Belgaum (1473), and recovered Goa in 1472, which had been lost by one of the earlier sultans to the raya of Vijayanagar, at a date not known exactly. The result of his operations was an increase of the Bahmanī dominions 'to an extent never achieved by former sovereigns'. The minister provided for the administration of the new territories by increasing the number of provinces to nine. Central control was strengthened by making many *parganas* into crown lands, by taking local appointments out of the hands of the provincial governors, and by accounting more rigorously for the numbers maintained in military contingents.

A disastrous famine, known as the 'famine of Bijapur' because it began in that state, devastated the Deccan in 1473 or 1474 and caused many deaths. The rains failed for two years, and when they came at last, in the third year, 'scarcely any farmers remained in the country to cultivate the lands'.

The title of Ghāzī. When Kondapalli (Condapilly) was surrendered early in 1481, previous to the raid on Kanchi, to be described presently, an incident occurred which illustrates the spirit of fanaticism characteristic of the Bahmanī kings.

The king [Firishta relates] having gone to view the fort, broke down an idolatrous temple and killed some Brahmans who officiated at it, with his own hands, as a point of religion. He then gave orders for a mosque to be erected on the foundations of the temple, and ascending the pulpit, repeated a few prayers, distributed alms, and commanded the *Khutba* to be read in his name. Khwāja Mahmūd Gāwān now represented that as his Majesty had

---

[1] The Persian words are ذَوقِ جهان , *zauk- jahān*. The numerical values of the letters total 865, the Hijrī year, corresponding to A.D. 1460–1; thus, *z* = 700, *au* (a) = 6, *k* = 100, *j* = 3, *h* = 5, *ā (alif)* = 1, and *n* = 50.

[2] H. K. Sherwani, *Mahmūd Gāwān*.

slain some infidels with his own hands, he might fairly assume the title of Ghāzī, an appellation of which he was very proud.

The virtuous minister, it will be observed, shared the beliefs of his master.

Raid on Kanchi or Conjeeveram. The most remarkable military exploit of the reign was the successful raid made on Kanchi or Conjeeveram, one of the seven Hindu sacred cities, during the course of a campaign against Vijayanagar in 1481. The remote position of Kanchi, forty-two miles south-south-west of Madras, had secured it from Muslim attacks, so that the inhabitants believed themselves to be perfectly safe. The sultan was encamped at Kondapalli near Bezwada, now in the Kistna (Krishna) District of Madras, when glowing accounts of the rich booty to be obtained in the holy city induced him to plan a surprise. The story is best told in the words of Firishta, as follows:

Muhammad Shāh accordingly selected six thousand of his best cavalry, and leaving the rest of his army at Kondapalli, proceeded by forced marches to Kanchi. He moved so rapidly on the last day, according to the historians of the time, that only forty troopers kept up with him, among which number were Nizām-ul-mulk Bahrī and Yūrish Khān Turk. On approaching the temple some Hindus came forth, one of whom, a man of gigantic stature, mounted on horseback, and brandishing a drawn sabre by way of defiance, rushed full speed towards the king, and aimed a blow which the latter parried, and with one stroke of his sword cleaved him in twain. Another infidel then attacked the king, whose little band was shortly engaged man to man with the enemy; but Muhammad Shāh had again the good fortune to slay his opponent, upon which the rest of the Hindus retired into the temple. Swarms of people, like bees, now issued from within and ranged themselves under its walls to defend it. At length, the rest of the king's force coming up, the temple was attacked and carried by storm with great slaughter. An immense booty fell to the share of the victors, who took away nothing but gold, jewels, and silver, which were abundant. The king then [12 March 1481] sacked the city of Kanchi, and, after remaining there for a week, he returned to his army.

Murder of Mahmūd Gāwān. Muhammad Shāh, a confirmed drunkard, gave way to his besetting sin more and more as time went on. His intemperance permitted the crime which disgraced and deservedly embittered the last year of his life. Khwāja Mahmūd Gāwān, his great minister, being a Persian, necessarily was counted as a 'foreigner', though he was on friendly terms with many Deccanis, and shared power fairly with them. He was hated, however, by the Brahman convert, Malik Hasan, governor of Telingana, who unceasingly sought his ruin. At last, early in April 1481, the plotters managed to lay before their intoxicated sovereign a treasonable letter falsely attributed to the minister, although an obvious forgery. The besotted sultan, without taking the slightest trouble to ascertain the facts, ordered the instant execution of his aged and faithful servant. When it was too late he found out the deceit practised on him and tried to drown his remorse in drink, until he killed himself by his excesses in March 1482.

Consequences of the crime. Meadows Taylor justly observes that the death of Mahmūd Gāwān was 'the beginning of the end', and that 'with him departed all the cohesion and power of the Bahmanī kingdom'. The minister was a devout Sunni Muslim, as ruthless as any one else in slaying and despoiling idolaters. Subject to that qualification, his character seems to deserve the praise bestowed upon it by Firishta, which is echoed by Meadows Taylor in language still more emphatic, and deserving of quotation, even though it may seem tinged with exaggeration:

Character of Mahmūd Gāwān. The character of Mahmūd Gāwān [Taylor observes] stands out broadly and grandly, not only among all his contemporaries, but among all the ancient Muhammadans of India, as one unapproachably perfect and consistent . . . his noble and judicious reforms, his skill and bravery in war, his justice and public and private benevolence have, in the aggregate, no equals in the Muhammadan history of India. . . . Out of the public revenues of his ample estates, while he paid the public establishments attached to him, he built and endowed the magnificent college at Bīdar, which was practically destroyed by an explosion of gunpowder in the reign of Aurangzēb, and which, while he lived at the capital, was his daily resort; and the grand fortresses of Ausā, Parēndā, Sholāpur, Dharūr [Dārūr], and many others attest alike his military skill and science.[1]

Mahmūd Shāh, 1482–1518; end of the dynasty. Little more remains to be said about the annals of the Bahmanī dynasty. The successor of Muhammad III was his son Mahmūd, a boy of twelve years of age, who lived and in a manner reigned until 1518, but never possessed real power. The provincial governors, one after the other, declared their independence, and only a small area round the capital, which became the separate sultanate of Bidar a few years later, remained under the nominal jurisdiction of Mahmūd. The actual government was in the hands of Qāsim Barīd, a crafty Turk, and after his death in those of his son, Amīr Barīd. It is unnecessary to relate the story of the murders, quarrels, and rebellions of Mahmūd's miserable reign. They may be read by the curious in the pages of Firishta and the *Burhān-i Ma'āsir*. After the death of Mahmūd four puppet sultans in succession were placed on the throne, until in 1526 Amīr Barīd felt that the time had come for the assertion of his right to rule on his own account.

Character of the dynasty. Before we proceed to notice some of the more prominent events in the complicated history of the five separate sultanates formed out of the fragments of the Bahmanī

[1] See map, p. 287. Ausā (Owsah) is 70 miles north-north-west of Gulbarga, Parenda is 70 miles west of Ausā, Sholapur is 70 miles north-west of Gulbarga, and Dārūr is about 22 miles east of Raichur. Burgess gives a photograph and plan of the ruined college (A.S.W.I., vol. iii, pl. xxviii, xxix). It is illustrated also in the *Ann. Rep. A. S. Nizam's Dominions* for 1914–15.

dominion, it will be well to pause for a moment in order to consider the nature of the achievement of the Bahmanī sultans of the Deccan, and to estimate the position in history to which they are entitled.

The story of the dynasty as it appears in the books is not attractive reading. Between 1347 and 1518 the throne was occupied by fourteen sultans, of whom four were murdered, and two others were deposed and blinded. With the exception of the fifth sultan, a quiet peaceful man, all the sovereigns who attained maturity were bloodthirsty fanatics. Humāyūn was a monster, comparable only with the most infamous tyrants named in history. Several of the sultans were drunken debauchees, and little is recorded about any member of the family which is calculated to justify a favourable opinion of his character. The only person mentioned who deserves much praise is the minister Mahmūd Gāwān, and even he was fanatical. It would be difficult to specify any definite benefit conferred upon India by the dynasty. No doubt, as Meadows Taylor points out, the Bahmanīs gave a certain amount of encouragement to purely Muslim learning, and constructed irrigation works in the eastern provinces, which incidentally did good to the peasantry while primarily securing the crown revenue. But those items to their credit weigh lightly against the wholesale devastation wrought by their wars, massacres, and burnings.

Misery of the common people. Our estimate of the character of the Bahmanī sultans and the effect of their rule upon the people committed to their charge need not be based merely upon inferences drawn from the story of their conspicuous doings. Observations on the conditions of life of the unregarded Hindu peasantry must not be looked for in the pages of Muslim historians, whether they deal with the north or the south. The scanty information recorded concerning the commonalty of India in ancient times is obtained almost wholly from the notes made by observant foreign visitors. Such a visitor, a Russian merchant named Athanasius Nikitin, happened to reside for a long time at Bidar and to travel in the Bahmanī dominions between the years 1470 and 1474 in the reign of Muhammad Shāh III. By a lucky accident his notes were preserved, and have been made accessible in an English version.

The merchant tells us that:

The Sultan is a little man, twenty years old,[1] in the power of the nobles. There is a Khorassanian Boyar [sc. Persian noble from Khurasan], Melik Tuchar [sc. Malik-ut Tujjār, 'Lord of the merchants', or 'merchant-prince', a title of Khwāja Mahmūd Gāwān], who keeps an army of 200,000 men; Melik Khan keeps 100,000; Kharat Khan, 20,000; and many are the khans that keep 10,000 armed men. The Sultan goes out with 300,000 men of his own troops.

The land is overstocked with people; but those in the country are very miserable, whilst the nobles are extremely opulent and delight in luxury.

[1] He was in his tenth year in 1463 (King, p. 98). The remark therefore applies to 1473 or 1474.

They are wont to be carried on their silver beds, preceded by some twenty chargers caparisoned in gold, and followed by 300 men on horseback, and by 500 on foot, and by horn men, ten torchbearers, and ten musicians.

The Sultan goes out hunting with his mother and his lady, and a train of 10,000 men on horseback, 50,000 on foot; 200 elephants adorned in gilded armour, and in front 100 horsemen, 100 dancers, and 300 common horses in golden clothing; 100 monkeys, and 100 concubines, all foreign.

The armies were armed mobs. It is obvious that such an over-grown establishment of armed men, women, and beasts, controlled by a selfish minority of luxurious nobles, must have sucked the country dry. There is no difficulty in believing the positive statement that the common people were 'very miserable'. The mass of the people in the Hindu empire of Vijayanagar was equally oppressed and wretched. The huge armies maintained were little better than armed mobs, extremely inefficient in warfare. Similar unwieldy hosts were maintained by the neighbouring states, Muslim and Hindu. Various recorded incidents prove that such masses of undisciplined men had little military value, and often were routed by quite small forces of active assailants. But, on the whole, the armed mobs of the Muslim sultans were a little more efficient than those of their Hindu opponents, and, in consequence, usually were victorious.

Fortresses and other buildings. It is characteristic of the nature of the rule of the Bahmanīs that Meadows Taylor, who judged the sultans with excessive partiality, should declare that the fortresses built by them are 'perhaps their greatest and most indestructible monuments, and far exceed any of the same period in Europe'. He mentions Gawilgarh and Narnāla, both in Berar, and especially the latter, as being choice specimens of the grandeur of design appropriate to mountain fortresses, and of work executed in good taste with munificent disregard of cost. The first gateway at Narnāla is decorated with elegant stone carving, which in Taylor's day was as perfect as it had ever been, and probably still is in the same condition. The works at Ausā and Parenda are commended for the military science displayed in their trace. The fortresses were equipped with huge guns built up of bars welded and bound together, of which several specimens still exist.

The buildings at Gulbarga are described as being heavy, gloomy, and roughly constructed. Those at Bidar, the capital from about 1430, are much superior in both design and workmanship. Enamelled tiles, a favourite Persian form of decoration, were applied to the Bidar edifices.

The Muslim population of the Deccan. The Bahmanī sultans failed in the atrocious attempt made more than once by members of the dynasty to exterminate the population of the Hindu states of the Deccan, or in default of extermination to drive it by force into the fold of Islam. They succeeded in killing hundreds of thousands of men, women, and children, and in making considerable numbers of 'converts'; but in spite of all their efforts the population continues to be Hindu in the main, the percentage of Muslims in the Nizam's former

SULTANS OF THE BAHMANĪ DYNASTY OF THE DECCAN

Name	Accession		Remarks
	A.H.	A.D.	
1. 'Alā-ud-dīn Hasan	748	1347	Full official title (according to the *Burhān-i Ma'āsir*) was Sultan 'Alā-ud-dīn Hasan Shāh al-walī al Bahmanī. He had been known previously as Zafar Khān. Died a natural death.
2. Muhammad I	759	1358	Son of No. 1. Died from the effects of 'an irreligious manner of living', presumably meaning drink.
3. Mujāhid	775	1373	Son of No. 2. Drank hard: murdered by No. 4.
4. Dāūd	779	1378	Son of brother of No. 2: murdered by a slave.
5. Muhammad II	780	1378	Brother of No. 4. Died a natural death. No wars or rebellions. Erroneously called Mahmūd by Firishta.
6. Ghiyās-ud-dīn	799	1397	Son of No. 5, and a minor. Blinded and deposed.
7. Shams-ud-dīn	799	1397	Brother of No. 6. Deposed and imprisoned, or blinded, according to Firishta.
8. Fīrūz	800	1397	Son of younger brother of No. 2. Deposed and strangled by No. 9.
9. Ahmad	825	1422	Brother of No. 8: changed capital to Bidar. Died a natural death.
10. 'Alā-ud-dīn II	838	1435	Son of No. 9. Died a natural death.
11. Humāyūn	862	1457	Son of No. 10, probably assassinated.
12. Nizām	865	1461	Son of No. 11, a minor. Died suddenly.
13. Muhammad III	867	1463	Brother of No. 12. Died from effects of drink.
14. Mahmūd	887	1482	Son of No. 13. Died a natural death in Dec. 1518, when the dynasty practically ended.

NOTE.—The names, genealogy, and order of succession are in accordance with the *Burhān-i Ma'āsir* and other authorities, supported by the coins. Firishta, who differs in certain matters, is in error. The dates also are given variously in the books; the most serious discrepancy, amounting to four years, being that concerning the death of No. 10, and the accession of No. 11. Many discrepancies occur in the minute details of dates which are not shown in the table. Kalīmullāh, the last nominal sultan, escaped to Bijapur, and thence retired to Ahmadnagar, where he died.

dominions and the Bijapur District being only about eleven. The origin of that section of the inhabitants, as noted by Meadows Taylor, is mainly a consequence of the Bahmanī rule, under which large numbers of Persians, Turks, Arabs, and Mughuls settled in the country and formed unions with native women. Many Hindu families also were forcibly converted, and the continuance of Muslim dynasties in large areas for centuries has kept up or even increased the proportion of the Muslim minority. The author cited was willing to credit the Bahmanī influence with 'a general amelioration of manners' in the Deccan, but that opinion might be disputed. The monuments of Hindu civilization certainly suffered severely.

AUTHORITIES

THE Persian histories are the leading authorities, FIRISHTA and others. The account of the dynasty in MEADOWS TAYLOR, *Manual of Indian History*[1] (Longmans, London, 1895), is based on Firishta, supplemented by local knowledge. Much additional material, completing the information from Persian books, has been printed by J. S. KING in *The History of the Bahmani Dynasty*, founded on the *Burhān-i Maʾāsir* (Luzac, London, 1900); reprinted from *Ind. Ant.*, vol. xxviii (Bombay, 1899), with additions from other chroniclers. The history is further elucidated by T. W. HAIG in 'Some Notes on the Bahmani Dynasty' (*J.A.S.B.*, part i, vol. lxxiii, 1904); in *Historic Landmarks of the Deccan* (Pioneer Press, Allahabad, 1907).

Some interesting material is obtained from the notes of ATHANASIUS NIKITIN, a Russian merchant, as edited in *India in the Fifteenth Century*, by R. H. MAJOR, Hakluyt Soc. (issued for 1858).

The inscriptions are treated by Haig, as above; and by HOROWITZ, *Epigraphia Moslemica* (Calcutta, 1909–10, 1912), s.v. Bidar, Gawilgarh, Gulbarga, and Kolhapur.

The coins are described and illustrated by O. CODRINGTON in *Num. Chron.*, 1898; and by H. N. WRIGHT, *Catal. of Coins in I. M.*, vol. ii (Clarendon Press, 1907). Both writers give references to earlier papers.

The architecture has been discussed to some extent by FERGUSSON, and also by BURGESS (A.S.W.I., vol. iii, London, 1878) and G. YAZDANI, *Antiquities of Bīdar*. The subject has been further examined by the ARCHAEOLOGICAL SURVEY OF THE NIZAM'S DOMINIONS: Annual Progress Reports, 1914–15 to 1922–3.

CHAPTER 2

The five sultanates of the Deccan, and Khandesh, from 1474 to the seventeenth century

The five sultanates. During the inglorious reign of Mahmūd Shāh Bahmanī (1482–1518), the provincial governors, as already mentioned, declared their independence one after the other, and set up five separate kingdoms or sultanates, namely, the Imād Shāhī dynasty of

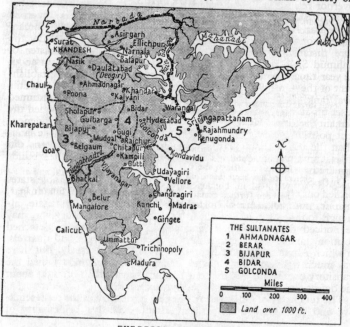

THE DECCAN SULTANATES

Berar; the Nizām Shāhī of Ahmadnagar; the Ādil Shāhī of Bijapur; the Barīd Shāhī of Bidar; and the Qutb Shāhī of Golkonda.

Imād Shāhī dynasty of Berar (Birār). The earliest defection was that of the province of Berar, the most northern portion of the Bahmanī dominions, and more or less equivalent to the ancient

Vidarbha, famous in Sanskrit literature. Berar was one of the four provinces into which the first Bahmanī sultan of the Deccan had divided his dominions. Late in the fifteenth century the province comprised two districts, namely, Gāwīl, the northern, and Māhūr, the southern. Early in the reign of Mahmūd Bahmanī, in the year 1484, according to most authorities, or 1490, according to others, the governor of Gawilgarh, a converted Hindu, named Fathullāh and entitled Imād-ul Mulk, proclaimed his independence, and made himself master of the whole province. He thus founded a dynasty, the Imād Shāhī, which lasted for four generations, until about 1574, when the principality was absorbed by Ahmadnagar. The details of its separate history, so far as recorded, are not of interest. The province was ceded in 1596 to Sultan Murād, son of Akbar. The imperial governor resided at first at Bālāpur, and later at Ilichpur (Ellichpur).

Barīd Shāhī dynasty of Bidar. The small principality governed by the Barīd Shāhī sultans was simply the residuum of the Bahmanī empire, consisting of the territory near the capital, left over after the more distant provinces had separated. Qāsim Barīd, minister of Mahmūd Shāh Bahmanī, was practically his own master from about the year 1492, which is given in some books as the date of the establishment of the dynasty. But he and his son Amīr long delayed to assume royal rank, and even after the death of Mahmūd in 1518 continued to set up and murder nominal Bahmanī sultans until 1527, when the formality was dispensed with, and Amīr openly assumed an independent position.[1] The dynasty lasted until about 1619 or a little later, when the territory was annexed by Bijapur. The Barīd sultans did little, if anything, deserving of remembrance; but some of their buildings are noteworthy.

Qutb Shāhī dynasty of Golkonda. The three considerable states formed out of the fragments of the Bahmanī empire were Ahmadnagar, Bijapur, and Golkonda (Gulkandah). The Golkonda sultanate, although founded the last of all, in 1518, and the latest survivor, may be noticed first, because it remained in a comparatively detached position, taking only a minor part in the endless wars and quarrels, in which Ahmadnagar and Bijapur intervened more freely. But there was much fighting with Bijapur, and in 1565 Golkonda joined the transitory confederacy of the four Muslim kings which brought about the defeat and destruction of the Vijayanagar Raj.

The territory of Golkonda. The new kingdom was the representative and successor of the ancient Hindu Kakatīya principality of

---

[1] According to Firishta, who depended on oral tradition for this dynasty, Amīr Barīd, who died in A.D. 1530 (A.H. 945), never called himself sultan or by any equivalent title. His son, Alī Barīd, 'is the first of this dynasty who adopted the style of shah or king; for though his grandfather Qāsim Barīd assumed regalia, he did not take the royal title'. Compare the case of the so-called Sayyid dynasty of Delhi, the members of which never assumed the royal title or struck coins in their own names.

Warangal,[1] which had been reduced by Ahmad Shāh Bahmanī early in his reign, about 1423. The territory was extensive, lying for the most part between the lower courses of the Godavari and Krishna rivers, and extending to the coast of the Bay of Bengal, along the face of the deltas. The western frontier was mostly identical with the eastern boundary of the Bidar principality. A northern extension was enclosed between the Godavari, Pen Ganga, and Wain Ganga rivers. The land was fertile, and the old irrigation works of Hindu times were maintained and extended by the sultans.

The sultans. The founder of the dynasty, a Turki officer, who assumed the title of Sultan Qulī Qutb Shāh, had been appointed governor of the eastern province by Mahmūd Gāwān. He withdrew from the Bahmanī court after the wrongful execution of that minister, but continued to recognize the sovereignty of Mahmūd Shāh until 1518, when he refused to submit any longer to the Barīd ascendancy, and declared his independence.

The first Qutbī sultan enjoyed a long life and prosperous reign, surviving until he had attained the age of ninety in 1543, when he was murdered at the instigation of his son Jamshīd. The parricide reigned for seven years. The crown was then (1550), after a short interval, offered to and accepted by a brother of Jamshīd named Ibrāhīm, who joined in the confederacy against Vijayanagar (1565), and died in 1580. His administration is reputed to have been good. In his time Hindus were freely employed in the service of the state and were permitted to attain high official rank. His son, Muhammad Qulī, lived until 1611, after which date the dynasty almost ceased to have a separate history, its affairs becoming entangled with those of the Mughul emperors of Hindostan. The state was finally annexed by Aurangzeb in 1687.

The capital. The capital had been moved from Warangal to Golkonda by the first sultan at the beginning of his reign. The new city was greatly developed in the reign of Ibrāhīm, but in 1589 it had become unhealthy. The court was then transferred to Bhāgnagar a few miles distant, which soon afterwards was called Hyderabad. The city thus created developed later as the capital of the Nizams and now has a population of about 750,000. Golkonda, largely in ruins, is best known for the tombs of the Qutb Shāhī kings.

The Nizām Shāhī dynasty of Ahmadnagar. Nizām-ul-Mulk Bahrī, the head of the Deccani party at Bidar, who had contrived the death of Mahmūd Gāwān, came to a violent end not long after. His son Malik Ahmad, governor of Junnār (Joonair) to the north of Poona, then revolted. In 1490 he defeated decisively the army of Mahmūd Bahmanī, and established himself as an independent sovereign. After a time he moved his court to a more convenient and strategically better position farther east, and so founded the city of

---

[1] Warangal is a corruption of Orukkal, meaning 'solitary rock', with reference to a prominent feature of the site of the old capital.

Ahmadnagar. The new sovereign having assumed the title of Ahmad Nizām Shāh, the dynasty established by him is called the Nizām Shāhī. Ahmadnagar is still a considerable town and the headquarters of a district in the Maharashtra state.

The main efforts of Ahmad Nizām Shāh for years were directed to the acquisition of the powerful fortress of Deogiri or Daulatabad, formerly the capital of the Yādava kingdom. Ultimately, he obtained the surrender of the place, in A.D. 1499, and thus consolidated his dominion.

The second and third sultans. The second sovereign, Burhān Nizām Shāh, who reigned for forty-five years (1508–53), was engaged in many wars with the neighbouring states, and made a new departure about 1550 by allying himself with the Hindu raya of Vijayanagar against the sultan of Bijapur. Some years earlier (1537) Burhān had himself adopted the Shia form of Islam. His successor, Husain Shāh, joined the confederacy which sacked Vijayanagar in 1565.

Later history. The subsequent history of the dynasty may be read in great detail in the pages of Firishta, who long resided at Ahmadnagar, but the incidents are not of much interest. Berar was absorbed in 1574. Chānd Bībī, the queen dowager of Bijapur, who had returned to Ahmadnagar, made a gallant and successful resistance to Akbar's son, Prince Murad, in 1596, purchasing peace by the cession of Berar. But war soon broke out again, and in August 1600 after Chānd Bībī had perished at the hands of the mob, the Mughul army stormed Ahmadnagar. Those events, which belong to the history of Akbar rather than to that of the minor kingdom, will be dealt with more fully when the story of his reign comes to be told. Akbar, although he formally gave Ahmadnagar the rank of a new Sūba or province, never obtained possession of more than a small portion of the kingdom. The remainder continued an obscure independent existence, and the state was not finally annexed until 1637 in the reign of Shāhjahān.

The Ādil Shāhī dynasty of Bijapur; the first sultan. Bijapur, the most important and interesting of the five sultanates or kingdoms, deserves more extended notice. The dynasty was known as the Ādil Shāhī, from the name of its founder, Yūsuf Ādil Khān, governor of Bijapur, who declared his independence in 1489, almost simultaneously with his colleagues in Berar and Ahmadnagar.

Yūsuf Ādil, so far as public knowledge went, was simply a Georgian slave who had been purchased by Khwāja Mahmūd Gāwān, and by reason of his own abilities and the discerning patronage of the minister had risen to high office at the Bahmanī court, ultimately becoming governor of Bijapur. But according to private information, accepted by Firishta on respectable authority, he was really a son of Sultan Murād II of Turkey, and had been brought up secretly in Persia. When the disguised prince was seventeen years old he seems to have found continued residence in Persia to be unsafe, and therefore allowed himself to be disposed of as a slave and sold in Bidar to the minister of the Bahmanī sultan. Firishta apparently was sati~fied as to the truth of the story.

Firishta's history. Firishta's history, written in a spirit of remarkable independence, presents an agreeable contrast when compared with Abu-l Fazl's too courtly *Akbarnāma*. But most of the wars and intrigues which seemed so important to the historian at the beginning of the seventeenth century are now seen to have had little or no effect on the development of India as a whole, and to be of only provincial interest. However, certain matters in the story of Bijapur and its rulers still deserve a place in the pages of even a short history of India.

Preference of Yūsuf Ādil Shāh for the Shia religion. Yūsuf Ādil Shāh waged wars against Vijayanagar and his Muslim neighbours with varying fortune. When residing in Persia in his youth he had learned to prefer the Shia form of Islam, and subsequently made a vow to profess publicly that faith. In 1502 he carried out his purpose, making the Shia creed the state religion, while giving free and untrammelled toleration to the Sunnis. A dangerous confederacy of neighbouring princes caused him to abandon this measure for a while, but later 'he renewed the public exercise of the Shia religion'.

Capture of Goa by the Portuguese. In those days Goa was a favourite residence of Yūsuf Ādil Shāh, who at one time thought of making the port the seat of his government. It was the rendezvous of the Muslims of the Deccan who used to embark there for the pilgrimage to Mecca. In February 1510 (A.H. 915) the king's officers negligently permitted the Portuguese commander, Albuquerque, to surprise the city and occupy it without the loss of a man. But the sultan, being determined to recover his much prized possession, prepared an overwhelming force and won back Goa in August of the same year 1510 (A.H. 916). Albuquerque's fleet, which was reduced to intense distress during the rainy season, received reinforcements in the autumn. The death of Yūsuf Ādil Shāh at the age of seventy-four, in October or November, weakened the defence, so that the Portuguese succeeded in storming the city after a hard fight.

Marriage with Marathi lady. Instances of Muslim princes in the Deccan marrying Hindu wives have been mentioned. Yūsuf Ādil Shāh early in his reign defeated a Maratha chieftain named Mukund Rāo, whose sister he espoused. She took the Muslim name of Būbūjī Khānam, and became the mother of the second sultan as well as of three princesses who were married to members of the royal families of the neighbouring Muslim states. Yūsuf Ādil Shāh freely admitted Hindus to offices of trust. The Marathi language was ordinarily used for purposes of accounts and business.

Character of Yūsuf Ādil Shāh. The first sultan or shah of Bijapur is given a high character by Firishta, who testifies on good authority that he was 'a wise prince, intimately acquainted with human nature', handsome, eloquent, well read, and a skilled musician.

Although he mingled pleasure with business, yet he never allowed the former to interfere with the latter. He always warned his ministers to act with justice and integrity, and in his own person showed them an example of attention to those virtues. He invited to his court many learned men and valiant officers from Persia, Turkistan, and Rūm, also several eminent artists, who lived happy under the shadow of his bounty. In his reign the citadel of Bijāpur was built of stone.

He lies buried, not at Bijapur, but at Gūgī or Gogī, farther to the east, near the grave of a saint whom he venerated.

No mausoleum was built over him; and in the precincts of the holy burying-ground his open tomb is as simple as many others, and an endow-ment, which has been preserved, still provides a covering of cotton chintz for it, renewed from year to year. Thus, as the people of Gogī assert, with an honourable pride, there are not as yet faithful servants wanting to the noble king to light a lamp at night at his grave, and to say *fatihas* for his soul's peace, while the tombs of the great Bahmanī kings and of all his enemies in life are desecrated.[1]

Ismāīl Shāh. The new king, Ismāīl, being a minor, the govern-ment was carried on by Kamāl Khān, an officer of the late ruler, as regent. He proved faithless, and conspired to seize the throne for him-self, but lost his life in the attempt. Like other kings of the period Ismāīl was fated to spend most of his time in fighting his neighbours. He recovered from Vijayanagar the Raichur Doab, the much disputed country between the Krishna and Tungabhadra. Ismāīl was so much pleased at the arrival of an embassy from the shah of Persia, who recognized Bijapur as an independent state, that he directed the officers of his army to wear the head-dress distinctive of the Shia sect. He rests beside his father, whom he resembled in character and accomplish-ments. The son, Mallū, who succeeded him, proved to be incurably vicious and incompetent. Accordingly he was blinded and deposed, the sceptre passing into the hands of his brother Ibrāhīm after a few months.

Ibrāhīm Ādil Shāh I. The new ruler, who assumed the title of Ibrāhīm Ādil Shāh, rejected foreign practices, including the use of the Shia head-dress, and reverted completely to Sunni ritual. He favoured the Deccanis, with their allies the Abyssinians, as against the Persians and other foreigners. Many of the strangers entered the service of Rāmarāja, the *de facto* ruler of Vijayanagar. At this time revolutions occurred at Vijayanagar which will be noticed more particularly in the history of that kingdom. In 1535 the Bijapur sultan accepted the in-vitation of the chief of one of the Hindu factions and paid a visit to Vijayanagar lasting a week. He departed enriched by an enormous present of gold coin, in addition to valuable horses and elephants. Subsequently the sultans of Bidar, Ahmadnagar, and Golkonda com-bined against Bijapur, which emerged victorious, thanks to the ability

---

[1] Meadows Taylor, *Manual,* p. 198.

of the minister, Asad Khān, whose reputation is scarcely inferior to that of Mahmūd Gāwān. It is needless to follow in detail the wars and intrigues which lasted throughout the reign. The sultan towards the end of his life abandoned himself to drink and debauchery, came to a dishonoured death in 1557, and was buried at Gogī by the side of his father and grandfather.

Alī Ādil Shāh. Alī Ādil Shāh, having succeeded his father, Ibrāhīm, began his administration by publicly resuming the Shia creed, professing it with a degree of intolerance which his ancestor had carefully avoided. In 1558, the sultan having made a transitory alliance with Rāmarāja, the combined Hindu and Muslim armies invaded the territory of Ahmadnagar, which they ravaged mercilessly—the Hindus taking the opportunity to avenge with pitiless savagery all the injuries which they had suffered from Muslim hands in the course of two centuries. The barbarous excesses committed by Rāmarāja and the insolence shown by him to his Muslim allies alienated Alī Ādil Shāh, who was advised that no single Muslim sovereign was capable of contending with success against the wealth and hosts of the arrogant Hindu prince. Ultimately all the four sultans of Bijapur, Bidar, Ahmadnagar, and Golkonda were convinced that their interests required them to sacrifice their rivalries and combine in an irresistible league in order to effect the destruction of the infidel. With a view to draw closer the bonds of alliance, Alī Ādil Shāh married Chānd Bībī, daughter of Husain Nizām Shāh of Ahmadnagar, whose sister was given to the son of the sultan of Bijapur.

Alliance against Vijayanagar. In December 1564 the four allied sovereigns established their joint headquarters at the small town of Talikota, situated about twenty-five miles to the north of the Krishna, in 16° 28′ N. lat. and 76° 19′ E. long.

The Vijayanagar government, in full confidence of victory, prepared to meet the threatened invasion by the assemblage of enormous levies numbering several hundred thousand men. Two large armies were sent forward under the command of Rāmarāja's brothers, Tirumala and Venkatādri, with orders to prevent the army of Islam from crossing the Krishna. But the allied princes by a simple stratagem got across by the ford of Ingaligi. The aged Rāmarāja then moved up from Vijayanagar with the main army, and encamped somewhere near the fortress of Mudgal, so often the subject of dispute between the Hindus and the Muslims.

Battle of Talikota. Battle was joined on 23 January 1565.[1] The forces on both sides being unusually numerous the fighting must have extended over a front of many miles. The Muslim centre was commanded by Husain Nizām Shāh of Ahmadnagar, who possessed a powerful park of artillery; Alī Ādil Shāh of Bijapur led the right wing; and the left wing was entrusted to Alī Barīd Shāh of Golkonda. 'The artillery, fastened together by strong chains and ropes, was drawn up

[1] Mr. Sewell correctly points out that the week-day was Tuesday, not Friday, as stated by Firishta.

in front of the line, and the war elephants were placed in various positions, according to custom. Each prince erected his particular standard in the centre of his own army, and the allies moved in close order against the enemy.'

Rāmarāja, then an old man, although in full possession of his faculties, commanded the centre opposed to the king of Ahmadnagar. His brother Tirumala encountered Alī Ādil Shāh of Bijapur, while his other brother, Venkatādri, fought against the princes of Bidar and Golkonda. After much strenuous fighting the Bijapur and Golkonda chiefs gave way and thought of retiring, but the Ahmadnagar sultan stood firm in the centre. Just then a furious elephant rushed at the litter in which Rāmarāja was seated, so that his frightened bearers let him drop. He was thus taken prisoner, and at once beheaded by Husain Nizām Shāh with his own hands. The head was placed on the point of a long spear so that it might be seen by the enemy. 'The Hindus according to custom, when they saw their chief destroyed, fled in the utmost disorder from the field, and were pursued by the allies with such success that the river was dyed red with their blood. It is computed by the best authorities that above one hundred thousand infidels were slain during the action and the pursuit.'

Results of the battle. The victory, known to history as the battle of Talikota, because the allies had assembled at that town, distant about thirty miles from the battlefield, was one of the decisive conflicts of Indian history. The Hindus made no attempt to dispute the verdict of the sword. The extensive Hindu empire of the south, which had lasted for more than two centuries, was largely dissolved, and the supremacy of Islam in the Deccan was assured. The noble city of Vijayanagar was blotted out of existence and remains desolate to this day. The dominions of both Bijapur and Golkonda were enlarged considerably.

League against the Portuguese; death of the sultan. In 1570 the sovereigns of Bijapur and Ahmadnagar again joined their forces and attempted to capture the settlements of the Portuguese, then at the climax of their power. But even the help of the zamorin of Calicut and the raja of Achin did not suffice to enable them to win success. The siege of Goa by a huge army was raised after ten months, although the defence had been maintained by only 700 European soldiers, supported by 300 friars and priests, 1,000 slaves, and some ill-equipped boats. Alī Ādil Shāh was killed in 1579 by a eunuch who had good reason for his act.

Ibrāhīm Ādil Shāh II. The heir to the throne, Ibrāhīm Ādil Shāh II, being a minor, was taken charge of by his mother, Chānd Bībī, while ministers ruled the kingdom. In 1584 the queen mother returned to her native city of Ahmadnagar, and never visited Bijapur again. We shall hear presently of her gallant doings in the conflict with Akbar. In 1595 the last fight between Bijapur and Ahmadnagar took place, and the Ahmadnagar monarch was killed. From that time the separate history of both states may be said to end, their annals becoming merged in those of the Mughul empire. Ibrāhīm Ādil Shāh II survived until 1626, when he died, leaving a great reputation as an able administrator. The testimony of Meadows Taylor, who was well acquainted with the country and local tradition, may be quoted:

Ibrāhīm Ādil Shāh died in 1626, in the fifty-sixth year of his age. He was the greatest of all the Ādil Shāhī dynasty, and in most respects, except its founder, the most able and popular.

Without the distraction of war, he applied himself to civil affairs with much care; and the land settlements of the provinces of his kingdom, many of which are still extant among district records, show an admirable and efficient system of registration of property and its valuation. In this respect the system of Todar Mull introduced by the Emperor Akbar seems to have been followed with the necessary local modifications.

Although he changed the profession of the State religion immediately upon assuming the direction of State affairs from Shīa to Sunnī, Ibrāhīm was yet extremely tolerant of all creeds and faiths. Hindus not only suffered no persecution at his hands, but many of his chief civil and military officers were Brahmans and Marāthās.[1] With the Portuguese of Goa he seems to have kept up a friendly intercourse. Portuguese painters decorated his palaces, and their merchants traded freely in his dominions. To their missionaries also he extended his protection; and there are many anecdotes current in the country that his tolerance of Christians equalled, if it did not exceed, that of his contemporary Akbar. He allowed the preaching of Christianity freely among his people, and there are still existent several Catholic churches, one at Chītapur, one at Mudgal, and one at Rāichūr, and others, endowed by the king with lands and other sources of revenue, which have survived the changes and revolutions of more than 300 years. Each of these churches now consists of several hundred members and remains under the spiritual jurisdiction of the Archbishop of Goa.

Ibrāhīm's dominions extended to the borders of Mysore. At the time of his death he left to his successor a full treasury and a well-paid army of 80,000 horse.

The splendid architectural monuments of his reign will be noticed presently.

It is not necessary to pursue the local history farther. The capital was taken and the country was annexed by Aurangzeb in 1686.

Fārūqī dynasty of Khandesh. Before quitting the subject of the Muslim kingdoms of the Deccan we may bestow a passing glance on the small kingdom of Khandesh in the valley of the Tapti, whose rulers were known as the Fārūqī dynasty. The principality, which did not form part of the Bahmanī kingdom, was established in 1388 at the close of the reign of Sultan Fīrūz Tughluq of Delhi, and took a share in the innumerable local wars. It was sometimes a dependency of Gujarat. The importance of the state resulted chiefly from its possession

---

[1] Ibrāhīm's partiality for Hindus led his Muslim subjects to give him the mocking title of *Jagad-guru*, or 'World-Preceptor'. Akbar conferred that title in all seriousness on his own favourite Jain instructor, and received it himself informally from Hindu admirers.

of the strong fortress of Asirgarh. The seat of government was Bur-hanpur. The surrender of Asirgarh to Akbar in January 1601 put an end to the dynasty and the independence of the state, which became the Sūba of Khandesh or Dāndēsh.

THE ĀDIL SHĀHĪ KINGS OR SULTANS OF BIJAPUR

Name	Accession	Remarks
	A.D.	
1. Yūsuf	1490	Had been governor under the Bahmanī king.
2. Ismaïl	1510	Son of No. 1.
3. Mallū	1534	Son of No. 2; deposed and blinded after six months.
4. Ibrāhīm I	1535	Brother of No. 3.
5. Alī	1557	Son of No. 4; assassinated. Destruction of Vijayanagar in 1565.
6. Ibrāhīm II	1580	Nephew of No. 5; good civil administration; fine buildings.
7. Muhammad	1626	Son of No. 6; became tributary to Shahjahan in 1636; Maratha aggression began.
8. Alī II	1656	Son of No. 7; war with Sivaji.
9. Sikandar	1673	Made captive by Aurangzeb, and dynasty extinguished in 1686.

Art and Literature. The monuments of the Bahmanī dynasty at Gulbarga and Bidar have been briefly noticed.

At Ahmadnagar the principal ancient building is the ruined Bhadr palace in white stone, built by the founder of the city, which possesses few other architectural remains of importance. The chief mosque at Burhanpur, the capital of the Fārūqī kings of Khandesh, erected by Alī Khān in 1588, is described as a fine building adorned with stone carvings executed in perfect taste. But Fergusson formed the opinion that the edifices of the town have 'very little artistic value'.

At Golkonda and Bijapur important schools of architecture developed, differing one from the other and from the styles of northern India. The precincts of the Golkonda fortress include a multitude of palaces, mosques, and other ancient buildings. The tombs of the Qutb Shāhī kings, which stand outside the fortress about half a mile to the north, are built of granite and characterized by narrow-necked domes of peculiar form.

The works executed to the orders of the Ādil Shāhī kings of Bijapur are 'marked by a grandeur of conception and boldness in construction unequalled by any edifices erected in India'. The gigantic walls of the city, begun by Yūsuf, the first sultan, and completed by Alī, the fifth sovereign, are six and a quarter miles in circumference, and still perfect for the most part.

The four leading builders at Bijapur were the kings Yūsuf (1490–1510), Alī (1558–80), Ibrāhīm II (1580–1626), and Muhammad Shāh

(^?6–56). The principal mosque, an admirably proportioned building, erected by Alī, is still perfect, and would accommodate 5,000 worshippers. The same sovereign constructed aqueducts for the supply of water to all parts of the city, and also built the spacious audience-hall or Gagan Mahall (1561). The richly decorated tomb of Ibrāhīm II is an exquisite structure; and the mausoleum of his successor, Muhammad (1626–56), built at the same time as the Tāj, is a marvel of skilful construction. The dome is the second largest in the world. The names of the architects employed do not seem to be recorded, and it is impossible to say whether they were foreigners or of Indian birth. The style shows traces of both foreign and native ideas.

Fine libraries are known to have existed at Ahmadnagar and Bijapur. One illuminated manuscript from the latter is in the British Museum. The excellent history of Muhammad Qāsim, surnamed Firishta, was written to the command of Ibrāhīm II of Bijapur. The author mentions many earlier writers whose works are not now extant.

The town of Bijapur, which long lay deserted and desolate, has revived in modern times, and is the prosperous headquarters of a district in the Bombay Presidency, with considerable trade and a population of about 25,000 persons.

AUTHORITIES

The Five Sultanates and Khandesh

THE principal authority is FIRISHTA, whose narratives are supplemented by observations recorded by SEWELL (*A Forgotten Empire*) and MEADOWS TAYLOR (*Manual of the History of India*). For relations with the Portuguese I have used FONSECA, *Sketch of the City of Goa* (Bombay, Thacker, 1878), a sound book based on the official records of the settlement. See also T. W. HAIG, 'The History of the Nizām Shāhī Kings of Ahmadnagar', in *Indian Antiquary*, 1920–3; 'Historic Landmarks of the Deccan', Allahabad, 1907; and G. YAZDANI, *Antiquities of Bīdar*.

The monuments are briefly described in FERGUSSON, *Hist. of Eastern and Ind. Archit.*[2], 1910, and other works there cited. The information about Bijapur is tolerably full, and the principal buildings there are in good condition. See also V. A. SMITH, *H.F.A.*, Oxford, 1911. A good detailed catalogue of the Bijapur buildings (with plan of city) will be found in the *Revised Lists of Antiquarian Remains in the Bombay Presidency*, 2nd ed., 1897 (vol. xvi, *A.S. India*, New Imp. Ser.). All works on Bijapur are superseded by the magnificent volume *Bijāpur and its Architectural Remains, with an Historical Outline of the 'Ādil Shāhī Dynasty*, by HENRY COUSENS, Bombay Government Central Press, 1916, pp. xii, 132, The coinage is described in the monograph by Mr. Cousens, pp. 127, 128, pl. cxv. The known specimens, issued by five of the Sultans, comprise three gold and two or three hundred copper coins, besides the curious *lārins*, made of stamped silver wire.

The ARCHAEOLOGICAL SOCIETY OF HYDERABAD has plenty of unpublished material of all kinds on which to work. The first number of the *Journal* contains an interesting article on Warangal.

CHAPTER 3

The Hindu empire of Vijayanagar, from A.D. 1336 to 1646

Special interest of the history. Although the history of the Hindu empire of Vijayanagar is closely entwined with that of the Muslim Bahmanī empire and the later sultanates of the Deccan for more than two centuries, it is impracticable to combine the two histories in a single narrative. Separate treatment is inevitable, but a certain amount of repetition cannot be avoided. The story of the Hindu monarchy which proved a barrier to the armies of Islam is one of singular interest, and might be narrated with a fullness of detail rarely possible in Indian history. The multitude of relevant inscriptions, numbering many hundreds, is extraordinary. Several European and Muslim travellers from the fourteenth to the sixteenth century have recorded the historical traditions of the empire with vivid descriptions of the system of government and the glories of the magnificent capital. The study of the polity, manners, customs, and religion of the Vijayanagar empire merits particular attention, because the state was the embodiment of the Telinga or Telugu and Kanarese forms of Hinduism which differed widely from the more familiar forms of the north. The sources of our knowledge are not confined to inscriptions and the notes of foreign observers. The Muslim historians who lived in the Deccan, headed by Firishta, give valuable information; and much may be learned from critical examination of the monuments and coins. A remarkable school of art was developed at Vijayanagar, and literature, both Sanskrit and Telugu, was cultivated with success.

Foreign relations of Vijayanagar. The external history of the Vijayanagar empire is mainly that of wars with the various Muslim dynasties of the Deccan. But from the middle of the fifteenth century both parties occasionally found it convenient to forget their principles and to enter into unholy temporary alliances. In the end the Muslims, who were more vigorous, better mounted, and better armed than the Hindus, won the long contest. Their destruction of the city of Vijayanagar in 1565 effectually put an end to the Hindu empire of the south as such. But the victory did not immediately increase very largely the territory under Muslim rule. The peninsula to the south of the Tungabhadra continued to be essentially Hindu, governed by a multitude of Hindu chiefs, uncontrolled by any paramount power. While the foreign relations of Vijayanagar were in the main concerned with the Muslim sultanates, the Hindu empire also had important dealings with the Portuguese, who first arrived on the Malabar coast in 1498, and established themselves permanently at Goa late in 1510. We are indebted to Portuguese authors for the best accounts of the polity and manners of the great Hindu state.

Origin of the kingdom or empire. In 1323 Pratāparudra, the Kākatīya ruler of Warangal, was defeated and overthrown by Ulugh Khān, the general of Sultan Ghaiyās-ud-dīn. Two brothers, Harihara and Bukka, treasury superintendents of the defeated raja, thereupon fled to the court of Kampili and there took service. Three years later Kampiladeva was in his turn overthrown for having sheltered the rebel refugee Garshāsp, and his two officers Harihara and Bukka were carried prisoner to Delhi.

In 1328–9 Muhammad bin Tughluq's withdrawal was the signal for Hindu resurgence in the Deccan, notably that of Kāpaya Nāyaka the leader of the Telingana Hindus, who by 1336 built up a kingdom on the east coast. In the same years there were rebellions against Malik Muhammad, the governor of Kampili, who had soon to call on Delhi for help. The sultan—so Nuniz and Baranī say—decided to appoint a new governor, with local influence and chose Harihara and Bukka, now converts to Islam. They advanced with an army and took Gutti and later Anegondi. By 1336 the area subdued was quite extensive.[1]

The rebellion of Ahsan Khān in Ma'bar led the sultan to move south in 1334–5, but at Warangal both he and his army were smitten by plague. Rumours of the sultan's death caused revolts in the north and the expedition was abandoned. This in turn brought further Hindu risings, and Harihara now joined with Kāpaya Nāyaka in throwing off the Muslim yoke. Continuing disorders in the sultanate enabled the brothers to establish the nucleus of the Vijayanagar state. 'Malik Maqbul, the naib-wazir, fled to Delhi', writes Baranī, 'and the Hindus took possession of Warangal, which was thus entirely lost, and fell into the hands of the Hindus. Devgir and Gujarat alone remained secure.'

Early chiefs ; Harihara and Bukka. The traditional date for the foundation of Vijayanagar on the southern bank of the Tungabhadrā, facing the older fortress of Anegondi on the northern bank, is A.D. 1336. The building of it was finished in 1343. It is certain that ten years later the brothers were in a position to claim control over 'the whole country between the Eastern and the Western Oceans'.

Harihara established order within the kingdom, and organized it into new subdivisions of villages and *sthala*, each under a *karnam*. The *karnams* were normally Brahmans. Agriculture he encouraged by rewards to those who cleared forest lands, and easy terms for the cultivators.

Bukka, who had been governor of the Western Telegu districts, with Gooty as his headquarters, was increasingly associated with his brother in his rule, and, on the death of the latter in 1354–5, succeeded to power. Bukka ruled until his death in 1377. Most of his life was spent in waging war against the Bahmanī kings, notably Muhammad Shāh (1358–73).

[1] For the view that Harihara and Bukka were chieftains under the Hoysala or Ballala kings of the Mysore country see H. Heras, *Beginnings of Vijayanagar*.

PLATE 17

b. Shahjahan

a. Aurangzeb

PLATE 18

b. Amar Singh of Mewar and his sons

a. Raja Man Singh

Harihara II, 1377–1404. His reign coincided roughly with that of Muhammad Shāh II, the fifth of the Bahmanī sultans, and the only peaceable man of his dynasty. Harihara consequently was free to extend and consolidate his dominion over the whole of south India. He began by uniting the Vijayanagar kingdom, hitherto a confederacy under five brothers, replacing his cousins by his own sons. One of these sons, Devarāya, was responsible for the slow advance towards the Krishna as north-east boundary of the kingdom, which was secured by the expulsion of the Reddis of Kondavīdu. There was expansion elsewhere —Goa, Kharēpatan, Chaul, and Dabhol were taken, and Trichinopoly and Kanchi included within his dominions. He was tolerant of various forms of religion, but gave his personal devotion to Śiva-Virūpāksha.

Devarāya I. On Harihara's death, Virupāksa first seized power but was quickly ousted by the Yuvaraja, or heir designate, Bukka II, who was in turn overthrown by Devarāya after some two years' rule.

This period of disorder was utilized by the active Sultan Fīrūz, who in 1406 conquered several districts, momentarily entered the capital, and secured both tribute and a daughter of Devarāya. At the same time the Reddis of Kondavīdu, who are known to have been allied with the Bahmanis, recaptured the eastern districts lost to Harihara II. Attempts to use divisions among the Reddis only led to further defeats for Devarāya, and the establishment of the sultan as overlord of Telingana.

Devarāya II. Devarāya I died in 1422, and was briefly succeeded by his son Rāmachandra. He in his turn was succeeded by Vijaya— known to have suppressed a rebellion in western Udayagir in 1421— whose reign extended from 1422 to 1425–6. For part of this period the Yuvarāja, Devarāya II, shared in the administration.

During his reign (1425/6–46) Devarāya was able to absorb the distracted Reddi lands of Kondavīdu, and thus to establish the Krishna as his north-east boundary. By 1444 he had even advanced to Rajahmundry. He also established his supremacy over all Kerala, except Calicut—of whose ruler the visiting 'Abdur-Razzāq wrote, 'although he is not under his (Devarāya's) authority, nevertheless he is in great alarm and apprehension from him'. In the north, however, Devarāya had to meet the attacks of Fīrūz Shāh's brother and successor, Ahmad Shāh (1422–35). The Hindu kingdom of Warangal was finally overthrown by him in 1425. To face this threat, Devarāya II seems to have considerably extended the recruitment of Muslim troops, recognizing his lack of well-mounted cavalry and archers.

Decline of the dynasty. In 1447, after the reign of Vijaya II, Mallikārjuna came to power. He was unable to control the nobles and was subject to vigorous attack from Sultan 'Alā-ud-dīn II and from the Orissa ruler Kapilēsvara who, by 1449, had overrun Rajahmundry and Kondavīdu. In 1463 the Uriya forces, masters since 1460 of Warangal, raided as far south as Kanchi.

In 1465 Mallikārjuna was succeeded by his cousin Virūpāksa II. He is described by Nuniz as 'given over to vice, caring for nothing but women, and to fuddle himself with drink'. The successes of this period were won by a noble of Chandragiri, Sāluva Narasimha, who had taken advantage of the death of Kapilēsvara to push his conquests from Udayagiri to the southern bank of the Godaveri. Many of these gains were lost later to Sultan Muhammad Shāh III.

The first usurpation. Virūpāksa II was murdered by his eldest son in 1485, who was in turn assassinated by a worthless younger brother. Sāluva Narasimha thereupon seized power. But it was only with much difficulty that the weakened central authority was restored, for although the imbecile Sultan Mahmūd II could not attack, the Uriya King Purusōthama did so. By 1489 he had retaken the Godaveri delta whence, crossing the Krishna, he invaded Kondavīdu. Narasimha was taken prisoner in a battle for Udayagiri, which was surrendered as the price of his liberty.

Nevertheless Narasimha did restore the authority of the government. The garrisoning of Honavar, Bhatkal, and other Malabar ports also served to strengthen the army by permitting the trade in Arabian and Persian horses to be resumed, after having been closed by the loss of Goa, Chaul, and Dabhol.

The second usurpation. Narasimha died in 1490–1, and was succeeded by his son, Immadi Narasimha, a minor. The regent, Narasa Nāyaka, a Tuluva, usurped real power, and eventually made the boy a state prisoner. In this period came the first of many struggles for the Raichur Doab between Vijayanagar and the newly founded kingdom of Bijapur. The regent was also much occupied by rebellions, but he did achieve successes in the south. He died in 1503.

His son and successor, Vīra Narasimha, soon threw off the mask of regency and had Immadi brutally murdered. His reign (1505–9) was actively filled by suppression of the revolts of the nobles, resistance to 'Ādil Shāhī attacks, and reassertion of control over the western ports.

His successor, a half-brother, Krishnadevarāya, was the greatest of the dynasty. He reigned from 1509 to 1529 and was thus a contemporary of Henry VIII of England.

Within six months of his accession he had met the attack of Sultan Mahmūd of Bidar and thrown him back wounded. Yūsuf 'Ādil Khān, attempting to stem Krishnadevarāya's advance, was defeated and killed. In 1510 he again advanced north, besieging Raichur, and thence moving to Gulburga and Bidar.

With the north secure, Krishnadevarāya was able to turn south, and there he overthrew the rebels of Ummattur, whose territory was made into a new province with Sriringapattanam as its capital. Thereafter he turned against the Uriya ruler, Pratāparudra, from whom he wrested Kondavīdu and the lands up to the Krishna. From Bezwada he pushed westwards into Telingana, and then, in 1516–17 to beyond the Godaveri.

His most famous fight took place on 19 May 1520, and resulted in the recovery of the much disputed fortress of Raichur from Ismā'īl 'Ādil Shāh of Bijapur. The Hindus gained a great victory in a contest so deadly that they lost more than 16,000 killed. The story of the fight is vividly told by the contemporary Portuguese chronicler, Nuniz. The raya, a man of a generous and chivalrous temper, used his victory with humanity and moderation. In the course of subsequent operations he temporarily occupied Bijapur, which was mostly destroyed by his soldiers tearing down buildings for fuel; and he razed to the ground the fortress of Gulburga, the early capital of the Bahmanīs. He died in 1529.

Description of the raya by Paes. Paes gives a good personal description of Krishnadevarāya:

This king is of medium height, and of fair complexion and good figure, rather fat than thin; he has on his face signs of small-pox. He is the most feared and perfect king that could possibly be, cheerful of disposition and very merry; he is one that seeks to honour foreigners, and receives them kindly, asking about all their affairs whatever their condition may be. He is a great ruler and a man of much justice, but subject to sudden fits of rage, and this is his title:

'Crisnarao Macação, king of kings, lord of the greater lords of India, lord of the three seas and of the land.'

Character of Krishnadevarāya. The dark pages of the sanguinary story of the medieval kingdoms of the Deccan, whether Hindu or Muslim, are relieved by few names of men who claim respect on their personal merits. The figure of Krishnadevarāya stands out as one such. A mighty warrior, he

was in no way less famous for his religious zeal and catholicity. He respected all sects of the Hindu religion alike, though his personal leanings were in favour of Vaishnavism.... Krishna Rāya's kindness to the fallen enemy, his acts of mercy and charity towards the residents of captured cities, his great military prowess which endeared him alike to his feudatory chiefs and to his subjects, the royal reception and kindness that he invariably bestowed upon foreign embassies, his imposing personal appearance, his genial look and polite conversation which distinguished a pure and dignified life, his love for literature and for religion, and his solicitude for the welfare of his people; and, above all, the almost fabulous wealth that he conferred as endowments on temples and Brahmans, mark him out indeed as the greatest of the South Indian monarchs.[1]

It is permissible to wonder, however, how far such lavish endowment was compatible with solicitude for the peasant.

In his time the Vijayanagar empire comprised substantially the same area as the Presidency of Madras, with the addition of Mysore and the other states of the peninsula.

Achyutarāya. Krishnadevarāya was succeeded by his brother Achyutarāya, a man of weak and tyrannical character, lacking even in

---

[1] Krishna Sastri in *Ann. Rep. A.S. India* for 1908–9, p. 186.

personal courage. Early attacks by Pratāparuda and the Golkonda ruler were staved off, but he soon lost the fortress of Mudgal and Raichur to Ismā'īl 'Ādil Khān, for he was hampered by the efforts of Rāmarāja to place an infant son of Krishnadevarāya on the throne. Rāmarāja, the son of Krishnadevarāya's minister Sāluva Timma, for a while got Achyutarāya into his power, but the prisoner escaped and by the dearly bought mediation of Ibrāhīm 'Ādil Shāh secured his position until his death in 1542.

Achyutarāya was succeeded by his son Venkata I, but on the infant's murder by an uncle, Rāmarāja·was able to seize power in the name of Krishnadevarāya's young son, Sadāsiva. In this process of seizing power, Rāmarāja destroyed many of the old nobility and replaced the Brahman officials by his own relations and adherents. He also considerably increased the importance of the Muslim element in the army.

Rāmarāja also instituted a policy of interfering in the perpetual struggles of the Muslim kings in the Deccan—and was most successful. In 1543 Rāmarāja made an alliance with Ahmadnagar and Golkonda in order to effect a combined attack on Bijapur, which was saved from destruction by the abilities of the minister Asad Khān. Fifteen years later (1558) Bijapur and Vijayanagar combined to attack Ahmadnagar. The territory of that state was so cruelly ravaged by the Hindus, and Rāmarāja treated his Muslim allies with such open contempt, that the sultans were convinced of the necessity for dropping their private quarrels and combining against the arrogant infidel.

Alliance of the four sultans. In 1564 the combination was duly effected. It seems probable that 'Ālī 'Ādil Shāh at first stood neutral, and was only drawn in when the allies had been checked. The set-back enabled them to spread false rumours that they wished for peace, and in the pause the 'Ādil Shāh and the Muslim commanders in Rāmarāja's army were won over. 'Ālī 'Ādil Shāh was to the last an uncertain ally, for he is said to have hastened to Husain Nizām Shāh, when the capture of Rāmarāja was reported, 'with the design of securing the release of the accursed infidel'.

The battle itself saw enormous forces engaged upon both sides. Estimates of the forces at the command of Rāmarāja vary, but it seems certain that his vast host numbered between half a million and a million men, besides a multitude of elephants and a considerable amount of artillery. On the other side, the sultan of Ahmadnagar brought on the ground a park of no less than 600 guns of various calibres. The total of the allied army is supposed to have been about half that of the Vijayangar host.

The battle was fought on 23 January 1565. At first the Hindus had the advantage, but they suffered severely from a salvo of the Ahmadnagar guns shotted with bags of copper coin, and from a vigorous cavalry charge. Their complete rout followed on the capture of Rāmarāja, who was promptly decapitated by the sultan of Amadnagar with his own hand. The princes fled from the city with countless treasures loaded upon more than 500 elephants, and the proud capital lay at the mercy of the victors who occupied it almost immediately.

The plunder was so great that every private man in the allied army became rich in gold, jewels, effects, tents, arms, horses, and slaves; as the sultans left every person in possession of what he had acquired, only taking elephants for their own use.

Ruin of Vijayanagar. The ruin wrought on the magnificent city may be described in the words of Sewell, who was familiar with the scene of its desolation. When the princes fled with their treasures,

then a panic seized the city. . . . No retreat, no flight was possible except to a few, for the pack-oxen and carts had almost all followed the forces to the war, and they had not returned. Nothing could be done but to bury all treasures, to arm the younger men, and to wait. Next day the place became a prey to the robber tribes and jungle people of the neighbourhood. Hordes of Brinjāris, Lambādis, Kurubas, and the like pounced down on the hapless city and looted the stores and shops, carrying off great quantities of riches. Couto states that there were six concerted attacks by these people during the day.

The third day saw the beginning of the end. The victorious Musalmans had halted on the field of battle for rest and refreshment, but now they had reached the capital, and from that time forward for a space of five months Vijayanagar knew no rest. The enemy had come to destroy, and they carried out their object relentlessly. . . . Never perhaps in the history of the world has such havoc been wrought, and wrought so suddenly, on so splendid a city; teeming with a wealthy and industrious population in the full plenitude of prosperity one day, and on the next seized, pillaged, and reduced to ruins, amid scenes of savage massacre and horrors beggaring description.

The pathetic language of the Hebrew prophet lamenting the ruin of Jerusalem applies accurately to the Indian tragedy:

How doth the city sit solitary, that was full of people! how is she become as a widow! she that was great among the nations, and a princess among the provinces, how is she become tributary! . . . The young and the old lie on the ground in the streets: my virgins and my young men are fallen by the sword. . . . How is the gold become dim! how is the most fine gold changed! the stones of the sanctuary are poured out in the top of every street.[1]

Rāmarāja's brother, Tirumala, who along with Sadāsiva, the nominal king, took refuge at Penugonda, himself usurped the royal seat some few years after the battle. This third usurpation, the beginning of the fourth dynasty, may be dated in or about 1570. The most remarkable king of the new dynasty was the third, by name Venkata I, who came to the throne about 1585. He seems to have moved his capital to Chandragiri, and was noted for his patronage of Telugu poets and Vaishnava authors. It is unnecessary to follow the history of his successors, who gradually degenerated into merely local chiefs. In 1639 a

[1] Lam. i. 1; ii. 21; iv. 1.

Nāik subordinate to Chandragiri granted the site of Madras to Mr. Day, an English factor. In 1645 that transaction was confirmed by Ranga II, who was the last representative of the line with any pretensions to independence. Much of the Deccan was overrun by the Muslims and passed under the sovereignty of the sultans of Bijapur and Golkonda, who in their turn were overthrown by Aurangzeb in 1686 and 1687.

The most important of the principalities formed by Hindus in the far south out of the fragments of the Vijayanagar empire was that of the Nāyaks of Madura. Tirumala Nāyak is justly celebrated for his buildings, which exhibit much dignity of design and splendour in execution.

The city in the fourteenth century. The grandeur of the city, the splendour of the buildings, the wealth of the bazaars, the volume of trade, and the density of the population are amply attested by a series of witnesses beginning in the fourteenth century, when Vijayanagar was only a few years old, down to the date of its irremediable ruin, and also by survey of the existing remains. The historian Firishta admits that as early as 1378 the rayas of Vijayanagar were greatly superior in power, wealth, and extent of country to the Bahmanī kings. Goa was then temporarily in possession of the raya, and his capital drew much wealth from commerce passing through the ports of the western coast.

Bukka II (1399–1406) improved and enlarged the fortifications of Vijayanagar. His most notable work was the construction of a huge dam in the Tungabhadra river, forming a reservoir from which water was conveyed to the city by an aqueduct fifteen miles in length, cut out of the solid rock for a distance of several miles. Firishta's account of the ceremonial at the marriage between Firūz Shāh Bahmanī and the daughter of Devarāya I gives some idea of the magnificence of the capital in 1406.

Nicolo Conti's description, 1420. The earliest foreign visitor whose notes have been preserved was an Italian named Nicolo Conti, who was at Vijayanagar about 1420, in the reign of Davarāya II. He estimated the circumference of the city to be sixty miles, and was much impressed by the strength of the fortifications, which were carried up the hills so as to enclose the valleys at their base. The traveller observes that the king had 12,000 wives, of whom no less than 2,000 or 3,000 were required to burn themselves with him when he died. Indeed the savage custom of *sati* was terribly common in the empire. The sacrifice was effected by burning in a pit, or, among the Telegus, by burial alive.

'Abdur-Razzāq in 1443. The next visitor was the learned 'Abdur-Razzāq of Herat, who was sent by Sultan Shāhrukh, son of Timur, as ambassador to the zamorin of Calicut. While the envoy was residing at Calicut a herald brought intelligence that the king of Vijayanagar required that he should be sent instantly to his court. The zamorin, although at that time not directly subject to the authority of the raya, dared not disobey. 'Abdur-Razzāq accordingly sailed to Mangalore, 'which is on the borders of the kingdom of Bījanagar', and thence travelled by land to his distant destination, through the country now known as Mysore.

At Belur he admired greatly a magnificent temple, which he dared not describe 'without fear of being charged with exaggeration'. Presumably he saw the fine structure erected in A.D. 1117 by the Hoysala King Bittiga, which still exists and has been surveyed by the archaeological department of Mysore.[1] Towards the end of April 1443 the traveller arrived at Vijayanagar. 'The city', he observes, 'is such that eye has not seen nor ear heard of any place resembling it upon the whole earth. It is so built that it has seven fortified walls, one within the other.' The writer goes on to illustrate his description by a comparison with the citadel of Herat.

The seventh fortress is placed in the centre of the others, and occupies ground ten times greater than the chief market of Hirāt. In that is situated the palace of the king. From the northern gate of the outer fortress to the southern is a distance of two statute *parasangs* [about 7 or 8 miles], and the same with respect to the distance between the eastern and western gates. Between the first, second, and third walls there are cultivated fields, gardens, and houses. From the third to the seventh fortress, shops and bazaars are closely crowded together. By the palace of the king there are four bazaars, situated opposite one to another. On the north is the portico of the palace of the Rāi.[2] At the head of each bazaar there is a lofty arcade and magnificent gallery, but the palace of the king is loftier than all of them. The bazaars are very long and broad, so that the sellers of flowers, notwithstanding that they place high stands before their shops, are yet able to sell flowers from both sides. . . . The tradesmen of each separate guild or craft have their shops close to one another. The jewellers sell their rubies and pearls and diamonds and emeralds openly in the bazaar.

In this charming area, in which the palace of the king is contained, there are many rivulets and streams flowing through channels of cut stone, polished and even. . . . The country is so well populated that it is impossible in a reasonable space to convey an idea of it. In the king's treasury there are chambers, with excavations in them, filled with molten gold, forming one mass. All the inhabitants of the country, whether high or low, even down to the artificers of the bazaar, wear jewels and gilt ornaments in their ears and around their necks, arms, wrists, and fingers.

Account by Paes in 1552. We have another detailed description recorded by Domingos Paes, a Portuguese, about 1522, in the reign of Krishnadevarāya, just after the capitulation of Raichur, when the empire was at the full height of its glory. His account, which is obviously

---

[1] There is no need to suppose that any place other than Belur is meant. It is eighty or ninety miles by road from Mangalore.
[2] This sentence is from the version in Sewell. The rendering in E. & D. does not give sense. The rest of the quotation is from E. & D.

truthful, may be accepted with confidence. It is well worth reading in full as translated by Sewell.

Size of the city; the palace. Paes found a difficulty in estimating the size of the city, because the hills prevented him from seeing the whole at once. So far as he could judge, it was as large as Rome. The houses were said to exceed 100,000 in number. If that guess be near the truth, the population cannot have been less than half a million. The numerous lakes, water-courses, and orchards attracted his admiration. As to the people, he could only say that they were countless. He considered Vijayanagar to be 'the best provided city in the world . . . for the state of this city is not like that of other cities, which often fail of supplies and provisions, for in this one everything abounds'. Paes was shown round a large part of the palace enclosure, which contained thirty-four streets. He saw one room which was 'all of ivory, as well the chamber as the walls from top to bottom, and the pillars of the cross-timbers at the top had roses and flowers of lotuses all of ivory, and all well executed, so that there could not be better—it is so rich and beautiful that you would hardly find anywhere another such'.[1]

The court. The ceremonial of the court was extremely elaborate. The royal words, as at the Mughul court, were carefully noted down by secretaries, whose record was the sole evidence of the commands issued. Nuniz, another Portuguese who visited Vijayanagar thirteen years later than Paes, declares that

no written orders are ever issued, nor any charters granted for the favours he (the king) bestows or the commands he gives; but when he confers a favour on any one it remains written in the registers of these secretaries. The king, however, gives to the recipient of a favour a seal impressed in wax from one of his rings, which his minister keeps, and these seals serve for letters patent.

In that respect the practice differed widely from that followed in the northern courts, where regular office routine was observed. The king always dressed in white. On his head he wore 'a cap of brocade in fashion like a Galician helmet, covered with a piece of fine stuff, all of fine silk, and he was barefooted'. His jewels, of course, were the finest possible.

The army. The army in the king's pay is said to have numbered 'a million fighting troops, in which are included 35,000 cavalry in armour', but this would be the total force called out in emergency. The standing army was probably no more than one-tenth of this figure. Paes declares that in 1520 Krishnadevarāya actually assembled for the operations against Raichur 703,000 foot, 32,600 horse, and 551 elephants, besides an uncounted host of camp-followers, dealers, and the rest. The efficiency of the huge army described was not proportionate to the numbers of the force. The soldiers were in terror of the Muslims, and their action against a fortress like Raichur in the absence of efficient siege artillery was ludicrou¹y feeble. The men are described

---

[1] Compare the 'ivory palaces' of Psalm xlv. 8.

as being physically strong and individually brave. Sometimes they fought gallantly, but the army as an organized force was inefficient.

Administration. The raya was assisted by a council of shifting composition and power. As usual, some offices tended to become hereditary or to be concentrated in one office—that of Pradhani. To counter this, Krishnadevaraya suggested that new men should be advanced to break the control of too powerful ministers, and that too much trust should be put in no one since 'the people employed by the king for the collection of revenue and discharging other duties are both friends and enemies according to circumstances. . . .' There was a large secretariat and the usual officers of a royal household are mentioned.

The empire was divided into a small number of great provinces, often under members of the royal family, and into further subdivisions. The Nāiks—nobles or tributary rulers—held these subdivisions on condition that they provided a fixed contingent of troops and a certain amount of revenue. Nuniz gives us detailed observations for about 1535, and Paes states that the governors were expected to pay over to the treasury half of their gross revenue, and to defray all the expenses of their households, contingents, and government from the other half. The provincial governors and Nāiks could do much as they pleased within their territories, though they were themselves at the mercy of the king, who was a most absolute autocrat.

The ruler's attitude in respect of law and order is summed up in Krishnadevaraya's trenchant, 'The king maintains the law (*dharma*) by killing.' The extreme ferocity of the punishments inflicted for offences against property was well designed to protect the rich against the poor.[1] 'The punishments they inflict in this kingdom', Nuniz states, 'are these: for a thief, whatever theft he commits, howsoever little it be, they forthwith cut off a foot and a hand; and if his theft be a great one he is hanged with a hook under his chin. If a man outrages a respectable woman or a virgin he has the same punishment, and if he does any other such violence his punishment is of like kind. Nobles who become traitors are sent to be impaled alive on a wooden stake thrust through the belly; and people of the lower orders, for whatever crime they commit, he forthwith commands to cut off their heads in the market-place, and the same for a murder unless the death was the result of a duel. . . .'

Land revenue assessment. The assessment varied according to the type of land under cultivation—whether wet, dry, or garden land. The revenue was taken either in cash or kind as it suited the ruler at the time, but the burden on the peasant was in any case crushingly heavy. Nuniz states that they 'pay nine-tenths to their lord'. Such a

---

[1] Knox, *An Historical Relation of the Island Ceylon, in the East Indies* (London, 1681), gives terribly realistic drawings of 'the execution by an eliphant'; 'one impaled on a stake'; and of 'the manner of extorting their fine'. The last-named plate shows a poor man crouching with a heavy stone on his back, while his rich creditor stands over him.

proportion of the gross produce seems improbable, but what is clear is that to the observer the demand seemed inordinately high. Evidence of village revolt against the burden and the observations of later travellers tend to confirm Nuniz. All agree that while the nobles lived in luxury, the mass of the people went all but naked and lived in hovels.

Wilks and later authorities also refer to the multitude of vexatious cesses levied upon peasant and merchant alike. Trade was hampered by heavy city dues and by the existence of numerous toll-stations upon the roads. 'At the end of the century, too, the missionaries insist on the need for passports in this part of India in order to avoid infinite trouble regarding dues and taxes.'

Duelling. Nuniz states that 'great honour is done to those who fight in a duel, and they give the estate of the dead man to the survivor; but no one fights a duel without first asking leave of the minister, who forthwith grants it'. The usage was not confined to Vijayanagar. Duels fought with swords were common among the Nayars of Malabar until recent times, probably as late as the nineteenth century. The practice was imitated by the Muslims of the Deccan early in the sixteenth century, much to the horror of Firishta, who denounces 'this abominable habit' as being unknown in any other civilized country in the world.

Legalized prostitution. Prostitution was a recognized institution and an acceptable source of revenue. The women attached to the temples, as Paes informs us, 'are of loose character, and live in the best streets that are in the city; it is the same in all their cities, their streets have the best rows of houses'.

'Abdur-Razzāq gives further details on the subject. 'Opposite the mint', he writes, 'is the office of the Prefect of the City, to which it is said 12,000 policemen are attached; and their pay, which equals each day 12,000 *fanams*, is derived from the proceeds of the brothels.'

An interesting comparison might be made between the statements of the Persian envoy and the regulations in the *Arthaśāstra* concerning the city prefect and the courtesans in Maurya times. Then, as at Vijayanagar, the public women played an essential part in court ceremonial.

Laxity in diet. Although vegetarian Brahmans were numerous at Vijayanagar and greatly pampered by the authorities, the diet of the general population and of the kings departed widely from the Brahmanical standard. Animal food was very freely used. Paes dwells with pleasure on the variety of meat and birds procurable in the markets. The sheep killed daily were countless. Every street had sellers of mutton, so clean and fat that it looked like pork. Birds and game animals were abundant and cheap; those offered for sale included three kinds of partridges, quails, doves, pigeons, and others, 'the common birds of the country', besides poultry and hares. The same author mentions that pork also was sold and that pigs kept in certain streets of butchers' houses were 'so white and clean that you could never see better in any country'.

His statements are confirmed by Nuniz, who writes that:

These Kings of Bisnaga eat all sorts of things, but not the flesh of oxen or cows, which they never kill in all the country of the heathen because they worship them. They eat mutton, pork, venison, partridges, hares, doves, quail, and all kinds of birds; even sparrows, and rats, and cats, and lizards, all of which are sold in the market of the city of Bisnaga.

Everything has to be sold alive so that each one may know what he buys—this at least so far as concerns game—and there are fish from the rivers in large quantities.

That was a curious dietary for princes and people, who in the time of Krishnadevarāya and Achyutarāya were zealous Hindus with a special devotion to certain forms of Vishnu. The kings of the first dynasty preferred to honour Śiva.

Bloody sacrifices. The numerous bloody sacrifices, similar to those still performed in Nepal, were equally inconsistent with the ordinary practice of Vaishnava religion. Paes mentions, that all the sheep required for the market supply of mutton for Hindu consumption were slaughtered at the gate of one particular temple. The blood was offered in sacrifice to the idol, to whom also the heads were left. The same writer states that on a certain festival the king used to witness the slaughter of 24 buffaloes and 150 sheep, the animals being decapitated, as now in Nepal, by a single blow from a 'large sickle' or *dāo*. On the last day of the 'nine days' festival' 250 buffaloes and 4,500 sheep were slaughtered.[1] Such practices prove clearly that the Hinduism of Vijayanagar included many non-Aryan elements. At the present day lizards and rats would not be eaten by anybody except members of certain debased castes or wild jungle tribes.[2]

The government of Vijayanagar Telinga and foreign. Doubts may be felt as to whether the founders of Vijayanagar had been in the service of the Hoysala king or in that of the raja of Warangal, but it is certain that they were foreigners in the Kanarese country, the Carnatic, properly so called. Wilks believed that Bukka and his brethren were fugitives from Warangal:

This origin of the new government at once explains the ascendancy of the Telinga [Telugu] language and nation at this capital of Carnatic, and proves the state of anarchy and weakness which had succeeded the ruin of the former dynasty. The government founded by foreigners was also

---

[1] Bishop Whitehead states that in the Telugu country as many as 1,000 sheep are sometimes sacrificed at once on the occasion of an epidemic (*Village Deities*, Madras, 1907, p. 136, as corrected in 2nd ed., Oxford University Press, 1916, p. 56). All the practices mentioned in the text seem to be Telugu or Kanarese. The modern Tamils usually are becoming averse to bloody sacrifices. The Kanarese still offer them freely.

[2] e.g. the Vaddas, who are numerous in Mysore, and said to come from Orissa, will eat any animal food, except beef or tortoise. 'Sheep, goats, pigs, squirrels, wild cats, lizards, and mice are equally welcome to them' (*Ethnogr. Survey of Mysore* Prelim. Issue, No. XI, p. 10, Bangalore, Govt. Press, 1907). Sewell (p. 13) suggests that the kings may have belonged to the Kuruba tribe or caste, who are shepherds and blanket-weavers primarily. For the Kurubas see *Ethnogr. Survey*, No. I, 1906

supported by foreigners; and in the centre of Canara a Telinga court was supported by a Telinga army, the descendants of whom, speaking the same language, are to be traced at this day nearly to Cape Comorin, in the remains of the numerous establishments, resembling the Roman colonies, which were sent forth from time to time for the purpose of confirming their distant conquests, and holding the natives in subjection. The centre and the west, probably the whole of the dominions of the late dynasty, including the greater part of the modern state of Mysoor, were subdued at an early period; but a branch of the family of Bellal [= Hoysala] was permitted to exercise a nominal authority at Tonoor until 1387, in which year we begin to find direct grants from the house of Vijeyanuggur as far south as Turkanamby beyond the Caveri. The last of thirteen rajas or rayeels of the house of Hurryhur [Harihara I], who were followers of Śiva, was succeeded in 1490 by Narsing Raja, of the religious sect of Vishnoo, the founder of a new dynasty, whose empire appears to have been called by Europeans *Narsinga*, a name which, being no longer in use, has perplexed geographers with regard to its proper position.

Narsing Raja seems to have been the first king of Vijeyanuggur who extended his conquests into *Drauveda* [Drāvida, the Tamil country], and erected the strong forts of Chandragerry and Vellore; the latter for his occasional residence, and the former as a safe place for the deposit of treasure; but it was not until about 1509 to 1515 that Kistna Rayeel [Krishna Rāya] reduced the whole of Drauveda to real or nominal subjection.

The fact that the kings and nobles of Vijayanagar were foreigners lording it over a subject native population would explain the severity of the government. It should be observed, however, that the Telugu or Telinga people themselves are noted for their submissiveness to official authority.[1]

Patronage of literature. The rayas of Vijayanagar, although their title was Kanarese in form, gave their patronage to Sanskrit and Telugu literature. Sāyana, the celebrated commentator on the Vedas, who died in A.D. 1387, was minister in the early part of the reign of Harihara II, and his learned brother Mādhava served Bukka. The first dynasty had close associations with the great monarchy of Sringēri. The achievements of Sāluva Narasimha, the founder of the second dynasty, were enthusiastically celebrated by Telugu poets. Krishnadevarāya, himself a poet and author, was a liberal patron of writers in the Telugu language. His poet laureate, Alasāni-Peddana, is regarded as an author of the first rank. The tradition of the court was carried on by Rāmarāja and the other rayas of the fourth or Aravīdu dynasty. Rāmarāja and his brothers were themselves accomplished scholars, and under their protection a great revival of Vaishnava religion was accomplished.

Architecture and art. The kings of Vijayanagar from the beginning of their rule were distinguished as builders of strong fortresses, immense works for irrigation and water supply, gorgeous palaces, and temples decorated with all the resources of art, both sculpture and paint-

[1] Wilks, reprint, vol. i, p. 9. See the good article 'Telugu' in Balfour, *Cyclopaedia*, based on Caldwell's works. The dates given by Wilks require some slight correction.

ing. They evolved a distinct school of architecture which used the most difficult material with success, and were served by a brilliant company of sculptors and painters. Enough of the sculpture survives to show its quality, but the paintings necessarily have disappeared. The descriptions recorded by the Portuguese authors and 'Abdur-razzāq permit of no doubt that the painters in the service of the kings of Vijayanagar attained a high degree of skill. The scenes from the Rāmāyana, sculptured in bas-relief on the walls of Krishnadevarāya's chapel royal, the Hazāra Rāma-swāmī temple, built in 1513, are much admired. No adequate account of the buildings and sculptures at Vijayanagar has yet been prepared.

THE RAYAS OF VIJAYANAGAR

Name	Accession	Remarks
	A.D.	
Chiefs, not of royal rank		
HARIHARA I, son of Sangama	1336	Traditional date for foundation of Vijayanagar.
BUKKA (BHUKKA, or BUKKANA) I, his brother and three other brothers, sons of Sangama; succession apparently disputed	1354	Bukka I died 1377.
Rayas of royal rank		
First dynasty: descendants of Sangama		Worshippers of Śiva Virūpāksa.
HARIHARA II, son of Bukka I	1377	
BUKKA II, son of Harihara II	?1404	A brother named Virūpāksa also a claimant.
Disputed succession		
DEVARĀYA I	1406	
VĪRA VIJAYA	1422	
Disputed succession		
DEVARĀYA II (alias Immadi, Pratāpa, or Praudha); at first associated with Vīra Vijaya; became sole ruler	1425	Empire prosperous and extensive.
MALLIKĀRJUNA, son of Devarāya II	1447	Sāluva Narasimha minister in power from about 1455.
VIRŪPĀKSA	1465	Decay of empire.
PRAUDHADEVARĀYA (Padea Rao)	1485	
Second or Sāluva dynasty		Worshippers of Vishnu.
SĀLUVA NARASIMHA	1486	
IMMADI NARASIMHA, alias Tammaya (Dharma) Rāya; son of Narasimha Sāluva	?1492	Power in hands of Narasa Nāyaka.
Third or Tuluva dynasty		
NARASA NĀYAKA succeeded as regent by his son Vīra Narasimha	1503	

The Rayas of Vijayanagar (cont.)

Name	Accession	Remarks
	A.D.	
VĪRA NARASIMHA murders Immadi and assumes power		
KRISHNADEVARĀYA	1509	
Battle of Raichur	1520	Climax of the empire.
ACHYUTA; brother of Krishnadevarāya	1529	
VENKATA I, son of Achyuta, succeeds but is murdered	1542	
SADĀSIVA, son of another brother of Achyuta	1542	Nominal king; Rāmarāja in power.
Battle of Tālikota	1565	Break-up of empire.
Death of Rāmarāja; confusion	1565	
Fourth dynasty; Āravīdu or Karnāta		
TIRUMALA, brother of Rāmarāja	c. 1570	Capital at Penugonda, now in Anantapur District.
RANGA, son of Tirumala	c. 1573	
VENKATA I, brother of Ranga	1585	Capital removed to Chandragiri.
Other princes		
RANGA	1642	Local chief.
Practical end of dynasty	1646	Ranga's inscriptions continue to 1684.

NOTE.—Dates and many details, especially those relating to disputed successions, are often doubtful.

SYNCHRONISTIC TABLE

Vijayanagar		Bahmanī		Bijapur
Harihara I, &c.	1336			
Bukka I	1354			
		'Alā-ud-dīn I	1347	
		Muhammad I	1358	
		Mujāhid	1373	
		Dāūd	1378	
Harihara II	1377	Muhammad II	1378	
		Ghiyās-ud-dīn	1397	
		Shams-ud-dīn	1397	
		Fīrūz	1397	
Bukka II	?1404			
Devarāya I	1406			
Vīra Vijaya	1422	Ahmad	1422	
Devarāya II	1425			
		'Alā-ud-dīn II	1435	
Mallikārjuna	1447			

Vijayanagar		Bahmanī		Bijapur	
		Humāyūn	1457		
		Nizām	1461		
		Muhammad III	1463		
Virūpāksa	1465				
Praudhadevarāya	1485				
		Mahmūd	1482		
Sāluva Narasimha	1486				
				Yūsuf	1490
Immadi Narasimha	?1492				
Vīra Narasimha	1503				
Krishnadevarāya	1509				
				Ismaīl	1510
Achyuta	1529				
				Mallū	1534
				Ibrāhīm I	1535
Sadāsiva	1542				
				Alī	1557
Tirumala	c. 1570				
Ranga	c. 1573				
				Ibrāhīm II	1580
Venkata I	1585				
Others	—			Muhammad	1626
Ranga	1642				

AUTHORITIES

THE leading authorities used are SEWELL, *A Forgotten Empire (Vijayanagar)*, London, 1900, which alone gives the Portuguese narratives; and three articles, chiefly based on inscriptions and Telugu literature, by H. KRISHNA SASTRI in *Ann. Rep. A.S. India* for 1907–8, 1908–9, and 1911–12. Early discussions of the subject will be found in H. H. WILSON's *Introduction to the Descriptive Catalogue of the Mackenzie MSS.*, 1828, reprint 1882; and in WILKS, *Historical Sketches . . . History of Myscor*, 1810–14, reprint, 1869. The account in MEADOWS TAYLOR's *Manual*, good when written, is no longer up to date. I have also consulted S. KRISHNASWAMI AIYANGAR, *A Little Known Chapter of Vijayanagar History*, Madras, S.P.C.K. Press, 1916; RICE, *Mysore and Coorg from the Inscriptions*, London, 1909; the same author's *Mysore Gazetteer*, revised ed., London, 1897; and many articles in the *A.S. Progress Reports of the Southern Circle* (Madras); *Indian Antiquary*, &c.

The coins are described by HULTZSCH, *Ind. Ant.*, vol. xx (1891); and V. A. SMITH, *Catal. Coins in I.M.*, vol. i, Oxford, 1906. The art of the dynasty is briefly noticed in *H.F.A.* New inscriptions are published continually. Many dates and other matters of detail remain unsettled, and cannot be disposed of until somebody takes the trouble to write a bulky monograph. The small book (144 pp., 8vo) by A. H. LONGHURST, Superintendent, Archaeological Department, Southern Circle (Madras Government Press, 1917), entitled *Hampi Ruins described and illustrated*, has 69 illustrations, and is good as far as it goes.

More recent works on the subject which offer varying interpretations include the following: H. HERAS, *The Aravidu Dynasty of Vijayanagar* and *Beginnings of Vijayanagar*; R. SEWELL and S. K. AIYANGAR, *Historical Inscriptions of Southern India* K. AIYANGAR, *Sources of Vijayanagar History*; N. V. RAMANAYA, *Vijayanagar Origin of the City and Empire*; *Vijayanagar Sexcentenary Commemoration Vol.*; B. A. SALETORE, *Social and Political Life in the Vijayanagar Empire*.

BOOK VI

The Mughul Empire

CHAPTER 1

The beginnings of the Mughul empire; Babur, Humayun, and the Sūr dynasty, A.D. 1526–56

BABUR, Zahir-ud-din Muhammad, king of Kabul, whose aid Daulat Khān invoked against Sultan Ibrāhīm of Delhi, was the most brilliant Asiatic prince of his age, and worthy of a high place among the sovereigns of any age or country. As a boy he inherited a fragment of that Timurid empire which briefly had stretched into India. This fragment was Farghana, the upper valley of the Syr Darya, whose revenues supported no more than a few thousand cavalry. With this force of helmeted, mail-clad warriors, attached to him only by personal loyalty or temporary interest, Babur began his career of conquest. He joined in the family struggles for power, thrice winning and thrice losing Samarqand, alternately master of a kingdom or a wanderer through the hills.

But in this period two new powers, the Safavis in Persia and the Usbegs in central Asia, were rising. Between these two powers the brilliant but divided Timurid princes were broken and squeezed until Babur was forced through the Kabul bottleneck into India. As he entered Kabul he pushed before him the Arghūn dynasty, and as they were shunted south, so other trans-Indus tribes were driven into their present homes.

In 1504 Babur made himself master of Kabul and so came into touch with India. The wealth of India tempted him into more than one raid—and the disturbing arrival of the Usbegs suggested the expediency of another. But his real hope was still of Samarqand, and the defeat of Shaibānī Usbeg in 1510 by Shāh Ismā'īl allowed him to realize his ambition. With Persian aid he mastered Samarqand in 1511, only to find that unhappily 'in thus gaining the needed ally he lost his subjects', who hated the Persian Shia. After hovering hopefully north of the Hindu Kush for two years, Babur at last gave up his hopes of central Asia, and turned instead towards India.

Pricked on by the need to provide employment for the many exiled rulers at his court, Babur swept down in 1517 and 1519 from the Afghan plateau to the plains of India. These were reconnaissances. His entry into the Punjab in 1523, on the invitation of Daulat Khān Lodī, the governor of that province, and ʿĀlam Khān, an uncle of Sultan Ibrāhīm, was intended to be a serious invasion. Usbeg pressure upon Balkh, however, compelled Babur to retire, so that his final invasion was not begun until November 1525.

Invasion of India. Even then his total force, including the Badakhshan troops under Humayun, and camp followers, did not exceed 12,000 men, a tiny army with which to attempt the conquest of Sultan Ibrāhīm's realm, and the vast mass of Hindu India behind the Afghan dominions. The enterprise, indeed, seemed to be rash, and Babur candidly admits that many of his troops were 'in great tremor and alarm'. Yet the bold attack succeeded.

Battle of Panipat, 1526. The hostile armies came to grips on 21 April 1526, on that plain of Panipat where the prize of India has been so often the reward of the victor. Babur possessed a large park of artillery, the new-fangled weapon then coming into use in Turkey and Europe, but previously unknown in northern India. Its power had already made itself felt at the siege of Bajaur. Carts, 700 in number, drawn by bullocks, were lashed together by chains, so as to form a barrier in front of the enemy,[1] gaps being left sufficient for the cavalry to charge through. On the other side, Sultan Ibrāhīm brought into the field an immense host believed to number at least 100,000 men, supported by nearly 100 elephants. Although the exact numbers drawn up by Babur in battle array are not stated, there is no doubt that they were immeasurably outnumbered by the enemy. But the Afghan sultan, 'a young inexperienced man, careless in his movements, who marched without order, halted or retired without method, and engaged without foresight', was no match for Babur, a born general, and a veteran in war although his years were few. The battle, which raged from half-past nine in the morning until evening, again demonstrated the inherent weakness of an ill-compacted Hindu host when attacked by an active small force under competent leadership, and making full use of bold cavalry charges. The decisive movement, the furious cavalry wheel round the flank of the enemy, delivering a charge in his rear, was exactly the same as that employed by Alexander against Pōros at the battle of the Hydaspes, and had the same result. When the sun set Sultan Ibrāhīm lay dead on the field, surrounded by 15,000 of his brave men. 'By the grace and mercy of Almighty God', Babur wrote, 'this difficult affair was made easy to me, and that mighty army, in the space of half a day, was laid in the dust.'

Occupation of Delhi and Agra. Delhi and Agra were promptly occupied, and the immense spoil was divided among all ranks of the victorious army with lavish generosity. But the heat was oppressive,

---

[1] Mrs. Beveridge rejects the earlier interpretation of ʿarāba as meaning guns; but the word may be rendered 'gun-carriages'.

grain and fodder scarce, and 'on these accounts, not a few of my Begs and best men began to lose heart [and] objected to remaining in Hindustan. . . .' Like Alexander, Babur sought to rouse their pride by a stirring address, and, unlike his great predecessor, succeeded in persuading his men to follow the path of glory, and despise the dangers which beset them in a strange land.

Rana Sanga. Babur had next to face a power more formidable than that of the sultan—the Hindu power led by Rana Sangrām Singh, head of the premier Rajput state, Mewar. His grandfather, Rana Kumbha, between 1419 and 1469, had broken the Muslim kingdom of Malwa, and defeated the effort of Gujarat to re-establish it. Of Rana Sanga, Shaikh Zain wrote, 'There was not a single ruler of the first rank in all these great countries like Delhi, Gujarat, and Mandu who was able to make head against him.' The rana had hoped that Babur would break the Lodī power for him, and then withdraw as Timur had done. But when Babur settled at Delhi, the rana moved to attack him.

He commanded an enormous host, composed of the contingents of 120 chiefs, and including 80,000 horse with 500 war elephants. The small army of Babur was much dispirited at the prospect of the unequal fight: 'a general consternation and alarm prevailed among great and small'. To counteract this despair, Babur strongly fortified his camp, publicly renounced his drinking of wine, and made another rousing speech. 'The Most High God has been propitious to us, and has now placed us in such a crisis, that if we fall in the field, we die the death of martyrs; if we survive, we rise victorious, the avengers of the cause of God. Let us, then, with one accord, swear on God's holy word, that none of us will ever even think of turning his face from this warfare . . .'.[1] An advance was ordered, and on 16 March 1527 battle was joined near Khānua, a village almost due west from Agra. The tactics which had won the victory at Panipat were repeated, with the same result. The rout of the Hindu host was complete and final, although the gallant rana escaped from the field and survived until 1529.

Battle of Ghāgra. After the rains, Babur moved to attack Chanderi, held for the rana by Medinī Rāo, 'a pagan of great consequence'. It was stormed on 29 January 1528, and the garrison annihilated. The Afghan chiefs of Bihar and Bengal were the next enemies to be attacked. They suffered defeat in 1529 on the banks of the Gogra (Ghāgra) near the junction of that river with the Ganges above Patna.

Death of Babur. In December 1530 Babur died. He left an empire which included Badakhshan, Afghanistan, the Panjab, Delhi, the open plain of Bihar and territories stretching southwards to a perimeter marked by the forts of Biyana, Ranthambhor, Gwalior, and Chanderi. Much of the empire lay beyond the Indus, many of the troops were drawn from beyond its boundaries, and the ties which held it together were only those of personal loyalty to Babur. An extract from the

[1] Erskine, vol. ii, p. 286.

memoirs suggests how frail those ties were, 'in a country where there are seven or eight chiefs, nothing regular or settled can be looked for'. The seven or eight chiefs referred to prove to be the Begams, each the centre of a family which might try to replace Babur or his sons. The Indian portion of the empire, surrounded by powerful states, was itself honeycombed with the estates of minor chiefs. There was little uniformity of administration, for districts were under the almost absolute control of grantees, the heads of families or tribal leaders. Babur, as leader of a band of foreign adventurers, could only hold the main strong points, and elsewhere rely on the passivity of the Hindu masses.

Character of Babur. Babur the man is revealed to us in his memoirs, which, originally written in Turki, were transcribed by Humayun personally, and were translated into Persian by the Khān Khānān under the direction of Akbar. Good English versions were made by Erskine and Leyden in 1826, and later by Mrs. A. S. Beveridge. Babur emerges as immensely likeable, a very vigorous, artistic personality, as able to 'rough it' over the Hindu Kush in winter as to write most excellent Turki verses. His zest was an inspiration to his followers, with whom he shared both hardships and a convivial appreciation of fine gardens or of wine. To the last India was for Babur 'a country of few charms', pleasant only in having ample wealth. 'They very recently brought me a single musk-melon. While cutting it up I felt myself affected with a strong sense of loneliness, and a sense of my exile from my native country; and I could not help shedding tears while I was eating it.'

Humayun's task. Babur left an empire barely held by force of arms, and lacking any consolidated civil administration. The struggle of his descendants to establish a firmly seated dynasty with a fairly complete control of northern India lasted from his death at the close of 1530 until 1576 when Akbar had been on the throne for twenty years. In 1530 Humayun was twenty-three years old, and had served an apprenticeship as governor of Badakhshan. But, although a cultivated gentleman not lacking in ability, he was deficient in the sustained energy of his versatile father. He could not keep the loyalties of his nobles, who found other centres of power in his three brothers, the eldest of whom, Kamran, was in charge of Kabul and Qandahar at Babur's death and treacherously added the Panjab to his possessions soon after. His addiction to opium partially explains his failure.

Wars with Gujarat and Sher Khān. In 1535 Humayun made a brilliant raid into Gujarat and exhibited his personal valour by forming one of the storming party which escaladed the strong fortress of Champaner (north-east of Baroda). He was unable long to maintain such dash. As his chronicler put it, 'The Emperor Humayun remained for a year at Agra, and took his pleasure.' At the end of that time Malwa and Gujarat had been lost.

Meanwhile Sher Khān Sūr, an Afghan chief, was busily consolidating his power in South Bihar. In 1537 Humayun moved against him, but spent so long in the taking of Chunar, that Sher Khān had time to capture Gaur and its immense treasures and escape with them. Only then did Humayun advance to Gaur where he passed months in idle pleasure 350 miles from his base, Benares. When the emperor's brother, Hindal, deserted his post on the line of communications, Sher Khān proceeded to close the trap, and utterly defeated Humayun at Chausa on the Ganges. Nearly a year later, in May 1540, Sher Khān again defeated Humayun still more decisively opposite Kanauj; and then pursued the fleeing Mughuls to Lahore. Here Humayun's brothers again displayed their selfish jealousy, and Humayun became a homeless wanderer, first in Sindh, then in Marwar, and finally in Sindh again. In the midst of his misery his son Akbar was born at Umarkot on 23 November 1542.

Humayun, after narrowly escaping the forces of his brother at Qandahar, reached Persia in 1544, and was granted asylum by Shāh Tahmāsp. He thought it well to declare himself a Shia in the shah's presence, but even so it was only after some hesitations, and upon promise that Qandahar, when conquered, should be handed over to Persia, that the shah provided military aid. With this Qandahar was taken in 1545—and treacherously retained by the Mughul—and thence a successful attack was launched upon Kamran, who had re ained control of Kabul. A misplaced and sentimental generosity towai : the brutal Kamran led to some years' further conflict, until in 15 the nobles forced Humayun to blind his brother.

Second reign and death of Humayun. Humayun, when relieved from his brother's opposition, was able to invade India where four Sūr claimants were struggling for power. He occupied Delhi and Agra in July 1555, and so regained his father's capital cities. But he was not permitted to consolidate his conquest or to establish a regular civil government. He was still engaged in making the necessary arrangements when an accidental fall from the staircase of his library at Delhi ended his troubled life in January 1556. His second reign had lasted barely seven months.

Reign of Sher Shāh. It has been convenient to give a rough outline of Humayun's adventures as a continuous story. Attention must now be directed to the proceedings of his Afghan rivals.

Sher Shāh's grandfather had been one of those Afghans who, in Sultan Buhlūl's day, 'came as is their wont like ants and locusts to enter the king's service'. His father, improving the family fortunes, served under Jamāl Khān first in the Panjab, then as a *jagīrdār* of 500 horse in the *pargana* of Sasaram in Jaunpur. Sher Shāh received his training as an administrator in the very practical management of his father's *parganas*, before entering first Babur's service, in 1527, and then that of Jalāl Khān Lohānī. By 1533 he had ousted Jalāl Khān from the Lohānī possessions, and by a reputation as a good paymaster had built up a strong army. While Humayun was busy in

Gujarat, Sher Khān was securing land and a great ransom from Bengal, and when the emperor did turn east, he was already too late. After the flight of the Mughuls, Sher Shāh consolidated his kingdom, holding down the Gakhars by a new fort at Rohtas in the Panjab, pruning the Bengal province and dividing it into several governorships in order to prevent attempts at independence, and making vigorous efforts to subdue Rajputana, Malwa, and Bandelkhand. He disgraced himself by ordering the treacherous massare of the garrison of Raisin in central India, and was killed in 1545 while directing the siege of Kalanjar in Bandelkhand.

Sher Shāh's government. Sher Shāh was something more than the capable leader of a horde of fierce, fanatical Afghans. He had a nice taste in architecture, manifested especially in the noble mausoleum at Sahasram in Bihar which he prepared for himself. He built a new city at Delhi and a second Rohtas in the Panjab. He also displayed an aptitude for civil government and instituted reforms, based to some extent on the institutions of 'Alā-ud-dīn Khiljī, which were developed by Akbar.

He maintained his authority by means of a powerful central army, said to have comprised 150,000 horse, 25,000 foot, and 5,000 elephants. He sought to make himself rather than the clan leaders the focus of loyalty, personally inspecting, appointing, and paying the men. He likewise made himself accessible to their appeals against a local governor or commander. He prevented fraudulent musters by branding the horses in government service—a system imitated by Akbar—and 'munsifs were appointed for examining the brands in the armies on the frontiers'. He also anticipated that monarch in a system of land revenue, assessment based on the measurement of the land, and if he had lived longer might have enjoyed a reputation equal to that of Raja Todar Mal, Akbar's famous minister. Justice of a rough and ready kind was administered under his strict personal supervision, and the responsibility of village communities for crimes committed within their borders was enforced by tremendous penalties. No man could expect favour by reason of his rank or position, and no injury to cultivation was tolerated. Sher Shāh, like Aśoka and Harsha, accepted the maxim that 'it behoves the great to be always active'. His time was divided by stringent rules between the duties of religion and those of government. He followed the example of the best Hindu sovereigns by laying out high roads, planting trees, and providing wells and sarāis for the accommodation of travellers. He reformed the coinage, issuing an abundance of silver money, excellent in both fineness and execution. That is a good record for a stormy reign of five years.

Islām Shāh ; Muhammad 'Ādil Shāh. When Sher Shāh died the choice of the nobles fell on his second son, Jalāl Khān, who ascended the throne under the style of Islām Shāh, often corruptly written and pronounced as Salīm Shāh. His brief and disturbed reign ended in 1553. He issued many regulations, but did not share his father's

..ity. After an interval of disputed succession the throne was usurped
by Muhammad 'Ādil Shāh, or 'Adalī, brother of a consort of Islām
Shāh. He was inefficient, and left the control of his affairs in the hands
of Hēmū, a clever Hindu tradesman. The right to the sovereignty was
contested by two nephews of Sher Shāh, whose fate will be related in
a later chapter.

CHRONOLOGY

First battle of Panipat	21 April 1526
Babur proclaimed as padshah	27 April 1526
Battle of Khanua (Kanwāha), defeat of Rana Sanga	March 1527
Battle of the Ghaghra (Gogra) river	1529
Death of Babur; accession of Humayun	Dec. 1530
Humayun in Bengal	1538
Defeat of Humayun at Chausa	June 1539
Final defeat of Humayun at Kanauj	May 1540
Birth of Akbar at Umarkot	23 Nov. 1542
Death of Sher Shāh; accession of Islām Shāh	1545
Death of Islām Shāh; Muhammad 'Ādil Shāh ('Adalī) acc.; other claimants	1553-4
Restoration of Humayun	June 1555
Death of Humayun	Jan. 1556

AUTHORITIES

THE main original authority for Babur is his book of *Memoirs*, transl. by LEYDEN and
ERSKINE, 1826, and by Mrs. A. BEVERIDGE. Contemporary accounts of Humayun are
the *Memoirs* of JAUHAR, transl. by STEWART, 1832; *Life and Memoirs of Gulbadan
Bēgam*, Akbar's aunt, transl. by Mrs. A. BEVERIDGE, R.A.S., 1902; and *Memoirs* of
BĀYAZĪD BIYĀT, abstracted in *J.A.S.B.*, part i, for 1898, p. 296. Other leading
Persian authorities for the period are the *Akbarnāma* of ABU-L FAZL, transl. by H.
BEVERIDGE, and various authors in E. & D., vols. iv, v; also FIRISHTA, transl. by
BRIGGS. ERSKINE's *History of India under Babar and Humāyūn*, 2 vols., 1854, is a
valuable work on a large scale. LANE-POOLE's *Bābar*, in Rulers of India, 1898, is an
excellent and well-written little book. FERNAND GRENARD, *Baber, first of the Moguls*,
transl. and adapted by WHITE and R. GLAENZER is also excellent. The skeleton of the
Sūr history is presented by E. THOMAS in *Chronicles of the Pathān Kings of Delhi*
(1871). The story of the Sūr kings needs to be worked out critically in detail. A
biography of Sher Shāh, by Professor K. QANUNGO, was published at Calcutta in 1921.
See also PARAMATMA SARAN, 'The date and place of Sher Shāh's birth', *J.B.O.R.S.*,
1934. The latest work on the period is Dr. ISHWARI PRASAD's *Life and Times of
Humayun*, 1955.

The early European voyages to and settlements in India; the East India Company from 1600 to 1708

The foreigners and the Mughul empire. Inasmuch as the influence of European settlers on the coasts made itself felt in Indian politics from the beginning of the sixteenth century, it is desirable to take a comprehensive although summary view of the steps by which the western powers acquired a footing in India before we enter upon the detailed history of the Mughul empire, as established by Akbar and maintained for a century after his death.

The Arab monopoly of Indian trade. We have seen how extensive was the trade, both overland and maritime, maintained between India and the Roman empire during the first three centuries of the Christian era, how that trade almost ceased in the fourth century, and revived to some extent in the fifth and sixth centuries. The Arab conquest of Egypt and Persia in the seventh century definitely closed the direct communication between Europe and India. Thenceforward all Indian wares which reached the West passed through Muslim hands, and so were transmitted from the markets of the Levant to Venice, which acquired enormous wealth and influence by its monopoly of Eastern commerce.

Portuguese exploration of African coast. The Portuguese kings of the fifteenth century looked with envy on the riches of Venice, and eagerly desired to obtain a share in her profitable trade. Prince Henry the Navigator devoted his life to the discovery of a direct sea route from Portugal to India, and, when he died in 1460, his adventurous captains had succeeded in passing the river Senegal on the west coast of Africa. But much further effort was needed before the circumnavigation of Africa could be accomplished. Ultimately the feat was performed by Bartholomeu Diaz de Novaes, who was driven by storms considerably to the south of the Cape, and made land half-way between the Cape of Good Hope and Port Elizabeth. He sailed up the eastern coast sufficiently far to satisfy himself of its north-easterly trend and to be convinced that the long-sought route had been opened. He returned to Lisbon in December 1488.

Vasco da Gama reaches India. This discovery was followed up ten years later by Vasco da Gama who sailed in July 1497 with four tiny ships, and worked his way round Africa. At Malindi, north of Zanzibar, one of the wealthy Arab trading settlements of this coast, he obtained experienced pilots for the run to India. On 20 May 1498 he anchored near Calicut. The Hindu ruler, the zamorin, owed his prosperity to his port's position as an entrepôt, and he was prepared to welcome the Portuguese. The Arab traders, however, did what they could to hamper their new competitors. After visiting Cochin and Cannanor, Vasco da Gama turned for home, reaching Lisbon in late August 1499.

The Portuguese were fortunate in the time of their arrival. In Egypt the Mamelukes were soon to be threatened by the Turks, and in Persia a new dynasty was still building its power. North India was much divided, though Gujarat was in the strong hands of Mahmūd Bīgarhā, while in the Deccan the Bahmanī kingdom was disintegrating. None of the great powers had a navy, or thought in terms of naval power. In the Far East the navigation of Chinese ships was limited by imperial decree. The Arab shipowners and merchants, who had dominated the commerce of the Indian Ocean, had nothing to oppose to the drive and unity of the Portuguese.

End of trade at Calicut. On da Gama's triumphant return the king of Portugal sent out a larger fleet under Cabral, the discoverer of Brazil. He brushed with the Arabs at Calicut, but secured his cargo at Cochin and Cannanor. In 1502 Vasco da Gama, when the zamorin refused to exclude the Arab merchants in favour of the Portuguese, turned on such Arab shipping as he could find with a mixture of commercial greed and hostility to all such 'Moors', and completed the rupture with the zamorin.

De Almeida. The first viceroy (1505–9) Dom Francisco de Almeida had to face a greater danger than the hostility of the zamorin. The Mameluke sultan of Egypt, urged on by Venice, now attempted to stop Portuguese interference with their lucrative trade by building a fleet in the Red Sea and entering the Indian Ocean. De Almeida, a seasoned crusader against the Moor in North Africa, was sent out with a large fleet in response to this threat. Though in 1507 a Portuguese squadron was surprised by the combined Egyptian and Gujarati fleet off Diu, and the viceroy's son was killed, de Almeida utterly crushed the enemy next year. He pointed the moral of his victory: 'As long as you may be powerful at sea you will hold India as yours; and if you do not possess this power, little will avail you a fortress on shore.'

Albuquerque's strategy. Affonso de Albuquerque, who succeeded Almeida, with the rank of governor, held wider views. His purpose was to found a Portuguese empire in the East. Before he died he had given Portugal the strategic control of the Indian Ocean by securing bases covering all the entrances to that sea—in East Africa, off the Red Sea, at Ormuz, in Malabar, and at Malacca. From these bases the strongly built, ocean-going Portuguese ships overawed the slighter Arab shipping. A system of licences for native shipping and control of the major ship-building centres long upheld Portuguese domination at sea. (Neither the Red Sea nor the Persian Gulf afforded timber for building warships.)

Acquisition of Goa. In 1510 Albuquerque effectively occupied the island of Goa, the principal port in the dominions of the sultan of Bijapur, the first bit of Indian territory directly governed by Europeans since the time of Alexander the Great. All Muslims were excluded from office.

Malacca. The valuable trade which came from the Spice Islands or Moluccas passed, along with that from China and Japan, through the Straits of Malacca. In those days the town of Malacca on the coast of the Malay peninsula, with its good if shallow harbour, was the principal emporium for this trade. In 1511, therefore, its possession carried with it the control of a vast commerce, for Singapore did not become important until the nineteenth century. Albuquerque, in nine days' fighting, cleared the city. It was held by the Portuguese for 130 years. His hope that 'if we take this trade of Malacca away out of their hands, Cairo and Mecca will be entirely ruined, and to Venice will no spices be conveyed, except what her merchants go to buy in Portugal' were for a time largely fulfilled. From Malacca he explored the Spice Islands, where trading posts were established.

Attempt on Aden. In 1513 Albuquerque sought to muzzle Arab trade through the Red Sea by an attack on Aden. He failed, but raids on shipping—and the preoccupation of the Mamelukes with the advancing Ottoman Turks—allowed the Portuguese to dominate the approaches for some years.

Occupation of Ormuz. Albuquerque was more successful in the Persian Gulf. Shortly before his death in 1515 he occupied the island of Ormuz and built a fortress there. At that time the port rivalled Malacca in importance as a centre of international trade. The Portuguese held it until 1622 when they were ousted by a Persian force supported by English ships from Surat. From that date Ormuz declined, and its trade passed to the new port of Bandar Abbas, not far distant.

Portuguese administration in India. The Portuguese Crown had been responsible for pushing forward the exploration of the African coast, and had sent out Vasco da Gama in the face of general opposition. When success crowned these efforts, the sole direction, both political and commercial, was naturally assumed by the Crown. This control was hampered by a division of authority, and particularly by the establishment of a special office responsible for the members of the great and wealthy religious orders and other clerics. The union with Spain (1580–1640) increased the number of authorities, though the *Conselho da India*, established in 1604, did good service. In the seventeenth century financial crises further undermined administration.

In India the head of the administration was the viceroy, who served for three years, with his secretary and, in later years, a council. His authority was weakened at times by conflict with the ecclesiastical authorities, by having no say in appointments, and by preoccupation with the lining of his own pockets. Next in importance came the *Vedor da Fazenda*, responsible for revenue and the cargoes and dispatch of fleets. The fortresses, from Africa to China, were under captains,

assisted by factors, whose power was increased by the difficulties of
communication and was too often used for personal ends. Indeed the
lack of control from Portugal and Goa when combined with the union
of political and commercial control in a single office was a perpetual
threat to honest administration.

The larger centres were granted the privileges of towns in Portugal
and had municipal councils—some, as in Goa and Macau, of considerable importance. There was a High Court at Goa and a hospital which
compelled the admiration of all. Also copied from home institutions
was the *Santa Casa da Misericordia* whose beneficent activities 'in
succouring widows and orphans and in helping the poor and needy
should be set against the greed, corruption, and despotism so graphically described by Diogo do Couto and his foreign contemporaries'.[1]

Military and naval power. At the opening of the sixteenth century, the Portuguese navy led the world in the rig of ships, navigational
techniques, and gunnery. The effort put forth—some 800 ships sent
east in the century—was remarkable. But the long absence of any
serious competition led to poor design and unwieldy ships, and the
rate of loss at sea rose alarmingly. Mortality on shipboard was very
high, and fresh crews had to be recruited for each voyage, while at a
time when the English and Dutch were learning ocean navigation,
travellers report declining standards of seamanship on Portuguese
vessels.

The national militia of Portugal was no basis for the army in India.
And while the population of Portugal was actually declining, and while
another great Portuguese empire was being opened up in Brazil, forces
for India could only be maintained by recruitment in India. Some
troops with officers of noble blood did come out in the annual fleets,
but in the main reliance was placed in those who had settled in the
Indies and married there. Albuquerque, recognizing the strength
which such settlers represented, had encouraged mixed marriage. The
stubborn resistance of so many settlements to the Dutch, who early
became masters at sea, testifies to the valour of the *casados* and their
slaves.

Religious policy. The Portuguese, crusading against the Moor in
North Africa, carried with them to the East something of the same zeal
and the same hostility to all Muslims. But their motives had always
been mixed, and once in India those of commerce early became dominant. So, though the Portuguese Crown had been made by the Pope
patron of all missions and churches in the Indies, it was not until the
advent of the Jesuits in 1542 that any great missionary activity was displayed. Their influence at the Mughul court will be examined in subsequent chapters. A like effort was made by the society in China and
Japan. The introduction of the Inquisition in Goa after 1560, with its
cruel persecution, served only to undo much of the good work done by
the Jesuits and the Mendicant Orders.

[1] C. R. Boxer in *Portugal and Brazil*, ed. H. V. Livermore, p. 223.

Portuguese commercial activity. It was the trade in spices which led the Portuguese to India, and in the early years it offered great profits, for the Arab middlemen had taken enormous profits between the Spice Islands and Venice. But ultimately the Portuguese gained most, as individuals certainly, from their participation in the carrying trade of the Indian Ocean and the China Sea. The position has been thus summed up: 'the Portuguese were able to deprive the Muslim traders of the Indian Ocean of a large share of the trade in Indian textiles and piece-goods, Persian and Arabian horses, gold and ivory from East Africa, as well as from spices from Indonesia, Ceylon, and Malabar. Moreover they extended their carrying trade into the China Sea, where Arab merchants had not penetrated since medieval times, save in insignificant numbers. Voyages between the principal ports in these areas (Macau–Nagasaki; Malacca–Siam; Ormuz–Goa, for example) were much shorter and easier than the long haul round the Cape of Good Hope. Money and goods invested in such "ventures" brought in both quicker and safer returns than did cargoes shipped to Europe. The comparative value of gold and silver in India, China, and Japan varied in a fluctuating ratio which enabled the Portuguese at Goa and Macau to make a handsome profit by acting as bullion-brokers trading in these precious metals.'[1]

The Portuguese decline. The emergence of powerful dynasties in Egypt, Persia, and north India and the appearance as neighbours of the turbulent Maratha power reduced the local advantages of the Portuguese in India. Political fears roused by the activities of Jesuit missionaries, and hatred of persecution such as the Inquisition practised, caused reaction against Portuguese spiritual pressure. Greed, selfishness, and corruption weakened the administration. But the system still worked and produced wealth. It was destroyed by the Dutch and English, two nations with wider resources and greater compulsions to expand than the Portuguese in the Indies felt to resist. The follies of King Sebastian's North African campaign, the embroilment in Spain's campaigns in Europe, and after 1624 the heavy drain of men to defend Brazil and Africa against the Dutch—all these successively weakened Portugal's ability to resist. The leakage of information about the route to the Indies to the Dutch and English, who were learning ocean navigation off Newfoundland or in the White Sea, destroyed an earlier monopoly of knowledge, as the losses in the Arzilla expedition and the Armada destroyed an earlier preponderance in shipping. Portugal was too small a nation permanently to sustain the role of 'Lord of the Conquest, Navigation, and Commerce of Ethiopia, Arabia, Persia, and India'.

Dutch and English rivalry with the Portuguese The Dutch and English almost simultaneously took measures to contest the claim of Portugal to the monopoly of Oriental commerce, and from the moment they appeared on the scene at the beginning of the seventeenth

[1] Ibid., p. 222.

century the Portuguese were unable to resist them effectually. One after another most of the Indian settlements fell into their hands, and, in the first instance, passed into Dutch possession. Goa, it is true, escaped actual capture, although it was often blockaded by Dutch fleets; but its importance in relation to India had dwindled so steadily after the destruction of Vijayanagar in 1565 that in the seventeenth century it did not much matter who held it.

The Dutch settlements. The United East India Company of the Netherlands was founded in 1602 from an earlier group of competing provincial companies. It commanded very large financial resources and was very closely linked with the state. After a brief exploratory period, headquarters were founded in Batavia, whence the policy was actively pursued of securing the trade to the Spice Islands and then of the pepper trade. This involved the exclusion of the English who had also founded factories in Java and the Moluccas. The Massacre of Amboyna was but an incident in this process of exclusion.

In India, whither the Dutch turned in search of the piece goods which were the staple article of trade throughout the Malay Archipelago, the Mughuls and the rulers of Golkanda were too powerful for the Dutch to be able to seek a monopoly by force. They settled at Pulicat, north of Madras, in 1609, and later at Masulipatam, Surat, and in Persia. Their command of the spice trade, the wealth of the company, and the ability of their factors enabled them to secure a major share in the trade of all these areas, but not to exclude their English rivals.

Danish settlements. The Danish settlements demand a passing notice. A Danish East India Company was established in 1616, and four years later (1620) the factory at Tranquebar on the east coast was founded. The principal settlement of the Danes at Serampore near Calcutta dates from 1755. The Danish factories, which were not important at any time, were sold to the British government in 1845.

French settlements. The French appeared late on the scene, their official organization, 'La Compagnie des Indes Orientales', having been established in 1664. Their principal settlement, Pondicherry, founded ten years later, still is a moderately prosperous town. The French never succeeded in capturing a large share of the Indian trade, and their settlements never received sufficient steady support from home. The Republic handed over its last possessions to the Indian state in 1954.

The struggle between the English and French for supremacy in the peninsula during the second half of the eighteenth century will be narrated in due course as part of the general history of India.

First Charter of the East India Company. The glorious victory over the Spanish Armada in 1588 stimulated British maritime enterprise, and suggested plans for claiming a share in the lucrative commerce of the Eastern seas. Those plans assumed definite form on the last day of 1600, when Queen Elizabeth granted a charter with rights of exclusive trading to 'the Governor and Company of Merchants of London trading into the East Indies'.

The separate voyages. The early 'Separate Voyages' organized by the Company were directed chiefly to the Spice Islands rather than to India. They were called Separate Voyages because each venture was financed and fitted out by a group of individuals from within the Company, who wound up the voyage on the return of their ships, and divided the profits among themselves. A ship of the Third Voyage reached Surat in 1608, but Portuguese influence was strong, and it was not until 1612, when Captain Best successfully beat off violent Portuguese attacks, that the Gujarat officials would grant to the English the right to trade at Surat. Early in 1613 this right was confirmed by an imperial *farman*. Surat thus became the seat of a presidency of the East India Company, which in time developed into the Presidency of Bombay.

English capture of Ormuz. In 1615 the English again defeated the Portuguese at sea, and their capture of Ormuz in 1622, with the aid of a Persian military force, further weakened the Portuguese power, already endangered by Dutch attacks elsewhere. Thenceforward they had little to fear from Portugal.

Embassy of Sir T. Roe. In 1615 James I sent Sir Thomas Roe as his ambassador to the Emperor Jahangir. During his stay of about three years in India, Sir Thomas, although he could not obtain all he asked for, succeeded in securing important privileges for his countrymen. From time to time British adventurers established many factories or trading stations at various points along the western coast, including one at Anjengo in Travancore. But their activity was not confined to that coast, the more easily accessible.

Settlements on Bay of Bengal. In the course of a few years they made their way into the Bay of Bengal and founded factories. The earliest was at Masulipatam, established in 1611, but others followed, such as Armagaon, built about 1625, the first fortified English post in India.

Foundation of Madras. Business at Masulipatam and Armagaon was hampered by the exactions of local officials, and experience showed that the piece goods required for export to Bantam and Persia were to be had at cheaper rates farther south. The chief at Armagaon, Francis Day, therefore secured from a local Hindu chief the grant of a strip of land just north of the friendly, decaying, Portuguese settlement of San Thomé. The grant was afterwards confirmed by the raja of Chandragiri, the representative of the old sovereigns of Vijayanagar; by it the English were permitted to erect fortifications, and the revenues were divided between them and the Nayak. Thus England acquired her first proprietary holding on Indian soil, and the foundation of the Presidency of Madras was laid. A fort was quickly built (to the dismay of the thrifty directors at home) and named Fort St. George. This gave to Madras its official designation as the Presidency of Fort St. George.

In 1647 the district fell into the hands of Golkonda, but happily the English were on good terms with the general, Mīr Jumla, and secured his confirmation of their position.

Foundation of Calcutta. The destruction in the 1660's of Portuguese and Arakanese pirates, who had infested the head of the Bay of Bengal, by Shayasta Khān opened a new area of trade to the Dutch and the English. Bengal offered new products such as silk and saltpetre, and trade in these rapidly grew. In 1688, however, Sir Josiah Child's foolish war with Aurangzeb ended in the expulsion of the English. When the Nawab Ibrāhīm Khān invited them back, they chose not Hugli, the Mughul centre of commerce, but a mud-flat with a deep-water anchorage, the site of Calcutta. As at Madras the choice was dictated by the need for security. There the delta of the evil-smelling Cooum, here extensive swamps, provided protection. So Job Charnock, truculent, masterful, but 'always a faithful man to the Company', doggedly set to work to build and fortify the settlement of Calcutta. In 1696 was built Fort William—so named after King William III—and the Presidency of Fort William or Bengal was established.

Acquisition of Bombay. Bombay was acquired by the Crown in 1661 as part of the dowry of Catharine of Braganza, queen of Charles II. The cession was made by the Portuguese in order to secure English support against the Dutch. A few years later the king, who had failed to appreciate the value of the acquisition, granted the island to the East India Company in return for the trifling sum of ten pounds a year.

Gerald Aungier. The real founder of the city was the early governor, Gerald Aungier (1669–77), who foresaw the future greatness of his charge, declaring that it was 'the city which by God's assistance is intended to be built'. Aungier, although rarely mentioned in the current general histories, was one of the noblest of the founders of the Indian empire. He is described as being 'a chivalric and intrepid man . . . a gentleman well qualified for governing', who made it his 'daily study to advance the Company's interest and the good and safety of the people under him'. His grave at Surat, to which Bombay was subordinate in his time, is marked by a tablet, affixed in 1916.[1]

Bombay became the headquarters of the English in western India instead of Surat, when Maratha raids had upset the commercial life of Gujarat. The Bombay territory, however, did not attain much importance until the time of Warren Hastings. The noble harbour could not be fully utilized until the passage of the Western Ghats had become practicable.

The United Company. Towards the close of the seventeenth century the East India Company encountered much opposition in England, which resulted in the formation of a rival body entitled 'The English Company Trading to the East Indies'. The old company was brought to the brink of ruin. But its directors were full of fight, and

[1] *Prog. Rep. A.S.W.I.*, 1916–17, p. 42.

declared that 'two East India Companies in England could no more subsist without destroying one the other, than two kings, at the same time regnant in one kingdom'.

After much bitter and undignified quarrelling in both England and India an agreement was arranged in 1702. The difficult financial questions at issue were finally set at rest in 1708 by the award of Lord Godolphin, with the result that the rivals were combined in a single body styled 'The United Company of Merchants of *England* trading to the East Indies'. The United Company thus formed is the famous corporation which acquired the sovereignty of India during the century extending from 1757 to 1858.

Failure of Portuguese, Dutch, and French. The Portuguese, who had the advantage of the start in the race for the control of the Indian trade, lost everything from causes sufficiently obvious, which have been already indicated. The Dutch, though they carried on a very vigorous trade in India, had their main centre in Java, whence they could gather riches by their monopoly of the trade of the Archipelago and Spice Islands. The French entered the field too late and failed to show sufficient enterprise or to receive adequate backing from their government at home. The English proved their superiority at sea against all comers from an early date. Their commercial affairs in India were looked after by agents often of dubious character, but always daring, persistent, and keen men of business, though often ill supported by the home government.

During the time of the Great Mughuls the British territory in India was of negligible area, comprising only a few square miles in the island of Bombay, Madras city, and three or four other localities. But even then the prowess of their sea captains had made their nation a power in Indian politics. Half a century after the death of Aurangzeb, when rich Bengal was acquired, nothing, not even an Act of Parliament, could stop the masters of the sea and the Gangetic valley from becoming the rulers of India.

CHRONOLOGY

Vasco da Gama arrived at Calicut	May 1498
Portuguese conquest of Goa	1510
Death of Albuquerque	1515
Trade of Goa injured by destruction of Vijayanagar	1565
Union of crowns of Spain and Portugal	1580
Defeat of the Spanish Armada	1588
Charter to E. I. Co. of merchants of *London*	31 Dec. 1600
United E. I. Co. of the Netherlands	1602
Accession of Jahangir	1605
Third 'Separate Voyage'; Capt. Hawkins at Surat.	1608
Joint stock voyages began; English factory established at Surat;	
Portuguese defeated at sea	1612
Embassy of Sir Thomas Roe	1615–18
Danish settlement at Tranquebar	1620

AUTHORITIES

INNUMERABLE books might be cited. The slight sketch in this chapter is based chiefly on the summary in *I.G.* (1907), chap. ii; H. MORSE STEPHENS, *Albuquerque* (Rulers of India, 1892), an excellent book; WHITEWAY, *The Rise of Portuguese Power in India* (Westminster, 1899); and a most valuable survey by C. R. BOXER, in *Portugal and Brazil*, ed. H. V. LIVERMORE, which is furnished with a very full bibliography, Oxford, 1953. P. KAEPPELEN, *La Compagnie Indes orientales et François Martin*, Paris, 1908, and S. P. SEN, *The French in India* (Calcutta, 1947), give the full picture of early French efforts. ANDERSON, *The English in Western India* (Bombay and London, 1854); RAWLINSON, *British Beginnings in Western India* (Clarendon Press, 1920); STRACHEY, *Keigwin's Rebellion* (Clarendon Press, 1916), a first-rate and most entertaining book; PENNY, *Fort St. George, Madras* (London, 1900); and BRUCE, *Annals of the E. I. Co.* (London, 1810).

Numerous references will be found in the works mentioned. For the history of the English settlements in India see *Letters Received by the East India Company*, 1602–17 (London, 1896–1902), and Sir WILLIAM FOSTER's *English Factories in India*, 1618–77 (Clarendon Press, 1906–36). The home affairs of the Company are dealt with in the *Calendar of State Papers, East Indies*, 1513–1634, by Mr. W. N. SAINSBURY, and *Court Minutes of the East India Company*, 1635–79, by Miss E. B. SAINSBURY and Mr. FOSTER (Clarendon Press, 1907–38). For foundation of Madras see W. FOSTER, *The Founding of Fort St. George* (Eyre & Spottiswoode, 1902); and H. D. LOVE, *Vestiges of Old Madras* (Murray, 1913).

CHAPTER 3

Akbar, 1555–1605

Humayun's sons. When Humayun died he left two sons, Akbar, the elder, aged thirteen, and Muhammad Hakim, the younger, who was more than two years junior to his half-brother. The Kabul province remained nominally in the charge of the younger prince, and, although regarded officially as a dependency of Hindustan, was ordinarily administered as an independent principality. Akbar, at the time of his father's death, was in camp with his guardian, Bairām Khān the Turkoman, engaged in the pursuit of Sher Shāh's nephew, Sikandar Sūr, who had collected a force in the Panjab and sought to win the crown for himself.

Enthronement of Akbar. Arrangements having been made to conceal Humayun's decease for a time sufficient to allow of the peaceful proclamation of Akbar's accession, the enthronement of the heir was duly effected at Kalānaur, in the Gurdaspur District, on 14 February 1556. The brick platform and seat used in the ceremony still exist and are now reverently preserved. But the enthronement ceremony merely registered the claim of Humayun's son to succeed to the throne of Hindustan. The deceased monarch never had had really assured possession of his kingdom, and during his brief second reign of a few months was in the position of an adventurer who had secured a momentary military success. He could not be regarded as an established legitimate sovereign. The representatives of his great rival Sher Shāh had claims quite as strong as those of Akbar to the lordship of Hindustan.

Two Sūr claimants. At that moment the effective claimants representing the Sūr dynasty were two nephews of Sher Shāh. The first of the two, king Muhammad Shāh ʿĀdil or ʿAdalī, had actually succeeded for a time in establishing himself as the successor of Sher Shāh's son, Islām Shāh, who had died in 1554. But at the time of Humayun's fatal accident he had retired to the eastern provinces and was residing at Chunar, near Mirzapur. Sher Shāh's other nephew, Sikandar, as already mentioned, was in the Panjab engaged in operations on his own behalf.

Hēmū, a third claimant. King ʿAdalī's interests in the north were in the charge of his capable Hindu minister and general, Hēmū, a trader or Baniya by birth, who had already won many victories for his master. Hēmū, advancing through Gwalior, occupied both Agra and Delhi, thus gaining a very important advantage. Tardī Beg, who had been entrusted by the protector, Bairām Khān, with the defence of

Z

Delhi, failed in his duty, and allowed the city to fall into the enemy's hands. For that offence he was executed by order of Bairām Khān. The punishment, although inflicted in an irregular fashion without trial, was necessary and substantially just.

Hēmū, after his occupation of Delhi, bethought himself that he was in possession of a powerful army, many elephants, and much treasure, while his sovereign was far away in Chunar. He came to the conclusion that he had better claim the throne for himself rather than on behalf of 'Adalī. Accordingly, he secured the support of the Afghan contingents by liberal donatives, and ventured to assume royal state under the style of Raja Bikramajit or Vikramāditya, a title borne by several renowned Hindu kings in ancient times. He thus became Akbar's most formidable competitor, while both 'Adalī and Sikandar Sūr dropped into the background for the moment.

Second battle of Panipat. Bairām Khān, with Akbar, advanced through Thanesar to the historic plain of Panipat, where, thirty years earlier, Babur had routed and slain Sultan Ibrāhīm Lodī. Hēmū approached the same goal from the west. The Hindu general, although he had the misfortune to lose his park of artillery in a preliminary engagement, possessed a powerful host of 1,500 war elephants on which he relied, and was in command of troops far superior in number to those of his adversary.

The armies met in battle on 5 November 1556. At first Hēmū was successful on both wings. Probably he would have been the victor but for the accident that he was hit in the eye by an arrow and rendered unconscious. His army, when deprived of its leader, the sole reason for its existence, dispersed at once. Bairām Khān and Akbar, who had left the conduct of the battle to subordinate officers, rode up from the rear. Their helpless dying opponent was brought before them. The Protector desired his royal ward to earn the coveted title of Ghāzī by slaying the infidel with his own hand. The boy, naturally obeying the instruction of his guardian, smote the prisoner on the neck with his scimitar, and the bystanders finished off the victim. The commonly accepted story that young Akbar exhibited a chivalrous unwillingness to strike a wounded prisoner is a later, courtly invention.

Famine, 1555–6. During the years 1555 and 1556 the upper provinces of India, and more especially the Agra and Delhi territories, suffered from an appalling famine due primarily to the failure of rain and much aggravated by the long continued operations of pitiless armies. Hēmū had displayed the most brutal indifference to the sufferings of the people, and had pampered his elephants with rice, sugar, and butter, while men and women ate one another. He deserved his fate.

End of the Sūr dynasty. The victors pressed the pursuit of the broken foe and promptly occupied both Agra and Delhi. During the year 1557 the pretensions of the Sūr family to the sovereignty of Hindustan came to an end. Sikandar Sūr, who surrendered, was

generously treated and provided with a fief in the eastern provinces.
King 'Adalī made no attempt to dispute the verdict of the sword at
Panipat. He remained in the east, and was killed in a conflict with the
King of Bengal. Akbar's position as the successor of Humayun was
thus unchallenged, although he had still much fighting to do before he
attained a position as good as that occupied by his father during his
first reign.

Progress of reconquest. In the course of the years 1558–60 the
recovery of the Mughul dominion in Hindustan progressed by the
occupation of Gwalior, the strong fortress of central India, Ajmer,
the key of northern Rajputana, and the Jaunpur province in the east.
An attempt on the Rajput castle of Ranthambhor failed for the moment,
to be renewed successfully a few years later. Preliminary arrangements
for the conquest of Malwa were interrupted by the events connected
with Akbar's assumption of personal rule and the dismissal of Bairām
Khān, his guardian and Protector.

Dismissal of Bairām Khān. Early in 1560 the young sovereign,
then in his eighteenth year, began to feel galled by the tutelage of his
guardian, who was a masterful man, prone to exert his authority without much regard for other people's feelings. Akbar's natural impatience
was encouraged by Hamīda Bāno Bēgam, his mother; by Māham
Anaga, chief of the nurses and ranking as a foster-mother of the
sovereign; by her son, Adham Khān; and by Shihāb-ud-dīn, her relative, the governor of Delhi. All those personages, who had much influence over Akbar, disliked Bairām Khān for reasons of their own. In
the spring of 1560 Akbar dismissed the Protector from office and announced his intention of taking the reins of government into his own
hands. Bairām Khān, after some hesitation, submitted to the royal
commands, and started for Mecca as ordered. But, on second thoughts,
being angered because he was hustled on his way by an ungrateful
upstart named Pīr Muhammad, he rebelled, although in a half-hearted
fashion. He was defeated in the Panjab and again compelled to submit.
Akbar treated the ex-regent with generosity and allowed him to proceed on his journey towards Mecca with all ceremonial honour.
Bairām Khān reached Pātan in Gujarat, where he was murdered by a
private enemy in January 1561. His little son, Abdurrahīm, was saved,
and lived to become the principal nobleman in the empire. The intrigue
against the regent was engineered by a court clique who desired his
destruction. They were supported by the orthodox, who, ranged against
him as a Shia, had also been violently offended by his choice of Shaikh
Gadāī as *Sadr-us-Sudūr*. Akbar at that time was under petticoat
government and had little concern with state affairs. His personal conduct in the affair shows a generous temper, so far as appears. The
faults of Bairām Khān certainly deserved indulgence from Akbar, who,
like his father, was indebted for his throne to the loyalty of the Turkoman.

Petticoat government, 1560–2. The next two years are the m...

discreditable in Akbar's life. The young monarch, as his biographer repeatedly observes, 'remained behind the veil', and seemed to care for nothing but sport. He manifested no interest in the affairs of his kingdom, which he left to be mismanaged by unscrupulous women, aided by Adham Khān, Pīr Muhammad, and other men equally devoid of scruple. The conquest of Malwa, entrusted to Adham Khān and Pīr Muhammad, was effected with savage cruelty to which Akbar made no objection, though he did angrily demand the spoils they retained. The fortress of Mirtha (Merta) in Rajputana was taken in 1562.

Emancipation of Akbar. The emancipation of Akbar from a degrading tutelage came in May 1562. His appointment in the previous November of Shams-ud-dīn Atga Khān as prime minister was extremely distasteful to Māham Anaga and her friends, who feared that their ill-used power might slip from their hands. Adham Khān one day swaggered into the palace where the prime minister was at work and stabbed him to death. Akbar, hearing the noise, came out from an inner apartment and narrowly escaped injury from the ruffian murderer. But a stunning blow from the heavy royal fist felled the traitor, who was then hurled from the battlements, thus suffering in a summary fashion the just penalty of his crime. Pīr Muhammad also died this year after rashly invading Khandesh—'the sighs of the orphans, of the weak, and of the captives did their work with him'. From that time Akbar was a free man, although the final emancipation was deferred until two years later (1564), when his mother's brother, a half-insane monster named Khwāja Muazzam, was removed. Akbar's policy for the forty-one remaining years of his reign was his own.

Reforms. In 1555 the ruler of the small state of Amber, Raja Bihār Mal, who earlier had submitted to Babur and Humayun, was presented to Akbar and well received. In 1561, however, the *jagīrdār* of Ajmer attacked him, reduced him to great straits, and took his son as hostage. The raja's complete destruction was only prevented by an order from court, and to secure his position the raja offered a daughter in marriage to Akbar. At Sambhar he married the princess, who became the mother of the Emperor Jahangir, and received into his service Mān Singh, the grandson, by adoption, of Bihār Mal. In the same year Todar Mal entered the imperial revenue service. The happiness of the marriage and the excellence of the Rajputs' loyal services led to the adoption by Akbar of the position of ruler over both Hindus and Muslims alike. Marriages with princesses of other Rajput states followed in later years. At this period (1562–4) Akbar effected several important changes. He abolished the taxes on Hindu pilgrims at Muttra; forbade the enslavement of prisoners of war, thereby reversing the policy of Fīrūz Shāh Tughluq; and also remitted the *jizya* or poll-tax on non-Muslims if Abu-l Fazl can be believed. (Badāūnī refers to the assessment of *jizya* in 1575, and puts its abolition in 1579.) The reforms were his own doing, carried out many years before he came under the influence of

Abu-l Fazl and the other persons whose names are associated with his later policy in matters of religion.

The ambition of Akbar. Akbar, one of the most ambitious of men, who loved power and wealth, brooking no rival near his throne, now set himself to effect the systematic subjugation of north-western and central India, to be followed later by the conquest of the west, east, and south. His designs were purely aggressive, his intention being to make himself the unquestioned lord paramount of India, and to suppress the independence of every kingdom within the reach of his arm. He carried out that policy with unflinching tenacity until January 1601, when the mighty fortress of Asirgarh, his last acquisition, passed into his hands. Circumstances beyond his control prevented him from continuing his career of conquest until his death in October 1605.

He began by encouraging a great noble, Āsaf Khān I, governor of Kara and the eastern provinces, to destroy the independence of Gondwana, equivalent to the northern portion of the present Madhya Pradesh, then governed by the dowager Rani Durgāvatī, an excellent princess, with whose administration no fault could be found. She was driven to her death, her country was overrun, and the wealth accumulated in the course of centuries was plundered. Injudicious flatterers of Akbar have printed much canting nonsense about his supposed desire to do good to the conquered peoples by his annexations. He never canted on the subject himself, or made any secret of the fact that he regarded as an offence the independence of a neighbour. 'A monarch', he said, 'should be ever intent on conquest, otherwise his neighbours rise in arms against him. The army should be exercised in warfare, lest from want of training they become self-indulgent.' Throughout his reign he acted consistently on those avowed principles.

Rebellions. The acquisition of the leading fortresses was an essential preliminary for securing the firm grasp of the imperial government on Hindostan or upper India. Gwalior, Chunar, and Mirtha had been acquired early in the reign. The next object of attack was Chitor in the territory of the Sīsōdia rana of Mewar in Rajputana, better known as the Udaipur state. Some delay in the execution of the padshah's ambitious projects was caused by the outbreak of several rebellions in the eastern provinces headed by a family group of Uzbeg officers, who disliked Akbar's Persianized ways and would have preferred Kamran's son, his cousin, to occupy the throne. In 1565 Akbar felt bound, as a matter of state necessity, to order the private execution of that cousin in order to prevent him from being used as a pretender. The act was the first of the long series of similar executions which have stained the annals of the Mughul dynasty. The rebellions of Khān Zamān and the other Uzbeg chiefs came to an end in 1567, leaving Akbar free to prepare for the siege of Chitor. He deeply resented the independent position assumed by the rana, who was acknowledged universally to be the head of the Rajput clans. His family never allowed a daughter to enter the Mughul palace. Udai Singh, the reigning rana in 1567, was a coward, unworthy of his noble ancestry, but his personal unworthiness did not prevent his brethren from organizing a gallant defence.

Siege of Chitor. The siege of Chitor, the most famous and dramatic military operation of the reign, lasted from 20 October 1567 to 23 February 1568, and would have lasted much longer had not Akbar by a lucky shot killed Jai Mal, the chieftain who was the soul of the defence, having assumed the place which the recreant rana should have occupied. The garrison abandoned all hope when deprived of their leader. The women were immolated on funeral pyres to save them from dishonour, a dread rite known as *jauhar* and usually practised by Rajputs when hard pressed. The clansmen of the regular garrison threw themselves on the Mughul swords and perished fighting. Akbar was so enraged by the fierce resistance that he massacred 30,000 of the country people who had taken part in the defence.

The gates of the fortress were taken off their hinges and removed to Agra. The huge kettledrums which used to proclaim for miles around the exit and entrance of the princes, and the massive candelabra which lighted the shrine of the Great Mother, also were carried away to adorn the halls of the victor. Chitor was left desolate, so that in the eighteenth century it became the haunt of tigers and other wild beasts. In these latter days it has partially recovered, and the lower town is now a prosperous little place with a railway station.

Fate of Rajputana. The fall of Chitor, followed in the next year (1569) by that of Ranthambhor, made Akbar master of Rajputana, although not in full sovereignty. The clans of Mewar never submitted to him, and he had to fight them from time to time during the greater part of his reign. But no doubt remained that the Mughul had become the paramount power over his Rajput neighbours. Most of the princes were content to receive official appointments as salaried dignitaries of the empire, and several gave daughters in marriage to the emperor. Rajputana or Rajasthan was reckoned as a province or *Sūba* with the headquarters at Ajmer, and the chivalry of the clans for the most part became devoted soldiers of the padshah.

The strong fortress of Kalanjar in Bundelkhand to the south of the Jumna opened its gates in 1569, the year in which Ranthambhor was taken.

Akbar was thus left at liberty to indulge his ambition in other directions, and to extend his conquests as far as the Arabian Sea on the west and the Bay of Bengal on the east.

Akbar's love of art. The activity of Akbar's versatile mind was never limited to the business of war and conquest. As early as his seventh regnal year he had taken pains to requisition the services of Tārsēn, the best singer in India, and he always retained an intelligent interest in music. Every form of art also attracted him, and as a boy he had learned the elements of drawing and painting under two renowned artists. He commemorated the gallantry of Jai Mal and Pattā, the heroes of Chitor, by causing their effigies to be carved and set on stone elephants placed at the gate of the Agra fort.

Buildings. He loved building and possessed excellent taste in architecture. The magnificent stone-faced walls of the Agra Fort were begun in 1565, and hundreds of buildings modelled on the designs of Bengal and Gujarat architects were erected within the precincts. Most of them were pulled down by Shahjahan, whose canons of taste differed. The palace-city of Fathpur-Sikri, twenty-three miles to the west of Agra, was begun in 1571, and finished about six or seven years later.

Akbar's sons. Akbar, having had the misfortune to lose at least two infant children while living at Agra, came to regard that place as unlucky. A famous Muslim holy man, Shaikh Salīm Chishtī, who dwelt among the rocks at Sikri, promised the emperor three sons who should survive. The prophecy was fulfilled. The eldest, born in August 1569, and named Prince Salim, in honour of the saint, became the Emperor Jahangir in due course. Murad, the second prince, born in 1570, died from the effects of intemperance about six years prior to his father's decease. The third son, Daniyal, met the same fate some four years later than his brother.

Fathpur-Sikri. The emperor, believing that the neighbourhood of Sikri, where the saint dwelt, would be lucky for himself, resolved to build a vast mosque there for the use of the Shaikh, and beside it a palace and royal residence, equipped with all the conveniences thought necessary in that age and adorned with all the resources of art.

After the conquest of Gujarat in 1573 the new city was named Fathābād or Fathpur, 'Victory town'. In order to distinguish it from many other places of the same name it is usually known as Fathpur-Sikri. The great mosque is still perfect, and several of the more important palace buildings, now carefully conserved, are almost uninjured. They are constructed of the local red sandstone, a fine durable building material. Artists from all countries accessible to Akbar were collected to decorate the buildings with carving and frescoes. Most of the carving has escaped damage, but few fragments of painting survive.

Fathpur-Sikri was occupied as the capital of the empire for only about fifteen years, when Akbar went north and quitted his fantastic city for ever, excepting a passing visit in 1601. The latest building of importance is the Buland Darwāza or Lofty Portal of the mosque, erected in 1575-6, probably as a triumphal arch to commemorate the conquest of Gujarat.

Gujarat. The rich province known as Gujarat, lying between Malwa and the Arabian Sea, had been held by Humayun for a short time, and long before had been subject to the sultanate of Delhi in the days of the Khiljīs and Muhammad bin Tughluq. Akbar, therefore, could advance reasonable claims to the recovery of the province, which in one case, invited aggression by its wealth Just then, too, the government had fallen into disorder and the intervention of Akbar was actually asked for by a local chief.

Conquest of Gujarat. The campaign began in July 1572. Surat was taken after a siege, and Akbar gave brilliant proof of his personal courage and prowess in a hard-fought skirmish at Sarnāl.[1] When the emperor, as he may now be called, started for home in the April following, he believed that the newly conquered province had been securely annexed and might be left safely in the charge of his officers. But he was hardly back in Fathpur-Sikri when he received reports of a formidable insurrection headed by certain disorderly cousins of his known as the Mīrzās, who already had given much trouble, and by a noble named Ikhtiyār-ul-Mulk. Akbar, who was then in his thirty-first year and in the fullest enjoyment of his exceptional powers, bodily and mental, rose to the occasion. He prepared a fresh expeditionary force with extraordinary rapidity, looking after everything personally, and sparing no expense. He declared that nobody would be ready to start sooner than himself, and made good his promise. Having sent on a small advanced guard, he rode out of his capital on 23 August with some 3,000 horsemen, rushed across Rajputana at hurricane speed and reached the outskirts of Ahmadabad, nearly 600 miles distant, in eleven days all told—nine days of actual travelling—a marvellous feat of endurance. The emperor, with his tiny force fought 20,000 of the enemy near Ahmadabad on 2 September 1573, and gained a decisive victory. He was back again in his capital on 4 October, Gujarat having then become definitely part of the empire. The province was disturbed many times afterwards, but the imperial supremacy was never questioned until 1758 when the Marathas occupied Ahmadabad.

The conquest of Gujarat an epoch. The conquest of Gujarat marks an important epoch in Akbar's history. The annexation gave his government free access to the sea with all the rich commerce passing through Surat and the other western ports. The territory and income of the state were vastly extended, so that the viceroyalty of Gujarat became one of the most important posts in the gift of the sovereign Akbar now first saw the sea and came into direct contact with the Portuguese, thus introducing new influences operating upon his mind The province became the practising ground for Raja Todar Mal, the able financier, who made his first revenue 'settlement' on improved principles in Gujarat.[2]

Reforms. The conclusion of the conquest gave Akbar and his advisers an opportunity for introducing several administrative reforms The government made a determined effort to check the extensive frauds continually practised by the officials or *mansabdārs*, who wer

---

[1] Near Thāsrā in the Kaira District, Bombay.

[2] The word 'settlement' in this technical sense is a translation of the Persian term *bandobast*. It includes all the processes necessary for the assessment of the 'land revenue' or crown rent, that is to say, the state's share of the produce of the cultivated land or its cash equivalent.

bound each to supply a certain number of mounted men. The expedient principally relied on was known as the 'branding regulation', based on precedents set by ʿAlā-ud-dīn Khiljī and Sher Shāh. Elaborate rules were laid down for branding every horse in the service of the government and thus making fraudulent musters of cavalry more difficult. The measure met with so much covert opposition from influential persons whose interests were affected that the success attained was only partial.

Akbar sought to diminish the power of the *jāgīrdārs*, or holders of revenue-assignments, and to enhance the authority of the crown by 'converting *jāgīrs* into crown-lands (*khālsa*)', that is to say, by dividing the imperial territory into convenient jurisdictions under the direct administration of salaried officials. Fīrūz Tughluq had favoured the system of paying his officers by assigning to each a district, from which the assignee collected the land revenue and cesses which otherwise would have been paid to the state. Akbar perceived clearly that that system tended to increase the power of local magnates and predisposed them to rebellion, while being also injurious to the fiscal interest of the central government. He was fond of money and always keen to increase his income. He therefore gave up the practice of assigning *jāgīrs* or fiefs, so far as possible, and preferred to appoint officials remunerated by definite salaries.

The consequent increase of officialdom, if it was to become an efficient instrument of government, involved the establishment of a bureaucracy or graded service of state officials. Akbar accordingly regularized the previously existing system of *mansabdārs*, or office-holders, and classified them in thirty-three grades. His arrangements will be described more particularly later. Here the fact is to be noted that all the above-mentioned measures of administrative and financial reform were worked out in the interval between the conquest of Gujarat in 1573 and the invasion of Bengal in 1575. The regulations were further perfected in subsequent years.

Conquest of Bengal. Akbar needed no pretext to induce him to undertake the extension of his empire eastward and the subjugation of Bengal which long before had been subject to the sultanate of Delhi. But the adventure was forced upon him by the rashness of Dāūd Khān, the young Afghan king of Bengal, who openly defied Akbar and believed himself to be more than a match for the imperial power. His father, Sulaimān Kararānī, had been careful to give formal recognition of the padshah's suzerainty, while preserving his practical independence. In 1574 Akbar undertook the chastisement of the presumptuous prince. He voyaged down the rivers, and drove Dāūd from Patna and Hajipur in the height of the rainy season, when Hindu custom forbade active operations. But Akbar cared for weather conditions as little as Alexander of Macedon had done, and insisted on the campaign being pressed, much against the inclination of his officers. He himself returned to Fathpur-Sikri. Dāūd was defeated early in 1575 at Tukarōī in the Balasore District. The battle would have been decisive and ended the war but for the ill-judged lenity of old Munim Khān, the commander-in-chief, who granted easy terms and allowed Dāūd to recover strength. Another campaign thus became necessary, and Dāūd was not finally defeated and killed until July 1576, in a battle fought near Rajmahal. From that date Bengal lost its independence.

Orissa was not annexed until 1592.

Defeat of Rana Partāp Singh. In this year (1576), which saw the annexation of Bengal, Kunwar Mān Singh of Amber, whose sister by adoption was married to the emperor, inflicted a crushing defeat on the brave Rana Partāp Singh of Mewar, the son of the craven Udai Singh. The battle was fought at the entrance of the Haldīghāt Pass, near the town of Gogūnda, and is spoken of indifferently by either name. The rana was driven to take refuge in remote fastnesses, and the strongholds of his kingdom passed into the hands of the imperialists. But before his death in 1597 he had recovered most of them. Ajmer, Chitor, and Mandalgarh always remained in possession of the padshah's officers.

The empire in 1576. The conquest of Bengal in 1576, twenty years after his accession, made Akbar master of all Hindustan, including the entire basins of the Indus and Ganges, excepting Sind on the lower course of the Indus, which did not come into his possession until many years later. He had thus become sovereign of the most valuable regions of India, extending from the Arabian Sea to the Bay of Bengal and from the Himalayas to the Narbada; besides the semi-independent Kabul province. The territories under his rule, with their huge population, fertile soil, numerous manufactures, and vast commerce, both internal and sea-borne, constituted even then an empire richer probably than any other in the world. The subsequent additions to his dominions, comprising Kashmir, Orissa, Sind, Kandahar, Khandesh, and a portion of the Deccan, with the complete absorption of the Kabul province, merely rounded off the compact empire which had been gradually acquired and consolidated in the first twenty years of his reign.

The 'House of Worship'. From 1575 Akbar ordinarily left the command of armies in the field to his trusted officers, Mān Singh, Todar Mal, Abdurrahīm, or others. Early in that year, when he returned from Patna, he busied himself with building in the gardens of the palace at Fathpur-Sikri near the mosque a handsome edifice called the House of Worship ('Ibādat Khāna) to be used as a debating-hall for the discussion of questions of religion and theology in which he was deeply interested. During the first three years, until 1578 or 1579, the discussions were limited to the various schools of Muslim theology. Even then they were sometimes embittered. From 1579 to 1582, when the debates came to an end, representatives of other religions were admitted and the disputants met in the private apartments of the palace. The site of the House of Worship has been utterly forgotten and no trace of the building, which was large and highly decorated, has been discovered. The probability is that Akbar pulled it down when he had no longer any use for it.

More reforms. The emperor during the years 1575 and 1576 also devoted much attention to the development of his administrative reforms, both those already mentioned and others. The record department was organized, and a record room was built at Fathpur-Sikri. The grading of the *mansabdārs* was made more systematic, and a plan was devised for dividing the older provinces into artificial districts each yielding a quarter of a million of rupees in land revenue. That plan was a failure and the government soon reverted to the use of the recognized sub-districts called *parganas*.

The mint was reorganized in 1577-8, and placed in charge of the celebrated artist Abd us-Samad, who had been Akbar's drawing-master twenty years earlier. The mint was a well-managed department, and Akbar's coinage was both abundant in quantity and excellent in quality.

The First Jesuit Mission. Akbar became personally acquainted with European Christians for the first time in 1572, when he met certain Portuguese merchants at Cambay. In the next year, 1573, he extended his intercourse with the foreigners at Surat and adjusted terms of peace with Antonio Cabral, the envoy from the viceroy at Goa. In 1576 and 1577 the emperor obtained some imperfect knowledge of the Christian religion from Father Julian Pereira, vicar-general in Bengal, and from other sources, but only sufficient to make him eager to attain more accurate information. Antonio Cabral, who again visited him at the capital in 1578, not being qualified to answer all the imperial inquiries, Akbar resolved to obtain from Goa theological experts who should be able to resolve his doubt and satisfy his intense curiosity. In September 1579, accordingly, he dispatched to the authorities at Goa a letter begging them to send two learned priests capable of instructing him in the doctrines of the Gospels. He assured his expected guests of the most honourable reception and effectual protection.

The church authorities at Goa eagerly accepted the invitation, which seemed to open up a prospect of converting the emperor to Christianity, and with him his court and people.

The two principal missionaries selected, Father Rodolfo Aquaviva and Father Antonio Monserrate, both Jesuits or members of the Society of Jesus, were remarkable men, highly qualified for their task in different ways. Aquaviva won respect by a life of extreme asceticism. Monserrate, a person of much learning, was directed to prepare a history of the mission; and obeyed the command by writing an excellent Latin treatise, which ranks as one of the principal authorities for the reign of Akbar. The priests travelled from Daman and Surat through Khandesh, the wild Bhil country, Malwa, Narwar, Gwalior, and Dholpur to Fathpur-Sikri, where they arrived on 28 February (O.S.) 1580, and were received with extraordinary honour. The emperor's second son, Prince Murad, then about ten years of age, was made over to Father Monserrate for instruction in the Portuguese language and Christian morals.

The 'Infallibility Decree'. When Akbar returned triumphant from Gujarat in 1573, a learned, although rather heretical, Muslim theologian named Shaikh Mubārak greeted him by expressing the hope that the padshah might become the spiritual as well as the temporal head of his people—in fact, pope as well as king. In 1579 he felt free to give practical effect to the theologian's hint. Shaikh Mubārak prepared a formal document, which may be conveniently called the Infallibility decree, authorizing the emperor to decide with binding authority any question concerning the Muslim religion, provided that the ruling should be in accordance with some verse of the Quran. The measure professed to be 'for the glory of God and the propagation of Islam'. It had no connexion with any other religion. The decree, which was forced upon the acceptance of the Ulamā, or Muslim doctors of divinity, obviously rendered superfluous the inter-Muslim discussions in the House of Worship, which ceased accordingly.

A little earlier in the same year (1579) Akbar had startled and offended religious people by displacing the regular preacher at the mosque, and himself mounting the pulpit, where he recited verses composed by Faizī, the elder son of Shaikh Mubārak. About the same time he began to show many indications that he had lost faith in the creed of the Prophet of Mecca. The Jesuits, when coming up from the coast at the beginning of 1580, were informed that the emperor had even forbidden the use of the name of Muhammad in the public prayers.

Muslim alarm and revolt. The excessive favour shown by the sovereign to his Jesuit visitors, his obvious lack of faith in Islam, and his partial compliance with the ritual of Parsis and Jains, who shared the royal condescension along with the Christian priests, grievously alarmed his Muslim subjects and produced important political effects.

The Bengal rebellion. The Muslim chiefs in Bengal and Bihar, mostly of Afghan origin, were specially alarmed by Akbar's conduct, which was interpreted, and not without reason, as an attack upon the Muslim religion. They were also irritated by his administrative measures, the resumption of grants in Bihar, the reduction of special pay for Bihar and Bengal, and the branding regulations, as carried out with considerable harshness by his officers, and for those reasons determined on rebellion. The Qazi of Jaunpur boldly issued a formal ruling, affirming the lawfulness of rebellion against Akbar as an apostate, an act of high treason for which he paid with his life.

The rebellion broke out in January 1580, and continued for five years. The rebels aimed at replacing Akbar by his orthodox half-brother Muhammad Hakim of Kabul, who supported their movement by an invasion of the Panjab. But the Bengal insurgents were separated from their ally by hundreds of miles, and the emperor rightly judged that they might be left to his officers, who would dispose of the trouble in time, as they did.

The expedition to Kabul. He resolved to meet in person the graver danger threatened from Kabul. He equipped an overwhelming force with the utmost care, and marched from the capital in February 1581. Muhammad Hakim, a feeble, drunken creature, fled from the Panjab, and offered little resistance to the advance of Akbar, who entered Kabul in August. His brother kept out of the way and never met him. The emperor was back safely in his capital on 1 December. He permitted Muhammad Hakim to remain as ruler of the Kabul territory until his death from drink in 1585, when his territories passed under the direct government of the padshah.

A critical year. The year 1581 was the most critical in the reign of Akbar, if his early struggles be omitted from consideration. When he marched from Fathpur-Sikri in February, nearly all the influential Muslims were opposed to him, subtle traitors surrounded his person, and the eastern provinces were in the possession of rebels. Defeat by Muhammad Hakim would have involved the loss of everything—life included. Akbar took no chances. He cowed the traitors by one terrible execution, the solemn and deserved hanging of Khwāja Shāh Mansūr, his finance minister, and overawed his brother by a display of irresistible force. We are fortunate enough to possess an accurate detailed narrative of the Kabul campaign, written by Father Monserrate, tutor of Prince Murad, who accompanied his pupil and the emperor.

When Akbar came home his demeanour showed that he had been freed from a great terror, and that he now felt himself thoroughly secure for the first time in his life. From the beginning of 1582 nobody dared to oppose him. He could do literally what he pleased. He enjoyed and used that liberty to the end of his life twenty-three years later.

The Dīn Ilāhī. He promptly took advantage of his freedom by publicly showing his contempt and dislike for the Muslim religion, and by formally promulgating a new political creed of his own, adherence to which involved the solemn renunciation of Islam. The new religion, dubbed the Divine Monotheism (*Tauhīd Ilāhī*) or Divine Religion (*Dīn Ilāhī*), rejected wholly the claims of Muhammad to be an inspired prophet, and practically replaced him by the emperor. Abu-l Fazl, Shaikh Mubārak's younger son, who had been introduced at court in 1574, became the high priest of the new creed, and the stage manager of the rather ridiculous initiation ceremonies. Many time-serving courtiers professed to become Akbar's disciples, surrendering to him life, property, honour, and religion, as the vows required, but the so-called religion never enlisted any considerable following, and it may well be doubted if a single person ever honestly believed in it. Abu-l Fazl, a man of immense learning and endowed with a singularly powerful intellect, certainly was far too intelligent to believe. But he was base enough to play the hypocrite's part and reap no small profit thereby, as the confidential secretary and adviser of the sovereign. Akbar's freak in professing to invent a new eclectic religion, compounded out of selections from several of the old religions, has received far more attention from most European historians than it deserves on its merits.

Akbar's rejection of Islam. From 1582, when the new religion was solemnly promulgated at a council, and indeed from a date considerably earlier, Akbar was not a Muslim, although on occasion he performed acts of conformity from motives of policy. He told Monserrate distinctly early in 1582 that he was not a Muslim, and that he paid no heed to the *kalima*, or Muslim formula of the faith. In that year and subsequent years he issued a stream of regulations openly hostile to Islam and inculcating practices learned from the Parsi, Hindu, and Jain teachers whom he received with marked favour and to whom he listened with profound attention. His conduct at different times justified Christians, Hindus, Jains, and Parsis in severally claiming him as one of themselves. But his heart was never really touched by any doctrine, and he died as he had lived for many years, a man whose religion nobody could name. The authors who affirm that he formally professed Islam on his death-bed appear to be mistaken.

Fantastic ordinances. Regulations aimed at Islam, and amounting along with others to an irritating persecution of that religion, wholly inconsistent with the principle of universal toleration, included the following: No child was to be given the name of Muhammad, and if he had already received it the name must be changed. The erection of new and the repair of old mosques were prohibited. The *sijdah*, or prostration, hitherto reserved for divine worship, was declared to be the due of the sovereign. The study of Arabic, Muslim law, or commentaries on the Quran was discouraged.

Hindu prejudices were humoured by the prohibition of beef, garlic, and onions as food.

Stringent restrictions on the use of flesh meat imposed by a series of enactments seem to have been mainly due to Jain influence, though the idea of Hindu asceticism may also have played a part, as Badāūnī suggests.

The worship of the sun, fire, and light, with sundry ritual observances enforced at court, were chiefly the result of Parsi teaching. Akbar's mode of life, on the whole, ceased to be that of a Muslim, and constantly approached the Hindu ideal of *dharma*, as modified by a Zoroastrian or Parsi tinge.

Akbar's audacity. The prestige resulting from the defeat of his brother in 1581, the suppression of the Bengal and Bihar rebellions, and the fate suffered by opponents of his policy enabled Akbar to do all the strange things mentioned above, and yet to escape assassination or even any open display of disaffection. The necessary backing of force, or the threat of force, which stood behind the audacious imperial policy, was supplied by the Rajput contingents under the command of the rajas of Amber (Jaipur), Marwar (Jodhpur), and other states. But Akbar never was reduced to the necessity of relying wholly on Hindu support. Many Muslim nobles continued to serve him to the end, whether they liked his proceedings or not.

Result of forty years' war. Whatever might be his religious vagaries, Akbar never forgot his worldly ambitions. He secured the important strategical position at the confluence of the Ganges and Jumna by building the Allahabad fort in 1583. Three years later, in 1586, he made war on Kashmir and by an act of gross treachery annexed the country, simply because the local sultan presumed to withhold complete submission to the master of Hindostan. Southern Sind was similarly absorbed in 1590; Orissa was conquered by Mān Singh in 1592; Baluchistan, with the coast region of Makran, was added to the empire in 1594; and Qandahar was surrendered by its Persian governor a year later.

Thus, in 1596, every part of India to the north of the Narbada, besides the vast territories of Kabul, Ghazni, and Qandahar, with their dependencies, acknowledged the might of Akbar. No man within that enormous area presumed to call himself independent, unless an exception be made in favour of certain tribes on the frontiers and in the hills. In 1586 the Yūsufzī and allied tribes of the north-western frontier succeeded in closing the Khyber for a period and in defeating one of Akbar's armies and killing Raja Bīrbal, one of his dearest and most intimate friends. The emperor could afford to overlook such minor military mishaps, and might well feel proud of the results gained by forty years of war.

Ambitious projects. The soaring ambition of Akbar was not bounded by the Narbada, or even by the limits of India and Afghanistan. He avowed his hopes both of regaining the ancient dominions of his ancestors in central Asia beyond the Oxus, and of bringing under his control all the sultanates of the Deccan. Moreover, he ardently desired to expel the Portuguese from his province of Gujarat, and vainly supposed that he could do so without the help of a fleet. But he never succeeded even in coming near to an attempt on Transoxiana, and his attacks on the Portuguese settlements were complete failures. His restricted conquests in the Deccan fell far short of his expectation. Before the campaign in the Deccan is described it will be convenient to revert to Akbar's curious relations with Christianity and more especially with the Jesuit missionaries.

Akbar and the Jesuits. The first Jesuit mission of Aquaviva and Monserrate ended in 1583 with the withdrawal of Aquaviva. The hopes of Akbar's conversion which had been entertained at Goa were grievously disappointed. A second mission sent in 1590 at the emperor's urgent request was recalled in 1592, having effected nothing. The third mission, also dispatched in compliance with a pressing invitation arrived in 1595 at Lahore where the court then resided, and became a more or less permanent institution, not without its effect on secular politics. The leading members were Fathers Jerome Xavier and Emmanuel Pinheiro. Their letters, of which many have been printed, are first-class authorities for the latter part of Akbar's reign. The missionaries, although they did not succeed in converting either the sovereign or his nobles, or indeed in making many converts of any kind, won from Akbar the right to make convers if they could, and obtained from him extraordinary privileges. Both he and his son Prince Salim professed veneration for the Virgin Mary and for Christian images. It is clear that the attention lavished on the priests was not the outcome of genuine religious fervour, but was dictated chiefly by the desire to secure Portuguese military help. Akbar in 1600 made special efforts to obtain the loan of the foreigners' superior ordnance for the siege of Asirgarh, which he could not breach with his own guns; while the prince, meditating rebellion, and in reality indifferent to religion, was equally eager to enlist their aid against his father. In 1601 Akbar sent a final embassy to Goa without any pretence of seeking religious instruction, but got no satisfaction from the wily Goan authorities, who understood the game perfectly. The Jesuits on their part combined patriotic politics with missionary zeal and acted as unofficial agents of the Portuguese government, or rather of the government of Spain, with which Portugal was then united.[1] Their considerable influence is attested by the report of an Englishman, John Mildenhall, who, seeking trading facilities, visited Akbar in the last years of his life.

Famine. A terrible famine, as bad as any recorded in the long list of Indian famines, desolated the whole of Hindostan or northern India and Kashmir for three or four years from 1595 to 1598. The historians barely notice the calamity, the fullest description being that recorded by a minor author in these few words: 'A kind of plague also added to the horrors of this period, and depopulated whole houses and cities, to say nothing of hamlets and villages. In consequence of the dearth of grain and the necessities of ravenous hunger, men ate their own kind. The streets and roads were blocked up with dead bodies, and no assistance could be rendered for their removal.' Some slight relief measures were adopted, but even the proverbial good fortune of Akbar could not either prevent or remedy the effects of long continued failure of rain.

The Deccan campaign. Akbar attempted in 1590 by means of diplomatic missions to induce the rulers of Khandesh in the valley of the Tapti, and of the more distant sultanates of Ahmadnagar (including Berar), Golkonda, and Bijapur, to recognize formally his suzerainty and consent to pay tribute. He did not trouble himself about the small principality of Bidar, which continued to exist until some years after his death. The imperial envoys obtained no substantial success except in Khandesh, which promised obedience. The other states politely evaded Akbar's demands. He therefore determined on war.

Operations, which began in 1593, were impeded by internal dissen-

[1] The union of the crowns of Portugal and Spain was effected in 1580, and lasted until Dec. 1640.

PLATE 19

a. Delhi: Quwat-ul-Islam Masjid

b. Delhi: Moth-ki-Masjid

PLATE 20

a. Delhi: Qil'a a-i-Kuhna Masjid in the Purana Qila

b. Delhi: Jami Masjid from the courtyard

sions on both sides. The imperialist generals, Prince Murad, and Abdurrahīm, the Khān Khānān, could not agree, while the states of the Deccan continued to quarrel among themselves.

A gallant princess, named Chānd Bībī, defended the city of Ahmadnagar with valour equal to that shown by Rāni Durgāvatī in Gondwana thirty years earlier, but in 1596 was constrained to accept a treaty by which the province of Berar was ceded to the emperor. War soon broke out again, which was terminated in August 1600 by the death of Chānd Bībī and the fall of Ahmadnagar.

Akbar goes south. Meantime, the sultan of Khandesh, Mīrān Bahādur Shāh, had repented of his submission and resolved to fight, relying on the strength of his fortress of Asirgarh, which was defended by renegade Portuguese gunners.

Akbar, who had been detained in the Panjab for thirteen years on account of his fear of an invasion by the Uzbegs, was relieved from that anxiety by the death early in 1598 of Abdullah Khān Uzbeg, the able ruler of Transoxiana. He perceived that the effective prosecution of the Deccan campaign was hopeless without his personal supervision. Accordingly, he marched from Lahore to Agra late in 1598, and in July of the following year was able to resume his advance southwards. He placed Prince Salim in charge of the capital and Ajmer with orders to complete the subjugation of the rana of Mewar. But the prince, who already meditated rebellion, ignored his father's commands, so that the rana was left in peace.

Meantime, in May 1599, Prince Murad had died of delirium tremens in the Deccan, and so had removed one competitor from Salim's path. No rival now remained except Daniyal, a drunken sot.

About the middle of 1599 Akbar crossed the Narbada, and occupied Burhanpur, the capital of Khandesh, without opposition. He then proceeded to make arrangements for the investment and siege of Asirgarh, which was only a few miles distant from Burhanpur and could not be left in enemy hands. It was one of the strongest fortresses in the world at that date, and so amply furnished with water, provisions, guns, and munitions that its defenders might reasonably expect to hold out for years.

Siege of Asirgarh. The emperor soon found that the task which he had set himself was beyond his military powers. His artillery was unable to breach the walls and he failed to obtain Portuguese guns. After the siege had gone on for about eight months, from April to December 1600, he resolved to try treachery. He inveigled Bahādur Shāh into his camp for the purpose of negotiation, swearing by his own head that the king would be allowed to return in safety. But Akbar, who was pressed for time, shamelessly violated his oath and detained Bahādur Shāh, hoping that the garrison would surrender after the usual Indian fashion when deprived of their leader. Bahādur had, however, ordered Yaqut, the African commander to ignore all orders to surrender. The siege dragged on until 17 January (O.S.) 1601, when the gates were opened by golden keys, or, in other words, Akbar corrupted the Khandesh officers by heavy payments. Akbar was unable to wait, because Prince Salim had already begun his rebellion and it was indispensable that his father should return to the capital. Asirgarh, won by perfidy and bribery, was the last conquest of Akbar, whose hitherto unbroken good fortune no longer attended him. The remaining years of his life were rendered miserable by the treachery of his eldest son, the child of so many prayers, by the scandalous death of Prince Daniyal, and other sorrows.

Three new provinces. The emperor made all possible haste in organizing the administration of the newly acquired territories, which were formally constituted as three *subas* or provinces, namely, Ahmadnagar, Berar, and Khandesh. But the Ahmadnagar *suba* had little more than a formal existence, because the greater part of the kingdom remained in the hands of a member of the local royal family. Prince Daniyal was appointed viceroy of southern and western India—that is to say, of the three new *subas*, with Malwa and Gujarat. Akbar arrived at Agra on 23 August 1601.

Submission of Prince Salim. Prince Salim continued in open rebellion, holding court as a king at Allahabad. In August 1602 he inflicted a terrible blow upon his father's feelings by hiring a robber chief named Bīr Singh Bundēla to murder Akbar's trusted friend and counsellor, Abu-l Fazl, whom the prince hated and feared. A temporary and insincere reconciliation between father and son was patched up by Salima Begam in 1603. But no real peace was possible until after the death of Prince Daniyal, which occurred in April 1604, when he died from the effects of drink, like his brother Murad. Salim being then the only son left, Akbar became really anxious to arrange terms with him. The one other possible successor was Salim's son, Prince Khusru a popular and amiable youth, whose claims were favoured by Raja Mān Singh and Azīz Kokā.

In November 1604 Salim was persuaded to come to court, probably under threats that, if he refused, Khusru would be declared heir apparent. His father received him with seeming cordiality. He then drew him suddenly into an inner apartment, slapped him soundly in the face, and confined him in a bathroom under the charge of a physician and two servants, as if he were a lunatic requiring medical treatment. After a short time, the length of which is variously stated, Akbar released his son, restored him to favour, made him viceroy of the provinces to which Daniyal had been appointed, and allowed him to reside at Agra as the acknowledged heir apparent.

The prince was cowed by his father's rough handling and gave no further trouble.

Death of Akbar. In September 1605 Akbar became ill with severe diarrhoea or dysentery, which the physicians failed to cure. While on his death-bed and unable to speak he received Salim and indicated by unmistakable gestures that he desired his succession. The emperor

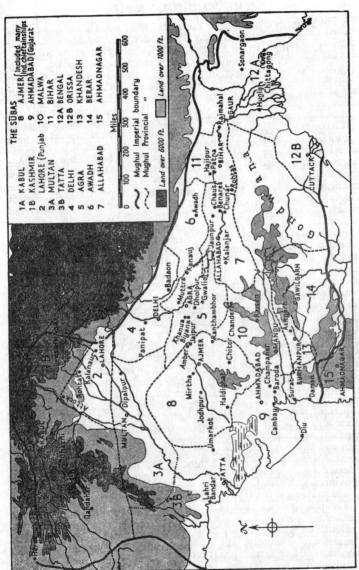

THE MUGHUL EMPIRE IN 1600

THE SŪBAS

1A KABUL
1B KASHMIR
2   LAHORE (Punjab
3A MULTAN
3B TATTA
4   DELHI
5   AGRA
6   AWADH
7   ALLAHABAD
8   AJMER (Included many Ind. chieftainships
9   AHMADĀBAD (Gujarat
10 MALWA
11 BIHAR
12A BENGAL
12B ORISSA
13 KHANDESH
14 BERAR
15 AHMADNAGAR

Miles
0   100 200 300 400 500 600

~~~ Mughul Imperial boundary
···· Mughul Provincial "
Land over 6000 ft.
Land over 1000 ft.

passed away in silence, after midnight, early on Thursday morning, 17 October (O.S. = 27 N.S., and Wednesday night by Muslim reckoning). The symptoms of Akbar's fatal illness, so far as recorded, are consistent with the administration of a secret irritant poison, but the evidence is not sufficient to permit of a definite judgement on the question whether or not he died a natural death. He was buried at Sikandara near Agra in the mausoleum which he had begun, and which his successor rebuilt to a fresh design. His funeral was hurried and poorly attended. 'Thus', observes Du Jarric, the eminent Jesuit historian, 'does the world treat those from whom it expects no good and fears no evil. That was the end of the life and reign of King Akbar.'

Desecration of Akbar's grave. Unhappily, he was not allowed to rest in peace. The Jats of the neighbourhood, whose revolt began in 1688 during the absence of Aurangzeb in the Deccan, attacked the mausoleum in 1691, breaking in the massive bronze gates, tearing away the costly ornaments, and destroying everything which they could not carry off. Their wrath against their Mughul oppressors led them to a still more shocking outrage. 'Dragging out the bones of Akbar, they threw them into the fire and burnt them.'

Succession of Salim. The intrigues of Raja Mān Singh and Azīz Kokā to set aside Prince Salim and raise his son Prince Khusru to the throne having failed, largely owing to Rajput resistance, Prince Salim was allowed to take his father's place without further opposition.

Akbar's personal qualities. Akbar was of middle stature, probably about 5 feet 7 inches in height, compactly built, and possessed of immense bodily strength, which he enjoyed using. His complexion was dark rather than fair, and his voice was loud. He looked every inch a king, and observers were specially impressed by his eyes, which have been vividly described by a Jesuit friend as 'vibrant like the sea in sunshine'. His naturally hot temper, usually kept under strict control, blazed out in wrath at times, as when he felled Adham Khān, or ordered an unlucky lamplighter to be thrown from the battlements because he had fallen asleep when on duty. His storms of passion subsided as suddenly as they arose, leaving no bitterness behind them. His manners were charming, and his sympathetic condescension to humble folk won all hearts. He was, as Bartoli neatly says, 'great with the great, and lowly with the lowly'. He honestly desired to do justice, and did it to the best of his ability in the stern fashion of his times, taking precautions against the too hasty execution of his sentences. Cruelty for its own sake gave him no pleasure, but he occasionally sanctioned barbarous punishments which shock the modern reader.

Intellectually, he was a man of boundless curiosity, and endowed with extraordinary versatility of mind. People said that there was nothing that he knew not how to do, and he loved doing mechanical work in wood or metal with his own hands. The founding of cannon and the manufacture of matchlocks specially interested him. His mechanical tastes and his habits of minute observation gave him a singular mastery over the details of departmental administration, which he combined happily with exceptional breadth of view. Every department, whether of his vast household or of the imperial government, came constantly under his watchful eye, and he spared himself no labour. He rarely slept more than three hours at a time and seemed to be almost incapable of fatigue.

Formal illiteracy. Although when a boy he had steadily refused to learn his lessons, and was the despair of successive tutors, so that to the end of his days he could not decipher a written word or sign his own name, he was, nevertheless, well read and well informed in many subjects, after an unsystematic fashion. He loved to have books of history, theology, poetry, and other kinds read to him, and his prodigious memory enabled him to learn through the ear more than an ordinary man could learn through the eye. He was thus able to take an active part in the discussion of literary and abstruse subjects with such skill that the listener could hardly believe him to be illiterate in the formal sense. His special taste was for endless debates on the merits of rival religions, which he examined from a strangely detached point of view.

Religious history. Akbar was brought up as a Sunni Muslim, and, as he himself confessed, gladly persecuted heretics during the early years of his reign. Shaikh Mubārak, father of Faizī and Abu-l Fazl, then narrowly escaped execution. But it is probable that Akbar even in boyhood was never thoroughly orthodox. One of his tutors introduced him to the works of the Persian Sufi mystics, and he evinced at an early age a strong liking for the society of Hindu holy men, whose speculations were much akin to those of the Sufis. Akbar was a mystic all his life, and on several occasions saw visions which seemed to bring him into direct communion with the Unknown God. He suffered from some form of epileptic disease, which may be regarded as the physical explanation of many of his peculiarities, including the melancholy which constantly oppressed him, and constrained him to seek relief in an unceasing round of diversions.

His religious history may be divided into three periods. Until 1575, or possibly until 1578, he was a convinced Muslim of the Sunni sect, regular in his observance of the prescribed ritual, a zealous builder of mosques, and a constant suppliant at the tombs of the saints. His last recorded mosque-building was the noble Buland Darwāza or Lofty Portal at Fathpur-Sikri erected in 1575–6. He continued to attend public worship regularly until 1578, and made his last pilgrimage to the shrine at Ajmer in 1579. His substantial orthodoxy in the eyes of the world was not compromised by his leaning to Sufi mysticism, which he shared with many learned doctors of the law.

From 1579, the year in which he ascended the pulpit and issued the Infallibility Decree, his belief in Islam was weak and shaky. By the beginning of 1582, after his victorious return from Kabul, that belief had wholly disappeared. He tried then the hopeless experiment of inventing a new religion to suit the whole empire, desiring that Hindus and Muslims should worship in unison the One God, recognizing the padshah as His vicegerent on earth and the authorized exponent of His will.

The gradual changes in Akbar's religious views, largely brought about by his own thinking over the Sufi studies of his boyhood and the diversity of creeds among his people, were furthered by the suggestions of Shaikh Mubārak, and the later confidential intercourse with the Shaikh's sons, Faizī and Abu-l Fazl, which began about 1575. Other influences co-operated with their teaching. Jains, Parsis, Hindus of various kinds, and Christians all took their share in modifying the opinions of the emperor and determining the lines of his policy.[1]

Toleration in theory and practice. The avowed principle of both Abu-l Fazl and Akbar was universal toleration (*sulh-i kul*). During the latter half of the reign that principle was fully applied in favour of Hindus, Christians, Jains, and Parsis, who enjoyed full liberty both of conscience and of public worship. But it was violated in respect of Muslims, who were subjected to irritating persecution. That failure of Akbar to act up to his own boasted principles is the principal blot on his public character to my mind.

Treatment of Hindus. Akbar's new policy in relation to his Hindu subjects was not determined mainly by his personal fancies or beliefs in matters of religion. At an early age he perceived the political necessity that the padshah should be the impartial sovereign of all his subjects, irrespective of creed. His marrying of Hindu princesses, abolition of pilgrim dues, and ready employment of Hindus were all measures taken while he was still a sincere practising Muslim. Marriages between a Muslim king and the daughters of Hindu rajas were not a novelty. Several of the Deccan sultans had formed such alliances, which were not unknown at Delhi; but Akbar contracted his marriages in a different spirit, and accepted his Hindu male connexions as members of the royal family. No pressure was put on the princes of Amber, Marwar, or Bikaner to adopt Islam, and they were freely entrusted with the highest military commands and the most responsible administrative offices. That was an entirely new departure, due to Akbar himself, not to Abu-l Fazl or another. The policy afforded the strongest support to the throne in the reigns of Akbar and his son, and continued to bear fruit even in the reigns of his grandson, Shahjahan, and his great-grandson, Aurangzeb. But Aurangzeb's ill-judged policy of worrying Hindus gradually estranged the Rajput chieftains and largely contributed to the rapid dissolution of the empire which occurred after his death.

The Hindu queens, who were given Muslim titles and received Muslim burial, probably adopted Muslim modes of life to some extent, but contemporary pictures prove that they were allowed to practise

---

[1] Neither Akbar nor Abu-l Fazl ever enjoyed an opportunity of meeting learned Buddhists. The statements made in several books that Buddhists joined in the debates on religion are erroneous.

their own religious rites inside the palace.[1] No doubt their society must have had some effect upon Akbar's religious opinions and practice.

Administration. The organization of the government undoubtedly was immensely improved by Akbar, who was the real founder of the Mughul empire. The autocracy or absolute power of the padshah remained unshaken, and the merits of the government depended mainly on the character of the supreme ruler. He broke the power of the wazir and divided his duties between the heads of departments. He chose, transferred, dismissed his great officials without respect for rank, race, or creed. He created regular departments with written regulations within which officials could freely work without dependence upon the royal whim. He developed an improved system for the assessment and collection of the revenue, with the help of Raja Todar Mal, who, I think, was on the whole the ablest and most upright of the great imperial officers.

The administration was framed on military lines. The governor of a province, the *sūbadār*, or *sīpāhsālār*, maintained a court modelled on that of his sovereign, and possessed practically full powers so long as he retained office. Subject to his liability to recall he was an absolute autocrat. All officials, administrative as well as military—and the roles were often exchanged—were called *mansabdārs*, as in Persia, the word simply meaning 'office-holder'. The *mansabdārs* were divided into thirty-three classes, each member of each class being supposed to furnish a certain number of cavalry to the imperial army. The three highest grades, 'commanders' of from 7,000 to 10,000, were ordinarily reserved for the princes. The other *mansabs* ranged from ten to 5,000. But the numbers used for grading purposes did not agree with the actual facts. In the years before 1580 Akbar attempted to secure contingents from his *mansabdārs* which should be equal to their nominal rank. But this, like the branding regulations, was partly frustrated by the interested opposition of all his officials. At the end of the reign a double rank was used, one element, the *zāt*, or personal rank, denoting the grade of the official within the imperial service, the other, the *suwar*, showing what contingent must in fact be produced. Pay scales were so devised as to encourage the official to secure a high *suwar* rank in relation to his *zāt* rank. The permanent regular army was very small. The greater part of the imperial forces consisted of contingents furnished by the rajas and *mansabdārs*, each under its own chief.

Every considerable official exercised general administrative and judicial powers, especially in criminal cases. Civil disputes ordinarily were left to the Qazis, to be settled under Quranic law. No regular judicial service existed, except in so far as the Qazis formed such, and each governor or other person in authority did what he pleased, subject to the risk of imperial displeasure. No code existed, and no written judgements were delivered. Officers were instructed to pay little heed

[1] *H.F.A.*, p. 332.

to witnesses or oaths, and to rely rather on their own discernment and knowledge of human nature. Even capital punishment was inflicted at discretion, and might assume any form.

Revenue system. Raja Todar Mal, following the precedent set by Sher Shāh, carried out in many parts of the empire an improved system of 'settlement', or assessment of the land revenue, based on fairly accurate measurement and a classification of the kind of soil, whether newly broken waste, or old tillage, combined with consideration of the crop grown and the mean prevailing prices. He thus increased the imperial revenue and gave the peasant a certain amount of security. The revenue was collected directly from the individual cultivator, so far as possible. In modern technical language the 'settlement was ryotwar'. Akbar, who preferred cash rents, took the equivalent of one-third of the gross produce instead of the one-sixth prescribed by the Hindu scriptures. The cultivators were supposed to be compensated by the abolition of a crowd of cesses. But we do not know how far the orders for such abolition were acted on, and have hardly any information concerning the actual working of Todar Mal's revenue system in the days of Akbar. The comparative peace which the imperial arms assured must have tended to create a considerable amount of agricultural prosperity. Trade certainly was brisk, and in ordinary years food was extraordinarily cheap.

Famines. Famines, however, occurred. We hear of several. The one of 1555–6 at the beginning of the reign was extremely severe; and that of 1595–8, when Akbar's career of conquest was almost completed, seems to have been one of the worst in the long list of Indian famines. It lasted for three or four years, and must have caused serious effects, of which there is no record.

Akbar's friends. Akbar, after his early years, chose his friends and great officers from among both Hindus and Muslims with a leaning in favour of the former.

His most intimate Muslim friends were the brothers Faizī and Abu-l Fazl, sons of Shaikh Mubārak. Faizī, who cared little for wealth or office, devoted himself chiefly to literary pursuits. Abu-l Fazl, a man of profound learning, untiring industry, and commanding intellect, resembled Francis Bacon, his junior contemporary, in combining the parts of scholar, author, courtier, and man of affairs. He was a faithful servant of Akbar, 'the King's Jonathan', as the Jesuits called him, and was for many years his confidential secretary and adviser.

Raja Mān Singh, nephew and adopted son of Raja Bhagwān Dās of Amber was one of Akbar's best generals and governors. He is said to have ruled the eastern provinces with 'great prudence and justice'.

Raja Todar Mal, who had no advantages of birth, made his way to the top of the imperial service by sheer merit and ability. He was a good commander in the field as well as an unrivalled revenue expert. He was free from avarice, and was, perhaps, the ablest man, excepting Abu-l Fazl, in the service.

Many other notable personages adorn the annals of the reign. The Jesuit Fathers, especially Aquaviva, Monserrate, and Jerome Xavier, must be reckoned as among the intimate friends of Akbar, who had a genuine liking for them personally, quite apart from political motives.

Literature and art. A long, prosperous, and victorious reign encouraged literature and art, which were in brisk demand at a magnificent court, where they received intelligent patronage from Akbar. Important histories in Persian were composed by Abu-l Fazl, Nizām-ud-dīn, Badāūnī, and other authors. The *Āīn-i Akbarī*, or *Institutes of Akbar*, compiled by Abu-l Fazl, as the result of seven years' labour, gives a wonderful survey of the empire. Among the poets or versifiers writing in Persian Faizī was considered the best. But the greatest author of the time, Tulsī Dās the Hindi poet, does not seem to have been known to Akbar personally. His noble work, the Hindi Rāmāyana, or *Rāmcharitmānas*, is familiar to all Hindus in Upper India.

The ancient art of Indian painting, which had always continued to exist, although examples dating between the seventh and the sixteenth centuries are extremely rare, received a new direction from Akbar, who induced the Hindu artists to learn Persian technique and imitate Persian style. The works produced in a spirit of mere imitation were not altogether successful, but an Indo-Persian school developed gradually, and became rich in coloured drawings of high merit. The portraits of the Mughul period, which are especially deserving of commendation, attained their highest degree of perfection in the reign of Shahjahan. The art of Akbar's time is cruder and more conventional. The frontispiece of my work *Akbar the Great Mogul* reproduces accurately the earliest known Indo-Persian painting, dating from about 1557 or 1558. The next earliest extant specimens are the fragments of fresco at Fathpur-Sikri, executed about 1570. Most of the ancient Hindu paintings appear to have been applied to walls in either fresco or tempera, or a combination of both processes, and necessarily were lost when the buildings fell to ruin or were destroyed.

The architecture of Akbar's reign is characterized by a happy blending of Hindu and Muslim styles, which is a reflex or expression in stone of his personal feelings and convictions. Abu-l Fazl truly remarks in an elegant phrase that 'His Majesty plans splendid edifices, and dresses the work of his mind and heart in the garment of stone and clay'. The best collection of his architectural achievements is to be seen at Fathpur-Sikri, but other notable buildings of Akbar's time exist elsewhere.

CHRONOLOGY

Leading dates only

Death of Humayun	Jan. 1556
Enthronement of Akbar	Feb. 1556
Second battle of Panipat; famine	Nov. 1556
Dismissal of Bairām Khān	1560

AUTHORITIES

THE principal contemporary authorities are of three kinds, namely, (i) *Āin-i Akbarī* by ABU-L FAZL, a survey of the empire and imperial system, as translated and annotated by Blochmann and Jarrett, Calcutta, 1873, 1891, 1896: vol. i has been revised by D. C. PHILOTT (1939) and vol. iii by Sir J. SARKAR (1948); (ii) three histories in Persian, namely, (1) the *Akbarnāma* by ABU-L FAZL, translated by H. Beveridge; vol. i, Calcutta, 1907; vol. ii, Calcutta, 1912, vol. iii, Calcutta, 1939, (2) the *Tabakāt-i Akbarī* by NIZAM-UD-DIN, translated by Dowson in E. & D., vol. v; and (3) the *Muntakhab-ut Tawārīkh* by ABD-UL QADIR AL BADĀUNI, vol. ii, translated by Lowe, as corrected by Cowell, Calcutta, 1884; and (iii) accounts by various Jesuit writers. Sir E. MACLAGAN, *The Jesuits and the Great Mogul*, 1932. The Latin work, *Mongolicae Legationis Commentarius* by Father ANTONIO MONSERRATE, S.J. (1582), ed. by Rev. H. Hosten, S.J., Calcutta, 1914, is of high importance.

Full details about those works and all minor authorities will be found in the author's book, *Akbar the Great Mogul*, A.D. 1542–1605, Clarendon Press, 1917. For the economic condition of India during this period see *India at the Death of Akbar*, by W. H. MORELAND (London, 1920). More general works on the Mughuls are IBN HASAN, *The Central Structure of the Mughal Empire*, 1936, and PARAMATMA SARAN, *The Provincial Government of the Moghuls*, 1941. See also, I. H. QURESHI, *Administration of the Mughal Empire*, Karachi 1966, and IRFAN HABIBH, *The Agrarian System of Mughal India*, 1963.

CHAPTER 4

Jahangir

Accession of Jahangir. Jahangir's enthronement at Agra took place on 3 November (N.S.) 1605, a week after his father's death. He assumed the style of Nūr-ud-dīn Muhammad Jahāngīr Pādshāh Ghāzī, the first name meaning 'light of the faith' and the third 'world-seizer'. He had secured his succession by making two solemn promises, one that he would protect the Muslim religion, the other that he would not cause any harm to the persons who had supported Khusru's claims. Both undertakings were honourably kept. The Muslims were gratified by his changed attitude to the Jesuit Fathers, whom he neglected as if he had never seen them, while the active adherents of Khusru, including Raja Mān Singh, received honours and dignities. He also issued various orders by way of reforms, the most important being the abolition of many transit and customs duties. But, as Sir Henry Elliot has shown, such orders had little practical effect.

Rebellion of Prince Khusru. Prince Khusru, who was extraordinarily popular, and had many well-wishers, could not bring himself to resign hopes of the crown which at one time had seemed to be within his grasp. According to one account he feared that his father might take the precaution of blinding him. Whether actuated by ambition or by fear or by both motives, he slipped out of the Agra Fort on 6 April 1606 (O.S.), and having collected a considerable force of troopers and obtained funds by capturing a treasure convoy hastened to the Panjab. His father pursued him with the utmost energy, dispensing with all the usual imperial hindrances to rapid movement. The governor of Lahore refused to open his gates to the prince, who, after some fighting, was captured while attempting to cross the Chenab on 27 April, exactly three weeks after his escape from Agra. Jahangir, who never again displayed such energy, then pitched his camp in a garden near Lahore, and proceeded to take deliberate and fearful vengeance.

Two of Khusru's principal followers were cruelly tortured by being enclosed in raw hides, one in that of an ox and the other in that of an ass; and in that fashion, seated on asses, were paraded through the city. One of the men died; the other, who barely escaped with his life, was afterwards pardoned. On Wednesday 7 May 200 or 300 of the prince's adherents were either hung from the trees or impaled on the prepared stakes set up along each side of the road. Jahangir, mounted on a splendidly caparisoned elephant, rode between the ranks, followed by his wretched son riding on a small unadorned elephant, with

Mahābat Khān behind him, to point out the names of the writhing victims.[1]

Guru Arjun. When Khusru was fleeing before his father, and in dire distress, he had asked the Sikh Guru, Arjun, at Tara-Taran for assistance. The holy man, moved it is said, merely by compassion, gave the fugitive 5,000 rupees. When the report came before the emperor Jahangir summoned the Guru, and after hearing his dignified reply fined him 200,000 rupees. The Guru, having refused to pay a single cowree, was savagely tortured for five days until he died (June 1606). The punishment, it will be observed, was inflicted as a penalty for high treason and contumacy, and was not primarily an act of religious persecution.[2] A second plot to raise Khusru to the throne led to the blinding of the prince, but not completely; he subsequently re-recovered the sight of one eye to some extent. Sultan Parviz, the emperor's second son, was recognized as heir apparent.

Popular love of Khusru. Sir Thomas Roe and his chaplain Terry sometimes met Khusru when his captivity had been relaxed (about 1616) and he used to follow his father on the march under a strong guard.

For that Prince [Terry writes] he was a gentleman of a very lovely presence and fine carriage, so exceedingly beloved of the common people, that as Suetonius writes of Titus, he was *amor et deliciae, &c.*, the very love and delight of them; aged then about thirty-five years.[3] He was a man who contented himself with one wife, which with all love and care accompanied him in all his streights, and therefore he would never take any wife but herself, though the liberty of his religion did admit of plurality.

After his death the beloved prince, as we learn from Mundy, was regarded as a martyred saint. On the way to his final resting-place in the Khusru Garden near Allahabad, each spot where the bearers of his body halted was marked by a shrine, consisting of a cenotaph, surrounded by a little garden, watered and tended by a fakīr or two. His figure, shadowy though it be, is one of the most interesting and pathetic in Indian history.

Sher Afgan. In 1607 an incident occurred which had important consequences as leading to the marriage of Jahangir with Nurjahan, who became the power behind the throne and practically sovereign of Hindostan. The lady, whose personal name was Mihr-un Nisa, was the daughter of a Persian refugee who had entered Akbar's service. She was given in marriage to ʿAli Qulī, surnamed Sher Afgan, the 'tiger-thrower', who received from Jahangir after his accession the *jāgīr* of

---

[1] The date is that given by Mr. H. Beveridge. The detail about Mahābat Khān (Zamāna Beg) is from de Laet. Authors differ concerning the number of victims. The smallest number, namely 200, is given by Du Jarric.

[2] For the full story from the Sikh point of view see Macauliffe, *The Sikh Religion* (1909), vol. iii, pp. 84–100.

[3] He was younger than the chaplain supposed, having been born in August, A.D. 1587 (A.H. 995). Khāfī Khān dates his birth two years later, and may be right.

Bardwan in Bengal. Sher Afgan fell under the suspicion of complicity with the Afghan rebels in Bengal, and the emperor sent his own foster-brother, Qutb-ud-dīn Koka, to remove Sher Afgan and forward him to court. When Qutb-ud-dīn attempted to carry out his orders an affray occurred, in the course of which both he and Sher Afgan were killed. The lady was brought to court and became an attendant on Salima Begam. In 1611 she attracted the emperor's attention and was married to him. She acquired at once unbounded influence over him, and freely made use of it to advance the interests of her family. Her father, who received the title of Itimād-ud-daulah, and her brother, ennobled as Āsaf Khān, became the leading personages in the court, while all her other connexions were well looked after. It is said that at first she desired to unite her daughter by Sher Afgan with Khusru. When that could not be done she married the girl to Jahangir's youngest son, Shahryar. The power of the family was further increased in 1612 by Prince Khurram's marriage to Āsaf Khān's daughter. Her earlier title of Nurmahall, 'Light of the Palace', was soon altered to Nurjahan, 'Light of the World', with allusion to the imperial style of Nur-ud din Jahangir. For many years she wielded the imperial power. She even gave audiences at her palace, and her name was placed on the coinage.

Favours to the Jesuits. The temporary alienation of Jahangir from the Jesuit Fathers ceased in 1606 when his favours to the priests were renewed. After some difficulty they were allowed to retain their elegant and commodious (*elegans et scitum*) church at Lahore, as well as the *collegium*, or priests' residence. At Agra about twenty baptisms took place in 1606, and when Jahangir was on his way to Kabul he accepted a Persian version of the Gospels and permitted the Fathers to act publicly with as much liberty as if they were in Europe. When the emperor returned to Agra he took two of the priests with him, leaving one at Lahore to look after the congregation there. Church processions with full Catholic ceremonial were allowed to parade the streets, and cash allowances were paid from the treasury for church expenses and the support of the converts. The zeal for Islam which Jahangir had displayed at the beginning of his reign gradually diminished, and he openly declared that he wished to follow in his father's footsteps. Of his eighteen wives, seven were Hindus.

Christian pictures. The Jesuits' exertions were directed principally to the conversion of the emperor himself. Certainly his conduct gave them some reason to hope that he might be brought within the Christian fold. He showed an extraordinary fancy for pictures of religious subjects from the Old and New Testaments, the Apocrypha, and the Lives of the Saints. At Agra his throne was surrounded by paintings of John the Baptist, Saint Anthony, and Saint Bernardin of Siena. Various halls, rooms, and courts in the palace were similarly decorated. It is no wonder that Jahangir was popularly reputed to have become a Christian, and that the Jesuits entertained 'good hope of his conversion'. They recognized that the practice of polygamy was one of the principal obstacles to his acceptance of the Christian faith, and tried in vain to persuade him that it was his duty to repudiate all his wives save one.

Embassy to Goa. In 1607 Jahangir expressed a desire, as his father had done, to send a mission to the king of Spain and the pope, but was persuaded to restrict the embassy to visiting the viceroy of Goa. The ambassador selected was Muqarrab Khān, an intimate friend of the emperor, a keen sportsman and skilled surgeon. In accordance with Jahangir's special request Father Pinheiro accompanied the ambassador as a colleague. They started from Lahore, where the court then was, in September 1607, and reached Cambay in the April following, 1608. At that time the envoys could not present their credentials at Goa, because the viceroy designate had not arrived. As a matter of fact he never arrived, and the government of Portuguese India was carried on by Archbishop de Menezes until 27 May 1609, when Don Andreas Hurtados de Mendosa took charge and held office until 5 September of that year.

Captain W. Hawkins. Meantime, Captain William Hawkins, of the ship *Hector*, had arrived at Surat in August 1608, bearing a letter from James I, king of Great Britain, to Jahangir, asking for the grant of trade facilities. Hawkins, in spite of strenuous opposition from Father Pinheiro and the Portuguese authorities, succeeded in reaching the court of Jahangir, who accepted his gifts, valued at 25,000 gold pieces, and gave him a most favourable reception. Hawkins was able to converse with the emperor in Turki, without the aid of an interpreter. He was appointed to be a commander (*mansabdār*) of 400, with a salary of 30,000 rupees (which, it is said, was not paid), and was married to the daughter of an Armenian Christian named Mubārak Shāh (Mubarikesha).

Portuguese hostility. When Mendosa, the new Viceroy at Goa, heard that Hawkins and other Englishmen had been granted privileges infringing on the commercial monopoly claimed by the Portuguese, he treated the imperial concession as a hostile act and considered himself to be at war with Jahangir, whose ambassador he refused to receive. That hasty action greatly disturbed the merchants on the coast, and alarmed Jahangir, who revoked his concessions to the English. Father Pinheiro, who had gone on to Goa, was then employed by the viceroy as a plenipotentiary to negotiate with Muqarrab Khān, hostilities were stopped, and English ships were refused admission at Surat.

Hawkins quitted the court in 1611, baffled by the intrigues of the Portuguese and the instability of the imperial policy. He recorded interesting notes of his experience, which have been preserved by the diligence of Purchas, and will be quoted presently in part.

Bengal and the Deccan. In 1612 the rebellion of Usmān Khān in Bengal, which had begun in Akbar's time, and had been complicated by the activities of Hindu rajas and zamindars, was at last ended by the death of the rebel leader from wounds received in a stiff fight. The success of Islam Khān was made lastingly fruitful by Jahangir's policy of conciliation. 'Nuruddin Ghazi pardoning them their former trespasses, attached them to himself by the bonds of bounty . . . so that by their praiseworthy exertions they raised themselves to the rank of Grand Umara, and were deemed worthy to be admitted to the Im-Imperial company.'[1] From the beginning of the reign hostilities in the Deccan had never wholly ceased. A feebly conducted war against the forces of the Ahmadnagar sultanate, then administered by an able Abyssinian, named Malik Ambar, went on continually without results worthy of notice. At this period the quarrels among the imperialist generals became so acute that the Khān Khānān (Abdurrahīm), who had been recalled, was again sent to see if he could do anything effectual. But Jahangir never succeeded in obtaining a firm control over any campaign in the Deccan.

English victory at sea. The same year, 1612, was marked by the entrance of British naval forces into Indian politics. At the end of November one English ship, the *Dragon*, commanded by Captain Best, 'assisted onely', as Purchas relates, 'with the *Osiander* a little ship (scarcely a ship, I had almost called her a little Pinnasse)', successfully fought a Portuguese fleet comprising four huge galleons, with five- or six-and-twenty frigates. It is not surprising to read that 'the great Mogoll, which before thought none comparable to the Portugall at Sea, much wondered at the English resolution, related to him by *Sardar Chan*'. The Mughul empire was then, as always, powerless at sea.

War with Portuguese. About a year later (1613) the Portuguese used their naval superiority as compared with the weakness of the Mughul government to seize four of the imperial ships, imprisoning many Muslims, and plundering the cargoes. The outrage naturally was 'very disagreeable' to Jahangir, who ordered Muqarrab Khān, then in charge of Surat, to obtain compensation. From English sources we learn that the principal ship plundered was called the *Remewe*, and that it was said to have carried 'three millions of Treasure, and two women bought for the Great Mogol'. Jahangir's mother had a large interest in the cargo, and lost heavily.

The Portuguese acts of piracy resulted in war with the imperial government, whose officers attacked Daman. All accessible Portuguese residing in the Mughul dominions were seized, and even Father Jerome Xavier was sent in custody to Muqarrab Khān, 'to do with him as he shall see good'. The public exercise of the Christian religion was forbidden, and the churches were closed. The Portuguese were still 'in deep disgrace with the king and people' early in 1615, when William Edwards from Surat arrived at court bearing a letter from King James I. Although he was not formally accredited as an ambassador, he was at first honourably received by Jahangir, who perceived that the

---

[1] 'Makhzan i-Afghāna' by Ni'mat-Ullah, tr. B. Dorn in *History of the Afghāns*.

English could now be used as a counterpoise to the Portuguese. Some years earlier the emperor had questioned Hawkins about the force needed to take Diu, and was told that the place could be reduced by fourteen British ships supported by a land force of 20,000 men.

Submission of Mewar. In 1614 the war against Mewar, pressed ever more vigorously in successive campaigns by Mahābat Khān and ʿAbdullah Khān (Firūz Jang), ended with the submission of Rana Amar Singh and his son Karan to Prince Khurram (Shahjahan), who had pursued the brave Rajputs until they were reduced to extremity. Jahangir was delighted by a success which Akbar had failed to achieve, and was willing to soften the humiliation of defeat by exceptionally courteous treatment of his gallant adversaries. After some time the emperor did special honour to them by directing artists at Ajmer to fashion full-sized marble statues of the rana and his son. The commission having been executed with all speed, the statues were removed to Agra and erected in the garden below the audience-window (*jharo-khā*). Mewar was required to contribute to the imperial army a contingent of 1,000 horse, and Karan had to accept the dignity of a 'commander of 5,000'. The reigning rana was never compelled to attend court in person, and no Sīsōdia bride ever graced the imperial harem. With the exception of those concessions to the dignity of the premier chieftain of Rajasthan, the rana became as other rajas, and officially was regarded as a mere zamindar or *jāgīrdār*.

In July of the same year, 1614, Raja Mān Singh died in the Deccan. No less than sixty of his women committed suttee by fire.

Plague. Bubonic plague, a disease not previously recorded with certainty in India, appeared in the Panjab early in 1616, at the close of Jahangir's tenth regnal year. The epidemic was marked by the symptoms unhappily familiar since the disease reappeared at Bombay in 1896. Rats and mice were first affected, and the mortality was severe, especially among Hindus. The pestilence, which spread to almost every locality in northern and western India, lasted for eight years. In 1619, while it was raging in Agra, Fathpur-Sikri, twenty-three miles distant, escaped. Another outbreak, apparently of the same disease, occurred in the Deccan in 1703 and 1704.[1]

Embassy of Sir Thomas Roe. The informal missions of Hawkins and Edwards, sent for the purposes of promoting the nascent trade between England and the East, and abating Portuguese pretensions, were quickly followed by the formal embassy of Sir Thomas Roe, the duly accredited ambassador from James I to Jahangir. The envoy, a gentleman of good education, a polished courtier, and trained diplomatist, was well qualified for the task assigned to him, which was the negotiation of a treaty giving security to English trade. Roe arrived at Surat, or rather Swally Road, in September 1615, and marched up country as soon as practicable to the court of Jahangir, then at Ajmer.

[1] *I.G.* (1907), vol. iv, p. 475. For the plague in the Deccan see *Storia do Mogor*, vol. iv, p. 97.

The chaplain whom he had brought out with him having died almost immediately, the ambassador summoned from Surat to take his place a young English clergyman named Edward Terry, a ship's chaplain in the fleet of 1616. The world is indebted to Terry for an account of his experiences, which is far superior to that of Roe as a description of the country and government. The chaplain was a good observer and extra-ordinarily sympathetic in his attitude towards the people of India, whether Hindu or Muslim. Roe's *Journal* is chiefly useful as a faithful record of the manner in which business was done at a court saturated with intrigue, treachery, and corruption. Jahangir, half fuddled with strong drink and opium, had not the strength of will to resist the wiles of his designing queen, her equally unscrupulous brother, Āsaf Khān, and the subtlety of Prince Khurram (Shahjahan). The ambassador's pen-picture of that prince is memorable. 'I never saw', he writes, 'so settled a countenance, nor any man keep so constant a gravity, never smiling, nor in face showing any respect or difference of men; but mingled with extreme pride and contempt of all. . . .'[1]

Princes Khusru and Khurram. Roe confirms his chaplain's testimony to the virtues and popularity of Prince Khusru, whose life even then was unceasingly threatened by his brother, Prince Khurram, with the privity of Nurjahan and Āsaf Khān. The ambassador, who was in a good position for learning the facts, records that

Sultan Khusru, the eldest brother, is both extremely beloved, and honoured of all men (almost adored) and very justly for his noble parts.

In another passage he amplifies his judgement by saying:

If Sultan Khusru prevail in his right, this kingdom will be a sanctuary for Christians, whom he loves and honours, favouring learning, valour, the discipline of war, and abhorring all covetousness, and discerning the base customs of taking, used by his ancestors and the nobility. If the other win, we shall be losers; for he is most earnest in his superstition, a hater of all Christians, proud, subtile, false, and barbarously tyrannous.

The event proved the correctness of the shrewd ambassador's predic-tion, as well as the soundness of his estimate of Shahjahan's character, which has been so grievously misunderstood by modern historians.

Roe went home in 1619. Although he had failed to obtain the formal treaty desired, he secured considerable concessions to his countrymen and laid a solid foundation for the East India Company's trade.

The Deccan war. The aggressive war in the Deccan, where the principal opponent of the imperialists was Malik Ambar, the able Abyssinian minister at Ahmadnagar, dragged on throughout the reign. No decisive result ever was obtained, and good reason existed for believing that Abdurrahīm, the Khān Khānān, was in collusion with Malik Ambar. In 1616 the fort at Ahmadnagar was surrendered, and Prince Khurram was allowed to obtain a show of success. He was

---

[1] The spelling has been modernized, but the old punctuation retained.

extravagantly rewarded with the title of Shahjahan, and the enormous emoluments attached to the command (*mansab*) of '30,000 personal, with 20,000 horse'. Malik Ambar lived until 1626, when he died at an advanced age.

Surrender of Kangra. The most notable military achievement of Jahangir's reign was the surrender to his authority in November 1620 of the strong fortress of Kangra, which had defied even Akbar. Jahangir was extremely proud because an officer of his had been able to reduce a stronghold which had baffled his father. A little later the emperor visited the conquest, and gratified the sentiment of the Muslims, while outraging that of the Hindus, by erecting a mosque and slaughtering a bullock within the precincts of the fort. Other minor conquests of this period included the diamond area of Khokhara Khurda—which carried the Orissa border to that of Golcanda, and Kishtwar, on the borders of Kashmir.

Murder of Prince Khusru. The 'tragical end' of the 'troublesome life' of Prince Khusru came in January 1622. Nearly six years earlier, in 1616, Jahangir, for reasons not stated, had transferred his son from the custody of a faithful Hindu named Ani Rāi to that of Āsaf Khān, the mortal enemy of the prince. Later, in or about 1620, the prisoner was made over to his brother, Prince Khurram, at the instigation of Āsaf Khān and Nurjahan. The inevitable result followed in the beginning of 1622. Jahangir records his son's death without comment or expression of regret, merely stating that 'a report came from Khurram that Khusru, on the 8th (? 20th) of the month, had died of the disease of colic pains (*kūlanj*) and gone to the mercy of God'.

Loss of Qandahar. In June of the same year, 1622, Shāh Abbās, the energetic king of Persia, retook Qandahar. He had tried without success to induce Jahangir to give up the place voluntarily. When diplomacy failed he took it by force without much trouble. Jahangir, who was grievously perturbed by the loss, planned a great expedition for the recovery of the town, and desired his son Shahjahan to take the command. But at the time, the emperor was in bad health, and Shahjahan was determined not to imperil his succession to the throne by absence on the Persian frontier.

Rebellion of Shahjahan. Instead of obeying his father's orders he went into open rebellion. Prince Shahryar was then appointed to take charge of the Qandahar expedition, but nothing came of the appointment, all the energies of the government being devoted to the suppression of the rebellion. A plan to bring from Agra to Lahore the whole of the immense treasure in gold and silver coin accumulated from the beginning of Akbar's reign was dropped when Shahjahan gave indications that he intended to intercept the convoy. It is impossible to refuse some sympathy to the outraged father when he laments the ingratitude of the once best-beloved son, and moans: 'What shall I say of my own sufferings? In pain and weakness, in a warm atmosphere that is extremely unsuited to my health, I must still ride and be active, and in this state must proceed against such an undutiful son.' But he thanks 'God that has given me such capacity to bear my burdens'. He lamented more especially that the rebel had compelled the postponement of the recovery of Qandahar, and thus had 'struck with an axe the foot of his own dominion, and become a stumbling-block in the path of the enterprise'. Several nobles were executed for high treason, and Sultan Parviz, Shahjahan's elder brother, was summoned to take his proper place at his father's side as heir apparent. Jahangir was justly disgusted because Abdurrahīm, the Khān Khānān, an old man of seventy, and loaded with marks of imperial favour, had joined the traitors.

In 1623 a battle fought at Balōchpur, to the south of Delhi, resulted in the death of the Brahman, Raja Bikramājīt, on whom Shahjahan chiefly relied, and in the consequent defeat of the rebel army at the hands of the imperialists under Mahābat Khān. Shahjahan was driven through Malwa into the Deccan, and thence across Telingana into Bengal, which province, with Bihar, he occupied. Another defeat by Mahābat Khān sent the rebel back to the Deccan, where he tried to make friends with his old enemy Malik Ambar and the other rulers of the south. In 1625 a sort of peace was patched up between the prince and his father. Shahjahan surrendered Rohtas and Asirgarh, and sent his eldest son Dara Shikoh and Aurangzeb his third to court as hostages. But he never appeared there in person, remaining absent in Rajputana or the Deccan.

Mahābat Khān. In the year following, 1626, strange events occurred. Mahābat Khān, who had become one of the principal personages in the empire, and had taken so active a part in the pursuit of Shahjahan, found himself in danger of destruction owing to the hostility of Nurjahan. He therefore marched north with 5,000 Rajput troops towards the imperial camp. Jahangir and his consort were encamped on the Jhelum on their way to Kabul, and were about to cross the river with the rearguard when Mahābat Khān surrounded their tents with his Rajput horsemen, and captured the emperor. Nurjahan was not detained, and escaped over the river. Her attempts to recover her husband by force having failed, she managed by stratagem to effect her purpose at Kabul. Mahābat Khān was then obliged to fly and join Shahjahan, who was hard pressed, and thinking of escape to Persia. But he was encouraged by the death in October at Burhanpur of his drunken brother, Parviz, the only serious rival for the succession to the throne.[1] Hardly anything is on record concerning the personal qualities of Parviz beyond the fact that he drank too much.

Death of Jahangir. Jahangir, who had been ailing for several years, died after a short illness while encamped at Chingiz Hatlī, a village near Bhimbhar at the foot of the hills on the road to Kashmir,

---

[1] Long afterwards Aurangzeb in a letter accused his father of the murder of both his brothers: 'How do you still regard the memory of [your brothers] Khusrau and Parviz, whom you did to death before your accession and who had threatened no injury to you?' (Sarkar, *Hist.*, vol. iii, p. 155).

from which he was returning. His death occurred in November 1627, but his successor Shahjahan was not able to take his seat on the throne until the following February, for the reasons which will be explained in the next chapter.

His personality. As appears from the foregoing narrative, the prominent public events of Jahangir's reign were few. The loss of Qandahar was not balanced by any substantial increase of territory elsewhere, and there can be no doubt that the empire was weaker as a military power in 1627 than it was when Akbar died in 1605. The administration generally was conducted on the lines laid down by Akbar, and the reign of Jahangir may be regarded as a continuation of that of his father, marked by a certain amount of deterioration due to Jahangir's personal inferiority when compared with his illustrious parent. His considerable natural abilities were marred by habitual and excessive intemperance, which added artificial ferocity to his innate violent temper. When angry, and especially if the security of his throne was threatened, he was capable of the most fiendish cruelty, having men flayed alive, impaled, torn to pieces by elephants, or otherwise tortured to death. Hawkins and Roe were much disgusted by such savagery. Mere passionate caprice, even when no question of treason arose, sometimes induced him to commit shocking barbarities. For instance, he relates without shame the following anecdote:

> On the 22nd, when I had got within shot of a nilgaw, suddenly a groom and two bearers appeared, and the nilgaw escaped. In a great rage I ordered them to kill the groom on the spot, and to hamstring the bearers and mount them on asses and parade them through the camp, so that no one should again have the boldness to do such a thing.

After this I mounted a horse and continued hunting with hawks and falcons, and came to the halting place.

Jahangir's authentic *Memoirs*, either written by his own hand or dictated to a scribe, cover nineteen years of his reign and offer a wonderfully life-like picture, a strange compound of tenderness and cruelty, justice and caprice, refinement and brutality, good sense and childishness. Terry truly observes: 'Now for the disposition of that king, it ever seemed unto me to be composed of extremes: for sometimes he was barbarously cruel, and at other times he would seem to be exceeding fair and gentle.' He was capable of feeling the most poignant grief for the loss of a grandchild, and often showed pleasure in doing little acts of kindly charity. His writings are full of keen observations on natural objects. He went to Kashmir nearly every hot season, and recorded a capital description of the country, carefully drawing up a list of the Indian birds and beasts not to be found in the Happy Valley. He loved fine scenery, and would go into ecstasies over a waterfall. He thought the scarlet blossom of the *dhāk* or *palās* tree 'so beautiful that one cannot take one's eyes off it', and was in raptures over the wild flowers of Kashmir.

He was a skilled connoisseur in the arts of drawing and painting, and a generous patron of artists. He had himself some skill with the brush, and drew parts of the decorative designs on the walls of the palace at Agra. He appreciated music and song, and had nice taste in architecture. The unique design of Akbar's tomb was prepared in accordance with his ideas.

Jahangir prided himself especially on his love of justice, and his reputation for that quality still endures in India. When recording the capital sentence passed by himself on an influential murderer, he remarks: 'God forbid that in such affairs I should consider princes, and far less that I should consider Amīrs.'

The fearful penalties which he inflicted were imposed without respect of persons.

Religion. His religion is not easy to define. Grave Sir Thomas Roe roundly denounced him as an atheist, but this verdict, like that of Mullā Ahmad, may express no more than the reaction of men accustomed to religious intolerance and therefore suspicious of tolerance. He sincerely believed in God, although he did not frankly accept any particular revelation or subscribe to any definite creed. The strange partiality which he showed for Christian images and ritual, and his intimacy with the Jesuit priests, did not induce him to accept the doctrines of the Church. Probably his favour to the priests was accorded chiefly from political motives, in order to secure Portuguese support and trade. The moment hostilities with Goa began the Christian churches were closed. He had not the slightest desire to persecute anybody on account of his religion. It is true that he passed severe orders against the Jains of Gujarat, whom his father had so greatly admired, but that was because for some reason or other he considered them to be seditious.

While he loved talking to philosophical ascetics, whether Hindu or Muslim, he did not imitate his father in adopting Hindu practices, nor did he follow Zoroastrian rites. His personal religion seems to have been a vague deism, either that taught by heretical Muslim Sufis, or the very similar doctrine of certain Hindu sages. Ordinary Hinduism he spoke of as a 'worthless religion'. Jahangir, like his contemporaries, James I of England and Shah Abbās of Persia, believed tobacco to be a noxious drug and forbade its use.

The material for discourse on Jahangir's interesting personality is so abundant that it would be easy to write at large on the subject. The reader perhaps will find what has been said more than enough.

The court. The court ceremonial was much the same as in the days of Akbar. Jahangir showed himself publicly three times a day. At sunrise he appeared on a balcony facing east, at noon on one facing south, and a little before sunset at a third facing west. On each occasion he received petitions and dispensed justice as he conceived it. Other state business was transacted chiefly between seven and nine o'clock in the evening in the private audience-hall, known as the *Ghusl-khāna* or 'bath room', to which only privileged persons were admitted. Roe and

Terry frequently attended such audiences. Before the evening had passed Jahangir often was dead drunk. Many anecdotes about his intemperance are on record.

The New Year festivities after the Persian manner, and the formal weighings of the sovereign against gold and other precious things on his birthday, calculated according to both the solar and lunar calendars, were duly observed.

The selfish luxury and ostentation of the court and nobles had increased since Akbar's time, and constituted a terrible drain on the resources of the country. The pay of the higher officials was scandalously extravagant, even if allowance be made for certain deductions. Hawkins, who received the comparatively small post of a 'commander of 400', had a nominal salary of 30,000 rupees a year, then worth more than £3,000 sterling. It must be noted, however, that there was often a great disparity between the realizable and the nominal value of the revenue assignments. Of this Hawkins had bitter experience. Even so the rewards were sufficient to attract able men from far beyond the empire's borders. Moreover, by the escheat of a noble's property at death to the crown, considerable sums were regularly recovered. The salary of a modern viceroy was a mere pittance when compared with the sums paid to the greater nobles. No money to speak of was spent on useful public works or on education. All considerable expenditure was designed for the glory of the sovereign or his chief courtiers.

The central control of administration was slacker under Jahangir than it had been under his father, and in the revenue department the system of payment by *jāgīr* gained ground. English records suggest that imperial control did not always extend far from the towns and main lines of communication. The great distances involved made it difficult to check tyranny by provincial officials, though, as Hawkins points out, and the records confirm, such misbehaviour was firmly dealt with when discovered.

Literature and art. Literature, chiefly in the Persian language, was encouraged. Jahangir himself could write sufficiently well. In addition to his *Memoirs* several historical works of some merit were composed, and he gave his patronage to the completion of a valuable dictionary entitled the *Farhang-i Jahāngīri*. Art, as already mentioned, really interested Jahangir. His book is full of references to the subject, which it would be desirable to collect and discuss. The two most eminent painters of the reign were Abu-l Hasan, honoured with the title of Nādir-uz-zamān, 'Wonder of the Age', and Ustād, or Master, Mansūr, who bore a synonymous title. The extant works of both those artists justify the enthusiastic praise bestowed upon them by their employer. The tomb of Itimād-ud daulah at Agra, the mausoleum of Akbar at Sikandara, and Jahangir's own sepulchre at Lahore testify to the good taste of the emperor and the skill of his architects.

CHRONOLOGY (O.S.)

Death of Akbar	17 Oct. 1605
Enthronement of Jahangir	24 Oct. 1605
Rebellion of Khusru	Sunday, 6 April 1606
Capture of Khusru	Sunday, 27 April 1606
Embassy to Goa	1607–9
Hawkins at court	1608–11
Marriage with Nurjahan	May 1611
End of Usmān Khān's rebellion in Bengal	1612
Capture of four ships by Portuguese of Goa	1613
Submission of Rana Amar Singh and Karan	1614
Sir Thomas Roe's embassy	1615–18
Bubonic plague began (lasted eight years)	1616
Conquest of Kangra	Nov. 1620
Death of Khusru	Jan. 1622
Loss of Qandahar to the Persians	June 1622
Rebellion of Prince Khurram (Shahjahan)	1622
Shahjahan defeated and put to flight	1623, 1624
Submission of Shahjahan	1625
Mahābat Khan seized Jahangir	1626
Death of Sultan Parviz	Oct. 1626
Death of Jahangir	28 Oct. 1627

AUTHORITIES

THE leading authority is the annotated version of JAHANGIR's authentic *Memoirs* (R.A.S. 1909, 1914), in two volumes, by ROGERS and BEVERIDGE, dealing with nineteen years of the reign. The other principal Persian histories are discussed and partly translated in E. & D., vol. vi. GLADWIN, *History of Hindostān, Reign of Jahāngīr* (vol. i, all published, Calcutta, 1788), a sound book, is chiefly valuable for the life of the emperor as Prince Salim in Akbar's reign.

The European authorities are numerous and copious. One of the most important and least known is DU JARRIC, *Thesaurus Rerum Indicarum*, vol. iii, 1616; Book I, chaps. 16–23 incl., to the end of 1609. The observations of HAWKINS and many minor travellers will be found in PURCHAS, *Pilgrimes* (ed. Maclehose, 1905, or in other reprints), and in FOSTER, *Early Travels in India, 1583–1619* (Oxford University Press, 1921). The best edition of Sir THOMAS ROE's *Embassy* is that by FOSTER, Hakluyt Soc., 1899, 2 vols. His chaplain TERRY may be read in the reprint of *A Voyage to East India*, London, 1777. The *Travels* of PETER MUNDY (vol. ii, ed. Temple, Hakluyt Soc., 1914) give the history as current about 1630, shortly after Jahangir's death, and include numerous accurate personal observations on the state of the country. The narrative of President VAN DEN BROECKE (1629), translated from a chronicle and printed in DE LAET's book (1631), is full and seems to be generally accurate. Some additional facts may be collected from certain printed volumes of the records of the E. I. Company from *Jahāngīr's India*, tr. from the Dutch of F. PELSAERT by W. H. MORELAND and P. GEYL, and from *Voyage of Thomas Best* (1612–14) ed. by Sir W. FOSTER. TOD gives the story of the Rajput campaigns from the Hindu point of view. BENI PRASAD, *History of Jahāngīr*, 1922, with a full bibliography. The coins are described in the official catalogues of the B.M., I.M., and Lahore Museum. The art of the reign is noticed by FERGUSSON; in *H.F.A.* (1911); in E. W. SMITH's *Akbar's Tomb* (Allahabad, 1909); in P. BROWN, *Indian Painting under the Mughals* (Oxford, 1924), and in various publications of the ARCHAEOLOGICAL SURVEY.

CHAPTER 5

Shahjahan and the War of Succession; climax of the Mughul empire

Disputed succession; executions. In October 1627, when Jahangir died on his way down from Kashmir, two of his sons survived him. Prince Khurram or Shahjahan, the elder, was then far away in the Deccan and could not arrive in Hindostan for many weeks. Prince Shahryar, the younger son, who was available at headquarters, probably at Agra, thus possessed an advantage as against his rival. Both the princes claimed the throne, and neither had any thought of yielding to the other. Shahryar, who was married to the daughter of Nurjahan by her first husband, Sher Afgan, hurried off to Lahore to join his mother-in-law; and assumed imperial rank. Shahjahan was married to Mumtaz Mahall, daughter of Nurjahan's brother, Āsaf Khān, who desired his son-in-law to succeed. In order to effect that purpose Āsaf Khān secured possession of Shahjahan's young sons, and set up, much against his will, the unfortunate Prince Khusru's son, Dawar Bakhsh nicknamed Bulākī, as a stop-gap padshah, until Shahjahan could arrive. He was, in fact, as the chronicler observes, 'a mere sacrificial lamb'. Shahryar, whose lack of brains had earned for him the contemptuous sobriquet of *Nā-shudanī*, or 'Good-for-nothing', was incapable of contending against Āsaf Khān, and was promptly blinded. Shahjahan, a man of a different kind, able and ruthless, hurrying up from Junnar in the Deccan with all possible speed, sent orders for the execution of all his male collateral relatives. The atrocious instructions were carried out thoroughly, except that if the accounts of the European travellers are to be believed the titular emperor, Dawar Bakhsh, was permitted to escape to Persia, where he lived as a pensioner of the shah. All the other male relatives were killed, one way or another. No doubt exists as to the wholesale character of the executions, which were carried out pitilessly, and, as Tavernier has justly remarked, have 'much tarnished' the memory of Shahjahan, who does not deserve pity on account of the fate which overtook him with tardy steps.

Rebellions of Khān Jahān Lodī and Bundēlas. In 1628 Jujhār Singh the Bundēla chief revolted, alarmed by threats to inquire into the acquisitions of his father, Raja Bīr Singh, Jahangir's criminal favourite. He was forced to submit, and to pay heavily in money and lands for his rebellion. For several years he served with distinction in the Deccan. But the grant of high rank and the title of raja whetted his ambition, and he defeated, and treacherously slew, the neighbouring chief of Chauragarh, despite Shahjahan's orders to desist, or at least to share the loot. Imperial forces thereupon defeated and pursued him until he was killed in the jungle by the Gonds. Orchha was systematically ravaged.

More serious was the revolt of the powerful Afghan, Khān Jahān Lodī, the governor of the Deccan. He had supported Dawar Bakhsh, and had sought to seize Mandu in his interests, but after Shahjahan's accession he was forgiven and confirmed in his Deccan post. He failed, however, to recover the Balaghat which he had sold earlier to the Nizam Shāh. He was therefore recalled to court, whence despite Shahjahan's written assurances, he fled, fearful for his own safety, to Ahmadnagar. After a long, but carefully planned campaign, he was driven from the Deccan, cut off from the Afghans of the Panjab, and killed at Sihonda (U.P.) in 1631.

The peacock throne. Shahjahan had a passion for the collection of jewels, and took extraordinary pleasure in the display of costly magnificence at court. Immediately after his formal enthronement in 1628 he determined to glorify himself by the construction of a throne more splendid and costly than that of any other monarch. The enormous stores of the imperial jewel-house were increased by extensive purchases of rare gems, and the combined accumulation was devoted to the decoration of the celebrated peacock throne, constructed under the superintendence of Bēbadal Khān in the course of seven years (1628–35). The throne was in the form of a cot bedstead on golden legs. The enamelled canopy was supported by twelve emerald pillars, each of which bore two peacocks encrusted with gems. A tree covered with diamonds, emeralds, rubies, and pearls stood between the birds of each pair. The gorgeous structure, which cost at least a hundred *lakhs* or ten million rupees, equivalent then to a million and a quarter pounds sterling, continued in use until 1739, when it was carried off to Persia by Nādir Shāh.

Famine of 1630–2. The prodigal expenditure and unexampled splendour of the court, which occupy so prominent a place in most of the current descriptions of Shahjahan's rule, had a dark background of suffering and misery seldom exposed to view. In the fourth and fifth years of the reign (1630–2), while the emperor usually was encamped at Burhanpur in Khandesh, intent on his aggressive schemes directed against the sultans of the Deccan, an appalling famine of the utmost possible severity desolated the Deccan and Gujarat.[1] The official historian, Abdul Hamīd, contrary to the frequent practice of writers of his kind, makes no attempt to disguise the horror of the calamity, which he describes in a few phrases of painful vividness.

The inhabitants of these two countries [the Deccan and Gujarat] were reduced to the direst extremity. Life was offered for a loaf, but none would buy; rank was to be sold for a cake, but none cared for it. . . . Destitution at last reached such a pitch that men began to devour each other, and the flesh of a son was preferred to his love. The numbers of the dying caused obstruc-

1 The famine extended to Persia and many parts of India.

tious on the roads, and every man whose dire sufferings did not terminate in death and who retained the power to move wandered off to the towns and villages of other countries. Those lands which had been famous for their fertility and plenty now retained no trace of productiveness.

The details of the horrible picture are set out even more fully in the plain, unadorned notes kept by an English traveller, Peter Mundy, a merchant, who journeyed on business from Surat to Agra and Patna and back again while the famine and consequent pestilence were raging. At Surat the sickness was so deadly that out of twenty-one English traders seventeen died. For a large part of the way between Surat and Burhanpur the ground was strewn so thickly with corpses that Mundy could hardly find room to pitch a small tent. In towns the dead were dragged 'out by the heels, stark naked, of all ages and sexes, and there are left, so that the way is half barred up'. Meantime, the camp of Shahjahan at Burhanpur was filled with provisions of all kinds.

So far as Mundy saw nothing to help the suffering people was done by the government, or by the grasping and unfeeling Hindu grain merchants, but the author of the *Bādshāh-nāmah* states that the emperor opened a few soup-kitchens, gave a *lakh* and a half rupees in charity spread over a period of twenty weeks, and remitted one-eleventh of the assessment of land revenue. The remissions so made by 'the wise and generous Emperor' in the crown lands amounted to 70 *lakhs*. The holders of *jāgīrs* and official commands were expected to make similar reductions. The facts scarcely justify the historian's praise of the 'gracious kindness and bounty' of Shahjahan. The remission of one-eleventh of the land revenue implies that attempts were made to collect ten-elevenths, a burden which could not be borne by a country reduced to 'the direst extremity', and retaining 'no trace of productiveness'. We are not told how far the efforts to collect the revenue succeeded; and as usual are left in the dark by the Persian authorities concerning the after effects of the famine. The English and Dutch, however, relate the long disturbance to trade and the production of commercial crops caused by the famine. They say, also, that government revenue demands gravely hampered recovery.

Life and death of Mumtaz Mahal. The marriage of Shahjahan to the lady named Arjumand Bano Begam, and entitled Nawab Aliya Begam, or alternatively Mumtaz Mahal, 'the ornament of the palace', has been mentioned as having been the main reason determining the adhesion of her father Āsaf Khān, the richest and most powerful noble in the empire, to the cause of Shahjahan and his consequent opposition to his sister the dowager empress Nurjahan, the widow of Jahangir and mother-in-law of Prince Shahryar. The marriage, which had taken place in the year 1612, when Prince Khurram (Shahjahan) was twenty years of age, had been successful to a degree rare in polygamous households. The prince had had two children born to him by an earlier consort. His remaining children, fourteen in number, eight sons and six daughters, were all borne to him by Mumtaz Mahal between the years 1613 and 1631. Husband and wife were devotedly attached to each other, and during her lifetime nothing is heard of the scandalous licentiousness which dishonoured Shahjahan's later years. All the four sons who contested the throne in 1658 were her offspring, as were the two daughters, Jahanara and Roshan Rai (Roshanara), who respectively supported the causes of Dara Shikoh and Aurangzeb.

In June 1631 Mumtaz Mahal died in childbirth at Burhanpur, at the age of thirty-nine. Her body was interred there temporarily, and after six months, when her mourning husband quitted the Deccan, was transferred to Agra, where it was placed in a provisional sepulchre in the gardens of the Tāj, the unrivalled monument to her memory which Shahjahan began in 1632.

Little is known of the personal character of Mumtaz Mahal. She must have possessed uncommon charm to be able to secure for so many years her husband's errant affections, and to merit a memorial such as no other lady in the world has ever won. She appears to have been a devout Muslim, as most of the ladies of the imperial family were.

The Portuguese at Hugli. Portuguese traders, who had settled on the river bank a short distance above Sātgāon in Bengal in or about 1579, under the protection of an imperial *farmān*, had gradually strengthened their position by the erection of substantial buildings, so that the trade migrated from Sātgāon to the new port, which became known by the name of Hugli (Hooghly).[1] They had a monopoly of the manufacture of salt. If the intruders had confined their energies to the business of trade they might, perhaps, have remained undisturbed, in spite of the injury which they inflicted on the provincial customs revenue. They maintained a custom house of their own, and were specially strict in enforcing the levy of duty on tobacco, which had become an important article of trade since its introduction at the beginning of the seventeenth century. The Mughul officers were so little skilled either in sieges or in naval matters that they would have been disposed to submit to the loss of revenue rather than fight the foreigners, who were well armed and expert in the management of ships. But the arrogant Portuguese were not content to make money quietly as merchants. They engaged in a cruel slave trade and habitually bought or seized children, both Hindu or Muslim, whom they brought up as Christians. They were rash enough even to offend Mumtaz Mahall by detaining two slave girls whom she claimed.[2] The misdoings of the Portuguese had been brought to the notice of Shahjahan before his accession. After the establishment of his throne he appointed Qāsim Khān as governor of Bengal, with instructions to exterminate the foreigners. The necessary preparations, which began in A.D. 1631 (A.H. 1040), were continued in the following year.

---

[1] The name, which is spelt in old records as Ogolim, &c., probably is a corruption of *O golim* or *goli*, meaning 'the godown' or 'storehouse'. *O* is the Portuguese definite article (Hosten, in *Bengal Past and Present*, vol. x (1915), pp. 89–91).

[2] 'Filles', not 'daughters' as sometimes erroneously translated.

Siege and capture of Hugli, 1632. The siege of Hugli, begun on 24 June 1632, ended three months later in the capture of the place. The town, often described erroneously as a fortress, was situated on an open plain along the banks of the Ganges, and was exposed on all sides. It had neither wall nor rampart, but only an earthen embankment which they had thrown up, a thing of little value and still lesser strength. The governor of Bengal was so much afraid of European skill in gunnery and the management of ships that he collected a huge army, said to number 150,000 for the attack on the weak settlement. The Portuguese soldiers consisted of only 300 Europeans, with 600 or 700 native Christians. The tiny garrison held out for exactly three months until 24 September, when the inhabitants embarked to go down the river. Most of the ships were lost, but a few reached Saugor Island, where a pestilence destroyed a large proportion of the survivors. The imperialists had nearly 1,000 fatal casualties. More than 400 prisoners were taken and brought to Agra, where they were offered the choice between conversion to Islam, and confinement or slavery under the most severe conditions. The persecution of Christians as such lasted until December 1635, after which date it gradually died down. Some of the Portuguese were allowed to reoccupy Hugli, but the town never recovered its former prosperity.

The detailed story is best told by the Spanish friar, Manrique, and by Father John Cabral, S.J., an eyewitness, who wrote a full account in 1633.

The action of Shahjahan quenched the hopes for the conversion of the royal family and Mughul India which had been encouraged by the proceedings of Akbar and Jahangir.

Destruction of Hindu temples. The excessive Muslim zeal which induced Shahjahan to undertake a distinct persecution of Christians as such, in continuation of his legitimate warfare against the slave-raiders of Hugli, prompted him in the same year (1632) to take severe action against his Hindu subjects, who, like the Christians, had ordinarily, although not invariably, experienced at the hands of Jahangir the same toleration which they had enjoyed in Akbar's reign. Jahangir had raised no objection to the erection of new temples, which is opposed to strict Muslim law. Shahjahan now resolved to put a stop to the practice, and gave orders that at Benares, and throughout all his dominions in every place, all temples that had been begun should be cast down. It was now reported from the province of Allahabad that seventy-six temples had been destroyed in the district of Benares. No record of the destruction in other parts of the empire has been preserved, but it must have been considerable.

Shahjahan's Deccan policy. Shahjahan, as has been seen, was engaged in the prosecution of operations for the annexation of the Deccan sultanates of Ahmadnagar, Golkonda, and Bijapur in the year 1631, when the famine occurred and his wife died. He then returned to Agra. It will be convenient to give in this place a connected summary view of the imperial plans and military operations in the Deccan during the earlier part of Shahjahan's reign.

The policy of Akbar, who avowedly aimed at the subjugation of all the kingdoms of the Deccan, had some success, for the entire kingdom of Khandesh and a small portion of that of Ahmadnagar proper, as well as Berar, then a dependency of Ahmadnagar, were absorbed into the imperial dominions during the years 1600 to 1605. But an able Abyssinian minister, Malik Ambar, succeeded in retaining or recovering the greater part of the kingdom, which was ruled in the name of a new sultan. Both Golkonda and Bijapur continued to enjoy real independence, and had obtained large accessions of territory in the south after the fall of the Hindu empire of Vijayanagar in 1565. Jahangir, while cherishing the same ideal as Akbar, made no considerable progress in the task of the subjugation of the Deccan. Shahjahan, who was stationed there at the time of his father's death in 1627, resumed the family designs of conquest as soon as possible after his accession, and did a good deal to realize them.

Early operations. In A.D. 1630 the imperialists were compelled to raise the siege of Parēndā, a strong fortress belonging to Ahmad nagar. In the same year Fath Khān, the minister of Ahmadnagar, and son of Malik Ambar, who had died at an advanced age in 1626, entered into communication with the imperial government and informed Shahjahan that in order to protect himself he had seized and confined his own sovereign, the Nizām Shāh. The emperor replied by instructions to kill the captive. Fath Khān complied, and placed on the throne a boy of the royal family, named Husain Shāh. Shahjahan, regarding Muhammad Ādil Khān, sultan of Bijapur, as contumacious because he desired to retain his independence, directed Āsaf Khān to require his submission, and, in the event of non-compliance, to conquer as much territory as possible and to lay the rest waste. In 1631 the imperial forces besieged Bijapur, but were compelled to withdraw owing to want of supplies, the country-side having been laid waste, partly by the Bijapuris in self-defence, and partly by the invaders. 'On whatever road they went they killed and made prisoners, and ravaged and laid waste on both sides. From the time of their entering the territories to the time of their departure they kept up this devastation and plunder. The best part of the country was trodden under.' That merciless warfare was not provoked by the government or people of Bijapur. It was ordered deliberately with the sole purpose of gratifying the emperor's ambition and lust for riches.

End of the Ahmadnagar kingdom. Shahjahan, on the completion of his operations, returned to Agra, where he occupied himself with the planning and building of the Tāj. He appointed Mahābat Khān, Khān Khānān, to be viceroy of Khandesh and the Deccan.

Malik Ambar's son, Fath Khān, proved as faithless to Shahjahan as he had been to his own sovereign. In 1631 he defended against the imperial forces the fortress of Daulatabad (Deogiri), which his father had fortified. But the explosion of a mine and the spread of disease among the garrison were sufficient to make him surrender.

He was taken into the imperial service and granted a liberal salary. The young prince whom he had set on the throne of Ahmadnagar was consigned to Gwalior for lifelong imprisonment, and the kingdom of the Nizām Shāhīs was ended (A.D. 1632; A.H. 1042).

In the following year (1633) the emperor went to the Panjab and Kashmir. Prince Shuja failed to take Parēndā, and Mahābat Khān, Khān Khānān, died.

Campaign of 1635–6. In 1635 Shahjahan resumed seriously his plans for the final reduction of the Deccan states, especially Bijapur, where the independent attitude of the wealthy Ādil Shāhī dynasty was a standing offence in his eyes. A minor complication was introduced by the operations of the Maratha chieftain, Shāhjī or Sāhū, who set up another Nizām Shāhī boy as the nominal sultan of Ahmadnagar. Shāhjī will be heard of often again, especially as being the father of the more famous Sivājī. The appearance of the Marathas on the stage of Mughul history may be dated from the early years of Shahjahan's reign, or from about 1630 to 1635.

The emperor sent written commands to the sultans of both Golkonda and Bijapur requiring them to recognize his suzerainty, to pay tribute regularly, and to abstain from support of Shāhjī and his allies of Ahmadnagar. The ruler of Golkonda (Hyderabad), unable to resist the might of the Mughul, complied humbly with all demands, reading the *khutba* and striking coins in the name of Shahjahan.

The Ādil Shāh of Bijapur was less complaisant, and, although willing to make some show of compliance, was determined to resist the imperial aggression. Shahjahan continued his ruthless policy, and 'the imperial order was given to kill and ravage as much as possible in the Bijapur territories'. Three armies converged on the country of the hapless sultan, burning, robbing, enslaving, and slaying without mercy or distinction. For instance, in one village 2,000 men were killed; and in another place 2,000 prisoners, male and female, were sold as slaves. Akbar's prohibition of enslaving prisoners of war, even if it was obeyed in his reign, which may be doubted, had been long forgotten, and exercised no restraint over his pitiless grandson.

Treaty with Bijapur, 1636. Although the capital city was saved by the desperate expedient of flooding the surrounding lands, effectual defence of the kingdom as a whole against the invading hosts was impracticable, and the Ādil Shāh was constrained to submit to terms only slightly less onerous than those imposed on Golkonda. The treaty, ratified by Shahjahan on 6 May 1636, required the sultan to yield obedience to the emperor; to pay a peace-offering of 20 *lakhs* of rupees; to respect the frontier of Golkonda, now a tributary state of the empire; and to abstain from aiding Shāhjī in hostile measures. The Ahmadnagar state was definitely blotted out of existence, its territories being divided between Shahjahan and the Ādil Shāh, whose independence was in a manner recognized by the imperial abstention from the demand for a regular annual tribute. The concession was more formal than real.

Aurangzeb appointed viceroy of the Deccan. The settlement so effected lasted for about twenty years. The peace was followed immediately by the appointment (14 July 1636) of the young Prince Aurangzeb, then nearly eighteen years of age, as viceroy of the Deccan. His charge comprised four provinces, namely:

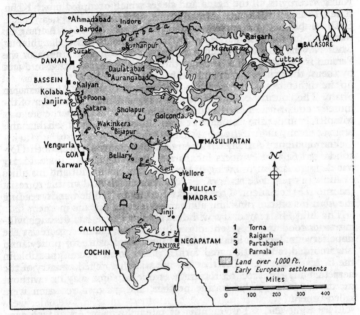

AURANGZEB AND THE MARATHAS

(1) Khandesh, in the valley of the Tapti; capital, Burhanpur; fortress, Asirgarh.

(2) Berar (Birār), lying to the south-east of Khandesh, and now attached to Madhya Pradesh; capital, Ellichpur (Īlichpur); fortress, Gāwīlgarh.

(3) Telingana, or the Telugu country; a wild, ill-defined region of hills and forests, situated between Berar and the Golkonda state; capital, Nāndēr; fortress, Kandhār (Kandahār); both in Hyderabad.

(4) Daulatabad, including the imperial portion of the late Ahmadnagar kingdom; capital, Aurangabad (formerly Khirki), a few miles

from Daulatabad, which was considered the principal of many important fortresses.

The four provinces together were reckoned to contain sixty-four forts, several of which were still in possession of Shāhjī or other hostile holders. The gross revenue was estimated at 5 'crores', or 50 million rupees, out of which Aurangzeb was expected to defray all expenses, civil and military.

Aurangzeb as viceroy, 1636–44. It is unnecessary to follow the young viceroy in all the fights and sieges which occupied much of his time. He annexed Baglana, a small principality in the hills near Nasik. Shāhjī submitted and surrendered certain forts. In 1637 Aurangzeb went to Agra for his marriage with Dilras Bano Begam, daughter of Shah Nawāz Khān, a nobleman belonging to a junior branch of the Persian royal family. She became the mother of three daughters and two sons, the princes Azam and Akbar.

The difficulties of Aurangzeb's first viceroyalty of the Deccan were many. The country could not pay its way, and the viceroy was continually embarrassed by the distrust shown by his father, who was completely under the influence of Dara Shikoh, his eldest son, and the lifelong enemy of Aurangzeb. A famous accident was associated with the termination of Aurangzeb's first term of provincial government. On 26 March 1644 the Princess Jahanara, Shahjahan's favourite daughter, was dangerously burnt owing to her light skirt having caught fire from a candle in the palace at Agra. In May Aurangzeb had visited Agra in order to see the patient. Three weeks after his arrival he was compelled to resign his official rank and allowances, retiring for the moment into private life. His temporary withdrawal from office has been usually misunderstood and represented as a hypocritical manifestation of religious fervour. He had incurred his father's displeasure for some cause not recorded, and anticipated formal punishment by resignation. In one of his letters he states that his life was threatened, and it seems clear that his enforced retirement was due in some way or other to the machinations of his hostile brother, and his own resentment at his treatment.

After eight and a half months of unemployment Aurangzeb was appointed to the difficult government of the province of Gujarat (16 February 1645). He conducted the administration to the emperor's satisfaction, and in January 1647 was transferred to a dangerous post as governor of Balkh and Badakhshan.

Qandahar. Qandahar, in virtue of its importance both as a strategical position and as the principal mart on the landward trade route between India and Persia, had been the subject of contention between the Persian shahs and the Indian padshahs since the time of Humayun, who held the city for a few years. The Persians recovered it during Akbar's minority, but lost it in April 1595, owing to the treachery of the governor who betrayed it to an officer of Akbar. In 1622,[1] during

[1] Raverty gives the date as Aug. 1622. Sarkar has 1623.

b. Agra: Taj Mahal from the river

PLATE 22

a. Agra Fort: Moti Masjid (Pearl Mosque)

Jahangir's reign, Shah Abbās the Great regained possession of the place, and Persia held it until 1638, when Alī Mardān Khān, threatened with an inquiry into his administration, betrayed it to a representative of Shahjahan. The traitor was rewarded by the immediate gift of a *lakh* of rupees, and subsequent lucrative office under Shahjahan, who attached high importance to the acquisition. He expended large sums on the fortification of the city and its dependencies. In the autumn of 1648 Shahjahan heard of Persian preparations for the attack on Qandahar, but was persuaded to defer sending adequate reinforcements until the spring when they were too late.

Mughul Central Asian policy. Shahjahan, like his father and grandfather, had always felt a strong desire to exercise complete control over the hilly region of Badakhshan and the more distant province of Balkh lying between the Hindu Kush and the Oxus whence, in 1622 and 1629, the Uzbegs had even attempted the conquest of Kabul. The Mughul emperors dreamed even of extending their sway over all the countries connected with the early glories of their family, and of bringing Transoxiana, and its capital Samarqand, under the sceptre of Hindostan. Depositions and revolts in the Uzbeg ruling house led to appeals for Shahjahan's intervention. Prince Murad Bakhsh, with Alī Mardān Khān, by July 1646 had Badakhshan and Balkh in their hands.

The prince, however, hated the country and asked to be recalled. The Oxus was left unguarded and the Uzbegs rallied. Aurangzeb restored the situation by a clear-cut victory over the Uzbegs in pitched battle, but his officers were all unwilling to serve in such a harsh area, and the Uzbeg ruler received help from Persia, so that in 1647 the imperial forces were compelled to evacuate Balkh. During the retreat they lost about 5,000 men in the passes.

First siege of Qandahar, 1649. Aurangzeb, after his failure in Balkh, was transferred to the governorship of the Multan province. The emperor moved to Lahore and Kabul in order to guard against a threatened invasion by the Uzbegs, who had been emboldened by their success in defeating the ill-conceived Balkh expedition. The reader may remember that similar fears had detained Akbar near the northwestern frontier for thirteen years from 1585 to 1598. Aurangzeb's stay at Multan was short. When news came in of the Persian designs on Qandahar the emperor determined to entrust Aurangzeb with the task of relieving the garrison. The prince made energetic preparations, but was sent too late; the city having been taken by the enemy long before he could arrive. The capitulation (11 February 1649) was due to the inactivity and incapacity of Daulat Khān, the commandant. Aurangzeb was directed to recover Qandahar before the Persians should have time to consolidate their hold. He combined his forces with the army under the command of Sadullāh Khān, the prime minister, and attacked the city in May, without effect. The expeditionary force, equipped merely as a reinforcement, was useless for besieging purposes, being destitute of heavy ordnance, while the

Persians were superior in military skill. The siege was raised on 5 September, and Aurangzeb endured for the second time the humiliation of failure as a general. A victory gained over the Persians at Shah Mīr on the Arghandab in August covered up the failure to retake Qandahar, and gave the Indian court an excuse for ceremonial rejoicing.

Second siege of Qandahar, 1652. Shahjahan would not abandon his design of retaking Qandahar, to which he rightly attached high importance. The next three years were spent by him and Aurangzeb, who had returned to Multan, in organizing a powerful army with a siege-train and large supply of munitions for the investment of the city. Aurangzeb was nominally the commander-in-chief, but the conduct of operations actually was in the hands of Sadullāh Khān, the prime minister, acting under the orders of Shahjahan at Kabul. Sadullāh Khān and Aurangzeb again combined their forces at the beginning of May 1652 near Qandahar and undertook the investment of the city. They had strict orders from the emperor not to attempt an assault until a practicable breach had been effected. All their efforts to effect such a breach failed, owing to the inefficiency of the Indian gunnery and the superior skill of the Persians. Early in July Shahjahan was constrained to order the abandonment of the siege, and Aurangzeb once more tasted the bitterness of defeat. His failure, although more his misfortune than his personal fault, finally destroyed his father's confidence in his powers.

Third siege of Qandahar, 1653. Prince Dara Shikoh, the emperor's favourite, who was shortly afterwards exalted by the title of Shāh Buland Iqbāl, or 'King of Lofty Fortune', bragged that he would soon redress his hated brother's failure. Immense exertions got together a fresh army and siege-train in the short space of about three months. But the elder prince's 'lofty fortune' did not help him. After operations lasting five months he too had to confess to failure, and raise the siege in September 1653.

The Mughul dynasty never again attempted to recover Qandahar, and the repeated defeats of the best armies which India could raise decisively established the military prestige of the Persians.

Cost of siege; imperial revenue. Trustworthy estimates place the cost of the three sieges of Qandahar (1649, 1652, 1653) at 12 'crores', or 120 million rupees, more than half of the annual income of the empire, which is stated to have been 22 'crores', or 220 million rupees, in 1648. During Shahjahan's reign the value of the rupee in English currency was usually taken at 2s. 3d. The imperial revenue, therefore, may be reckoned at 24¾ million pounds sterling, or, in round figures, as about 25 millions.

Demolition of walls of Chitor. Shahjahan obtained some cheap compensation for his conspicuous defeats by the Persians in the destruction of the new fortifications of Chitor, which Rana Jagat Singh had ventured to construct, in defiance of a prohibition recorded by Jahangir. The submission of the reigning rana was secured by a show of force, and a fortnight's work sufficed to demolish the walls of the fortress.

Aurangzeb again sent to the Deccan. Aurangzeb had not been a success as a general in the regions of the north-west, all his undertakings—the Balkh expedition, and the first and second sieges of Qandahar—having ended in disaster. He could not remain at court, where both his father and his elder brother were hostile, and it was necessary to place him somewhere at a distance. The emperor insisted on his resuming charge of the Deccan, to which he was reappointed immediately after his return from Qandahar. Towards the end of the year he took up his residence at the official capital, either in the fort of Daulatabad or in the neighbouring town of Aurangabad.

The remaining events of importance in the reign of Shahjahan, until the war of succession began in 1658, are chiefly concerned with Aurangzeb's proceedings in the Deccan.

Administrative difficulties. The financial and administrative difficulties which had beset Aurangzeb during his first term of office as viceroy of the Deccan were still more troublesome during his second term. The country had been ill governed by a succession of incompetent and frequently changed officers, who, far from repairing the damage wrought by the great famine and by war, had allowed the cultivated area to decrease, villages to be abandoned, and the people to be cruelly oppressed. Nothing like the nominal assessment of the land revenue could be collected, and in consequence both the imperial treasury and the provincial income suffered, while the *jāgīrdārs*, to whom the land revenue of certain districts had been assigned for their personal support and for the maintenance of their military contingents, were unable to meet their obligations. Aurangzeb was obliged to draw heavily on his cash reserves, and his requests to his father for pecuniary assistance were either absolutely rejected or granted with extreme reluctance. The prince did his best to restore cultivation and improve the revenue, but the results of bad government for many years could not be quickly remedied. While much improvement was effected, much remained to be done when the war of succession broke out.

Murshid Qulī Khān's 'settlement'. Aurangzeb was fortunate in commanding the services of an exceptionally skilled revenue officer named Murshid Qulī Khān. For fiscal purposes the Deccan was divided into two sections, namely, the *Pāinghāt*, or Lowlands, comprising Khandesh, or the Tapti valley, with part of Berar, and the *Bālāghāt*, or Highlands, comprising the rest of the viceregal jurisdiction. Murshid Qulī Khān, a Persian, originally in the suite of Alī Mardān Khān, came to the Deccan with Aurangzeb as diwan of the Highlands, and at the beginning of 1656 was promoted to be diwan of the whole Deccan. Before his time the management of revenue affairs had been marked by complete want of system. The assessment of the state demand was made in a rough-and-ready fashion by the imposition of a small charge on the land cultivated by each plough, without any attempt at survey or valuation. Murshid Qulī Khān extended to the Deccan Todar Mal's system of survey and assessment, or 'settlement', so far as possible; but was wise enough to make many local exceptions, and to preserve the old practice of fixing a lump sum for each plough-land, whenever a more scientific arrangement would not work in practice. He also was willing to accept payment in kind, and to arrange for the division of the crop by various methods. Advances of cash to the peasantry for the restoration of cultivation were freely made with good results. A capable observer noted in 1658 that then there was no waste land near Aurangabad.

The hostility of Dara Shikoh and the consequent estrangement of Shahjahan greatly complicated the difficulties of administration. The emperor was so dissatisfied with Aurangzeb that he offered the Deccan to his son Shuja, who did not care to accept a transfer from Bengal.

Aurangzeb's aggressive policy. Aurangzeb did not confine his attention to the problems of internal administration. He was an ambitious, aggressive ruler, eager to carry on the traditional policy of his dynasty and play the part of 'a great pike in a pond', as Chaplain Terry puts it. His main purpose was to destroy the independence of the sultanates of Golkonda and Bijapur, and to transfer to himself and his supporters the immense riches and resources of both kingdoms. Both the emperor and his son, as bigoted Sunni Muslims, took special pleasure in warring with the sultans of Golkonda and Bijapur, who adhered to the Shia faith, and looked for alliance and protection to the shah of Persia rather than to the padshah of Hindostan. The aggressive wars were waged ruthlessly, and when ultimately the sultans were dethroned they received no generous treatment from the victors. The defence of their independence by the two states is always described by the court historians as villainous contumacy.

Pretexts for invasion were never lacking. Golkonda had become avowedly a tributary state since 1636, and arrears were always due. Although the sense of dignity ('izzat) of the Bijapur sultan had been respected so far that he was not required to pay a fixed annual tribute, he was expected to make 'presents' every year, so that the distinction between his position and that of Golkonda was little more than a matter of form. Bijapur never paid anything that it could avoid paying. Other reasons for displeasure against the sultans were easily found when wanted.

Mīr Jumla. Aurangzeb's chief helper in his designs on the Deccan kingdoms, and a little later on the throne of Hindostan, was the Persian adventurer generally known as Mīr Jumla, a merchant from Ardistān. Following the example set by Mahmūd Gāwān under the Bahmanī dynasty in the fifteenth century, he began as a successful trader and quickly went on to make himself virtual master of the Golkonda or Hyderabad kingdom as prime minister of 'Abdullah Qutb Shāh. Not content with his position as the chief of the Qutb Shāh's servants, he carved out for himself a domain virtually amounting to an independent kingdom, by conquering and annexing the Karnatik, or Kanarese country under the rule of the raja of Chandragiri, the representative of the Vijayanagar dynasty. Mīr Jumla's dominion, about 300 miles long by 50 broad, yielded a revenue of 40 *lakhs* of rupees and supported a considerable army especially strong in its park of good artillery manned by European gunners.

The semi-independent position acquired by Mīr Jumla naturally aroused the jealousy of his nominal master, the Qutb Shāh, who attempted to bring his too powerful servant under his control. Mīr Jumla defended himself by intrigues with Bijapur, Persia, Shahjahan, and Aurangzeb. Ultimately he attached himself definitely to the Mughul service and accepted high office from Shahjahan, thus becoming a traitor to the Qutb Shāh.

Aurangzeb's treacherous policy. Aurangzeb forced hostilities on that unhappy and incompetent monarch, whom he was determined to destroy. His purpose is frankly expressed in written instructions under his hand addressed to his eldest son, Prince Muhammad Sultan, which were:

Qutb-ul-Mulk is a coward and will probably offer no resistance. Surround his palace with your artillery and also post a detachment to bar his flight to Golkonda. But before doing so, send a carefully chosen messenger to him, saying:

'I had been so long expecting that you would meet me and hospitably ask me to stay with you. But as you have not done so, I have myself come to you.' Immediately on delivering this message, attack him impetuously, and if you can manage it, lighten his neck of the burden of his head. The best means of achieving this plan are cleverness, promptitude, and lightness of hand.[1]

Such was the treachery which Aurangzeb and his father were not ashamed to employ against a Muslim king whose only offence was his independence.

Prince Muhammad Sultan presently entered Hyderabad, which was plundered by his soldiery in spite of orders forbidding excesses. The prince and his father, Aurangzeb, who were not above taking advantage of the irregular action of their troops, appropriated many valuables, including a library of precious manuscripts. Hyderabad, however, was so rich that much wealth remained to tempt another attack. The king, meantime, had shut himself up in the fortress of Golkonda a few miles distant.

Siege of Golkonda; peace. In February 1656 Aurangzeb began the siege of Golkonda, and progressed slowly, after the manner of Mughul generals when besieging strong places. Being resolved to annex the whole of the kingdom, the wealth of which he coveted, he rejected all proposals for peace. Shahjahan, however, who had reasons

[1] *Adab*, 187 *b*; in Sarkar, *History*, vol. i, p. 230.

of his own, was more accommodating, and accepted the sultan's proposals for peace on certain terms, promising complete pardon. Aurangzeb held back that letter in order to extort more favourable terms, and the emperor, having been referred to, sanctioned his son's action. A little later Shahjahan was induced by Prince Dara Shikoh and Princess Jahanara to put a summary stop to the war. Aurangzeb was compelled to raise the siege on 30 March. The Qutb Shāh agreed to pay a considerable indemnity and to cede a district. By a secret agreement with Aurangzeb the sultan also promised to make Prince Muhammad Sultan his heir.

Mīr Jumla prime minister. Mīr Jumla, who had joined Aurangzeb's camp with a powerful army, was now appointed prime minister of the empire in succession to Allāmī Sadullāh Khān who had recently died. The deceased minister, although unfortunate in his military adventures, was reputed one of the best Muslim administrators whom India has known.

The raja of Chandragiri, the representative of the great dynasty of Vijayanagar, tried to secure protection from the emperor, offering even to become a Muslim. But his efforts failed utterly and he was left to the tender mercies of Bijapur, Golkonda, and Mīr Jumla.

Foundation of Madras. The grant made early in 1639 of the site of Madras to an English factor, although unnoticed at the time, was one of the most important events in the reign of Shahjahan, as being the beginning of British territorial acquisition in India.

War with Bijapur. The sultan or king of Bijapur had taken advantage of the security afforded by the treaty of 1636 to extend his dominions to the east, south, and west. At the end of 1649 the powerful fortress of Jingi or Gingee, now in the South Arcot District, capitulated to him, and he also gained a certain amount of success against the Portuguese of Goa. The reigning sultan, Muhammad Ādil Shāh (1626–56), ruled a realm extending across the peninsula from sea to sea, maintained a magnificent court, and had raised his kingdom to a degree of wealth and power previously unattained. That fortunate sovereign died on 4 November 1656. The succession of his only son, a youth of eighteen years of age, naturally resulted in internal disturbances, which also offered an opportunity for the gratification of the ambition of the Mughul dynasty. Shahjahan readily granted his viceroy power to act as he thought fit. Aurangzeb invaded the kingdom with the help of the traitor Mīr Jumla at the earliest possible moment. Bidar fell at the end of March 1657, after a gallant defence; Mahābat Khān and Aurangzeb cruelly ravaged the Bijapur territory; and on 1 August Kalyani capitulated.

The complete conquest of the kingdom was in sight, when at Dara's prompting Shahjahan intervened and ratified a treaty of peace, by which the sultan agreed to surrender Bidar, Kalyani, and Parenda, besides certain other places, and to pay a large indemnity. The final operations in the Deccan undertaken by Aurangzeb were directed to checking the daring raids of young Sivājī, the Maratha leader, son of Shāhjī Bhonslā, who has been mentioned more than once. The dangerous illness of Shahjahan, which began early in September 1657, and resulted in the war of succession, put a stop to all thoughts of further conquest in the Deccan. The sultanates obtained a respite for nearly thirty years.

Disputed succession. Although the preferential claim of the eldest son of a Chagatāi Mughul sovereign to succeed his father on the throne was generally acknowledged, his absolute right was not established sufficiently to secure his position without dispute. Humayun, Akbar, Jahangir, and Shahjahan had all found themselves compelled to confront the rivalry of near relatives. Shahjahan desired to be succeeded by his eldest son, Prince Dara Shikoh, and took every practicable step to ensure the fulfilment of his desire. Unprecedented titles, honours, and wealth were lavished on the much loved senior prince, who was kept constantly near the imperial person, and, as Shahjahan grew old, was allowed to exercise most of the imperial prerogatives. The emperor's three other sons observed with unconcealed jealousy the favour bestowed on the eldest-born, and all three were resolved to contest his succession. Each thought himself capable of reigning, and was prepared to stake life and everything else on the issue of the conflict which was regarded as inevitable whenever their father should die. The fact that all the four sons were children of one mother, Arjumand Bano Begam, was no check on their ambitions. They all accepted the Timurid maxim that 'no one is a relation to a king', and well knew that mere abstention from contest would not save the life of any of the brothers after one of their number had taken his seat on the throne definitely. The struggle for the succession had to be fought out to the bitter end—*takht yā takhta*, which may be loosely rendered as 'crown or coffin', was the inevitable goal.

The long story of the war of succession has been vividly related by several contemporary authors, in Persian, French, and English, whose narratives have been digested critically in Professor Sarkar's work, the second volume being wholly devoted to the subject. In this place it is not practicable to give more than a summary outline of the tragic happenings.

The sons of Shahjahan. The four sons of Shahjahan were Dara Shikoh, Shuja, Aurangzeb, and Murad Bakhsh, all men of mature age in 1657, aged respectively 43, 41, 39, and about 33 years. All the four had had considerable experience in military and civil affairs on a large scale. The eldest, who remained with his father, was viceroy of the Panjab and other provinces on the north-west, which he administered through deputies. Shuja ruled the great territories of Bengal and Orissa. Aurangzeb controlled the Deccan, while Murad Bakhsh governed Gujarat and the west. Thus the four princes held the semi-independent government of regions, each of which had been a powerful kingdom, and could supply its ruler with abundant cash and many thousands of armed men. The gigantic hoard of treasure stored in the vaults of the Agra fort was to be at the disposal of the victor.

All the princes possessed the soldier's virtue of personal valour, which was displayed conspicuously by both Aurangzeb and Murad Bakhsh. Dara Shikoh's considerable natural abilities were neutralized by the violence of his temper and the intolerable arrogance of manner, which gained him hosts of enemies. Shuja, an agreeable man, with some skill as a general, was rendered ineffective by his love of pleasure, and his unreadiness to take instant action at the decisive moment. Murad Bakhsh was a passionate, headstrong, tyrannical man, the bravest of the brave, but drunken, dissolute, and brainless. It is needless to draw a formal sketch of the character of Aurangzeb, whose consummate ability as an unscrupulous intriguer and cool politician is apparent on the face of the narrative. Although his failures in Balkh and at Qandahar may be regarded as disparaging to his skill as a commander of armies, his imperturbable self-possession enabled him to emerge with success from most embarrassing tactical situations during the war of succession. His indomitable resolve to win the throne at any cost and by any means carried him through and gave him victory.

Religious hostility. The unorthodoxy of Dara Shikoh was an important factor in the struggle. That prince, while continuing to conform to the Sunni ritual and to be a professed Muslim of the Hanafī school, was deeply imbued with the pantheistic mysticism of the Sufis. He also associated gladly with Hindu philosophers and went so far as to take part in producing a Persian version of some of the Upanishads, which he declared to be a revelation earlier than the Quran.[1] He was so intimate with Father Buseo and other priests that he was believed by some persons to be within measurable distance of embracing Christianity. That attitude towards Islam infuriated Aurangzeb, who certainly was a devout Sunni Muslim, whatever judgement may be formed of his moral character. He regarded his eldest brother as a pestilent infidel, deserving of worse than death. Shuja, who professed the Shia faith, and Murad Bakhsh, who was reputed to be privately inclined to that form of religion, concurred with Aurangzeb in hostility to Dara Shikoh's latitudinarian views, and were glad to help their own causes by appeals to religious fanaticism. The Rajputs were the principal support of Dara Shikoh, and if Jaswant Singh of Marwar (Jodhpur) had not behaved with shameless treachery the eldest prince might have won.

Rebellion of Aurangzeb. During the autumn of 1657 endless plotting and counter-plotting went on. Shahjahan, whose health was partly restored, sought to secure the succession of his first-born son, and to prevent civil war if possible. Aurangzeb continually temporized and endeavoured to shirk the responsibility of open rebellion. He was

---

[1] For list of his works see 'Dara Shikoh as an Author' (*J.P.H.S.*, vol. ii, pp. 21–38); and Blochmann in *J.A.S.B.*, part 1, 1870, pp. 273–9. The spellings *Shikoh* and *Shukoh* are both legitimate.

anxious to secure the fruits of his military successes in the Deccan, but failed in that design, and was constrained to give his whole attention to the contest with his father and brothers in the north. Both Shuja and Murad Bakhsh forced his hand by assuming the imperial style and striking coins, each in his own name. Shuja was the first to enthrone himself, doing so at Rajmahal, then the capital of Bengal, in the autumn of 1657, immediately on receipt of the news of his father's dangerous illness. Murad Bakhsh took similar action at Ahmadabad, on 5 December, in opposition to the advice of his ally, Aurangzeb, who preferred to move with extreme caution. At the end of October Aurangzeb took the prudent precaution of seizing all the ferries over the Narbada, and so concealing the progress of events in the Deccan from his father and eldest brother, while securing his own passage into Hindostan. Late in December Shahjahan sent peremptory orders recalling Mīr Jumla to court. Aurangzeb countered that step by arresting his confederate and attaching his property. The circumstances indicate that probably Mīr Jumla connived at his own arrest. Certainly he did not resent it, nor did he fail to continue to give his ally invaluable support when released. Aurangzeb had thus become a rebel, and could no longer continue his temporizing policy. Mīr Jumla's fine park of artillery proved to be extremely useful. At the beginning of February 1658 Aurangzeb began to exercise imperial prerogatives by granting titles and making appointments to high offices. He crossed the Narbada on 3 April without opposition, and effected a junction with Murad's army in Malwa, in the neighbourhood of Ujjain. At that time the agreement between Aurangzeb and Murad Bakhsh, as solemnly recorded in writing, was to the effect that the empire should be divided, Murad Bakhsh receiving the Panjab, Kabul, Kashmir, and Sind, while Aurangzeb should take the rest. No provision was made for Shuja. A little later Aurangzeb seems to have pretended that he desired Murad Bakhsh to become sole emperor, but at the beginning of the war the policy of partition had been accepted formally.

Battle of Dharmat, 15 April 1658. Shahjahan experienced much difficulty in procuring generals to oppose princes of the blood-royal, especially inasmuch as he gave instructions that the lives of his rebel sons were to be spared if possible. The only prince available to lead an imperialist army at a distance was Dara Shikoh's elder son, Sulaiman Shikoh, who was sent to fight Shuja. Raja Jaswant Singh of Marwar (Jodhpur) and Qāsim Khān were induced to undertake the duty of stopping Aurangzeb and Murad Bakhsh. The hostile armies, approximately equal in numbers, met at Dharmat, fourteen miles south-south-west of Ujjain, on 15 April (o.s.), 1658, with the result that the imperialists were utterly defeated. Their disaster was due partly to the evils of divided command and jealousy between the Rajputs and the Muslims, and partly to the bad choice of ground made and the erroneous tactics pursued by the raja. Qāsim Khān did little to help his master's cause, and the gallant Rajput clans suffered most of the casualties.

Battle of Samūgarh, 29 May 1658. The rebel princes pressed on, securing the passage of the Chambal over a neglected ford. Dara Shikoh led out from Agra a superior and powerful force, which met the rebels at Samūgarh or Sambhūgarh, eight miles to the east of Agra Fort. The battle fought on 29 May, in the terrible heat of summer, was vigorously contested, and the Rajputs, although injudiciously handled, again did honour to the traditions of their race. Equal valour was displayed by Aurangzeb and Murad Bakhsh, who risked their lives without hesitation. The younger prince received three wounds in the face and the howdah of his elephant bristled with arrows. When the imperialists had suffered severely, and Dara Shikoh's elephant had become the mark of the enemy's guns so that it was in imminent danger of destruction, the heir apparent was persuaded to come down and mount a horse. That action settled the fate of the battle. His remaining troops broke when they saw the empty howdah, and Dara Shikoh fled to Agra with a few exhausted followers. His camp, guns, and all he possessed fell into the hands of the victors. Some accounts represent his defeat, and especially his descent from the elephant, as being due to the treacherous advice of Khalīlullah Khān, one of his generals, but the tactical errors committed by the imperialist commanders suffice to explain the disaster. The battle really decided the war of succession. All the subsequent efforts to retrieve the cause then lost, whether made by Dara Shikoh himself, by his son, Sulaiman Shikoh, or by Shuja and Murad Bakhsh, were in vain. Aurangzeb proved himself to be by far the ablest of the princes in every phase of the contest, which was not ended until two years later, in May 1660, when Shuja met his miserable fate.

Fate of Shahjahan and Murad Bakhsh. Aurangzeb lost no time. On 8 June he received the surrender of the Agra Fort with all its treasures, and made his father a prisoner for life. Father and son never met again. Murad Bakhsh rashly attempted open opposition and was silly enough to allow himself on 25 June to be inveigled into a manifest trap by his unscrupulous brother while encamped at Rūpnagar near Mathura. He was imprisoned first at Salīmgarh, Delhi, and then at Gwalior, where he was executed in December 1661. Aurangzeb, who, like Henry VIII of England, preferred to kill his victims with all the forms of law when possible, instigated a son of Alī Naqi, the diwan whom Murad Bakhsh had murdered in Gujarat in 1657, to claim the price of blood under Quranic law. The prince, after trial by a Qazi, was duly declared deserving of death and beheaded in his prison.

Fate of Shuja and Prince Muhammad Sultan. Aurangzeb went through an informal ceremony of enthronement, equivalent to the coronation in European monarchies, on 21 July, but refrained from inserting his name in the *khutba* or 'bidding prayer', and from issuing coins. He devoted all his energies to the pursuit of Dara Shikoh, who was hunted through Delhi and Lahore as far as Multan by Aurangzeb, who was then, in September, obliged to turn back in order to meet the danger threatening him by reason of Shuja's advance from Bengal, and the operations of Dara Shikoh's son, Sulaiman Shikoh. The latter had defeated Shuja at Bahādurpur near Benares in February 1658, but was too far away to be able to help his father in time. Shuja, who was strong in artillery, and had a large fleet of boats, recovered from his defeat, and during the autumn entertained high hopes of success. But on 7 January 1659 his army was routed at Khajwah in the Fatehpur District by a superior force under Aurangzeb in person, and he never again had any real prospect of vanquishing his enemy. Mīr Jumla pursued the prince unrelentingly with an army fivefold the strength of his; and drove him across Bengal to Dacca and thence over the Arakan frontier in May 1660. He and all his family were slaughtered by the Arakanese, but the exact details were never ascertained, and false reports that Shuja still lived continued to be current for some years.

Aurangzeb's eldest son, Prince Muhammad Sultan, having quarrelled with Mīr Jumla, had foolishly joined Shuja for a time and married his daughter. He paid the penalty by lifelong imprisonment and death by private execution in 1676 or 1677.

Fate of the sons of Dara Shikoh. Sulaiman Shikoh, having been forced to take refuge in the hills of Garhwal in August 1658, was received hospitably by the raja of Srinagar in that principality, which must not be confounded with the town of the same name in Kashmir. The raja honourably kept faith with his hunted guest, but his son yielded to the pressure applied by the emperor, and betrayed the prince in December 1660. The young man, who was singularly handsome, was brought in chains before his uncle, who solemnly promised that the prisoner would not be tortured by the slow poison of *postā*, or infusion of opium-poppy heads. The promise was shamelessly violated, and Sulaiman Shikoh's body and mind were gradually wrecked by the daily administration of the deadly draught in the state prison at Gwalior. His jailers finished him off in May 1662.

His younger brother, Sipihr Shikoh, was spared, and married a few years later to his cousin, the third daughter of Aurangzeb. The same treatment was accorded to the son of Murad Bakhsh, named Izid Bakhsh, who was married to the emperor's fifth daughter. Aurangzeb, while not shrinking from any severity deemed necessary to secure his throne, had no taste for indiscriminate, superfluous bloodshed; and, when he felt his power established beyond danger of dispute by the sons of his brothers, was willing to allow the youths to live. His subsequent dangers came from the side of his own sons.

Flight and defeat of Dara Shikoh. The sad story of Dara Shikoh remains to be completed. We left him at Multan in September 1657, when Aurangzeb turned back in order to dispose of Shuja, while his officers pursued Dara Shikoh with untiring energy. The prince, who 'seemed doomed never to succeed in any enterprise', fled down the course of the Indus with an ever-diminishing force, and would not make a stand even at the strong fortress of Bhakkar, where a faithful eunuch guarded his treasure and some of his ladies. At this point, acting under the influence of unjust suspicions, he dismissed Dāūd Khān, one of his most faithful followers. Dāūd Khān was constrained to quit his ungrateful master and enter the service of Aurangzeb, who welcomed him and raised him to high office.

Dara Shikoh forced his way with difficulty through the Sihwan gorge, and so reached Tatta (Thathah). Driven thence he crossed the Indus delta and the terrible Rann, and so entered Cutch (Kachchh) where he was kindly received. But he dared not stay, and pressed on into Kathiawar and Gujarat. At Ahmadabad he found a friend in the governor Shāh Nawāz Khān, who opened the gates of the city to him, and enabled him to occupy Surat. At that moment the unlucky prince, who had collected a considerable force, seemed to have a chance of success. If he had adopted the advice of the counsellors who recommended retirement to the Deccan, he might have become a dangerous rival of his brother. Unfortunately, delusive hopes of alliance with Shuja and Jaswant Singh, the treacherous raja of Marwar, tempted him to advance to Ajmer in reliance upon Rajput help. His programme was announced as being the release of Shahjahan, not the assumption of royalty by himself. Jaswant Singh had promised to bring his Rathors to the standard of the prince, but he yielded to the seductions and gold of Aurangzeb, and broke his plighted word.

Dara Shikoh, when forced to fight, even without the expected Rathor contingent, made the best of his situation by entrenching himself in a strong, well-chosen position at the Pass of Deorāi, to the south of Ajmer. The battle raged for three days, 12–14 April 1659, and ended in the rout of the prince, whose position had been turned by a body of hill-men in the imperialist service.

Betrayal of the prince. The hapless Dara Shikoh now resumed his flight. Speeding across Rajputana he again reached Cutch, once more traversed the waterless Rann, and entered Sind hoping to reach Qandahar, and so find asylum in Persia. With extreme folly, and in opposition to urgent remonstrances, he placed himself in the power of a faithless Afghan named Jīwan Khān, chief of Dādar, a place nine miles to the east of the Bolan Pass. The treacherous host promptly betrayed his guest on 9 June. It is some satisfaction to know that the traitor did not long enjoy the reward of his baseness. He and his retinue of about fourteen persons were stoned to death in a field near Sirhind by order of Aurangzeb. Manucci experienced 'great pleasure' at seeing the corpses, and notes that the Muslims with him 'uttered a thousand curses' over the body of Jīwan Khān. The same author points out that Aurangzeb was careful to destroy every person who had laid hands on any member of the imperial family.

Death of Nadira Begam. The only excuse for the obstinate folly of Dara Shikoh on this occasion is to be found in the fact that he was not then in his right mind, by reason of the death of his cousin, Nadira Begam, the wife of his youth, and the mother of his sons. Throughout his dreadful journeyings, in heat, hunger, thirst, and every form of misery, that loving woman had borne her husband company. Her much-tried strength failed as they approached Dādar, and when the prince threw himself on the hospitality of Jīwan Khān he cared little whether he lived or died. 'Death was painted in his eyes. . . . Everywhere he saw only destruction, and losing his senses became utterly heedless of his own affairs.'

The Timurid princes, notwithstanding their polygamous habits and the freedom of their relations with women, often showed a capacity for feeling the passion of conjugal love in its utmost intensity. Akbar's strange nature does not seem to have been disturbed by any such deep passion. His attitude towards women was much like that of Napoleon. But Jahangir, Shahjahan, Dara Shikoh, and even Aurangzeb knew what it meant to love a wife. A beautiful album in the India Office Library is a pathetic memorial of Dara Shikoh's love. It bears the inscription in his handwriting: 'This album was presented to his nearest and dearest friend, the Lady Nadirah Begam, by Prince Muhammad Dara Shukoh, son of the Emperor Shahjahan, in the year 1051 (= A.D. 1641–2).'[1]

Betrayal of Dara Shikoh. The rest of the tragic story is soon told. The captive prince, with two daughters and his second son, Sipihr Shikoh, a boy of fourteen, was made over to Bahādur Khān, who brought the party to Delhi. Aurangzeb indulged his spite by parading his brother, clad like a beggar-man, on the back of a small, dirty she-elephant through the streets of Delhi. The learned French physician François Bernier witnessed the sad procession.

I took [he writes] my station in one of the most conspicuous parts of the city, in the midst of the largest bazaar; was mounted on a good horse, and accompanied by two servants and two intimate friends. From every quarter I heard piercing and distressing shrieks, for the Indian people have a very tender heart; men, women, and children wailing as if some mighty calamity had happened to themselves. *Gion-kan* (Jīwan Khān) rode near the wretched *Dara*; and the abusive and indignant cries vociferated as the traitor moved along were absolutely deafening. I observed some *Fakires* and several poor people throw stones at the infamous *Patan*; but not a single movement was made, no one offered to draw his sword with a view of delivering the beloved and compassionated *Dara*.

His execution. A council was held to determine the prisoner's fate. His sister Roshan Rai (Roshanara) clamoured for his blood and was supported in her unnatural contention by most of the councillors. Bernier's patron, Dānishmand Khān, seems to have been the only person who opposed the capital sentence. The court theologians readily humoured Aurangzeb's liking for proceeding by legal forms, and passed sentence of death against Dara Shikoh, as being a heretic. A popular riot on 30 August, directed against Jīwan Khān, the traitor, determined Aurangzeb no longer to delay the execution. On the night

[1] H.F.A., p. 458, pls. cxix, cxx, cxxi.

of that day brutal murderers tore away Sipihr Shikoh from his father's embrace, and, after a violent struggle, beheaded Dara Shikoh. The corpse was again paraded through the city and buried without ceremony in a vault under the dome of Humayun's tomb.

Captivity and death of Shahjahan. Shahjahan, meanwhile, continued to be closely confined in the Agra Fort, under the special care of a tyrannical eunuch, who frequently gratified the malice of his perverted nature by inflicting galling petty indignities upon the captive monarch. Except for such torturing humiliations and the continuance of strict confinement to the fort the prisoner was not physically ill treated. His lascivious tastes were gratified by the provision of female attendants, and his daughter Jahanara was allowed to minister to her father. Shahjahan lived until 22 January (o.s.) 1666, when he died a natural death at the age of seventy-four. Towards the close of his life he became extremely devout, detaching himself from worldly affairs, and occupying his time with religious exercises.

Character of Shahjahan. Shahjahan has received from most modern historians, and especially from Elphinstone, treatment unduly favourable. The magnificence of his court, the extent and wealth of his empire, the comparative peace which was preserved during his reign, and the unique beauty of his architectural masterpiece, the Tāj, have combined to dazzle the vision of his modern biographers, most of whom have slurred over his many crimes and exaggerated such virtues as he possessed. As a son he failed in his duty, remaining in rebellion for years. He exterminated his collateral male relations, beginning with his elder brother, Khusru, in order to clear his own path to the throne. As a father he displayed undue partiality for his first-born son, and showed little capacity for control over his family. The brightest feature in his character as a man is his intense love for Mumtaz Mahall the mother of fourteen of his sixteen children. Probably he restrained his passions during her lifetime, but she died early in his reign (1631), and there is no doubt that during the remaining thirty-five years of his life he disgraced himself by gross licentiousness. He had little skill as a military leader. The loss of Qandahar and the triple failure to recover that important position prove the inefficiency of the organization and command of his army.

The justice of Shahjahan. Flatterers have recorded the most extravagant eulogies on his supposed justice, but examination of concrete facts suggests that it was rather crude in its operation. Shahjahan, like his father, took a horrid pleasure in witnessing the shocking punishments inflicted. Thieves, we are told, were never pardoned.

Administration. The severity exhibited by the emperor was imitated by his provincial governors, who never dreamed of studying the causes of crime, being content to attempt its repression by a policy of indiscriminate massacre. When Peter Mundy, one of the most prosaic and matter-of-fact observers conceivable, travelled to and from Patna in the years 1630 to 1633, early in the reign, he found the neighbourhood of Patna unsafe, because 'this country, as all the rest of India, swarms with rebels and thieves'. Multitudes cf *chōr mīnārs*, or masonry pillars studded with the heads of alleged criminals, were found 'commonly near to great cities'. Each *mīnār* contained from thirty to forty heads set in plaster. At a place in the Cawnpore District the traveller counted 200 such pillars. When he returned some months later 60 more had been added. The 260 pillars in that small area recorded the massacre of at least 8,000 persons within a short time.

Shahjahan did succeed, however, in restoring efficiency in the *mansabdārī* system, which had deteriorated in the later years of Jahangir's reign. Though unable to reduce the inflated *mansabs* of the nobles, he did cut their rates of pay and exacted a definite, stated quota of troops from them.

State of the country. Other travellers bear similar testimony to the harshness of the administration. Bernier, who travelled and resided in the empire at the close of Shahjahan's reign, and the earlier part of that of his successor, was a highly trained observer, in the service of a great noble of the court, who was reputed the most learned man of Asia. Bernier, while deeply interested as a student in what he saw, was free from personal bias for or against either Shahjahan or Aurangzeb. He speaks of the actual state of the country at the most brilliant period of Mughul rule, when the dynasty was fully established, rich beyond compare, and undisturbed by foreign aggression. His pessimistic observations appear to apply specially to the upper provinces. The fertility and commerce of Bengal excited his enthusiastic admiration.

Bernier's gloomy impressions. The traveller's gloomy impressions are illustrated by the following passages. Having spoken of the despotic tyranny of local governors, he declares that it was

often so excessive as to deprive the peasant and artisan of the necessaries of life, and leave them to die of misery and exhaustion—a tyranny owing to which those wretched people either have no children at all, or have them only to endure the agonies of starvation, and to die at a tender age—a tyranny, in fine, that drives the cultivator of the soil from his wretched home to some neighbouring state, in hopes of finding milder treatment, or to the army, where he becomes the servant of some trooper. As the ground is seldom tilled otherwise than by compulsion, and as no person is found willing and able to repair the ditches and canals for the conveyance of water, it happens that the whole country is badly cultivated, and a great part rendered unproductive from the want of irrigation. The houses, too, are left in a dilapidated condition, there being few people who will either build new ones, or repair those which are tumbling down (p. 226).

The country is ruined by the necessity of defraying the enormous charges required to maintain the splendour of a numerous court, and to pay a large army maintained for the purpose of keeping the people in subjection. No adequate idea can be conveyed of the sufferings of that people. The cudgel and the whip compel them to incessant labour for the benefit of others; and driven to despair by every kind of cruel treatment, their revolt or their flight is only prevented by the presence of a military force (p. 230).

Thus do ruin and desolation overspread the land (p. 231).

A *Persian*, in speaking of these greedy Governors, Timariots [= *jāgirdārs*] and Farmers of Revenue, aptly describes them as men who extract oil out of sand. No income appears adequate to maintain them, with their crowds of harpies—women, children, and slaves (p. 236).

This picture of an excessive state demand is largely borne out by the early revenue *farmāns* of Aurangzeb, translated by Sarkar in his *Studies in Mughal India*. Similar ruin and tyranny had been the fate of the Deccan during the years from 1644 to 1653, in the interval between the first and the second viceroyalty of Aurangzeb. When one pitiless governor of that time, Khān-i Daurān, died, his death was hailed as a divine deliverance.

Climax of the Mughul empire. Whatever be the view taken of the personal character of Shahjahan or the efficiency of his administration, it can hardly be disputed that his reign marks the climax of the Mughul dynasty and empire. During the space of thirty years (1628–58) the authority of the emperor was not seriously challenged, and the realm was never invaded by any foreign foe. Although the loss of Qandahar and the failure of three attempts to retake it proved military inefficiency and encouraged Persian pride, those events had little effect on India, where the strength of the army amply sufficed to uphold the imperial system.

Art. In the realm of architecture and other forms of art it is unquestionable that the works of the highest quality in the Mughul period belonged to the reign of Shahjahan. The puritan Aurangzeb cared for none of those things. His buildings are insignificant, with one or two exceptions, and the drawings and paintings of his time show deterioration on the whole. Many of Shahjahan's artists survived into the reign of his son, and some of their productions executed during that reign are not distinguishable from earlier works; but, generally speaking, the atmosphere of Aurangzeb's court was unfavourable to the arts.

Indo-Persian architecture. The Indo-Persian architecture of Akbar and Jahangir, beginning with the noble mausoleum of Humayun, and including Fathpur-Sikri, Sikandra, the tomb of Itimād-ud-daula (1628), and many dignified buildings at Lahore and other places, has great merits. It is generally more massive and virile than that of Shahjahan, but the world is agreed in preferring the Tāj, with its feminine grace, to all its predecessors or successors.

It is impossible to give either descriptions or criticisms of particular buildings in this book. Generally speaking it may be said that the edifices of Shahjahan are characterized by elegance rather than by strength, and by the lavish use of extraordinarily costly decoration. Marble was preferred to the red sandstone favoured by Akbar and Jahangir. The dainty *pietra dura* inlay, borrowed from Florence, and executed in semi-precious stone regardless of expense, was largely substituted for the simpler white marble mosaic or the sandstone carving of the earlier reigns.

PLATE 23

b. Bijapur: Ibrahim Rauza Mosque

PLATE 24

a. Jaunpur: Atala Devi Mosque

b. Bengal: Bara Sona Masjid

The Hindu features so prominent in the buildings of Akbar and Jahangir were much diminished, although never wholly discarded.

The new city of Delhi called Shahjahanabad, with its gorgeous palace, was occupied by the court in 1648 some ten years after the beginning of the works. The Tāj, begun in 1632, was completed with all its appurtenances nearly twenty-two years later, in 1653; but the central mausoleum was ready in 1643. The lovely Pearl Mosque (Moti Masjid) at Agra was finished in 1653, the year which saw the completion of the accessories of the Tāj. The middle of the seventeenth century, therefore, may be taken as the date at which Indo-Persian architecture attained the summit of excellence.

Drawing and painting. The arts of drawing and painting reached their highest point at the same time. The somewhat crude imitations of Persian work current in Akbar's days had gone out of fashion. The artists of Shahjahan allowed themselves to be largely influenced both by the old Hindu tradition and by study of European pictures. A certain amount of shading was introduced, and a subdued scale of colour was preferred. Many of the artists were endowed with unsurpassed keenness of vision and steadiness of hand. Some were able to use with success a brush consisting of a single squirrel's hair. The portraits of Shahjahan's time, which are free from the stiffness common in the preceding and succeeding ages, are wonderfully life-like and often perfectly charming.

Hindu architecture. The erection of new Hindu temples, frequently of immense size and cost, was freely permitted, or even encouraged, by both Akbar and Jahangir. For instance, Raja Bīr Singh, the murderer of Abu-l Fazl, was allowed to squander 33 *lakhs* of rupees (= £247,500 at 1s. 6d.) on the Kēsava Deva temple at Mathurā, 'one of the most sumptuous edifices in all India'. Aurangzeb destroyed the building utterly in 1669, and replaced it by a mosque. In 1632 Shahjahan had prohibited the erection of new temples. No important Hindu building, religious or secular, dates from his reign so far as I am aware.

Literature. The most valuable part of the literature written in Persian continued to be the historical. Among the many works noticed by Elliot and Dowson or Sarkār the *Bādshāh-nāma* of Abdul Hamīd and the *Muntakhab-ul-Lubāb* of Khāfī Khān (Muhammad Hāshim of Khwāf)[1] may be mentioned specially.

None of the numerous Hindi poets can compare with Tulsī Dās in influence or importance. The most eminent is Bihārī Lāl, the ingenious author of the *Satsāi*, completed in 1662.

---

[1] That is the real meaning of 'Khāfī'. Khwāf is in Khurasan.

CHRONOLOGY (o.s.)

Reign of Shahjahan

Death of Jahangir	Sunday, 28 Oct. 1627
Enthronement of Shahjahan	Feb. 1628
Famine in Gujarat and Deccan	1630–2
Destruction of Khān Jahān Lodi	1631
Death of Mumtaz Mahall	17 June 1631
Siege of Hugli	24 June–24 Sept. 1632
Destruction of new Hindu temples	1632
End of the kingdom of Ahmadnagar	1632
Treaties with Golkonda and Bijapur	1636
Aurangzeb appointed viceroy of Deccan	July 1636
Marriages of Aurangzeb and Dara Shikoh	1637
Acquisition of Qandahar	1638
Grant of site of Madras to Mr. Day	1639
Accident to Princess Jahanara, and temporary disgrace of Aurangzeb	1644
Campaign in Badakhshan and Balkh	1645–7
Transfer of capital from Agra to Delhi (Shahjahanabad)	1648
Qandahar taken by Persians; first siege by Aurangzeb	1649
Second siege of Qandahar by Aurangzeb	1652
Third siege of Qandahar by Dara Shikoh	1653
Aurangzeb reappointed to Deccan	1652
Demolition of walls of Chitor	1654
Murshīd Qulī Khān appointed diwan of the Deccan; siege of Golkonda by Aurangzeb; death of Sadullāh Khān and appointment of Mīr Jumla as prime minister; death of Muhammad Ādil Shāh of Bijapur	1656
Invasion of Bijapur	Mar. 1657

War of Succession

Illness of Shahjahan	Sept. 1657
Battle of Bahādurpur, defeat of Shuja	Feb. 1658
Battle of Dharmat, defeat of Jaswant Singh	15 Apr. 1658
Battle of Samūgarh, defeat of Dara Shikoh	29 May 1658
Captivity of Shahjahan and Murad Bakhsh	June 1658
Informal enthronement of Aurangzeb	21 July 1658
Battle of Khajwah, defeat of Shuja	5 Jan. 1659
Battle of Deorāi, defeat of Dara Shikoh	12–14 Apr. 1659
Formal enthronement of Aurangzeb	June 1659
Execution of Dara Shikoh	Aug. 1659
Death of Shuja	May 1660
Betrayal of Sulaiman Shikoh	Dec. 1660

AUTHORITIES

THE biography of Shahjahan has been written by BANĀRSI P. SAKSENA, *History of Shāh Jahān of Dihlī*, Allahabad, 1932, with full bibliography. K. R. QANUNGO has written a study of *Dara Shukuh*, Calcutta, 2nd ed. 1952. The events, as viewed in relation to the biography of Aurangzeb, are discussed critically by Professor JADUNATH SARKAR in *History of Aurangzēb*, vols. i–v (Calcutta, 1912–19). For translations of the leading Persian authorities see E. & D., vol. vii. The European authorities used include the travels of BERNIER (transl. and ed. Constable and V. A. Smith, Oxford

University Press, 1914); OLEARIUS, trans. Davies (London, 1669); MANUCCI, transl. and ed. Irvine (London, Murray, 1907, 1908); *Travels of Sebastian Manrique*, ed. by C. E. Nuord and H. Hosten. Hakluyt Soc. 1926, 1927. MUNDY, ed. Temple, vol. ii and iii (Hakluyt Society, 1914 and 1919); and J. J. A. CAMPOS, *History of the Portuguese in Bengal*, Calcutta, 1919. TAVERNIER, transl. and ed. V. Ball (London, Macmillan, 1889).

The following works also have been consulted: DE LAET, *De Imperio Magni Mogolis, sive India Vera*, including the *Fragmentum Historiae Indicae* by President VAN DEN BROECKE (Elzevir, 1631, two impressions), transl. and ed. by Hoyland and Banerjee 1928; HOSTEN, 'A Week at the Bandel Convent, Hugli', in *Bengal Past and Present*, vol. x (Calcutta); *Journal of the Panjāb Historical Society* (*J.P.H.S.*, Lahore and Calcutta); Sir C. LYALL's article on 'Bihārī Lāl' in *Encycl. Brit.*[11]; W. H. MORELAND, *From Akbar to Aurangzeb*; ABDUL AZIZ, *The Mansabdāri System and the Mughul Army*.

The art of the reign is discussed in *H.F.A.* The coins are described in the official catalogues of the B.M., I.M., and Lahore (Panjāb) Museum, as well as in other publications.

The published inscriptions are listed in HOROWITZ, *Epigraphia Indo-Moslemica* (Calcutta, 1912).

CHAPTER 6

Aurangzeb Alamgir (1658–1707)

Second enthronement of Aurangzeb. The fate of Aurangzeb's father, brothers, and nephews has been related in the last preceding chapter, although some of the events took place in 1659 and 1660, after his formal assumption of the imperial dignity and titles. He re-entered Delhi in May 1659 and was enthroned for the second time in June with complete ceremonial. His name was then read in the *khutba*, and coins were issued with his superscription (A.H. 1069). He assumed the title of Alamgir, by which he is usually designated in the writings of Muslim authors. His earlier title of Aurangzeb, being more familiar in English, has been retained in this work.

The new sovereign at once showed his respect for Muslim usage by discontinuing the Ilāhī era of Akbar, and reverting completely to the Muslim lunar calendar, notwithstanding its inconveniences in practice.

Nominal remission of taxes. Like many other newly installed rulers he sought the goodwill of his subjects by abolishing oppressive imposts, which were especially vexatious at the time by reason of a famine of intense severity.[1] He remitted nearly eighty taxes and cesses of various kinds, and issued strict orders prohibiting their collection. But the leading historian of the reign records distinctly that, with one or two exceptions, 'the royal prohibition had no effect', and the local officers continued to collect for their own benefit nearly all the prohibited taxes. In fact, when Khāfī Khān wrote in the reign of Muhammad Shāh, the local officers and landholders used to exact more than ever by way of transit duties, so that goods in transit often had to pay more than double their cost price.

Mīr Jumla's war with Assam, 1661–3. Aurangzeb's success against his rivals had been due in large measure to his alliance with Mīr Jumla. After his accession that officer did further good service by hunting down Shuja and bringing him to his miserable end. The emperor was glad to keep Mīr Jumla at a distance from the capital as governor of Bengal. During the wars of succession, Mughul Kāmrūp, capital Gauhati, was overrun both by the troops of the vassal raja of Cooch Behar, and by the Āhoms, who eventually prevailed. Mīr Jumla was ordered to punish both rajas. Cooch Behar was rapidly overrun, the raja fled, and the kingdom was annexed in December 1661. The army, with a vast flotilla of boats, then pressed up the Brahmaputra valley, seizing fort after fort, destroying the Āhom

---

[1] See Tod, vol. i, p. 310, for a vivid description of the horrors of the famine as experienced in Mewar in Samvat 1717 = A.D. 1660–1.

fleet, and entering the capital, Garhgaon, just before an early onset of the rains in March 1662.

Immense spoils were secured, but the Āhom king escaped. Mīr Jumla therefore held his ground during the rains. Though isolated by floods, harassed by the Āhoms, and swept by an epidemic, the Mughuls held firm under Mīr Jumla's magnificent leadership. In October he resumed the offensive and so hounded the raja that he bought peace with a heavy fine in gold, silver, elephants, and territory. A princess for the imperial harem and hostages were also surrendered.

The withdrawal was as skilfully handled as the advance, but Mīr Jumla, who had shared in every hardship, died just before reaching Dacca, 10 April 1663.

The new territory, held only for four years, was lost by the disgruntled Raja Rām Singh of Amber. Even Gauhati was lost in 1681. The raja of Cooch Behar was reinstated by Shāyista Khān in 1664, but later much of the kingdom was permanently annexed.

Shāyista Khān in Bengal. Mīr Jumla was succeeded in the government of Bengal by Aurangzeb's maternal uncle, Shāyista Khān, who was transferred from the Deccan in consequence of the events to be related presently. Shāyista Khān continued to govern Bengal for about thirty years (excepting an interval of less than three years, from 1677 to 1680), and died at Agra in 1694, when over ninety years of age. Early in his rule he cleared out the Portuguese pirates who infested the waterways of the Brahmaputra delta, and compelled the King of Arakan to cede the Chittagong (Chatgaon) district (1666).

Respite of the Deccan. In 1657, when the serious illness of Shahjahan became known, Aurangzeb, who was then viceroy of the Deccan, was within measurable distance of effecting the destruction of the sultanates of Bijapur and Golkonda, which he ardently desired. The ensuing war of succession gave those much harried states a respite and enabled them to prolong their existence for nearly thirty years. But, meantime, Bijapur suffered many losses from the operations of Siyājī, a young Maratha chieftain, son of Shāhjī Bhonslē, originally an officer of the Ahmadnagar state, who had transferred his services to Bijapur a few years before the Nizām Shāhi kingdom was annexed to the empire.

Early life of Sivājī. Sivājī, who was born in 1627, began operations in a small way as a robber chief in Bijapur territory while still a boy, and took his own line, without consulting his father, in whose *jāgīr* the irregular proceedings took place. Shāhjī, however, who could not escape suspicion of having abetted his unruly son, suffered in consequence four years' confinement at Bijapur, and was in imminent danger of losing his life. The young adventurer, when only nineteen years of age, made his first important advance by gaining possession of a hill-fort named Torna, about twenty miles to the south-west of Poona. He gathered round him the men of the hills in the Western Ghats called Māwalis, who are described as an 'uncouth, backward, and stupid race', but who proved hardy, brave, and intensely devoted to their new leader. They knew every path and rock in their native wilds and could pit their knowledge of woodcraft against the military training of their Muslim enemies. Fort after fort yielded to the young chieftain, who built other strongholds on his own account. He next turned his attention to the Konkan, the rich strip of broken ground between the crest of the mountains and the sea. One of his officers gained possession of the important town of Kalyan in that region. In 1655 Sivājī directed the treacherous murder of the raja of Jāolī, who had refused to join him in rebellion.

End of Afzal Khān and his army. A Bījāpur *farmān* of 1645 notes that 'Shivaji Rāje has turne disloyald to the Shah', but the illness of Muhammad Shāh from 1646, and troubles in the Carnatic, long distracted attention. But, in 1659, while Aurangzeb was still busy securing his throne, they thought that the time had come to suppress the audacious rebel. An imposing army, numbering about 10,000 men and equipped with mountain guns, was organized and dispatched under the command of Afzal Khān, a brave and experienced officer. Sivājī, not being capable of meeting his foe in the field, opened negotiations through a Brahman envoy, who was sent to the Muslim general. The Brahman and Sivājī arranged a plot to inveigle Afzal Khān into an interview at which he could be killed with little risk to the Maratha. Afzal Khān fell into the trap readily, and, accompanied only by two officers, advanced close to Partābgarh and met Sivājī, who also had two companions. When Afzal Khān embraced him in the customary manner, Sivājī wounded him in the belly with a horrid weapon called a 'tiger's claw', which he held hidden in his left hand, and followed up the blow by a stab from a dagger concealed in his sleeve. The treacherous attack succeeded perfectly; Sambhājī Kāvjī beheaded the dying Khān, and the Marathas ambushed in the surrounding jungles destroyed the Muslim army. Among the immense amount of spoil taken 4,000 good horses were specially welcome.[1]

Shāyista Khān. Bījāpur only partially succeeded in retrieving the disaster, and Sivājī was left free to turn his arms against the more formidable Mughul power. In 1660 Aurangzeb, although still much occupied personally in the north, found it necessary to send Shāyista Khān, his maternal uncle, to the Deccan. The new commander won important initial successes, but could not fully get to grips with his swiftly moving foe. Shāyista Khān retired to Poona for the rainy season, taking precautions which he fondly imagined were sufficient to secure him from attack. But the cunning Maratha was too much for him. Sivājī himself, attended by a few trusty followers, managed, perhaps with the connivance of Jaswant Singh, to penetrate into the lodging of Shāyista Khān, who narrowly escaped death and was thankful to get off with the loss of three fingers and of his son. The humiliated

[1] For the details I follow chiefly Sarkar, *Shivaji and His Times*, Calcutta, 1919, S. N. Sen's *Siva Chhatrapati*, 1920, and Grant Duff.

general was obliged to ask for his recall. His request was granted, and he was posted to Bengal, as already stated. In 1664 the rich port of Surat was plundered with ruthless cruelty.

Prince Muazzam and Raja Jai Singh. Aurangzeb replaced Shāyista Khān by his own son, Prince Muazzam, with whom was associated in the command Raja Jai Singh of Jaipur. Skilful diplomacy and a swift success in capturing the most important fort of Purandar enabled Jai Singh to force Sivājī to accept a treaty, in June 1665, by which he gave up twenty-three forts and extensive lands, acknowledged himself to be a Mughul vassal, and promised a contingent of 5,000 horse. The raja, who had always maintained more or less friendly relations with Sivājī, then persuaded him to surrender to the imperial authority in 1666. The Maratha went to court under Jai Singh's protection and was received by Aurangzeb at Agra, but refused to comply with the rules of etiquette, and resented being treated merely as 'a commander (*mansabdār*) of 5,000', instead of as a sovereign prince. He was, consequently, kept under surveillance, from which he managed to escape with the connivance of Rām Singh, a son of Jai Singh, returning in safety to his own country in December 1666 after many adventures. His absence had lasted nine months.[1]

Raja Jai Singh died in 1667, while still in the Deccan, having been poisoned by his son, Kirat Singh, probably at the instigation of Aurangzeb, who publicly rejoiced at the news of the raja's death. He felt that the decease of his leading Hindu officer gave him greater liberty in his policy of persecution. He availed himself of the liberty so gained by destroying the large temple at Mathura.

Prince Muazzam and Raja Jaswant Singh. The replacement of Jai Singh by Raja Jaswant Singh of Marwar (Jodhpur), who had served previously in the Deccan, did not effect any improvement in the situation of the imperialists. Both the raja and his colleague Prince Muazzam accepted large sums of money from Sivājī and deliberately abstained from effective operations. They even persuaded Aurangzeb to grant Sivājī the title of raja in 1667.[2] The Maratha power continued to increase steadily, and the newly appointed raja was left at liberty to devote the years 1668 and 1669 chiefly to the organization of the internal arrangements of his government. In 1670 active hostilities were resumed, and in December of that year Sivājī's officers exacted from the local authorities of certain places in Khandesh written promises to pay to Sivājī or his deputies one-fourth of the yearly revenue due to government. 'Regular receipts were promised on the part of Sivājī, which should not only exempt them from pillage, but

[1] According to some authorities Aurangzeb received Sivājī at Delhi, but Agra certainly is correct. The *Tārikh-i Marāthah* MS. in the I.O., as I learn from an unpublished essay by Mr. Zāhir-ud-dīn Fārūkī, states that Sivājī displayed extreme conceit, refused to make obeisance, struck the chamberlain, and actually sat down in the imperial presence. Other accounts of the incident exist. Sivājī certainly considered himself to have been insulted at the audience.

[2] Grant Duff, ed. 1826, vol. i, p. 220.

ensure them protection. Hence we may date the first imposition of Maratha *chauth* on a province immediately subject to the Mughuls.'[1] That scandalous submission to blackmail is conclusive proof of the feebleness of Aurangzeb's government even early in his reign. His administration, in truth, never was everywhere successful at any date during the half-century of his rule. In October of the same year Sivājī had again plundered the city of Surat for three days in a leisurely fashion, but was not able to damage the European factories.

Jat rebellions. Grave disorders occurred close to the capital. Early in 1669 the Jat peasantry of the Mathura District rebelled under the leadership of a man named Gokulā, and killed the imperial *faujdār* or commandant, a zealous Muslim, who had carried out Aurangzeb's persecutory policy. A big battle ensued in which the rebels lost 5,000 and the imperialists 4,000 men. Severe measures restored quiet in the following year, but the trouble was renewed in 1681 and again in 1688, from which date it continued to the end of the reign.[2] We have seen how in 1691 the rebels inflicted the gravest possible affront on their enemy the emperor by plundering the sepulchre of his ancestor Akbar and burning his bones. When such scenes could occur close to Agra it is no wonder that the control of the government over the Deccan provinces was feeble.

Satnāmī insurrection. In this connexion mention may be made of an insurrection by the members of a Hindu sect called Satnāmī which occurred in the fifteenth year of the reign, A.D. 1672.[3] The sectarians are described by Khāfī Khān as 'a gang of bloody miserable rebels, goldsmiths, carpenters, sweepers, tanners, and other ignoble beings', who had their headquarters at the town of Narnaul, now in the Patiala district. The insurgents, who numbered about 5,000, took possession of Narnaul, and being persuaded that they were proof against human weapons fought with desperation. After some slight early success they were defeated with great slaughter, few escaping the sword.

Afghans and Sikhs. Nearly at the same time the imperial troops were engaged in difficult operations against the Afghan tribes. Despite extensive annual subsidies to the tribal leaders, coupled with such punitive raids as that of Shamsher Khān up the Panjshir river in 1667, first the Yusufzais and then the Afridis rose. The former overwhelmed Muhammad Āmīn Khān, governor of Kabul, at ʿAlī Masjid in 1672, the latter destroyed Shujāʿat Khān's force at the Karapa pass in 1674. These defeats led Aurangzeb to move to near Peshawar in 1674, whence for a year and a half he supervised successful military and diplomatic measures. His choice of Amīr Khān as governor of Kabul, 1677–98,

---

[1] Grant Duff, p. 249.
[2] Professor J. Sarkar in *Modern Review*, April 1916, pp. 383–92.
[3] Elphinstone gives the name erroneously as Satnāmī, and in the margin of ed. 5 the date is stated wrongly as 1676. The term *satnāmī* means 'devotees of the true Name', *sc.* God.

ensured a long period of comparative calm. Tegh Bahādur, the ninth Sikh guru, was executed in 1675 because he refused to accept Islam.

Coronation of Sivājī. Continued success emboldened Sivājī to claim for himself a dignity more exalted than the rank of a titular raja conferred at the pleasure of Aurangzeb. He aspired to the position of an independent king ruling in his own right, and not in virtue of delegation by a suzerain. In pursuance of his ambition he took his seat on the throne at his fortress of Raigarh in June 1674, with all possible solemnity, and established a new era dating from his enthronement.[1]

Southern conquests of Sivājī. In 1676 Sivājī planned and began to execute operations, described by Grant Duff as 'the most important expedition of his life'. His design was to recover the southern *jāgīrs* which had been held under the Bijapur government by his father and were still partly in the hands of Sivājī's younger brother, Vyankājī (Venkajee). Sivājī, at the head of a powerful force, visited Golkonda (Hyderabad), where he succeeded in inducing the sultan to become his ally and lend him a train of artillery. Proceeding south he took the strong fortress of Jinji (Gingee) in South Arcot, with Vellore and other important places, compelling his brother to surrender a half-share in the Tanjore principality. On his way home Sivājī captured Bellary, and a little later entered into alliance with his old enemy the sultan of Bijapur, thereby relieving the pressure exercised on the kingdom by the Mughul armies. The success of the Maratha leader had been secured in large measure by Aurangzeb's entanglement in the hostilities with the Afghan tribes on the north-western frontier, which lasted until 1678, when peace was arranged.

Sarkar remarks with justice that

ruinous as the Afghan war was to imperial finances, its political effect was even more harmful. It made the employment of Afghans in the ensuing Rajput war impossible, though Afghans were just the class of soldiers who could have won victory for the imperialists in that rugged and barren country [Rajputana]. Moreover, it relieved the pressure on Shivaji by draining the Deccan of the best Mughal troops for service on the N.W. frontier.

Death of Sivājī. The victorious career of the Maratha chieftain was ended by his death after a short illness at Raigarh in the fifty-third year of his age. His decease, which was concealed for a time, probably occurred on 5 April (o.s.) 1680.[2] Before proceeding with the narrative of the events of Aurangzeb's reign, it is desirable to give a short account of the institutions of Sivājī, and to attempt an apprecia-

[1] See the account of Oxinden, an eyewitness, inserted in Fryer's book *A New Account*, &c., vol. i, pp. 198–210.

[2] 5 Apr. is the date according to Grant Duff and Orme. Mānkar (p. 111) states the Hindu equivalent date as Sunday, Chait 15, 1602 Saka, in the Rudra year. But, according to chronological tables, 5 Apr. 1680 was Monday. Fryer gives 1 June; but Crooke in his note thereon (vol. iii, p. 167) quotes Irvine's discovery of contemporary French evidence that the date was 17 Apr. (N.S.).

tion of the qualities which enabled him to become the creator of a new nation and to take a commanding part in the history of his times.

The Maratha country. Mahārāshtra, or the Maratha country, in which the Maratha language is the prevailing tongue, is most compendiously defined by Elphinstone as 'lying between the range of mountains which stretches along the south of the Narbada [*sc.* the Satpura], parallel to the Vindhya chain, and a line drawn from Goa, on the sea-coast, through Bidar to Chanda on the Warda. That river is its boundary on the east, as the sea is on the west.'

The prominent feature of the country is the range of the Western Ghats. The mountains are so formed that the flat summits are protected by walls of smooth rock, constituting natural fortresses, which various princes, throughout many centuries, had converted by elaborate fortification into strongholds almost impregnable against the means of assault available in ancient times. Most of the hill-tops are well provided with water.

The Maratha people. The Maratha people do not play a conspicuous part in early history.

The Brahmans of Mahārāshtra, especially the Chitpāwan section of the Konkan—the narrow strip of broken, rugged country between the crest of the Ghats and the sea—are an extremely intelligent class, to which the peshwas belonged.

The bulk of the people would be classed according to the theory of Manu as Sudras. Elphinstone's description is the best:

Though the Marathas had never appeared in history as a nation, they had as strongly marked a character as if they had always formed a united commonwealth. Though more like to the lower orders in Hindostan than to their southern neighbours in Kanara and Telingana, they could never for a moment be confounded with either. They are small sturdy men, well made, though not handsome. They are all active, laborious, hardy, and persevering. If they have none of the pride and dignity of the Rajputs, they have none of their indolence or want of worldly wisdom. A Rajput warrior, as long as he does not dishonour his race, seems almost indifferent to the result of any contest he is engaged in. A Maratha thinks of nothing *but* the result, and cares little for the means, if he can attain his object. For this purpose he will strain his wits, renounce his pleasures, and hazard his person; but he has not a conception of sacrificing his life, or even his interest, for a point of honour. This difference of sentiment affects the outward appearance of the two nations; there is something noble in the carriage even of an ordinary Rajput, and something vulgar in that of the most distinguished Maratha.

The Rajput is the most worthy antagonist—the Maratha the most formidable enemy; for he will not fail in boldness and enterprise when they are indispensable, and will always support them, or supply their place, by stratagem, activity, and perseverance. All this applies chiefly to the soldiery, to whom more bad qualities might fairly be ascribed. The mere husbandmen are sober, frugal, and industrious, and though they have a dash of the national cunning, are neither turbulent nor insincere.

The chiefs, in those days, were men of families who had for generations filled the old Hindu offices of heads of villages or functionaries of districts, and had often been employed as partisans under the governments of Ahmadnagar and Bijapur. They were all Sudras, of the same cast with their people, though some tried to raise their consequence by claiming an infusion of Rajput blood.

Sivājī's environment. Such was the country to which Sivājī belonged, and such were the people whose virtues and vices he shared. His father, Shāhjī, a member of the Bhonslē family or clan, was one of the class of chiefs mentioned by Elphinstone, and, as already noted, had passed from the service of Ahmadnagar to that of Bijapur. Sivājī's mother, Jījī Baī, came from a family of higher social rank. She was an intensely devout Hindu, and by her example and teaching did much to stimulate the zeal of her famous son in defence of Brahmans, cows, and caste, the three principal objects of Hindu veneration. The devotion of the young chief was fostered by the Marathi poets, Rāmdās and Tukārām, with whom he lived on terms of close communion. The former was his chosen guide, philosopher, and friend; while the latter, who refused to come to his disciple's court, impressed on the mind of Sivājī the mystic doctrines which form the main subject of Hindu poetry.

There is one Truth in the world: there is one Soul in all Being. Pin thy faith to This Soul, see thyself mirrored in Rāmdās: Do this, O Prince, and thou and the whole world shall be blest therein; thy fame will pervade the Universe, saith Tukā.

The more practical Rāmdās pointed out to his royal pupil the duties of kingship as he conceived them:

Gods and Cows, Brahmans and the Faith, these are to be protected: therefore God has raised you up. .

In all the earth there is not another who can save the Faith; a remnant of the Faith you have saved. . . .

When the Faith is dead, death is better than life; why live when Religion has perished? Gather the Marāthās together, make religion live again: our fathers laugh at us from Heaven![1]

The poet's pious opinion that 'Treachery should be blotted out' reads strangely when contrasted with his ode of congratulation on the treacherous murder of Afzal Khān. But the Marathas, including Sivājī and the mother whom he adored, believed with one accord that their patron goddess sanctioned the execution of their oppressor even by treacherous means, which rightly shock the conscience of more scrupulous critics. The suggestion made in some of the Maratha writings that Afzal Khān tempted fate by meditating the assassination of Sivājī is not in accordance with the ascertained facts. The troops of the Muslim general were kept out of the way, while the forest round the meeting-place swarmed with hidden Marathas awaiting their chief's signal.

The power of Sivājī over his people rested at least as much on his

---

[1] Rawlinson, *Shivājī the Marāthā*, 1915, pp. 113–22.

intense devotion to the cause of Hinduism as on his skill in the special kind of warfare which he affected, or on his capacity for organization. Indeed, it is safe to affirm that his religious zeal was the most potent factor in arousing the sentiment of nationality which inspired his lowly countrymen to defy the Mughul legions.

One of those countrymen proudly declares that 'the king was no doubt an incarnation of the Deity. . . . No such hero was ever born, nor will there be any in the days to come.'

Sivājī's special virtues. The foregoing observations go a long way towards explaining the personal influence wielded by Sivājī and his conspicuous success, both as a robber chief in the early part of his career and as the responsible ruler of a kingdom in his latter years. But they do not exhaust the subject. Sivājī possessed and practised certain special virtues which nobody would have expected to find in a man occupying his position in his time and surroundings.

It is a curious fact that the fullest account of those special virtues is to be found in the pages of the Muslim historian, Khāfī Khān, who ordinarily writes of Sivājī as 'the reprobate', 'a sharp son of the devil', 'a father of fraud', and so forth. Nevertheless Khāfī Khān honours himself as well as Sivājī by the following passage:

In fine, Fortune so favoured this treacherous worthless man that his forces increased, and he grew more powerful every day. He erected new forts, and employed himself in settling his own territories, and in plundering those of Bijapur. He attacked the caravans which came from distant ports, and appropriated to himself the goods and women. But he made it a rule that wherever his followers went plundering, they should do no harm to the mosques, the Book of God, or the women of any one. Whenever a copy of the sacred Quran came into his hands, he treated it with respect, and gave it to some of his Musalmān followers. When the women of any Hindu or Muhammadan were taken prisoners by his men, and they had no friend to protect them, he watched over them until their relations came with a suitable ransom to buy their liberty. Whenever he found out that a woman was a slave-girl, he looked upon her as being the property of her master, and appropriated her to himself. He laid down the rule that whenever a place was plundered, the goods of poor people, copper money, and vessels of brass and copper, should belong to the man who found them; but other articles, gold and silver, coined or uncoined, gems, valuable stuffs and jewels, were not to belong to the finder, but were to be given up without the smallest deduction to the officers, and to be by them paid over to Sivājī's government.

His army differed from all other Indian armies of the period, and even from the Anglo-Indian armies of Wellesley's time, in its complete freedom from the curse of female followers. 'No man in the army was to take with him wife, mistress, or prostitute; one who infringed this rule was to lose his head.' Discipline was strictly maintained, and death was the penalty for either disobedience of orders or grave neglect of duty.

Organization of the army. The army, which originally consisted of infantry only, was organized in a sensible fashion with a due gradation of officers, ascending, in the infantry, in units of ten, under *nāik*, *jumledār*, and *hazārī*, and in the cavalry, in units of twenty-five, under *havīldār*, *jumledār*, and *hazārī*. The commander-in-chief was styled *sarnobat* or *senāpati*. When cavalry was introduced there was sometimes a separate chief for that arm. The troopers comprised *bārgīrs*, mounted by the state, and *silāhdārs* (*sillidars*), who provided their own horses. The proportion of *silāhdārs* who were partly outside Sivājī's control was steadily reduced during the reign. Sivājī disliked the *jāgīr* system, and preferred to pay his officers' salaries from the treasury. The garrisons of the forts were carefully constituted, and special precautions were taken against the risk of the commandants being corrupted. The forts played a very important part in Sivājī's kingdom, and required all possible care. Regular drill was not practised, but in that respect Sivājī's army was no worse than that of any rival power, while it excelled all others in simplicity of equipment and mobility. The army retired into quarters for the rainy season, when military operations in Mahārāshtra are almost impossible.[1] The campaigning season began in accordance with Hindu practice by a grand review held at the Dasahra festival in October, and lasted until about April.

A considerable fleet was built and stationed at Kolaba, in order to check the power of the Sīdī or Abyssinian pirate chiefs of Janjira and to plunder the rich Mughul ships.

Civil administration. Some of the revenue of the Maratha state was derived from simple robbery, and a large portion came from payments made by districts under the government of other powers which desired protection from plunder. The army was organized primarily for plunder, rather than the extension of territory directly administered. The principal blackmail payment was called *chauth*, or 'the fourth', being one-quarter of the authorized land revenue assessment of the district claiming protection. We have seen how as early as 1670 a portion of Khandesh, although imperial territory, was compelled to submit to the payment of *chauth*. Sometimes an extra tenth, called *sardēshmukhī*, was extorted. The aim of the ruler was of course to extend the payment of *chauth* which came to the state, rather than to plunder, for it was difficult to secure a share of plunder in the soldiers' hands. The details were purposely made as intricate as possible, so that nobody except the professional Maratha Brahman accountants could understand them. All clerical and account work was in Brahman hands. The fighting Marathas, including Sivājī himself, ordinarily refused to learn the arts of reading, writing, and ciphering, which they considered unworthy of a soldier.

The kingdom or principality under the direct rule of Sivājī at the time of his death in 1680, although considerable, was not very extensive. The home territory consisted of a long narrow strip comprising chiefly the Western Ghats and the Konkan between Kalyan, now in the Thana District, and Goa, with some districts to the east of the

[1] The older European writers call the rainy season in western India 'the winter'.

mountains, the extreme breadth from east to west being about a hundred miles. The provinces or districts in the far south, and shared with Sivājī's brother, Vyankājī (Venkajee), were scattered in a fashion not easily definable. Sivājī's civil institutions applied only to the territories under his direct rule.

The government. The government of the kingdom was conducted by the raja, aided by a council of eight ministers, of whom the chief was the peshwa, or prime minister. The other members held departmental charges, such as finance, foreign affairs, and so forth. They included a shāstrī, or officer whose duty it was to expound Hindu law, to deal with matters of religion, criminal jurisdiction, and astrology. The whole administration was largely influenced by Mughul practice, though Hindu terminology was employed. The eight ministers usually were actually employed on military business, the work of their offices at the capital being performed by deputies. Each district officer similarly had eight principal subordinate officials, to deal with correspondence, accounts, and the treasury.

Civil disputes were settled in the immemorial Hindu fashion by a *panchayat*, or jury of neighbours.

Revenue system. The revenue system was based on the practice of Dādājī Konadēo, Sivājī's early instructor. Farming of the revenues was stopped, and the assessment was made on the crop, the normal share of the state being two-fifths. But the raja's districts had suffered terribly from constant war, and Sivājī never had sufficient leisure to complete his revenue arrangements as a working system. The English traveller, Dr. Fryer (1673), paints an unpleasant picture of his government as in actual operation. Writing from Goa he speaks of Vengurla, now in the Ratnagiri District, as being under the 'tyrannical government of Sivājī'; and with reference to Karwar, the important port in North Kanara, then recently occupied by the Marathas, observes:

It is a general calamity and much to be deplored to hear the complaints of the poor people that remain, or are rather compelled to endure the slavery of Sivājī. The Desāis [headmen of districts or petty chiefs] have land imposed upon them at double the former rates, and if they refuse to accept it on these hard conditions (if monied men) they are carried off to prison, there they are famished almost to death; racked and tortured most inhumanly till they confess where it is. They have now in limbo several Brahmans, whose flesh they tear with pincers heated red-hot, drub them on the shoulders to extreme anguish (though according to their law it is forbidden to strike a Brahman). This is the accustomed sauce all India over, the princes doing the same by the governors when removed from their offices, to squeeze their ill-gotten estates out of them; which when they have done, it may be they may be employed again. And after this fashion the Desāis deal with the Kunbīs [an agricultural caste]; so that the great fish prey on the little, as well by land as by sea, bringing not only them but their families into eternal bondage. However, under the King of Bijapur the taxations were much milder, and they lived with far greater comfort.[1]

---

[1] *A New Account*, ed. Crooke, vol. ii, p. 3, but printed in modern fashion.

The robber state. Similarly, when the first sack of Surat occurred in 1664, an Englishman named Smith saw Sivājī seated in a tent and employed in ordering the cutting off the heads and hands of those who concealed their wealth. No reason exists for branding that statement by an eyewitness as 'a gross exaggeration'.[1] Sivājī, when gathering plunder, behaved as Indian dacoits and banditti always have done, and still do, although his barbarities were mitigated by certain chivalrous practices already noted, which may be ascribed with probability to the teaching of Tukārām. Hindus are prone to worship power as such, and Sivājī's brilliant success alone would have sufficed to win popular veneration. When that success was combined with intense devotion to the gods, reverent liberality to Brahmans, and protection to cows, the brave and victorious leader was well qualified to be considered an incarnation of the deity. But the fact that Sivājī possessed and practised certain unexpected virtues must not obscure the truth that he was in the first instance a robber chieftain, who inflicted untold misery on innocent people, Hindus and Muslims alike, merely for the sake of gain, using without scruple all means to attain his ends. The Maratha state at any stage, whether during Sivājī's lifetime, or in its later developments under the peshwas and the chiefs who replaced them as leaders, never served any good purpose or conferred any benefit upon India, except in so far as it gratified Hindu sentiment in the particular ways above stated.

Prohibition of histories. It is now time to quit the Deccan for a while and return to Aurangzeb in Hindostan. Some transactions in that region have been already noticed. A foolish order of the emperor in the eleventh year of the reign (A.D. 1668–9) put a stop to the compilation of the official annals maintained so carefully by his predecessors, and also forbade the publication of histories by private persons. The motive for the order seems to have been a morbid humility. Khāfī Khān, the principal authority for the reign, was seriously embarrassed in his pursuit of historical truth by the effects of the prohibition, experiencing much difficulty in determining the order of events during forty years. The period extending from the eleventh to the twenty-first regnal year in particular presented special difficulties.

The narratives of contemporary European travellers and the researches of modern scholars have done much to clear up the obscurity of which Khāfī Khān complained, but uncertainty as to the precise order of events still remains.

Aurangzeb a puritan. Aurangzeb was a Muslim puritan. He desired that his empire should be a land of orthodox Sunni Islam, administered in accordance with the rules laid down by the early Khalifs.[2] His conscience impelled him to take up that position, and

---

[1] Rawlinson, p. 98 note. The statement is quoted by Grant Duff (vol. i, p. 199 note) from a most minute description in the records of the E. I. Company in London. See *Times Lit. Suppl.*, 20 Mar., 15 May 1919.

[2] See, for instance, letter xciv in Bilimoria's translation.

he was willing to incur any political danger or loss of revenue rather than forgo his ideal. Authors who accuse Aurangzeb of sanctimonious hypocrisy and feigning religious sentiments which he did not feel in his heart are mistaken, in my judgement. Although his religion did not hinder him from committing actions in the field of statecraft which are repugnant to the moral sense of mankind, his creed, as a creed, was held in all sincerity, and he did his best to live up to it. He resembled most other autocrats in assuming that the rules of morality do not apply to matters of state. There is no reason to suppose that he felt any remorse for his treatment of his father, and it is certain that his conscience was perfectly easy concerning the penalties which he inflicted on his brothers, sons, and other relatives. The safety of the state, as identified with the maintenance of his personal authority, was sufficient justification in his eyes for acts which we are disposed to call unfeeling crimes. Those acts in no way conflicted with his religious convictions.

Destruction of temples. In 1669, when he had been firmly seated on the throne for some ten years, and Raja Jai Singh was dead, he felt himself at liberty to act on his theory of government more thoroughly than he had been able to do at first. We are informed by a credible author that on 18 April 1669 (Zulk'ada, 17, A.H. 1079) the emperor was shocked by the receipt of reports that in the provinces of Thathah, Multan, and Benares, but more especially in the last named, Brahmans dared to give public lectures on their scriptures which even attracted Muslim students from distant places. Such open propaganda of Hindu idolatry seemed to Aurangzeb a scandal. Accordingly, commands were issued 'to all the governors of provinces to destroy with a willing hand the schools and temples of the infidels; and they were strictly enjoined to put an entire stop to the teaching and practice of idolatrous forms of worship'. Five months later the local officers reported that in accordance with the imperial command the temple of Bishannáth (*sic*) at Benares had been destroyed.

After a short interval (in Ramazán of the year A.H. 1080) Aurangzeb had the satisfaction of learning that the magnificent temple of Késava Déva at Mathura, one of the noblest buildings in India, had been levelled with the ground. The foundation of a large and costly mosque was laid on the site.

Glory be to God [exclaims the historian] who has given us the faith of Islam, that in the reign of the destroyer of false gods, an undertaking so difficult of accomplishment has been brought to a successful termination! The vigorous support given to the true faith was a severe blow to the arrogance of the rajas, and like idols they turned their faces awe-struck to the wall. The richly-jewelled idols taken from the pagan temples were transferred to Agra, and there placed beneath the steps leading to the Nawáb Bégam Sáhib's mosque, in order that they might ever be pressed under foot by the true believers. Mathurá changed its name into Islámábád, and was thus called in all official documents, as well as by the people.[1]

---

[1] The dates for the demolition of temples are precisely fixed by the *Ma'ásir-i Álamgíri* in E. & D., vol. vii, p. 183. Aurangzeb's mosque, the Álamgíri Masjid, is the

Aurangzeb was far too intelligent to be blind to the political consequences of his action. He deliberately threw away the confidence and support of the rajas in order to carry out his religious policy, thinking the spiritual gain to outweigh the material loss.

Beginning of the Rajput war. Raja Jaswant Singh of Marwar (Jodhpur), after his failure in the Deccan, had been sent in disgrace to the west of the Indus, a region abhorred by Hindus, and was appointed to the small post of commandant of Jamrud at the mouth of the Khyber. Towards the close of 1678 he died. The emperor thought that his disappearance offered a good opportunity for further progress in the policy of abasing the rajas and Hindus generally. Two posthumous sons of Jaswant Singh were born at Lahore. One died, the other was brought to Delhi. When Aurangzeb gave orders for the child to be transferred from his mother to the imperial harem, Durgā Dās rescued the child, the gallant Rajput guard sacrificing their lives to effect the escape of the baby Ajit Singh. The mother claimed the protection of Mewar (Udaipur), which was readily granted by the reigning rana, Rāj Singh. War then began between the imperialists and the clans of Mewar and Marwar, but Amber (Jaipur) continued to support the imperial cause. Aurangzeb moved to Ajmer early in 1679 and usually resided there for more than two years, until September 1681.[1]

Reimposition of the *jizya*. The death of Jaswant Singh emboldened the imperial bigot to reimpose the hated *jizya*, or poll-tax on non-Muslims, which Akbar had wisely abolished early in his reign. Aurangzeb's objects are defined by Khāfī Khān as the curbing of the infidels and the demonstration of the distinction between a land of Islam and a land of the unbelievers.

A nobly worded protest, too long to quote in full, but deserving of commemoration by extracts, was sent to the emperor about this time.

The writer, having recited the tolerant conduct of Akbar, Jahangir, and Shahjahan, proceeds:

Such were the benevolent intentions of your ancestors. Whilst they pursued these great and generous principles, wheresoever they directed their steps, conquest and prosperity went before them; and then they reduced many countries and fortresses to their obedience. During your majesty's reign, many have been alienated from the empire, and further loss of territory must necessarily follow, since devastation and rapine now universally prevail without restraint. Your subjects are trampled under foot, and every province of your empire is impoverished, depopulation spreads, and difficulties accumulate. . . .

If Your Majesty places any faith in those books by distinction called divine, you will there be instructed that God is the God of all mankind, not the God of Muslims alone. The Pagan and the Muslim are equally in His

most prominent building in Benares, and occupies the site of the Saiva Visvesvara temple destroyed in 1669, erroneously called Bishannāth by the Muslim author. The name of Islāmābād has been long disused. For the temple of Kēsava Dēva see Growse, *Mathurā*[3], Allahabad, 1883.

[1] The detailed chronology of the Rajput war is given by Sarkar, vol. iii, App. ix.

presence. Distinctions of colour are of his ordination. It is He who gives existence. In your temples, to His name the voice is raised in prayer; in a house of images, when the bell is shaken, still He is the object of adoration. To vilify the religion or customs of other men is to set at naught the pleasure of the Almighty. When we deface a picture we naturally incur the resentment of the painter; and justly has the poet said, 'Presume not to arraign or scrutinize the various works of power divine.'

In fine, the tribute you demand from the Hindus is repugnant to justice; it is equally foreign from good policy, as it must impoverish the country; moreover, it is an innovation and an infringement of the laws of Hindostan.[1]

The testimony of the writer to the general misery caused by the misgovernment of Aurangzeb during the earlier years of his reign deserves particular notice. Rajputana suffered all the horrors of war in their most extreme form; because the rana, who had retired to the western hills, devastated the plains in order to hamper the progress of the invader, while the Mughul armies destroyed the little that was left.

Many temples were demolished. For example, in May 1679, Khān Jahān Bahādur received warm praise from Aurangzeb for bringing from Jodhpur several cartloads of idols taken from temples which had been razed. During the campaign of 1679-80 enormous damage was wrought among the shrines of Rajputana. At or near Udaipur 123, and at Chitor in the same state, sixty-three temples were overthrown. The friendly state of Amber (Jaipur) was treated with equal severity and suffered the loss of sixty-six temples. Many other figures will be found in Sarkar's *History*. Nor was the ruin confined to new or recent structures.

Aurangzeb employed all his three adult sons, the Princes Muazzam, Azam, and Akbar, in the Rajput war, with poor success and several serious reverses. Marwar (Jodhpur) was formally annexed to the empire late in 1679, but the conquest was far from complete, and fighting in that territory continued without interruption for nearly thirty years longer.

Revolt of Prince Akbar. Prince Akbar, although supposed to be his father's favourite son, smarted under his father's censure, and dreaming of a throne for himself to be won by Rajput swords, he went

---

[1] The authorship of the letter lies between Rana Rāj Singh, favoured by Tod, and Sivājī, to whom Professor Sarkar ascribes it (*Mod. Review*, Allahabad, 1908, p. 21) on the authority of R.A.S. MS. No. 71. The writer is said to have been Nīl Prabhu Munshi, a Brahman adviser of Sivājī. The chief, who was illiterate, could not have composed and dictated such a document.

The rate of the *jizya* assessment in Bengal, according to Stewart (p. 308 n.) was 6¼ per *thousand* on all property. Christians paid 1¼ per cent. on their trading in addition. The sick, lame, and blind were excused. The following quotation explains Stewart's statement about the tax on Christians. 'As for the three European Companies, they flatly refused to pay it (the *jizya*), on which Aurangzebe, while exempting them from the impost, obtained its equivalent by raising the duties on Europe goods to 3¼ per cent., instead of the 2 per cent. which had hitherto been allowed them by special charter' (Strachey, *Keigwin's Rebellion*, p. 45).

over to the enemy on the first day of 1681. He addressed singularly outspoken remonstrances in reply to a letter from his father, written probably early in January 1681. Aurangzeb had endeavoured to win back his son by a combination of promises with threats, and in the course of his argument exposed his real sentiments concerning his gallant Rajput subjects by describing them as 'Satans in a human shape . . . beast-looking, beast-hearted, wicked Rajputs'.

Akbar responded by urging his personal claims to consideration, and repelling his father's foul abuse of the clans.

All sons have equal claims to the property of their father. . . . Verily, the guide and teacher of this path [*sc.* of rebellion against a father] is Your Majesty; others are merely following your footsteps. How can the path which Your Majesty himself chose to follow be called 'the path of ill-luck?'

The writer recalls how Akbar had conquered the realm of Hindustan with the help of the Rajputs, and continues:

Blessings be on this race's fidelity to salt, who without hesitation in giving up their lives for their master's sons, have done such deeds of heroism that for three years the emperor of India, his mighty sons, famous ministers, and high grandees have been moving in distraction against them, although this is only the beginning of the contest.

The prince proceeds to expound the oppression of the government, the misery of the Deccan as well as of other provinces, and the universal official corruption.

The clerks and officers of state have taken to the practice of traders, and are buying posts with gold and selling them for shameful considerations. 'Every one who eats salt destroys the salt-cellar.'

Akbar continued with admonitions to his father to retire from the world, and 'make his soul', to use the Irish idiom. He added bitter personalities in verse:

What good did you do to your father
That you expect so much from your son?
O thou that art teaching wisdom to mankind
Administer to thine own self what thou art teaching to others!
Thou art not curing thyself,
Then, for once, give up counselling others.

A caustic pen was not enough to save the prince, who was no match for his wily father. Decisive action at the right moment would have overwhelmed Aurangzeb, who was almost destitute of troops for a short time. Akbar allowed the opportunity to slip, and spent his time in unseasonable pleasures. When he was ready to attack it was too late, reinforcements having reached the emperor. The Rajputs deserted him, and he was forced to ride hard for the Deccan, escorted by a small retinue of faithful followers, and guided by Durgadās, the devoted servant of the Rāj. Sivājī having died in 1680, Akbar took refuge with his son Raja Sambhājī, but ultimately was constrained to quit India and retire to Persia. His subsequent designs aimed against his father came to naught, and he died in exile in 1704.[1]

Hostilities with Mewar were ended in June 1681 by a treaty which provided for the cession of certain territory by the rana in lieu of the payment of the *jizya*, the demand for that odious impost being dropped. War in Marwar, as already mentioned, continued for thirty years until 1709, when Aurangzeb's successor, Bahadur Shah, formally and finally acknowledged the rights of Jaswant Singh's son, Ajīt Singh, as raja and ruler of Marwar.

Although Aurangzeb always commanded a certain amount of service from several of the Rajput clans, his unwise fanaticism alienated the two principal states, and deprived his throne of the loyal support gladly tendered to his wiser ancestors.

Aurangzeb goes to the Deccan. In 1681 Aurangzeb resolved to proceed to the Deccan in person, hoping that the presence of the sovereign might remove the danger threatening from Akbar's presence, secure the long-deferred conquest of the sultanate, and curb the growing insolence of the Marathas. The recent death of Sivājī seemed to offer a favourable opportunity. The Mughul generals, as Bernier observes, used to 'conduct every operation . . . with languor and avail themselves of any pretext for the prolongation of war which is alike the source of their emolument and dignity. It is become a proverbial saying that the Deccan is the bread and support of the soldiers of Hindostan.' Fryer quotes the same saying, observing that the policy of Aurangzeb was 'frustrated chiefly by the means of the soldiery and great Amirs (Ombrahs), who live lazily and in pay, whereupon they term the Deccan (Duccan) "the bread of the military men"'. The emperor left Ajmer in September, and arrived at Burhanpur in November 1681. In the year following he moved to Aurangabad; and in 1683 pitched his camp at Ahmadnagar, from which place he marched in 1685 to Sholapur. Those years were spent in the unsuccessful attempt to capture Prince Akbar and in sundry operations against the Marathas. But by 1685, when the Marathas had suffered considerably, the emperor had decided to turn upon Golkonda. This campaign was entrusted to Prince Muazzam, who came to terms with the enemy, which were accepted officially but disapproved privately by the emperor.

Surrender of Bijapur. The investment of Bijapur ended in October 1686 by the surrender of the city and of the young king, Sikandar, who became a prisoner for life. The independence of the state and the existence of the Ādil Shāhī dynasty thus came to an end. Sikandar's death in prison fifteen years later was, as usual, attributed to poison. The noble city remained desolate for many years, but has now recovered some small measure of prosperity. The buildings of

[1] For the correct date see E. & D., vol. vii, p. 196, and Sarkar, *History*. Beale and other writers wrongly give the year as 1706. The quotations from Akbar's letter are taken from Sarkar's article in *The Modern Review*, Jan. 1915, pp. 44–48.

the kings rival and in some respects surpass the Mughul monuments of northern India.

Capture of Golkonda. Abu-l Hasan, king of Golkonda or Hyderabad, had incurred Aurangzeb's wrath in a special measure because he had employed Brahman ministers and had sent money to Sambhājī. The dissoluteness of his private life was alleged as another reason for treating him with the utmost severity. When the final attack on the fortress of Golkonda came in 1687 the king gave up his evil ways, and played a man's part by conducting a gallant defence, with the aid of a brave and faithful lieutenant named 'Abdur Razzāq. Aurangzeb and his generals tried every means known to them—mines, bombardment, and escalade—without success; their troops suffered dreadful losses. The fortress, like Asirgarh in Akbar's time, was so amply provided with food and munitions that it was prepared to hold out indefinitely. The emperor, therefore, following the precedent of his ancestor, had recourse to bribery, and gained admittance through the treachery of one of the officers of the garrison, who opened a gate. 'Abdur Razzāq, fighting to the last, fell covered with seventy wounds. Aurangzeb, admiring his courage and fidelity, placed him under the care of surgeons, who succeeded in effecting his cure. After about a year he accepted unwillingly a post in the imperial service.

Khāfī Khān states that Aurangzeb received the captive king 'very courteously' and provided him with a 'suitable allowance' for his maintenance in the fortress of Daulatabad.

The fall of Golkonda in October 1687 closed the story of the Qutb Shāhī dynasty.

Impolicy of the conquest. Aurangzeb had thus attained what he considered to be the main purpose of the campaign, and had won the prize which had seemed to be within his grasp thirty years earlier, but had then eluded him. All historians agree in pointing out the impolicy of the destruction of the sultanates, which annihilated the only Muslim governments in the south, let loose a swarm of discharged soldiers to plunder the country, and freed the Maratha chiefs from any fear of local rivalry. Aurangzeb did not yet fully understand the strength of his Maratha enemies, whom he despised.

Execution of Raja Sambhājī. In 1689 his troops captured Sivājī's successor, Sambhājī, with his Brahman minister, Kalusha, while they were roistering at Sangameshwar. The raja, when offered his life in return for his forts, is said to have used abusive language to his captors. It is certain that he, his minister, and ten or twelve other persons were executed with horrid barbarity, their tongues being torn out and many other tortures inflicted. Aurangzeb personally ordered those atrocities, which stain his memory. Sambhājī's son, a boy of seven years of age, whose real name was Sivājī, but who is ordinarily known by the nickname of Sāhū or Shāhū, seized when Raigarh fell, was spared, appointed a *mansabdār* of 700, and brought up in the imperial palace.

Farthest advance of Mughul power. The capture and execution of Sambhājī naturally aroused hopes that the Maratha resistance would collapse. The imperialists actually did obtain a certain measure of success, and in 1691 were able to levy tribute even on Tanjore and Trichinopoly in the far south. That year, accordingly, may be taken as marking the most distant advance of the Mughul power.

Arrest of Prince Muazzam. Aurangzeb's eldest surviving son, Prince Muazzam or Shah Alam, had shown a sentiment of tenderness towards the sultans of both Golkonda and Bijapur, whose utter destruction he regarded as impolitic. He seems to have gone so far as to have entered into treasonable correspondence with his father's enemies and to have furnished supplies to Bijapur during the investment of that city. His arrest for those alleged offences was effected in March 1687. He remained in confinement, at first of the severest kind, but later much relaxed, for more than seven years until April 1694, when he was released and appointed governor of Kabul. During the period of Prince Muazzam's imprisonment, his next brother, Prince Azam, believed himself to be the heir apparent and chosen successor of his father. He was much disappointed by the unexpected end of his brother's detention, which was arranged by the old emperor with his accustomed cunning. The immediate motive for the release of the eldest prince was an attempt of Prince Akbar to invade India with Persian help, and make a bid for the crown. He advanced with 12,000 Persian horsemen to the neighbourhood of Multan, but was obliged to retire when confronted by a superior force under Shah Alam (Prince Muazzam).

A fatuous campaign. After the execution of Sambhājī the Maratha government was carried on by his brother, Raja Rām, who retired to Jinjī in the south. When he died a few years later (1700), his widow Tārā Bāī, an able and energetic woman, administered the affairs of the state as regent, and gave the Mughuls no peace. Her capital was Sātārā. The natural expectation that the death of three rajas within a few years should weaken the Maratha resistance was completely falsified. The central authority was weakened, and for payments from the treasury was substituted the more feudal system of payment by grant of *jāgīrs*, but national resistance continued. From about 1698, if not earlier, Aurangzeb's prolonged campaign may be described as a complete failure. Although he seemed to be still physically strong, he had lost the capacity for controlling his subordinates, who wasted time and money in the most unblushing manner. Zulfiqār Khān, son of Asad Khān, the prime minister, and supposed to be one of the best imperial generals, deliberately played with the siege of Jinji for some seven years and purposely allowed Raja Rām to escape. Prince Kambakhsh, the emperor's youngest and favourite son, hearing rumours of his father's death, entered into traitorous correspondence with the enemy, whom he even thought of joining, so that Zulfiqār Khān was obliged to send him to his father under arrest, a liberty which Aurangzeb privately resented.[1] Plague and cholera desolated the Deccan for about eight years, floods more than once swept through the imperial camp, and hardly any pretence of fighting was maintained. Only Mu'tabar Khān, in the northern Konkan achieved any lasting successes. Aurangzeb, with almost incredible fatuity, devoted his energies to the capture of individual forts, and, as a rule, was content to buy them from the commandants. Khāfī Khān gives a long list of forts so acquired, and mentions only one or two as having been honestly stormed. It seems clear that Aurangzeb towards the end of his unduly prolonged life was in his dotage and quite incapable of effective executive action, although still retaining his old cunning.[2] Khāfī Khān discreetly observes that Prince Azam had noticed 'the altered temper of his father, whose feelings were not always in their natural state'. Aurangzeb had never trusted anybody, and had tried to look after all the affairs of a great empire in person. The affairs of the rest of India slipped from his grasp almost completely, and the gigantic hoards of treasure amassed by his father were squandered without result.[3]

Thus the too cunning old autocrat wasted the last twenty-six years of his reign. The Deccan, from which he never returned, was the grave of his reputation as well as of his body.

Dr. Gemelli-Careri's description. One of the most interesting of the many narratives by European travellers who visited India during the reign of Aurangzeb is the account of the camp and court of the aged emperor in the Deccan early in the year 1695 as recorded by the learned Italian lawyer Dr. Gemelli-Careri. Aurangzeb was then, in March and April, encamped at Galgala or Galgali, on the northern bank of the Krishna (Kistna), about fourteen miles distant from the town of Mudhol.[4]

The enclosure of the royal tents alone measured about three miles, and the whole camp, with a circumference of some thirty miles, had a population of half a million. The separate bazaars or markets numbered 250, and every class of goods, even the most costly, was on sale.

The traveller was accorded the honour of a private audience in the morning before the public reception, which began about ten o'clock. Aurangzeb received him courteously, questioning him about his travels and the war with the Turks in Hungary. The emperor, who was then approaching the age of eighty, was bowed by the weight of years, and leant on a crutched stick, but was able to write his orders on

---

[1] See letter clxxiv in Bilimoria for the treason of Prince Kambakhsh. Gemelli-Careri calls the prince Sikandar, apparently in error, confounding him probably with the ex-sultan of Bijapur.

[2] 'One cannot rule without practising deception. . . . A government that is joined to cunning lasts and remains firm for ever, and the master of this [art] becomes a king for all time. . . . It is contrary to the Quran to consider stratagem as blameable' (Sarkar, *Anecdotes of Aurangzĕb*, p. 96).

[3] In letter clxiii (Bilimoria) Aurangzeb expressly says that the expenses of the Deccan war were 'defrayed from the treasury of Northern India'.

[4] Sarkar, *Anecdotes*, p. 52.

petitions without using spectacles. He was of small stature, with a large nose, and white rounded beard. His coat and turban were of white cotton, his sash or waistband of silk, all quite inexpensive, but his head-dress was adorned by a gold band and a great emerald surrounded by smaller stones. The traveller confirms the Muslim accounts of the extraordinary austerity of Aurangzeb's personal habits. He slept little, spent hours in devotion, confined himself to vegetable diet, and often fasted. His attendants marvelled how a man of his age could endure the hard conditions to which he subjected his body.

The public reception was conducted with the pomp customary at the Mughul court. Aurangzeb never either compelled other people to adopt his ascetic personal habits, or allowed any diminution in the accustomed magnificence of his surroundings. His letters show that he was extremely jealous in his care of the royal prerogative and watchful to prevent the slightest infringements of etiquette.

Death of Aurangzeb. The last or almost the last petty success of the imperialists was won in 1705 by the capture of the fort of Wākin-kera which had been evacuated by the enemy. About the same time the health of Aurangzeb broke down, and he was seized with fainting fits which rendered him temporarily unconscious. Whenever he grew a little better he gallantly fought his disorder and forced himself to make a public appearance. At last, 'slowly and with difficulty', he marched back to Ahmadnagar, where he had encamped twenty-four years earlier, filled with hopes of conquest and glory. Now, when he nerved himself to sit in the hall of audience, he was 'very weak and death was clearly stamped upon his face'. The fever increased, but he still attended scrupulously to the prescribed times of prayer. On the morning of Friday, 21 February (O.S.) 1707, when one watch of the day had gone, and the prayers and creed had been duly recited, his weary spirit was released. His embalmed body was carried to the village of Rauza or Khuldābād near Daulatabad, and there laid to rest in holy ground beside the tombs of famous saints. He left written instructions that his obsequies were to be conducted with studied austerity. His tomb is a perfectly plain block of plastered masonry on an open platform.[1]

Aurangzeb's ideal. Thus Aurangzeb died as he had lived, striving to attain the ideal of a strict Muslim ascetic of the school of Hanīfa. He endeavoured to follow the Law and Traditions in every detail of his personal conduct and habits. He learned the whole Quran by heart after his accession, and was well versed in the works of theologians, especially those of the Imām Muhammad Ghazzāli.[2] He was careful to educate his children, including his daughters, in sacred lore. He

[1] The tombs at Rauza ('the garden', sc. of Paradise) are described by Haig, *Historic Landmarks of the Deccan*(1907), pp. 56–58. *Khuld* means 'paradise', with allusion to Aurangzeb's posthumous title *Khuld-makān*, 'whose abode is in paradise'.

[2] Abū Hāmid Muhammad Zain-ud-dīn of Tūs near Mashhad (A.D. 1058–1111), a renowned philosopher, mathematician, and astronomer.

abstained scrupulously from the slightest indulgence in any prohibited food, drink, or dress; and, although well skilled in the theory of music, refused to enjoy the pleasures of that art from an early date in his reign. Every ritual prescription of prayer, fasting, and almsgiving was obeyed exactly, even at the risk of his life. He desired all judicial proceedings to be conducted in precise accordance with Muslim law. He excluded Hindus from holding office so far as possible, cast down their temples, and harassed them by insulting regulations because he believed that he was bound to do so by the precedent of the early Khalifs. For the same reason he enforced the levy of the *jizya*, and in his latest years refused to allow the least relaxation in the collection of the tax, even for the purpose of securing supplies for his own camp.[1] It is not to be wondered at that such conduct has won him the reverence of Muslims.

Failure as a sovereign. But when he is judged as a sovereign he must be pronounced a failure. The criticism of Khāfī Khān emphasizes equally his merits as an ascetic and his demerits in the practical government of an empire:

Of all the sovereigns of the House of Timur—nay, of all the sovereigns of Delhi—no one, since Sikandar Lodī, has ever been apparently so distinguished for devotion, austerity, and justice. In courage, long-suffering, and sound judgement he was unrivalled. But from reverence for the injunctions of the Law he did not make use of punishment, and without punishment the administration of a country cannot be maintained. Dissensions had arisen among his nobles through rivalry. So every plan and project that he formed came to little good; and every enterprise which he undertook was long in execution and failed of its object.

The censures of the friendly Muslim critic do not exhaust the list of Aurangzeb's defects as a ruler. His intense suspiciousness, already mentioned, poisoned his whole life. He never trusted anybody, and consequently was ill served. His cold, calculating temperament rarely permitted him to indulge in love for man or woman, and few indeed were the persons who loved him. His reliance on mere cunning as the principal instrument of statecraft testified to a certain smallness of mind, and, moreover, was ineffective in practice. His proceedings in the Deccan during the latter part of his life show a great decline in his ability as a general. In fact, nothing in the history of Aurangzeb justifies posterity in classing him as a great king. His tricky cunning was mainly directed, first to winning, and then to keeping the throne. He did nothing for literature or art. Rather it should be said that he did less than nothing, because he discouraged both.

Aurangzeb's death-bed letters. The famous letters to his son, written shortly before his death, express the weariness of an aged man who had lived too long, had failed in cherished plans, and was tormented by morbid fears about his fate in the next world—fears based upon his theological creed, and perfectly sincere.

[1] Sarkar, *Anecdotes*, p. 142.

The following collection of passages includes extracts from all the three letters, which are nearly identical:

I know not who I am, where I shall go, or what will happen to this sinner full of sins. Now I will say good-bye to every one in this world and entrust every one to the care of God. My famous and auspicious sons should not quarrel among themselves and allow a general massacre of the people who are servants of God. . . . My years have gone by profitless. God has been in my heart, yet my darkened eyes have not recognized his light. . . . There is no hope for me in the future. The fever is gone, but only the skin is left. . . . The army is confounded, and without heart or help, even as I am; apart from God, with no rest for the heart. . . . When I have lost hope in myself, how can I hope in others? . . . You should accept my last will. It should not happen that Muslims be killed and the blame for their death rest upon this useless creature. . . . I have greatly sinned and know not what torment awaits me. . . . I commit you and your sons to the care of God and bid you farewell. May the peace of God be upon you.

The sternest critic of the character and deeds of Aurangzeb can hardly refuse to recognize the pathos of those lamentations or to feel some sympathy for the old man on his lonely death-bed.

Transactions with European nations. The transactions in which European nations, chiefly the English, were prominently concerned lie so much apart from the general current of events in the reign that it is convenient to notice them separately, rather than in their chronological setting. But it is not possible to go into details of the incidents, which were numerous and complicated.

The Portuguese, in the days of Aurangzeb, were of so little account that the dealings between them and his government may be passed by. The struggle for the eastern maritime trade then lay between the English and the Dutch. But the Hollanders devoted their attention chiefly to the commerce with the Indian Archipelago and Spice Islands, though quietly developing a very prosperous trade in their Indian factories. The small settlements on the coasts made by the French and Danes during the reign did not seriously concern the Mughul empire.

The English factory at Surat was gallantly defended against Sivājī and his Maratha robbers on two occasions, in 1664 and 1670. Sir George Oxinden's brave repulse of the marauders on the first occasion won appproval and honours from Aurangzeb.

Disputes concerning customs duties between the English traders on the Hugli and Nawāb Shāyista Khān, the governor of Bengal,[1] had the curious result of bringing about a semi-official war between England and the Mughul empire. The authorities of the East India Company in London ordinarily were averse to acquisition of territory or to fortifying their factories, but Sir Josiah Child, the masterful chairman or governor of the Company, who was ambitious, aimed at laying 'the foundation of a large, well-grounded, sure English dominion in India

---

[1] See the *Diary of William Hedges*, ed. by Sir H. Yule, for an account of these disputes.

for all time to come'. In 1685 he persuaded King James II to sanction the dispatch of ten or twelve ships of war with instructions to seize and fortify Chittagong. The expedition, rashly planned and unfortunate in execution, was an utter failure. Subsequently, in 1688, the English found themselves obliged to abandon Bengal altogether.

Sir John Child, the president of Surat, acting under instructions from home, defied Aurangzeb's power on the western coast, with the result that the factory at Surat was seized, and orders were issued by the emperor to expel all Englishmen from his dominions. Ultimately terms were arranged on both sides of India. Ibrāhīm Khān, the successor of Shāyista Khān as governor of Bengal, invited Job Charnock, who had been chief of the settlement on the Hugli, to return. The invitation was accepted. On 24 August 1690 Charnock hoisted the English flag on the banks of the Hugli and laid the humble foundation of the small settlement destined to develop into the city of Calcutta.

The scandalous quarrels between the old East India Company of London and the New English Company, which lasted from 1698 to 1702 and to some extent later, were brought prominently to the notice of Aurangzeb, who could not make out which Company was the genuine one. His great officers profited largely by receiving heavy bribes from both associations, but the queer story is too long and intricate for brief narration.

After the ignominious failure of the warlike policy of the two Childs and the complete fusion of the rival companies in 1708, the English merchants kept clear of politics and fighting for almost half a century.[1]

Administration. In the latter years of Aurangzeb's reign the fifteen provinces (sūbas) of Akbar's time had increased to twenty-one. Thathah (Tatta), or Southern Sind, Kashmir, and Orissa, formerly included respectively in Multan, Kabul, and Bengal, had been separated, and the provinces of the Deccan had become six instead of three.

The system of administration, while substantially the same as in Akbar's days, was worse in operation, because Aurangzeb failed to keep a firm hand over his subordinates, and when he grew old was unable to make his authority respected. From his reign must be dated the wide extension of the practice of farming the revenues, and an increase in the demand which led to the flight or passive resistance of the peasants.

Several authors have taken much trouble to compare various statements of the revenue of the empire at different times, but the figures on record cannot be forced to yield trustworthy results. I therefore refrain from quoting or discussing them. The army, which made a brave show on paper or in camp, was of little military value. Manucci's estimate that 30,000 good European soldiers could sweep away the imperial authority and occupy the whole empire seems to be fully justified by

---

[1] Mr. Strachey has proved that the two Childs, Sir Josiah and Sir John, were not brothers. They were not even related (Keigwin's Rebellion, Clarendon Press, 1916, App. A).

the facts. The navy was utterly inefficient. The assertion of one of the Persian historians that Aurangzeb renounced the practice of confiscating the estates of deceased notables is contradicted decisively by the emperor's letters. The few letters translated by Bilimoria give three instances of such confiscation being ordered by Aurangzeb under his own hand. When Amīr Khān, governor of Kabul, died the authorities were instructed to seize everything belonging to him, so that 'even a piece of straw' should not be left (letter xcix). Similar orders were given concerning the estates of Shāyista Khān, the emperor's maternal uncle, and Mahābat Khān (letters cxxviii, cxlvi). The receipts from such confiscations were exceedingly large, and the treasury was not in a position justifying the surrender of revenue, 'because', as the emperor wrote, 'the royal treasury belongs to the public'.

CHRONOLOGY

Leading dates only

(For dates of war of succession see above, p. 124

Formal enthronement of Aurangzeb; murder of Afzal Khān by Sivājī	1659
Cession of Bombay by Portuguese to English	1661
Mīr Jumla's expedition to Assam	1661–3
Aurangzeb's illness; first sack of Surat by Sivājī; foundation of French *Compagnie des Indes*	1664
Death of Shahjahan; annexation of Chittagong by Shāyista Khān	1666
Prohibition of Hindu worship; demolition of temples; first Jat rebellion	1669
First levy of *chauth* on Mughul territory; second sack of Surat by Sivājī	1670
Satnāmī insurrection	1672
Enthronement of Sivājī as independent raja	1674
Sivājī's expedition to the south	1676
Death of Raja Jaswant Singh	1678
Reimposition of the *jizya*	1679
Death of Sivājī	1680
Rajput war; rebellion of Prince Akbar	1680–1
Second Jat rebellion; Aurangzeb goes to the Deccan	1681
Sir Josiah Child's war	1685–6
Annexation of Bijapur	1686
Annexation of Golkonda	1687
Total withdrawal of the English from Bengal	1688
Execution of Raja Sambhājī	1689
Return of the English to Bengal and foundation of Calcutta	1690
Greatest southern extension of imperial authority	1691
Indecisive war in the Deccan	1692–1705
Union of the rival East India Companies	1702–8
Retreat of Aurangzeb to Ahmadnagar	Jan. 1706
Death of Aurangzeb	21 Feb. (o.s.) 1707

AUTHORITIES

COPIOUS extracts from KHĀFĪ KHĀN and other writers in Persian are translated in E. & D., vol. vii. Professor JADUNATH SARKAR gives a summary history of the reign and many interesting details in *Anecdotes of Aurangzib and Historical Essays* (Calcutta, 1912). His full-scale *History of Aurangzib* was completed, in five volumes, in 1925. His *Shivājī and His Times* (Calcutta, 1919) is extremely useful, though lacking an index. For a rather crude version of selected correspondence, BILIMORIA, *Letters of Aurangzebe* (London (Luzac) and Bombay, 1908), is useful. A leading authority for Maratha affairs is GRANT DUFF, *History of the Mahrattas* (1826, and reprints). That work, being founded on personal knowledge and manuscripts now lost, ranks as an original source. The most recent major work in English is the *New History of the Marathas* by G. S. SARDESAI. Professor SUREN-DRANATH SEN's *Siva Chhatrapati*, published by the Calcutta University, 1920, has been followed by his *Administrative System of the Marathas* and *Military System of the Marathas* in 1925 and 1928. Professor RAWLINSON's sketch, *Shivājī the Marāthā* (Clarendon Press, 1915), is of interest for the translations from Rāmdās and Tukārām. ELPHINSTONE knew the Maratha country and people so intimately that his narrative counts as a primary authority for some purposes. Many European travellers illustrate the story of the reign. The most serviceable works are those of BERNIER (ed. Constable and V. A. Smith, Oxford University Press, 1914); FRYER (ed. Crooke, Hakluyt Society, 1909, 1912, 1913); *Indian Travels of Thevenot and Careri*, ed. Surendranath Sen, 1949. *Storia do Mogor*, by N. MANUCCI, has been translated and edited by W. Irvine, in 4 vols., 1907–8. TOD, *Annals of Rajasthan* (popular ed.); STRACHEY, *Keigwin's Rebellion* (Clarendon Press, 1916), and other books have been consulted. STANLEY LANE-POOLE's *Aurangzíb* (R. I., 1896), the most readable account of the whole reign, requires considerable correction in certain details. A very detailed, if uncritical, study is S. N. BHATTACHARYA, *History of the Mughal N.E. Frontier Policy*, Calcutta, 1928.

W. IRVINE's *Army of the Indian Mughals* despite its title, is concerned very largely with the events of Aurangzeb's and his successors' reigns.

It may be well to note that the spelling Aurangzíb represents the Persian and Aurangzēb the Indian pronunciation.

CHAPTER 7

The later Mughuls; decline of the empire; the Sikhs and Marathas

War of succession; Bahadur Shah. The practical certainty that his sons would fight for the throne of Hindustan as soon as he should die weighed heavily on the heart of Aurangzeb, who attempted to prevent the inevitable war of succession by admonitions which have been already quoted. He cannot possibly have believed in their efficacy. He also left behind him a memorandum suggesting a partition of the empire, but could not have had any real expectation that his heirs would accept that solution of the difficulty. The same reasons which had brought about the war of succession between Aurangzeb and his brothers forced his sons to fight. The eldest, Prince Muazzam, also called Shah Alam, was far away in Kabul, and so for the moment at a disadvantage. The second, Prince Azam, and the third, Prince Kambakhsh, who were both at hand in the Deccan, lost no time in asserting their claims. Each promptly proclaimed his accession, and struck coins in his own name. The immediate objective of all the three claimants was the seizure of Agra with its hoards of treasure. Whoever could first obtain possession of the cash in the Agra vaults would be able to buy unlimited support. Prince Muazzam, aided by an able officer named Munim Khan, moved down from Kabul with all speed, and met the army of his brother Azam at Jājau to the south of Agra on 10 June 1707. Kambakhsh, who had occupied Bijapur and Golkonda or Hyderabad, was not able to leave the Deccan. The hotly contested battle at Jājau ended in the defeat and death of Prince Azam. Shah Alam secured the Agra treasure, which he distributed liberally among the nobles and soldiery. He assumed the style of Bahadur Shah.

The new emperor then made arrangements to keep the Rajput chiefs quiet, and marched south to meet Kambakhsh, who was defeated near Hyderabad and died of wounds early in 1708.[1]

Release of Shāhū. Bahadur Shah, acting on the astute advice of Zulfiqār Khān, released Shāhū (Sivājī II), the great Sivājī's grandson, who had been educated at court, and sent him back to his own country, then under the government of Tārā Bāī, the widow of the young prince's uncle, Raja Rām. The expected civil war among the Marathas which ensued prevented them from troubling the imperial government, thus justifying Zulfiqār Khān's counsel.

[1] No sympathy need be wasted on either Azam or Kambakhsh, who were both unfit to rule. The former is described as being 'very choleric, a debauchee, rough and discourteous to everybody, also avaricious' (Irvine, Manucci, vol. iv, p. 462). The latter was a half-insane tyrant, who behaved with 'outrageous cruelty', doing acts to his servants, companions, and confidants such 'as before eye never saw; nor ear heard'.

News of Sikh rebellion. Bahadur Shah, when returning from the Deccan, committed the government of the south to Zulfiqār Khān, who passed on the duties of administration to Dāūd Khān, a ferocious Afghan ruffian, concerning whose barbarities Manucci relates many horrible stories.[1] When the emperor reached Ajmer in 1710 he received reports that the towns of Sonepat, Sadhawa, and Sirhind had been sacked by the Sikh sectaries under a leader known as Banda ('the slave'), and sometimes described as the False Guru, who had committed innumerable atrocities. The news received was so serious that Bahadur Shah resolved to proceed in person against the rebels. In order to render the situation intelligible it is necessary to narrate briefly the origin and early development of the Sikh movement.

The early Sikh gurus. The Sikhs, or 'disciples', originally were a pious sect of Hindus following the precepts of their first *guru* or prophet named Nānak, who lived from A.D. 1469 to 1539. He resembled Kabīr and many other sages in his teaching which laid stress on the unity of God, the futility of forms of worship, and the unreality of caste distinctions. The first four gurus were merely leaders of a peaceable reformed sect, with no thought of either military organization or political power. In 1577 Akbar, who liked the Sikh teaching so far as he knew it, granted to the fourth guru the site of the tank and Golden Temple at Amritsar, and so established that town as the headquarters of the Sikh faith.

The fifth guru, Arjun, combined business with spiritual guidance, and acquired wealth from the offerings of the faithful. He was tortured and executed in 1606 by order of Jahangir, not on account of his religious teaching, but because he refused to pay the fine imposed on him for having assisted Khusrū. The Ādi Granth, or original Sikh Bible, was compiled in 1604 at the dictation of Arjun.

Hargobind. Hargobind, the sixth head of the sect (1606–45), when presented at his installation with the turban and necklace of his predecessors, refused to accept them, saying: 'My necklace shall be my sword-belt, and my turban shall be adorned with a royal aigrette.' He thus began the transformation of a sect of quiet mystics into a fierce military order or brotherhood. He was driven into the wild country of the Siwaliks by Jahangir, and, after the death of that emperor, constantly fought the officers of Shahjahan until he died in the hills in 1645.

Tēgh Bahādur. Tēgh Bahādur, the ninth guru, served under Rām Singh in Assam, but on his return to the Panjab was roused by Aurangzeb's persecution to revolt. Captured in 1675, he rejected the demand of Aurangzeb that he should embrace Islam, and in consequence was executed (1675).

Govind Singh. The tenth and last guru, Govind Singh (1675–1708), was the real founder of the Sikh military power, which he

---

[1] Meadows Taylor describes the brute as 'an officer of great distinction, ability, and bravery'. Elphinstone, too, gives no indication of the man's real character.

organized to oppose the Muslims. He bound the Sikh fraternity together by instituting or adopting two sacraments, perhaps suggested by Christian example. The ceremony of *pāhul* or baptism consists essentially of drinking consecrated water stirred by a sword or dagger. The communion rite was specially designed to break caste. The communicants seated in a circle partake of a mixture of consecrated flour, butter, and sugar, and thus set themselves free from the restrictions of caste. The brotherhood so constituted was termed the Khālsa or Pure, and may be compared with the Templars and other military orders of medieval Europe. The Sikhs are not, and never have been, a nation in any intelligible sense. The members of the order are only a fraction of the population in the districts where they reside, and at the present day many Sikhs describe themselves as Hindus. In fact, the distinction between Hinduism and Sikhism is not well defined, the observance of the sacraments often being neglected by men who are recognized as Sikhs. Guru Govind required the members of the brotherhood to abjure tobacco, which he detested. 'Wine', he said, 'is bad; Indian hemp (*bhang*) destroyeth one generation; but tobacco destroyeth all generations.' The initiated members of the brotherhood were also commanded to wear the 'five *K*'s', meaning five things of which the Hindi or Panjabi names begin with that letter—namely, long hair, short drawers, an iron bangle or discus, a small steel dagger, and a comb. Those commands are not all fully observed now, and modern Sikhism owes its continued existence chiefly to the influence of the corporate spirit of the Sikh regiments. A supplementary *Granth* or Bible containing the compositions of Govind was compiled after his death.

After a life of war and banditry against the hill rajas and local Mughul officers—in which he lost his two sons who were executed by the governor of Sirhind—he decided to support Bahadur Shah (Shah Alam) in the war of succession, and consequently accepted service under that prince when he gained the throne. Govind, who was murdered at Nander in the Deccan by an Afghan in 1708, was the last of the gurus. Since his decease the holy Granth has been regarded as the representative and successor of the gurus.

Banda. Banda, an impostor-Govind, took his revenge upon Wazīr Khān of Sirhind with appalling ferocity and completeness. Irvine draws a lively picture of his proceedings.

The scavengers and leather-dressers and such-like persons, who were very numerous among the Sikhs, committed excesses of every description. For the space of four days the town [Sirhind] was given up to pillage, the mosques were defiled, the houses burnt, and the Muhammadans slaughtered; even their women and children were not spared. . . .

In all the parganahs occupied by the Sikhs, the reversal of previous customs was striking and complete. A low scavenger or leather-dresser, the lowest of the low in Indian estimation, had only to leave home and join the Guru, when in a short time he would return to his birthplace as its ruler, with his order of appointment in his hand. As soon as he set foot within the boundaries, the well-born and wealthy went out to greet him and escort him

PLATE 25

b. Delhi Fort, the Diwān-i-'Ām, the throne

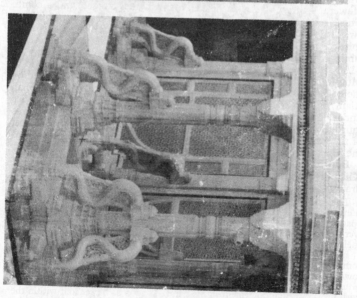

a. Sheikh Salim Chisti's Tomb at Fatehpur Sikri, near Agra·

PLATE 26

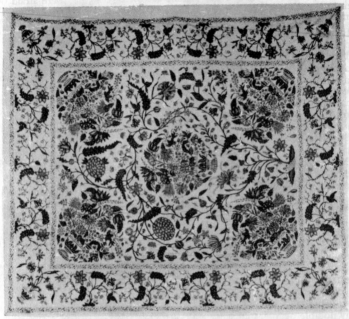

a. Bronze statue of Khrishna Devarāya
b. Eighteenth-century bedspread

home. . . Not a soul dared to disobey an order, and men, who had often risked themselves in battle-fields, became so cowed, that they were afraid even to remonstrate. Hindus who had not joined the sect were not exempt from those oppressions.

Bahadur Shah and Munim Khān succeeded in defeating the Sikhs and driving them into the hills, but Banda escaped.

The Rajputs. On Aurangzeb's death Ajīt Singh had expelled the Mughul governor from Jodhpur. In 1708 he was defeated by Bahadur Shah. But when the emperor turned to deal with Kam Bakhsh in the Deccan, Ajīt Singh, with Durgā Dās, Jai Singh, Raja of Jaipur, and Amar Singh of Mewar again drove the Mughuls from Jodhpur and also from Amber. The emperor, occupied by the Sikh war, could only make peace with the rebel Rajputs, and confirm the rajas in their states.

Death of Bahadur Shah. Bahadur Shah, then an old man in his sixty-ninth year, died in 1712. The prolonged repression which he endured under his father had destroyed his spirit. Although he had no vice in his character, and possessed a generous forgiving disposition, he could not govern, and justly earned the nickname of *Shāh-i be khabar*, the 'Heedless King'.

War of succession; Jahandar Shah. His four sons engaged in the customary war of succession. Azim-ush-shan, governor of Bengal, and the best of the four, was killed in battle with the other three, who then fell out among themselves. Jahandar Shah, the eldest and worst of them, a worthless profligate, became emperor.

Farrukhsiyar. After a disgraceful reign of eleven months he was defeated at Agra, owing to the Turani-Persian jealousies of his nobles, and murdered by his minister Zulfiqār Khān. Farrukhsiyar, son of Azim-ush-shan, ascended the degraded throne (1713). He executed many notable people, including Zulfiqār Khān, and established a state of terror in the court. During the scandalous reign of Farrukhsiyar, who was a good-for-nothing and shameless debauchee, the power of the government was mostly in the hands of two brothers, Abdullah and Husain Ali, Bārha Sayyids, whose clan had been eminent in the imperial service since the days of Akbar. They deposed Farrukhsiyar, who had half-heartedly plotted against them throughout his reign, in 1719, and put him to death in a horrible way.

The short reign of Farrukhsiyar was marked by a futile attempt to re-impose the *jizya*, and by the capture of Banda, who was executed with tortures. About 1,000 of his followers were killed in large batches (1715).

In the same year the East India Company, worried by the exactions of the Bengal provincial government, sent two factors to Delhi in order to seek redress. The envoys took with them £30,000 worth of gifts, and in the course of two years obtained valuable trade concessions and exemptions from customs duties. Their success was due partly to the fact that an English surgeon named William Hamilton cured the emperor of 'a malignant distemper', and partly to the fears of the Delhi government that the British fleet might hold up the Surat trade.

Muhammad Shah. After the cruel murder of Farrukhsiyar the Sayyid king-makers placed on the throne several phantom emperors.[1] They quickly disappeared and were replaced by another named Muhammad Shah (1719), who despite his rejection of the services and good advice of Nizam-ul-Mulk, and despite his readiness to set faction against faction, even to the point of calling in the Marathas, retained his life and dignity until 1748. He got rid of Sayyid Husain Ali by assassination, and imprisoned Abdullah.[2]

Break-up of empire. In 1722 Āsaf Jāh (Chīn Qilīch Khān) became wazir. He found it impossible to bring the government into order, and in the year following retired to his province the Deccan, where he became independent and founded the dynasty of the Nizam, with effect from 1724.

In the same year Saādat Khān, the progenitor of the kings of Oudh, became ruler of that province, which he governed in practical independence. Similarly, ʿAlī Vardī Khān, the governor of Bengal (1740–56), forwarded an irregular tribute only and ceased to recognize in practice the sovereignty of the emperor. The Rohillas, an Afghan clan, made themselves masters of the rich tract to the north of the Ganges, which consequently became known as Rohilkhand. Thus, in the space of seventeen years after the death of Aurangzeb, the empire was breaking up. The process of decay was continued in subsequent years. The capital was the scene of incessant intrigues and treasons, unworthy of record or remembrance.

New system of Maratha government. Meantime, momentous changes had been effected after long struggles in the Maratha government, which resulted during Muhammad Shah's lifetime in the Marathas becoming the most considerable power in India. The excellent system of internal administration instituted by Sivājī had not survived that chief. It fell to pieces, as we have seen, in the hands of his son, Sambhājī. During the civil war between different parties of Marathas which followed on the return of Shāhū to his native country, after his release by Bahadur Shah, a new system of government was gradually evolved.

The first peshwa, Bālājī Visvanāth. Raja Shāhū, who had to defend his position as raja against a rival claimant, leant for support chiefly on a Brahman from the Konkan, named Bālājī Visvanāth, who held from 1714 the office of peshwa, as the second minister was called in the early Maratha administration.[3] By reason of his personal qualities Bālājī Visvanāth made the office to count in practice as the first,

---

[1] Their names are Rafi-ud-darajat, Rafi-ud-daulat (Shahjahan II), Nekusiyar, and Ibrahim. The 'reigns' of the first three fall between 18 Feb. and 27 Aug. 1719. Ibrahim claimed the throne in 1720, from 1 Oct. to 8 Nov., and struck coins, now very rare. See the genealogy at the end of this chapter.

[2] The confused struggles of his reign are dealt with in the second volume of W. Irvine's *Later Mughals.*

[3] In Sivājī's time the pratinidhi did not exist, and the peshwa was the first minister.

and not the second. When he died in 1720 his official position was inherited by his son, Bājī Rāo, a man still abler than himself. The appointment of peshwa thus became hereditary, and soon overshadowed the raja, who sank into a purely ornamental position, exactly as the Mahārājādhirāj of Nepāl did in modern times. After Shāhū the descendants of Sivājī dropped out of sight so completely that all readers of history think of the Maratha government in the eighteenth century as that of the peshwas. Their dynasty, as we may call it, comprised seven persons, and may be regarded as having lasted from 1714 to 1818, a little more than a century. Shāhū, who survived until 1749, granted his minister full powers in 1727.

Chauth and *Sardeshmukhi.* Bālājī Visvanāth, as minister of Shāhū, had succeeded in introducing a certain amount of order into the Maratha administration, and had made elaborate arrangements for collecting the assignments of revenue from provinces belonging to other powers on which his government chiefly lived. The Marathas of those days administered only comparatively small districts directly, preferring to raise contributions from provinces governed, nominally at all events, by the emperor of Delhi or other potentates of that confused and anarchical time. In 1720 Muhammad Shah, confirming arrangements made by Sayyid Husain Ali, recognized by treaty the authority of Raja Shāhū, admitted his right to levy the *chauth*, or assessment of one-fourth of the land revenue over the whole Deccan, and permitted him to supplement that levy by an additional tenth of the land revenue called *sardeshmukhi.*

Bālājī Visvanāth claimed that those levies should be calculated on the revenue as fixed either by Todar Mal in Akbar's, or by Malik Ambar in Shahjahan's time, well knowing that no such amount of revenue could be raised from a ruined country. He thus secured the advantage of always keeping a bill for arrears in hand. He had, however, to accept the semi-independence of the greater chiefs, achieved during the minority of Raja Rām's sons, by which they were assigned spheres of action wherein they collected *chauth* on their own authority, though paying something to the royal treasury. Large numbers of fiefs continued to be granted by the peshwas whose control, through civil officers, of the military chiefs was thus further weakened.

The second peshwa, Bājī Rāo. Bājī Rāo (1720) inherited the instrument of extortion so cunningly devised by his father, and used it with supreme skill. He resolved to establish the power of his nascent nation by reorganizing the army, and directing it against the northern territories of Hindustan held by the nerveless hands of Muhammad Shah. He also made arrangements by which he checked the growing power of Āsaf Jāh as ruler of the Hyderabad territories. The quarrels between Āsaf Jāh and Bājī Rāo ended in the rivals coming to terms (1731).

Origin of the Gaikwar, Sindia, and Holkar. We may take note that at the period in question the ancestors of the later great Maratha chiefs, namely, the Gaikwar of Baroda, Sindia of Gwalior, and Holkar of Indore, became prominent personages and laid the foundations of the fortune of their families, which by strange chance survived at the final settlement in 1818 of the rivalry between the Marathas and the British. The ancestor of the Gaikwar was an adherent of a defeated opponent of Bājī Rāo, whom the peshwa treated with politic generosity; the progenitors of Sindia and Holkar were men of humble origin who became officers of Bājī Rāo and rose gradually in his service.

Maratha appearance before Delhi. The Marathas, having made themselves masters of Gujarat, Malwa, and Bundelkhand, made a startling demonstration of the weakness of the empire and of their own power by evading the imperial army and suddenly appearing in the suburbs of Delhi in 1737. They did not attempt to occupy the capital, and returned to the Deccan to meet Āsaf Jāh, who had again taken the field against them. The Nizam, as we may now call him, was no match for his nimble enemy and was forced to make a formal cession of Malwa to the Marathas.

Weakness of the empire invited attack. Bājī Rāo, Elphinstone observes,

took possession of his conquests; but before he could receive the promised confirmation from the emperor, the progress of the transaction was arrested by one of those tremendous visitations, which for a time render men insensible to all other considerations.

The empire was again reduced to the same state of decay which had on former occasions invited the invasions of Tamerlane and Bābar; and a train of events in Persia led to a similar attack from that country.

Nādir Shāh; battle of Karnal. Nādir (or Tahmāsp) Qulī Khān, 'the greatest warrior Persia has ever produced', had overthrown the Safavī dynasty in 1736, and been acclaimed king of that country under the style of Nādir Shāh. When established on his throne he easily found pretexts for the invasion and plunder of the rich and defenceless Indian plains. Advancing in 1739 through Ghazni, Kabul, and Lahore, he met with no real obstruction until he had approached the Jumna, within 100 miles of Delhi, when he encountered the imperial army entrenched at Karnal, not very far from the field of Panipat. After a fight lasting two hours the imperialists were routed, some 20,000 being slain, and immense booty falling into the hands of the conqueror. Muhammad Shah made no attempt at further resistance, but attended Nādir Shāh in his camp, where he was received courteously. Both kings entered Delhi together, and good order was preserved until a false report of Nādir Shāh's death gave occasion to a rising of the inhabitants, in the course of which several hundreds of the invaders were killed. Nādir Shāh took terrible vengeance. Seated in the Golden Mosque of Roshan-ud-daula, situated in the main street of the city, he commanded and watched for nine hours the indiscriminate massacre of the people in uncounted thousands. At last he yielded to the prayers of Muhammad Shah and stayed the carnage, which ceased instantly.

Nādir Shāh then proceeded systematically and remorselessly to collect from all classes of the population the wealth of Delhi, the accumulation of nearly three centuries and a half. After a stay of fifty-eight days he departed for his own country laden with treasure of incalculable richness, including the world-famed peacock throne of Shahjahan. He annexed all the territory to the west of the Indus and the now extinct Hakrā river (nāla of Sankrah) under the provisions of a treaty dated 26 May 1739. Afghanistan was thus severed from the Indian monarchy.

Anarchy; Ahmad Shah of Delhi. Nādir Shāh left the Mughul empire bleeding and prostrate. No central government worthy of the name existed, and if any province enjoyed for a short time the blessing of tolerably good administration, as was the case in Bengal, that was due to the personal character of the noble or adventurer who had secured control over it. Very few indeed of the prominent men of the time possessed any discernible virtues. It is not worth while to relate the intrigues which occupied the corrupt and powerless court of Delhi. Maratha affairs will be noticed presently. Here it will suffice to note that in 1748 Muhammad Shah was succeeded peaceably by his son Ahmad Shah.

Ahmad Shāh Durrānī. A month before the death of Muhammad Shah his army, under the command of the heir apparent, Prince Ahmad, and the wazir Qamr-ud din, had repulsed at Sirhind on the Sutlaj Ahmad Shāh Durrānī, the Afghan chief who had succeeded Nādir Shāh in the eastern portion of that monarch's dominions. But, notwithstanding his repulse, the Durrānī was strong enough to exact tribute from the Panjab.

After the accession of Ahmad Shah to the throne of Delhi his Durrānī namesake came back and obtained the formal cession of the Panjab from the helpless Indian government, which was distracted by civil war.

Āsaf Jāh, the founder of the Nizam's dynasty, died at a great age in 1748. His grandson Ghāzī-ud-dīn ousting Safdar Jang of Oudh, became wazir at Delhi in 1752. That nobleman blinded and deposed Ahmad Shah in 1754, replacing him by a relative who was styled Alamgir II.

Two years later Ahmad Shāh Durrānī invaded India for the third time, and captured Delhi, which again suffered from the horrors of massacre and pillage (1757). Mathura, too, was once more the scene of dreadful slaughter. In the summer of 1757 the Durrānī returned to his own country.

We must now revert to Maratha affairs.

Bālājī, third peshwa. Bājī Rāo, the second peshwa, who had become the ruler of the Marathas with hardly any pretence of dependence on the nominal raja, engaged in war with the Nizam after his return from his Delhi raid in 1737. He died in 1740, leaving three sons, the eldest of whom, Bālājī Rāo, succeede' him as peshwa, although not without much opposition from other Maratha chiefs. In 1750 Bālājī consolidated his authority, making Poona his capital, and becoming the head of a confederacy of chiefs. Raghujī, the most prominent rival chief, had meantime added to his Nagpur territories the province of Cuttack or Orissa.

Maratha occupation of the Panjab. In 1758, when Raghoba or Raghunāth, the brother of the peshwa, having taken possession of Lahore, had occupied the whole of the Panjab, it seemed as if the Marathas were destined to become the sovereigns of India. That prospect seriously alarmed the Muslim rulers. Shujā-ud-daula, nawab of Oudh, accordingly combined with the Rohilla Afghans, who had settled in Rohilkhand a few years earlier, against the aggressive Hindus. Ahmad Shāh Durrānī, too, was not content that the Panjab, which he had held for a time, should be in Maratha hands. In 1759 he returned to India and reoccupied that province. Alamgīr II, the nominal emperor of Delhi, was murdered at this time, and succeeded by Shah Alam, or Prince Gauhar Ali, then in Bengal. The new emperor was recognized later by Ahmad Shāh Durrānī.

Maratha power at its zenith. The Maratha power was now, as Elphinstone observes, 'at its zenith. Their frontier extended on the north to the Indus and Himalaya, and on the south nearly to the extremity of the peninsula; all the territory within those limits that was not their own paid tribute. The whole of this great power was wielded by one hand . . . and all pretensions of every description were concentrated in the peshwa.'

Elphinstone's statement requires correction in so far that the 'one hand' which directed the Maratha government was that of Sadāshiv (Sadāsiva) Bhāo, the peshwa's first cousin, and was not that of Bālājī himself, who was addicted to sensual indulgence and 'left the entire management of all the affairs of government' to his cousin, a man well trained in the conduct of business and the hero of the overwhelming victory over the Nizam at Udgir (3 February 1760).

Sadāshiv Bhāo, having organized a regular well-paid army, including a large train of artillery, and 10,000 infantry, disciplined more or less completely after the European manner and under the command of a Muslim general named Ibrāhīm Khān Gardī, believed himself qualified to dispute the sovereignty of India with the Durrānī.

Renewed invasion of Upper India. In 1760 the Maratha government decided to renew the invasion of Upper India and to attempt the achievement of Maratha supremacy. The command of the enterprise having been denied to the peshwa's brother, Raghunāth Rāo, the peshwa's son, Viswās Rāo, a lad of seventeen, was appointed titular generalissimo, 'according to the ancient custom of the Mahrattas', with Sadāshiv Bhāo as his adviser. The Bhāo, to use his ordinary designation, was actually in full control of the whole army. All the Maratha contingents under their various chiefs were summoned to the standard, and the promise of the aid of the Jats of Bharatpur under their leader Sūraj Mal was secured.[1] Both sides, that is to say, the Muslims, Ahmad Shāh Durrānī with his allies the Rohillas on one side, and the Marathas on the other, negotiated for the adhesion of Shujā-ud-daula, the young ruler of Oudh.

The Maratha commander obtained possession of Delhi without difficulty and quartered his host there during the rainy season of 1760. The Durrānī encamped at Anūpshahr, on the Ganges, now in the Bulandshahr District. Shujā-ud-daula mounted guard over his own frontier. When the rains had ended and the Dasahra festival had passed Ahmad Shāh Durrānī managed to bring his army across a dangerous ford of the Jumna on 23 and 24 October, and thus placed himself between Delhi and the Marathas. The Maratha commander failed to take advantage of the opportunity thus offered to him.

The armies in contact. A few days later the advanced guards of the two armies came into contact, and at the end of October the Bhāo fixed his headquarters at Panipat, enclosing his whole camp as well as the town with a ditch 60 feet wide and 12 feet deep. His guns were mounted on the rampart.

The Durrānī camped about eight miles from the Maratha lines on a front of about seven and a half miles, defending his encampment by an *abattis* of felled trees. He pitched a small red tent for himself at some distance in front of his lines, and devoted incessant care to the inspection of his troops and defences. The Marathas cut his communications, thereby causing severe distress in the Afghan camp. In mid-December a bold and successful attack on the force of Gobind Pundit, which was operating on the lines of communication, opened up the sources of supply and delivered Ahmad Shāh from all danger of starvation.

The enormous crowd shut up in the Maratha entrenchments then began to feel the pressure of hunger. Several engagements took place, but afforded no relief to the starving host. The Bhāo made desperate efforts to negotiate, going so far as to offer Ahmad Shāh peaceful possession of the Panjab up to Sirhind. The Durrānī was inflexible. He agreed with the Rohilla leader that 'the Marathas are the thorn of Hindostan', and that 'by one effort we get this thorn out of our sides for ever'.

Ahmad Shāh declared that the Hindustani chiefs, all of whom desired to make terms, might negotiate or do what they pleased. He understood, he said, the business of war, and would settle the matter finally in his own way.

The Marathas were thus reduced to the 'last extremity' and forced to fight. As the Bhāo said, 'The cup is now full to the brim and cannot hold another drop.'

Third battle of Panipat. He was constrained to take the offensive. At dawn on 13 January 1761 the Maratha army advanced eastwards

---

[1] The Jats took no part in the battle. They withdrew in disgust at the arrogance and folly of the Bhāo.

and battle was joined.[1] The fighting was fierce, and up to noon the balance of advantage rested with the Hindus. An hour later reinforcements pushed forward by the shah delivered a charge, which produced a terrible effect. Between two and three o'clock the peshwa's son, Viswās Rāo, was wounded and unhorsed. About three o'clock,

all at once, as if by enchantment, the whole Mahratta army at once turned their backs and fled at full speed, leaving the field of battle covered with heaps of dead. The instant they gave way, the victors pursued them with the utmost fury; and as they gave no quarter, the slaughter is scarcely to be conceived, the pursuit continuing for ten or twelve *coss* [more than twenty miles] in every direction in which they fled.

Such was the third battle of Panipat, a conflict far more determined and sanguinary than either of the battles fought on the same ground in the sixteenth century.[2]

Numbers engaged and killed. The forces engaged were large on both sides, but the Marathas possessed a superiority. Kāsī Raja Pundit, who was present at the battle and made exact inquiries based on the shah's muster rolls, states that Ahmad Shāh's army consisted of 41,800 cavalry, 38,000 infantry—say, in all, 80,000 in round numbers, supplemented by something like four times as many irregulars. That estimate evidently includes mere camp followers. He says that the Marathas had 55,000 cavalry, besides 15,000 Pindāris, but reckons their infantry at only 15,000. They certainly were immensely superior in artillery. Elphinstone supposes that the total number of men within their lines may have been about 300,000. It is not known how many camp followers they had. The number of Hindus slaughtered was thought to approach 200,000. Thousands of prisoners were destroyed, 'so that in the Durrany camp (with an exception of the shah and his principal officers) every tent had heads piled up before the door of it'.

Nearly all the Hindu leaders of note were slain. The body of Viswās Rao was found and identified, but some slight doubt remained as to the correctness of the identification of the head and trunk said to be those of the Bhāo. Sindia and Holkar both escaped, as did the Brahman, famous in after years as Nānā Fadnavīs. The losses were reported to the peshwa in enigmatical language easily interpreted: 'Two pearls have been dissolved, twenty-seven gold mohurs have been lost, and of the silver and copper the total cannot be cast up.' The casualties on the side of the victors are not recorded.

Causes of the Maratha defeat. Ahmad Shāh had won by patient, skilled generalship. The Bhāo had lost by reason of blind pride and obstinacy. He trusted in his guns and disciplined infantry, scornfully rejecting the wise words of the chiefs who counselled him to fight in

[1] The 'black mango-tree' which marked the battlefield is now replaced by a simple masonry memorial with railing (*Prog. Rep. A.S., N. Circle,* 1910–11, *Muhammadan and British Monuments,* pl. xv).

[2] Battles of Panipat: (1) Babur and Ibrāhīm Lodī, 1526; (2) Akbar and Hēmū, 1556; (3) Ahmad Shāh and Marathas, 1761.

the old and well-tried Maratha fashion, and to free himself from the encumbrance of the women and followers. His fate was determined from the moment when he shut himself up in his lines with a multitude whom he could not feed.

The shah's ambition baulked. The shah had planned his ably conducted campaign with the purpose of seizing the empire of Hindustan. His ambition was baulked, as that of Alexander had been long before, by the mutiny of his soldiers. The Durrānīs mutinied in a body and passed completely out of his control, demanding payment of their arrears for two years past and immediate return to Kabul. Ahmad Shāh was powerless against such opposition and had to go home. Shujā-ud-daula, the nawāb of Oudh, who had taken no active part in the battle, although nominally on the side of the shah, also slipped away to his own dominions.

Effects of the battle on India. The effects of the battle on the political state of India are well summarized by Elphinstone, who observes that 'the history of the Mughul empire here closes of itself', and states that

never was a defeat more complete, and never was there a calamity that diffused so much consternation. Grief and despondency spread over the whole Maratta people; most had to mourn relations, and all felt the destruction of the army as a death-blow to their national greatness. The pēshwā never recovered from the shock. He slowly retreated from his frontier towards Pūna, and died in a temple which he had himself erected near that city. The wreck of the army retired beyond the Nerbadda, evacuating almost all their acquisitions in Hindostan. Dissensions soon broke out after the death of Bālājī, and the government of the pēshwā never recovered its vigour. Most of the Maratta conquests were recovered at a subsequent period; but it was by independent chiefs, with the aid of European officers and disciplined sepoys. The confederacy of the Maratta princes dissolved on the cessation of their common danger.

Causes of decline of Mughul empire. The Mughul empire, like many despotisms, had shallow roots. Its existence depended mainly on the personal character of the reigning autocrat and on the degree of his military power. It lacked popular support, the strength based upon patriotic feeling, and the stability founded upon ancient tradition; nor were there any permanent institutions to steady the top-heavy structure. Akbar, the real founder of the empire, was a man truly great, notwithstanding his frailties, and during his long personal reign of forty-five years (1560–1605) was able to build up an organization strong enough to survive twenty-two years of Jahangir's feebler rule. Shahjahan, a stern, ruthless man, kept a firm hand on the reins for thirty years, and was followed by Aurangzeb, who maintained the system more or less in working order for almost fifty years longer. Thus, for a century and a half, from 1560 to 1707, the empire was preserved by a succession of four sovereigns, the length of whose reigns averaged thirty-four years, a very unusual combination. Even Jahangir, the weakest of the four, was no fool. The three others were men of unusual ability.

Akbar's exceptional gifts made him a most successful general, and enabled him to construct a military machine much superior to anything of the kind possessed by other Indian states. That machine failed in the time of Shahjahan when used against the Persians, but was still good enough to keep India fairly quiet during the first half of Aurangzeb's reign. The mechanism thenceforward steadily deteriorated. Moreover the strain of continued widespread war broke down the revenue administration of the empire. The last of the Great Mughuls attained an age far beyond the limit of efficiency; his sons, benumbed by the crushing weight of parental control, lost all capacity for government; excessive luxury enervated the nobles, and gradually brought the army to the condition of a helpless mob. Then the hardy, frugal Marathas pricked the bubble, and proved by experiment the worthlessness of the glittering imperial host. The long absence of Aurangzeb in the Deccan undermined the foundations of government, which degenerated in every department. Lack of control engendered oppression; and oppression begat poverty, entailing financial ruin, which was intensified by reckless spending and the lack of honest administration. The powerful Hindu support of the throne, won so cleverly by Akbar, was weakened by the erroneous policy of Shahjahan and, in still greater degree, by the austere fanaticism of Aurangzeb. The prolonged anarchy involved in the repeated wars of succession was a potent influence in bringing about the ruin of the imperial fabric. Long before Aurangzeb's death the military power of the state had become contemptible, and the authority of the emperor could be defied with impunity. When the breath left his body no man remained in India who was fit to take the helm of the ship of state, which soon drifted on the rocks. The collapse of the empire came with a suddenness which at first sight may seem surprising. But the student who has acquired even a moderately sound knowledge of the history will be surprised that the empire lasted so long rather than because it collapsed suddenly.

It would be easy to expand such observations, and to indicate other causes, as, for example, the neglect of sea-power, which contributed to the ruin of the Mughul empire; but it is needless to work out the theme in further detail. Every attentive reader of the story can fill in the outline in his own fashion.

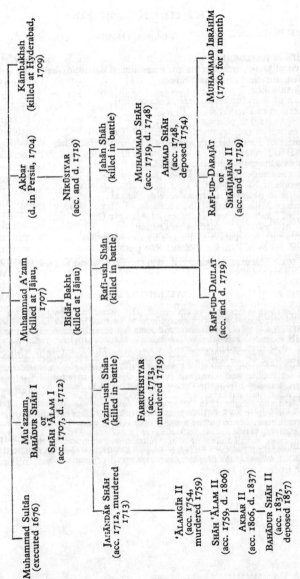

The Later Mughuls (principal names only)

AURANGZĒB 'ĀLAMGĪR

Muhammad Sultān (executed 1676)

Mu'azzam, BAHĀDUR SHĀH I or SHĀH 'ĀLAM I (acc. 1707, d. 1712)

Muhammad A'zam (killed at Jājau, 1707)

Bidār Bakht (killed at Jājau)

Akbar (d. in Persia, 1704)

Nikūsiyar (acc. and d. 1719)

Kāmbakhsh (killed at Hyderabad, 1709)

Jāhāndār Shāh (acc. 1712, murdered 1713)

Azīm-ush Shān (killed in battle)

FARRUKHSIYAR (acc. 1713, murdered 1719)

Rafī-ush Shān (killed in battle)

RAFĪ-UD-DAULAT (acc. and d. 1719)

RAFĪ-UD-DARAJĀT or SHĀHJAHĀN II (acc. and d. 1719)

Jahān Shāh (killed in battle)

MUHAMMAD SHĀH (acc. 1719, d. 1748)

AHMAD SHĀH (acc. 1748, deposed 1754)

MUHAMMAD IBRĀHĪM (1720, for a month)

'ĀLAMGĪR II (acc. 1754, murdered 1759)

SHĀH 'ĀLAM II (acc. 1759, d. 1806)

AKBAR II (acc. 1806, d. 1837)

BAHĀDUR SHĀH II (acc. 1837, deposed 1857)

LEADING DATES

Death of Aurangzeb	21 Feb. (O.S.) 1707
Battle of Jājau; defeat of Azam; accession of Bahadur Shah .	June 1707
Defeat and death of Kambakhsh	Jan. 1709
Sikh rebellion	. 1710
Death of Bahadur Shah; war of succession	. 1712
Accession of Farrukhsiyar	. 1713
Bālājī Visvanāth peshwa	. 1714
Execution of Banda; mission from E. I. Co..	. 1715
Murder of Farrukhsiyar; accession of Muhammad Shah	. 1719
Bājī Rāo I peshwa	. 1720
Independence of the Deccan and Oudh	. 1724
Marathas appeared under Delhi	. 1737
Invasion of Nādir Shāh	. 1739
Bālājī Rāo peshwa; independence of Bengal . . .	. 1740
Death of Muhammad Shah; accession of Ahmad Shah of Delhi	. 1748
Ahmad Shah deposed; accession of Alamgir II . . .	. 1754
Sack of Delhi by Ahmad Shāh Durrānī	. 1756
Temporary occupation of Panjab by the Marathas . .	. 1758
Third battle of Panipat; Mādho Rāo peshwa . . .	. 1761

NOTE. The events connected with the French and English settlements are treated separately.

AUTHORITIES

ELPHINSTONE enters into much detail. His narrative is based on the *Siyar-ul Mutākhirīn*; KHĀFĪ KHĀN's history, now to be read in E. & D., vol. vii; GRANT DUFF's *History of the Mahrattas*; and some few other books. A mass of minute and usually accurate information will be found in IRVINE's articles in *J.A.S.B.*, part 1, for 1894, 1896, 1898, and in his *Later Mughals* (1707-39), a two-volume work edited and continued by Sir Jadunāth Sarkār, Calcutta, 1921-2. He supplies references to all original authorities, printed and manuscript. The leading original authority for the battle of Panipat and connected events is the lucid narrative of Kāsi (Casi) Rājā Pandit, translated from the Persian and published in *Indian Historical Quarterly*, 1934. A full study has been made in T. S. SHEJWALKAR, *Panipat, 1761*. The history of the Sikhs may be studied in CUNNINGHAM, *History of the Sikhs* (1849 and 1853), or compendiously in Sir LEPEL GRIFFIN, *Ranjit Singh* (Rulers of India, 1898), an excellent little book. Several other works on the subject exist. The extensive treatise by MACAULIFFE, entitled *The Sikh Religion* (6 volumes, Oxford, 1909), is the only authoritative detailed account of the religion and scriptures of the sect. The four volumes of Sir J. SARKAR's *Fall of the Mughal Empire*, completed in 1950, and T. G. P. SPEAR's *Twilight of the Mughals*, 1951, are excellent later works.

PART III

THE RISE OF THE BRITISH
DOMINION, 1740-1818

by

PERCIVAL SPEAR

INTRODUCTION

THE British period of Indian history is usually reckoned to begin in 1757 with the battle of Plassey. It is sometimes predated to 1740, the opening year of the War of the Austrian Succession, which precipitated the Anglo-French struggle for supremacy in India, and sometimes postponed to 1761, the year of Panipat or even to 1774, the year of Warren Hastings's assumption of the new governor-generalship established by the Regulating Act. Any date must be 'somewhat arbitrary in marking a political transition which in fact took nearly eighty years to accomplish. The date of Plassey no more obviously marked a political revolution to contemporaries than the fall of Constantinople in 1453 marked a cultural and intellectual one to fifteenth-century Europe. But both are convenient as marking a point in time after which an awareness of large changes developed from the status of a minor speculation to that of a major concern. An Indian political observer before 1740 was mainly occupied with Mughul imperial politics and their complementary Maratha affairs. Between 1740 and 1757 he was concerned with Mughul-Afghan-Maratha affairs in the north and the Anglo-French struggle in the south, while after Plassey and still more after 1761, the year both of Panipat and the final defeat of the French in the south, he concentrated his attention on the rising British power with sidelong glances at the Marathas and Haidar Ali. It was then that the idea of political revolution, as distinct from mere political change, became uppermost in men's minds.

During this period of Indian history it is specially necessary to avoid the mistake of interpreting the past in terms of the future. What has occurred in time cannot be undone, but it does not necessarily follow that nothing else could have happened, or that the actual course of events was the only possible or even probable outcome of the interplay of historical forces and personalities. It was not clear to most Indian observers before the years 1756–61, as it is obvious to us, that the Mughul empire was already moribund. Indeed, its partial revival under Mirza Najaf Khan postponed the full realization until about 1785. Nor was it clear then to the same observer that the Maratha confederacy must crumble and that British supremacy was inevitable. To contemporary minds, unaware of the relative strength of the various factors involved, all was uncertainty and anything might emerge.

It is therefore worth considering the causes which secured so decided a success for the British in this apparently doubtful field, a success maintained with so few interruptions that the rise of the British star to its zenith seems, at a distance indeed, to resemble the serene motion of a celestial body.

The cause to which this success is most commonly attributed is superiority of arms and military science. The British in the first place (after the defeat of the French) enjoyed unquestioned supremacy at sea. They could come and go as they would, repair their losses, and strike at the interior from several points at will. The moment of greatest peril was when reinforcements were cut off for a time during the American War of Independence. Sea-power was decisive in the sense that British supremacy could not have been obtained without it. But it would not have sufficed in itself if the British had not possessed the resources with which to exploit this advantage. Sea-power was a necessary preliminary to success, but not in itself the cause of that success.

The British undoubtedly possessed superiority in arms and military tactics. Their cannon and their small arms were superior in quality to those generally in Indian use, and all their officers were trained in military tactics and strategy. Compared to them the Indian troops, both rank and file and leaders, were amateurs, greatly gifted though some of them might be. Amateurs can be great generals, as the case of Cromwell proved, but even he could do little until he had trained the New Model as his instrument. Thus the genius of men like Haidar Ali was often frustrated by the lack of trained subordinates and of material with which to carry out their plans. Indian leaders early began to pay European military science the compliment of imitation. These efforts failed ultimately it is true but not before the Sikhs had produced a military machine which was in some respects superior to that of British India. The failure of European military science in Indian hands was due to other than military causes. European military science was an important contributory cause of the British success, but not in itself a decisive one.

The factor of leadership has often been stressed. It is true that the British (like the French) produced men of rare distinction, from the conquistador type in the person of Clive to the military genius of Wellington, from the subtle statesmanship of a Warren Hastings to the ardent empire-building of a Wellesley. If they had not existed the enterprise could not have succeeded, but their existence alone was not enough. The Indian states also had leaders of brilliance. Madhu Rao Sindia, Haidar Ali Khan, Mirza Najaf Khan, Nana Fadnavis, several of the Peshwas, and Ranjit Singh would take high rank in any assembly of soldiers and statesmen. The British had a greater advantage in the ranks of secondary leaders, for their scientific training produced a general level of competence not equalled on the Indian side. But even this advantage was not decisive in itself, and it tended to be reduced as special training, often with European aid, was developed by the Indian princes.

An advantage which has been more justly stressed was that of military discipline. From the time of Alexander the cult of discipline has given to men an often decisive advantage over superior numbers of brave but unregulated troops. The habit of obedience, the willingness to face danger and suffer hardship to order, the power of restraint, and the inner cohesion which discipline breeds, provide a morale far superior to anything which personal or clan loyalty, the spirit of adventure or personal bravery can produce of themselves. The Portuguese had been able to secure and maintain their hold upon India with their scanty forces by its aid, and they were only driven out by troops whose discipline was more effective. It was this quality which gave both French and English their early sensational successes. Discipline not only meant that groups of men would act with cohesion and steadiness at the command of one; it also meant that the leadership was reliable as well as skilful, and integrated with the overall direction of affairs. Reliability is promoted by any system wherein each man depends for his promotion upon his professional conduct and is assured of his maintenance so long as he is loyal. The habitual loyalty, even in the face of reverses, of European officers, was a frequent cause of comment in Indian society from the time of the Portuguese onwards. The system of personal attachments which prevailed in India from the emperor downwards, and was only partially modified by the *mansabdari* system even in its hey-day, made loyalty a purely personal thing and as such dependent upon the fates of individuals and the turns of fortune's wheel. The impulse to independent action was often great and the risks of unquestioned obedience considerable.

But even more valuable to the British was the civil discipline of the Company's servants. An undisciplined state possessing disciplined troops may have far more anarchic possibilities than one resting solely upon a complex system of personal loyalties, as the fate of the Sikh kingdom showed. A group of chiefs broke up within ten years a powerful kingdom through lack of inner cohesion and the existence of a fine military machine only made the collapse more violent and complete. The Mughuls organized a joint military-civil imperial service in the *mansab* system, which prevented this particular danger, but they did not change the traditional personal basis of government. The Company, on the other hand, possessed a hierarchy of civil officials which in its way was as effective and disciplined as its military forces. They possessed not only a group of men dependent on the Company for their prospects and accustomed to obey orders, but men observing certain standards of conduct, possessing a pride of service and an *esprit de corps*. These standards proved very elastic, it is true, for a few years in the mid-eighteenth century. But the very consequences of this laxity served to prove the value of the Company's civil discipline as a whole. The Company could not have survived if the conditions of the early sixties had not been corrected; it was the restoration and reinforcement of this discipline which made possible the British supremacy of the nineteenth century. It should not be thought that civil discipline can be achieved merely by grading ranks and paying regular cash salaries. Until the time of Cornwallis the cash salaries of the Company's servants were negligible. There must not only be a recognized superior capable of enforcing its orders, but a body of standards and principles whose authority is recognized by all in some degree. Civil discipline must have a moral content as well as an effective legal sanction. In this the Company's servants were strong, for they carried with them English law as well as English commercialism, and English patriotism as well as individualism.

But without resources in money as well as men the British could not have succeeded even with the help of civil and military discipline, and of naval and military superiority. They might have gone no farther than the Portuguese in the sixteenth century or the Dutch of our own day. There is a limit to the achievements of the disciplined administrator as of the disciplined soldier. But what the British lacked in men they made up in financial resources, which enabled them to replace losses with equanimity and to attract and maintain Indian auxiliaries with regularity. For those, and they were many, whose rule was to be true to their salt, there was an adequate supply to be true to. The chronic embarrassment of the eighteenth-century Indian statesman was lack of means. Governments oppressed their peasantry not of choice but from necessity. The Marathas were 'rapacious' because their natural resources were meagre. Armies marched and countermarched as often to collect revenue as to defeat the foe; before a general could plan a battle he had first to forestall a mutiny. In consequence the British possessed a cohesion and resilience which first astonished and then depressed their Indian contemporaries. The legend of British invincibility was built up on an ability to replace losses and to pay troops regularly. The British could do this because during the eighteenth and nineteenth centuries they enjoyed an expanding economy based on developing trade which provided surplus resources. This development was accelerated by the onset of the Industrial Revolution, but it was well in train before. Akbar's revenue in 1605 was stated from official accounts to be about £17,500,000;[1] the Company's gross revenue in 1792 was £8,225,000 from a smaller area exhausted by war.[2] Added to the contrast of military and civil techniques was the disparity of economic systems. India, with her agricultural subsistence economy could not compete with the commercialism of the West. Britain, for all her paucity of numbers, was in fact stronger in resources than any one Indian power and equal to all of them put together. When it is remembered that the Indian powers never were united, the success of the British ceases to seem either extraordinary or unaccountable.

A final factor in the British success was the nature of their objectives. There was no head-on collision between British imperialism and Indian society, and in consequence there was no resistance à outrance or to the death. Indian society, whether in its Hindu or Muslim forms, was centred round religio-social systems which showed little trace of

---

[1] De Laet's computation. See V. Smith, *Akbar the Great Mogul*, 2nd ed., p. 379. The rupee was probably worth rather more than two shillings.
[2] From returns of gross revenue, printed by order of the House of Commons, 22 June 1855. R. Dutt, *Economic History of India*, 5th ed., i. 399.

political nationalism in its modern sense. The affections of the people were fastened upon social and religious ideals rather than upon political freedom. Freedom for the Hindu was a matter of inner release, for the Muslim of freedom to worship the true God in the right way. No doubt both Hindu and Muslim preferred their own rulers to others but what both would die for was their religious ideals and social patterns. The Mughul empire was accepted by Hindus as long as it was both tolerant and strong. The Portuguese made no headway in India because they attacked both parties where they felt most deeply, in the religious sphere. The British came for trade and went into politics to preserve their trade. They eschewed religion. So to the Hindu they were preferable to the Muslim and to the Muslim more acceptable than the Hindu. And this was the case in spite of general dislike of most British customs and many British individuals. The British attack was a glancing blow which left the vital centres of Indian life untouched. Religious toleration and social non-interference were more powerful weapons than the rupees of the Company or the guns of its troops.

The British period is now a completed whole and can be viewed with more detachment and balance than was possible before 1947. We see it now, not, as did nineteenth-century historians, as the consummation to which all Indian history had been moving, but as one episode among many in the long story of India. But this does not deprive it of significance. In one sense it is true, it represents one more example of an alien domination which blossomed, bloomed, and faded as others had done before it. But the incompleteness of such a view can be seen the moment the India of 1947 is compared with that of 1757. The India which saw the British depart differed far more from the India which saw the conquest of Bengal than the India of Plassey differed from the India of Babur or Alberuni. At first the rise of the British dominion bore a recognizable resemblance to the rise of the Mughul empire. A sensational start was followed by setbacks and a period of uncertainty and confused politics, and this in turn was succeeded by a rapid consolidation of power in the hands of masterful leaders. The reunited India of 1818 could be compared in many ways with the northern India of Akbar's later years. The old life was restored under a new imperial umbrella. The new rulers, it is true, were more alien than the former ones; their habits were more strange, their manners more aloof, their arrogance more marked. But then something happened. The new rulers reorganized the country more efficiently than before; they were self-consciously tolerant; they studied to preserve rather than destroy. But almost in spite of themselves new thoughts, new ideas, and new ways of life came into the country, with results which have proved incalculable in their range and depth. It is here that we can find the significance of the British connexion with India. The British were the harbingers of the West. At times unconsciously, at times with optimistic zeal, and at times with reluctance or dislike, they were the vehicles of western influence in India. That is why their influence in India has proved creative, and why their period will be looked back on as formative for the India that is yet to be. The British provided the bridge for India to pass from the medieval world of the Mughuls to the new age of science and humanism.

While Britain's supreme function has been that of a cultural germ carrier, this has by no means been her only significant work. Britain's first achievement was the restoration of the unity of India and the re-establishment of order. Though in themselves operations which may be called mechanical, they were necessary preliminaries for all that was to follow. The introduction of the English language provided a vehicle for western ideas, and English law a standard of British practice. Along with English literature came western moral and religious ideas, and the admission of missionaries provided, as it were, a working model of western moral precepts. In the economic sphere again, the British played the part of 'carriers'. They were the agents for the entry of the new machine age into India, and their provision of a railway system provided the nervous system of the country's new economic life. If they were responsible for the decay of the old handicrafts, they made possible the development of mechanized industry and brought India within the orbit of the new world economy. In the British period it became clear that India would not go wholly western; the years since independence have made it clear that she will not remain wholly eastern. Whatever the final form assumed by Indian culture, it will be original and significant and the process which led to it will have been deeply influenced by the British.

In 1740 all such developments were far in the future. India was not yet aware that an age was coming to an end. In the north the Mughul empire, though shaken by Nadir Shah's incursion of the previous year, was still a going concern. Nadir Shah's advance to Delhi had been a large-scale raid rather than a regular invasion, and as such it had been less destructive and less dislocating in its effects. In fact the Mughul government appeared to have recovered a measure of stability in the north after the dissensions and confusions of the second decade of the century. In thirteen years there had been four outbreaks of full-scale civil war; this was not to recur for another twelve years. Though Kabul was lost, the Panjab, Sindh, and Kashmir were firmly held and so were Gujarat and the Ganges valley to the Bay of Bengal. Bengal itself, though semi-independent, still acknowledged the emperor and sent him tribute. The Rajput states were quiescent. The Mughul government still presented an imposing front to the world, and only close observers suspected how far the inevitable dry rot of decay had advanced. Short-sighted opportunism had taken the place of statesmanship; compromise of leadership; loyalty to the emperor was giving ground to personal ambitions and no new principle had appeared to take its place. The troubles of the north-west were drying up the stream of recruits whose fortunes depended upon imperial favour and whose vigour helped to sustain its burdens.

Farther south the picture was less favourable. The Deccan provinces of the empire had become separated from the main body under Āsaf Jāh, the first Nizam and last of Aurangzeb's officers. The Maratha tide was flowing through the gap across central India threatening Gujarat and the Rajputs to the north and west, Bengal and Orissa to the east. Hyderabad itself was threatened on two sides. Maratha methods of swift raids, indiscriminate plunder, and quick withdrawals proved crippling to the countryside, and their levy of *chauth* or one-fourth of the revenue, as the price of immunity, ruinous to the finances. The whole Deccan was in the grip of a slow economic strangulation, which had begun with Aurangzeb's campaigns with their destruction of the natural political breakwaters of the Deccan kingdoms.

On the west the Maratha power was centred in Poona, the seat of the Peshwa. Though the limits of Maratha authority were but vaguely defined, and the mechanism of government but loosely integrated, the Peshwa's writ ran throughout the Maratha dominions. There was still a Maratha empire rather than a Maratha confederacy. The Maratha power was visibly growing and constituted, on the Indian side, the one dynamic factor in an otherwise apparently static situation. But the Marathas, though plainly confident and aggressive, were not yet clearly imperially minded. They were a threat to the Mughul supremacy rather than a rival for the Mughul dominion.

South of the Kistna the coastal province of the Carnatic extended to the Maratha principality of Tanjore. This was a dependency of the Nizam who maintained his authority until his death in 1748. The coast of Malabar was still largely cut off from the rest of India by the tangle of tropical jungle and hill which constitutes the Western Ghats; here the Zamorin of Calicut still ruled, while the extreme south was shared between the Rajas of Cochin and Travancore. Malabar was no longer the exchange centre for the spice trade between East and West, for the spice ships from the East Indies by-passed it on their way to the Cape and Europe, while the newer trade in cloths, dyes, and saltpetre was centred elsewhere. Only a restricted and local trade in spices survived, controlled by a number of subordinate European factories. Between Malabar and the Carnatic lay the Hindu state of Mysore, which had achieved a modest modicum of power on the ruins of the Vijayanagar empire and through the vicissitudes of Mughul-Maratha wars. But it lacked native vigour and would only achieve a brief glory under alien leaders.

To complete the picture we must add the European factories and settlements. Portuguese Goa was a museum of sixteenth-century imperialism, more plentifully supplied with churches than trade and with monks than soldiers. Bombay was a British possession but as yet the heir-apparent rather than actual successor to the wealth of Surat. The British settlements of Madras and Calcutta were prosperous and populous but centres of trade rather than of political power. French Pondicherry fulfilled the same function to a lesser degree. Other European stations, such as French Chandernagar, Dutch Chinsura and Negapatam, and Danish Tranquebar, were trading-posts without political significance.

Foreign trade was active and profitable, but it must be remembered that it formed but a fraction of India's whole economic life. The products of the interior could only reach the seaports in bulk where good communications existed, and these at that time consisted of river lines. In general the economic life of India was stagnant or in decline. There was little productive expenditure because the surplus revenue in the country was absorbed by the cost of military operations. Production was actually decreasing because of the wide extent of these same operations, of the insecurity they created, and the devastation they wrought. The general standard of life was falling for the same reason. There was increasing concentration on the effort to keep things as they were rather than on improvement or development. In the later years of Aurangzeb men looked back with regret upon the spacious days of Shahjahan; by 1740 it was Aurangzeb's time to which men looked back and the survivors of his reign, like the Nizam-ul-Mulk who were regarded as the surviving giants of a greater age.

The general cultural life of the country shared in the general malaise. The promotion of culture depended largely upon patronage, and great men were too occupied with power politics and the problem of survival to have much time or means to encourage the arts. There was little growth and a general slow decay. Mughul building showed a continuance of the same ideas with decreasing means and a gradually deteriorating taste. Compare, for example, Safdar Jang's tomb in Delhi (1756) with the Jama Masjid 100 years earlier. Master masons and craftsmen were still to be found but they lacked adequate support or intelligent direction. The same was true of painting. Exquisite work could still be done, but patronage was erratic and the flashes of brilliance transitory. Hindu art suffered equally with the Muslim from the inhibitions of expense and neglect. Only in the extreme south did the tradition of great building linger and in the deserts and hills of the north that of tasteful painting continue. In intellectual and religious life the same conditions prevailed. Islam had its learned men but no new school of thought. No new philosophic system and no new religious cult like the *bhakti* movements of the fifteenth to the seventeenth centuries appeared within Hinduism. Syncretistic movements like that of Guru Nānak, the founder of Sikhism, or the *Kabirpanthis*, the followers of Kabir, had either developed into military bodies whose sword was their creed or become bodies of quietists in the process of being transmuted into new castes. Indeed, the one sign of positive development in this field was the tendency of ascetics to develop into military bands. Groups of armed ascetics, valiant for their Lord, roamed and often terrorized the countryside, specially in the north.

Social life shared in the general restriction of society. Those features of Hindu life which tended to decline or be discouraged in settled periods were increasingly in evidence. Suttee, frowned upon by the Mughuls, revived as their power declined. Infanticide was encouraged by economic stringency as security diminished. Such customs as *purdah* or female 'seclusion' tended to increase among Hindus as well as Muslims for the same reason. Education, beyond the rudiments of letters, and the cultivation of the arts, became more and more confined to the great and then mainly to their youth. India, in nearly all the departments of life, was increasingly living upon its past. There was a lack of purpose and vigour in the cultural field, of hope and enterprise in the economic sphere, while in public affairs there was a bewildering array of cross purposes. There was energy, ability, and intellect in abundance, but they were directed to mutually contradictory ends or wasted in sterile endeavours. In Chinese phrase the signs were many that for the Mughuls in India the Mandate of Heaven was exhausted.

AUTHORITIES

JAMES MILL's *History of British India* (1817), completed by H. H. Wilson to 1835 (1840), remains outstanding among the old general histories, for all its one-sidedness and occasional wrongheadedness, though it has not lived up to Macaulay's comparison with Gibbon. Smaller works of this class are the histories by E. THORNTON, J. C. MARSHMAN, and W. BEVERIDGE. The outstanding general modern work is the *Cambridge History of India*, vols. v and vi (1929 and 1932), edited by H. H. Dodwell, which, though uneven in quality and unbalanced in planning, is in general authoritative and contains exhaustive bibliographies. Its best chapters deal with the eighteenth century and with administration. Amongst the smaller general histories may be mentioned P. E. ROBERTS, *History of British India* (3rd ed., 1952), a balanced and scholarly survey, E. THOMPSON and G. T. GARRETT, *Rise and Fulfilment of British Rule in India*, 1934, a sensitive and nervous study, giving more attention to economic and cultural aspects and the rise of Indian nationalism, and Sir A. LYALL, *Rise of the British Dominion in India* (3rd ed., 1896), a fair-minded imperialist interpretation. The cultural aspect is dealt with in the co-operative work *Modern India and the West* (1941), edited by L. S. S. O'MALLEY. The same author has written a history of the Indian civil service, whose work has also been described by P. WOODRUFF in *The Men who ruled India* (2 vols., 1953–4). There is as yet no modern economic history of India. R. C. DUTT's two volumes are now fifty years old and V. ANSTEY, *Economic Development of India* (3rd imp., 1949), is a study rather than a history. An Indian survey of the period is to be found in Part III of an *Advanced History of India* by R. C. MAJUMDAR, H. C. RAYCHAUDHURI, and K. K. DATTA (1946). An original and challenging Indian interpretation of the British period is to be found in K. M. PANIKKAR, *Asia and Western Dominance* (1953). Finally may be mentioned the Rulers of India series (29 vols.) which, though old, still contains much material of value, and W. W. HUNTER, *Gazetteer of India*, including the first four general volumes, which remains an invaluable work of reference. For detailed references to parliamentary papers, &c., and manuscript sources the reader should consult the *Cambridge History of India* and for treaties, &c., see Sir C. V. AITCHESON, *Treaties, Sanads*, &c. (14 vols., ed. 1931). An Indian counterpart to the *Cambridge History of India* may now be consulted in vols. ix and x of *The History and Culture of the Indian People*, edited by Dr. R. C. Majumdar. They are entitled respectively *Indian Paramountcy and Indian Renaissance, 1818–1905. Parts I and II* (1963 and 1965).

BOOK VII

The Rise of the British Dominion, 1740–1818

CHAPTER 1

English and French

THE force which precipitated the new age in India was quite unconnected with that country itself. In 1740 the Emperor Charles VI died, and according to the Pragmatic Sanction agreed upon by most of the European powers, his daughter Maria Theresa succeeded to his hereditary dominions in Austria and elsewhere. But Frederick, the newly acceded King of Prussia, thought the moment opportune to seize the coveted province of Silesia and marched in October 1740. The surprised Hapsburgs proved more resilient than expected and the result was the War of the Austrian Succession, not to be concluded by the treaty of Aix-la-Chapelle until 1748. The act which inaugurated *realpolitik* in Europe introduced a new age in India. France supported Prussia, and Britain, already involved in a colonial war with Spain in the War of Jenkins' ear, was at war with France in 1742. Colonial rivalry with the twin Bourbon powers reinforced considerations of the Balance of Power in Europe to make such a decision inevitable. Since Britain and France had important positions and interests in India, this conflict naturally spread thither. In former wars, it is true, the two Companies had agreed upon neutrality, but then the French were too weak to excite much jealousy, nor were they in a position to send great armaments to the East. But now their Indian trade formed an important part of French colonial interests and these were, in the eighteenth century, the main cause of rivalry between the two countries. So while the French, being the weaker party, offered to continue the neutral tradition, the British declined.

The position of the English Company had outwardly changed but little since the union of the old and new Companies in 1709. It was organized into the three independent Presidencies of Bombay, Fort St. George in Madras, and Fort William in Bengal. Surat was subordinate to Bombay (from 1709) and Fort St. David to Madras. Bombay had been a British possession since 1662 and possessed a dockyard (controlled by a succession of Parsis). Both Madras and Calcutta were settlements which had grown up round the nucleus of a fortified factory, and the status of both was regulated by the result of Surman's embassy to Delhi from 1714 to 1717. Attached to each settlement were a number of satellite factories, like those of Patna, Dacca, and Kasimbazar in Bengal, Vizagapatam and Cuddalore to Madras, and the Gujarat and Malabar factories to Bombay. All these presidencies were the sites of substantial Indian cities. The population of Bombay was rising steadily and had reached 70,000 by 1744; that of Calcutta was about 100,000, while Madras, for long the leading settlement, had contained about 300,000 inhabitants since the beginning of the century. The Company had enjoyed a steady prosperity since 1709 based on an increasing turnover but limited by its subordinate position in a still powerful empire. Its position was further strengthened by the extension of its trade to China. From the time of the union of the companies its dividends had never dropped below 7 or exceeded 10 per cent. Its trade was chiefly in indigo (from Gujarat and Bengal), saltpetre (from Bengal and Bihar), spices from Malabar, and cotton goods of all kinds. The Company's servants supported themselves by private trade within India and overseas trade eastwards, and this again being limited by local conditions was steady rather than sensational. The time for dazzling profits was not yet.

Compared to this story of solid prosperity the history of the French Company had been modest and chequered. The French first turned their eyes eastwards in the time of Henry IV, when France, like England and the Netherlands, was hostile to a Spain which had absorbed Portugal and her eastern possessions. But their first efforts were exploratory and the trading sequels abortive. It was not until the genius of Colbert looked eastwards that the *Compagnie des Indes Orientales* was formed in 1664. In 1674 the settlement of Pondicherry on the Coromandel coast was secured, but the Company's fortunes languished during Louis XIV's European wars. A succession of prudent heads and a reorganization in 1723 wrought a transformation; by 1740 the Company could challenge comparison though not parity with the English. Pondicherry had been fortified and subordinate stations opened at Chandernagar in Bengal, Masulipatam on the Coromandel coast, and in Malabar. French India was backed by the French possessions of Mauritius (the Isle de France) and Réunion (the Isle de Bourbon) in the southern Indian Ocean; Colbert's political curiosity (which helped to inspire the reports of Bernier) had long been forgotten, and the French Company was as peaceful in intent and as commercial in outlook as the English.

Compared to the English East India Company the French enterprise was a mushroom growth. Though its strength was substantial it was by no means equal to that of its prospective rivals. The English Company had three well-established seats of power in India, one of which possessed a dockyard and excellent harbour; the French had only one on the exposed Coromandel shore. The French had a harbour and sea base at Mauritius (their headquarters) but this was distant and ill supplied with stores. The British were more than compensated by the possession of Bombay, their copious mercantile marine and their naval power. Though both Companies were prosperous the French volume of trade was much less and their resources correspondingly weaker. The value of French exports from India increased between 1728 and 1740 nearly ten times,[1] but in the same year British imports from India were more than twice as great.[2] To the advantage of finance the English Company added those of unified direction by an independent mercantile corporation, itself backed by important interests in the city of London. It possessed long traditions and much experience; it could call on capital and make its influence felt in Parliament. The French Company on the other hand owed its existence largely to state action; its resuscitation in 1723 left it with twelve directors and four inspectors nominated by the Crown and only eight syndics to represent the shareholders. It was essentially a state enterprise whose fortunes depended upon the attention or neglect of ministers. Both companies depended upon the sea link with Europe, and here again the British held the lead. The result of a conflict must depend in the last resort upon sea-power and British naval power was not only greater than the French but backed by growing resources. Only in the matter of leadership were the French unquestionably superior. Lenoir and Dumas had built up the Company and in Dupleix they were to find one of those superior minds whose insight clarifies the issues of politics and whose activity often determines them.

In 1740 the political scene in south India was uncertain and confused. The Nizam Āsaf Jāh, the last representative of the Aurangzeb school of public duty and integrity, was old and fully occupied by the rising Maratha power in the western Deccan; his subordinates were already speculating upon the consequences of his death. South of the mass of the Hyderabad territory with its coastal Coromandel strip lay no powerful Hindu state to maintain a balance of power. Instead there existed in the interior Mysore, the ghost of the old Vijayanagar empire, on the west coast the Malabar states with Cochin and Travancore, and on the east the principalities of Trichinopoly, Madura, and Tanjore. The age and preoccupations of the Nizam encouraged ambition, and the weakness of the Hindu states invited attack. Thus the last flickers of Muslim expansionism united with the first signs of Hyderabad decline to set the stage for the plans of adventurers. There was one other factor in the situation, the Marathas. The Tanjore kingdom had a Maratha raja, a relic of the Maratha invasion of the south (in Aurangzeb's time); the existence of this state, together with the claim to *chauth* or one-fourth of the revenue, dating from the same period, gave the Peshwa of Poona an excuse for interference whenever it suited him.

The Nawab of the Carnatic, Dost Ali, busied himself with expansion in preparation for a bid for independence on the Nizam's death. First

[1] From £89,000 to £880,000.   [2] £1,795,000.

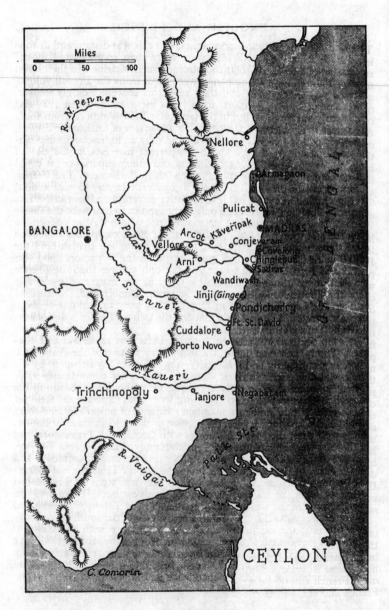

THE CARNATIC

Trichinopoly and then Madura fell to his son Safdar Ali and his son-in-law Chanda Sahib. But attacks on Maratha Tanjore were less successful. In 1740 and 1741 the Marathas moved down from the north; Dost Ali was killed, Trichinopoly taken, and Chanda Sahib captured. Safdar Ali succeeded his father only to be murdered by his cousin Murtaza Ali in late 1742. At this point the Nizam intervened, retook Trichinopoly, and replaced Murtaza by an officer of his own, Anwar-ud-din Khan, early in 1743. This was the situation on the eve of European intervention in south Indian affairs. The new Nawab of the Carnatic was but insecurely seated in his government, and was beset by partisans of the displaced family. In the background hovered the two great powers of the Nizam and the Marathas, powerful enough to intervene but too preoccupied to sustain their agents continuously. 'The whole country was in a state of uncertainty, expecting some great event, though none knew what.'

When news of the outbreak of war arrived late in 1742 Dupleix had just become Governor of Pondicherry. For the moment he was powerless because the French fleet had been recalled; in accordance with the French directors' wishes he proposed neutrality to the three English presidencies, but even though the English merchants would have welcomed it, such an understanding could not bind the king's ships on either side and so the war was joined. The War of the Austrian Succession in India depended entirely upon sea-power. Besides Dupleix the French possessed another leader of genius in La Bourdonnais, the Governor of Mauritius. In the absence of a French naval squadron he improvised a fleet of French Indiamen and country craft, manned them partly with local sailors, and sailed for the Coromandel coast. There he met the British fleet whose commander Barnett had been succeeded by the unenterprising Peyton. An indecisive action in June 1746 led both sides to port to refit, Peyton to Ceylon and La Bourdonnais to Pondicherry. On his return Peyton was so impressed by the appearance of the French that he retired to the Hugli, thus leaving the way open for an attack on Madras. Madras was in no condition, physically or morally, to stand a siege and capitulated within a week on 21 September. The French had achieved a great and unexpected success, but the effect was spoilt by the quarrel which immediately ensued between their leaders. La Bourdonnais was disposed to ransom the town which would have excluded Dupleix and his friends from any share of the profits. The quarrel was unsettled when a storm in early October dispersed La Bourdonnais's squadron, whereupon Dupleix seized and plundered the town.

Dupleix now tried to complete the elimination of the British by the capture of Fort St. David. But his efforts were rendered fruitless by the return of a British fleet under Griffin. In mid-1748 British reinforcements intended for the recovery of Madras arrived with a new fleet under Boscawen. Pondicherry in its turn was besieged, but once more French enterprise was aided by British ineptitude in securing a French success. Before the see-saw could change again came news of the treaty of Aix-la-Chapelle. Madras was restored to the British in exchange for Cape Breton Island in America and outwardly the *status quo* was restored.

But the restoration concealed a profound change in the politics of south India. The British now held Madras by European treaty and soon obtained release of the old quit-rent of 1,200 pagodas a year from one of the rival nawabs. The French had acquired a high reputation for enterprise and military skill, and had been strengthened in a military sense by detachments of La Bourdonnais's fleet which had been left behind when the admiral left. Thirdly, the Nawab of the Carnatic had been unable to intervene effectively. This was not for want of appeals from the Europeans or inclination on his part. Both sides had in fact appealed to him when it suited them, Dupleix against the British navy and the British against the French attack on Madras. The nawab responded with surprising promptitude, but his troops arrived to find Madras in French hands. Skirmishes before its walls and on the Adyar provided the first concrete evidence of that greatly increased superiority of European arms and tactics which was to prove decisive in Indian politics during the next fifty years.

There followed Dupleix's bold bid for south Indian empire. If circumstances favoured the man, here was a man fitted to make the most of circumstances. Like Clive, Dupleix began his career in commercial service. But unlike Clive, he did not find fame in deserting the counting-house for the field. He rose regularly in the French Company's service and reached Pondicherry by promotion from Chandernagar. His genius was diplomatic and political rather than military. A supple mind and an active imagination easily converted a skilful merchant into a subtle politician. But Dupleix was more than a politician. He possessed that insight of statesmanship which can divine a change in the balance of political forces when it is actually taking place rather than years later, when it has become obvious to all. It was this quality which enabled him to penetrate the inherent weakness of the south Indian political system and the consequent decisive importance of the tiny European forces in the country. In the Indian politics of the time all was policy, power politics, and personal ambition; there was no emotional bar, such as patriotism might have provided, against invoking the help of the foreigner. Consequently interference could be freely indulged in, and the technical advantages enjoyed by the European would bring victory to whichever side they were given. In the absence of conviction, of national and religious feeling, politics were a matter for lords and their followers; the longest-ranged guns, the quickest-firing musket, the steadiest soldiers would decide the issue. The makeweight had become the balance, the client could become the master.

Dupleix is thus described by Ananda Ranga Pillai, for many years his *dubash* or secretary. Dupleix's

method of doing things is not known to anyone, because none else is possessed of the quick mind with which he is gifted. In patience he has no equal. He has peculiar skill in carrying out his plans and designs in the management of affairs and in governing; in fitting his advice to times and persons; in maintaining at all times an even countenance; in doing things through proper agents; in addressing them in appropriate terms; and in assuming a bearing at once dignified towards all.

His faults were those of an over-sanguine temperament, which led him to hope too often and too long to snatch advantages from critical situations, and of an intelligence which relied too much on artifice in dealing with opponents. His love of display impressed and endeared him to the south Indians, but his autocratic temper made it difficult for him to work with equals and was a fruitful source of quarrels. Dupleix dazzled but he also divided. He left no school to continue his work, but only a void place which no one could fill. His impact was that of the flood which destroys rather than the rain which fertilizes.

The essence of Dupleix's policy lay in using his diplomatic skill and military advantages to secure a local Indian authority amenable to himself. By this means he would satisfy the French Company by ruining British trade, and by making the Indian authorities dependent on himself he would become the *de facto* ruler of south India. The French Company, like its British counterpart in the time of Wellesley, had no other wish than for a quiet life, but as later, their doubts for a time were silenced by the brilliance of their agent's success. Events played into Dupleix's hands at the moment of the signing of the peace. The aged Nizam died in 1748 and was succeeded by his second son, Nasir Jang. But the succession was disputed by a grandson in the person of Muzaffar Jang. At the same moment Chanda Sahib was released by the Marathas and appeared in the Carnatic with their support. Dupleix supported both claimants and provided the help which secured the defeat and death of Anwar-ud-din Khan at Ambur near Vellore in August 1749. Anwar's son Muhammad Ali retired to Trichinopoly, where in October the British began to send him help. The Madras government had already interfered in Tanjore politics a few months before, but it was their October action which really cast the die for their large-scale interference in Indian affairs.

Muzaffar Jang was now confronted with the full forces of Nasir Jang, who spent most of 1750 in the Carnatic. Muzaffar submitted and Dupleix prepared to make an agreement when Nasir was assassinated. Dexterously turning these events to his advantage Dupleix secured the recognition of Muzaffar as Nizam, sending Bussy with a French force to support him in Hyderabad, and receiving in return large grants and a vague title as ruler of India south of the Kistna.[1] Muzaffar was shortly killed in his turn, but Bussy's force secured the accession of Salabat Jang and maintained him in power. The Nizam was henceforward dependent on the French. Dupleix was now at the height of his fame, and free to complete his designs in the Carnatic.

[1] This was a title rather than an office, which superseded neither the rulers of Madura, Tanjore, or Mysore, nor even Chanda Sahib as governor of the Carnatic.

The only remaining obstacles were the British in Madras and Muhammad Ali in Trichinopoly. The first clash occurred with a British force under Gingens sent to strengthen Muhammad Ali. From this moment Dupleix's fortune began to wane. The French arrived before Trichinopoly in September 1751, but meanwhile Clive had created a diversion by seizing the capital city of Arcot in August with 210 men. The famous siege of fifty days in September and October divided the French efforts and gave Muhammad Ali time to procure allies. Mysore, Tanjore, and the Maratha chief Morari Rao restored the balance of forces of which the generalship of Clive and Stringer Lawrence took full advantage. Trichinopoly was first relieved and the French general Law with Chanda Sahib was then cooped up in the island of Srirangam and forced to surrender in June 1752. Chanda Sahib was executed by Muhammad Ali, his British allies failing to intervene. Dupleix refused to admit defeat and with infinite resource continued the struggle. He even besieged Trichinopoly a second time in 1753. But early in 1754 he was obliged to open negotiations with the British and meanwhile the French Company had decided upon his recall. Godeheu, a director of the Company, was sent out in August to supersede Dupleix and restore peace. The French retained their territorial possessions and their special position in Hyderabad, but their bid to control the Carnatic and rival the British had failed. What was in theory another practical restoration of the *status quo* did not, however, leave things as they were. The British had greatly strengthened both their position and reputation in the south and the French legend of superiority had been discredited. Above all, the relative positions of European and Indian powers in the south had been reversed. Both European nations had intervened actively in Indian politics; it had become evident that the countenance of Indian authority was no longer necessary for European success; rather Indian authority itself was becoming dependent on European support. Muhammad Ali in the Carnatic and Salabat Jang in Hyderabad were both clients rather than patrons.

Dupleix no doubt suffered from misfortune. Except for Bussy he was generally ill-served by his military lieutenants, and he had to contend with talent in the person of Lawrence and genius in that of Clive. But the causes of his failure lay deeper than this. It was rather his early success which should excite our wonder than his later failure. His system was unsupported from home and in consequence depended upon constant success in order to silence the criticism of the French directors. Success required not only the defeat of the British but the management of the ever-changing politics of south India. As soon as it was seen that the British could withstand the French, his south Indian allies broke into disarray. Above all, Dupleix lacked the financial resources to sustain a long campaign and satisfy his allies. Dupleix's bid for power was a *tour de force* which was bound to fail as soon as the real limitations of his resources came to be realized.

The French enjoyed but a brief respite before the third and decisive

PLATE 27

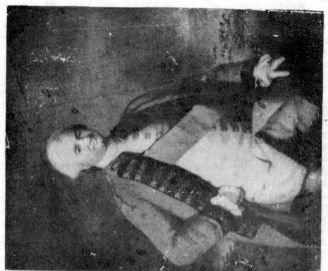

b. Clive

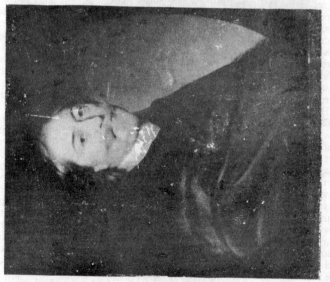

a. Sir Thomas Roe

Warren Hastings (Old Age)

phase of the Anglo-French struggle commenced. The Seven Years War broke out in Europe in 1756. Its cause was the Austrian desire to recover Silesia, but though this time the alignment of the powers was different, Britain and France were again on opposite sides. At the time neither side in south India was in a position to renew the struggle. The French Company was still exhausted and discredited. Clive had returned to Madras in 1755 with a plan to attack Bussy in Hyderabad. This had been delayed on account of Bombay's failure to co-operate, and the Company's disaster in Bengal had then called him away to the north. The French could do nothing until reinforcements arrived, and this gave time for Clive to consolidate his position in Bengal whence he could send to Madras, if not men, the no less necessary financial resources. In a sense the war was lost for the French before it began. Since both sides were supported from Europe, sea-power again became vital. The French had to control both elements if they were to succeed.

The main French armament arrived early in 1758 convoyed by a fleet under d'Aché. Its leader was the Comte de Lally, a brave but headstrong soldier, who was bold when he should have been cautious and cautious when he should have been bold. He was armed with full powers, being both governor and commander-in-chief. But he was unable to inspire loyalty in his subordinates, and above all proved unable to work with the experienced and sagacious Bussy. At first all went well. An indecisive action between d'Aché and Pocock had the result of leaving the coast clear of British ships. Lally marched at once to Fort St. David which he took much sooner than expected, on 2 June. His next step should have been to attack Madras, but here his troubles began. Pocock reappeared on the coast and d'Aché declined to meet him. Lally must wait for the change of season before Madras would be clear of British ships and he resolved to use the time by extorting an old debt from the Raja of Tanjore. He impetuously marched ahead of his artillery and supplies so that he could only sit down before Tanjore when he arrived; he terrorized the countryside by the execution of six temple Brahmans so that he could not obtain supplies; finally he raised the siege on hearing of the defeat of d'Aché off Karikal. The monsoon season now drew on, and Lally prepared to besiege Madras. But Governor Pigot and Colonel Lawrence had used their respite to good effect. The resolute defence of the two from October 1758 to March 1759 redeemed its former feeble showing. Lally was still hesitating to storm a difficult breach when a squadron of British ships appeared. Lally then raised the siege, leaving his military reputation behind in the trenches.

At the same time the French suffered another blow. Lally had recalled Bussy from Hyderabad, but on second thoughts had allowed the French garrison in the Northern Sarkars to remain. As a way of helping Madras without losing control of his troops Clive sent Colonel Forde to Vizagapatam in the autumn of 1758. While Lally was before Madras Forde defeated the French, and before he could march north had captured Masulipatam and made peace with the Nizam. Forde returned to Calcutta in October 1759, having safeguarded Bengal, but Lally had lost a body of veteran troops seasoned in Indian warfare. The whole episode is a good example of the way in which the correct use of sea-power can double the striking power of an army. The campaign dragged on without decisive result until the arrival of Coote with reinforcements. In January 1760 Lally was decisively defeated by Coote at Wandiwash, Bussy being taken prisoner. There only remained the reduction of Pondicherry. After eight months of blockade, endured gallantly but in an atmosphere tense with recrimination, Lally surrendered on 16 January 1761.[1] The French power in India was at an end.

The defeat of the French was partly due to the character of Lally. His impetuosity, his inability to work with colleagues or to inspire confidence among the civilians undermined the morale of the French; his errors of judgement and his failure to understand or conciliate the local population were equally costly. But behind these personal faults lay the two factors of sea and financial power. Lally could not recover after Wandiwash because he had no finance; he had no finance because he could get no supplies from France. The British, on the other hand, could feed Madras from Bengal as well as supply it from home, and by moving their men in ships they could make one man do the work of two. Lally blundered, but without the aid of sea-power he would not have been destroyed.

French power in India was never again formidable. Pondicherry was restored at the conclusion of peace in 1763, but as an open town. For a moment the sea victories of de Suffren in 1782–3 promised a revival of French power, but peace came before any advantage could be taken of them. French influence remained but it was confined to individuals and backed by no fleets or armies. Raymond at Hyderabad, de Boigne and Perron with Sindia worried but did not seriously menace the British. For a time the spectre of Napoleonic invasion exercised the mind of Lord Minto, but the Moscow campaign ended for ever the French dream of empire in India.

AUTHORITIES

ROBERT ORME's *History of Military Transactions . . . in Indostan* (1803) remains a basic authority for this period, along with R. O. CAMBRIDGE, *Account of the War in India* (1761). The standard modern account is by H. H. DODWELL, in his *Dupleix and Clive* (1920). Clive's part is covered by the biographies detailed in the next chapter, and the naval side by H. W. RICHMOND, *The Navy in the War of 1739–48* (3 vols., 1920) and *The Navy in India, 1763–83* (1931), and Sir J. S. CORBETT, *England in the Seven Years War* (2 vols., 1907).

On the French side P. CULTRU, *Dupleix* (1901) has been superseded by ALFRED MARTINEAU's *Dupleix et l'Inde française* in 4 volumes (1920–8). More recent studies are VIRGINIA THOMPSON, *Dupleix and his Letters* (1933), and W. H. DAGLEISH, *Company of the Indies in the Time of Dupleix* (1933). A. R. Pillai's Diary has been published in 12 volumes (Madras, 1904–28), ed. J. F. PRICE and H. H. DODWELL, and a single-volume edition has been edited by Professor C. S. SRINIVASACHARI (1940).

Two recent and scholarly studies are S. P. SEN's *The French in India: First establishment and struggle* (1947) and *The French in India 1763–1816* (1958).

[1] On his return to France Lally was tried for treason and executed.

CHAPTER 2

The British in Bengal

THE East India Company first established a factory in Bengal in the year 1650–1. A flourishing trade soon developed. The ill-advised attempt of the Company to free itself from Mughul control in 1686 by taking Chittagong ended in the founding of Calcutta by Job Charnock in 1690 on the swamp-girdled site of Sutanati. A local rebellion provided a pretext for fortifying the factory in 1696 and four years later it became the seat of a presidency under the name of Fort William in Bengal. Though the last of the three main centres of British trade to be established, the British establishments in Bengal soon became some of the most lucrative and important. They tapped a richer and extensive hinterland provided with excellent communications by water, and furnished with goods in rising demand in Europe. There was not only a flourishing trade in cotton goods, silk goods and yarn, and sugar, but also in saltpetre, for which the constant wars in Europe furnished a steadily growing demand. Bengal was less disturbed by war than Madras or Bombay or Surat, and felt the effects of the weakening of imperial authority later. In 1717 Surman's embassy to the court of Farrukhsiyar achieved a signal diplomatic success. Imperial *farmans* granted free trade to the Company in Bengal, subject to an annual payment of Rs. 3,000, and in the Hyderabad lands, subject to a quit rent for Madras; more land around Calcutta was rented and the right of settlement in the interior accorded; all dues at Surat were commuted for an annual payment of Rs. 10,000; and free currency was granted to the Company's rupees which were minted in Bombay. These arrangements governed the Company's relations with the empire for the next forty years. But as the imperial authority declined, the Company's officials were increasingly concerned with the local *subadar* or Nawab of Bengal rather than with the emperor. Fort William was completed in 1716, but its walls were soon encumbered with warehouses; the Maratha ditch (now the Circular road) was begun in 1742 on an alarm of a Maratha incursion, but it was perhaps fortunate that its strength was never tested. The Company's servants were peppery and prosperous but very unwarlike.

At the time of Aurangzeb's death Murshid Quli Khan (Jafar Khan) was deputy governor for the Prince Azim-ush-Shan. On the accession of that prince's son as Farrukhsiyar in 1713, Murshid Quli Khan was confirmed in office. He added Bihar in 1719 and died in 1727. His son Shuja-ud-daula held office until his death in 1738 and added Orissa to his other two provinces. The governorship of the three provinces now practically became a local dynasty; the only remaining ties with Delhi were imperial investiture and the remission of 52 *lakhs* a year as the annual tribute or *peshkash*. From 1719 at least Bengal may be said to have enjoyed substantial local autonomy. Shuja-ud-daula's son Sarfaraz proved incapable and was overthrown by Alivardi Khan, his deputy in Bihar, in 1740. Though Alivardi obtained confirmation from Delhi he had struck a severe blow at local stability by raising the hopes of adventurers within and without. Most of his fifteen years of rule was occupied in putting down rebellions or repelling Maratha incursions. The Marathas left an indelible impression on the popular mind. The Bengali poet Gangaram thus described them:

The *bargis*[1] came up and encircled them (the fleeing villagers) in the plain. They snatched away gold and silver, rejecting all else. Of some people they cut off the hand, of some the nose and ears; some they killed outright. They dragged away the beautiful women, tying their fingers to their necks with ropes. . . . After looting in the open, the *bargis* entered the villages. They set fire to the houses, large and small, temples and dwelling places. After burning the villages they roamed on all sides plundering. Some victims they tied with their arms twisted behind them. Some they flung down and kicked with their shoes. They constantly shouted 'Give us rupees, give us rupees, give us rupees'. When they got no rupee, they filled their victims nostrils with water and drowned them in tanks. Some were put to death by suffocation. Those who had money gave it to the *bargis*; those who had none gave up their lives.

Alivardi died on 21 April 1756, after a long illness. He had no sons and his chosen successor was his grandson Siraj-ud-daula, the son of his youngest daughter who had married a nephew. Siraj, a youth of barely twenty, found himself in no easy position. All the three nephews of Alivardi (his brother's sons) had predeceased him. But Siraj had to reckon with the jealousy of his cousin Shaukat Jang, governor of Purnea, and his aunt Ghasiti Begam, supported by her *diwan* Rajballabh. To these internal complications were added the state of the foreign settlements in Bengal. Europe was then on the eve of the Seven Years War, and French and British were visibly preparing for the contest. French, Dutch, and British were all objects of suspicion, but the British were clearly the strongest of the three. They enjoyed free trade under the Mughul *farman* of 1717 and they had given some ground for complaint by overstepping their extensive privileges. Both they and the French had begun to fortify their settlements in anticipation of war with each other. The French desisted before Alivardi's actual death, but the British prevaricated and increased growing suspicion by giving asylum to a political fugitive. Siraj had also to fear rising Hindu restlessness with minority Muslim rule in what was now practically an independent state.

Siraj-ud-daula was an impulsive but vacillating youth, with many of the vices commonly attributed to princes and little of the judgement or resolution which can redeem them. Denied by his youth the

---

[1] *bargi*: a corruption of *bargir* a horseman supplied with mount and arms by government.

experience to cure his faults and by circumstances the security which would in time have provided it, he acted on a series of contradictory impulses which combined to compass his ruin. He first secured the person of Ghasiti Begam and then marched against his cousin at Purnea. But on the receipt of a letter from Drake, the Governor of Fort William, he turned about, caused the English factory at Kasimbazar to be seized, and then marched on Calcutta. It then became clear that reports of new fortifications were ludicrously optimistic and the spirit of the factors was the reverse of aggressive. Calcutta was invested on 16 June. Three days later the governor, the commandant, and most of the council joined the women and children on board ship on the river, and dropping downstream left the distracted garrison to its fate. Under Holwell, the junior member of council, resistance was prolonged for a day and then Calcutta surrendered. There followed a search for treasure and the incident of the Black Hole.[1] With characteristic imprudence Siraj did nothing to follow up his victory, leaving Drake and the fugitives to languish at Fulta, succoured only by a reinforcement of 230 men in July. Instead he confined himself to eliminating his only dynastic rival, Shaukat Jang.

The news of this disaster reached Madras at the moment when an expedition against the French in Hyderabad was under active preparation. The happy obduracy of the senior royal officer resulted in the command being given to Robert Clive, then the deputy Governor of Fort St. David. Clive turned with delight from the bickerings of the Madras Council to the hazards of war. He had no doubts and no fears. He set out on 16 October with 900 European and 1,500 Indian troops, conveyed by Admiral Watson with five men-at-war and five transports. Fulta was relieved in December and Calcutta recovered on 2 January 1757. This roused the nawab to measures he should have taken long before, but an indecisive engagement again disheartened him; by another volte-face he concluded peace and an alliance on 9 February. Calcutta was restored and the Company's privileges renewed with the addition of permission to fortify the town and coin money.

Siraj's incompetence has already been sufficiently indicated, and his fall was now only a matter of time. He was surrounded by disaffected Hindu officers, supported by the banking house of the Seths, and was faced with resolute and skilful men. Clive's first care was to deal with the French. Their post at Chandernagar, unlike Calcutta in the previous year, was well fortified, and Bussy was in the Northern Sarkars within 200 miles of Calcutta. He was helped by the news of Ahmad Shah Durrāni's capture of Delhi (January 1757) which once more caused Siraj to hesitate in supporting the French lest he should need British aid in resisting the Afghans. By the end of March and with the aid of Watson's ships Chandernagar was in British hands. Siraj was now isolated. Unlike his grandfather, Siraj was unfriendly to his officers; with the death of Shaukat Jang he had thrown off all

[1] See note at end of chapter p. 479.

restraint while his opponents had lost hope of peaceful redress. It was not therefore necessary for the English leaders to concoct a conspiracy; they had only to decide as to which conspiracy to support. Clive's position was still precarious. The French were still in strength in Hyderabad and his forces and the ships of Watson might at any time be recalled to meet pressing dangers in the south. The nawab could not but be hostile, and the great disparity between the numbers and strength of his forces could not be fully known. These were the reasons which caused Clive to welcome a possible change of government and to resort to deceit rather than to open warfare.

The first overtures to the British had been made in the previous autumn while they were still at Fulta. It was not until Mir Jafar, an elderly brother-in-law of Alivardi Khan, and the recently dismissed *bakshi* of the nawab, became willing to join the Seths and Hindu officers that Clive took action. There followed the treaty by which Mir Jafar promised to confirm the Company's privileges, to pay a million pounds as compensation for the loss of Calcutta and half a million more to its European inhabitants. By private agreement, in addition, there were to be large consolations for the chief Company officers.

It was thought that the nawab's treasury contained forty millions of which the go-between, the Sikh financier Amin Chand (Omichand), thought himself entitled to 5 per cent. This proportion was thought to be unreasonable and Amin Chand's threat of exposure of the plot was countered by devising a second copy of the treaty doctored for his benefit. The secret was out by the beginning of June in any case, but the nawab, irresolute to the last, not only failed to seize Mir Jafar but asked for his help instead.

Clive left Calcutta on 22 June: his army of 800 Europeans and 2,200 Indians faced the nawab's motley and disaffected 50,000. In spite of previous south Indian experience Clive was doubtful of the issue, and showed on the eve of the battle almost the only sign of irresolution in his life. The battle was little more than a cannonade, and was settled first by Kilpatrick's unauthorized advance and then by Siraj's headlong flight. Mir Jafar, like Stanley at Bosworth, looked on from a distance, appearing cautiously next day to reap the expensive fruits of his circumspect treachery. On the 28th Clive installed him on the *masnad* at Murshidabad and four days later Siraj, captured by the new nawab's son Miran, was executed. A new era had begun.

It should not be thought that the full import of the revolution then begun was yet realized. Legally and to most outward appearances the old order continued. There had been revolutions before and the assistance of foreigners was well understood. The English were not even the first Europeans to interfere in Bengali politics, for the Portuguese had done it long before them. The nawab continued to administer Bengal and Bihar as the emperor's deputy, and the Company continued to trade by imperial permission. Its privileges were enhanced and its prestige increased. But few on either side accepted the momentary power of the Company as permanent, and in fact it was seven years before this fact was generally recognized. In the eyes of contemporaries Clive was an English Bussy controlling an Indian state by force of character and dint of superior military genius and technique;[1] he was more fortunate than Bussy in that his stage was the richest region of India and that he was relatively untroubled with formidable enemies. It was the events of the next ten years which turned a paramount influence into a new régime. Bengali dissensions had avoided the necessity of proving European military superiority by hard fighting as in the south; the demonstration was therefore yet to come.

Clive's immediate task was to establish Mir Jafar in po er, and to secure the resumption of normal trade. The whole position was prejudiced at the outset, however, by the financial provisions of the treaty. The fabled treasures of Murshidabad turned out to be no more than a million and a half pounds. Clive was forced to agree to the settlement of Mir Jafar's debts by instalments and Mir Jafar found his resources strained to accomplish even this. The result was to undermine the far from firm union of the Muslim nawab with local Hindu officers. Mir Jafar looked longingly to the provincial treasuries to fill the financial void in the capital. Clive, therefore, was faced with the triple task of protecting the Hindu officers from their Muslim superior, of defending Mir Jafar from external attack, and of protecting himself from European intervention. With immense energy he accomplished all three. He put down revolts against Mir Jafar's authority, sustained Ramnarayan in his charge of Patna, and gave sanctuary to the diwan Rai Durlabh when he could no longer maintain himself in Murshidabad. With equal incisiveness he dealt with the other danger. In 1759 Ali Gauhar, the heir to the Mughul throne (later Shah Alam II), laid siege to Patna hoping to strengthen his claims at Delhi by acquiring control of Bihar and Bengal. Ramnarayan proved loyal and defended himself until Clive could send help when Ali Gauhar retired to Oudh. The third danger came from the Dutch in Chinsura. Alarmed by and jealous of the English successes the Dutch hoped to play on the nawab's restiveness at his dependence upon the Company by sending an armament from Batavia. Although England was at peace with Holland, Clive, by a series of adroit and bold moves, placed them in the position of aggressors, destroyed their expedition, and exacted compensation. Henceforth the Dutch confined themselves to commercial activity and disappeared as a factor in Indian power politics.

Clive left Calcutta in January 1760 in a blaze of personal glory. He had excelled Bussy in his own field; in three years he had made a position unassailable which Bussy had precariously maintained for nine. But it was clearly a highly unstable one, depending on the genius of a single forceful personality. Clive had become the indispensable

[1] His Persian title, by which he was popularly known, was Sabat Jang, 'the tried in battle'. It was procured by Mir Jafar from the emperor.

power behind and on occasion against the throne, and on his withdrawal there must either be an Indian reaction or the conversion of a dominating influence into explicit authority. In fact both occurred during the most confused and most sordid five years of the British period of Indian history. It will be convenient to trace the thread of power politics before examining the web of corruption with which it was entangled.

The first step was the replacement of Mir Jafar by his son-in-law Mir Kasim. Mir Jafar had always hoped to free himself from the Company's meshes, but he lacked the resolution to oppose Clive or the skill to build up his strength. All he succeeded in achieving was an impression of unreliability, of being a nuisance without being a danger. On the Company's side there was no one with the address to maintain the tension between nawab and Company but many to see in an unstable situation the chance of financial gain. The Company found itself in financial straits and pressed by puzzled directors who thought that the most industrious province in India ought not to be a tax on their resources. The nawab offered an easy target by falling into arrears with his subsidies. To Clive succeeded the plausible and shallow Holwell and to Holwell the honest and capable but rather ineffective Henry Vansittart from Madras. Local greed pushed him along the path of aggression and local jealousies neutralized his instincts of integrity. The death of Mir Jafar's son Miran in July opened the question of the succession. Mir Kasim was proposed as *diwan* or deputy nawab; Mir Jafar after his usual vacillation refused to trust himself to the power of his kinsman and retired to Calcutta with an English guard.

The new nawab was a very different man from his father-in-law. Able and ambitious, though suspicious and unwarlike, he was an adept in the cynical and pitiless politics of the time, and determined to assert his independence at the earliest opportunity. In him the Indian reaction was ably embodied. But he had mortgaged his fortunes as the price of office. The three districts of Burdwan, Midnapur, and Chittagong were assigned to the Company for the maintenance of their troops, the outstanding debts of Mir Jafar were to be repaid, and £200,000 paid in cash to the Calcutta Council. There were now two powers in Bengal, each determined to assert themselves, and each urgently requiring funds which they could only obtain at the other's expense. A clash was inevitable, and that it was postponed for three years is evidence both of the ability of the new nawab and the divided counsels of Calcutta.

The nawab first dealt with the emperor, who had again been repulsed in Bihar, and whose restoration to Delhi the Calcutta authorities proposed to assist. Mir Kasim suspected that this might end in the transfer of Bengal to the Company (as happened five years later) and by adroit diplomacy he both obtained his own investiture from Shah Alam and induced him to leave Bihar. He then, with Vansittart's support, procured the removal of Clive's protégé at Patna, Ramnarayan, and so possessed himself of the resources and treasure of Bihar. He next began to raise a force of disciplined troops, the most effective of all bargaining counters, and, to secure himself from undue interference from Calcutta, transferred his capital from Murshidabad to Monghyr. All these measures required money and it was on this rock that the first attempt of an Indian state to get on equal terms with the West foundered. To pay his way the nawab must make full use of the commercial tolls on the Bengal trade. To keep up their remittances to England, the Calcutta merchants must increase their receipts, and to amass the private fortunes which the successes of Clive seemed suddenly to have placed within their grasp, the same merchants must not allow their new-found economic freedom to be abridged. The imperial *farman* of 1717 had exempted the Company from all export and import duties on their foreign trade, but the private trade of the Company's servants was subject to the ordinary internal tolls. In 1757 Clive obtained from Mir Jafar the practical exemption of this private internal trade from duty without an express provision in the treaty. Naturally the private trade of the Company's servants grew apace while that of the Indian merchants dwindled. Thus Mir Kasim found his revenue declining at the moment he wished to increase it. Early in 1762 Vansittart agreed to an *ad valorem* duty at 9 per cent. on European traders' private goods as against a duty of 40 per cent. for others, and admitted the right of the local *faujdars* or police officers to adjudge disputes. At this the Calcutta Council revolted; the duty was reduced from 9 to 2½ per cent. on salt only and the right of the nawab's officers to interfere was rejected. The nawab retaliated by abolishing the duties altogether. Between the Company's servants' determination 'to do themselves justice' and the nawab's resolve to be master in his own house there could be no compromise, and war was now inevitable. The conflict was precipitated at Patna where an irascible English chief and an embittered nawab provoked each other beyond endurance. A regular campaign ensued during the summer of 1763, during which the nawab's new army was defeated in four pitched battles. Losing all control Mir Kasim executed his commander-in-chief, murdered Ramnarayan, the Seths, and his British prisoners in Patna, and then fled to Oudh. Mir Jafar was now restored but the war was not yet over. Mir Kasim enlisted the support of Shuja-ud-daula, the Nawab Wazir of Oudh, who was joined by the wandering emperor. An interval ensued during which both sides recruited their strength, the English commander Adam died in Calcutta, and his successor Hector Munro severely repressed the first Indian military mutiny. Fighting was resumed in the autumn of 1764 and the campaign concluded by the resounding victory of Baksar on 22 October. Shah Alam once more joined the British camp, Shuja-ud-daula fled to Rohilkund while Oudh was overrun, and Mir Kasim disappeared into obscurity. Plassey was a cannonade but Baksar a decisive battle. It was this battle, the culmination of an obstinate campaign, which determined the British mastery of Bengal. Hitherto they had been rivals and manipulators of existing authority; their power was fortuitous and hedged with doubt; the issue was still open. It was now unchallenged and about to receive imperial recognition; henceforth its full extent was only partly concealed for a time by surviving legal fictions. Plassey marked the beginning of the British expansion in Bengal; Baksar determined the success of the enterprise. The period was rounded off by the death of Mir Jafar in 1765. He had been restored on condition of reimposing the old duties on Indian merchants, with 2½ per cent. on salt for the British, along with further presents to the governor and council. The council (disregarding Muslim law) raised his second son Najm-ud-daula to the *masnad* in preference to his grandson, and strengthened their hold by stipulating that the government should be carried on by a deputy of their own choosing. His name was Muhammad Reza Khan; his appointment marked the virtual end of independent Indian rule in Bengal.

We may now turn to the nature of the régime which had achieved so marked a success in so short a time. Sir Alfred Lyall described these years as 'the only period which throws grave and unpardonable discredit on the English government'. Clive was still more forthright. 'I will only say that such a scene of anarchy, confusion, bribery, corruption and extortion was never seen or heard of in any country but Bengal, nor such and so many fortunes acquired in so unjust and rapacious a manner.' It was, however, Clive himself who had started the moral collapse of the Bengal civilians. Before 1756 the Calcutta civilians had been neither better nor worse than their kind elsewhere. They carried on the Company's business with efficiency and enterprise; they used the energy remaining from their not overweighty public duties to prosecute private trade on their own account. They were expected to do this, and indeed could not have lived on the meagre salaries allotted by the Company. But they were restrained from excesses both by the power of the local government, vigilant to safeguard the interests of the merchants and peasants, upon whom its own revenue depended, and by an ingrained respect for constituted authority, even when shaken by the blows inflicted on the Mughul government by Persian, Maratha, and Afghan. The unknown power of the nawab and the provisions of the *farman* of 1717 together kept their private commercial activities within reasonable bounds. The events of 1757 transformed the situation. The sudden transformation of plodding merchants into the arbiters of Bengal politics dazzled and unbalanced men already smarting from loss and indignity. The two restraints were removed almost simultaneously; the nawab became a suitor for British favour instead of the regulator of British activity, and the imperial government dissolved in the clash of Maratha and Afghan, only to be revived in the person of a wandering fugitive. The merchants were merchants still; they suddenly found avenues to undreamed of wealth open before them, and they lacked the inner restraint which alone could promote moderation or justice. They were neither exceptionally evil nor unusually weak, but they were overwhelmed with the unfamiliar temptations which now crowded upon them.

The first step was taken by Clive himself in negotiating the treaty of 1757 with Mir Jafar. Before Plassey, it was privately agreed that in addition to the official compensation, £400,000 should be given to the army and navy and £150,000 to the select committee of six. The members of council received £50,000 to £80,000 each. Clive received in all £234,000. In addition he received a *jagir* worth about £30,000 a year on his own plea that the dignity of an imperial noble (a status procured for him by Mir Jafar from the emperor) required a revenue grant to maintain it. These were the grants which caused Clive 'to be astonished at his own moderation'. The discovery that the nawab's treasury contained only 1½ millions sterling instead of the 40 millions which were rumoured led to no abatement in the demands. Mir Kasim won the support of Calcutta by promising to pay Mir Jafar's arrears, and paid a further £200,000 to the council. Najm-ud-daula was forced to pay another £139,000 odd to the same council. With such examples at the top it is not surprising that the lesser men scrambled to make quick fortunes. Their first means was the reception of more modest presents from humbler men. The most prized posts were up-country agencies such as the residency of Murshidabad or the headship of factories like that of Patna. Here there were the greatest number of moneyed men with the strongest motives for the corrupt use of their wealth. But the new power of the Company put every young factor in the way of receiving presents, if not for benefits received, then in the hope of favours to come. The second method was private participation in the internal trade of the country. The Company's servants enjoyed unlimited credit. They could both command whatever capital was needed and live, even at Madras, at the rate of £5,000-6,000 a year. This proved so profitable that once experienced, as a result of Clive's arrangements with Mir Jafar, the servants were willing to risk war and the possible resultant bankruptcy of the Company itself rather than give it up. This open private trading duty free in competition with Indian merchants paying 40 per cent. *ad valorem* was made more extensive and profitable by intimidation exercised through agents or *gomastahs*. The British held that the right to private internal trade carried with it the right 'to do themselves justice'. Mir Kasim's attempt to enforce discipline through his *faujdars* was one of the immediate causes of the Company's breach with him. Ellis of Patna employed bodies of up to 500 sepoys in order to deal with the nawab's agents. In addition to all this there were lucrative contracts to be worked. Thus the light of commercial greed, ignited by sudden and unexpected opportunity and fanned by unbridled power divorced from responsibility, became a devouring flame which could only be checked by drastic intervention from England. It was not effectively quenched until the time of Cornwallis and continued to smoulder until the time of

Bentinck seventy years later. Men made fortunes, returned to England, lost them, and returned to India for more. Some idea of the fevered atmosphere of these years can be obtained from the unpublished journal of James Rennell. Appointed Surveyor-General of Bengal in 1764 at the age of twenty-two, he reported an allowance of £900 and perquisites of £1,000 a year; 'I can enjoy my friends, my bottle and all the necessaries of life for £400. Besides, when I get acquainted with the trade of this part of India, I shall make much greater advantages as I shall always be able to command a capital.' He hoped to return in a few years with £5,000 or £6,000. With favourable conditions £30,000 to £40,000 was possible. This was on the eve of Clive's return. By 1769 he only hoped to retire on £120 a year. By 1771 he thought it would soon 'be high time to decamp'. He actually retired in 1777 at the age of thirty-five. Lives of fevered activity and dissipated gaiety were only too often, as the Calcutta cemeteries bear eloquent witness, cut short by death. But the personal tragedies which formed the background of fortune-making must not obscure the greater tragedy of the demoralization of the Company's service and the misery of all Bengal.

The directors had taken alarm at the decline of the Bengal remittances as early as 1758. There was more criticism of the revolution of 1760. But the hands of the directors were largely tied by dissensions in the newly important Court of Proprietors. A staid Company meeting had now become the final arbiter of a supposedly wealthy Indian province; a scramble for office ensued leading to uncertainty of tenure and divided counsels. The very class of men whom it was vital for the Company to control could make their influence felt in this direction by using their new wealth to buy Company stock with its accompanying votes. This development resolved itself into a duel between Clive who sought to use his new wealth to secure control and then reform the Indian administration and Sulivan, once his friend, a clear-headed man of business immersed in the intrigue and jobbery of the time. On the news of Mir Kasim's overthrow alarm deepened to consternation; it was not profits only, but the Company's existence which now seemed to be in question. The news coincided with Clive's triumph over his opponents in the Court of Proprietors, and the result was vigorous action. Clive (now an Irish peer) was appointed Governor and Commander-in-Chief of Bengal, and was empowered to act, if necessary, over the head of council, with a select committee of four.[1] At the same time the practice of receiving presents was drastically curtailed and Clive was given authority to regulate the trade in salt, betel-nut, and tobacco, lately seized from the nawab, in the general interest.

Clive set sail in June 1764 and arrived in Calcutta on 3 May 1765. Within two days he had appointed his select committee and with an act of characteristic vigour had begun his second administration which constitutes his chief claim to fame as a statesman. The poacher had

[1] Colonel Carnac and Henry Verelst, already in Bengal, Sumner and Sykes, who sailed with Clive.

turned gamekeeper without loss of vigour or finesse. For the moment he wielded unquestioned authority. His second governorship showed what could be accomplished by public spirit and vigour when home and local authorities were in concert, as his first showed what vigour and ambition alone could achieve in the absence of all restraint.

On arrival Clive found that the immediate crisis which had led to his appointment had passed. Baksar had removed the imperial danger but not settled the imperial question. Vansittart had promised Oudh to the emperor, but Shuja-ud-daula was at large up-country and the fate of Allahabad had still to be settled. Najm-ud-daula had succeeded his father Jafar, but the Company had virtually taken over the revenue administration by the appointment of Muhammad Reza Khan as *naib* or deputy nawab. From Calcutta to the Delhi doab there was no one who could withstand the Company's arms, and no one but the Company who could resist an invader. Yet the wielder of all this power was still only a commercial corporation controlling directly only Calcutta and three districts close by. It will be convenient to deal with Clive's external policy first; then with the settlement of Bengal; and finally with his reform of the Company's services.

Clive's first decision was perhaps the most difficult of all to take. He had to decide where to stop. At the moment there was no visible limit to the British power, and if he had marched to Delhi, replaced Shah Alam on his throne, and taken for the Company the power of regent (*vakil-i-matlaq*, the title later assumed by Sindia), or *wazir*, no one could have stopped him. There were not wanting those who advocated this course. But Clive realized that this short cut to empire might easily have proved a blind alley. He could certainly have marched to Delhi, but Najib-ud-daula with his Rohillas and the Sikhs of the Panjab, not to mention the Jats of Bharatpur and the enigmatic Marathas of the Deccan, were made of sterner stuff than the peoples of the Gangetic plain. Difficulties would have multiplied and the enterprise must soon have ended in frustration or disaster. Only a lifetime of vigorous action and the expenditure of treasure which the Company could not possibly sustain could have brought success, and then the result would not have been a commercial empire based on Calcutta, but a northern realm engrossed in Deccan and north-western politics. Clive wisely decided to limit the Company's influence to the old double *sūba* of Bengal and Bihar, leaving Oudh as a buffer between the Company, the Marathas, and possible northern invaders. This involved the difficult question of the emperor, whose return to Delhi Clive was unable to sponsor but whose complete abandonment would have cut off the authority on whom the Company depended for a legitimate title. 'I take the Shah's authority', wrote an English agent seventeen years later, 'to be of as much importance as an Act of Parliament in England if supported by as strong a force.'[1] If Clive could not implement that

---

[1] Major Browne, Memorandum on the Affairs of Delhi. India Office. Home Miscellaneous Series, vol. 336.

authority throughout the empire, he also could not afford to dispense with it in Bengal. Accordingly, the emperor's claim to the direct control of Oudh was discountenanced, but he was given the districts of Kora and Allahabad with a subsidy or tribute of 26 *lakhs*.[1] In return Shah Alam conferred upon the Company the *diwani* of Bengal. Oudh was restored to Shuja-ud-daula on payment of an indemnity of 50 *lakhs* and a defensive alliance concluded by which his defence was guaranteed provided he bore the expense of the necessary troops. This suited Shuja well, with the Marathas in mind; he did not realize that his new friends would eventually prove more deadly than his supposed enemies. This treaty provided a model for the system which Wellesley later developed by which Indian princes saved themselves from their enemies at the price of enmeshing themselves in the threads of the Company's spider's web.

We may now turn to the settlement of Bengal. The grant of the *diwani* regularized the revenue settlement with Najm-ud-daula, and marked the first great step towards the direct administration of Bengal by the Company. In order to understand the import of this and later developments, it is necessary to explain certain principles of Mughul administration. The powers of government were theoretically divided into the *diwani*, or power of collecting revenue and administering civil justice, and the *nizamat*, or power of commanding troops and dispensing criminal justice. From the time of Akbar it was the Mughul custom to place these powers in different hands as well as to rotate the officials from province to province. From the later years of Aurangzeb's reign governors began to be allowed to remain at their posts and to be succeeded by their sons; this development soon brought with it the combination of the two powers in the same hands. Alivardi enjoyed this double privilege and had been followed by his successors, who thus, to the Company, appeared as the sole rulers of the three provinces. The new grant meant that the Company became the *diwan* of the emperor empowered to collect revenue and administer civil justice. The *nizamat* power remained nominally with the nawab, but he had by treaty handed over its exercise to the Company's nominee, Reza Khan. The Company appointed as its deputy *diwan* the same Muhammad Reza Khan. He was thus the Company's deputy for revenue collection and the nawab's deputy for criminal justice and the control of troops. But since the Company in fact possessed the sole military power in the region and nominated the nawab's deputy, Reza Khan was in effect the deputy of the Company for the whole administration. This was a dual system in a double sense. In theory the authority (under the emperor) was divided between Company and nawab; while in practice the administration was divided between English controllers and Indian agency. It is this latter feature which was the essence of the Dual System which Hastings ended seven years later. It was an improve-

[1] Shuja had little to complain of, because he had himself only recently seized Allahabad from the legitimate governor, Muhammad Quli Khan.

ment in that the Indian deputy was now directly responsible to the Company and the Company for the deputy; it left the door wide open to abuses because all depended upon the integrity and vigilance of the Calcutta Council. Later developments consisted in the gradual taking over by the Company of revenue collection and justice by its own British agents. The Dual System is more correctly named the Indirect System, which was gradually transmuted into the Direct System.

In dealing with the Company's own administration Clive showed a vigour so great that those who remembered his previous record thought at first that it could not last and that he was malignantly determined to prevent others from amassing the fortune that he had already achieved. On the matter of presents he was fortified by explicit instructions; on that of the internal trade the Company had whittled down its original prohibition to an authority to regulate in the general interest. Clive first asserted his authority. The select committee assumed full powers. All resignations were accepted and some enforced, and the vacant places filled from Madras. Recalcitrant officials soon found that the only practicable courses were submission or return to England. Next, the orders on presents were enforced. Every servant was required to sign a covenant binding them to hand over to the Company all presents in excess of Rs. 4,000, and only to accept presents of Rs. 1,000 and upwards with the president and council's consent. The question of the internal trade was more difficult. The salaries of the Company's servants were well known to be inadequate in themselves; if the liberty of private trade as well as of receiving presents was withdrawn, they would not be left with reasonable means of subsistence. There would be wholesale evasion and the last state of things would be worse than the first. The obvious course would have been to couple the prohibition of private trade with a large increase of official salaries. But to this he could not induce the directors to agree. Clive attempted to meet this situation by regulating the private trade so as to provide the effect of regular salaries. He formed a Society of Trade to administer the salt monopoly in which the Company's servants received shares according to their rank. Under this arrangement the governor received £17,500, a colonel and a member of council £7,000 a year, and others in proportion. But the directors regarded this as disobedience to their orders and another form of corruption. Two years later the system was abolished and replaced by a system of commissions on the revenues of the province under which most of the officials received even more.[1] This system had the further disadvantage that the amounts fluctuated with the revenue figures so affording an inducement for the extortion of revenue. When to this system is added the fact that clandestine private trade continued (at least after Clive's departure) by a sort of general tacit consent, and that the secret reception of presents continued as well, it will be seen that the financial reform of the services was far from complete. Irregularities were reduced but still rampant,

[1] *Reports of the House of Commons*, vol. iv, p. 460.

and that is why Cornwallis found so much to do twenty years later. For this comparative failure the directors were partly responsible, since they vetoed the solution of adequate salaries and adopted the less satisfactory of the two alternative systems.

With equal vigour Clive dealt with military allowances or *batta*. Here the position was more difficult, for it was not a question of dealing with illicit gains but of reducing legitimate allowances improperly prolonged. *Batta* signifies an allowance for special service and was originally designed to cover the extra cost of field service as distinct from garrison duty. The practice began at Madras during the French wars, when the nawab subsidized British troops in his service in this way. It naturally spread to Bengal, but when hostile territories came within the Company's control double *batta* for field service continued to be drawn for what had now become garrison duty. Clive allowed officers in cantonments to draw half *batta*, those on field service within Bengal full *batta*, and those outside its borders double *batta*.[1] The officers felt the greatest indignation, and they could plead that their pay was more rigidly determined than that of the civilians, making little allowance for the upward trend of prices, and that they were denied in large measure the opportunities open to civilians for unofficial additions. Encouraged by one of the brigade-commanders, Sir Robert Fletcher, a mutinous movement was set on foot. This 'White Mutiny' was more dangerous than the civilian opposition, but Clive met it with equal vigour. At the same time he used a legacy of 5 *lakhs* from Mir Jafar to form a fund to make provision for officers in need when compelled to retire early. This was the forerunner of later pension schemes.

Clive retired from his second governorship in February 1767. He left the Company with defined territories recognized in law and secure for the present from attack, controlled by a docile army and chastened civilians. He had scotched rather than killed the snake of corruption, but he had taken the first long step towards an ordered and honest administration in Bengal. There was much still to be done, but there was never a return to the anarchy of the early sixties. How much of this was due to Clive himself was shown by what happened after his departure.

By the irony which commonly pursues the great, his greatest achievement was the prelude to his eclipse. The gathering criticism of the Company broke in a storm of reproach when it became clear in 1772 that the Company was threatened with bankruptcy. Parliamentary inquiry threw the glare of publicity on the actions of his first governorship and this led to Burgoyne's parliamentary attack in 1773. The attempt collapsed, ending with the unanimous resolution 'That Robert, Lord Clive, at the same time rendered great and meritorious service to his country.' But the strain proved too great for a mind prone to depression; Clive took his own life on 2 November 1774.

Clive had been praised as a soldier turned statesman. His real claim

[1] For a captain the respective rates were Rs. 3, 6, and 12 a day.

to fame is neither as statesman nor soldier but as a dynamic leader of men. He had, says Roberts, 'a certain rough-hewn, almost elemental force and a tireless energy which made him a true pioneer of empire'. He had the gift of inspiring others, the ability to improvise and the strength to persevere in all circumstances. His piercing vision saw ends so clearly that the question of means often seemed unimportant. He was fundamentally honest, but his one-track mind could only see one issue at a time and his egotism prevented him from seeing the inconsistency of courses suggested by immediate necessities. He had a genius for emergencies and a talent for dictatorship. He lacked larger views or the art of management needed for giving to conquest a foundation of justice. He was the first and greatest of the English *conquistadores*, but for statesmanship we must look to his profounder successor.

NOTE ON THE BLACK HOLE

THE incident of the Black Hole has been given only a passing mention in the text in order to place it in proper proportion to the whole story.

We owe the traditional story of the Black Hole to the descriptive powers of J. Z. Holwell, the defender of Calcutta and a plausible and none too reliable man. For fifty years little notice was taken of the incident, but it then became convenient material for the compilers of an imperialist hagiology. The transition in progress can be seen in H. H. Wilson's note to Mill's notes on his account in pp. 117-18 of vol. iii of his *History of India* (ed. 1858). The emphasis upon the incident grew so great that the Black Hole became, along with Plassey and the Mutiny, one of the three things which 'every schoolboy knew' about India.

For many years it has now been agreed that the incident was not due to the deliberate action of Siraj-ud-daulah, and that on the part of his agents it was the result of ignorance and carelessness rather than of cruelty and vindictiveness. As such it should be regarded as a deplorable incident rather than as a deliberate atrocity. The attempt to prove that the incident never occurred has not proved convincing, though the details of Holwell's account may well owe something to his imagination. The fact remains that 123 people who defended Calcutta have to be accounted for, and that the evidence for their death in battle is more slender than for their death in the Black Hole. In my judgement something like the Black Hole incident as described by Holwell actually occurred, though the numbers involved and details are not certain, as the combined result of ignorance, apathy, and confusion on the part of the nawab's agents, in the confused circumstances of the overrunning of the fort.

The interested reader will find a good account by H. E. Busteed in his *Echoes of Old Calcutta* and a judicious summing up of the controversy over its actual occurrence by H. H. Dodwell in the *Cambridge History of India*, vol. v, p. 156. The term Black Hole was the current term for the local lock-up or temporary gaol.

AUTHORITIES

THE Indian background is given by MIRZA GHULAM HUSAIN in his *Siyar-ul Mutaqherin*, vol. i, trans. Briggs (1832), and vols. ii and iii by HAJI MUSTAPHA (RAYMOND), Calcutta'(1789), a work of great ability compared by Macaulay to BISHOP BURNET'S

History of his own Times. N. N. GHOSE, *Memoirs of Nubkissen* (1901), deals with the Indians who worked with the British. The best modern general works are H. H. DODWELL, *Dupleix and Clive*, and P. E. ROBERTS, *British India* (1952); both authors were specialists on this period. Orme is authoritative on the conquest and H. VANSITTART, *Narrative of the Transactions in Bengal from 1760-64* (1766) the best contemporary account of those years. For the years 1756-7 S. C. HILL's monumental *Bengal in 1756-7* (1905) may be consulted. Clive's part is dealt with in lives by Sir J. MALCOLM (3 vols., 1836), Sir G. W. FORREST (2 vols., 1918), and A. DAVIES (1939). Forrest is detailed but uncritical; the best study is by Davies. CHARLES CARACCIOLI's *Life* (1775-7) is a libel written in the interests of the mutinous officers of 1766. There are studies of *Mir Qasim* (1935) and *Verelst's Rule in India* (1929) by N. L. CHATTERJI, and of *Mir Jafar Khan* by A. C. ROY (1953).

The economic side of the picture is given by S. C. SINHA in his *Early Economic Annals in Bengal* (1927) and N. K. SINHA in his *Economic History of Bengal* (1956), while Sir W. W. HUNTER deals with the famine of 1770 in his *Annals of Rural Bengal*. The internal politics of the Company are dealt with in masterly fashion by LUCY SUTHERLAND in her *East India Company in 18th Century Politics* (1952), in which Lawrence Sulivan appears in a more favourable light than previously.

See also K. K. DATTA, *Studies in the History of the Bengal Subah, I, Social and Economic* (1936).

RECENT PUBLICATIONS

AN important book on the economic side of the British in Bengal is by P. J. MARSHALL, *East Indian Fortunes: The British in Bengal in the 18th Century* (Oxford, 1976), New studies of Clive are by P. SPEAR, *Master of Bengal: Clive and his India* (1975), and N. C. CHAUDHURI, *Clive of India: A Political and Psychological Essay* (1975).

CHAPTER 3

Afghans, Mughuls, and Marathas

FROM 1760 to 1785 central and northern India were wholly in Indian (or non-European) hands and some account must now be given of their condition. The period is marked by a three-cornered struggle for power; it is darkened by a gradual decline of prosperity, civil order, and even of civilization, and it is complicated by the tendency of all three parties to break up into their constituent units. Political society displayed that characteristic of malignant growth, a tendency to the indefinite increase of cells with all their attendant strains on the body social. The India which the British surveyed at the end of the century was a very different place in numbers and level of life as well as in outlook to the India of the eve of Nādir Shah's invasion. During this period the spendthrift process begun by Mughul civil wars and Maratha incursions developed to the extent of turning the great prosperity of the seventeenth century into the Great Anarchy of the later eighteenth. The British administrators of the early years of the nineteenth century surveyed only the ruins of past grandeur. Men like Malcolm and Metcalfe realized that this was so; men like Mill and Macaulay assumed that this was the usual state of Indian affairs. The British public believed their publicists rather than their public servants. So came to be created the Victorian Anglo-Indian myth, that all Indian government had always been corrupt and inefficient and that all Indians must for ever be incapable of self-government. Like the earlier myth of boundless Indian riches, this belief was the result of facile conclusions drawn from premises based on half-knowledge. In the earlier case the fallacy had arisen from the geographical limitation of attention to the courts rather than the countryside; in the latter it came from the temporal limitation of view to the mid and late eighteenth century instead of the Mughul period as a whole.

The centripetal tendency was at work in all the three main parties. The Afghans split off from the Persians, and splinter groups from the predominant Durrānīs; later the Durrānī chiefs themselves fell out and massacred each other. The Mughul empire was not only troubled by the ambitions of local governors and court intrigues, but by the rise of new aspirants to power in the wild Sikhs of the Panjab, the rustic Jats, and the Rohilla Afghans. The Marathas themselves, in some ways the most united of the three, had no sooner laid the apparent foundations of empire than they began to be afflicted by the ambitions of military chiefs on the frontiers and the intrigues of rival factions at Poona. ' Delhi and Hyderabad resided the traditions of empire without the

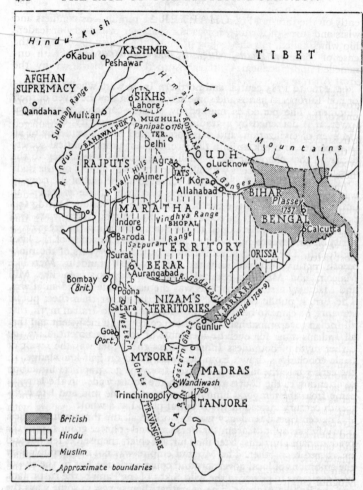

INDIA, 1761

means or the spirit for maintaining them; in Afghanistan was to be found the vigour to achieve victory without the means or the knowledge to gather its fruits; amongst the Marathas existed both the means and the vigour for achieving empire along with the spirit of the guerilla and the *condottiere* which frustrated each effort when apparently on the threshold of success. In all the tumultuous conflicts and twists and turns of fortune, it was not character or bravery or leadership which failed, but the feeling of unity, the ability to combine, the sense of common destiny. Great energy and skill united with untramelled individualism to replace ordered administration by the Great Anarchy.

There is no easy way through this jungle of political and military growth. The most that can be done is to trace in broad outline the fortunes of the three main parties, to note the principal occasions on which they crossed each other's paths, and how in the final result each managed to frustrate the hopes of the others. In sum the three parties did the work of the British for them. During the half-century following 1740 between them they threw away Indian independence. In these years India defeated herself.

The first of the three was the Persians and Afghans. Nādir Shah captured and sacked Delhi early in 1739 and returned to Persia laden with loot equal to three years revenue as well as the treasure of the Peacock Throne. But disappointment dogged his footsteps from this time forward; his temper soured to vindictiveness and finally crossed the verge of insanity. When he was assassinated in 1747 he was the most hated man of his age. His death was the signal for the break-up of Persia. The troubles began which ended with the emergence of the *Kajar* dynasty; the ever-turbulent Afghans broke away to form a new succession state. Henceforth the Afghan thread replaces the Persian in the woof of the Indian tapestry. The net result of Nādir Shah's incursion into India was the permanent loss of Kabul.

The Afghans found a leader of genius in Ahmad Shah Abdali. He would have remained the ruler of a vigorous people in a barren country but for one of the periodical eras of political confusion in the Indian plains. Like Babur in the last period of the kind, he had the ability t conquer, but unlike Babur he lacked the political sagacity and the skilful agents to make good his conquest. Babur had adventurers from Persia and Turkistan to draw on as well as Afghan chiefs. For the most part they were untroubled by fanaticism and used to dealing with diverse people and creeds. The Mughuls were 'kings by profession' and their officers imperialists by instinct; the Afghans were turbulent and fanatical hillmen who knew how to conquer but not how to conciliate. They could die for a cause, but not compromise for it. Ahmad Shah's first attempt on the empire failed at Sirhind in 1748. If the Mughul empire had continued to be vigorous, no more would have been heard of him east of the Indus. But the Emperor Muhammad Shah died the same year to be succeeded by his son Ahmad Shah. Under his nerveless control Delhi dissensions revived and Ahmad Shah Abdali was not slow to take advantage of them. In 1749 he again appeared, but was bought off by the governor of Lahore. In 1751-2 he appeared again and captured Lahore after a four months' siege. This time the imperial government itself bought him off by the session of the Panjab and Multan. By 1756 the empire was further weakened by civil war and political assassinations. This time Ahmad Shah took and sacked Delhi and appointed the Rohilla chief Najib Khan (entitled Najib-ud-daula) as the guardian of the new emperor. The local forces then rallied and called in the Hindu world from the Deccan to redress the balance of the Muslim world in the north. Ahmad Shah entered India for the fifth time in 1759 and found himself confronted not so much with the Mughuls as with the resurgent power of the Hindus represented by the Marathas. The moves and counter-moves of the next eighteen months culminated in the battle of Panipat on 14 January 1761. By skilful movements Ahmad had cut off the Maratha forces from their base in the south and compelled them to fight when depressed by inaction and starved of supplies. The resounding victory which he gained appeared to lay Hindustan at his feet. The Marathas were scattered and confounded, the surviving Mughul chiefs divided and of little power, the English Company still distant in Bengal. But at this moment his troops clamoured for arrears of pay and a return to Kabul. They lacked the tenacity of Babur's Mughul *begs* and Hindustan the wealth which had existed in Babur's day. There is nothing more eloquent of the enfeebled state of the empire than that Afghans should return to their hills because Delhi could not provide them with pay. Ahmad Shah was compelled to lay aside the sceptre within his grasp, saving his face by the nomination of Shah Alam as a vassal emperor and of Najib-ud-daula as his minister. In fact he had abdicated the empire; his Indian territories were henceforth confined to the Panjab and Sind. He never returned to Delhi and his own kingdom was to break up in its turn within half a century.

In 1740 the Mughul empire had emerged from the shock of Nādir Shah's expedition apparently almost unabated in size and dignity, like a whale surfacing with undiminished bulk after some stunning blow. The Emperor Muhammad Shah still sat on his throne, the Mughul authority was accepted as legitimate throughout India except by the Marathas, and half accepted even by them. The courtiers bowed and the trumpets blew. The internal injuries sustained by recent shocks remained largely concealed, and for a few years a deceptive calm prevailed in Indian affairs. The attempt to recover Malwa failed, but the Marathas were repulsed from Bengal by Alivardi Khan. The northwest, except Kabul, remained intact, the Nizam was firmly entrenched in the Deccan. A number of provincial governors were even induced to pay visits of respect to Delhi. This calm ended with the repulse of the Afghans and Muhammad Shah's death in 1748. Though lacking in courage, energy, and decision he had a certain subtlety combined with a sense of dignity, and a certain persistence running through his vacillations which raised him above the level of a puppet. But his son Ahmad had neither dignity nor sense. The result was a series of internal commotions which ruined the empire.

The Wazir Qamr-ud-din Khan had been killed at Sirhind and the

Nizam-ul Mulk died at Burhanpur within a few months of Muhammad Shah. The stage was thus cleared for new characters. They were younger, more vigorous, and no less able, but lacking in their elders' discretion and sense of obligation to the imperial idea. The new Wazir was Safdar Jang, the governor of Oudh since his father-in-law's death in 1739. He disposed of offices without reference to the emperor, who retorted, with the encouragement of his queen, by forming a court party headed by the eunuch Javid Khan. Javid Khan was assassinated and the emperor then turned to a young grandson of the old Nizam, Ghazi-ud-din, Imad-ul-Mulk. Imad-ul-Mulk was a youth of eighteen of great bravery and remarkable talents but devoid of scruple, principle, or direction. In the hands of this desperate pilot the empire finally foundered. In 1753 Imad succeeded in ousting Safdar from Delhi after a six months' war in which old Delhi,[1] then more populous than Shah-jahanabad, was ruined. Within a few months he fell out with the emperor, deposed and blinded him, and raised the elderly son of Jahandar Shah to the throne with the title of Alamgir II. The new sovereign was devout and serious minded but quite unused to public affairs, so that Imad-ul-Mulk was in complete control.

Having thus secured himself in power the minister turned his thoughts to restoring the imperial fortunes. An attempt to recover the Panjab on Ahmad Shah Abdali's fourth invasion of India culminated in the sack of Delhi in January 1757. Imad-ul-Mulk had already called in the Marathas during his struggle with Safdar Jang; he now called them in again against Ahmad Shah. From this moment they became principals in north Indian power politics. It was their forces which recovered Lahore in 1759 and their armies which faced Ahmad Shah on his fifth return to India. Imad-ul-Mulk, who had forfeited all trust by his deceit and all respect by his violence, became a puppet in his turn. His eclipse in public esteem was completed by the murder of the blameless Alamgir in 1759. His son, Ali Gauhar, had escaped a similar fate by flight from Delhi the year before. When Ahmad Shah retired from Delhi after Panipat, his supporter the Rohilla chief Najib-ud-daula secured control of Delhi and Imad-ul-Mulk disappeared into obscurity.[2]

In this welter of conflict, massacre, and bad faith the empire ended as an effective power. It continued to provide a legal framework for Indian politics and as an idea lasted on to the Mutiny. But though the Mughul *raj* was over, a Mughul state in the Delhi district persisted for another quarter of a century. It is conveniently distinguished from the old empire by the name of the kingdom of Delhi. The Delhi rulers retained the imperial forms and customs, but they were essentially local princes with limited horizons. The kingdom had its ups and downs and at times was comparatively formidable. It virtually ended as an independent power with the advent of Sindia in 1785, though its extinction is usually dated from the blinding of Shah Alam in 1788.

[1] i.e. the city stretching from the Delhi Gate to the Purana Qila.
[2] He is said to have died in 1800.

Najib-ud-daula ruled Delhi from 1761 to 1770. In theory he was the deputy of both Ahmad Shah and the new emperor Shah Alam; though he never broke with either, he was in practice an independent princeling. The disappearance of Ahmad Shah on the one hand and the exhaustion of the Marathas on the other provided him with an opportunity of which he made full use. He was harassed by Sikh forays in the north and Jat insurgence in the south; he was strong enough to defeat but not to subdue either. His death was followed by Shah Alam's return to Delhi and the rule of the Persian adventurer Mirza Najaf Khan. Shah Alam was crowned emperor in 1759 while a fugitive in Bihar. Though by no means brilliant he was the most talented and personable of the later Mughul emperors and in happier times he might have had a prosperous reign. The French adventurer Jean Law, who knew him well, thus described him.[1]

The *Shahzada* passed for one of those who have had the best education and who have most profited by it. This education consists particularly in the knowledge of religion; of the Oriental tongues, and of history, and in the writing of one's academic exercises well. In effect, all that I could perceive decided in his favour. He is familiar with the Arabic, Persian, Turki, and Hindustani languages. He loves reading and never passes a day without employing some hours in it. . . . He is of an enquiring mind, naturally gay and free in his private society, where he frequently admits his principal military officers in whom he has confidence.

For several years Shah Alam endeavoured to make imperial bricks without the straws of money or loyalty by borrowing troops with which to assert his authority over his nominal lieutenants. His attempt to recover Bengal with the help of Shuja-ud-daula of Oudh (the successor of Safdar Jang) was finally foiled in 1764 at Baksar. There followed the settlement with Clive by which he obtained control of Kora and Allahabad and some tribute from Bengal. The death of Najib in 1770 compelled him to choose between permanent seclusion in Allahabad under British protection or a last attempt to restore the imperial fortunes with all its attendant risks. His decision to return to Delhi was inconvenient to the British but creditable to his honour and spirit. Because the Company would not assist his project he accepted Maratha aid and in consequence lost his foothold down country. But the prophesied Maratha tutelage did not occur. That was mainly due to the ability of Mirza Najaf Khan who was the effective ruler of the Delhi kingdom from Shah Alam's return in January 1772 until his own death ten years later. The Sikhs were repulsed, the Jats suppressed, Agra recovered, and the Marathas held at arm's length. At his death he controlled a broad band of territory stretching from the Sutlej to the Chambal and from Jaipur to the Ganges.

Najaf Khan's death in 1782 coincided with a famine comparable with the Bengal famine of 1770. One-third of the rural population is said to have perished and the country had not fully recovered at the

[1] J. Law, *Mémoire sur l'empire mogul*, p. 329.

time of Fortescue's revenue report on the Delhi territory in 1820. The misery and poverty thus created encouraged a renewal of dissension and there was now no capable leader left on whom the emperor could lean. In 1785 Mahadji Sindia was invited to Delhi and his position legalized with the title of deputy *Vakil-i-Mutlaq* or Regent of the Empire. In 1787 Sindia's defeat at Lalsont in Rajputana weakened his hold on the north and before he could recover the Rohilla Ghulam Qadir (grandson of Najib-ud-daula) had seized Delhi and blinded Shah Alam in a fit of frenzied frustration at his failure to find expected treasure in the palace. The deed excited general horror throughout India. Ghulam was defeated and executed by Sindia and the emperor restored. He lived to welcome the British in 1803, but henceforward he was a pensionary, pitied, respected, and disregarded. The Delhi kingdom became a Maratha province.

The only other centre of political power in the north was Oudh. Failing in his attempt to take Bengal under imperial cover, Shuja-ud-daula turned to the Company from whom he obtained Allahabad by purchase and with whose help he subdued he Rohillas. But the price of this act and of security from the Marathas was a British brigade stationed on the borders of his dominions, with the result that Oudh passed into the orbit of the new political system now developing in Bengal. In the rest of north-west India there was no defined power at all. Sind recognized the Afghan supremacy and Gujarat, like Malwa, was under Maratha control. The collection of Rajput states no longer acknowledged Mughul supremacy, but remained disunited, disorganized, and distracted by Maratha interference. The Panjab gradually slipped from the erratic Afghan grasp to become a prey to war bands led by robber chiefs. The most prominent of these were the Sikhs, now relieved from Mughul menace and Afghan threat. The Panjab anarchy paved the way for the rise of the later states and prepared the way for Ranjit Singh.

The third of the contending claimants for the *masnad* of India now demands our attention. The Marathas have usually been regarded as more vigorous, more capable, and more united than the Mughuls in the eighteenth century. It is certain that they were much more vigorous, and that they produced many leaders of the highest ability. But their fate and that of India would have been very different if they had possessed even a modicum of unity. They equalled their competitors in courage and ability, and surpassed them in the possession of something like national spirit, but in ability to work together and to subordinate ambition to the common weal they were no better than the late Mughul or adventuring Afghan. They had the great handicap of lacking imperial tradition. What little they had came from their own recent experience or was borrowed from their opponents. Sivājī gave them a pattern of military glory and fearless patriotism but no code of imperial conduct. Shāhū's long residence at Aurangzeb's court introduced some tincture of Mughul manners, but not political conceptions in the grand

manner. In the early eighteenth century the Marathas faced the opportunities of empire building with the minds of raiders; when they took
to the business in earnest a generation later these efforts were stultified
by the desire of each part to be greater than the whole.

Sivājī had left a compact kingdom which had won its independence
and levied contributions on the surrounding districts. In the next
twenty years the fight for independence was converted into a struggle
for existence. This epic struggle included a feat comparable to that of
the Chinese communists in the thirties, that of the traversing of hostile
provinces and the founding of a fresh centre of resistance at Gingi in
the Carnatic. Emphasis has usually been laid on the Maratha feat of
breaking the back of Aurangzeb's empire; it should not be forgotten
that Aurangzeb on his side achieved the extinction of Sivājī's compact
and well-organized kingdom. The loose organization, the wide discretion of lieutenants, and the widespreading movements of the
leaders which this struggle made necessary permanently changed the
nature of the Maratha polity. The loose, self-destructive confederacy
of later days was born of the indomitable wanderings of the Maratha
chiefs in the last years of the seventeenth century. The unitary political
principle was then lost; what remained was a bounding energy and
enterprise and brilliant local leadership. For Sivājī guerilla warfare and
chauth or blackmail levies was a tactic; for his successors a rule of life.
The Marathas became the land Vikings of India without ever quite
equalling the constructive achievement of the Norman kingdoms.
Aurangzeb achieved his final triumph nearly a hundred years after his
death when the Maratha confederacy collapsed through its own dissensions.

The period after 1707 which saw the revival of the Maratha kingdom
also saw the rise of the Maratha prime ministers or Peshwas. Raja
Shāhū reigned until 1749 and was never a cipher in the government.
But he had spent his youth as a Mughul hostage, and what he had
acquired in taste he had lost in energy. He was one of those rulers like
Charles VII or Louis XIII of France who lack the vigour to govern
themselves but possess the wisdom to choose and maintain those who
can. A remarkable Chitpavan Brahman family performed the service
with such success that the imperial sceptre seemed for a time to be
within their grasp. Bālājī Vishvanāth, the founder of the family,
rescued Shāhū from his enemies and restored order within Maharashtra itself. His son Baji Rao I turned his face northwards. The father
had obtained the *chauth* of the six Deccan provinces; the son obtained
the outright cession of Malwa in 1738 after a series of successful campaigns and a daring raid to the gates of Delhi. A foothold was secured
in Gujarat. During this period the chiefs whose families later broke up
and in some cases survived the Maratha empire first distinguished
themselves. Malhar Rao Holkar and Ranoji Sindia were prominent in
Malwa, Damaji Gaekwar in Gujarat, and Raghujī Bhonsla in Berar.

Baji Rao died in 1740 at the early age of forty-two, but his son succeeded to his office and proved equally able. Under him the Maratha power reached its zenith. It became an empire *within* India and bade fair to become the empire *of* India. Yet the sprouting of the first seeds of disintegration could already be seen in the antagonism of Bālājī and Raghujī Bhonsla of Berar. Raghujī invaded Bengal and actually annexed Orissa in 1751. But the larger prize eluded him not only because of the vigorous resistance of Alivardi Khan but also because of a Maratha threat in his rear. Bālājī's plans were interrupted by the death of Raja Shāhū in 1749. He had never approved of the policy of northward expansion at the expense of the Mughuls, whose vassal he always believed himself to be. His removal was a gain to Maratha imperialism, but it also involved succession questions which delayed expansion. Bālājī turned for a time to the Deccan, now lacking the strong hand of the Nizam, and to the Carnatic where confused politics invited interference. But Bussy upheld the feeble hands of the Nizam Salabat Jang so that his efforts in that quarter were indecisive. It was in the north that a dramatic opening came. First Safdar Jang invited Maratha help against the Bangash Afghans who had invaded Oudh. The Afghans were defeated and Rohilkhund occupied. Then Imad-ul-Mulk invited their help against Safdar Jang in 1753. Their assistance was the decisive factor in the civil war of that year. When Ahmad Shah sacked Delhi early in 1757 Imad called them in again. Ragunath Rao occupied Lahore in 1758. The Poona court was intoxicated with expansionist dreams and there was talk of 'flying over the walls of Attock'. The Abdali's *riposte* came in 1759–60 when he drove the Maratha army with loss into Rajputana and once more occupied Delhi. Maratha honour as well as imperialism was now engaged and the die was cast for the Panipat campaign. The finest armament ever collected by the Marathas was dispatched under the Peshwa's uncle Sadāshiv Rao, known as the Bhao Sahib, the victor of Udgir over the Nizam.

The battle of Panipat on 14 January 1761 was not only a defeat but a catastrophe for the Maratha cause. The Peshwa's eldest son and heir, the Bhao Sahib, and all the leading chiefs were killed. The Peshwa himself died of vexation within six months. Outwardly the Marathas soon appeared to recover themselves. The young Peshwa soon asserted himself and proved that he possessed his father's ability; by 1767 Maratha troops were again across the Chambal. But the Peshwa's power had been dealt a blow from which it never recovered. From this moment the tendency of military chiefs to become territorial magnates became too strong to be resisted. Dissensions at Poona increasingly palsied the central direction, while imperial ambitions grew apace among the generals. At the moment when one of them, Mahadji Sindia, proved stronger than the rest and fit to rule, he died prematurely in 1794. It was against this background that the Marathas collided with the nascent British power in western India.

From 1761 there are two main themes in Maratha affairs. The first is the disintegration of authority at Poona. The young Madhu Rao I proved his ability and for a time, with the help of Nana Fadnavis, succeeded in maintaining central control. His early death in 1772 reopened intrigues for the succession which brought in the Company's intervention. The two leading figures were Raghunath Rao (Raghoba) and Nana. But even after Raghunath had retired into obscurity Nana was never able to secure unquestioned power. Sindia had overcome him when he died; thereafter the new Peshwa Baji Rao II's erratic personality prevented any settled administration. There was thus never a strong government in Poona between the death of Madhu Rao Peshwa in 1772 and the treaty of Bassein thirty years later.

The second is that of the development of the Maratha succession states. The Gaekwar's family established themselves in Gujarat with their capital at Baroda. The Bhonslas similarly established themselves at Nagpur with a realm stretching to Orissa. Towards the north Holkar and Sindia at first shared and then disputed Maratha primacy. From 1761 to 1795 the Rani Ahalya Bai maintained a static and almost idyllic régime at Indore. With endless patience and infinite resource Mahadji Sindia built up a power for himself which dominated the north for a time and appeared to reanimate the Mughul skeleton by covering it with Maratha flesh. In addition to Maratha lieutenants, his instruments were mercenary troops, hired adventurers, and above all the disciplined batallions of the French officer de Boigne. In the seventies he emancipated himself from Poona. Thereafter, he used his trained troops as the decisive counters in his effort to become dominant in the Delhi kingdom and secure supremacy in Rajputana. Lalsont weakened his hold and led to Shah Alam's blinding, but he recovered and was stronger than before. His dominion stretched from the Sutlej to the Narbada: he was the recognized Mughul agent as deputy Regent of the Empire. But his ambition was still to control Poona, and in 1792 he marched thither to assert his claims against Holkar and Fadnavis in the Poona court. His death in 1794 left his dominions to the far less capable Daulat Rao, while his disciplined troops passed to the correspondingly inferior Perron. Thus by 1790 the Afghan power had withdrawn, the Mughul power had disintegrated, and the Maratha had split into fragments, the strongest and most promising of which was about to lose its leadership.

AUTHORITIES

THE *Siyar-ul-Mutaqherin*, particularly vols. i and iii, provides useful background. FRANCKLIN's *History of the Reign of Shah Aulum* (1798) is a near contemporary account. For the empire from 1707 to 1739, including Nādir Shah's invasion, W. IRVINE, *Later Mughuls* (2 vols., 1921–2), completed by Sir J. SARKAR, is authoritative. Sir J. SARKAR, *Fall of the Mughul Empire* (4 vols., 1932–50), carries the story with equal thoroughness to the British occupation of Delhi in 1803. H. G. KEENE, *Fall of the Mughul Empire* (1887) is a useful summary. T. G. P. SPEAR, *Twilight of the Mughuls* (1951) covers the Delhi kingdom and carries the Mughul story to 1858.

For the Afghan and Persian sides of the story the reader may consult Sir P. SYKES, *History of Persia* and *History of Afghanistan* (1920 and 1940).

The classic account of the Marathas is J. GRANT DUFF's *History of the Marathas*

(3 vols., 1826). A modern account is by C. A. KINCAID and D. B. PARASNIS, in their *History of the Maratha People* (3 vols., 1918–25, 1 vol., 1931). The latest study is by G. S. SARDESAI, *New History of the Marathas* (3 vols., 1946). There are valuable studies by M. G. RANADE, *Rise of the Maratha Power* (1900), now somewhat dated, and by G. S. SARDESAI in *Main Currents of Maratha History* (1926), an able book.

For European adventurers see H. COMPTON, *European Adventurers in Hindustan* (1892)

CHAPTER 4

The Maratha Polity

WE have seen that the Marathas rather than the Persians or Afghans were the successors of the Mughuls as the holders of imperial power. The Persian attempt proved to be nothing more than a high-sounding raid while the Afghans of Ahmad Shah Abdali lacked the resources to sustain and the genius to exploit their victory. The Maratha succession proved to be an abortive one, but they controlled a larger part of India for a longer period than anyone else during the Anglo-Mughul inter-regnum, and their contribution to the life of India should therefore be examined.

The rise of Sivājī has been dealt with in an earlier chapter;[1] here we are concerned with the Maratha administration. The whole Maratha movement is often conceived as a Hindu reaction against the encroaching Muslim power and it has therefore been assumed that the Maratha institutions also embodied this spirit. But while the Maratha spirit, fed by crusading sentiments and cemented by the *bhakti* movement with its emphasis on the unity of all men, was certainly an expression of a renascent and militant Hinduism, the institutions with which that spirit clothed itself were affected by the traditions and influences of the time and place. The student will therefore find the Maratha administrative framework by no means as wholly Hindu as the self-conscious militant Hinduism of Sivājī himself might suggest. The Marathas, ever realists, were willing to use anything which had proved itself useful and to borrow anything which appeared valuable from any quarter.

In the mid-seventeenth century there was a collapse of authority in western India from whose ruins the Maratha kingdom arose. The Nizam Shāhī realm of Ahmadnagar was absorbed into the Mughul empire in 1632, and the Bijapur kingdom showed signs of increasing weakness. The absence of central control permitted the tyranny of the petty chiefs or *watandars*; every man's hand was turned against every man. It was a period of treachery and rapine, when the blood feud flourished and chiefs were uncontrolled. Wolves prowled in Poona.

The people who lived in the Mawal valley were in many respects worse than wild beasts. The blood feud was the order of the day and rapine formed the normal state of things. Almost every *watan* had two or more claimants and they fought to the bitter end. In his blind fury the Maratha *watandar* felt no pity for his rival's widow and orphan children. But even the apparent destruction of the family would not bring the feud to an end. The loyalty of an old adherent would often save a pregnant lady or an infant heir in some village or mountain fastness far away from their native hamlet. The child

[1] Book VI, Chap. 6.

would never be allowed to forget the wrongs of his family. When grown up he was sure to avenge his dead relations and plundered house. The anarchy of the time has left its mark on the family papers of the old *deshmukhs* and nowhere do we get a more terrible account of these feuds in all their horrors and bloodshed than in the papers of the Jagdales of Masur and the Jedhes of Rohid-khore. The Jagdales could not even count on the fidelity of their own servants.[1]

Internally, therefore, the rise of Shāhjī and consolidation of his realm by Sivājī may be seen as the restoration of order out of chaos. The Maratha country was first rescued from anarchy and then organized into a compact and centralized kingdom. Sivājī's first care was to curb the power of the old police and revenue officers who had become hereditary and who were known as *deshmukhs* and *deshpandes*, or collectively as *mirasdars*. They were not destroyed but their rights and dues were defined and fixed while their duties were confided to new royal officials known as *karkuns*. Some of the forts of these local chiefs were destroyed and they subsided into the position of privileged spectators of the changing scene. On this basis Sivājī organized his kingdom. At the head stood the king with the eight chief officers of state or *Ashta Pradhan*. Sivājī's innovation here was to form them into an advisory council which can be compared more closely to the Tudor Privy Council than to the Viceroy's Executive Council or a modern cabinet. The chief minister was the Peshwa or *Mukhya Pradhan* who held the seal and was responsible for general administration. The council included the commander-in-chief (*Senapati*), the *Amatya* or *Mazumdar*, a sort of finance minister, the foreign secretary (*Sumanta*), the chief justice (*Nyayadhish*), and the chief religious officer (*Pandit rao*). These officers were directly dependent on the king in Sivājī's time, having no heredi-tary rights and no land grants or *jagirs* for their maintenance. They were assisted by a staff of secretaries who formed the nucleus of a state bureaucracy.

The three pillars of the traditional Indian state have always been the peasants who paid the land revenue, the main source of income, the administrators of justice and order, and the army which defended society. In revenue matters the country was divided into a number of districts or *prants* which, with their subdivisions may be compared to the Mughul *parganas* and *sarkars*. The general system of assessment was based on that of Malik Amber in Ahmadnagar who recognized four kinds of soil, fixed a permanent cash payment, and abolished revenue farmers in favour of direct dealings between the district offi-cers and the village headman or *patels*. Sivājī added an accurate survey which was carried out by Annaji in 1678, the abolition of many small local cesses or duties, and the encouragement of the settlement of waste land by various means. The peasant was cherished by the state: 'he knew what he had to pay and he seems to have been able to pay without any great oppression'.[2] Order and justice were left in the

---

[1] S. N. Sen, *Administrative System of the Marathas*, 2nd ed., pp. 29–30.
[2] Kennedy, *History of the Great Mughuls*, vol. ii, p. 125.

villages to the village officers and panchayats. All civil suits were decided by this means, while criminal matters were dealt with by the royal officers. In the towns justice was administered by the *Nyayadhish*, the Maratha equivalent of the Mughul *Qazi*. The army had both stationary and mobile departments. The former comprised the hill-forts, of which there were about 240, with an average garrison of 500. They could not have all been fully garrisoned at one time and many must have normally had mere token forces. But collectively they formed storehouses in time of peace, refuges in case of invasion, and an ensurance against surprise. They were the core of the Maratha defence and proved themselves against Aurangzeb. For their maintenance Sivājī devised an ingenious mixture of classes, placing a Maratha *havaldar* in charge of the gates, a Brahman *sabnis* in charge of the accounts and muster roll, and a Prabhu *karkun* in charge of the stores. The mobile army consisted first of the feudal array of the *watandars*, an undependable and motley host; the essential portion, however, was the cavalry (*bargiri*) and infantry directly maintained by the state. They were carefully graded and grouped and controlled with a strictness which was remarkable for the times. In addition there was the *silahdar* cavalry whose members provided their own horses and arms, a sort of yeoman horse, and the freebooters who were allowed to attach themselves to any expedition, whose Marathi name was *pendhara*, and who were the forerunners of the later dreaded Pindaris.

Land was classed in Maratha eyes as *swarajya*, or homeland under direct rule, which was organized into sixteen districts, and *moglai* or land under alien, generally Mughul rule. Like the early Islamic distinction between *dar-ul-Islam* and *dar-ul-harb*, this latter was legitimate prey. Here could be levied the two exactions known as *sardesh-mukhi* and *chauth*. *Sardeshmukhi* was a levy of a tenth of the revenue assessment claimed on the legal fiction that Sivājī was *Sardeshmukh* or overlord. *Chauth* was a levy of one-fourth of the revenue assessment as a fee for non-molestation. It was, says Dr. Sen, 'a tribute exacted from the weak by the strong'; it resembled danegeld more nearly than anything else in English experience.[1] Such distinctions could be made out and such claims put forward only in a region where political authority was weak and boundaries confused. These reveal the secret of Sivājī's financial success, for it was by these means that war was made to pay.

From this brief description we can proceed to consider the distinctive features of the new Maratha state. Compared with the complicated structure of Shahjahan's empire it is clear that it is simple and almost rudimentary. But it possessed several interesting features which were of significance for the future. The Maratha state was conceived in anarchy, born in war, and nurtured in conflict; there was therefore no

---

[1] Neither Dr. Sen nor Sir J. Sarkar agrees with Justice Ranade's claim that the payment of *chauth* implied a claim to protection from others besides the Marathas. In later days it did not even ensure the payer against rival Maratha armies.

time for neat ideological constructions. It is therefore not surprising to find that for all the conscious Hindu revivalism associated with Sivājī, Maratha institutions were very mixed in origin. We have seen that while the village organization was traditional the land revenue system was largely borrowed from Malik Amber's practice in Ahmadnagar. The district officers and even the great officers of state resemble their Mughul counterparts, and the Sanskritic title of even the first minister could not prevail against the more popular designation of Peshwa. Maratha institutions were never wholly Hindu and cannot be represented as a revival of the Hindu past against an intrusive Muslim present. The mixture of ideas was illustrated in the symbolism at Sivājī's coronation in 1674.

The coverings of the royal seat were a grotesque combination of ancient Hindu asceticism and modern Mughul luxury: tiger skin below and velvet on top. On the two sides of the throne various emblems of royalty and government were hung from gilded lanceheads. On the right stood two large fish-heads of gold with very big teeth and on the left several horses' tails (the insignia of royalty among the Turks) and a pair of gold scales, evenly balanced, (the emblem of justice) on a very costly lancehead. All these were copied from the Mughul Court. At the palace gate were placed on either hand pitchers full of water covered with bunches of leaves, and also two young elephants and two beautiful horses, with gold bridles and rich trappings. These were auspicious tokens according to Hindu ideas.[1]

It next seems clear that the administration, if authoritarian in the pattern of the times, was paternal and efficient in the *swarajya* or home territory. It did not press too hardly on the people, and with its army and hill-forts was well adapted for defence. It also seems clear that the state was more than a personal monarchy of the usual type. There was a real attempt to integrate the classes and to invest the state with an ethos beyond that of personal loyalty to the sovereign. One sign of this was Sivājī's ingenious use of the principal communities in the garrisoning of the hill-forts. Another was his patronage of the *bhakti* cult, with its emphasis on the spiritual unity of all believers. But there was a limit to this process on account of the jealousies subsisting between the intellectual and privileged Brahman, the martial Maratha, and the sturdy Prabhu. An emotional bond was found in the pose of the patriotic and religious defence of the motherland against invasion and desecration. Sivājī was the defender of *desh* and *dharma*. A further motive was found in the appeal to greed implied in the policy of plundering raids and the exaction of *chauth* and *sardeshmukhi*. Events showed that these centripetal measures were not in themselves sufficient to hold the Maratha people together. More and more reliance was placed on what may be called expansionism, which diverted attention from inner tensions by external conquest.

But the sympathy which the religious aspect of the Maratha state might have drawn from Hindus was dissipated by the aspect of plunder

[1] Sir J. Sarkar, *Shivaji*, 2nd ed., pp. 248-9.

which was applied as ruthlessly to Hindus as to Muslims. The peaceful Bengali and the martial Rajput were equally subjected to it and equally welcomed deliverance from Maratha hands. This defect in the ideology of the Marathas condemned them to a provincialism in outlook which prevented them from rising to the level of their later opportunities. They could think imperially in military terms but not in terms of administration. They could guide and they could conquer, but they could not conciliate. The instinct to plunder was the internal defect as the failure to combine was the later external defect of the Maratha system.

When Sivājī died in 1680, the unitary state which he had created rapidly broke up. His son and successor Sambhājī led the way by disbanding the *Ashta Pradhan* Council. His capture and execution in 1689 completed the process, and for a number of years the Maratha state was precariously directed by Raja Ram from Gingi in the far south. It was the enduring result of Aurangzeb's Deccan campaigns to have broken beyond repair Sivājī's construction. When Shāhū occupied his grandfather's throne after the settlement with the emperor Bahadur Shah, there was a change both of sentiment and circumstances. Shāhū had been brought up in the Mughul court and accepted the Mughul claim to paramountcy. He was never happy in the role of Mughul rebel, held a *mansab* of 10,000, and was glad to regularize the conquest of Malwa by an imperial grant from Delhi. He dreamt no dreams of Hindu empire. On the other hand Sivājī's centralized machine had broken down so that Shāhū found himself largely in the hands of military chiefs basing their power on grants of land or *jagirs*. The Maratha monarchy might easily have broken up had not the situation been saved by the Bhat family who became the hereditary Peshwas and heads of the new Maratha state. The first step in the transition of power was taken in 1714 when Bālājī Vishvanāth Bhat was appointed Peshwa. At that time the Peshwa was inferior in status to the *Pant Pratinidhi*, whose office had been created by Raja Ram at Gingi. The next step was Shāhū's decision to expand northward (the Peshwa's proposal) rather than southward (the Pant Pratinidhi's proposal). The success of this policy consolidated the Peshwa's position as the leading minister and enabled the Bhat family to secure the hereditary succession to the office. A further factor was the brilliance of successive Peshwas through three generations and beyond the death of Shāhū. Finally Shāhū's lack of an heir, his distrust of his great-nephew Ram Raja, and his failing energy in his later years all contributed to the passing of authority from the house of Sivājī to the Peshwas. By 1750 the kingdom of Sivājī had become a confederacy headed by the Peshwa.

The nominal head of the new confederacy continued to be the descendant of Sivājī. But he now lived in straitened and undignified seclusion in Satara. He still gave robes of honour for the Peshwaship and other important offices, and enjoyed some public esteem, but he possessed no powers and depended on the Peshwa for the necessities of life. The real head was now the Peshwa, and in relation to him also a dualism speedily developed. He held his position in theory as deputy of the Raja of Satara, and in fact as controller of Maharashtra. To the old ministers and officers he was therefore but a *primus inter pares*, predominant by reason of superior might rather than right. This feeling lingered on until the end of Baji Rao II's reign. It provided a check on the Peshwa's power in Maharashtra, a check which left the later Peshwas almost helpless when they had lost control over their own subordinates like Sindia and Holkar. But to his own subordinates he was a superior and dictator. These subordinates were the officers who carried out the Maratha expansion northwards and eastwards under the Peshwa's direction. So long as he could retain control of them his power overshadowed that of the old title holders of the south. But they were, in fact, too successful. Long absences necessarily gave them independence of action while large acquisitions of territory gave them independent resources. Thus it was that the Sindias and Holkars, the Gaekwars and the Bhonslas gradually came to rival the Peshwa in power though they always recognized his superior status. The parting of the ways when, broadly speaking, the Peshwa may be said to have passed from the position of a director of a number of generals to that of the head of a military confederation of equal powers may be fixed at Panipat in 1761. Both the Peshwa's heir and cousin were killed and the Peshwa himself died of vexation at the news of the disaster. The revival brought about by Madho Rao I died away with the succession disputes which followed his death in 1772. Not only did the Peshwaship suffer a blow to its prestige from which it never recovered, but the Maratha armies were never the same. A hundred thousand Marathas were said to have perished in the battle. Henceforward the number of auxiliaries and mercenaries in the Maratha forces notably increased with a corresponding decline in Maratha cohesion and national spirit. Since they were paid for by local exactions of the Maratha chiefs the control of the distant Peshwa correspondingly decreased. Before 1761 we can say that in general the commanders of the Maratha armies in the north were agents of the Peshwa, though with a large degree of independence of action. After 1772 we can say that the northern generals were in fact independent chiefs, though still subjected to some interference from Poona and recognizing the Peshwa's nominal headship of the Maratha confederacy. The nature and extent of this process can be seen in the pains which Mahadji Sindia took to obtain Mughul confirmation for his territorial gains culminating in his appointment as deputy Regent of the Empire. Though he was careful to reserve the actual regency for the infant Peshwa the procedure clearly pointed to eventual freedom from Poona. If Aurangzeb shattered the hope of a centralized Maratha Hindu empire by breaking up Sivaji's kingdom, Ahmad Shah Abdali destroyed the prospect of an imperial Peshwaship. Mughul and Afghan between them turned the scale against a revived Hindu *raj*.

Another development which further undermined the already weakened Peshwaship was the organization by Sindia and Holkar of disciplined forces equipped with artillery and officered extensively by European adventurers. These forces were under no control from Poona; they gave their masters both independence of action in their chosen fields and also a decisive voice in the affairs of Poona itself. A final cause for the eclipse of the Peshwaship was a long minority which transferred power to a minister. Thus when we come to the time of Nana Fadnavis in the latter years of the eighteenth century we find that the royal deputy has himself a deputy, but that this deputy no longer owes his position so much to solid popular or military backing as to the diplomatic address with which he can play one party off against another. Instead of internal disputes being incidents in a united policy of action, common action such as that which led to the victory over the Nizam at Kharda in 1795 has become but an interlude in the internal struggle for power. Nor was it given to the Marathas to reach a decision in this last internal struggle. The most hopeful of the competitors, Mahadji Sindia, seemed about to gain control when he defeated Holkar in 1792. But his death in 1794 restored the balance. His successor was incapable and Holkar was unbalanced. Jaswant Rao Holkar's victory over the Peshwa in 1802 precipitated British intervention.

The early Peshwas were themselves aware of the danger of disintegration and endeavoured to avert it by a number of precautions. All *sanads* or grants were issued in Shāhū's name, thus emphasizing the subordination of all to the titular head of the state. A careful balance of power between the various chiefs was maintained by a judicious selection of both the amounts and locations of the various land grants. As far as possible a single chief was not given control of a solid block of territory. Control was also maintained over the distribution of *chauth* and *sardeshmukhi*. It was not appropriated by the collectors themselves, but divided between the Peshwa, the *Pant Pratinidhi*, and the *Pant Sachiv*. Distant generals were given land grants in the Swarajya or homeland which would be forfeit in case of disobedience. Audit officers from the central treasury travelled with the Maratha armies and the final accounts from all provinces had to be passed at Poona. These checks remained real so long as the Peshwas retained their energy and a formidable force of their own. After Panipat the observance of these rules became more and more formal until they finally died away altogether.

When we speak of the late Maratha administration we are thus really inquiring into the nature of the late Maratha constitution. Its imprecise nature makes it easy to assume either that the Peshwa was the effective head of a far-flung empire or that he was simply the leading member of a group of five independent powers. In fact it was only for short periods that he was either. When the peculiar nature of the late Maratha polity and of the Peshwa's position within it is realized, it will be seen that the only Maratha administration which was specially

Maratha in genius was that of the *swarajya* land in Maharashtra itself. The outlying territories were either merely subject to the exaction of *chauth* or were administered along traditional lines by the local Maratha rulers. Most of the chiefs were too busy expanding their territories to have time to invent new administrative systems, and in the north the Mughul tradition was too strong to give them much desire to do so. Mughul influence can be discerned in Maratha states as much as Maratha influence in former Mughul lands.

Within Maharashtra itself matters were, of course, different. We have Elphinstone's description of the administration of the Peshwa's territories as he observed it when resident in Poona in the time of Baji Rao, and surveyed it after 1818.[1] In general, the picture is not unlike that of Sivājī's time. The village communities flourished; the hereditary officers continued to be excluded from power though they retained their dues. The district officers were now called *mamlatdars*; there was the same system of check and balance between the officers of the Peshwa who possessed executive authority, and the hereditary officers, like the *deshmukhs* and *darakhdars* who held in effect watching briefs over their doings. There was the same jealousy on the part of the southern landholders who held themselves to be the equals of the Peshwa as direct feudatories of the Raja of Satara, and on whom the last Peshwa's hand fell heavily. But there was a large increase of the *jagir* system in payment for military services which meant the transfer of local administration from the Peshwa's agents to those of the *jagirdar*. Elphinstone held that the system worked well apart from the vagaries of Baji Rao II, and retained as much as he could of it for some years.

When we look at the Maratha political and administrative system as a whole we are constrained to admit that while this system in Maharashtra was both effective and reasonably benevolent, it was neither wholly Maratha or strikingly original, nor offered any serious alternative to the Mughul system at its best. Both based themselves on the village, both insisted on careful assessment and moderate collection and both employed a system of checks and balances. It was good of its kind without being revolutionary. The Maratha political system was vitiated by the division of authority, first between Raja and Peshwa, and then between the Peshwa and his generals. The Marathas lacked an imperial spirit because they were nurtured in defiance rather than imperial ambition and rose to greatness through guerilla tactics rather than regular warfare. These tactics imply inferiority and the Marathas never quite got over the feeling that they were temporary freebooters who must take what they could while they could. So the detested *chauth*, instead of being discarded in favour of regular methods as they rose to dominion, became an essential part of their system. If would-be imperialists behave as plunderers and robbers they cannot expect their *imperium* to

[1] M. Elphinstone, *Report on the Territories lately conquered from the Peishwa*, 22.

be popular. So it was with the Marathas. Their dominion passed unregretted from every part of India save Maharashtra. They have only been popular as the defenders of religious and civil liberty against the Muslim and the foreigner. The rest of India has preferred to admire this work from a distance. In Indian history as a whole Maratha rule proved to be a provincial round peg in an imperial square hole.

AUTHORITIES

THERE is much material not only in British India records but in the records of the Peshwa's *daftar* at Poona and other Marathi sources. Messrs. V. K. RAJWADE, D. B. PARASNIS, P. V. MAVJI, and G. C. WAD have published extensive but by no means exhaustive selections in Marathi and Sir G. W. FORREST in English. For details see the *Cambridge History of India*, vols. iv and v. In addition may be mentioned M. ELPHINSTONE, *Report . . . on the Peshwa's Territories* (1822), and R. JENKINS, *Report . . . on the Nagpur Territories* (1827).

Pioneer work in the administrative field was done by Justice M. G. RANADE. His three works, *Rise of the Maratha Power, Miscellaneous Writings,* and *Introduction to the Peshwa's diaries* (all Poona, 1900) are still valuable. The study which at present holds the field is S. N. SEN, *Administrative System of the Marathas* (1925). N. S. TAKAKHOV and K. A. KELUSKAR have a chapter on administration in their *Shivaji Maharaj* (1921) and there is a chapter by S. M. EDWARDES in the *Cambridge History of India*, vol. v, ch. 23.

CHAPTER 5

The Age of Hastings

THE years 1767–72 in Bengal were covered by the governorships of Verelst and Cartier. Their terms were marked by no administrative change save the appointment of 'Supervisors' of the revenue in 1769; they covered instead a gradual revival in more discreet forms of the abuses which Clive had sought to repress. But in the life of the province an epoch was marked by the famine of 1769–70. One-third of the population was said to have died and one-third of the cultivated lands to have become waste.[1]

The husbandmen sold their cattle; they sold their implements of agriculture; they devoured their seed grain; they sold their sons and their daughters, till at length no buyer of children could be found; they ate the leaves of trees and the grass of the field; and in June 1770 the Resident at the Durbar affirmed that the living were feeding on the dead. Day and night a torrent of famished and disease-stricken wretches poured into the great cities. At an early period of the year pestilence had broken out. In March we find smallpox at Moorshedabad, where it glided through the Viceregal mutes and cut off the Prince Syfut in his palace. Interment could not do its work quick enough, even the dogs and jackals, the public scavengers of the East, became unable to accomplish their revolting work, and the multitude of mangled and festering corpses at length threatened the existence of the citizens.[2]

The speculative buying of rice and its retail at high prices, in which Company's servants were thought to share, did not make matters better. In spite of the distress the revenue was collected with 'cruel severity'. Five per cent. only was remitted in 1770 and 10 per cent. added in the year following. It is against this background that must be set accounts of the splendour of Calcutta life in the seventies and of the frolics of Hickey and his friends just after. Shuja was not without insight when he declined to entertain any commercial treaty with Clive, preferring to deny himself the advantages of the lucrative Bengal trade.

The famine had several important effects. It meant that Bengal and Bihar, for the first time in centuries, were seriously underpopulated for two generations. It dealt a heavy blow at the whole social system. Many of the *zamindars*, or hereditary farmers of the revenue, were ruined as the result of inability to collect the regular assessments from a reduced and enfeebled peasantry. Hunter dates the ruin of two-thirds of the old aristocracy from this time.[3] The loss both of artisans and

---

[1] Sir W. W. Hunter, *Annals of Rural Bengal*, pp. 53–54; Letter from the President and Council to the Court of Directors, 3 Nov. 1772, para. 6.
[2] Ibid., p. 26. [3] Ibid., p. 57.

cultivators caused a steady decrease in the Company's profits and so hurried on the financial crisis of 1772 which led to state interference in the Company's affairs.

Warren Hastings became Governor of Bengal early in 1772. He was then not forty years old, and had first gone to India twenty-two years before. Unlike Clive, he had risen regularly up the rungs of the civilian ladder from the position of writer. In 1756 he became resident of Murshidabad and as a member of Vansittart's Council he had steadily opposed the policy of the majority. He was described by Lord North in 1773 as one who 'though of flesh and blood, had resisted the greatest temptations'. His hands were admitted to be clean, yet it was a striking commentary on the times that he could return to England at the age of thirty-two after fourteen years service with a fortune of £30,000. In 1769 he returned to India as second-in-council at Madras, where his good conduct earned him promotion to Bengal. He had shown skill, courage, and integrity but had as yet no sign of that enigmatic greatness which was to make him a standing puzzle and centre of controversy in Anglo-Indian history. His apparent task was the consolidation of the Company's rule in Bengal, and to this he looked forward with no sense of elation. But destiny had reserved for him a far greater one. It was the preservation of the British possessions from deadly danger without and bitter schism within. He found the Company a commercial corporation turned revenue farmer; he left it one of the great powers of the Indian sub-continent.

At first Hastings's course was clear. He found himself at the head of a council of twelve or thirteen and subject to a majority vote in all matters save foreign affairs which were controlled by himself and two others. But the mandate of the directors was definite, the mind of the new governor lucid and vigorous and his methods tactful and adroit, while the servants were now resigned to the idea of some regulation. Their tactic of opposition was circumvention rather than defiance. It thus came about that the first years of Hastings's administration ran more smoothly than any period since Plassey. The foundation was thus laid on which Hastings and British India were able to stand during the years of stress which followed.

The directorial instructions by which Hastings was guided included a large discretion of which he made full use. 'We now arm you with full powers', wrote the directors, 'to make a complete reformation.' His first care was to deal with the *diwani* or revenue administration. For seven years this had been carried on by Muhammad Reza Khan and Shitab Rai as deputies for the Company which was now the imperial diwan for Bengal and Bihar. These men were deposed and their offices abolished. The Company 'stood forth as diwan', and undertook the collection of the revenue by its own agents. In practice this meant the direct control of the whole civil administration, for civil justice went with tax collection. English collectors were appointed for each district, to be supervised by a Board of Revenue in Calcutta. A preliminary revenue settlement was made for five years, the lands being farmed out by public auction. This arrangement was far from perfect, but it at least provided a framework which could be improved with fuller knowledge. The new collectors at once stumbled on a major difficulty. This was to protect the *zamindar* from unreasonable government demands on the one hand, while protecting the cultivator from extortion by the *zamindars* on the other. The essence of the problem was the '*zamindars'* secret'—of the difference between the amount collected from the peasant by the *zamindar* and the amount actually paid by him to government. Hastings, whose genius did not lie in revenue matters, never probed this secret, and it took many years of trial and error before new methods elsewhere led to new systems. Along with the new collectorates were established a network of civil courts with an appeal court in Calcutta. These measures were rounded off by a number of others. The first was a reduction of the nawab's allowance from 32 to 15 *lakhs* a year.[1] This was a direct order from the Court, but it speaks much both for Hastings's management and previous conditions that under the new system the nawab actually received more for his personal expenses than he had done under the old. The second was the removal of the treasury from Murshidabad, where it had been controlled by juniors, to Calcutta, where it could be supervised by senior servants. Lastly the nawab's household was reorganized and placed in charge of Mir Jafar's widow, Munni Begam.

There remained the commercial reforms. The ghost of the *dastaks* or free passes for the goods of the Company's servants was finally laid by their abolition in 1773. The flow of trade was stimulated by the suppression of all custom houses except at the five main centres.[2] Duties on all goods except the monopolies of salt, betel-nut, and tobacco were lowered to a uniform $2\frac{1}{2}$ per cent. for Indian and European alike. By these measures trade was encouraged, unfair competition prevented, and extortion reduced.

Warren Hastings accomplished so much in less than three years that it is easy to claim that he accomplished all. If the reforms had really been complete the work of Cornwallis would not have been necessary. But men of the next generation like Malcolm and Elphinstone repudiated the standards of the seventies and eighties. In fact Hastings accomplished a great deal in a short space of time and beginning from a very low level. He showed what could be done by a determined and skilful man with steady support from home. But while his work marked the end of the period of the greatest abuses, it was only the beginning of really constructive administration. The emoluments of the Company's servants were as yet neither fixed nor certain; private trading and taking of presents continued under cover of outward conformity to rule. Commerce was not yet fully separated from administration. The new revenue and judicial systems were tentative and far from perfect.

---

[1] It was reduced from 53 to 41 *lakhs* in 1766 and to 32 in 1769.
[2] Calcutta, Hughli, Murshidabad, Patna, and Dacca.

Hastings himself, with his usual insight, compared his work at this period to an unfinished building. Another five years of constructive endeavour might indeed have made Cornwallis's mission superfluous. But as so often happens in public affairs time, the gipsy man, would not wait; instead Hastings had to face the Marathas without and Philip Francis within.

The herald of this confused and baffling period was the Regulating Act of 1773. The relations of the Company with the state will be considered separately;[1] it is only necessary for clarity here to explain the provisions which affected administration in India itself. The Act created the new post of Governor-General of Fort William in Bengal, and a council of four. The governor-general was given a superintending authority over the other two presidencies and thus Calcutta became the effective capital of British India. In addition the Crown was empowered to set up a Supreme Court of Justice in Calcutta, consisting of a chief justice and three judges. Liberal salaries were provided.[2] The first governor-general, Warren Hastings, and his four councillors were named in the Act to hold office for five years. The enhanced dignity of the head of the government, however, was not marked by any increase in authority. The governor-general had one vote in his council, and a casting vote in the event of a tie. The government was still the Governor-General *and* Council and not yet the Governor-General-*in*-Council.

Hastings's internal difficulties were the direct consequence of this Act. It will now be convenient to trace them briefly before considering his external policy and internal measures. The four councillors named in the Act were General Sir John Clavering, Colonel Monson, Philip Francis, and Richard Barwell. Only the last of these was a Company's servant and resident in India. His father had been governor of Bengal; he was a typical Company's servant and after some early suspicion became a regular supporter of Hastings. Clavering was an honest, passionate, and somewhat limited man subject to strong prejudices. Monson was more able and more controlled; he had served with credit for five years in southern India and his attitude was perhaps the most impressive of the four. Neither of these two would probably have embarked upon a permanent vendetta but for the wayward genius of the last member of the quartet, Philip Francis. With real gifts of character and eminent talents he possessed a vindictiveness of temper which the Bengal climate was only too likely to encourage, and strong opinions derived from recent Indian discussions in England; he was in Macaulay's words 'a man prone to mistake malevolence for public virtue'.[3] He went to Bengal convinced of the rottenness of the administration and openly hoping for the reversion of the governor-generalship

[1] Chap. 6.
[2] The governor-general, £25,000, councillors, £10,000, the chief justice, £8,000.
[3] Francis's authorship of the *Letters of Junius* has never been conclusively proved, but general literary consent ascribes them to him.

'which I believe to be the first station in the world attainable by a subject'. It was not surprising that such a council should be subject to dissensions. What made the contest memorable was the vindictive skill with which Francis achieved ascendancy over two colleagues in order to thwart the governor-general and the tempered tenacity and resource with which Hastings countered his efforts. Both sides would have been more than human if they had never fallen below the highest levels of conduct during the struggle, and both sides had their full share of humanity.

The three non-resident councillors arrived in Calcutta in October 1774, and immediately joined issue with their chief on the manner of their reception. For two years Hastings found himself steadily outvoted in his council and unable to use his casting vote. Many of his measures were reversed and a less resilient or more sensitive man would have broken down under the strain. But he held on grimly and it was the opposition which broke. In September 1776 Colonel Monson died; the bitter debates on every question continued, but the decision went with the governor-general's casting vote. Early in 1777 Hastings's agent in England, misinterpreting ambiguous instructions, reported his offer to resign. Clavering was appointed to succeed him, but Hastings repudiated his agent and was supported by the Supreme Court. The strain of this episode was perhaps too much for Clavering for he died in August of the same year. To Monson succeeded Wheler who at first generally voted with Francis, and to Clavering Sir Eyre Coote in 1779, who though difficult of temper, never fell under Francis's spell. An attempted accommodation in 1780 lead to a duel in which Francis was disabled, and shortly afterwards, disappointed in his ambition of becoming governor-general himself or at least of displacing Hastings, he returned to England. Hastings had regained general control from the time of Monson's death in 1776, but acrimonious debates with their strain and constant burden of anxiety continued until Francis actually left. Even then Hastings knew that his enmity would pursue him in England. It was thus only during the last five years of his governorship that Hastings experienced something like undisputed supremacy, and by that time he had grown too weary to enjoy it. He had come through the fire, but not unscathed by the flames. These facts should be remembered in judging Hastings's acts as a whole. The climax of the whole struggle was the case of Raja Nand Kumar. In March 1775 Nand Kumar accused Hastings of accepting a large bribe from Munni Begam in return for her appointment as guardian of the young Nawab Mubarak-ud-daula.[1] The charge was welcomed by the majority, who immediately resolved 'that there is no species of peculation from which the governor-general has thought it reasonable to abstain'. Hastings refused to meet his accuser in council and dissolved the meeting, whereupon the majority ordered him to repay the amount into the Company's treasury. Hastings now brought a charge of con-

[1] Rs. 354,105.

spiracy against Nand Kumar. While this was pending Nand Kumar was arrested at the instance of a Calcutta merchant on a charge of forgery unconnected with the previous controversy. He was tried before the new Supreme Court, found guilty, and executed. Thereafter the charges against Hastings were dropped and never revived.

This case has exercised the ingenuity of commentators ever since, and it is unlikely that a full explanation will ever be forthcoming. The one thing which seems certain is that there was a miscarriage of justice for which the blame cannot be fastened on any one man. Here we must confine ourselves to noticing a few salient points. Forgery was not a crime punishable by death in the current criminal law of Bengal derived from the Muslim code, and the application of English penalties in Indian cases was opposed to a well-established Indian legal tradition. The Supreme Court had not been six months in the country and possibly acted in ignorance of the prevalent opinion; thus far Nand Kumar was unfortunate. On the other hand the charge of forgery would have come up against Nand Kumar at the time it did even if he had preferred no charge against Hastings. It is at least arguable that Nand Kumar played the game of the majority as an insurance against the unknown risks of the Supreme Court. The majority failed to make any effort on Nand Kumar's behalf after his sentence, and callously watched him go to his death. The Supreme Court was a patently independent body as its later proceedings showed; in order to prove improper influence by Hastings it would be necessary to prove that he had tampered not only with Chief Justice Impey, but also with three other judges, or that the three judges were wholly subservient to Impey, which they were known not to be. There is no evidence that Hastings had anything to do with the case against Nand Kumar, on the one hand, and no sign of any magnanimous plea to the Court for a commutation of the death sentence to one of imprisonment on the other. There the matter must rest, a mystery to be solved only when the hidden motives of the chief actors are laid bare. Historically the incident is the supreme example of the absurdity and injustice of attempting to apply English legal methods to Indian conditions. The Supreme Court wished to impress on the Indian mind the seriousness of the crime of forgery; it actually very successfully convinced men that it was dangerous to attack the governor-general.

The new council was Hastings's major embarrassment, but the Supreme Court was also a cause for anxiety. The avowed purpose of the Court was to administer justice to the Company's servants and to deal with complaints against them. But the extent of its jurisdiction was undefined, its sense of dignity and its appetite for power robust, and its members quite impervious to the special conditions in which they had to work. In consequence the Court appeared arbitrary and unpredictable to Indian eyes, interfering and capricious to those of the Company's officers. Friction with the government culminated in the Patna case of 1777–9 and the Kassijura case of 1779–80. The council denied the jurisdiction of the court over the Raja of Kassijura and the court accused the council of contempt of court. Hastings attempted to break the deadlock by inducing Impey to accept the presidency of Sadr Diwani Adalat or Company's court of appeal. The device had great practical advantages, for it solved the problem of clashing jurisdictions and averted the danger of the establishment of a kind of administrative law over and above the accepted law of the land. But it involved contradictions and practical difficulties which the opponents of both men did not fail to point out. In 1782 Impey was recalled and left India the next year. An attempt to impeach him four years later broke down on the first charge. Impey was headstrong, obstinate, and unimaginative, but he was a man of integrity as well as ability. On Impey's side this episode was an honest attempt to mend evils largely caused by his own difficult temper. It is significant that though the double system was restored, there was never again enough friction to generate an equal amount of heat.

We may now turn to Hastings's foreign policy. His policy was throughout a defensive one. He was at first concerned with the defence of Bengal and Bihar. The Regulating Act made him responsible for the Company's dominions throughout India, and in that capacity he found himself saddled with conflicts with the Marathas in the west, and the Nizam and Mysore in the south, with whose inception he had nothing to do. The keynote of the Company's attitude was defensive; they were well aware that wars absorbed revenue and so reduced their annual investment. They were always ready to suspect their servants of hoping to enrich themselves with the spoils of conquered provinces. But the application of this policy involved two very real difficulties. The first arose from the confused state of Indian politics. Power was uncertain, jurisdiction undefined, and successions disputed all over India. The north lived under the shadow of a return of the Afghans. The emperor had nearly all of the rights and hardly any of the powers of government. Hyderabad, Mysore, and the Marathas had all been subject to disputed succession and civil commotion. At no point were the Company's boundaries clearly defined either by physical features or the presence of a stable power beyond the official line. It was therefore not possible to sit back and adopt a rigid policy of non-interference. There must be active concern in neighbours' affairs for fear of what the next-door-neighbour-but-one might do. The second difficulty was the complement of the first. The Indian rulers were quite as aware of their own insecurity as the Company itself. They had also as high an opinion of the Company's military prowess. The Company's aid was therefore the refuge of every state which thought itself threatened, or of any state nursing ambitious designs against a neighbour. The Company's concern in its neighbours' affairs was thus fully matched by the neighbours' interest in the disposition of the Company. The handling of such a situation without major commitments in Indian politics would have required all the talents of Hastings at his strongest and most clear sighted. In fact he had to cope with situations which others had created, superintend two unwilling presidencies, who were also subject to direct interference from London, and at a critical moment to face the complications of European war as well. On the whole Hastings must be given the credit not only for preserving British India intact in the face of difficulty and great peril, but also from refraining from further interference in the affairs of the Indian states.

Until late 1774 Hastings was only responsible for Bengal and Bihar. Clive's settlement of 1765, by which Shuja-ud-daula of Oudh and Shah Alam at Allahabad were the twin buffers to absorb the shocks of possible Afghan and Maratha collisions, had worked well for five years. No Afghan appeared and the Marathas were recovering from Panipat. In 1769, however, the Marathas recrossed the Narbada. Two years later they induced Shah Alam to return under their protection to Delhi, where the death of Najib-ud-daula had produced a political vacuum. The price was the cession of Kora and Allahabad. This imperial action, while justifiable from Shah Alam's point of view,[1] exposed Oudh to Maratha raids and uncovered the flank of the Company. The Marathas immediately raided Rohilkhand, whose ruler Hafiz Rahmat Khan applied to Shuja-ud-daula for help. Thus Hastings found himself both threatened with the passing of a key fortress out of friendly hands, and asked for help by an ally who was himself being importuned by a state threatened by the common enemy of all three. At a stroke the Company's interests were extended to a point 800 miles from Calcutta. Out of this situation grew the Rohilla war of 1774.

Rohilkhand was a fertile tract lying to the north-west of Oudh between the Ganges and the Kumaon hills. Its population was mainly Hindu, but since 1740 it had been overrun and now was ruled by migrant Afghans of the Rohilla tribe and Pathans who had originally quitted their homeland before the sword of Nādir Shah. Shuja-ud-daula agreed in 1772 to assist the Rohillas if attacked by the Marathas in return for a payment of 40 *lakhs*. The next year the Marathas returned, were faced by the nawab supported by a British brigade, and retired. The Rohillas then evaded payment. In September 1773 Hastings concluded the treaty of Benares with Shuja. Allahabad and Kora were ceded to him in return for a payment of 50 *lakhs* of rupees; in addition over 2 *lakhs* a month were to be paid for the British brigade when used in the defence of the nawab's territories. A secret article pledged the use of the brigade against the Rohillas, when called on, in return for another 40 *lakhs*. At the same time the payment of the emperor's subsidy or tribute was formally stopped.[2] The following February the call came. The Rohillas were overthrown at Miranpur Katra, and their dominions incorporated with Oudh, except for a fragment which was allowed to survive at Rampur. Hastings's object was to increase his security by augmenting the buffer state of Oudh, whose

---

[1] T. G. P. Spear, *Twilight of the Mughuls*, pp. 18–19.
[2] Twenty-six *lakhs* a year. It had not actually been paid since 1770.

control was secured by the presence of a British brigade. Shuja-ud-daula was anxious to exploit the Company's support to increase his dominions; between the two motives the Rohillas were sacrificed. A further financial motive on the part of Hastings is clearly visible; in one year he obtained more than a *crore* of rupees (£1,125,000) for the Company's treasury. In remedying the threatened loss of Allahabad Hastings showed courage and resource. The emperor could not complain of the loss of payments from a power whose gift of a province he had offered to an enemy. In strengthening Oudh he was again on firm ground. There remains the support of Shuja against the Rohillas with whom the Company had no quarrel. This proved to be one of the principal indictments against Hastings at his impeachment. Here it is sufficient to say that whatever the merits of the case, it was no more high handed than some of the acts of Wellesley or some of the later proceedings in Sind. It was not so much the act as the actor which made the Rohilla war a *cause célèbre* of Anglo-Indian history. We may here complete the story of Hastings's political dealings with Oudh by noting the transfer of Benares from Oudh to the Company by the council majority in 1775.

Hastings had next to deal with the far more complicated question of the Marathas in western India. Here he had to reckon with the intractable temper of the Bombay Council and the unpredictable twists of Maratha internal politics. Bombay and Madras approved of every part of the Regulating Act except that which concerned themselves, the superintendence of Calcutta. They also retained the right of direct correspondence with London so that, in the not improbable event of disagreement with Calcutta, they had, as it were, a private wire to the directors by which they could state their case. The other element in the situation was the divisions in the Maratha camp, where the tortuous intrigues of Poona were only matched by the shifts and balancings of the commanders in the field. Maratha power had seemed, in the fifties, to be sweeping forward to fill the vacuum being created by the steady ebb of Mughul vigour. The dream was ended at Panipat in 1761, where the flower of the Maratha array with its leader, the Peshwa's uncle, went down before the Afghan Ahmad Shah, and after which the Peshwa himself died of vexation in June. His son was a minor, and from the disputes which ensued sprang directly the conditions which led to British intervention. The decade which followed saw the young Peshwa's rise to manhood, his assertion of independent power at Poona, and consequent dismissal of his uncle Raghunath Rao (popularly known as Raghoba),[1] and the rise of Nana Fadnavis,[2] chief accountant from 1763. Under his vigorous lead the Marathas recrossed the Chambal in 1769; but three years later he died, confiding his brother Narayan Rao to the care of Raghunath. Within two years

[1] In Indian circles he was usually referred to as Dada Sahib.
[2] His real name was Balaji Janardhan. *Phadnavis* or *Fadnavis* was the title of his office.

Narayan had been murdered and Raghunath had been driven from Poona by a council of regency acting in the name of Narayan's posthumous son. Raghunath was a brave but ill-advised and unlucky man; it was his misfortune that his star came into conjunction at this moment with that of the Regulating Act. On his expulsion from Poona Raghunath turned for support to the British in Bombay. The Bombay Council, without considering their obligations to Calcutta, demanded Salsette and Bassein as the price of support. They were refused, but they nevertheless seized Salsette on the rumour of Portuguese action. In March 1775 the council concluded the treaty of Surat with Raghunath, by which they promised 2,500 English troops to restore Raghunath to Poona in return for Salsette and Bassein, the expenses of the campaign with 6 *lakhs* in addition, and a promise to refrain from raids in Bengal and the Carnatic.

At this stage the Calcutta Council interfered. With unwonted harmony they united in condemning the Bombay action. But the majority then ordered the withdrawal of the forces which had already gained some success, while Hastings, with perhaps some fellow-feeling for the man on the spot, was in favour of recognizing the *fait accompli*. Colonel Upton was sent to make a settlement. In 1776 the Surat treaty was replaced by the treaty of Purandhar by which peace was restored on the payment of 12 *lakhs* with the retention of Salsette; the cause of Raghunath was abandoned, and he himself pensioned. Again interference occurred, this time from London. The directors, in spite of all their censures of interference with weak states, now advocated intervention in a strong one. Hastings was authorized to revive the Surat treaty and in 1778 used his casting vote to sanction a fresh patronage of Raghunath. For this error of judgement Hastings paid dearly in four years of inconclusive war at a time when the British power in India was about to be tested to its utmost. An overconfident march towards Poona ended in the envelopment of the army and the disgraceful convention of Wadgaon (13 January 1779). The price of retreat was the restoration of all conquests, the stopping of the Bengal force, and the handing over of all hostages. Carnac and Cockburn had, of course, no power to agree to such terms. They were repudiated and the war went on, but the British never recovered from its effects. The war continued to the end an affair of shifts and turns lacking an overall plan and any competent direction.

At the start Hastings had dispatched a force (under Leslie, later succeeded by Goddard) which was to march across central India and provide the decisive factor in the campaign.[1] It arrived in Surat in February 1779 after a brilliant march. But the feats which win fame do not always win wars. One month earlier Wadgaon had crippled the power and ruined the prestige of Bombay. Goddard's force proved to

---

[1] This was less hazardous than might appear at first sight. The road was open to Allahabad, and thence the route lay through the dominions of the Bhonsla who was friendly to the British.

be a makeweight to restore the balance instead of the decisive factor in the campaign. The war dragged on for two more years, with military action and diplomacy interwoven in almost equal proportions. Goddard was successful in Gujarat, but his attempted march on Poona was repulsed with heavy loss. Popham's escalade of Gwalior was an episode of brilliance rather than decision. But in the course of 1781 Madhu Rao Sindia made peace after suffering defeat. He now acted as an intermediary with Nana, having his own views about the future of the Poona government. The treaty of Salbai, in May 1782, ended the unhappy war. The Peshwa pensioned Raghunath, the Gaekwar's lands in Gujarat and Sindia's west of the Jumna were restored, together with all territories occupied since the treaty of Purandhar. In other words Salsette was the sole dividend of eight years of war and diplomacy which began by an aggressive interference in Indian politics on the part of the Bombay Council. In this mingled frustration and impolicy too many took part for it to be possible to fix the full responsibility. The Bombay Council, with their gratuitous support of a Maratha political refugee and their ineffective measures, must perhaps bear the chief burden of blame. The directors added contradictory instructions and various soldiers military blunders. Hastings's contribution was an error of judgement in sanctioning a renewal of the war, and thereafter measures like the dispatch of Goddard's and Popham's forces, and much skilful diplomacy in dividing his foes, which restored the fortunes of the day. Events in India at this time cannot be judged from the importance attached to them in public discussions in England. Prejudice, financial interest, *amour propre*, and party spirit combined to focus attention on some periods and places to the exclusion of others equally worthy of attention. Thus Bengal affairs were much more canvassed than those of Madras where comparable conditions continued for longer, and the Rohilla war excited far greater criticism than the Maratha, which lasted many times as long and was begun less excusably. The historian's task is to restore, as far as may be, the balance of truth disturbed by propaganda and controversy. Looked at in this light, the first Maratha war must be regarded as unnecessary in its inception and unfortunate in its handling.

Just as the Maratha war was proving an embarrassment Hastings found himself confronted with the supreme crisis of his career. As with the Marathas, the occasion was not of his making and we must judge him by the manner in which he met it rather than by the mode of its occurrence. The War of American Independence began in 1775; in 1778 it developed into a European coalition bent upon the ruin of British overseas power. The strain of the American war reduced the possibility of reinforcing India, and the hostility of France and Spain rendered the dispatch of any help difficult. British sea-power was strained to its uttermost, and France was thus provided with an opportunity of recovering lost ground. Hastings met the situation in characteristic fashion. On hearing the news of the surrender of

General Burgoyne at Saratoga during the debate on the Maratha war he remarked: 'if it be really true that the British arms and influence have suffered so severe a check in the western world, it is the more incumbent upon those who are charged with the interest of Great Britain in the East to exert themselves for the retrieval of the national honour'. But worse was to follow. For many years the Madras Presidency had been in a chronic state of misrule. There had never been another Clive to carry reforms there with a strong hand, nor had the directors exerted themselves to this end as they had in Bengal. Less was at stake and the evils were less obvious though no less real. In 1775 Lord Pigot was sent out to effect the restoration of Tanjore and the reform of the service, and next year was imprisoned by his own council. One unnecessary war with the new ruler of Mysore had already occurred. Though the Nizam, the Marathas, and Haidar Ali of Mysore were mutually suspicious and ready to injure one another, the Madras Council by its tactlessness allowed them to form a coalition, and by its folly failed to provide for the consequent emergency. In July 1780 Haidar Ali burst into the Carnatic; Baillie's brigade was destroyed, Munro of Baksar retreated with ignominy; within a few months Arcot had fallen and the whole province been overrun. But Hastings was not dismayed. He set about reinforcing Madras on the one hand and dividing his foes on the other. He suspended the Governor of Madras and sent Sir Eyre Coote (now commander-in-chief in Bengal) to Madras with all possible supplies and reinforcements. In the following January he dispatched Pearce on his overland march from Bengal to Madras. At the same time his diplomacy was active. The Raja of Berar was detached in central India and Sindia in the north. In 1782 peace was made with the whole Maratha confederacy (as we have seen). There then remained Haidar Ali to deal with, for the Nizam was never a formidable foe. Coote checked Haidar at Porto Novo in July 1781. He then joined Pearce north of Madras and re-established mastery over the Mysore forces in two more pitched battles, Pollilore and Solingar. The war now assumed a more equal aspect. Haidar Ali had met his match on land, but he was assisted by the arrival of a French fleet under the fighting Admiral de Suffren. In sixteen months he fought five battles with the brave but less skilful Hughes, which though indecisive in detail, gave the French for some months the freedom of south Indian waters. The great harbour of Trincomali, newly taken from the Dutch, was captured, and a body of French troops landed which joined Haidar in taking Cuddalore. The great Bussy was on the way, but he only arrived after long delays in April 1783. By then the moment for a decisive stroke had passed. Coote and Haidar were both dead, and Haidar's son Tipu had marched to the west coast in order to besiege Mangalore. Madras affairs were now in the capable hands of Lord Macartney, while the news of the peace in Europe made it clear that Tipu could no longer hope for a decisive result. Both sides were exhausted, and though Hastings thought that

PLATE 29

a. Fort St. George, Madras

b. Government House, Calcutta

further efforts should have been made, and a better result obtained, the treaty of Mangalore in 1784 restored peace on the basis of a mutual cession of conquests.

Thus in the south, as in the west, the war apparently ended very nearly where it began. The British had barely held their ground. But in fact it meant very much more than this. Though handicapped by internal dissensions in their principal settlements, involved in a disastrous struggle in America, and in deadly peril from a European coalition at home, the British had met and withstood a union of the principal Indian powers and had emerged relatively stronger than at the beginning. The Indian powers had done their utmost at the most favourable conjunction of events and had failed. The Company with all its defects had proved to be stronger than any Indian state. Henceforth the Company was not merely a power in India, but the strongest of the Indian powers. From primacy it was but a step to supremacy.

The conclusion of the peace of Mangalore enabled Hastings to leave the Company's possessions in 1785 as tranquil as he had found them as well as far stronger than before. In the north the cases of the Begams of Oudh and Chait Singh of Benares have still to be mentioned. Inasmuch as they played an important part in Hastings's impeachment, they will receive fuller notice; here it is enough to say that they both showed that the velvet glove was wearing thin. They reveal a coarsening of Hastings's fibre, which, considering all that he had gone through is hardly surprising, but which is nevertheless undeniable. Pressing financial need combined with fading scruples united to produce incidents which it has become ever more difficult to justify with the passage of time.

Hastings's governorship was marked by other features than those of war and politics. His long residence in Bengal in the shadow of the Mughul cultural tradition had kindled oriental tastes and allowed time for the acquisition of oriental learning. Hastings with his air of authority, his long tenure of office, his cultural interests, and his understanding of the people, came nearer to the heart of India than any of the other pre-Mutiny rulers. His name became a legend, passing into popular folklore, his exploits were celebrated in popular verse. Almost alone of the early rulers, he showed an awareness of cultural as well as political and commercial issues. He sought to understand Indian culture as a basis for sound Indian administration. Hastings knew Persian (the diplomatic language) and Bengali (the local language) well and had a working knowledge of Urdu with some Arabic. He encouraged Halhed in his work on Hindu law, based on a Persian translation from the Sanskrit made by ten pundits. He encouraged William Wilkins in his Sanskrit studies and patronized his translation of the *Gita*. When Sir William Jones, already a Persian and Arabic scholar, joined the Supreme Court, Hastings encouraged his interest in Sanskrit and supported the foundation of the Asiatic Society of Bengal in 1784. He was equally interested in Islamic culture and founded the Muslim *Madrasah* or College of Arabic studies at Calcutta in 1781. He encouraged Rennell in the production of his *Bengal Atlas* (1781) and sent two expeditions to Tibet. By his patronage of learning and the arts, by his political vigour and subtlety, and by his continuance of the traditional methods of administration by means of corruption kept within bounds, Hastings placed himself in the line of the great Indian monarchs. No British ruler before Lawrence was as much in tune with the country he governed and no one was better loved.

Hastings's achievement may be summed up by saying that he proved an effective warden of the Company's marches during a period of unexampled difficulty. He faced his external enemies with unflinching courage and unfailing resource, and his internal opponents with extraordinary patience and firmness. He laid the foundation of the administrative structure upon which others were to rear a stately edifice, and through all this activity he found time to cultivate that interest in cultural things which was to lead in a still greater return from the Indian side. He found Calcutta a counting-house and left it a seat of empire. But having said so much we must not hide the other side of the medal. His revenue measures were tentative and far from wholly successful; his political skill was marred by a certain lack of moral tone and a streak of hardness, more Prussian than English, which grew with the years. His correspondence developed a speciousness and lack of candour which became habitual. If inflexible purpose marked the course of his actions, he also showed at times a cold hostility which could freeze to an icy hate. The thin pursed lips which set off the intellectual brow tell their tale of suppressed feeling and smouldering resentments. It could almost be said that he never said a foolish thing or ever did a generous one. This aloof and self-centred quality created suspicion in many who met him; even Barwell began by distrusting him. In his personal administration he did little to deserve the censure of the older school of Anglo-Indian historians, but neither did he deserve the encomiums of later generations. Hastings can best be understood by remembering that he went to India at the age of seventeen, that much of his early service was up-country, and that he lived through the whole period of Plassey, Mir Jafar, and Mir Kasim in Bengal. His standards were high in his own estimation, and judged by the level of the times. But they were neither the standards of the nineteenth-century administrators nor of the best men in English public life of his day. It would be as foolish to deny the fact as it would be unjust to revive prejudiced stories of exceptional turpitude. Warren Hastings is in any view a complex and puzzling character. The task of interpreting him has been made far more difficult by the controversies which his name and the passions which Bengal excited. Behind this eloquence and prejudice the real man disappeared like reality beneath the mask of *maya*. The achievement of Hastings is an established fact; his character remains something of an enigma.

NOTE ON CHAIT SINGH OF BENARES
AND THE BEGAMS OF OUDH

THE cases of Chait Singh of Benares and the Begams of Oudh formed the most damaging counts against Hastings at his impeachment. It was indeed the Chait Singh case which changed the mind of Pitt and so precipitated the actual trial. Sheridan's 'Begam speech' has generally been considered the most eloquent oration delivered in Parliament. The passion and prejudice unloosed at the actual trial, however, and the hazy knowledge of Indian conditions possessed by most of the participants has resulted in the respective parties being over-blamed and over-praised to the confusion of the judgement of posterity. The most judicious accounts are those of Sir Alfred Lyall in his *Warren Hastings* (Rulers of India), H. H. Dodwell in the *Cambridge Shorter History of India*, and P. E. Roberts in his *History of British India* and in the *Cambridge History of India*, vol. v.

Chait Singh was Raja of Benares but his status was that of a *zamindar* or collector of revenue, not of a ruling prince. But he was a *zamindar* with a difference in that he had a compact territory and considerable powers. Until 1775 he was a dependent of the Nawab Wazir of Oudh, but by the treaty of that year his allegiance was transferred to the Company. His annual tribute, or the revenue which he was expected to hand over, was 22½ *lakhs* of rupees (£225,000). This was a substantial amount and may be compared with the 52 *lakhs* which constituted the Bengal provincial payment to Delhi in the early eighteenth century. On the transfer of Benares to the Company an undertaking was given that the demand would not be increased 'on any pretence whatsoever'. In 1778, when the French war combined with the Maratha and Mysore entanglements to make the British position critical, Hastings thought himself justified in demanding (not requesting) a special sum of 5 *lakhs* for war expenses. The demand was repeated in 1779 and enforced by a threat of military action. In 1780 the demand was again renewed. This time the raja sent 2 *lakhs* to Hastings as a bribe. Hastings took the 2 *lakhs* which he used for the Company's forces, but did not relax his demand. The raja was then required to furnish 2,000 horsemen, which were reduced to 1,000. When the raja produced 500 with 500 matchlockmen Hastings proceeded to Benares, determined to exact a fine of 50 *lakhs*. The raja was put under arrest in his own palace. His own troops then rose and the small British force involved was massacred owing to the accident that they had not been provided with ammunition. From then on Hastings behaved with the utmost coolness. He retired to Chunar, brought up reinforcements, recovered Benares, and drove Chait Singh from the country. His dominions were conferred upon a nephew with a tribute increased to 40 *lakhs*. Making all allowance for the necessities of a perilous situation, and the irritation of a prevaricating prince who had intrigued with the governor-general's enemies in the council, it is difficult not to regard Hastings's behaviour as both high-handed and vindictive. The Company's power was vindicated but not its good faith. Others (like Wellesley and Napier) were as high-handed without being impeached, but from the historian's point of view, the possible excess of blame by contemporaries cannot affect the issue of the actuality of guilt.

The Begams or princesses of Oudh were the mother and grandmother of the Nawab Wazir of Oudh, Asaf-ud-daula. They held valuable *jagirs* or grants of land and had inherited other wealth under the will of Shuja-ud-daula. The nawab was in chronic arrears with his subsidy payments to the

Company and turned a wistful eye towards this family endowment. In 1775 the widow of Shuja, at the behest of the British resident, agreed to pay 30 *lakhs* to her son in addition to 25 already given (approximately £560,000) on condition that both he and the Company desisted from further demands. Hastings opposed the giving of this pledge but was outvoted by the council. In 1781 Asaf-ud-daula, being hard-pressed for money by Hastings who was himself hard-pressed for public funds, suggested that he might be released from his undertaking and Hastings consented. But the nawab was soon daunted by the vigour of the ladies' remonstrances and desired to draw back. The rest of the story is one of relentless pressure to keep the nawab up to the mark, exercised both on the nawab himself and on two successive British residents. (Middleton, his own nominee, and Bristow a Francis man.) British troops were sent to support the nawab, the eunuch stewards of the Begams were imprisoned for nearly a year and subjected to fetters, starvation, and the threat of the lash. In February 1782 Middleton wrote 'no further rigour than that which I exerted could have been used against females in this country', and in June Bristow added the opinion of the officer commanding the troops, 'all that force could do has been done'. By these means 100 *lakhs* (£1 million sterling) were eventually secured, the nawab's debts paid and the Company's finances restored.

The Begams were not left penniless, or even uncomfortable. Nor was their title to their riches quite certain. But there is no doubt that faith was broken, that the Company's government interfered in what was essentially a domestic and intimate situation in the nawab's own household, that the Begams were severely treated and their dependants bullied and ill-used. There also seems no doubt that Hastings's was the moving spirit egging on reluctant British residents and officers. When due allowance has been made for the dire necessities of Hastings's position at the time and the strains to which he was subjected, the fact remains that in both these cases Hastings sank below not only modern codes of conduct but the accepted Indian standards of the time.

AUTHORITIES

FOR the period 1772–4 M. E. MONCKTON-JONES, *Warren Hastings in Bengal 1772–74* (1918), is authoritative. Sir JOHN STRACHEY has dealt with the Rohilla war in his *Hastings and the Rohilla War* (1892).

For the governorship as a whole, apart from numerous state papers and voluminous manuscript sources may be mentioned Sir G. W. FORREST, *Selections from the State Papers in the Foreign Dept. of the Govt. of India, 1772–85* (3 vols., 1890), and *Selections from the State Papers of the Governors-General: Warren Hastings* (2 vols., 1910). There are many lives of Hastings, the fullest being the first by G. R. GLEIG, (3 vols., 1841), which roused Macaulay's ire, and the latest by KEITH FEILING (1954), a closely packed study drawn from partly new sources. A good modern biography is by A. DAVIES (1935) and among studies may be mentioned those by Sir A. LYALL (1908) and PENDEREL MOON, *Warren Hastings and British India* (1947). The best recent authority is P. E. ROBERTS, in his *History of British India* and the *Cambridge History of India*, vol. v. S. C. GRIER, *The Letters of Warren Hastings to his wife* (1905), and H. H. DODWELL (ed.), *Warren Hastings's Letters to Sir J. Macpherson* (1927), reveal a more personal side.

For the Nand Kumar case see Sir J. STEPHEN, *The Story of Nuncomar and the Impeachment of Sir Elijah Impey* (2 vols., 1905), and H. BEVERIDGE, *Maharaja Nuncomar* (1886), taking different sides. For Oudh and Chait Singh see C. C. DAVIES, *Warren Hastings and Oudh* (1939). The case for Sir Philip Francis can be seen in J. PARKES and H. MERIVALE, *Memoirs of Sir Francis* (2 vols., 1867). For Maratha affairs consult the *Cambridge History* or the history of Kincaid and Parasnis. For the impeachment see the *Lives* and the *Cambridge History of India*, vol. v, chap. xvii, and P. J. MARSHALL, *The Impeachment of Warren Hastings* (1965).

H. E. BUSTEED, *Echoes of Old Calcutta* (4th ed., 1908), is an admirable study of the times and T. G. P. SPEAR, *The Nabobs* (1932), deals with the social life of the British. See also W. HICKEY, *Memoirs* (4 vols., 1913). LUCY SUTHERLAND, *East India Company in 18th century politics*, is again invaluable for the London scene. See Sir C. ILBERT, *The Government of India* (3rd ed., 1916), for the Regulating and Pitt's Acts

RECENT PUBLICATION

P. J. MARSHALL's *Impeachment of Warren Hastings* (Oxford, 1965) is a searching analysis of the subject.

CHAPTER 6

The Company and the State

THE East India Company, which found itself the master of Bengal in 1757, was the result of the fusion, in 1702 (completed in 1708), of the rival 'old' and 'new' Companies, which had for a time disputed the English trade with India, each with the backing of a royal charter. 'The United Company of Merchants of England trading with the East Indies' was henceforth the only body of English merchants entitled to carry on the English trade. It was governed in London by a court of twenty-four directors, who were elected annually by the body of shareholders, known as the Court of Proprietors. The working capital of the Company known as East India stock was provided by the proprietors as shareholders on the joint-stock plan. The profits were steady and the annual dividend declared between 1711 and 1755 varied between 8 and 10 per cent. The day-to-day administration was carried on by the directors, usually referred to as 'the Court', which for this purpose was divided into a number of committees.

In India the Company was essentially a commercial concern, and any political activities were incidental to its commerce. The Company administered the solitary British possession of Bombay and held its other factories and settlements under grants from the local powers. The three main settlements of Madras, Calcutta, and Bombay were administered separately by local councils dealing direct with the home authorities. In each settlement there was a hierarchy of merchants rising through the grades of writer and factor to those of junior and senior merchants. The council consisted of senior merchants and had as its head a president who was also governor of the settlement. These councils controlled all the commercial operations, which consisted mainly in selling English goods in the local markets and with the proceeds and the help of bullion exported from England making up the 'investment' of goods for dispatch to England. The salaries paid were nominal,[1] it being understood that the Company's servants were free to augment them by engaging in the internal trade in India or in the external trade to the Far East. The one thing which they were forbidden was to infringe the Company's monopoly by engaging in the trade with England. The method of appointment was nomination by the directors, writers usually going to India at the age of fifteen.

The even tenor of the Company's merchants' way was first disturbed

---

[1] The annual salary of a writer was £5, of a factor £15, and of a junior merchant £30. The chief of Dacca in 1744 received £40. L. S. S. O'Malley, *The Indian Civil Service*, p. 9.

by the French wars which began in 1744. It is obvious that such a system was bound to be shaken to its roots by the sudden acquisition of political power in Bengal. This brought with it previously undreamt of opportunities of making fortunes. Having the whole weight of political power within the state at their back, and often themselves holding important political positions, these men found easy roads to fortune in three ways. They received presents and considerations for favours public and private, past, present, and to come, they held lucrative contracts, such as the salt monopoly or the supply of clothing to the troops, and they enjoyed unfair competition with the local merchants as a result of the *dastak* system started by Mir Jafar and confirmed by Vansittart's Council at the cost of war with Mir Kasim. Parliamentary reports showed that between 1757 and 1766, £2,169,665 had been given to the Company's servants in the form of presents (without counting Clive's *jagir*) and £3,770,833 paid in compensation for losses incurred.[1]

This sudden affluence of the Company's Bengal servants had a variety of results. It started a stream of returned 'Indians' to England who became the 'Nabobs' of eighteenth-century England, scandalizing society by their ostentation and creating jealousy by their wealth. Their influence began to be felt by 1760 and they were a parliamentary force by 1767. The dramatist Foote guyed them in his play *The Nabob* in 1770. Politicians did not see why the state should not share in this new-found wealth and moralists began to doubt the means by which it was acquired; Burke was later to become their spokesman (while dipping the family finger into the Indian dish). At the same time the cost of frequent campaigns raised expenses and the maladministration reduced revenue. The Company therefore found itself not nearly so well off as its servants. But when retrenchment was proposed it met two obstacles within the Company itself. There was a reluctance on the part of directors to take strong action since those concerned in irregularities were their own nominees, often their own relations or connexions, or the clients of highly placed persons in England whom they did not wish to offend. The directors were therefore bold in exhortation but hesitant of action. Similarly, while firm in deprecating the assumption of further political responsibility they were apt to condone the accomplished fact if it promised an increase of resources. There was, secondly, an eagerness on the part of the proprietors (or shareholders) to share in the new prosperity, which took the form of a demand for increased dividends. In 1766 the dividend was raised to 10 per cent., and the next year to 12½ per cent.

The total effect of these influences was to produce the financial crisis which led to the passing of the Regulating Act in 1773. In 1766 Parliament first concerned itself with Indian questions and the demand was voiced that the Crown should take over the Company's possessions. This opposition was bought off in 1767 by an undertaking to pay

[1] *Reports of the House of Commons 1772*, vol. iii, pp. 311–12.

£400,000 a year to the state in return for the continued enjoyment of the Company's new possessions and revenues.[1] This extra burden proved too great in the then condition of the Company. The directors in vain endeavoured to avert disaster. Their first attempt was the dispatch of Vansittart to Bengal from Madras in 1760, but he was over-borne by the majority of the council. The next measure was the dispatch of Clive for his second term in 1765, but the effort died away with his return in 1767. In 1769 three 'supervisors', Vansittart, Forde, and Scrafton, were dispatched with plenary powers, but their ship was never heard of after leaving the Cape of Good Hope. In 1772 Hastings was appointed Governor of Bengal with a mandate for reform, but a financial crisis had already arrived. The court was compelled to ask Lord North for a loan of a million pounds to avert bankruptcy. The mounting public criticism now found vent in the appointment of select and secret parliamentary committees which produced between them eighteen hostile reports. These were the prelude to the assertion of parliamentary control over the Company's affairs, which led on, step by step, to the assumption of full sovereignty by the Crown in 1858. We can trace three broad themes in this process; the separation of trade from administration within the Company itself, the gradual assertion of state control over the political affairs of the Company itself in India, and a similar process in the control of the Company in London. The main steps of these processes can be followed in a series of great parliamentary enactments, which commence with the Regulating Act of 1773, continue with Pitt's India Act of 1784 and the periodical Charter Acts of 1793, 1813, 1833, and 1853, and end with the final Act of 1858. We shall consider the first two of these measures in turn and then trace the three themes mentioned above to their conclusions.

In 1773 two Acts were passed. The first relieved the financial embarrassments of the Company by granting a loan of £1,400,000 at 4 per cent. interest. The second was the Regulating Act, so called because it was an Act 'to regulate' the affairs of the Company in India. The Act first dealt with the affairs of the Company in England. The tumultuous proceedings of the Court of Proprietors were restrained. Rival factions made and unmade directors at the annual elections, and shares were bought in order to obtain voting power;[2] Indian policy was influenced and sometimes determined by the intrigues of city groups wholly devoid of responsibility. The qualification for a vote in the Proprietors' Court was raised from £500 to £1,000. Annual elections of directors were replaced by the election of six directors a year for a four-year term with a disqualification for a year before election

---

[1] Clive believed that the grant of the *diwani* of Bengal to the Company in 1765 would bring £2 million a year to the Company as revenue surplus.

[2] The practice of dividing holdings of East India stock in order to increase the number of votes in the Court of Proprietors was known as 'splitting votes'. See L. Sutherland, *E. India Co. and the State*.

for a second term. This ended the scandal by which a body of commercial shareholders had dictated policy in a great country. The Act then dealt with the Bengal government. A Governor-General of Fort William in Bengal was appointed for five years, together with four councillors who were all named in the Act. Future appointments were to be made by the Company. The Governor-General was given supervisory authority over the other two presidencies and thus the first step towards unitary control was taken. Finally, a Supreme Court consisting of a chief justice and three puisne judges was set up.

The importance of the Regulating Act is that it marks the first assertion of parliamentary control over the Company and registers the first concern of Parliament for the welfare of the people of India. But in itself it was a temporizing measure full of defects which contributed much to the difficulties of Warren Hastings as the first Governor-General. The Governor-General had no casting vote and so could be overruled by his council as Philip Francis and his friends succeeded in doing for two years. The general superintendence of the other presidencies was vague and no provision was made for its enforcement. The Supreme Court was neither given any definition of the law it was to administer or of those to whom it was to apply. Once the machine had been set going the government in England could only intervene again by further legislation. Apart from the assertion of the principle of responsibility the best thing that can be said of the Act was that it increased contact with India and knowledge of its affairs by the dispatch of mature judges and councillors to the East.

The Regulating Act was the first measure passed in a period of more than twenty years during which Indian affairs were a major topic in the British Parliament. Its defects were soon manifest, but remedial measures were delayed by the crisis of the American War of Independence. In 1780 the Company's privileges ran out under the Act of 1744, but the government of Lord North, still reeling under the shock of Saratoga, was unwilling to bring forward any radical proposal. Instead the Company's privileges were extended to 1791 with three years' notice from that date. The Company's dividend was at the same time limited to 8 per cent. But Parliament was not now to be thus put off. In 1781 two parliamentary committees were appointed, one presided over by Burke, to examine the administration of justice, and one by Dundas, to consider the causes of the wars in the Carnatic. The prophet of reform and its practical manager both found congenial subjects for their labours. At the same time Lord North's ministry was tottering to its fall, ushering in a period of political instability which only ended with Pitt's victory at the general election of 1784. For the first time India became a dominant issue of English politics. It provided a main political issue during the Fox-North coalition in 1783 and provided King George III with an excuse for dismissing the ministry at the end of the year. It formed the subject-matter of the first measure of Pitt's long ministry and made his reputation both as an administrator and legislator. It continued to agitate Parliament through the years of Warren Hastings's impeachment, providing opportunities for the assertion of moral principle and the expression of political idealism. England inoculated herself with Indian wealth to develop within her the anti-body of political integrity.

Three constructive proposals emerged from this period. The first was Dundas's Bill, a centralizing measure which never received serious discussion. The second was Fox's India Bill, the occasion of the fall of the Fox-North coalition. Fox proposed to supersede both the proprietors and the directors with seven commissioners appointed by the Crown and irremovable except by an address from either House of Parliament; the leading shareholders were to be represented by nine assistant directors. The solid objection to this proposal was that it would have transferred the whole patronage as well as the direction of policy to seven persons knowing nothing of India, owing their appointment to political influence, and subject to political pressure. Political patronage would have replaced the personal jobbery of the directors and India might well have become the scene of greater corruption than before.

The third measure was Pitt's India Bill which actually passed into law in August 1784. Pitt rejected the outright taking over of the management of the Company's Indian possessions by the Crown, which had first been proposed by Clive in 1759. He equally rejected the crude subordination of Company to Parliament proposed by Fox. He left open the question of the sovereignty of the Company's possessions in India. At the same time it was clear that the Company was incapable of meeting its new responsibilities without assistance and supervision. Pitt's remedy was a double or joint government of Company and Crown. The directors themselves were left in being and retained control of commerce and patronage. But the Court of Proprietors lost the power of modifying or rescinding any proceeding of the directors which had been approved by the new Board of Control. This meant in effect that their power to influence political decisions in India was ended; the proprietors thus passed unhonoured from the Indian political scene. It was in the political sphere that the new dual system was effective. The directors themselves, unhindered by the Court of Proprietors except in the matter of their election, formed one-half of the partnership and the new Board of Control the other. This body consisted of six unpaid privy councillors, one of whom was the president with a casting vote. In fact, under the masterful direction of Dundas and with the backing of Pitt, the president soon became in effect minister for the affairs of the East India Company. The board had no patronage and did not interfere in commercial matters, but it had power 'to superintend, direct and control all acts, operations and concerns which in anywise relate to the civil or military government or the revenues of the British territorial possessions in the East Indies'. The board approved all dispatches (which it could modify or reject) and could even insist on its own orders being transmitted without the directors' consent. In matters of secrecy the board dealt with a secret committee of three directors whose proceedings were unknown to the rest of the Court.

In India the same system of indirect control was applied and there was a similar tightening up. The Governor-General was appointed by the directors but could be recalled by the Crown as well as the Court. The experiment of appointing English public men to the governor-general's council was abandoned, and the council itself reduced to three of whom the commander-in-chief was to be one. The control of Calcutta over the subordinate presidencies in matters of war, revenue, and diplomacy was tightened, and the local councils were in their turn reduced to three members each. At the same time the Act declared that 'to pursue schemes of conquest and extension of dominion in India are measures repugnant to the wish, honour and policy of this nation'. The Governor-General and Council were expressly forbidden to declare war or enter into aggressive designs without the explicit authority of the Court or the secret committee. Pitt's India Act was rounded off by amending acts of which the most important gave the governor-general power to override his council and also made it possible for the offices of governor-general and commander-in-chief to be united in the same person. The first of these measures was made a condition by Lord Cornwallis of his acceptance of the office of Governor-General. It made the governor-general the effective ruler of British India under the authority of the board and the Court, and prevented any repetition of the embarrassments from which Hastings had suffered. The Governor-General *and* Council now became the Governor-General *in* Council and as such he remained until 1947.

The dual system thus set up lasted until the Mutiny in 1857. The apparent weakness of duality proved in practice to be the secret of its success. The home government at the time lacked the means for providing an efficient civil service in India. At the same time the Company unaided lacked the strength for enforcing probity and efficiency in its servants. The dual system left the administration in the hands of those who were familiar with it, but provided a supervisor at home with parliamentary backing in the shape of the Board of Control, and another in India in the person of the Governor-General whose authority was above local influence and beyond local challenge. Disputes there were, but the directors had the good sense to realize that the last word lay with the ministry of the day. Compromise was therefore the usual outcome of disagreement. Despite theoretical appearances, the partnership worked. But as the British stake in India grew, the government's influence increased and the directors' political power correspondingly declined. There were frequent compromises on appointments to the governor-generalship. The directors could block an unwanted candidate as in the case of Metcalfe. But it was only with difficulty that they secured the recall of Wellesley, and their recall of

Ellenborough in 1844 was only successful because Peel's ministry had already lost confidence in him. We can say that the essential result was to give the home government a continuous influence on, and ultimate control of, Indian policy. The days of the irresponsible exploitation of India were over; in its place the responsibility of Parliament for the government of India and the welfare of the people of India was not only clearly defined but also made possible of enforcement. The planning genius of Pitt and the practical management of Dundas were more effective than the generous rhetoric of Fox in making effective the professed idealism of Burke.

The assertion of the moral responsibility of Parliament for the welfare of India was the essential theme of the impeachment of Warren Hastings. The motives of its managers were mixed from the personal spite of Sir Philip Francis to the crusading zest of Burke, and even Burke was not free from personal rancour. Yet behind the invective and passion which accompanied it lay the conviction that moral principles must prevail in Indian as much as in British public life, and that what was wrong in the West could not be right in the East. It was this feeling which caused Pitt to withdraw that support of Hastings in the case of Chait Singh of Benares which he had given on the issue of the Rohilla war. Hastings was arraigned before the House of Lords on twenty-three charges. The proceedings opened amidst great excitement at Westminster Hall in 1787. They dragged on for six years and ended with Hastings's acquittal on all the counts. By that time the country had entered on the long French revolutionary wars and public interest had long since flagged. Though acquitted Hastings was financially crippled and debarred from further employment or public honours. He spent the rest of his long life in retirement at his beloved Daylesford, emerging finally to receive the spontaneous tribute of the Commons which rose in his honour when he finished giving evidence at its bar in connexion with the charter discussions of 1813. It must be admitted that only very rough and rather brutal justice was done, but justice of a kind there was. Though the faults of many lesser men transcended those of Hastings as his ability exceeded theirs, it was fitting that the responsibility for misgovernment and acts of high-handedness should be fixed upon the head rather than on lesser men. At the same time the greatness of his services as well as the gravity of his shortcomings required recognition. It would have been as unjust roundly to condemn him as wholly to absolve him for all the acts of his government. Justice required that he should be both blamed and praised and this was in fact what occurred though the prosecution was tainted with vindictiveness and the length of the trial imposed cruel hardship. As a form of justice the proceedings were discreditable and rang the death knell of impeachment as a legal form. But the arraignment of Hastings and the ending of all his further prospects gave warning to the Company's servants in general that no lesser man could expect his actions to go without scrutiny or his faults without reproof;

his acquittal and the parliamentary esteem which later came to him demonstrated that merit and ability in serving the state, even though speckled with wayward actions, would not go unnoticed either.

The Company's existing charter ran out in 1794 with a warning three years earlier. Consideration of the terms for the renewal of the charter involved the focusing of attention on Indian affairs in a way not known in later times. Parliamentary committees took evidence and made reports to the Houses and the subsequent debates which took place occupied much time and attracted much attention. For the rest of the Company's existence the charter was regularly renewed for twenty-year periods. What amounted to a grand inquest on Indian affairs and the conduct of the Indian government thus took place periodically. It formed the preliminary for legislative changes which can thus be conveniently distinguished and the discussions provided ample and convenient evidence of the gradually changing climate of opinion in Britain and its effect upon Indian policy. We may now pass the subsequent Charter Acts in brief review before distinguishing their effect upon the several strands of government. The Act of 1793 was passed when Pitt was at the height of his power, when Britain was just embarking upon the French revolutionary wars and when Cornwallis had just completed his first successful governor-generalship. It was in effect a vote of confidence in the new system, and in consequence the changes made were few. Consolidation, not innovation, was the keyword. The advocates of free trade and Wilberforce's plea for the countenance of Christian missionaries were both repulsed, and the Company was confirmed in its commercial privileges.

In 1813 the French wars still continued but the end was in sight. There had been alarm at Wellesley's aggressive policy with its financial repercussions and concern at the administrative shortcomings in the administrative and judicial spheres. Inquiry began in 1808, and was more prolonged and exhaustive than before. But the reports produced were more informed, and the discussions they provoked were less passionate than previously. The Fifth Report of 1812 on the revenue and judicial system of Bengal became a classic of Indian administration. The Act of 1813 showed how much the climate had changed in twenty years in spite of the deadening influence of war conditions. The Company obtained another twenty years lease of life. But the advocates of free trade succeeded in breaking the Company's monopoly of Indian trade, thereby opening a new chapter in Indian economic history. The immediate effect was not apparently very great, but from this change flowed the later commercial and industrial developments which have placed India in the forefront of industrial countries. The apostles of welfare, led again by William Wilberforce, secured the admission of Christian missionaries, a church establishment of a bishop and three archdeacons, and a resolution 'that it is the duty of this country to promote the interest and happiness of the native inhabitants of the British dominions in India and that such measures ought to be adopted as may tend to the introduction amongst them of useful knowledge and of religious and moral improvement'.[1] Here again the immediate effect was small, but the way was pointed to developments of the utmost importance.

The discussions which led to the Act of 1833 again began in an atmosphere of financial stringency caused by the expenses of the first Burman war. But the success of Bentinck's economies blunted the weapons of the Company's critics and perhaps helped to prolong its life. Before the Act was passed the Whigs had come to power and opened a new era in British politics. The great Reform Bill became law in 1832 and liberal and Benthamite ideas were in the ascendant. The Company disappeared as a commercial agency in India, remaining only as a political agent for the Crown. Their possessions were to be held 'in trust for His Majesty, his heirs and successors, for the service of the Government of India'. Centralization advanced another step. The new ideas of law bore fruit in the conferment of definite legislative powers and the establishment of a Law Commission, of which Macaulay was the most prominent member, to codify in a single system the five existing systems of law.[2] The eventual fruit of this commission was the Indian Penal Code, which came into force in 1860, and the Codes of Civil and Criminal Procedure. Thus the Act formed the starting-point for the development of Indian public law as known today. Similarly, the legislative powers conferred on the Governor-General and his council sitting with a fourth or legislative member (Macaulay was the first of these) formed the starting-point of the legislative development which lead straight to the sovereign parliaments of the Indian union and the Pakistan republic. The final Act (before the Mutiny) of 1853 was passed in the hey-day of Dalhousie's rule and involved only one or two changes. It continued the Company as a government agency. It arranged for the completion of the Law Commission's work.[3] The most important departure was the abolition of the Company's patronage by the introduction of open competition for entry into the covenanted service. Thus the Indian Civil Service, the creation of Cornwallis in its general character, assumed its modern form. The tree of the Company had now clearly lost its sap; its political fruit of the government of India hung overripe from the branches ready to drop into the lap of the Crown as soon as a passing breeze of crisis should shake them.

We can now turn to the broad themes mentioned previously. As the Company was organized as a commercial hierarchy, the early adminis-

---

[1] The thirteenth and last resolution which was the basis of the Act of 1813.

[2] C. P. Ilbert, The Government of India, pp. 83–84. These systems were (1) the body of English statute law as far as applicable, introduced by the charter of George I; (2) all later English Acts expressly extended to any part of India; (3) the regulations of the Governor-General's council, 1793–1834 (for Bengal only); (4) Madras Regulations; (5) Bombay Regulations.

[3] By appointing British commissioners to codify the work of the Indian commissions.

trators were simply merchants seconded to political duties. Many performed both at once and few suffered their commercial interests to atrophy. A decisive step was taken by Cornwallis when he separated the commercial and revenue departments. Thereafter men opted for either the commercial or revenue branch and became either merchants or administrators, but not both. The goal of the merchant was a commercial residency, which lasted until the end of the Company's Indian trade in 1834.[1] These stately merchant princes, possessing the dignity without the rapacity of the old 'Nabobs', were a picturesque by-product of the Company's evolution. The Company as a whole retained its monopoly of both the Indian and China trades until 1813 with some minor encroachments by private traders after 1793. In 1813 it lost the Indian monopoly but retained that of China, whose tea trade had long provided the bulk of its profits.[2] In 1833 it lost the Indian trade altogether and the *monopoly* of the China trade; in 1853 this also ceased, leaving the Company a political husk which hardly concealed the actual control of the Crown.

The state's control of the Company's political affairs steadily increased after 1783. The first factor was the personality of Dundas himself, whose diligence and skill in managing men firmly established the Board of Control as the final arbiter of political decisions. The withdrawal of the Crown's right to consent to the appointment of the Governor-General in 1786 did not in practice affect the steady growth of the board's power and the right was in any case restored in 1813. The superior political experience and greater breadth of view of the presidents gradually overbore the more extensive local knowledge of the directors. Their power of appointment soon came to be that of objecting to men they disliked rather than insisting on men they wanted. The breaking of the commercial monopoly in 1813 and the extinction of the Indian trade in 1833 cut the ground from beneath the directors' feet by depriving them of any independent body of support. When in 1853 six of the twenty-four directors were nominated by the Crown they were further undermined from within and it was clear that the end was near. The Crown was the effective ruler of India in all but name from 1834,[3] the Company being its local managing agency.

The control by the state of the Company's affairs in India itself was initially effected by its control of the Governor-General. The first step was the reduction of the council to three including the commander-in-chief, and the rule that the other two members should be Company's servants. The next was the appointment of a man high in British public life to the supreme office and the power given to him (by the

---

[1] For an account of the latter-day commercial resident see W. W. Hunter, *Annals of Rural Bengal.*

[2] For the interaction of tea and opium in China see M. Greenberg, *British Trade and the opening of China 1800–42* (1951).

[3] The Act of 1833 came into force in 1834.

Amending Act of 1786) of overriding his colleagues. The Governor-General was thus raised above local controversy and prejudice and elevated above his colleagues both in dignity and legal authority. The relation of Warren Hastings to his councillors was exactly reversed; the former colleagues became in effect subordinates.[1] When the Governor-General was also commander-in-chief, as was the case with Cornwallis, Lord Hastings, and Bentinck (from 1833), his position was indeed formidable. The power of the governor-general was gradually enlarged by increasing his authority over the two subordinate presidencies. In 1793 his superintending powers were underlined and further defined, and he automatically superseded a governor on visiting another presidency. An example of this was Wellesley's sojourn in Madras in 1798–9. In 1834 his paramount authority was emphasized by the change in his title form from Governor-General of Fort William in Bengal to that of Governor-General of India. His power of making 'regulations' for the presidency of Bengal was extended to formal law-making powers by means of legislative Acts for the whole of British India in 1834. A governor-general was virtually impregnable so long as he was supported by the London cabinet and behaved with reasonable prudence. Even Ellenborough would not have been recalled had he not lost the confidence of his former colleagues in Peel's ministry.

AUTHORITIES

FOR the preliminary period and an outline to 1861 the masterly work of Sir C. ILBERT, *The Government of India* (1922), may be consulted. See also chaps. x, xviii, and xxxii in the *Cambridge History of India*, vol. v. For the relations of the British with the Mughuls see PERCIVAL SPEAR, *Twilight of the Mughuls* (1951). A. BERRIEDALE KEITH, *Constitutional History of India* (1936) is a good constitutional history.

For Company politics and Company–state relations see L. SUTHERLAND, *East India Co. and the State* (1952), and C. H. PHILIPS, *The East India Company 1784–1834* (1940), both most valuable works. C. H. PHILIPS's edition of the *Correspondence of David Scott* (2 vols., 1951) is also revealing.

P. AUBER, *Analysis of the Constitution of the E. India Co.* (1826), is useful. L. S. S. O'MALLEY, *The Indian Civil Service 1601–1930* (1931), is careful and accurate; P. WOODRUFF, *The Founders* (1953) is more personal and colourful. Sir W. W. HUNTER, *Annals of Rural Bengal* (1868), gives a good picture of the Company's commercial establishments in their later days.

For the Nabobs in Britain see J. M. HOLTZMAN, *The Nabobs in England 1760–65* (1926).

---

[1] The cases of those Company's servants (Shore and Barlow) who became governor-generals (apart from acting appointments) on the whole served as exceptions to prove the rule. They lacked something of authority and tended to see the situation through local spectacles.

CHAPTER 7

Cornwallis

THE rule of Lord Cornwallis marks an epoch in the history of the British enterprise in India. Not only is there a change of persons and of method, but also a change of outlook and of atmosphere. Internally the commercial colour of the Company's government faded from this time forward, and with it went the grosser forms of corruption which had stained its servants and the accompanying connivance and collusion which had existed in the courts both of directors and proprietors. Sound government in the interests of the inhabitants was henceforth the touchstone of policy rather than an enlargement of the Company's investment or an increase in territorial revenues. That sound government, it is true, was conceived along traditional lines of an administration which collected the taxes and left the people as much as possible to themselves. But if not yet a conscious 'welfare state', the Company's internal government from this time forward can fairly be described as a justice state, whose ideal was defined by an unknown eulogist who thus addressed Shahjahan when in public procession—'Hail, O King, thou owest a thanksgiving to God. The King is just, the ministers are able and the secretaries honest. The country is prosperous and the people contented.'[1] Externally the Cornwallis régime also marked a change. The change proved to be a stopping-place rather than a change of direction but it was nevertheless effective and significant. The haphazard expansionism of the preceding thirty years was replaced by a steady determination of the home authorities, now seconded by the men on the spot, to limit commitments and eschew imperialism. For the next twelve years policy was self-consciously unaggressive. The old directorial urge for revenue which led to the condonation of the seizure of Tanjore, which urged Bombay to take Bassein as well as Salsette whenever practicable, which condemned the Rohilla war because it was waged by Hastings rather than because it was aggressive, was now replaced by the settled policy of the British government itself working both through its Board of Control and the remodelled directorate. The Cornwallis period saw the replacement of financial and commercial by political motives within and of makeshift imperialism by planned isolationism without the Company's dominions.

With the advent of Cornwallis a fresher air began to blow through Government House. His appointment was the result of the long series of discussions and debates which began in 1781 as soon as public

[1] Ibn-i Hasan, *Central Structure of the Mughul Empire*, p. 360

attention ceased to be focused on the American problem. The culminating points were the debates on the two India Bills and practical results were registered in Pitt's India Act of 1784. For our purpose we may say that this Act marked the determination of the British Parliament to assume responsibility for the Company's dominions,[1] and defined the means by which this was to be accomplished. An essential part of the plan was the appointment to the governor-generalship of a British public servant who would be independent of local interests, and vested with adequate authority. The post was twice offered to Cornwallis before he finally accepted it,[2] and for his benefit a special Act was passed permitting him to be governor-general and commander-in-chief at the same time and allowing him when necessary to override a majority in his council. Cornwallis was forty-eight at the time of his arrival in India. He had already a distinguished military career behind him. He was a man of such solid and accepted ability that his reputation survived the surrender of Yorktown in America in 1781. Above all, he possessed a massive integrity before which corruption and small-mindedness withered, and he was the personal friend of Pitt, the Prime Minister, and of Dundas, the President of the Board of Control. He was incorruptible without being sour and clear headed without being brilliant. His rule of bluff common sense and of genial simplicity was neither faultless nor always wise, but it imported a new spirit into British Indian affairs which was never again wholly lost.

During the eighteen months which passed between Hastings's departure and the arrival of Cornwallis the government was carried on by Sir John Macpherson. He was an official of the old school, and his rule was described by the studiously moderate Cornwallis as a 'system of the dirtiest jobbing'.[3] Cornwallis never spoke a word in criticism of Warren Hastings, but more damaging than the rhetoric of Burke were the measures which he found it necessary to take. In his cleansing and reformatory work he found able assistants from the Company's servants. There was John Shore, his chief lieutenant in revenue matters, and Jonathan Duncan, later Governor of Bombay, who came second in Cornwallis's estimation. There were the cousins Charles and James Grant, the former of whom became Chairman of the Directors and his son a President of the Board of Control, and Charles Stuart the commercial expert. But in the main he had to rely on his own judgement and strength in carrying through measures which necessarily affected long-established vested interests. That he did so much at the cost of so little friction is witness as much to his personality as to the powers with which he had been vested. A less vigorous man would have been

[1] The sovereignty of the Crown over the Company's dominions in India was explicitly declared by the Charter Act of 1813.
[2] The explicit offer to Cornwallis was made after Lord Macartney had made unacceptable conditions for acceptance.
[3] *Correspondence of Charles, first Marquess Cornwallis*, ed. C. Ross, 3 vols., vol. i, p. 371.

PLATE 30

b. Wellesley

a. Cornwallis

baffled by obstruction; a more imperious one like Ellenborough would have made confusion worse confounded.

The instructions with which Cornwallis was armed covered three main heads in internal affairs. He was to settle the administration on a regular basis, cutting down extravagance and suppressing corruption; he was to settle the system of revenue collection moderately and permanently; and he was to reform the judiciary, retaining the Indian framework while informing it with the spirit of British justice, and securing even-handed justice between Indian and European.

His first task was purification. Within a few months of his arrival the whole Board of Trade was suspended and most of the members subsequently dismissed for irregularities. A regiment was discovered for which full pay had been drawn for several years, but which only existed on paper.[1] Almost all the thirty-five collectors were, he believed he had good reason for thinking, deeply engaged in the forbidden private trade, 'and by their influence as collectors and judges of Adalat became the most dangerous enemies to the Company's interest'.[2] The Governor-General was pressed by influential men in England, including the Prince of Wales, to sanction 'infamous and unjustifiable jobs'.[3] Hickey records in his journal how offices were bought and sold. Cornwallis had the integrity to reprobate and the strength of mind and weight of dignity to resist such importunities, and they were never so unashamed again. The rule against private trade in the public branch of the service was sternly enforced, offenders being sent home. These cleansing acts would only have had a temporary effect had not Cornwallis gone to the root of the evil by regularizing the emoluments of the Company's servants. In pre-Plassey times the Company had paid nominal salaries and expected their servants to support themselves by private trade which did not interfere with the Company's investment. The first attempt to find a substitute for private trade in the new conditions was Clive's Society of Trade. This was superseded by a somewhat larger scale of salary with commissions at a fixed rate on the revenue. The salaries were too low and the commissions too high,[4] and the possible abuses which this system might encourage are obvious. It must also be remembered that no pensions were paid on retirement; in consequence many servants did not retire when they should, because they were too indebted to afford to do so, while everyone wished to amass capital sufficient to support themselves in dignity and ease in England. The temptation to make haste by illicit means was inevitably strong. Cornwallis was strong enough to induce a reluctant Company to abolish the commissions and to substitute for them generous fixed salaries. These salaries were attached to posts for which minimum

---

[1] Ibid.   [2] H. Beveridge, *Comprehensive History of India*, vol. ii, p. 575.
[3] *Cornwallis Correspondence*, vol. ii, p. 51.
[4] The outstanding case was that of the resident of Benares. His salary was Rs. 1,000 a month (£1,350 a year); his commission £40,000 a year, with, according to Cornwallis, other perquisites as well.

terms of service were prescribed. Thus the old evil of great offices held by junior servants was ended. With this basis he was able to take a strong line on the already forbidden but still extensively practised private trade. Thus were laid the foundations of a civil service generously paid, imbued with a high sense of public duty, and possessed of an impressive integrity, which governed India during the nineteenth century. Its work was done on the whole with notable efficiency and its standard of conduct was one of the highest in its contemporary world.

The reformation of the public service had, however, other facets which proved to be less pleasing. The day of public selection of public servants had not yet dawned. Nomination by the directors therefore continued to be the avenue of entry. The worst jobbery was prevented by the higher standards of service exacted in India with home support. A real misfit was not any longer able to make a fortune and return quickly, and would soon be returned without one. But the limited method of choice tended to produce a caste and family spirit within the service. Its strength may be gauged from the jealousy which greeted the appearance of the 'competition-wallah' after 1853. The hereditary traditions of Indian service produced some splendid examples of family service; it also produced a strongly exclusive and obstinately conservative outlook. It was this spirit which obstructed the admission of Indians to the higher services and which prevented the service as a whole from reading the signs of the new nationalist times in the late nineteenth century. Another unfortunate consequence of Cornwallis's measures was the exclusion of Indians from all higher government posts. Cornwallis had as poor an opinion of Indian probity as of British. 'Every native of Hindustan, I verily believe, is corrupt', he wrote. But while he had the means of improving the standards of European officials, he saw no way in the case of their Indian counterparts. Therefore he refrained from appointing them to responsible posts, or removed them when possible with the shining exception of Ali Ibrahim Khan, the incorruptible judge of Benares. This policy received legislative sanction in the Charter Act of 1793 which limited the tenure of all posts worth more than £500 a year to covenanted servants of the presidency concerned. Since no Indians were members of the covenanted service, they were not eligible for appointment. Subsequent admission to higher offices was the result of special enactments until admission to the covenanted services became a limited reality as well as a theory after 1853. The exclusion of Indians had certain important effects. The large ministerial Indian class, both Hindu and Muslim, found themselves excluded from public life in the Company's dominions. Public ability ceased to bloom when denied the sun of opportunity. Thus grew the legend that public ability did not and never had existed in India, that proficiency in commerce and the law were the summit of modern Indian achievement. Secondly, European and Indian gradually ceased to rub shoulders in public affairs. Within the Company's territories personal relations, outside the sphere of commerce, tended more and more to be that of master and servant, the governor and the governed. Up-country equality of status continued and with it good fellowship and mutual respect. When status becomes unequal opinion grows unbalanced. So developed that contempt for things and persons Indian which was already prevalent in Calcutta in the time of Lord Hastings, and which produced the shallow half-truths of Mill and Macaulay and the downright contempt of lesser men.

In order to follow the administrative reforms of Cornwallis some idea of the state of affairs as he found it on his arrival is necessary. The administration was divided into the commercial and revenue branches. The commercial branch was responsible for the Company's annual commercial investment. This originally took the form of silk, wool, cotton goods, and indigo. Later saltpetre was added and, from 1770, raw cotton. Until 1756 this was partly paid for by specie sent from England; thereafter it was met by the revenue of Bengal. The investment was controlled by the Board of Trade and was actually made by a number of commercial residents by means of contracts. The revenue or general branch controlled the civil administration, which in practice meant the collection of revenue and the administration of civil justice (criminal justice still being managed by the nawab through his deputy Muhammad Reza Khan). Revenue control was exercised by a Board of Revenue at Calcutta, and the work of collecting land and local customs dues performed by British collectors. The opium trade was a government monopoly let out on contract to Indians while the salt trade had since 1780 been controlled directly from Calcutta, the price being fixed every year by the Supreme Council. European officials had now become familiar figures in the districts, most of which had a collector and a judge, and some a commercial resident besides.

Hitherto service in both branches of the government had been interchangeable. It is easy to see how habits and outlooks legitimately acquired in the commercial field might prejudice good administration in the political. Cornwallis's first care was to separate the two. In 1789 all the Company's servants were allowed to opt for one or other branch and there remained. The Company's commercial system took the form it retained until the abolition of its trade in 1834. A reformed Board of Trade directed operations. The annual investment remained in the hands of the commercial residents, who had no political powers and worked on the agency system. They were remunerated by commissions on the value of the investment (the money annually entrusted to them) and they were allowed private trade. This was a recognition of the fact that in their case it was a practice impossible to stop. But this practice ceased to be a serious evil because they were deprived of political power, not only while holding a particular office, but throughout their careers. To adapt Macaulay's phrase about Impey, they became rich and quiet, leaving it to their political colleagues to become famous. The public half of the government was now divided into the general (civil and military matters) and the revenue departments, which also included civil justice. We can now consider Cornwallis's successive reformation of the revenue and judicial systems.

As in all mainly agricultural communities, the chief source of the public revenue in India was land. The system of landholding, the methods of assessment, and collection of land revenue were therefore of fundamental importance both to the administration and to the people themselves. In India the systems of land tenure were regulated by age-old custom and it was their methods of assessment which were subject to change and regulation. The people looked for lenient assessments and honest collection, the government for accurate information and reliable collection. The interests of the cultivator and of good government in fact largely coincided, but if government were pressed for money or distracted by internal dissension, long-term maxims of justice would be put aside; superintendence would become lax; the agents of collection would be pressed or allowed to do their own pressing on the cultivators of the soil, with the inevitable results of harsh demands, punitive measures of collection, and rural misery.

The system in vogue when the British were granted the *diwani* of Bengal in 1765 was that known as the *zamindari*. The peasant paid a fixed share of his produce (in cash or kind) to tax-collectors known as *zamindars* (landholders). The share was traditionally one-third of the gross produce, and might be more or less. The *zamindar* paid over nine-tenths of what he received to the state, retaining a tenth as remuneration for his exertions. By custom the *zamindar* had acquired an hereditary right. He paid a fine or fee on his succession, but could only dispose of his holding by state permission. Failure to pay the full *jama* or assessment was visited by fines, imprisonment, or floggings but not by confiscation. In addition to his revenue rights and duties, the *zamindar* regulated the occasional taxes imposed by the provincial government and was responsible for public order in his district. The *zamindars* of Bengal thus formed a provincial aristocracy. They were revenue collectors, magistrates, local magnates, and men of substance. But they were not landowners or a landed aristocracy in the British sense. They were an official aristocracy of hereditary rent-collecting and magisterial magnates. Their estates resembled those of British landlords in appearance, but were essentially different in texture. This system had its own checks and balances. The *zamindar* was too close to the peasant to be deceived about his capacity to pay. If the *zamindar* was too rapacious the peasant could leave his estate for another's or band together against extortion. The *zamindar* had only his own levies to rely upon, and severe repression therefore defeated its own object by ruining the *zamindar*.

At first the British acted through Indian agency and the system went on undisturbed. When Hastings took over the management in 1772 a series of experiments began, which proved the least successful part of his administration. A quinquennial settlement was tried, farming the revenues to the highest bidder, though the great famine was only two years past. Then annual settlements were tried with resulting unsettlement, loss of confidence, and rural stagnation. Revenue farming became a matter of speculation amongst Calcutta financiers and the ancient personal connexion between tax-collector and cultivator was broken in the anxiety to increase receipts and preoccupation with revenue returns. The whole rural life of the Bengal Presidency was disturbed by the regulation of demand by people ignorant of conditions and by the displacement of the old hereditary agents. Nor did the appearance of British collectors improve matters. They lacked both knowledge of and interest in the countryside; they were bewitched with the dream of fortune-making; they were, taken as a whole, the unfeeling agents of the impersonal calculating machine at Calcutta.

The Parliament which turned its attention to this problem was an assembly of landlords. They felt an affinity with the *zamindars* and they too easily assumed them to be tropical replicas of themselves. It was therefore natural that Pitt's Act of 1784 should insist on the abandonment of annual leases and direct the preparation of 'permanent rules' for revenue collectors. Cornwallis was himself a great landowner of the better type. The solution of the problem was thus in a sense predetermined before the facts were studied. But the facts *were* studied. Hastings himself set on foot the first inquiries and it was under his *aegis* that John Shore and Charles Grant acquired their knowledge. Cornwallis intensified this process, and contributed himself, with his instinct for the land, a far more understanding spirit than that of his great predecessor. In 1789, as a result of Shore's researches, a settlement for ten years was made. In 1793, at the end of his term, Cornwallis urged Dundas to sanction the permanence of the settlement. Shore opposed this step, but the famous ten-days' study of Pitt and Dundas at Wimbledon decided against him. On 22 March 1793 the Permanent Settlement was decreed. The *zamindars* were regarded as landowners; they were to pay, as previously, nine-tenths of the revenue collection to government through the collectors and the lesser holders, or *taluqdars*, direct through the sub-collectors. The cultivators or ryots were to be protected from oppression by the British collectors.

This settlement has been variously praised and blamed; it is for us to assess its results on the life of the three provinces. The first result was a further period of unsettlement caused by the fact that the new assessment was too high for the existing state of cultivation. Many old-established *zamindars* could not meet their obligations. Instead of being imprisoned or flogged they were more humanely but ruthlessly sold up, and their places taken by moneyed men from Calcutta. Thus the character of the *zamindar* body suffered a large change; the body which emerged into permanence about 1800 was a very different set of families to those who had existed in 1765. The personal tie between *zamindar* and peasant was in many cases broken, and the absentee landlord became common. The subsequent result was the re-establishment of stability in the Bengal countryside. The class of *zamindars* was largely a new one, but it was a stable class. It was bound by strong ties of interest to the ruling power. The settlement was made when there was still a large margin of cultivable land lying waste. Security led to this land being taken up, with an increase of population and of cultivation. The increased rents went to swell the coffers of the new *zamindars'* families, since the government assessment was fixed. The nineteenth-century *zamindar* thus reaped the whole agricultural increment of Bengal and became wealthy as well as secure. Some, like the Tagores and the Laws, used their wealth for the public good and the promotion of the arts. Others preferred the Irish model of absentee landlordism. As the *zamindars* gained in status, the peasants sank, for they were now legally regarded as rent-paying tenants and as such subject to eviction. Their customary occupational rights were forgotten and they shared little in the new prosperity. Not till 1859 did the Bengal Land Act do something to protect their interests. As the personal link with the *zamindar* was broken by the break up of the old families, so the functional link was impaired by the withdrawal of the *zamindar's* police and revenue powers. Henceforth the *zamindar* was a revenue collector only and the peasant a rent-payer only. The Permanent Settlement restored rural order in Bengal and provided the conditions of agricultural development, but it replaced the organic ties between the two classes of rural society by an impersonal cash-nexus. The two classes were henceforth unrelated and hostile. Order and progress were secured but social justice was not done. If annual settlements were too flexible, a permanent settlement was too rigid; between the two it took forty years to find the mean of a long-term settlement for thirty years.

The Permanent Settlement was set into the frame of Cornwallis's reorganization of the district and judicial administration of Bengal. Cornwallis found the foundations of the district administration laid by the reforms of 1786, which set up thirty-five districts headed by British collectors and supervised by a Board of Revenue, and he proceeded to build thereon. The Board of Revenue was reorganized; the thirty-five districts were reduced to twenty-three; each collector was provided with two European assistants. The collector's former stipend of Rs. 1,200 a month, which in fact he supplemented by private trade,[1] was raised to a subsistence salary of Rs. 1,500. In addition he was given a commission 'in the nature of reward' of 1 per cent. on the revenue collected. In the case of the largest district, Burdwan, this was reckoned at Rs. 27,500 a year. At the same time he was strictly forbidden to engage in private trade of any kind and this rule was vigorously enforced. The commission system might have led to abuse if the collectors had continued to be responsible for making annual assessments as

---

[1] Private trade by collectors and other specified officers had been forbidden along with the reception of presents by the Regulating Act of 1773. See Sir C. Ilbert, *The Government of India*, 3rd ed., p. 49.

well as collecting revenue, but as soon as the demand was fixed the collectors' expectations were regularized, and the last great bar to integrity was removed. Thus the framework of the typical British district administration was laid.

The collector was given magisterial powers, and at first presided over the old civil and new revenue courts as well. But this apotheosis did not last. By a system of trial and error Cornwallis reformed the whole system of civil and criminal justice. For civil justice district or *zillah* courts were instituted which dealt with both civil and revenue matters. Above them were four provincial courts at Calcutta, Murshidabad, Dacca, and Patna, with a final appeal in important cases to the Supreme Council sitting as the *Sadr Diwani Adalat*. At the same time the system of criminal justice was brought into line. Hitherto this had been in the hands of the nawab, whose deputy, Muhammad Reza Khan, presided over the *Sadr Nizamat Adalat* at Murshidabad and whose local agents or *darogas* held local courts in the districts. Cornwallis solved the problem of dual authority by causing the dismissal of Muhammad Reza Khan and himself assuming the criminal judicial functions of the deputy nawab. The court was brought from Murshidabad to Calcutta, where the Governor-General and council sat with Indian advisers. In the districts the *darogas* were superseded by four courts of circuit stationed at the four provincial capitals. Over each two civil servants presided assisted by Indian advisers, and they made circuits through their divisions twice a year. Under these arrangements the collector was limited to his magisterial and collecting duties. The civil courts were administered by district judges and the criminal courts by the judges of the courts of circuit. Thus a beginning was made in separating the Company's judicial from its revenue service, as its revenue service had already been separated from the commercial. The Bengal district pattern with its twin luminaries of collector and judge emerged, which was to remain substantially unchanged through the British period. The separation between the judicial and administrative classes was complete; though it was later modified in other areas and even in Bengal itself, it always remained substantial.

The system was completed by two further measures. The rule of law was expressed in unmistakable terms.

The collectors of revenue and their officers, and indeed all the officers of Government, shall be amenable to the courts for acts done in their official capacities, and Government itself, in cases in which it may be a party with its subjects in matters of property shall submit its rights to be tried in these courts under the existing laws and regulations.[1]

This rule, which was never departed from, laid the foundation of the civil liberty of the subject which was the essential basis for the later addition of the political liberty of self-government. At this point, more than at any other, did new British diverge from old Mughul India, and the seeds of the future were planted amid the still flourishing crop of

[1] *Cornwallis Correspondence*, vol. ii, p. 558.

past practice. The second measure was the establishment of police. First in Calcutta and then in the districts police were established for the maintenance of order. As a consequence the *zamindars* were relieved of their police duties. Salutary for the towns, it was less obviously beneficial in the districts where it separated the *zamindars* still farther from the people and tended to make government more distant and more olympian. Law remained largely unaltered, the civil code being customary and the criminal continuing to be the Islamic code shorn of those penalties such as mutilation, which offended the more humane instincts of the age. Finally the whole system as it stood was embodied in May 1793 in a single set of regulations, known as the Cornwallis Code.

The constructive work of Cornwallis was one of which any man might have been proud. Though the Permanent Settlement had serious defects, it gave tranquillity to the countryside and stability to the government; though the reorganization of the services was marred by the exclusion of senior Indians, it established a service distinguished for both efficiency and integrity; though the courts were blocked before long by massive arrears of business, they were capable of improvement and embodied the great principles of the separation of powers and the rule of law. Taking it all in all, Cornwallis had set the Company's ship of state on a new course, and had brought in justice and integrity to redress corruption and power politics.

AUTHORITIES

THERE is no full life of Cornwallis, and the reader must be content with W. S. SETON-KARR, *The Marquis Cornwallis* (Rulers of India, 1898). But C. ROSS (ed.), *Correspondence of Charles, 1st Marquis Cornwallis* (3 vols., 1859), is most valuable. Sir G. FORREST, *Selections from the State Papers of the Government of India: Lord Cornwallis* (2 vols., 1926) is much taken up with military affairs. The best modern summaries of Cornwallis's work are to be found in the *Cambridge History of India*, vol. v, chap. xxvi, by LILIAN PENSON, and in A. ASPINALL, *Cornwallis in Bengal* (1931). For revenue matters see also F. D. ASCOLI, *Early Revenue History of Bengal and the Fifth Report 1812* (1917) and W. K. FIRMINGER, *Fifth Report on East India Affairs* (3 vols., 1917). J. MILL's discussion in his *History* is trenchant and well informed.

CHAPTER 8

The South, 1780–1801

THE south has always been in some degree isolated from the north; it pursues its individual way and maintains its distinctive character even in the days of the telegraph, the railway, and the aircraft. It has always had a power situation of its own, albeit ultimately subordinate to that of the north, and its peculiar features have always required, even if they have not always received, separate and considered treatment. It is therefore desirable to see the south through its own spectacles during the formative years of the British dominion.

At the time of the break-up of the Tughluq empire in the fourteenth century the south established its own power system. It was based upon a balance between the Hindu empire of Vijayanagar to the south of the river Kistna and the Muslim Bahmanī kingdom, and later its successors, to the north. This lasted for two centuries until the collapse of Vijayanagar on the field of Talikota in 1565. Thereafter the two Muslim kingdoms of Bijapur and Golkonda divided most of the Deccan between them, leaving a fringe of Hindu chiefs in the extreme south and along the Malabar and Konkan coasts. The Hindu chiefs were saved by Mughul encroachments from the north and Maratha emergence to the west, and in the late seventeenth century the whole system was overthrown by one of the periodic assertions of northern authority. Aurangzeb's conquest of the Deccan kingdoms was more thorough than 'Alā-ud-dīn's, but it was hardly more lasting. From the beginning Mughul power in the Deccan was drained by the running sore of Maratha activity in the Western Ghats, and it was soon to be paralysed by wars of succession, by Maratha advances northwards, and by foreign incursions from the north-west. From 1720 the Mughul garrisons were in effect left to their own devices, and there emerged a revised version of the balance of power of the fourteenth and fifteenth centuries. This time it was a triple instead of a twin balance, the new and disturbing element being the Maratha power to the west. The Muslim power in the Deccan redeployed itself under the first Nizam and last Mughul governor to form the virtually independent state of Hyderabad, the Peshwas of Poona grew formidable in the west and the Hindu power in the south emerged once more as the state of Mysore. Hyderabad, including the whole coastline from Orissa to Tanjore, was the largest and the Peshwa's the most powerful state. The development of the new geopolitical pattern in the south was interrupted by the Anglo-French struggle in the mid-century which left at its close a fourth power controlling the western seaboard and the Carnatic plain.

At the same time the Hindu state of Mysore was transmuted into a Muslim power by the adventurer Haidar Ali, being made formidable by his talents. The wars of the next twenty years served to emphasize the power of the four by securing the eclipse of lesser states. The Nawab of the Carnatic sank to be an ingenious but helpless debtor in the hands of the Company; Tanjore was equally dependent. The ancient Malabar rulers including the Zamorin of Calicut, whose ancestors had warred with the Portuguese, were absorbed by Mysore and only Travancore maintained a precarious independence.

At the close of the second Mysore war in 1784 the leading power in the south, apart from the Company, was Mysore itself. It owed this position partly to the genius of its late ruler Haidar Ali, and partly to its central position on the Deccan plateau which enabled its rulers to move on interior lines to threaten the Company in Madras, the Nizam in Hyderabad, and the Peshwa in Poona by turns. The Marathas would indeed have been stronger if they had been united. But since the thirties much of their energy had been diverted by the glittering prospect of northern empire. The Marathas might have had northern empire or southern dominion but their strength was insufficient for both. Further, they were no longer a united people, but rapidly splitting into five states nearly as jealous of each other as they were aggressive towards others. The fame of Mysore was maintained by Haidar's son Tipu, who inherited most of the talents of his father without his judicious and cautious temper. Restless and erratic but brilliant in tactics and fertile in expedients, he kept the south in continual alarm and was regarded, until the day of his death, as the most formidable power with which the Company had to deal. Against his personal defects, his intolerance, and his maltreatment of prisoners must be set his incessant activity, his military genius which frequently baffled British generalship by the speed of his movements and the rapidity of his changes of front, and his skill as an administrator which kept his territories loyal under the severest tests and was acknowledged by their British invaders. His name dominates the writings of the time; his destruction gave to Wellesley a resounding prestige which carried him through six more years of wars and of mounting expense and criticism.

Cornwallis came to India forbidden, under Pitt's India Act, to declare war on country powers or conclude treaties for that purpose without the consent of London. No man was more anxious than Cornwallis to obey these injunctions, but he could not evade the commitments which his predecessors had entered into. In the south he found himself the victim of the divided control of pre-Regulating Act days, when Madras was a law unto itself and often a singularly injudicious one. In 1765 the district of Guntur in the northern Sarkars had been assigned to Basalat Jung, a brother of the Nizam, as a *jagir* or fief for his life. Its resumption by the Madras government in 1779 was one of several factors which prompted the Nizam to join Haidar Ali and the Marathas in a triple attack on Madras in that year. Hastings secured the Nizam's neutrality by handing back Guntur. Basalat Jung died in 1782, but the Nizam evaded the surrender of the district. It was Cornwallis's demand, under the treaty of 1765, for the return of Guntur, which led to war with Tipu Sultan. The Nizam complied but made a counter-demand under the treaty of Masulipatam of 1768, for troops for the reduction of the district of Balaghat. This district was now in the possession of Mysore, and had been recognized as such by a treaty made by the same Madras government only a year after its treaty of Masulipatam with the Nizam. Further, Mysore's possession of Balaghat had been confirmed by the treaty of Mangalore which ended the war with Tipu (the second Mysore war) in 1784. Madras had double-crossed itself and made it impossible for Calcutta to behave with honour to all parties. In this dilemma, which sorely vexed him, Cornwallis chose the friendship of the party he judged least dangerous to the Company. He recognized the treaty of 1768 with the Nizam as binding as being prior to those of 1769 and 1784. In a letter he promised to hand over Balaghat should it ever come into the possession of the Company; he undertook to supply troops to the Nizam provided that they were not used against any power in alliance with the Company; and he supplied a list of such powers from which the name of Tipu Sultan was excluded. Cornwallis comforted himself with the reflection that war with Tipu was bound to come and that his action was only hastening the inevitable. War with Tipu may indeed have been inevitable, and not merely on account of Tipu's bad faith. His restless and ambitious temper was bound to see in the Company the principal threat to his power, and his previous experience of the Madras government could have fostered in him no great opinion of European good faith. Further, he lacked his father's insight into the depth of the Company's reserves of power or the restraint to bide his time until a more convenient season. But the action of Cornwallis lowered the diplomacy of the Company to the level of the contemporary country powers; its boasted integrity was no better than the duplicity of the Nizam or the shifts of the Marathas. The misfortune was not that the Company fell below the diplomatic standard of the day but that it did not rise any higher. It sank below the level which it claimed to maintain and which, from the time of Warren Hastings, it had in some measure achieved. If Cornwallis had declined to lend troops to the Nizam in time of peace, or had retained the name of Tipu in the list of the Company's friends, his action might not have been wholly consistent and might not have prevented eventual war, but it would have been an honourable attempt at compromise between conflicting obligations. As it was, Tipu, in the manner of the time, regarded the omission of his name as a signal that an attack was being prepared and took care to strike the first blow.

Tipu precipitated the war by an attack on Travancore, which was in alliance with the Company, at the end of 1789. Cornwallis countered by forming a league with the willing but ineffective Nizam and the ever-ready Marathas. At first Tipu's agility in manœuvre and skill in cutting off supplies was too great for the slow-moving and heavily cumbered Madras army under General Medows. At the end of 1790 Cornwallis himself took command. He took Bangalore, but though he defeated Tipu in the field and arrived within sight of Seringapatam, his agile adversary was able to compel a second retreat by cutting off supplies. A third advance brought final success and Cornwallis was able to dictate peace terms under the walls of Seringapatam in March 1792. One-half of Tipu's territories were annexed, and indemnity of over £3 million (330 *lakhs*) was exacted, all prisoners were released, and two of Tipu's sons were handed over as hostages. Wisdom after the event suggested that it would have been better to have annexed the whole state whereby another war would have been prevented, or, as an alternative, to have restored the ancient Hindu dynasty. But the political horizon did not present the same perspective to the observer of 1793 as to the historian of 1956, or even the statesman of 1800. Tipu had run even Cornwallis close. Cornwallis was in an exposed situation, with sickness in his camp, treachery suspected among his allies, and the hot weather upon him. A single check on the walls of Seringapatam would have made his position critical. The man of Yorktown had no mind to add a Saratoga to his record. Half-annexation was accepted as a prudent measure of safeguard, but full annexation would have disturbed the Indian allies and aroused public opinion at home. Pitt's India Act still forbade the acquisition of fresh territories. Further, the territory was too large to be administered with any prospect of efficiency. Madras had not impressed with its handling of the Carnatic and full annexation might well have left the last state of Mysore worse than the first. The alternative of restoring the Hindu dynasty was proposed by Medows. But there could be no certainty that a discredited family, even with the aid of the minister Purnea, could maintain itself in so large an area against Marathas and the Nizam without, and the discontented elements which would remain within. Cornwallis adopted what seemed to be the sensible compromise of drawing the dragon's teeth while leaving him his lair.

The effect of the annexation was virtually to surround Mysore with British territory, except on the north-west and north-east, where the Marathas and the Nizam made gains. The taking of Malabar and Coorg cut Tipu off from the western sea, the retention of Baramahal deprived him of the passes through which his father had descended to devastate the Carnatic. Tipu was confined and shut in, and for all his will for revenge might have remained quiet if events in Europe had not raised false hopes in his restless mind.

Peace continued for five years during the administration of Sir John Shore. Cornwallis's last act in the south was to propose a mutual guarantee between Peshwa and Nizam against attack from Tipu. When the Marathas demurred the Nizam turned to Cornwallis for security. Cornwallis would give no more than general assurances of support, which were esteemed even less in India than in the Europe of that time, or since. When Shore explicitly declined any definite commitment, the Nizam turned to an able French officer, Raymond, for the training of his army. The Nizam was not deceived as to the intentions of the Marathas. The Maratha confederacy had long since developed from a co-operative enterprise to a permanent family quarrel. In 1795, by a sudden twist in the bewildering maze of Maratha politics, the five units united for the purpose of plundering the Nizam. Although the Nizam was as much an ally as Travancore had been when succoured by Cornwallis in 1789, Shore refused all help. Such were the shifts to which a faithful observance of the non-interference policy drove honest men. As a result the Nizam was heavily defeated at Kharda in March 1795. A state of virtual vassalage was only avoided by a renewal of Maratha disputes which caused the Poona minister Nana Fadnavis to buy the Nizam's support in a disputed succession to the Peshwaship at the price of most of the fruits of Kharda.

The curtain was rung down on the struggle for power in the south by Lord Mornington, soon to become the Marquis Wellesley. Apart from the weakness of the Nizam, the restlessness of the Marathas, and the implacability of Tipu, a new factor in the situation had appeared in the form of the French Revolution. Since 1793 Britain had been at war with France and since 1797 alone in the struggle. France was known to have designs on the East; as Wellesley set sail for India Bonaparte was preparing his expedition to Egypt. To forestall France in all quarters was even more important than to counteract the Afghans in the north-west. When, therefore, Wellesley learned that Tipu in his anxious search for allies had sent agents to the French island of Mauritius, that the governor there had rashly proclaimed a French alliance with Mysore, that Tipu had planted a tree of liberty at Seringapatam, and that a handful of French troops had landed on the Malabar coast, he thought that instant and drastic action was called for. He removed to Madras and made characteristically thorough preparations while seeking to isolate his foe. The Nizam was the first object of his attention. Knowing himself to be weaker than Tipu and the Marathas as well as the Company Nizam Ali proved willing to conclude the first of Wellesley's subsidiary treaties. In September 1798, after delicate negotiations skilfully conducted by Malcolm and Kilpatrick, the Nizam agreed to dismiss Raymond and his French officers, to receive in their stead four batallions of Company's troops, and to increase the subsidy for their support from ½ to 2 *lakhs* of rupees a month. He gained security but he lost control of foreign relations. The Peshwa was next approached. Too wily to fall into the trap of a subsidiary treaty and too suspicious to co-operate fully with the British, he remained aloof but neutral. When preparations were complete Tipu was called upon for an explanation of the Governor of Mauritius's proceedings and his reply was duly interpreted as a signal for war. A double attack was launched from Madras and Bombay;

within two months Seringapatam was besieged. After Tipu had refused a demand for the cession of half his territory and the payment of £2 million as an indemnity, the city was stormed on 6 May 1799 and Tipu killed, fighting bravely in the breach. Though as determined upon war as any twentieth-century dictator Wellesley was surprised at the completeness of his success. His real object was the removal of the French menace to India which he exaggerated but in which he sincerely believed, and the establishment of British hegemony in the south. He was prepared for some annexation, but now found himself with the whole of Tipu's still extensive dominions at his disposal. His dilemma was that of Cornwallis, for where were the British administrators for such an area to come from? In addition the Nizam was entitled to half the territory annexed and this would unduly aggrandize him. The solution was to restore the Hindu royal family still living in seclusion in Mysore, whose heir was a child five years of age. An area rather larger than the old dominions of Mysore was allotted to the child raja, with Tipu's Brahman minister Purnia as the *de facto* ruler. The arrangement was sealed by a subsidiary treaty on the new model, which, in addition to the usual provisions, enabled the Governor-General to interfere in the internal administration of the country and even to take over its direct management in the interests of good government. This was to prove important later. The Company annexed Kanara in the west, thus completely encircling Mysore with British territory, Coimbatore in the south, and Seringapatam with other land in the east. The Nizam received land adjacent to his state, but soon surrendered it in settlement for the support of his subsidiary force. Under Purnia the new Mysore state enjoyed a continuity of administration until 1811, while the districts transferred to the British were soon to receive the attention of the humane and industrious Munro.

British supremacy in the south was now established and it only remained to tidy up, as it were, the loose ends. The Carnatic was still under the nominal control of its nawab, with the proviso that the British could assume the administration in time of war. The plausible and pliable but none the less tenacious Walajah had died in 1795, to be succeeded by his less able son, Umdut-ul-Umara. It was irksome to Wellesley to give up anything, let alone the most fertile province of the south; on Umdut's death in 1801 he revealed correspondence with Tipu which he considered had placed him and his father 'in the condition of public enemies of the British Government in India'. He selected Azam-ud-daula, a grandson of Muhammad Ali, as titular nawab and took over the actual administration.[1] At almost the same time a disputed succession in the Maratha principality of Tanjore[2]

---

[1] In 1853 Dalhousie abolished the title of Nawab of the Carnatic. The head of the family has since been designated the Prince of Arcot and accepted as the premier noble of the Madras Presidency.

[2] The Tanjore dynasty was a survival of the Maratha wars of Aurangzeb's time. The raja descended from Sivājī's father, Shāhjī. The pension lapsed in 1855 on the failure of heirs.

enabled Wellesley to take over that administration in return for a pension of 4 *lakhs* of rupees (£40,000) a year. The British dominion south of the Kistna was now complete.

It remains to note something of the internal history of the Madras Presidency during the previous twenty years. The presidency never fully recovered during this period from the results of the Anglo-French wars. The Company's servants were demoralized, first on the model of Bengal, by the corrupting influence of the princes whose fortunes depended upon European aid, secondly by the opportunities for quick returns provided by wars with its relaxing of supervision and stimulation of spending, and thirdly by the presence of the greatest single centre of corruption in the Nawab of the Carnatic. The Anglo-French wars had left Muhammad Ali with formal independence and the title of Nawab Walajah,[1] but they had been waged in his name largely with Company's funds, with the result that he was deep in debt. During the sixties the Company's debt had been reduced but a fresh one was contracted with the servants of the Company themselves. Then came the Mysore and Maratha wars, with the result that the nawab plunged deeper still into debt while his embarrassments were aggravated by persistent maladministration. Official pressure to reform the administration and private demands for arrears of interest steadily mounted, but the nawab soon detected the possibilities of playing off creditors and Company against each other, well knowing that in many cases they were the same persons. It was the official interest of the Company to reform the Carnatic administration and this pointed to the taking over of the state and the funding of the public and private debts on reasonable terms. But this was against the interest of the private creditors, who would lose their exorbitant rates of interest, and against the private interests of many officials themselves who were also private creditors. It was to the interest of these men to keep the question of the nawab's debts simmering, as it were, but never to allow it to come to the boil when drastic action would be necessary; or to change the metaphor, to top the nettle from time to time by such measures as the reduction of interest, rather than to grasp it firmly at the root.[2] The nawab showed much address and persistence in using private interest to influence public causes and thus exercised an influence in the Company's affairs which was as unhealthy as it was tenacious. The leader of the private creditors was the Company's merchant Paul Benfield, who, if not necessarily the most unscrupulous, was certainly the most successful and notorious. He and his friends did not neglect to maintain an interest both with the Company and in public life in England. Benfield himself was a member of Parliament for many years and the Indian interest was a force to be reckoned with in England as well as in India. The nawab was the sworn enemy of the Raja of

---

[1] By the treaty of Allahabad, 1765.

[2] The internal interest on the private debt was reduced by stages from 36 per cent. to 10 per cent., but as fast as one set of debts were regularized, a fresh crop appeared.

Tanjore and his influence reached its height in 1776 when Lord Pigot on attempting the restitution of Tanjore to its Hindu raja was deposed and imprisoned by a group of Benfield's friends.

The affairs of Madras reached their nadir in 1780 when Haidar Ali's irruption into the Carnatic found the Madras government entirely unprepared and quite unable to deal with the crisis. With the arrival of Lord Macartney as governor in that year there began a steady improvement. Macartney was able and upright but he was handicapped by the dispatch from Bengal, before his arrival, of an agent to watch over the implementing of a treaty negotiated between Hastings and Muhammad Ali in Calcutta. Macartney went to Madras as a supporter of Hastings, but the fluctuations of the Company's London politics lead to misunderstandings which bred distrust between the two. Macartney rejected the Calcutta treaty but imposed one on the same lines upon the nawab in 1781. The nawab assigned the revenue to Macartney in person for five years. But the actual transmission of the revenue was successfully obstructed by the nawab's agents. Macartney then himself assumed the power of appointing renters, and introduced considerable reforms. His work was first threatened by a change in Hastings's attitude and then undone in 1785 by orders from home cancelling the assignment of the nawab's revenues to the Company. These changes were not unconnected with the activities of Benfield's friends in London. Macartney resigned and went home to argue his case but the Madras interest was for the moment too strong.

But such a state of affairs was too unsatisfactory to last for long even in Madras. In 1787 a fresh treaty was concluded with the nawab, by which he was to pay four-sevenths of his revenue to the creditors, and to place the sole military power with the Company. During Tipu's war Cornwallis went a step further. In 1790 he took over the Carnatic and found control so conducive to the conduct of the war that by a fresh treaty in 1792 it was arranged that the Company should take over the whole administration in time of war. Still scope was left for the nawab's ingenuity and the creditors' activities. It was left to Wellesley, helped by the welcome occasion of the last Mysore war, to retain the administration which he had taken over, to select a new nawab who agreed to accept a pensionary status, and to arrange for the liquidation of the debt. Only then was the official air cleared from the taint of corruption and the ground cleared for serious civil administration.

AUTHORITIES

THE internal affairs of Madras are dealt with in detail by H. D. Love, *Vestiges of Old Madras* (4 vols., 1913). For the Nabobs' debts see the *Cambridge History of India*, vol. v, in chaps. xv and xxi. A valuable and revealing document is the *Private Correspondence of Lord Macartney* ed. C. C. Davies (Camden Series, 1950) which has a good introduction.

For Haidar and Tipu see the *History of Hyder Naik* by Husain Ali Khan Kirmani (trans. Miles) 1842, the *Lives of Haidar Ali and Tipu Sultan* by Ghulam Mohammad (1855), and L. B. Bowring, *Haidar Ali and Tipu Sultan* (1899). The latest work on Mysore is by C. HAYAVARDANA RAO, *History of Mysore 1399–1799* (3 vols., 1943–8), an exhaustive and learned study. There is also a modern *History of Tipu Sultan* by M. H. KHAN (1952). All these writers have been bemused by the wars and there has as yet been no proper assessment of Mysore administration. The best study of Mysore is still MARK WILKS, *Historical Sketches of the South of India* (3 vols., 1810–17). For the final episode WELLESLEY's *Despatches* may be consulted.

For English life in Madras see H. H. DODWELL, *The Nabobs of Madras* (1926).

F. BUCHANAN, *A Journey through Mysore . . .* (3 vols., 1807), gives a detailed description of the state of Mysore just after the conquest. See also A. DAS GUPTA, *Malabar in Asian Trade* (1967).

CHAPTER 9

Shore and Wellesley

LORD CORNWALLIS had been appointed governor-general because it was considered that only a personality from British public life high above local jealousies and ambitions could control the Company's servants in Bengal. He himself hoped that such public men would always be found, but when the time came no 'very proper man of distinction', in George III's words, could be found to undertake the task. Dundas, the President of the Board of Control, for a time thought of going out himself, but in the end the choice fell upon Sir John Shore. Shore had been collaborator of Cornwallis in his work of reform and reorganization, and the esteem in which he was held was such that Cornwallis thought that an exception might be made in his favour. Shore justified every estimate of his ability and integrity, but like a too faithful chief-of-staff, felt embarrassed when entrusted with supreme authority. His handling of affairs showed a caution which verged on irresolution and a faithfulness to non-intervention which verged upon disregard for obligations.

Shore succeeded in 1793 during the high noon of the non-intervention, non-aggressive policy laid down by Pitt's India Act in 1784. At the time the Act was passed it was believed that many Indian wars had been the result of the ambition and cupidity of the Company's own servants. Therefore any declaration of war or annexation had been forbidden without the consent of Parliament. This firm directive was supported by other considerations. It was believed that the Indian powers were not in themselves aggressive and if left to themselves they would, as it were, sort themselves out and thereafter strike a balance with the British power in India. Mysore, the Nizam, and Madras would divide the south; the Marathas would settle their own disputes and then be balanced by Afghans and Sikhs in the north and by Bengal to the east. Thus tranquillity of a sort would be restored to India and trade would proceed. There was the further consideration that all danger from France or other European powers had now been removed. A trading company had no business to rule for the sake of ruling provided that it could make its profits without it. Parliament from concern for the Indian people and the directors from concern for their profits were determined to curb the high-spirited instincts of the men on the spot.

This system worked well enough under Cornwallis for the reason that the assumptions upon which it was based held good. Danger from France remained in abeyance and in the first years of the revolution seemed likely to be suspended for many years. The Maratha disputes continued and seemed likely to result in the supremacy of their ablest and most judicious leader, Mahadji Sindia. The Sikhs were growing in power in the distracted Panjab, with the Afghans in uncertain but not threatening strength beyond. Only in the south did Cornwallis find himself involved in war and there the exception could be explained on the ground of Tipu's well-known restlessness and of the clumsiness of Cornwallis's attempt to reconcile two mutually contradictory obligations.

It is now easy to see that the continued success of non-intervention depended upon the continued validity of these assumptions. The French must continue to be remote and the Maratha disputes evolve into an hegemony which would be constructive and non-aggressive. But when Shore assumed office in 1793 the facts of politics had already begun to upset the logic of politicians. It was Shore's misfortune to strive to maintain a policy whose bases were being steadily shorn away by unexpected political events. It was his weakness not to perceive the new forces which were developing and to adapt the accepted policy to meet them. The changes were broadly two. In Europe during these years a distracted France apparently in dissolution was becoming a dynamic revolutionary France with a leader of genius about to show his interest in the East by an expedition to Egypt. In India the expected Maratha evolution was cut short by the death of Mahadji Sindia in the prime of life in 1794. Thereafter fresh dissensions destroyed all prospects of stability in central India and gave rise to renewed aggression in order to divert attention from internal stress. The hope of Indian tranquillity was seen to be vain and non-intervention a blindness to the facts.

On Sindia's death Nana Fadnavis regained his influence in Poona and thought to cement it by an attack on the Nizam. The Nizam had already sought a defined guarantee of security from Cornwallis and later from Shore, but though these had been refused he was listed as a friend of the Company and was as much an ally as the Raja of Travancore had been when Cornwallis came to his rescue against Tipu in 1790. He had, moreover, earned this friendship by the cession of Guntur and by his help in the war against Tipu. In spite of this Shore held aloof and thus gave colour to the belief that his real motive was fear of the Marathas. Indian confidence in British good faith was shaken, and the unease was increased by the Nizam's resounding defeat at Kharda in 1795. Had the Marathas remained united the position would indeed have been serious, but they immediately dissolved into contending factions and the Nizam himself shortly recovered much of his lost ground as the price of support for Nana at Poona. The immediate effect was the Nizam's employment of Raymond and other French officers to train a body of disciplined troops.

In Oudh Shore was more successful. The state was already under the Company's protection with troops stationed within its borders. He could therefore afford to be vigorous without fear of parliamentary censure. In 1797 the Nawab Asaf-ud-daula died and a reputed son, Wazir Ali, was recognized as his successor. On realizing that Wazir Ali was both illegitimate and incapable, Shore intervened to replace him by a brother of Asaf, the capable but unfortunate Saadat Ali. A new treaty was enacted, which included the cession of the fort of Allahabad, the complete control of foreign relations, and the raising of the annual subsidy to 76 *lakhs* of rupees in return for a guarantee of all the nawab's dominions. The presence of the Afghans under Zaman Shah at Lahore, of whom the Company had been unduly sensitive since the days of Ahmad Shah Durrānī, possibly contributed to this stiffness. It was a presage of Wellesley's own later policy.

Shore's Indian career was ended by one of the periodic combinations of the Bengal officers at the end of 1795. They had been angered by Cornwallis's reductions of inflated allowances and now took action against his gentler and less influential successor. The news of his concessions determined the directors upon his recall. Cornwallis was persuaded to return but withdrew on learning that Dundas in his turn had made concessions he deemed inadmissible. Thereupon Lord Mornington was appointed Governor-General.

The new governor-general at the time of his appointment was thirty-seven years of age. He was small of stature but keen of face, imperious in temper, talented, energetic, and of boundless ambition. A classical scholar in his youth, he had been a M.P. for several years and one of the East India commissioners since 1795. He had the rare political insight which detects changes in political balance at the times of their occurrence but lacked the final political virtue of nicely balancing means with ends, of knowing the limit to which one's resources will stretch. His insight encouraged him to attempt and his ability accomplished a series of dazzling triumphs, but his lack of self-limitation in dealing with both foes and colleagues led first to a series of checks and then to recall. With an imaginative sweep greater than his illustrious brother Arthur, he fell short in the quality of judicious poise. He was well fitted to impress the authority of the home government upon the Company's servants, 'repelling all approaches to familiarity with a degree of vigour amounting to severity', but quite unwilling to be controlled in his turn by his directorial and ministerial colleagues.

The changes brought about during the seven years of Wellesley's leadership were so great that they are rightly considered to mark an epoch in the development of the British power in India. But Mornington's appointment marked no conscious revolution in the policy of the British in India. There was rather a change of political climate and a change of emphasis; both suited the ardent and enterprising temper of the new ruler, who was able to effect a revolution before the realization of what he was doing resulted in his recall. A change of political climate had occurred both in India and Europe. It was becoming clear that the Indian powers would not of themselves develop a pattern of power politics which would produce a balanced international system. A concert of Indian powers would never match the eighteenth-century concert of Europe. Commerce demanded tranquillity for its conduct and the maintenance of permanent armaments eat into profits. Those who had looked to balance began therefore to consider supremacy as the political aim of the British in India; and even within the Company itself there were those who defended a forward policy on the ground that it would be more economical in the long run.[1] Even more marked was the change of climate with regard to Europe. The days were past when the French Revolution was believed to have heralded the beginning of a new era, and when Pitt had clung to peace till the last possible moment. Revolutionary France was now believed to menace liberty in England and the established order everywhere. The first coalition had come to an inglorious end with the treaty of Campo Formio in October 1797, and young General Bonaparte was known to be preparing a large expedition for an unknown destination. The British governing class were nervous with apprehension and tense with resolution. After the Italian campaign of 1796 no move by the French was incredible and every measure to forestall them welcome. Wellesley's first measures evoked a warm response from all who were disillusioned by the continuance of Indian anarchy and alarmed by the phenomenal growth of French power. And these included both Pitt and Dundas.[2]

It was in this favourable atmosphere that Wellesley was able to pursue his own policy without apparent disharmony with the home authorities. His personal policy was simple; all traces of French influence must be swept from India in order to allow no foothold to an invading army, and since Indian anarchy encouraged such footholds, on this and on general grounds non-intervention and balance must be replaced by British supremacy in India. At first his ideas of the practicable went no farther than 'forward against the French'; it was the dazzling success of his first move which encouraged him to proceed towards the larger aim.

Wellesley's (for by this name we shall henceforth know him)[3] two main instruments of policy were war and diplomacy leading to the subsidiary treaty. In practice the subsidiary treaty was often but the prelude to war, but this was a reversal of intended procedure which he never failed to accept. These were supplemented by *diktats* by which feeble princes were bowed off the *masnad* into well-pensioned retirements. Wellesley himself never had any doubts as to the legality or morality of his proceedings because he was convinced that in the large view British supremacy was in the interests of the people of India as a

[1] e.g. David Scott of the directorate.
[2] On 18 June 1798 the secret committee informed Wellesley that Bonaparte's armament had left Toulon on 19 May. On 18 Oct. Wellesley heard of the invasion of Egypt and on 31 Oct. of Nelson's victory of the Nile.
[3] Mornington was created Marquess Wellesley on the defeat of Tipu.

whole. With a curious blindness to its democratic implications, he sacrificed princes for the good of the people. On each issue as it arose he was comforted by a generous talent for convincing himself that his opponents were wholly in the wrong. The most striking of these instruments was the subsidiary treaty. As with most of Wellesley's measures it was not in itself wholly novel. The originality lay in the use he made of it. Clive concluded the first subsidiary treaty with Shuja-ud-daula of Oudh in 1765, and Hastings and Cornwallis had developed it. But whereas these men concluded their treaties for a limited purpose with a particular prince, Wellesley regarded them as part of the technique of supremacy. The treaties with Oudh were defensive, treating Oudh as an outwork of Bengal against the Marathas and Afghans; the treaties of Wellesley were offensive, placing advanced posts of British troops in the heart of purely Indian territory. They were the prelude to British control of non-Company India and they provided vantage-points for winning the wars which they provoked.

The nature of the subsidiary treaty was simple and it proved as effective as it was simple. A prince in danger from his neighbours was encouraged to turn to the British for help. The British guaranteed his independence against all comers, and to make the guarantee effective, stationed a detachment of Company's troops within the state, which was pledged to march against any invader. The prince undertook to pay and supply these troops either in cash or by alienating a portion of his territory to British control. In the primary purpose of giving a prince security these treaties proved completely successful, but they also had secondary effects. The prince was secure against his Indian enemies but also irrevocably attached to his British friends. The princely fly was firmly enmeshed in the British political web, and any hope of escape was idle. The people for their part were spared recurrent invasions and the harrowing scenes which accompanied armies on the march at this period, but they had no resource against the vagaries of the ruler himself. The efficiency of these treaties in undermining the independence of their beneficiaries was such that one is prompted to ask why any ruler was ever induced to agree to them. The answer is that some (like the Peshwa Baji Rao) were too short-sighted or distressed to consider ultimate consequences when concluding them, while others (like the Nizam) preferred certain dependence with a treaty to certain extinction without one. Opportunism was universal at this time, and while most princes realized the strength of the British at the moment, few had much conception of the secret springs of power which would make that strength still greater. The most distressed still hoped that some turn in events might yet restore their fortunes.

We can now turn to the actual conduct of affairs by Wellesley. Wellesley arrived in May 1798 and within a few weeks heard of the proceedings of Tipu's agents on the Isle de France (Mauritius). With a mind brimming with anti-Jacobinism and fearful of Bonaparte's designs his first impulse was to levy instant war. But the proverbial unreadiness of the Madras government proved a much more effective hindrance than their customary counsels of caution. Wellesley then proceeded to prepare armies in Madras and Bombay with characteristic thoroughness, himself moving to Madras at the end of the year. The delay thus incurred was turned to good account by the diplomatic isolation of Tipu. In September 1798, as already described, the first of Wellesley's subsidiary treaties was concluded with the Nizam. Attempts also made to secure the Peshwa secured his neutrality if not his signature. The success of the war which followed surpassed Wellesley's expectations and left him with the whole of Mysore at his disposal. In this predicament he showed good sense in restoring half of Tipu's state to the heir of the dispossessed Hindu Rajas of Mysore. This first success, complete and resounding as it was, echoed through India and Britain alike. At a stroke the prestige of the Company in India was restored and elevated to a fresh peak; in Britain this success, following Nelson's victory of the Nile, provided a much-needed tonic. It was in a way even more effective than Nelson's fleet, for the British were accustomed to victory at sea but had become sadly unused to it by land. The extravagant language used both about Wellesley and his achievement revealed not only the over-estimation in which Tipu had been held, but the depression of spirits into which the British had fallen.

The prestige thus gained by Wellesley sustained him against all criticism until his armies were checked by Holkar. He was now master of the south with the Nizam in his train and had no Indian power of substance to deal with except the distracted Maratha confederacy. There followed a series of *diktats* whose manner even the most convinced admirers have found difficult to justify. There was first the Carnatic itself. Amongst the papers captured at Seringapatam was correspondence with both Muhammad Ali and Umdut-ul-Umara. Wellesley was convinced that the Carnatic should be under British control and it did not require a very detailed scrutiny to convince him that he had now been given just cause for seizure. On the death of Umdut-ul-Umara in 1801 his eldest son was set aside in favour of a grandson of Muhammad Ali who was recognized as nawab on condition that he resigned the administration to the Company. One-fifth of the net revenue was set aside for his support and the whole of his debts taken over by the Company. This liquidation of the double government was both overdue and salutary, making sound administration possible for the first time, but it would have been better if Wellesley had based his actions on the people's needs rather than on their princes' pretended crimes. Shortly before, a disputed succession in Tanjore provided a pretext for taking over this state from the descendant of Sivājī's brother. The justification of misgovernment here was lacking but that of insignificance was greater. In the same year, 1799, on the death of the Nawab of Surat, the successor of the Mughul governors of the chief Mughul port, he pensioned the new nawab and assumed the government. Surat's value as a fort and as a strategic point between the Deccan and Gujarat was here the justification.

Wellesley now turned his attention to Oudh. Since 1765 this most prosperous of Mughul provinces had been regarded as a buffer state between Bengal on the one hand and the Marathas and Afghans on the other. Hastings had stationed one brigade in Oudh and Cornwallis had increased it to two. But the more efficiently Oudh was protected the less able it became to take care of itself. Under the listless though cultured sway of Asaf-ud-daula,[1] the army fell into disarray and the finances into confusion, while the state became the happy hunting ground of European concession hunters and adventurers. At the end of the century a series of events again focused attention on Oudh. While the Maratha menace had receded owing to the struggle for supremacy in the Deccan, the Afghan menace was revived by the two visits of Zaman Shah to the Panjab in 1796 and 1798. He never proceeded farther than Lahore and his force was moderate; but it consisted almost wholly of cavalry, and there was no organized force to meet it between the Sutlej and the Ganges. The fact of mobility and the memory of Ahmad Shah gave Zaman Shah a disproportionate importance in the eyes of contemporary politicians and Wellesley was not slow to take advantage of the fact. At this time Asaf had died and the ephemeral Wazir Ali had been replaced by the careful and cautious Saadat Ali at the price of a fresh treaty dictated by Sir John Shore. But the Afghan provided a pretext for interference which the murder of the resident Cherry by Wazir Ali and his short-lived revolt strengthened. Saadat Ali was unable to deal with his rival and showed hesitation and nervousness. Wellesley demanded disbandment of his troops and an increase in the subsidiary force. An offer by the nawab to abdicate 'could not, in his Lordship's opinion be too much encouraged'. When the offer was withdrawn on the knowledge that the succession would go not to the nawab's son but to the Company, this action was made an excuse for further demands. Eventually, on the new plan (first tried out on the Nizam in 1800) of exacting territory in lieu of payment for a subsidiary force, the nawab was deprived of the broad and fertile belt of land between the Ganges and the Jumna and in Rohilkhand which amounted to one-half of his territory. The state of Oudh reremained compact, prosperous, and disorderly, but it was now, except along the northern Himalayan border, entirely surrounded by British territory. It became a domestic problem of the Company and ceased to be a factor in Indian high politics. The nawab, with the encouragement of Lord Hastings, proclaimed himself king in 1819 to the dismay of most Muslim opinion which regarded the act as one of disloyalty to the emperor at Delhi. Thenceforward the rhythm of disorder, remonstrance, and promised reform continued until the final annexation of

---

[1] Asaf was a great builder, his major achievement being the great *Imambara* of Lucknow.

1856. The ceded districts were settled by the governor-general's brother Henry, later Lord Cowley.

So far Wellesley had been carried along on the momentum of the destruction of Tipu with its assumed ensurance against French attack. The doubts of the directors were stifled by the support of the ministry and the acclaim of the public. He now approached the decisive phase of his grand design. So long as the Marathas were outside his system there could be no British supremacy in India; so long as British desired or Marathas feared such supremacy, there could neither be peace on the principle of balance, nor armed neutrality on the principle of mutual fear. At first events seemed once again to play into Wellesley's hands. The Maratha coalition which defeated the Nizam at Kharda dissolved at the moment of victory. The suicide of the young Peshwa Madhu Rao Narayan in October 1795 opened the way to fresh dissensions. In the confusion which followed the ablest politician was Nana Fadnavis. But he had no troops of his own and died in 1800. The new Peshwa Baji Rao II, the son of the ill-fated Ragunath Rao or Rhagoba, possessed all his father's irresolution with none of his charm and few of his talents. Incapable of firm leadership or of inspiring devotion he stumbled from shift to shift and was a congenial subject for Wellesley's technique. The two strongest Maratha leaders were Sindia and Holkar. Daulat Rao Sindia had inherited his uncle's French-trained and led army under Perron, but lacked his ability and was almost as irresolute as Baji Rao himself. In the house of Holkar the successor to the politic Tukoji and the saintly Ahalya Bai was the brilliant but erratic Jaswant Rao, a man cast in the mould of an Italian *condottiere*. He could lead and he could dare and until his reason gave way he moved across the north Indian scene like a blazing and erratic comet. But he had no disciplined army behind him and the day of the light-armed, lean-limbed horsemen who had baffled Aurangzeb were gone. There was no time for these contending forces to sort themselves out before a collision took place with the waiting British power.

After the death of Nana in 1800 'with whom', said the resident, 'departed all the wisdom and moderation of the Maratha government', Maratha politics resolved themselves into a struggle between Sindia and Holkar for the control of the Peshwa Baji Rao. That hapless and vicious prince joined Sindia against Jaswant. The murder of Jaswant's brother made compromise impossible. In October 1802 he defeated Sindia and Baji Rao at Poona and raised to the Peshwaship Amrit Rao, brother by adoption to Baji Rao. Baji Rao was now in dire straits. He fled to Bassein and there accepted in desperation a subsidiary treaty at Wellesley's hands. He accepted a subsidiary force of six battalions, resigned his claims on Surat, accepted British arrangements with the Gaekwar, and promised to abstain from war or relations with foreign powers without British knowledge and consent. He was forthwith restored by Arthur Wellesley to Poona.

The treaty of Bassein was Wellesley's master stroke. It gave the

British the supremacy of the Deccan as Seringapatam had given them south India. If it did not yet convert the British empire in India to the empire *of* India, it brought the issue close to decision, for the remaining Maratha powers had lost the key position of their system, the control of the Maratha homeland. By implication it made war with these powers inevitable since they could not accept the new situation without accepting the ultimate supremacy of the Company. The shock of being face to face with the British power produced a momentary movement to unity. But the Peshwa's hands were tied. The Gaekwar was neutral and Holkar, unready and jealous, retired to Malwa. This left Sindia and the Raja of Berar who had joined forces and crossed the Narbada. This gave Wellesley his chance to demand their withdrawal and on their refusal to declare war in August 1803. The campaign was planned in two parts; in the Deccan to defeat and separate the combined forces and in Hindustan to break up Sindia's disciplined troops under General Perron at Aligarh. Arthur Wellesley's victories of Assaye and Argaon broke the power of the Bhonsla raja and Lake's capture of Delhi and defeat of Perron's army at Delhi and Laswari subdued Sindia.

The treaties of Deogaon with the Bhonsla and of Surji Arjungaon with Sindia ended the war before the end of the year and marked the summit of Wellesley's success. Both states received residents at their courts, recognized the treaty of Bassein, and banished Europeans other than the British from their service. The Company gained Cuttack from the Bhonsla, thus joining in a continuous belt of territory Bengal with Madras. From Sindia the gains were even greater. The Doab or river plain between the Jumna and the Ganges, which had supported Perron's army, together with Delhi and Agra, passed to the British, and the Doab became the 'conquered province' of the Bengal Presidency. The Emperor Shah Alam was taken under protection, though Wellesley was careful to make no formal treaty or recognize imperial claims. All Sindia's lands in the Deccan and Gujarat were annexed and his control in Rajputana loosened. The map of modern India was taking shape.

But Wellesley's position was not so strong as it looked. Holkar was unsubdued, and the two subsidiary treaties did not include subsidiary forces; above all vast distances faced small forces set to control numbers of embittered but not yet hopeless men. Wellesley had buried his fangs in the Maratha prey and could not now withdraw them. The attempt to negotiate with Holkar soon broke down and war broke out in April 1804. Monson's defeat near Kotah and retreat to Agra, the siege of Delhi, and above all Lake's failure to storm Bharatpur broke the spell of Wellesley's magic. The Maratha chiefs began to stir again. His enemies in the Company at last obtained the consent of the ministry for his recall. The race for empire was halted in the last lap.

Thus ended in gloom and frustration the most brilliant period in Anglo-Indian annals to that time. Wellesley had shown what a man of vigour, decision, and clear purpose could affect in a world of dissensions, doubts, and fears. He had divined the weakness of the Indian powers and had applied an effective remedy with great skill as well as great resolution. Throughout, his acts showed vigour and clearsightedness; in the case of the Marathas he displayed virtuosity in planning and co-ordination as well as great skill in threading his way through the tortuous maze of Indian diplomacy. He had the defects of his virtues, an impatience with all that stood in his way, of public rights as well as of public vices, a vigour which ran to high-handedness, a pride which verged on insolence, a tendency to underrate genuine difficulties, a subordination of means to ends. He must be judged in terms of power rather than of rights or public morality. He believed that India was ripe for unification and that this great end made irrelevant all minor wrongs. In fact, he was so nearly right that he may almost be excused his error. But it may be questioned whether the attempt to hustle history really benefited the people of India. His final campaign broke down authority in central India without putting anything in its place; to that extent he must share with others more usually blamed the responsibility for the Pindari scourge.

AUTHORITIES

For Shore, apart from the general histories, see Lord TEIGNMOUTH, *Correspondence of John, Lord Teignmouth* (2 vols., 1843), and H. FURBER (ed.), *The Private Record of an Indian Governor-Generalship* (1933). In these letters to Dundas Shore, while nervous and anxious to please, shows himself to be not incapable of firmness.

For Wellesley Mill is a stern but well-documented critic and Marshman an enthusiastic admirer, calling him the Akbar of the Company's dynasty. There is an admirable modern study by P. E. ROBERTS, *India under Wellesley* (1929). The standard life by R. W. PEARCE, *Memoirs and Correspondence of . . . Richard, Marquess Wellesley* (3 vols., 1846), is only partly concerned with India. But W. H. HUTTON, *Marquess Wellesley* (Rulers of India, 1897) is a good short study. The basic authority is MONTGOMERY MARTIN (ed.), *Despatches, Minutes and Correspondence* (5 vols., 1836). Shorter versions are the *Wellesley Papers* (Anon.) (2 vols., 1914), and S. J. OWEN (ed.), *Selections from Despatches, &c.* (2 vols.), 1877. The first volume contains a survey of Wellesley's administration. The same editor's *Selections of the Despatches of the Duke of Wellington* (1880) may also be used.

For the Marathas see GRANT DUFF or KINCAID and PARASNIS. For home politics see P. E. ROBERTS, op. cit., and C. H. PHILIPS, *East India Company 1784-1834* (1940). See also S. N. QANUNGO, *Jaswant Rao Holkar* (Lucknow, 1955).

RECENT PUBLICATION

IRIS BUTLER's *The Eldest Brother* (1973) is a fascinating re-appraisal of Lord Wellesley, in both his public and private lives, based on new material.

CHAPTER 10

Interlude: Barlow and Minto

IN assessing the reasons for change in Indian policy regard must always be had to conditions in Europe and Britain as well as in India. The directors were subject to commercial and parliamentary opinion as well as mindful of profits abroad; the ministers of the day were sensitive to public opinion and the changes in the international scene. Many factors contributed to the recall of Wellesley and they operated as much in Britain as in India. A section of the directors had supported, or at least acquiesced, in the early stages of the forward policy because they believed that supremacy was the surest way to peace and revival of trade. But their tolerance turned to opposition as expenses grew, nearly doubling the Company's debt in seven years.[1] They were affronted by Wellesley's failure to keep them informed and outraged by his unconcealed contempt. The majority objected to his advocacy of private trade. But it was the ministry not the Company which took the decisive step. Pitt and Dundas at first sustained Wellesley because they believed that the French threat to India was real. Ministers grew lukewarm when wars continued after that threat had been clearly removed. When the French war was renewed in 1804 and England was threatened with invasion Pitt and Dundas (back in office) grew fearful that Wellesley was attempting a task beyond his own strength and beyond British capacity to maintain. The checks of Kotah and Bharatpur confirmed this fear, which explains the promptness of the recall which followed. Britain could not afford an indefinite Indian war in the year of Trafalgar and Austerlitz.

The eight years of marking time which followed should not be regarded as a mere return to the non-intervention principles of Pitt's India Act. It was now generally agreed that there could be no stable Indian balance of power and no decorous concert of Indian powers. Supremacy in some form was the only solution, but the time was not ripe. Napoleon was a more pressing danger than Marathas or Pindaris. The Indian problem was 'put on ice' until the French problem should have been solved. The ardent followers of Wellesley on the spot saw only the devastation of uncontrolled India, and their impatience was both marked and natural. This tension underlay much of the literature and controversy of the period. It was a conflict between what was desirable to British minds in India and what was possible in view of British commitments in Europe. It was an interlude in rather than a

---

[1] From £17 to 31 million between 1799 and 1806.

reversal of the forward policy. The fort must be held until the final sortie could be made.

Wellesley's successor was Cornwallis, now in his sixty-seventh year.[1] His aim was to replace the Company's dominions within the limits of the practicable, but by no means to restore the *status quo*. This meant in practice withdrawal from entanglements with Sindia and Holkar but no disturbance of the position at Hyderabad, Lucknow, or Poona. The measures he proposed erred in one direction as Wellesley had erred in another, but he died at Ghazipur on 5 October while on his way to enforce his views. His successor was Sir John Barlow, a Company's servant and the right-hand man of Wellesley, who showed, like Shore before and Lawrence after him, the permanent official's tendency to caution when vested with supreme responsibility. To him fell the task of drawing in, as it were, the Company's horns, and this work he performed faithfully. In November 1805 Sindia's treaty was revised. Gwalior and Gohad were restored to him and his northern boundary fixed at the river Chambal. He was given a free hand throughout the non-British Deccan and in Rajputana. Holkar, who had been pursued to the Panjab by Lake, was similarly confined to the south of the Chambal but he also had a free hand beyond these bounds. The British retained the Jumna *doab* with Agra and Delhi and its territory where the British stood in a vague but undefined relationship to the Mughul emperor and professed to rule in his name. Elsewhere Barlow maintained the *status quo*, suppressing a nascent intrigue of the Nizam with the Marathas and resisting an attempt by the directors to annul the treaty of Bassein. The south was ruffled by the mutiny of Indian troops at Vellore, fostered by changes in regulations which were thought to reflect upon religion and encouraged by the vicinity of the exiled Mysore princes. It was not comparable to the later Mutiny because the discontent was wholly military, but it cost Lord William Bentinck his governorship of Madras. This was perhaps its most significant result, because that influential nobleman[2] never rested from demanding reparation until he attained the governor-generalship in 1827.

On the whole Barlow did his work efficiently and well. It was no light thing to rein in troops in full career and to control a bevy of politicals flushed with annexations. The value of his work was to reduce the Company's commitments at a time when they could not be indefinitely extended or even maintained at their existing limits, and to do it without provoking a counter-attack from the still independent powers or encouraging those under the Company's control to make a fresh bid for independence. The weak side was the abandonment of commitments to many Rajput states and in particular Jaipur, which in consequence suffered much from renewed Maratha depredations in

[1] He was the oldest governor-general to take office and shared with Curzon a second appointment.

[2] Lord W. Bentinck was a younger son of the 3rd Duke of Portland, Prime Minister from 1807 to 1809.

the next few years. But if it is accepted that, because of the European situation the strength to protect them was not available, it is difficult to see what else could have been done. The Rajput states were so far gone in decay that they could only have proved a liability which at that time the Company could not afford to meet. But Barlow suffered from the pens of those who served him grudgingly and who themselves, as in the case of Charles Metcalfe, came to much the same conservative views when they attained to age and responsibility.

Barlow was recalled on the morrow of his confirmation as Governor-General as the result of a ministerial reshuffle in London. His successor was Lord Minto, who had been one of the managers of Warren Hastings's impeachment and so could be supposed to eschew aggressive designs. He went with genuine reluctance as a believer in marking time but he was too intelligent not to realize quickly that non-intervention could now at best be but watching and waiting. His period of office coincided with the height of the Napoleonic struggle; events in Europe forbade any diversion of strength for a forward move in India; events in India forbade any backward one. His first and principal care was the revived French menace. His arrival in India coincided with the final collapse of the Third Coalition with the defeat of Russia and the treaty of Tilsit. Together Russia and France controlled all Europe and threatened Asia. Napoleon had never given up the dream of Eastern conquest. He toyed with the project of a Franco-Russian expedition through Persia until diverted to Spain and Austria. In addition France still held the Île de France and the Île de Bourbon in the southern Indian Ocean, and controlled the Dutch East Indies through her supremacy in Holland. Minto set out to cement the cracks in the Company's north-western front and then to attack the remaining centres of French power. With much patience and skill and greater discretion than Wellesley he sought to achieve the first of these ends by a series of embassies. Sir John Malcolm was sent on two embassies to Persia to counteract French influence. There he clashed with a royal embassy under Sir Harford Jones. The upshot of much undignified wrangling was a Crown treaty pledging the Shah to resist the French which Minto was feign to accept with what grace he could muster.[1] Mountstuart Elphinstone went to the Afghan Shah Shuja at Peshawar but the treaty concluded proved abortive because the Shah was shortly overthrown. The third and most successful of these embassies was that of the young Charles Metcalfe to the Sikh ruler Ranjit Singh of Lahore.[2] Ranjit had recently established his rule west of the Sutlej and was casting his eyes on the Sikh states to the east, of which Patiala was the chief. The temporary decline of the French menace enabled Minto to take a stronger line than he had originally intended; by the treaty of Amritsar in April 1809 Ranjit Singh obtained a free hand west of the Sutlej in return for undertaking not to interfere to

[1] From these journeys Malcolm obtained the materials for his *History of Persia*.
[2] For an account of the rise of the Sikh power see Book VIII, Chapter 4.

the east. This was the most important event of the period. This treaty lasted until the first Sikh war in 1845, bringing stability to the whole Panjab; Sikh energies were directed westwards and southwards against Afghans and Sindhis instead of east against the Company; the Delhi territory was secured and Charles Metcalfe's reputation made.

This diplomacy was skilful, and in the case of the Sikhs far-reaching in importance. But the danger it was designed to meet was averted by European events which took Napoleon first to Spain, then to Vienna, and finally to Moscow. The recession of the danger enabled Minto to deal with the remaining strongholds of French power in the East. The Dutch colony of the Cape of Good Hope had been finally taken in 1806. When the French seized Portugal the British occupied Goa, and in 1809 Macao in China. In 1810 strong expeditions were sent to the southern French isles, whence the ill-fated proclamation of the Mysore alliance had emanated and which were now nests of skilful French privateers. Both were captured, Bourbon to be returned in 1815 and renamed Réunion, and the Île de France to be retained under its early Dutch name of Mauritius. Minto then turned his attention to the Dutch possessions in the East Indies. In 1810 Amboyna and the Moluccas were seized; in 1811 an expedition under Sir Samuel Auchmuty, with which Minto himself sailed, wrested Java from the French-controlled Dutch after severe fighting. Minto left Stamford Raffles in charge of the government and thus opened a chapter which was brief though lively in the case of Java itself, but led on to the great adventure of Singapore and so to a new phase of British expansion in the East. The seed of the British empire in south-east Asia was carried on Minto's Java-bound transports.

In India itself the Marathas showed no sign of recovery and indeed sank deeper in distress. The desire of every prince to regain or to retain independence was balanced by their financial plight which now threatened bankruptcy. The only other Hindu states were the Rajputs, who were quite incapable of combination, and Ranjit Singh's new Sikh kingdom in Lahore, which had renounced its interest in affairs east and south of the Sutlej. In order to supplement the meagre collections in their own territories, the Maratha chiefs turned their arms against one another and against the Rajput chiefs; the result was increased misery and greater financial stringency. The natural leader of the Marathas was the Peshwa, but while he never ceased to intrigue industriously, the confidence he inspired was so slight and the distaste for his harsh treatment of his own people so great that there was no general move in his favour. Raghuji Bhonsla lay inert at Nagpur, and the Gaekwar had admitted a subsidiary force in 1805. Daulat Rao Sindia was in financial straits and lacked the energy or ability to take the heroic measures needed to restore his fortunes. There remained the brilliant if wayward Jaswant Rao Holkar who alone had the ability to revive the Maratha cause. But he was struck down by insanity in 1808 and died three years later leaving his state in greater disorder than the rest.

Jaswant's incapacity removed the last restraint on the Pindaris; they now emerged as a positive factor in Indian power-politics as well as an ingredient in the mounting misery of central India. According to Malcolm, they were known as early as the latter part of Aurangzeb's reign as auxiliaries to the Marathas. They started their career as adventurers who attached themselves to Maratha chiefs, themselves pursuing predatory warfare against the Mughul power. They were more elusive, less coherent, and even more ruthless than the Marathas themselves. They were the jackals to the Maratha leopards. They differed from the Marathas in having no bonds of caste or creed, no homeland, and no national pride. They came from all communities and latterly were matched by bands of Pathan freebooters. Their only tie was the leader, their only object plunder, and their means of increase recruits from the population which they had themselves plundered and disrupted. They fed on social and political disintegration; they arose, in Malcolm's words, 'like masses of putrefaction in animal matter, out of the corruption of weak and expiring states'. When the Maratha chiefs were strong, they were the jackals of the chase, limited in numbers and kept in some sort of subordination; when the great chiefs were weak their leaders like Chithu, Wasil Khan, and Karim Khan turned their estates into states, recruited their numbers from landless men and disbanded soldiers who roamed the country, and became an independent force in politics. They can be compared to the 'Free Companies' who scourged Italy in the later Middle Ages.

The Pindaris were neither encumbered by tents nor baggage; each horseman carried a few cakes of bread for his horse. The party which usually consisted of two or three thousand good horse with a proportion of mounted followers, advanced at the rapid rate of forty or fifty miles a day, neither turning to the right nor left till they arrived at their place of destination. They then divided, and made a sweep of all the cattle and property they could find; committing at the same time the most horrid atrocities, and destroying what they could not carry away. They trusted to the secrecy and suddenness of the irruption for avoiding those who guarded the frontiers of the countries they invaded; and before a force could be brought against them, they were on their return. Their chief strength lay in their being intangible. If pursued, they made marches of extraordinary length (sometimes upwards of sixty miles) by roads almost impracticable for regular troops. If overtaken, they dispersed, and reassembled at an appointed rendezvous; if followed to the country from which they issued, they broke into small parties. Their wealth, their booty and their families, were scattered over a wide region, in which they found protection amid the mountains, and in the fastnesses belonging to themselves and to those with whom they were either openly or secretly connected; but nowhere did they present any point of attack; and the defeat of a party, the destruction of one of their cantonments, or the temporary occupation of some of their strongholds, produced no effect, beyond the ruin of an individual freebooter, whose place was instantly supplied by another, generally of more desperate fortune, and therefore more eager for enterprise.[1]

A word should be added of the parallel bands of Pathans, whose most noted leader was Amir Khan. They were an equal terror to the countryside, but, unlike the Pindaris, they had regular infantry, organized horse and artillery. Nominally in the service of Holkar, they formed a peripatetic military state. They were more formidable in battle, but being more encumbered were less swift in their movements. They were the special scourge of Rajputana as the Pindaris were of the Deccan.

Thus the shadows lengthened over independent India, and the way was prepared for the passive acceptance of the hated foreign rule, because every form of Indian alternative had become insupportable. Minto's six years of watching and waiting made it clear that while the situation might still be watched it would not wait much longer.

AUTHORITIES

FOR this period H. H. WILSON's continuation of James Mill's *History* is valuable. Sir J. MALCOLM's *Political History* (1826) is also useful, Malcolm being an actor as well as an observer. For Minto see Countess of MINTO, *Lord Minto in India* (1880). The embassies are dealt with by J. W. KAYE in his *Life of Lord Metcalfe*, 2 vols. (2nd ed., 1858), and *Life of Sir J. Malcolm* (2 vols., 1856), as well as by E. THOMPSON in his *Charles, Lord Metcalfe* (1937). The Kabul Mission is given in Sir T. E. COLEBROOKE, *Life of Mountstuart Elphinstone* (2 vols., 1884). ELPHINSTONE himself has contributed his *Account of the Kingdom of Cabaul* (1815). Sir L. GRIFFIN, *Ranjit Singh* (Rulers of India, 1911) is useful for the Sikhs at this time.

For central India see Sir J. MALCOLM's classic *Memoir of Central India* (2 vols., 3rd ed., 1832), which includes an account of Ahalya Bhai, and for the princes, E. THOMPSON, *The Making of the Indian Princes* (1943).

CHAPTER 11

Hastings and Hegemony

EVENTS now moved swiftly to the final act of the drama. India was about to be united under the British because every alternative had been tried and found wanting. The process was quicker than in the case of the Mughuls because the British had greater resources than they and because the local powers were weaker. It involved more dislocation, though it was quicker in evolution, because there was a more complete breakdown of authority in India and there was a greater gulf between the habits and ideas of British and Indians than there was between Mughuls and Indians. So far as the process had gone it appeared to observers, and certainly to Indian observers, to be but a new exercise in power politics, the seizure of the Indian *raj* by one more alien people who in their turn would have their day of glory, their decline and fall. The eight years which had just passed had served, in Indian eyes, as a filling up of the cup of misery until it was ready to overflow.

It was at this juncture that Lord Moira, who will for convenience be designated by his later title of Lord Hastings from the start,[1] appeared in India. Lord Minto had never sat secure in the governor-general's seat because he lacked that essential of strength, the firm support of one party in the state.[2] Cornwallis had been strong in the support of Pitt and Dundas, and Wellesley could safely defy the directors as long as the ministry supported him; Shore and Barlow had been weak because only the directors supported them cordially and not even they consistently. Minto was a Whig appointed to office as a part of a political bargain during the short-lived Ministry of All the Talents. Neither Tory ministry, Whig opposition, nor the Company were strongly in his favour. He kept his place by avoiding too great a divergence from the non-intervention policy, by his successful moves against the French, and by his skill in the conduct of Indian diplomacy. He was not the client of any group; he satisfied and displeased each in turn but not to the extent of recall. Minto's conduct in office represented among other things a very skilful feat of political balance, which should be remembered when considering the tendency to minimize his merits. But by 1812 his term was run. The intrigues which surrounded the formation of the Liverpool ministry on the assassination of Spencer Perceval found the Prince Regent seeking a lucrative

---

[1] He was the 2nd Earl of Moira, and was created Marquess of Hastings in 1817 for his success in the Nepal war.

[2] C. H. Philips, *The East India Company, 1784–1834*, p. 177.

place for his elderly friend Lord Hastings and the directors anxious to remove Sir George Barlow from Madras. Some sort of bargain was struck;[1] Minto was recalled to an earldom and died on his way to rejoin his wife in Scotland.

Lord Hastings was in his fifty-ninth year. He was a soldier who had risen to the rank of general, but his chief claims to fame had been his friendship with the Prince Regent and his reputation for prodigal expenditure. He had opposed Lord Wellesley's policy and he now found himself called upon by circumstances to complete it. Something in the Indian air seemed to suit this fashionable *bon viveur*. The not very successful soldier showed himself to be a strategist of outstanding talent (he was his own commander-in-chief), the ex-courtier became a statesman of large and generous views; the one-time gambler proved a careful steward of the Company's affairs and the man of fashion revealed a real concern for the welfare of the people.

On his arrival Hastings complained that his predecessor had left him with seven quarrels on his hands, 'each likely to demand the decision of arms'. The most serious of these was the Pindari menace, with its intricate connexion with the still independent and distracted Maratha states. But the solution of the problem was postponed by the emergence of a new and more urgent one, that of the Gurkhas of Nepal. It was perhaps well that this was so, for the delay gave Hastings time to survey the situation and to prepare a comprehensive plan which embraced in one wide sweep the whole problem of Indian disorder. He thus settled at one stroke a question which might have required several unco-ordinated campaigns. The only part played by the hills during the eighteenth century had been to provide a refuge for the Sikhs after they had been crushed by the Mughuls in 1717. Through most of their length ancient little kingdoms continued in self-sufficing simplicity and with fluctuating fortunes. The only visitors were pilgrims to the Hindu shrines and the chief article of commerce was ice for the courts. The eastern portion of these hills, stretching 700 miles from Sikkim to the Sutlej, and running back about 100 miles from the plains to the great snowy range, now marched with the Company's lands except for the surviving portion of Oudh. The original Mongolian inhabitants had been conquered by a Hindu race in the fourteenth century and had to some extent intermarried. In 1768 the Gurkha tribe had secured the valley of Khatmandu and from this central position had steadily en-croached both east and west. Kumaon, Garwhal, and the Simla hills had fallen to them in the first years of the nineteenth century, but at the Sutlej their farther advances were blocked by the new Sikh power. The Gurkhas then turned their attention to the plains and at once clashed with the British. The Company now had to pay for Wellesley's Oudh annexations, for it was in the ceded Gorakhpur and Basti Dis-tricts that the main aggressions took place. The Gurkhas were ejected

[1] Ibid., pp. 177–8.

from the posts they had occupied, but a fresh attack in Butwal in 1814 determined Hastings on a regular campaign.

A four-pronged attack was organized along the extended frontier; 34,000 men were employed against 12,000 Gurkhas. In addition negotiations were opened with the dispossessed hill-rajas to the west. The result was sensational; at the end of 1814 three of the forces were thrown back with heavy loss and only Sir David Ochterloney in the west made any progress. All India held its breath, watching intently; and envoys hurried to and fro between the Maratha courts. With remarkable coolness Hastings reinforced his mountain troops while relaxing no precaution in the plains. Though the British were again checked in the centre and east Ochterloney took Jaitak and Gardner Almora in April 1815, thus liberating the whole region from the Sutlej to the Kali river. The Gurkhas then opened negotiations which dragged on all through the summer rains when operations were impossible. A treaty was concluded but not ratified, and operations reopened at the beginning of 1816. This time Ochterloney, now in supreme command, penetrated the deadly *Terai* and marched directly on Khatmandu. A month's operations convinced the Gurkhas that they could not hope to withstand the Company's troops when properly handled. In March they accepted the treaty of Sargauli which they had formerly repudiated and which Hastings was glad to confirm without further penalty. The clouds were gathering to the south and he was anxious to free his hands. By this treaty the Gurkhas accepted a British resident at Khatmandu; they surrendered most of their claims to the *Terai* or forest belt along the southern border. They also surrendered their recent gains between the Gogra and the Sutlej, where they had appeared as the unwelcome conquerors of ancient principalities, whose harshness was still a living memory in recent times. Thus Kumaon, Garwhal, and the Simla hill states passed to the British and the way was prepared for that unique feature of British India, the hill station. Kennedy, the agent for the Simla hill states, set up his headquarters at Sabathu, and from there discovered the beauties and fresh breezes of the Simla ridge.[1] Charles Metcalfe sang the praises of Kasauli in 1827 and Bentinck's residence in Simla on medical advice during the summers of his great northern tour fairly set development in motion. When Auckland followed his example the career of 'the Hills' as providing sanatoria for invalids, places of recreation for the weary and the idle, and summer seats for governments, was assured. India was won in the sweltering plains of Bengal and the Carnatic; it was administered for nearly a century with the help of the air of the pine-scented breezes of the Himalayas.

This clash was enough to convince the Gurkha people of the strength of the British power. It also left both sides with a lively appreciation of each other's qualities. Their mutual respect was the foundation for the

---

[1] Lieut. Ross built a thatched wooden cottage in 1819 and Kennedy the first permanent house in 1822.

friendly relations which persisted throughout the British period. The Gurkhas were now confined to their own homeland. For many years they were absorbed in internal dissensions which led to the rise of the Rajput Rana family and their seizure of the premiership of the state in 1846. From that time the king remained a cipher until his re-emergence into the political limelight in 1949. Their land remained closed to Europeans with few exceptions; trade contacts with India were severely restricted and there was little internal development until the twentieth century. But the Gurkha found an outlet for their enterprise in service with the British. The Gurkha contingent became a regular feature of the British Indian army and distinguished itself in every campaign from the Mutiny onwards. Their military lustre never shone more brightly than during the Burma campaign against the Japanese. The tactical skill of Ochterloney, the planning and judicious moderation of Lord Hastings reaped a rich harvest in the permanent security of the Himalayan frontier and the addition of a devoted corps of hardy and courageous soldiers to the British power in India.

Lord Hastings was now free to deal with central India. We get a very different impression of his methods compared with those of Lord Wellesley. No longer does the eager imperialist seek to force the hand of history by precipitate aggressions, treating the weak with a rigour deserved by the strong, to a voluble commentary of explanation and reproach. Instead we observe a statesman devising means to meet a dangerous situation adequate in range, planning, and resources, but always related to the scale of the problem before him, never pushing beyond the range of the possible or far beyond the bounds of just; as anxious to conserve as to destroy and never seeking to strike before the moment was ripe. He enjoyed the wisdom of age without its loss of vigour, and an imperial vision without the haste or the ruthlessness which so often goes with it. With unhurried deliberation he planned each move, leaving the door of co-operation as well as of war open at each step. It is for this reason that it can be said that if it had been possible for the Maratha confederacy to enter into a working relationship with the British, it would have been done in the time of Lord Hastings. The Maratha power finally fell under the weight of its own ineptitude.

The situation in central India was never more confusing than in 1814. The one factor common to all parties was a dislike and distrust of the British. Sindia was restless and hostile but fearful and slow moving; the Peshwa scheming but irresolute; Holkar still torn with internal feuds; between them all roamed Amir Khan and his Pathans, while from within issued, like wild dogs from between the feet of their nominal masters, the Pindaris to slay, to burn, to plunder, and to disappear. In 1812 they raided the Mirzapur District and they were now, in their cantonments at Nemawar on the Narbada river, planning still more extensive expeditions. In the cold weather of 1814–15 they twice traversed the Nizam's dominions from end to end, plundered portions of the Madras Presidency and returned unscathed with £100,000 worth of booty, leaving a trail of devastation in their wake. By turning on British or British-protected territories they converted a distant nuisance and source of confusion into an active menace, and thus made counter-measures inevitable. They reckoned on their mobility to elude the slow-moving disciplined troops of the Company, but they left out of account the factor of combination. One disciplined force would have been as useless as Aurangzeb's army against the Marathas; several acting in isolation would have been little better. But the British were now able to organize a net of co-ordinated strong points, so that the Pindaris' success in eluding one force provided information for their interception by another. Their lack of fighting ability enabled very small forces to scatter any Pindaris intercepted, and the hostility of the countryside enabled these forces to be thinly spread. In the season of 1816–17 the net was more widely cast; the Pindari *luhburs* were harried and cut up and returned crestfallen to Nemawar. The scene was now laid for their final extinction. The news of the Madras raids converted London to the necessity of action and Hastings could plan a comprehensive drive for the cold weather of 1817–18.

Meanwhile the Marathas had not been idle. A threat by Sindia against Bhopal in early 1815 was called off on a demonstration of British support, and an attack by Amir Khan on Jaipur in 1816 withdrawn for the same reason. But the real centre of interest was at Poona. In July 1815, while the Gurkha war still remained undecided, the envoy of the Gaekwar of Baroda, Gangadhar Sastri, was murdered at the temple of Pandurpur. It was clear that the murder had been planned by Trimbakji the Peshwa's favourite who held Ahmadabad from the Peshwa and was much concerned in the disputes which the Sastri had come to settle under a safe conduct. The resident at Poona was Mountstuart Elphinstone, who conducted the British case with faultless skill even when he had to divine the Governor-General's wishes owing to the pressure of events and delays in the official post. He insisted on the arrest of Trimbakji and his transfer to the British for detention in Salsette. This was accomplished in September by a nicely calculated mixture of conciliation, understanding, and pressure. By the following spring the Nepal war was over and Hastings received a political windfall which perhaps proved the decisive factor in the whole complicated Maratha-Pindari affair. In March 1816 Raghuji Bhonsla II of Nagpur died and his nephew Appa Sahib, in order to secure his position as regent for Raghuji's imbecile son Parsaji, proposed a subsidiary treaty which had been declined by his uncle only two years before. Hastings was well served by his 'politicals'; Jenkins at Nagpur made a worthy third to Elphinstone at Poona and Metcalfe at Delhi. The treaty was ratified in July whereby a subsidiary force was introduced into Nagpur and a Maratha contingent organized under British advice. The net was tightening, and Hastings could proceed to his grand designs for ensnaring the whole Pindari group while intimidating the remaining Maratha powers in a single operation.

During the early months of 1817 the design took shape. More than 100,000 troops were employed, arranged in two great groups. To the north in Hindustan four divisions were stretched along the Ganges–Jumna line from Rewari in the west (under Ochterloney) through Agra and Etawah to Kalinjar nearly due south of Cawnpore. Each of these was a self-contained army, capable of acting on its own and fending for itself. In addition there were two observation corps at Rewa and in south Bihar. Hastings himself took command of this group, taking station with the Etawah force. To the south in the Deccan there were also four divisions under the command of Sir Thomas Hislop. They were stationed at Hushangabad on the Narbada, at Hindia on the same river to the west, in Berar and Khandesh. There was a reserve at Adoni in the Madras Presidency under Sir Thomas Munro. Sir John Malcolm was placed under Hislop as his political adviser. In Gujarat a further division was prepared whose function was to cut off bands which might retreat thither from the east or north-west. In addition there were the subsidiary forces at Poona and Nagpur, strong points, as it were, in areas of doubtful allegiance.

The campaign was to open at the end of the rains of 1817. The various forces were to advance south, west, and north, driving the Pindari bands before them from their haunts in the Narbada valley. The co-operation of the various bodies would make forays between them into British territory difficult and a return to their own country hazardous. Even Pindaris could not subsist permanently without a refuge for their families and a retreat for recuperation. At the same time the powers of central India, Sindia, Holkar, Bhopal, and lesser states were to be invited to co-operate with the alternative of war. Amir Khan was to be offered the lands he occupied as the price of dis-bandment and disarmament. The Peshwa and the Bhonsla would be saved from the temptation to intervene, it was hoped, by the presence of their resourceful residents with subsidiary forces at their backs. Such a plan, with its widely scattered forces, isolated posts, and distant reserve, might seem foolhardy in the face of a resolute and active opponent, enjoying the advantage of interior lines. The young Bona-parte with troops to match would have made short work of such a scheme. But there was no young Bonaparte, or any sign of one, nor was there the troops to match. Those that could move could not fight and those that could fight would not move. Among the leaders there was irresolution alternating with exasperation and despair. They shared no fixed common purpose, they had no common feeling save dislike of the British and only fitfully was the Maratha portion of them moved by feelings of national pride. The plan was in fact nicely calculated to the purpose in view and adapted to the conditions it had to meet. Hastings knew that he had to deal with a large number of disparate units whose suspicion of each other was nearly as great as their dislike of the British, who could be overawed or defeated in detail if dealt with simultaneously by a concerted movement, but who would, on account of their mobility and variety, be capable of re-forming and regrouping indefinitely if dealt with one by one. There was no real danger in separation of forces provided co-ordination existed, and this Hastings was able to maintain with the help of the singularly able group of officers he had gathered round him.

Hastings was an adaptable as well as a comprehensive planner, and it was this quality which ensured the success of the plan. While it was still being revolved a new turn was given to events by the romantic escape of Trimbakji from his prison at Thana in Salsette in October 1816.[1] By the spring he was raising troops while the Peshwa was denying the fact and protesting his inability to secure him by turns. Elphinstone demanded his arrest and the conclusion of a more drastic treaty in place of that of Bassein. After weeks of tension Baji Rao again faltered and the treaty of Poona was concluded in July 1817. Trimbakji was renounced, his territory was surrendered to support the Peshwa's contingent provided for by the treaty of Bassein but never yet formed, and foreign agents were dismissed from the Peshwa's court. Above all, the Peshwa formally renounced the headship of the Maratha confederacy. This condition undoubtedly exasperated Baji Rao, but it was judged that the disadvantage of this was outweighed by the discredit it would bring him among the surviving and more formidable Maratha princes. While these events were proceeding the imbecile Bhonsla Parsaji was murdered in February 1817. Appa Sahib, now ruler beyond dispute, no longer felt the need of British support and began to chafe against the bonds of the subsidiary treaty in his turn.

In October 1817 Hastings began to move. Sindia was given the option of co-operation against the Pindaris and of abrogating the stipulation in the treaty of Surji-arjangaon for non-interference in the affairs of the Rajput states or of war. After the usual agonized hesitations he agreed on 5 November. As a result the way was cleared for relations with the Rajput states which they eagerly embraced. Within a few months Metcalfe at Delhi made treaties with nineteen of them, including Jaipur, Udaipur, and Jodhpur. At the same time Bhopal accepted a subsidiary treaty and Amir Khan agreed to disarm in return for confirmation in his existing territories as Nawab of Tonk. So far success had been brilliant. But on the day that Sindia signed his treaty the wavering Peshwa finally decided to strike. Elphinstone behaved with the utmost coolness. An attack on the Poona force was beaten off at Kirki and in face of a counter-attack the Peshwa retreated southwards. Within a few days Appa Sahib in his turn attacked his subsidiary force and met defeat on the Sitabaldi hills.[2] It was now the turn of Holkar. The Regency was inclined to accept terms similar to those

---

[1] Trimbakji was guarded by British troops for greater security. The escape was arranged by a Maratha *syce* or groom who wove directions into Marathi songs sung outside the prisoner's window.

[2] He was restored and then deposed again at the instance of Hastings. For some time he conducted a guerilla campaign and finally found asylum and obscurity at the court of Ranjit Singh.

offered to Sindia, but the Pathan war party gained control. The Regent Tulsi Bai was murdered and the army joined battle at Mahidpur, only to be defeated like the rest on 21 December. By the end of the year the whole Maratha confederacy was in ruins, the chiefs defeated or in subordination. There only remained the mopping up of the Pindaris and the remnants of the Maratha forces. After two defeats at Ashti and Koregaon and many twists and turns the Peshwa surrendered to Sir John Malcolm on 2 June. The Pindaris moved hither and thither with their usual speed, but though some slipped through the tightening net, the bands were dispersed for ever. The game had become too dangerous to play any longer. Chithu, the most daring of their leaders, fell to a tiger in the jungle to which he had fled. The campaign ended with the fall of Asirgarh in March 1819.

We can now describe the settlement of 1818. The breach with the Peshwa was beyond recall. His dominions were annexed and he himself, through the generosity of Malcolm, much regretted by Hastings, settled at Bithur on the Ganges with a pension of 8 *lakhs* of rupees a year. There he survived until 1851, leaving his claims and his grievances to his adopted son, the Nana Sahib.[2] The nominal head of the Marathas, and descendant of Sivājī, was restored to the principality of Satara. With this exception the Peshwa's dominions became part of the presidency of Bombay. This now ceased to be a seaport district and became the province of Marathas and Gujaratis (with the Sindhis to follow). Bombay city itself began its career as the port of western India, to be successively helped by the increasing size of shipping which made Surat less accessible, by the development of railways, which overcame the obstacle of the Western Ghats, and by the development of the modern cotton industry. While Marathi pundits mused in Poona, Gujarati and Parsi merchants flocked to the developing emporium. Commerce came into its own in the west, as it had already done in the east, but in this case European and Indian were on equal terms. In becoming the gateway of the east Bombay was also to become the outpost of the west. Farther east the child Raghujī III, grandson of Raghujī II, was substituted for the injudicious Appa Sahib in Nagpur. Berar was attached to Hyderabad in reward for the assistance of the Nizam's contingent and Saugor was detached to become the Saugor and Narbada territory, soon to be the centre of the campaign against the thags. Amir Khan settled down to respectability as the Nawab of Tonk while adjacent Bhopal was relieved of fears from Sindia and the Pindaris. Sindia preserved his state at the price of his supremacy in Rajputana and lands around Ajmir. With enough intelligence to understand the strength of the British power, but not enough to co-operate or the energy to oppose in time, Daulat Rao Sindia saved his state and his family fortunes by a hair's breadth. The Holkar state, shorn of Tonk and all influence, was suffered to remain, and under the able ministry of Tantia Jog began to revive. The Rajput states were happy in their relief from Marathas and Pathans. They were not required to entertain subsidiary forces, but watch was maintained by British posts at Ajmir in the centre, at Delhi to the east, and in Gujarat to the south. Alone of the Maratha princes the Gaekwar gained territory as a reward for his fidelity.

It is incorrect to say that the Maratha confederacy was crushed, because it had been in dissolution since 1802 and largely by its own act. What really happened in 1818 was the substitution of British authority in central India for no authority at all, and the extension of paramountcy over the ancient Rajput states. The pages of Malcolm's report on central India at this time are eloquent of the devastation which prevailed and the exhaustion which the British discovered. A seat of anarchy was removed and in the course of it several disorderly states brushed aside. The larger consequence of the whole episode was the establishment of the hegemony of the Company throughout India up to the Sutlej river. To the east and north its frontiers had reached their natural limits in the Assam hills and the Himalayas, with only Nepal separating them in parts from the snowy range itself. To the west the Thar desert and the Rann of Cutch provided another natural barrier. Only in the Panjab could the frontier be said to be open, and there the human barrier of Ranjit Singh's Sikh kingdom stood firm and friendly. Elsewhere the principal surviving Indian states were islands in a sea of British territory, either surrounded completely as in the case of Oudh and Mysore, or so fenced in, as in the case of Hyderabad and Sindia's state, as to make concerted action impossible. Apart from these states the only large blocks of Indian-ruled territory were the tracts of central India from Nagpur to Orissa and Rajputana. At Nagpur itself was a subsidiary force, and the rest of the tract was so full of hill and jungle as to constitute no danger. The Rajputs were rendered harmless by their temporary exhaustion and permanent jealousies, and were effectively watched by the British posts as already described. The settlement of 1818 restored the unity of India to a degree more effective than had existed under the great Mughuls, the main difference being that whereas the British power was firm in the south but stopped short at the Sutlej, the Mughul had been firm in the north-west as far as Kabul, but had faltered in the Deccan. As the Mughul power wrecked itself in trying to stretch to Cape Comorin the British power was to strain itself in trying to reach Kabul. Henceforth India was a unit again and we can divide our attention between domestic and foreign developments.

Lord Hastings was fortunate in possessing a band of loyal and skilful lieutenants both military and political. In Elphinstone, Malcolm, Metcalfe, Munro, and Jenkins he had officers of real distinction who would have graced any service, and who had the gifts both of harmonious co-operation and independent command. But the major credit for this success must be given to Hastings himself. His political insight and strategical grasp were nicely matched; his gift for spacious planning was balanced by a faculty for vigorous action, and in all his arrangements he showed the flexibility which is the mark of distinguished leadership. The observer cannot fail to notice another quality that stamps his work with greatness. Never dazzled by the extent of his resources or the brilliance of his prospects, he always sought to proportion his means to his end. His treatment of Nepal, the Marathas, and the Rajputs showed that he was no lover of annexation for its own sake, even though he was better equipped to undertake it than Wellesley had been. His conduct was determined but not minatory; conciliation mingled with his firmness. He was as conciliatory as Cornwallis without his occasional muddle-headedness; if he was severe in holding princes to their engagements, he was also strict in observing them himself. It is difficult to see what alternative there was to the policy he pursued because the Marathas themselves ruled out the possibility of an Indo-British partnership in central India, on the analogy of the Nepal settlement of the Himalayas. Hastings enhanced the British reputation for vigour and ability by the success of his comprehensive measures. But even more valuable to the stability of the British power was his practice of the virtues of public justice and conciliation. It was this which removed the memory of Wellesley's aggressive and bullying tactics and did much to strengthen belief in British justice and good faith.

AUTHORITIES

For Hastings himself there is a compact study by Major ROSS-OF-BLANDENSBURG, *The Marquess of Hastings* (Rulers of India, 1893), and there is his own *Private Journal*, edited by his daughter, the Marchioness of Bute (2 vols., 1858).

H. H. WILSON devotes a whole volume of his continuation of Mill's *History* to Hastings (vol. viii of the whole work). An authoritative contemporary study is by H. T. PRINSEP, *History of the Political and Military Transactions in India during the Administration of the Marques of Hastings* (2 vols., 1825). Various aspects of the period are dealt with in the lives of Metcalfe, Malcolm, and Elphinstone already mentioned and in G. R. GLEIG, *Life of Sir T. Munro* (3 vols., 1830), and Sir A. J. ARBUTHNOT, *Sir Thomas Munro* (2 vols., 1884).

For the Indian states see M. S. MEHTA, *Lord Hastings and the Indian States*, a careful study, as well as Edward Thompson's work already mentioned. J. TOD, *Annals and Antiquities of Rajasthan* (1st ed., 1829-32), gives the Rajput background while R. JENKINS, *Report on the territories of Nagpur* (1827), along with Malcolm's study of central India covers the whole of central India. There is no history of the Nepal war; *Papers relating to the Nepaul war* (printed by the E. I. Company) (1824) and P. LANDON, *History of Nepal* (2 vols., 1928) should be consulted. H. G. KEENE, *Hindustan under freelances 1770-1820* (1907) deals with the military adventurers of the north.

RECENT PUBLICATION

J. PEMBLE's *The Invasion of Nepal: John Company at War* (Oxford, 1971) is a lively and important work.

BOOK VIII

Completion and Consolidation, 1818-58

CHAPTER 1

General—From Hastings to Dalhousie

THE year 1818 marks the beginning of a new phase in the history of British India. The period of internal wars and struggles for supremacy is over; India can be treated as a unity once more in a way not possible since 1740. The Company's administration had become in effect the government of India: in the ensuing period we can divide events into foreign policy and internal administration. Abroad the note was one of rounding off dominion, while at home it was that of restoration and organization; the new feature was that it now became possible to speak of an 'at home' and 'abroad'. Along with this external rounding off and internal consolidation went the first signs of that cultural transformation which has since become a major Indian development. At first it took the form mainly of innovations or changes based upon western ideas, but the beginnings of an Indian response, which was later to vitalize the whole process, have also to be noted. The period now to be dealt with covers approximately thirty years from 1818 to 1848. Dalhousie's rule, which in some ways marks the consummation of these tendencies, is so intimately connected with the upheaval which followed it that it will be treated in a separate section. The plan to be followed will include some description of the India with which the British were confronted in 1818, and of their ideas for dealing with it. It will then trace the thread of high policy at the centre and thereafter treat with specific subjects, such as the Company's foreign policy, its organization of the administration and social, economic, and cultural developments.

The state of India in 1818 differed widely from its condition under Akbar or Shahjahan or even up to the death of Muhammad Shah in 1748. The political system of the country was in ruins. Not only had the former unifying authority collapsed, but the chief rival for its heritage had in its turn split into a number of rival factions. The British in this sense were not so much heirs of the Mughuls as the legatees of anarchy. The Marathas had divided into factions of whom the most hopeful was that of Sindia. With the death of Mahadji in 1794 his successors had lost their grip while their most energetic rivals, the Holkars, had in turn allowed their power to dissolve in family strife. The Sikhs had usurped power without providing order in the north, while the once vigorous state of Oudh had subsided into corrupt senility. All over Rajputana ancient princely houses had failed either to keep the Marathas at bay or to control their own feudatories. With the rise of the Pindaris and the paralysis of the Marathas it can be said that virtual anarchy prevailed from the Thar desert to the borders of Orissa and from the Sutlej to the upper waters of the Kistna. When the British came to Delhi in 1803 they found the villages to be fortified posts, only paying revenue at the point of the bayonet, and the city itself divided into wards for the purpose of plunder by village gangs in the neighbourhood. It was not safe to visit the ruins without an escort for fear of bandits lurking behind walls, nor to travel unprotected on the main road from Delhi to Agra. Robber chiefs and local rulers were interchangeable terms and Metcalfe officially listed some of the neighbouring chiefs as the 'Plunderers' of this or that. Malcolm's report on central India and Tod's account of Rajputana told the same story. British rule or supremacy was accepted without enthusiasm or much hope, but with resignation as the only alternative to an indefinite continuance of anarchy.

Along with political loss of control and purpose went administrative collapse. None paid revenue unless compelled, and the business of administration became a scramble somehow to secure enough money to stave off military mutinies by meeting a proportion of the chronic arrears of pay. Officers inevitably took what they could for themselves in the process. The cultivator had no hope of improvement and much fear of extortion on every hand, together with the ever present risk of plunder, torture, and death from marauding bands. The merchants dwelt in constant danger of loss from dacoits or armies on the march and of extortion from hard-pressed governments. Not even their loans to the ephemeral governments of the day were safe. The well-ordered administration of Mughul times had disappeared, surviving only, if at all, in the records of the local hereditary village officials and in the traditions of the old governing families.

The social and cultural state of the country declined along with its political fortunes. The state of the country was in nothing more clearly revealed than in the spread of social diseases whose germs always lurk within civilized societies ready to multiply and break forth should favourable conditions arise. The most obvious of these was dacoity, of which the Pindaris were the supreme example. The dislocation of society drove adventurous, hopeless, or embittered spirits to a lawless life. They formed the material for princely armies or robber bands, each of whom recruited from the other as fortunes rose and fell. The landless or uprooted man looking for a leader and reckless from despair was a typical figure of the time. A specialized form of these men were the thags, robbers and ritual murderers, who rose to prominence in these times and spread across central India to the terror of travellers and peaceful men. Suttee, or widow-burning, increased in vogue as the hand of restraining authority grew weak. As reason seemed to have lost its hold so superstition increased its sway. Astrology, always a popular adjunct of Indian life, rose to the status of a directing force. Pathological aspects of social life like infanticide and of religion, like hook-swinging, self-immolation, and throwing oneself before the processional car of a god, grew apace. Even religious devotees suffered from the general degeneration. Many ascetics, threatened like ordinary citizens with plunder and death, took to arms and formed bodies variously described as *nagas*, *bairagis*, *sannyasis*, or *gosains*. They can be traced back to the reign of Akbar, but their number increased with the general disorder. Examples are the Gosains under Himmat Bahadur who served Mahadji Sindia, and the Dadu-panthis in the service of Jaipur.[1] The Sikhs were the supreme manifestation of this movement and the only body to achieve both statehood and the status of an independent religion.

Intellectual and cultural activities inevitably came to a standstill, for there was neither the security to encourage it nor the means to support it. Men of learning depended upon princely patronage and this patronage was now monopolized by soldiers and diplomatists. The tradition was maintained in the Sanskrit *tols* and the Muslim *madrasahs* but originality was lost and its influence on the community at large declined. There was little sign during these years of new thought or of creative religious achievement. Living religion retreated to the quietist sects, whose devotees haunted temples of Krishna or Kali, or retired to the banks of the Ganges at Benares or the Godavari at Nasik. Here and behind the *purdah* of many devout homes much true devotion lived on, but it had nothing to offer to the turbulence of the times save abstraction and retreat.

The arts of life suffered in the general malaise. Architecture, like learning, could not thrive without patrons. Temples and mosques gave place to forts. No great and few good buildings were erected after 1750. In Delhi the decline can be traced from the great mosque of Shah-jahan through the decadent but still imposing tomb of Safdar Jang (1756) to the insubstantial and uninspired buildings of the nineteenth century. Only in Oudh was the building tradition maintained, and here confusion of styles and elaboration of repetitive detail betrayed confusion of mind and loss of inspiration. Painting, in its Mughul and Rajput forms, suffered a similar eclipse and by the nineteenth century only survived as a living school in the foothills of the Panjab. The local languages were rich in folksong but the only major literary development was the growth of Urdu under the patronage of the later Mughul emperors.

[1] See W. G. Orr, 'Armed Religious Ascetics in N. India', *Bulletin of John Rylands Library*, vol. xxiv, no. 1, Apr. 1940.

Throughout Indian India there was little sign of fresh cultural development, or glimmer of creative activity.[1] The most that could be done was to hold fast to tradition, the most that was hoped for was a return to former times. Indian society like the Mughul dynasty had lost the 'mandate of heaven'. Courage, energy, ability, devotion, and loyalty existed as ever in profusion but these qualities either wasted themselves in fruitless efforts and forlorn hopes or were enlisted in negative causes or destructive enterprises.

If we turn to British India we find superficially a somewhat different picture. Wherever the British went they restored order; commerce was possible, the revenue was punctually collected, and the courts functioned regularly. But man cannot live by peace alone any more than solely by bread. This peace was accompanied by no cultural revival, and save in Calcutta by few signs of intellectual activity. Indians were excluded from all responsible public life with the result that the best men stood aloof and estranged and power was largely exercised by the irresponsible agents of ignorant masters. The new rulers had passed through their first phase of naïve corruption, but their good intentions and growing experience had not yet made up for their former mistakes and ignorance of local conditions. In consequence their administration seemed aloof though efficient and cold and distant if no longer harsh. The British were splendid but alien. Mirza Ghulam Hussain complained of British 'aloofness, absorption in their own concerns and surrounding themselves with sycophants'.[2] When Bishop Heber was in Lucknow in 1824 he asked a jamadar who was complaining of the Oudh government whether he would not be better off under the British. 'Miserable as we are, of all miseries keep us from that', was the reply, and the reason, 'the name and honour of our nation would end.'[3] The British had to rescue an exhausted society from anarchy and threatened dissolution, organize it and their own dominions with due regard to justice and local conditions, to revive, if they could, the feeble spark of cultural life and to break down by some means the wall of partition which divided ruler from ruled, foreigner from native. Such was the scene upon which the more thoughtful of the Company's servants gazed on the morrow of Hastings's 'crowning mercy' in 1818. They were neither dazzled, jubilant, nor even elated at their success, for they were too conscious of the magnitude of their charge.

The young officers of Wellesley's day had found his exuberant imperialism and aggressive leadership much to their taste and their disappointed diatribes against his two immediate successors have not yet quite ceased to influence historical opinion. Their successors in juniority showed an equal zest in acquisition; Edward Thompson has well described the excitement of these men at the time of the last

[1] Note should, however, be taken of Shah Wali-ullah and his school of Muslim theologians at Delhi, whose work had important repercussions. See Book X, ch. 5.
[2] Siyar-ul Mutaqherin, vol. iii, pp. 170–1.
[3] Bishop Heber, *Narrative of a Journey* ..., vol. i, p. 405.

Maratha war, their feeling of being on the threshold of a new era with a world about to be conquered. Their seniors, on the other hand, had seen enough of wars and devastations and had become aware of the inherent strength of the society it had become their fate to control through its temporary weakness. Their note was that of caution. The former acolytes of expansionism were now counsellors of moderation. They believed that they were sitting on a social and religious volcano, quiescent and apparently burnt out for the moment, it is true, but liable to erupt into fresh activity at any moment. Metcalfe, writing like an old man at the age of thirty-three, emphasized his belief in the 'precariousness' of the British dominion; Elphinstone, steeped in the classics with the coolest of heads, feared 'that the belief that our Indian Empire will not be long lived is reason and not prejudice'; Malcolm, for all his soldierly optimism, considered 'that in an empire like that of India we are always in danger'; while Munro considered 'innovation the ruling vice of our government'. They saw danger from foreign invasion, danger from a military mutiny, and danger from a religious explosion. If none of these things happened the people might so far develop as to replace the British in control. 'This', said Elphinstone, 'would be the most desirable end to British rule', but it seemed 'at an immeasurable distance'.

The British dominions in India were now more extensive than Akbar's in 1600, for if his empire reached to Kandahar, Kabul, and Badakhshan it had stopped short at the Narbada. All India to the Sutlej and the Rajput deserts was now under British control; beyond lay the Sikh kingdom of Ranjit Singh, the loosely knit states of the Amirs of Sind, and the manifestly dissolving Afghan kingdom. The only stable government of the three was that of Lahore, but the Sikhs were themselves a minority and their régime really a military dictatorship by one community over two others. Two themes thus emerged during the next thirty years. One was that of foreign policy, which had as its motif the rounding off or completion of the British dominion within the limits of Hindustan. The other was the organization of the existing British supremacy and possessions into a new empire.

It was here, within the limits of British India, that a great policy decision had to be made. Granted the fact of dominion, how was the new *raj* to be administered? The simple solution of alien exploitation had already been ruled out as a result of the Bengal experience. India was to be administered for the benefit of the Indians. But what kind of administration? The solution which appealed to many on the spot was a virtual revival and continuance of the Mughul empire. The Company would replace the Mughul and his umara, would restore the administration along traditional lines, and would protect the country with their new model army. Trade would flow more freely than before, culture, the arts, and religion would revive under judicious patronage; new British would be old Mughuls writ large. This was the outlook of Warren Hastings and his friends and was implicit in the general internal policy from that time on. Of course there would be 'improvements' such as the substitution of European for Indian agency in government, of British for Muslim criminal law and methods of administering justice. The whole tenor of British internal policy to 1818 was in the direction of a revived and improved benevolent despotism.

If India could have been wholly insulated from Europe and shielded from the ferment of ideas prevailing there, such a course might have been practicable. But even if ideas could have been prevented from taking wing to the East, the men on the spot were controlled by men in Britain who were themselves subject to them. The foreign rulers' ideal that everything should continue in its familiar groove was therefore shattered almost as soon as it was formed. The British agents were influenced by the currents of thought prevailing in Britain and their policy was shaped accordingly. To the views of men like James Forbes or Scott Waring who admired Hindu institutions and desired their revival and continuance were opposed the ideas of the progressive and religious schools of thought in Britain. The Age of Enlightenment included a belief in reason and a belief in progress; as embodied in the Utilitarian school it developed a missionary fervour and a belief that its principles were applicable everywhere. Its mouthpiece in Indian matters was James Mill, whose *History of India* was begun in 1809 and published in 1817. The latter was manifested in the Evangelical movement with influential leaders in William Wilberforce, the friend of Pitt, and Charles Grant in the Company's direction. For them Christian morals were applicable everywhere. They had a sacred mission, they believed, to introduce the Gospel into India, for Britain was now the trustee of India's moral welfare. These two schools of thought found little to praise in Indian life and thought. So much of Indian life was bound up with religion and tradition; to the Utilitarian this was superstition or the denial of reason; to the Evangelical not only this but also idolatrous or the denial of God.

Three broad tendencies of thought can be distinguished in the discussions of Indian policy during these years. There was first the Tory or conservative view, of whom the orientalist H. H. Wilson was perhaps the most distinguished exponent. Without altogether denying the possibility of improvements, they recommended extreme caution; they were impressed by the value and strength of Indian institutions; they desired above all their restoration and maintenance, seeing no possibility of their early collapse, and they were acutely conscious of the danger of provoking a violent reaction by unwise interference or hasty innovations. They wished to foster Sanskrit and Arabic learning, they opposed Christian missions, and they considered such measures as the prohibition of suttee as playing with fire. The second may be called the Liberal Tory view. It was to this school that the great administrators Metcalfe, Munro, Malcolm, and Elphinstone belonged in various degrees. They accepted the desirability of improvements and of the introduction of western ideas and values, but they were also convinced of the value of the traditional institutions and the strength of traditional feeling. Cautious innovation was their watchword. They looked to an eventual integration of old and new.

Let us [said Malcolm] proceed on a course of gradual improvement, and when our rule ceases, as cease it must, (though probably at a remote period) as the natural consequence of our success in the diffusion of knowledge, we shall as a nation have the proud boast that we have preferred the civilisation to the continued subjection of India. When our power is gone, our name will be revered; for we shall leave a moral monument more noble and imperishable than the hand of man ever constructed.[1]

The third school of thought may be called the radical with its rationalist and religious wings. Bentham and James Mill were the most influential rationalists with Macaulay, Lord William Bentinck, and Charles Trevelyan as followers; Wilberforce and the Clapham sect were the leaders of the religious Evangelicals. They advocated bold innovations, because they believed that prejudice must give way to reason and falsehood to truth. The light of reason and the light of the Gospel, once transferred to India, would shine of themselves. The Indians would convert themselves and the new order would begin.

It should not be thought that these schools represented distinct parties; they were rather tendencies in influencing those who determined policy whether in Parliament, the Court of Directors, or in the governing class at large. Temperament and chance modified logical distinctions. It may be said in general that there was a group for moving as little as possible, a group for making definite and planned innovations along western lines, and a series of gradations between the two. Through all the discussions can be detected the assumption that western civilization was on the march while Indian culture was static if not moribund; any changes that were made therefore must be in a westernizing direction. Secondly it should be noted that reform and innovation were now part of the English mental atmosphere. 'Improvement' was a magic word which even Tories applied to agriculture; few Englishmen could undertake anything without considering what improvements might be made.

The decisions which these schools of thought sought to influence were modified not only by their opinions but by the force of events, the weight of experience, and the prevailing assumptions of the British governing class. The force of events ruled out any serious attempt to sustain masterly inactivity; in many areas the confusion was such that there were virtually no precedents to follow. In many matters, as those of the criminal law or methods of administration, existing practice offended the humanitarianism, the conscience, or the sense of fitness of the West. In other cases new situations, such as the breakdown of authority in Bengal in the sixties, were such that they called for new remedies. And those remedies, where they were not simply restorative, like the attempt to revive village *panchayats*, were always inspired by

[1] Sir J. Malcolm, *Memoir on Central India*, vol. ii, p. 304.

western ideas and modes. On the other hand the full application of the radical policy was equally interdicted by experience and common sense. Official opinion, which could not be lightly disregarded, was generally against it, and was reinforced from time to time by such events as the Vellore mutiny of 1806. In sum a policy like Malcolm's was in fact pursued. At first the emphasis was upon continuity and the necessity of caution; from the time of Bentinck it was upon the desirability of innovation without forgetting the need for caution. Not until Dalhousie's time was confidence sufficient to drive ahead without recking much of consequence. This mood was sobered by the Mutiny which induced a caution sustained long after other forces had arisen which made such an attitude first unnecessary, then harmful, and at last dangerous.

These new forces were the Indian response to western ideas and innovations. Prior to 1818 there had been little response to the western challenge other than the military. Princes knew much of western cannons and western discipline, but nothing of western science or the rights of man.[1] It was in Bengal that the larger aspects of the western spirit first became known to the Indian mind. The widespread knowledge of English provided an ideological bridge; ideas flowed over in the persons of British lawyers and officials, missionaries, and disinterested men of learning like Sir William Jones. The radicals believed that these seeds would quickly sprout to replace the weeds of Indian tradition and were disappointed at the slowness of the process. A later generation virtually despaired and talked of the unchanging East. But the essential fact is that these ideas did begin to take root in the very years of which we are speaking. The germination and growth was much slower than expected, but the process had been set in motion, and as it developed it determined the great transformation which is modern India today. It is this process which marks the difference between mid-twentieth-century independent India and fifth-century Britain after the withdrawal of the Romans. In the one case there was an organic development from within, in the other a superimposed culture which remained exotic and alien. This movement owed its origin to the group of Bengalis of whom Ram Mohan Roy was the leading figure. During the second and third decades of the century they were working out the first Indian response, not to western power or diplomatic cunning but to western civilization as a whole. At the very time that Lord Hastings was completing the central edifice of British power in India, Ram Mohan Roy was tracing the lines of the first synthesis between East and West in India which was to transform that power by a process of internal development and finally peacefully to replace it.

AUTHORITIES

THE following works are suggested as sources for a survey of India at the completion of the British hegemony. Bishop R. HEBER, *Narrative of a Journey through the Upper*

[1] With the partial exception of Tipu.

Provinces of India (2 vols., 1828), V. JACQUEMONT, *Letters from India* (2 vols., 1834) (the north only), for general description; J. TOD, *Annals and Antiquities of Rajasthan* (3 vols., 1829–32) for Rajputana; Sir J. MALCOLM, *A Memoir of C. India* (2 vols., 1832), R. JENKINS, *Report on the Territories of Nagpur* (1827), M. ELPHINSTONE, *Report on the territories lately conquered from the Peshwa* (1822) for central and western India; M. WILKS, *Historical Sketches of Mysore* (3 vols., 1810–14), F. BUCHANAN, *A Journey from Madras through Mysore* ... (3 vols., 1807) for south India; W. W. HUNTER, *Annals of Rural Bengal*, and MONTGOMERY MARTIN, *The History, antiquities, statistics ... of Eastern India* (3 vols., 1838) for Bengal; *Selections from the Records of the Delhi Residency and Agency* (1911) for the Delhi territory (chap. vi) and the Simla hills (chap. viii); W. G. OSBORNE, *The Court and Camp of Runjeet Singh* (1840) and C. MASSON, *Travels*, &c. (1842) for the Panjab.

For the state of Hinduism see Abbé J. A. DUBOIS, *Hindu Manners, Customs and Ceremonies* (3rd ed., Oxford, 1906) and the writings of RAM MOHAN ROY, T. E. COLEBROOKE, and H. H. WILSON; for the state of Islam, Mrs. MEER HASSAN ALI, *Observations on the Mussulmanns of India* (2nd ed., Oxford, 1915) and G. A. HERKLOTS, *Islam in India* (new ed., Oxford, 1921), and for Christianity C. BUCHANAN, *Christian Researches in India* (1810). For English life see E. EDEN, *Up the Country* (ed. E. Thompson, Oxford, 1930).

CHAPTER 2

The Political Thread. Lord Hastings to Hardinge, 1818–48

WE have seen the policy that led to the reunification of India in 1818 determined by the interaction of events and persons in India and Britain. In India the gainful and impetuous Company's servants were too much for the peaceful but also gainfully-minded directors. The ill-restrained urge for personal gain almost produced corporate bankruptcy and so provoked state intervention. From the time of Pitt's India Act onwards (and indeed ineffectively still earlier) the state was both humane and unaggressive in intention, but the steady dissolution of the Indian political system together with revived fears of French intervention produced a state of feeling in which it seemed less ruinous to move forward than to remain static. Wellesley moved too fast and too far, thus provoking a reaction, and it was left to Lord Hastings to complete the process with a kind of majestic instancy.

The interaction of interests and views continued into the new period. But it is to be noted that the vital decisions of policy were increasingly made in London rather than in Calcutta. The stream of policy, like the stream of ideas at this time, flowed from the West. Professor Philips has noted that no governor-general could hope to do much without the firm support of the ruling faction in Britain. Minto was embarrassed by its absence, and it is a part of the greatness of Warren Hastings that he accomplished so much with so insecure a basis of support in London. In general the rulers of achievement were those with strong support at home like Cornwallis, Wellesley (in his early years), Bentinck, and Dalhousie. This helps to explain why the rulers who were promoted officials from Shore to John Lawrence tended to be static and cautious in their conduct. Their appointments were largely gestures of esteem and they could not rely for support for new measures on a solid political body in London. We can now turn to the political thread from 1818 to 1848.

The justification of Lord Hastings's measures was their success. His debts made him anxious to retain office and his prestige and judgement made the home authorities willing to retain him. The final years of his rule are liable to be obscured by the drama of his early years. They were in fact studded with incident and developments of significance for the future. Looking abroad we have first to notice the acquisition of Singapore. On the final defeat of France in 1815 the island of Java, which had been governed by Sir Stamford Raffles for four years, was handed back to Holland as part of the peace settlement. A promising experiment in Indonesian administration thus came to an end, but the fact cannot be overlooked that Holland was an ally of the British and that Java had been seized in 1811 because it had been occupied by the French while Holland was a victim of French aggression. Lord Hastings, however, saw the advantage of securing the sea route to China and the Far East. In 1819 he allowed Raffles to occupy the island of Singapore at the extremity of the Malay peninsula. Its position was a strategic one, its harbour was capacious and its occupants at that time Malay fishermen. Dutch objections were eventually countered by the exchange of the British settlements in Sumatra for the surviving small Dutch stations in India. Thus a new enterprise of the British in the East was set on its course; the port of call has become the centre of a highly productive region and shows signs of becoming another dominion. In 1867 Singapore became a Crown colony and so passes from our purview.

In India Hastings took one of those half-measures which was so out of character that it revealed the nervousness and perplexity of the British in dealing with the Mughul emperor. Their legal claim to Bengal still rested on the imperial grant of 1765. Wellesley had carefully avoided either recognizing Mughul suzerainty in 1803 or repudiating it. In fact he signed no treaty with Shah Alam, but promised him liberty and maintenance. To the emperor the Company was still officially a favoured son; by the Company the emperor was beginning to be regarded as a nuisance. In 1816 the presentation of *nazars* on behalf of the government, a symbol of inferior status, was stopped. But the issue of the Company's coinage stamped with Shah Alam's titles continued until 1835. At the same time Hastings encouraged the Nawab Wazir of Oudh, as a reward for loans during the wars, to assume the title of King of Oudh. It was thought thus to divide the Muslim allegiance, the Nawab Wazir being the political head of the Shias and the emperor being a Sunni. In fact this action brought little credit to the Nawab Wazir, being widely regarded as an act of rebellion. The Nizam pointedly refused to follow his example.

Lord Hastings showed a surer touch in dealing with other internal incidents. When the chief of Hathras defied the British in his fort in 1817 Hastings brought up such a weight of artillery as not only to reduce the fort itself but also to give notice that no aristocratic recalcitrance would be permitted. The lesson of Bharatpur in 1805 had been learnt. On the conclusion of the Maratha war the nest of sea pirates which still lingered on the coast between Kolhapur and Goa was dealt with. In 1820 they were finally dispersed and a scourge to commerce of the west coast which had existed since the days of Graeco-Roman commerce disappeared for good. A Muslim religious outbreak at Bareilly in Rohilkund was suppressed and an agrarian revolt in Orissa in 1816 was treated with a characteristic blend of firmness and conciliation.

In internal administration Lord Hastings must be given the credit of taking the first steps towards the development of the country. His tours opened his eyes to the ruined nature of the countryside. In 1818 he gave orders for the repair of the Mughul canal system, whose waters had ceased to flow in the troubles of the mid-eighteenth century. In 1820 the water flowed again into the city of Delhi and thereafter commenced the great system of British irrigation. He commenced the restoration of roads, which, with the returning security of the countryside, had more than a purely military value. In Bengal he advocated the development of education, giving private support to English schools and becoming a patron of the new Hindu college in Calcutta.

These measures were gestures which showed the direction in which enlightened minds were moving. But in the vital matter of judicial and revenue administration he made a more positive mark. Measures were taken to reduce the block of legal suits and the rigid separation of the executive and judicial functions was modified by combining the office of collector and district magistrate. A beginning with Indianization was made by enhancing the status of subordinate Indian judicial officers. In the revenue department he set on foot the settlement of the new conquered and ceded provinces which bore fruit in the elaborate Regulation VII of 1822. In the south Munro was engaged in restoring the *ryotwari* system of land settlement under the Charter Act of 1813 after the encroachment of the Cornwallis system at the instance of Wellesley. In 1820 he became Governor of Madras. In Bombay Elphinstone became governor in 1819 and with deft and careful hands eased the transition from old to new in the newly acquired Peshwa's territories.

Hastings's closing years were clouded by the controversy over the Nizam's financial relations with the house of Palmer and Co. in whose Hyderabad branch he was personally interested.[1] He failed to intervene after irregularities had been exposed by the new resident, Charles Metcalfe, and might well have been recalled but for his personal friendship with George IV.[2] But this is the only touch of regency morals which Hastings took with him to India and cannot obscure the magnitude of his services in other directions.

At the time of Hastings's retirement Canning, disappointed with his prospects in England, accepted the Governor-Generalship. But the suicide of Lord Castlereagh in August 1822 diverted him to the Foreign Office and British India lost thereby a lively chapter in its history. Lord Amherst was a friend of Canning and was brought in by a political shuffle in London rather than by any particular merits. The directors approved him for his China mission in 1816 and because he was thought to be a man of peace, and Canning excused him as amiable. He wrote to Huskisson: 'I agree with you perhaps in thinking the appointment which takes place not a very *strong* one; but . . . Amherst is at least blameless. . . . Upon the whole he is as good a *barren* choice as could have been made.'[3] On this occasion Lord William Bentinck made a fruitless attempt to secure the appointment.

---

[1] The wife of Sir T. Rumbold, a partner in the firm, was his ward.
[2] C. H. Philips, *The East India Co. and the State*, pp. 225–8.   [3] Ibid., pp. 239–40.

During a seven-months' interregnum India was administered by john Adam, the senior member of council. His brief reign was signalized by the expulsion of John Silk Buckingham, the editor of the *Calcutta Journal*, for undue freedom of criticism of public officials. Thus another feature and issue of modern life appeared on the Indian scene. Amherst arrived in August 1823. He had been told that there was now no occasion for further wars and that a period of peace was expected. But he had no sooner arrived than a fresh war cloud emerged which dominated his four and a half years of office. Within a month the Burmans occupied the island of Shahpuri off Chittagong; this was followed by aggression in Assam and war followed. The Burmans had been pursuing a course of expansion during the previous seventy years somewhat similar to that of the Gurkhas, and like the latter, they had no idea of the force against which they were now pitting themselves. The war dragged on till February 1826, bringing much loss and expense and little credit to the Company. The treaty of Yandaboo began the transfer of Burman territories to the British which was completed in 1886.[1] During the course of the war the dispatch of Indian troops by sea led to the military mutiny of Barrackpore in October 1824, which nearly caused Amherst's recall and would have actually done so but for political complexities at home. The checks in Burma led to unrest in India and this found an outlet in the defiance of Bharatpur on the occasion of a disputed succession. After his usual vacillation, which caused the retirement of Ochterloney, Amherst permitted Metcalfe to take measures for the final reduction of the fortress in 1826. Amherst retired in March 1828 and, perhaps in gratitude for his departure, was awarded an earldom for his pains. Like his contemporary 'goody' Goderich, he was a well-meaning man with no faults but the inability to rise to the height of sole responsibility.

Amherst's successor was a very different man. If Lord William Bentinck had a fault, it was not that of being colourless. He had been recalled from Madras in 1807 on account of the Vellore mutiny, for which the unwisdom of the Madras commander-in-chief had later been admitted to have been mainly responsible, and he never ceased to wish to redeem his reputation. He had served as a soldier in Spain (where Wellington disliked him) and he had represented Britain in Sicily and Genoa where his conduct gave some colour to the charge of impulsiveness.[2] He was an advanced Whig in politics, a supporter of reform, and a disciple of Bentham. He owed his appointment to the support of the directors, to the death of Liverpool who disapproved of him, and to the approval of Canning who had unexpectedly become prime minister. Even then he was only the sixth choice. Canning died shortly after the appointment, and before he reached India the high Tory and critical Wellington was prime minister. His career would probably have been brief and unhappy but for the advent of Lord

[1] See Book IX, Chapter 3.
[2] For these episodes see J. Roselli, *Lord William Bentinck and Sicily*, Camb., 1956.

Grey's reform ministry in 1830, which provided him with steady support in the ministry as well as the direction.[1]

The directors supported Bentinck because he was a man of peace, a man of discipline,[2] and a man of economy. The Company's finances were once again embarrassed, as a result of the Burman war, and they were afraid to face the impending discussions for the renewal of the charter on a deficit budget. But the real significance of Bentinck was that he was a man of the left, who carried within himself the ideas of the new age just coming into power. By carrying out the directors' mandate for economy and by the good fortune of the advent of the reform ministry to power, he was able to give Indian policy a twist towards welfare and western innovation which it never afterwards altogether lost. The phrase 'We have a great moral duty to perform in India' was coined by the brilliant Ellenborough, but it was the man he sought to recall who gave it content and meaning.

Bentinck's first duty was to economize, and it was the hazards which surrounded economizers in India which made the directors welcome a general as their agent. His economy measures were extensive and severe but it was the comparatively minor measure of the abolition of double batta[3] in the Bengal army which gained him the title of the 'clipping Dutchman' and an opprobrium which even yet has not quite faded.[4] In dealing with military discontent which ran to personal discourtesy and an attempt at social ostracism he displayed a combination of tact with firmness of which his earlier career had not given much promise. Age had tempered his zeal with discretion and sobered impulse to the point where it enabled him to act where others had only talked. The economies were personally distasteful to him and he privately denounced the batta reduction as pettifogging and ineffective. In all he saved £1½ million by economies in the civil and military service and left the treasury which he had found with a deficit of £1 million a year with a surplus of £1½ million. Thus far he had the directors' enthusiastic support, but when he wished to use this surplus for Indian welfare, their ardour cooled. In India the government became again a going concern and in England the direction was able to face Parliament in more confident mood. The continued existence of the Company after the Charter Act of 1833 was in no small measure due to Bentinck's financial measures.

Bentinck's second great achievement was that of judicial and revenue reform. In the former department he abolished Cornwallis's provincial

[1] For friction with Wellington's ministry see T. G. P. Spear, 'Ellenborough and Bentinck', *Proceedings of Indian History Congress, 1939.*

[2] Bentinck was a full general.

[3] *Batta* was an allowance to troops when on active service. The area covered by *batta* was not reduced as the area of British authority extended. Hence the periodical disputes about its reduction. The new rule allowed half *batta* only in the case of troops stationed within 400 miles of Calcutta.

[4] An example of this is the legend that Bentinck proposed to sell the Taj Mahal for the price of its marble. See T. G. P. Spear, 'Bentinck and the Taj', *Roy. Asiatic Soc. Journal.*

courts of appeal and circuit which had been largely responsible for the huge arrears of cases. Persian as the Court language was displaced by the local languages in the lower and English in the higher courts. Indian ability was recognized by the increase in the powers and salaries (and so status) of the Indian judges. This measure was the more readily agreed to since it contained an element of financial economy. Where principle was still disputed finance had opened a way. In the sphere of revenue he was faced by the complaint that the system laid down by Regulation VII of 1822 had proved too elaborate and ingenious. At the end of 1830 he set out on his great northern tour, spending the summer in Simla and the winter in the plains, in order to inform himself at first hand of the situation. The result was the launching of the revenue settlement of the north-west provinces under the auspices of R. M. Bird. Taking ten years to complete, its principle was that of a semi-permanent settlement for thirty years which would both encourage the tenant to make improvements and enable the state to reap some of the benefits. It respected existing rights, being made with large land-holders, cultivators, or village communities according to the locality. A secondary result was the discovery of the value of the hills as a place for work as well as for convalescence. His example was quickly followed, so that he may be said to have inaugurated that characteristic feature of British India, hill station life.

Bentinck's third great achievement was that of social and intellectual reform. His most resounding measure was the prohibition of suttee or the burning of widows on the funeral pyres of their husbands.[1] This evil custom, frowned on by the Mughuls, had increased in Bengal under British administration and its prohibition had been considered by every Governor-General since Wellesley. Bentinck acted where others had talked and found, when it came to the point, that the opposition was surprisingly weak. Also important was the campaign undertaken by Col. Sleeman from 1830 against the *thugs*. These groups of robbers and ritual murderers, who formed both a plundering brotherhood and a religious cult, had also increased in central and northern India during the Time of Troubles. To these measures may be added the suppression of ritual child-sacrifice at Saugar island in Bengal and the active discouragement of infanticide. These steps marked a new feature of British rule; for they avowedly interfered with social and religious customs. The ground of interference was the universal law of humanity; it was now maintained that not even religious sanction could stand against the universal moral law.

From the correction of abuses Bentinck turned to positive innovation. The principle of encouraging learning and education had been embodied in the Charter Act of 1813. Bentinck gave the policy a new force and direction by laying down that the content of the learning encouraged should be western knowledge and the medium of instruction English. In this he was fortified but not anticipated by

[1] See further Book VIII, Chapter 7, pp. 647-8.

Macaulay, who had joined the council as law member in 1834 under the Charter Act of 1833. In 1829 he had written to Metcalfe of 'the British language, the key to all improvements' and in 1834, before Macaulay's arrival, 'general education is my panacea for the regeneration of India'.[1] The substitution of English for Persian as the language of the higher courts and of government business gave a powerful even if utilitarian fillip to the study of English and the spread of western knowledge. To this great measure may be added other examples of his forward-looking mind: the abolition of transit duties in 1835, the development of steam transport by river and ocean, the beginnings of tea and coffee cultivation and of iron and coal production, the planning of a network of roads, projects for drainage, and of irrigation canals,[2] and the abolition of flogging in the Indian army.

In his relations with the states and with foreign powers Bentinck continued the policy of non-interference and non-aggression which he had inherited. In the case of the states he had to face the increasing embarrassment which that policy was bringing to the government. The security with which rulers were endowed within and without and the lack of any field for talent or legitimate ambition led to irresponsibility, indolence, and decadence. Bentinck found no solution to this problem. He forbore as long as possible and only interfered when misgovernment had gone beyond a certain point of bearing. In Mysore Wellesley's raja proved incompetent and vicious. In 1831 the administration was taken over (as provided by treaty) and remained in British hands for fifty years. The Raja of Coorg was deposed in 1834 on account of his cruelty and the state annexed 'in consideration of the unanimous wish of the people'. The little state of Cachar was also annexed at the wish of the people, later to become a nest of tea gardens. Oudh staved off the fate of Mysore by promises of reform. Elsewhere, as in Jaipur and Gwalior, disturbances stopped short of the need of intervention. Beyond the border peace was maintained, but in 1831 the first measures were taken to open up the Indus for navigation and a commercial treaty was made with Ranjit Singh at Lahore. Bentinck was the first Governor-General to envisage a Russian menace to India, but it is safe to say that both his and Metcalfe's methods of meeting it would have been very different from Auckland's.

Bentinck announced his retirement at a moment of political change. During the year between his departure in March 1835 and the arrival of his permanent successor Sir Charles Metcalfe acted as Governor-General. He had been continuously in India since 1800 and had been Bentinck's right-hand man during most of his government. A liberal in sentiment, he was too experienced to desire foreign adventure and too rooted in habit to be radical in action. His liberalism, however, prompted him to one bold act. He repealed the rule of John Adam

[1] Bentinck Papers, Bentinck to Metcalfe, 16 Sept. 1829; and to Mancy, 1 June 1834.
[2] The Grand Anicut in Madras was cut in 1835–6.

requiring printers to obtain a licence before publishing a newspaper. This so alarmed the directors that he forfeited his chance of permanent appointment.[1] His year of office was in effect a year's extension of the Bentinck régime.

The governor-generalship was first offered to Mountstuart Elphinstone who declined it on grounds of health. The short-lived Tory government then appointed Lord Heytesbury. But the Whigs returning to office before he had sailed, cancelled the appointment in favour of Lord Auckland, a good Whig and a nephew of Lord Minto. Auckland was an able and conscientious man, not to be compared with Amherst, but he lacked the personality to dominate a situation and was prone to be influenced by spirits more ardent than his own. He had a vein of moral weakness, which led him to acts which still seem, in perspective, to be wholly out of character. His appointment was regarded as a 'safe' one, but his sponsors forgot that the quality which consists of lack of positive faults is apt to prove most dangerous in times of crisis. There is no position like that of sole ruler and no conditions like those of India more apt to reveal the feet of clay beneath the dignified figures of party politicians.

Auckland was faced with foreign problems not of his choosing as Bentinck found states' problems not of his devising. In intention he desired to continue Bentinck's internal régime and up to a point he succeeded. He broadened and sweetened the western rigour of the new education by providing some encouragement for Eastern as well as Western studies; he developed the irrigation policy inaugurated by Bentinck, and he made the first large-scale efforts to deal with the famine which visited northern India in 1837-8. In 1770 the government had looked helplessly on while Bengal was devastated; in 1838 nearly 40 *lakhs* were spent on relief measures. But the lack of good communications prevented the sovereign remedy for large-scale famine, the quick import of grain from a distance, from being supplied on a sufficient scale, and at least 800,000 people are thought to have died. He also implemented the directors' orders abolishing the pilgrims' tax and all signs of official connexion with temples or religious festivals. Thus the neutrality of the state towards religion was given that absolute character which it preserved for the rest of the British period. Towards the states his conduct was not so blameless. The Raja of Satara was necessarily deposed in favour of his brother for intrigue and the Nawab of Karnal deposed altogether for attempting to wage war against the Company. But when the directors disallowed a treaty which Auckland sought to force on the new King of Oudh in 1837, he failed to inform the king of the fact. This lack of candour is an instance of a new vein of Machiavellianism which appeared in British Indian policy at this time and disfigured it for some years.

The shadow of Afghanistan has covered Auckland's administration

[1] Metcalfe resigned the service in 1837 but lived to be Governor of Jamaica in 1839 and Governor-General of Canada in 1843.

so darkly that not even the charm and liveliness of his sister's descriptive writing have been able to lift it. The Afghan episode will be dealt with in Chapter 3; here it is sufficient to point out its connexion with British policy as a whole. The full story of the Afghan war has not been revealed because the parts played by the British Cabinet and Foreign Office are not yet fully known. But it should be remembered that Auckland had not one set of mentors but two. Apart from the eager politicals egging him on from Kabul and in Simla there was Lord Palmerston in the full tide of his masterful diplomatic career. It was Palmerston's object to undo the treaty of Unkiar Skelessi by which Russia had achieved a stranglehold on Turkey in 1833. He not only considered the possibility of Russia putting pressure on Britain through Afghanistan but the counter policy of putting pressure on Russia through the same region. A pro-British power in Afghanistan could influence affairs in Persia in which Russia was deeply interested, and in Turkistan beyond the Pamirs, across which the Afghan dominion spread into Badakhshan.

By the thirties Russian influence in Persia was such that the Persian siege of Herat with Russian help seemed to be a direct threat to India. It is significant that the siege was raised in 1838 on a protest from Palmerston. Russian sensitivity in the east to pressure from the West may well have encouraged Palmerston and the Whig government to persevere with the Afghan adventure even though its principle justification had now ceased to exist. A pro-British Afghan state would be a threat to the Russian position in central Asia just as much as a Russian-dominated Afghanistan would be a threat to India.

Be that as it may, the decision to move forward in the north-west, taken in 1838, determined the character of Indian government for the next period of years. From 1818 to 1839 India was substantially at peace. Only one war of importance occurred beyond her borders, and that was demonstrably forced upon the government. Internally disturbances had been occasional and limited in character; the keynote of the period was peace, retrenchment, and reform. During these years the foundations of modern India were being laid and the seeds were being sown of that Indo-British cultural synthesis which later provided the inner force of the Indian national movement. There followed ten years of successive wars, each leading on to the other in a logical sequence of aggression. The peace which followed was uneasy, being disturbed by the second Burman war abroad, by annexations and rising discontent at home. Not till after the storm of the Mutiny did India again settle down to peace and constructive administration. By then the spirit of the government was very different to that of the optimistic liberalism of the thirties. Constructive effort did not disappear altogether, but it was subordinated to power politics. A harder tone crept into the voice of authority. Indians had not only to complain of an 'aloofness' caused by British 'absorption in their own concerns' but also of a pride of race and achievement which judged Indians to be inferior in both culture and character and saw no hope of improvement or regeneration.

The conduct of the Afghan adventure depended upon the maintenance of the Sikh alliance and the overawing of the suspicious but ineffective Amirs of Sind. The death of Ranjit Singh endangered the one and the loss of Afghanistan made it the more necessary to maintain a hold of the other. Lord Ellenborough, who was on his way to succeed Auckland before the news of the Kabul disaster was received, was not the man to meet a difficult situation with restraint or effect a withdrawal with prudence. A brilliant orator with flashes of real insight, he was vain and pompous, overbearing and irascible. He longed for glory which the situation did not permit and resented not only opposition but advice. His experience as Wellington's President of the Board of Control had fired his lively imagination and whetted his ambition for power. He was chosen by Peel's Conservative government in spite of his faults on account of his experience and ability. In two and a half years his changes of policy, his overbearing temper, and his theatrical gestures alienated nearly every responsible authority in the country. The withdrawal from Afghanistan was marred by contradictory orders and the farcical episode of the return of the supposed gates of Somnath from Ghazni.[1] Thereafter he superseded Outram in Sind, appointed Sir Charles Napier to sole military and political authority, and encouraged him in the measures which led to the defeat of the Amirs and the annexation of the country. Napier proved such an apt pupil that even Ellenborough entertained doubts of his conduct before the end.[2] Ellenborough's final exploit was the overthrow of Sindia's army in December 1843. The measure in itself was a prudent precaution in view of the threatening aspects of affairs in the Sikh Panjab; but its execution exemplified Ellenborough's weakness for using the maximum of force with the minimum of tact. A comparison with Lord Hastings's methods in 1817 illustrate the Governor-General's lack of judgement and the hardened tone of the Indian government. This exploit filled the cup of the directors' fears and indignation, and emboldened them to use their constitutional right of recall for the last time.

Ellenborough had little time for domestic affairs. But there is one measure for which he must be given his meed of credit. In 1843 slavery was finally abolished in India. The method adopted was to declare that the status of slavery did not exist and thus avoid the problems of compensation that so vexed the process of emancipation in the West Indies.

Ellenborough's successor was Sir Henry Hardinge, a seasoned soldier who had fought at Waterloo and a statesman who had held office as Secretary-at-War and Chief Secretary for Ireland.[3] His main

---

[1] The great temple of Somnath in Kathiawar was sacked by Mahmud of Ghazni in 1025.

[2] See Lambrick, *Sir Charles Napier and Sind.*

[3] He was also Ellenborough's brother-in-law, a fact which sweetened for Ellenborough the pill of supersession.

PLATE 31

Ram Mohan Roy

7. Dalhousie

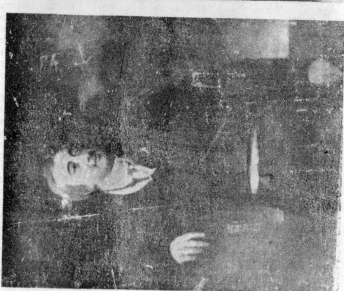

a. Lord William Bentinck

pre-occupation was the first Sikh war with its aftermath, which broke out in December 1845, within eighteen months of his arrival. But he was able to devote attention to internal matters as well. He developed the great irrigation system of the Ganges, and made the first plans for an Indian railway system. He supported education. In line with Bentinck he promoted the suppression of suttee and infanticide in Indian states and he undertook the suppression of human sacrifice in the hill tracts of Orissa. Under the lead of John Campbell the custom was stamped out between 1847 and 1854.

This period of thirty years can be divided at the year 1839. The first twenty-one years was a period of peace disturbed only by the first campaign in distant Burma and the brief alarm of the Bharatpur defiance. It was the longest period of tranquillity that India had known since Aurangzeb left Delhi for the Deccan in 1680. But it was not only a period of passive peace; it was also a period of active and vital reform. It saw the broad organization of the whole fabric of British administration in India. Before 1818 we can speak of the British *power in* India; after 1839 it is more correct to speak of the British *empire of* India. A dynamic force within the country had become its ruling authority. But the actions of the British did not stop short at organization. There were, in addition, a series of innovations which laid the foundations for the development of the India of the twentieth century. These innovations were all in a westernizing direction. Though presented as additions or alternatives to existing institutions, they constituted in effect a challenge to the past. The significance of these measures of the British was matched by that of the first responses made to the challenge by Indians in Bengal. These centred on Ram Mohan Roy and his group in Calcutta.

The last nine years of this period presented a marked contrast to the earlier years. The administrative reforms, the cultural innovations, and the economic projects went on as before, though arousing less public attention and pursued with less obvious enthusiasm. Their place in the public eye was taken by the series of campaigns, Afghan, Sindhi, Maratha, and Sikh which engrossed the attention of government, soldiers, administrators, and non-officials alike. A certain hardening was perceptible in the whole tone of the British government, indeed in the attitude of Europeans generally to India. The advocates of 'westernism' became more strident and aggressive, the conviction grew that nothing good was to be found in the Indian past, and that all reform must be *western* reform. The earlier faith of men of high position in a quick and favourable response to the ideas of the West, along with the patience and willingness to wait, faded into indifference and scepticism. India had little to contribute to the future from her own past it was more and more widely believed, and no serious intention of abandoning it in favour of the western present. The attitude of trusteeship for an old and embarrassed estate tended to change to an attitude of ownership of a derelict property. The series of wars and annexations deepened both the sense of superiority and of being conquerors which had long been prevalent among junior, subordinate, and commercial Europeans. The sense of trusteeship, where it continued to exist, was no longer that towards a ward in chancery, until a minor's coming of age, but that to a ward permanently absent or incapable. In the eyes of the governing class both in England and India, India ceased to be the scene of an impending cultural transformation, to become a conquered territory peopled by communities wedded obstinately to obscure and archaic cultures, strange in their habits, mysterious in their thoughts and hostile to all change. The myth of spontaneous reform was giving place to the counter-myth of the unchanging East.

AUTHORITIES

THERE are lives of the Governor-Generals in the Rulers of India Series by A. T. RITCHIE, and R. EVANS, *Lord Amherst* (1894), D. BOULGER, *Lord William Bentinck* (1897), L. J. TROTTER, *Lord Auckland* (1905), Viscount HARDINGE, *Lord Hardinge* (1900). For Ellenborough, Lord COLCHESTER, *History of the Indian Administration of Lord Ellenborough* (1874) gives Ellenborough's letters to the queen and the Duke of Wellington, and A. H. IMLAH has published a biography (1939). See also Sir A. LAW, *India under Ellenborough* (1926), Lord COLCHESTER (ed.), *Lord Ellenborough's Political Diary*.

C. H. PHILIPS, *The East India Company*, is valuable until 1834 and Marquis CURZON, *British Government in India* (2 vols., 1925), useful for the whole period. Of the general works both Marshman and Wilson's continuation of Mill's *History* are useful for Amherst and Bentinck. Thereafter Marshman is a contemporary document. From modern works P. E. ROBERTS (*British India*) and the *Cambridge History of India*, vol. v, may be recommended.

RECENT PUBLICATIONS

J. ROSELLI's *Lord William Bentinck, The Making of a Liberal Imperialist* (1974) is a subtle and important biography. See also *The Correspondence of Lord William Bentinck, 1828–35* (2 vols.) edited by C. H. PHILIPS (Oxford, 1977). This selection, in two large volumes, is vital for an understanding of Bentinck and his work.

CHAPTER 3

Foreign Policy 1818–48: Burma and the north-west

THE establishment of the Company's dominion in 1818 brought with it a new problem of external relations as well as of internal development and treatment of the surviving Indian princes. The new frontiers were the Himalayas to the north, the Sutlej and the Rajput deserts to the north-west and west, and the tangled Assam hill tracts to the north-east. The only power in the north was the Gurkha kingdom of Nepal, with whom Lord Hastings had already tried conclusions and with whom the settlement of the treaty of Khatmandu was to outlast the British period. The Gurkhas were to prove an asset rather than a liability. To the north-west, between the Sutlej and the Indus, lay the Sikh kingdom of Ranjit Singh. Relations were regulated by the treaty of Amritsar in 1809 which allowed the Sikhs to expand westwards and northwards at the price of leaving Sind and the Cis-Sutlej Sikhs alone. In Sind the five disorderly Amirs of Sind held sway, emancipated for the moment from both Mughul and Afghan dominion, but incapable in themselves of either serious aggression or concerted defence. Beyond lay the Afghan kingdom, at this time torn by feuds between the Barakzai brothers and the old Abdali dynasty and rivalries amongst the brothers themselves. 1818 was the year when the eldest of the brothers was murdered by Kamran Shah and Ghazni was seized by Dost Muhammad Khan. Beyond was Persia, just emerged from the shadow of the Franco-Russian alliance of Tilsit in 1807, which had cost her Georgia, and further threatened by a Russia refreshed and strengthened by victory. Russia enjoyed all the prestige of the vanquisher of Napoleon, but she had lately been an ally and her proceedings in eastern Europe and Asia Minor had not yet caused the finger of alarm to be pointed at large-scale maps of Asia. Continuing our tour, the seaboard of India was now secure with the defeat of the French and the annexation of the Île de France (now Mauritius).[1] Though Java had been restored to the Dutch, the Dutch were themselves dependent on British sea-power. In addition the founding of Singapore in 1819 provided the British with a strategical strongpoint of incalculable value. There only remained the north-eastern frontier where a tangle of hill and jungle separated the plains of eastern Bengal from the rising power of the kings of Ava in the Irrawaddy valley and the Siamese kingdom in the basin of the Mekong.

If we look at the situation as a whole we shall observe that the British

---

[1] Mauritius was its original Dutch name after Prince Maurice of Orange, successor to William the Silent.

now controlled two of the three areas necessary for the secure domina·
tion of southern Asia. Command of the sea precluded maritime attack
and secured control of the eastern border of the region, the East Indian
archipelago. The Dutch here were virtually British agents since their
power depended on the sufferance of British sea-power. The British
hold over the Indian land mass was now nearly complete. The only
thing they lacked which their Mughul predecessors had enjoyed was
the control of the north-western rampart giving access to Persia and
central Asia on the one hand and to the Indus valley and India on the
other. The early Mughuls enjoyed this advantage by virtue of their
possession of Kabul and Kandahar, covering the approaches to the
Indian passes and opening a way to Persia through Herat, and of
Badakhshan covering the approach to Kabul through the Hindu Kush
range. It was therefore clear that the main energies of the British
would necessarily be concerned with the problem of establishing a
similar position on this side. It was long thought that control of the
passes and the Afghan plateau was essential to Indian security; Shahjahan's loss of Kandahar was cited as the first great blow to the empire
and Nādir Shah's seizure of Kabul as the beginning of the end. In fact,
whatever truth this contention may have had for the Mughuls, it did
not apply to the British with the same force, because the British had
two resources denied to their predecessors. They possessed sea-power,
and with it the ability to reinforce the land mass from overseas as well
as from within, and they had in western military discipline and artillery
the modern equivalent of the central Asian horsemen and Turkish
artillery. They had the resources to repel an attack on the borders of
India even if they had not the strategical position to prevent the attack
being made. That position could only be modified if Russia advanced
with sufficient troops to restore the balance of military force on the
Iranian plateau. In 1818 Russia was still far off, but it was these considerations which gave Russian policy its enigmatic and sometimes
sinister significance for Indian statesmen during the nineteenth century. If Russia appeared on the Iranian and Afghan plateau in strength
she would threaten the British position in India. But could she, and
would she? The solution of the strategical problem therefore resolved
itself into securing a defensible line without necessarily advancing as
far as the Hindu Kush and the Persian deserts. It was around the
answers to these questions that the controversies of Indian foreign
policy revolved, and it was the problem of a practicable defensive line
which exercised the minds of soldiers and statesmen. By 'practicable
line' is meant one which gave reasonable security and which could both
be achieved and maintained within the limits of the diplomatic, military, and financial resources available. And it must always be remembered that the problem could not be worked out in a political vacuum,
but was complicated by the presence of virile and warlike tribes, and
of intriguing and on occasion powerful states in the area concerned.

During his five-year march to Indian supremacy Lord Hastings had always kept a wary eye on Ranjit Singh in the Panjab who seemed to be emulating Mahadji Sindia in building up a powerful state based on the loyalty of a minority community and organized on western military lines with a leavening of European leadership. When he had therefore completed his work without interruption from the north and enjoyed four further years of peace he not unreasonably drew the conclusion that India could look forward to a period of external calm. Scarcely had his successor Amherst arrived in Calcutta, however, when he was faced with a threat from the north-east. Burma had long been the seat of a Buddhist kingdom whose dynasties had shared fully in the common vicissitudes of oriental kingdoms. In the year of Plassey Alompra, the founder of a new dynasty, conquered the province of Pegu and so added the Irrawaddy delta to his upper Burman realm of Ava. The Thais of Siam were next defeated, their capital Ayuthia destroyed in 1768 and Tennasserim annexed (1766). King Bodawpaya added Arakan in 1785, Manipur in 1813, and Assam in 1816. As successors of the kings of Arakan the Burmans called on Lord Hastings to surrender Chittagong, Dacca, and Murshidabad in 1818. But a defeat by the Siamese and Hastings's disinclination to engage in fresh wars induced the respective parties neither to repeat or to resent the demand. As a prelude to their career of expansion the Burmans had repelled invasions from China in 1765-9, and since China was then regarded by them as the leading power in the world their pride and confidence were inflated accordingly. The Burmans were arrogant, isolated, and ignorant. They had no conception of the nature of western civilization and suffered acutely from the megalomania which is apt to come from prolonged success within narrow confines.

The first Burman war thus started as one of the simplest cases of aggression in modern times. 'Brought into contact with the English they felt no fear: Ava was the centre of the universe, its arms invincible, its culture supreme.' 'From the king to the beggar they were hot for a war with the English.' In September 1823 they attacked the island of Shahpuri near Chittagong and made hostile moves on the Assam border. British demands for satisfaction being designedly ignored, war was declared by Amherst in February 1824. The war lasted for two years and brought little credit to either side. The Burmans suffered for their ignorance and folly, the British for their obstinacy and lack of adaptability. The British planned to seize Rangoon by sea and advance up the Irrawaddy. This sound strategy was put into force on the brink of the rains in May, with the result that the army found itself cooped up in an unhealthy swamp, unable to move and decimated by sickness. Subsidiary expeditions through Manipur and Arakan were baffled by the climate and the difficulty of the country. The Burmans had a leader of genius in Bandula, but after his death in April 1825 their only hope lay in the climate and the terrain. As the British learnt to adapt themselves to the new conditions the defeat of the Burmans became certain. Tenasserim was taken from the sea in the autumn of 1824. The final advance in the autumn of 1825 brought the King of Ava to terms and peace was signed at Yandaboo, sixty miles from Ava, in February 1826. The Burmans ceded Arakan and Tenasserim, withdrew from Assam and Cachar, and recognized the independence of Manipur. They agreed to pay an indemnity of £1 million sterling, to conclude a commercial treaty, and admit a British resident.

The second Burman war broke out in 1852 as the result of commercial disputes. The British resident at Ava had previously been withdrawn with the result that disputes in Rangoon were handled by bellicose governors on the one hand and tactless ships' captains on the other. Dalhousie was averse to annexation in this direction and war was actually precipitated by the hastiness and mutual misunderstandings of subordinates on both sides. Once war was declared Dalhousie took care to avoid the mistakes of Amherst's general Sir Archibald Campbell and he showed unusual restraint when his measures proved completely successful. The people of lower Burma, who were only partly Burman, welcomed the British as deliverers; the health of the troops was better than in many cantonments; the battle casualties were 377 and the cost less than £1 million sterling. Dalhousie annexed Pegu but refused to advance farther. King Pagan was succeeded by King Mindan under whose judicious rule friendly relations were maintained until the accession of King Thibaw. This war marked the real beginning of the British period in Burma because the earlier annexations had only been on the fringes of the real Burman dominion.

We now turn to the north-west. Until the end of the century the British were more concerned with the south of India than the north. Wellesley diverted their attention to the Marathas in the centre. It was their defeat and the capture of Delhi, the gateway of the north-west, that first brought the British into contact with the new problems that awaited them. Palm-trees and mango groves were now replaced in their imaginations by sandy wastes and arid mountains; the elephant by the camel. We may start our survey by noting the one point which continued fixed for over thirty years in the shifting scene of northern politics. This was the treaty of Amritsar in 1809 concluded by Charles Metcalfe with Ranjit Singh as the fruit of one of Lord Minto's missions. This fixed the line of the Sutlej as the boundary between Sikh and British influence; henceforward the Sikhs on the east side of the river, or the Cis-Sutlej states, were under British protection. From this agreement flowed in due course the Patiala and Eastern Panjab States Union or P.E.P.S.U. Until Ranjit Singh's death in 1839 the tract from the Sutlej to the Indus was in strong and friendly hands. The Lahore kingdom in fact was one of the few really successful buffer states in history.

The dissolution of authority to the south and west of the Panjab should next be noted. Sind had been subject to the Mughuls from 1591 to 1750. It then passed to the new Afghan Shah, Ahmad Shah Abdali. In 1783 Mir Fath Ali Khan Talpura overthrew the last of the Kaloras and thereafter, as the hand of the Afghan Shah Taimur grew weaker, became virtually independent. Tribute continued to be claimed but was usually withheld. Sind was parcelled out between three main branches of the clan, the Shahdadpur family ruling central Sind from Hyderabad, the Mirpur or Manikani family at Mirpur and the Sohrabanis at Khairpur. Mir Fath Ali Khan died in 1802 and thereafter central Sind was subdivided between his son, brothers, and nephews, one of their number being vaguely acknowledged as rais or chief. There were thus three main branches, one of whom was subdivided into four. These were the Amirs of Sind, and since the Afghans were too distracted to reassert their overlordship, the Amirs too indolent to strive for supremacy and too foolish to unite, the country was virtually divided into a number of independent but petty states.

In Afghanistan the dissolution came not by natural increase but by battle and murder. Ahmad Shah Abdali was chief of the Sadozai clan of the Abdali tribe whose name he changed to Durrānī. He ruled from Kandahar and aimed at uniting all Afghans under his sceptre. When he died in 1773 his rule extended to Kafiristan and the Oxus on the north, to Kashmir, the Sutlej, and the Indus on the east, to the sea on the south, and to Persia and Khorasan to the west. In modern terms it stretched over Pakistan and Afghanistan and parts of what are now Persia and Russian Turkistan. It was a short-lived revival of the realm of the Ghaznavids and the Ghorids. Ahmad Shah left eight sons of whom the second, Taimur, became Shah. In his time the Sikh power grew in the Panjab and Sind was lost. Distrusting the Durrānīs he leaned on Payandah Khan, chief of the Barakzai clan. Taimur, on his death in 1793, left twenty-three sons, while Payandah Khan in his turn left twenty-one in 1799. Such fruitfulness was too much for stability and amid the interlocking rivalries of the several brothers and the two families the Durrānī empire perished. Zaman Shah, after a march to Lahore in 1798, was deposed and blinded. His brother Mahmud Shah seized the throne with the aid of Payandah Khan's eldest son, the king-maker Fath Khan. In 1803 he was discarded in favour of the ill-fated Shuja-ul-Mulk (another son of Taimur Shah), to be restored by Fath Khan in 1809. The Durrānīs were now bound to Barakzai tutelage. A final explosion occurred in 1818; Fath Khan was murdered but Mahmud Shah and his son Kamran were confined to Herat; Kamran succeeded Mahmud in 1829 and acknowledged Persian suzerainty. The rest of the country was parcelled out among the Sadozai brothers. The ablest of these was Dost Muhammad Khan. He held Ghazni and gradually rose to eminence during twenty years of struggle and intrigue. To Ghazni he added Jalalabad and in 1826 seized Kabul and proclaimed himself Amir. He lost Peshawar to the Sikhs in 1834, but easily repulsed an attempt by Shah Shuja in the same year to recover the family throne.

The dissolution of authority in the north-west promoted the security of the British in India, but they were haunted by fears of more distant threats. The first of these was the French in the time of Napoleon. His Egyptian expedition, and his known fascination with the East thereafter, caused the British to transfer the French threat in their minds from the south of India to the north-west. This directed their attention to Persia as the nearest stable power who might stand in the way of a French advance. In 1801 Wellesley sent the young John Malcolm to Persia where he concluded commercial and political treaties. But Persia was more concerned with Russia on her border, who had seized Georgia in 1801, than France on the Atlantic, and introduced French agents to counteract the Russians. The *entente* between Napoleon and the Tsar Alexander at Tilsit in 1807 reversed the Persian tendency to look to France as a counterpoise to Russia and drove her back into the arms of Britain. Minto strove to take advantage of this by sending Malcolm to Teheran on a second mission, only to find that the London Foreign Office had also dispatched its own agent in Sir Harford Jones. An undignified episode ended in the conclusion of a treaty in 1809 by Jones by which Persia undertook to deny any European power a passage through Persia and to help British India if attacked. Britain undertook to aid Persia in the event of an attack by a European power either with troops or with a subsidy and a loan of officers. At the same time Elphinstone's mission to Peshawar produced a treaty with Shah Shuja which proved abortive because of his fall immediately afterwards. It was hoped by these means to turn Persia into a buffer between the Franco-Russian menace and India. But Britain and India were both too distant, Persia too weak, and Russia too near for the policy to prove successful. The amount of aid and comfort required by Persia was beyond the powers of a Britain standing at bay against a French-controlled Europe and a British India still absorbed by the Maratha problem. In 1811 Russia again attacked and by the treaty of Gulistan in 1813 excluded Persian vessels from the Caspian. British officers were lent and Persia hoped thus to strengthen her army against the Russians. The turning-point came when Shah Fath Ali was compelled by popular feeling to attack Russia in 1826. Defeat made it clear that the army was no better and led to a humiliating peace in 1828. Henceforth Russian influence grew at the expense of the British. Russia hoped to control central Asia through Persia and Persia to recover her lost prestige in that direction. In 1832 Khorasan was conquered on this plan and in 1834 the pro-Russian Muhammad Mirza succeeded his grandfather as Shah.

At the same time Russia's position in Europe was much strengthened by her defeat of Turkey in the war of 1828-9, which involved accessions in Asia Minor as well as the practical independence of the Danubian principalities (the modern Rumania). She followed this up by the treaty of Unkiar Skelessi in 1833 which came near to establishing a Russian protectorate over Turkey. Russia would protect the Sultan from Muhammad Ali of Egypt, of course at a price; the process of weakening from without had been replaced, as in Persia, by the process of undermining from within. It looked as though, before long, the Russians would control the whole of the Near and Middle East. The warning voices of a Russian threat to India, which had first been raised in the late twenties, were now heard in high places. The treaty of Unkiar Skelessi was the signal for Lord Palmerston's diplomatic counter-offensive which led to the virtual independence of Muhammad Ali and his confinement to Egypt, the humiliation of France at Palmerston's hands in 1840, and the gradual replacement of Russian by British influence in Turkey. The support of the Turkish empire against Russian encroachment now became, and remained during the rest of the century, a major British interest. It is in the interaction of British policy towards Russia in the Near and Middle East that the explanation of much that happened in the two Afghan wars is to be found. If, argued Palmerston, Russia could alarm the British in India by moves in Persia, why should not the British in India alarm the Russians by moves in Afghanistan? Similarly the Russians could bring pressure to bear on the British in Europe by making their flesh creep in India. Both sides, the one through the possession of interior land lines, and the other through sea-power, were able to threaten the other in either direction. Events in one theatre cannot therefore be understood without reference to events in the other; the Afghan wars were essentially a part of the general Eastern Question.

There is one other consideration, frequently forgotten by the framers of policy, which should always be remembered. This was the feelings of the Afghans themselves. Through all their turbulence and feuds there shone one passion above all others—an objection to outside interference. In this respect the Afghans are the Spaniards of Asia. There is evidence that Dost Muhammad would have preferred the British to the Russians as did his son Sher Ali later. But both much preferred their own independence to either. Disregard of this facet of the Afghan character caused much harmful exaggeration of the Russian danger in the minds of British Indian 'politicals'.

When Lord Auckland arrived in India in April 1836 he found a difficult position confronting him. The Persians were threatening Herat under Russian influence, Dost Muhammad was asking for aid against Persia and Ranjit Singh, who had taken Peshawar in 1834, while Ranjit Singh himself was an ally of the Company. Auckland had hoped for a peaceful reign devoted to internal development. His course of action was determined in the first instance by a despatch from the secret committee of the directors, dated 25 June 1836, a portion of which may be quoted. The Governor-General was instructed to

judge as to what steps it may be proper and desirable for you to take to watch more closely, than has hitherto been attempted, the progress of events in Afghanistan, and to counteract the progress of Russian influence in a quarter which, from its proximity to our Indian possessions, could not fail, if it were once established, to act injuriously on the system of our Indian alliances, and possibly to interfere even with the tranquillity of our own territory.

British territory.

Cis-Sutlej states under British protection.

----- Approx. boundaries.

INDIA, 1836

The mode of dealing with this very important question, whether by dispatching a confidential agent to Dost Muhammad of Kabul merely to watch the progress of events, or to enter into relations with this chief, either of a political, or merely, in the first instance, of a commercial character, we confide to your discretion, as well as the adoption of any other measures that may appear to you desirable in order to counteract Russian advances in that quarter, should you be satisfied from the information received from your own agents on the frontier, or hereafter from Mr. McNeill, on his arrival in Persia, that the time has arrived at which it would be right for you to interfere decidedly in the affairs of Afghanistan.

Such an interference would doubtless be requisite, either to prevent the extension of Persian dominion in that quarter or to raise a timely barrier against the impending encroachments of Russian influence.

The immediate consequence was the dispatch of Alexander Burnes on an ostensibly commercial mission to Kabul, but really to talk politics.[1] He arrived in Kabul in September 1837, and two months later the famous siege of Herat by the Persians began. Matters thus reached a crisis, and a decision of policy was imperative. Dost Muhammad must be aided against the Perso-Russian menace, or another set up in his stead, or Afghanistan left to its fate. Dost Muhammad was at first eager for an alliance. But his price was the recovery of Peshawar from Ranjit Singh, whose loss in 1834 had just been confirmed by the bloody battle of Jamrud. Auckland rightly refused to desert a profitable Sikh alliance for a doubtful Afghan one. But he also refused to exercise any influence with Ranjit Singh for a diplomatic arrangement which would have saved the face of both parties. Burnes in consequence had nothing to offer Dost Muhammad who now turned to the Russians as his only other resource.

Auckland, assuming that Afghan overtures to Russia automatically involved Afghan hostility to British India, proceeded to the second stage of his policy. His minute of 12 May 1838 defined three possible courses.[2]

The first to confine our defensive measures to the line of the Indus, and to leave Afghanistan to its fate; the second to attempt to save Afghanistan by granting succour to the existing chiefships of Caubul and Candahar; the third to permit or to encourage the advance of Ranjit Singh's armies upon Caubul, under counsel and restriction, and as subsidiary to his advance to organise an expedition headed by Shah Shooja, such as I have above explained.

If Auckland had adopted the first alternative, which he thought 'would be absolute defeat', no ill would have happened as events very shortly proved. If he had chosen the second the result would have been the same. If the third had been persevered in the result would have been similar, because Ranjit Singh had no real intention of committing his forces to the bleak Afghan plateau, particularly in someone else's cause. His choice of the third course was not disastrous in itself but

---

[1] It was Burnes's correspondence at this time which was garbled in the interests of Auckland's government in the Blue Book of 1843.
[2] J. W. Kaye, *History of the War in Afghanistan*, vol. i, p. 320.

led to disastrous consequences. First it involved Auckland in a battle of wits as to who should do the military work, a contest which revealed the depth of his diplomatic incompetence and dependence on the views of his political advisers, particularly Sir William Macnaghten. The result of the contest was the Tripartite Treaty of June 1838. The object of the treaty was to restore Shah Shuja to the *masnad* of Kabul. Ranjit Singh was confirmed in all his dominions and was to send Muslim troops to Kabul if called upon by the Shah. Similarly the Shah would assist the Sikhs if required. Sind was to be free 'for ever' from Afghan rule. In other words Shah Shuja was to have Kabul at the price of Sind with Sikh military and British financial support. Auckland was still uncommitted to military action.[1] But Ranjit's success consisted in the fact that he was not committed to military action with the British, but only with the resourceless exile Shah Shuja. He had only to sit still in order to force the British to act themselves or see the whole enterprise collapse. Ranjit Singh had outwitted Auckland. He sat still. Auckland now took the next of his fatal steps. It was determined in Simla that the British should do the work and this decision was justified in a dispatch to the directors dated 13 August 1838.

Before the final plunge Auckland was given one more opportunity of withdrawing in time. The London cabinet had protested direct to Persia and followed this up by the occupation of Karak. On the news of this action the Shah raised the siege of Herat, whose defence had been inspired by the courage and skill of Eldred Pottinger, in August 1838. But though doubts had been expressed at home, and the Duke of Wellington said that advance into Afghanistan would mean 'a perennial march into that country', Auckland persisted. His manifesto announcing the invasion was published on 1 October, before he knew that Herat was safe. But on 8 November he announced both the raising of the siege and perseverance in the plan.

We can now summarize Auckland's errors which led to an aggressive and dangerous war without even the justification of necessity. He first overlooked the fact that Afghan love of independence was even greater than their love of turbulence, and was thus the most effective of all safeguards against Russian domination. His ignorance of Middle Eastern conditions might excuse him on this score, but could not absolve him from responsibility for the others. The next mistake was his failure to put pressure on Ranjit Singh to come to terms with Dost Muhammad over Peshawar. Then followed the decision to replace the exile of thirty years' standing, Shah Shuja, who shared James I's reputation of never saying a foolish thing and never doing a wise one, on the throne of Kabul. Next came the virtual release of Ranjit Singh from a major part in the work by the terms of the Tripartite Treaty. From this flowed the decision that the British should undertake the main burden themselves and the final step of persevering in the project

[1] In itself the Tripartite Treaty was only 'a new and enlarged version of that made between Ranjit Singh and Shah Shuja in 1833'. *Camb. History of India*, vol. i, 195

when all reason for it had vanished with the saving of Herat. Auckland saw himself as a diplomatic potter moulding the political clay of Afghanistan; but he was in fact the clay and his political advisers the potters.

The iron of war now succeeded the gentler movements of diplomatic pens and it only remains to record the first deceptive success, the later disaster, and the final recovery. The army of the Indus was formed during the summer of 1838. It moved forward in December 1838, 21,000 strong including Shah Shuja's contingent of 6,000. At first all went well. Kandahar was taken in April 1839, Ghazni stormed in July, and Kabul entered in August. Dost Muhammad was a fugitive. But then the difficulties began. Shah Shuja proved unpopular and unable to win sufficient adherents to hold the country. In consequence the Bengal troops under General Cotton had to remain as auxiliaries. In fact they became an occupying force and a kind of double Afghan and British government resulted. Shah Shuja could only maintain himself at the price of foreign and infidel aid and this rendered an already unpopular régime an odious one. The result was a state of permanent unrest and sporadic revolt. Such a situation could only have one ending. In 1840 a revolt of the Ghilzais was suppressed and in November Dost Muhammad himself surrendered. But the country remained disturbed and the occupation costs steadily mounted.[1] The home government ordered retrenchment and this was unwisely effected at the expense of the stipends to Afghan chiefs. The Ghilzais rose again and interrupted communications with Peshawar. On 2 November 1841 a concerted revolt began with the murder of Burnes in Kabul city. Then began the oft-told tale of ineptitude and irresolution which converted defeat into disaster and tragedy. The commanding general Elphinstone was infirm and imbecile (his appointment in spite of his own protests was another of Auckland's mistakes); the political agent Macnaghten resolute but too confident of the power of money and diplomacy in such a crisis; the troops disheartened and exposed in the open cantonments instead of being esconced in the citadel of the Bala Hissar. Macnaghten was murdered in conference by Akbar Khan; on 2 January 1842 a treaty of evacuation was signed. On 6 January 16,000 men marched out of the cantonments and on the 13th Dr. Brydon reached Jalalabad as the only survivor. The rest had fallen to the Ghilzais and the rigours of the Afghan winter. In April 1842 the everluckless Shah Shuja was murdered by a nephew.

Such a disaster had never previously befallen a British-Indian army. But though Auckland was at first dismayed and despairing the disaster was not in fact complete. Kandahar, Ghazni, and Jalalabad were still in British hands and the Sikh alliance, in spite of the death of Ranjit Singh two years earlier, held good in a passive way. At this juncture Lord Ellenborough, who had been actually appointed Governor-General the previous November, arrived in February 1842. It was

---

[1] They were reckoned to amount to at least £1,250,000 a year.

clear that Afghanistan would have to be evacuated. The only question was how this could be done with the least damage to British prestige both within and without India. Ellenborough's moves were erratic. He first proposed to evacuate the country after inflicting 'some signal and decisive blow' on the Afghans. The news of the fall of Ghazni so shook him that he ordered evacuation forthwith. But Generals Nott at Kandahar and Pollock who had reached Jalalabad from Peshawar stood their ground, pleading lack of transport. Ellenborough realized that he had made a mistake, but strove to conceal it beneath sonorous phrases. In July 1842 he repeated the order but in a note allowed Nott at Kandahar to 'retreat', if he considered it feasible, by way of Kabul and the Khyber instead of the Bolan, while Pollock at Jalalabad was allowed to co-operate with him. The onus of action was thus thrown upon the generals, and they asked for nothing more. General Pollock defeated Akbar Khan in two battles and took Kabul on 16 September. The next day he was joined there by General Nott who had marched from Kandahar by way of Ghazni. The European prisoners were rescued. The vindication of British Indian arms was only sullied by the blowing up of the great *bazar* of Kabul. On 12 October Kabul was evacuated and the army retired by way of the Khyber Pass. With them they took by express desire of Lord Ellenborough the gates of Mahmud of Ghazni's tomb which were thought to be those which Mahmud had removed from the temple of Somnath in Gujarat in A.D. 1025. In fact they were of a common pattern and later date. With this brilliance and this anti-climax the first Afghan war ended. Dost Muhammad was now allowed to return to his country. He soon reasserted his authority and died in 1863, at the age of eighty, still in possession of power. The passivity of Russia during the first campaign and the later disasters showed how grossly the Muscovite menace had been miscalculated.

AUTHORITIES

For Burma see G. E. HARVEY, *History of Burma to 1824* (1925), D. G. E. HALL, *Dalhousie-Phayre Correspondence 1852–56* (1932) and *Early English Intercourse with Burma* (1928), H. H. WILSON, *Documents Illustrative of the first Burmese war* (1827), Sir W. LEE-WARNER, *Life of the Marquis of Dalhousie* (2 vols., 1904), and Major J. J. SNODGRASS, *The Burmese War* (1827).

For the north-west ELPHINSTONE's *Account of the Kingdom of Cabaul* (1815) is a good starting-point. J. W. KAYE, *History of the War in Afghanistan* (3 vols., first published in 1851) remains the principal authority. The garbled Afghan Blue Book of 1839 may be compared with the revised issue of 1859 after Kaye's exposure of the suppression of important passages in Burnes's letters. Sir A. COLVIN, *John Russell Colvin* (Rulers of India, 1905) seeks to clear his father of responsibility for the war. For Afghan and Persian affairs see Sir P. SYKES, *History of Persia* (2 vols., 1920) and *History of Afghanistan* (2 vols., 1940). See also A. BURNES, *Travels into Bokhara . . .* (3 vols. 1834) and *Cabool; being a personal narrative* (1842).

CHAPTER 4

Sind and the Panjab

I. Sind

BECAUSE of its isolated position, Sind had, up to this time, played little part in the affairs of India as a whole. It was long a Mughul province, chiefly famous as containing (at Umarkot) the birthplace of Akbar. Its trade through the port of Tatta was restricted to the products of the Panjab and southern Afghanistan. For this reason the British, through the East India Company, had had little contact with the country; the prospects were not good enough. A factory was reopened at Tatta in 1758, but only to be closed again in 1775. The means rather than the will for trade was lacking. As the north-western region became more settled, interest in commercial possibilities revived and a mission to the new Talpura *amirs* was sent in 1799. But if the country was more settled the rulers were more suspicious than before and the mission came to an abrupt conclusion.

With the turn of the century political motives stimulated the Company's hitherto rather languid interest. The French bogey descended on the country. Henceforward the British had a double interest in Sind, as a possible seat of trade as conditions grew more settled, and as a counter in the power politics of the north-west. In 1809 Sind received one of Lord Minto's diplomatic missions whose fruit (after one envoy had been recalled for exceeding his instructions) was a treaty with the Amirs undertaking not to allow the French a foothold in the country. The treaty was renewed in 1820 with the proviso that no European or American settlements should be allowed. In 1825 a punitive expedition against the Khosas led to the visit of James Burnes[1] to Hyderabad. He published the first account of Sind in English, and from this time dated ideas of turning the Indus into a great highway of commerce. So great a river should not flow by unused, seems to have been the argument, though where the commerce was to come from, since most of its course ran through deserts, and the Panjab was still unirrigated, seems to have been less distinctly understood. Lord Ellenborough's easily kindled imagination took fire at the thought of the rolling waters of the Indus;[2] in 1831 Alexander Burnes journeyed up the river to offer to Ranjit Singh a gift of English cart-horses.[3] 'Alas',

[1] Brother of Alexander, the more famous Kabul envoy.

[2] Ellenborough was President of the Board of Control 1828–30 and urged Bentinck to undertake this mission.

[3] The cart-horses were regarded by Ranjit Singh with more curiosity than appreciation, being larger than any breed known in the Panjab, but unsuitable for riding. They died of overfeeding.

remarked a Sindi Sayyid, 'Sind has now gone since the English have seen the river', and so the event proved.

British interest in Sind having now been stimulated by a modicum of knowledge, the country became a plaything in the tripartite political manœuvres of the Sikhs, the British, and the Afghans. The Amirs were deeply suspicious of all three, but they were helpless against any of them separately and could only hope to play one off against the others. The immediate danger came from Ranjit, who proposed the partition of the country to Bentinck at Rupar. That pacific statesman declined, and the British thus became the virtual protectors of the Amirs from the Sikhs from 1831 to 1838. The outcome of Ranjit's proposal was the treaty of 1832, negotiated by Colonel Henry Pottinger, the first resident. By this treaty the Indus was thrown open to commerce with the proviso that no armed vessels or military stores should pass through.[1] The fears of the Amirs were expressed and soothed in the article which ran, 'the two contracting parties bind themselves never to look with the eye of covetousness upon the possessions of each other'. The essential case against later British policy in Sind rests in the first place on the unilateral violation of this treaty by the British.

So matters rested until 1838. When Lord Auckland decided that the British must bear the burden of restoring Shah Shuja to his throne the only possible route (the Panjab being ruled out by the presence of the Sikhs) lay through Sind and the Bolan pass. The treaty of 1832 was therefore brushed aside and in addition the Amirs were commanded to pay arrears of tribute to Shah Shuja though they held covenants issued by the Shah himself in 1833 releasing them from all further claims. Further, a new treaty was dictated in 1839 (and later revised in favour of the British) compelling them to pay 3 *lakhs* a year for a subsidiary force. They were told that 'neither the ready power to crush and annihilate them nor the will to call it into action were wanting, if it appeared requisite however remotely for the safety and integrity of the Anglo-Indian empire or frontier'. This was perhaps the least excusable of all Auckland's dubious actions at this time; to such depths can a weak man (in moral scruple as in will power) be driven in the effort to conceal the effect of earlier misjudgements. Sind thus became the military base for the campaign against Dost Muhammad.

Reparation could still have been made by withdrawal from the country at the conclusion of the Afghan 'incident'. But the incident ended in disaster. Further, an Amurath to Amurath succeeded in Ellenborough's succession to Auckland. The victories of Nott and Pollock were after all but the parting shots in a disastrous adventure. Ellenborough thirsted for some glory more positive than the subdued credit of a victorious retreat. There therefore followed the final episode of the annexation. On the excuse that the Amirs had shown themselves unfriendly during the Afghan affair (how could they have been anything else?) it was proposed to retain at least Karachi (occupied in

[1] Tariffs were settled by a supplementary treaty in 1834.

1839), Sukkur, and Bukkur. Before James Outram, the resident at Hyderabad and a man of the highest character, could arrange this, he was superseded by Sir Charles Napier, who was given supreme military and political control, in September 1842. This eccentric swashbuckler possessed as few scruples as Auckland but had at least the honesty to avow it. 'We have no right to seize Sind', he wrote in his diary, 'yet we shall do so and a very advantageous, useful, humane piece of rascality it will be.' New terms were presented to the Amirs, involving the cession of territory, the provision of fuel for steamers on the Indus, and the loss of coinage rights. Napier then acted as though the Amirs intended to reject the terms, seized the land demanded and razed the desert fortress of Imamgarh. The Amirs eventually signed at Outram's per-suasion while absolving themselves of the consequences. A tumultuous attack on the Hyderabad residency gave Napier his cue; the Amirs were duly defeated at Miani in February 1843; they were then exiled and Sind annexed.[1] Napier remained four years to govern the country in rude but vigorous fashion. Outram returned to raise his voice in England against the policy but though he found support from the directors, it was too late to undo the past. It only remained to atone, by the administration of Sind, for the manner of its taking.

The whole Sind incident is one of the least creditable episodes in British history during the nineteenth century. There was the unblush-ing violation of the 1832 treaty; there were the dictated terms of the succeeding years under a naked show of force, and there was the cynical provocation of the final struggle. In more recent times these actions would have been labelled 'fascist', and in this case the newer title would have been more accurate than the old. But an appreciation of this public injustice should not blind us to the larger issues involved. Sind, like the rest of India, was fated by the current of the time to come under the transforming influence of the West. The process might have occurred spontaneously from within, as in the case of Turkey or Siam, or through protection, as in the case of the Indian states, or through annexation. The imbecility of the Amirs ruled out the first of these alternatives. The cynicism of Auckland and Napier presented the third in its most objectionable form. The issue was not whether western influence should penetrate Sind, but how it should do so; we can deplore the manner of its imposition while recognizing that Sind could not for ever remain isolated from the world, and that it was not in her own best interests that she should do so.

II. The Panjab

The rise of the Sikh movement, its entry into politics, and conversion into a military sect has been described in earlier pages in this book.[2] At the end of Aurangzeb's reign it seemed that Sikhism was dead as a military menace to the Mughuls. The tenth Guru, Govind, died in

[1] The Mir of Khairpur alone escaped.
Part II, pp. 431–3.

1708. But his sons had been killed in battle and he named no spiritual successor. His follower Banda prolonged the struggle until 1716 when he was captured and executed and the revolt finally suppressed with great severity by Abdul Samad Khan. His surviving followers escaped to the hills where they lurked for a generation. Numerous small hill-forts in the foothills of the Himalayas from the Jumna to the Ravi attest to their outlaw existence during this period.

The Sikhs, it was thought, had been hammered out of existence. But the hammering did not in fact reduce them to pulp, but hardened a remnant to tempered steel. It is worth noting the transformation which this 'crisis experience' produced in the Sikh community. In one aspect the Sikh transformation was the well-known one of the meta-morphosis of peaceful *panths* or sects into bands of armed ascetics. But in the case of the Sikhs it was more than this, for not only the ascetic *Akalis* went armed, but the whole community. Guru Govind retained the old theology but altered the whole genius of the Sikh body. From a religious movement it became a separate religion, from a sect a distinct community and from a passive religious group a dynamic socio-political movement. Thus the worship of the one God and the disavowal of caste remained; the Muslim practice of meat eating was even added at this time. But a series of innovations strengthened the sense of brotherhood within, of separateness without, and above all, the sense of mission. The initiation ceremony encouraged new entrants and marked off the Sikhs from others; the greeting 'Hail Guru', the leaving of the hair unshaven, the title of Singh (lion or champion) encouraged the sense of separateness; the five 'Ks' provided as it were talismen of unity which appealed to high and low alike.[1] With the death of Guru Gobind political power passed to the *Khalsa* or whole con-gregation of the Sikhs, and spiritual authority to the Sikh scripture or *Granth Sahib*. This work now took the place of the Guru as God's representative among men and as such was the only object entitled to worship. Though the Sikhs as a body had now become permanently anti-Muslim in sentiment, it is interesting to notice the extent to which they borrowed from Islam even while they were striving against it. The emphasis on the unity of the Godhead, the repudiation of idolatry, and the disavowal of caste were loans taken before the breach with the Mughuls. But the custom of meat eating and the various devices to increase the sense of brotherhood were all added in the midst of the conflict. And may we not see in the title of 'Singh' the emphasis on struggle, and in the concept of martyrdom the influence of the Muslim doctrine of *jehad* or holy war?

The remnant which survived in the Panjab hills was thus a body which, though apparently leaderless as well as stateless, was held together by a body of doctrine which made them look upon themselves

---

[1] The five 'Ks' were *kesh*, unshorn hair and beard; *kungha*, carrying a comb in the hair; *kuchcha*, the wearing of shorts; *kara*, the wearing of a steel bangle on the right wrist; *kirpan*, carrying a sword. See K. Singh, *The Sikhs*, pp. 29–32.

as a Chosen People and by a ritual of daily life which underlined their separateness both to themselves and to others. Nothing was heard of them in the plains until Nādir Shah's march to Delhi in 1738–9. From that time the loosening of authority in the Panjab encouraged Sikh groups to reappear in the plains. The troubles of the fifties were their opportunity and after Panipat in 1761 there was virtually no one to oppose them. Their advance was thus rapid but disorderly. No strong chief existed to check them, but no accepted leader directed their movements. They spread over the Panjab as a number of war bands gaining converts and recruits as they proceeded and gradually forming into a number of embryo states. In the next thirty years the Sikh body was grouped into twelve loosely knit tribes or *misls*, each named after a leader or some local peculiarity, and predominantly Jat by race. The only outward link was an annual assembly or *Sarbat Khalsa* held at Amritsar, and an annual meeting of chiefs at *Gurumatta* which fell into abeyance after 1773 and last met in 1805. In this desultory and roving manner the Sikhs spread as far south as Karkhauda, twenty miles from Delhi, and as far north as the Indus.

The time was now ripe for crystallization into political unity. The need produced the man. Lahore was first occupied by the Sikhs in 1764, but their tenure was subject to periodical interference. The Patiala state was founded by Amar Singh in 1767 and became the chief Sikh power to the east of the Sutlej. In 1792 Ranjit Singh succeeded to the headship of the *Sukerchakia misl* at the age of twelve. Only a youth of exceptional ability could hold his place for long in such tumultuous times. In this respect Ranjit bears comparison with Akbar, who succeeded his father Humayun at the age of thirteen. His great chance came on Shah Zaman's last visit to the Panjab in 1798. On his retirement in 1799 he confirmed Ranjit in the possession of Lahore, thus casting the halo of legitimacy over what was already his in fact. Though superfluous in a material sense, such a title was of great value in terms of prestige. Ranjit could pose as the legitimate ruler to Muslims and as the favoured of the leading power in the region to his own Sikhs. Henceforward his progress was rapid. In 1801 he defeated the most powerful of the Sikh *misls*, the Bhangis. In 1802 Amritsar was his and he thus controlled, as it were, both the London and the Canterbury of the Sikh nation. In 1806 he took Ludhiana, but his further progress eastwards and southwards was then stopped by the British. Metcalfe's mission and the treaty of Amritsar in 1809 which followed marked a crisis in Ranjit's career, and his manner of dealing with it confirmed both his judgement and foresight. He realized the power of the Company without the bitter experience of defeat, he extracted the utmost advantage from his sacrifice of Cis-Sutlej claims, and he used the occasion to fasten discipline upon his brave but unruly followers. The visit of Holkar to Lahore as a fugitive in 1805 marked the beginning of the disciplined Sikh army; the ease with which Metcalfe's sepoy bodyguard repulsed an *Akali* attack enabled Ranjit to impress on his followers the value of discipline and so to extend it. In 1818-19 he took Multan to the south-west and Kashmir to the north; in 1833 Ladakh was added and in 1834 Peshawar. Farther advance southwards, at the expense of the Amirs of Sind, was prevented by the British and westwards into Afghanistan by Dost Muhammad. But Peshawar was held in 1837 against the Dost's counter-attack. When Ranjit died at the age of fifty-nine in 1839 he was the undisputed master of a compact and well-knit kingdom possessing the only army in India capable of meeting the Company's forces on equal terms.

Ranjit with Ram Mohan Roy were the most remarkable Indians of their generation.

Here are two contemporary descriptions; the first by Charles Masson,[1] who visited Ranjit in the eighteen-twenties, and the second by W. G. Osborne,[2] who saw him in 1838.

In person, the Maharajah is a little below the middle size, and very meagre. His complexion is fair, and his features regular, with an aquiline nose. He carries a long white beard, and wants the left eye. Though apparently advanced in years, I believe he has not completed fifty. On the right side of his neck a large scar is visible, probably the effect of a wound. In his diet he is represented to be abstemious, but he has always been perniciously prone to copious cups of the strongest spirits, which, with his unbounded sensuality, has brought on him premature old age, with a serious burthen of infirmities: for some ailment, he makes daily use of laudanum. Simple in his dress, which is of white linen, he wears on his arm the celebrated diamond Koh-i-Nūr, of which he deprived Shah Sujah ul Mulk.

Ill-looking as he undoubtedly is, the countenance of Runjeet Singh cannot fail to strike everyone as that of a very extraordinary man; and though at first his appearance gives rise to a disagreeable feeling almost amounting to disgust, a second look shows so much intelligence, and the restless wandering of his single fiery eye excites so much interest, that you get accustomed to his plainess, and are forced to confess that there is no common degree of intellect and acuteness developed in his countenance, however odd and repulsive its first appearance may be.

His height is rather below the usual stature of the Sikhs, and an habitual stoop causes him to look shorter than he really is. He is by no means firm on his legs when he attempts to walk, but all weakness disappears when he is once on horseback. He has still a slight hesitation of speech, the consequence of a paralytic stroke about three years ago; but those about him assert that his health is much improved within the last twelvemonth. His long white beard and moustachoes give him a more venerable appearance than his actual age would lead you to expect; and at fifty-eight years of age he is still a hale and hearty old man, though an imaginary invalid. . . .

It is hardly possible to give an idea of the ceaseless rapidity with which his questions flow, or the infinite variety of subjects they embrace. 'Do you drink wine? How much? Did you taste the wine I sent you yesterday? How much

[1] C. Masson, Narrative ... in Baluchistan, Afghanistan and the Panjab, vol. i, p. 443.
[2] W. G. Osborne, The Court and Camp of Runjeet Singh, pp. 81-83 and 79-80.

did you drink? What artillery have you brought with you? Have they got any shells? How many? Do you like riding on horseback? What country horses do you prefer? Are you in the army? Which do you like best, cavalry or infantry? Does Lord Auckland drink wine? How many glasses? Does he drink it in the morning? What is the strength of the Company's army? Are they well disciplined?

The Panjab state was neither a traditional Indian territorial state and monarchy, nor merely a dictatorship of one community over another. The Sikhs were as much the leading partners in the state as the Marathas were in Sindia's or Holkar's territories, but they were not communal dictators like the early dynasties of the Delhi sultans. There was an element of partnership with other communities, even if it was only subordinate partnership, and this included the Muslims as well as various kinds of Hindus. At the same time Ranjit did not claim the despotic sway of a traditional monarch over his own Sikhs. To the end, though taking the title of Maharaja, he claimed to be no more than the general of the Khalsa. He was, in some sense, its elected chief, and like Augustus Caesar, he was careful never to push his pretensions too far and always preferred the substance to the shadow of power. We can perhaps best describe the Sikh state as a communal régime with the lesser communities in the position of junior partners. They were subordinate, but they were not trampled on. As the régime grew more stable and time passed, there were glimmerings of a nascent Panjabi nationalism. This faded away in the troubles of the eighteen-forties, to make an equally abortive appearance in the first half of the next century. Too much depended on one man for such feelings to take firm root in the time available.

It is clear that the first pillar of the Lahore state was Ranjit Singh himself. To an average military skill he united a diplomatic guile which even the tangled politics of the time rarely produced. But it was the presence of other qualities as well which made him such an outstanding figure. He had an Elizabethan faculty for bemusing both friends and foes as to his real intentions. Very shrewd in his assessment of character, he knew whom to trust and when and how far. He was able to make all hopes and fears revolve round himself; he never allowed any one man a position of dominating power, nor drove anyone to acts of desperation or despair. He balanced individuals and communities against each other with uncanny skill. Muslims, Dogras, Brahmans, and Europeans were used to set off his Sikhs, and his new army, composed of all these, was devoted personally to himself. In consequence each leader reckoned that he had as much to lose as to gain by his disappearance. He walked secure in a court of ambitious and ruthless men and no one dared to touch him even when he lay helpless and speechless with paralysis. He dominated his contemporaries by intellect as well as by craft. The activity of his mind showed itself, as in the case of Akbar, in an immense curiosity. 'His conversation is like a night-mare', wrote Victor Jacquement about 1830. 'He is almost the first inquisitive Indian I have seen; and his curiosity balances the apathy of the whole of his nation. He asked a hundred thousand questions of me, about India, the British, Europe, Bonaparte, the world in general and the next, hell, paradise, the soul, God, the devil and a myriad of others of the same kind.'[1]

The next pillar of the state, which gave to it its remarkable stability during Ranjit Singh's life, was the principle of integration. The dominance of the ruling race was sweetened, as in the case of Akbar, by the co-operation of other communities. The principle of religious toleration was observed and the avenue to honour and confidence was open to all. The Fakir Aziz-ud-din was one of Ranjit's most trusted confidential advisers; Brahmans and Dogras with other Hindus, and Europeans[2] were high in his confidence. Unlike contemporary Afghanistan, there was no permanent state of sporadic rebellion. The rivalries were personal and they were pursued within the orbit of a struggle for the leader's favour.

The third and most obvious pillar (after the personality of Ranjit Singh himself) was the army. At the end of his reign the armed forces directly controlled by Ranjit totalled about 75,000 men, and there were in addition the contingents of dependent chiefs, such as the Dogras of the hills. More than half of this number constituted the *fauj-i-ain* or regular army, which was organized on the European plan, and indeed included many Europeans in its officer cadre. The infantry owed much to the Italian General Ventura and consisted of both Sikhs and Panjabi Muslims. The cavalry, 12,000 strong, was organized by the French General Allard. It was said to be less efficient than the infantry, but was a capable and effective force. The glory of the Sikh regular army was the artillery, first organized by the French General Court and Colonel ·Gardner. Both the infantry and the artillery were unrivalled for steadiness; if the former was the equal of its British-Indian counterpart the latter was probably superior. These forces constituted the material strength of the Sikh power and as long as they held together and were capably led, they had no superior in the sub-continent.

The other pillars of the state were less imposing and of less intrinsic strength. The revenue and judicial administration was a fair imitation of the Mughul model and served well enough in an almost wholly agricultural country. But there was little attention to commerce or development. It is true that there was a public works department which was responsible for 300 miles of canals, but in general there was little realization of the economic possibilities of the country or any attempt to exploit them. The army in fact overshadowed the rest of the administration, monopolizing the manpower, engrossing the revenue, and canalizing ambition. The best men went into it, the wealth of the country was absorbed by it. After satisfying its needs there were no funds for constructive works. The Panjab therefore suffered the nemesis

---

1 V. Jacquement, *Letters from India*, vol. i, p. 395.
2 General Avitabile, a Neapolitan, was for many years Governor of Peshawar.

which overtook every state in the nineteenth century which tried to support a modern state on an agricultural economy; there was nothing else which could be supported. The Panjab state was imposing but its roots were shallow.

Ranjit Singh's policy was expansion within the limits of the possible. The political limit was the power of the British, recognized in the treaty of Amritsar of 1809, and the physical the cold of the northern mountains and the Afghan plateau which his Sikh soldiers never found congenial. Ranjit Singh went first to his fellow Sikhs, but he did not stop there and he was quite prepared to leave some Sikhs unredeemed if they were outside one of his self-imposed limits. Thus the Cis-Sutlej Sikhs were left as undisturbed by intrigue as by arms during his reign. On the other hand, having mastered all the Sikhs beyond the Sutlej he went on to take Kashmir in the north, Peshawar in the west, and Multan in the south-west. He cast covetous eyes on Shikarpur, the gateway of Sind, and would have been ready to absorb the whole of that country but for the British veto. But he had no desire to expand beyond the passes, because he knew the reluctance of the Sikhs to face the rigours of the Afghan winter and, better than Auckland and Macnaghten, the difficulty of maintaining a permanent foothold in Afghanistan itself. In the negotiations for the Tripartite Treaty he readily gave up his claim to Jalalabad in return for a subsidy of 2 *lakhs* from Shah Shuja. For him Afghanistan was a buffer against attack from farther afield, to be kept from dangerous strength by fomenting divisions.

The death of Ranjit Singh in June 1839 was the signal for the rapid collapse of the Sikh state. There was no one strong enough to control the uncouth but ambitious chiefs, and those ruthless men were themselves too shortsighted and egotistic to form an aristocratic union. The regular army was soon in control. There followed the Sikh anarchy, leading direct to the Sikh wars. Ranjit Singh's only legitimate but slow-witted son Kharak Singh was murdered in 1840 and his son Nao Nihal Singh accidentally killed the next day. Sher Singh, a reputed son, succeeded, to be murdered in his turn in late 1843. Tumults and assassinations followed in quick succession. Sher Singh's successor was the boy Dulip Singh, another reputed son, with his mother Rani Jindan as Regent. Sher Singh's decision to deal only with deputations and not individuals led to the growth of the *punches* or military committees, which soon came to be the real seats of power. They debated policy while leaving discipline and command to the officers. They had the power but not the discretion of the Puritan army committees in England, and, above all, there was no Oliver Cromwell to guide them. There could only be one answer to political anarchy and factional military leadership. If the army could not be controlled it must be disbanded or its energies diverted in war. No one dared to attempt the former and so the latter was the only resource. Anti-British feeling and suspicion of British intentions were on the increase; respect for British

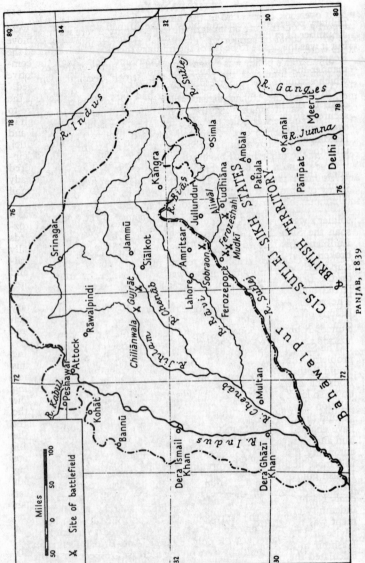

PANJAB, 1839

military power had received a blow in the Afghan war, and there were a number of minor disputes. The army was therefore willing to move but it was the desire to be rid of the military menace which induced the Regent Rani Jindan, Lal Singh the Wazir, and Teja Singh the commander-in-chief to countenance the move. It was the same motive which accounted for the irresolution with which the war was waged.

On the British side the danger of war had long been apparent as the crisis in the Panjab grew chronic and steadily deeper. The desire to secure his rear in the event of war had weighed with Ellenborough in overthrowing Sindia's army in 1843. Auckland, Ellenborough, and Hardinge had all increased the forces between Meerut and the Sutlej, until they reached a total of 40,000 men and 94 guns. Since the disciplined Sikh forces now numbered about 60,000 with several hundred guns, this cannot be considered provocative. Like many unsteady régimes, the Sikh government had the choice of war or internal turmoil and it chose war.

The Sikh army crossed the Sutlej on 11 December 1845. It was a soldier's war, brief and bloody. In the two battles of Mudki and Firozshah the Sikh thrust on Firozpur was driven back; a dash towards Ludhiana was thrown back at Aliwal and the Sikh army was finally broken up at Sobraon on 10 February 1846. There was little generalship on either side. Mutual distrust paralysed the Sikh command and on the British side the commander-in-chief, Sir Hugh Gough, preferred bull-headed frontal attacks to tactics and the use of artillery. The result was desperate fighting and severe battles. The military lessons of the war were the fighting value of the Sikh soldier which came as a revelation to many on the British side and the old Napoleonic lesson of the importance of artillery.

The Sikh state now lay prostrate and its disposal became a pressing problem. One solution was to annex the Panjab outright. But this would both have removed a hitherto useful buffer against aggression from the north-west and severely taxed British strength in holding down so large an area filled with a martial and disaffected people. The solution of a subsidiary force on the Maratha plan was rejected on the ground that it would probably lead to further conflict. In fact it might have enabled Mulraj's rebellion in 1848 to have been nipped in the bud and so saved much blood and treasure and perhaps some Panjabi autonomy. The actual solution was an attempt to revive the Sikh state in a more healthy form by pruning away its militarism and providing British guidance. By the treaty of Lahore of 9 March 1846, the Sikh army was limited to 20,000 infantry and 12,000 cavalry. The Jallandhar *doab*, Kashmir, and its dependencies were ceded to the British and an indemnity of £500,000 sterling was exacted. The Maharaja's government was recognized and a British resident established in Lahore to advise it. The settlement was completed by the handing over to Kashmir to the Dogra chief of Jammu, Golab Singh, who had nicely calculated the precise moment for abandoning the cause to which he owed all his fortune, for £1 million sterling. The effects of this ill-omened act have not yet ceased to operate.

The resident appointed under the treaty was Sir Henry Lawrence. On grounds of personality and sympathy with traditional chiefs no better choice could have been made. Yet his very zeal for reform was one of the factors which shattered his dream of re-creating the Sikh state on modern and humane lines. Sikh militarism was scotched, not destroyed; Sikh nationalism looked to a revival rather than regeneration from within and therefore regarded all reforms as so much western interference. At first matters went well. Within a year Lawrence was using Sikh troops to help crush a revolt in Kashmir. But at the end of 1846 the regency had to be replaced by a regency council of eight *sardars* with Lawrence himself as their president and the British garrisons were continued for another eight years. This was done at the request of friendly chiefs, but necessarily deepened the fissure between extremist patriots and those who were now regarded as fellow travellers with the foreigner. The very merits of Lawrence's vigorous rule strengthened the extremist party. In attacking such abuses as suttee, female infanticide, ferocious punishments, and vexatious taxes he was held to be attacking traditional life in general. The common people heard him gladly, but the *sardars* muttered in private and bided their time.

The departure of Lawrence on leave at the end of 1847 perhaps hastened but did not cause an outbreak which was as nearly as possible inevitable. But his absence may well have been responsible for converting what began as a local defiance in a distant stronghold into a national rising. In April 1848 Diwan Mulraj, the Governor of Multan, took up arms after two British officers, who had been sent to install his Sikh successor, had been murdered. Lord Dalhousie had only been three months in office and accepted General Gough's advice that punitive operations should be delayed till the autumn. Though young Herbert Edwardes attacked Mulraj with what local levies he could gather he could not assault the fortress or prevent the spread of the revolt. The crisis came in September when a large Sikh force sent by the resident and the Lahore Durbar under Sher Singh went over to Mulraj. A local and very natural rising had become a national revolt. Dalhousie then acted with the vigour he never afterwards lost. On 10 October he declared, 'unwarned by precedent, uninfluenced by example, the Sikh nation has called for war, and on my words, Sirs, they shall have it with a vengeance'.[1] Lord Gough was again in command and crossed the Ravi on 16 November. The two inconclusive and costly battles of Ramnagar and Chillianwalla[2] led up to the decisive battle of Gujarat.

[1] Vengeance is here used in the sense of the French 'à outrance', or 'to the limit', and not in the common sense of taking revenge.

[2] The losses on this occasion (2,446 casualties, 4 guns, and 3 colours) so stirred public feeling in London that Napier was sent out to replace Gough. Gough won Gujarat before Napier could arrive.

For once Gough made full use of his artillery; the Sikh army was shattered beyond hope of recovery and its remnant surrendered at discretion in March 1849.

The Panjab was now annexed outright by Dalhousie on his own responsibility.[1] He could get no clear lead from London, and while some authorities like Ellenborough and Henry Lawrence were against it, others like John Lawrence were in favour. The choice really lay between annexation and administration for a time on the Mysore model. Against this latter could be argued the fact that the Panjab was a frontier tract instead of lying deep within British territory; the same risks could not therefore be taken. A second national rising could not be risked. Dalhousie had no use for effete monarchies or oriental tradition; all that he knew of the old Sikh government he considered to be bad; for him annexation was a matter of common sense and common humanity. Opinion in general, then born along on the flowing tide of western self-confidence, was with him, and if efficient administration was to be taken as the sole criterion of government, the case was irresistible. But something is lost in corporate personality every time a nation loses its independence. The modern spirit had to come to the Panjab with all its material benefits and spiritual unrest. But if it had come by the free action of a reforming party within rather than by the compulsion of an alien rule, the conversion would have been more complete in the long run though it might have been slower in the beginning. Much that later happened in the Panjab might then have been avoided, including the division of India. The Sikhs by their own folly threw away the first chance of a Panjab organically integrated into a healthy plural society, Dalhousie by his over-confidence the second. Henry Lawrence had been too hasty with his reforms but his prescription was on the right lines.

AUTHORITIES

For Ellenborough's part in Sind the works of Lord COLCHESTER and Sir A. LAW may be referred to. The country on the eve of conquest is described in JAMES BURNES, *Narrative* . . . (1839). The great Sind controversy may be studied in Sir W. NAPIER, *The Conquest of Scinde* (1845), *Sir Charles Napier's Administration of Scinde* (1851), and the *Life of Sir C. Napier* (4 vols., 1857) on the one side and in Sir J. OUTRAM, *Conquest of Scinde, a Commentary* (1846) and Sir F. J. GOLDSMID, *James Outram* (2 vols., 1881) on the other. H. T. LAMBRICK, *Sir Charles Napier and Sind* (1952) is an exhaustive and authoritative modern study.

M. A. MACAULIFFE, *The Sikh Religion* (6 vols., 1909), is the standard work on Sikhism. A useful modern compendium on Sikhs and Sikhism in general is by K. SINGH, *The Sikhs* (1953). J. D. CUNNINGHAM, *History of the Sikhs* (Oxford, 1918) remains the best descriptive work on the Sikhs up to 1846. See also G. C. NARANG, *The Transformation of Sikhism*. For the Panjab in general see SYAD MOHAMMAD LATIF, *History of the Punjab* (1891) and for European adventurers H. L. O. GARRETT and C. GREY, *European Adventurers in the Panjab* (Lahore, 1929).

Of printed records there are nine volumes of selections from the Panjab Government Records, several Parliamentary Papers, HARDINGE's *Despatches* and DALHOUSIE's *Private Letters*. Dalhousie's part is given in his *Life* by LEE-WARNER (1904)

[1] Dulip Singh was pensioned. He later lived in England as a country gentleman.

and his *Private Letters* (1910). Henry Lawrence's part may be studied in the *Lives* by H. B. EDWARDES, and H. MERIVALE (1872), and by J. L. MORISON (1934), and John's in the *Life* by S. B. SMITH (3rd ed., 1883).

There is a lively description of Ranjit Singh in V. JACQUEMENT, *Letters from India* (1834) and of the Court in W. G. OSBORNE, *Court and Camp of Runjeet Singh* (1840). There are studies of Ranjit by Sir L. GRIFFIN (1911) and N. K. SINHA. For the Sikh state see N. K. SINHA, *The Rise of the Sikh Power* (1936), and H. L. CHOPRA, *The Punjab as a Sovereign State*.

RECENT PUBLICATIONS

H. T. LAMBRICK's *Sind, A General Introduction*, 2nd ed. (Karachi, 1976) is valuable and W. H. McLEOD's *Evolution of the Sikh Community* (Oxford, 1976) an excellent introduction.

CHAPTER 5

Government and People: Organization of Power

WITH the conquest of the Panjab the shape of British India was virtually complete. The British were the masters of India from the Indus to the Bay of Bengal. We may now ask ourselves in what way they proposed to administer these vast territories. They had begun as the heirs of the moribund Mughul empire and continued as the legatees of the Maratha confederacy. They had begun to pride themselves on being the harbingers of western civilization to India, but for the present they believed that India must long remain dependent. How did they propose to govern the country in the interim? We have already traced the steps by which the Company was first supervised and then superseded by the Crown, and its commercial character gradually whittled away. It remains to consider the organization which gradually developed during this period, what the term Company Bahadur meant to the people at large.

We may first note the development of the central executive. Most empires in India began with a single controlling and conquering head who devolved power as he extended and established his dominion. Sometimes, as with the Maratha Peshwa, the agent of the leader became the effective ruler and devolution proceeded to the point of division and even dissolution. In the case of the British, authority began by being separate and only slowly became united. There were three presidencies each directly subordinate to the Company in London, and this state of affairs lasted until the Regulating Act of 1773. The Governor-General at Calcutta was then given a very general authority over the two presidencies. In 1783 this was extended to give him control over 'all such points as shall relate to any transaction with the country powers, or to war or peace, or to the application of the revenues or forces of such presidencies in time of war'. This was underlined by a provision of the Act of 1793 superseding the authority of a governor when a Governor-General visited one of the subordinate presidencies. Wellesley made use of this provision when preparing for the last Mysore war. From this time, therefore, there was a unified direction of major policy tempered only by the old privilege of the Governors of Madras and Bombay of corresponding directly with the home authorities. The freedom of Madras and Bombay shrank to that of a considerable degree of internal autonomy.

The Governor-General himself, as we have seen, became the effective master of his own house when the number of his councillors was reduced to three by Pitt's India Act and the Act of 1786 gave him power to override his council. This power not only enabled him to dominate his council in person but also to act without it. The Governor-General could proceed up-country and send back decisions which the councillors could protest against but not reverse. In a country so vast, with communication so slow and a capital so distant from the frontiers, decisions were often necessary before all the necessary information could be conveyed to Calcutta and debated there. The system of government 'from the stirrup' as Ellenborough called it, was seen at its best when Lord Hastings directed the operations of the Pindari and last Maratha wars in person in 1817–18, and during Lord William Bentinck's great up-country tour of 1830–3. Its dangers in case of a susceptible or irresolute ruler were revealed during Lord Auckland's sojourn in Simla during 1838. The manifesto of 1 October 1838 announcing the Afghan expedition was issued without the knowledge of the councillors, who could only remonstrate at not having an opportunity of recording their views before its publication. So long as the Governor-General was supported by the President of the Board of Control, no power or person could resist him in India. Distance and the disinclination to force a crisis gave the Governor-General considerable freedom even from home control as the case of Lord Ellenborough showed. From the time of Cornwallis the Governor-General was the effective 'great Mughul' of India.

The Governor-General's internal authority increased with the expansion of the Bengal Presidency. After Tipu's fall the limits of the Madras Presidency were practically fixed. Bombay found its limit with the fall of the Peshwa in 1818 except for the addition of Sind in 1843. All the expansion north and westwards from Calcutta fell to the direct control of the Governor-General as did the control of the Rajput and central Indian states when they became dependent on the British. When we add Hyderabad to the list it will be seen that the control not only of external policy, but of the dependent states and the major portion of British Indian territory, fell directly to the Governor-General. His power of legislation, as of administration, was first limited to his own presidency. But the Charter Act of 1833 gave him, as 'Governor-General of India in Council' (no longer Governor-General of Fort William in Bengal) power to pass legislative Acts for the whole of British India with the sole extra help of a fourth or legislative member of council.[1] Cornwallis first received the power and Wellesley added the trappings of the Mughul. The popular instinct rightly saw in the Governor-General the supreme arbiter of Indian destiny.

The essential instruments of the Governor-General's will were the civil service and the army. Together they performed for the British raj the functions of Akbar's *mansabdars*. The *mansabdars* were in origin military officers some of whom exercised civil functions. It is significant

[1] He was not to be a member of the Company's service. The first of these members was Macaulay.

of the whole tenor of British administration that these two branches from the first were kept distinct and that there were constant protests against the practice of appointing military officers for civil duties. At first the civil officers were merely those of the Company's commercial factors who were detailed for revenue and other civil duties. The real start of the civil service was made by Cornwallis, when he separated the commercial and revenue branches of the administration, enforced the rules against receiving presents and carrying on private trade, and secured the payment of adequate salaries. At the same time he began the practice of excluding Indians from all high office.[1] This was given a legal basis in the Charter Act of 1793, which confined all posts worth more than £500 a year[2] to the covenanted servants of the Company. The Company's servants had been ill-paid, corrupt, and mixed up with commerce, while many responsible posts had been held by Indians. From this time the service was well-paid, honourable, and confined to administration, while Indians were not only excluded from the covenanted service, but also from all higher posts. The character of the service was broadly fixed for the rest of the Company's life.

The Company's servants became the best paid civil service in the world. With nothing more than their official emoluments they could live well and retire with a competence. But they never forgot that they had once lived better and could make fortunes. Hence arose the tension which lingered through the British period between civilians bewailing successive 'clippings' as the reward for faithful service and an English public critical of a pomp and extravagance which they believed had continued from the days of Clive and the 'nabobs'. The large-scale corruption of older days disappeared and the service soon attained a high standard of duty and probity. A kind of lesser corruption, which consisted in finding loopholes in the regulations and making money by clandestine presents, irregular allowances, fictitious sales, and the like, lingered on until Bentinck's day.[3] But as the young men who entered the service from the turn of the century rose to responsibility these things disappeared for good. The jobbery and corruption of a Potts, a Grand, or a Macpherson gave place to the industry and high-minded integrity of a Metcalfe, an Elphinstone, or a Lawrence. This was not only due to administrative reform or the stimulus and example of men like Cornwallis and Wellesley. It was also promoted by the Company's greater care in appointment. Though the system of nomination by directors continued, the process was less haphazard and the preparation for duty more studied. Wellesley forced the pace by founding his College of Fort William in 1801. The directors managed to quash this project but only at the price of establishing their own East India College at Haileybury. There cadets received a general education and some

---

[1] With the outstanding exception of Ali Ibrahim Khan, the Judge of Benares.
[2] About Rs. 500 a month at the rate of exchange then.
[3] An illustration of this was the Colebrooke case in Delhi. See T. G. P. Spear, *Twilight of the Mughuls*, pp. 167–81.

tincture of Eastern knowledge and left England both more mature and better prepared for their life work in India.

The last characteristics of the civil service were its family nature and its 'Englishness'. Its family character derived from the practice of nomination. The directors could no longer send impossible friends and relations because of the Haileybury bar. But they could still send friends and relations. This had both good and bad effects. A tradition of hereditary service grew up, which gave to India some of its most devoted foreign servants; on the other hand, the civil service tended to become a close corporation, possessive in its attitude and conservative in its outlook. Every Governor-General had to reckon with the senior Company's servant, convinced of the folly of all innovation. The 'Englishry' of the service derived from the fact that Indians were in practice excluded from it. Men like Purnea of Mysore, Nana Fadnavis of Poona, and Salar Jung of Hyderabad were admitted to combine great ability with integrity, but there was no avenue of employment for their kind in the Company's service. This was the result, not of a race but a patronage bar, because nominations were in the directors' hands. As things were, the only way to introduce Indians would have been to appoint some Indian directors. In 1833 the new liberal Parliament declared that 'no native . . . shall, by reason only of his religion, place of birth, descent, colour or any of them, be disabled from holding any place, office or employment under the Company'. But nomination remained for twenty years longer; when open competition replaced it in 1853 the examinations were held in Britain and it was not until 1864 that the first Indian entered the Indian civil service.[1] Where principle was unavailing against vested interest, however, the more mundane motives of convenience and economy found a way. Wellesley and Lord Hastings took the first steps towards promoting Indian agency, and Lord William Bentinck threw open to Indians three judicial grades up to the position of subordinate judge. This was the real beginning of the great Indian judicial tradition.

If the civil service was the right hand of the Governor-General, the army was his left. As in the case of the civil administration each presidency army was at first independent. In the early days a company of Europeans, a body of topasses, and a number of undisciplined peons sufficed. Their chief business was to grace processions to the Company's garden, to fire salutes whenever possible, to keep order in the settlement, including the young roystering factors, and to put on a brave show should a local potentate or Mughul magnate draw uncomfortably near. The real start of the Company's armies came during the Anglo-French wars when Stringer Lawrence embodied the Madras European Regiment[2] and raised a number of Indian companies. From that time the armies of the three presidencies developed independently. The Acts of 1773 and 1783 gave the Governor-General an overall

---

[1] He was Satyendra Nath Tagore.

[2] Later the 1st Madras Fusiliers. Clive had his first commission in this regiment.

control, but the armies remained separate till the Mutiny. But as the Bengal Presidency expanded, its army grew with it and came in time to overshadow the others by reason both of its numbers and the greater wealth of fighting material at its disposal.

In considering the British forces in India we must distinguish between the royal and Company troops. Royal regiments were first sent in particular crises to aid the Company and later were permanently stationed in the country. They were the most efficient and most reliable force in India, being remote from local feelings and controversies. They were a source of much jealousy since their officers enjoyed precedence over Company's officers of the same rank, and were fully conscious of their position. They were, in fact, the ultimate resource of the Governor-General and it was primarily to them that the restoration of authority was due in 1857-8.

The Company's armies consisted of both Europeans and Indians. The European branch was at first poor both in its officers and other ranks with a few shining exceptions. But it gradually improved in tone and efficiency to bear comparison with the royal regiments. At the close of the Mutiny it numbered 16,000 men. By far the larger proportion of the army consisted of the Sepoy regiments. In 1830 these numbered 187,000 and in 1857 200,000. The army, from early days, was officered by Europeans. By the reorganization of 1796 the European officers equalled in numbers those of the royal regiments. Since they had Indian company commanders as well, there was in fact a pool of officers available for other duties. At a time when the civil service had still barely taken shape and the Company's territories were rapidly expanding, there was a need for men of resource and ability outside the covenanted ranks. Hence arose the practice of seconding officers for civil and diplomatic duties. Wellesley used as many as he could and the 'soldier-civilian' and 'soldier-political' became important elements in the Company's services. Civil work being well paid and offering chances of distinction was eagerly sought after. These men were the cause of much jealousy among the civilians, who regarded them as interlopers, and among their own brethren who looked on them as deserters in the pursuit of ambition. On the credit side it can be said that they provided a valuable link between the civil and military departments and introduced a useful element of flexibility; on the debit side was the fact that many of the best officers were thus drained away from the officer cadre. The occasional lapses of European military leadership were not wholly unconnected with this loss of good men. The officers of the Company's army, both European and Indian, were first recruited from the ranks of the Company's writers (like Clive), from foreign sources, and from royal regiments. They were a motley collection, inferior to the royal officers both in morale and technique. But as the army developed their quality improved to produce such leaders as Sir John Malcolm, Sir Thomas Munro, Generals Nott, Pollock, Sale, and Havelock. If they lacked, as a body, some of the patriotic ardour of the king's troops, they yielded nothing in *esprit de corps* and professional skill. Their advantage over royal officers was knowledge of the country, their disadvantage a certain provincialism, and narrowing of their sense of the possible.

The Indian troops formed the bulk of the Company's army. The regular pay, the comparatively good conditions, and the prestige of the Company's name made it easy to raise troops. The general success of the Company's arms and the care taken to defer to local custom retained their loyalty and fed their pride. The Company's Indian troops were undoubtedly the most efficient army in India and probably in all Asia[1] in the early nineteenth century. Only the Sikhs ran them close. At the same time it remained a fact that they were a collection of mercenaries. The men were loyal to their salt, and usually proud of their leaders. But fighting was for them a professional matter and they had no spark of supra-regimental or national pride. All hopes of high promotion were denied them and between them and their leaders a great cultural gulf was fixed. Since they could not identify themselves with the régime by helping to control it, they tended to express their feelings of self-respect or *izzat* by a fanatical devotion to traditional customs. Hence developed a certain brittle quality in the Indian troops. They were brave and steadfast in battle, loyal and well behaved in the camp, but they were liable to see in small changes and unconsidered actions insults to their customs or subtle plots against their deepest feelings. Loyalty was therefore always conditional and as the wind of innovation grew stronger from the West it became more difficult to maintain those conditions. Thus the career of victory of the Company's forces were chilled by an undercurrent of mutiny such as those of Vellore in 1806 and of Barrackpore in 1824. These were more serious than the parallel 'white mutinies' of the Company's Europeans, because of the numbers involved and the intimate connexion of the troops with the country. The Company's Indian troops were a sharp and shining sword for the Governor-General, but also a two-edged one.

The armed forces were completed by a number of irregular corps, raised to keep pace with the expansion of the British territories. One of the first of these was Skinner's Horse. Others were the Gurkha battalions raised after the Gurkha wars, and the Panjab Frontier Force with the famous Corps of Guides.

Subsidiary to the army was the police. In Mughul times local security was the responsibility of the village community through its headman and the effective district police were the local governor's military forces. The British subdivided the army into soldiers and police as they had formerly subdivided the imperial service into civil and military. The police system really began with Cornwallis. He appointed a superintendent of police for Calcutta in 1791 and extended this system to the districts in the next year. A *daroga* or superintendent was allotted to each district and the *zamindars* were relieved of their police

[1] Counting Russia as in Europe.

duties. The hereditary village police became *chokidars* or watchmen and the village authorities incidentally lost much of their prestige. The new police increased the authority of the central government by providing a force under its direct control in every part of its possessions. But they also increased its unpopularity by their oppressions and exactions. They were badly paid and used their extensive powers to recoup themselves both in cash and self-esteem. They were loyal and effective up to a point, but they were corrupt and heavy handed.

As for the police [wrote Bentinck][1] so far from being a protection to the people, I cannot better illustrate the public feeling regarding it, than by the following fact, that nothing can exceed the popularity of a recent regulation by which, if a robbery has been committed, the Police are *prevented* from making any enquiry into it, except upon the requisition of the persons robbed: that is to say, the shepherd is a more ravenous beast of prey than the wolf.

The Governor-General had his army to protect (and enlarge) the state, his police to maintain order, and his civil officers to collect revenue and administer affairs. He had also to dispense justice to the people. He had to consider both the kind of justice which ought to be dispensed and also the machinery for its administration. In Mughul times each community enjoyed its own personal law, which was administered according to its own customs. Revenue questions were settled by revenue officers. For criminal law the Islamic code was enforced on all, and administered through *Qazis* appointed by the emperor and governors. This was tempered by the right of the rulers, jealously guarded by the Mughuls, and exercised by Alivardi Khan, to do justice themselves. At first the Company continued this policy, allowing the Nazim of Bengal (or his deputy, for many years Muhammad Reza Khan) to superintend the courts. Then came the irruption of the Supreme Court in 1774, which administered English law because it knew no other and the limits of whose jurisdiction were undefined. The Act of 1781 restricted English law to English persons, and defined this Court's authority. Cornwallis, through his regulations, pruned the Islamic criminal law of its harsher features[2] and so made Indian law more humane for a time than its British counterpart. But as British judges replaced Indian, the absence of a definite code, and the reliance which had in consequence to be placed on experts in local law, became more and more irksome. The beginning of modern Indian public law came in 1833 with the creation of the Indian Law Commission which in due time (1861) produced the Indian Penal Code and later the codes of criminal and civil procedure.

After the question of the content of law came that of its administration. Until the dismissal of Muhammad Reza Khan in 1790 criminal justice remained in the hands of the nawab. From this time the civil and criminal courts were both controlled by the Company. There was a

[1] Bentinck MSS. Lord William to Charles Grant, 21 Dec. 1832.
[2] Such as mutilation of limbs for small offences.

central criminal court in Calcutta and four 'courts of circuit' which made tours twice a year from Calcutta, Murshidabad, Patna, and Dacca to try cases too serious for the district courts. On the civil side the local *Diwani adalats* were renamed district or *zillah* courts backed by appeal courts at the same four centres. The two systems were linked at the district level by giving the same judicial officer both civil and criminal power. The system was regular and imposing, but it had two defects; the judges were English and often both junior and ill-acquainted with the language of the proceedings. They were therefore often unduly influenced by their expert advisers. Both the new land settlements and the new hope of obtaining justice without fear of executive interference tended to multiply suits. There thus arose a judicial block which amounted to a denial of justice. By 1812 arrears of cases in the Bengal courts amounted to 163,000. Justice was intended to be done, but the legal process was at first cumbrous to a degree. A further effect of the new system may also be noticed. Though the law was Hindu or Muslim, the procedures of the new courts were British, and the assumptions which underlay the judicial interpretations of the judges were British also. This added a further element of uncertainty to that already created by the inexperience and ignorance of the judges themselves. The elaborate procedures created a class of legal middlemen or pleaders to advise perplexed clients. The great legal profession of India thus had its birth but it is not surprising that the average suitor was bemused by the intricacy of the whole legal machine and saw in the legal process a lottery rather than the working of remote and passionless justice.

Apart from defending the country, maintaining order and administering justice, the government had to make its will effective throughout its dominions. Its most important will was the financial one, and revenue collection was its most important positive activity.[1] Its agents in this respect were the local officers. British India was divided into districts, which corresponded roughly with the *sarkars* of Mughul times. Macpherson created thirty-five districts for Bengal and Bihar, which Cornwall is reduced to twenty-three; Madras had from twenty to twenty-six, and Bombay about thirteen, with three for Sind. In each district there was a collector, whose business was to collect the revenue, a judge to administer justice, and a magistrate to maintain order. In general the collector was the head of the district though for most of this time in Bengal the judge took precedence. Bentinck introduced commissioners to supervise the district officers, but the essential unit of administration remained the district. Not until the end of the period were subordinate governorships created with the title of Chief Commissioners, as in the case of the Panjab in 1853 and Oudh in 1856. These men were subordinate governors, exercising their authority direct from the Governor-General.

The district officers were governed by the Cornwallis Code of Regulations of 1 May 1793. The aim of the regulations was to make

[1] For revenue systems see the next chapter.

permanent Cornwallis's work by defining it. 'They dealt with the commercial system, with civil and criminal justice, with the police and with the land revenue. While restating the existing position, they contemplated further changes. . . .' The regulations were intended to ensure ordered administration and prevent any return to the chaos and abuses of the past. In this they succeeded but they easily became in their turn a cast-iron mould hindering measures to meet new situations. In particular they were unsuited for detailed application to newly acquired, unsettled, or disorganized regions. Hence arose the distinction between regulation and non-regulation provinces. The Bengal Presidency, in its expansion up to the Jumna, was generally subjected to the regulations. But other areas were specifically excepted, the rule being that the *spirit* of the regulations should be observed so far as local conditions permitted. Thus the Delhi territory acquired in 1803, Assam, Arakan, and Tenasserim in 1824, the Saugar and Narbadda territories in 1818, and the Panjab in 1849, became non-regulation provinces. Collectors in these areas were known as deputy commissioners and a very practical consequence was the freedom to appoint military officers to perform civil duties.

The last problem of power confronting the British was that of the control of the dependent Indian states. We have seen how the Company's hope of forming an element in an Indian concert of powers faded and how the plan of a ring fence (never very enthusiastically entertained) foundered on the rocks of central Indian anarchy. The wars of Lord Hastings left the Company supreme in India surrounded by a number of dependent states. How were they to be treated? Lord Hastings's system consisted in extending the subsidiary system to certain Maratha states and assuming feudal powers of control over a medley of smaller ones. In territorial terms it amounted to a putting on ice, as it were, of numbers of states in their then momentary extent and boundaries. Like so many Lot's wives, the Indian states were petrified in their last backward look at independence. The first fact which emerged from Lord Hastings's work was that of paramountcy. The doctrine was preached by Metcalfe but not explicitly claimed for fear of raising difficult legal questions of legitimacy and Mughul pretensions. Nevertheless, it was a fact from this time, and the government acted as though it was a fact. But if paramountcy was a fact, there were also degrees of subordination. First came such states as Hyderabad and Sindia which possessed an independent origin and claimed an independent status; until 1829 the Nizam used the royal 'we' in correspondence and was addressed in terms implying superiority. Then came states of similar origin like Oudh which had sunk lower in the scale of dependence as a result of treaties. Thirdly there were the treaty states, whose being derived from a specific treaty or which by treaty recognized the claims of the Company to the traditional paramountcy of the holders of imperial power. Mysore exemplified the first of these subdivisions and the Rajput states the second. Then came the lesser chiefs who were confirmed in their possessions as part of the general settlement. These were both old as in the case of the Kathiawar chiefs and new as in that of Amir Khan, the Nawab of Tonk, and the rulers of Firozpur and Jhansi. Lastly came the 'sanad' chiefs, petty princes who simply transferred allegiance from one overlord to another. The most tenacious of independence was Hyderabad. In 1801 the new Nizam obtained confirmation of his accession from the court of Delhi and later refused the title of king on the ground that it would be an act of rebellion against the pensionary emperor; not until 1926 was the paramountcy of the government of India explicitly asserted by Lord Reading.

Over all these states the government of India asserted the right of controlling external relations whether by the provisions of specific treaties or by the general claim of overlordship. The larger were controlled in fact as well as in theory by the existence of subsidiary forces controlled by the Company though paid for by the state. There was also a generally recognized right to interfere in crises such as disputed successions. But a clear distinction was drawn between internal and external interference. The supreme government was as loth to interfere in the internal affairs of a state as it was determined not to allow any independence in its external relations. This was the policy of non-interference, around which centred most of the states' problems up to the time of Dalhousie. It may be said that in general non-interference held the field in state relations up to 1848, but circumstances forced departures from the rule in a number of instances.

These circumstances arose from the effects of the government's policy as a whole. One effect was to secure each prince from all danger of external invasion and overthrow, and the next to secure him (through the presence of a subsidiary force) from all danger of revolution and indeed from all personal risk save that of assassination. The rulers thus lacked the stimulus to activity of fear from dangers without and within; they also lacked the spur of ambition through their studious isolation by the new alien government. Rajput and other princes could rise high in the Mughul service, hold governorships and command armies. Jaswant Singh was one of Akbar's inner council and Raja Jai Singh the Mughul officer who brought Sivājī to terms with Aurangzeb. But no such avenues to honour existed with the British; princes had to stay in their states or be nowhere. Thus there was no incentive to glory or to caution, and the natural result was apathy, irresponsibility, and vice. Another effect of the government's policy was economic embarrassment. The subsidiary forces were paid for by contributions from the states concerned. The princes concerned, for reasons of *izzat* if nothing else, also maintained armies of their own. They were thus saddled with two forces, the one efficient but expensive and beyond their control, and the other more numerous and dependent, but both inefficient and expensive. These forces (as in Oudh) were dangerous to disband and ruinous to maintain. The result was a financial strain which the states could not bear. Some resorted to loans, as in Hyderabad, which only made things worse. Cessions of territory in lieu of subsidy brought only temporary relief, since the local pressure on an apathetic prince's patronage soon unbalanced the budget again.

The advocates of the policy of non-interference had therefore to struggle with evils which were rooted in the new system and not the result of any one individual's shortcomings. Conscientious residents might reform and exhort, but they could only palliate the symptoms and not remove the causes of the malady. That is why some of the warmest advocates of non-interference like Bentinck had to interfere on a large scale. For in practice non-interference always stopped short at a certain point. At first it was danger to the Company's security which prompted action, as in Lord Hastings's dealings with the Maratha states. As humanitarian principles grew stronger it was manifest abuses and injustice which prompted action, and as the conviction of the superiority of British administration increased, mere mismanagement sufficed. After the pacification of 1818 the first important case of interference occurred in Hyderabad. Here the loans of the financial house of Palmer & Co. had secured a stranglehold on the state's finances, and the reforming zeal of the resident Metcalfe forced the hand of a reluctant Governor-General. The case of Bharatpur in 1826 arose out of a disputed succession and resolved itself into an old-fashioned defiance of the paramount power. Lord William Bentinck was a firm believer in non-intervention. But he found himself compelled to take over the administration of Mysore in 1831 owing to the excesses of the raja. Characteristically, he stopped short of outright annexation so that the state could be handed back to Indian control in 1881 to become one of the model states of later days. Coorg was annexed outright in 1834 at the request of the inhabitants, who could no longer bear the abnormalities of the ruling family, and so was Jaintia in Assam following the sacrifice of three British Indian subjects to Kali. In these measures the humanitarian as well as the reforming motive can be seen. They all had the justification that actual violence had occurred or grave injustice been committed. Short of this Bentinck held his hand. There were dissensions and mismanagement but no actual violence in Hyderabad, Indore, Gwalior, Jaipur,[1] and Baroda. In Oudh he insisted on reform but stopped short of taking over the government. Auckland annexed only the small state of Karnul in Madras, and the tale of interference (before 1848) was concluded by Ellenborough's destruction of the Sindian army in 1843. In this case the danger which might come from the presence of a hostile army in the rear in the event of a Sikh war was a leading motive and Ellenborough refrained from annexation. We can thus say that during the period 1818–48 the British sought to control Indian India by a policy of external isolation, by military control through subsidiary forces and

[1] Violence occurred in Jaipur just after Bentinck's departure when the assistant resident was murdered.

well-placed cantonments, and by internal non-interference. The policy may be summed up as isolation and non-interference tempered by annexation. The states were not so much pillars of British supremacy as its divided and discredited opponents.

AUTHORITIES

AN excellent summary of constitutional and administrative history is to be found in the first volume of the *Montagu-Chelmsford Report* (1918). Good general pre-Mutiny studies are J. W. KAYE, *The Administration of the East India Co.* (1853) and G. CAMPBELL, *Modern India* (1853). The legal framework is admirably summarized in Sir C. ILBERT, *The Government of India* (1898, 3rd ed., 1915), while P. AUBER, *Analysis of the Constitution of the East India Co.* (1826) gives the London end.

For the civil service see L. S. S. O'MALLEY, *The Indian Civil Service 1601-1930* (1931) and for a more intimate study of the service in action, P. WOODRUFF, *The Founders* (1953). For the army see A. BROOME, *History of the Rise and Progress of the Bengal Army* (1850), W. J. WILSON, *History of the Madras Army* (5 vols., 1882), and the *Cambridge History*, vol. vi, chap. ix. The police have fewer memorials, but the *Report of the Indian Police Commission* (1902) may be consulted.

For the law see H. COWELL, *History and Constitution of the Legislative Authorities of British India* (1905), chapters in the *Cambridge History*, vol. vi, and L. S. S. O'MALLEY (ed.), *Modern India and the West* (1941).

For district administration see chapters in the *Cambridge History*, vols. v and vi, Woodruff supplying the human side as before.

For the states see Sir W. LEE-WARNER, *The Native States of India* (1910), K. M. PANIKKAR, *Evolution of Indian Policy towards Indian States 1774-1858* (1929) and Sir C. AITCHESON, *Collection of Treaties ... relating to India* (14 vols., ed. 1931).

RECENT PUBLICATION

R. E. FRYKENBERG, *Guntur District, 1788-1848* (Oxford, 1965) is a vital work, opening up new perspectives.

CHAPTER 6

The People and the Government—The Village, the Land, and Trade

HAVING noted the measures by which the new government cemented its hold on the country, we can now consider the effect which it had on the people themselves. The official in Calcutta saw a congeries of peoples with a baffling variety of customs divided by ancient animosities and modern tensions. The cultivator in the village at first saw only a new kind of tax collector, more implacable if not more rapacious than before. It would be a great mistake to suppose, however, that the population of India was merely a uniform peasant 'mass'. The bulk of the people certainly lived in the villages, but they were woven into a series of intricate social patterns. Position depended as much upon caste as on wealth and as much upon landholding as upon either. The unit of society was the village; there were no Indian towns with corporate traditions like those of Europe. Indian towns were either the shadows of rulers like Delhi, Hyderabad, or Lahore, or export centres like Surat, Madras, and Bombay, or places of pilgrimage like Benares and Mathura. The village in general was a closely knit social and self-sufficing economic unit, which had shown extraordinary resilience through ages of invasion. The impact of government on the people meant essentially the impact of government on the village. The village society was thus described by Metcalfe.[1]

The village Communities are little Republics, having nearly everything they want within themselves, and almost independent of any foreign relations. They seem to last where nothing else lasts. Dynasty after dynasty tumbles down; revolution succeeds to revolution; Hindu, Pathan, Mughul, Mahratta, Sikh, English, are masters in turn, but the village communities remain the same. In times of trouble they arm and fortify themselves; a hostile army passes through the country; the Village Community collect their cattle within their walls, and let the army pass unprovoked; if plunder and devastation be directed against themselves and the force employed be irresistible, they flee to friendly villages at a distance, but when the storm has passed over they return and resume their occupation. If a country remains for a series of years the scene of continual pillage and massacre, so that the villages cannot be inhabited, the villagers nevertheless return whenever the power of peaceable possession revives. A generation may pass away but the succeeding generations will return. The sons will take the place of their fathers, the same site for the village, the same position for the houses, the same lands will be reoccupied by the descendents of those who were

---

[1] The village in Metcalfe's mind was the north and central Indian village. But the description was valid everywhere for its emphasis on the tenacity of the village unit.

driven out when the village was depopulated; and it is not a trifling matter that will drive them out, for they will often maintain their post through times of disturbance and convulsion, and acquire strength sufficient to resist pillage and oppression with success.

The essential contact between the village and the outside world was through the revenue collector. He might be a direct nominee of government or the agent of a local lord or rent collector; in any case the impulses of government were felt through his agency. There was next the occasional intervention of judicial officers in the case of serious crimes. Before the British period these occasions were rare and sporadic. In general the village elders were left to settle the ordinary disputes of property while the caste councils settled a large range of personal matters. The elders were held responsible for major personal crimes and offences like cattle stealing. But they were to a large extent their own police and brought offenders to justice in their own way. The third visitants of the pre-British village were the armies of the local governors or rebel leaders or local robber chiefs. During the hey-day of the empire these were in the main limited to the marches of large armies, whose movements, if devastating, were fairly regular. In later days as confusion grew the numbers of these bodies increased though their size declined. They covered more territory and at last their movements were largely dictated by the prospect of wringing money from villages to buy a few more months' service from mutinous troops. The reply of the village was submission when unavoidable, flight when the visitation seemed likely to be short-lived, and resistance if at all practicable. It was the era of the fortified village all over the Deccan and the north, old *sarais*, walled gardens, or other enclosures being used where possible or mud walls erected for the purpose.

The first effect of British administration was the elimination of these military locusts and their aftermath, the plundering band and the *dacoit*. The Pindari scourge and the Sikh bands were the last organized bodies of rural plunderers. Once these had been disposed of there only remained *dacoits* as the residuary legatees of the great anarchy. Dacoity was put down firmly and finally by the Company's officers in each area as it came under their control. In the Delhi District disorganization had reached such a pitch that the city itself was divided into wards for plunder by bands in the neighbourhood; the revenue officers had to go out with regular infantry and guns and were sometimes received with such 'briskness' as 'temporarily to stagger them'. The restoration of peace and security to the countryside was pure gain to the villagers.

The second effect of British administration upon village life was a steadily increasing interference from outside. This came about from both their revenue and judicial activities.[1] At first the old revenue system was left untouched, annual sums being collected according to

[1] The transfer was less obvious in Bengal because the *zamindari* system continued. The change was largely one of personnel, arising from the coming in of new men as *zamindars*, and it was not for the better.

the existing methods of assessment and collection. Then came fact-finding officers and after them experimental modes of assessment; finally, there was measurement and calculation and an established demand based on the information collected. The net result of all this activity was the gradual transfer of authority within the village from the village elders to agents of government. In the north-west, for example, the village elders had bargained with the agents or *amils* of government or local chief, and having agreed upon the total assessment for the year had themselves divided the amount to be paid among the various cultivators and seen to its collection. Eventually revenue officers not only measured and assessed the village land, but divided the demand among the cultivators. The elders were consulted at the stages of assessment and division of demand, but not to the exclusion of the general body of cultivators. They were accorded a complimentary respect by the officials but their authority was undermined because their power over the cultivators was taken away. The same process occurred in judicial matters. As police were organized in the districts they took cognizance of crimes which had formerly been largely left to the discretion of the village officials. The cases which arose, both revenue and criminal, were dealt with in district courts presided over by alien and often youthful officials and employing a strange and cumbrous procedure. From the villagers' point of view, anything might come out of a case at a local court. Whereas in medieval England the royal courts attracted cases from the baronial ones by offering better justice, in Company India the new courts attracted cases by offering the chance of success to bad cases. The legal process was looked upon as a lottery, and men with bad cases preferred a chance of success in a distant court to the probability of failure amongst those who knew them. In this sphere also the authority of the village elder was undermined.

Thus it came about that while the British administrators of the early nineteenth century with one voice earnestly desired to restore the vigour of the village community, their measures had the effect of depressing it even where it was still working well. In some parts of India the old village autonomy had already disappeared and in others only the wrecks of it were left; where it was in health it slowly decayed, and where it was non-existent or feeble it failed to revive. The basic reason was, in the case of healthy villages, the transfer of authority to new central agents, and where it was in decay, the removal of usurping authorities in favour not of the village elders but of those same central agents. Thus in Madras the local *zamindars* and *polygars* lost their authority, not to revived village councils but to revenue, judicial, and police officials. The British hymn of praise to the traditional *panchayat* turned out to be a funeral dirge. Efficiency triumphed at the expense of local autonomy and organic village life.

But the position of the village elders and their *panchayats* was only one facet of the face of Indian rural life. There remained the cultivator in general. He now enjoyed freedom from violence and war but he was still concerned with his security of tenure, the amount he had to pay to government, and the manner of his paying. Land revenue was the traditional mainstay of Indian governmental finance, and government's claim to a share of the annual produce was a universally accepted obligation. In the times of the Mauryas and Guptas it was said to be a sixth of the total or gross produce;[1] under Akbar it was fixed at a third while in the Deccan it was as high as a half. These amounts were tempered by the difficulty of collection in a widely scattered society which produced a perennial and well-understood gap between demand and actual payment. There was an infinite diversity of practice and no figure of proportion can be taken to have applied universally and always. After their early days in Bengal, the British set themselves to evolve a system both effective and fair, and in the main and in the long run they were conspicuously successful. The revenue system which they evolved stands as a whole today; the only large change since independence has been the abolition of the Permanent Settlement in Bengal and the *zamindari* system connected with it. Both of these had been much modified by a series of measures before 1947 and the abolition of the former was in preparation.

The first great area of revenue settlement was Bengal and Bihar, where hereditary *zamindars* acted as go-betweens between government and cultivator. These men were not landholders in the northern sense but hereditary tax-collectors, often on a large scale. After a number of experiments by Warren Hastings, who was not conspicuously successful as a revenue officer, the question was settled by Cornwallis with his Permanent Settlement in 1793. This measure has already been described in Book VII, Chapter 7, and a brief reference must suffice here. The *zamindar* tax-collectors were recognized as *zamindar* landlords in the English sense. The amounts of their annual payments were fixed once and for all and they were left free to retain the balance between their payments to governments and collections from their tenants. As a consequence they enjoyed the whole benefit of increased cultivation which was the result of security from 1770 onwards. But the demand was at first too high for many of them to meet in the wasted state of the country. Instead of the old method of beatings and bargainings as a prelude to an agreed payment short of the demand, the new government substituted sale of estates to realize arrears. The result was a large change in the personnel of *zamindars* and the substitution of many Calcutta financiers for long-settled families. Thus the Permanent Settlement brought in numbers of absentee landlords in place of resident *zamindars*, snapping the personal link between them and the cultivators. A harsher tone spread into rural life and the cultivator got little benefit from the spread of cultivation except a bare livelihood for more people. The effect of the change was reminiscent of the change

[1] One-sixth is the share mentioned in the Laws of Manu, rising to one-fourth in times of war or other emergency.

in sixteenth-century England from the easy-going monastic landlords to the pushing new men of Henry VIII. During the nineteenth century efforts were made to protect the tenant from the landlord. They were not without effect, but the system remained intact throughout the British period. Its political advantages, specially in its earlier days were considerable, but socially the loss was substantial.

The Permanent Settlement and the *zamindari* system were extended to Benares and Orissa and to the Northern Sarkars in 1802–5. But by then the manifest defects of the system in practice had begun to raise doubts. The result was that in the settlement of the Madras Presidency, which only became a practical issue with the taking over of the Mysore and Carnatic lands in 1799–1801, a wholly different procedure was adopted. This was the *ryotwari* system or method of settlement direct with the cultivator, which is associated with the name of Sir Thomas Munro. He advocated it as the result of his settlement work in the early years of the last century. He came to know village life and its problems intimately and became convinced of the evils both of uncontrolled landlords and of final once-for-all settlements. At this time the *zamindari*, *ryotwari*, and village settlement systems all existed within the presidency. During his governorship of Madras the *ryotwari* system became the rule, but it only acquired its modern methodical form from 1855. The essence of the *ryotwari* plan is that the settlement is made direct with the *ryot* or cultivator, and that the settlement is temporary, not permanent. The connexion of these two features is a matter of fact rather than of logic, and the temporary principle was only finally accepted in 1883. After measurement and assessment according to the nature of the soil and crop, a settlement was made with each individual cultivator for a period of years, the standard being thirty. The holdings were necessarily small, the average in recent times being $6\frac{1}{2}$ acres. Once the settlement was made the holder enjoyed free tenure so long as he paid his legal dues, and the rate could not be varied until the end of the fixed term of years. Any improvements in or increase of cultivation, or upward move of prices therefore directly benefited him. He could sell or alienate his land, and he could be sold up on failure to pay his dues, but there were remissions of demand in times of famine or drought, and no action could be taken without due process of law. The share of the government was eventually fixed at half the estimated *net* value of the crop, that is, after deducting the expenses of cultivation and other incidentals. The *ryotwari* system had the great advantage of removing the *zamindar* middleman between government and cultivator, who too often acted as a screen behind which oppression could go on undetected. On the other hand it left the cultivator at the mercy of the government officers with their zeal for full collection and tendency to over-assess through ignorance or disregard of the old devices for reducing the full nominal demand. Roughly we may say that the cultivator gained security and freedom from oppression in the first half of the century, but suffered from over-assessment. In the second half this defect was removed through a more understanding administration, so that the cultivator grew more prosperous as well as being secure. Individual justice was done but there was clearly no room for the village community.

In Bombay the *ryotwari* system was followed with local variations. Both in Gujarat and the Deccan the British took over going concerns from the Marathas. At first they continued the existing systems and then gradually modified them according to the *ryotwari* principle. In Gujarat the local officers or *mamlatdars* had bargained with the village *desais* and *patels* who had then been left to raise the agreed sums in their own way without interference. From 1816 onwards the *ryotwari* system was gradually introduced. The part played by the *patel* was gradually eliminated and his place taken by the *talati* or village accountant, who was appointed directly by the Bombay government. In the Deccan Elphinstone endeavoured to retain the best features of the Maratha system while abolishing such imposts as *chauth*. The *patel* was retained under the *mamlatdar*, who was in turn supervised by British district officers. Civil cases from the villages were referred to *panchayats* while criminal ones went to the collector. In time a complete survey and measurement was made of every holding. The demand, however, was fixed district by district and then divided among the holdings according to a complicated table of soils and types of crop. As in Madras the settlement was for thirty years. There was thus elasticity for the cultivator but little discretion for the *patel*. It may be said in fact that the general effect of the settlement in both these areas was to stabilize the position of the cultivator, making improvement possible and profitable, but to depress the status of the village officers and the village community. In Gujarat the *patel* faded out altogether while in the Deccan he was closely supervised by the *mamlatdar* and lost the discretion of dividing the demand amongst his villagers. As in Madras justice for the individual was purchased at the price of organic life for the village community. The functions still left to the *panchayats* by Elphinstone were insufficient to outweigh the loss by the village officers of discretion in revenue matters. When the turn of Sind came the same *ryotwari* plan was adopted with the usual local variations.

In the great area of the north-west, beyond Bengal and Bihar, the British succeeded to the disordered administration of Oudh and the chaotic conditions of the Delhi region. Benares was permanently settled by Shore, so that the region consisted of the ceded districts of Oudh, the conquered (from the Marathas) districts between the Ganges and the Jumna, the Delhi territory, and later the whole of the Panjab. Here there were two types of holding, the estates of the great land-owners or *taluqdars*, many of ancient lineage, and village communities. At first much confusion prevailed. Settlements were made for short periods and over-assessment was general. The first great step was the decision in 1811 not to proceed with a permanent settlement. The next step was Holt Mackenzie's minute of 1819 which became the basis of Regulation VII of 1822. But it was Lord William Bentinck in his great northern tour who set in motion the scientific settlement of the whole region. Between 1833 and 1853 R. M. Bird and James Thomason carried through a work which was a monument of patient labour and detailed investigation. The settlement was temporary, the usual period of thirty years being favoured, and there was the usual detailed measurement as a prelude to assessment. But the settlement was made with village-communities, as in the Delhi District, or with separate estates or *mahals* as in many parts of the later United Provinces. Hence it was known as the *mahalwari* system. At first the village elders apportioned the demand amongst their members, but later the demand, having been agreed as a whole with the elders, was divided among the cultivators according to the measurements of the detailed survey. The Panjab in its turn was settled broadly on the same lines. In this settlement or series of settlements much greater care was taken to safeguard the position of the village communities, which were indeed much more robust than in most other parts of India. But the turning of the *patwari* or village record-keeper into a paid government official, the ever-increasing reliance on scientific surveys both for general assessment and detailed distribution of the demand, and the diversion of legal cases to the new courts, all tended to sap the strength of village institutions. In the north, as elsewhere, the villager tended to look increasingly away from the elders towards authorities outside the village in the matters which most intimately affected his well-being. The process was slower than elsewhere and may perhaps be described as a gradual withering away rather than as a speedy or sudden disappearance. The settlement in the Central Provinces after the annexation of the Nagpur state in 1853 was on similar lines.

We can now sum up the broad effects of the British land revenue operations. In the Permanent Settlement areas they produced a country of great landed estates, where the link between the landlord and the cultivator tenant was tenuous both personally and in interest. The efforts to protect tenants from exploitation were never more than partly successful, and there were the evils of a large tenantry and a growing body of landless men. Elsewhere the general justice of the settlements has been attested by the absence of any large movement for change. The process of assessment and collection became familiar and then fixed by repetition and soon became hallowed as custom. The revenue procedure acquired the prestige of Todar Mal's *bandobast* in Akbar's day; it became part of the settled order of things. At first the new system displayed a number of evils. There was the general tendency to over-assessment, even with conscientious officers like Metcalfe and Munro. This arose from imperfect information, from a failure to relate properly the report of the former state of a region with its existing condition, from a failure to appreciate the *tentative* nature of all figures of traditional demand, and from a natural desire to gain credit with one's superiors by enhancing the revenue yield. Along with

over-assessment went over-collection, or the insistence on realizing
the revenue demand in full. It was difficult for the British revenue
collectors, with their precise and unimaginative minds, influenced by
the trend of an age which gloried in science and accuracy, to realize
that all revenue figures of the past were symbols of desire and submission rather than exact statements of demand and payment. There
was also much misunderstanding of rent-free tenures which were
found abounding in every part of the country. The grant of these
tenures was the customary way of supporting religion, learning, and
culture generally, which were all closely linked together. In the
eighteenth century they increased rapidly and were often unsupported
by past proof of gifts or by the nature of present usage. Nevertheless
there was a substratum of value in these grants, and the tendency to
sweep them all away as wasteful or harmful caused much misery and
more resentment. But the desire to do justice ran like a redeeming
thread through the government's revenue policy. These abuses were
errors of judgement and knowledge rather than lapses of virtue, and
they steadily gave way before the advance of knowledge and experience.
From the time of Bentinck in the north and the governorships of
Elphinstone and Munro in the west and south, they tended to decrease
and disappear.[1] The general result was that the land tax became a
steadily decreasing burden on agriculture. The demand declined from
a third or more of the gross produce to a sixth or less. In 1925 it was
reckoned that while prices had risen 117 per cent. between 1903 and
1924, the land tax had risen not more than 20 per cent., and this
fact was agreed in 1931 by a Congress committee of inquiry.[2] There
was a steady increase of cultivation along with a large increase of population.

But there were other defects in the system which were more deep-
rooted. One was the sustained policy of selling up holdings for arrears
of tax. This was thought to be a humane departure from the old system
of coercion with its *zabardasti* or bullyings and beatings. But in fact it
was a cruel kindness, for it meant that many a landholder preserved
his skin at the expense of his land. We have already seen the effect of
this policy in displacing the old *zamindars* of Bengal. The process
went on everywhere; its tendency was to swell at every time of difficulty the number of landless men on the one hand, and the indebted-
ness of the survivors on the other. Many preferred virtual serfdom to
the moneylenders to the outright loss of their holdings. A further evil
associated with the *ryotwari* system of smallholdings was the fragmentation of holdings. This was the result of increasing population
lacking other means of support together with the system of equal
division among descendants, and it is difficult to see how it could have
been avoided altogether. But where holdings became too small to

---

[1] The proceedings of the Inam Commission under Dalhousie were an exception to
this rule.

[2] The Tax Inquiry Committee of 1925.

provide subsistence for a family the result was much the same as if the land had been lost altogether.

On the credit side must first be set the general sense of justice which the new systems gradually infused throughout the countryside. This was associated with the new security, the new certainty of demand, the gradually established moderation of that demand, and the scientific adjustment of demand to the different types of soil, climate, and crop. Next comes the great increase of cultivation. Instead of landlords travelling long distances to tempt tenants to cultivate their land, the more familiar practice of tenants begging for waste plots, or men going out to marginal lands in search of a livelihood grew up. By 1880 shortage of cultivators had been replaced by shortage of land. Along with increase of cultivation went increase of population. The estimated 100 million people in Akbar's India and 130 million in 1800 had become 206 million at the first census in 1872.[1] More people and more cultivation were both cause and effect of each other, but neither would have been possible if the land system had not been both flexible and reasonably just.

Though India was dominantly an agricultural country it was not wholly so; the artisan and the craftsman, the trader and the merchant, and government's policy towards them, have also to be considered. Setting aside village industries for village needs and luxury industries for the wealthy few, India's customary industrial activity was comprised in the word cotton. The flourishing trade in cotton piece goods of Mughul times continued during most of the eighteenth century. Most of the cotton export was channelled through the East India Company which found a ready market for re-export to Europe after the home market in England was closed to it by commercial jealousy.[2] But by the end of the century the picture had changed. In 1740 England had begun to export her own cotton hand-made piece goods to Europe; by 1800 she was exporting machine-made cotton goods to India. At the same time the re-export trade to Europe for Indian cottons dried up with the long-continued French wars. The European market was thus closed to India at the same time that the Indian market was invaded by cotton machine goods from Lancashire. The principle of free trade ruled out any hope of protection for the Indian handicraft industry, and there thus began the long decline of the old Indian handicraft weaving industry. Weavers fell into distress and then returned to the land. By the time of the Mutiny India's ancient and famous cotton industry had shrunk to the production of homespun or *khaddar* for the villager and to a limited quantity of the finest 'counts'. The machine goods of Lancashire together with the free trade policy had killed the Indian cotton industry. From that time Indian exports changed their character from finished articles like cotton and silk piece

[1] This was generally considered to have been an under-estimate. The estimate for Akbar's India is W. H. Moreland's and for 1800 my own.
[2] In the early eighteenth century.

goods and quality materials like indigo to raw materials in bulk. Changes in methods of transport such as the introduction of steamships and railways and the opening of the Suez Canal in 1869 made this development possible.

If the handicraftsmen fell on evil times, however, for all traders the period was one of enlargement. The new security and the increased intercourse with Europe encouraged both internal and external trade. Internally, at least, the new economic doctrines were beneficial, for they brought about the abolition of inland transit duties in 1835 to the great benefit of all traders. The turning-point in commercial development was the Charter Act of 1813, which abolished the East India Company's monopoly of commerce. This was a response to the demand from the new manufacturers for more markets for their goods as well as the old commercial demand for freedom. The new private merchant now took the place of the Company in the organization of Indo-British trade. But development was not at first as rapid as had been expected. The new traders lacked capital and even when the French wars ended this did not flow to the east because more tempting fields lay to hand in Europe and America. The period from 1813 to 1858 was therefore one of preparation on the part of both the private merchant and the government.

The private merchant found himself free from Company control but soon realized that the Company was not the cause of all commercial evil in India. He lacked capital for development and he lacked the means for large-scale operations which the nature of the country required. His working capital came largely from the savings of the Company's officers. The merchants evolved the managing agency system for the conduct of their affairs whereby one firm would undertake a variety of different functions. An incidental result was that the whole European community shared in any commercial slumps such as the collapse of the agency houses in the early thirties. With this limited capital the private merchants could trade but they could not launch out in new directions or find the means for overcoming the large natural obstacles to big-scale development. Hence arose a cry for government assistance in removing hindrances to commercial action. Give us the conditions and we will produce the profits was the argument. The Company's role as monopolist was to be converted into that of industrial assistant.

It would not be too much to say that in 1813 the Company, as the ruler of India, had no economic policy. So far as it had one indeed, it was to have no policy, for it was increasingly influenced by the new *laissez-faire* theories. But pressure from India and at home forced it into economic action in the name of economic liberty. Its measures can be broadly described as 'enabling action', action designed to enable private traders to develop their activities. The period can be subdivided into that of experiment, which lasted to the mid eighteen-thirties and that of positive action, which lasted to the Mutiny and beyond. There was, of course, considerable overlapping of these dates. The first tentative steps were taken by Lord Hastings with his measures to reopen the Mughul irrigation canals. In 1825 the Company helped in the establishment of an iron works. Lord William Bentinck made a number of experiments. A great believer in good communications he lamented that Metcalfe 'had no idea of a good road'. One of the first efforts in this direction was the building of the road from Bombay to Poona in 1830. Bentinck introduced steam navigation on rivers and thus made possible the opening up of Assam. He gave a further push to irrigation projects and considered draining schemes in Bengal. In 1834 he sent for tea seeds from China and started government tea gardens and also encouraged coffee cultivation.

But large developments were held back by the great natural obstacles. In India this was partly a matter of finance but mainly a matter of communications. Local finance was strengthened by the establishment of three presidency banks. But further capital could not be obtained until there was a prospect of a good return and a suitable subject for investment. The provision of means of transport would create a prospect of good returns for commercial capital, and the provision of the means provided a field of investment for the industrial investor. The solution of the transport problem is the key to modern Indian economic development. So long as that problem was unsolved, mere size defeated most schemes of development. You cannot feed large-scale industry or distribute mass-produced products by bullock wagons or hitch modern industry to a camel. The government's first enabling measure was therefore to improve the means of transport. Steam navigation was introduced on the rivers. The next measure was the provision of good roads. In 1839 the Grand Trunk road from Calcutta to Delhi was commenced and this was followed by links between the major cities of British India. It was now possible for goods to be moved but there was still only the bullock wagon to move them. The third and decisive step was the introduction of railways. This was the work of Lord Dalhousie and in some respects may be regarded as his greatest. The first agreements were signed in 1849 and the whole programme of railway development was defined in his famous minute of 1853. By the time of the Mutiny some 200 miles of track had been constructed; the mutiny experience emphasized their military as well as commercial value and thereafter development was rapid.

The advent of railways was decisive for Indian economic development in a number of ways. Firstly they not only provided a track along which goods could be transported, but carriages to transport them. Henceforth fuel could be brought to the centres of power and production and the products of those centres could be distributed cheaply and widely. The chronic transport bottle-neck of Indian industry was broken. The way was thus paved for the development of large-scale industries. It was no accident that the development of the jute and cotton, the coal and iron, and the plantation industries progressed slowly before 1850 and occurred in quick succession thereafter. Transport is the life-blood of industry and without railways it lacked the arteries through which to flow. Secondly railways made it possible to deal with famines in a way never possible before. The essence of famine relief is the provision of supplies from outside the famine area in time, and this was now made possible by the railway. Thirdly the construction of railways commenced a new phase of capital import into India and popularized the joint-stock method organizing trade and finance. Finally the railways gave to the people of India a new mobility of which they took full advantage and so formed an important factor in building up the new India. The iron rail has been called a stake which pierced the heart of the village community and slowly drained its life blood away;[1] it was also a pile driven into the marsh of a static community upon which a new and forward-looking society could be founded.

AUTHORITIES

For conditions before 1750 see W. H. MORELAND, *India at the death of Akbar* (1920), and *Agrarian System of Muslim India* (1929). For the village system see B. H. BADEN-POWELL, *The Indian Village Community* (1896), and for the relations of village with governments, J. W. KAYE, *Papers of Lord Metcalfe* (1855), Sir G. W. FORREST, *Selections from . . . Mountstuart Elphinstone* (1884), Sir A. J. ARBUTHNOT, Sir *T. Munro* (2 vols., 1881). T. G. P. SPEAR, *Tw. . . ʰt of the Mughuls* (1951), describes village life in the L ʰi territory.

For land and revenue B. H. BADEN-POWELL, *Land Systems of British India* (3 vols., 1892) is authoritative. There is a digest published in 1894. See also W. K. FIRMINGER (ed.), *Fifth Report . . . to the House of Commons, 1812* (3 vols., 1917).

For commerce and industry see BAL KRISHNA, *Commercial Relations between England and India 1601–1757* (1924), S. C. SINHA, *Economic Annals of Bengal* (1927), N. K. SINHA, *Economic History of Bengal* (1956), H. FURBER, *John Company at Work* (1948), V. ANSTEY, *Economic Development of India* (1949), and L. H. JENKS, *Migration of British Capital 1815–1875* (London, 1938). For railways see Book IX, Chapter 4.

[1] J. Buchanan, *Development of Industrial Enterprise in India.*

CHAPTER 7

Social Policy and Cultural Contacts

NOTHING would have surprised the founders of the East India Company more than to have been told that they would one day be held responsible for the moral and material progress of the whole country. The British went to the country as traders and some of them (like Sir Thomas Roe) became interested observers of its life. But even when they began to take part in internal politics they were concerned with nothing more than questions of power. The acquisition of Bengal turned their attention to the revenue, but they looked upon it as the means of power for the Company and of private enrichment for themselves. It was the private excesses of the Company's servants and indignation against the possessors of ill-gotten gains that first attracted attention to the welfare of India. The principle that the welfare of the governed must be an object of government was enunciated by Burke in the debates which preceded the Regulating Act. It may be said to have been statutorily accepted by Pitt's India Act in 1784 and to have been publicly emphasized and responsibility for it enforced by the proceedings of Warren Hastings's impeachment.

But this concept of welfare was one of justice in the acts of government rather than of the positive promotion of the happiness and welfare of the people. We see the first signs of this in Wilberforce's proposal in 1793 to give governmental aid to Christian activity. But in 1807 it was still possible for Sir John Barlow to define the objects of the government in India without mentioning the subject of welfare. A turning-point in this, as in economic matters, came with the Charter Act of 1813 with its clause setting aside a *lakh* of rupees a year for the advancement of the arts and sciences. Wars supervened and it was not until the liberal wind blew fresher in the twenties that the matter became a major concern of government. In 1828 the Tory President of the Board of Control, Lord Ellenborough, wrote to Lord William Bentinck, 'We have a great moral duty to perform to the people of India', and the Whig Governor-General fully reciprocated the sentiment.

It was during these years that the principle of the moral duty of the government to promote the welfare of the people was accepted by the governing class in England. But it was not so easy to decide the kind of welfare which was to be promoted. Was it to be Hindu, Muslim, or British welfare, traditional or modern welfare? The first opinion was that the government's duty lay in restoring the old society and fostering the development of that society along traditional lines. This found support among many Company servants who had acquired a taste and respect for oriental learning and culture. They were reinforced by the growing interest in oriental culture, Hindu as well as Islamic, which developed during the latter part of the eighteenth century. Sir William Jones, who discovered the connexion between Sanskrit and the Aryan languages, William Wilkins the Persian scholar, and Horace Hayman Wilson were leaders in this movement. They would give peace and security, justice and mercy, but interfere with local society as little as possible and leave it as far as possible to its own devices. Men like the Abbé Raynal and James Forbes found much merit in the ancient ways of life as well as depth in traditional thought.

Against this conservative and static view were set the radical views of a forward looking school. The civilizations of the East had long been regarded with respect, if not with approval, by the men of the West. They were admitted to be powerful and talented if erring and sometimes hostile. Jesuit reports represented Akbar as the philosopher king of the East and in the eighteenth century came a wave of Sinophilism from the same sources. China was widely regarded for a time as the leading civilized state. This was never, perhaps, a majority view, but if the European was regarded as the most advanced civilization, it was only a *primus inter pares*. But the rationalist movement of the eighteenth century now changed all this. Its devotees believed that reason had given Europe the key to indefinite progress, that this principle, and the sciences which sprang from it, made European civilization different in kind as well as in degree to all others. Thus was laid the intellectual foundation of the European superiority complex of the nineteenth century. These views developed in England into the vigorous Utilitarian school. Adam Smith in economics, Jeremy Bentham in ethics and law, James Mill in logic and philosophy attacked old positions and advocated new remedies with a robust vigour born of a conviction that the forces of progress were on their side. Their view of India was supplied by James Mill in his *History*, which was begun in 1808 and published in 1817.[1] Mill found little good in Indian institutions; reason lay dormant beneath the debris of centuries; Indian thought was puerile, its religion superstitious, its customs hidebound or harmful. The remedy was to introduce reason and European knowledge. Indians would see the light and reform themselves.

The rationalists were reinforced by the influence of the Evangelical Christians. These men repudiated the scepticism of the rationalists, but they agreed with them in their humanitarianism. For them Christianity was not only a herald of salvation for the individual, but of mercy for the suffering and the oppressed. The Evangelicals, with Wilberforce at their head, were foremost in such social works as the abolition of slavery and the improvement of prisons. When they turned to non-Christian countries they became advocates of Christian missions. In India they found much ground for concern. Indian reli-

[1] J. Mill, *History of British India*, Books II and III.

gion was superstitious and rampant with idolatry; much evil existed and there was ignorance of the truth. Their zeal for souls made them eager for action. They therefore joined with the rationalists as westernizing innovators in Indian affairs.

Between the conservatives and the radicals, in the British way, stood a large group, both in India and Britain, with a foot in both camps. These were the men who accepted the liberal or Christian gospels in varying degrees, desired to introduce western culture into India but preached patience and caution. The great administrators were mostly of this school; before 1828 they were looking forward to gradual changes and after that date they tended to counsel caution. Malcolm's prescription, 'let us, therefore, calmly proceed in a course of gradual improvement', may be taken as the watchword of these men.

It was by these influences that British social policy in India was shaped. Before 1813 the conservative vein was generally ascendant; between 1813 and 1828 the conservative and liberal veins contended and precept was more prominent than practice; from 1828 the liberal view gathered strength though tempered by caution and the limits of available resources. We may define it broadly in this way. There was first an attack on abuses considered to violate the universal moral law. No plea of religion restrained action in these cases; only caution counselled delay on occasion for fear of the consequences. Then there was the introduction of European institutions, science, knowledge, and thought, in a word, the transfer of western culture to India. The voices of experience and caution secured a ban on deliberate interference with existing institutions except those that came under the first heading. But all improvements, moral and intellectual as much as material, were to derive from the West. The West was to be placed side by side with the East, and it was hoped and believed that the East would prefer the new to the old.

It now remains to follow the working out of this general attitude. The attack on breaches of the universal moral law was begun by Lord Wellesley, when in 1803 he suppressed the sacrifice of children in worship on Saugor island at the mouth of the Hughli. It is an interesting commentary on the state of opinion at that time that this action was criticized as an unjustified interference with Hindu customs. Wellesley was also aware of the evil of suttee or the practice of widows accompanying the bodies of their husbands to be burnt on the same funeral pyre with them. But fear of Hindu opinion restrained him. For the next twenty-five years the custom was under review, but each governor-general postponed action. Lord Minto tried to mitigate the evil by making rules designed to prevent coercion,[1] but this was interpreted as a kind of government sanction and the number of recorded cases in Bengal rose. The main areas were in the Panjab and Rajputana among Sikhs and Rajputs, and in Madura and the Ganges valley among the Brahmans. In the Panjab and among the Rajputs it was an

[1] Instruction of 5 Dec. 1812.

aristocratic custom, but among the Brahmans it was more widespread. In the decade 1817–26 the recorded number of cases in Bengal varied between 500 and 850 a year. The victims were rarely volunteers and the circumstances were usually sordid and evil. In 1829 Bentinck acted where others had called for reports[1] and suppressed suttee by Regulation XVII of 1829. Suttee, unlike child sacrifice, had ancient though not undisputed warrant in the *Shastras* and it was feared that its suppression might outrage the feelings of orthodox Hindus. But the opposition led by Raja Radhakant Deb went no further than to organize a petition of protest and carry an appeal to the Privy Council which was dismissed in 1833. The Bombay and Madras governments followed Bentinck's lead and steady pressure secured its gradual abolition in the Indian states. The last case of a suttee on the death of a ruler occurred at Udaipur in 1861.

There quickly followed the suppression of *thagi* in central and upper India. This was armed robbery and murder carried out in the name of religion. The *thags* used a regular ritual in their murders and believed themselves to be serving the goddess Kali by so doing. The practice had long existed but had grown to be a menace to society with the collapse of authority in central India at the turn of the century. Bentinck took their suppression in hand in 1830, the work being carried through by Sir William Sleeman with the help of men like Meadows Taylor. No petitions attempted to stay this work for its practical advantage was too obvious. Another measure of this class was the abolition of slavery, which became an anachronism in India after its abolition in the rest of the British empire in 1833. Slavery in India as an abuse had not the dramatic qualities of suttee or *thagi*. There were no chain gangs as in the West Indies and no middle passage. But its practice was widespread and deep-rooted and its evil very real. It was abolished by Lord Ellenborough's government in 1843 (Act V) by refusing to recognize slavery as a legal status.

We now turn to the class of western innovations which were superimposed, as it were, upon the existing body of customs and laws in India. The principle of equality of the subject before the law is one which lies at the root of the whole body of English law. It was equally absent from the body of Hindu custom with its special privileges for Brahmans and disabilities for the exterior castes or depressed classes. The principle was laid down by the Charter Act of 1833 in the matter of qualification for government office, thus condemning by anticipation the colour bar of which so much was heard later. It has been explained that this had little immediate effect in practice. But Bentinck went farther. He modified the Hindu law of inheritance to make it possible for a convert from Hinduism to inherit the family property. It was the first invasion of the principle of equality into the domain of Hindu personal law. A further influence in this direction was the whole

[1] It should be remembered, however, that Metcalfe when resident of Delhi, 1809–18, abolished suttee within the Delhi territory by administrative order.

system of Indian public law. The inspiration for all changes was British and the machinery of courts and legal procedure came from the same source.

These innovations, though of great importance, were subtle in their nature and slow in revealing their effects. But the next series of innovations were much more obvious in their nature and more striking in their immediate results. The first of these was the introduction of Christian missions. The early missions of the eighteenth century worked from non-British stations, like the Danes in Tranquebar and William Carey with his band of British Baptists at Serampore. They could only get a footing in the Company's territory by becoming Company's chaplains as David Brown and Henry Martyn did in Bengal and the Swartz for a time in Madras. From 1813 free entry was allowed. There followed the establishment of a network of British missions to be reinforced shortly by the Americans. The missionary with his black cloth and hat, his church and his band of converts became a familiar sight in many an up-country station. The missionaries embodied, as it were, the Evangelicals' views about India.[1] They engaged in many types of activity from pure evangelism to educational and medical work and the conduct of colleges in the great cities. They were wholly unsupported by government but could not fail to gain some prestige from their personal and racial connexions with the ruling class. In the person of Alexander Duff, the founder of the Scottish Churches College in 1830, they made a striking impact on Bengali society. They constituted an overt challenge to Hinduism and Islam, permitted though not patronized by the government. Though they could not change society except by persuasion, they formed an important channel by which western values and western knowledge were poured into India and spread through the spray of many mission stations all over the country.

The next change of importance was the government's action about language. Hitherto Persian had been the language of diplomacy throughout India and of proceedings in the higher courts. Here again Bentinck led the way. By a series of enactments beginning from 1835 English and the vernacular languages replaced Persian as the language of record and legal proceedings. It also became the language of government business. English was already being studied for its practical advantage as Persian long had been, and now, in the course of a few years, it became essential for a public career. The study of English involved some acquaintance at least with the ideas of its literature, so that these measures were also westernizing in their effects.

The most momentous of all these changes was the new education policy. At first the Company had patronized the old learning so far as it had patronized anything. Warren Hastings established the Calcutta *Madrasa* for the study of Arabic and Persian in 1781 and Jonathan Duncan the Benares Sanskrit College in 1794. The Act of 1813 pro-

[1] They were by no means all Evangelicals in theology.

vided that a *lakh* of rupees should annually be 'set apart and applied to the revival and improvement of literature and the encouragement of the learned Natives of India and for the introduction and promotion of a knowledge of the sciences among the inhabitants of the British Territories in India'.[1] After ten years a Committee of Public Instruction was set up and began to encourage ancient learning, the modern sciences, and the teaching of English. Gradually the advocates of 'useful learning', encouraged from the India House where James Mill was high in influence, grew more positive and more aggressive. The value of Indian learning and literature was questioned altogether. The controversy came to a head over a minor point;[2] it provoked Macaulay's famous and heavily overcharged minute and led to Bentinck's fateful decision. Bentinck ruled that 'the great object of the British government ought to be the promotion of European literature and science. . . .' He directed that all available funds 'be henceforth employed in imparting to the Native population knowledge of English literature and science through the medium of the English language'.[3] This decision excluded all support for oriental learning and was modified by Lord Auckland in 1840.[4] But two great decisions had been made. The main object of the government's educational efforts would be the encouragement of education whose content would be western 'literature and science' and whose medium of instruction would be English. As a result of these decisions there arose a network of English schools and colleges, supported directly by the government and a few missionary bodies and then extended through private agency by means of the grant-in-aid system. Along with the change over to English as the medium of government's legal and administrative business it made an acquaintance of the English language and western ideas essential to anyone who aspired to any sort of distinction in public life and to a large extent in private business also. The new educational system became a formidable agent of westernizing influences. Bentinck thus became a major apostle of the West in India.

And what of the Indian attitude to these measures? Hitherto the effect of European influences on Indian life and thought had been superficial and fleeting. In Mughul times there had been some interest in European art as known through the Portuguese Jesuit missions and some curiosity about European thought.[5] But these did not survive the isolationist influences of Aurangzeb's time. In the eighteenth century the aristocratic Indian world no longer had much leisure for cultivating the arts of peace. Its chief interest in Europe was political and its chief

---

[1] Stat. 53, Geo. III, cl. 155, Sect. 43.
[2] The proposal to make English a compulsory subject at the Arabic College in Calcutta.
[3] Resolution of 7 Mar. 1835.
[4] Minute of 24 Nov. 1839. See H. Sharp, *Selections from the Educational Records of the Govt. of India*, i. 170–80.
[5] Mughul miniatures exist showing European influences, and European craftsmen were employed.

loans were military. Artillery and firearms, tactics and discipline were the object of their curiosity. Other things which interested them were European wines, horses, carriages, and similar incidental externals of life. There was some borrowing of architectural forms, with curiously hybrid results in the town-houses of Calcutta and the palaces of Lucknow. Corinthian pillars and saracenic arches jostled uneasily together. There was some disposition to sit for European painters as Daniell's portrait of Mahadji Sindia shows. But of intellectual contacts or influences there were few. Tipu's tree of liberty was a political stunt; and the only real contact was between men like Warren Hastings and Colonel Palmer on the one hand and Beneram Pandit and Tufazul Husain Khan on the other. But this, though interesting, was not fruitful, and grew less with the years. The aristocratic world of India remained largely impervious to western influences.

A change, when it came, emerged from a quarter half-way between the British and Indian worlds, and between the old aristocratic world and the new middle class which had begun to cluster round the British. This was the group of 'go-betweens' in Bengal between the British and the people. They were men of business, but many of them were also of good family and cultivated tastes. These men were in constant contact with the ablest Europeans in India. They developed an interest, not so much in European arms or viands or ways of living, as in western thought and ideas. This interest was by no means wholly cultural. It was both practical and theoretical. There was the desire to acquire mastery of the English language for the worldly advantages it would bring, and there was the wish to know the secret of the men of the West, who had so swiftly and decidedly achieved dominion in India. By the early years of the nineteenth century both these movements were in perceptible motion in Bengal. Each tended to feed the other, and both found a champion in Ram Mohan Roy, a Brahman from Krishnagar. On the British side a new class was appearing which in its turn acted as a half-way house between the official world and the new middle class. There were the judges and lawyers connected with the Supreme Court of whom the most distinguished was the Sanskrit scholar Sir William Jones. There were the missionaries, led by William Carey and his band of Baptists at Serampore, and there was the rationalist influence, embodied in the person of David Hare, the free thinking watchmaker.

These forces provided the elements for a creative movement, and the man of the moment appeared in Ram Mohan Roy. Born in 1770, he left his home in disgust at a suttee in his family, and for seven years wandered in the traditional manner seeking truth. His pilgrimage led him as far as Tibet and as deep as the doctrines of the Upanishads, of Buddhism, Islam, and Christianity. In the course of time he mastered ten languages including Sanskrit, Arabic (to study the Quran), Hebrew (for the Old Testament), Greek (for the New), Persian, and English. There followed a period of government service when he was *sherista-*

dar to Digby of Rungpur and acquainted himself with European thought. In 1814 he returned to reside in Calcutta and take up the role of reformer. The next sixteen years were filled with tireless activity. He advocated the study of the English language and of western knowledge and thought, he attacked Hindu idolatry and abuses like suttee and criticized the caste system; he championed freedom of opinion and was a pioneer of Indian journalism. His career was crowned by his journey to England in 1830 whither he went to plead the cause of the pensionary Mughul emperor[1] and oppose the petition to the Privy Council against the abolition of suttee, and there he died in 1833.[2] His positive achievements were a share in founding the Hindu college or *Vidyala* in 1816, the foundation of the first modern Indian newspaper, and the foundation of the *Brahmo Samaj*, or divine society, a reforming theistic religious group. He was persuasive enough to convert a Baptist missionary to Unitarianism and to make the first inroad from within upon the massive structure of Hindu orthodoxy.

By the time of Ram Mohan Roy's death there had arisen in Calcutta movements aiming variously at the reform of Hinduism from within, a synthesis between East and West and the outright rejection of Hinduism. The reforming movement came to be lead by Devendranath Tagore; the radical tendency, stimulated by Derozio and impelled by the Presbyterian Alexander Duff, lead to a number of notable conversions to Christianity.[3] The same tendency, though in a more subdued tone, can be traced in Bombay after 1820 and later in Madras. But the most interesting development outside Calcutta was in pre-Mutiny Delhi where Muslim intellectuals led by Maulvi Nazir Ahmad and including Altaf Husain, Hali, and centred in the Delhi College, studied western thought with enthusiasm. The seed of the new India had been sown, and the first seedlings were sprouting.

AUTHORITIES

FOR a general treatment of this subject L. S. S. O'MALLEY (ed.), *Modern India and the West* (1941), is recommended. T. G. P. SPEAR, *India, Pakistan, and the West* (1949) may serve as an introduction to the subject. A. YUSUF ALI, *A Cultural History of India* (Tarporewala, 1940), though confused, is interesting and full of information. K. M. PANIKKAR, *Asia and Western Dominance* (1953), treats the subject from a critical angle.

For early cultural approaches see Lord TEIGNMOUTH, *Life of Sir W. Jones* (1805), and J. FORBES, *Oriental Memoirs* (4 vols., 1813). The humanitarian approach can be studied in the works of Burke and the Christian Evangelical in Sir R. COUPLAND, *Wilberforce* (2nd ed., 1945). The social measures of Bentinck's period are described in vol. ix of MILL and WILSON's *History*, and in C. BOULGER, *Lord William Bentinck* (1897). For suttee see E. THOMPSON, *Suttee* (1928); for *thagi* the works of Sir W. SLEEMAN and MEADOWS TAYLOR, for infanticide, R. W. MORE, *Hindu Infanticide* (1860), and for slavery *Parliamentary Papers*. See also S. E. STOKES,

---

[1] It was from the Emperor Akbar II that he received the title of raja.
[2] At Stapleton, near Bristol, on 27 Sept. 1833. A monument in Hindu style, to his memory, stands close to the entrance of Arno's Vale cemetery.
[3] The most notable was that of Madhu Sudhan Datta.

For education, apart from general works, A. MAYHEW, *The Education of India* (1926), may be used. ADAM's *Reports* (ed. A. Basu, 1941) give a picture of the indigenous system in Bengal and C. E. TREVELYAN, *The Education of the People of India* (1838), the reformer's viewpoint. The part played by missions is given in K. S. LATOURETTE, *History of the Expansion of Christianity* (7 vols., 1938–45). There are new studies by K. INGHAM, *Reformers in India* (1956) and M. M. ALI: *The Bengali Reaction to Christian Missionary Activities 1833–1857* (Chittagong, 1965).

For the Indian response see the works of O'MALLEY and YUSUF ALI already quoted. Also studies of Ram Mohan Roy by N. C. GANGULY (1936) and AMAL HOME (1933), and the *English works of Ram Mohan Roy*, ed. J. C. C. GHOSE (2 vols., Calcutta, 1885). See also K. BALLHATCHET, *Social Policy and Social Change in Western India, 1817 to 1830* (1957). Miss S.D. Collets's *Life and Letters of Raja Rammohun Roy* has now been edited in a third edition with an authoritative commentary by D.K. Biswas and P. C. Ganguli (Calcutta 1962), embodying much recent research.

RECENT PUBLICATION

D. KOPF, *British Orientalism and the Bengal Renaissance, 1773–1835* (California, 1969) provides some valuable insights.

CHAPTER 8

Dalhousie

THE accession of Dalhousie introduced a new period in the history of British India. For ten years events had been dominated by the Afghan aggression and its consequences. Now, apart from the early and brief final campaign in the Panjab, and the distant operations in Burma, peace descended upon India once more. But it was a dynamic not a static state of affairs, and for the inhabitants it was hardly more restful than war. The previous peaceful age of Bentinck and Metcalfe had also been active and forward-looking it is true; in many ways the innovations which then took place were more radical than those of Dalhousie. But they affected the people as a whole less. It was an age of beginnings rather than of accomplishments, of aspiration rather than of major achievement, and there still lingered at that time some feeling of restoration after the anarchy which had preceded 1818. By Dalhousie's time these memories had faded, and it was obvious that the government was pressing forward along new paths towards unknown goals.

Bentinck's reign had made it clear that innovation and reform would be on western lines. But Auckland had tempered the western wind with some concessions to tradition and then war had arisen to absorb the government's energies. Such projects as irrigation and land settlement proceeded, but the rulers were too busy elsewhere to raise the *tempo* of ideological aggression. Dalhousie came to India as a convinced westernizer. He hoped that his chief duties would 'consist in suggesting and carrying out those great measures of internal improvement which you are so desirous of promoting'. These measures would be western measures carried out by western agency. Dalhousie was influenced by the flowing tide of materialist utilitarianism even though he never proclaimed himself to be one and was in fact a professed Presbyterian. He believed that the promotion of civilization meant the promotion of western reforms, that western administration and western institutions were as superior to Indian as Western arms had proved more potent. With less of Macaulay's belief in the possibility of Indian internal regeneration he shared to the full Macaulay's belief in the value of western models. His temperament suited his convictions and combined with the growing self-confidence of the British in India to impart a certain arrogance to official benevolence and a certain hardness to the tone of the government. The consciousness of conquest competed with the sense of moral mission and increasingly combined with the latter to produce a sense of ingrained superiority. The old

sense of caution and humility in the presence of the problems of a sub-
continent was now submerged in the flood of military success, and by
the self-confidence of a people who believed that their civilization was
superior to all others in actual achievement, and by virtue of its discovery of the secret of progress, increasing its lead year by year.

Dalhousie was not thirty-six when he landed in Calcutta. He was
short and stocky in appearance, but he had a commanding presence,
abounding energy, and an imperious temper. He refused cabinet office
on his return from India partly on the ground that he did not feel able
to work harmoniously with equal colleagues. He had achieved distinction in Peel's cabinet in dealing with the railway boom as Vice-Presi-
dent of the Board of Trade and he joined to aristocratic hauteur Scotch
practicality and business sense. Almost the only gift denied him was
good health, but his will sustained him through massive labours which
wore out his constitution. He died in 1860 at the age of forty-eight.

Within three months of Dalhousie's arrival he was faced with a fresh
crisis in the Panjab with the revolt of Diwan Mulraj at Multan. The
delay during the summer of 1848 which enabled a desperate act of
defiance to become a national revolt, the campaign which ended at
Gujarat in March 1849, and the decision to annex that he did not feel able
on in Chapter 4 above. But Dalhousie did not stop short at annexation;
he personally supervised the organization of the new province. In a
very real sense he was the father of the British Panjab as it existed from
1849 to 1947. His first instrument was a board of administration of
which Henry Lawrence was the head, with John Lawrence and Mansel
(replaced in 1851 by Robert Montgomery) as junior members. Dalhousie found John more congenial than the imaginative and unmethodi-
cal Henry. But he felt unable to pass over the elder brother and so
surrounded him with a board instead of giving him sole authority. To
Henry was given the political work of dealing with the chiefs and disarming the country; to John the settlement of the land revenue and to
Mansel the organization of the judiciary. For two years the board was
famous alike for the ardour of its reconstructive work and the heat of
its disputes. In 1851 the two brothers agreed that they could not
profitably continue to work together; Dalhousie seized the occasion to
send Henry to Rajputana as agent-general and to give John sole
authority as Chief Commissioner of the Panjab.

Dalhousie thought that John 'taking him all in all . . . was the better
man'. But more than temperament stood between the brothers in this
most famous of British-Indian official quarrels. John had served his
earlier years in the Delhi territory where village communities were
strong and sturdy *zamindars* of moderate means dealt direct with the
government. He was the friend of the cultivator, and had little use for
the Sikh chiefs of the Panjab whom he regarded as oppressors of their
people and as upstarts and little better than the baronial tyrants of
King Stephen's reign. Henry's early service, on the other hand, had
been in the north-western provinces where he had to deal with local

chiefs and landowners whose family trees stretched back a thousand years. He respected tradition and desired to preserve it if possible. Thus Henry wanted to work *through* the chiefs while John was quite prepared to work without them or in spite of them. It was the issue of reform from within with the consent and support of the aristocracy, or from above by authority and direct administrative action. Henry had opposed annexation in accordance with his principles while John was in favour of it. But it must not be supposed that Henry was in favour of the *status quo* or the old ways against his brother's reformism. Both were convinced reformers and westernizers; indeed, it was Henry's zeal for reform between the two wars that aroused Sikh opposition and helped to produce the situation which led to the second war and annexation. Reformism was the link between the two brothers; their final parting resulted from differences over methods rather than measures.

It was thus John Lawrence who completed the reorganization of the Panjab with his fifty-six picked subordinates and became the working head of 'the Panjab school'. Dalhousie was its founder and director behind the scenes, Henry Lawrence its 'suffering servant', admired but not followed, and Kipling later its poet and eulogist.[1] It early acquired an *ethos* of its own, and through the facts of its foundation by one Governor-General, the elevation of its first head to be another, its inspired publicity, the strategical importance of the province and its physical relation to the summer capital acquired an influence and reputation out of all proportion to its numbers. As men in Wellesley's or Lord Hastings's time sought the political service as the avenue to fame, in later years they aspired to entry in the Panjab branch of the civil service. The first principle of the Panjab school was direct rule. The government must deal direct with the people and all go-betweens, whether chiefs, tax-collectors, or urban Panjabis, were suspected and discouraged. Along with this went the doctrine of the 'personal touch'. Officers must move among the people knowing their virtues and vices, undeviating in their justice and unsparing of their strength. This had been learnt by John Lawrence himself in his Delhi territory days and was never altogether lost. Along with this personal touch and high sense of duty went a sense of mission. The best men of Metcalfe's day believed themselves to be the instruments of Providence. But Providence for them was inscrutable and they were by no means certain where it was leading. The men of the Panjab school had no such doubts. They had divined the purposes of the Providence they served; they went forward confident in their mission to rule, to civilize, and to modernize in the western way. They loved the Panjabi with his hearty manners, his addiction to sport, his simple 'man's man' outlook, and they were certain that God had sent them to rule him for his good.

Along with this moral and personal dynamism went other qualities.

[1] The officials of Kipling's Indian tales were mostly men of the Panjab and the Frontier.

There was a touch of ruthlessness in the Panjab official illustrated by Dalhousie's phrase, 'Unwarned by precedent, uninfluenced by example, the Sikh nation has called for war, and, on my word, sirs, they shall have it with a vengeance'. It can be traced through the Panjab treatment of the mutineers down to the Amritsar episode of 1919. The Panjab school was confident and convinced of its mission, but never quite sure of its position. Its work had a brittle quality which added perhaps to its brilliance, like polished metal, but which made it uncertain under strain and told against its permanent survival. Its great achievement was the modernization of the Panjab and its transformation into the most prosperous portion of India; its defect the failure to implant and to develop among the people the seeds of an integrated plural society. The reward of its virtues was the making of the Panjab the leader of India, the penalty of its faults the tragedy of partition.

The team which worked under John Lawrence until 1859 was not hampered by the regulations which had been developed for more settled parts of the country. The Panjab was the supreme example of the non-regulation province. A simpler code of civil and criminal procedure was drawn up and individual officers were given wide personal discretion. Working along these lines great progress was quickly made. The people were disarmed and the north-west frontier fortified. Roads were built everywhere, the most conspicuous example being the Grand Trunk road from Lahore to Peshawar. Then the welfare of the people was vigorously promoted. The land tax was reduced by about half and village settlements effected on the lines of those made in the neighbouring Delhi territory. The old abuses of slavery, *thagi*, and dacoity were suppressed. Trade was encouraged by the abolition of internal transit duties. Finally great projects of irrigation were commenced, which were to make the Panjab the garden of India. The immediate result was a release of energy for peaceful pursuits, or perhaps we should say a transfer of this best of Panjabi commodities from war to peace. The short-term reward was great. By 1857 the new system had so far won the martial people that when the Mutiny came the province remained tranquil and loyal while the Sikhs actively assisted in its suppression.

The only other large-scale war in which Dalhousie was engaged was in Burma. This has already been dealt with in Chapter 3 above and it only remains to note its results. Dalhousie showed caution in its conduct and wise restraint in limiting annexation to lower Burma. He bestowed the same care in the organization of this territory as in the case of the Panjab. He found an eastern Lawrence in Sir Arthur Phayre and maintained the same close touch in his organizing measures.

The next great scene of Dalhousie's activity was the Indian states. The first period of British relations with the states has been described by Sir W. Lee-Warner as that of the 'ring fence', which lasted until the Hastings's settlement of 1813–18. States were treated as foreign and there was no internal interference. The second period was that of 'subordinate isolation' lasting until Dalhousie's time, and the third was that of 'subordinate union' which was the result both of Dalhousie's measures and the reaction which they provoked. In this second period the British government claimed paramountcy which meant that the states were both unable to engage in aggression and protected from external attacks. A consequence was that the rulers were both insulated from internal sedition and shut out from any share in all-India affairs. Many princes lost interest in the routine of local administration so that abuses multiplied while their subjects had no remedy. The government was reluctant to intervene, but was pressed by the rising tide of humanitarian opinion. The result was non-interference tempered by occasional annexation for extreme misgovernment, such as Bentinck's action in Coorg and Mysore and his threat to Oudh in 1831.

When Dalhousie arrived misgovernment was more widespread and humanitarian opinion stronger than ever before. To this situation he added his own personal equation and the result was the annexation policy, of which the famous doctrine of lapse was only a part. Dalhousie believed that British administration was immensely better than the contemporary Indian; he regarded the states as obsolete in the new India he envisaged, and he was very sensitive to the charge of princely misgovernment, which he considered a slur on the name of British rule in India. He was neither ruthless nor deaf to ancient rights, but other things being equal, he considered that annexation was desirable when possible. 'His predecessors had acted on the principle of avoiding annexation if it could be avoided; Dalhousie acted on the general principle of annexing if he could do so legitimately.'

The first part of his annexation policy was 'the doctrine of lapse'. We can take as our starting-point the general assumption of paramountcy which provided ground for interference in any state in certain circumstances. One of these circumstances was the succession to the *gadi* or throne. The Paramount Power insisted on the right of recognizing the succession, with its corollary of regulating it in doubtful or disputed cases, as had been done in the cases of Bharatpur and Gwalior. But what if there was no recognized natural heir? Hindu law provided for this contingency by the practice of adoption, those so adopted becoming for all legal purposes the heirs of their adoptive fathers. Dalhousie claimed that since succession had to be recognized by the Paramount Power, princely adoptions could only be valid if ratified by the supreme government. If that was withheld, the state would pass by 'lapse' to the Paramount Power. There were two qualifications to this rule. The first was that it only applied to Hindu princes amongst whom adoption was recognized as customarily legal, and the second was a distinction between states directly dependent on the British and those with an independent pre-existence. Dependent states were those whose creation or recognition was directly due to the British, the status being defined by treaty, or who had formerly been dependent on some state which had been annexed by the British.[1] In practice the line was by no means always easy to draw, but its existence meant that even the most radical application of the doctrine of lapse would not have involved the extinction of the whole of Hindu princely India. Nevertheless, though the distinction was a real one, Dalhousie's operation of the doctrine of lapse was sufficiently extensive to create misgivings among all Hindu princes while his actions on other pretexts extended the uneasiness to the Muslim princes as well.

The states which suffered from the process were Satara in 1848, Jaitpur and Sambalpur in 1849, Baghat in 1850, Udaipur in 1852, Jhansi in 1853, and Nagpur in 1854. The proposal to annex Karauli was disallowed by the home government. Baghat and Udaipur were restored by Lord Canning. Jaitpur was a tiny state of 165 square miles. Sambalpur was a disorderly one on the banks of the Mahanadi in what is now the state of Madhya Pradesh. The important cases were Satara, Jhansi, and Nagpur. Satara had been revived by Lord Hastings in 1818 for the benefit of Sivājī's direct descendants; it came well within the class of 'dependent' states, but its annexation irritated Maratha sentiment. Jhansi in Bundhelkhund had been dependent on the Peshwa and then on the British. The refusal to recognize the raja's last-minute adoption infuriated his high-spirited rani, who later, after some reluctance, played a prominent part in the Mutiny. Nagpur was one of the three large surviving Maratha states with a population of 4 millions. Here again the state was undeniably dependent but its annexation inevitably both irritated Maratha sentiment and injured the interests of a large governing class. In all these cases annexation was justified from Dalhousie's point of view but was a cause of deep discontent to those immediately affected and of resentment to a much wider circle.

The second plank, as it were, in Dalhousie's annexation platform was misgovernment. He regarded misgovernment as a justification for taking over states additional to the doctrine of 'lapse'; in his view the benefit of direct administration for the people at large far outweighed the evils of any injury done to an effete governing class and the resentment which it might cherish. But misgovernment alone, if sufficiently prolonged and profound, justified annexation in Dalhousie's view. This covered the case of Oudh. From the death of Saadat Ali in 1813 the state administration had steadily deteriorated, and only the obstinate loyalty of the Nawabs and Kings of Oudh (from 1818) had prevented the solemn warnings of Bentinck in 1831 and Hardinge in 1847 from going further. The Rajput *taluqdars* were undisciplined and refractory, the court extravagant, dissolute, and incompetent. Sleeman's report on its condition in 1851 painted a vivid picture of disorder and chronic misrule.[2] Dalhousie himself proposed to take

---

[1] Examples of the first were Tonk, Firozpur, Satara, and Mysore; of the second, Jhansi; of independent states Gwalior and the Rajput states generally.

[2] W. H. Sleeman, *Diary of a Journey through Oudh*. Dalhousie's private letters show that the directors' decision represented his real desires.

over the administration, leaving titular sovereignty with the king. But the directors overruled him, insisting on outright annexation. The taking over of the administration had much to commend it, but the manner of its achievement left Muslim princes with the same uneasy feelings as their Hindu brethren. A further case of veiled annexation increased their misgivings. In 1853 the Nizam's tardiness in paying for the Hyderabad contingent led to the assignment of the revenue of Berar for the upkeep of the force.

The third plank of the annexation platform was the abolition of titular sovereignties which Dalhousie regarded as obsolete. The title of Nawab of the Carnatic was abolished on the ground that it was a personal and not an hereditary one.[1] The titular Rajaship of Tanjore was abolished in 1855 when the last raja died without male heirs. On the death of the ex-Peshwa Baji Rao in 1853 the pension secured for him by Malcolm was refused to his adopted son, the Nana Sahib. Finally, Dalhousie wished to abolish the imperial title at Delhi. The home authorities overruled him in this, but he made the recognition of the aged Bahadur Shah's heir dependent on his agreement to forgo the imperial name and withdraw his family from the imperial palace. When heirs were lacking, Dalhousie abolished titles; when they were plentiful he made abolition a condition of recognition of family headship against rival relatives.

Apart from conquering and organizing two provinces, annexing large tracts, and abolishing the gilded survivals of the past, Dalhousie engaged in incessant reforming and constructive activity. In many ways he was the founder of modern India, for he was the first to envisage a modernized and westernized India as a practical proposition rather than as a far-off dream. Even self-government was not beyond his vision,[2] though the prospect was more distant than it was to Macaulay. He carried out the first major reorganization of the Calcutta secretariat, and obtained the appointment of a lieutenant-governor to relieve the Governor-General from the direct administration of the overgrown province of Bengal. He suppressed the old military board and set up the Public Works Department as the agent for carrying out his great programme of public works. These works comprised the extension of irrigation projects, such as the Ganges canal,[3] which had already been begun. They included a great roads programme, thereby fulfilling Bentinck's hopes, of which the most striking monument was the Grand Trunk road from Calcutta to Peshawar. Above all, Dalhousie was the father of the Indian railways. The man who worked day and night to deal with the British railway boom of the forties was well fitted to introduce railways to India. Railways for India had been discussed since 1844, but except for the sanction of certain experimental lines, caution and obstruction had hitherto been successful. It was said that

---

[1] The head of the family was given the title of Prince of Arcot in 1867.
[2] See W. Lee-Warner, *Life of the Marquis of Dalhousie*, vol. i, p. 124.
[3] Completed in 1854.

the climate was against them, that there were no engineers to build them, that Hindus would not travel on them and that they would not pay. Dalhousie's minute of 1853 convinced the home authorities of the need and feasibility of railways and laid down the main lines of their development. He envisaged a network connecting the main internal centres with the ports and providing both for strategical needs and commercial development. Before he left India 200 miles were in operation and had proved a success. Along with the planning of railways, which were to revolutionize Indian transport, went the introduction of the telegraph and the reform of the postal service. The first telegraph line from Calcutta to Agra, a distance of 800 miles, was opened in 1854. It was extended to Lahore and Peshawar by 1857. The postal system was reformed, a uniform half-anna rate being provided for all letters and stamps substituted for cash payments. Before his time it had cost a rupee to send a letter from Calcutta to Bombay.

Lastly, Dalhousie's rule saw great developments in education. Hitherto the Bengal government had tended to concentrate on higher and the Bombay government on primary education. The Dispatch of 1854, said to be the work of Sir Charles Wood, but which had the full support of Dalhousie, formed the basis of large developments. A fresh emphasis was laid upon primary education. At the same time the development of high schools and colleges was encouraged by the grant-in-aid system which encouraged private bodies to launch out on their own under suitable rules. The whole system was to be crowned by a number of universities, the first three of which came into existence in the year of the Mutiny. Dalhousie's special contribution was the establishment of an engineering college at Roorkee and he thus ranks as the father of technical as distinct from professional education in India.[1] There was scarcely a branch of administration, from the conserving of forests to the improvement of jails, which did not feel his reforming hand.

When we look at Dalhousie's administration as a whole we cannot fail to recognize the work of a masterly as well as a masterful mind. In some respects Dalhousie's was not an attractive personality. He seemed cold and unfeeling to some, harsh and overbearing to others; only rarely did the human warmth of a man eaten up by his passion for improvement emerge to inspire his closest confidants. He was almost morbidly sensitive to criticism and fiercely determined to dominate; he lacked imaginative sympathy with tradition and the Indian point of view. But for all that he was filled with a vision of the modern India that was to be; he exhausted his strength in the service of that India and did more, perhaps, than any single man to bring it about. Wellesley had acquired much territory and displayed singular drive and purpose but Dalhousie spent more energy in organizing than in acquiring. Bentinck had the vision of a westernized India, but while he could do little more than set up a few signposts, Dalhousie laid down the roads

[1] The Calcutta Medical College should not be forgotten in this connexion.

of progress. Curzon was a great systematizer but Dalhousie created what Curzon sought to perfect. The creative and comprehensive nature of his work surpassed that of all his nineteenth-century peers, and for a greater mind among the British rulers of India we have to go back to the most subtle and enigmatic of all, Warren Hastings. His weakness was that of going too far too fast. He was a sick man in a hurry. He was the apostle of a westernized India with all an apostle's zeal and faith. He lacked sympathetic understanding, the intuitive knowledge of how his measures would appear to those they affected. For this he paid the penalty of the Mutiny disaster, but he had also provided the antidotes of a contented Panjab, of railways, and of telegraphs.

AUTHORITIES

THERE is a small but able study of Dalhousie by W. W. HUNTER in the Rulers of India Series (1905), and a large and able *Life* by Sir W. LEE-WARNER (2 vols., 1904). J. A. BAIRD (ed.), *Private Letters of the Marquis of Dalhousie* (1910), is valuable and revealing. So is D. G. E. HALL (ed.), *The Dalhousie-Phayre Correspondence 1852-56* (1932), for Burma. A contemporary study is that of E. ARNOLD, *Dalhousie's adminis-tration of British India* (2 vols., 1861).

For the Panjab see the works of BOSWORTH SMITH and S. E. MORRISON on the Lawrences already quoted, and for the states Sir W. LEE-WARNER and K. M. PANIKKAR's works quoted under Book VIII, Chapter 5, for Oudh see W. H. SLEEMAN, *Journey through the Kingdom of Oudh* (2 vols., 1858). For education see A. MAY-HEW's work quoted under Chapter 7 above and for railways V. ANSTEY, *Economic Development of India* (3rd ed., 1949).

CHAPTER 9

The Mutiny

BOTH the nature and causes of the Mutiny are still a subject of lively dispute. It has been considered, and not only by Indian historians, as a national rising and even as 'the first war of independence'. Outram regarded it as a Muslim conspiracy exploiting Hindu grievances. It has been regarded as an aristocratic plot whose gunpowder was prematurely touched off by the spark of the Meerut outbreak. And it has been asserted to have been a purely military outbreak produced jointly by the grievances and indiscipline of the Indian troops and the folly of the British military authorities. It is in fact an anachronism to describe the Mutiny as the first essay towards modern independence. It was rather, in its political aspect, the last effort of the old conservative India. The princes had opposed the Company both with their own methods, like the Marathas, and with western military technique like Sindia and the Sikhs, and had failed. They had then retired into brooding isolation. Conservative India hoped to live its own secluded life under the princes within and British collectors outside the states, and for a few years after 1818 it seemed that it might continue undisturbed if politically impotent. But first westernization alarmed the orthodox in British India and then annexation followed the princes in their fastnesses. However negative its attitude conservative India could not escape the challenge of the West. That challenge was as inevitable as it was sincere. It was bound to cause irritation and perplexity to a community attached to an age-old system of life. It was bound to sow suspicions that the new measures were deliberately undermining the old and that they portended ruin and disgrace. The speed of the introduction of these measures after 1848 increased the irritation and created the social and political background which made it possible for military grievances to convulse a whole country. But for it the soldiers themselves would have been less fanatical. The classes which supported the troops were those who had lost something or whose interests lay in the past like the Oudh *taluqdars*, the Jhansi *sardars*, the Nana's circle, the Mughul princes, or the Maulvi of Fyzabad. The new groups, which were the product of western influence, were not only quiet but actively loyal.[1]

The factors which promoted the unrest which made a large-scale military revolt possible were many in number. There was the political factor which affected mainly the old ruling class but also Indian sentiment in general. Men, whether Hindu or Muslim, cherished their

[1] See Devendranath Tagore's autobiography.

traditional institutions and thought nominal independence a necessary part of their communal self-respect. The comfort of national self-esteem outweighed, in general sentiment, the inconveniences of local rule, even in the notorious case of Oudh. The career of expansion indulged in since 1838 made men wonder where the British would stop, and when a halt seemed to have come after the second Sikh war, the effect was spoilt by Dalhousie's annexations. These in turn alarmed the whole princely order and their dependants. Each state annexed and each court extinguished meant, perhaps, the removal of a centre of oppression and corruption. But even if this was so, it meant also further contraction of the area where Indians could hold high office, where men of good family could look forward to a career of honour in the public service. It meant also the creation of another group of resentful and perhaps desperate people who would seize any opportunity of expressing their feelings which might come their way. The Rani of Jhansi and her followers were one of these because she believed that she had been robbed of her ruling rights in defiance of recognized Hindu law. So also was the Nana Sahib at Bithur, though with far less reason, because he thought that he had a claim to the title of Peshwa and the pension of Baji Rao. Similar feelings existed in the princely circle of Delhi in anticipation of the lapse of the imperial title and the removal of the family to Mahrauli. The unease amongst the Gwalior *sardars*, which culminated in the revolt of Sindia's army, can be ascribed to the same general cause. They had no special grievance but caught the fever of unrest from events around them. The Oudh *taluqdars* saw danger to their estates as well as to their political position. The impeccable but blind Coverley Jackson fanned their fears by disbanding the royal army and starting inquiries into *taluqdari* titles.

These political fears were supplemented by the alarm felt by the whole order of large landholders, the *jagirdars* of previous days. The Permanent Settlement in Bengal had led to the displacement of many old-established *zamindari* families, but two generations had passed since the principal evictions and the new families, like the holders of Henry VIII's monastic lands under Elizabeth, were now well-established and firm supporters of the new order. But Bentinck's resumption of rent-free tenures, profitable as it was to the state and salutary in many respects, dispossessed many landholders for no other reason than loss of title deeds, and left all those affected with a sense of grievance. The *Imam* commission of the fifties was an inquiry of the same sort in the Bombay Presidency which led to the confiscation of 20,000 estates. Where would the British stop? To the fact of conquest many of them added an aggressive and superior air which could not fail to be both offensive and alarming. Their type of talk is illustrated by one of Sir Charles Napier's typical outbursts: 'Were I Emperor of India for twelve years, she should be traversed by railways and have her rivers bridged. . . . No Indian Prince should exist. The Nizam should no more be heard of. . . . Nepal would be ours. . . .'

The impact of western innovations was calculated to alarm both Hindu and Muslim religious sentiment in general and the professional religious classes in particular. Among Hindus there was an under-current of disapproval of such reforms as the suppression of suttee and infanticide and such innovations as the teaching of European science and medicine, the promotion of western education at the expense of oriental learning, and the introduction of railways and the telegraph. Hindu learning was publicly disparaged, Macaulay's minute on educa-tion being the most obvious example, while Christian missions were permitted and approved, if not officially countenanced. Widows were legally permitted to remarry and converts from Hinduism to inherit property. Was not this evidence of a design to subvert the ancient religion and all that made life worth while? The impalpable pressure of western ideas was making itself felt upon Hindu society as a whole.

These feelings were perhaps stronger and more widespread in Hindu than in Muslim society, but they were by no means absent from the latter as well. Muslim *maulvis* had lost their favoured position in the criminal courts. Muslims in general preferred British to Hindu rule, but only so long as tradition was respected; and they preferred their own to either. So orthodox opinion was rendered uneasy by such activities as western education and Christian missions and such inno-vations as railways and telegraphs just as the Hindus were. The annexa-tion of Oudh meant the imposition of infidel rule on the faithful. Shias were outraged by the fall of the King of Oudh, and Sunnis dis-tressed by the steady denigration of the Mughul emperor. It was no accident that one of the leaders in Oudh was the Maulvi of Fyzabad. To the Muslim orthodox Victorian reformers were but old infidels writ large.

All these factors united to spread a general disquiet through northern and central India outside Bengal. It was a foreboding of the end of the old familiar age and a fear of the unknown future. But it was no state of exasperation (save in a few isolated pockets) which only required some provocative incident to start a popular revolt. The most we can say is that it provided a social soil in which army discontent could germinate and grow. The soldiers found society in general sympathetic because society shared in a vague way the apprehensions of the soldiers themselves. The relations of the civilian to the military community was something like that of Tory rural England towards the Jacobites in 1745. They sympathized with their feelings; they half-hoped for their success, but there were too many people with too much to lose for many to stir until they knew which side fortune would favour. The soldiers on their side could feel the popular sympathy, and, like the Jacobites, counted too easily on this sympathy being expressed in action. In support of this analysis we can point to the general quietness of the countryside during the earlier stages of the Mutiny, and the apathy except in some areas like Oudh during the later. For this divorce of action from sympathy it may be suggested that the new land settlements from the times of Munro and Elphinstone in the south and west, and of Bentinck and Bird in the north, were responsible. The peasants were passively contented, having more to lose than gain from a revolution.

There are two further points to notice. The Madras and Bombay Presidencies were hardly touched by the Mutiny, whose area of influence was the north and centre. The armies of the two presidencies were similarly almost free from the contagion. There was also little evidence of deliberate conspiracy. Sir John Lawrence held that there was none, but this can hardly be sustained in view of the established fact of circulating *chapatis* and the readiness of the Nana Sahib to seize the occasion. On the other hand there was clearly no ready-made plan in Delhi to direct a revolt when the mutineers arrived there. Two embryo and rival *rajs* were set up and there is no evidence of co-ordination between them.

We can now turn to the army. In 1857 the total military strength of the Company was 238,000 of whom 38,000 were Europeans. Each presidency had its own army and it was only that of Bengal which was seriously affected. The Bengal army numbered 151,000 of whom nearly 23,000 were Europeans. About 13,000 of these latter were in the Panjab beyond the Sutlej or in the Cis-Sutlej districts. There were hardly any European troops between Meerut and Bengal except at Dinapur near Patna. The low proportion of British troops was the result of withdrawals for the Crimean and Persian wars.

The Bengal army, unlike those of Madras and Bombay, contained a large number of high-caste men, Brahmans and Rajputs, and on that account had always been more difficult to control. Forty thousand men, or nearly one-third of the whole, came from Oudh, forming a compact interest within the army, and a large number of these were Brahmans, subject to all the current Brahman prejudices and fears. There had been no mutiny in Madras since that at Vellore in 1806 but four had occurred in the Bengal army in the previous thirteen years. The pride of the troops had been inflated by a long series of military successes, their feelings seared by the rigours of the Afghan campaigns and taunts of losing caste beyond the Indus from their down-country brethren. Discipline was undeniably lax and long before Bentinck, himself commander-in-chief as well as Governor-General, had called the Bengal army 'the most expensive and inefficient in the world'. The situation called for both firm and tactful handling, but after Napier, whose energy was mostly misplaced, there was no commander-in-chief with the perception to recognize and the weight to deal with the situation.

To this general picture may be added two particulars. In 1856 the General Service Enlistment Act required every recruit to serve wherever required instead of in India only as previously. This impinged on caste feelings about travelling overseas. And then came the greased cartridges. The cartridges for the new Enfield rifle were said to be smeared with the fat of cows and pigs, thus nicely outraging the feelings of both Hindus, to whom the cow was sacred, and Muslims, to whom the pig was unclean.[1] The story spread like wildfire and was denied vigorously and in good faith by the officers. But animal fat had in fact been used in the Woolwich arsenal, so that the denial only confirmed the Hindu soldiers' belief that some plot was afoot. The withdrawal of the cartridges on the discovery of the facts came too late to allay suspicion and indignation for it was thought to be only a sign of weakness and alarm at the unmasking of a nefarious design. Had the general atmosphere been calm and unruffled no general outbreak would have occurred. But it was brooding, anxious, and suspicious. Here, said the soldiers, is concrete confirmation of so much we have vaguely heard talked about. No doubt their feelings were exploited by interested parties, but it was the feelings themselves which finally convulsed them in desperate action.

Dalhousie retired in February 1856 believing that he had restored India to that unruffled tranquillity in which he had expected to find her eight years earlier. Lord Canning, his successor, was the son of the brilliant lieutenant of Pitt and later Foreign Secretary, and had been Postmaster-General in the Aberdeen and Palmerston ministries. He had the high-mindedness of his father without his brilliance, his industry without his restless ambition and sudden intuitions. He was judicial in temper and diffident in decision. But if slow in coming to conclusions he was firm in holding them and he possessed a reserve of moral strength which eventually infused and dominated his whole character. His reflective nature invited criticism in times demanding quick decisions which his moral courage enabled him to resist; his detached temper both enraged men who were carried away by passion and enabled him to pursue his solitary path to the end. His nickname of 'Clemency' was a title first of derision and finally of honour. 'If he lacked the daring resolution', says Roberts, 'the imperious will, and the personal force of Dalhousie, he displayed a splendid constancy under taunts and misrepresentation, and he possessed a curious power of detaching himself from the influence and passions of the moment in solving intricate problems.'[2]

Canning's first care was a Persian crisis. In 1856 the Persians occupied Herat, then controlled by Dost Muhammad. Afghanistan was now a friendly power and a force was accordingly sent to the Persian Gulf which induced the Persians to make peace and evacuate Herat in May. This incident was of importance because it cemented Indo-Afghan friendship and helped to secure Afghan neutrality in the crisis which shortly followed. Canning's next care was affairs in Oudh, where the proceedings of Outram's successor as Chief Commissioner, Coverley Jackson, were causing increasing unrest. Jackson was replaced by Sir Henry Lawrence in March 1857, too late to prevent but in time to ensure the defeat of the outbreak in Oudh.

From the beginning of 1857 military unrest was clearly increasing. In January the cartridges (which had not now to be bitten and for which the men provided their own grease) were refused at Dumdum near Calcutta. In March a regiment was disbanded at Barrackpur. Outbreaks of incendiarism occurred and rumours flew. The actual outbreak occurred on 10 May at Meerut. Some troops refused the cartridges and were placed in irons. Their comrades of three regiments released them during service time on a Sunday evening, shot their officers, and made off for Delhi although there were over 2,000 European troops at Meerut. Delhi had no European troops. The Indian garrison joined the mutineers; the city was seized and by nightfall the aged Emperor Bahadur Shah had become their reluctant and bewildered leader.[1]

The course of the Mutiny falls into three periods. The first covers the terrible summer of 1857 when the problem was to prevent the conflagration from spreading and to hold on until reinforcements could arrive. The second centres round the operations for the relief of Lucknow in the autumn of the year. The third saw the set campaigns of Sir Colin Campbell and Sir Hugh Rose in the first part of 1858 which finally broke the rebel strength. There was a final phase of 'mopping up' operations which may be said to have ended with the capture of Tantia Topi in April 1859. It was a time of heroic constancy and great courage on the part of the government forces, who were never entirely British, and of equally desperate but ill-regulated valour on the part of the mutineers. Dark deeds were done on both sides, on the one side in the abandon of the release of long-suppressed passions, on the other in the rage of reprisal and blind vengeance. No good purpose would be served by detailing horrors on either side. It is sufficient for our purpose to say that the best men on either side were above them, that they were regretted by all when the fever of hate and fear had abated, and that their memory on both sides long remained a living obstacle to the restoration of harmonious relations.

A pause occurred after the fall of Delhi on 11 May while the commander-in-chief, General Anson, was collecting troops and transport at Ambala. Before his force could reach Delhi, the troops at Nasirabad in Rajputana, Nimach in Gwalior, at Lucknow, Cawnpore, and Benares in the United Provinces, rose together with the Rani of Jhansi in Bundelkhand. Everywhere officers were shot and Europeans massacred; everywhere vacillation as to the next step and lack of ready-made leaders showed the absence of well-planned conspiracies. Only in Cawnpore and Jhansi did the Nana Sahib and the Rani provide any immediate and aristocratic leadership. By mid-June therefore

[1] He was eighty-two years of age.

British authority had practically ceased in a broad band of territory stretching from the borders of Rajputana to the neighbourhood of Patna in Bihar. Only the fort of Agra, the residency of Lucknow, and entrenchments at Cawnpore were held while a mobile force was on its way from Ambala to Delhi. For the rest the countryside waited on the course of events without displaying any marked leanings to either side. The British had, as it were, two bastions of strength, in the Panjab and in Bengal. The problem was to hold these, to rescue the beleaguered garrisons, and to prevent the spread of the movement until reinforcements could arrive from Europe. In Bengal there was no danger; in the Panjab the situation was saved by the iron nerve of Sir John Lawrence and his picked team of enterprising officers. Here there was the triple danger of Afghan interference, of a Sikh rising, and of sepoy mutiny. Dost Muhammad remained loyal to his treaties, a delayed effect of his respect for British arms acquired in the first Afghan war. The Sikhs remained quiet and indeed actively helped in the operations. They had nothing to gain from a revival of the Mughul power at Delhi; for them the memory of Aurangzeb and his immediate successors was even more bitter than that of Dalhousie. The measures of the new government had also contented many more than it had alienated. The sepoy danger was met by prompt disarming and the way cleared for the organization of a mobile column under the redoubtable John Nicholson.

From the moment of hearing the news of the capture of Delhi both Canning and Lawrence realized that there lay the key to victory. Its recovery was a vital preliminary to the crushing of the revolt. The prestige of the old empire, with its Hindu as well as Muslim affiliations, made Delhi a rallying-point for all. Many in India still considered the titular emperor to be the rightful sovereign of the country and his nominal headship of the movement laid a strain upon all classes as well as upon Muslim princes in particular. General Anson at once organized a force which established itself on the Ridge before Delhi in late June.[1] But it was too weak to storm the city and for a time was more besieged than besieging. During July and August the force maintained itself with desperate valour and increasing confidence while Lawrence secured himself in the Panjab and then took the hazard of sending Nicholson, followed by a siege train, to Delhi. The nature of the hazard can be judged from the fact that Lawrence at one time thought of abandoning Peshawar and was only restrained by the entreaties of Herbert Edwardes and the command of Canning. In September the city was assaulted and carried after six days of desperate street fighting. Bahadur Shah surrendered on the promise of his life and the mutineer forces, about 30,000 strong, scattered to the villages or made their way down country to Lucknow. Nearly a quarter of the British force

[1] General Anson died of cholera at Karnal, and his successor Barnard soon followed him on 5 July. Reed resigned through ill-health and the command devolved on Sir Archdale Wilson.

became casualties and Nicholson was killed. But the traditional capital had been recovered by the men on the spot without the aid of a man from overseas. From that moment the suppression of the Mutiny as a whole was only a matter of time. The largely innocent inhabitants of Delhi, to whom the advent of the mutineers had been as much a calamity as the Marathas and Afghans before them, suffered acutely in the reprisals and punitive measures which followed.

But this result could not have been achieved if large rebel forces had not been tied up in and around Lucknow. Here the second epic of resistance against huge odds was enacted. Wheeler at Cawnpore surrendered on 26 June after three weeks of gallant resistance. Nana Sahib stained his own and the Maratha name by breaking his word and murdering his prisoners including 125 women and children. At Lucknow Sir Henry Lawrence was besieged in the residency from 1 July and died of his wounds three days later. But his work lived after him. His spirit inspired the garrison and his wise measures enabled it to resist until relief came. On 11 June the fortress of Allahabad was secured by Neill, a man cast in the mould of Nicholson, but who dimmed his glory by deeds of dark vengeance. On 7 July General Havelock set out from Allahabad with 2,000 men to achieve the first relief of Lucknow. He reached Cawnpore to find the prisoners murdered by the Nana's orders in a fury of frustration. In twelve pitched battles between 7 July and 25 September he fought his way into the residency. The back of the Mutiny had been broken before any reinforcements from Britain could reach the scene of action.

But the revolt was by no means over and much greater efforts were needed before the mutineers, rendered desperate by the prospect of defeat and condign punishment, were finally scattered. The second phase consisted in the second relief of the Lucknow residency. The relieved garrison, now commanded by Outram, was still too weak to attack Lucknow and was again besieged. In November Sir Colin Campbell finally relieved the residency and then returned to defeat the Gwalior contingent of 20,000 men under Tantia Topi, who had hitherto remained inert at Kalpi. On 1 March, joining forces with Outram, he recovered Lucknow and pressed the remnants of the rebel forces back into the Terai bordering Nepal.[1] Nana Sahib went with them and disappeared in the border jungles.

The third phase was the central Indian campaign. In many ways it showed the mutineers at their best though their cause was by then hopeless. The reckless courage of the rani and the skill of Tantia relieved the gloom of a hopeless struggle in a discredited cause. In March 1858 Sir Hugh Rose captured Jhansi after defeating Tantia's relieving force. The struggle seemed over with the victory of Kunch in May when the rani and Tantia doubled back to Gwalior, won over

[1] This phase was prolonged by Canning's proclamation forfeiting the *aluqdars'* lands except for six specifically mentioned and others who could prove their loyalty. Many then rose and maintained a guerrilla resistance for many months.

the raja's personal forces, and seized the fortress-capital. Two more battles were needed to break up this force in one of which the rani in a soldier's dress met a soldier's end. With the fall of Gwalior on 20 June the Mutiny was virtually over and there only remained minor operations.[1] Canning proclaimed peace on 8 July 1858.

It must always remain an object of wonder that forces so small should defeat opponents so numerous animated by such desperate courage in so short a time. But in fact the forces arrayed on each side were not so unevenly balanced as appeared at first sight. While at first the balance of material factors weighed heavily on the side of the rebels, the balance of moral factors lay equally clearly on the side of the British. They only needed time to convert their moral assets into material terms, and this their determination and confidence in themselves, no less than their courage, enabled them to do. The passions of the mutineers were centred on their grievances, not on larger ideals. They knew what they disliked, but not what they would wish to set up in its stead. So they gained little advantage from successes and nothing but despair from their defeats. Their resistance was made desperate by the knowledge that they had burnt their boats, that they had committed the unforgivable military sin. However courageous their resistance it was therefore despairing rather than purposeful. They fought to the end, because there was nothing to make them fight another day, and because the chance of death from surrender was equal to that from continued battle. Where the populace joined in, as round Saharanpur and Bareilly, it was on account of particular grievances rather than from any large vision of a new India. Those who had any such vision, as had some Muslims and the Nana Sahib's circle, looked backwards rather than forwards with the result that their programmes clashed. The British, on the other hand, enjoyed gifted and determined leadership; they had a compact discipline based upon a robust national pride. They had a long record of success and the hope of reinforcements to sustain them, and above all they had abounding self-confidence springing from the belief that they represented the irresistible forces of progress in the modern world. Seen in this light the result is not so difficult to understand. The pity of it was that the issue should have been put to the test of battle, to be decided at the cost of so much blood, and of the flowing of so many tears.

In the summer of 1858 northern India lay inert and lacerated. The wisdom of Canning and the strength of men like Sir John Lawrence restrained and soon ended the punitive measures and clamours for vengeance which followed the wake of the armies. But much remained to be done. Most of the rebel leaders were killed in battle like the Rani of Jhansi, or disappeared like the Nana and Bakht Khan of Delhi, or were executed like Tantia Topi. The Emperor Bahadur Shah had been promised his life. After a trial of doubtful legality he was exiled

[1] Tantia Topi was betrayed in April 1859 and hung for complicity in the Cawnpore massacre.

to Rangoon where he died in 1862 at the age of eighty-seven. The Mughul family lost its royal status. Delhi and Lucknow slowly returned to a normal life, but Delhi with its territory lost its semi-independent position and was attached to the Panjab. A number of implicated princelings lost their states and their lives. In Oudh Canning's confiscatory proclamation was not withdrawn, but its application was left to the discretion of the new Chief Commissioner Montgomery, and its rigour mitigated by a system of regrants.

These were the immediate and local results; there followed a number of measures of great importance. The East India Company ended its long career as the ruling power in India; a new attitude was adopted towards the princes; the army was reorganized; a beginning was made in associating Indians with the supreme government of their country. The new age was ushered in and its intended spirit defined in the Queen's proclamation of 1 November 1858. If good can come out of evil the Mutiny can claim the credit for most of these measures. There remained the psychological gulf between the peoples of India and Britain. This gulf was not created by the Mutiny as we have seen. The forces of separation had outstripped those making for harmony in the previous twenty years. The spirit of superiority and social pride had surpassed that of co-operation and the hope of self-government. This spirit was reinforced by that of fear on the British side and the resentment which it aroused was deepened by the memory of defeat and vengeance on the Indian. In this sense the Mutiny was a calamity whose effects only time could heal. Happily the progressive forces of reform and co-operation were not consumed but only obscured by the smoke of passion. They had received a severe set-back, but the next fifty years showed that it was a check rather than a final halt.

AUTHORITIES

THE best single-volume study remains T. R. E. HOLMES, *History of the Indian Mutiny* (1883, 5th ed., 1904). A large-scale work is J. W. KAYE and G. B. MALLESON, *History of the Indian Mutiny* (ed. Longmans, 6 vols., 1897). The first two volumes are by Kaye, the next three by Malleson. The sixth volume completes the work and adds an index to the whole. Sir G. W. FORREST, *History of the Indian Mutiny* (3 vols., 1904–12), rambles and contains much material already published elsewhere. For published documents see the *Cambridge History of India*.

Of the numerous monographs, studies, &c., only a few can be mentioned. Those are studies in the Rulers of India Series of *Canning* by Sir H. S. CUNNINGHAM (1903), *Lord Lawrence* by Sir C. V. AITCHESON (1905), and *Colvin* by Sir A. COLVIN (1912). Col. G. B. MALLESON is the best authority for military matters. E. THOMPSON, *The Other Side of the Medal* (1925), should be consulted for perspective in outrages. For causes, SAYYID AHMAD KHAN, *The Causes of the Indian Revolt* (Benares, 1873), should be consulted as well as the general histories. For Cawnpore see Sir G. O. TREVELYAN, *Cawnpore* (1805), for Delhi on the Indian side, T. G. P. SPEAR, *Twilight of the Mughuls* (1951), for Lucknow, M. JOYCE, *Ordeal at Lucknow* (1938), and for the Panjab, BOSWORTH SMITH, *Life of Lord Lawrence*. In 1957 there appeared a standard reassessment by S. N. SEN, *1857* (1957). R. K. MAZUMDAR, *The Sepoy Mutiny and Revolt of 1857* (1957), uses new material in dealing with certain episodes.

RECENT PUBLICATION

M. MACLAGAN's *Clemency Canning* (1962) is a full study of Canning in India, based on private papers.

BOOK IX

Imperial India, 1858–1905

CHAPTER 1

Canning and Reorganization

AFTER the Mutiny came reorganization. The first of these measures was
the abolition of the East India Company. Since 1833, as we have seen,[1]
the Company had lost its commercial connexion with India. From
1853 it had ceased to be a commercial corporation at all with the ending
of its China trade. Six of its directors were actually nominated by the
home government and the directors' monopoly of appointments had
been broken by the introduction of competitive examinations. The
Company had already become a husk of its former self. It was in fact
a corporate agency to whom the local management of affairs in India
was entrusted. It had little influence on high policy and its last convulsive assertion of authority went back to the recall of Lord Ellenborough.
The justification of its continued existence, so far as it had one, was in
supplying local knowledge for the benefit of the President of the Board
of Control, and in keeping the details of Indian administration and
patronage from the contagion of party politics. For all that, it had
become an anomaly, and public anomalies are apt only to continue so
long as no special occasion arises to prompt review and reform. The
Company itself argued ably in its own favour through the pen of John
Stuart Mill, but the current of opinion was against it.

The Government of India Act of 1858 deprived the Company of the
Indian government.[2] The place of the President of the Board of Control was taken by a Secretary of State for India, who now became, in
subordination to the cabinet, the fountain of authority as well as the
director of policy in India. To supply the local knowledge which the
directors claimed to give a Council of India was set up. This consisted
of fifteen members, appointed at first for life but later for periods of
between ten and fifteen years. Eight members were appointed by the
Crown and seven at first by the directors and afterwards by co-option
by the council itself. This body tended to represent official experience

[1] Book VIII, Chapter 6.
[2] The Company itself was formally dissolved from 1 Jan. 1874 by Act of Parliament.

and since the members were usually men who had retired from a life-time of service in India, embodied the official experience of the past generation. At first this fact provided a useful link between past and present, but when India really began to move forward in the latter years of the century, it became a handicap. It meant that the Secretary of State's immediate advisers were not in a position to judge accurately the new currents of opinion because they had arisen or developed since their time. Initially, however, the change was to the good; the influence of British 'interests' in British-Indian counsels was reduced, and the weight of administrative experience increased. A man no longer had influence in the direction of Indian affairs through the accident of having inherited business connexions with India or even Company stock, or because he was himself a successful trader with the country.

The arguments urged in favour of the Company as a ruler in its commercially disembodied form as an administrative corporation were that its long tradition and family spirit held the loyalty of its servants as an impersonal Crown could never do; that detailed superintendence by the directors ensured that due regard would be paid to local circum-stances, essential in a place like India, and that the directors' control of patronage kept the administration above the welter of party politics and jobbery. All these arguments had at one time had force, but the cogency of each had grown less with time. The Crown was certainly less personal than the Company and under the Hanoverians the loss by transfer would have been a severe one. But India was now a subject of continuous attention in the governing circle in London; the best men were sent to India not exceptionally as in the case of Cornwallis but as a matter of course. The Crown itself, in the person of Queen Victoria, took an interest in Indian affairs more personal than that of most directors, and she contrived to convey that interest, in some almost magic way, both to her civil and military servants and to the people of India at large. As for the family spirit of the old days, a blow had already been struck by the introduction of the competition system. The change checked a certain tendency to turn the Indian services into a closed caste circle, which lost in enterprise and originality what it gained in fraternalism. The old families were not excluded by the new system, but only their less capable members.

The argument of the local knowledge of the directors was met by the institution of the India Council which has been already discussed. The contention that the existence of the Company kept Indian affairs out of the bounds of party politics had once had great force. When jobbery was the rule in British politics, it was bound to extend to India if politicians controlled jobs. But jobbery was no longer the rule in British politics, whose tone had been transformed during the previous fifty years. The directors themselves were not guiltless in the matter of jobs. As for day-to-day interference it was now generally realized that too much was at stake in India for irresponsible meddling to be tolerated by either party.

Looking at the transfer as a whole we may agree that the change involved some loss of personal feeling, of the informality and intimacy which lingered round the East India House. But this was more than compensated by the more forward-looking spirit which pervaded the new India Office. The relics of commercialism and the ledger-book attitude to which directors clung to the last disappeared for ever. The nostalgic tendency to envisage Indian government as mere tax collecting and police work with its reluctance to embark on new ventures was also swept aside. The government as a whole was now consciously looking forward to a modernized India, not unconsciously harking back to a Mughul tranquillity, and the people became aware, as they had not been before, that their welfare was the concern of the rulers over the water. The royal courts and the royal law had once been the terror of the Bengali; the person and declarations of the new queen were to become the focus of Indian loyalty and the fountain of Indian hope.

We now turn to India, where Canning continued to hold the reins of power for four more years. Canning was industrious, deliberate, and reflective; he lacked the executive force of Dalhousie or Wellesley or the deeper insight of Warren Hastings. But his lack of brilliance was compensated by integrity and his slowness by tenacity; above all he possessed a high seriousness which imparted to his government a moral quality which was all his own. He was not at his best at the onset of the Mutiny because his qualities did not match the precise needs of the hour. He was firm and tenacious rather than bold or inspiring. But the initial crisis surmounted, his stature steadily grew as his strongest qualities were increasingly called forth by the course of events. The tenacious resister, the patient planner, the far-sighted conciliator increasingly came into his own. No one was better fitted to restrain the inflamed passions of his countrymen or to convince the Indian countryside that defeat was not to be synonymous with vengeance. Looked at in the cool light of posterity, many governmental acts of the time still seem severe; it is only by remembering the heat of the passions aroused that the extent of both Canning's and Lawrence's achievements can be measured. Their work and their difficulties are sufficiently attested by their private correspondence. Canning was awarded his nickname of 'Clemency' in Calcutta in disgust at his stand against vengeance; the intended insult, as such things so often do, became his recognized title of honour.

Canning's refusal to countenance indiscriminate vengeance was as noble and far-sighted as it was difficult. But in Oudh a certain fatality dogged his steps. His Oudh proclamation of March 1858 was interpreted by the *taluqdars* as an act of general confiscation; they thereupon took to arms and prolonged guerrilla warfare until the end of the year. The incident ended Lord Ellenborough's last tenure of the Presidency of the Board of Control.[1] Canning characteristically retrieved his

---

[1] Lord Ellenborough condemned the proclamation in a public dispatch without consulting the cabinet.

mistake, not by withdrawing the proclamation, but by entrusting its enforcement to Sir Henry Montgomery as Commissioner of Oudh. As a result of his tactful suasion and with the help of regrants, most of the chiefs recovered their estates on submission. For India as a whole the Queen's proclamation of 1 November 1858 set the tone for the new era of authority and conciliation, of piety and benevolence. Mercy and justice, welfare and improvement now took their stand on the royal word.

In India the change from Company to Crown was largely a matter of nomenclature. The machine continued to work in much the same way and the same men continued to work it. Administrative changes at the centre were nevertheless considerable and changes of policy were still more significant. In every measure the touchstone was how to avoid the mistakes which led to the catastrophe. In this natural anxiety to discover and rectify errors can be perceived the tendency, so common at such periods, to forget the needs of the present in remedying the failures of the past. Thus the government thought more of quieting the old classes of the society than of attaching the new and rising elements to itself. The loyalty of these groups had been signal and it was now assumed as an axiom until subsequent neglect goaded them into discontent.

For the moment, however, the new measures seemed conciliatory and wise. The Governor-General retained his legal title, but added the honorific of Viceroy as the personal representative of the Crown. There was here gain in intimacy as well as of pomp, for the Governor-General was henceforth the personal representative of the sovereign rather than the temporary figurehead of an impersonal corporation. At first it was proposed to make the Governor-General a supreme bureaucrat served by secretaries. But wiser counsels prevailed. By the Indian Councils Act of 1861 the Executive Council was retained and expanded to contain a fifth ordinary member in addition to the commander-in-chief, who continued to sit as an extraordinary member but rarely attended. To this council was introduced the 'portfolio' system whereby members were placed in charge of specific departments instead of sitting as a board of consultants to discuss each question as it came up on its merits. Business ordinarily went from the members to the Viceroy and only matters of general import or in doubt or dispute were referred to the council as a whole. Much time and effort were thus saved and the shape of the central government began to assume its modern form. The system also permitted the appointment of experts for specific subjects such as finance. The Governor-General's position as head of a cabinet of departmental chiefs began to approach somewhat to that of a prime minister. But since he retained his overriding powers it more nearly conformed to that of an American president unhampered by an independent legislature.

The Legislative Council of 1853 was substantially modified. The two judges and four provincial representatives who had formed under Dalhousie a kind of toy Parliament, modelling its procedure and spirit on that of Westminster, were replaced by from six to twelve additional members nominated for two years by the Governor-General, at least one-half being non-officials. No rule was laid down for their selection but in practice Dalhousie's desire to secure Indian representation was achieved by this means. At the same time the powers of the council, which Canning had found to be inconveniently independent,[1] were confined to the consideration of measures specifically laid before them. It was thus hoped to reduce the isolation of the supreme government from the people while removing a spurious parliamentary opposition in the guise of judges and provincial officials. At the same time legislative powers were restored to Madras and Bombay for provincial purposes.

The next subject of reconstruction was finance. The government of India's finances had hitherto been jointly controlled by the Governor-General and his council. But the Mutiny, by cutting off some sources of revenue and imposing new expenses, had added £42 million to the Indian debt to make a total of £98 million. In 1859–60 there was a deficit of over £7 million. India was steadily passing from the old self-contained rural economy of Mughul times into the orbit of world economic forces. Something more was needed than the old rule of thumb methods and the principles of Micawber finance. The new place on the Viceroy's Council was filled by the appointment of the financier James Wilson in 1859. In the nine months between his arrival in Calcutta and his death he remodelled the system of financial administration, outlined important economies, imposed an income tax for five years, and introduced the practice of annual budgets and statements of accounts. His work, as completed by his successor Samuel Laing, included a uniform tariff of 10 per cent., a convertible paper currency, and additions to the salt duty. Against previous belief Laing, taking into account the great productive assets of the country, maintained that 'the revenue of India is really buoyant and elastic to an extraordinary degree', an opinion justified by later experience. By these means and helped by good seasons the annual deficit disappeared in 1864. The work of Wilson and Laing marks the beginning of modern Indian finance.

Land was the next object of attention. The lot of the cultivators of Bengal under the Permanent Settlement had long been an object of concern. The settlement had given the value both of the unearned increment of the land and of increased cultivation to the *zamindars*, and it had made the cultivators in effect their tenants-at-will.[2] In 1859 an attempt was made to remedy this with the Bengal Rent Act. The Act applied to the whole of the north-west[3] as well as Bengal proper,

---

[1] The judges were held to be the chief offenders in this respect.
[2] The Court of Directors declared in 1858: 'The rights of the Bengal ryots had passed away *sub silentio* and they had become, to all intents and purposes, tenants-at-will'.
[3] Except the Panjab and Oudh.

gave occupancy rights to all cultivators who could prove possession for twelve years, and limited the raising of rents. The Act was far from a complete success and instigated much litigation; but if it is too much to describe it as a peasant's Magna Carta, it at least proved a landmark in protecting cultivators from the vagaries of the great *zamindars* and *taluqdars*. A further question was then mooted, nothing less than the extension of the Permanent Settlement from Bengal and parts of Madras and the North-West Provinces to the whole of India. It was believed that the cultivators of the great estates were now protected by the new Rent Act; elsewhere permanency would give to peasants settled under the *ryotwari* and village systems the whole value of un-earned increment and of increased cultivation. It was argued that famine mortality was connected with the system of temporary settle-ments with its danger of over-assessment. Were not the peasants left with too small a margin to have a reserve for bad times? The view won impressive support, including Sir Bartle Frere and Samuel Laing in India and Sir John Lawrence at home, and was actually accepted in principle by Sir Charles Wood in 1862. But its enforcement was first shelved and then finally abandoned. The greater efficiency of settlement operations and the partial nature of the success of the Bengal Rent Act combined to raise doubts sufficiently potent to arrest action. The real solution of the famine problem was to come later.

After the problem of a contented peasantry came that of discon-tented princes. Had not the uneasiness caused by the strict application of the doctrine of lapse and the series of annexations been at least a contributory cause of the Mutiny? On the other hand the loyalty of the Nizam and his minister Sir Salar Jung, of Sindia and his minister Sir Dinkar Rao, of the Rajput and Sikh chiefs had proved of the highest value. Loyal chiefs were rewarded by titles and gifts of money or lands. But far more important was the new policy which was now formulated. Canning had described the princes as the 'breakwaters of the storm which would otherwise have swept over us in one great wave'. Henceforward they were to be regarded as subordinate partners rather than dependent chiefs awaiting extinction or autonomous rulers cut off from the main stream of Indian life. The first step in the new policy was the assumption of sovereignty by the Crown. All states were now to be subject to royal paramountcy as in Mughul times. The new link was more definite and more personal than the Company's vague assertion of an impersonal supremacy. Two implications were contained in this step. First, as integral parts of the empire they were to be cherished rather than ignored with a bias to extinction. Their territories were guaranteed and the right of adoption conceded. Secondly, paramountcy carried with it the right of interference. The cherisher of princes could insist on good behaviour in a way that the Company with its aloof disdain could not. The influence of the resident was now actively exercised in promoting good government. Princely maladministration became an imperial concern as it had not generally been before to be visited, not by annexation but by periods of British administration. Princes were encouraged to interest themselves in affairs around them and to throw their states open to western influences by such measures as the building of roads and railways and the promotion of education and modern industries. A first step was thus taken in the integration of princely British-India; if the process appeared to halt half-way after a promising beginning it was not the fault of the beginning itself. From being a collection of isolated potentates the princes became an order with a stake in the new régime.

The Bengal army had to be reorganized from the bottom. Some 120,000 out of 128,000 Indians in the Bengal army had been involved in the Mutiny and had been killed or scattered. There were left eleven regiments which had not mutinied, some remnants of others, some irregular corps, and the Company's European troops, which numbered about 16,000. The Bengal army had thus virtually disappeared. On the other hand the form of organization in three presidency armies had helped to prevent the spread of the mutiny to the south, because each army had developed its own traditions and *esprit de corps*. Questions of caste did not weigh heavily with the Bombay sepoy and the outlook of the Madrasi was quite different to that of the up-country Brahman. The existing form of organization into three presidency armies was therefore retained, in spite of its anomaly in a centrally organized India. It was not until 1895 that the three forces became the unified Indian army under a single commander-in-chief, separate 'commands' replacing the old independent 'armies'.

The first problem of reorganization was the fate of the Company's European troops. With the passing of the Company's rule they automatically passed under the Crown. They need not, for that reason, have been disbanded, and Canning desired to retain a local European army. But he was overruled by the home government which decided on complete amalgamation. All ranks were offered service on the new terms, but these aroused discontent because many men had acquired domestic ties in India which transfer to England might break and the officers thought they would not be so well off in the royal regiments. What was rather imaginatively termed the last white mutiny was allayed by the grant of bounties to the 10,000 men who took their discharge and the offer of service with Indian regiments to the officers.

The Indian portion was re-formed on new principles. Before the Mutiny there had been about 238,000 Indian troops to 45,000 Europeans in all three presidencies. The proportion of Indian to European was now fixed at fifty-fifty in the Bengal army and two to one in the other two. When the reorganization was complete in 1863 the Indian troops numbered 140,000 and the Europeans 65,000. The spirit of caution was further shown by the disbandment of the Indian artillery (except for a few mountain batteries) which had proved so formidable in the hands of the mutineers. There were those who advocated a return of the 'mixed' system of regiments in use in the eighteenth century, whereby each regiment contained men of all classes. But neither the spirit of tradition or prophecy prevailed; instead the 'class' system of community regiments was adopted and lasted for the rest of the period. Two Indian battalions were brigaded with one European so that no important station would be without its European complement of troops. As before Indian regiments continued to be officered by Europeans. A change was also made in the proportion of classes recruited. The number of Rajputs and Brahmans from the United Provinces was reduced and that of Gurkhas, Sikhs, and Panjabis increased. This process was extended later in favour of the martial races of the north-west and in preference to those in the south. From 1893 Pathan, Sikh, and Panjabi units were increased at the expense of the south; by 1910 only thirteen battalions were recruited from the Madras Presidency.[1] There was no need, it is true, to maintain large forces in the south and northerners were better fitted to defend the northern passes. The effect was to make the army less representative in its composition, if not less national, and to emphasize both its professional aloofness from the life of the country and the martial character of the Panjab.

The Mutiny crisis necessarily brought to a halt the programme of social and material improvement which Dalhousie had pursued so energetically. But it was only for a moment and there was no more basis in Canning's time for John Bright's description in 1862 of British rule as 'a hundred years of crime against the docile natives of India' than there had been from the time of Lord William Bentinck onwards. The development of education as a result of Sir Charles Wood's dispatch of 1854 went forward with hardly a break. The first three Indian universities of Calcutta, Madras, and Bombay were founded while the Mutiny was actually in progress, and the rapid expansion of private colleges as a result of the grant-in-aid system began soon after. Public works, which added to the security of the country, had immediate priority and of these railways were the chief. There is no doubt that the great expansion in railway construction in the sixties was directly stimulated by the crisis and as such was one of its main compensations. The railway network has proved to be the nervous system of modern India. In 1859 and 1860 disturbances between European indigo planters and the Bengal peasants enabled Canning with home support to correct a system by which the cultivator was often compelled to grow indigo against both his will and his interests. By his efforts to organize relief during the north Indian famine of 1861 Canning foreshadowed the later development of the great Famine Code. The mortality of the most affected districts was estimated at less than 10 per cent. instead of the third or half of the population in the great famines of the eighteenth century. Finally the great law reform, which had been in progress since the passing of the Charter Act of 1833, reached completion. The Penal Code, the work of the Law Commission commenced

[1] In 1857 the number was 41.

under the lead of Macaulay, was enacted in 1860 and was followed by the Code of Criminal Procedure in the following year. Along with some reorganization of the law courts and the judges, a proportion of whom were to be members of the Indian civil service,[1] these codes form the basis of the Indian legal system today.

For all his lack of brilliance and periodical misjudgements, Canning not only weathered the storm of the Mutiny but achieved the even more difficult feat of weathering the peace. Along with John Lawrence he did more than anyone to reconcile the Indian people with the government and to convince them that welfare and not vengeance or police rule was its larger aim. His resolute stand against Calcutta cries for vengeance and his disregard of abuse gave to Indian eyes in Lord Elgin's words 'to acts which carried justice to the verge of severity the grace of clemency'. In the abstract and in the light of after events Canning could have well been more clement, but in the setting of his times his actions marked high moral courage and great tenacity of purpose. The administration was reorganized and tentative steps taken to bring it into closer touch with the people. The princes were rewarded, reconciled, and reassured as to their future. Only in the case of the new class of westernized Indian was nothing done to mark their loyalty by associating them more closely with the administration which had called them into existence and with whose future their fortunes were linked. Their attachment was taken for granted and they were in fact hardly thought of. But as in the case of the liberals and nationalists at the Vienna settlement it was with them that the future lay. The new government had restored the situation; its motto may be described as one of paternal efficiency. But every restoration conceals some change. In this case the change was one from the dynamic view looking to eventual self-government by a westernized India prevalent in the thirties, to a static view of watchful and solicitous parental care without any large hope of development. Material progress there was to be, and there was never an explicit denial of the larger aim. But there was an implicit understanding that self-government was a matter for future ages if at all. Even Dalhousie had cherished the earlier ideal, but the British now settled down to an imperial stewardship amongst an inexplicable people which was not to experience its first doubts until the eighties or to be seriously modified until the first World War had come upon them. The pride of achievement remained but the hope of Indian freedom lay dormant.

AUTHORITIES

For Canning himself there is only H. S. CUNNINGHAM's little book at present. It is hoped that a work based on his private papers may soon be forthcoming. For concise treatment of reorganization the *Cambridge History of India*, vol. vi, which is strong on the administrative side, may be consulted in chaps. xi, xii, xix-xxii. The *Gazetteer of India*, vols. iii and iv, are also useful. The constitutional side is dealt

[1] By the Indian High Courts Act of 1861.

with by Sir C. ILBERT, *The Government of India, a Historical Survey* (1922) and A. BERRIEDALE KEITH, *Constitutional History of India* (1937). Mill's defence of the East India Company will be found in the *Parliamentary Papers* for 1857–8, vol. xliii. He also deals with the subject in his *Responsible Government* (ed. Oxford 1946). See also A. WEST, *Sir Charles Wood's Administration . . . 1859–66* (1867) and Sir J. STRACHEY; *India, its administration* (1911).

RECENT PUBLICATION

M. MACLAGAN's *Clemency Canning* (1962) is again valuable.

CHAPTER 2

The Political Thread—Elgin to Elgin

THE period between the retirement of Lord Canning and that of Lord Curzon is usually regarded as the high noon of the British imperial power in India. There is much truth in this view for thereafter its power was never wholly uncontested or its prospects unclouded. For the first half of the period British rule was not even questioned. The old states had passed into obscurity, the old order had made its passionate convulsive protest and lay inert and resourceless; the new order beginning to emerge was recognized by only a few discerning spirits and its significance under-estimated by many of them. There was no one left to offer a serious challenge to the British power and the British were now on their guard against provoking fresh outbursts of wounded popular sentiment. Efficiency and order, benevolence and development, were the keynotes of the first half of the period. The politics of the north-west, the control of the frontiers, the development of welfare measures like education, irrigation, and prevention of famine were the topics of the day. The apotheosis of this period was the proclamation of the queen as Empress of India in 1876. Yet what the British power gained in stability and pomp it was losing in organic vitality and purpose. The government of India was increasingly regarded as a white man's burden rather than as a call to creative effort or the preparation for a new era. The exhilaration which Wellesley's young men had experienced in setting in order previously unknown and desolated regions and the sober but large hopes of these same men in later life had faded, and so had the rather naïve expectations of the reformers of Bentinck's time. The pride of conquest which had succeeded in the forties had led to disillusionment; the moral earnestness of the Panjab school was fortified by duty rather than by hope. India had not responded to the magic wand from the West; the thought of any response on a large scale was relegated to the distant and incalculable future. By 1880 Lord Northbrook, a very cautious Whig, could complain that hardly anyone in India could bring himself to believe any Indian to be capable of responsibility. Twenty-five years before Dalhousie himself was proposing the appointment of an Indian as one of the new legislative councillors. With vision and hope laid aside there remained the task of keeping order and dealing justice, of devising improving measures and exercising fostering care. In many ways it was a satisfying work, but it lacked the inspiring and exciting flavours of earlier periods and it bred a different type of official. Thus the sixties and seventies, though prosperous and materially creative, were spiritually somewhat barren.

In the second half of the period, though the same general conditions prevailed, there was a perceptible change in the atmosphere. Democratic liberalism had received a fresh impetus from the radicalism of Chamberlain and the moral fervour of Gladstone. Conscience and political principle united to direct fresh attention to India and revive almost forgotten dreams of political freedom. But while this new current of thought existed and made its impact on India before 1900 it was a minority opinion in both countries. Gladstonian liberalism went into eclipse for twenty years with the defeat of home rule and the new ideas had not more than a scanty following amongst officials in India itself. The viceregal backing which obtained under Bentinck was lacking except for a time under Ripon, and there was never a 'pressure group' of young civilians such as that constituted by Charles Trevelyan, Macaulay, and their friends.

It is important to remember that the close connexion between English thought and action in India not only continued but was strengthened during this period. With the closing of Haileybury College there was less community of outlook amongst the young civilians actually coming to the country. But there was a tighter control of policy at the top, and a quicker transmission of ideas. The telegraph was nearly as fatal to the independence of the Viceroy as it was to the prospects of the mutineers. No Dalhousie could annex a Panjab again without reference to the home authorities on the plea of the necessity for a quick decision. The opening of the Suez Canal in 1869 quickened the flow of ideas both by enabling literature to move more freely to India and by encouraging Europeans to more frequent resort to India. Thus the influence of English ideas continued to be the main factor in the formation of basic policy with the difference that local experience on the whole was less powerful to modify or to hinder. The influence of English ideas of property was revealed in the Permanent Settlement which Indian experience only partially modified. Utilitarian ideas of rent played an important part in the settlement of the north-west and ideas of western efficiency dictated the annexation policy. Foreign policy was controlled more from London than from Calcutta and education, and indeed all philanthropic measures, were wholly western in inspiration. On the whole the advocates of the Indian point of view, whether as defenders of suttee or champions of princely rights, fought a losing battle. English policy during this time was mainly a reflection of London opinion with the Viceroy tending increasingly to become the cabinet's executive agent. Only towards its close did Indian opinion begin to make its first modest but significant contributions. And then it was not *traditional* Indian opinion so much as sunburnt Gladstonianism.

Lord Canning, like Dalhousie, wore himself out in the public service and returned home only to die. His reward was to lie with his father in Westminster Abbey. His successor was one of those imperial handymen of whom Lord Macartney (of China fame) was the first

Indian example, Lord Lansdowne perhaps the most conspicuous and Lord Willingdon the last. He was Governor of Jamaica at the age of thirty-one and as Governor-General of Canada in succession to Metcalfe did much to establish parliamentary government by the quiet creation of constitutional precedent. His record in the second China war was more contentious, but it was while on his way thither in 1857 that he showed his power of decision by diverting his whole force to India on receiving Canning's call for help. Elgin was able, independent, and cautious, but his career was cut short by death at Dharmsala after only twenty months of office. In retrospect his term may be said to have continued Canning's régime as Metcalfe continued Bentinck's. The chief event of his time was the Ambela campaign against *Wakhabi* fanatics on the fringes of the Hindu Kush to the west of the Indus. The surprise of Elgin's death forestalled the usual political manœuvres for office and the fact that the Ambela campaign was still in suspense induced the home authorities to look favourably on Indian experience as a qualification. In these circumstances Sir John Lawrence was an obvious choice and he joined Warren Hastings, Shore, and Barlow in the group of 'official' Governor-Generals.

Sir John Lawrence was then fifty-two and of Indian reputation and experience. His labours had transformed an always forceful into a rugged and rather obstinate personality; in the words of P. E. Roberts he was masterful, somewhat obstinate in temperament, and 'exacting in his relations with his subordinates, though, if they did him good service, he loyally supported them'. Men expected action on Panjab lines, but Lawrence considered that tranquillity was the need of the moment. He concentrated on internal development while insisting on external caution. In administration he disappointed where he was expected to excel through over-attention to detail; in policy he excelled where less was expected by a Bismarckian ability to combine moderation with strength.

In essence the rule of Lawrence was a continuation of the Canning period, but it was a continuation clearly marked with the Lawrence stamp. The policy of public works, particularly of railways and irrigation, was pushed forward with vigour. He introduced into Indian finance the principle of raising money for productive works by loan, but even so the annual expenditure rose by nearly £10 million or nearly 20 per cent.[1] The fact that the definition of a productive work had later to be more finely drawn cannot obscure the importance of the decision itself or the courage required to make it. His special care for the peasantry was shown by the passing of Panjab and Oudh Tenancy Acts of 1868, which were essentially the sequels of Canning's Bengal Tenancy Act of 1859. The Panjab Act gave occupancy rights to all tenants who had held land for a specified period and became 'the bulwark and charter of a contented peasantry'. The Oudh Act gave to the

[1] From £45½ million to £54½ million. In the circumstances a net deficit of £2½ million over five years cannot be regarded as ruinous.

cultivator something of the security which Canning and Montgomery had given to the *taluqdars*. One-fifth of the peasants were given occupancy rights at fair rents, allowance for improvements was made, and equitable control of rent rates attempted. This measure was carried through in the teeth of opposition from vested interests and was perhaps the most constructive achievement of the viceroyalty. Two famines visited India during Lawrence's term. The first in Orissa in 1866 cost nearly a million lives owing to the great difficulties of communications, the failure of the Bengal government to take adequate action, and Lawrence's failure to override them in time. The second, in Rajputana and Bundelkhand in 1868-9, found him better prepared and was notable for the enunciation of the principle that the prevention of starvation must be the supreme guide to official action.

In external relations Lawrence maintained Dalhousie's policy of non-intervention. The circumstances of Dost Muhammad's death in 1863 and a prolonged struggle for the succession and of Russian encroachment on the central Asian Khanates made this attitude controversial. As in the case of Canning an epithet coined in derision became a hallmark of distinction; the 'masterly inactivity' which was taken for political myopia or obstinacy was proved by later events to have been true foresight. Rarely has a statesman been so completely and quickly vindicated by time as Lawrence was in Afghanistan.

On Lawrence's retirement Disraeli appointed his Chief Secretary for Ireland, Lord Mayo, then aged forty-six. The appointment was thus a party one, and could have been cancelled by the Liberals who came into office before he sailed. Gladstone's restraint in not following the precedent of the Melbourne Whigs in the case of Lord Heytesbury in 1835 confirmed the bipartisan nature of Indian government. Mayo's appointment was a characteristic Disraelian leap in the dark to many but the greatness of the opportunity revealed the extent of his talents. His ability and industry were adorned with charm to make his government one of the most successful in the series.

Mayo had first to deal with the financial deficit left by Lawrence. This he achieved with the help of the Strachey brothers by increasing the salt duty and income tax and by enforcing economies. The changes culminated in the substitution of fixed block grants over a period of five years to the provincial governments for annual grants earmarked for special purposes. An incentive was thus provided for economy since savings in one department or year could be used in another instead of reverting to the central exchequer. As a result 'he found a serious deficit and left a substantial surplus; he found estimates habitually untrustworthy, he left them thoroughly worthy of confidence'. He showed his imagination by increasing the powers of the town committees permitted by the Act of 1850, and thus taking an important step in developing local self-government, and by founding the first college at Ajmir for the education of chiefs and nobles. It was the beginning of princely reforms by persuasion, and the logical corollary of the recognition of the princes as an integral part of the empire.

Abroad Mayo continued the established policy of non-intervention. He exercised his charm in the friendly management of Sher Ali at the meeting at Ambala in 1869 and afterwards and in helping to secure Russian recognition of the Oxus as the northern Afghan frontier.

Mayo's government promised to rise from distinction to brilliance when it was cut short by the dagger of a Pathan fanatic at the conclusion of a visit to the Andamans in February 1872. Gladstone appointed as his successor Lord Northbrook, the head of the banking Baring family and at the time Under-Secretary for War. Able, unexpensive and shrewd, he may be described as the business man in the viceregal chair. He had all the qualities needful save the personal magnetism of his predecessor, of which his régime was essentially a less inspired continuation. India was prosperous save for one year of famine and overseas trade was increasing with the opening of the Suez Canal. Though a Liberal he was no doctrinaire free trader and he resisted the reduction of tariff duties below a general level of 5 per cent. on the ground of the special circumstances of India. Though he lacked the imagination to encourage the setting up of rural municipalities in Bengal he realized the danger of allowing Lancashire trading interests to appear to override those of India. His careful measures prevented serious famine in Bengal and Bihar in 1873-4 and he dealt firmly though not dexterously with the Gaekwar of Baroda's alleged attempt to poison his resident.

The return of the Conservatives to power under Disraeli in 1874 marked the beginning of a period when Indian affairs re-entered for a time the orbit of British party politics. The two parties had increasingly different conceptions of Indian policy and Viceroys were shuffled accordingly. They differed primarily on foreign affairs in relation to Afghanistan and Russia and secondarily on the question of the introduction of western institutions. New radicals wished to go further than old Whig relished or old Tory would allow. Northbrook was left undisturbed by the incoming Conservatives but rifts soon developed on the subject of further tariff reductions and Lord Salisbury's proposals for sending an envoy to Kabul. Northbrook resigned a year before his time without waiting for recall. The new Viceroy, Lord Lytton, was the avowed agent of Disraeli and Salisbury. Talented and handsome, witty of speech and bohemian in habit, with something of the literary flair of his novelist father, he hid his fundamental seriousness beneath a cloak of nonchalance which many mistook for frivolity. He had the knack, by speech even more than by action, of arousing Gladstonian moral indignation and came to be regarded as an evil only less than that of his greater chief. He began under suspicion and ended under a cloud. For all that he accomplished much and succeeded in importing some refreshing imagination into Indian policy-making and some unconventionality into the social purlieus of Simla.

Lytton's Afghan policy, which shadowed his name most deeply, will be dealt with separately, but it was in fact only one facet of an eventful government. His first problem was the prolonged famine of 1876–8 which cost the lives of more than 5 million people in British India alone. Some of his methods were criticized, but he showed his grasp and imagination by the appointment of the Famine Commission under Richard Strachey which proved the precursor of the great Famine Code. In finance he called Sir John Strachey from the north-west provinces and with his help evened out the salt duties, thus making the great customs cactus hedges unnecessary, and reduced other inland duties. In this field also he ran into controversy by abolishing, under direction from London, the customs duty on the coarser kinds of cotton cloth. This draught of the pure milk of free trade was thought by the nascent Indian opinion and many officials to be really Lancashire's tit-for-tat against the rising Bombay cotton industry. Lytton's imagination was shown in the establishment of the statutory civil service of nominated Indians to whom one-sixth of the posts hitherto reserved for the covenanted service were to be thrown open. This was the first serious attempt to fulfil the promise of the Charter Act of 1833 repeated by the Royal Proclamation of 1858. He also proposed an Indian peerage and privy council to match the queen's assumption of the imperial title. Less imaginative but almost equally abortive was the Vernacular Press Act of 1878, which imposed restrictions on the vernacular press not applied to the English. Though some Indian papers were already published in English the hand of racial discrimination was detected by the rising and sensitive westernized class.

When Gladstone returned to power in 1880 Lytton resigned without waiting for recall. He must be accounted as a brilliant failure even apart from the Afghan policy, for though his imagination taught him the importance of sentiment, it failed to show him how to use it. His actions widened the gulf between British and Indian for they aroused distrust where they were meant to impress or to soothe. The severe but genuine paternalism of Lawrence, made genial and friendly by Mayo and remaining sincere though frigid under Northbrook, died away under Lytton to be replaced, in the ears of the Indian public, by the jingling of spurs and tramp of jack-boots. The paternalist had become an alien public authority. Lytton's successor, Lord Ripon, was a man of entirely different stamp. Industrious and able, with a deep moral earnestness,[1] he was staid and uninspiring; the impression he made was due to his moral rather than his personal qualities. Nevertheless he was the first man of major cabinet rank to be appointed since Canning and he came, like Lytton, with a mission. He was a convinced Liberal of the forward school and may be described as Gladstone's agent in India as Lytton was Disraeli's. But whereas Lytton outran his master's wishes Ripon lacked the strength to keep pace with Glad-

[1] It required both conviction and courage at that time for a public man to declare himself a Roman Catholic, as Ripon did in 1873.

PLATE 33

a. The Residency, Delhi

b. Dilkusha, near Delhi

PLATE 34

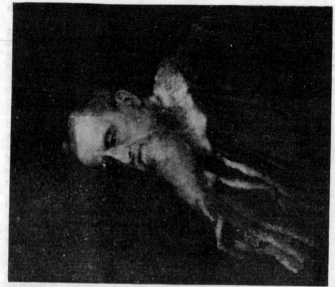

b. Lord Ripon

a. John Lawrence

stone's. The fault of Lytton was that he insisted too much, of Ripon that he persisted too little.

Gladstone considered it to be 'our weakness and our calamity' that 'we have not been able to give to India the benefits and blessings of free institutions'. Ripon set out with the intention of making a beginning in that direction. In doing so he had to encounter the hostility of the commercial Europeans, the fears of officials 'who have strongly ingrained in their minds . . . that no one but an Englishman can do anything'. It was the beginning of the change from paternalism to partnership and such changes are notoriously difficult. Ripon succeeded in creating representative local government boards in districts and *tahsils* and in largely extending municipal committees. But his attempt in the Ilbert Bill to enable Indian sessions judges to try Europeans,[1] a practice already permitted in the presidency towns, raised a storm of non-official European protest which received much covert sympathy within the services. After much ill feeling had been aroused Ripon bowed to the storm by agreeing that Europeans might claim a jury, half of whom would be Europeans. In trying to remove one racial distinction he thus succeeded in creating another one; neither party was satisfied and the racial cleavage he had come to close was wider at his departure than on his arrival. But if Ripon's conduct in this matter was not impressive, his general attitude was of the highest importance. The new Indian middle class felt that though the administration was against it, a tide of opinion in Britain was on their side, as they had not felt under Lytton. The dull resentment against Lytton was replaced by hope for the future as well as by admiration for Ripon himself. The fruit of this hope was the Indian National Congress. Ripon's real significance to India was that his failure even more than his successes caused the precipitation in political form of the new Indian westernizing movement. Indians would now oppose government but in the name of western principles; they would demand self-government, but in the forms of western institutions. To the British the new movement had given notice of its existence; it might be belittled, but its existence could no longer be denied.

Other aspects of Ripon's rule have been obscured by the drama of the Ilbert controversy. Ripon behaved as an orthodox Liberal should. He reduced the salt tax and removed the last protective duties; he repealed Lytton's Vernacular Press Act and encouraged the development of primary and secondary schools; he restored Mysore to its raja on his coming of age in 1881 and he made a modest beginning with factory legislation. As an administrator he may be called a tepid Dalhousie as in politics he was a timid Gladstone. But whether timid or tepid, he should not be assessed merely on his shortcomings. By carrying the Liberal spirit to India he began the transition from paternalism to partnership which culminated in 1947. His rule must therefore rank in

[1] In 1873 it had been enacted that a British European subject could only be tried by a European magistrate or sessions judge.

importance with that of Canning, Dalhousie, Bentinck, and Wellesley, even though his personality may have been less arresting than theirs.

When Ripon retired in December 1884, amid unexampled expressions of Indian goodwill, Gladstone's second ministry was staggering towards its fall. It was a time for consolidation rather than forward moves. Ripon's successor Lord Dufferin, was a distinguished member of the regiment of imperial handymen, well fitted by his tact and suavity to assuage the bitter feelings aroused by the Ilbert controversy, and by diplomatic experience and personal distinction to head the Indian government. Few Viceroys have so exactly fulfilled expectations and gone so little beyond them. A diplomatist rather than an administrator or politician his rule might be described as an imperial embassy rather than an orthodox government and in this sense it was highly successful. His main preoccupation was with external affairs where he dealt with the Panjdeh incident of 1885 in Afghanistan and annexed upper Burma in 1886. In India he gave a cautious countenance to the National Congress while not reopening the Ilbert question, and equally cautiously prepared for constitutional reform. He used the new confidence and loyalty of the princes to set up the Imperial Service Corps, state forces available for service overseas. Perhaps even more significant than this proof of princely contentment was the fact that the new corps were officered by Indians and only inspected by British commanders. In a sense they formed the cradle of the modern Indian army. Dufferin's liberalism was shown in three Tenancy Acts, affecting Bengal, Oudh, and the Panjab, which carried previous attempts to protect tenants a stage further.

Lord Dufferin's term covered the home rule crisis in England and saw Lord Salisbury firmly in power at the head of a Unionist ministry. A new wind now began to blow in the British outlook on Indian affairs. The rift in principles of policy narrowed again to differences of expediency, a process helped by the spread of imperialism within the Liberal ranks and the moderation of successive Salisbury governments. Dufferin found no difficulty in working with the new government and on his retirement was given the embassy at Rome. His successor was another imperial handyman in the person of Lord Lansdowne, who had already been Governor-General of Canada and was to become a distinguished Foreign Secretary and deputy-leader of the Conservative party. He was one of the last of the great aristocratic Whigs to whom public duty was a natural vocation, reserve and discretion a second nature. So complete was the mask of quality that it is not easy to perceive the real man behind the veil of classic poise. Without the charm of Mayo or urbanity of Dufferin, the brittle brilliance of Lytton or the moral earnestness of Ripon he was as able but more agreeable than Northbrook and as influential as Ripon. A great gentleman presided over the land, treating men and things alike in the grand manner with courtesy, dignity, and detachment.

The restored continuity in Indian party policy was shown by the completion, under Lansdowne, of a modest constitutional reform proposed by the Liberal Dufferin.[1] It was Riponism in a minor key. Its details are described elsewhere but its significance lay in the introduction of virtual election for the return of certain Indian members to the Legislative Council and the enlargement of the council's powers to include a discussion on the annual budget. It amounted to a careful revival of Dalhousie's little Parliament on a broader basis. The value of the elective principle, hedged about as it was, lay in providing the first opportunity for the new India to take part in the central Indian government. This was the arena of G. K. Gokhale a few years later. Lansdowne's other internal concern was the fall in the exchange value of the rupee, which fell from about 2s. in 1870 to its lowest point of 1s. 1d. in 1891. This occurred from 1873 owing to the demonetization of silver in Germany and the Latin union. The value of silver declined relative to gold and this hit India hard because she was indebted to a gold standard country in Britain. Exports were stimulated but the cost of imports was ruinous. Before the fall was finally checked in 1895 the income tax had been reimposed and the salt tax enhanced. The rest of Lansdowne's attention was devoted to Afghan and frontier questions which are dealt with separately.

Lansdowne retired during Gladstone's brief fourth ministry. The ministry was divided and no one was anxious to undertake an office with little chance of backing from home and no mandate to fulfil. Lord Cromer declined the Viceroyalty and Sir H. Norman retired after accepting, on grounds of age. Thus the mantle fell on Lord Elgin, who could claim that his father had been Viceroy before him. For two more years the calm induced by Lord Dufferin continued. Then India was struck by plague and famine. Large portions of south, central, and northern India were stricken with famine; but though the famine was on the largest scale the new methods limited deaths to three-quarters of a million, chiefly in areas like the Central Provinces where communications were still primitive. Bubonic plague, which devastated Europe as the Black Death in the fourteenth century and London in 1665 as the Plague, spread across China in the nineties and came from Hong Kong to Bombay in 1896. Jahangir accurately described the symptoms in 1616, but since then there had been no large outbreak. The efforts to prevent the spread of the disease disturbed orthodox sentiment and lead to rioting. It was at this time that B. G. Tilak became prominent. Since that time the disease has been endemic in India but has not again attained such alarming proportions.

In the thirty-six years from 1862 to 1898 we can see the government of India passing through the phase of paternalism, incipient imperialism, and dictatorship, and tentative moves towards partnership. The dominant thread is the paternal one; at the end of the period the government could be described as paternalism tempered by consultation. In the economic field India was subjected to the whole free trade

[1] The Indian Councils Act of 1892.

gospel and experienced the evil as well as the good effects of her entry into world markets. Unobtrusively but steadily she was building up modern industries. Above all, beneath the imposing façade of imperial rule the ferment within Indian society was developing apace, and had reached the point when it had assumed a visible political shape.

AUTHORITIES

P. E. ROBERTS in his *History* gives a good political summary of this period. A most acute study is by H. H. DODWELL, *A Sketch of the History of India 1858–1918* (1925). E. THOMPSON and G. T. GARRATT, *British Rule in India* (1934) deal well with the effects of the Mutiny and show awareness of new trends. A. B. RUDRA, *The Viceroy and Governor-General of India* (1940), is a study of the Viceroy's position.

There are studies of many of the leading figures of this period of which the following may be mentioned: R. SMITH, *Life of Lord Lawrence* (2 vols., 1883), D. PAL, *The Administration of Sir J. Lawrence in India 1864–69* (1952), and Sir C. AITCHESON's study; Sir W. W. HUNTER, *Life of Lord Mayo* (2 vols., 1876) and a study in the Rulers of India Series; B. MALLET, *Northbrook, a Memoir* (1908), B. BALFOUR, *Lord Lytton's Indian Administration* (1899), Lady G. CECIL, *Life of Lord Salisbury*, vols. i and ii (1921), S. GOPAL, *Viceroyalty of Lord Ripon* (1953), Sir A. LYALL, *Life of Lord Dufferin* (1905), Sir G. W. FORREST, *The Administration of Lord Lansdowne* (1894); Sir G. CHESNEY, *Indian Policy* (1870).

RECENT PUBLICATIONS

S. GOPAL's *British Policy in India, 1858–1905* (Cambridge, 1965) is a valuable general survey. Vol IV, *The Evolution of India and Pakistan, 1858–1947*, edited by C. H. PHILIPS *et al.* (1962) of the series *Select Documents on the History of India and Pakistan*, is an invaluable source book. See also B. B. MISRA, *The Bureaucracy in India* (New Delhi, 1976).

CHAPTER 3

Foreign and Frontier Policy 1862–98

The North-West. The post-Mutiny period saw certain changes in the general geopolitical situation which were the determining causes of both the second Afghan and third Burman wars. After 1857, as before, two of the three prerequisites of Indian security were satisfied. Britain continued to control the sea and the East Indies continued to be controlled by the virtual British auxiliaries, the Dutch. They were, indeed, extending their direct control over the outer East Indian islands, and to that extent making security more secure. But both East and West a change was creeping over the general situation. The eastern change was brought about by the appearance of France. The western change was the more important and will be dealt with first. To the north-west of India security has been historically best achieved by a balance between a strong Indian and a strong Iranian power. India has never in fact controlled the whole Iranian plateau; a strong power there has therefore proved a source of security because it held in check the potential power of central Asia. The traditional cradle of empires may be described as a reservoir of power whose human springs have periodically gushed forth floods, unpredictable in their appearance and uncertain in their force. It was clearly to the interest of India, provided that she herself possessed a strong centre of power, to have as a north-western neighbour a power capable of stemming any ordinary overflow from the central Asian reservoir. With the fall of the Safavids and the death of Nadir Shah in Iran and the collapse of the Mughuls in India this condition ceased to be fulfilled; and when the British reintegrated the Indian empire by 1818 they found confronting them beyond the Indus a distracted Afghanistan and a still weak Persia under the Kajar dynasty. Beyond lay Russia. But her time was not yet. In the twenties and thirties she turned south-west towards Turkey and Constantinople and was sufficiently met by Palmerstonian diplomacy. Between her and the Afghans lay the central Asian Khanates. They were the reason that Auckland's failure to control Afghanistan had no untoward results on the security of India. There was no one as yet to take advantage of it. Russia's eyes were still set on Constantinople. In 1844 she agreed with Britain to regard the central Asian Khanates as a neutral zone between the two empires, thus leaving the Indian government free 'to repair the wire' to Dost Muhammad with the Dost inclined to assist in the process. In these circumstances Persia was in no position to be aggressive while Britain had neither the will nor power (with the Afghans in between) to subjugate Persia. When Persia seized Herat from its local ruler in 1856 she was quickly induced to retire by Outram's expedition to the Persian Gulf. During these years the Iranian power problem was not solved, but remained in abeyance.

Such a situation could not last and was in fact ended by the Crimean war of 1854-6. The Russian advance towards Constantinople was again checked, but at the same time the understanding over the Khanates was broken. This is the beginning of the second phase of Indian north-western policy during the nineteenth century. In surveying this period there are two considerations which should be borne in mind. The first is that the control of Indian foreign policy was far closer than in the earlier period. From the time that the Red Sea cable was laid in 1870 there was little independent action by Calcutta save for a short period under Lytton and to some extent by Curzon, until Hardinge could write in 1907, 'recently we have left the Government of India entirely out of our account'. The second is that the London cabinet had always in mind, in dealing with Russia, the situation in Europe and the Near East as well as in the Middle East and in central Asia.

Russia could give no help to Persia in 1856 because of her recent defeat in the Crimea. But the Mutiny suggested that Britain was not so strong in India as she had been supposed to be. Thereafter Russia returned to her traditional policy of moving in a direction where resistance was not likely to be great when baulked in her designs elsewhere. The sixties, which were years of recovery, internal reform, and diplomatic quiescence in Europe, saw the beginning of her advance in Asia. In short, she began to move into the central Asian reservoir. The internal springs of that reservoir were drying up, not so much from internal rottenness as from poverty and depopulation induced by the physical desiccation of the region. The Khanates, without modern sources of knowledge or power, were suffering from a creeping paralysis for which there was no remedy. That is why the Tartar Khans, who had once overspread Russia itself, fell easy victims in their turn in the latter part of the nineteenth century. In 1866 Bokhara became a dependent ally; in 1868 Samarkand was acquired and in 1873 Khiva followed. A new province of Russian Turkistan was formed and the Russian base moved a thousand miles from Orenburg to Tashkend. Only Merv now remained between north-eastern Afghanistan with Herat and the Russian empire.

It is now time to turn to Afghan affairs. In the absence of Russian interference the policy of non-intervention begun by Lord Ellenborough had borne good fruit. Dost Muhammad, not yet master of Herat, was glad to have British neutrality and hoped for British support against Persia. Dalhousie concluded a treaty of friendship in 1855 and help was given in the Herat incident. The Dost refrained from taking Peshawar during the Mutiny; he finally captured Herat in 1863 and died a few days later at the age of eighty. There followed a war of succession in the Mughul style but complicated by the fact that the

Dost had sixteen sons instead of the Mughul's usual three or four. John Lawrence resolutely refused to interfere; his policy was described with equal warmth by friends and critics as 'masterly inactivity', but it was in fact only a rather frigid continuation of the existing policy of non-interference. Lawrence saw in each claimant a turbulent *sardar* and found it difficult to disguise his general disapproval of all chiefs. When in 1868 Sher Ali finally defeated his rivals, he was duly recognized as Amir. He had already been provided with a subsidy as soon as his rivals appealed to Persia and Russia for help. Lord Mayo added warmth to Lawrence's correctitude and so wrought on Sher Ali at his Ambala interview in 1869 that the Amir passed on to him the letters that began to arrive from 1870 onwards from the Russian Governor-General Kauffmann. The complement of the non-interference policy was in Lawrence's eyes an understanding with Russia about the integrity of Afghanistan. The Russian advance in Turkistan and the concern which it gave the Amir provided a fresh opportunity. The first Gladstone ministry secured Russian recognition of Sher Ali's possessions south of the Oxus in 1869 and acceptance of his control over Badakshan in 1873.

If the European situation had remained stable this understanding might have settled the Afghan question for many years. But affairs in Europe did not remain static and soon gave to the Russian advance and usual policy of pinpricks a deeper significance. Sher Ali, alarmed by the steady Russian approach, sent an envoy to Simla on the morrow of the fall of Khiva in 1873 to ask for a closer alliance. But Northbrook could offer no more than Mayo's vague promises and henceforth Sher Ali thought it politic to be less frigid towards Russian advances and assurances. Events now moved rapidly. In 1874 Disraeli became prime minister with Lord Salisbury as Secretary of State. In 1875 revolt broke out in the European provinces of Turkey. In 1876 Russia took up the cause of the rebels and moved forward once more. At the beginning of 1878 she was at the gates of Constantinople dictating a peace which would have made her mistress of the Balkans through an inflated but puppet Bulgaria. Britain insisted on revision at the risk of war, succeeding, through Bismarck's intervention, at the Congress of Berlin. The Conservative leaders were deeply suspicious of Russian intentions and therefore viewed her central Asian proceedings with critical eyes. They had in mind both the protection of Afghanistan from Russian attack and a threat through Afghanistan on Russian central Asia as a means of pressure on Russia in Europe. From 1876 they had as their agent in India Lord Lytton, who possessed a schoolboy zest and was to prove 'plus royaliste que le roi'.

The method adopted to further these ends was to put pressure on Sher Ali rather than on Russia direct. Salisbury suggested in early 1875 the dispatch of a British envoy to Kabul with a simultaneous strengthening of Indian forces on the frontier. Northbrook demurred and on the proposal being repeated as an instruction, retired early in the next year. With Lytton's arrival the proposal was made to the Amir and the occupation of Quetta was secured by treaty with the Khan of Kalat in 1876. On his side the Amir was determined to accept no British resident. The unhappy precedent of his father's time was before him, and in any case it was the general belief in the East that the advent of a British resident at a durbar commonly foreshadowed the end of its independence. He feared the British in refusing and his own subjects in accepting. He was between two fires. Early in 1877 he finally declined the British embassy. But as the crisis in Europe deepened the Russians became more pressing and in July 1878 the Russian General Stolietoff arrived without resistance in Kabul, just as the Congress of Berlin ended. With the Berlin settlement just concluded the proper reply would have been to demand the withdrawal of Stolietoff directly from St. Petersburg. Instead Lytton was allowed to announce the dispatch of a British envoy. From this point control of events virtually passed from London to their impetuous Indian agent because his restraint would have involved a cabinet crisis which the government could not afford to face.

The repulse of the envoy (Sir Neville Chamberlain) at Ali Masjid was followed by invasion. The usual successes brought about the flight of Sher Ali in ominous repetition of the events of 1839. Too late he discovered that the Russians had no help to give. Sher Ali died early in the following year and peace was made by the treaty of Gandamak with his son Yakub in May 1879. Once more brilliant success proved but the descent to the valley of disappointment. By the treaty Kurram, Pishin, and Sibi were assigned to British control, a resident was established at Kabul with agents elsewhere, and the Amir undertook to conduct his foreign relations in accordance with British advice. In return the British engaged to support Yakub against aggression and pay an annual subsidy of 6 *lakhs* of rupees. It seemed that Afghanistan had now at last become an Indian protected state. But the treaty had thought of everything except the people with whom it was concerned. Within six weeks of his arrival in July the new envoy, Cavagnari, was murdered with his escort in a popular rising. This brought Generals Roberts to Kabul and Stewart to Kandahar while Yakub Khan joined the British camp and became a state prisoner in India.[1] During the winter Roberts was besieged at Sherpur to be joined by Stewart at Kabul in the spring. Lytton's policy was in ruins. The web of policy, he wrote, 'so carefully and so patiently woven, has been rudely shattered'. He had now no resource but to recognize such chiefs as could be found. In Kandahar Sher Ali Khan, as representative of the old Sadazai house, was recognized, while at Herat, Ayub Khan, a son of the Amir Sher Ali, had established himself. There remained Kabul. At the beginning of 1880 there appeared in Balkh, Abdur Rahman, son of Sher Ali's brother and former rival Afzal Khan.[2] He had long been in Russian Turkistan and used by the Russians as a potential

[1] He died at Dehra Dun in 1923.   [2] Afzal reigned in Kabul in 1866-7.

threat to exercise pressure on Sher Ali. Abdur Rahman was a man of forty, 'short and stoutly built, with bluff but pleasant manners and an easy smile, self-possessed and clear-minded'. A master of statecraft had appeared. Lytton clutched at this 'ram caught in a thicket' (which he had not caught); there was now a man to deal with and the arrival of Ripon enabled the tangled skein of Afghan politics to be unravelled at last.

Abdur Rahman was recognized in July 1880 as Amir of Kabul on the sole conditions of having 'no political relations with any foreign power except the English', and confirming the cession of Kurram, Sibi, and Pishin. In return the British promised an annual subsidy and abandoned the claim to post a resident at Kabul. Next Ayub Khan's eruption from Herat and defeat of the Kandahar force in June was countered by Roberts's classic march of 313 miles from Kabul in twenty days and victory at Kandahar. British troops now withdrew from Kabul and the next year from Kandahar, taking Sher Ali Khan with them. In September 1881 the defeat and flight of Ayub Khan completed the consolidation of the new Amir's power which he retained until his death in 1901.

On the whole the second Afghan war must be adjudged an unnecessary one. If Lawrence's attitude to Afghan chiefs savoured too much of his distaste for Sikh *sardars* his policy of non-interference was yet sound in principle when read with its corollary of a direct understanding with Russia. The policy of making Afghanistan a forward bastion of British power in Asia neglected too many fundamentals to have any hope of success. The country was too arid to support an army and too hostile to dispense with one. The distances which precluded large Russian concentrations in Afghanistan equally forbade large British movements beyond the Hindu Kush. Above all, it went against the known Afghan passion for independence which made the position of every force and the life of every envoy precarious. British control of Afghanistan would have meant Russian concentrations on the Oxus followed by the building up of British armies at Kabul and Herat. The policy would have been financially ruinous in any case; it was fortunate for India that the Afghan rising demonstrated its unsoundness before it exacted the penalty of bankruptcy. The only gain from the whole episode was the substitution of Abdur Rahman for Sher Ali. The ease with which a settlement was made with a refugee from Russian territory threw into sharp relief the unwisdom of supposing that every Afghan chief was a secret friend of Russia. They were no more friends of Russia than of Britain; they were friends of Afghan independence.

A final diplomatic brush completed the Afghan settlement. The Russian defeat of the Turkomans in 1881 and the capture of Merv led to fresh fears in Britain or 'mervousness' as the Duke of Argyll called it. Both powers agreed to a joint commission to demarcate the frontier, but an acute situation arose when the Russian General Komaroff drove the Afghans from Panjdeh and threatened the Zulfiqar Pass. Fortunately at the moment Abdur Rahman was visiting Dufferin at Rawalpindi. The cool nerve of the one and the tact of the other backed up by the resolute attitude of the second Gladstone ministry prevented war. Abdur Rahman was willing to barter Panjdeh for the vital Zulfiqar while the Russians had no mind to risk a general war. Negotiations were resumed and the boundary agreement, which still holds good, was concluded in 1887.

The Frontier. Something must now be said of the frontier created by the annexation of Sind and the collapse of the Sikh kingdom to which the Afghan wars added prominence as well as importance. In dealing with the frontier the distinction must always be remembered between the Baluchis and the Pathans, peoples very different in custom and situation, who required separate treatment. The first problem in Sind was defence against marauding Baluch bands. Sir Charles Napier's military system relied upon a system of fortified posts. But the posts were too few and the commanders not enterprising enough to deal with a mobile foe. From 1848 John Jacob devised a system of mobile defence by patrols which provided the security needed for increasing the cultivated area. In the Panjab the problem was far more difficult because of the greater length of the line involved, the variety of tribes, the number of tribesmen, and the long tradition of conflict. It is important to remember that the problem was not new. The British inherited from the Sikhs who in turn succeeded the Mughuls. The Mughul method had been to keep open the passes by subsidies; it was indeed the withdrawal of these which made easy Nadir Shah's march into India after his capture of Kabul in 1738. The British were unfortunate in their predecessors. There was a natural antipathy between Sikh and Pathan, the sturdy plainsman and wiry hillman, which was increased by the religious feud. Generals Avitabile and Hari Singh ruled Peshawar and Hazara by terror and controlled their areas just so far as their bullets would carry. The British therefore found resentment and defiance added to the natural turbulence of the tribesmen. Until the seventies non-interference was tried; the remission of the old capitation tax, free trade, and the offer of military service to tribesmen was tempered by punitive expeditions, blockades, and fines. Thus the tribal belt of 25,000 square miles continued in uneasy and perplexing proximity to the British power.

The second Afghan crisis led to the next development of policy. In 1876 the treaty of Jacobabad with the Khan of Kalat extended the treaty of 1854 and secured Quetta as a military base. Thereafter Sir Robert Sandeman developed a system of subsidies in return for duties performed and based on close personal relations with the chiefs and *jirgas* or tribal gatherings, which proved highly successful. It was not, however, suitable for export and failed when applied to the more democratic Mahsuds, whose chiefs could not answer for their people.

There remained the frontier proper stretching from the Hindu Kush to the district of Dera Ismail Khan where the various Pathan tribes held sway. There were four possible lines of defence. The first was the

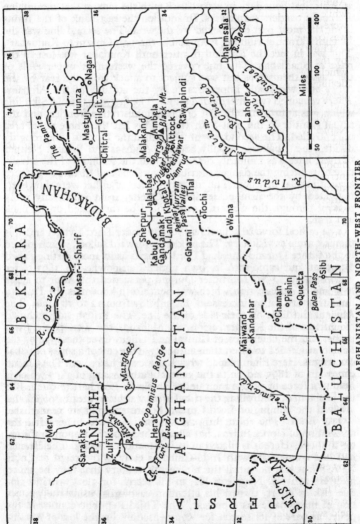

AFGHANISTAN AND NORTH-WEST FRONTIER

river Indus itself, favoured by Lawrence. This has never in fact been an historical boundary in accordance with the maxim that mountains are better barriers than rivers. In addition the east bank of the Indus is for the most part overlooked by the west. The second line was the 'scientific frontier running from Kabul through Ghazni to Kandahar'. This was in fact the Mughul frontier until Kandahar was lost in the reign of Shahjahan. This line covered the western or upper ends of the passes themselves but was subject to attack from the rear by the tribes and was made impracticable by the attitude of the Afghans. There remained two intermediate lines. The first was the old Sikh line which was approximately that of the administrative frontier, and the actual frontier in the post-Sikh years. This left the whole tribal area uncontrolled. The second, eventually called the Durand line, roughly divided the tribal area equally between Afghans and British. Neither of these lines was militarily defensible, but the second had the advantage of reducing the danger of tribal incursions and threats to defence against regular invasion. The military defects of either were, however, mitigated by the firm possession of Quetta, from which any army passing through the western passes could be threatened on its flank and rear.

The radical forward school had its day under Lord Lytton and was then set aside as visionary. The moderate forward school, which looked to the future Durand line, had Lord Roberts as its most distinguished exponent and came into its own under Lansdowne. In 1893, after various hitches,[1] Sir Mortimer Durand persuaded the Amir to agree to a line of demarcation which was henceforth known as the Durand line, in return for an increase of his subsidy from 12 to 18 *lakhs*. The Afghans did little on their side of the line. The British side included the Afridis of the Khyber region, the Mahsuds, the Waziris, the Swat tribes, and the chiefships of Chitral and Gilgit. Over these tribes the British proceeded to assert their authority at the cost of a series of tribal campaigns. Here Elgin reaped what Lansdowne had sown. The Chitral campaign of 1895 led on to the general Pathan rising of 1897 which it needed a force of 35,000 men under Sir Bruce Lockhart to quell. But the problem of controlling the tribal areas was by no means solved and awaited the coming of Lord Curzon before entering its next phase.

The East. The third Burman war of 1885, which heralded the annexation of Upper Burma, has already been touched upon in Chapter 2 above. Here it is placed in its international setting. The French had had connexions with Indo-China as early as the reign of Louis XIV, but it was not until the nineteenth century that they began to interfere actively. Napoleon III, in his search for glory without undue risk or effort, turned his attention eastwards, using the protection of missionaries as a pretext. The Third Republic continued the policy as part of its search for 'compensation' for the loss of Alsace-

---

[1] Abdur Rahman found that ill health and other preoccupations prevented him from receiving Roberts before he left India.

Lorraine and its former position in Europe. The French empire of Indo-China was thus built up. The French proceedings were narrowly watched by Britain who saw in them a possible threat to the eastern flank of the Indian empire. Unlike Holland, France was in no way dependent upon Britain, but in many respects her rival, while her fleet was next in importance to the British itself. It was French action which hastened the annexation of Upper Burma. In January 1885 the French concluded a public treaty, and followed it up by appointing a consul. A few months later a secret letter, signed by the French foreign minister at the same time as the treaty, and promising the import of arms from Tonkin, was discovered. These proceedings, in which Britain detected a threat to her position in Burma, rather than the grievances of the Bombay-Burma Trading Corporation, were the real cause of Dufferin's action. A final flutter occurred with the French ultimatum to Siam in June 1893. Lord Rosebery, who was then Foreign Secretary, while urging the Siamese government to accede to the French demands, refused to submit to a French blockade of Bangkok, which was accordingly raised. For a few hours, according to Rosebery, the issue of peace or war hung in the balance. Siam for the future came to be accepted as a buffer state between the British and French spheres of influence. If French action precipitated the end of Burman independence it at the same time secured that of Siam by bringing into operation the British balance as a counter to further aggression.

Indians overseas. No survey of India's external relations would be complete without paying some attention to the movement of Indians overseas during the Victorian period and the problems to which it gave rise. The record of Indians overseas has a long and honourable history stretching back beyond the beginning of the Christian era. There were undoubtedly commercial contacts with the Near East, overland to Persia and central Asia, by sea to the Persian Gulf and the Arab ports. The first millennium of the Christian era was the great age of Indian expansion in all its forms and this has been dealt with in greater detail in Part I. There were active commercial contacts with the Graeco-Roman world; there was a commercial colony in Alexandria as the Romans had theirs at Muziris and Arikimedu in south India; and 'Indian gymnosophists' or *yogis* were known to the Christian Fathers of the second century. Overland Indian traders and Buddhist priests penetrated into central Asia and along the silk route to China, carrying their wares, their art, and their religion with them. The desiccated cities and monasteries of central Asia bear witness to Indian artistic activity and the art and cults of China to their religious influence. Indian influence was also extensive in Tibet though there was little colonization there. But the major Indian external activity was overseas in south-east Asia. Here India sent representatives of commerce, the arts, and cults and established political kingdoms, as well as cultural spheres of influence. It was overseas that Buddhist art reached its zenith at Borobudur and Hindu art its culmination at Angkor.

With the slackening of the outward thrust from India these cultural outposts lost their positive vigour. The combined result of the Hun and Muslim incursions dried up the stream of Indian intercourse and Hindu ideas, but Indian influence continued in its own right and has persisted in some degree to the present day. In the medieval period there was little of either physical or cultural export, for India was not overpopulated and Indian society was too preoccupied in resisting external pressure at home to think of renewing it abroad. Little remained of former movements but commercial activity in the Near and Middle East and in East Africa. Hindu society in general so lost the habit of foreign adventure that overseas travel came to be regarded as inconsistent with caste.

The situation continued virtually unchanged until the late eighteenth century when close contacts with Europeans revived the desire to proceed overseas. Mirza Abu Talib Khan was one of the first to proceed to England in 1785, while the Brahman Ram Mohan Roy effectively challenged the orthodox taboo on overseas travel by his visit to England in 1830. Even so at the end of the century Surendranath Bannerjee and Mahatma Gandhi both encountered orthodox resistance to their student voyages. So far the movement was one of re-establishment of contact by individual Indians with the outside world. It continues today in the steady stream of students, officials, and business men who proceed overseas to all the countries of the world.

But contacts do not amount to colonization. The larger movement, which has led to the establishment of Indian settlements all over the world began (apart from a slight movement to Burma in the eighteenth century) in the thirties of the nineteenth century. It was prompted by a social and economic revolution in the western world, and helped by certain supporting factors in the Indian situation. The revolution was the abolition of slavery within the British colonial empire and the economic repercussions which followed. Formerly slaves had worked the sugar plantations but now they showed reluctance to work as free labourers, so that only a few years of apprenticeship lay between the planters and apparent ruin. There therefore began an urgent search for an alternative labour supply in the West Indian islands of Jamaica and Trinidad, in British Guiana in South America, and in Mauritius in the south Indian Ocean. In India there were factors making for a response. The decline of the handicraft industry caused by the introduction of machine-made cotton goods had caused unemployment both in Bengal and Madras. From time to time from the thirties onwards to the end of the century, famines created temporary distress which encouraged thoughts of overseas work. And from about 1870 the growth of population, with its consequent fragmentation of holdings and increase of landless labourers, began to press upon the means of subsistence. The first departures to Mauritius were privately arranged but both the Indian and home governments soon found that intervention and regulation were necessary. Thus grew up the indenture system, the main